PAGE 40

ON THE ROAD

YOUR COMPLETE DESTINATION GUIDE
In-depth reviews, detailed listings and insider tips

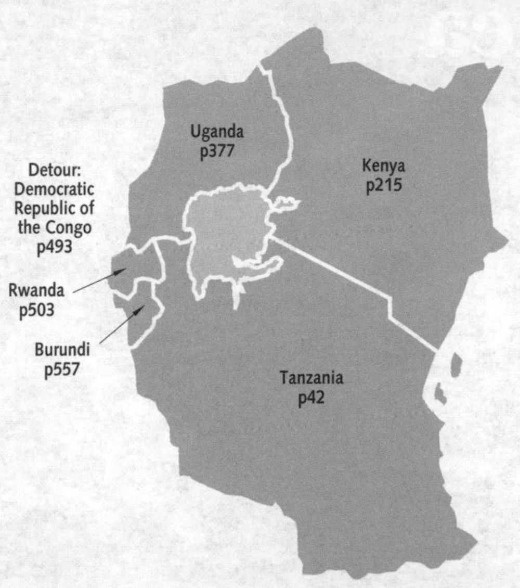

PAGE 637

SURVIVAL GUIDE

VITAL PRACTICAL INFORMATION TO HELP YOU HAVE A SMOOTH TRIP

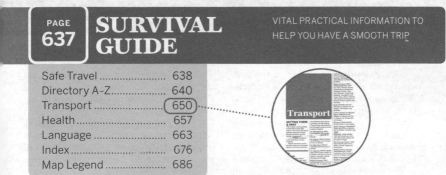

Safe Travel 638
Directory A–Z.................. 640
Transport 650
Health 657
Language 663
Index 676
Map Legend 686

welcome to East Africa

Wildlife & Nature

Mention East Africa and one of the first things that comes to mind is safaris. Wildebeest stampede across the Serengeti Plains. Chimpanzees swing through the treetops in Tanzania's lushly forested Mahale Mountains National Park and Rwanda's Nyungwe Forest National Park. Elephants stand silhouetted against the distant profile of Mt Kilimanjaro in Kenya's arid Tsavo National Park. Lions pad through the high grass in Tanzania's Ngorongoro Crater. And shoebill storks perch near Uganda's Murchison Falls. Wherever you go in the region, there are unparalleled opportunities to experience wildlife and nature at their most untamed.

Gorillas

The mist-covered Virunga mountains, on the borders of Rwanda, Uganda and the Democratic Republic of the Congo (DRC; formerly Zaïre), are home to the world's last remaining mountain gorillas, and seeing these gentle giants at close range is a highlight. To get here, you will need to work, trekking up slippery, steep, densely vegetated slopes. But the thrill of suddenly finding yourself admitted into the gorillas' world more than compensates.

Beaches & Islands

East Africa's Indian Ocean coastline is magical, with its tranquil islands and sleepy villages steeped in centuries of Swa-

Gentle gorillas, stampeding wildebeest, snowcapped peaks, paradisiacal beaches and an amazing array of tribal cultures – all this and more await you in East Africa, one of Africa's most enticing corners.

(left) Maasai warriors
(below) Elephants in Tarangire National Park (p131), Tanzania

hili culture. Travel back in time to the days when this part of the world was at the centre of a far-flung trading network, extending inland to the jungles of the Congo and eastwards to Persia, India and beyond. Relax on white-sand beaches, dive amid colourful fish and corals or sail on a dhow (ancient Arabic sailing vessel), with its sails billowing. Inland, laze on the shores of Lake Tanganyika, or explore the islands of Lake Victoria.

Captivating Cultures

Wherever you go, don't miss the chance to get to know East Africa's people. Explore the Masai Mara National Reserve guided by a red-shawled Maasai warrior. Experience the energy and artistry of Burundi's famous dancers, Les Tambourinaires. Stand in solidarity with victims of the genocide at the sobering Kigali Memorial Centre. Begin to understand the realities of daily life that lead to tragedies such as the overloading and subsequent sinking of the *Spice Islander* ferry between Zanzibar and Pemba. Take advantage of opportunities for cultural and community-based tourism. Immerse yourself in the everyday beauty, realities and vibrancy of East African life. In the end, it is East Africans themselves, with their warmth, hospitality and their unique way of looking at life, who are at the heart of the region's legendary allure.

› East Africa

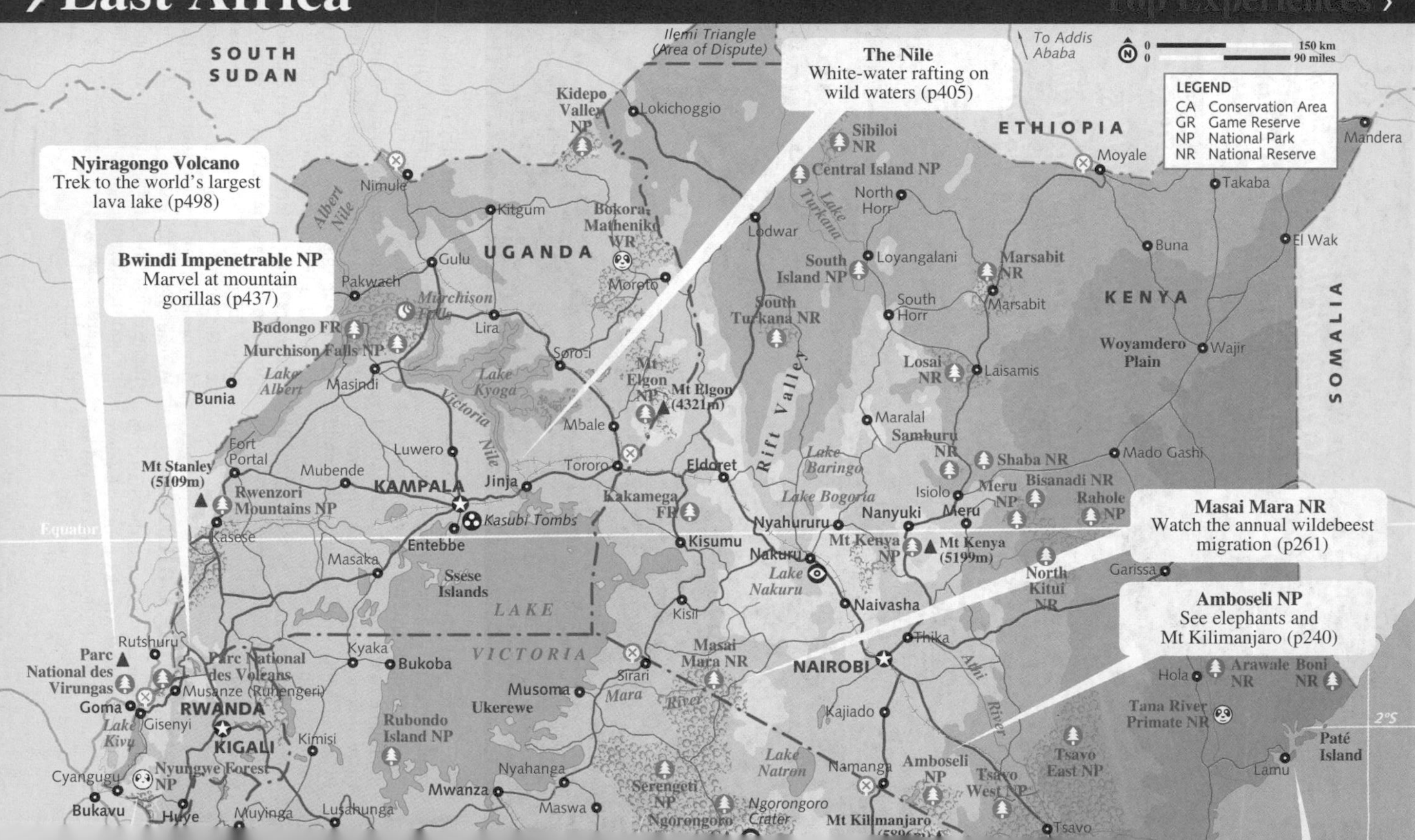

Nyiragongo Volcano
Trek to the world's largest lava lake (p498)
Bwindi Impenetrable NP
Marvel at mountain gorillas (p437)
The Nile
White-water rafting on wild waters (p405)
Masai Mara NR
Watch the annual wildebeest migration (p261)
Amboseli NP
See elephants and Mt Kilimanjaro (p240)
LEGEND
CA Conservation Area
GR Game Reserve
NP National Park
NR National Reserve
150 km
90 miles
SOUTH SUDAN
ETHIOPIA
UGANDA
KENYA
SOMALIA
RWANDA
KAMPALA
NAIROBI
KIGALI
LAKE VICTORIA

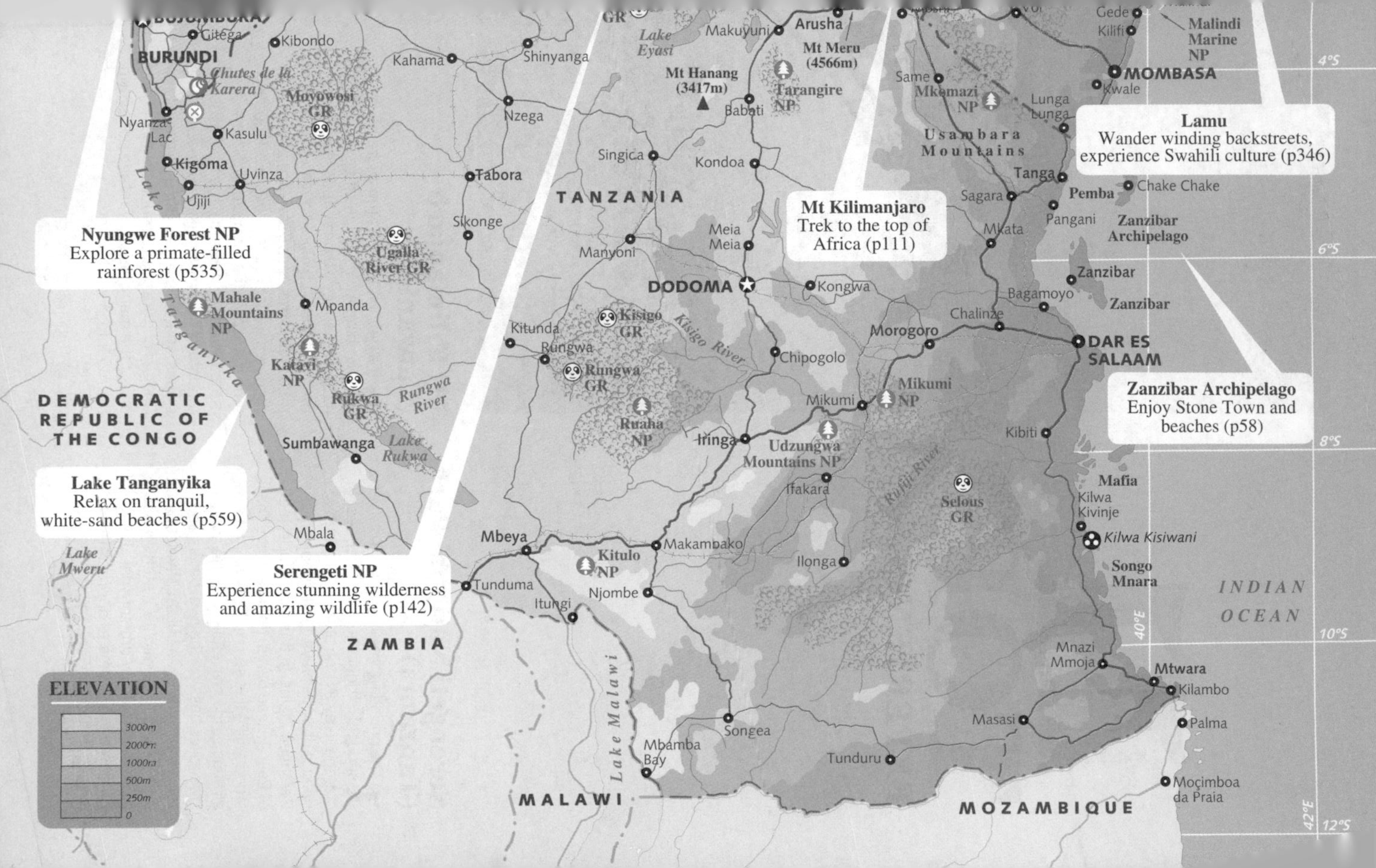
Nyungwe Forest NP
Explore a primate-filled rainforest (p535)
Lake Tanganyika
Relax on tranquil, white-sand beaches (p559)
Serengeti NP
Experience stunning wilderness and amazing wildlife (p142)
Mt Kilimanjaro
Trek to the top of Africa (p111)
Lamu
Wander winding backstreets, experience Swahili culture (p346)
Zanzibar Archipelago
Enjoy Stone Town and beaches (p58)
ELEVATION
3000m
2000m
1000m
500m
250m
0
BURUNDI
DEMOCRATIC REPUBLIC OF THE CONGO
TANZANIA
ZAMBIA
MALAWI
MOZAMBIQUE
INDIAN OCEAN
DODOMA
DAR ES SALAAM
MOMBASA
Gitega
Kibondo
Kahama
Shinyanga
Chutes de la Karera
Moyowosi GR
Nzega
Nyanza-Lac
Kasulu
Kigoma
Uvinza
Ujiji
Tabora
Sikonge
Ugalla River GR
Mpanda
Mahale Mountains NP
Katavi NP
Rukwa GR
Rungwa River
Lake Rukwa
Sumbawanga
Mbala
Lake Mweru
Lake Tanganyika
Lake Eyasi
Makuyuni
Arusha
Mt Meru (4566m)
Mt Hanang (3417m)
Tarangire NP
Babati
Singica
Kondoa
Manyoni
Meia Meia
Kongwa
Kitunda
Rungwa
Kisigo GR
Kisigo River
Rungwa GR
Ruaha NP
Chipogolo
Iringa
Mikumi
Mikumi NP
Udzungwa Mountains NP
Ifakara
Ilonga
Mbeya
Tunduma
Kitulo NP
Makambako
Njombe
Itungi
Lake Malawi
Mbamba Bay
Songea
Tunduru
Masasi
Same
Mkomazi NP
Usambara Mountains
Lunga Lunga
Tanga
Sagara
Mkata
Pemba
Chake Chake
Pangani
Zanzibar Archipelago
Zanzibar
Bagamoyo
Chalinze
Morogoro
Rufiji River
Selous GR
Kibiti
Mafia
Kilwa Kivinje
Kilwa Kisiwani
Songo Mnara
Mnazi Mmoja
Mtwara
Kilambo
Palma
Moçimboa da Praia
Gede
Kilifi
Malindi Marine NP
Kwale
4°S
6°S
8°S
10°S
12°S
40°E
42°E

11 TOP EXPERIENCES

Serengeti National Park (Tanzania)

1 The pounding hooves draw closer, and suddenly, thousands of wildebeest stampede by as one of Africa's greatest natural dramas plays itself out on the Serengeti Plains. In this most superlative of East African parks, time seems to have stood still. A lion sits majestically on a rock, giraffes stride gracefully into the sunset, crocodiles bask on the riverbanks and secretary birds gaze quizzically at you from the roadside. The wildlife-watching here is outstanding at any time of year. Just be sure to allow enough time to appreciate all the Serengeti has to offer.

Mt Kilimanjaro (Tanzania)

2 It's difficult to resist the allure of climbing Africa's highest peak, with its snow-capped summit and views over the surrounding plains. And hundreds of trekkers do this each year, with a main requirement for success being adequate time for acclimatisation. But there are also other rewarding ways to experience the mountain. Take a day hike on the lush lower slopes, spend time learning about local Chagga culture or sip a sundowner from one of the many nearby vantage points with the mountain as a backdrop.

ANDREW PEACOCK/LONELY PLANET IMAGES ©

Zanzibar's Stone Town (Tanzania)

3 Zanzibar's Stone Town never loses its touch of the exotic. First, you'll see the skyline, with the spires of St Joseph's Cathedral and the Old Fort. Then, wander through narrow alleyways that reveal surprises at every turn. Linger at shops scented with cloves, watch men wearing *kanzu* (white robe-like garment) play *bao* (game), and admire intricate henna designs on the hands of women in their *bui-bui* (black cover-all). Island rhythms quickly take over as mainland life slips away.

(top) General store, Stone Town, Tanzania

Wildlife Migration, Masai Mara (Kenya)

4 Studded with flat-top acacia trees, the rolling savannahs of the Masai Mara National Reserve support some of the highest concentrations of wildlife on the planet, and are the stage on which the legendary wildebeest migration is played out. From August, the Mara's plains are flooded with literally millions of these ungainly animals along with herds of zebras, elephants and giraffes. Trailing this veritable walking buffet are prides of lions, solitary cheetahs and packs of laughing hyenas. Yes, come August in the Mara, it's most definitely *game on*.

6

TOM COCKREM/LONELY PLANET IMAGES ©

Elephants of Amboseli National Park (Kenya)

5 There's possibly no better place in the world to watch elephants than at Amboseli National Park in Kenya's south. A big part of the appeal is the setting – Africa's highest mountain, snow-capped Mt Kilimanjaro, provides the backdrop for seemingly every picture you'll take here. Just as significantly, Amboseli was spared the worst of Kenya's poaching crisis: these are elephants who are remarkably tolerant of the human presence (allowing you to get *really* close), and their tusks are among the biggest in Kenya.

Wandering Lamu Backstreets (Kenya)

6 Lamu is surely the most evocative destination on the Kenyan coast. With no cars around, the best way to get to know this graceful town is by wandering its backstreets, admiring the grand old Swahili doors, peeking into hidden courtyards bursting with unexpected colours, slipping into an easy chair and sipping on fruit juices, and accepting all invitations to stop and shoot the breeze (chat). Do all this and the backstreets of Lamu will become a place you'll dream of forever.

...la Tracking at ...ndi Impenetrable ...ional Park (Uganda)

...Nothing can really prepare you for that first moment as you stand just metres ...ay from a family of mountain gorillas. It's an ...terly humbling experience. Particularly that ...rst glimpse of the silverback, whose sheer size and presence will leave you in awe. Or the glee you'll feel as you watch adorable fuzzy black babies clowning about and tumbling from trees. The term 'once in a lifetime' is bandied about a lot, but gorilla tracking in Bwindi is a genuine experience that you'll forever cherish.

White-Water Rafting on the Nile (Uganda)

8 With rapids that go by names like A Bad Place or Dead Dutchman, the idea of being flung head-on into surging torrents of water sounds like a nightmare. But for those who've experienced it, it's one of the most exciting things they've done in Africa. Taking place along the source of the Nile River, things start off as a leisurely paddle. This is, of course, the calm before the storm. Next thing you know you're looking up at a towering wave that mercilessly smashes upon you. It's breathtaking stuff and a ridiculous amount of fun.

7

8

ARIADNE VAN ZANDBERGEN/LONELY PLANET IMAGES ©

ROBERT HARDING PICTURE LIBRARY LTD/ALAMY ©

Nyungwe Forest National Park (Rwanda)

9 With no less than 13 species of primates, a rich tapestry of birdlife and a degree of biodiversity seldom found elsewhere, Nyungwe Forest National Park has been identified as one of Africa's most important conservation areas. The vast forest is home to habituated families of chimpanzees and a huge troop of colobus monkeys made up of more than 400 individuals. Whether hiking through this equatorial rainforest in search of our evolutionary kin or just in search of a waterfall, Nyungwe is guaranteed to bring out your inner Tarzan.

Lake Tanganyika Beaches (Burundi)

10 As unlikely as it may seem, some of the region's best inland beaches are those found on the Burundian shores of Lake Tanganyika. After years of internal conflict, peace is slowly taking hold. Infrastructure is limited and the situation precarious, but intrepid travellers are once again throwing down their beach towels and sipping their daiquiris on the sandy shores first made famous by the explorers Stanley and Livingstone. (top right) Saga Beach, Lake Tanganyika, Burundi

Nyiragongo Volcano (the DRC)

11 After destroying half of Goma in 2002, the Nyiragongo Volcano is now open for business and one of the hottest (no pun intended) sights in Africa. Those who make the five-hour scramble to its summit are rewarded with amazing views of the world's largest lava lake. Trekkers can sleep in cabanas perched on the crater's rim and spend an eerie night under a sky smudged red by the fiery lights below.

need to know

Buses

» Buses, often overcrowded and far from luxurious, are the most widely used form of transport. Prices are inexpensive for the distance travelled.

Trains

» Main routes (Nairobi–Mombasa, Dar es Salaam–Mbeya and Dar es Salaam–Kigoma) are ageing and slow, but offer a glimpse into daily life.

When to Go

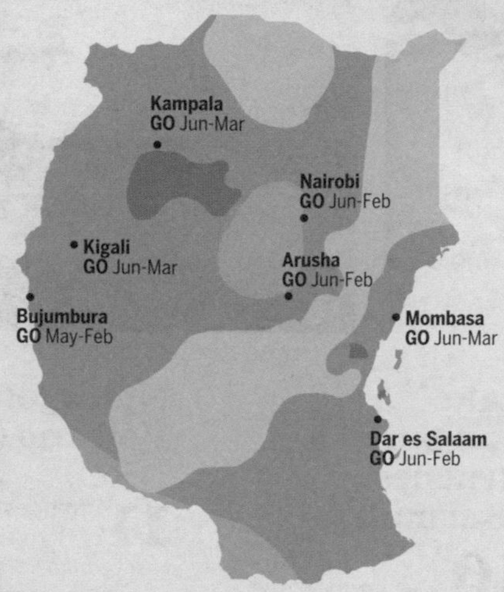

High Season (Jun–Aug)

» Much of the region is cooler and dry.

» Hotels in popular areas are full, many with high-season prices.

» Animal-spotting is easiest, as foliage is sparse and animals congregate around water sources.

Shoulder Season (Sep–Feb)

» An ideal travel time, with greener landscapes and fewer crowds.

» Peak-season prices from mid-December to mid-January.

Low Season (Mar–May)

» Heavy rains in much of the region make secondary roads muddy, some areas inaccessible and landscapes green.

» Some hotels close; others offer low-season discounts.

Your Daily Budget

Budget Less Than US$50

» Room in basic budget guesthouse US$10 to US$20

» Ask about low-season room and safari discounts

» Local-style meals are tasty and cheap

Midrange US$50 - US$200

» Double room in a midrange hotel US$50 to US$150

» Budget extra for safaris, gorilla tracking and vehicle rental

» Meals in Western-style restaurants

Top End Over US$200

» Upmarket hotel room from US$150

» All-inclusive safari packages from US$250 per person per day

Driving

» Driving is on the left in Tanzania, Kenya and Uganda, and on the right in Rwanda and Burundi.

Ferries

» Apart from the newer ferries to Zanzibar, most boats in the region are ageing and decrepit, but they are a real adventure.

Bicycles

» Bicycles are ideal for exploring one area in depth.

Planes

» Useful for coverin East Africa's large distances in one shor relatively hassle-free hop.

Websites

» **Lonely Planet** (www.lonelyplanet.com/africa) Destination information, hotel bookings and traveller forum.

» **BBC News: Africa** (www.bbc.co.uk/news/world/Africa) East Africa's pulse.

» **Kamusi Project** (www.kamusi.org) Living Swahili dictionary.

» **East Africa Living Encyclopedia** (www.africa.upenn.edu/NEH/neh.html) Country information.

» **Integrated Regional Information Network** (www.irinnews.org) Regional humanitarian news.

Money

ATMs in cities and towns; credit cards not accepted for payment but vital to access ATMs. Cheques difficult to change. US dollars and euros get best exchange rates.

» Burundi Franc (BFr)

» Kenya Shilling (KSh)

» Rwanda Franc (RFr)

» Tanzania Shilling Franc (TSh)

» Uganda Shilling (USh)

Visas

» Visas are required by most travellers for all countries.

» Single-entry, one-month visas are available at international airports and most land borders.

» A single-entry visa for Kenya, Tanzania or Uganda allows you to visit either of the other two countries (after meeting their visa requirements) and then return to the original country without needing a new visa.

Arriving in East Africa

» **Jomo Kenyatta Airport (Nairobi)**
Taxis to centre – KSh1200-1500
Shuttle to/from Arusha (Tanzania) – US$30

» **Julius Nyerere Airport (Dar es Salaam)**
Taxis to centre – Tsh20,000-30,000

» **Kilimanjaro Airport**
Taxis (Tsh50,000) and shuttle (Tsh10,000) to Arusha or Moshi

» **Entebbe Airport**
Taxis to Kampala – USh60,000-80,000

» **Overland**
Cross-border buses link Tanzania, Uganda and Kenya, and Rwanda with Burundi

What to Take

» **Binoculars & a field guide** Essential for wildlife watching and birding.

» **Torch** You'll be without electricity in the bush.

» **Mosquito repellent, net & prophylaxis** Always sleeping under a net; follow your doctors' recommendations regarding malaria prophylaxis.

» **Zoom lens** For wildlife shots; also bring spare batteries and extra storage chips.

» **Sleeping bag & waterproof gear** Expect cold, wet conditions on the mountains.

» **Travel insurance** Be sure emergency air medical evacuation is included; also check diving and other 'dangerous activities' coverage.

» **Wind- & waterproof jacket** For chilly, damp highland areas.

» **Yellow fever vaccination certificate** Required if you're crossing land borders.

if you like...

Primates

Tanzania, Uganda and Rwanda are the most accessible places on the planet to see primates. Soulful encounters with endangered mountain gorillas and chimpanzees are the major draws, but golden monkeys and the charismatic colobus also have their devotees.

Bwindi Impenetrable National Park Almost-guaranteed sightings of eastern mountain gorillas (p437)

Parc National des Volcans Eastern mountain gorillas and golden monkeys (p519)

Kibale Forest National Park Thirteen species, including red colobus and L'Hoest's monkey (p423)

Semuliki National Park Nine species, including De Brazza's monkey (p424)

Queen Elizabeth National Park Chimpanzees in beautiful Kyambura Gorge (p432)

Nyungwe Forest National Park Chimpanzees and Angolan colobus monkeys (p535)

Gombe National Park Chimps where Jane Goodall made them famous (p165)

Mahale Mountains National Park Up-close chimpanzees in stunning setting (p165)

Big Cats

Of all the predators on the prowl, it's the big cats that most people come to see. Lions sleeping under (or up!) a tree, a lone leopard draped along a branch, a cheetah accelerating across the savannah – these are some of East Africa's most unforgettable experiences.

Masai Mara National Reserve Arguably the best place to spot all three cats, especially from July to October (p261)

Serengeti National Park One of the best places in Africa to see all three cats (p142)

Ngorongoro Conservation Area The continent's highest lion density in Africa (p137)

Tsavo East National Park A good spot for relatively easy sightings of all three (p247)

Lake Nakuru National Park Resident leopards and lions in Kenya (p256)

Queen Elizabeth National Park Leopards and tree-climbing lions in Uganda (p432)

Murchison Falls National Park Lions and leopards in northwestern Uganda (p460)

Lake Manyara National Park Leopards and tree-climbing lions in Tanzania (p133)

Rhinos & Elephants

The African elephant and the rhinoceros are the enduring icons of the continent, whether as a symbol for the gravitas of its wildlife or the natural world's resilience in the face of humankind's onslaught.

Amboseli National Park As close as you'll ever get to a big-tusked elephant, with Mt Kilimanjaro in the background (p240)

Ruaha National Park Some of East Africa's largest herds, with 12,000 elephants in total (p176)

Tsavo East National Park Kenya's largest elephant population with over 11, 000 (p247)

Tarangire National Park Large dry-season elephant herds in one of Tanzania's most underrated parks (p131)

Lake Nakuru National Park One of the best places in Kenya to see the highly endangered black rhino (p256)

Nairobi National Park The world's densest concentration of black rhinos (p221)

Ngorongoro Conservation Area Perhaps the best chance to see rhinos in Tanzania (p137)

JULIET COOMBE/LONELY PLANET IMAGES ©

» Orphaned baby elephant being fed, Tsavo East National Park (p247), Kenya

Hiking & Trekking

With its combination of soaring Rift Valley mountains with accessible summits, snaking forest trails and flatland savannah, East Africa has a range of trekking experiences to suit most time frames and fitness levels. More than that, exploring East Africa on foot often takes you away from the crowds to some of Africa's most beautiful corners.

Mt Kilimanjaro Trek to the roof of Africa (p111)

Mt Kenya Africa's second-highest mountain with arguably better views (p291)

Rwenzori Mountains National Park Fabulous high-altitude trekking in mist-soaked forests (p428)

Mt Elgon A vast volcano with quieter hiking trails (p412)

Usambara Mountains Trails wind through pretty villages and even prettier landscapes (p98)

Crater Highlands Enjoy rugged beauty and Rift Valley vistas with a Maasai guide (p139)

Hell's Gate National Park Trails bisect towering gorges with wildlife nearby (p253)

Islands

The islands of East Africa's Indian Ocean coastline capture the essence of the region's appeal – a marvellously relaxed approach to life, idyllic palm-shadowed beaches and an unmistakeably Swahili sensory experience, from the aroma of spices to the haunting call to prayer from island mosques. And for an utterly different experience, Lake Turkana has a volcanic island of rare beauty.

Zanzibar A magical name for a magical place, from Stone Town to perfect beaches (p58)

Pemba Hidden white-sand coves and an intriguing culture (p85)

Mafia Island Paradise with a marine park and few visitors (p186)

Lamu Archipelago Manda, Manda Toto and Paté Islands are simply superb (p354)

Wasini Island One of Kenya's little-known jewels and a real step back in time (p336)

Central Island National Park Other-worldly volcano rising above the extraordinary Lake Turkana (see the boxed text, p319)

History & Ruins

It has been said that the history of Africa resides in the belly of the termite, but East Africa's Swahili coast is an exception. It was here, at the confluence of empires and trade routes, that settlements built to last were erected. The powerful kingdoms of ancient Uganda also left their mark, particularly around Kampala.

Gede Ruins Ancient Swahili trading post in Kenya, with ancient palaces, mosques and important archaeological finds (p342)

Kilwa Kisiwani Imposing and predominantly 15th-century Arab ruins in Tanzania (p193)

Mnarani Medieval Swahili port with fine mosques and massive baobab trees (p339)

Kasubi Tombs Ancient royal tombs of the Buganda kings with other sites nearby (p379)

Zanzibar Palaces Crumbling reminders of Zanzibar's past grandeur (p59)

Kondoa Rock Art Sites Beguiling ruins of a very different (and more ancient) kind (p149)

Kigali Memorial Centre Sobering monument to Rwanda's tragic recent history (p506)

» Coco Beach (p52), Dar es Salaam, Tanzania

Beaches

East Africa's coastline is utterly gorgeous and no amount of overdevelopment in some areas can take away from that. The large resorts are easy to avoid, and remember that people come here for a reason – there are some near-perfect beaches, including some with stunning, remote stretches of sand that have yet to be discovered. They're the sorts of places that you'll always remember as your own slice of paradise.

Takaungu Fishing village, empty sand and Indian Ocean perfection (see the boxed text, p339)

Zanzibar's East Coast White sand and offshore reefs (p75)

Watamu Seven kilometres of unspoiled beach with a lovely fishing village nearby (p339)

Pemba Lovely white-sand coves with plenty of space to spread your towel (p85)

Tiwi Beach The alter ego to nearby Diani Beach resorts and its equal in beauty (p331)

Diving & Snorkelling

Reefs proliferate all along East Africa's coastline and the diving and snorkelling here ranks among the best in Africa. It's not quite the Red Sea, but casual divers and snorkellers will find more than enough to marvel at, from abundant marine life to an exceptional array of coral. Most snorkelling is done by diving off the back of a dhow (ancient Arabic sailing vessel) – very cool.

Manda Toto Island Snorkelling here is highly favoured among devotees of Kenya's Lamu archipelago (p354)

Kisite Marine National Park Snorkel with dolphins; diving is also possible (p337)

Watamu Marine National Park Fabulous reefs, fish and sea turtles (p340)

Diani Beach Professional dive schools and even a purpose-sunk shipwreck (p332)

Zanzibar Archipelago Coral reefs and shipwrecks offshore from Stone Town (see the boxed text, p85)

Pemba Divers in the know swear about Pemba's reefs (p85)

Lake Tanganyika Endemic fish and fabulous cichlids (p169)

Creature Comforts

East Africa does luxury extremely well. And nothing quite lends itself to our need for pampering than the experience of returning from a day's safari to luxury accommodation, spa and massage packages and impeccable standards of personal service.

Finch Hatton's Safari Camp, Tsavo West National Park Dress for dinner and eat from bone china in the African wilds (p247)

Tortilis Camp, Amboseli National Park Fine Kilimanjaro views from this ecolodge with extraordinary family rooms (p240)

Basecamp Masai Mara, Masai Mara National Reserve Ecolodge close to the world's greatest wildlife spectacular (p265)

Grumeti Serengeti Tented Camp, Serengeti National Park The Serengeti's premier address (p143)

Kyambura Game Lodge, Queen Elizabeth National Park Luxury safari chic with a reasonable price tag (p435)

Sabyinyo Silverback Lodge, Parc National des Volcans Exclusive base for visiting Rwanda's gorillas (p528)

month by month

Top Events

1. **Annual wildebeest migrat**, July to October
2. **Migrating bird species**, November to March
3. **Festival of the Dhow Countries**, July
4. **Kwita Izina**, June
5. **International Camel Derby**, August

January

January is one of the most popular months for visiting East Africa, with animals congregating around waterholes and the bird migration well and truly underway. Days are usually warm and dry.

February

High season continues; days are hot and dry. The same principles apply as in January, with excellent wildlife-watching around waterholes and countless bird species on show.

Maulid Festival

This annual celebration of the Prophet Mohammed's birthday rouses the Swahili coast from its slumber as Muslims from up and down the coast converge on Lamu, Zanzibar and other Swahili ports. See p646 for festival dates.

Zanzibar Song & Dance

Zanzibar gets even more rhythm than usual with the three-day Sauti za Busara festival (www.busaramusic.org). Swahili songs from every era fill the night, and dance troupes take over the stages of Stone Town and elsewhere on the island.

Wildebeest Births

The annual wildebeest migration mid-year may grab the headlines, but the species' great calving, a similarly epic yet also heart-warming sight, occurs in February in Tanzania's Serengeti National Park.

March

March is traditionally when East Africa's big annual rains begin, flooding many areas and making wildlife-viewing difficult. Prices are low if the rains are late.

April

Unless the rains have failed entirely, this is one month to avoid. The inundation that should have begun in March continues to batter the region into submission. Getting around is difficult.

June

East Africa emerges from the rains somewhat sodden but ready to make up for lost time. The annual migration of wildebeest and zebra in their millions is usually well underway.

Gorilla Naming Ceremony

Rwanda stages the Kwita Izina (see boxed text p523; www.kwitizina.org), otherwise known as the Gorilla Naming Ceremony, a countrywide event that honours the country's newborn gorillas with local community events and gala balls. Watch out for the odd celebrity conservationist in Kigali (Rwanda).

Rhino Charge

This charity cross-country rally in aid of Rhino Ark (www.rhinoark.org) and various other worthy conservation causes pits mad motorists who must reach the finish line in the straightest line possible, whatever the crazy obstacles. The location changes annually.

y

wildebeest migration n full swing, and , too, is the annual igration of two-legged visitors who converge on Kenya's Masai Mara and Tanzania's Serengeti. Weather is fine and warm, with steaming conditions on the coast.

Wildlife Spectacular

Wildebeest cross the Mara River en masse, passing from Tanzania's Serengeti National Park to Kenya's Masai Mara National Reserve, with predators following in their wake. It's one cliché that just happens to be true: this is the greatest wildlife show on earth.

Festival of the Dhow Countries

Arguably East Africa's premier cultural festival, this Zanzibar extravaganza in early July runs over two weeks with live performances, literary events with an East African focus, and the Zanzibar International Film Festival (www.ziff.or.tz).

Kenya Music Festival

The country's longest-running music festival (see p223), and one of East Africa's most prestigious, is held over 10 days in Nairobi, drawing some worthy international acts.

Camel Racing

Maralal's International Camel Derby (see boxed text, p315) is at once serious camel racing and a chance to join the fun. It's a huge event.

August

The mid-year high season continues with the Serengeti and the Mara the focus, although other parks are also rewarding. Europeans on holiday flock to the region so prices go up and room availability goes down.

September

The weather remains fine and tourist numbers drop off slightly, even though the Serengeti, the Mara and Rwanda's Parc National des Volcans are still filled to bursting with wildlife. Prices remain high.

Royal Ascot Goat Racing

Kampala's expats dress in their finest and funniest for the Royal Ascot Goat Races (www.thegoatraces.com). It all happens on the shores of Lake Victoria and is the biggest event on the *muzungu* (white person) social calendar.

October

The short rains begin but rarely disrupt travel plans. Wildebeest are still in the Mara until mid-October, it's the best season for diving and snorkelling, and visitor numbers start to fall.

Gorilla Tracking

Although the dry-season months of June to September are the prime months for gorilla tracking in Uganda, the short (and not-so-disruptive) rains in October and November see permit prices drop; permits are also much easier to obtain.

November

The short rains occur almost daily, but disruptions are minimal. Migratory birds arrive in their millions; it's an aerial version of the Serengeti and the Mara wildebeest migration and, for some, every bit as spectacular.

East African Safari Rally

This classic car rally (www.eastafricansafarirally.com) held in late November is more than 50 years old, and there's more than a whiff of colonial atmosphere about it. The rally traverses Kenya, Tanzania and Uganda and is open only to pre-1971 vehicles.

December

A reasonable month in which to visit, with lower prices and fine weather. Plenty of migratory birds in residence, and much of the region is swathed in green.

itineraries

Whether you've got six days or 60, these itineraries provide a starting point for the trip of a lifetime. Want more inspiration? Head online to lonelyplanet.com/thorntree to chat with other travellers.

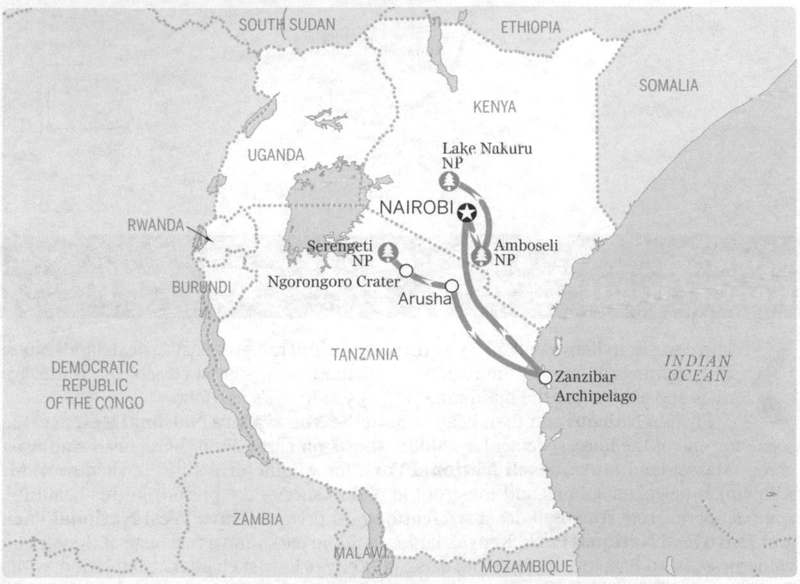

Two Weeks

Classic East Africa

This itinerary samples the best that East Africa has to offer, combining some of Africa's best wildlife watching with beaches and the Swahili coast. To manage this itinerary in two weeks, you'll need to travel some parts of the journey by air.

After arriving at Tanzania's Kilimanjaro International Airport and **Arusha**, head to **Serengeti National Park** and **Ngorongoro Crater**. Then, catch a flight to the **Zanzibar Archipelago** for diving, snorkelling and relaxing. While you're there, take in the charm and historical attractions of Zanzibar's old **Stone Town**.

Fly from Zanzibar to **Nairobi**, but don't linger in the Kenyan capital any longer than you have to; instead head straight out on safari again. If you've already visited the Serengeti, you could probably skip the Masai Mara National Reserve and make a beeline for **Amboseli National Park** for peerless Mt Kilimanjaro views and some of Africa's best elephant-viewing, before travelling northeast (via Nairobi) to see the rhinos and flamingos of **Lake Nakuru National Park**.

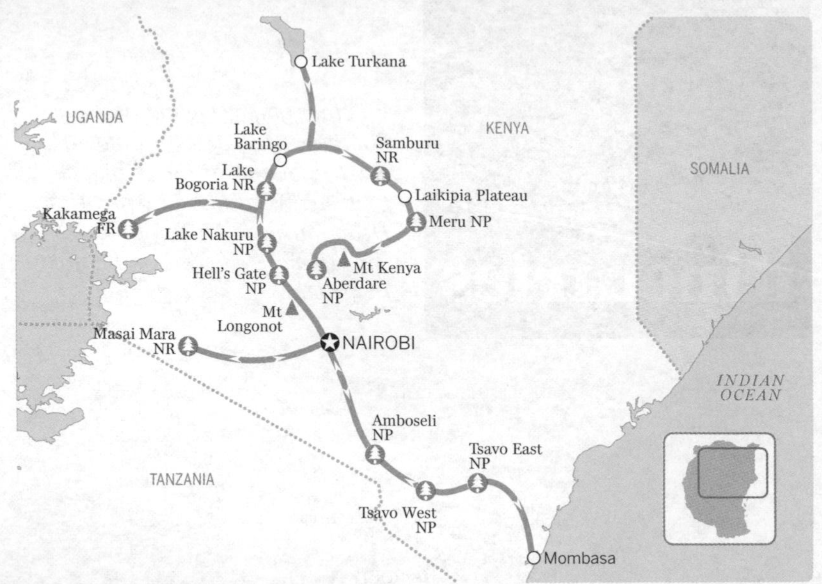

Three Weeks
Kenya Circuit

Three weeks in Kenya will take you through the full range of East African landscapes, with sightings of most of the region's charismatic mega-fauna possible en route; gorillas and chimps are the main missing links in Kenya's portfolio.

Fly into **Nairobi** and then head west to the **Masai Mara National Reserve**, the scene for one of the most spectacular wildlife shows on earth. From here, head southeast across Maasai land to **Amboseli National Park** for wildlife drives in the shadow of Mt Kilimanjaro; elephants, lions and most of the plains' species are present in this beautiful, compact park. From Amboseli, it's a straightforward drive to **Tsavo West National Park** and **Tsavo East National Park**, Kenya's largest wildlife parks and a real taste of the African wilderness. Tsavo East has all three big cats and Kenya's largest elephant population, while Tsavo West boasts all of the Big Five – see them all in one day and you've hit the safari jackpot. From here, you could head down the highway to the ancient Swahili port of **Mombasa**, one of the truly great port cities on earth; this is a good option if you're en route to Tanzania or on a journey up the coast.

But we recommend returning north to explore the heart of Africa's Great Rift Valley. Climbing **Mt Longonot** takes you to the rim of a lost world and affords fine Rift Valley views, while **Hell's Gate National Park** promises weird rock formations and the rare chance to walk among the wildlife. Rhinos cavort with flamingos and massed pelicans in **Lake Nakuru National Park**, while birders will never want to leave **Lake Baringo** and the **Lake Bogoria National Reserve**; the latter hosts more flamingos. If you're heading to Uganda, make **Kakamega Forest**, a Kenyan outpost of the great rainforests of Central Africa, your next stop. Otherwise, press on into the deserts of the north, focusing your explorations on **Lake Turkana**.

Returning south, the **Samburu National Reserve** has a certain gravitas, and don't miss the conservation success story that is the **Laikipia Plateau**. One of Kenya's most underrated parks is **Meru National Park**, while some seriously large beasts lurk in the undergrowth of the **Aberdare National Park**. You're almost done, but climbing **Mt Kenya** is a worthy end to your explorations of the country.

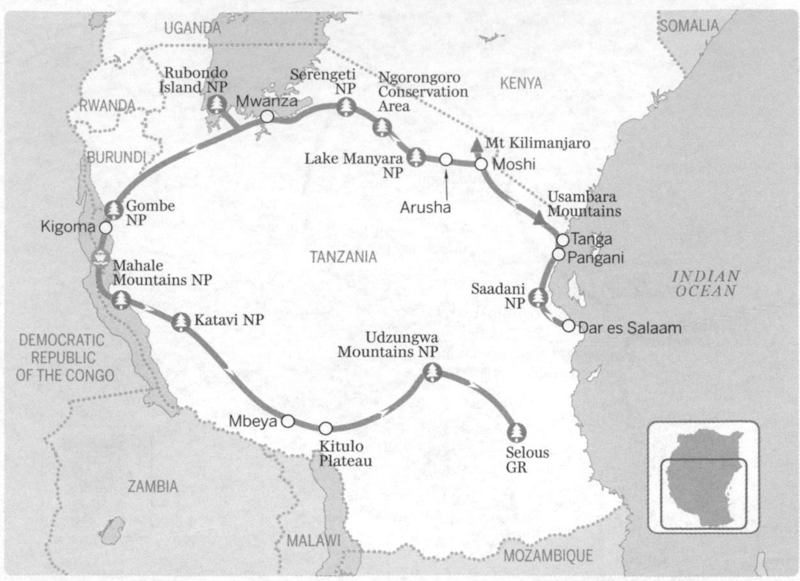

Four Weeks
Tanzanian Trails

Tanzania is the soul of East Africa and this route through the country ranges across the country's enduring highlights. As with the Kenya itinerary, we've saved the coast for its own itinerary.

Starting from **Dar es Salaam**, one of Africa's more agreeable larger cities, head up the coast to **Saadani National Park**, a manageable prelude to the grander national parks of the Tanzanian interior. Further north, **Pangani** is an old Swahili trading post surrounded by lovely beaches. **Tanga** has a sleepy colonial air; if you're coming from Mombasa in Kenya, this may be your first staging post in the country. Best of all, the nearby **Usambara Mountains** promise green hiking trails through pretty villages.

As you shadow the Kenyan border travelling northwest, you can start to tick off some of Tanzania's (and East Africa's) signature sights. **Moshi** (another possible first stop if you're coming from Kenya) is the perfect place to plot your attempt on the summit of Africa's highest peak, the iconic **Mt Kilimanjaro**. Not far away, **Arusha** (connected by bus to Nairobi) is your gateway to a triumvirate of the country's most beautiful and significant protected areas: **Serengeti National Park** (for vast quantities of wildlife), **Ngorongoro Conservation Area** (for stunning Rift Valley landscapes and lions) and **Lake Manyara National Park** (for tree-climbing lions, if you're lucky).

If you can tear yourself away, **Mwanza** and **Lake Victoria** offer a welcome change of pace; birders won't want to miss **Rubondo Island National Park**. Once in this part of Tanzania, it's straightforward to continue on into Uganda, but if you're sticking with Tanzania a while longer, **Gombe National Park** is all about chimpanzees. From **Kigoma**, board the MV *Liemba* and cruise down Lake Tanganyika to **Mahale Mountains National Park**, where chimpanzees are also the major draw; these two parks receive a fraction of the visitors compared to those of the northern safari circuit. The same can be said for **Katavi National Park**.

As you return east, consider breaking up the journey in **Mbeya**, the **Kitulo Plateau** or **Udzungwa Mountains National Park**. But whatever you do, finish your journey in the **Selous Game Reserve** for the rare opportunity to explore the Tanzanian wilderness on foot or by boat.

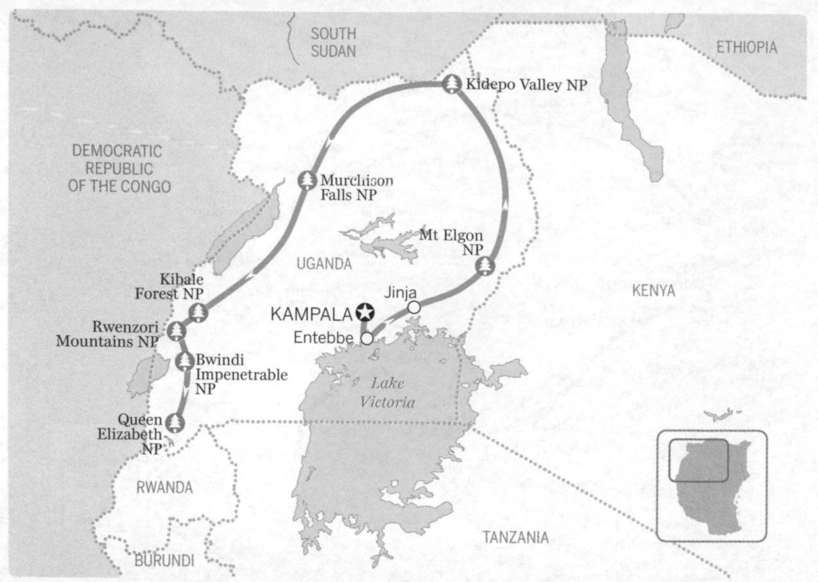

Three Weeks

Ugandan Odyssey

Uganda is East Africa's unsung star, a country that combines many of the attractions you'll find elsewhere in the region, but with gorillas thrown in and far fewer visitors to spoil the view.

First stop, **Kampala** which, unlike Nairobi, makes an appealing introduction to this corner of East Africa. It's a good place to get your bearings, visit a handful of stellar cultural sites and start planning your foray out into the Ugandan wilds. From here, it's a short hop to **Entebbe**, with its attractive Lake Victoria beaches, and **Jinja**, which makes a convincing claim for the title of Africa's adrenaline sports capital. Throw in the **source du Nil (source of the Nile)** and some curious architecture and **Jinja** is one of East Africa's more well-rounded towns. Away to the northeast, **Mt Elgon National Park** is a challenging but immensely rewarding centre for high-altitude trekking; once in the area, don't miss the vertiginous **Sipi Falls**. If you're linking up with a Kenyan itinerary, Busia is a convenient launch pad for Western Kenya. If not, check the security situation and, assuming you get the all clear, travel north to **Kidepo Valley National Park**, a remote and beguiling park that receives very few visitors. It's the only park in Uganda where all three big cats are present.

Depending on the prevailing security situation, you may need to return to Kampala. Otherwise, push on to the northwest to **Murchison Falls National Park**, arguably Uganda's finest park; watch out for chimps, lions, leopards and so much more. Tracking south, pause for a few days amid the **crater lakes** south of Fort Portal, and on no account miss the rainforests of **Kibale Forest National Park**, with 13 primate species and some of the best chimpanzee tracking in East Africa. In the same area, you're spoiled for choice when it comes to uplifting landscapes, some of whose names carry the unmistakeable rhythms of African magic – the **Rwenzori Mountains National Park** is a mist-shrouded introduction to the rainforests of Central Africa, **Queen Elizabeth National Park** has extraordinarily rich bird life, tree-climbing lions and a slew of other mega-fauna, and **Bwindi Impenetrable National Park** is one of the best places in the world to see mountain gorillas. From this part of the country, it's an easy hop across the border into Rwanda.

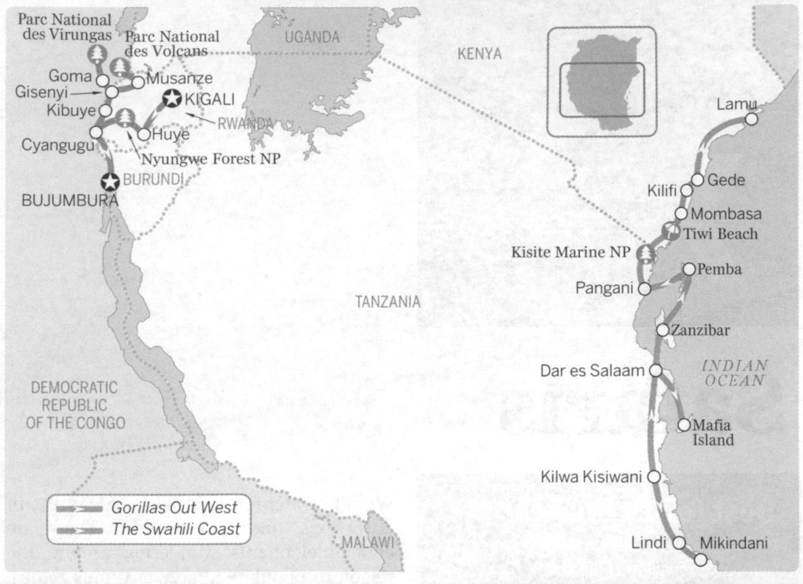

Two Weeks
The Swahili Coast

Warning: this itinerary could take far longer if you find your own slice of paradise and never want to leave.

From **Dar es Salaam**, travel south to the ruins at **Kilwa Kisiwani**, and further south still to pretty, palm-fringed **Lindi**, and tiny **Mikindani**, a charming Swahili village. Returning north, **Mafia Island** is like Zanzibar without the crowds. And yet, there's nowhere on earth quite like **Zanzibar**, the essence of East Africa's Indian Ocean coast. **Pemba**, its northern neighbour, is an adventurous detour. Your last Tanzanian port-of-call is **Pangani**, while just across the Kenyan border, **Kisite Marine National Park** is home to crocs along the banks of mangrove-lined rivers, dolphins crashing through the surf and humpback whales from August to October. Just before you arrive in the roiling Swahili port city of **Mombasa**, pause in **Tiwi Beach**, a tranquil white-sand paradise away from the resorts. Continuing north, stop in the charming town of **Kilifi** and at the **Gede Ruins**, an ancient Swahili city. But **Lamu**, a Swahili heritage gem, is the main event; a dhow (ancient Arabic sailing vessel) trip out into the wonderful **Lamu archipelago** is a must while here.

Two Weeks
Gorillas Out West

Although this itinerary focuses on Rwanda, Burundi and the Democratic Republic of the Congo (DRC), it can link up seamlessly with the national parks of southwestern Uganda or the chimpanzee-rich protected areas of Tanzania's far west, allowing you to mix and match itineraries with ease.

Rwanda's capital **Kigali** has a lush, mountainous setting and lively nightlife, with the sobering counterpoint of a genocide memorial. Next, head southwest via **Huye (Butare)** to **Nyungwe Forest National Park**, with its chimpanzees and other primates, and then via **Cyangugu** to the scenic inland beaches on Lake Kivu around **Kibuye** and **Gisenyi**. From here, it's a short hop to **Musanze (Ruhengeri)** and the mountain gorillas of **Parc National des Volcans**. Returning to Gisenyi, cross the frontier into the DRC, where **Goma** serves as a gateway to the **Parc National des Virungas**, where you can track gorillas and chimpanzees, or stare down into the seething crater of the **Nyiragongo Volcano**. Returning to Rwanda, a detour into Burundi (security situation permitting) and its capital **Bujumbura** makes for an agreeable introduction to one of Africa's least-known countries.

Safaris

Best for Primates

Mahale Mountains National Park (Tanzania)
Gombe National Park (Tanzania)
Nyungwe Forest National Park (Rwanda)

Best for Elephants

Tarangire National Park (Tanzania)
Amboseli National Park (Kenya)
Ruaha National Park (Tanzania)
Tsavo East National Park (Kenya)

Best for Rhinos

Lake Nakuru National Park (Kenya)
Ngorongoro Crater (Tanzania)

Best for Birding

Kakamega Forest Reserve (Kenya)
Lake Baringo (Kenya)
Rubondo Island National Park (Tanzania)
Selous Game Reserve (Tanzania)
Murchison Falls National Park (Uganda)
Semuliki National Park (Uganda)

Best Times to Go

Dry season (July through September) for spotting the Big Five
Rainy season (March through May) for birding
Dry and shoulder seasons (June through January) for chimpanzee tracking

Wildlife watching tops East Africa's list of attractions, and little wonder. There are enough elephants wandering around the region to populate a large city, plus zebras, wildebeest, giraffe, lions and more. National parks range from the dense mountain forests of Bwindi Impenetrable National Park and Nyungwe Forest National Park to the flat, acacia-studded plains of the Serengeti–Masai Mara ecosystem. Throughout, the sheer number and variety of animals combined with the evocative topography ensure that wildlife watching is always rewarding.

An East African safari can also be expensive. This chapter provides an overview of the factors to consider when planning a safari; many apply in equal measure to organised treks. At the budget end, reliability is a major factor, as there's often only a fine line between operators running no-frills but good-value safaris, and those that are either dishonest or have cut things so close that problems are bound to arise. At the higher end of the price spectrum, ambience, safari style and the operator's overall focus are important considerations. Gorilla tracking is covered separately (see p32).

Planning A Safari

Choosing an Operator

A good operator is the single most important variable for your safari, and it's worth spending time thoroughly researching those you're considering. Competition among sa-

KATO & TATO

The **Kenyan Association of Tour Operators** (KATO; www.katokenya.org) and the **Tanzanian Association of Tour Operators** (TATO; www.tatotz.org) serve as local regulatory bodies. Reputable safari companies in Kenya and Tanzania will be registered members. While they're not always the most powerful of entities, going on safari with one of their members (both have member lists on their websites) will at least give you some recourse to appeal in case of conflict or problems. They're also good sources of information on whether a company is reputable or not, and it's well worth checking in with them before finalising your plans.

Uganda's equivalent, the **Association of Uganda Tour Operators** (AUTO; www.auto.or.ug), has no policing power, but does screen prospective new members to confirm they are at least competent.

Other good sources of information on tour operators include:

» **Tanzania Tourist Board Tourist Information Centre** (☎027-250 3842/3; www.tanzaniatouristboard.com; Boma Rd, Arusha)

» **Uganda Tourist Board** (www.visituganda.com)

» **Kenya Professional Safari Guides Association** (www.safariguides.org)

fari companies is fierce and corners are often cut, especially at the budget level. Some companies enter wildlife parks through side entrances to avoid park fees, while others use glorified matatu or dalla-dalla (minibus or pick-up truck) drivers as guides, offer substandard food and poorly maintained vehicles, or underpay and poorly treat their staff. There are also many high quality companies who have excellent track records. Operators recommended in this guidebook enjoyed a good reputation at the time of research, as do many others that couldn't be listed due to space considerations. However, we can't emphasise enough the need to check on the current situation with all of the listed companies and any others you may hear about. Following are some things to keep in mind when looking for an operator:

» Do some legwork (the internet is a good start) before coming to East Africa. Get personal recommendations, and once in the region, talk with as many people as you can who have recently returned from a safari or trek with the company you're considering.

» Be sceptical of price quotes that sound too good to be true, and don't rush into any deals, no matter how good they sound.

» Don't fall for it if a tout tries to convince you that a safari or trek is leaving 'tomorrow' and that you can be the final person in the group. Take the time to shop around at reliable outfits to get a feel for what's on offer. If others have supposedly registered, ask to speak with them.

» In Tanzania and Kenya, check with the Tanzanian Association of Tour Operators (TATO) or Kenyan Association of Tour Operators (KATO), and in Uganda with the Association of Uganda Tour Operators (AUTO), to find out whether the operator you're considering is licensed. See p25 for contact details.

» Don't give money to anyone who doesn't work out of an office, and don't arrange any safari deals at the bus stand or with touts who follow you to your hotel room. Also be wary of sham operators trading under the same names as companies listed in this or other guidebooks. Don't let business cards fool you either; they're easy to print up and are no proof of legitimacy.

» Go with a company that has its own vehicles and equipment. If you have any doubts, don't pay a deposit until you've seen the vehicle (and tyres) that you'll be using. Also be aware that it's not unknown for an operator to show you one vehicle, but then on the actual departure day, arrive in an inferior one.

» Especially at the budget level, there's often client swapping between companies whose vehicles are full and those that aren't. You could easily find yourself on safari with a company that isn't the one you booked with; reputable companies will inform you if they're going to do this. Although getting swapped into another company's safari isn't necessarily a bad thing, be sure that the safari you booked and paid for is what you get, and try to meet the people you'll be travelling with before setting off.

» Unless you speak the local language, be sure your driver can speak English.

» Go through the itinerary in detail, confirming what is expected and planned for each stage of the trip. Be sure that the number of wildlife drives per day and all other specifics appear in the written contract, as well as the starting and ending dates and approximate times. Normally, major problems such as complete vehicle breakdown are compensated for by adding additional time onto your safari. If this isn't possible (for example, if you have an onward flight), reliable operators may compensate you for a portion of the time lost. However, don't expect a refund for 'minor' problems such as punctured tyres or lesser breakdowns. Also note that park fees are non-refundable.

Safari Style

While price can be a major determining factor in safari planning, there are other considerations that are just as important:

» **Ambience** Will you be staying in or near the park? (If you stay well outside the park, you'll miss the good early morning and evening wildlife-viewing hours.) Are the surroundings atmospheric? Will you be in a large lodge or an intimate private camp?

WHAT TO BRING

» Binoculars

» Field guides

» Good-quality sleeping bag (for camping safaris)

» Mosquito repellent

» Mosquito net (many lodges and tented camps have nets, but you may need one for budget guesthouses)

» Rain gear and waterproofs for wet-season camping safaris

» Sunglasses

» Camera and extra batteries, memory and zoom capacity

» Extra contact lens solution and your prescription glasses (the dust can be irritating)

» Toilet paper, snacks and extra water for budget safaris

» For walking safaris, bring lightweight, long-sleeved shirts and trousers in subdued colours, a head covering, and sturdy, comfortable shoes

» **Equipment** Mediocre vehicles and equipment can significantly detract from the overall experience. In remote areas, lack of quality equipment or vehicles and appropriate back-up arrangements can be a safety risk.

» **Access & activities** If you don't relish the idea of spending hours on bumpy roads, consider parks and lodges where you can fly in. To get out of the vehicle and into the bush, target areas offering walking and boat safaris.

» **Guides** A good driver/guide can make or break your safari. With operators trying to cut corners, chances are that staff are unfairly paid, and are not likely to be knowledgeable or motivated.

» **Community commitment** Look for operators that do more than just give lip-service to ecotourism principles, and that have a genuine, long-standing commitment to the communities where they work. In addition to being more culturally responsible, they'll also be able to give you a more authentic and enjoyable experience.

» **Setting the agenda** Some drivers feel that they have to whisk you from one good 'sighting' to the next. If you prefer to stay in one strategic place for a while to experience the environment and see what comes by, discuss this with your driver. Going off in wild pursuit of the 'Big Five' means you'll miss the more subtle aspects of your surroundings.

» **Extracurriculars** In some areas, it's common for drivers to stop at souvenir shops en route. While this gives the driver an often much-needed break from the wheel, most shops pay drivers commissions to bring clients, which means you may find yourself spending more time souvenir shopping than you'd bargained for. If you're not interested, discuss this with your driver at the outset, ideally while still at the operator's office.

» **Less is more** If you'll be teaming up with others to make a group, find out how many people will be in your vehicle, and try to meet your travelling companions before setting off.

» **Special interests** If birdwatching or other special interests are important, arrange a private safari with a specialised operator.

Booking

Booking (and paying for) a safari before arriving in East Africa is advisable if you'll be travelling in popular areas during peak season or if your schedule is tight or inflexible. Only prebook with operators that you have thoroughly checked out, and take particular care if prebooking at the budget end of the spectrum. Confirm that the operator you're

TIPPING

Assuming service has been satisfactory, tipping is an important part of the East African safari experience (especially to the drivers/guides, cooks and others whose livelihoods depend on tips), and it will always be in addition to the overall safari price quoted by the operator. Many operators have tipping guidelines. Depending on where you are, for camping safaris this averages from about US$10 to US$15 per day per group for the driver-guide/cook, more for upscale safaris, large groups or an especially good job.

Another way to calculate things is to give an additional day's wage for every five days worked, with a similar proportion for a shorter trip, and a higher than average tip for exceptional service. Wages in East Africa are low, and it's never a mistake to err on the side of generosity when tipping those who have worked to make your safari experience memorable. Whenever possible, give your tips directly to the staff you want to thank.

considering is registered with the relevant national regulatory body (see p25) and get as much feedback as possible from other travellers.

If cutting costs and maintaining flexibility are priorities, then it can work out better to book your safari once you are in East Africa. Allow at least a day to shop around, don't rush into any deals, and steer clear of any attempts at intimidation by touts or dodgy operators to get you to pay immediately or risk losing your place in a departing vehicle.

Costs

» Camping safaris cater to shoestring travellers and to those who are prepared to put up with a little discomfort and who don't mind helping to pitch the tents and set up camp. Safaris based in lodges or tented camps cost more, with the price usually directly proportional to the quality of the accommodation and staff, and the amount of individualised attention you'll get.

» Most safari quotes include park entrance fees, accommodation and transport costs to/from the park and within the park, but confirm before paying. Drinks (alcoholic or not) are generally excluded, although many operators provide one bottle of water daily. Budget camping safari prices usually exclude sleeping bag rental (US$5 per day to US$20 per trip). For group safaris, find out how many people will be sharing the vehicle with you (the prices listed here are based on a group size of four), and how many people per tent or room.

» If accommodation-only prices apply, you'll need to pay extra to actually go out looking for wildlife, either on wildlife drives, boat safaris or walks. There is usually the opportunity for two of these 'activities' per day (each about two to three hours). Costs range from about US$25 per person for a walk up to US$200 or more per day per vehicle for wildlife drives.

» There isn't necessarily a relationship between the price paid and the likelihood of the local community benefiting from your visit. Find out as much as you can about an operators' social and cultural commitment before booking.

» Kenya is generally the cheapest place in the region for safaris, although increased park fees mean it is now considerably more costly than it used to be. Tanzania is the most expensive. In Uganda, most companies rely heavily on pricier lodge and hotel accommodation; where camping is involved, it's usually the luxury tented variety. That said, there are an increasing number of good midrange deals both inside and outside the national parks.

Budget

Most budget safaris are camping safaris. To minimise costs, you'll camp or stay in basic guesthouses, travel in relatively large groups and have no-frills meals. In some areas the camping grounds may be outside park boundaries to save on park entry fees and high park camping fees; however, this means you'll lose time during prime morning and evening wildlife viewing hours shuttling to and from the park. Most budget safaris also place daily kilometre limits on the vehicles, meaning your driver may be unwilling or unable to follow certain lengthier routes.

In Tanzania, expect to pay US$150 to US$200 per person per day for a budget safari with a registered operator. And the cost in Kenya will be slightly lower. Genuine budget camping safaris are few and far between in Uganda, although a few companies offer reasonably priced three-day trips

SAFARI ITINERARIES

Wherever you plan to take your safari, don't be tempted to try to fit too much into the itinerary. Distances in East Africa are long, and moving too quickly from park to park is likely to leave you tired and unsatisfied. Instead, try to stay at just one or two parks, exploring in depth and taking advantage of nearby cultural and walking opportunities.

Tanzania

NORTHERN CIRCUIT

» **Half-Week**

» Any of the northern parks alone

» Ngorongoro Crater together with Lake Manyara or Tarangire National Parks

» **One Week to 10 Days**

» Lake Manyara or Tarangire National Parks plus Ngorongoro Crater and the Serengeti

» Serengeti National Park, Ngorongoro Crater and Lake Natron

» Serengeti and Rubondo Island National Parks

» One or two of the northern parks plus cultural tourism programs around Arusha or hiking in the Usambara Mountains

SOUTHERN CIRCUIT

» **Half-Week**

» Any one of the following: Mikumi, Saadani or Ruaha National Parks or Selous Game Reserve

» **One Week**

» Selous Game Reserve and Ruaha National Park

» Ruaha and Katavi National Parks

» Selous Game Reserve and the Mafia or Zanzibar islands

» Mahale Mountains National Park plus Lake Tanganyika

» Katavi National Park and Lake Tanganyika

» **10 Days**

» Ruaha, Katavi and Mahale Mountains National Parks

» Kaavi and Mahale Mountains National Parks plus Lake Tanganyika

to Murchison Falls and Queen Elizabeth National Parks for about US$70 to US$100 per person per day, camping or sleeping in dorms.

To save money, bring drinks with you, especially bottled water, as it's expensive to buy in and near the parks. Snacks, extra food and toilet paper are other worthwhile take-alongs. During the low season, it's often possible to find lodge safaris for close to the price of a camping safari.

Midrange

Most midrange safaris use lodges, where you can expect to have a comfortable room and to eat in a restaurant. In general, you can expect reliability and reasonably good value in this category. A disadvantage is that the safaris may have a packaged-tour atmosphere, although this can be minimised by carefully selecting a safari company and accommodation, and giving attention to who and with how many other people you travel. Expect to pay from about US$200 to US$250 per

Kenya

» **Half-Week**

» Masai Mara National Reserve

» Lake Nakuru National Park

» Amboseli National Park

» Tsavo National Park

» **One Week**

» Masai Mara National Reserve or Amboseli National Park plus Lakes Nakuru, Bogoria and Baringo

» Samburu and Buffalo Springs National Reserves

» **10 Days**

» Rift Valley lakes plus Masai Mara, Amboseli or Tsavo

» Rift Valley lakes plus Samburu and Buffalo Springs National Reserves

» Samburu and Buffalo Springs National Reserves plus Marsabit National Park and Lake Turkana

» Meru National Park or Shaba National Reserve plus Marsabit and Lake Turkana

Uganda

Most safaris last one week to 10 days and focus on the southwest, usually combining a gorilla visit in Uganda or neighbouring Rwanda with wildlife watching in Queen Elizabeth and Murchison Falls National Parks and chimp visits in Kibale Forest National Park.

Rwanda

It's easy to visit the highlight parks – Parc National des Volcans, Nyungwe Forest National
Park and Parç Nacional de l'Akagera – within one week to 10 days. Most organised safari packages are short (less than a week), and concentrate on trips to Parc National des Volcans.

WESTERN PARKS

» **Half-Week**

» Katavi National Park

» Gombe National Park

» Rubondo Island National Park

» **One Week**

» Mahale Mountains and Katavi National Parks

person per day in Kenya and Tanzania for a midrange lodge safari. During low season, always ask about special deals. In Uganda, plan on anywhere from US$100 to US$150 per person per day.

Top End

Private lodges, luxury tented camps and sometimes private fly camps are used in top-end safaris, all with the aim of providing guests with as authentic and personal a bush experience as possible while not foregoing the comforts. For the price you pay (from US$250 or US$300 up to US$800 or more per person per day), expect a full range of amenities, as well as top-quality guiding, a high level of personalised attention and an intimate atmosphere.

When to Go

Getting around is easier in the dry season (July to October), and in many parks this is when animals are easier to find around waterholes and rivers. Foliage is also less dense,

FIELD GUIDES

» *The Kingdon Field Guide to African Mammals* by Jonathan Kingdon

» *The Safari Companion: A Guide to Watching African Mammals* by Richard Estes

» *Field Guide to the Birds of East Africa* by Terry Stevenson & John Fanshawe

» *Birds of Kenya and Northern Tanzania* by Dale Zimmerman, Donald Turner & David Pearson

» *Lonely Planet's Watching Wildlife East Africa* (not a field guide, but full of tips on spotting wildlife, maps of East Africa's parks and background information on animal behaviour and ecology)

making wildlife easier to spot. However, as the dry season corresponds in part with the high-travel season, lodges and camps in some areas get crowded and accommodation prices are at a premium.

Apart from these general considerations, the ideal time to make a safari very much depends on which parks and reserves you want to visit and your particular interests. For example, the wet season is the best time for birdwatching in many areas, although some lowland parks may be completely inaccessible during the rains. Wildlife concentrations also vary markedly, depending on the season. See the country chapters for more information.

If you're timing your safari around specific events, such as the wildebeest migration in the Serengeti–Masai Mara ecosystem, remember that there are no guarantees, as seasons vary from year to year and are difficult to predict in advance.

Types Of Safari

Organised Vehicle Safaris

Four to six days is often ideal. At least one full day will normally be taken up with travel, and after six you may well feel like a rest. If you pack too much distance or too many parks into a short period, you'll likely feel as if you've spent your whole time in transit.

Minivans are the most common safari transport throughout Kenya and northern Tanzania, but if you have a choice, go for a good 4WD instead – preferably one with a pop-up style roof (versus a simple hatch that flips open or comes off), as it affords some shade. Minivans accommodate too many people for a good experience, the rooftop opening is usually only large enough for a few passengers to use at once, and at least some passengers will get stuck in middle seats with poor views.

Whatever the vehicle, avoid crowding. Most price quotes are based on groups of three to four passengers, which is about the maximum number of people most vehicles can hold comfortably. Some companies put five or six passengers in a standard 4WD, but the minimal savings don't compensate for the extra discomfort.

Other Safaris

There are many options for walking, cycling and other energetic pursuits, sometimes on their own, and sometimes in combination with a vehicle safari. At all parks, any out-of-vehicle activities in areas with large wildlife must be accompanied by an armed ranger.

Walking, Hiking & Cycling Safaris

At many national parks, you can arrange walks of two to three hours in the early morning or late afternoon, with the focus on watching animals rather than covering distance. Following the walk, you'll return to the main camp or lodge, or to a fly camp.

Multi-day or point-to-point walks are available in some areas, as are combination walking-hiking-cycling itineraries with side trips by vehicle into the parks to see wildlife. Popular areas in Kenya include Mt Kenya National Park, Mt Elgon National Park and the Cherangani Hills for trekking and hiking and Hell's Gate National Park for cycling.

In Tanzania, places where you can walk in big game areas include Selous Game Reserve and Ruaha, Mikumi, Katavi, Tarangire, Lake Manyara, Serengeti and Arusha National Parks. There are also several parks – including Kilimanjaro, Mahale Mountains and Gombe National Parks – that can only be explored on foot. Short walks are easily arranged in Rubondo Island National Park. Multi-day walks are possible in Ngorongoro Conservation Area, Serengeti National Park and Selous Game Reserve, and cycling is possible in the area around Lake Manyara National Park.

In Uganda, opportunities include everything from tracking gorillas and chimpanzees to birdwatching walks in Bwindi Impenetrable and Kibale Forest National Parks, to wildlife walks in Queen Elizabeth, Kidepo Valley and Lake Mburo National Parks, to climbing Mt Elgon or trekking in the Rwenzoris.

Boat & Canoe Safaris

Like walking safaris, boat safaris are an excellent way to experience the East African wilderness, and offer a welcome break from dusty, bumpy roads. Good destinations include along the Rufiji River in Tanzania's Selous Game Reserve, with boat safaris of two to three hours' duration; and in Uganda, Queen Elizabeth National Park, or the launch trip up the Victoria Nile to the base of Murchison Falls.

Camel Safaris

Most camel safaris take place in Kenya's Samburu and Turkana tribal areas, with Maralal a logical base. Although you may see wildlife along the way, the main attractions are the journey itself, the chance to immerse yourself in nomadic life and to mingle with the indigenous people. You can either ride the camels or walk alongside them. Most travelling is done in the cooler parts of the day, and a campsite is established around noon. Most operators provide camping equipment or offer it for retail. There ar[e] also camel safaris in Maasai areas near Arusha National Park; see p123.

Balloon Safaris

The main places for balloon safaris are Kenya's Masai Mara National Reserve, and Tanzania's Serengeti National Park. Everything depends on wind and weather conditions, spotting animals can't be guaranteed and flight time is generally limited to a maximum of one hour. But the captains try to stay between 500m and 1000m above ground, which means that if animals are there you'll be able to see them. Most balloon safaris are followed by a champagne breakfast in the bush.

Do-It-Yourself Safaris

It's possible to visit most of East Africa's parks with your own vehicle, without going through a safari operator, though it's less commonly done than in some southern African safari destinations. But unless you're experienced at bush driving and self-sufficient for repairs and spares, the modest cost savings are generally offset by having someone else handle the logistics.

For most areas, you'll need a 4WD. In addition to park admission fees, there are daily vehicle fees and, in some areas, a mandatory guide fee. You'll need to carry extra petrol, as it's not available in most parks, as well as spares. Carrying a tent is also recommended.

Gorilla Tracking

Best for Gorillas

Bwindi Impenetrable National Park (Uganda)
Parc National des Volcans (Rwanda)
Parc National des Virungas (the DRC)

Best for Independent Travellers

Mgahinga Gorilla National Park (Uganda)
Parc National des Virungas (the DRC)

Dry Season

When December to February and June to August
Advantages Generally dry weather
Disadvantages Permits more difficult to obtain

Wet Season

When March to May and September to November
Advantages Fewer visitors so permits easier to obtain; permits cheaper at Bwindi Impenetrable National Park; generally easier to track gorillas
Disadvantages Can be extremely wet

Cheapest Permits

US$350: Bwindi Impenetrable National Park (Uganda), March to May, September and October
US$400: Parc National des Virungas (the DRC)

Planning Your Trip

Coming face to face with mountain gorillas is one of life's great experiences. No bars, no windows – you're a humble guest in their domain. Nothing quite prepares you for the moment when you come upon a gorilla family in the wild; the first glimpse of black as a juvenile jumps off a nearby branch, a toddler clings to its mother's back and a giant silverback rises to size you up. To make the most of this life-changing experience, planning ahead is essential.

For more information on gorillas, see p627.

When to Go?

Any time you can. The experience will be incredible no matter when you go, but there are advantages to different times of the year.

It's generally easier to track gorillas in the rainy seasons (April to May and September to November) because they hang out at lower altitudes. You may also get better photos in the rainy season, assuming it isn't raining at the time you're with the gorillas, because they love to sunbathe after getting wet. Then again, you'll need to be wearing some serious wet-weather gear.

The busiest times on the mountains are December to February and July to August. Scoring permits takes more effort during these months, but that won't matter if a tour company is handling things for you.

Booking Ahead

Permits are required to visit the gorillas and booking ahead is always a good idea, particularly if you're planning to visit Uganda's Bwindi Impenetrable National Park and Rwanda's Parc National des Volcans from December to February or July to August. If you aren't travelling in these months and you only have a very small window of opportunity, you should still make a reservation as far in advance as possible to be safe.

To make a phone booking for Rwanda, you need to pay a deposit by bank transfer, while in Uganda you'll need to provide all the money up front. If you can't get a permit on your own, you'll need to go through a tour operator, which is often a good idea anyway. In the Democratic Republic of the Congo (DRC), you can book online.

Required Fitness Levels

With the combination of mud, steep hills and altitude, gorilla tracking is hard work. Although gorillas sometimes wander near the visitor centres and might be found quickly, you're far more likely to be hiking for two to four hours, and some trackers have wandered across the mountains for an entire day.

What to Bring

For the most part, you don't need anything special beyond the usual outdoor essentials such as sunscreen, insect repellent, and food and water (enough for the whole day, just in case). Good boots are important. Some people like rubber boots because they keep the mud and fire ants at bay, but they have no ankle support. Plan for rain no matter what month you're tracking (you'll be in a rainforest after all). It's also often chilly in the morning, so you might want a warm top.

You may have to trudge through thorns and stinging nettle, so trousers and long-sleeve shirts with some degree of heft may save you some irritation. For the same reason, garden gloves can come in handy.

Finally, bring your passport with you on tracking day; you'll need it during registration.

Costs

For most of the year, demand for gorilla-tracking permits far outstrips supply: permits in Uganda cost US$500; in the DRC it's US$400 and in Rwanda it's US$750.

The price includes park entry, guides and armed escorts, while porters are available for a little extra. These people are paid very little, and work hard, and so they will expect a small tip.

Where to Track Gorillas

Bwindi Impenetrable National Park (Uganda)

Home to around half of the world's eastern mountain gorilla population, Bwindi Impenetrable National Park remains one of the top spots to track mountain gorillas. The evocatively named park lives up to its name, with stunning scenery comprising dense, steep virgin rainforest. And yes, it means tracking can occasionally be hard work, but with the aid of a good walking stick (or a porter to lend a hand), you'll get there without too

GORILLA LOCATIONS

COUNTRY	LOCATION	DAILY PERMITS AVAILABLE	COST (US$)	HABITUATED GORILLA GROUPS
Uganda	Bwindi Impenetrable NP (p437)	64	500 (350 Mar-May, Oct & Nov)	9
Uganda	Mgahinga Gorilla NP (p450)	8	500	1
Rwanda	Parc National des Volcans (p519)	80	750	10
the DRC	Parc National des Virungas (p497)	26	400	6

RULES FOR GORILLA TRACKING

» Anyone with an illness cannot track the gorillas. In Rwanda you'll get a full refund if you cancel because of illness and produce a doctor's note, while in Uganda, you'll get back half.

» Eating and smoking near the gorillas is prohibited.

» If you have to cough or sneeze, cover your mouth and turn your head.

» Flash photography is banned; turn off the autoflash.

» Speak quietly and don't point at the gorillas or make sudden movements; they may see these as threats.

» Leave nothing in the park; you shouldn't even spit.

» Keep a few metres back from the gorillas and follow your guide's directions promptly and precisely about where to walk.

» When faced by 200kg of charging silverback, never, ever run away...crouch down until he cools off.

» Children under 15 years of age aren't allowed to visit the gorillas.

much difficulty. And while visibility often isn't as good as it is in the open spaces where the Virunga gorillas hang out, in Bwindi you'll get just as close to them and they're more likely to be seen swinging from the trees.

For more information, see p437.

Arranging Permits

Even though the number of tracking permits has increased to around 64 per day, it can still be difficult to get them. There are nine mountain gorilla groups spread across four areas of the park.

Permits, which cost US$500, must be booked at the **Uganda Wildlife Authority** (UWA; ☎0414-355000; www.ugandawildlife.org; ⏲8am-5pm Mon-Fri, 9am-1pm Sat) headquarters in Kampala or through a Ugandan tour operator. It's theoretically possible to arrange permits online via a bank transfer, but UWA are notoriously tricky to get in touch with via email.

At the time of research, discount permits were available for US$350 for the low season months between March to May, October and November; whether this remains a permanent fixture is yet to be determined.

Mgahinga Gorilla National Park (Uganda)

Mgahinga Gorilla National Park encompasses Uganda's share of the Virunga volcanoes, which sit squarely on the tri-nation border. This park is popular with independent travellers because reservations aren't possible more than two weeks in advance, due to the only habituated gorilla group's tendency to duck over the border into Rwanda or the DRC. Of course, the down side of this is that it means they can't always be tracked. It often takes longer to find the gorillas here than in Bwindi, but the walking is usually (but not always) much easier.

For more information, see p450.

Arranging Permits

Reservations for the eight places available daily are only taken at the **Mgahinga Gorilla National Park Office** (☎0486-430098; Main St; ⏲8am-5pm) in Kisoro. The US$500 fee is paid at the park headquarters on the morning of your tracking.

Parc National des Volcans (Rwanda)

Rwanda's Parc National des Volcans ranks up there with Uganda's Bwindi Impenetrable National Park as one of the best places in East Africa to see gorillas. Part of its appeal is that this is where Dian Fossey was based and where the film about her work was made. Also, the towering volcanoes form a breathtaking backdrop. Tracking here is usually easier than in Bwindi because the mountains offer a more gradual climb, and the visibility is often better too; remember, however, that the trekking here is still extremely strenuous. One other thing to remember is that visitors here, unlike in Bwindi, are assigned gorilla groups on tracking day, not when reservations are made, so those who aren't in such good shape will get one of the groups requiring the least amount of walking.

For more information, see p520.

Arranging Permits

There are 10 habituated gorilla groups meaning 80 tracking permits (US$750 per person) are available each day.

You can book a permit with the **Office Rwandaise du Tourisme et des Parcs Nationaux** (ORTPN; ☎252-502350; www.rwandatourism.com; 1 Blvd de la Revolution; ⏲7am-5pm Mon-Fri, 7am-noon Sat & Sun) in Kigali or through a tour operator (p516 and p556).

Parc National des Virungas (the DRC)

The DRC is once again (at the time of writing at least) a viable alternative to see mountain gorillas. After decades of conflict, the Virungas and surrounding region reopened to tourism in 2008. Assuming that the security situation is safe, the DRC receives far fewer visitors than Uganda's Bwindi Impenetrable National Park or Rwanda's Parc National des Volcans. Given that permits are much easier to come by here (and they are cheaper), this is probably the easiest place for independent travellers to see the gorillas. And the setting is stunning.

For more information, see p497.

Arranging Permits

You can buy permits (US$400) and arrange transport and accommodation directly through the website of **Institut Congolais pour la Conservation de la Nature** (ICCN, the Congolese Wildlife Authority; ☎0991715401; www.visitvirunga.org; www.gorillacd.org) or via its **Goma Office** (⏲8.30am-5pm Mon-Fri, 8.30am-12pm Sat).

Travel with Children

Best Regions for Kids

Tanzania

Tanzania combines fabulous safari destinations – the Ngorongoro Conservation Area, a true place of the imagination, and the Serengeti National Park in particular – with a lengthy Indian Ocean coastline; safari lodges and beach resorts (especially in Zanzibar) are often family friendly.

Kenya

Like Tanzania, Kenya combines stirring safaris with fabulous coastline. The Masai Mara National Reserve during the wildebeest migration (July to October) is an extraordinary spectacle; other national parks such as Nairobi, Amboseli and Lake Nakuru are more manageable in size. Anywhere along the coast can be good for families, although Lamu is probably our pick.

Uganda

With wildlife-rich national parks and a slew of water-based activities at Entebbe and Jinja, Uganda can be a good destination if your kids are older. Remember that minimum age requirements (usually 12 or 15 years old) apply for chimp and gorilla tracking.

East Africa is a wonderful destination in which to travel as a family. Yes, there are vaccinations to worry about, distances can be large and there are some regions you'll want to avoid (such as Burundi and the Democratic Republic of the Congo). But if you're prepared to spend a little more and take comfort over adventure, it is possible. Loads of families simply cast their worries aside and have the holiday of a lifetime.

East Africa for Kids

Health & Safe Travel

Africa's list of potential health hazards is formidable, although a little preparation can ameliorate most risks – talk with your doctor before departure, take special care with hygiene once you're on the road and make sure your children always sleep under a mosquito net. In beach areas, keep in mind the risks of hookworm infestation in populated areas, and bilharzia infection in lakes. The scarcity of decent medical facilities outside major towns is also a concern. And when it comes to safety, the rules that apply to adults also apply to children. For more information, see p638 and p657.

Safaris & Cultures

The safari could have been custom-built for older children, but younger kids may not have the patience to sit for long periods in a car. Driving up to within touching distance of elephants, watching lion cubs gambolling across the plains, or a cheetah accelerating across the savannah – these are experiences that will stay with your kids for a lifetime. Children also find it so much easier to break down the cultural barriers than adults do: watching your child play in the dust with a Maasai boy or girl of their own age is an unforgettable experience.

Beach Holidays

Beach holidays are a sure-fire way to keep the kids happy, and factoring in some beach time to go with the safari can be a good idea. Kenya's and Tanzania's beaches alone should be sufficient, but some of the watersports on offer, and other pursuits such as snorkelling, may be suitable for children, depending on their age. And packing a picnic lunch and sailing out to sea on a dhow (ancient Arabic sailing vessel) is fun family time.

Planning

What to Bring

Canned baby foods, powdered milk, disposable nappies and the like are available in most large supermarkets, but they are expensive. Bring as much as possible from home, along with child-friendly insect repellent (this can't be bought in East Africa). A blanket to use as a makeshift nappy-changing area is another good idea. Child seats for hire cars and safari vehicles are generally not available unless arranged in advance.

For protection against malaria, bring mosquito nets for your children and ensure that they sleep under them.

Accommodation

Although some wildlife lodges have restrictions on children under 12 years, most lodges can handle most practicalities with aplomb, whether it's the extra bed or cot, or serving buffet meals for fussy eaters; some lodges even have children's playgrounds and almost all have swimming pools.

Budget hotels are probably best avoided for hygiene reasons. Most midrange accommodation should be acceptable, though it's usually only top-end places that cater specifically for families. Camping can be exciting, but make sure little ones don't wander off unsupervised.

Children under two years usually stay for free in most hotels. Children between two and 12 years are usually charged 50% of the adult rate; you'll also get a cot thrown in. Large family rooms are sometimes available, and some places also have adjoining rooms with connecting doors.

CHILDREN'S HIGHLIGHTS

National Parks & Reserves

» **Masai Mara National Reserve (p261)** Africa's charismatic megafauna in abundance

» **Serengeti National Park (p142)** Ditto

» **Ngorongoro Conservation Area (p137)** Stunning scenery with lots of lions

» **Lake Nakuru National Park (p256)** Lions, leopards and monkeys

Beaches

» **Zanzibar (p58)** Intriguing island culture and glorious beaches

» **Lamu (p346)** Indian Ocean port

» **Pangani & around (p95)** Terrific beaches on Tanzania's north coast

» **Entebbe (p398)** White-sand beaches on Lake Victoria's shore

Activities

» **Kisite Marine National Park (p337); Zanzibar (p58)** Swim with the dolphins

» **Manda Toto Island (p354), Pemba (p85); Lake Tanganyika (p169)** Do some snorkelling

» **Zanzibar (p58); Lamu (p346)** Take a dhow trip

» **Jinja (p403)** Enjoy white-water rafting for teens

Restaurants

Hotel restaurants occasionally have high chairs, and it's easy enough to find items suitable for young diners. Avoid uncooked, unpeeled fruit and vegetables, meat from street vendors and unpurified water. Supermarkets stock boxes of fresh juice, and fresh fruit is widely available.

Transport

Safari vehicles are usually child-friendly, but travelling between towns on public transport is rarely easy. Car sickness is one problem, as are bathroom stops. Functional seatbelts are rare even in taxis and accidents are common; a child seat brought from home is a good idea if you're hiring a car or going on safari.

countries at a glance

East Africa is a vast region, and getting around takes time. It's better to focus on getting to know one or two areas in depth, rather than trying to take in too much on one visit.

If it's wildlife you're after, head to the savannah parks of Kenya or Tanzania to see large numbers of elephants, giraffes and zebras, or to northwestern Uganda for wildlife watching by the thundering Murchison Falls.

Uganda and Rwanda are the places to go for gorillas, while western Tanzania is one of the best places anywhere for observing chimpanzees in the wild.

Burundi offers fascinating cultures and tranquil inland beaches, and both Kenya and Tanzania have miles of Indian Ocean coastline.

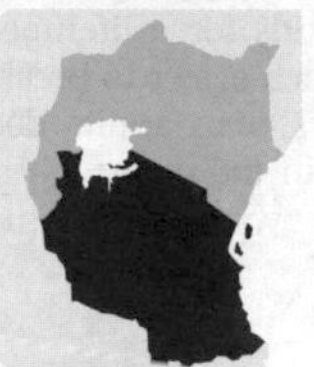

Tanzania

Wildlife ✓✓✓
Beaches ✓✓
Culture ✓✓

Wildlife

Whether you're watching wildebeest on the Serengeti Plains or floating past hippos and crocs in Selous Game Reserve, the variety of wildlife in Tanzania is unsurpassed.

Beaches & Islands

Let yourself be seduced by miles of Indian Ocean coastline, magical archipelagos, swaying palms, and fine diving and snorkelling. Once you get hooked, it's likely you'll never want to leave.

Culture

Tanzania has a rich array of tribal traditions and long Swahili roots. To get to know the cultural melange, travel off the beaten track. Cultural tourism programs offer an accessible introduction.

p42

Kenya

Wildlife ✓✓✓
Beaches ✓✓
Culture ✓✓

Wildlife

From the plains of Masai Mara National Reserve to the landscapes of Amboseli National Park, Kenya offers superb and affordable wildlife watching against stunning natural backdrops.

Beaches & Islands

Kenya's coast is enchanting, whether you're relaxing on the beaches around Mombasa or wandering sleepy lanes on Lamu island. Come for a week, but wind up staying much longer.

Culture

The beaded Turkana and the red-robed Maasai are just a sampling of Kenya's vibrant tribal mix. Getting to know the different peoples and rich traditions is a highlight, no matter which part of the country you visit.

p215

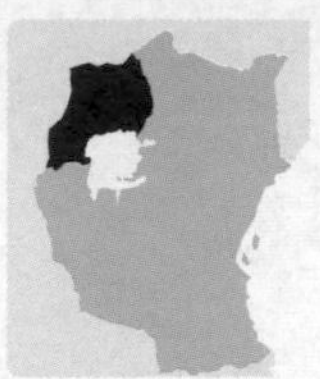

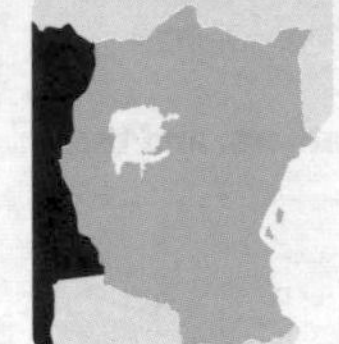

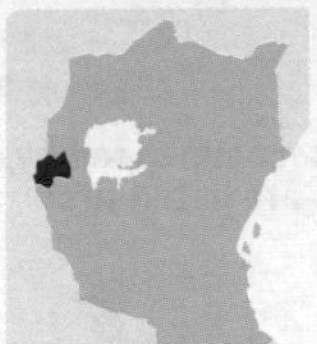

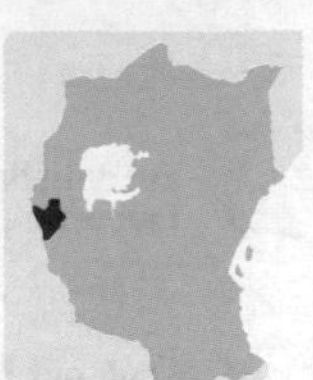

Uganda

Gorillas ✓✓✓
Wildlife ✓✓
Rafting ✓

Gorillas
The steep mountain slopes of Uganda's Bwindi Impenetrable National Park are home to almost half of the world's surviving mountain gorillas, and a visit here is a highlight.

Wildlife
Uganda is overshadowed as a wildlife destination by neighbouring Kenya and Tanzania, but it has much to offer. Lovely Murchison Falls National Park and wild Kidepo Valley National Park are just two of the many attractions.

White-Water Rafting
Uganda's upper Nile stretch, with its Class IV and Class V rapids, is a challenging white-water rafting destination. Or, take a family float trip for a gentler introduction.

p377

Detour: the DRC

Primates ✓✓✓
Nature ✓✓
Adventure ✓✓✓

Primates
The gorillas of Parc National des Virungas are the main attraction. Get ready for hard, sweaty tracking work, and magical encounters once you find them. Virungas park is also home to chimpanzees, and visits to the park's habituated Tongo population should soon be possible.

Nature
Climb to the top of Nyiragongo Volcano for views down into the world's largest lava lake. Plan to overnight on the crater rim, to see the fiery glow of lava light up the night sky.

Adventure
Whether it's meeting gorillas, trekking up Nyiragongo volcano or just getting into the country, everything about the DRC is an adventure.

p493

Rwanda

Landscapes ✓✓
Culture ✓✓
Gorillas ✓✓✓

Landscapes
The 'Land of a Thousand Hills' has endless mountains and stunning scenery. Lake Kivu offers lovely inland beaches, while Nyungwe Forest National Park protects extensive tracts of montane rainforest.

Culture
Rwanda has moved far from its troubled history, and getting to know its vibrant cultural backdrop is a highlight of local travel.

Gorillas
The bamboo- and rainforest-covered slopes of the Virunga volcanoes are home to some of the last remaining sanctuaries of the endangered eastern mountain gorilla. A hike here in search of silverbacks is an unforgettable experience.

p503

Burundi

Beaches ✓✓
Bujumbura ✓
Culture ✓✓

Inland Beaches
Burundi's fine beaches, with their powdery white sands and gentle waves, are some of the best to be found in inland Africa. Saga Beach (Plage des Cocotiers) just outside Bujumbura is a good place to start your relaxing.

Bujumbura
Burundi's steamy capital – with its wide boulevards, imposing public buildings and busy Lake Tanganyika port – is the focal point for most visitors to the country.

Culture
Burundi's famous dance troupe, Les Tambourinaires, and the irrepressible *joie de vivre,* which you'll sense on the streets of Bujumbura, are but introductions to the country's vibrant culture and traditions.

p557

❯ **Every listing is recommended by our authors, and their favourite places are listed first.**

❯ **Look out for these icons:**

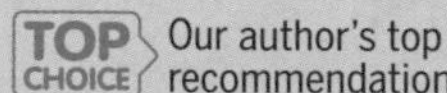

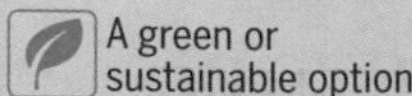

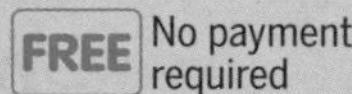

TANZANIA 42
DAR ES SALAAM 46
AROUND DAR ES SALAAM 56
Pugu Hills 56
Northern Beaches 57
ZANZIBAR ARCHIPELAGO 58
Zanzibar 58
AROUND ZANZIBAR 75
Beaches 75
PEMBA 85
Chake Chake 87
Northern Pemba 90
NORTHEASTERN TANZANIA 91
Bagamoyo 92
Saadani National Park 94
Pangani 95
Tanga 96
USAMBARA MOUNTAINS 98
Amani Nature Reserve .. 99
Lushoto 100
NORTHERN TANZANIA .. 103
Moshi 103
Marangu 110
Mt Kilimanjaro National Park 111
Arusha 114
Arusha National Park 127
Tarangire National Park 131
Lake Manyara National Park 133
Lake Natron 135
Karatu 136
Ngorongoro Conservation Area 137
Serengeti NationalPark 142
CENTRAL TANZANIA 146
Dodoma 146
Kondoa Rock-Art Sites 149
LAKE VICTORIA 151
Musoma 151
Mwanza 152
Rubondo Island National Park 157
Bukoba 158
WESTERN TANZANIA 160
Tabora 161
Kigoma 162
Gombe National Park ... 165
Mahale Mountains National Park 165
Mpanda 167
Katavi National Park 167
Sumbawanga 168
SOUTHERN HIGHLANDS 169
Morogoro 169
Mikumi National Park ... 171
Iringa 173
Ruaha National Park 176
Mbeya 179
Lake Nyasa 182
Songea 184
SOUTHEASTERN TANZANIA 185
Mafia 186
Selous Game Reserve 188
Kilwa Masoko 192
Mtwara 194
Mikindani 196
UNDERSTAND TANZANIA 197
SURVIVAL GUIDE 201

KENYA 215
NAIROBI 217
SOUTHERN KENYA 240
Amboseli National Park 240
Tsavo West National Park 243
Tsavo East National Park 247
Voi 249
THE RIFT VALLEY 249
Lake Naivasha 250
Hell's Gate National Park 253
Nakuru 255
Lake Nakuru National Park 256
Lake Bogoria National Reserve 257
Lake Baringo 259
WESTERN KENYA 260
Masai Mara National Reserve 261
Lake Victoria 266
Kericho 272
Kakamega Forest 274
Eldoret 276
Kitale 279
Mt Elgon National Park 281

See the Index for a full list of destinations covered in this bo

On the Road

CENTRAL HIGHLANDS ... 283
Nyeri & Around ... 283
Aberdare National Park ... 287
Nyahururu (Thomson's Falls) ... 289
Mt Kenya National Park ... 291
Naro Moru ... 297
Nanyuki ... 297
Meru ... 301
Meru National Park ... 302
NORTHERN KENYA ... 305
Isiolo to Ethiopia ... 305
Maralal to Turkana's Eastern Shore ... 313
Marich to Turkana's Western Shore ... 317
THE COAST ... 320
Mombasa ... 320
Tiwi Beach ... 331
Diani Beach ... 332
Shimoni & Wasini Island3 ... 336
Malindi ... 342
Lamu ... 346
UNDERSTAND KENYA ... 355
SURVIVAL GUIDE ... 362

UGANDA ... 377
KAMPALA ... 379
AROUND KAMPALA ... 398
Entebbe ... 398
Ngamba Island Chimpanzee Sanctuary ... 401
EASTERN UGANDA ... 403
Jinja ... 403
Mt Elgon National Park ... 412
Sipi Falls ... 414
SOUTHWESTERN UGANDA ... 416
Fort Portal ... 417
Rwenzori Mountains National Park ... 428
Queen Elizabeth National Park ... 432
Bwindi Impenetrable National Park ... 437
Kabale ... 443
Lake Bunyonyı ... 445
Kisoro ... 448
Mgahinga Gorilla National Park ... 450
Ssese Islands ... 455
NORTHWESTERN UGANDA ... 457
Ziwa Rhino Sanctuary ... 457
Masindi ... 458
Murchison Falls National Park ... 460
NORTHEASTERN UGANDA ... 467
Kidepo Valley National Park ... 469
UNDERSTAND UGANDA ... 471
SURVIVAL GUIDE ... 484

DETOUR: DEMOCRATIC REPUBLIC OF THE CONGO ... 493
Goma ... 494
Parc National Des Virungas ... 497
UNDERSTAND THE DRC ... 500
SURVIVAL GUIDE ... 501

RWANDA ... 503
KIGALI ... 505
NORTHWESTERN RWANDA ... 515
Musanze (Ruhengeri) ... 515
Parc National des Volcans ... 519
Gisenyi ... 525
SOUTHWESTERN RWANDA ... 530
Huye (Butare) ... 530
Nyungwe Forest National Park ... 535
Cyangugu ... 540
Kibuye ... 540
EASTERN RWANDA ... 542
Parc National de l'Akagera ... 542
UNDERSTAND RWANDA ... 545
SURVIVAL GUIDE ... 550

BURUNDI ... 557
BUJUMBURA ... 558
AROUND BUJUMBURA ... 564
UNDERSTAND BURUNDI ... 564
SURVIVAL GUIDE ... 566

Tanzania

Includes »

Dar es Salaam 46
Zanzibar Archipelago 58
Pemba 85
Usambara Mountains 98
Mt Kilimanjaro National Park 111
Arusha National Park 127
Ngorongoro Conservation Area 137
Serengeti National Park 142
Lake Victoria 151
Kigoma 162
Southern Highlands 169
Selous Game Reserve 188

Best of Nature

» Serengeti National Park (p142)

» Ngorongoro Crater (p137)

» Selous Game Reserve (p188)

Best of Culture

» Arusha area Cultural Tourism Programs (p123)

» Usambara Mountains (p98)

» Zanzibar's Festivals (p68)

Why Go?

Tanzania is *the* land of safaris, with wildebeest stampeding across the plains, hippos jostling for space in rivers, massive elephant herds kicking up the dust on their seasonal migration routes and chimpanzees swinging through the treetops.

But, it's not just the wildlife that enchants visitors. Tanzania's Indian Ocean coastline is magical, with its tranquil islands, long beaches and sleepy coastal villages steeped in centuries of Swahili culture. Coconut palms sway in the breeze, dhows glide by on the horizon, and colourful fish flit past spectacular corals in turquoise waters.

More than anything, though, it is Tanzania's people who make a visit to the country so memorable, with their characteristic warmth and politeness, and the dignity and beauty of their cultures. Chances are that you'll want to come back for more: most Tanzanians would say '*karibu tena*' (welcome again).

When to Go

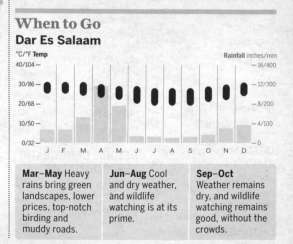

Dar Es Salaam

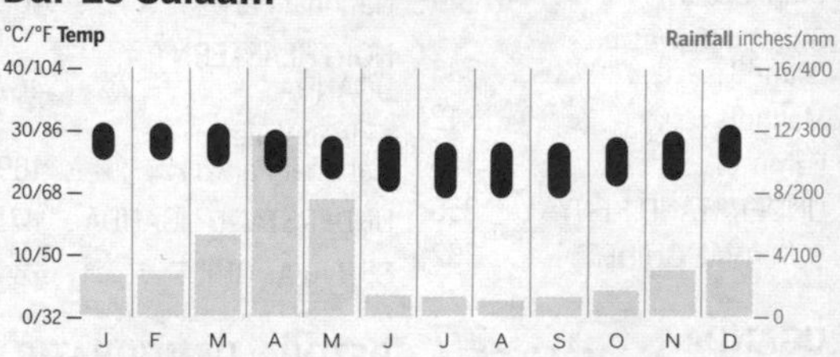

Mar–May Heavy rains bring green landscapes, lower prices, top-notch birding and muddy roads.

Jun–Aug Cool and dry weather, and wildlife watching is at its prime.

Sep–Oct Weather remains dry, and wildlife watching remains good, without the crowds.

Itineraries

One Week With Arusha as a starting point, spend the first part of the week visiting one or two of the northern parks. Some possibilities: Serengeti National Park and Ngorongoro Crater, or Ngorongoro plus Lake Manyara National Park and Tarangire National Park. With the remaining time, do a cultural tourism program around Arusha. Alternatively, by flying between Arusha and Zanzibar, you could visit one or two of the northern parks, and then relax for a few days on the beach.

Two Weeks Starting in Dar es Salaam, travel northwards to Pangani, Tanga and the nearby beaches. From Tanga, continue to Lushoto and the western Usambaras for some hiking. Make your way northwards via Marangu or Moshi to Arusha, and a flight out from Kilimanjaro International Airport or the bus to Nairobi.

TRANSPORT IN TANZANIA

Tanzania has an extensive, albeit adventuresome bus network and good domestic flight connections.

» Away from main routes (which are paved), expect lots of bumping and dust (or mud, during the rains).

» Distances and travel times are long. Don't try to squeeze too much in, and consider an internal flight or two.

» Trains are sloooww... Take them for glimpses into local life, rather than for efficiency.

» Never travel at night, especially on buses.

» Keep your luggage with you in the main part of the bus, and try to sit on the shadier side.

» Buy bus tickets the day before to minimise bus station chaos and dealings with touts on the morning of travel. Only buy your ticket from a proper office, not from a tout outside.

» Be prepared for hair-raising speeds.

Cultural Tips

» **Take time** for greetings and pleasantries.

» **Before entering** someone's house, call out *hodi* (May I enter?), then wait for the inevitable *karibu* (welcome).

» **Don't eat** or pass things with the left hand.

» **Respect authority** Losing your patience is always counterproductive; deference and good humour will see you through most situations.

» **Avoid** criticising the government.

» **Receive gifts** with both hands, or with the right hand while touching the left hand to your right elbow.

» **Ask** Always ask before photographing people.

AT A GLANC

» **Currency** Tanz Shilling

» **Languages** Swah English

» **Money** ATMs in major towns; credit cards not widely accepted for payment; Visa card essential for national parks.

» **Visas** Available at most land borders and major airports.

Fast Facts

» **Area** 943,000 sq km

» **Capital** Dodoma (legislative), Dar es Salaam (economic)

» **Country code** ☎255

Exchange Rates

Australia	A$1	Tsh1686
Canada	C$1	Tsh1597
Euro Zone	€1	Tsh2095
Japan	¥100	Tsh1963
New Zealand	NZ$1	Tsh1299
UK	UK£1	Tsh2507
USA	US$1	Tsh1593

Set Your Budget

» **Budget hotel room** Tsh20,000

» **Two-course dinner** Tsh12,000

» **Beer** Tsh1500

» **Bus fare Dar es Salaam to Arusha** Tsh25,000-30,000

» **Serengeti National Park Entry Fee** US$50 per person per day

...nts

...at ...ythms on ...geti Plains ...where in ...a's **northern** ... (p103)

...scale **Mt Meru** ... **Mt Kilimanjaro** ...11), or hike their ...wer slopes

3 Watch an Indian Ocean moonrise, loose yourself in Zanzibar's Stone Town and explore Pemba's hidden corners on the **Zanzibar Archipelago** (p58)

4 Discover colourful markets, hike through rolling hills and see elephants in Ruaha park in Tanzania's **Southern Highlands** (p169)

5 Visit **Lake Victoria** (p151) for fine birding and tranquil Rubondo Island park

6 Hike in the Usambaras or relax on the coast in **northeastern Tanzania** (p91)

7 Discover Swahili culture, boat past grunting hippos and dive and snorkel in **southeastern Tanzania** (p185)

8 See chimpanzees up close, watch wildlife in Katavi and explore Lake Tanganyika's shoreline in **western Tanzania** (p160)

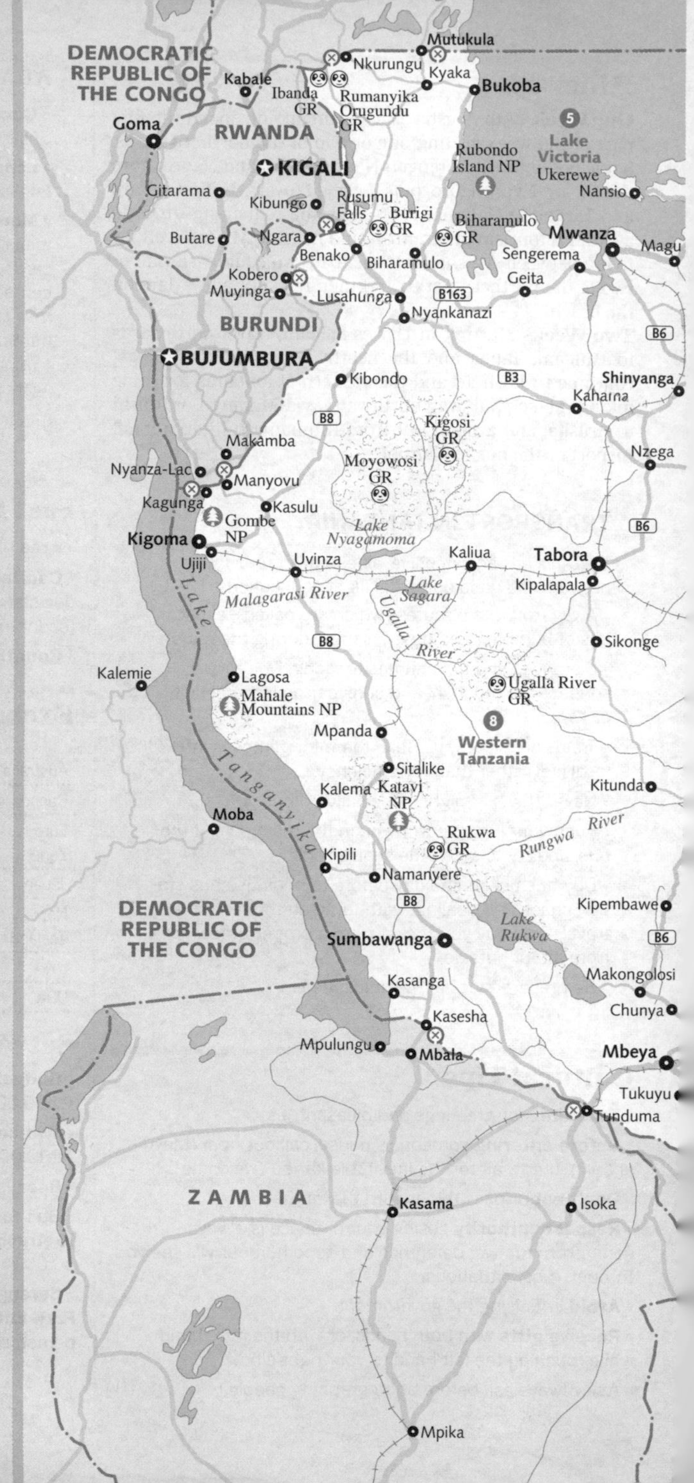

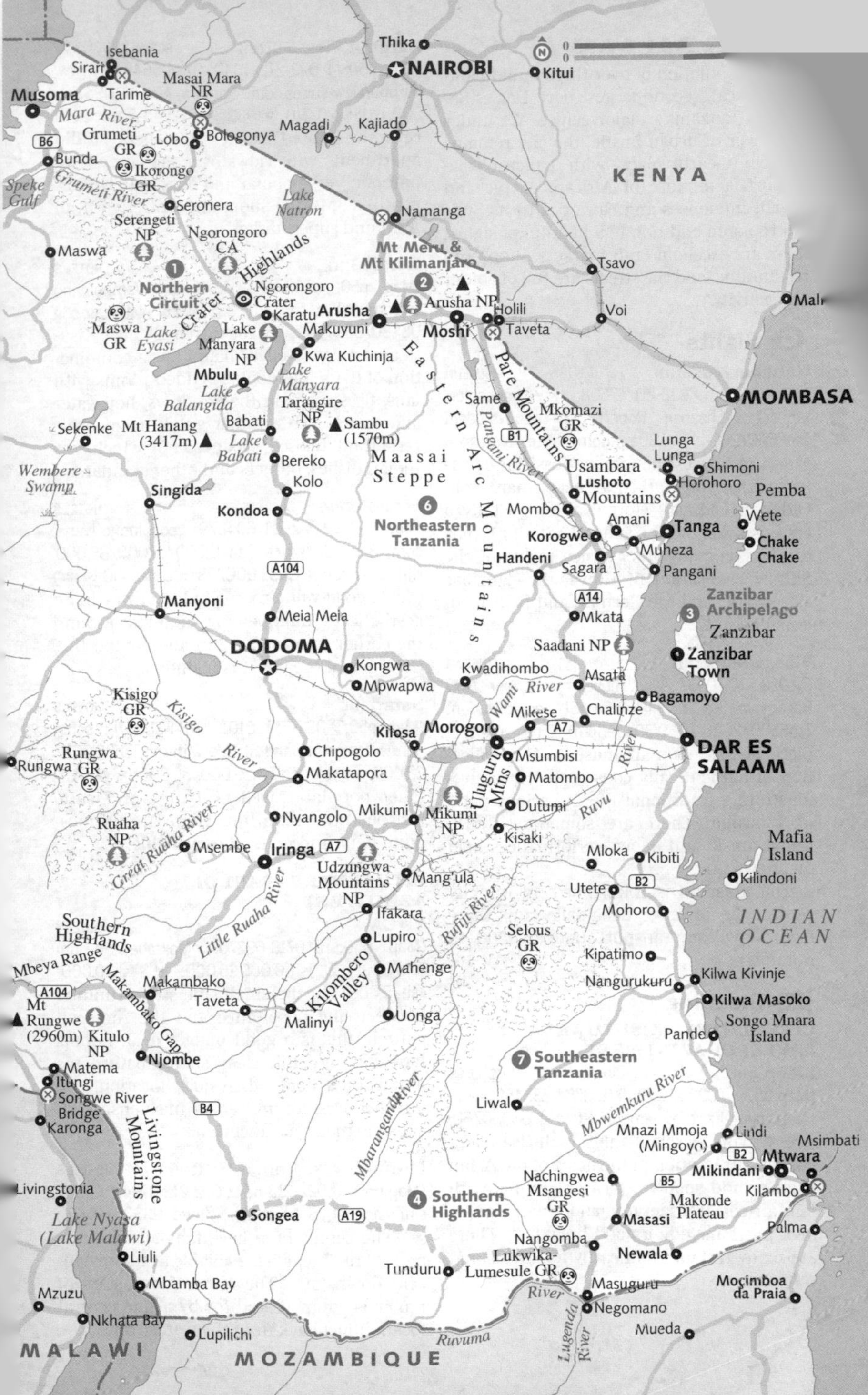

Thika
NAIROBI
Kitui
Isebania
Sirari
Tarime
Musoma
Masai Mara NR
Mara River
Grumeti GR
Lobo
Bologonya
Magadi
Kajiado
B6
Bunda
Ikorongo GR
KENYA
Speke Gulf
Grumeti River
Lake Natron
Seronera
Namanga
Serengeti NP
Ngorongoro CA
Crater Highlands
Maswa
Mt Meru & Mt Kilimanjaro
Tsavo
Northern Circuit
Ngorongoro Crater
Arusha NP
Holili
Mali
Karatu
Arusha
Moshi
Taveta
Voi
Maswa GR
Lake Eyasi
Lake Manyara NP
Makuyuni
Kwa Kuchinja
Eastern Arc Mountains
Pare Mountains
Mbulu
Lake Manyara
MOMBASA
Lake Balangida
Tarangire NP
Same
Mkomazi GR
Sekenke
Mt Hanang (3417m)
Babati
Sambu (1570m)
B1
Lake Babati
Bereko
Maasai Steppe
Pangani River
Lunga Lunga
Wembere Swamp
Usambara
Shimoni
Lushoto
Horohoro
Kolo
Mountains
Pemba
Singida
Kondoa
Northeastern Tanzania
Mombo
Wete
Amani
Tanga
Korogwe
Chake Chake
Muheza
Handeni
Sagara
Pangani
A104
A14
Zanzibar Archipelago
Manyoni
Meia Meia
Mkata
Zanzibar
Saadani NP
DODOMA
Zanzibar Town
Kongwa
Kwadihombo
Msata
Mpwapwa
River
Bagamoyo
Kisigo GR
Wami
Mikese
Chalinze
Kisigo River
Kilosa
Morogoro
A7
DAR ES SALAAM
Rungwa GR
Chipogolo
Msumbisi
Makatapora
Matombo
Uluguru Mtns
Ruvu River
Mikumi
Dutumi
Ruaha NP
Nyangolo
Mikumi NP
Great Ruaha River
Kisaki
Msembe
Iringa
Mafia Island
Udzungwa Mountains NP
Mloka
Kibiti
Mang'ula
Kilindoni
Utete
B2
Little Ruaha River
Rufiji River
Mohoro
Ifakara
INDIAN OCEAN
Southern Highlands
Selous GR
Lupiro
Kipatimo
Mbeya Range
Kilombero Valley
Mahenge
Kilwa Kivinje
Makambako Gap
Nangurukuru
A104
Makambako
Kilwa Masoko
Mt Rungwe (2960m)
Taveta
Malinyi
Uonga
Songo Mnara Island
Kitulo NP
Pande
Njombe
Southeastern Tanzania
Matema
Itungi
Songwe River Bridge
Mbwemkuru River
B4
Liwale
Karonga
Livingstone Mountains
Mbarangandu River
Lindi
Mnazi Mmoja (Mingoyo)
Msimbati
B2
Mtwara
Nachingwea
Mikindani
Msangesi GR
B5
Kilambo
Livingstonia
Southern Highlands
Makonde Plateau
Lake Nyasa (Lake Malawi)
Songea
A19
Masasi
Palma
Nangomba
Liuli
Lukwika-Lumesule GR
Newala
Tunduru
Mbamba Bay
Masuguru
Mocimboa da Praia
Mzuzu
River
Negomano
Nkhata Bay
Ruvuma
Mueda
Lupilichi
Lugenda River
MALAWI
MOZAMBIQUE

...pulation of over three million and ...ca's second-largest port, Dar es Salaam... Tanzania's major centre. Yet under ...eer of urban bustle, the city remains ...wn-to-earth place, with a picturesque ...ort, a mixture of African, Arabic and ...ian influences and close ties to its Swa...i roots. In addition to a handful of sights, ...nere are excellent craft markets, shops and restaurants, and the streets are full of colour and activity.

Sights

National Museum MUSEUM
(Map p50; 022-211 7508; www.houseofculture.or.tz; Shaaban Robert St; adult/student Tsh6500/2600; 9.30am-6pm) The National Museum houses the famous fossil discoveries of *zinjanthropus* (nutcracker man) from Oldupai (Olduvai) Gorge (although only a copy is available for general viewing), plus displays on many other topics, including the Shirazi civilisation of Kilwa, the Zanzibar slave trade, and the German and British colonial periods.

Village Museum MUSEUM
(022-270 0437; www.museum.or.tz; cnr New Bagamoyo Rd & Makaburi St; adult/student Tsh6500/2600; 9.30am-6pm) The centrepiece of this open-air museum is a collection of authentically constructed dwellings illustrating traditional life in various parts of Tanzania. There are sometimes traditional music and dance performances held on afternoons.

The museum is 10km north of the city centre; the Mwenge dalla-dalla runs there from New Posta transport stand (Tsh300, 45 minutes).

Sleeping

CITY CENTRE – KISUTU AREA & WEST OF AZIKIWE ST

Sleep Inn HOTEL $$
(Map p50; 022-212 7340/1, 0784-233455; www.sleepinnhoteltz.com; Jamhuri St; s/d US$50/60) This excellent-value high-rise has a convenient location in the heart of the Asian Quarter and spotless, pleasant rooms with fan, air-con, refrigerator and small double bed. Rates include a good breakfast. There are many restaurants nearby for meals and refreshments.

Harbour View Suites BUSINESS HOTEL $$
(Map p50; 022-212 4040, 0784-564848; www.harbourview-suites.com; Samora Ave; s US$110-200, d US$120-210) Well-equipped, centrally located business travellers' studio apartments with views over the city or the harbour. Very popular and often full. Underneath is JM Mall shopping centre, with an ATM and supermarket.

Jambo Inn HOTEL $
(Map p50; 022-211 4293; www.jamboinnhotel.com; Libya St; s/d US$20/26, with air-con US$30/36) In the extremely busy Kisutu area, this travellers' haunt has a combination of twin- and double-bedded rooms with fans, fly screens in the windows, hot water and there's also a rather good, inexpensive restaurant (closed Wednesday), which has Indian dishes, burgers and other standards.

Econolodge HOTEL $
(Map p50; 022-211 6048/9; econolodge@raha.com; Band St; s/d/tr Tsh20,000/27,000/35,000, with air-con Tsh33,000/38,000/45,000) Clean, good-value rooms hidden away in an aesthetically unappealing high-rise around the corner from Safari Inn and Jambo Inn. Continental breakfast is included.

Safari Inn HOTEL $
(Map p50; 022-213 8101, 0784-303478; safari-inn@lycos.com; Band St; s/d with fan Tsh22,000/28,000, with air-con Tsh26,000/35,000) Another popular travellers' haunt in Kisutu, just behind Jambo Inn. There are no mosquito nets, and no food is available.

CITY CENTRE – EAST OF AZIKIWE ST

YWCA HOSTEL $
(Map p50; 0713-622707; Maktaba St; dm Tsh7000; s Tsh10,000-15,000; d Tsh20,000-Tsh25,000) On the small side street running between the post office and the Anglican church, this is a good budget deal. Rooms have fan and sink, clean shared bathrooms and a convenient, albeit noisy location. The attached restaurant serves inexpensive local-style meals at lunchtime.

Luther House Centre Hostel HOSTEL $
(Map p50; 022-212 6247, 022-212 0734; luther@simbanet.net; Sokoine Dr; s/tw/d US$35/40/45) The rooms here have fans and air-con, and there's breakfast available at the restaurant downstairs. The rather faded state of repair is compensated for by a fine central location just back from the waterfront.

YMCA HOSTEL **$**
(Map p50; ☎022-213 5457, 0755-066643; Upanga Rd; r Tsh25,000) No-frills rooms in a small compound around the corner from the YWCA, and marginally quieter (though the step up in price from the YWCA isn't justified). There's a canteen with inexpensive meals.

Dar es Salaam Serena Hotel HOTEL **$$$**
(Map p50; ☎022-211 2416; www.serenahotels.com/serenadaressalaam; Ohio St; r from US$220; P❄@📶🏊) Spacious rooms and expansive gardens, plus a pool and a fitness centre.

Southern Sun HOTEL **$$$**
(Map p50; ☎022-213 7575; www.southernsun.com; Garden Ave; r from US$205; P❄@📶) Modern rooms and the standard amenities, including a business centre that's open until 10pm. It's on a quiet, leafy side street near the National Museum and next to Standard Chartered Bank.

UPANGA

Swiss Garden Hotel B&B **$$**
(☎022-215 3219; www.swissgardenhotel.net; Mindu St; s/d from US$78/98; P❄@) A cosy B&B in a quiet, leafy neighbourhood, with helpful hosts and small, spotless rooms. Meals can be arranged. It's in Upanga, just off United Nations Rd.

Palm Beach Hotel HOTEL **$$**
(☎022-213 0985, 0713-222299; www.pbhtz.com; Ali Hassan Mwinyi Rd; s/d/tr US$95/120/130; P❄@📶) This Dar es Salaam institution (look for the bright-blue art deco architecture) has spacious, good-value, well-equipped rooms and a restaurant.

MSASANI PENINSULA & OYSTERBAY

Msasani Slipway Apartments APARTMENT **$$**
(☎022-260 0805, 0784-324044; slipway@coastal.cc; Msasani Slipway; r/apt from US$90/120; P❄) Furnished apartments in a good location and just opposite the Msasani Slipway (reception is next to Barclays Bank).

Sea Cliff Hotel HOTEL **$$$**
(☎022-260 0380/7, 0752-555500; www.hotelseacliff.com; Toure Dr; r in village annex/main bldg from US$170/300; P❄@📶🏊) Sea Cliff has an excellent, breezy setting overlooking the ocean at the northern tip of Msasani Peninsula. Rooms are in the main building, or in the less appealing and view-less 'village', next door adjoining the shopping mall.

Coral Beach Hotel
(☎022-260 1928, 0784-783858; w -tz.com; s/d from US$140/170; P❄ quiet hotel (part of the Best Weste catering to business travellers.

OTHER AREAS

TEC Kurasini Training & Conference Centre HO
(☎022-285 1077; tec@cats-net.com; Nelson M dela Rd; s/d/tr Tsh22,000/45,000/66,000, s in n wing with air-con Tsh30,000; P@) A church-ru place with simple, quiet rooms with fan, and a canteen for meals. It's just southeast of the city centre off the port access road (about Tsh5000 in a taxi).

Eating

Most restaurants in the city centre are closed on Sunday.

CITY CENTRE – KISUTU AREA & WEST OF AZIKIWE ST

Akberali Tea Room INDIAN **$**
(Map p50; cnr Morogoro Rd & Jamhuri St; snacks from Tsh200) This tiny place oozes local flavour. Look for the sign 'A Tea Room'. It's just down from Barclays Bank, and just a few minutes on foot from the Kisutu area hotels.

Patel Brotherhood INDIAN **$**
(Patel Samaj; Map p50; off Maktaba St; meals Tsh5000-7000; ⏲lunch & dinner) This large compound is a favourite evening spot for local Indian families, with tasty, good-value Indian veg and non-veg meals (thali, chicken *biryani* and more). Evenings, a Tsh1500 per person entry fee is charged. From Maktaba St opposite Holiday Inn, make your way through the large car park towards the bright blue roof.

Al Basha LEBANESE **$$**
(Map p50; ☎022-212 6888, 0787-909000; Bridge St; snacks from Tsh4000, meals Tsh8000-9500; ⏲breakfast, lunch & dinner) This popular eatery has delicious hummus and other Lebanese dishes, plus burgers and subs. It's next to Heritage Hotel, and diagonally opposite the Extelecoms House.

Chef's Pride EUROPEAN **$**
(Map p50; Chagga St; meals from Tsh1500; ⏲lunch & dinner, closed during Ramadan) This long-standing and popular local eatery features standard fare, plus pizza, Indian and vegetarian dishes, and even some Chinese cuisine.

...alaam

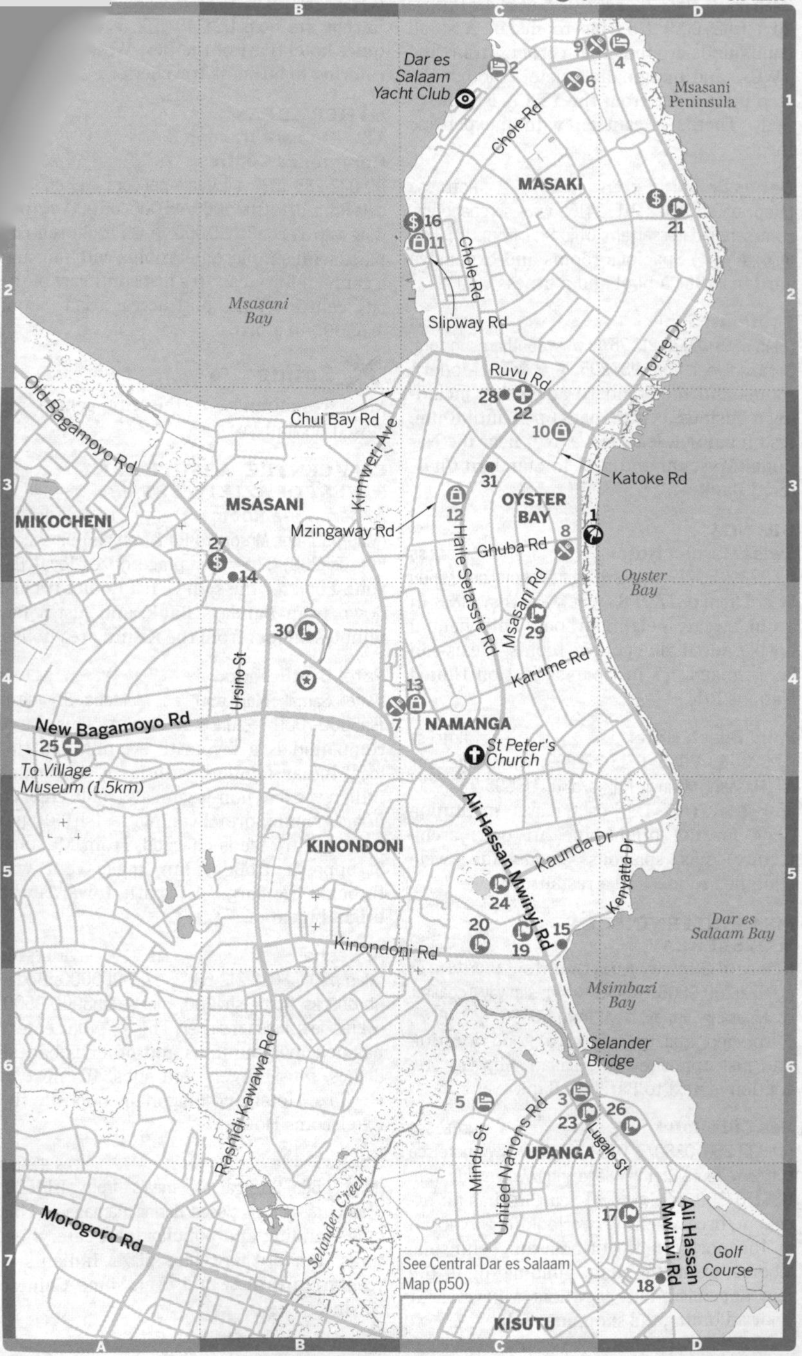

0 — 1 km
0 — 0.5 miles

Dar es Salaam Yacht Club
Msasani Peninsula
Chole Rd
MASAKI
Msasani Bay
Slipway Rd
Ruvu Rd
Toure Dr
Old Bagamoyo Rd
Chui Bay Rd
Kimweri Ave
Katoke Rd
MIKOCHENI
MSASANI
OYSTER BAY
Mzingaway Rd
Haile Selassie Rd
Ghuba Rd
Oyster Bay
Msasani Rd
Ursino St
Karume Rd
New Bagamoyo Rd
NAMANGA
To Village Museum (1.5km)
St Peter's Church
Ali Hassan Mwinyi Rd
KINONDONI
Kaunda Dr
Kenyatta Dr
Dar es Salaam Bay
Kinondoni Rd
Msimbazi Bay
Selander Bridge
Rashidi Kawawa Rd
Mindu St
United Nations Rd
Lugalo St
UPANGA
Selander Creek
Morogoro Rd
Ali Hassan Mwinyi Rd
Golf Course

See Central Dar es Salaam Map (p50)

KISUTU

1 2 3 4 5 6 7 8 9 10 11 12 13 14 15 16 17 18 19 20 21 22 23 24 25 26 27 28 29 30 31

Dar es Salaam

Sights
1 Coco Beach C3

Sleeping
2 Coral Beach Hotel C1
Msasani Slipway Apartments .... (see 11)
3 Palm Beach Hotel C6
4 Sea Cliff Hotel D1
5 Swiss Garden Hotel C6
Triniti Guesthouse .... (see 29)

Eating
Azuma .... (see 11)
6 Épi d'Or C1
Fairy Delights Ice Cream Shop .... (see 11)
Msasani Slipway .... (see 11)
7 Rohobot Ethiopian Restaurant B4
8 Sweet Eazy Restaurant & Lounge C3
9 Village Supermarket C1
Waterfront Sunset Restaurant & Beach Bar .... (see 11)

Drinking
Coco Beach .... (see 1)
Waterfront Beach Bar .... (see 11)

Entertainment
Alliance Française .... (see 15)

Shopping
10 Makutano Centre for Tanzanian Art & Craft C3
11 Msasani Slipway ....
Msasani Slipway Weekend Craft Market .... (
12 Tingatinga Centre ....
13 Wonder Workshop ....

Information
A Novel Idea .... (see 11,
14 A Novel Idea B3
A Novel Idea .... (see 8)
15 Alliance Française C5
16 Barclays Bank C2
Burundian Embassy .... (see 23)
17 Democratic Republic of the Congo Embassy D7
18 Flying Doctors & Amref D7
19 French Embassy C5
20 Indian High Commission C5
21 Irish Embassy D2
22 IST Clinic C3
23 Italian Embassy C6
Kearsley Travel .... (see 9)
24 Kenyan High Commission C5
25 Premier Care Clinic A4
26 Rwandan Embassy D6
27 Standard Chartered ATM B3
28 Travel Partner C3
29 Ugandan High Commission C4
30 US Embassy B4

Transport
31 Dalla-Dalla Junction & Taxi Stands C3
Travel Partner .... (see 28)

CITY CENTRE – EAST OF AZIKIWE ST

YMCA TANZANIAN $
(Map p50; ☎022-213 5457; Upanga Rd; meals about Tsh2500; ⊙lunch & dinner) The YMCA canteen serves filling, inexpensive local food.

Kibo Bar EUROPEAN $$$
(Map p50; ☎022-211 2416; Dar es Salaam Serena Hotel, Ohio St; sandwiches Tsh11,000, meals Tsh15,000-20,000; ⊙lunch-11.30pm) Design-your-own sandwich station at lunchtime on weekdays at at this upmarket sports bar.

City Garden TANZANIAN $$
(Yami Yami; Map p50; cnr Pamba Rd & Garden St; meals Tsh9000-15,000; ⊙lunch & dinner) A lunch buffet (Monday to Friday) and à la carte dining, featuring standards such as grilled fish/chicken and rice. There's a shady outdoor seating area, and it's one of the few places in the city centre open93 on Sunday.

Steers BURGERS $
(Map p50; cnr Samora Ave & Ohio St; meals from Tsh2000; ⊙8am-11pm) Burgers and fast food.

MSASANI PENINSULA & OYSTERBAY

Épi d'Or CAFE $$
(☎022-260 1663, 0786-669889; Haile Selassie Rd and cnr Chole & Haile Selassie Rds; light meals from Tsh8000; ⊙8am-7pm Mon-Sat) This French-run bakery-cafe has a mouth-watering selec-

Central Dar es Salaam

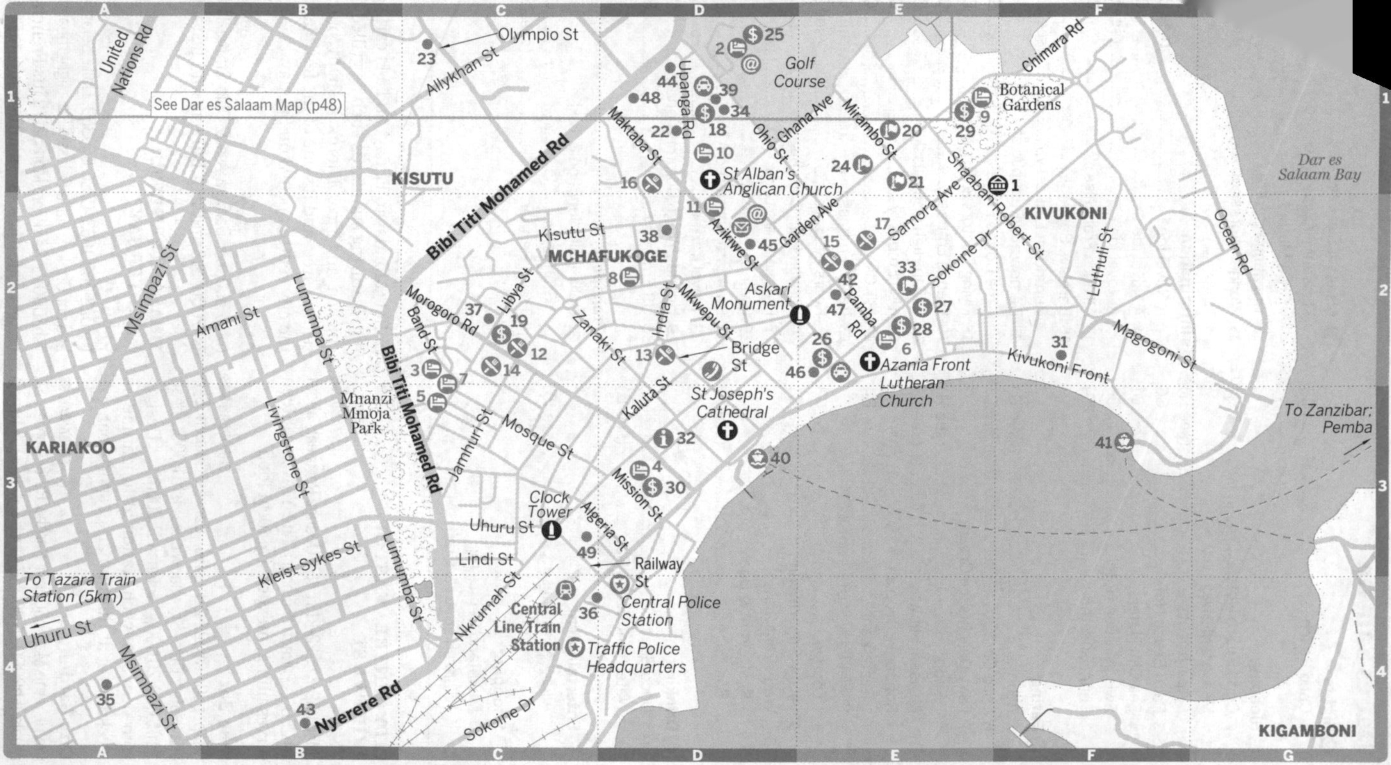

See Dar es Salaam Map (p48)

Central Dar es Salaam

Sights

1 National Museum F1

Sleeping

2 Dar es Salaam Serena Hotel D1
3 Econolodge C2
4 Harbour View Suites D3
5 Jambo Inn C3
6 Luther House Centre Hostel E2
7 Safari Inn C2
8 Sleep Inn D2
9 Southern Sun E1
10 YMCA D1
11 YWCA D2

Eating

12 Akberali Tea Room C2
13 Al Basha D2
14 Chef's Pride C2
15 City Garden E2
Kibo Bar .... (see 2)
16 Patel Brotherhood D1
17 Steers E2
YMCA .... (see 10)

Information

18 Barclays Bank D1
19 Barclay's Bank C2
20 British High Commission E1
21 Canadian High Commission E1
22 Coastal Travels D1
Dutch Embassy .... (see 20)
German Embassy .... (see 20)
Kearsley Travel .... (see 9)
Malawian High Commission .... (see 33)
23 Marine Parks & Reserves Unit C1
24 Mozambique High Commission E1
25 NBC ATM D1
26 NBC Bank E2
Rickshaw Travels .... (see 2)
27 Stanbic Bank E2
28 Standard Chartered Bank E2
29 Standard Chartered Bank E1
30 Standard Chartered Bank D3
31 Surveys & Mapping Division Map Sales Office F2
32 Tanzania Tourist Board Information Centre D3
33 Zambian High Commission E2

Transport

Air Uganda .... (see 4)
34 Avis D1
British Airways .... (see 2)
Coastal Aviation .... (see 22)
35 Dalla-Dallas to Kisarawe A4
36 Dalla-Dallas to Temeke C4
37 Dar Express Booking Office C2
Egyptair .... (see 2)
38 Emirates Airlines D2
39 Ethiopian Airlines D1
40 Ferries to Zanzibar Archipelago D3
41 Ferry to Kigamboni & Southern Beaches F3
42 Fly540.com E2
43 Green Car Rentals B4
Kenya Airways .... (see 44)
44 KLM D1
Linhas Aéreas de Moçambique .... (see 4)
45 New Posta Transport Stand D2
46 Old Posta Transport Stand E2
47 Precision Air E2
48 South African Airways D1
49 Stesheni Transport Stand C3
Swiss International Airlines .... (see 6)

tion of freshly baked breads, pastries, light lunches, paninis, banana crêpes, and tasty Middle Eastern dishes, plus great coffees. It's at the northern end of Chole Rd.

Rohobot Ethiopian Restaurant ETHIOPIAN **$$**
(☎0713-764908, 0774-265126; meals from Tsh8000; ⊙lunch & dinner) This small place in the walled courtyard of a private home rivals Addis in Dar for the city's best Ethiopian cuisine. It's signposted opposite Wonder Workshop.

Sweet Eazy Restaurant & Lounge EUROPEAN **$$$**
(☎0755-754074; www.sweeteazy.com; Oysterbay Shopping Centre; meals Tsh12,000-23,000) A wide menu choice, featuring seafood and meat, and live music Thursday evenings. Seating indoors or on a raised deck. Very popular.

Msasani Slipway EUROPEAN **$$**
(☎022-260 0893; www.slipway.net; off Chole Rd) The eateries here include **Fairy Delights Ice Cream Shop** (cones from Tsh4000), **Azuma** (meals from Tsh15,000; ⊙dinner), with Japanese cuisine and **Waterfront Sunset Restaurant & Beach Bar** (meals from Tsh12,000; ⊙lunch & dinner), with good seafood and meat grills and pizzas, and great sunset views.

DON'T MISS

CULTURAL TOURISM IN DAR ES SALAAM

The highly recommended **Investours** (www.investours.com; adult/student US$50/35) offers regular tours to Mwenge Carvers Market that give visitors the chance to meet locals, get a glimpse into their lives and invest in their business ideas. Following the tour, all fees are pooled and given to an investor of the visitors' choice as an interest-free micro-loan to help them expand their business. It's an excellent way to get to know the 'real' Dar es Salaam while benefiting the local community.

Kigamboni Community Centre (☎0788-482684, 0753-758173; www.kccdar.com; Kigamboni; ⏰Mon-Sat) is an impressive locally initiated and locally run community centre providing education, talent development and vocational training for Kigamboni-area youth. For visitors, it offers reasonably priced walking and cycling tours, 'day-in-the-life' tours, Dar city tours, plus traditional dance, drumming, acrobatic, cooking and Swahili lessons. To get here, take the ferry to Kigamboni, get a *bajaji* (tuk-tuk) and ask them to take you to the centre (most drivers know it); it's opposite Kigamboni police station next to Kakala bar.

The locally run **Afriroots** (☎0732-926350, 0787-459887; www.afriroots.co.tz) offers a range of bicycle and walking tours in and around Dar es Salaam that are a fine way to get acquainted with local life.

Village Supermarket SUPERMARKET **$$**
(Sea Cliff Village, Toure Dr) Pricey but wide selection of Western foods and imported products.

Drinking

MSASANI PENINSULA & OYSTERBAY

Waterfront Beach Bar BAR, RESTAURANT
(Msasani Slipway) Sundowners with prime sunset views.

Coco Beach BEACH
(⏰Sat & Sun) This beach is packed with locals on weekends, and an amenable setting for an inexpensive beer and snacks.

Entertainment

Traditional Music & Dance

Alliance Française DANCE, MUSIC
(www.ambafrance-tz.org; Ali Hassan Mwinyi Rd) Traditional and modern dance, music and more at the monthly Barazani multicultural nights. The schedule is on its website.

Village Museum TRADITIONAL DANCE
(☎022-270 0437; www.museum.or.tz; cnr New Bagamoyo Rd & Makaburi St) *Ngoma* (drumming and dancing) performances from 4pm to 6pm on Saturday and Sunday.

Shopping

Wonder Workshop ARTS & CRAFTS
(Wonder Welders; ☎022-266 6383, 0754-051417; www.wonderwelders.org; Karume Rd, Msasani) At this excellent workshop, disabled artists create world-class jewellery, sculptures, candles, stationery and other crafts from old glass, metal, car parts and other recycled materials. It's off Haile Selassie Rd; turn left at Karume Rd, and follow the signs.

Mwenge Carvers' Market ARTS & CRAFTS
(Sam Nujoma Rd; ⏰8am-6pm) This market, opposite the Village Museum, and just off New Bagamoyo Rd, is packed with vendors, and you can watch carvers at work. Take the Mwenge dalla-dalla from New Posta transport stand to the end of the route, from where it's five minutes on foot down the small street to the left. The best way to visit Mwenge is with Investours.

Tingatinga Centre ARTS & CRAFTS
(www.tingatinga.org; Morogoro Stores, Haile Selassie Rd, Oysterbay; ⏰8.30am-5pm) This centre is one of the best places to buy Tingatinga paintings and watch the artists at work.

Makutano Centre for Tanzanian Art & Craft ARTS & CRAFTS
(Makutano House; ☎0784-782770, 0684-006840; www.makutanotz.com; Katoke Rd; ⏰9.30am-6.30pm Mon-Sat, 10am-4pm Sun) Makutano promotes local arts and crafts, holds regular exhibitions and has crafts for sale.

Msasani Slipway Weekend Craft Market ARTS & CRAFTS
(Msasani Slipway, Msasani Peninsula; ⏰Sat & Sun) Prices are slightly higher here than else-

where in town, but quality is g... atmosphere calm.

A Novel Idea BOOKS
Msasani Slipway (☎022-260 1088; Msasani Slipway, Msasani Peninsula); Shoppers' Plaza (Old Bagamoyo Rd); Steers (Map p50; cnr Ohio St & Samora Ave); Oysterbay Shops (Toure Dr) Has a wide selection of books.

Information

Dangers & Annoyances

Dar es Salaam is safer than many other cities in the region, notably Nairobi, though it has its share of muggings and thefts, so take the usual precautions. Watch out for pickpocketing, especially at crowded markets and bus and train stations, and for bag snatching via vehicle windows. Stay aware of your surroundings, minimise carrying conspicuous bags or cameras and leave your valuables in a reliable hotel safe. At night, always take a taxi rather than taking a dalla-dalla or walking, and avoid walking alone on the path paralleling Ocean Rd, on Coco Beach (which is only safe on weekend afternoons, when it's crowded), and at night along Chole Rd. With taxis, use only those from reliable hotels or established taxi stands. Avoid hailing taxis cruising the streets, and never get in a taxi that has a 'friend' of the driver or anyone else already in it.

Note that most shops in the city centre are closed on Sundays.

Emergency

Central police station (Map p50; ☎022-211 5507; Sokoine Dr) Near the Central Line Train Station.

Flying Doctors & Amref (☎in Nairobi emergency 254-20-315454/5, 254-20-600090; www.amref.org; Ali Hassan Mwinyi Rd) For emergency evacuations; see p643 for details.

IST Clinic (☎022-260 1307/8, 24hr emergency 0754-783393; www.istclinic.com; Ruvu Rd; ⏲8am-6pm Mon-Fri, to noon Sat) A Western-run fully equipped clinic, with a doctor on call 24 hours. From Chole Rd, look for the small Ruvu Rd signpost just south of and diagonally opposite the Slipway turn-off.

Immigration Office

Ministry of Home Affairs (Wizara ya mambo ya ndani; ☎022-285 0575/6; www.moha.go.tz; Uhamiaji House, Loliondo St; hvisa applications 8am-noon Mon-Fri, visa collections until 2pm) In Kurasini area, just off Kilwa Rd, & about 3.5km from the city centre.

Internet Access

Post Office Internet Café (Map p50; Main Post Office, Maktaba St; per hr Tsh1500; ⏲8am-7pm Mon-Fri, 9am-3pm Sat)

Tsh... Sat, 9am-1pm Su...

Media

Dar Tourism (www.dartourism.com)

Dar es Salaam Guide Free monthly with restaurant and club listings, embassy listings, airline schedules etc; available from hotels, travel agencies and the tourist information centre.

Medical Services

IST Clinic (☎022-260 1307/8, 0784-783393, 24hr emergency 0754-783393; istclinic@istclinic.com; Ruvu Rd; ⏲8am-6pm Mon-Fri, to noon Sat) See listing under Emergency.

Premier Care Clinic (☎022-266 8385, 022-266 8320; www.premiercareclinic.com; New Bagamoyo Rd) Western standards and facilities; next to Big Bite restaurant.

Money

Forex bureaus give faster service and marginally better exchange rates. There are many scattered around the city centre on or near Samora Ave (all open standard business hours), or try the following:

Forex Bureau (International Arrivals Area, Julius Nyercre International Airport; ⏲for all flights) Straight ahead when exiting customs; cash only.

Galaxy Forex Bureau (International Arrivals Area, Julius Nyerere International Airport; ⏲6am-11pm) Cash and sometimes travellers cheques; to the right as you exit customs.

Dar es Salaam Serena Forex Bureau (Map p50; Dar es Salaam Serena Hotel, Ohio St; ⏲8am-8pm Mon-Sat, 10am-1pm Sun & public holidays) Cash and travellers cheques (receipts required).

Electron Bureau de Change (Msasani Slipway; ⌚9.30am-6.30pm Mon-Sat, 10am-2pm Sun) Changes cash and travellers cheques (receipt required).

There are ATMs all over the city, including the following:

Barclays Bank Dar es Salaam Serena Hotel (Map p50; opposite Dar es Salaam Serena Hotel, Ohio St); Msasani Slipway (Msasani Slipway Apartments); Kisutu (Map p50; cnr Morogoro & Libya Sts)

National Bank of Commerce Azikiwe St (Map p50; cnr Azikiwe St & Sokoine Dr); Dar es Salaam Serena Hotel (Map p50; in lobby of Dar es Salaam Serena Hotel, Ohio St)

Stanbic Bank (Map p50; Sukari House, cnr Ohio St & Sokoine Dr)

Standard Chartered Southern Sun (Map p50; Garden Ave); JM Mall (Map p50; Samora Ave); NIC Life House (Map p50; cnr Ohio St & Sokoine Dr)

Post

Main post office (Map p50; Maktaba St; ⌚8am-4.30pm Mon-Fri, 9am-noon Sat)

Telephone

The **Telecom Office** (Map p50; cnr Bridge St & Samora Ave; ⌚7.30am-6pm Mon-Fri, 9am-3pm Sat) behind the Extelecoms House sells top-up cards for domestic and international calls from any landline phone.

Tourist Information

Tanzania Tourist Board Information Centre (Map p50; ☎022-212 0373, 022-213 1555; www.tanzaniatouristboard.com; Samora Ave; ⌚8am-4pm Mon-Fri, 8.30am-12.30pm Sat) Just west of Zanaki St, with free tourist maps and brochures and city information.

Travel Agencies

For safari and tour operators, see p54. For flight and hotel bookings, try the following:

Coastal Travels (Map p50; ☎022-211 7959/60; www.coastal.cc; Upanga Rd) Especially good for travel to Zanzibar, and for flights linking northern and southern safari circuit destinations. Also offers reasonably priced city tours, day trips to Zanzibar and Mikumi National Park excursions.

Kearsley Travel (www.kearsleys.com) Southern Sun (Map p50; ☎022-213 1652/3; Garden Ave); Sea Cliff Village (☎022-260 0467; Toure Dr)

ℹ Getting There & Away

Air

Julius Nyerere International Airport has two terminals. Most regularly scheduled domestic flights and all international flights depart from Terminal Two (the 'new' terminal, and the first one you reach coming from town), while many flights on small planes and most charters depart from Terminal One (the 'old' terminal), about 700m further down the road.

SAFARI OPERATORS

The following do southern-circuit safari bookings, and combination itineraries involving Mikumi, Ruaha and Katavi National Parks, Selous Game Reserve, and Zanzibar and Mafia islands.

Afriroots (☎0732-926350; www.afriroots.co.tz; budget) Backpacker-oriented biking, hiking and cultural tours.

Authentic Tanzania (☎0786-019965, 0784-972571; www.authentictanzania.com; midrange)

Coastal Travels (☎022-211 7959, 022-211 7960; safari@coastal.cc; Upanga Rd; midrange) A reliable, long-established outfit with its own fleet of planes, and safari camps and lodges in Ruaha, the Selous and on Mafia island; offers frequent 'last-minute' flight-and-accommodation deals.

Foxes African Safaris (☎in UK 44-01452-862288, in Tanzania 0784-237422; www.tanzaniasafaris.info; midrange to top end) Runs lodges and camps in Mikumi, Ruaha and Katavi National Parks, on the coast near Bagamoyo, in the Southern Highlands and in Selous Game Reserve; organises combination itineraries using plane and road.

Hippotours & Safaris (☎0754-267706; www.hippotours.com; midrange to top end)

Tent with a View (☎022-211 0507, 0713-323318; www.saadani.com; upper midrange) Runs lodges in Selous Game Reserve, Saadani National Park and Zanzibar; midrange and upmarket combination itineraries in these and other areas.

Wild Things Safaris (☎0773-503502; www.wildthingsafaris.com; budget and midrange)

For flights to Zanzibar, try Coastal Aviation, ZanAir and Tropical Air.

Air India (☎022-215 2642; cnr Ali Hassan Mwinyi & Bibi Titi Mohamed Rds)

Air Uganda (Map p50; ☎022-213 3322, 0756-886323; www.airuganda.com; 1st fl, JM Mall, Samora Ave)

British Airways (Map p50; ☎022-211 3820, 022-284 4082; Dar es Salaam Serena Hotel, Ohio St)

Coastal Aviation (Map p50; ☎022-211 7959/60, 022-284 3293; aviation@coastal.cc; Upanga Rd) Also at Terminal One, Julius Nyerere International Airport.

Egyptair (Map p50; ☎022-213 6665/3, 0717-737800; Ohio St) At Dar es Salaam Serena Hotel.

Emirates Airlines (Map p50; ☎022-211 6100; Haidery Plaza, cnr Kisutu & India Sts)

Ethiopian Airlines (Map p50; ☎022-211 7063; Ohio St) Opposite Dar es Salaam Serena Hotel.

Fly540 (Map p50; ☎022-212 5912/3, 0752-540540, 0765-540540; www.fly540.com; Samora Ave) Near the corner with Ohio St.

Kenya Airways (Map p50; ☎022-211 9376/7; Upanga Rd) Located with KLM.

KLM (Map p50; ☎022-213 9790/1; Upanga Rd)

Linhas Aéreas de Moçambique (Map p50; ☎022-213 4600; 1st fl, JM Mall, Samora Ave) At Fast-Track Travel (www.fasttracktanzania.com).

Precision Air (Map p50; ☎022-213 0800, 022-212 1718, 022-284 3547, 0784-402002, 0787-888407; cnr Samora Ave & Pamba Rd) Also at Terminal Two, Julius Nyerere International Airport.

South African Airways (SAA; Map p50; ☎022-211 7044; Raha Towers, cnr Bibi Titi Mohamed & Ali Hassan Mwinyi Rds)

Swiss International Airlines (Map p50; ☎022-211 8870; Luther House Centre Hostel, Sokoine Dr)

Tropical Air (☎022-284 2333, 0773-511679; Terminal One, Julius Nyerere International Airport)

ZanAir (☎022-284 3297, 024-223 3670; Terminal One, Julius Nyerere International Airport)

Boat

For ferry connections to Pemba, see p212.

TO/FROM ZANZIBAR

There are 'fast' ferry trips (on *Kilimanjaro I and II* and *Sea Bus*) daily between Dar es Salaam and Zanzibar, departing at 7am, 9.30am, 12,30pm and 3.45pm. All take about two hours and cost US$35/40 regular/VIP (VIP gets you a seat in the air con hold). There are also several slow ferries. The main one is *Flying Horse*, which departs daily at 12.30pm (one way US$25) and takes almost four hours.

Ferry departures from Zanzibar are daily at 7am, 9.30am, 12.30pm, 3.30pm (all 'fast' ferries) and 10pm (*Flying Horse*, arriving before dawn the next day).

The only place at the Dar es Salaam ferry port to buy legitimate tickets is the tall blue-glass building at the southern end of the ferry terminal area on Kivukoni Front opposite St Joseph's Cathedral. The building is marked 'Azam Marine – Coastal Fast Ferries', and has official ticket offices and a large waiting area inside. Avoid the smaller offices just to the north of this building. Don't fall for touts at the harbour trying to collect extra fees for 'doctors' certificates', departure taxes and the like. The only fee is the ticket price (which includes the US$5 port tax). Also, avoid touts who want to take you into town to buy 'cheaper' ferry tickets, or who offer to purchase ferry tickets for you at less expensive resident rates.

Depending on the season, the ferry crossing can be choppy, and most lines pass out sea sickness bags at the start of each trip. If you're travelling with the night ferry, it may be worth paying extra for the VIP section to avoid being awash in the seasickness of your fellow passengers on the deck, although the fresh air is arguably better than the air-con of VIP.

Bus

Except as noted, all buses depart from and arrive at the main bus station at Ubungo, 8km west of the city centre on Morogoro Rd. It's a sprawling place with the usual assortment of bus station hustle and touts. Keep an eye on your luggage and your wallet and try to avoid arriving at night. Ask your taxi driver to take you directly to the ticket office window for the line you want to travel with. Avoid dealing with the touts. Dalla-dallas to Ubungo (Tsh300) leave from New Posta and Old Posta transport stands, as well as from various other spots in town. Taxis from the city centre cost from Tsh10,000. If you're coming into Dar es Salaam on Dar Express, you can usually stay on the bus past Ubungo until the bus line's town office, which is worth doing as it will be less chaotic and you'll have a cheaper taxi fare to your hotel. This doesn't work out leaving the city, since departures are directly from Ubungo. Tickets can be booked at Ubungo, and, for Dar Express, at its office on Libya St.

Dar Express (Map p50; Libya St, Kisutu) Daily buses to Arusha (Tsh25,000 to 30,000) departing every 30 to 60 minutes from 6am to 10am from Ubungo bus station.

Following are sample prices for bus travel from Dar es Salaam. All routes are serviced at least once daily.

Buses to Kilwa Masoko and Mtwara depart from south of the city. See the Southeastern Tanzania chapter for details.

For information about connections between Dar es Salaam and Kenya, Uganda, Zambia and Malawi, see p651.

DESTINATION	PRICE (TSH)
Arusha	Tsh25,000-30,000
Dodoma	Tsh15,000-20,000
Iringa	Tsh15,000-20,000
Kampala	Tsh95,000
Mbeya	Tsh30,000-35,000
Mwanza	Tsh40,000
Nairobi	Tsh45,000-50,000
Songea	Tsh 40,000

Car & Motorcycle

See p213 for information on car rental.

Train

For information about Tazara trains between Dar es Salaam, Mbeya and Kapiri Mposhi (Zambia), see p214. The **Tazara train station** (off Map p50; ☎022-286 5187, 0713-225292; www.tazara.co.tz; cnr Nyerere & Nelson Mandela Rds; ⏲ticket office 7.30am-12.30pm & 2-4.30pm Mon-Fri, 9am-12.30pm Sat, in theory) is about 6km southwest of the city centre (Tsh8000 to 10,000 in a taxi). Dalla-dallas to the train station leave from either New or Old Posta transport stands, and are marked Vigunguti, U/Ndege or Buguruni.

For more on Central Line trains between Dar es Salaam and Kigoma, see p214. **Tanzanian Railways Corporation (Central Line) train station** (Map p50; ☎022-211 7833; www.trctz.com; cnr Railway St & Sokoine Dr) is in the city centre just southwest of the ferry terminal.

ℹ Getting Around

To/From the Airport

Julius Nyerere International Airport is 12km from the city centre. Dalla-dallas (marked U/Ndege) go to the airport from New Posta transport stand. In heavy traffic the trip can easily take over an hour, and there's no room for luggage. Taxis to central Dar es Salaam cost Tsh15,000 to Tsh20,000 (Tsh25,000 to Tsh30,000 to Msasani Peninsula).

Car & Motorcycle

Most rental agencies offer self-drive options in town; none offer unlimited kilometres. Rental agencies include the following:

Avis (☎022-211 5381, 022-212 1061/2; www.avis.com) Airport (Julius Nyerere International Airport); Amani Towers (Map p50; Ohio St, opposite Dar es Salaam Serena Hotel)

Green Car Rentals (Map p50; ☎022-218 3354, 0713-227788; www.greencarstz.com; Nyerere Rd) Next to Dar es Salaam Glassworks.

Travel Partner (☎022-260 0573; www.travelpartner.co.tz; Chole Rd) Near the Slipway turn-off.

Public Transport

Dalla-dallas (minibuses) go almost everywhere in the city for Tsh200 to Tsh500. First and last stops are shown in the front window, but routes vary, so confirm that the driver is going to your destination. Centre city terminals include the following:

New Posta transport stand (Map p50; Maktaba St) At the main post office.

Old Posta transport stand (Map p50; Sokoine Dr) Down from the Azania Front Lutheran Church.

Stesheni transport stand (Map p50; Algeria St) Off Samora Ave near the Central Line Train Station; dalla-dallas to Temeke bus stand also leave from here; ask for 'Temeke *mwisho*'.

Taxi

Taxis don't have meters. Short rides within the city centre cost from Tsh3000. Fares from the city centre to Msasani Peninsula start at Tsh10,000.

Taxi stands include those opposite the Dar es Salaam Serena Hotel (Map p50), on the corner of Azikiwe St and Sokoine Dr (Map p50) and on the Msasani Peninsula on the corner of Msasani and Haile Selassie Rds.

For a reliable taxi driver, recommended also for airport pick-ups, contact **Jumanne Mastoka** (☎0784-339735; mjumanne@yahoo.com). Never get into a taxi that has others in it, and always use taxis affiliated with hotels, or operating from a fixed stand and known by the other drivers at the stand.

AROUND DAR ES SALAAM

Pugu Hills

Pugu Hills, which begins about 15km southwest of Dar es Salaam and extends past Kisarawe, is lightly wooded, with two small forest reserves, and offers an escape from the urban scene.

Pugu Hills Nature Centre (☎0754-565498, 0754-394875; www.pugukwakiki.com; admission Tsh5000, camping per person with own/rented tent US$10/15, d bandas US$80-100;) is a great, tranquil place on a hillside backing onto the Pugu Forest Reserve with four spacious, en suite bungalows, an area to pitch your tent and a restaurant. Advance bookings are essential for all visits, day or overnight.

Getting There & Away

Dalla-dallas to Kisarawe (marked either Kisarawe or Chanika) leave from New Posta dalla-dalla stand, and from Libya St in Kariakoo. You can also get them on Nyerere Rd at the airport turn-off. For Pugu Hills Nature Centre, ask the driver to drop you at the Pugu Kajiungeni petrol station (about 7km before Kisarawe, and about 12km past the airport). Continue straight along the Kisarawe road for about 200m, to the end of a tiny group of shops on your left, where there's a dirt path leading up to Pugu Hills (about 15 minutes further on foot); ask for Bwana Kiki's place.

Offshore Islands

The uninhabited islands of Bongoyo, Mbudya, Pangavini and Fungu Yasini, just off the coastline north of Dar es Salaam, were gazetted in 1975 as part of the Dar es Salaam Marine Reserve system.

Bongoyo, about 7km north of Dar es Salaam, is the most popular of the islands, with a small stretch of beach offering snorkelling and swimming (which is not tide dependent, as on the mainland) and some short walking trails. Basic grilled fish meals and sodas are available, and snorkelling equipment can be rented.

A boat goes to and from the island several times daily (except during the long rains) from **Msasani Slipway** (☎022-260 0893; www.slipway.net; per person return Tsh12,000, plus US$10 marine reserve entry fee; minimum four people). The departure and ticketing point is the Waterfront Beach Bar.

Northern Beaches

The jetty-studded coastline about 25km north of Dar es Salaam and east of New Bagamoyo Rd lacks Zanzibar's tropical ambience and beauty but is a popu. getaway.

Sights & Activities

Diving & Snorkelling
(☎0754-783241; www.seabreezemarine.org, ing around the coral gardens near Bon and Mbudya islands, and diving certifica courses (PADI), can be arranged year-rou at the long-standing Sea Breeze Marine ne to White Sands Hotel.

Kunduchi Wet 'n' Wild WATER PARK
(☎022-265 0050, 022-265 0545; http://wetnwild.kunduchi.com; adult/child Tsh7000/5000; ⏲9am-6pm) Next to Kunduchi Beach Hotel & Resort.

Water World WATER PARK
(☎022-264 7627, 022-264 7620; adult/child Tsh5000/4000; ⏲10am-5.30pm Tue-Sun, women only Wed) Similar to Kunduchi Wet 'n' Wild, but somewhat smaller and quieter. Next to White Sands Hotel.

Sleeping & Eating

All hotels charge an entry fee for day visitors on weekends and holidays, averaging Tsh3000 to Tsh5000 per person.

Kunduchi Beach Hotel & Resort HOTEL $$$
(☎022-265 0544/8, 0688-915345; www.kunduchi.com; s/d from US$144/164;) This former government hotel is set on the best stretch of beach with a long row of attractive beach-facing rooms, expansive green grounds and a restaurant.

White Sands Hotel HOTEL $$$
(☎022-264 7620/1; www.hotelwhitesands.com; s/d US$150/175, deluxe apt from US$160;) This large, somewhat hectic and popular place is on the beach, with rooms in two-storey rondavels, plus self-catering apartments and a restaurant with weekend buffets (per person about Tsh25,000).

Silver Sands Beach Hotel HOTEL $
(☎022-265 0428, 0713-297031; camping Tsh5000, r Tsh50,000;) This dilapidated place is set on a quiet stretch of beach and is a respectable low-budget choice. The camping facilities have hot water (usually), and there are basic but adequate rooms.

Getting There & Away

White Sands Hotel is reached via a signposted turn-off from New Bagamoyo Rd. About 3km further north along New Bagamoyo Rd is the

…rn-off for Kunduchi Beach and … Beach hotels.

… transport, take a dalla-dalla from … transport stand in Dar es Salaam to … Tsh300). Once at Mwenge, take a 'Teg…a-dalla to Africana Junction (Tsh200), …m there a motorcycle (Tsh500), *bajaji* …000) or taxi (Tsh2000) the remaining …ple of kilometres to the hotels. It's also pos…le to get a direct dalla-dalla from Kariakoo to …egeta. For Kunduchi Beach and Silver Sands, once at Mwenge, take a 'Bahari Beach' dalla-dalla to 'Njia Panda ya Silver Sands'. From here, it's Tsh500 on a motorcycle or *bajaji* the remaining distance. Don't walk, as there have been muggings along this stretch of road.

Taxis from Dar es Salaam cost about Tsh40,000 one way. All hotels arrange airport pick-ups.

Driving, the fastest route is along Old Bagamoyo Rd via Kawe.

Southern Beaches

The long, white-sand beach ('South Beach') south of Kigamboni, around Mjimwema village, is the closest spot to Dar es Salaam for camping and chilling.

Sleeping & Eating

Mikadi Beach BACKPACKERS **$**
(0754-370269; www.mikadibeach.com; camping Tsh8000, d Tsh60,000, without bathroom Tsh40,000;) This chilled place has a backpacker-friendly vibe, a convivial bar and meals. Accommodation is in no-frills twin-bedded beach *bandas*, and there are warm (salt-water) showers.

Sunrise Beach Resort HOTEL **$$**
(022-282 0222, 0755-400900; www.sunrisebeachresort.co.tz; camping Tsh8000, tw in tent Tsh25,000, standard/sea-view/executive d Tsh45,000/90,000/150,000) Sunrise has straightforward, closely-spaced rooms just in from the sand plus air-con 'executive' rooms in two-storey brick rondavels to the back of the property. There's also a row of canvas tents on the sand.

Kipepeo Beach & Village BUNGALOW **$$**
(0754-276178; www.kipepeovillage.com; camping US$5, s/d beach bungalow US$15/25, s/d/tr cottage US$60/80/110) Kipepeo, 8km south of the ferry dock, has raised cottages with balconies about 300m back from the beach. Closer to the water, but enclosed behind a fence and a bit of a walk to the nearest bathroom, are makeshift thatched bungalows without windows, and a camping area. Breakfast is included only in cottage rates.

Getting There & Away

The Kigamboni (Magogoni) ferry (per person/vehicle Tsh100/1000, five minutes) runs throughout the day between the eastern end of Kivukoni Front in Dar es Salaam and Kigamboni village. Once on the other side, catch a dalla-dalla heading south and ask the driver to drop you off at Mjimwema village (Tsh300) from where it's a 1km walk to Sunrise or Kipepeo. For Mikadi Beach, they can drop you directly at the entrance. *Bajajis* from Kigamboni charge about Tsh3500 to Kipepeo and Sunrise, less to Mikadi Beach.

ZANZIBAR ARCHIPELAGO

Step off the boat or plane onto the Zanzibar Archipelago, and you'll be transported through the miles and the centuries – to ancient Persia, to Oman's caliphs and sultans, to India, with its heavily laden scents.

On Zanzibar, Stone Town's alleyways wind past Arabic-style houses with brass-studded wooden doors. Along the coast, local life moves to the rhythm of the tides and the winds of the monsoon.

Across the deep waters of the Pemba channel lies hilly, verdant Pemba, the archipelago's seldom visited 'other' island. Coastal mangrove swamps open onto stunning white-sand coves, and neat farm plots cover the hillsides.

Yet, there is another side to life on the archipelago. Overdevelopment is suffocating the coast and mass tourism makes the archipelago's allure ever more elusive. While the magic remains, you'll have to work much harder to find it.

Zanzibar

POP 990,000

The winding alleyways are still there, and the carved doors. The east coast beaches are as lovely as ever. But, Zanzibar has changed. It's due in part to the masses of visitors who descend on the island during the high season. In part, it's due to the seemingly endless proliferation of new hotels, most built with apparently no thought for the surrounding community and ecosystems. Whatever the reason, the sense of stepping back in time, the island's once-legendary ability to transport the visitor through centuries and cultures, is lesssened. Is the magic completely gone? Probably not, although it's certainly more difficult to find.

Zanzibar Town, on the western side of the island, is the heart of the archipelago, and the first stop for most travellers. The best-known section by far is the old Stone Town *(Mji Mkongwe)*, surrounded on three sides by the sea and bordered to the east by Creek Rd.

Sights

It's easy to spend days wandering around and getting lost in Stone Town's jumble of alleyways although you can't get lost for long because, sooner or later, you'll end up on either the seafront or Creek Rd.

While the best part of Stone Town is simply letting it unfold before you, it's worth putting in an effort to see some of its major features.

Beit el-Ajaib (House of Wonders) MUSEUM
(Map p62; Mizingani Rd; adult/child US$4/1; 9am-6pm) One of the most prominent buildings in the old Stone Town, this elegant edifice is now home to the **Zanzibar National Museum of History & Culture**. Inside it houses exhibits on the dhow culture of the Indian Ocean (ground floor) and on Swahili civilisation and 19th-century Zanzibar (1st floor). Just inside the entrance is a life-size *mtepe*, a traditional Swahili sailing vessel made without nails, the planks held together with only coconut fibres and wooden pegs.

Beit el-Sahel (Palace Museum) MUSEUM
(Map p62; Mizingani Rd, adult/child US$4/1; 9am-6pm) Just north of the Beit el-Ajaib is this palace, which served as the sultan's residence until 1964, when the dynasty was overthrown. Now it is a museum devoted to the era of the Zanzibar sultanate.

Outside is the Makusurani graveyard, where some of the sultans are buried.

Old Fort HISTORIC BUILDING
(Map p62) Just south of the Beit el-Ajaib is the Old Fort, a massive, bastioned structure originally built around 1700 on the site of a Portuguese chapel by Omani Arabs as a defence against the Portuguese. Now it houses the Zanzibar Cultural Centre and the offices of the Zanzibar International Film Festival (ZIFF). Inside, an open-air theatre hosts music and dance performances. There's also a helpful tourist information desk that arranges tours and has schedules for performances, and a restaurant.

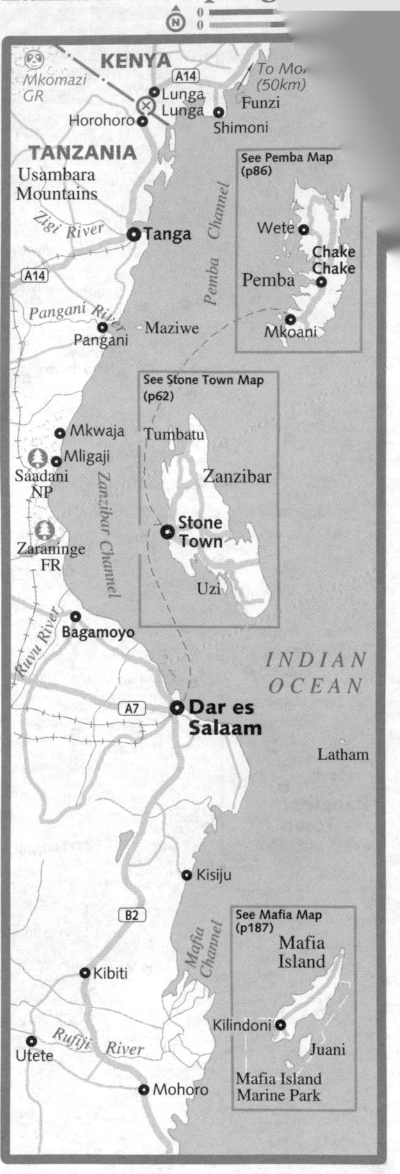

Anglican Cathedral & Old Slave Market HISTORIC BUILDING
(Map p62; admission Tsh5000; 8am-6pm Mon-Sat, noon-6pm Sun) Constructed in the 1870s by the Universities' Mission to Central Africa (UMCA), this was the first Anglican

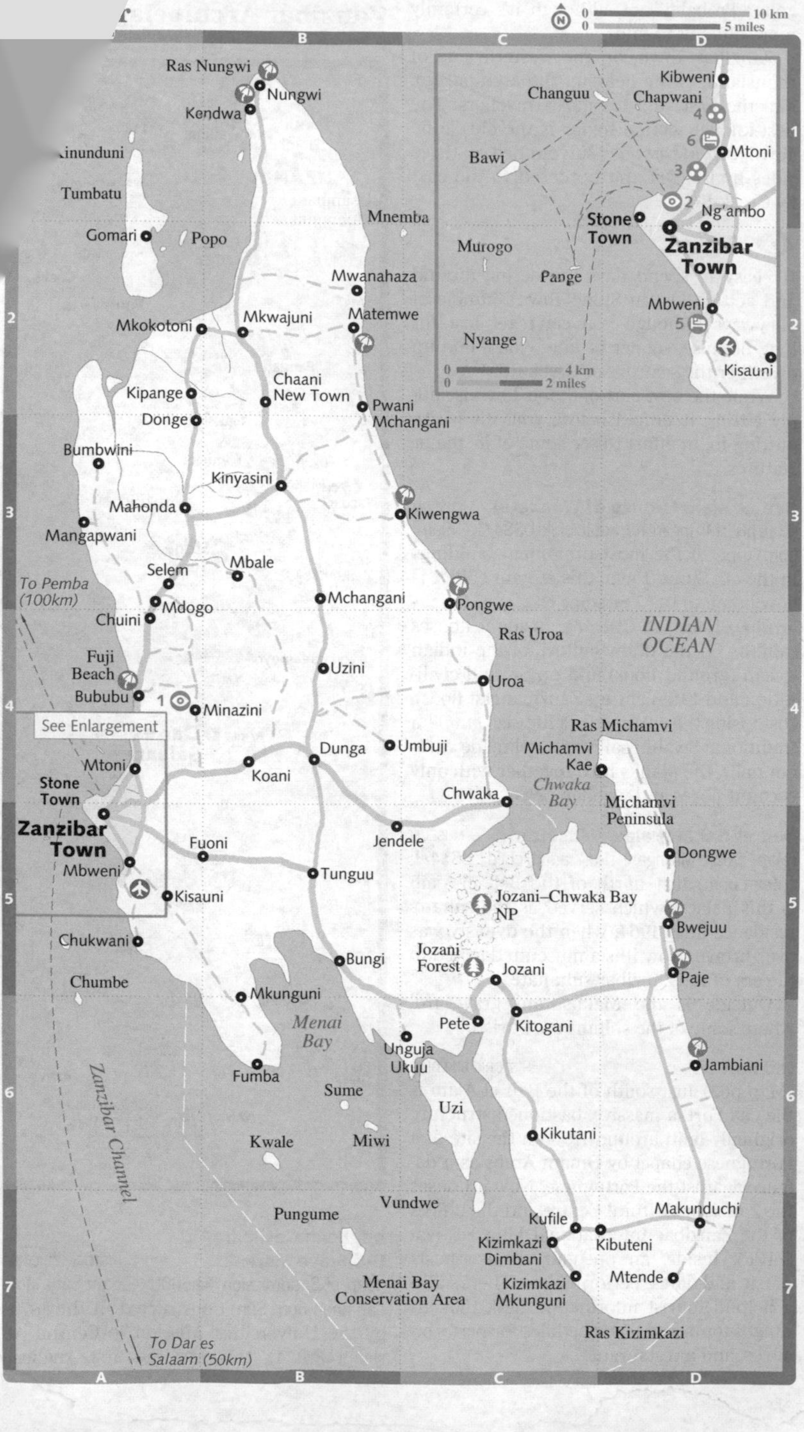

10 km
5 miles

Ras Nungwi
Nungwi
Kendwa
Kinunduni
Tumbatu
Gomari
Popo
Mnemba
Mwanahaza
Mkwajuni
Matemwe
Mkokotoni
Chaani New Town
Kipange
Donge
Pwani Mchangani
Bumbwini
Kinyasini
Mahonda
Kiwengwa
Mangapwani
Selem
Mbale
To Pemba (100km)
Mdogo
Chuini
Mchangani
Pongwe
Ras Uroa
INDIAN OCEAN
Fuji Beach
Bububu
Uzini
Uroa
1
Minazini
See Enlargement
Ras Michamvi
Umbuji
Dunga
Michamvi Kae
Mtoni
Koani
Stone Town
Chwaka
Chwaka Bay
Michamvi Peninsula
Zanzibar Town
Jendele
Fuoni
Mbweni
Dongwe
Tunguu
Kisauni
Jozani–Chwaka Bay NP
Bwejuu
Chukwani
Jozani Forest
Bungi
Jozani
Paje
Chumbe
Mkunguni
Menai Bay
Pete
Kitogani
Unguja Ukuu
Jambiani
Fumba
Zanzibar Channel
Sume
Uzi
Kwale
Miwi
Kikutani
Pungume
Vundwe
Makunduchi
Kufile
Kizimkazi Dimbani
Kibuteni
Menai Bay Conservation Area
Kizimkazi Mkunguni
Mtende
Ras Kizimkazi
To Dar es Salaam (50km)

Kibweni
Changuu
Chapwani
4
6
Mtoni
Bawi
3
2
Ng'ambo
Stone Town
Zanzibar Town
Murogo
Pange
Mbweni
5
Nyange
Kisauni
4 km
2 miles

Zanzibar

Sights

1 Kidichi Persian Baths A4
2 Livingstone House D1
3 Maruhubi Palace D1
Mbweni .... (see 5)
4 Mtoni Palace D1

Sleeping

5 Mbweni Ruins Hotel D2
6 Mtoni Marine Centre D1

Eating

Mcheza Bar .... (see 6)
Mtoni Marine Centre .... (see 6)

Drinking

Mcheza Bar .... (see 6)

cathedral in East Africa. It was built on the site of the old slave market alongside Creek Rd. Although nothing remains of the slave market today, other than some holding cells under St Monica's Hostel next door, the site is a sobering reminder of the not-so-distant past. Services are still held at the cathedral on Sunday mornings; the entrance is next to St Monica's Hostel.

St Joseph's Cathedral CHURCH
(Map p62; Cathedral St) One of the first sights travellers see when arriving at Zanzibar by ferry are the spires of the Roman Catholic cathedral. Despite this, the church is deceptively difficult to find in the narrow confines of the adjacent streets. (The easiest route: follow Kenyatta Rd to Gizenga St, then take the first right to the back gate of the church, which is usually open even when the front entrance is closed to the public.) There's a brief summary of the mission's history just inside the entrance. The church is still in use.

Hamamni Persian Baths HISTORIC BUILDING
(Map p62; Hamamni St; admission Tsh5000) Built by Sultan Barghash in the late 19th century, these were the first public baths on Zanzibar. Although there's no longer water inside, they're still worth a visit, and it doesn't take much imagination to envision them in bygone days.

Livingstone House HISTORIC BUILDING
(Map p60) Located about 2km north of town along the Bububu road, Livingstone House was built around 1860 and used as a base by many of the European missionaries and explorers before they started ... to the mainland. Today it's mo... bered as the place where David ... stayed before setting off on his la... tion. You can walk from town, or t... dalla-dalla.

Old Dispensary HISTORIC B...
(Map p62; Mizingani Rd) Located near the ... the Old Dispensary was built at the tur... the 20th century by a wealthy Indian me... chant, and later renovated by the Aga Kha... Charitable Trust. It currently houses shops and offices.

Victoria Hall & Gardens HISTORIC BUILDING
(Map p62; Kaunda Rd) Diagonally opposite Mnazi Mmoja hospital, this imposing building housed the legislative council during the British era. It's not open to the public, but you can walk in the small surrounding gardens. Opposite is the **State House** (Map p62), also closed to the public.

Mbweni HISTORIC SITE
(Map p60) About 5km south of Zanzibar Town, Mbweni was the site of a 19th-century UMCA mission station that was used as a settlement for freed slaves. In addition to the small and still functioning St John's Anglican church, dating to the 1880s, you can see the ruins of the UMCA's St Mary's School for Girls, set amid lush gardens on the grounds of Mbweni Ruins Hotel (p70).

Maruhubi Palace RUINS
(Map p60) This once-imposing palace, 4km north of Zanzibar Town, was built by Sultan Barghash in 1882 to house his large harem. In 1899 it was almost totally destroyed by fire, although the remaining ruins hint at its previous scale. The ruins are just west of the Bububu road and signposted.

Mtoni Palace RUINS
(Map p60) The ruins of Mtoni palace, built by Sultan Seyyid Said as his residence in the early 19th century, are located just northeast of Maruhubi Palace. Today nothing remains of Mtoni's grandeur other than a few walls, although you can get an idea of how it must have once looked by reading Emily Said-Reute's *Memoirs of an Arabian Princess*. To get here, continue north on the main road past the Maruhubi Palace turn-off for about 2km, from where the ruins are signposted to the west.

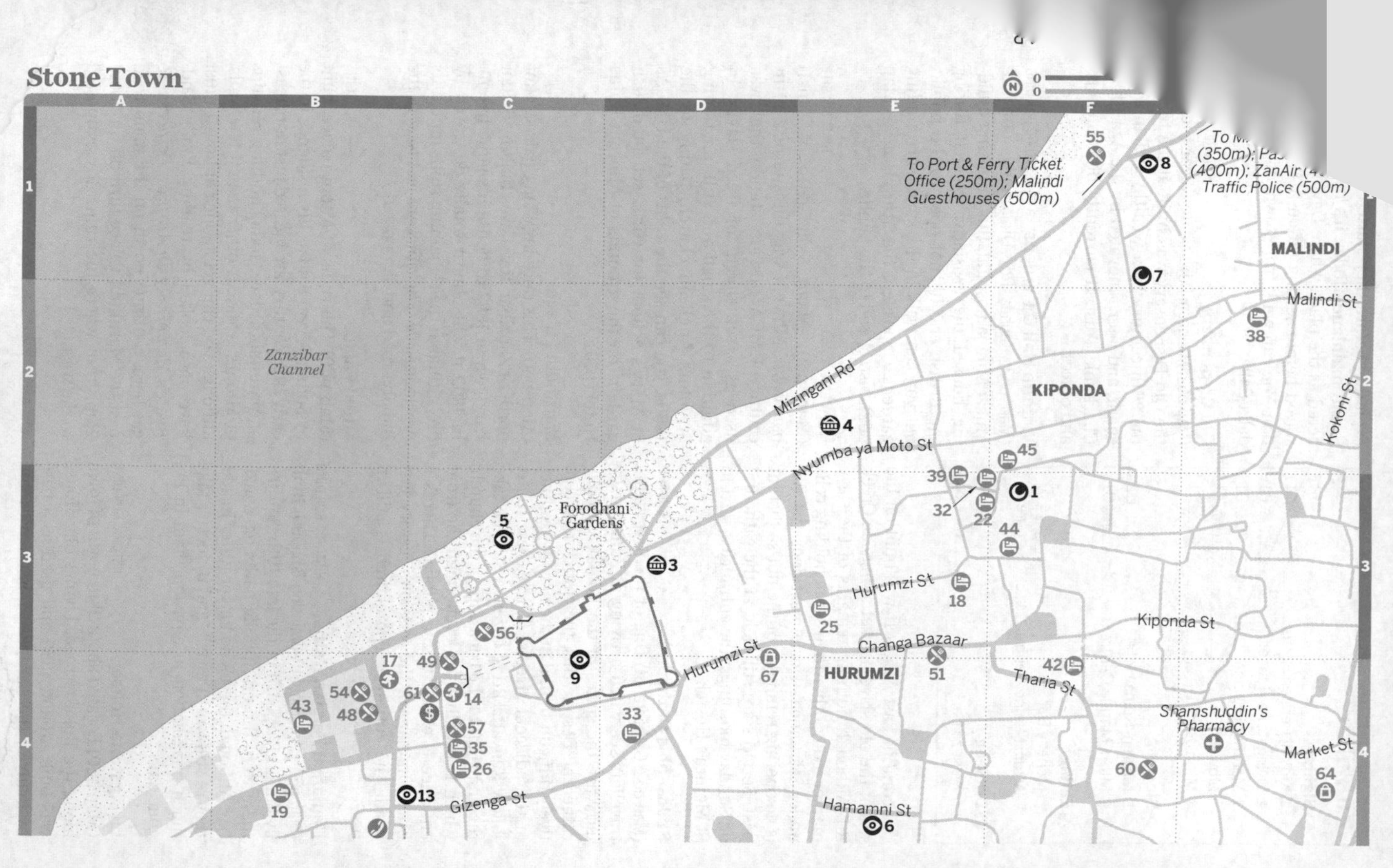
Stone Town
Zanzibar Channel
To Port & Ferry Ticket Office (250m); Malindi Guesthouses (500m)
Traffic Police (500m)
MALINDI
Malindi St
KIPONDA
Kokoni St
Mizingani Rd
Nyumba ya Moto St
Forodhani Gardens
Hurumzi St
Kiponda St
Changa Bazaar
HURUMZI
Tharia St
Shamshuddin's Pharmacy
Market St
Gizenga St
Hamamni St

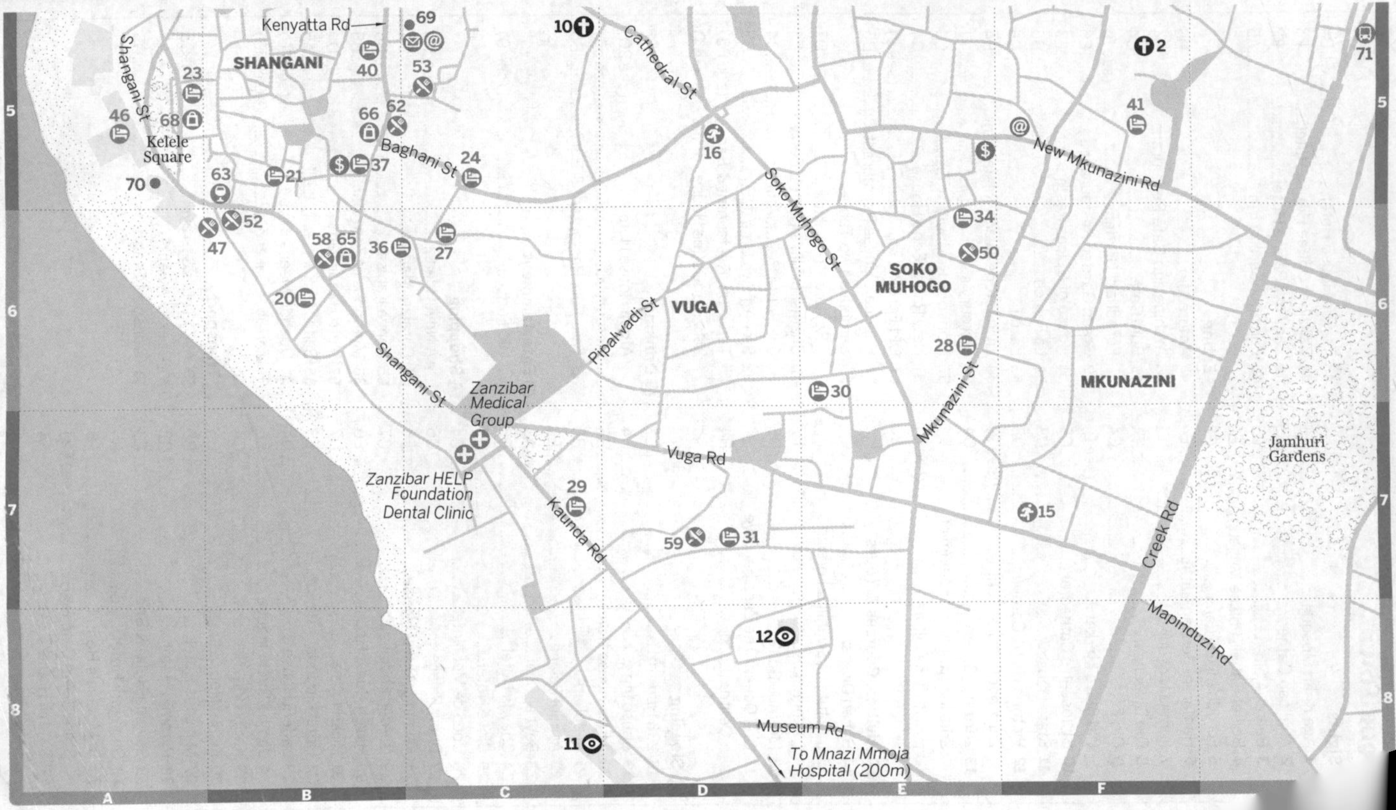

Kenyatta Rd
SHANGANI
Shangani St
Kelele Square
Baghani St
Cathedral St
Soko Muhogo St
New Mkunazini Rd
SOKO MUHOGO
VUGA
Pipalvadi St
Shangani St
Zanzibar Medical Group
Zanzibar HELP Foundation Dental Clinic
Vuga Rd
Kaunda Rd
Mkunazini St
MKUNAZINI
Jamhuri Gardens
Creek Rd
Mapinduzi Rd
Museum Rd
To Mnazi Mmoja Hospital (200m)

...one Town

Sights
1 Aga Khan Mosque ... F3
2 Anglican Cathedral ... F5
3 Beit el-Ajaib ... D3
4 Beit el-Sahel (Palace Museum) ... E2
5 Forodhani Gardens ... C3
6 Hamamni Persian Baths ... E4
7 Ijumaa Mosque ... F1
8 Old Dispensary ... F1
9 Old Fort ... C4
Old Slave Market ... (see 2)
10 St Joseph's Cathedral ... C5
11 State House ... C8
12 Victoria Hall & Gardens ... D8
Zanzibar Cultural Centre ... (see 9)
13 Zanzibar Gallery ... C4
Zanzibar National Museum of History & Culture ... (see 3)

Activities, Courses & Tours
14 Bahari Divers ... C4
15 Institute of Swahili & Foreign Languages ... F7
16 Mrembo Spa ... D5
17 One Ocean/The Zanzibar Dive Centre ... B4

Sleeping
18 236 Hurumzi ... E3
19 Abuso Inn ... B4
20 Africa House Hotel ... B6
21 Al-Johari ... B5
22 Asmini Palace ... E3
23 Beyt al-Chai ... A5
24 Chavda Hotel ... C5
25 Clove Hotel ... E3
26 Coco de Mer Hotel ... C4
27 Dhow Palace ... C6
28 Flamingo Guest House ... E6
29 Garden Lodge ... C7
30 Haven Guest House ... E6
31 Hiliki House ... D7
32 Hotel Kiponda ... E3
33 Jafferji House & Spa ... D4
34 Jambo Guest House ... E6
35 Karibu Inn ... C4
36 Kisiwa House ... B6
37 Mazsons Hotel ... B5
38 Pyramid Hotel ... G2
39 Seyyida Hotel & Spa ... E3
40 Shangani Hotel ... B5
41 St Monica's Hostel ... F5
Stone Town Café B&B ... (see 62)
42 Swahili House ... F4
43 Tembo House Hotel ... B4
44 Zanzibar Coffee House Hotel ... F3
45 Zanzibar Palace Hotel ... F2
46 Zanzibar Serena Inn ... A5

Eating
47 Amore Mio ... B6
48 Archipelago Café-Restaurant ... B4
49 Buni Café ... C4
Forodhani Gardens ... (see 5)
50 Green Garden Restaurant ... E6
51 House of Spices Restaurant ... E3
52 La Fenice ... B6
53 Lazuli ... C5
54 Livingstone Beach Restaurant ... B4
55 Mercury's ... F1
56 Monsoon Restaurant ... C3
57 New Radha Food House ... C4
Old Fort Restaurant ... (see 9)
58 Pagoda Chinese Restaurant ... B6
59 Sambusa Two Tables Restaurant ... D7
60 Shamshuddin's Cash & Carry ... F4
61 Silk Route Restaurant ... C4
62 Stone Town Café ... B5
Tatu Pub, Restaurant & Bar ... (see 63)
Zanzibar Coffee House ... (see 44)

Drinking
Africa House Hotel ... (see 20)
Mercury's ... (see 55)
63 Tatu Pub, Restaurant & Bar ... B5

Entertainment
Old Fort ... (see 9)

Shopping
A Novel Idea ... (see 18)
64 Darajani Market ... G4
65 Kanga Kabisa ... B6
66 Memories of Zanzibar ... B5
67 Moto Handicrafts ... D4
68 Saifa ... A5
Upendo Means Love ... (see 26)
Zanzibar Gallery ... (see 13)

Transport
69 Asko Tours & Travel ... C5
70 Coastal Aviation ... A5
71 Transport Stand ... G5

PAPASI

In Zanzibar Town you will undoubtedly come into contact with street touts. In Swah they're known as *papasi* (ticks). They are not registered as guides with the Zanzibar Tourist Corporation (ZTC), although they may carry (false) identification cards, and w a few can be helpful, others can be aggressive and irritating.

If you decide to use the services of an unlicensed tout, tell them where you want to go or what you are looking for, and your price range. You shouldn't have to pay anything additional, as many hotels pay commission. If they tell you your hotel of choice no longer exists or is full, take it with a grain of salt, as it could well be that they just want to take you somewhere where they know they'll get a better commission.

Another strategy is to make your way out of the port arrivals area and head straight for a taxi. This will cost you more, and taxi drivers look for hotel commissions as well, but most are legitimate and once you are 'spoken for', hassles from touts usually diminish.

Most *papasi* are hoping that your stay on the island will mean ongoing work for them as your guide. If you're not interested in this, explain (politely) once you've arrived at your hotel. If you want a guide to show you around Stone Town, it's better to arrange one with your hotel or a travel agency.

Kidichi Persian Baths HISTORIC SITE

(Map p60) These baths, northeast of Zanzibar Town, are another construction of Sultan Seyyid Said, built in 1850 for his Persian wife at the island's highest point. The decor, with its stylised birds and flowers, is typically Persian, though it's now in poor condition. Take dalla-dalla 502 to the main Bububu junction, from where it's a 3km walk east down an unsealed road. Look for the bathhouse to your right.

Mosques MOSQUE

Misikiti wa Balnara (Malindi Minaret Mosque) is the oldest of Stone Town's many mosques, originally built in 1831, enlarged in 1841 and extended again by Seyyid Ali bin Said in 1890. Others include the **Aga Khan Mosque**, and the impressive **Ijumaa Mosque**. It's not permitted to enter the mosques, as they're all in use, although exceptions may be made if you're appropriately dressed.

Forodhani Gardens GARDENS

(Jamituri Gardens; Map p62) One of the best ways to ease into life on the island is to stop by these recently renovated waterside public gardens in the evening, when the grassy plaza comes alive with dozens of vendors serving up grilled *pweza* (octopus), plates of goat meat, Zanzibari pizza (rolled-up, omelette-filled chapati), *mkate wa ufuta* (a thick, local version of naan), chips, samosas and more. The gardens are opposite the Old Fort.

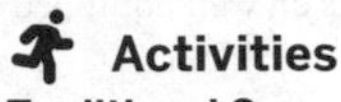

Activities

Traditional Spa

There are many traditional spas in Stone Town, where you can treat yourself to Zanzibari beauty rituals. One to try: **Mrembo** (www.mtoni.com/mrembo) has branches at Mtoni Marine (p70) and in Stone Town signposted past St Joseph's Cathedral.

Diving & Snorkelling

Bahari Divers DIVING

(Map p62; ☎0777-484873; www.baharidivers.com; Shangani St) A small outfit under new management primarily organising dives around the islands offshore from Stone Town and offering PADI certification courses.

One Ocean/The Zanzibar Dive Centre DIVING

(Map p62; ☎024-223 8374, 0748-750161; www.zanzibaroneocean.com; just off Shangani St) A PADI five-star centre with branches at Matemwe Beach Village (Matemwe) and many other locations along the east and southwestern coasts. It organises dives all around the island, for divers of all levels.

Tours

Spice Tours

While spices no longer dominate Zanzibar's economy as they once did, plantations still dot the centre of the island. It's possible to visit them on 'spice tours' - half-day excursions from Zanzibar Town that take in some plantations, plus some of the ruins described earlier and other sights of historical interest.

tours through your hotel, a ...nt or through the long-standing ...s **office** (024-223 4636; off Malawi ... posted just in from Ciné Afrique. ...or all tours are about US$12 per ... in a group of about 15, and include ... They depart about 9.30am and return ...bout 2.30pm (later, if a stop at Mangapwani beach is included). Book a day in advance (you'll be collected from your hotel), though it's usually no trouble to just show up in the morning.

Dhow & Island Tours

All the listings under Travel Agencies & Tour Operators (p74) arrange excursions to the offshore islands near Stone Town.

Safari Blue DHOW CRUISES
(0777-423162; www.safariblue.net) Organises day snorkelling excursions on well-equipped dhows around Menai Bay.

Sleeping

SHANGANI

Kisiwa House BOUTIQUE HOTEL $$$
(Map p62; 024-223 5654, 0777-789272; www.kisiwahouse.com; r US$165-220;) The lovely Kisiwa House (formerly Baghani House Hotel) has nine rooms that are full of character. Most are on the upper level and reached via a steep staircase (the one on the ground floor next to reception can be noisy). It's just off Kenyatta Rd.

Tembo House Hotel HOTEL $$
(Map p62; 024-223 3005, 0777-413348; www.tembohotel.com; s/d/tw/tr from US$100/120/120/155;) This attractively restored building has a prime waterfront location, including a small patch of beach (but no swimming), efficient management and comfortable, good-value rooms. There's a small pool, a restaurant (no alcohol) and a great buffet breakfast on the seaside terrace.

Dhow Palace HOTEL $$
(Map p62; 024-223 3012, 0777-878088; www.dhowpalace-hotel.com; s/d from US$80/110; Jun-Mar;) This is a classic place with old Zanzibari decor, a fountain in the tastefully restored lobby and comfortable, well-appointed rooms. It's just off Kenyatta Rd, and under the same management as Tembo House Hotel.

Abuso Inn HOTEL $
(Map p62; 024-223 5886, 0777-425565; abusoinn@gmail.com; Shangani St; s/d/tr/f US$55/75/90/100;) This family-run place diagonally opposite Tembo House Hotel has spotless, mostly quite spacious rooms with large windows, wooden floors and fan or air-con. Some rooms have glimpses of the water.

Coco de Mer Hotel HOTEL $$
(Map p62; 024-223 0852, 0785-099123; cocodemer_znz@yahoo.com; s/d/tw/tr US$40/60/60/70) Coco de Mer is conveniently located just off Kenyatta Rd, near the tunnel, and vaguely reminiscent of the Algarve, with white walls and tile work. Avoid the one closet-sized room on the 1st floor, and the downstairs rooms, many of which have only interior windows; otherwise rooms are pleasant and good value. The restaurant serves smoothies, sandwiches and light meals.

Mazsons Hotel HOTEL $$
(Map p62; 024-223 3694, 0713-340042; www.mazsonshotel.net; Kenyatta Rd; s/d from US$70/90;) The long-standing Mazsons has impressively restored lobby woodwork and a convenient location, which go some way to compensating for its rooms – modern and quite comfortable, though pallid. There's also a restaurant on-site.

Chavda Hotel HOTEL $$
(Map p62; 024-223 2115; www.chavdahotel.co.tz; Baghani St; s/d/tw from US$100/120/130;) Chavda is a quiet, reliable hotel with some period decor and a range of bland, carpeted rooms with TV, telephone and minibar. The rooftop bar and restaurant are open during the high season only, and there's a spa. It's just around the corner from Kisiwa House hotel.

Beyt al-Chai BOUTIQUE HOTEL $$
(Map p62; 0774-444111; www.stonetowninn.com; Kelele Sq; s US$75-265, d US$105-295) This converted tea house is an atmospheric choice, with just five rooms, each individually designed, and all with period decor. For a splurge, try one of the top-floor Sultan suites. Downstairs is a good restaurant.

Al-Johari BOUTIQUE HOTEL $$
(Map p62; 024-223 6779, 0777-242806; www.al-johari.com; Shangani; s/d from US$100/140;) This 15-room boutique hotel has modern rooms with a few Zanzibari touches, an air-con, glassed-in restaurant upstairs and a breezy rooftop bar with views. Take

DIVING

Tanzania's waters offers an array of hard and soft corals and a diverse collection of sea creatures, including manta rays, hawksbill and green turtles, barracudas and sharks. Other draws include the possibility for wall dives, especially off Pemba and the opportunity to combine wildlife safaris with underwater exploration. On the down side, visibility isn't reliable, and prices are considerably higher than in places such as the Red Sea or Thailand. Another thing to consider is that you'll need to travel, often for up to an hour, to many of the dive sites.

Planning

Diving is possible year-round, although conditions vary dramatically. Late March until mid-June is generally the least favourable time because of erratic weather patterns and frequent storms. July or August to February or March tends to be the best time overall.

Water temperatures range from lows of about 22°C in July and August to highs of about 29°C in February and March, with the average about 26°C. Throughout, 3mm wetsuits are standard; 4mm suits are recommended for some areas during the July to September winter months, and 2mm are fine from around December to March or April.

Costs & Courses

Costs are fairly uniform, with Pemba and Mafia island slightly pricier than elsewhere along the coast. Expect to pay from US$375 for a four-day PADI open water course, from about US$45/75 for a single-/double-dive package, and from about US$50 for a night dive. Discounts average about 10% if you have your own equipment, and for groups.

Where to Dive

Zanzibar is known for the corals and shipwrecks offshore from Stone Town, and for fairly reliable visibility, high fish diversity and the chance to see pelagics to the north and northeast. There are many easily accessed sites for beginning and mid-level divers.

Unlike Zanzibar, which is a continental island, Pemba is an oceanic island located in a deep channel with a steeply dropping shelf. Diving here tends to be more challenging, with an emphasis on wall and drift dives, though there are some sheltered areas for beginners, especially around Misali island. Most dives are to the west around Misali, and to the north around the Njao Gap.

Mafia offers divers fine corals, good fish variety, including pelagics, and uncrowded diving, often done from motorised dhows.

Also see p641.

the small road off Kenyatta Rd in front of Mazsons Hotel and follow it down a few hundred metres.

Zanzibar Palace Hotel HOTEL $$$
(Map p62; ☎024-223 2230, 0773-079222; www.zanzibarpalacehotel.com; Kiponda; s/d from US$160/180; ❄@📶) This small, atmospheric hotel has a mix of rooms in varying sizes. Some have separate sitting areas, some have small balconies, most have large raised or sunken-style bathtubs, and most have air-con. All have Zanzibari beds and period design.

Karibu Inn HOTEL $
(Map p62; ☎024-223 3058, 0777-417392; karibuinnhotel@yahoo.com; dm US$15, s/d/tw/tr US$30/40/40/60) The soulless Karibu's complete lack of atmosphere is compensated for by a convenient location in the heart of Shangani, within a five-minute walk of Forodhani Gardens. Accommodation is in dorm beds or clean, decent rooms with private bathroom. The upstairs rooms are brighter and better ventilated. Breakfast is served, but otherwise there is no food.

Shangani Hotel HOTEL $$
(Map p62; ☎024-223 3688, 024-223 6363, 0777-411703; www.shanganihotel.com; Kenyatta Rd; s/d/tr US$55/75/85; ❄) This unpretentious place opposite Shangani post office has bland but reasonably comfortable rooms, most with TV, fridge and fan. There's no food at the moment except breakfast.

FESTIVALS & EVENTS

» **Eid al-Fitr** Marking the end of Ramadan, with lanterns lighting the narrow passageways, families dressed in their best and a generally festive atmosphere. Many restaurants close down completely during Ramadan.

» **Sauti za Busara** (Voices of Wisdom; ☎024-223 2423; www.busaramusic.com) Held yearly in February and celebrates Swahili music and culture.

» **Festival of the Dhow Countries** and **Zanzibar International Film Festival** (www.ziff.or.tz) Held yearly in July, with film screenings, performing arts groups, village events and a generally festive atmosphere.

» **Mwaka Kogwa** The Shirazi New Year, celebrated in July and at its best in Makunduchi.

Zanzibar Serena Inn HOTEL **$$$**
(Map p62; ☎024-223 2306, 024-223 3587; www.serenahotels.com; s/d from US$325/475; ❄@📶🏊) The Zanzibar Serena, in the refurbished Extelecoms House has a beautiful setting on the water, plush rooms with all the amenities, and a business centre, although we've had some complaints about lackadaisical staff.

HURUMZI

Zanzibar Coffee House Hotel BOUTIQUE HOTEL **$$**
(Map p62; ☎024-223 9319; www.riftvalley-zanzibar.com; s US$70-160, d US$90-190; @) This small but excellent-value boutique-style hotel above the eponymous coffee house in Hurumzi has just eight rooms, most spacious, some with private bathroom and all decorated with Zanzibari beds and period decor. The price includes a spectacular rooftop breakfast (both the rooftop area and the breakfast).

Jafferji House & Spa LUXURY HOTEL **$$$**
(Map p62; www.jafferjihouse.net; Gizenga St; ste US$190-505; ❄📶) This restored family home, under the same management as the Zanzibar Gallery and Gallery Tours & Safaris, was just opening as this book was researched, with 10 top-of-the-line rooms (all named after famous Zanzibari figures, and authentically furnished), a rooftop spa, a cafe and a library.

Stone Town Café B&B B&B **$$**
(Map p62; ☎0778-373737; www.stonetowncafe.com; Kenyatta Rd; s/d US$70/80; ❄) Above Stone Town Café, this B&B has a handful of simple, spotless rooms, all with hot water bathrooms and cable TV.

Clove Hotel HOTEL **$$**
(Map p62; ☎0777-484567; www.zanzibarhotel.nl; Hurumzi St; s/d/f from US$40/65/80) Renovated several years ago, but now beginning to fade, Clove has decent but rather spartan rooms (check out a few) with fans. On the rooftop is a terrace with breakfast, drinks and views.

236 Hurumzi BOUTIQUE HOTEL **$$$**
(Map p62; ☎0777-423266; www.236hurumzi.com; Hurumzi St; s US$125, d US$165-250; @📶) Formerly Emerson & Green, this Zanzibar institution is in two adjacent historic buildings that have been restored along the lines of an *Arabian Nights* fantasy and are full of character. Each room (most reached by steep staircases) is unique and all are decadently decorated to give you an idea of what Zanzibar must have been like in its heyday. Service and standards were suffering on our last visit, but this will hopefully be soon remedied. It's several winding blocks east of the Old Fort.

KIPONDA

Pyramid Hotel HOTEL **$**
(Map p62; ☎024-223 3000; www.pyramidhotel.co.tz; s/d US$25/35, with air-con US$30/45; ❄@) This long-standing, atmospheric place notable for its steep staircasing has a mix of rooms, most with private bathroom, and all with Zanzibari beds and fan. Look at a few rooms as standards and size vary. There's a rooftop breakfast terrace.

Hotel Kiponda HOTEL **$$**
(Map p62; ☎024-223 3052; www.kiponda.com; Nyumba ya Moto St; s/d/tr US$30/50/65) This is another long-standing place with spotless, good-value rooms in an atmospheric building, and a convenient location, tucked away in a small lane near the waterfront. All rooms have private bathroom, except two that have a bathroom outside. There's a rooftop restaurant.

Seyyida Hotel & Spa BOUTIQUE HOTEL $$$
(Map p62; ☎024-223 8352, 0776-247744; www.theseyyida-zanzibar.com; r US$170-290; ❄@☎) Just up from Hotel Kiponda is this lovely, atmospheric 17-room boutique hotel. All rooms have satellite TV, some have sea views, and some have balconies. There's also one family room, a rooftop terrace restaurant and a spa.

Asmini Palace HOTEL $$
(Map p62; ☎0774-276464, 0777-478532; www.asminipalace.com; s/d/tr US$85/105/145; ❄☎) This friendly hotel in a restored building offers good-value rooms with Zanzibar beds, cable TV, mini-fridge and an elevator.

Swahili House HOTEL $$
(Map p62; ☎0777-510209; www.theswahilihouse.com; s/d US$141/156; ❄@) The multistorey Swahili House, formerly Hotel International, has had a facelift, and its rooms are now fresh and comfortable. Some have open bathrooms and large tubs, and all have fan, air-con and Zanzibari beds. There's a rooftop terrace, restaurant and bar, and steep staircases. It's just off Kiponda St, with a forex bureau opposite.

MALINDI

Warere Town House HOTEL $
(☎0782-234564, 0778-429336; www.warere.com; d with fan US$55, s/tw/d/tr with air-con US$35/65/75/90; ❄) Warere has good-value rooms (some with small balconies and all with hot water) plus a rooftop breakfast terrace and a trim gravel-grass entry area planted with bougainvillea. It's just a few minutes' walk from the port (staff will meet you), behind Bandari Lodge.

Malindi Guest House HOTEL $
(☎024-223 0165; www.malindiguesthouse.com; Funguni Rd; s/d/tr with air-con US$40/50/70, s/d without bathroom US$30/45; ❄) This long-standing guesthouse has whitewashed walls, well-maintained rooms with fan or air-con, and a small rooftop restaurant. Reconfirm the price you are quoted, as a sign at reception advertises that room rates may rise to US$75/80 per single/double, depending on demand.

Princess Salme Inn HOTEL $
(☎0777-435303; d without bathroom US$35, s/d US$35/50, d with air-con US$60; ❄@) Formerly Annex of Malindi Lodge, this friendly place between Bandari Lodge and Warere Town House has been spruced up a bit. The rooms are basic but clean, with Zanzibari beds and fans, and most sharing cold-water bathrooms.

Zenji Hotel HOTEL $$
(off Map p62; ☎0774-276468, 0776-705592; www.zenjihotel.com; Malawi Rd; s US$35, d from US$50 with bathroom from US$65; ❄@☎) In a busy location diagonally opposite Ciné Afrique, this small, spiffy hotel has a mix of clean, pleasant rooms, some with shared bathroom, and all with fan, air-con and Zanzibari beds. Downstairs is a cafe, and upstairs is a rooftop breakfast terrace.

Zanzibar Grand Palace HOTEL $$
(off Map p62; ☎024-223 5368/9; www.zanzibargrandpalace.com; Turkys Sq, just off Mizingani Rd; s/d/tr US$80/130/170; ❄☎) This large, 32-room multistorey place one block off Mizingani Rd near the ferry exit has a mix of comfortable twins and doubles, a rooftop restaurant with harbour views, a small cafe, and an elevator.

Bandari Lodge HOTEL $
(☎024-223 7969; bandarilodge@hotmail.com; s/d/tw/tr US$20/35/35/45) Bandari has straightforward, high-ceilinged, no-frills rooms with fan. Turn left as you exit the port; it's two minutes' walk ahead on the right-hand side.

Malindi Lodge HOTEL $
(☎024-223 2359; sunsetbungalows@hotmail.com; s/d without bathroom US$25/40; ❄) The long-standing Malindi Lodge has clean, albeit basic rooms near Ciné Afrique and the port, and diagonally opposite Mr Mitu's spice tours office. There are no fans.

MKUNAZINI

Jambo Guest House GUESTHOUSE $
(Map p62; ☎024-223 3779; info@jamboguest.com; s/d/tr without bathroom US$20/30/45; ❄@) Just around the corner from Flamingo Guest House, and also popular with backpackers, Jambo has free tea and coffee, clean rooms and decent breakfasts. Green Garden Restaurant, with cheap local meals, is just opposite.

St Monica's Hostel HOSTEL $
(Map p62; ☎024-223 0773; monicaszanzibar@hotmail.com; s/d US$40/50, s/tr without bathroom US$22/35/50) This old, rambling, atmospheric place next to the Anglican cathedral has spacious rooms, including some with a small verandah. Breakfast is served next door at St Monica's Restaurant.

Flamingo Guest House GUESTHOUSE $
(Map p62; ☎024-223 2850; www.flamingoguesthouse.com; Mkunazini St; s/d US$25/44, without bathroom US$12/24) Flamingo is no frills but cheap and fine, with straightforward rooms, all with fans, around a courtyard. There's also a common TV and a rooftop sitting/breakfast area.

Haven Guest House GUESTHOUSE $
(Map p62; ☎024-223 5677/8; s/d US$15/30) This long-standing place has straightforward, no-frills rooms and a convenient location just south of Mkunazini, between Soko Muhogo St and Vuga Rd.

VUGA

Garden Lodge GUESTHOUSE $
(Map p62; ☎024-223 3298; gardenlodge@zanlink.com; Kaunda Rd; s/d/tr US$30/40/60) This efficient, friendly, family-run place is in a convenient location diagonally opposite the High Court. Rooms are good value, especially the upstairs ones, which are bright and spacious, and all have hot water, ceiling fans and Zanzibari beds. There's a rooftop breakfast terrace, but otherwise no food.

Hiliki House GUESTHOUSE $$
(Map p62; ☎0777-410131; www.hikikihouse-zanzibar.com; Victoria St; d US$60 with bathroom US$80;) This converted private house has six atmospheric, well-appointed rooms, including one twin-bedded room, five doubles, and two rooms sharing bathroom. All have fan, air-con and shared sitting room.

OUTSIDE STONE TOWN

Mtoni Marine Centre LODGE $$
(Map p60; ☎024-225 0140; www.mtoni.com; club s/d US$85/110, palm court s/d US$125/165; @) This long-standing family-friendly establishment offers spacious, well-appointed 'club rooms', and more luxurious 'palm court' sea-view rooms with private balconies. There's a small beach, large gardens, a fantastic 25m infinity pool, a popular waterside bar and good dining in the main restaurant. It's 3km north of town along the Bububu road.

Mbweni Ruins Hotel LODGE $$$
(Map p60; ☎024-223 5478, 0775-016541; www.mbweni.com; s/d US$145/240; @) Mbweni is a quiet, genteel establishment set in lovely, expansive and lushly vegetated gardens about 5km from town, and several kilometres off the airport road. In addition to well-appointed rooms and a relaxing ambience, it has a very good restaurant and a bar overlooking the water and stands of mangroves – ideal for bird watching. The property was formerly the site of the UMCA mission school for the children of freed slaves.

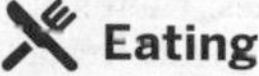

Eating

During the low season and Ramadan, many restaurants close or operate reduced hours.

SHANGANI

New Radha Food House VEGETARIAN $$
(Map p62; ☎024-223 4808; thalis Tsh10,000; breakfast, lunch & dinner;) This great little place is tucked away on the small side street just before the Shangani tunnel. The strictly vegetarian menu features thalis, lassis, homemade yoghurt and other dishes from the subcontinent.

Forodhani Gardens TANZANIAN $
(Map p62; meals Tsh3000-8000; dinner;) These waterside gardens (p65) are the place to go in the evening, with piles of grilled fish and meat, chips, snacks and more, all served on a paper plate or rolled into a piece of newspaper and eaten while sitting on benches or on the lawn. While prices are reasonable, overcharging is frequent, and with some vendors you'll need to bargain to get a fair price.

Silk Route Restaurant INDIAN $$
(Map p62; Shangani St; meals Tsh11,000-16,000; lunch & dinner Tue-Sun, dinner Mon;) This popular place has a large menu of tasty Indian cuisine, a good selection of wine and fine views over the water. It's just before the tunnel in Shangani, on the first floor.

Lazuli ORGANIC $$
(Map p62; ☎0776-266670; meals Tsh8000-10,000; lunch & dinner Mon-Sat) This informal little Zanzibari–South African place on a tiny courtyard just off Kenyatta Rd has freshly prepared curries, fresh juices, burgers, chapati wraps, salads, smoothies, pancakes and more.

Monsoon Restaurant ZANZIBARI $$
(Map p62; ☎0777-410410; Shangani St; lunch Tsh8000-16,000, dinner Tsh12,000-30,000; lunch & dinner) The impeccably decorated and atmospheric Monsoon has traditional-style dining on floor cushions, and well-prepared Swahili and Western cuisine served to a backdrop of live *taarab* (Zanzibari music combining African, Arabic and

Indian influences) on Wednesday and Saturday evenings. It's at the southwestern edge of Forodhani Gardens.

Amore Mio ITALIAN $$

(Map p62; Shangani St; ice cream from Tsh2000, light meals Tsh8000-15,000; ⏲high season) Across the road from La Fenice, Amore Mio has delectable ice cream, as well as well-prepared pasta dishes and other light meals, good coffees and cappuccinos, and fantastic views of the water.

Pagoda Chinese Restaurant CHINESE $$

(Map p62; ☎024-223 1758; meals Tsh9000-17,000; ⏲lunch & dinner) The 1st-floor Pagoda has tasty Chinese food, including a good-value set-menu lunch. It's diagonally opposite the Africa House Hotel.

La Fenice ITALIAN $$$

(Map p62; ☎0777-411868; Shangani St; meals Tsh15,000-38,000, pizzas Tsh9000-14,000; ⏲lunch & dinner) A breezy little patch of Italy on the waterfront, La Fenice has top-notch Italian cuisine and outdoor tables where you can enjoy your pasta while gazing out at the turquoise sea.

Archipelago Café-Restaurant CAFE $$

(Map p62; ☎024-223 5668; Shangani St; meals Tsh12,000-14,000; ⏲breakfast, lunch & dinner) This popular place has a fine, breezy location on a 1st-floor terrace overlooking the water, and a menu featuring such delicacies as vegetable coconut curry, orange and ginger snapper, and chicken pilau, topped off by an array of homemade cakes and sweets. Breakfast is served until 11am. There's no bar, but you can bring your own alcohol.

Stone Town Café CAFE $$

(Map p62; Kenyatta Rd; breakfast Tsh5000, meals Tsh6000-10,000; ⏲breakfast & lunch Mon-Sat) All-day breakfasts, milkshakes, freshly baked cakes, vegie wraps and good coffee.

Buni Café CAFE $$

(Map p62; Shangani St; snacks & light meals Tsh8500-15,000; ⏲breakfast, lunch & dinner) Just before the Shangani tunnel and around the corner from Monsoon restaurant, Buni has plain decor but good smoothies, paninis, fresh juices, salads, cakes, burgers and an outdoor porch where you can watch the passing scene.

Livingstone Beach Restaurant EUROPEAN $$$

(Map p62; ☎0773-164939; off Shangani St; meals Tsh17,000-32,000; ⏲lunch & dinner) This worn but popular place in the old British Consulate building has seating directly on the beach – lovely in the evening, with candlelight – and an array of pricey, well-prepared seafood grills and other dishes, plus a bar.

HURUMZI

House of Spices Restaurant ITALIAN $$

(Map p62; Hurumzi St; meals Tsh12,000-15,000; ⏲lunch & dinner Mon-Sat) This place (formerly Zee Pizza) has delicious Italian dining on a covered upper-floor terrace, with pastas, seafood and a pizza oven.

Old Fort Restaurant EUROPEAN $$$

(Map p62; ☎0777-416736; Old Fort; meals from Tsh15,000, fixed dinner menu plus traditional dance performance Tsh30,000; ⏲lunch & dinner) The chefs here serve up a well-prepared menu featuring grilled seafood and meat, salads, pasta dishes and more. For info on the accompanying traditional dance and drum performances, see p73.

Zanzibar Coffee House CAFE $$

(Map p62; ☎024-223 9319; coffeehouse@zanlink.com; snacks Tsh5000-Tsh12,000) This cafe below the hotel of the same name has a large coffee menu, plus milkshakes, fruit smoothies and freshly baked cakes.

KIPONDA

Mercury's EUROPEAN $$

(Map p62; ☎024-223 3076; meals Tsh8000-16,000; ⏲lunch & dinner) Named in honour of Queen vocalist Freddie Mercury, this scruffy but popular place is Stone Town's main waterside hang-out. On offer are seafood grills, pasta dishes and pizza, and a well-stocked bar and a terrace that's a favourite location for sipping sundowners.

MALINDI

Passing Show ZANZIBARI $

(Malawi Rd; meals Tsh2500-5000) Mingle with the locals and enjoy inexpensive pilaus and other standards at this Zanzibar institution opposite Ciné Afrique.

Al-Shbany ZANZIBARI $

(off Malawi Rd; meals from Tsh4000; ⏲breakfast & lunch) This is another local favourite, with delicious pilau and *biryani,* plus chicken and chips. It's on a small side street just off Malawi Rd and east of Creek Rd.

MKUNAZINI

Green Garden Restaurant EUROPEAN $$

(Map p62; meals Tsh9000-10,000; ⏲lunch & dinner) This no-frills, backpacker-friendly place opposite Jambo Guest House has outdoor and upstairs covered eating areas and a large menu featuring hummus, curries, pizzas, fish, milkshakes, smoothies and more.

VUGA

Sambusa Two Tables Restaurant ZANZIBARI **$$**
(Map p62; ☎024-223 1979; meals US$15; ⊙by advance arrangement) For sampling authentic Zanzibari dishes, it's hard to beat this small, family-run restaurant just off Kaunda Rd, where the proprietors bring out course after course of delicious local delicacies. Advance reservations (preferably the day before) are required; up to 15 guests can be accommodated.

DARAJANI

Shamshuddin's Cash & Carry SUPERMARKET **$**
(Map p62; Soko St) Just behind the Darajani market. For self-catering.

OUTSIDE STONE TOWN

Mtoni Marine Centre EUROPEAN **$$$**
(Map p60; ☎024-225 0117; mtonirestaurant@zanzibar.cc; meals Tsh15,000-38,000; ⊙dinner) Mtoni Marine's well-regarded main restaurant has a range of seafood and meat grills, and waterside barbecues several times weekly, sometimes with a backdrop of *taarab* or other traditional music.

Mcheza Bar PUB **$$**
(Map p60; meals Tsh12,000-20,000; ⊙lunch & dinner; Wi-Fi) Next door to Mtoni Marine Centre is this beachside sports bar, with a mix of booth and table seating, two big screens, plus burgers and pub food, seafood, South African steaks and a pizza oven.

Drinking

Stone Town isn't known for its nightlife, but there are a few popular spots.

Africa House Hotel BAR
(Map p62; www.theafricahouse-zanzibar.com; Shangani St) The upper-level terrace here is the spot for waterside sundowners.

Tatu Pub, Restaurant & Bar BAR
(Map p62; ☎0778-672772; www.tatuzanzibar.com; Shangani St) There's a well-stocked pub on the first floor, a pub-style restaurant on the second serving good, fresh seafood and meat dishes and salads, and a rooftop cocktail lounge on the third floor with ocean views. It's diagonally opposite Amore Mio.

Mcheza Bar PUB
(Map p60; ☎024-225 0117; mtonirestaurant@zanzibar.cc) A happening sports bar that draws mainly an expat crowd.

Mercury's PUB
(Map p62; ☎024-223 3076) Waterside sundowners plus live music some evenings.

Entertainment

Old Fort TRADITIONAL DANCE
(Map p62; admission Tsh6000) On Tuesday, Thursday and Saturday evening from 7pm to 10pm there are traditional *ngoma* (dance and drumming) performances at the Old Fort.

Shopping

Items to watch for include finely crafted Zanzibari chests, kanga (cotton wraps worn by women all over Tanzania), *kikoi* (the thicker striped or plaid equivalent worn by men on Zanzibar and in other coastal areas), spices and handcrafted silver jewellery.

A good place to start is Gizenga St, which is lined with small shops and craft dealers.

Moto Handicrafts HANDICRAFTS
(Map p62; www.motozanzibar.worldpress.com; Hurumzi St) Moto sells baskets, mats and other woven products made by local women's cooperatives using environmentally sustainable technologies.

Upendo Means Love CLOTHING
(Map p62; www.upendomeanslove.com; off Kenyatta Rd) Western-style clothes handmade by local women from kanga, *kikoi* and other traditional fabrics. It's next to Coco de Mer hotel.

Zanzibar Gallery SOUVENIRS
(Map p62; ☎024-223 2721; gallery@swahilicoast.com; cnr Kenyatta Rd & Gizenga St; ⊙9am-6.30pm Mon-Sat, to 1pm Sun) This long-standing gallery has a fine collection of souvenirs, textiles, woodcarvings, antiques and more.

Gallery Bookshop BOOKS
(☎0773-150180; gallery@swahilicoast.com; 48 Gizenga St; ⊙9am-6pm Mon-Sat, to 2pm Sun) A large selection of books and maps, including travel guides, Africa titles and historical reprint editions.

Memories of Zanzibar SOUVENIRS
(Map p62; Kenyatta Rd) Offers a large selection of jewellery, textiles and curios.

TAARAB MUSIC

No visit to Zanzibar would be complete without spending an evening listening to the evocative strains of *taarab*, the archipelago's most famous musical export. A traditional *taarab* orchestra consists of several dozen musicians using both Western and traditional instruments, including the violin, the *kanun* (similar to a zither), the accordion, the *nay* (an Arabic flute) and drums, plus a singer. There's generally no written music, and songs – often with themes centred on love – are full of puns and double meanings.

Taarab-style music was played in Zanzibar as early as the 1820s at the sultan's palace, where it had been introduced from Arabia. However, it wasn't until the 1900s, when Sultan Seyyid Hamoud bin Muhammed encouraged formation of the first *taarab* clubs, that it became more formalised.

A good time to see *taarab* performances is during the **Festival of the Dhow Countries** (p68) in July.

Saifa CLOTHING
(Map p62; http://sites.google.com/site/saifashop/; Kelele Sq) Screen-printed T-shirts and batik bags.

Kanga Kabisa CLOTHING
(Map p62; www.kangakabisa.com; off Kenyatta Rd) Diagonally opposite Africa House Hotel, with clothes made from kangas and *kikois*.

A Novel Idea BOOKS
(www.anovelideatanzania.com; Hurumzi St) Next to 236 Hurumzi, with a wide selection of books.

 Information

Dangers & Annoyances

While Zanzibar remains a relatively safe place, robberies, muggings and the like occur with some frequency, especially in Zanzibar Town and along the beaches.

Follow the normal precautions: avoid isolated areas, especially isolated stretches of beach, and keep your valuables hidden. At night in Zanzibar Town, take a taxi or walk in a group. Also avoid walking alone in Stone Town during predawn hours. As a rule, it's best to leave valuables in your hotel safe, preferably sealed or locked.

If you've rented a bicycle or motorcycle, be prepared for stops at checkpoints, where traffic police may demand a bribe. Assuming your papers are in order, the best tactic is respectful friendliness.

Internet Access

Azzurri Internet Café (Map p62; New Mkunazini Rd; per hr Tsh1000; ⌚8.30am-8.30pm) Around the corner from the Anglican cathedral.

Shangani Post Office Internet Café (Map p62; Kenyatta Rd; per hr Tsh1000; ⌚8am-8pm Mon-Fri, 8.30am-7pm Sat & Sun) This cafe also offers international telephone calls.

Medical Services

If you experience any serious ailments, accidents or emergencies, you should go straight to Dar es Salaam or Nairobi (Kenya) for treatment.

Shamshuddin's Pharmacy (Map p62; ☎024-223 1262, 024-223 3814; Market St; ⌚9am-8.30pm Mon-Thu & Sat, 9am-noon & 4-8.30pm Fri, 9am-1.30pm Sun) Just behind (west of) the Darajani market.

Zanzibar HELP Foundation Dental Clinic (☎0779-272600; www.zanzibarhelp.org; off Kenyatta Rd) An excellent, state-of-the-art clinic, with profits going to support dental care for the local community.

Zanzibar Medical Group (Map p62; ☎024-223 3134; Kenyatta Rd)

Money

There are several ATMs in Stone Town (though none to be found elsewhere); all ATMs will accept Visa and MasterCard. There's also a lot of forex bureaus in Stone Town (most are open until 8pm daily) where you can change cash, but not travellers cheques. Rates will vary, so shop around to compare; the rates for US dollars are generally better than those for British pounds and euros. Officially, accommodation on Zanzibar must be paid for in US dollars, and prices are usually quoted in dollars, but at the budget places it's often not a problem to pay the equivalent of the asking price in Tanzanian shillings.

Barclays (Map p62; Kenyatta Rd) ATM; next to Mazsons Hotel.

CRDB (New Mkunazini Rd, Mkunazini) ATM.

Maka T-Shirt Shop (Map p62; Kenyatta Rd) Changes cash.

NBC (Map p62; Shangani St) ATM.

Queens Bureau de Change (Map p62; Kenyatta Rd) Changes cash.

Post

Shangani post office (Map p62; Kenyatta Rd; ⌚8am-4.30pm Mon-Fri, to 12.30pm Sat)

Telephone

Robin's Collection (Map p62; Kenyatta Rd; ⌚9am-8pm Mon-Sat) International calls for about US$2 per minute; also good for flash drives and digital camera components.

Shangani post office (Map p62; Kenyatta Rd; ⌚8am-9pm Mon-Fri, 8.30am-7pm Sat & Sun) Operator-assisted calls from Tsh1500 per minute.

Tourist Information

Tourist Information Office (Map p62; Creek Rd; ⌚8am-5pm) About 200m north of Darajani market on the same side of the road, with tourist information and standard tours.

Travel Agencies & Tour Operators

All the following can help with island excursions, and plane and ferry tickets. Only make bookings and payments inside the offices, and not with anyone outside claiming to be staff.

Eco + Culture Tours (Map p62; ☎024-223 3731, 0755-873066; www.ecoculture-zanzibar.org; Hurumzi St) Located opposite 236 Hurumzi hotel; culturally friendly tours and excursions, including to Unguja Ukuu, Jambiani village and Stone Town, in addition to spice tours, all with a focus on environmental and cultural conservation.

Gallery Tours & Safaris (☎024-223 2088; www.gallerytours.net) Top-of-the line tours and excursions throughout the archipelago; it also can help arrange Zanzibar weddings, honeymoon itineraries and dhow cruises.

Madeira Tours & Safaris (Map p62; ☎024-223 0406, 0777-415107; www.madeirazanzibar.com; Baghani St) All price ranges; opposite Kisiwa House.

Sama Tours (Map p62; ☎024-223 3543; www.samatours.com; Hurumzi St) Reliable and reasonably priced.

Tabasam Tours & Safaris (Map p62; ☎0777-413385; www.tabasamzanzibar.com; Mizingani Rd) In Old Dispensary, first floor; midrange tours.

Tropical Tours (Map p62; ☎0777-413454, 0777-411121; http://tropicaltours.villa69.org; Kenyatta Rd) Budget tours.

Zan Tours (Map p62; ☎024-223 3042, 024-223 3116; www.zantours.com; Malawi Rd) Offers a wide range of quality upmarket tours on Zanzibar, Pemba and beyond. Its office is diagonally opposite Ciné Afrique.

ℹ Getting There & Away

Air

Coastal Aviation and ZanAir have daily flights connecting Zanzibar with Dar es Salaam (US$75), Arusha (US$235), Pemba (US$100), Selous Game Reserve and the northern parks. Coastal Aviation goes daily to/from Tanga via Pemba (US$130), and has good-value day excursion packages from Dar es Salaam to Stone Town for US$142, including return flights, lunch and airport transfers. Tropical Air flies daily between Zanzibar and Dar es Salaam, and Precision Air has connections to Nairobi (Kenya).

Airline offices in Zanzibar Town include the following:

Coastal Aviation (Map p62; ☎024-223 3489, 024-223 3112, 0777-232747; www.coastal.cc; Kelele Sq) At the airport, with a booking agent next to Zanzibar Serena Inn.

Kenya Airways (☎024-223 4520/1; www.kenya-airways.com; Room 8, Ground fl, Muzamil Centre, Mlandege St) Just north of town along the Bububu Rd in Mlandege.

Precision Air (☎024-223 4520/1, 0787-888417; www.precisionairtz.com; Room 8, Ground fl, Muzamil Centre, Mlandege St) Located with Kenya Airways.

ZanAir (Map p62; ☎024-223 3670; www.zanair.com) Just off Malawi Rd, opposite Ciné Afrique.

Boat

For information on ferry connections between Zanzibar and Dar es Salaam, see p212. For ferry connections between Zanzibar and Pemba, see p212. You can get tickets at the port (the ticket office is just to the right when entering the main port gate), or with less hassle through any of the listings under Travel Agencies & Tour Operators. The departure and arrivals areas for the ferry are a few hundred metres down from the port gate along Mizingani Rd. If you leave Zanzibar on the *Flying Horse* night ferry, take care with your valuables, especially when the boat docks in Dar es Salaam in the early morning hours.

Dhows link Zanzibar with Dar es Salaam, Tanga, Bagamoyo and Mombasa (Kenya). Foreigners are not permitted on dhows between Dar es Salaam and Zanzibar. For other routes, the best place to ask is at the beach behind Tembo House Hotel. Allow anywhere from 10 to 48 hours or more to/from the mainland; also see the boxed text, p653.

ℹ Getting Around

To/From the Airport

The airport is about 7km southeast of Zanzibar Town. A taxi to/from the airport costs Tsh15,000. Dalla-dalla 505 also does this route (Tsh500, 30 minutes), departing from the corner opposite Mnazi Mmoja hospital. Many Stone Town hotels offer free airport pick-ups for confirmed bookings, though some charge. For hotels elsewhere on the island, transfers usually cost about US$25 to US$50, depending on the location.

Car & Motorcycle

It's easy to arrange car, moped or motorcycle rental and prices are reasonable, although breakdowns are fairly common, as are moped accidents. Considering how small the island is, it's often more straightforward and not that much more expensive to work out a good deal with a taxi driver.

You'll need either an International Driving Permit (IDP; together with your home licence), a licence from Kenya (Nairobi), Uganda or South Africa, or a Zanzibar driving permit; there are police checkpoints along the roads where you'll be asked to show one or the other. Zanzibar permits can be obtained on the spot from the **traffic police** (cnr Malawi & Creek Rds). If you rent through a tour company, they'll sort out the paperwork.

Daily rental rates average from about US$25 for a moped or motorcycle, and US$40 to US$55 for a Suzuki 4WD, excluding petrol, with better deals available for longer-term rentals. You can rent through any of the tour companies or through **Asko Tours & Travel** (☎024-223 0712, 0715-411392; askotour@hotmail.com; Kenyatta Rd), which also organises island excursions. If you're not mechanically minded, bring someone along with you who can check that the motorbike or vehicle you're renting is in reasonable condition, and take a test drive. Full payment is usually required at the time of delivery, but don't pay any advance deposits.

Dalla-Dallas

Dalla-dallas piled with people and produce link all major towns on the island. They are open-sided and generally more enjoyable than their mainland Tanzanian counterparts. For most destinations, including the beaches, there are several vehicles daily, with the last ones back to Stone Town departing by about 3pm or 4pm. None of the routes cost more than Tsh2000, and all take plenty of time (eg about one and one half hours from Zanzibar Town to Jambiani). All have destination signboards and numbers. Commonly used routes include the following:

ROUTE NO	DESTINATION
116	Nungwi
117	Kiwengwa
118	Matemwe
206	Chwaka
214	Uroa
308	Unguja Ukuu
309	Jambiani
310	Makunduchi
324	Bwejuu
326	Kizimkazi
501	Amani
502	Bububu
505	Airport ('U/Ndege')

Private Minibus

Private tourist minibuses run daily to the north- and east-coast beaches, although stiff competition and lots of hassles with touts mean that a splurge on a taxi isn't a bad idea. Book through any travel agency the day before you want to leave, and the minibus will pick you up at your hotel in Stone Town between 8am and 9am. Travel takes from one to 1½ hours to most destinations, and costs a negotiable Tsh5000 to Tsh15,000 per person, depending on how full the minivan is. Don't pay for the return trip in advance as you'll probably see neither the driver nor your money again. Most drivers only go to hotels where they'll get a commission, and will go to every length to talk you out of other places, including telling you that the hotel is closed/full/burned down etc. Be sure you've confirmed your destination in advance.

Taxi

Taxis don't have meters, so you'll need to agree on a price with the driver before getting into the car. Town trips cost from Tsh3000, more at night.

AROUND ZANZIBAR

Beaches

Zanzibar has superb beaches, with the best along the island's east coast. While many are now overcrowded and overdeveloped, all offer a wonderful respite from bumping along dusty roads on the mainland. The east-coast beaches are protected by coral reefs offshore and have fine, white coral sand. Depending on the season, they may also have a lot of seaweed (most abundant from December to February).

Everyone has their favourites, and which beach you choose is a matter of preference. For a never-quiet party scene, head to central or west Nungwi in the far north (although for a beach, you'll need to go around the corner to Kendwa). East Nungwi has a narrow beach at low tide, and a much quieter ambience. Paje, on the east coast, is the island's other hub of beach and party activity.

Bwejuu and Jambiani on the east coast have some of the finest stretches of palm-fringed nd you'll find anywhere. Things here are also more spread out and calmer than in the north. For a quieter atmosphere, try Matemwe or Pongwe. If you're seeking the large resort scene, the main area is the beach north of Kiwengwa towards Pwani Mchangani, although Kendwa is coming close. The coast north of Bwejuu along Ras Michamvi is also quiet. Except for Kendwa, where you can take a dip at any time, swimming at all of the beaches is tide dependent, with the tide receding up to 1km or more at low tide in the east.

NUNGWI

This large village, nestled among the palm groves at Zanzibar's northernmost tip, is a dhow-building centre and one of the island's major tourist destinations. This is despite lacking any sort of substantial beach during much of the year, thanks to shifting tidal patterns and development-induced erosion.

Nungwi is also where traditional and modern knock against each other with full force. Fishers sit in the shade repairing their nets while the morning's catch dries on neat wooden racks nearby, and rough-hewn planks slowly take on new life as skilled boat builders ply their centuries-old trade. Yet you only need to take a few steps back from the waterfront to enter into another world, with blaring music, an internet cafe, a rather motley collection of guesthouses packed in against each other, interspersed with the occasional five-star hotel, and a definite party vibe. For some travellers it's the only place to be on the island (and it's one of the few places you can swim without needing to wait for the tides to come in); others will probably want to give it a wide miss. Most hotels and the centre of all the action are just north and west of Nungwi village, where it gets quite crowded. If partying isn't your scene, there are some lovely, quiet patches of sand on Nungwi's eastern side (where swimming is more tidal), and Kendwa (p78) is only a short walk, boat or taxi-ride away.

Activities

The best diving in the north is around Mnemba, which can be readily arranged from Nungwi, though it's a bit of a ride to get there. Leven Bank is closer and can be quite rewarding, but you'll need previous experience. Otherwise, there are various sites closer in that are good for beginners.

East Africa Diving & Water Sport Centre DIVING
(☎0777-420588; www.diving-zanzibar.com) Next to Jambo Brothers Beach Bungalows.

Zanzibar Watersports DIVING
(☎0773-235030; www.zanzibarwatersports.com) A PADI five-star centre based at Ras Nungwi Beach Hotel, with branches at Paradise Beach Bungalows and at Kendwa Rocks.

There is also kitesurfing and parasailing, both based near Paradise Beach Bungalows: **Kiteboarding Zanzibar** (www.kiteboardingzanzibar.com) and **Zanzibar Parasailing** (www.zanzibarparasailing.com).

Sleeping & Eating

WEST NUNGWI

Smiles Beach Hotel HOTEL $$
(☎024-224 0472; www.smilesbeachhotel.com; east-central Nungwi; s/d/tr US$90/120/150;) Smiles, at the quieter edge of west Nungwi, has well-maintained, well-appointed rooms in somewhat stern-looking two-storey tile-roofed blocks overlooking a manicured lawn and a small patch of beach. They're clean and good value, all with small sea-facing balconies, and with more space and quiet than at some of the other central hotels.

Flame Tree Cottages B&B $$
(☎024-224 0100, 0777-479429; www.flametreecottages.com; east-central Nungwi; s/d US$110/150;) The cosy Flame Tree offers simply furnished white cottages in a small garden just in from the beach in a quieter spot on the northeastern edge of Nungwi. All have fan, and some have a small kitchenette and mini-fridge. Breakfast is served on your verandah; dinner can be arranged with advance order.

Langi-Langi Beach Bungalows HOTEL $$
(☎024-224 0470, 0733-911000; www.langilangizanzibar.com; s/d from US$85/130; @) This appealingly named place is in the centre of Nungwi next to Amaan Bungalows, and just in from the water. Rooms are clean and fine, if undistinguished, and despite the crowded location, it's an amenable choice. There's a restaurant.

Nungwi Inn Hotel HOTEL $$
(☎024-224 0091, 0777-418769; www.nungwiinnhotel.co.tz; west Nungwi; s/d/tr US$45/60/85, with sea view US$55/75/100;) Located towards the southern end of the main hotel strip, Nungwi Inn has reasonable rooms in small whitewashed cottages scattered around

scruffy but rather spacious grounds, and a restaurant.

Safina Bungalows GUESTHOUSE $

(0777-415726; kihorinungwi@hotmail.com; s/d/tr US$30/50/70, with air-con US$40/70) Safina is a decent budget choice, with spiffy no-frills bungalows around a small, pretty garden, just in from the beach in the centre of Nungwi, and meals in a double-storey pavilion. It's just behind Z Hotel.

Amaan Bungalows HOTEL $$

(024-224 0024/6; www.amaanbungalows.com; central Nungwi; s US$60-120, d US$70-130;) This large, efficient place is at the centre of the action. There are various room types, ranging from small garden-view rooms with fan to nicer, spacious sea-view rooms with air-con and small balconies. Also in the crowded complex is a waterside restaurant-bar, internet access, moped rental, diving and fishing outfits and a travel agency.

Baraka Beach Bungalows BUNGALOW $

(0777-415569, 0777-422910; http://barakabungalow.atspace.com; s/d US$30/45) Small and friendly, between Cholo's, and Paradise Beach Bungalows, Baraka has no-frills stone-and-thatch cottages around a tiny garden, and a restaurant.

Paradise Beach Bungalows HOTEL $

(0777-260389, 0777-854182; www.paradisebeach.co.tz; dm US$20, s/d/tr US$30/50/70) This is a large, busy two-storey block in front of Baraka Bungalows on the water with 19 basic but reasonable value rooms, including some dorm beds. All have fan and hot water, and there's a restaurant. Only consider here if you want to be in the thick of things, as there's nowhere to quietly chill.

Union Beach Bungalows BUNGALOW $

(0773-176923, 0776-583412; http://unionbungalow.atspace.com; central Nungwi; s/d from US$40/50;) Union Beach has no-frills bungalows plus rooms in a two-storey block, some with air-con and fridge. Meals are available. It's next to Jambo Brothers.

Jambo Brothers Beach Bungalows BUNGALOW $

(0773-109343, 0777-492355; jambobungalows@yahoo.com; central Nungwi; s/d without bathroom US$20/30) This low-key place on the sand in northwestern Nungwi has been spruced up a bit, though rooms are still quite basic. There's a large waterside restaurant.

Cholo's Bar & Restaurant BANDA $

(banda per person without bathroom US$15) Very chilled out, with a few basic *bandas*, meals and a bar/music area that stays going until the wee hours.

Z Hotel BOUTIQUE HOTEL $$$

(0774-266266; www.thezhotel.com; s/d from US$170/220;) This boutique hotel is the most upmarket choice by far in this part of Nungwi (rivalled only by the less atmospheric Zanzibar Doubletree, further north). Rooms, all beautifully appointed, are in a three-storey block overlooking a small infinity pool and the water, and there's a timbered waterside restaurant. There's a minimum three-night stay.

NUNGWI VILLAGE

Nungwi Guest House GUESTHOUSE $

(0772-263322; www.nungwiguesthouseznz.com; Nungwi village; s/d/tr US$20/30/45) A good budget option in the village centre, with simple, clean en suite rooms around a small garden courtyard, all with fans. There's no food. Watch for the light-blue fish-painted walls and courtyard.

Romantic Bungalows BUNGALOW $

(0772-114469; lucas.chonde@yahoo.com; Nungwi village; r US$40, s without bathroom US$25) Behind Flame Tree Cottages and near Nungwi Guest House, with 10 no-frills twin-bedded rooms with fan in basic thatch cottages around a small garden and meals.

Baraka Bungalows Annex BUNGALOW $

(0777-415569, 0777-422910; http://barakabungalow.atspace.com; r US$35) Four quiet rooms away from the beach, diagonally opposite the entrance for Mnarani Beach Cottages. Baraka Aquarium and 'snake park' are also on the premises.

EAST NUNGWI

Mnarani Beach Cottages LODGE $$

(024-224 0494, 0777-415551; www.lighthousezanzibar.com; east Nungwi; s US$78-90, d US$120-200, tr US$195-225, all prices include half board;) Mnarani Beach Cottages is the first place you come to on the placid eastern side of Nungwi, just after the lighthouse (the name means 'at the lighthouse' in Swahili). The beach itself is a narrow, walkable strip at low tide, which disappears at high tide. Accommodation is in small, spotless cottages, larger family rooms, the two-storey Zanzibar House or a more private honeymoon cottage.

Ras Nungwi Beach Hotel HOTEL $$$
(☎024-223 3767; www.rasnungwi.com; east Nungwi; s/d full board from US$240/280; ⊙Jun-Mar; ❄@≋) This cosy, upmarket place has long been a standout in Nungwi, with a low-key ambience, airy sea-view chalets nestled on a hillside overlooking the sea, and less expensive 'garden-view' rooms in the main lodge. The hotel can organise fishing and water sports, and there's a dive centre.

Information

There's an internet cafe and forex bureau at Amaan Bungalows.

Getting There & Away

Bus 116 runs daily between Nungwi and Zanzibar Town (Tsh2000) along a sealed road.

KENDWA

About 3km southwest of Nungwi along the coast is Kendwa. It's a long, wonderfully wide stretch of sand, although the once-quiet ambience is now gone, thanks to a seemingly non-stop frenzy of hotel development and the incursion of Italian package tourism. That said, there is more space than at Nungwi, and amenable tidal patterns mean that there is swimming at all hours. For diving, there's **Scuba Do** (☎0777-417157; www.scuba-do-zanzibar.com) at Sunset Bungalows, with a full range of PADI courses.

Sleeping

Les Toits du Palme BUNGALOW $$
(☎0777-851474; d US$60-80, d with air-con & hot water US$100) Three basic wooden beach bungalows on the sand, and six more rooms up on a small cliff. Everything's no-frills, but it's one of the few quieter backpackers' chill spots left at Kendwa.

Sunset Bungalows BUNGALOW $$
(☎0777-414647, 0777-413818; www.sunsetkendwa.com; s/US$40-75, d US$55-95, tr US$60-95; ❄) This long-standing place has a mix of rooms on the beach and on the cliff top, some with air-con and all with bathroom with hot water, plus some cliff-top rooms in two-storey blocks. There's also a resident dive operator, and a large, popular beachside restaurant-bar with evening bonfires on the beach.

Kendwa Rocks BUNGALOW $$
(☎0777-415475; www.kendwarocks.com; s/d banda without toilet from US$28/41, s/d beach bungalows from US$55/69, s/d/tr stone cottages from US$41/76/97, cliff-top s/d from US$55/83, d ste from US$103; ❄) A Kendwa classic, although it has considerably expanded from its humble beginnings. Accommodation is in no-frills beach *bandas* sharing toilets, nicer self-contained bungalows on the sand, cool stone garden cottages and suites and rooms up on the cliff top. Full moon parties are an institution.

La Gemma del'Est HOTEL $$$
(☎024-224 0087; www.gemmadellest.com; per person full board from US$265; ❄@📶≋) This is the nicest of the larger resorts and Kendwa's quietest, most family-friendly place, with large grounds, a good beach, several restaurant-bars (including one on a jetty over the water), a gym, a spa and a huge pool.

Getting There & Away

You can walk to Kendwa from Nungwi at low tide in about 25 to 30 minutes, but take care as there have been some muggings. Alternatively, you can arrange boats with hotels in both Nungwi and Kendwa for the short jaunt. Via public transport from Stone Town, have dalla-dalla 116 drop you at the Kendwa turn-off, from where it's about a 2km walk to the beach.

MATEMWE

The long, idyllic beach at Matemwe has some of the finest sand on Zanzibar. It's also the best base for diving and snorkelling around Mnemba, which lies just offshore. In the nearby village, life moves at its own pace, with women making their way across the shallows at low tide to harvest seaweed, strings of fish drying in the sun, and cows and chickens wandering across the road.

Sleeping

Matemwe Beach Village LODGE $$
(☎0777-417250, 0777-437200; www.matemwebeach.net; r per person with half board US$80-135, asali ste with half board US$400; ❄@📶≋) This recommended beachfront place has a wonderful setting on a beautiful stretch of coast, a low-key ambience and spacious, airy, good-value bungalows with small verandahs. There's also a private beachfront honeymoon suite, plus several two-storey '*shamba* suites' and an open lounge area with throw pillows. One Ocean/The Zanzibar Dive Centre (p65) has a branch here.

Sunshine Hotel HOTEL $$$
(☎0774-388662; www.sunshinezanzibar.com; s/d US$140/210, garden apt s/d US$100/130, ste from US$280; @📶≋) This lovely new place on the beach next door to Zanzibar Retreat Hotel has approximately 14 rooms in two-storey blocks, all with louvered doors and standing and ceiling fans. All rooms look over the

small garden towards the beach. There are also two suites, a garden apartment, and a restaurant

Nyota Beach Bungalows BUNGALOW **$$**
(☎0777-484303, 0777-439059; www.nyotabeachbungalows.com; s/d/tr from US$40/75/100) Nyota has straightforward but atmospheric bungalows (including one two-storey bungalow) set amid the palms and papaya trees in a garden just back from the beach. There's a restaurant.

Matemwe Bungalows BUNGALOW **$$$**
(www.asiliaafrica.com/matemwe; ste per person full board US$337; ⊙mid-Jun–Easter; @≋) Matemwe Bungalows, about 1km north of Matemwe Beach Village, is a relaxing, upmarket place with a dozen spacious and impeccably decorated seaside bungalow suites. There are also more luxurious suites, including one for honeymooners with its own beach.

Sele's Bungalows BUNGALOW **$$**
(☎0777-413449; www.selesbungalowsznz.com; d from US$70, without bathroom from US$45, f US$120) This friendly, no-frills place just south of Matemwe Beach Village has six simple cottage-style rooms in a dhow-themed garden on the beach. The two family rooms are upstairs, open on one side and sharing toilet. The others (all doubles) have private bathroom, and all have fans. There's a small restaurant and a bar.

Azanzi HOTEL **$$$**
(☎0775-044171; www.azanzibeachhotel.com; r per person full board US$185-255; ❄@≋) The 35-room South African–owned Azanzi has attached 'standard' rooms snaking back from the beach in two long rows with a pool in the centre, plus some separate, spacious luxury villas. It's all comfortable and well located, but lacking space. Matemwe One Ocean has a base here for diving.

Zanzibar Retreat Hotel BOUTIQUE HOTEL **$$$**
(☎0776-108379; www.zanzibarretreat.com; s/d US$128/176; ❄@☜≋) A small, well-located place on the beach with just seven rooms, all well appointed and with Zanzibari beds, but on the small side and rather on top of each other. It is, however, good value considering the location.

Matemwe Baharini Villas Beach Resort LODGE **$$**
(☎0772-990021; www.baharinivillasznz.com; d US$80-100; ❄☜) This unassuming place is on the beach between Matemwe Beach Village and Matemwe Bungalows. There are 12 rooms, divided between two main houses ('villas') and a row of simple, beach-facing attached double bungalows. Furnishings and ambience are simple and functional, and there's a restaurant and an on-site PADI dive centre.

Mohammed's Restaurant & Bungalows BUNGALOW **$**
(☎0777-431881; r without bathroom US$40) This establishment has four very basic en suite bungalows, each with two large beds, in Mohammed's small garden just back from the beach. Grilled fish and other local meals can be arranged. It's a good budget deal.

Key's Bungalows BUNGALOW **$**
(☎0777-411797; www.allykeys.com; s/d US$40/50) This quirky backpackers' place on the beach at the north end of Matemwe village has a chilled beach bar and a handful of simple, clean rooms, some in a two-storey block, others separate, and meals.

Getting There & Away

Matemwe village is located about 25km southeast of Nungwi and is reached via a sealed road branching east off the main road by Mkwajuni. Dalla-dallas travel here daily from Stone Town (Tsh1500). Early in the day, they continue as far as the fish market at the northern end of the beach (and this is where you can catch them as well). Otherwise, the start/terminus of the route is at the main junction near Matemwe Beach Village hotel. The last dalla-dalla in both directions departs about 4pm, the first about 6am.

KIWENGWA

Kiwengwa village is spread out along a fine, wide beach, much of which is occupied by large, Italian-run resort hotels, although there are some quieter stretches to the north and south.

Sleeping

Shooting Star Lodge BOUTIQUE HOTEL **$$$**
(☎0777-414166; www.shootingstarlodge.com; s/d garden view US$130/200, s/d sea-view cottages US$170/300; ❄@≋) Classy and intimate, this small lodge is recommended, both for its location on a low cliff overlooking a beautiful, quiet stretch of beach, and for its excellent service and cuisine. There's a salt-water infinity pool, and a raised beachside bar. It's tranquil, calm and an overall fine place to unwind after a gruelling safari or three.

Bluebay Beach Resort RESORT $$$
(☎024-224 0240/1; www.bluebayzanzibar.com; s/d with half board from US$190/300;) One of the nicer of the large resorts along the Kiwengwa coastline, Bluebay has a more subdued atmosphere than its neighbours. Rooms have two large beds and all the amenities, and the grounds are expansive, green and serene.

Ocean Paradise Resort RESORT $$$
(☎0774-440990; www.oceanparadisezanzibar.com; per person half board US$120-170;) An agreeable choice if you're seeking a resort, with accommodation in spacious, round bungalows, a raised restaurant with commanding views over the water, large, green gardens dotted with palms and sloping down to the beach and a huge swimming pool.

Getting There & Away

Dalla-dalla 117 runs daily between Kiwengwa village and Stone Town along the sealed road.

PONGWE

This quiet arc of beach, about 5km south of Kiwengwa, is dotted with palm trees and backed by dense vegetation, and is about as close to the quintessential tropical paradise as you can get. Thanks to its position in a semi-sheltered cove, it also has the advantage of having less seaweed than other parts of the east coast.

The intimate and unassuming **Pongwe Beach Hotel** (☎0773-000556, 0784-336181; www.pongwe.com; garden/sea-view r US$170/190;) has 16 bungalows on a wonderful arc of beach. Most are sea-facing (three are garden view), spacious and breezy, the cuisine is good. It's justifiably popular, good value and often fully booked.

Set on the beach south of Pongwe village, **Santa Maria Coral Park** (☎0777-432655; www.santamaria-zanzibar.com; s US$30-40, d US$60-80, tr US$90-100) is a laid-back beach haunt with accommodation in no-frills thatched *bandas*, stone-and-thatch bungalows or a newer double-storey bungalow. All have fans, bathroom and (sometimes) hot water. There's a restaurant with basic seafood meals. The beachside bar has music and a bonfire in the evenings.

Dalla-dallas to Pongwe depart from Zanzibar Town's Mwembeladu junction; take dalla-dalla 501 from Darajani towards Amani stadium and ask to be dropped at Mwembeladu (Tsh300, 10 minutes), from where you can get dalla-dalla 233 to Pongwe-Pwani (Tsh1500, one hour), and walk the last short stretch.

PAJE

Paje is a wide, white beach at the junction where the coastal road north to Bwejuu and south to Jambiani joins with the road from Zanzibar Town. It's built-up, with a cluster of mostly unremarkable places all within a few minutes' walk of each other, and a party atmosphere. Paje is also Zanzibar's main kitesurfing centre; on fine days in season, the sea is filled with kitesurfers, often so much so that it can be difficult to find a quiet spot to swim. Contact **Zanzibar Kite Centre** (www.kitecentrezanzibar.com), just south of Kitete Beach Bungalows or **Airborne Kite Centre** (www.airbornekitecentre.com), just north of Arabian Nights Annex. For diving, there's **Buccaneer Diving** (www.buccaneerdiving.com) on the beach near Arabian Nights hotel. **Supaduka** (town entrance) has internet.

Sleeping

Kitete Beach Bungalows HOTEL $$
(☎024-224 0226, 0778-160666; www.kitetebeach.com; s/d main house US$30/50, new wing s/d from US$40/70) This friendly, good-value place on the beach has six clean, no-frills rooms with cold water showers in the original cottage building, and newer, very nice rooms next door in bright ochre-coloured double-storey bungalows, all with ceiling and standing fans and ocean views.

Paradise Beach Bungalows BUNGALOW $$
(☎024-223 1387, 0777-414129; http://paradisebeachbungalows.web.fc2.com/; s/d from US$50/60) This long-standing Japanese-run place is hidden among the palm trees in a quiet, relaxed beachside compound at the northern edge of Paje and slightly removed from the main cluster of hotels. Each room has two large beds, and there's also a restaurant.

Teddy's Place BUNGALOW $
(☎0776-110850; www.teddys-place.com; dm/s/d/tr US$15/28/35/45;) Teddy's has no-frills thatched huts on the sand back from the beach. Bathrooms are all shared (bring your own towel). There are also some dorm beds, a restaurant-bar and weekly 'hakuna kulala' (no sleep) parties. It's very popular with backpackers. It's about 300m south of the Paje roundabout.

Ndame Beach Lodge BUNGALOW $$
(☎0777-886611; www.ndamezanzibar.com; s/tw/d/tr/f US$50/70/75/90/130) The German-run Ndame Beach has no-frills, good-value adjoining bungalows on the beach, and a res-

taurant and bar. It's on the northern edge of Paje, en route to Bwejuu.

Sun & Seaview Bungalows BUNGALOW $$
(☎0718-102633; www.sunandseaviewbungalows.com; s/d/tr/q US$40/70/110/140) On offer here are 10 good-value attached cottage rooms plus one family cottage in a small beachside garden next to Paradise Beach Bungalows. It's at the far northern edge of Paje, and away from the main hotel cluster. All rooms have double bed, and there's a restaurant.

Paje by Night LODGE $$
(☎0777-460710; www.pajebynight.net; d US$90-115; ⏲Jun–mid-Apr; ❄) This chilled place, known for its noisy bar and its party vibe, has a crowded mix of no-frills standard and more spacious rooms, plus several double-storey four-person rustic 'jungle bungalows'. Air-con is available only in the larger rooms and jungle bungalows. There's a restaurant with a pizza oven. It's two minutes' walk back from the beach in Paje centre.

Arabian Nights Annex HOTEL $$
(☎024-224 0190, 0777-844443; www.zanzibararabiannights.com; s/d from US$130/140; ❄@≋) Well-located directly on the beach just up from the affiliated Arabian Nights is this nice, new annex, with clean, fairly spacious rooms in double-storey cement rondavels, a pool directly in front and a restaurant.

Arabian Nights HOTEL $$
(☎024-224 0190; www.zanzibararabiannights.com; s/d/tr from US$100/110/140; ❄@≋) Arabian Nights has closely spaced rooms in stone cottages just back from the beach, including some with sea view, and a restaurant. Standards have slipped since our last visit, and everything is looking a bit worn out, although rooms are still reasonable value for price.

ℹ Getting There & Away

Bus 324 runs several times daily between Paje and Stone Town en route to/from Bwejuu, with the last departure from Paje at about 4pm. The Makunduchi–Michamvi dalla-dalla also stops at Bwejuu; see the Makunduchi section.

BWEJUU

The large village of Bwejuu lies about 3km north of Paje on a long, palm-shaded beach. It's quite spread out, and quieter and less crowded than Paje and Nungwi, with a mellow atmosphere and nothing much more to do other than wander along the sand and listen to the breezes rustling the palm trees.

Sleeping & Eating

Evergreen Bungalows Bwejuu BUNGALOW $$
(☎024-224 0273; www.evergreen-bungalows.com; r US$70-90) North of Bwejuu village, the well-maintained Evergreen has spiffy two-storey beach bungalows, plus several single-storey 'palm garden' cottages back from the beach. All have bathrooms, although the palm garden cottages have only cold water. There's a restaurant and a dive centre.

Twisted Palms Lodge BUNGALOW $$
(☎0776-130275; www.twistedpalms.zanzibarone.com; s/d/tr US$40/50/60, s/d/tr/q on beach US$55/65/75/85) Twisted Palms is under new Italian management, which is working hard to make it a tranquil beach retreat. There are five, clean, bright cottages up on a hill just behind the road, each with one double and one twin bed. Directly on the beach are five more beachside cottages (two quads, two triples, one double). There's a dhow for excursions. Seafood meals are available.

Kilimani Kwetu BUNGALOW $$
(☎024-224 0235; www.kilimani.de; s/d US$40/60) This German-Zanzibari run place has four simple rooms in two attached cottages just across the road back from the beach, and a relaxing bar-restaurant area on the beach. The emphasis is on partnering and integration with the local community.

Palm Beach Inn LODGE $$
(☎024-224 0221; www.palmbeachinn.com; s/d/tr from US$50/60/85, f/ste US$120/250; ❄≋) This friendly Bwejuu institution, run by former Zanzibari MP Mama Naila and son Mahfoud, is worth considering for the insights it gives into local life (which you'll be right in the middle of) rather than for its comforts. Accommodation is in small, heavily furnished rooms in a crowded beachside compound. There are two newer, nicer sea-view suites and a good restaurant. The beach immediately in front isn't the best, but there's a pool, and you can walk to better beaches nearby.

ℹ Getting There & Away

Bus 324 goes daily between Stone Town and Bwejuu, and will drop you along the main road, from where it's about 500m down to the beach.

MICHAMVI PENINSULA

Beginning about 4km north of Bwejuu, the land begins to taper off into the narrow Michamvi Peninsula, where there are several upmarket retreats and a few budget places. The beach is lovely here, and comparatively quiet, though this will likely not last long.

Sleeping & Eating

Breezes Beach Club & Spa RESORT $$$
(☎0774-440883; www.breezes-zanzibar.com; per person half board from US$177; ❄@📶🏊) This long-standing place on the east side of the peninsula near Bwejuu receives consistently good reviews. Accommodation is in well-appointed rooms and suites in lovely gardens. There's diving, a gym and other activities. Advance bookings only – you won't get by the tight gate security without one.

Sagando Lodge BUNGALOW $
(☎0773-866395; r US$30) Just behind Michamvi Sunset Bay and just back from the beach, this is an amenable budget option, with a handful of single- and two-storey bungalows on the sand in a small, enclosed garden and meals on order.

Michamvi Sunset Bay RESORT $$$
(☎0777-878136; www.michamvi.com; per person half board s/d US$182/280) Formerly Michamvi Watersports, this large, South African-owned resort just north of Kae village and overlooking Chwaka Bay has an array of comfortable rooms with the standard amenities, a restaurant, and – uniquely for Zanzibar's east cost – sunset views over the water.

Getting There & Away

Dalla-dallas travel regularly from Stone Town (Tsh2000). There's also at least one, usually two or three dalla-dallas between Michamvi village and Makunduchi (Tsh1300).

JAMBIANI

Jambiani is a long village on a stunning stretch of coastline. The village itself, a sunbaked and somnolent collection of thatch and coral-rag houses, is stretched out over more than a kilometre. The sea is an ethereal shade of turquoise and is usually dotted with *ngalawa* (outrigger canoes) moored just offshore. It's quieter than Paje and Nungwi, and has a good selection of accommodation in all price ranges.

Sleeping & Eating

Blue Oyster Hotel HOTEL $$
(☎024-224 0163, 0787-233610; www.zanzibar.de; s/d/tr US$75/90/120, s/d/tr/q with sea view US$98/113/143/158) This German-run place, directly on the beach at the northern end of Jambiani, has pleasant, spotless, good-value rooms (some around a small inner courtyard, others beachfront) and a breezy terrace restaurant with good meals.

Red Monkey Lodge BUNGALOW $$
(☎024-224 0207, 0777-713366; www.redmonkeylodge.com; s/d/tr US$75/95/115) Located at Jambiani's far southern end, Red Monkey has nine rooms in clean, sea-facing bungalows set along a nice garden on the beach. There's a dhow bar, chill-out area, restaurant, diving and kitesurfing.

Coco Beach Hotel & Restaurant BUNGALOW $$
(☎0732-940154; www.cocobeachzanzibar.com; s/d/tr US$60/70/90) This place has five small whitewashed bungalows in an enclosed garden just back from the beach in Jambiani village, and a restaurant.

Casa Del Mar Hotel Jambiani HOTEL $$
(☎024-224 0400, 0777-455446; www.casa-delmar-zanzibar.com; d downstairs/upstairs US$86/106; 🏊) This small beachside place has 14 rooms in two double-storey blocks (the upper-storey rooms have lofts). They're in a small, lush garden in a tiny, enclosed beach area, with a restaurant and a terrace bar.

Jambiani White Sands BUNGALOW $$
(☎0777-450565; www.jambianiwhitesands.com; s/d US$45/55; 📶) This small place on the beach about 800m south of Jambiani centre has no-frills stone-and-thatch bungalows with fans and hot water, all behind a low fence, and meals. It's not the fanciest, but it's quite decent value for the price.

Kimte Beach Inn BUNGALOW $
(☎024-224 0212, 0778-832824; www.kimtebeachinn.com; dm US$20, s US$20-25, d US$40-50) At the southern end of Jambiani, this chilled Rasta-run place has basic, dark-ish rooms on the land side of the road (about half a minute's walk from the beach), meals and a popular beach bar with music and evening bonfires.

Coral Rock HOTEL $$
(☎024-224 0154; www.coralrockzanzibar.com; r US$85-159; ❄@🏊) The aptly-named Coral Rock is on a large coral rock jutting out into the sea at the southern end of Jambiani, just south of Kimte Beach Inn. Accommodation is in 14 reasonable whitewashed stone-and-thatch cottages with fan, air-con and small porches, and there's a bar overlooking the water.

Getting There & Away

Dalla-dalla 309 runs several times daily to Jambiani from Darajani market in Stone Town. The Makunduchi to Michamvi dalla-dalla (see the Makunduchi section) also stops at Jambiani.

MAKUNDUCHI

The main reason to come to Makunduchi is for the **Mwaka Kogwa festival** (p68), when this small town is bursting at its seams with revellers. The only accommodation is at **Zanzibar Blue Resort** (La Madrugada; ☎024-224 0348, 0777-276621; www.zanzibarblueresort.com; d with half board US$160; ❄📶≋), a tranquil beachside place with rows of two-storey attached rooms overlooking two pools.

Bus 310 runs to Makunduchi on no set schedule, with plenty of additional transport from both Zanzibar Town and Kizimkazi during Mwaka Kogwa. There's dalla-dalla service two or three times daily along this sealed road from Makunduchi to Michamvi (Tsh1300, one hour) via Jambiani (Tsh400) and Bwejuu (Tsh800), departing Makunduchi around 8.30am and Michamvi at 7.30am. Later departures are whenever the vehicle fills.

KIZIMKAZI

This small village consists of two adjoining settlements: Kizimkazi Dimbani to the north and Kizimkazi Mkunguni to the south. It has a small, breezy and in parts quite attractive beach broken by coral rock outcrops. However, the main reason people visit is to see the **dolphins** that favour the nearby waters, or to relax or go **diving** at one of the handful of resorts. Dolphin trips can be organised through tour operators in Stone Town from about US$25 per person, or with some of the hotels at Paje and Jambiani from Tsh20,000 per person. Most Kizimkazi hotels also organise tours (about US$50 per boat including snorkelling equipment). While the dolphins are beautiful, the tours, especially those organised from Stone Town, can be unpleasant, due to the hunt-and-chase tactics used by some of the tour boats. If you do go out, the best time is early morning when the water is calmer and the sun not as hot. If it's too windy, it's difficult to get in and out of the boats to snorkel.

Kizimkazi is also the site of a Shirazi **mosque** dating from the early 12th century. Inside, however, in the mihrab are inscribed verses from the Quran dating to 1107 and considered to be among the oldest known examples of Swahili writing. You'll need to take off your shoes, and you should cover up bare shoulders or legs. The mosque is in Kizimkazi Dimbani, just north of the main beach area.

Sleeping & Eating

Kizi Dolphin Lodge GUESTHOUSE $
(☎0777-422843, 0777-410253; www.kizidolphinlodge.com; Kizimkazi Dimbani; r US$50; ❄) This friendly two-storey budget establishment is about 500m back from the beach in Kizimkazi Dimbani; follow the dirt road uphill from the dalla-dalla stop for about 300m. There are five double rooms and one twin, all clean with fan and air-con. Meals and dolphin trips can be arranged.

Unguja Lodge LODGE $$$
(☎0774-477477; www.ungujalodge.com; Kizimkazi Mkunguni; per person half board from US$230; @📶≋) Unguja Lodge is a stylish place with 11 wonderfully spacious two-storey vil-

WATCHING THE DOLPHINS

If you want to watch the dolphins, heed the advice posted on the wall of the Worldwide Fund for Nature (WWF) office in Zanzibar Town, which boils down to the following:

» As with other animals, viewing dolphins in their natural environs requires time and patience.

» Shouting and waving your arms around will not encourage dolphins to approach your boat.

» Be satisfied with simply seeing the dolphins; don't force the boat operator to chase the dolphins, cross their path or get too close, especially when they are resting.

» If you decide to get in the water with the dolphins, do so quietly and calmly and avoid splashing.

» No one can guarantee that you will see dolphins on an outing, and swimming with them is a rare and precious occurrence.

» Remember – dolphins are wild and their whereabouts cannot be predicted. It is they who choose to interact with people, not the other way around...

las, all impeccably decorated and well-appointed, and some with sea views. They're set amid attractive gardens dotted with baobab trees. There's a good restaurant and an in-house dive operator. Very relaxing if you can afford it.

Kumi na Mbili Centre BUNGALOW **$**
(www.zanzibar-tourism.org; Kizimkazi Mkunguni; r Tsh40,000) This small centre, near the entrance to Kizimkazi Mkunguni, is part of an NGO-sponsored village development centre, and a good budget bet. There are a few no-frills twin-bedded rooms with fan, and meals on order.

Karamba LODGE **$$**
(0773-166406, 0777-418452; www.karambaresort.com; Kizimkazi Dimbani; s US$95, d US$140-200) Karamba, on the northern end of the beach in Kizimkazi Dimbani, has 12 detached whitewashed cottages lined up along a small cliff overlooking the sea. All are bright and en suite and some have appealing open-roof showers. There's a restaurant, and a beachside chill-out bar with throw pillows.

Getting There & Away

To reach Kizimkazi from Stone Town take bus 326 (Kizimkazi) direct (Tsh2000), or take bus 310 (Makunduchi) as far as Kufile junction, where you'll need to get out and wait for another vehicle heading towards Kizimkazi, or walk (about 5km). The last vehicle back to Stone Town leaves Kizimkazi about 4pm. As you approach from Stone Town go right at Kufile junction (ie towards Kizimkazi) and then right again at the next fork to Kizimkazi Dimbani. Kizimkazi Mkunguni is to the left at this last fork.

Jozani Forest

This cool and shady patch of green, now protected as part of Jozani–Chwaka Bay National Park, is the largest area of mature forest left on Zanzibar. Living among Jozani's tangle of vines and branches are populations of the rare red colobus monkey, as well as Sykes monkeys, bushbabies, Ader's duikers (although you won't see many of these), hyraxes, more than 50 species of butterflies, about 40 species of birds and several other animals. There's a nature trail in the forest, which takes about 45 minutes to walk.

Jozani Forest (adult/child with guide US$8/4; 7.30am-5.30pm) is 35km southeast of Zanzibar Town off the road to Paje, and best reached via bus 309 or 310, by chartered taxi, or with an organised tour from Zanzibar Town (often in combination with dolphin tours to Kizimkazi). The best times to see red colobus monkeys are in the early morning and late evening.

When observing the monkeys, take care not to get too close (park staff recommend no closer than 3m) both for your safety and the safety of the animals. In addition to the risk of being bitten by the monkeys, there's considerable concern that if the monkeys were to catch a human illness it could spread and rapidly wipe out the already threatened population.

Menai Bay & Unguja Ukuu

Menai Bay, fringed by the sleepy villages of Fumba to the west and Unguja Ukuu to the east, is home to an impressive assortment of corals, fish and mangrove forests, some idyllic sandbanks and deserted islets, and a sea-turtle breeding area. Since 1997 it's been protected as part of the **Menai Bay Conservation Area**. Unguja Ukuu is notable as the site of what is believed to be the earliest settlement on Zanzibar, dating to at least the 8th century, although there is little remaining today from this era.

The lovely **Fumba Beach Lodge** (0777-860504; www.fumbabeachlodge.com; s/d half board from US$217/366), 18km south of Zanzibar Town next to Fumba village, has accommodation in 26 spacious cottage-style rooms set in expansive grounds. There's a small spa built around a baobab tree (including a great Jacuzzi up in the tree) and a resident dive operator. It's also the base for Safari Blue (see p66). Although the beach at Fumba has a considerable amount of coral rock, the setting is beautiful and uncrowded, and the lodge makes an enjoyable change of pace.

Offshore Islands

CHANGUU

Also known as Prison Island, Changuu lies about 5km and an easy boat ride northwest of Zanzibar Town. It was originally used to detain 'recalcitrant' slaves and later as a quarantine station. Changuu is also known for its large family of **giant tortoises**, who were brought here from Aldabra in the Seychelles around the turn of the 20th century. There's a small beach and a nearby reef with **snorkelling**,

WORTH A TRIP

CHUMBE ISLAND CORAL PARK

The uninhabited island of Chumbe, about 12km south of Zanzibar Town, has an exceptional shallow-water coral reef along its western shore that abounds with fish life. Since 1994, when the reef was gazetted as Zanzibar's first marine sanctuary, the island has gained widespread acclaim, including from the UN, as the site of an impressive ecotourism initiative centred on an ecolodge and local environmental education programs. It's now run as **Chumbe Island Coral Park** (www.chumbeilsand.com), a private, nonprofit nature reserve.

Chumbe can be visited as a day trip, although staying overnight in one of the **eco-bungalows** (☎024-223 1040; www.chumbeilsand.com; s/d full board US$370/540) is recommended. Each bungalow has its own rainwater collection system and solar power, and a loft sleeping area that opens to the stars. Advance bookings are essential. Day visits (also by advance arrangement only) cost US$100 per person.

as well as the former house of the British governor, General Lloyd Matthews. There's accommodation at **Changuu Private Island Paradise** (☎0773-333241; www.privateislands-zanzibar.com; s/d half board US$310/440; ❄), with some rooms in the old converted Quarantine Area, and others in newly built bungalows on the island's quieter northwest side. Day trips to visit the tortoises cost about US$30 per person including lunch and island entry fee, but excluding boat transfer costs from Stone Town.

BAWI

Tiny Bawi, about 7km west of Zanzibar Town and several kilometres southwest of Changuu, offers a beach and **snorkelling**. For years marketed as a day out from Stone Town, it's now privately owned, and while snorkelling in the surrounding waters is possible, the island itself can only be visited by guests of **Bawe Tropical Island Lodge** (☎0773-333241; www.privateislands-zanzibar.com; per person-full board incl airport transfers US$510/680; ❄).

MNEMBA

Tiny Mnemba, just northeast of Matemwe, is the ultimate tropical paradise for those who have the money to enjoy it, complete with white sands, palm trees and turquoise waters. While the island itself is privately owned, with access restricted to guests of Mnemba Island Lodge, the surrounding coral reef can be visited by anyone. It's one of Zanzibar's prime **diving** and **snorkelling** sites.

The exclusive **Mnemba Island Lodge** (www.mnemba-island.com; per person full board US$1500) is a playground for the rich and famous, and is often rented out in its entirety.

OTHER ISLETS

Just offshore from Zanzibar Town are several tiny islets, many of which are ringed by coral reefs. These include **Nyange**, **Pange** and **Murogo**, which are sandbanks that partially disappear at high tide, and which offer snorkelling and diving (arranged through Stone Town dive operators).

PEMBA

POP 362,000

For much of its history, Pemba has been overshadowed by Zanzibar, its larger, more visible and more politically powerful neighbour to the south. Although the islands are separated by only 50km, very few tourists cross the channel. Those who do, however, are seldom disappointed because Pemba offers an authentic experience that's largely disappeared in the archipelago's other half.

Unlike flat, sandy Zanzibar, Pemba's terrain is hilly, fertile and lushly vegetated. In the days of the Arab traders it was even referred to as 'al Khuthera' or 'the Green Island'. Throughout much of the period when the sultans of Zanzibar held sway over the East African coast, it was Pemba, with its extensive clove plantations and agricultural base, that provided the economic foundation for the archipelago's dominance.

Much of Pemba's coast is lined with mangroves and lagoons; however, there are stretches of sand and some idyllic uninhabited isles where you can play castaway for a day. The healthy coral reefs, the steeply dropping walls of the Pemba Channel and an abundance of fish provide world-class diving: the best in East Africa.

…ke Zanzibar, where tourist infrastruc… well developed, Pemba is very much …kwater. Other than a few multistar re…, facilities range from fairly basic to non…stent. Pemba remains largely 'undiscov…ed' and you'll still have most things (even …e lovely beaches) more or less to yourself, which is a big part of the island's appeal.

Getting There & Away

Air

Karume airport is 6km east of Chake Chake. Five airlines (As Salaam, Coastal, Flightlink, Tropical, and Zan Air) fly Dar–Zanzibar–Pemba–Zanzibar–Dar at least once daily and all charge about US$100/140 from Pemba to Zanzibar/Dar es Salaam. Coastal adds a connection from Chake Chake to Tanga (US$100).

Boat

Ferries to/from Zanzibar and Dar es Salaam dock in Mkoani. Three companies were operating at the time of research: *Sea Bus*, *Sea Gull* and *Sepideh*. Several other ferries had been taken out of service because of questionable seaworthiness, but it's likely they'll find a way to start running again without making any significant safety

Pemba

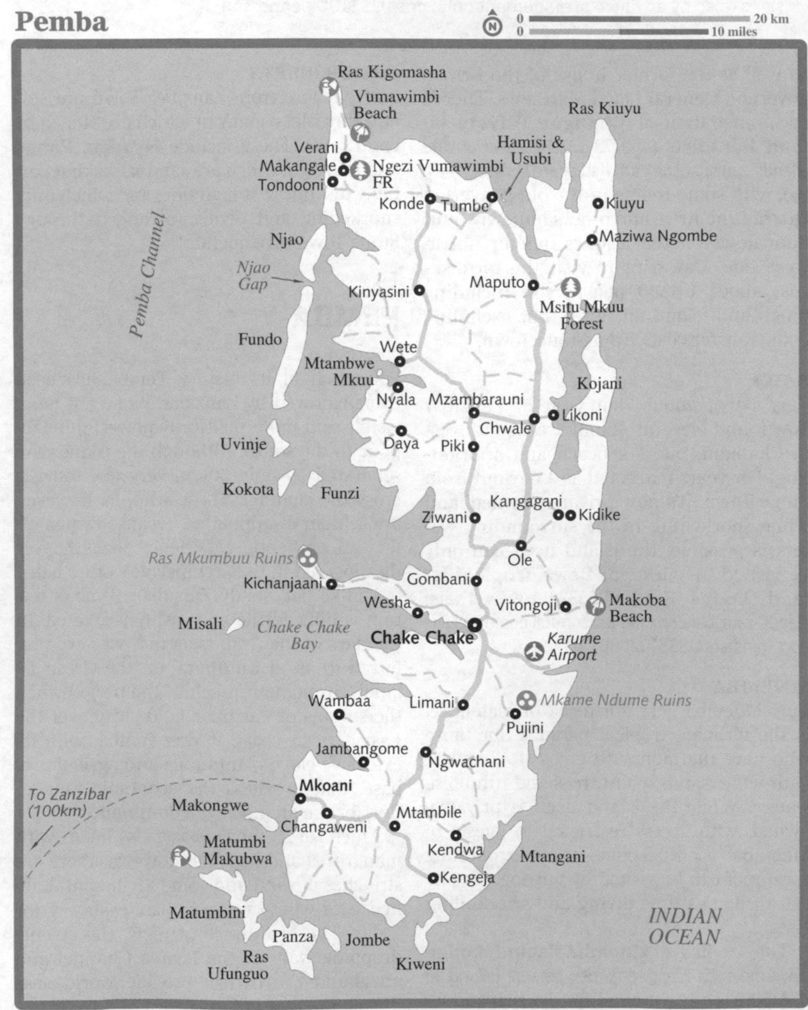

improvements so we recommend asking about particular ships before buying tickets.

Schedules exist more in theory than reality. *Sea Bus* (economy/1st class US$40/45) boats, the fastest and least likely to cancel, depart Dar daily at 7am and Zanzibar at 10am arriving in Pemba about 1pm. They leave Pemba at 8am. *Sea Gull* (economy/1st class US$20/30) runs only three times a week leaving Dar at 10am and Zanzibar at 10pm; it arrives in Pemba about 6am the next morning. It turns around from Pemba at 9.30am. Safeguard your luggage on the overnight trip. *Sepideh* (economy/1st class US$45/50), the least reliable, only travels between Zanzibar and Pemba. Boats leave Zanzibar at 8am and take about seven hours. Sometimes they turn around right away and sometimes wait until the next day to return. Tickets for all companies can be booked commission-free at various businesses in Chake Chake, Wete and Mkoani. It's usually possible to buy tickets last minute, but buying as early as possible is the best plan.

Normally there's an infrequent (less than weekly on average) boat between Wete and Tanga. Though it wasn't running at research time, service should resume again.

An immigration officer usually meets the boats to have arrivals from the mainland fill out a meaningless card. If you don't see them at the port and you aren't coming from Zanzibar, you're supposed to go the immigration office (500m up the hill in Mkoani) and sign in.

Getting Around

Crowded dalla-dallas (and a few comfortable coasters) plod down the main roads, most of which are sealed, but for many places you'll have to get off at the nearest junction and walk, wait for a lift, or try to negotiate an addition[illegible] the bus driver to deliver you. There are f[illegible] Cycling is an excellent way to explore Pem[illegible] distances are relatively short and roads ar[illegible] lightly travelled.

Chake Chake

Lively Chake Chake, set on a ridge over looking mangrove-filled Chake Chake Bay, is Pemba's main town and the best base for visiting the island's southern half, including Misali.

Sights & Activities

Pemba Museum MUSEUM
(adult/student US$5/3; 8.30am-4.30pm Mon-Fri, 9am-4pm Sat & Sun) Filling what's left of an 18th-century Omani-era **fort**, which was probably built on the remains a 16th-century Portuguese garrison, this is a small but well-executed museum with displays on island history and Swahili culture.

Pemba Essential Oil Distillery SPICE TOURS
(admission Tsh3000; 8am-3.30pm Mon-Fri) Visitors to this factory just out of town to the northeast can see the tanks where clove stems, cinnamon leaves, eucalyptus leaves, lemon grass and sweet basil are turned into essential oils. Check in at the office and someone will show you around.

Sleeping

Pemba Misali Sunset Beach RESORT **$$$**
(0775-044713; www.pembamisalibeach.com; Wesha Rd; s US$100-140, d US$120-160;)

PEMBA PECULIARITIES

Tourism in Pemba is different from anywhere else in the country; even Zanzibar. Keep the following in mind.

» Chake Chake has the island's only internationally linked ATM, so come prepared with enough cash.

» Despite the scarcity of tourists, prices are as high as (and sometimes higher than) those in Zanzibar.

» Most businesses operate from 8am to 3pm and many reopen from 7pm to 9pm. Outside Chake Chake few stores open on Sundays. Many also shut down for a few minutes at 1pm so the men can pop over to the mosque for prayers.

» Other than local brews (the most common of which is *nazi*, a fermented coconut wine), there's little alcohol available on the island once away from the expensive resorts.

» Unmarried couples are not allowed to share a room in most hotels in towns (no problems at the resorts) and you may be asked to produce a marriage certificate as proof.

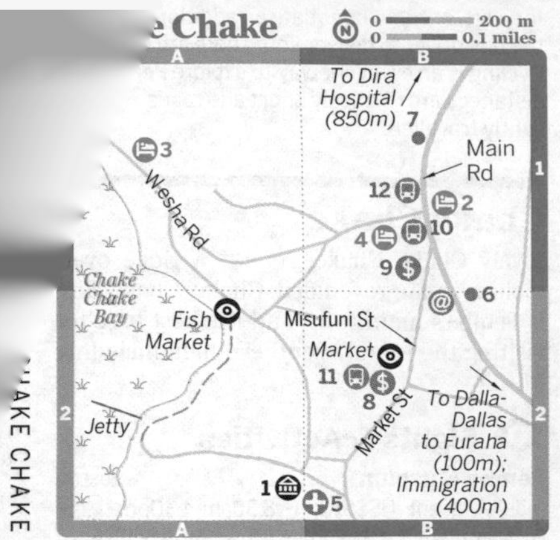

Out amid the mangroves just before Wesha, 7km from Chake Chake, this new resort is quite reasonably priced for Pemba. Its most expensive bungalows sit right on the white sand beach and diving, snorkelling and canoe trips through the mangroves are available. There is a discount for booking online. There's a good restaurant.

Le-Tavern HOTEL $
(☎0777-429057; Main Rd; s/d US$20/30, s without bathroom Tsh10,000) The cheapest rooms in town aren't much worse than those at Pemba Island Hotel, although they don't have hot water. Overall, it's Chake Chake's best value.

Pemba Island Hotel HOTEL $
(☎0777-490041; pembaislandhotel@yahoo.com; Wesha Rd; s/d/tw US$40/50/60; ❄📶) Clean rooms with cable TV and hot water, plus a rooftop restaurant. Nothing special, nothing wrong.

Pemba Clove Inn HOTEL $$
(☎0777-429057; Wesha Rd; s/d & tw US$75/105; ❄@🏊) Even the Zanzibar beds in some of the rooms aren't enough to give this place any ambience, but the rooms have the expected facilities for the price.

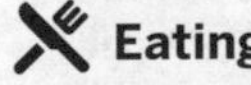 Eating

There's a small town-centre night market where you can get grilled *pweza* (octopus) and *maandazi* (doughnuts) and experience a slice of Pemban life.

Ahaabna TANZANIAN $
(top fl, Le-Tavern, Main Rd; meals Tsh5000-6000; ⏰lunch & dinner) Serves just one meal a day, either pilau or *biryani* with a choice of green bananas, chicken or fish, but for our money it's the best food in Chake.

Chake Chake

Sights
- 1 Pemba Museum A2

Sleeping
- 2 Le-Tavern B1
- 3 Pemba Clove Inn A1
- 4 Pemba Island Hotel B1

Eating
- Ahaabna .... (see 2)

Information
- 5 Chake Chake Hospital B2
- 6 Coral Tours B2
- 7 Imara Tours & Travel B1
- 8 PBZ Bank B2
- 9 Pemba Bureau de Change B1

Transport
- Dalla-Dallas to Mkoani .... (see 6)
- 10 Dalla-Dallas to Wesha B1
- 11 Dalla-Dallas to Wete, Konde & Vitongoji B2
- 12 Transport Stand B1

 Information

Medical Services

Dira Hospital (☎0777-424418; Wete Rd; Machomane; ⏰7am-9pm) A private clinic with pharmacy.

Internet Access

Adult Computer Centre (Main Rd; per hr Tsh1000; ⏰8am-4pm)

Money

Barclays Bank (Misufuni St) Best exchange rates on Pemba and ATM works with all major systems.

Pemba Bureau de Change (Misufuni St; ⏰8am-4pm) Behind the Neptune Tours sign, has worst exchange rates in Chake Chake, but best hours.

Travel Agencies & Tour Operators

Coral Tours (☎0777-437397; coralnasa@yahoo.com; Main Rd; ⏰8am-3pm & 7-9pm) Sells ferry tickets; plane tickets (only flights within Tanzania); hires cars, motorcycles and bicycles; and has knowledgeable guides for island tours at backpacker-friendly prices. They also sell small tourism maps and large topographical maps.

Imara Tours & Travel (☎0777-842084; www.imaratours.com; Main Rd; ⏰8am-4pm

Mon-Fri, 8am-3pm Sat & 9am-1pm Sun) Sells plane tickets for destinations worldwide, hires vehicles and offers expensive island tours.

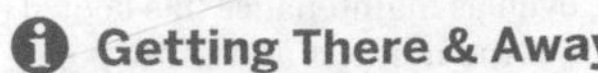

Getting There & Away

Most buses depart from points along Main Rd rather than the bus stand. Mkoani (Tsh1500, 1½ hours) dalla-dallas park near Coral Tours. Wete (Tsh1400, 1½ hours), Konde (Ths2000, two hours) and Vitongoji (Tsh500, 30 to 45 minutes) dalla-dallas park near PBZ bank while much less frequent ones for Wesha (Tsh1000, 30 minutes) are around the corner on Wesha Rd. Pujini (Tsh1000, one hour) is the only notable destination that uses the bus stand.

See p206 for flight details.

Getting Around

To/From the Airport

Dalla-dallas from Chake Chake to Furaha will drop you off at the airport (Tsh500, 20 minutes), but they don't come there to pick people up. They're quite infrequent, so leave early. A taxi to town costs Tsh10,000 to Tsh15,000.

Car & Motorcycle

There are a few taxis around Chake Chake, and cars and motorbikes can be hired through travel agencies. Prices are fairly standard: US$40 to Mkoani and US$70 from to Ras Kigomasha.

RAS MKUMBUU

Ras Mkumbuu is the long, thin strip of land jutting into the sea northwest of Chake Chake. At its tip are the **ruins** (adult/student US$5/3) of a settlement believed to be Qanbalu, the oldest known Muslim in Africa.

During the rainy season you'll like able to drive no further than Kichanja (Depu), leaving about a 3½km walk. Y could also go by boat from Wesha.

MKAME NDUME (PUJINI) RUINS

About 10km southeast of Chake Chake, near Pujini, are the atmospheric ruins (late 15th century to early 16th centuries) of what was either a fort or a palace of the infamous Mohammed bin Abdul Rahman, who ruled Pemba prior to the arrival of the Portuguese. Locally, Rahman is known as Mkame Ndume (Milker of Men) and for Pembans, his name is synonymous with cruelty due to the harsh punishments he meted out to his people.

Dalla-dallas from Chake Chake to Pujini (Tsh1000, one hour) are infrequent and the ruins are poorly signposted. A taxi from Chake Chake costs about Tsh30,000 return.

WAMBAA

Pemba's most exclusive property, **Fundu Lagoon Resort** (☎0774-438668; www.fundulagoon.com; s/d full board & non-motorised activities from US$540/780, discounts for long stays; ⊙mid-Jun–mid-Apr; @≋) is set on a low hillside overlooking the sea near little Wambaa town. The luxurious tents, some with their own private plunge pools, are tucked away amid the vegetation. Particularly notable is its bar, set over the water on a long jetty. Children under 12 are not allowed.

DON'T MISS

MISALI

A little patch of paradise surrounded by crystal waters and some of the most stunning coral reefs in the archipelago, a trip to Misali never disappoints. There are underwater and terrestrial nature trails, and you can arrange guides at the visitors centre. On the northeast of the island is **Mbuyuni beach**, with fine, white sand and a small visitor centre.

The island is part of the **Pemba Channel Conservation Area** (PECCA; adult/student US$5/3) which covers Pemba's entire west coast. All divers, snorkelers and beachgoers to Misali or any other place here must pay the admission fee.

To get to Misali on your own, head to Wesha (taxis cost Tsh10,000). Once in Wesha, you can negotiate with local boat owners to take you to Misali. If you can bargain well, you might find a boat for about US$70 return. There's no food or drink on the island, so bring everything with you. It's easier, and not much more expensive, to arrange excursions through hotels or travel agencies. Coral Tours in Chake Chake and Ocean Panorama Hotel in Mkoani and Sharook Guesthouse all charge under US$100 for two people including food, drinks and entry fees. Camping is not permitted.

NI

…ail Kiweni, marked as Shamiani on maps, is just off Pemba's southeastern …t. It's a remote backwater island with …isturbed stretches of sand, quiet water…ys and a nesting ground for sea-turtle …olonies. Offshore is some good **snorkelling**.

Pricey **Pemba Lodge** (0777-415551; www.pembalodge.com; per person full board US$220) is the only accommodation in these parts. Its five stilted bungalows are attractively rustic and free kayaks are available to explore the surrounding mangroves. Transfers cost US$30 from Mkoani and US$60 from the airport.

MKOANI & AROUND

Although it's Pemba's major port, Mkoani has managed to fight off all attempts at development and remains a small and rather boring town, redeemed only by its great guesthouse.

The friendly **Ocean Panorama Hotel** (0773-545418; www.zanzibaroceanpanorama.com; dm/s/tw/tr US$20/35/50/75; @) set up on a hill overlooking the sea in the distance has bright, clean rooms with decks and Zanzibar beds. Manager Ali has lots of information on Pemba and arranges good value trips, including snorkelling at Misali, Matumbini lighthouse (on Matumbi Makubwa island). To get here, head left when exiting the port and walk 700m up the hill.

Buses run regularly to Chake Chake (Tsh1500, 1½ hours), Wete (Tsh3000, two hours) and Konde (Tsh3500, 2½ hours) from in front of the port.

Northern Pemba

WETE

The rundown town of Wete, Pemba's second largest port, is a good base for exploring northern Pemba. It's also the easiest place to see Pemba flying foxes (p91) with a large colony hanging from some trees just uphill from the port. At night they fly off to the north past Annex of Sharook guesthouse.

Sleeping & Eating

Pemba Crown Hotel HOTEL $

(0777-493667; www.pembacrown.com; Bomani Ave; s/d US$25/35; ❄) Decent albeit soulless rooms, all with fan and air-con, in a low high-rise smack in the centre of town. It's Wete's best value. There's no restaurant.

Sharook Guest House GUESTHOUSE $

(0777-431012; www.pembaliving.com; s/d US$25/30) Prices have risen at this small guesthouse even as maintenance has lagged, but it remains the homiest and most popular in town with travellers. The friendly English-speaking owners know much about travel on the island, though their advice is usually weighted towards what makes them money: ie car, motorcycle and bicycle rental. There's no restaurant. Room rates are sometimes negotiable.

Annex of Sharook GUESTHOUSE $

(0777-431012; www.pembaliving.com; dm US$20, s/d US$30/50; ❄) Bigger and better than the original, but less cosy. There's a nice narrow view of the bay from the rooftop restaurant.

Information

Barky Bureau de Change (Bomani Ave; 8.30am-3.45pm Mon-Sat, 8.45am-12.30pm Sun) Best place in town to change money.

Raha Tours & Travel (0777-938004) Just off the main road, it's an auto spares store that also sells plane and ferry tickets.

Royal Tours & Travel (0777-429244; royaltours@live.com; Bomani Ave; 8am-3pm Mon-Sat, 8am-noon Sun) Books plane and ferry tickets hires vehicles and leads tours.

T-Net (Bomani Ave; per hr Tsh1500; 8.30am-3pm & 7-9pm) Pemba's best internet cafe.

Getting There & Away

There are two dalla-dalla routes (both use 606) between Wete and Chake Chake (Tsh1400, 1½ hours). Most vehicles use the faster eastern 'new' road (these are labelled in green) while some (red) travel via Ziwani along the 'old' road, which features more forest and some ocean vistas. There are also frequent dalla-dallas to Konde (Tsh1500, one hour).

A shuttle bus from Wete to Mkoani (Tsh3000) is timed to connect with most ferry departures and arrivals. It picks up passengers at various points around town and leaves Wete three hours before the boat departure.

TUMBE

The large village of Tumbe lies on a sandy cove fringed at each end by dense stands of mangroves. The beach north of the village is the site of Pemba's largest **fish market**, and if you're in the area it's well worth a stop to watch the bidding. There's no accommodation in Tumbe or nearby Konde. Dalla-dallas from Chake Chake to Konde pass Chwaka and Tumbe (Tsh2000, two hours). From Wete, you'll have to change vehicles in Konde for the final leg.

PEMBA FLYING FOX

Pemba's only endemic mammal is a large and critically endangered bat *(Pteropus voeltzkowi)* called *popo* in Swahili. They spend their days in trees rather than caves and the island's biggest roosting site, home to some 4000 bats, is in a burial forest at **Kidike** (☎0777-472941; adult/child Tsh7500/2600) about 10km northeast of Chake Chake. If you arrange things in advance, there are cooking classes, homestay (US$20 per person) and other cultural activities available. Kidike is 3.5km off the Chake–Wete road. Some people at the junction will hire their bicycles or you can wait for a lift.

NGEZI VUMAWIMBI FOREST RESERVE

The dense and wonderfully lush forest at Ngezi is one of the last remaining patches of the forest that once covered western Pemba. There are two nature trails tunnelling beneath the shady forest canopy, and off-trail walks are allowed. All visits must be done with a naturalist guide, some of who speak English.

The **visitor centre** (hikes can begin ⏲7.30am-3.30pm) is 4km west of Konde on the road to Kigomasha Peninsula. A taxi from Konde costs Tsh5000. Kervan Saray will deliver its guests here for free.

KIGOMASHA

With good resorts on the peninsula's west shore and the beautiful palm-fringed **Vumawimbi beach** stretching along the east, Kigomasha Peninsula, in Pemba's northwestern corner, has become the centre of Pemba's small tourist industry.

Not to be missed is **Ras Kigomasha lighthouse** at the peninsula's tip. Built in 1900, it's still actively maintained by its keeper. Scale the tiny staircase (for a Tsh3000 donation) for wonderful views. Vumawimbi beach itself is an isolated place; don't bring anything valuable and women shouldn't come alone. While a new resort is under development on the north end of the beach, for now bring food and drink with you.

Sleeping & Eating

Opened by the love-him-or-hate-him Raf, who's been running **Swahili Divers** (www.swahilidivers.com; Padi Five-Star) on Pemba since 1999, the almost luxurious and fully comfortable **Kervan Saray Beach Lodge** (☎0773-176737; www.kervansaraybeach.com; dm US$55 full board, s/d US$160/250; @📶❄) is a lovely, relaxing resort on the shore (there's a beach only half the year) near Makangale village. Accommodation is in a mildly Arabian-themed high-roof bungalow or a six-bunk dorm, and the restaurant serves a daily set menu (lunch and dinner for non-guests US$15). Diving, naturally, is the main activity, but snorkelling and kayaking are also on offer and they can take you anywhere on Pemba or even camping on deserted isles. Those intending a long stay will find some good packages on the website. Airport pick-up costs US$90 per vehicle.

Superbly situated above Panga ya Watoro Beach near the top of the peninsula, **The Manta Resort** (☎0776-718852/3; www.themantaresort.com/; s/d all-inclusive except excursions US$400/660; @📶❄) rests on a breezy escarpment with perfect ocean views. Accommodation is in rather ordinary (considering the price) thatched-roof cabins that have a safari tent layout. Spa treatments are free and diving, sea kayaking and fishing charters are possible. Day visits cost US$26, including a meal and a drink. Airport pick-up costs US$40 per person.

Getting There & Away

The only dalla-dallas on this road leave Makangale for Konde (Tsh1000, one hour) at 7am and return at 1pm. Sometimes a second truck follows a short time later. Hitching is usually slow going, as there's little vehicle traffic other than bikes.

NORTHEASTERN TANZANIA

Northeastern Tanzania's highlights are its coastline, its mountains and its cultures. These, combined with the area's long history, easy access and lack of crowds make it an appealing focal point for a Tanzania sojourn.

Step back to the days of Livingstone in Bagamoyo, relax on palm-fringed beaches around Pangani, or explore Saadani, a seaside national park. Inland, hike forested footpaths in the Usambaras while following the cycle of local market days.

amoyo

e mid-19th century, Bagamoyo was one ie most important settlements along the st African coast and the terminus of the ade caravan route linking Lake Tanganyi- a with the sea. In 1868 French missionaries established Freedom Village at Bagamoyo as a shelter for ransomed slaves.

From 1887 to 1891 Bagamoyo was the capital of German East Africa, and in 1888 it was at the centre of the Abushiri revolt, the first major uprising against the colonial government. In 1891 the capital was transferred to Dar es Salaam, sending Bagamoyo into a slow decline from which it has yet to recover.

Sights & Activities

Bagamoyo Town HISTORIC SITE

With its cobwebbed portals, crumbling German-era colonial buildings, **central Bagamoyo**, or *Mji Mkongwe* (Stone Town) as it's known locally, is well worth exploration. The most interesting area is along Ocean Rd. Here, you'll find the old **German boma**, built in 1897 and **Liku House**, which served as the German administrative headquarters. On the beach is the **German Customs House** (1895), Bagamoyo's **port**, where you can watch boat builders at work, and a busy **fish market** (on the site of the old slave market). There is a Tsh2000 per person fee levied to walk around the old town, payable at the Antiquities office at the **Caravan Serai Museum** (9am-6pm), just past CRDB bank at the town entrance. The fee also includes admission to the Caravan Serai Museum, which has a small display documenting the slave trade.

Holy Ghost Catholic Mission MUSEUM

(023-244 0010; adult/student Tsh2000/500; 10am-5pm) About 2km north of town and reached via a long, mango-shaded avenue is this mission, with the excellent **Catholic Museum**. In the same compound is the chapel where Livingstone's body was laid before being taken to Zanzibar Town en route to Westminster Abbey. The mission dates from the 1868 establishment of Freedom Village and is the oldest in Tanzania.

Sleeping & Eating

Travellers Lodge LODGE $$

(023-244 0077, 0754-855485; www.travellers-lodge.com; camping with shower US$12, s/d cottages from US$55/70; P) With its relaxed atmosphere and reasonable prices, this is among the best value of the beach places. Accommodation is in clean, pleasant cottages scattered around expansive grounds, some with two large beds. There's a restaurant and a children's play area. It's just south of the entrance to the Catholic mission.

Livingstone Beach Resort HOTEL $$

(023-244 0080/0059, 0756-932649; www.livingstonebeachresort.com; s/d US$80/130; P@) This pleasant place has whitewashed stone and makuti bungalows (some with a double bed, others with a double and a single) scattered around expansive palm-tree-studded grounds. In front is a tiny, mangrove-fringed beach. The restaurant-bar serves good Italian meals, coffees and cappuccinos.

Mary Nice Place GUESTHOUSE $

(0754-024015; maryniceplace@yahoo.co.uk; r Tsh25,000-35,000; P) A converted house with a small garden, no-frills rooms with fan and meals with advance order. It's signposted, just in from the road to the left shortly after passing the College of Arts.

Information

Money

CRDB At the town entrance; ATM to open soon.

National Microfinance Bank At the town entrance; changes cash.

NBC At the petrol station 500m before town along the Dar es Salaam road, with an ATM.

Tourist Information

Tourist Information Office (9am-6pm) At Caravan Serai Museum; good for guides and excursions, including town tours, museum tours and visits to Kaole ruins.

Getting There & Away

Bagamoyo is about 70km north of Dar es Salaam and an easy drive along good sealed road (the best routing for drivers is via Old Bagamoyo Rd through Mikocheni and Kawe).

Via public transport, there are dalla-dallas (minibuses) throughout the day from Mwenge (north of Dar es Salaam along the New Bagamoyo road, and accessed via dalla-dalla from New Posta) to Bagamoyo (Tsh2000, two hours).

Dhows to Zanzibar cost about Tsh5000, but before jumping aboard, read the boxed text on p653. You'll need to register first with the immigration officer in the old customs building. Departures are usually around 1am, arriving in Zanzibar sometime the next morning if all goes well.

Northeastern Tanzania

0 — 50 km
0 — 30 miles

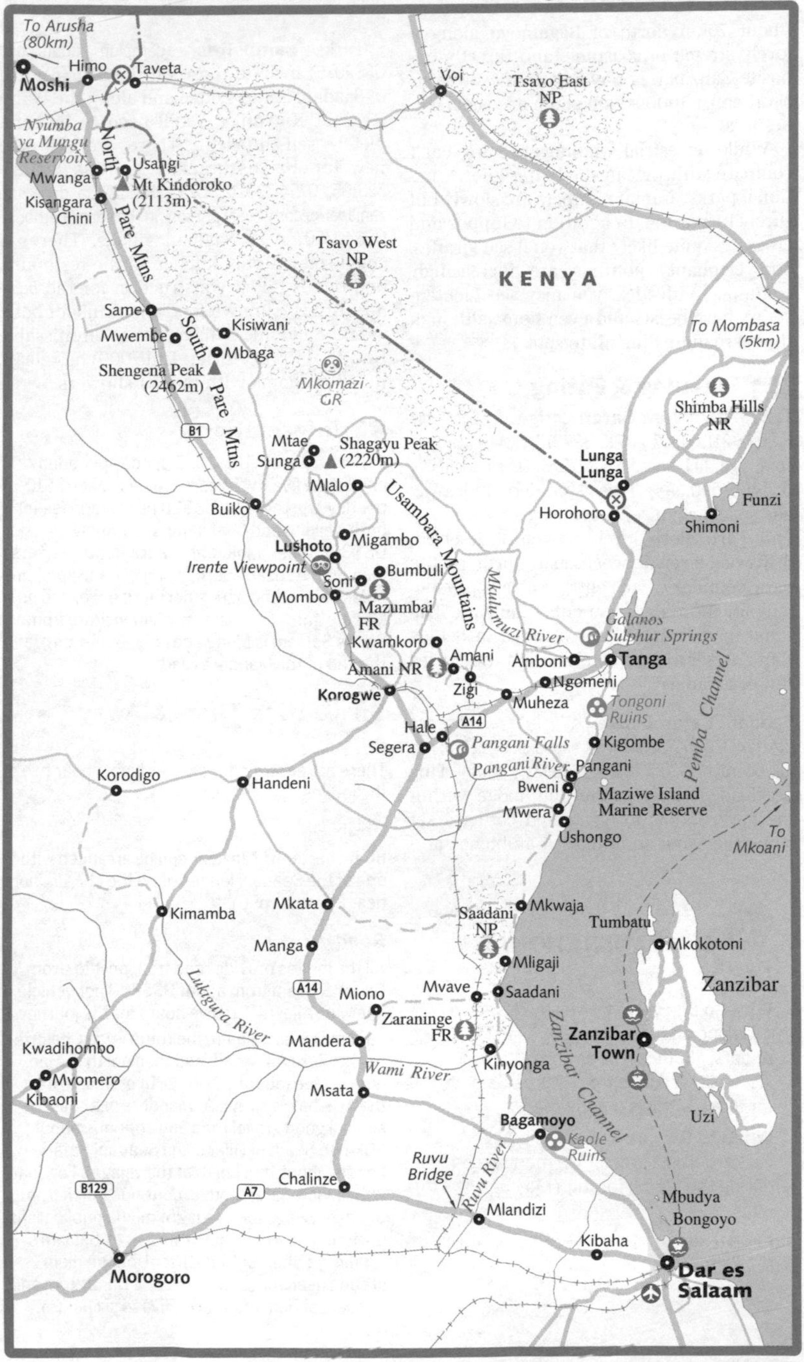

To Arusha (80km)
Moshi
Himo
Taveta
Voi
Tsavo East NP
Nyumba ya Mungu Reservoir
North Pare Mtns
Usangi
Mwanga
Mt Kindoroko (2113m)
Kisangara Chini
Tsavo West NP
KENYA
To Mombasa (5km)
Same
Mwembe
Kisiwani
Mbaga
South Pare Mtns
Shengena Peak (2462m)
Mkomazi GR
Shimba Hills NR
B1
Mtae
Sunga
Shagayu Peak (2220m)
Lunga Lunga
Mlalo
Usambara Mountains
Buiko
Horohoro
Funzi
Shimoni
Migambo
Lushoto
Irente Viewpoint
Bumbuli
Soni
Mombo
Mazumbai FR
Mkulumuzi River
Galanos Sulphur Springs
Kwamkoro
Amani
Amani NR
Amboni
Tanga
Zigi
Ngomeni
Korogwe
Muheza
Tongoni Ruins
Pemba Channel
A14
Hale
Segera
Pangani Falls
Kigombe
Pangani River
Pangani
Korodigo
Handeni
Bweni
Maziwe Island Marine Reserve
Mwera
Ushongo
To Mkoani
Kimamba
Mkata
Mkwaja
Saadani NP
Tumbatu
Mkokotoni
Manga
Mligaji
Zanzibar
A14
Miono
Mvave
Saadani
Lukigura River
Zaraninge FR
Mandera
Zanzibar Town
Kwadihombo
Mvomero
Kibaoni
Wami River
Kinyonga
Zanzibar Channel
Msata
Uzi
Bagamoyo
Kaole Ruins
Ruvu Bridge
Ruvu River
Chalinze
B129
A7
Mbudya
Bongoyo
Mlandizi
Kibaha
Morogoro
Dar es Salaam

Saadani National Park

About 70km north of Bagamoyo along a lovely stretch of coastline, and directly opposite Zanzibar, is tiny **Saadani** (www.saadanipark.org), a 1000-sq-km patch of coastal wilderness.

While terrestrial wildlife watching can't compare with that in the better-known national parks, animal numbers are slowly but surely increasing. In addition to hippos and crocs, it's quite likely that you'll see giraffes, and elephant spottings are increasingly common. With luck, you may see Lichtenstein's hartebeests and even lions, although these are more difficult to spot.

Sleeping & Eating

Tent With a View Safari Lodge LODGE **$$$**
(022-211 0507, 0713-323318; www.saadani.com; s/d full board US$275/390, all inclusive US$465/590; P) This secluded hideaway has spacious, raised treehouse-style *bandas* on a particularly lovely stretch of deserted, driftwood-strewn beach just north of the park boundary. Park entry fees are payable only for those days you enter the park. The same management runs a lodge in Selous Game Reserve, and combination itineraries can be arranged.

Saadani Safari Lodge LODGE **$$$**
(/fax 022-277 3294; www.saadanilodge.com; s/d full board US$285/480; Jun-Mar; P) This beachside retreat is the only lodge within the park. It has lovely tented cottages set along the sand, an upmarket ambience and an open-style restaurant and sundowner deck.

Park **campsites** (camping adult/child US$20/5) include those on the beach north of Saadani Safari Lodge and along the Wami River at Kinyonga. You'll need to be completely self-sufficient. There are also the new **Tanapa resthouse & bandas** (0785-555135, 0754-730112, 0787-336612; saadani@tanzaniaparks.com; per person in bandas/resthouse US$40/50) near Saadani village. There's a small self-catering kitchen in the resthouse, and one is under construction for the *bandas*. Bring your own food and drink for both.

In Saadani village, the unmissable **Saadani River Park** (r Tsh15,000) has clean, no-frills rooms with bucket showers.

Information

Park entry costs US$20/5 per day per adult/child aged five to 15 years, guides cost US$10 per day and there's a US$20 per person fee for both walking and boat safaris. Camping costs US$30/10 per adult/child. **Park headquarters** (saadani@tanzaniaparks.com; 8am-4pm) are at Mkwaja, at the park's northern edge, and near Madete gate. The main entry for visitors from Dar es Salaam is **Mvave gate** (6am-6pm), at the end of the Mandera road.

Getting There & Away

Air

There are airstrips for charter flights near two of the lodges.

Boat

Boat charter to Zanzibar can be arranged with one of the Saadani lodges or on the MV *Ali Choba* near Pangani (p96).

Road

All the lodges provide road transport to/from Dar es Salaam from about US$200 per vehicle, one way. Allow 4½ to five hours for the journey.

From Dar es Salaam, the route is via Chalinze on the Morogoro road, and then north to Mandera village (about 50km north of Chalinze on the Arusha highway). At Mandera bear east along a good gravel road and continue about 60km to Saadani village and Saadani Safari Lodge (about 1km north of the village). For Tent With a View Safari Lodge, continue north from Saadani village for about 25km. Via public transport, there's a daily bus from Dar es Salaam's 'Standi ya Shamba', just after Ubungo main station near Tanesco, departing Dar at 1pm and Saadani at 5am (Tsh9000, five to six hours).

SAADANI NATIONAL PARK

Why Go Enjoy a long, mostly deserted coastline and the chance to see elephants, giraffes, hippos and other wildlife; easily reached from Dar es Salaam for those without much time.

When to Go June-February; black cotton soil is a problem in many areas during the March through May heavy rains

Practicalities Drive, bus or fly in from Dar es Salaam; drive or bus from Pangani.

Coming from Pangani, take the ferry across the Pangani River, then continue south along a rough road via Mkwaja to the reserve's northern Madete gate. Transfers can be arranged with Saadani or Pangani (Ushongo) lodges for about US$150 per vehicle each way (1½ to two hours).

There's no vehicle rental in the park for a safari, unless you've arranged something in advance with the lodges, or through the **tourism warden** (☎0754-730112, 0787-336612; saadani@tanzaniaparks.com).

Until the ferry over the Wami River is rehabilitated, there is no direct road access to Saadani from Bagamoyo.

Pangani

About 55km south of Tanga is the small and dilapidated Swahili outpost of Pangani. It makes an intriguing step back into history, especially in the area within about three blocks of the river, where you'll see some carved doorways, buildings from the German colonial era and old houses of Indian traders. More of a draw for many travellers are the beaches running north and south of town.

Pangani's centre, with the market and bus stand, is on the corner of land where the Pangani River meets the sea. About 2km north is the main junction where the road from Muheza joins the coastal road, and where you should get out of the bus if you're arriving from Muheza and staying at the beaches north of town.

Sleeping & Eating

TOWN CENTRE

Seaside Community Centre Hostel GUESTHOUSE $
(☎0755-276422; s/d/tr Tsh25,000/35,000/60,000; P) This church-run place has clean, simple rooms with fan, and meals on order. It's about 1km from the bus stand (Tsh3000 in a taxi). As you enter Pangani from Tanga, shortly after the sealed road begins, a small road branches right to the bus stand and left to the hostel (watch for the small signpost), which is about 150m down to your right.

NORTH OF PANGANI

Capricorn Beach Cottages BOUTIQUE HOTEL $$
(☎0784-632529; www.capricornbeachcottages.com; s/d US$70/104; P@) This classy, low-key place on a lovely beach 19km north of Pangani has three spacious self-catering cottages set in large, lush grounds dotted with baobab trees. There's a grill area overlooking the water for catered barbecues or for cooking yourself, and the hosts go out of their way to be sure you're not lacking for anything – from a cooler and ice on the deck to local coffee beans in the refrigerator. There's also a clothing boutique, a pizza oven with delicious pizzas and a deli selling homemade bread, cheese, wine and other gourmet essentials.

Peponi Holiday Resort LODGE $$
(☎0784-202962, 0713-540139; www.peponiresort.com; camping US$5, s/d bandas with half board US$70/85, extra adult beds in family bandas with half board US$38; P@) The relaxing Peponi is set in expansive bougainvillea- and palm-studded grounds on a fine beach 20km north of Pangani. There's a shady campsite (bring supplies with you), spotless ablution blocks, simple, breezy double bungalows and spacious five-person chalets, all nestled among the palms. There's also a restaurant, a beach bar serving milkshakes, a small pool (for Peponi guests only) and a hand-crafted motorised dhow for excursions to a stunning nearby sand bank and snorkelling reef. Ask any bus running along the Pangani–Tanga coastal route to drop you at the Peponi turn-off, from where it's a two-minute walk.

Tinga Tinga Lodge LODGE $$
(☎027-264 6611, 0784-403553, 0786-364310; www.tingatingalodge.com; camping US$4, s/d US$50/60; P) This down-to-earth place south of Mkoma Bay has modest but spacious twin-bedded bungalows set slightly inland, just north of the main junction. There's a restaurant-bar gazebo overlooking the water, with swimming possible just below.

SOUTH OF PANGANI

All of the following accommodation options are located on Ushongo beach, about 15km south of the Pangani River.

Tides LODGE $$$
(☎0784-225812; www.thetideslodge.com; s/d half board from US$240/330, honeymoon ste US$380, 4-person family cottage US$540; P@) The lovely Tides has a prime seaside location, delightful, spacious cottages directly on the beach and excellent cuisine.

Tulia Beach Lodge LODGE $$
(☎027-264 0755, 0782-457668; www.tuliabeachlodge.com; s/d with half board US$65/110) This unassuming place has accommodation in straightforward, recently renovated cottages set just back from the beach and a restaurant.

Beach Crab Resort BACKPACKERS $
(☎0784-543700; www.thebeachcrab.com; camping Tsh5000, s/d safari tent without bathroom Tsh30,000/40,000, s/d bungalows Tsh110,000/150,000) This friendly backpackers has camping and tents just back from the beach. If you're not up for camping, there's no-frills self-contained bungalows with hot water on a hill just behind and a beachside bar-restaurant. To get here, follow signs to the Tides and continue 1.2km further south. Pick-ups can be arranged from Mwera (about 7km away and along the bus route from Tanga to Mkwaja village near Saadani) and from Pangani.

Information

The closest banks and ATMs are in Tanga. Staff at the **Pangani Cultural Tourism Program office** (⏰8am-5pm), in the yellow building at the bus stand, organises town tours (per person US$10) and river cruises (US$60 for up to three people).

Getting There & Away

Boat

The MV *Ali Choba* sails three times weekly between Ushongo (south of Pangani), Pangani and Zanzibar. The trip takes about 90 minutes, and costs US$250 per boat for up to four passengers, and US$45 per person for five or more passengers between Ushongo and Zanzibar (US$270 per boat or US$50 per person between Pangani and Zanzibar). Book through your hotel or **Emayani Beach Lodge** (www.emayanilodge.com), on the beach 2km north of the Tides.

Road

The best connections between Pangani and Tanga are via the rehabilitated coastal road, with about five buses daily (Tsh2000, 1½ hours). The first departure from Pangani is at about 6.30am, so you can connect with a Tanga–Arusha bus. There's also at least one daily direct bus between Pangani and Dar es Salaam (Tsh12,000).

For Ushongo and the beaches south of Pangani, all the hotels there do pick-ups from both Pangani and Tanga. There's also a daily bus between Tanga and Mkwaja (at the northern edge of Saadani National Park) that passes Mwera village (6km from Ushongo) daily at about 7am going north and 3.30pm going south. It's then easy to arrange a pick-up from Mwera with the lodges.

The vehicle ferry over the Pangani River from Pangani to Bweni village runs regularly between about 6.30am and 6.30pm daily (Tsh200/5000 per person/vehicle). From Bweni, taxis are scarce, but motorcycles charge about Tsh10,000 to the Ushongo hotels.

Tanga

POP 250,000

Tanga, a major industrial centre until the collapse of the sisal market, is Tanzania's second-largest seaport and its third-largest town behind Dar es Salaam and Mwanza. Despite its size, it's a pleasant-enough place with a sleepy, semicolonial atmosphere, wide streets filled with bicyclists and motorcycles, and faded charm.

Sights & Activities

The most interesting areas for a stroll are around Jamhuri Park overlooking the harbour, near which you'll find the old German-built **Clock Tower**, and the park and cemetery surrounding the **Askari monument** at the end of Market St.

FREE **Urithi Tanga Museum** MUSEUM
(☎0713-440068, 0784-440068; www.urithitanga.org; Independence Ave; ⏰9am-noon Mon-Fri) Tanga's old Boma has been rehabilitated, and now houses this museum, with historical photos and artefacts from the area.

Toten Island HISTORIC SITE
Directly offshore is this small, mangrove-ringed island (also called Island of the Dead) with the overgrown ruins of a mosque (dating at least to the 17th century) and some 18th- and 19th-century gravestones. Fifteenth-century pottery fragments have also been found on the island, indicating that it may have been settled during the Shirazi era. Organises excursions through the tourist information office.

Tanga Yacht Club SWIMMING
(☎027-264 4246; www.tangayachtclub.com; Hospital Rd, Ras Kazone; day admission Tsh2500) This place has a small, clean beach, showers and a restaurant-bar area overlooking the water (meals and drinks are purchased using a prepaid coupon system).

Sleeping

CENTRAL TANGA

Panori Hotel HOTEL $
(☎027-264 6044; www.panorihotel.com; Ras Kazone; s/d/tw/tr Tsh30,000/42,000/42,000/55,000; P ❄) This is a reliable choice – especially for those with their own transport –

with clean, straightforward rooms, all with fan and TV, a breezy garden and an outdoor restaurant. It's 3km from the town centre (Tsh7000 in a taxi from the bus stand). Take Hospital Rd east to Ras Kazone and follow the signposts.

Mkonge Hotel HOTEL $$
(027-264 3440; mkongehotel@kaributanga.com; Hospital Rd; s/d US$70/80, with sea view US$80/90; P ❄) The imposing Mkonge Hotel, on a grassy lawn overlooking the sea, has comfortable rooms (worth the extra money for a sea view), a restaurant and wonderful views.

Regal Naivera Hotel HOTEL $$
(027-264 5669, 0767-641464; www.regalnaiverahotel.com; r Tsh40,000-100,000; P ❄ ☎) This large, pink edifice in a quiet location one block in from Hospital Rd and behind Katani House has clean, modern rooms in varying sizes, all with double bed, fan, air-con and mini-fridge, and a restaurant.

Central City Hotel HOTEL $
(027-264-4476, 0718-282272; centralcityhotelltd@yahoo.com; Street No 8, Ngamiani; r Tsh40,000-50,000; P ❄) This is a bland but reliable and centrally located budget choice. Rooms have fan, air-con, hot water, mini-fridge and one double bed, and there's a restaurant. From the bus stand, take a right onto Taifa Rd ('Double Rd') to the roundabout. At the roundabout, go right onto Street No 8. Central City is down about 600m on your left.

OUTSIDE TANGA

Fish Eagle Point HOTEL $$
(0784-346006; www.fisheaglepoint.com; s/d full board from US$120/170; P) Affiliated with Outpost Lodge in Arusha, this place on a mangrove-fringed cove has spacious cottages in varying sizes, a dhow, snorkelling, sea kayaking, fishing and birding. Follow the Horohoro road north from Tanga for about 40km until the signposted turn-off, from where it's 10km further.

Eating

Patwas Restaurant INDIAN $
(Mkwakwani Rd; meals & snacks from Tsh3000; 8am-8pm Mon-Sat) An unassuming, friendly place with fresh juices and lassis, and good-value local-style meals. It's just south of the market.

Tanga Yacht Club EUROPEAN $$
(027-264 4246; www.tangayachtclub.com; Hospital Rd, Ras Kazone; admission Tsh2500, meals from Tsh8000; lunch & dinner) Tasty seafood and mixed grill.

SD Supermarket SUPERMARKET $
(Bank St) For self-caterers; behind the market.

Information

Internet Access

Kaributanga.com (Market St; per hr Tsh1000; 9am-9pm Mon-Thu, 9am-noon & 2-8pm Fri, 9am-2pm & 4-8pm Sat & Sun)

Money

Barclays (Independence Ave) ATM.

CRDB (Tower St) ATM.

Exim (Independence Ave) Next to Barclays; ATM.

NBC (cnr Bank & Market Sts) Just west of the market. Changes cash and travellers cheques; ATM.

Tourist Information

Tayodea Tourist Information Centre (027-264 4350; Market St; 8.30am-5pm) Information and English-speaking guides for local excursions; opposite NMB bank.

Getting There & Away

Air

There are daily flights on **Coastal Aviation** (027-264 6548, 0713-376265; Independence Ave) between Tanga, Dar es Salaam, Zanzibar and Pemba (one way between Tanga and Pemba/Zanzibar/Dar es Salaam US$70/100/130). Its booking agent is near Exim Bank, and at the airport. The airstrip is about 3km west of town along the Korogwe road (Tsh4000 in a taxi).

Boat

At the time of research, the ferry service between Tanga and Wete on Pemba was suspended, but it is likely to soon resume.

Bus

Buses for Dar es Salaam, Simba, Raha Leo and other lines depart daily every few hours from 6.30am to 2pm in each direction (Tsh12,000 to Tsh15000, five hours).

To Arusha, there are at least three departures daily between about 6am and 11am (Tsh13,000 to Tsh14,000, seven hours). To Lushoto (Tsh5000 to Tsh6000, three to four hours), there's a direct bus departing by 7am, or you can take any Arusha bus and transfer at Mombo.

Tanga

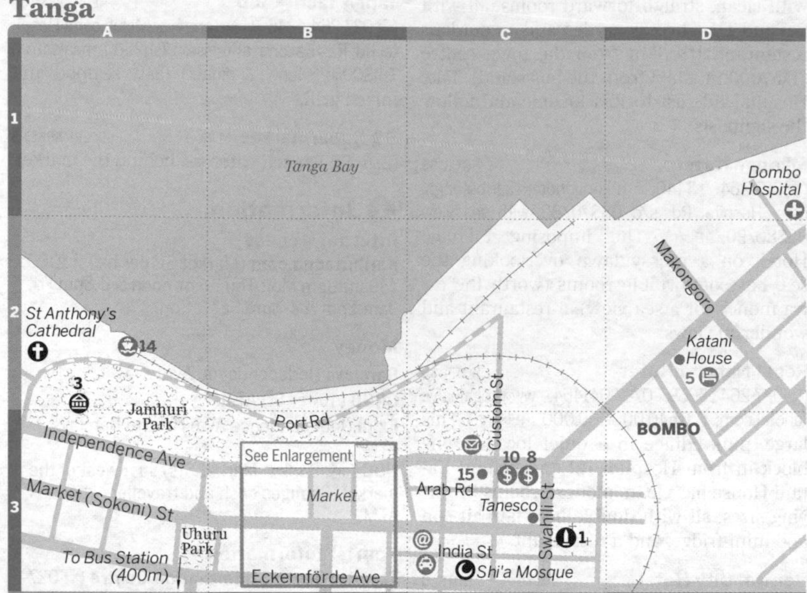

To Pangani (Tsh2000, 1½ hours), there are small buses throughout the day along the coastal road.

Getting Around

There are taxi ranks at the bus station, and at the junction of Usambara and India Sts. If you're keen on cycling, the tourist information office can help with bicycle rental. There are occasional dalla-dallas that run along Ocean Rd between the town centre and Ras Kazone.

Muheza

Muheza is a scrappy junction town where the roads to Amani Nature Reserve and to Pangani branch off the main Tanga highway.

GK Lodge (r Tsh10,000) has clean, basic rooms and no food. It's 1.2km from the bus stand: follow signs to Amani Nature Reserve; after crossing the railroad tracks, continue along the Amani road for 500m to the signposted right-hand turn-off.

Transport to Amani leaves from the bus stand just off the Tanga road. There are two buses daily to and from Amani, departing Muheza about 2pm (Tsh3000, two hours), and Amani at 6am. There are connections to Tanga (Tsh2000, 45 minutes) throughout the day, and direct daily buses in the morning to Lushoto (Tsh3000, three hours).

USAMBARA MOUNTAINS

With their wide vistas, cool climate, winding paths and picturesque villages, the Usambaras are one of northeastern Tanzania's delights. Rural life revolves around a cycle of bustling, colourful market days that rotate from one village to the next, and is largely untouched by the booming safari scene and influx of 4WDs in nearby Arusha. It's easily possible to spend at least a week trekking from village to village or exploring with day walks.

The Usambaras, which are part of the ancient Eastern Arc chain, are divided into two ranges separated by a 4km-wide valley. The western Usambaras, around Lushoto, are the most accessible, with a better road network, and are quite heavily touristed these days, while the eastern Usambaras, around Amani, are less developed.

Paths get too muddy for trekking during the rainy season. The best time to visit is from July to October, after the rains and when the air is clearest.

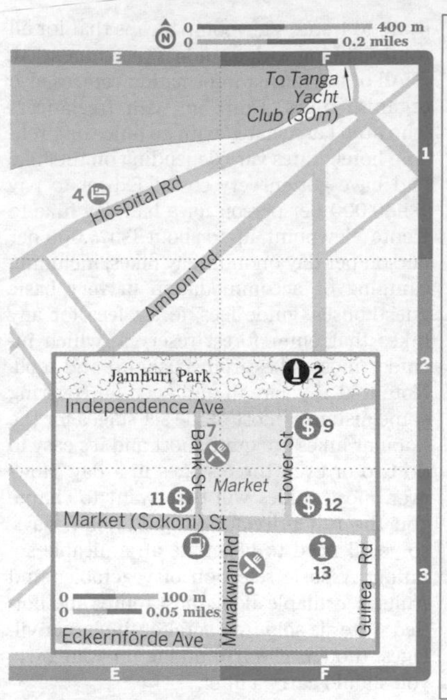

Tanga

Sights

1 Askari Monument ... C3
2 Clock Tower ... F2
3 Urithi Tanga Museum ... A2

Sleeping

4 Mkonge Hotel ... E1
5 Regal Naivera Hotel ... D2

Eating

6 Patwas Restaurant ... F3
7 SD Supermarket ... E2

Information

8 Barclays Bank ... C3
9 CRDB ... F2
10 Exim ... C3
11 NBC ... E3
12 NMB Bank ... F3
13 Tayodea Tourist Information Centre ... F3

Transport

14 Boats to Toten Island ... A2
15 Coastal Aviation ... C3

Amani Nature Reserve

This often-overlooked reserve is located west of Tanga in the heart of the eastern Usambaras. It's a peaceful, lushly vegetated patch of montane forest humming with the sounds of rushing water, chirping insects and singing birds, and is exceptionally rich in unique plant and bird species – a highly worthwhile detour for those ornithologically or botanically inclined. For getting around, there's a network of short walks along shaded forest paths that can be done with or without a guide.

Sleeping & Eating

There's **camping** (per person US$30) at both Zigi and Amani with your own tent and supplies.

Reserve Guesthouses RESTHOUSE $
(027-264 0313, 0784-242045; amaninaturereservebfd@yahoo.com; r per person with or without bathroom Tsh12,000; P) There are two reserve-run guesthouses: the Amani Conservation Centre Resthouse at Amani and the Zigi Rest House at Zigi. Both are reasonably good, with hot water for bathing and filtered water for drinking, and meals (breakfast/lunch/dinner Tsh3000/5000/5000), though it's a good idea to bring fruit and snacks as a supplement. The Zigi Rest House is directly opposite the Zigi information centre. To reach the Amani Conservation Centre Rest House, once in Amani continue straight past the main fork, ignoring the 'resthouse' signpost, to the reserve office. The resthouse is next to the office.

Emau Hill Forest Camp CAMPGROUND $
(0782-656526; www.emauhill.com; camping US$7, tented bandas per person with full board US$60, s/d cottage with full board US$105/150; mid-Jun–Mar; P) Emau has good camping, comfortable permanent tents sharing ablutions and a small cottage with bathroom, all in a wooded setting with fine birding. Continue 1.5km past Amani on the Kwamkoro road to the signposted turn-off, from where it's 3km further along a narrow bush track.

Information

There's an **information centre** (8am-5pm) at the old Station Master's House at Zigi with information about the area's history, animals and medicinal plants.

The **reserve office** (027-264 0313, 0784-242045; amaninaturereservebfd@yahoo.com; adult/child per visit, not per day US$30/10,

Tanzania-registered/foreign vehicle per visit Tsh5000/US$30) is at Amani. Fees for entry and guides (per person per day US$15) can be paid here or at Zigi.

Getting There & Away

Amani is 32km northwest of Muheza along a dirt road which is in fair condition the entire way, except for the last 7km, where the road is rocky and in bad shape (4WD only). There's at least one truck daily between Muheza and Amani (Tsh3000, two hours), continuing on to Kwamkoro, 9km beyond Amani. Departures from Muheza are between about 1pm and 2pm. Going in the other direction, transport passes Amani (stopping near the conservation centre office) from about 6am.

Lushoto

This leafy highland town is nestled in a fertile valley at about 1200m, surrounded by pines and eucalyptus mixed with banana plants and other tropical foliage. It's the centre of the western Usambaras and makes an ideal base for hikes into the surrounding hills.

Activities

Hiking

The western Usambaras around Lushoto offer wonderful walking. Routes follow well-worn footpaths that weave among villages, cornfields and banana plantations, and range from a few hours to several days. It's easy to hike on your own, though you'll need to master basic Swahili phrases, carry a GPS, get a map of the area and plan your route to go via the handful of villages where local guesthouses are available. This said, a spate of robberies of solo hikers, mostly en route to Irente Viewpoint, means that for all routes, hiking with a guide is recommended.

All of the tourist information centres also organise hikes. Don't go with freelancers who aren't associated with an office or a reliable hotel. Rates vary depending on the hike and have gotten very costly. Expect to pay Tsh30,000 per person for a half-day hike to Irente Viewpoint, up to about Tsh75,000 per person per day on multiday hikes, including camping or accommodation in very basic guesthouses, guide fees, forest fees for any hikes that enter forest reserves (which includes most hikes from Lushoto) and food. Note that if you're fit and keen on covering some distance, most of the set stages for the popular hikes are quite short and it's easy to do two or even three stages in a day. However, most guides will then want to charge you the full price for the additional days, so you'll need to negotiate an amicable solution. A basic selection of vegetables and fruits is available along most routes and bottled water is sold in several of the larger villages, though if you're hiking on your own, you should carry a filter.

Lushoto can get chilly and wet at any time of year, so bring a waterproof jacket.

Sleeping & Eating

IN & NEAR TOWN

St Eugene's Hostel GUESTHOUSE $

(☎027-264 0055, 0784-523710, 0763-623210; www.steugeneshostel.com; s/tw/tr/ste US$25/45/54/60; P) This quiet place has spacious, good-value rooms, all with hot showers, balconies and views over the hills and surrounding gardens. It's run by the Usambara Sisters and profits go to support their work with local children, including a school on the premises. Delicious meals are served, and homemade cheese and jam are avail-

HIKES FROM LUSHOTO

An easy walk to get started is to **Irente Viewpoint** (6km, allow two to three hours return), which begins on the road running southwest from the Anglican church and leads gradually uphill to the viewpoint, with wide views on clear days. It's impressive to see how abruptly the Usambaras rise up from the plains below. En route is **Irente Farm** (⏲8am-5pm Mon-Fri, 10am-5pm Sat & Sun), where you can buy fresh cheese, yoghurt and granola, and get accommodation.

There's also a lovely three- to four-day hike that you can do from Lushoto to **Mtae** through stands of pine and past cornfields, villages and patches of wild asters, a six-day walk to Amani Nature Reserve, plus many other possibilities. The tourist information centres have wall maps detailing some of the routes.

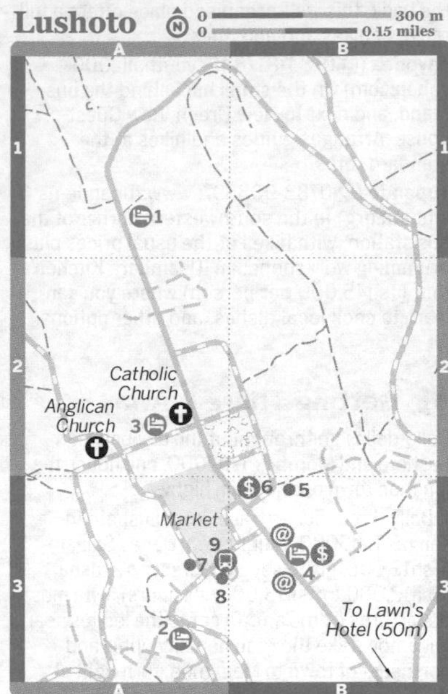

Lushoto

Sleeping

1 Kakakuona A1
2 Kialilo Green Garden Motel A3
3 St Benedict's Hostel A2
4 Tumaini Hostel B3

Eating

Makuti African Restaurant .... (see 4)
Tumaini Restaurant .... (see 4)

Information

5 Friends of Usambara Society B3
6 National Microfinance Bank B3
7 Tayodea A3
8 Tupande A3

Transport

9 Bus Stand A3

able for sale. St Eugene's is along the main road about 3.5km before Lushoto, on the left coming from Soni. Ask the bus driver to drop you at the Montessori Centre.

Tumaini Hostel HOSTEL $
(☎027-264 0094; tumaini@elct-ned.org; Main Rd; d/ste Tsh25,000/35,000, s/d without bathroom Tsh12,000/17,000; P) This hostel run by the Lutheran church offers simple twin-bedded rooms and hot-water showers in a two-storey compound overlooking tiny gardens. It's in the town centre near the Telecom building and just behind **Tumaini Restaurant** (☎027-264 0027; Main Rd; meals from Tsh6000; ⏰breakfast, lunch & dinner), which has banana milkshakes and well-prepared continental fare. Just behind, and under the same management, is **Makuti African Restaurant** (meals Tsh2000), with good local food.

Lawn's Hotel HOTEL $
(☎027-264 0005, 0784-420252; www.lawnshotel.com; camping with hot shower US$10, s/d US$40/50, d bungalow US$45; P@) This Lushoto institution is faded but full of charm, with vine-covered buildings surrounded by extensive gardens, spacious, musty rooms with dark-wood floors and fireplaces, and in need of a shake-out, plus some newer doubles and bungalows, a small library, a bar and restaurant. It's at the southern end of town and signposted; go left at the small traffic circle at the entrance to town, following the unpaved road up and around through the pine trees to the main entrance.

Kakakuona HOTEL $
(☎0754-006969; kakakuonainfo@yahoo.com; s/d/tw Tsh25,000/30,000/30,000; @) Just behind the post office, Kakakuona has clean, very good-value rooms with hot water and TV, and a nice terrace restaurant overlooking the valley.

Rosmini Hostel GUESTHOUSE $
(☎0785-776348; rosminihostellushoto@yahoo.co.uk; per adult Tsh25,000; P) This small, friendly church-run place has simple double-bedded rooms with hot-water showers, and meals with advance order. It's 1.8km before town, on the left when coming from Soni. Ask the bus driver to drop you.

St Benedict's Hostel GUESTHOUSE $
(camping Tsh10,000, s/d Tsh20,000/30,000) One larger double plus several smaller rooms, all no-frills, and meals with advance order. It's next door to the Catholic church.

Near the market and bus stand area there are many shoestring guesthouses, all with serviceable, but mostly scruffy and undistinguished rooms and hot-water buckets on request. **Kialilo Green Garden Motel** (☎0715-237381; s/d Tsh18,000/30,000) is a step above the rest, with small, clean rooms around the shared living room and eating area, and food with advance order. Head left when coming out of the bus park and cross the small footbridge. Kialilo is left and up the hill.

OUTSIDE TOWN

Swiss Farm Cottage LODGE $$
(☎0715-700813, 0714-970271; www.swiss-farm-cottage.co.tz; per person in standard/luxury bungalow US$25/40; P) A lovely, tranquil spot, complete with cows grazing on the grassy hillsides. It's about 15km from Lushoto past Migambo village, in an area well-situated for walking, and a good option for those with their own transport.

Mullers Mountain Lodge LODGE $$
(☎026-264 0204, 0784-500999; www.mullersmountainlodge.co.tz; camping US$5, s/d US$40/50, q without bathroom US$80, cottage US$100; P) An old family homestead set in sprawling grounds, with rooms in the main house or, for a bit more privacy, in nearby cottages (with two rooms sharing a sitting room), plus meals. There are also a few less appealing cement huts with shared bathroom and a large grassy camping area with a covered cooking area. It's 2km beyond Swiss Farm Cottage in a similarly fine walking area, and signposted.

Information

Internet Access

Bosnia Ultimate Shop Internet Café (per hr Tsh2000; 8.30am-6pm Mon-Fri, 9am-2pm Sat) Diagonally opposite Tumaini Restaurant, with many terminals.

Tumaini Restaurant Internet Café (per hr Tsh1500; 8.30am-6pm Mon-Fri, 9am-3pm Sat) Next to Tumaini Restaurant, with one terminal.

Garage

Rosmini Garage About 1.5km before town on the Mombo Rd.

Money

There's not yet an ATM in Lushoto that accepts international credit cards.

National Microfinance Bank (8am-3pm Mon-Fri) On the main road. Changes cash only.

Tumaini Bureau de Change (8.30am-5pm Mon-Fri, 9am-1pm Sat) Changes cash; next to Tumaini Restaurant.

Tourist Information

Friends of Usambara Society (☎027-264 0132, 0787-094725; www.usambaratravels.com) Just down the small road running next to the bank, this well-organised place offers a full range of hikes and activities.

Tayodea (☎0784-817848; youthall2000@yahoo.com) On the small hill behind the bus stand, and next to New Green View Guesthouse. Arranges guides and hikes at the standard rates.

Tupande (☎0783-908597; www.tupande-usambara.org) In the southwestern corner of the bus station, with hikes at the usual prices plus drumming workshops, an 'Usambara Kitchen' tour (Tsh45,000 per person) where you can learn to cook local dishes, and other options.

Getting There & Away

Dalla-dallas go throughout the day between Lushoto and Mombo (Tsh2000, one hour), the junction town on the main highway.

Daily direct buses travel from Lushoto to Tanga (Tsh6000, four hours), Dar es Salaam (Tsh12,000, six to seven hours) and Arusha (Tsh12,000 to Tsh13,000, six hours), with most departures from 7am. To get to the lodges near Migambo, take the road heading uphill and northeast of town to Magamba, turn right at the signposted junction and continue for 7km to Migambo junction, from where the lodges are signposted. Via public transport, there's a daily bus between Tanga and Kwamakame that goes to within around 2km of Mullers, departing Tanga at about 9am or 10am and reaching the Migambo area at around 2pm.

Around Lushoto

MTAE

Tiny Mtae is perched on a cliff about 55km northwest of Lushoto, with fantastic 270-degree views over the Tsavo Plains and down to Mkomazi National Park. Just to the southeast is **Shagayu Peak** (2220m), one of the highest in the Usambara Mountains.

About 3km before Mtae is the excellent **Mambo Viewpoint Eco Lodge** (☎0785-272150; www.mamboviewpoint.org; camping US$10, s US$50-80, d US$65-110; P), with stunning views, comfortable permanent tents and cottages. The owners offer a wealth of information on the area, and can sort out hikes, village stays and more.

If travelling by public transport you'll need to spend at least one night in Mtae as buses from Lushoto (Tsh5000, four hours) travel only in the afternoons, departing Lushoto by about 1pm. The return buses from Mtae to Lushoto depart between 4am and 5.30am en route to Dar es Salaam.

SONI

Tiny Soni lacks Lushoto's infrastructure, but makes a good change of pace if you'll be staying longer in the Usambaras. It's also the starting point for several wonderful walks, including a two- to three-day hike to the Mazumbai Forest Reserve and Bumbuli town.

Sleepy **Maweni Farm** (☎0784-307841, 0784-279371; www.maweni.com/lodge; s/d/f from €40/60/108, d without bathroom €36; P) is an atmospheric old farmhouse is set in lush, rambling grounds, with Kwa Mungu mountain rising up behind. The rooms (some in the main house and some in a separate block) are spacious and comfortable. There are also safari-style tents with private bathrooms, plus meals and guides for walks. Maweni is 2.9km from the main Soni junction along a dirt road, and signposted.

Getting There & Away

Soni is 12km south of Lushoto along the Mombo road, and easy to reach via dalla-dalla from either destination (Tsh1000 from Lushoto, Tsh1000 from Mombo).

MOMBO TO SAME

Mombo is the scruffy junction town at the foot of the Usambara Mountains where the road to Lushoto branches off the main Dar es Salaam–Arusha highway. As most buses from either Arusha or Dar pass at a reasonable hour, you should have no trouble getting a dalla-dalla up to Soni or Lushoto to sleep.

About 45km northwest of Mombo is **Pangani River Campsite** (camping per tent US$5), with hot-water showers and meals. It's 1.5km off the main road and signposted.

NORTHERN TANZANIA

For many visitors to Tanzania, it's all about the north. With snow-capped Mt Kilimanjaro, wildlife-packed Ngorongoro Crater, red-cloaked Maasai warriors and the vast plains of the Serengeti, northern Tanzania embodies what is for many the quintessential Africa. But there's much more to this majestic and mythical place and it would draw scores of visitors even if it didn't host these African icons.

Crater-capped Mt Meru is a climb that rivals its taller neighbour, dry-season wildlife watching in Tarangire National Park is as good as any other park in Africa, and the desolate Rift Valley landscape between Lakes Manyara and Natron will mesmerise you. Sleep in a coffee plantation, hunt with modern day nomads, ride camels, canoe with hippos...well, you get the point.

You couldn't possibly do it all in one trip, but you'll make a lifetime of memories no matter how much time you have.

Moshi

The noticeably clean capital of the densely populated Kilimanjaro region sits at the foot of Mt Kilimanjaro and makes a good introduction to the splendours of the north. It's a low-key place with an appealing blend of African and Asian influences and a self-

MOSHI TREKKING OPERATORS

The following Moshi-based companies focus on Kilimanjaro treks, although most can also organise day hikes on the mountain's lower slopes.

» **Ahsante Tours** (☎027-275 0248; www.ahsantetours.com; Karanga Dr; midrange) Kilimanjaro treks, plus cultural tours in Machame, Marangu and other areas.

» **Kessy Brothers Tours & Travel** (☎027-275 1185, 0754 803953; www.kessybrotherstours.com; Chagga St; budget) Kilimanjaro treks.

» **Moshi Expeditions & Mountaineering** (MEM Tours; ☎027-275 4234; www.memtours.com; Kaunda St; budget to midrange) Kilimanjaro treks.

» **Shah Tours** (☎027-275 2370/2998; www.kilimanjaro-shah.com; Sekou Toure Rd; midrange) Kilimanjaro and Meru treks, plus treks in the Ngorongoro highlands and on Ol Doinyo Lengai.

» **Zara Tanzania Adventures** (☎027-275 0233, 0754-451000; www.zaratours.com; Springlands Hotel, Tembo Rd, Pasua Neighbourhood; budget to midrange) Kilimanjaro treks.

Northern Tanzania

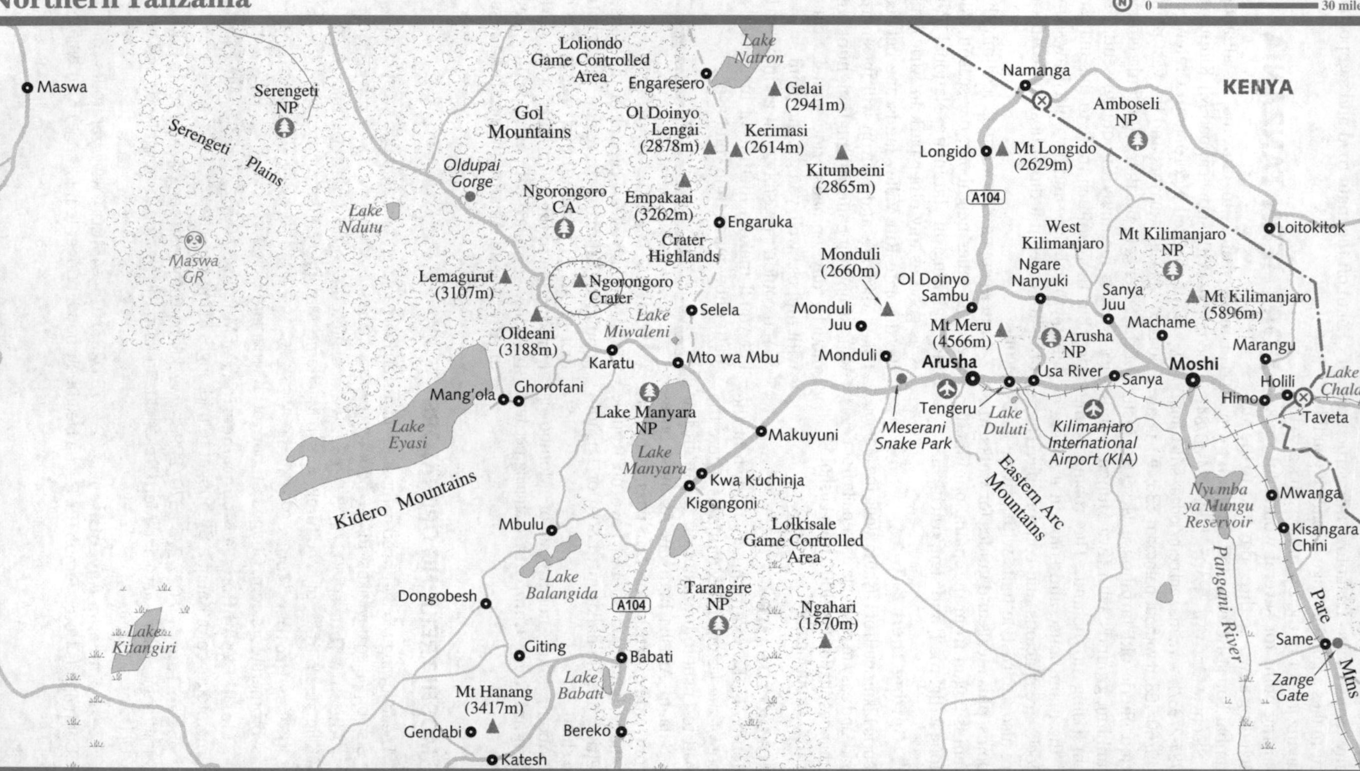

VOLUNTEERING IN MOSHI

If you're looking to do more in Moshi than just climb Kili, consider volunteering. Moshi is the easiest place in Tanzania to lend a hand since many groups looking for help post flyers on noticeboards around town. For those who'd prefer to have someone help them find a placement, **Honey Badger** (p107), **Hostel Hoff** (☎0787-225 908; www.hostelhoff.com; dm US$18) and the less cosy **Foot2Afrika** (Hostel Foot Prince; ☎0784-828835; www.foot2afrika.com; dm US$20) will set you up with a project that fits your skills and desires as long as you sleep at their hostels. All are for-profit enterprises, but they're locally based and while not cheap, they're much less expensive than the big international volunteering companies. They require a minimum stay of two weeks, one month and three weeks respectively and the prices for Hoff and Foot include breakfast and dinner (Hoff also does your laundry) while Honey Badger is more flexible about arrangements and has several options. Longer stays mean lower prices.

Ujamaa Hostel (p120) is a similar set-up in Arusha.

sufficient, prosperous feel, due in large part to it being the centre of one of Tanzania's major coffee-growing regions. It's also less expensive than nearby Arusha. Virtually all visitors are here to climb Mt Kilimanjaro.

Sights & Activities

Even inside the city, **Mt Kilimanjaro** is the main attraction and you'll probably be continually gazing north trying to catch a glimpse. Most of the time it will be hidden behind a wall of clouds, but nearly every evening after 6pm it emerges from the mist to whet your appetite for altitude. From December through June it's usually visible during the mornings too and during these months it's extra beautiful because it's topped by much more snow.

Trekking agencies and many hotels lead easy, scenic **walks** along the footpaths linking various villages on Kilimanjaro's lower slopes.

Sleeping

CENTRAL MOSHI

These places are all an easy walk from the bus station.

AA Hill Street Accommodation GUESTHOUSE $
(☎0754-461469; sajjad_omar@hotmail.com; Kilima St; s/d/tr Tsh20,000/25,000/35,000) Clean, quiet and pleasant rooms with fans in a convenient location a short walk from the bus station. Alcohol is not allowed on the premises and unmarried couples cannot share a room. There's no breakfast.

Buffalo Hotel HOTEL $
(☎027-275 2775; New St; r Tsh 25,000-35,000, without bathroom Tsh17,000, ste Tsh45,000; P ❄) The long popular Buffalo Hotel has straightforward double and twin rooms (the cheapest with fan; others with air-con) with cable TV. It's reasonably priced.

Kindoroko Hotel HOTEL $
(☎027-275 4054; www.kindorokohotels.com; Mawenzi Rd; s/d/f US$25/35/50; P) This longstanding and often busy place has small but otherwise good rooms featuring cable TV and hot water. It's a good meeting place, though the great Kilimanjaro views from the rooftop bar are only for guests.

Haria Hotel HOTEL $
(☎0763-019395; Mawenzi Rd; dm Tsh10,000, tw Tsh25,000, without bathroom Tsh20,000, ste Tsh35,000;) With bright, large and clean no-frills rooms with fans, it's worlds better than the more well-known and more expensive Kilimanjaro Backpackers a block away. There's a roof-top bar and restaurant serving a limited menu of local meals like chicken and chips at fair prices. Breakfast costs Tsh3000.

Zebra Hotel HOTEL $
(☎027-275 0611; New St; s/d/tr US$30/35/45; ❄) A new-ish high-rise with big rooms with hot water and cable TV. The restaurant has left the 8th floor, but you can still lounge about there taking in some of the best mountain views available in Moshi. There's no elevator, but if you're here to climb Kilimanjaro it shouldn't matter.

Moshi

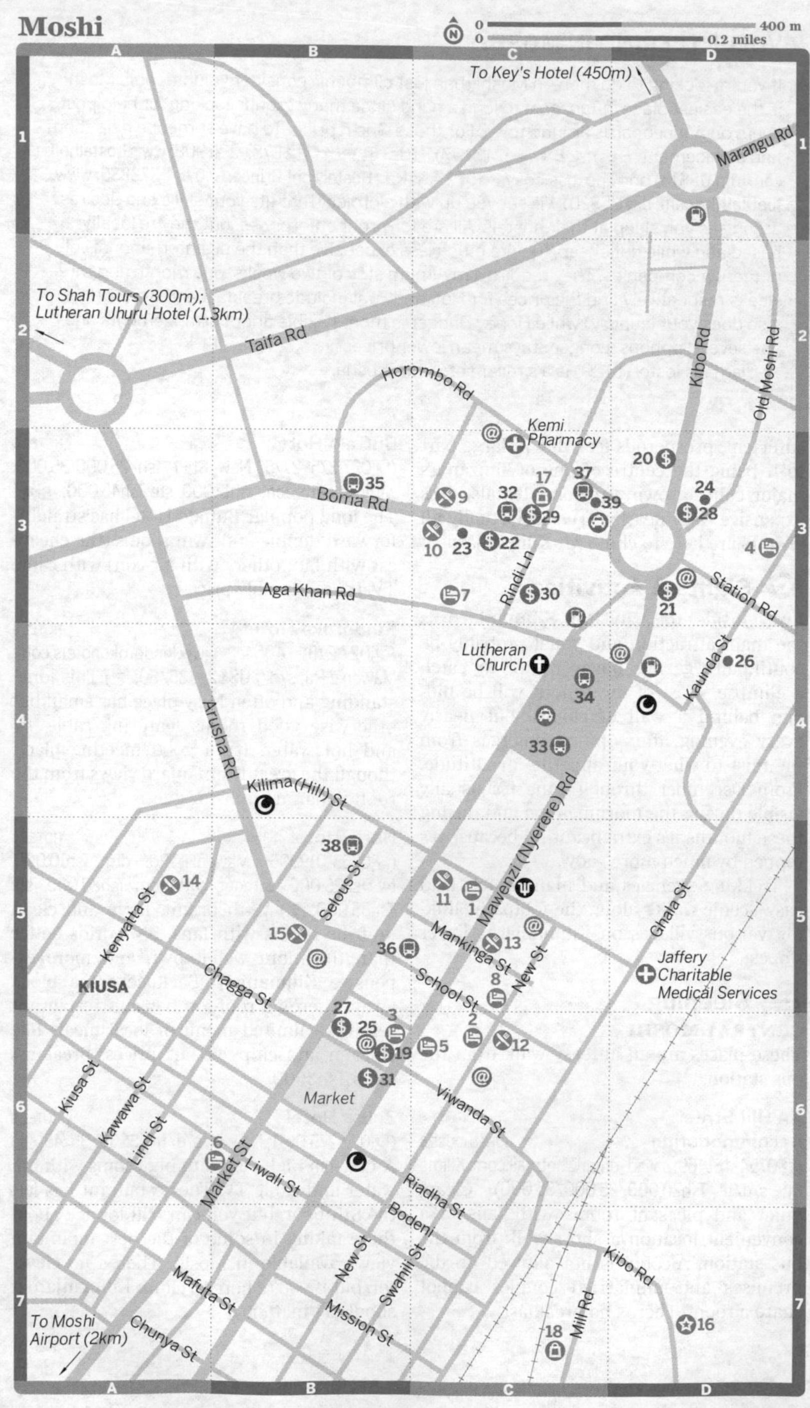

0 400 m
0 0.2 miles
A
B
C
D
1
2
3
4
5
6
7
To Key's Hotel (450m)
Marangu Rd
To Shah Tours (300m); Lutheran Uhuru Hotel (1.3km)
Taifa Rd
Horombo Rd
Kibo Rd
Old Moshi Rd
Kemi Pharmacy
Boma Rd
Aga Khan Rd
Rindi Ln
Station Rd
Lutheran Church
Kaunda St
Arusha Rd
Kilima (Hill) St
Mawenzi (Nyerere) Rd
Selous St
Kenyatta St
Mankinga St
New St
Ghala St
School St
Chagga St
KIUSA
Jaffery Charitable Medical Services
Market
Viwanda St
Kiusa St
Kawawa St
Lindi St
Market St
Liwali St
Riadha St
Bodeni
New St
Swahili St
Kibo Rd
Mafuta St
Mission St
Mill Rd
To Moshi Airport (2km)
Chunya St

Moshi

Sleeping

1 AA Hill Street Accommodation C5
2 Buffalo Hotel C6
3 Haria Hotel B6
4 Kilimanjaro Crane Hotel D3
5 Kindoroko Hotel C6
6 Lutheran Umoja Hostel B6
7 Parkview Inn C3
8 Zebra Hotel C5

Eating

9 Abbas Ali's Hot Bread Shop C3
10 Aleem's C3
11 Coffee Shop C5
12 IndoItaliano Restaurant C6
13 Milan's C5
14 Salzburger Café A5
15 Union Café B5

Entertainment

16 Club La Liga D7

Shopping

17 La Chance Bookshop C3
18 Shah Industries C7

Information

19 Barclays Bank B6
20 Classic Bureau de Change ....
21 CRDB Bank ....
22 Exim Bank C
23 Immigration Office C3
24 Kahawa Shamba Booking Office D3
25 Kilimanjaro Coffee Lounge Internet Café B6
26 Moshi Expeditions & Mountaineering D4
27 NBC ATM B6
28 NBC Bank D3
29 Stanbic Bank C3
30 Standard Chartered Bank C3
31 Trast Bureau de Change B6

Transport

32 Akamba C3
33 Central Bus Station C4
34 Dalla-Dalla Stand C4
35 Dar Express B3
36 Kampala Coach B5
37 Kilimanjaro Express C3
38 Metro Express B5
Precision Air .... (see 24)
39 Zara Tours C3

Kilimanjaro Crane Hotel HOTEL $$
(☎027-275 1114; www.kilimanjarocranehotels.com; Kaunda St; s US$40-50, d US$50-60; P❄@≋) You can't go so far as to say this aging midranger has a faded charm, but there is a tiny bit of character. Rooms have fans (air-con for an extra US$10), cable TV and large beds backing a small garden. There are great Kili views from the rooftop, but they've shut the bar that used to be there.

Parkview Inn HOTEL $$
(☎0754-052000; www.pvim.com; Aga Khan Rd; s/d/ste US$60/70/120; P❄@≈≋) No one would ever call this centrally located place attractive, but the modern rooms and swimming pool make it a good post-climb rest spot at the midrange level.

Lutheran Umoja Hostel GUESTHOUSE $
(☎027-275 0902; Market St; s Tsh18,000, d Tsh25,000, ste Tsh30-40,000, f Tsh50-60,000, s/d/tr without bathroom Tsh10,000/15,000/25,000; P@) The cheapest place in the city centre has clean, no-frills rooms around a small (mostly) quiet courtyard.

OUTSIDE THE CENTRE

Lutheran Uhuru Hotel LODGE $$
(☎0753-037216; www.uhuruhotel.org; Sekou Toure Rd; s US$30-45, d US$40-55, tw & ste US$60-75; P❄@≈) This alcohol-free place has spotless good-value rooms (the old rooms have fans and TVs, the new rooms have air-con and they say TVs will be installed) in leafy, expansive grounds, and a good restaurant (meals Tsh4000 to Tsh8000) with a broad menu. Rooms are wheelchair accessible and many have Kili views. It's 3km northwest of the town centre (Tsh3000 to Tsh4000 in a taxi) and an ideal choice for families.

Honey Badger GUESTHOUSE $$
(☎0787-730235; www.honeybadgerlodge.com; camping with own/hired tent US$5/10, dm US$10, s US$25-30, d US$40-50, tr US$60; P@≈≋) A large family-run place with cheap camping in an enclosed lawn and a variety of expensive rooms. Campers and dorm dwellers must pay US$3 to use the large pool. They offer a variety of tours and lessons (drumming, cooking etc) and volunteer opportuni-

[K]AHAWA SHAMBA COFFEE TOURS

[Th]e most popular coffee tour in town is offered by **Kahawa Shamba** (027-275 [0]64, 0767-834500; www.kahawashamba.co.tz; per person Tsh26,400, transport from Moshi [T]sh45,000), a laudable community-run venture that not only shows you how beans are grown, picked and roasted, but offers insight into the lives of the Chagga coffee farmers who live on Kilimanjaro's lower slopes. Meals with local families can be arranged, as can additional village and waterfall walks. It's easiest to book at Union Café, but there's also an office (in the unsigned white building by the blue gate) at the KNCU building just off Clock Tower roundabout. There was once (and may be again) interesting accommodation (US$120 per person full board) made to look like traditional banana-thatch Chagga houses, but with modern amenities.

ties can be arranged. It's 7km from town off the Marangu road.

Ameg Lodge LODGE $$
(027-275 0175, 0754-058268; www.ameglodge.com; off Lema Rd; s/tw/ste from US$50/88/149;) Spacious rooms in detached cottages – all with TV, small porches and fans – set around a large, grassy compound. There's also Moshi's best gym, and a restaurant. It's signposted just off Lema Rd in Shanty Town.

Key's Hotel HOTEL $$
(027-275 2250; www.keys-hotel-tours.com; Uru Rd; s/d/tr US$58/71/104, with air-con US$78/91/124;) Key's, about 1km northeast of the Clock Tower on a quiet side street, has been popular with travellers for years. Somewhat overpriced accommodation is in spacious, high-ceilinged rooms in the main building, or in small, dark rondavels out back. There's a restaurant and bar and nonguests can relax by the pool for Tsh5000.

Sal Salinero Villa HOTEL $$
(027-275 2240, www.salsalinerohotel.com; s/d/tr US$90/120/130;) Moshi's top address offers seven large rooms in a mock Italian villa with hardwood flooring, a winding staircase and public lounge plus 20 more modern-feeling cottages under palm trees. It's in the Shanty Town area, just off Lema Rd.

Eating & Drinking

TOP CHOICE **Milan's** INDIAN $
(Mankinga St; meals Tsh3500-5000; lunch & dinner;) This colourful all-vegetarian spot is our favourite Indian restaurant, and not only because the prices are so low: it's really delicious. There are also pizzas and a few Chinese choices.

Union Café CAFE $$
(Arusha Rd; meals Tsh4000-14,000; breakfast, lunch & dinner;) A stylish and historic shop with good pizzas, pastas and sandwiches, but this is one coffee shop that really is foremost about the coffee. It's run by the Kilimanjaro Native Cooperative Union representing tens of thousands of small-holding coffee farmers and they roast their own beans on-site. Locals also like it because they have a generator, which ensures wi-fi during power cuts.

Salzburger Café TANZANIAN, EUROPEAN $
(Kenyatta St; meals Tsh6800-9500; breakfast, lunch & dinner) The Alps meet Africa at this classic place, which comes complete with waiters sporting faux-leopard skin vests, Austrian *kneipe* (bar) decor and a selection of good, cheap dishes (try Chicken Mambo Yote), all with amusing menu descriptions.

IndoItaliano Restaurant INDIAN, ITALIAN $$
(New St; meals Tsh7000-14,000; lunch & dinner;) This very popular travellers destination has two big menus, Indian and Italian, and surprisingly both are quite good. The pavement terrace is a nice place to linger.

The Coffee Shop CAFE $
(Kilima St; meals Tsh2200-5000; breakfast, lunch & dinner Mon-Fri, breakfast & lunch Sat) A laid-back vibe, garden seating, good coffee, small book exchange and an assortment of homemade breads, cakes, yogurt, breakfast and low-priced light meals. Proceeds go to a church project.

Self-Catering

Aleem's (Boma Rd) is a well-stocked grocery. **Abbas Ali's Hot Bread Shop** (Boma Rd) is Moshi's best bakery.

Shopping

La Chance Bookshop BOOKS, MAPS
(Rindi Lane, Kibo Tower) East Africa books and national park maps.

Shah Industries LEATHER
(Mill Rd) Lots of interesting leatherwork, some of it made by people with disabilities.

Information

Immigration

Immigration office (Boma Rd; 7.30am-3.30pm Mon-Fri)

Internet Access

Dot Café (Horombo Rd; per hr Tsh1000) Well-run shop. Cheap Net2Phone international calls from Tsh250 per minute.

EasyCom (Ground fl, Kahawa House, Clock Tower roundabout; per hr Tsh1000; 7.30am-8pm)

Kilimanjaro Coffee Lounge Internet Café (Chagga St; per hr Tsh1500; 8am-8pm Mon-Sat, 10am-5pm Sun)

Internet Resources

Kiliweb (www.kiliweb.com)

Medical Services

Jaffery Charitable Medical Services (027-275 1843; Ghala St; 8.30am-5pm Mon-Fri, 8.30am-1pm Sat) Well-trained doctors, and a reliable laboratory.

Kemi Pharmacy (027-275 1560; Horombo Rd; 7am-7pm Mon-Sat, 10.30am-3pm Sun)

Kilimanjaro Christian Medical Centre (027-275 4377/80; Sokoine Rd; 24hr)

Money

All the big banks have branches in Moshi. They're shown on the map.

Classic Bureau de Change (Kibo Rd; 8am-4pm) One of the few bureaus open Sundays.

Trast Bureau de Change (Chagga St; 9am-5pm Mon-Sat, 9am-2pm Sun) Best rates for travellers cheques. Also open Sundays.

Tourist Information

The Coffee Shop, Kilimanjaro Coffee Lounge, Union Café and IndoItaliano restaurants have message boards.

Getting There & Away

Air

Kilimanjaro International Airport (KIA) is 50km west of town, halfway to Arusha. The only airline with a Moshi office is **Precision Air** (0787-800820; www.precisionairtz.com; Old Moshi Rd). See Arusha (p125) for flight details.

There's also the small Moshi airport just southwest of town, along the extension of Market St, which handles occasional charters.

Bus

Buses and minibuses run throughout the day to Arusha (Tsh2500, 1½ hours) and Marangu (Tsh1500, 1½ hours).

The best service to Dar es Salaam (seven to eight hours) is Dar Express, with several full luxury (Tsh30,000; air-conditioning and toilets) departures from Moshi between 7am and 10.30am. Metro Express (Tsh32,000, 10am) also has a full luxury bus while Kampala Coach (Tsh25,000, 1pm) and Kilimanjaro Express (Tsh28,000, 10am) have air-con ('luxury') buses. All of these buses use their own offices rather than the bus station (Kampala Coach and Metro Express near the market, Dar Express and Kilimanjaro Express near Clock Tower). Ordinary buses (Tsh18,000) and a few less-reliable luxury companies, such as Fresh Express, use the bus station. Dar Express's 7am bus sometimes arrives early enough for you to catch the afternoon ferry to Zanzibar, but don't count on it.

Dar Express, departing 6am, is also the best company to Mwanza (Tsh38,000, 12 to 13 hours). For Tanga (Tsh12,000 to Tsh15,000, five to six hours), there are many buses between 6.30am and 1pm. Simba line, with four-across seating, is probably the best.

For details on travel to Nairobi, Voi and Mombasa in Kenya, see p207.

The chaotic bus station is conveniently location in the middle of the city. There are many touts and arrivals can be quite annoying if you're new to this sort of thing. If they prove too much hassle you may want to take a taxi to your hotel, even if it's within walking distance. This is one good reason to travel with the companies that have their own offices. It's best to buy tickets the day before you'll travel.

Getting Around

To/From the Airport

Precision Air has a shuttle (Tsh10,000) to/from KIA for their flights (except Nairobi), departing from their offices a few hours before flight time. Taxi drivers are tough negotiators; try for US$30, but expect to pay more.

Taxi & Dalla-Dalla

There are taxi stands near the Clock Tower and at the bus station, plus you can find taxis by most hotels. The bus station to a city centre hotel should cost Tsh2000 and it's Tsh3000 to Shantytown. Motorcycle taxi drivers expect Tsh1000, even for a very short ride. Dalla-dallas run down main roads from next to the bus station.

Marangu

Nestled on the lower slopes of Mt Kilimanjaro, 40km northeast of Moshi, amid dense stands of banana and coffee plants, is the lively, leafy market town of Marangu. It has an agreeable highland ambience, cool climate and good selection of hotels, all of which organise treks. While you'll generally get slightly better budget deals in Moshi, Marangu makes a convenient base for Kili climbs using the Marangu or Rongai routes, and it's an enjoyable stop in its own right.

Marangu is also the heartland of the Chagga people, and there are many possibilities for walks and cultural activities. *Marangu* means 'place of water' and the surrounding area is laced with small streams and waterfalls (most with a small entry charge) to visit.

Sights & Activities

Most hotels can arrange **walks and cultural activities** in the area. At Kilimanjaro Mountain Resort, there's also the **Chagga Live Museum** (adult/child US$3/2; 10am-5pm), a small outdoor museum illustrating traditional Chagga life.

It's possible to do a **day hike** in Mt Kilimanjaro National Park from Marangu gate as far as Mandara Hut (about two hours up, one hour down; US$60 per person for park fees, plus US$10 per guide, arranged at the park gate).

Sleeping & Eating

Coffee Tree Campsite CAMPGROUND $
(0754-691433; kilimanjaro@iwayafrica.com; camping US$8, rondavel/chalet per person US$12/15; P) This place has expansive, trim grounds, hot-water showers, tents for hire, double rondavels and four- to five-person chalets. It's 700m east of the main road, signposted near Nakara Hotel. There's no food, but get meals at nearby Nakara Hotel or **John's Corner** (meals about Tsh4000) across the road.

Kilimanjaro Mountain Resort LODGE $$$
(0754-693461; www.kilimountresort.com; camping US$17, s/d/tw/tr US$121/182/182/266; P@) This stately old-style building is surrounded by gardens and forest 3km west of the main junction. It has spacious, well-appointed rooms (some with enormous beds), a restaurant (meals US$18) and the adjoining Chagga Live Museum.

MARANGU TREKKING OPERATORS

Most Marangu hotels organise Kilimanjaro treks; see p110. Also worth noting is Marangu Hotel's 'hard way' option that's one of the cheapest deals available for a reliable trek. For US$295/350 plus park fees for a five-/six-day Marangu climb, the hotel will take care of hut reservations and provide a guide with porter, while you provide all food and equipment. Marangu Hotel also offers 'hard way' deals on the other Kilimanjaro routes.

Fortune Mountain Resort LODGE $$
(0762-932686; www.equitanzresorts.com; s/d US$60/120; P) About 700m before the main junction, Fortune lacks the lush garden surroundings of some of the other lodges, but the rooms are beautiful, spacious, well-appointed (the honeymoon suite has a large, raised bathtub) and very comfortable. There's a restaurant.

Marangu Hotel LODGE $$
(0754-886092; www.maranguhotel.com; camping US$10; s/d/tr half board US$90/130/195; P@) This long-standing hotel is the first place you reach coming from Moshi. It has a pleasantly faded British ambience, pleasant rooms in expansive grounds, lovely gardens and a campground with hot-water showers. Room discounts are available if you join one of the hotel's fully equipped climbs.

Nakara Hotel LODGE $$
(0754-277300; www.nakarahotels.com; r per person US$60; P) This is a reliable establishment with reasonable twin or double-bedded rooms and a restaurant. It's in a quiet, leafy area just off the main road towards the park gate and signposted.

Capricorn Hotel LODGE $$
(0754-841981; www.thecapricornhotels.com; s/d cottages US$65/130, in main house US$100/200; P) With its dark wood and surrounding greenery, the Capricorn makes a pleasant impression, although prices are on the high side for Marangu. Breakfast costs US$12 per person extra. It's about halfway between the main junction and the park gate.

Bismarck Hut Lodge GUESTHOUSE $
(0754-318338; camping US$5, r per person without bathroom US$10-15; P) Along the road to

the park gate and shortly before the turn-off to Capricorn Hotel, the no-frills Bismarck has a few clean, basic rooms, a small camping area, two large, old resident tortoises and meals on order.

Information

Internet Access

Marangu Village Computer Literacy Centre (Main junction; per 15 min Tsh1500; ⌚8.30am-5.30pm Mon-Sat) Behind the post office.

Money

CRDB (Main junction) ATM; 100m before (downhill from) main junction.
NBC (Main junction) ATM; just uphill from the main junction.

Getting There & Away

Minibuses run throughout the day between Marangu's main junction ('Marangu Mtoni') and Moshi (Tsh1500, 1½ hours). Once in Marangu, there are sporadic pick-ups from the main junction to the park gate (Tsh1000), 5km further. For the Holili border, change at Himo junction.

Mt Kilimanjaro National Park

Since its official opening in 1977, Kilimanjaro National Park has become one of Tanzania's most visited parks. Unlike the other northern parks, this isn't for the wildlife, although it's there. Rather, it's to gaze in awe at a mountain on the equator capped with snow, and to climb to the top of Africa.

At the heart of the park is the 5896m Mt Kilimanjaro, Africa's highest mountain and one of the continent's magnificent sights. It's also one of the highest volcanoes and among the highest freestanding mountains in the world, rising from cultivated farmlands on the lower levels, through lush rainforest to alpine meadows, and finally across a barren lunar landscape to the twin summits of Kibo and Mawenzi. The lower rainforest is home to many animals, including buffaloes, elephants, leopards and monkeys, and elands are occasionally seen in the saddle area between Kibo and Mawenzi.

A trek up Kili lures around 25,000 trekkers each year, in part because it's possible to walk to the summit without ropes or technical climbing experience. Yet, non-technical does not mean easy. The climb is a serious (and expensive) undertaking, and only worth doing with the right preparation.

There are entry gates at Machame, Marangu (which is also the site of park headquarters), Londorosi and several other points. Trekkers using the Rongai Route should pay their fees at Marangu gate.

Trekking Mt Kilimanjaro

Mt Kilimanjaro can be climbed at any time of year. Though weather patterns are notoriously erratic and difficult to predict, during November and March/April, it's more likely that paths through the forest will be slippery, and that routes up to the summit, especially the Western Breach, will be covered by snow. That said, you can also have a streak of beautiful, sunny days during these times. Overall, the best time for climbing the mountain is in the dry season, from late June to October, and from late December to February or early March, just after the short rains and before the long rains.

Don't underestimate the weather on Kilimanjaro. Conditions on the mountain are frequently very cold and wet, and you'll need a full range of waterproof cold-weather clothing and gear, including a good-quality sleeping bag. It's also worth carrying some additional sturdy water bottles. No matter what the time of year, waterproof everything, especially your sleeping bag, as things rarely dry on the mountain. It's often possible to rent sleeping bags and gear from trekking operators. For the Marangu Route, you can also rent gear from the Kilimanjaro Guides Cooperative Society stand just inside Marangu gate, or from a small no-name shop just before the gate. However, especially at the budget level, quality and availability can't be counted on, and it's best to bring your own.

KILIMANJARO NATIONAL PARK

» **Why Go** Trekking on Africa's highest peak

» **When to Go** Year round

» **Practicalities** Must climb with a licensed guide; waterproof all gear and come prepared for cold, wet conditions

Kilimanjaro Area

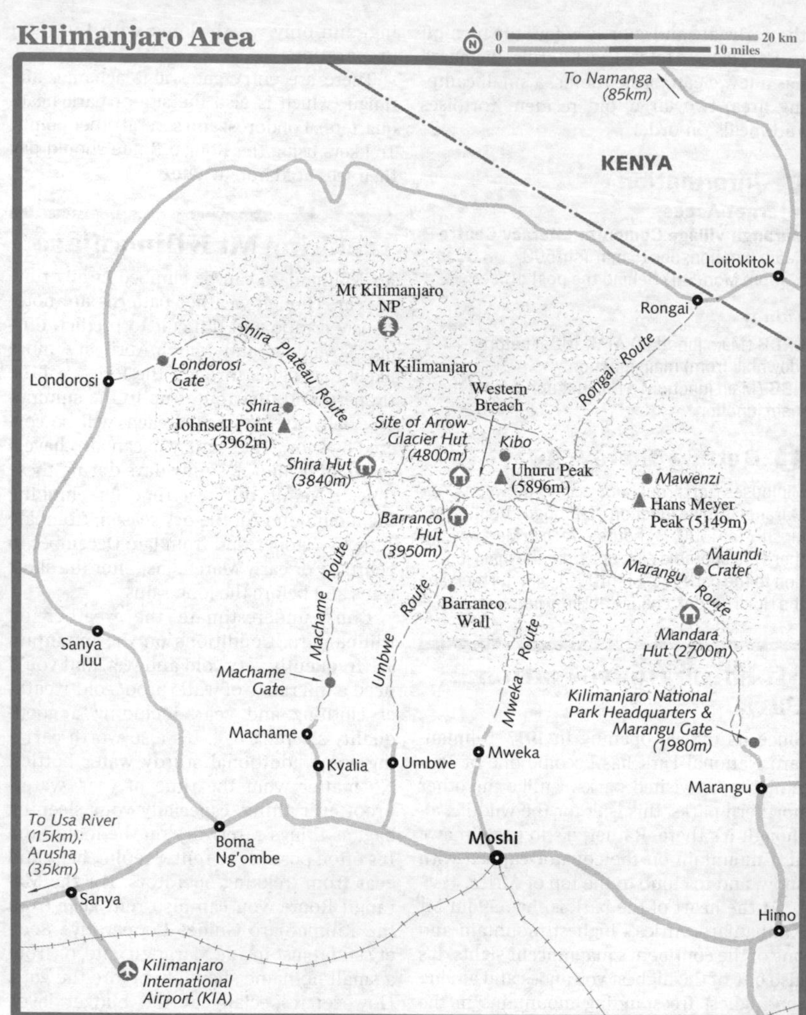

Apart from a small shop at Marangu gate selling a limited range of chocolate bars and tinned items, there are no shops inside the park. You can buy beer and soft drinks at high prices at huts on the Marangu Route.

Costs

Kilimanjaro can only be climbed with a licensed guide. Unless you're a Tanzanian resident and well-versed in the logistics of Kili climbs, the only realistic way to organise things is through a tour company. For operator listings and some tips see the Arusha, Moshi and Marangu sections, the trekking operators listing on p120 and the safari operators listing in the boxed text on p126. No-frills five-day/four-night treks up the Marangu Route start at about US$1100, including park fees, and no-frills six-day budget treks on the Machame Route start at around US$1400. Better-quality six-day trips on the Marangu and Machame routes start at about US$1500. The Umbwe Route is often sold by budget operators for about the same price as Marangu, and billed as a quick and comparatively inexpensive way to reach the top. Don't fall for this; the route should only be done by experienced trekkers and should have an extra acclimatisation day built in. Prices start at about US$1200 on the Rongai Route, and about US$1600 for a seven-day trek on the Shira Plateau Route. As the starting points for these latter routes are further from Moshi than those for the other routes, transport costs can be significant, so clarify whether they're included in the price.

Whatever you pay for your trek, remember that at least US$525 of this goes to park fees for a five-day Marangu Route climb, and more for longer treks (US$745 for a seven-day Machame-route climb). The rest of the money covers food, tents (if required), guides, porters and transport to and from the start of the trek. Most of the better companies provide dining tents, decent to good cuisine and various other extras to both make the experience more enjoyable and maximise your chances of getting to the top. If you choose a really cheap trip you risk having inadequate meals, mediocre guides, few comforts and problems with hut bookings and park fees. Also remember that an environmentally responsible trek usually costs more.

PARK FEES

Park entry fees (calculated per day, and not per 24-hour period) are US$60/10 per adult/child aged five to 15. Huts (Marangu Route) cost US$50 per person per night, and there's a US$20 rescue fee per person per trip for treks on the mountain. Camping costs US$50 per person per night on all routes. Park fees are generally included in price quotes, and paid on your behalf by the trekking operator, but you'll need to confirm this before making any bookings. Guide and porter fees (but not tips) are handled directly by the trekking companies. For anyone paying directly at the gate, all entry, hut, camping and other park fees must be paid with either Visa or MasterCard and your PIN.

Kilimanjaro National Park Headquarters (☎027-275 6602/5; info@tanzaniaparks.com; marangugate@yahoo.com; ⏲8am-6pm) is at the park gate in Marangu.

TIPPING

Most guides and porters receive only minimal wages from the trekking companies and depend on tips as their major source of income. As a guideline, plan on tipping about 10% of the total amount you've paid for the trek, divided up among the guides and porters. Common tips for satisfactory service are from about US$10 to US$15 per group per day for the guide, US$8 to US$10 per group per day for the cook and US$5 to US$10 per group per day for each porter.

Guides & Porters

Guides, and at least one porter (for the guide), are obligatory and are provided by your trekking company. You can carry your own gear on the Marangu Route, although porters are generally used, but one or two porters per trekker are essential on all other routes.

All guides must be registered with the national park authorities. If in doubt, check that your guide's permit is up to date. On Kili, the guide's job is to show you the way and that's it. Only the best guides, working for reputable companies, will be able to tell you about wildlife, flowers or other features on the mountain.

Porters will carry bags weighing up to 15kg (not including their own food and clothing, which they strap to the outside of your bag), and your bags will be weighed before you set off.

While most guides, including those working for the budget companies, are dedicated, professional, properly trained and genuinely concerned with making your trip safe and successful, there are exceptions. If you're a hardy traveller you might not worry about basic meals and substandard tents, but you should be concerned about incompetent guides and dishonest porters. Although it doesn't happen often, some guides leave the last hut deliberately late on the summit day to avoid going all the way to the top. Going with a reputable company, preferably one who hires full-time guides (most don't) is one way to prevent bad experiences. Also, insist on meeting the guide before signing up for a trip, familiarise yourself with all aspects of the route, and when on the mountain have morning and evening briefings so you know what to expect each day. The night before summiting talk to other climbers to be sure your departure time seems realistic (though note that not everyone leaves at the same time) and if not, get an explanation from your guide. Should problems arise, be polite but firm with your guide.

Maps

Topographical maps include *Map & Guide to Kilimanjaro* by Andrew Wielochowski and *Kilimanjaro Map & Guide* by Mark Savage.

Trekking Routes

There are six main trekking routes to the summit. Of these, the **Marangu Route** is the easiest and the most popular. A trek on this route is typically sold as a five-day, four-night return package, although at least one extra night is highly recommended to help acclimatisation, especially if you've just flown in to Tanzania or arrived from the lowlands.

Other routes on Kili usually take six days (which costs more, but helps acclimatisation) and pass through a wider range of scenic areas than the Marangu Route, although trekkers must use tents. The increasingly popular **Machame Route** has a gradual ascent, including a spectacular day contouring the southern slopes before approaching the summit via the top section of the Mweka Route. The **Umbwe Route** is much steeper, with a more direct way to the summit: very enjoyable if you can resist the temptation to gain altitude too quickly. Unfortunately, some trekking companies now push attractively priced five-day four-night options on the Umbwe Route in an effort to attract business. Although the route is direct, the top, very steep section up the Western Breach is often covered in ice or snow, which makes it impassable or extremely dangerous. Many trekkers who attempt it without proper acclimatisation are forced to turn back. An indication of its seriousness is that until fairly recently, the Western Breach was considered a technical mountaineering route. It has only gained in popularity recently because of intense competition for business and crowding on other routes. The bottom line is that you should only consider this route if you're experienced and properly equipped, and travelling with a reputable operator. Reliable operators will suggest an extra night for acclimatisation.

Another thing to watch out for is operators who try to sell a 'short' version of the Machame Route, which ascends the Machame Route for the first few stages, but then switches near the top to the final section of the Umbwe Route and summits via the Western Breach. This version is a day shorter (and thus less expensive) than the standard Machame Route, but the same considerations outlined in the preceding paragraph apply here, and you should only consider this combination if you're experienced, acclimatised and properly equipped.

The **Rongai Route**, which has also become increasingly popular in recent years, starts near the Kenyan border and goes up the northern side of the mountain. It's possible to do this in five days, but six is better. The attractive **Shira Plateau Route** (also called the Londorosi Route) is somewhat longer than the others, but good for acclimatisation if you start trekking from Londorosi gate (rather than driving all the way to the Shira Track road head), or if you take an extra day at Shira Hut.

Trekkers on the Machame and Umbwe routes descend via the Marangu Route or the **Mweka Route**, which is for descent only. Some Marangu treks also descend on the Mweka Route.

Officially a limit of 60 climbers per route per day is in effect on Kilimanjaro. It's currently not being enforced, except on the Marangu Route, which is self-limiting because of maximum hut capacities. If and when this limit is enforced, expect the advance time necessary for booking a climb to increase, with less flexibility for last-minute arrangements.

Arusha

POP 300,000

Cool, lush and green, Arusha is one of Tanzania's most developed and fastest-growing towns and the seat of the East African Community, a revived attempt at regional collaboration. It sprawls near the foot of Mt Meru at about 1300m altitude and enjoys a temperate climate throughout the year. Arusha's location is convenient for all Northern Circuit parks, and as such, it's the safari capital of Tanzania and a major tourism centre; with all the bad and good that brings.

Prices are high and the chorus of *hi how are you?, hey myfriend, what are you looking for? want something special? good price*, and *remember me?* lead many tourists to fits of exasperation. On the other hand, Arusha's food and facilities are excellent. For travellers making an extended trip across Tanzania it can make a nice break from the rigors of the road. For first-timers to Africa, it provides a gentle introduction.

Orientation

Central Arusha is divided by the small Naura River valley. To the west are the bus stations,

TAKE YOUR KILI CLIMB SERIOUSLY

Whatever route you choose, remember that ascending Kilimanjaro is a serious undertaking. While many thousands of trekkers reach Uhuru Peak without major difficulty, many more don't make it because they suffer altitude sickness or simply aren't in good enough shape. And, every year some trekkers and porters die on the mountain. Come prepared with appropriate footwear and clothing, and most importantly, allow yourself enough time. If you're interested in reaching the top, seriously consider adding at least one extra day onto the 'standard' climb itineraries. Although the extra US$150 to US$250 may seem a lot when you're planning your trip, it will seem insignificant later on if you've gone to the expense and effort to start a trek and then can't reach the top. Don't feel badly about insisting on an extra day with the trekking companies: standard medical advice is to increase sleeping altitude by only 300m per day once above 3000m; which is about one-third of the daily altitude gains above 3000m on the standard Kili climb routes offered by most operators.

It's also worth remembering that it's not essential to reach Uhuru Peak, and you haven't 'failed' if you don't. If time (or money) is limited choose other treks and you can experience several different mountain areas for the price of a single Kili climb. Consider trekking up to an area such as the Saddle, the top of the Barranco Wall or the Shira Plateau to appreciate the splendour and magnificence of the mountain without the gruel of summiting.

the main market and many budget hotels. To the east are most of the airline offices, craft shops, midrange and upmarket hotels, and other facilities aimed at tourists; many clustered around Clock Tower roundabout (a 20-minute walk from the central bus stand) where the two main roads (Sokoine Rd to the west and Old Moshi Rd to the east) meet.

Dangers & Annoyances

After Zanzibar, Arusha is the worst place in Tanzania for street touts. Their main haunts are the bus stations and Boma Rd, but they'll find you just about anywhere. Read Confessions of a Flycatcher (p119) and the Choosing an Operator and Safari Scams & Schemes boxed texts in the Safaris chapter (p24) before arriving so you'll be ready.

At night, take a taxi if you go out. It's not safe to walk after dusk except around the market area. Even during the daytime, try to avoid carrying a bag or anything that could tempt a thief.

Sights & Activities

The best thing to do in Arusha, besides arrange your safari and/or trek, is
cultural tourism program (p123
surrounding countryside. If you
ested in a city walking tour
how to cook Tanzanian food
make drums, stop by Via Via

Natural History Museum MUSEUM
(Boma Rd; adult/student US$5/2; 9am-6pm Mon-Fri, 9.30am-6pm Sat & Sun) This museum inside the old German *boma*, completed in 1900, has three parts. The best is the wing dedicated to the evolution of humans since much of what we know about it came from fossils unearthed in Tanzania. There are also displays on insects, the history of Arusha during the German colonial era, and many wildlife photos and mounts.

FREE **Warm Heart Art Gallery** GALLERY
(0754-672256; www.warmheartart.com; Pemba Rd; 10am-8pm) A mix of art for sale and show, there are changing exhibitions and three artists in residence rooms out the back. It's also home to the **Rock Art Project** where you can get information about the Kondoa Rock-Art Sites.

Arusha Declaration Museum MUSEUM
(Makongoro Rd; adult/student Tsh8000
9am-5pm) Half the spa
cussed little mus
dom)

and east of Colonel Middleton Rd (a -minute walk from the bus stand), whose usty streets host many cheap guesthouses and local restaurants/bars.

Hotel Flamingo GUESTHOUSE $
(☎0754-260309; flamingoarusha@yahoo.com; Kikuyu St; s/d US$20/30) This low-key place has sparse but very clean rooms. There's a little lounge, breakfast is reasonable and the staff is friendly.

Arusha

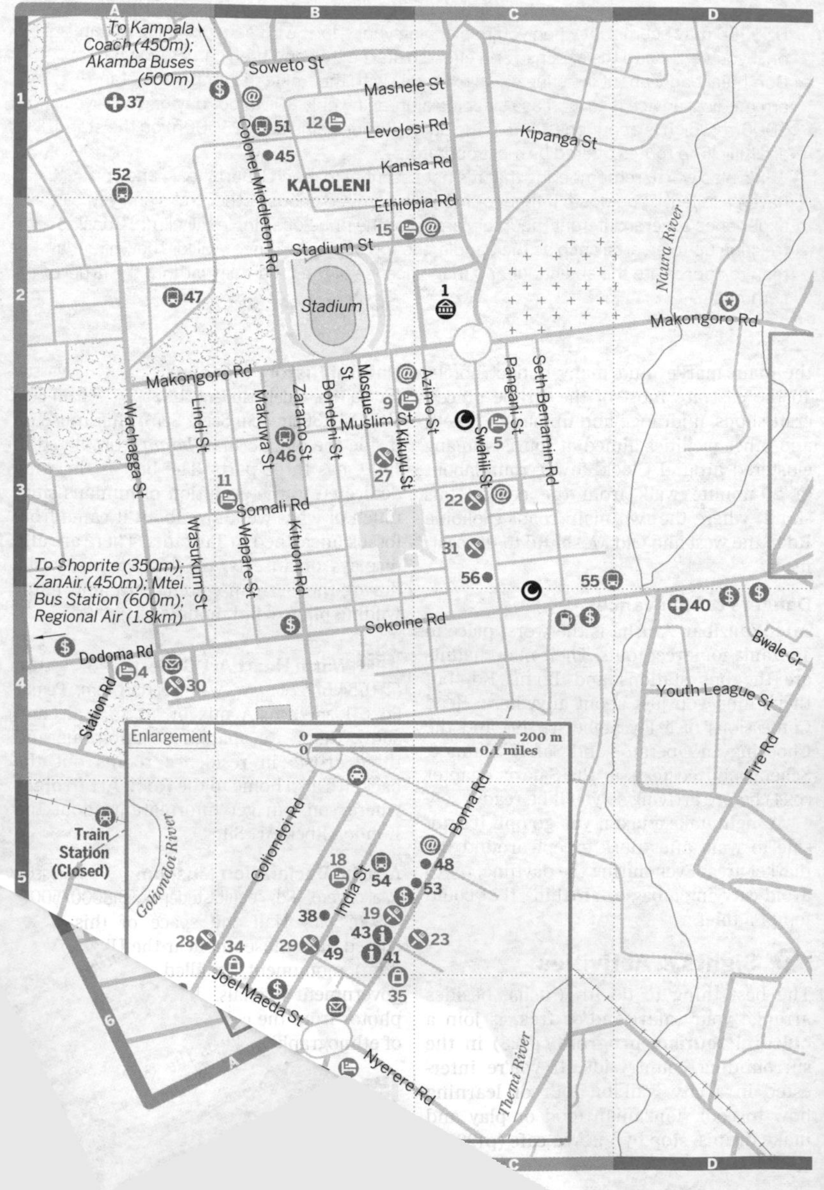

Raha Leo GUESTHOUSE $
(☎0753-600002; Stadium St; s/tw without bathroom Tsh15,000/20,000, s/d Tsh20,000; P) Undistinguished although adequate double and twin rooms around an open-air lounge. With hot-water and cable TV it's one of the best values in town.

Joshmal Hotel HOTEL $
(☎0784-729289; Wapare St; s/d/tw/ste Tsh40,000/50,000/60,000/70,000; P❄) Although this hotel is rather boring, its rooms are actually better than some other higher-priced high-rises in this area. And it has big Mt Meru views.

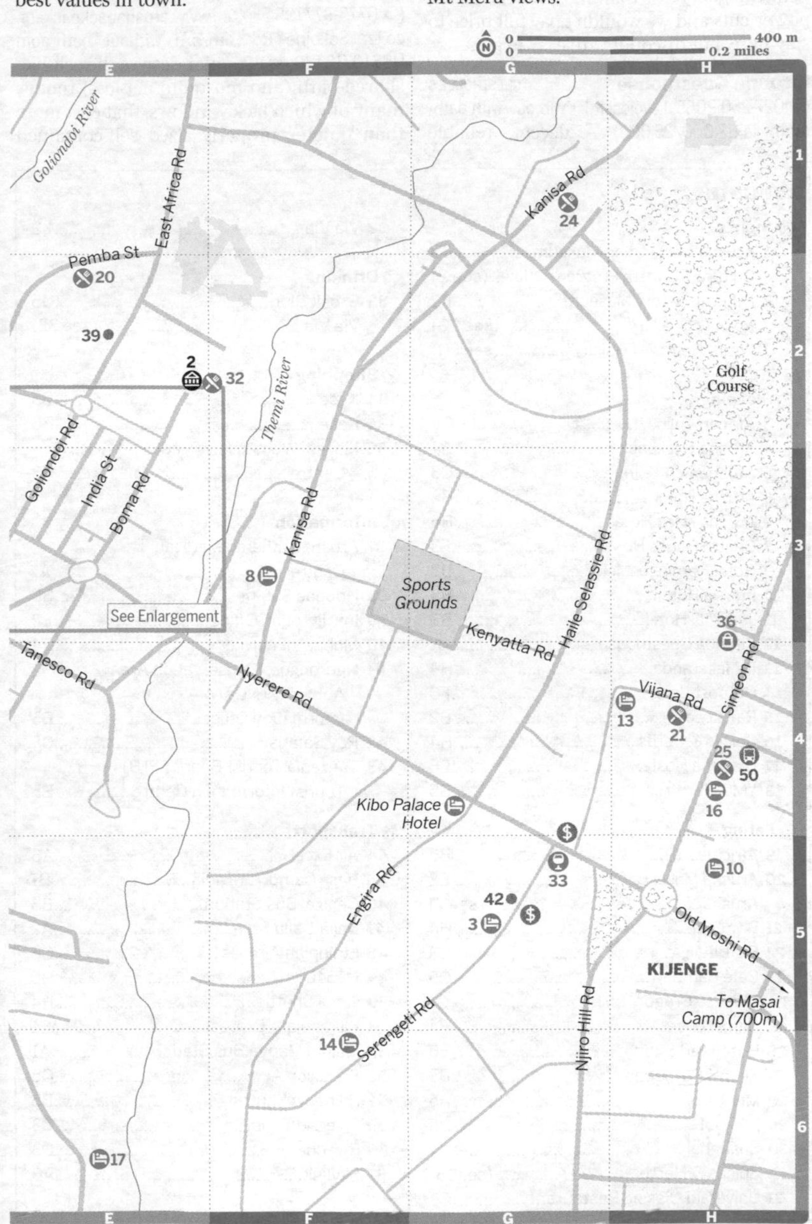

Arusha Centre Inn HOTEL $
(☎027-250 0421; Livingstone Rd; s/d US$25/30; @) Unremarkable but clean and fairly spacious rooms. The three storeys ring a courtyard and there's a wanna-be posh restaurant in front with good food. This hotel is stingier with the generator than most hotels during power cuts and we wouldn't pay full price to stay here, but discounts are easy to get.

Kitundu Guesthouse GUESTHOUSE $
(☎027-250 9065; Levolosi Rd; r without/with bathroom Tsh12,000/25,000) A decent, reliable choice. Though it's pricier than some similar and even better guesthouses (such as Raha Leo) around here, the others don't offer Mt Meru views. You might be able to get a discount if you're travelling alone.

Arusha Backpackers BACKPACKERS $
(☎0773-377795; www.arushabackpackers.co.tz; Sokoine Rd; dm/s/d without bathroom US$10/12/20; @) Popular despite the cell-like shared-bath (and mosquito net-less) rooms, many of which lack windows, that cost more than quieter properly sized self-contained

Arusha

Sights

1 Arusha Declaration Museum C2
Cultural Tourism Program Office.. (see 2)
2 Natural History Museum E2
Rock Art Gallery .... (see 20)
Warm Heart Art Gallery .... (see 20)

Sleeping

3 African Tulip G5
4 Arusha Backpackers A4
5 Arusha Centre Inn C3
6 Arusha Hotel B6
7 Arusha Naaz Hotel B6
8 Centre House Hostel F3
9 Hotel Flamingo B3
10 Impala Hotel H5
11 Joshmal Hotel B3
12 Kitunda Guesthouse B1
13 Le Jacaranda H4
14 Outpost Lodge F6
15 Raha Leo B2
16 Spices & Herbs H4
17 Ujamma Hostel E6
18 YMCA B5

Eating

19 Africafe B5
20 Arusha Masai Café E2
Arusha Naaz Hotel .... (see 7)
21 Bay Leaf H4
22 Big Bite C3
23 Café Bamboo C5
24 Chinese Dragon G1
25 Damascus H4
26 Hot Bread Shop B6
27 Khan's Barbecue B3
28 Meat King A5
29 Mirapot B5
30 Shanghai A4
Spices & Herbs .... (see 16)
31 Universal Classic Restaurant C3
32 Via Via F2

Drinking

33 Greek Club G5
Via Via .... (see 32)

Shopping

34 Kase B5
35 Kase B6
36 Maasai Women Fair Trade Centre H3

Information

37 Arusha Lutheran Medical Centre A1
38 Hoopoe Safaris B5
39 Immigration Office E2
40 Moona's Pharmacy D4
41 Ngorongoro Conservation Area Authority (NCAA) Information Office B5
42 Roy Safaris G5
43 Tanzania Tourist Board (TTB) Tourist Information Centre B5

Transport

44 Air Excel A6
45 Base Camp Tanzania B1
46 Central Bus Station B3
47 Dalla-Dalla Stand A2
48 Ethiopian Airlines C5
49 Fly540 .... B5
50 Jamii Shuttle H4
51 Kilimanjaro Express B1
52 Makao Mapya Bus Station A1
53 Precision Air C5
54 Rainbow Shuttle B5
55 Riverside Shuttle C3
56 Rwandair C3
57 Skylink A6

LOCAL KNOWLEDGE

OTHUMAN: CONFESSIONS OF A FLYCATCHER

How did you begin working as a flycatcher? I've been doing this for six years. Before, I was at the beach in Zanzibar. I was a captain for the glass-bottom boat. My mother was scared about the boat sinking, so she told me not to go to Zanzibar again. I came to Arusha because I have an uncle here. I suffered for about one year, but the companies learned to trust me.

What do you tell tourists? The flycatcher will try to be a friend of the tourist. I think if I can be a friend and help the tourist, get them the Tanzanian price, they will come to my company. Sometimes when we walk with tourists and they want to buy a batik or SIM card, people try to cheat them and we tell them the right price. Also, when the thieves see a tourist with a flycatcher they don't come because we help tourists. Maybe if it is a little bit dark, like 7pm, if they see the tourist with a flycatcher they don't do nothing.

If he lets us help him, then we give them the [business] card and say go ask tourist information about this company. If I hear a company takes money and don't do the tour we tell the police. We help tourists. Sometimes [the tourists] don't have a group. We know all the companies in Arusha, and we know where there is a group looking for more people. Some tourists go into one office and buy the safari, but if they are trusting me I try to tell them to compare. Go to four or five offices.

Do you ever lie? Just a few flycatchers lie. You say I have tour going tomorrow and then [the company doesn't]. If I do that they might leave me. Sometime I do lie about trip leaving tomorrow. I say yes they have it. And I take them to any company just to get them in the door. Sometimes the safari company will lie too. The tourists shop around and they pay to the company, but the group is not full so then [the manager] will take the money but put them in another company.

The companies know there are bad flycatchers and they want to work with good ones. The bad flycatchers talk bad to the tourists, talk rubbish. Maybe they can say, 'Give me money; I want to buy food for the trip and hire a tent. Just give me $100 and I'll buy your food and rent the tent.' If the tourist is honest they trust him and give him the money and then the guy runs away. We never take money from the tourist.

How do you choose which people to talk to? Normally in the morning we go to the tourist information. I talk to the tourist. If you have a book in the hand, like Lonely Planet, or they have Arusha city map we know this is safari. If they are complicated; maybe they tell us 'no thank you', or 'we don't want a safari' or tell us to go away, we follow them from far. They say 'I'm not looking for safari', but we know which ones are. We see them shop around. If they go to tourist information then we know this is safari. When they say no, we just say 'OK'. For me, normally my friend is in the back and I send my friend to talk to them. We are three – like a team. If the first one talks to them and they refuse, then the second one goes and tells them about another company. If it gets to number three, then maybe we have to start to try to confuse them.

How much commission do the safari companies give you? I don't want a commission, I want a job. We live as a cooker or as a porter so when we bring someone somewhere we get work on the safari or go up the mountain. Or commission, but I want the work more than the commission. Me, I work as a cook. [If I get the company customers] they just put me on the list and then I go another time. The big companies don't give us a job or a commission.

The Maasai [Mt Meru] Market gives us 5% and we get commission from tanzanite companies. The hotels in Arusha don't give us commissions like in Zanzibar, so we never take them to a bad place.

Do you like being a flycatcher? Me I don't like it, but I don't have a job. If I get a job then I leave this. But because I don't have a job I do it. Another company gives me a good salary for cooking. But they don't have much work. It's hard work, but there's nothing to do and we are not thieves.

Othuman, age 45

ARUSHA TREKKING OPERATORS

If you're organising a Kilimanjaro trek in Arusha, look for operators that organise treks themselves rather than subcontracting to a Moshi- or Marangu-based operator. Many of the safari operators listed in the boxed text on p126 also organise treks. In addition, try the following:

» **Dorobo Safaris** (027-250 9685, 027-254 8336; daudi@dorobo.co.tz, dorobo@habari.co.tz; midrange) Community-oriented treks in and around the Ngorongoro Conservation Area and wilderness treks in Tarangire park border areas and in the Serengeti.

» **Kiliwarrior Expeditions** (www.kiliwarriors.com; top end) Upmarket Kilimanjaro climbs, treks in the Ngorongoro Conservation Area and safaris.

» **Summits Africa** (www.summits-africa.com; upper midrange & top end) Upmarket adventure safaris, including treks in the Ngorongoro Conservation Area and to Lake Natron with the option to climb Ol Doinyo Lengai, West Kilimanjaro walking safaris, multiday fully equipped bike safaris and combination bike-safari trips.

rooms elsewhere. And the rooftop restaurant has lost its Mt Meru view.

CLOCK TOWER & EASTERN ARUSHA

Most of the following are in the green, leafy and overall quieter eastern part of town, while a few are in the thick of the action around the Clock Tower.

TOP CHOICE **Outpost Lodge** LODGE $$
(0715-430358; www.outposttanzania.net; Serengeti Rd; s/d/tr US$52/70/84; P@) The rooms are nothing special, albeit with attractive stone floors, but the lush grounds and communal poolside restaurant-lounge with couches, board games and fresh-squeezed juices more than compensate. It's in a quiet residential area off Nyerere Rd.

Spices & Herbs GUESTHOUSE $
(0754-313162; axum_spices@hotmail.com; Simeon Rd; s/d US$35 tw US$45; P@) The 19 rooms behind this popular Ethiopian restaurant are simple but warm, with woven grass mats and wooden wardrobes adding character not often found at this price level. An excellent budget choice; it's the best value spot in eastern Arusha.

Ujamaa Hostel HOSTEL $
(0753-960570, 0763-830608; www.ujamaahostel.com; Fire Rd; dm incl breakfast, dinner & laundry US$17, d without bathroom US$38; P) Focussing on volunteers, but open to all, Ujamma is the most communal spot to lay your head in Arusha. Besides the clean dorms with shelves, lockable draws and hot-water baths, there's a TV lounge, book exchange, plenty of travel advice and a quiet backyard. They can hook you up with a variety of volunteer opportunities (minimum two-week commitment) in Arusha including an orphanage and a special needs school.

Centre House Hostel GUESTHOUSE $
(0754-089928; Kanisa Rd; dm/d Tsh15,000/35,000; P@) On the grounds of a Catholic high school, the no-frills Centre House Hostel also has a communal atmosphere due to the large number of long-term volunteers who stay here. Dorm rooms have either two or four beds while the self-contained rooms have cable TV. Both have hot water. Meals are available by request. The gate shuts at 11pm unless you've made previous arrangements.

Le Jacaranda GUESTHOUSE $$
(027-254 4624; www.chez.com/jacaranda; s/d/tr US$50/55/75; P@) This French-owned place set off Nyerere Rd has a variety of spacious rooms whose frumpiness is mostly hidden by the African themed art. There's a lush garden with minigolf and a restaurant (Tsh8000 to Tsh18,000) serving a variety of cuisines: but not French.

Arusha Naaz Hotel HOTEL $$
(027-257 2087; www.arushanaaz.net; Sokoine Rd; s/d/tr US$45/60/75;) Naaz is short on atmosphere, but otherwise good value, with comfortable 1st-floor rooms in a convenient location by the Clock Tower. Rooms are not all the same, so check out a few first; we think those around the triangular courtyard are best. Reception is in the walkway next to the mall.

African Tulip HOTEL $$$
(0783-714104; www.theafricantulip.com; Serengeti Rd; s/d/tr/ste US$190/230/300/310; P@

(🛜🏊) On a green, quiet side street, this lovely place successfully merges an African safari theme with a genteel ambience. The large rooms have all the mod-cons. It's owned by Roy Safaris.

Arusha Hotel HOTEL **$$$**
(☎027-250 7777; www.thearushahotel.com; Clock Tower roundabout; s US$250-300, d US$300-360, ste s/d US$400/450; P❄@🛜🏊) One of the first hotels in Arusha (though it barely resembles its former incarnation) and now one of the best, it's smack in the city centre, but the large lush garden in the back gives it a countryside feel. Though the smallish rooms should have more flash considering the price, the facilities (including a gym, casino and 24 hour room service) and staff are top notch.

YMCA GUESTHOUSE **$**
(India St; s/d without bathroom Tsh15,000/20,000) The five small rooms here are similar in quality to Centre House Hostel. Cheap meals (Tsh2500 to Tsh3500) are available all day.

Impala Hotel HOTEL **$$**
(☎027-254 3082; www.impalahotel.com; Simeon Rd; s US$90, d US$110-150 tr US$155, ste US$230; P❄@🛜🏊) Filling a gap between the small family-run guesthouses and the big luxury hotels, the nothing-special Impala offers okay rooms (be sure you get one of the newer ones) and abundant services like a forex bureau and 24 hour restaurant.

OUTSIDE THE CITY CENTRE

TOP CHOICE **Karama Lodge** LODGE **$$**
(☎0754-475188; www.karamalodge.com; s/d/tr US$100/135/190; P@🛜🏊) Truly something different. On a forested hillside in the Suye Hill area just southeast of town, Karama offers proximity to both nature and the town centre. Accommodation is in 22 rustic and very lovely stilt bungalows, each with a verandah and views to both Kilimanjaro and Meru on clear days. There are short walking trails nearby and a creative restaurant (Tsh8000 to Tsh14,000) which caters to vegetarians. It's signposted north of Old Moshi Rd.

Moyoni Lodge LODGE **$$**
(☎0784-841555; www.moyoni-lodge.com; Visiwani Rd; s/d US$65/100, d without bathroom US$30; P@) On the northern edge of Arusha, this small lodge's jungle-like grounds give a strong sense of escape. The seven sizable regular rooms are cleverly decorated with banana leaves and other materials and there are also two backpacker rooms. Meals are available, though choices are limited. A taxi from town costs about Tsh6000.

Onsea House LODGE **$$$**
(☎0787-112498; www.onseahouse.com; s/d US$240/290; P🛜🏊) Run by a Belgian chef whose eye for the little things is what really makes this lovely bed and breakfast such a great place. The regular rooms and the outer *bandas* in the gardens each have their own themes, plus there is a small restaurant (lunch/dinner US$30/60) of course. Very tranquil and very classy. It's about 1km off the Moshi road on the edge of town.

Kigongoni LODGE **$$$**
(☎0732-978876; www.kigongoni.net; s/d/tr incl guided walks US$172/244/305; P@🛜🏊) Kigongoni's tranquil hilltop perch about 5km past Arusha gives it an almost wilderness feel. Spacious cottages are scattered around the forest, some quite a hilly walk from the cosy common areas. A portion of the lodge's profits support mentally disabled children in the area. It's about 5km beyond Arusha toward Moshi.

L'Oasis Lodge LODGE **$$**
(☎075-755 7802; www.loasistanzania.com; s/d/tr US$75/100/145, backpacker r per person without bathroom US$25; P@🛜🏊) Offering a good balance between proximity to town and relaxing surroundings, this clued-in place north of the city centre has a mix of African-style rondavels and airy stilt houses set around peaceful gardens (but skip the outrageously overpriced 'backpacker' rooms across the road), plus a good restaurant. Discounts for Peace Corps, VSO and other long-term volunteers are available.

Moivaro Coffee Plantation Lodge LODGE **$$$**
(☎0754-324193; www.moivaro.com; s/d/tr US$185/250/335; P@🛜🏊) Very near, but seemingly far from Arusha, with cosy cottages, each with its own fireplace, and extensive gardens, this place is justifiably popular as a pre- and post-safari stop. With 42 rooms, it can get pretty busy.

Meserani Snake Park CAMPGROUND **$**
(☎027-253 8282; www.meseranisnakepark.com; camping incl admission to snake park US$10; P) This overlander-oriented place has good facilities, including hot showers, a bar cum restaurant with cheap meals and a vehicle

repair shop. It's 25km west of Arusha along the Dodoma road.

Masai Camp CAMPGROUND $
(☎0754-507131; Old Moshi Rd; camping US$5, banda per person with shared bathroom outside US$10, s/d with shared bathroom US$15/25; P@) A regular stop for overland trucks, it's noisy and dusty, but facilities are good. Around the expansive grounds you'll find hot showers, pool tables, a restaurant, and a happening bar. Don't plan on sleeping on Friday or Saturday since the disco goes all night.

Eating

CITY CENTRE WEST

Shanghai CHINESE $
(Sokoine Rd; meals Tsh3500-12,000; lunch & dinner;) Very good Chinese-owned restaurant with fast service and a Far East meets the Wild West decor. It's hidden behind the post office.

Big Bite INDIAN $$
(Swahili St; meals Tsh8000-12,000; lunch & dinner Wed-Mon;) One of the oldest and most reliable Indian restaurants in Arusha. Don't let the modest premises fool you.

Khan's Barbecue BARBECUE $
(Mosque St; mixed grill from Tsh6000; from 6.30pm) This Arusha institution ('Chicken on the Bonnet') is an auto-spares store by day and the best known of many earthy roadside barbecues around the market area by night. It lays out a heaping spread of grilled, skewered meat and salads.

Universal Classic Restaurant TANZANIAN $
(off Swahili St; meals Tsh2000-5000, buffet Tsh5000; breakfast, lunch & dinner Sun-Fri) A bigger than average selection of local foods. Either order from the menu or walk the line and sample a bunch from the buffet tray.

CLOCK TOWER AREA

Café Bamboo INTERNATIONAL $
(Boma Rd; meals Tsh6000-12,000; breakfast, lunch & dinner;) Bamboo has a bigger menu of light Tanzanian and European meals, plus some less-successful Asian options.

Arusha Masai Café PIZZERIA $
(Pemba St; meals Tsh6500-12,000; lunch & dinner) This simple garden spot makes what many will tell you is Arusha's best pizzas (and we can't disagree) in their little stone oven. Warm Heart Art Gallery (p115) is located here.

Via Via CAFE $$
(Boma Rd; meals Tsh7000-18,000; lunch & dinner Mon-Sat) Cultured and laid-back with the best soundtrack of any restaurant in Arusha, this place along the river behind the Natural History Museum has coffee, salads and sandwiches plus more substantial meals like pastas and grilled fish. There's a decent bar and live music.

Mirapot TANZANIAN $
(India St; meals Tsh2500-4000; breakfast & lunch Mon-Sat) Very friendly little spot for local meals like beans and rice and *kuku nazi* (coconut chicken).

Arusha Naaz Hotel TANZANIAN $$
(Sokoine Rd; buffet Tsh9000; lunch daily) All-you-can-eat lunch buffet and large snack counter.

Africafe CAFE $$
(Boma Rd; meals Tsh7500-18,000; breakfast, lunch & dinner) European cafe vibes; and prices. The menu is heavy on sandwiches and there's good bakery.

Hot Bread Shop BAKERY, FAST FOOD $
(Sokoine Rd; meals Tsh3600-7300; breakfast & lunch;) A limited menu of cheap Indian and Chinese fast food plus plenty of its namesake, all priced cheap. Also has an internet cafe.

EASTERN ARUSHA

TOP CHOICE **Damascus** MIDDLE EASTERN $$
(☎0782-372273; Simeon Rd; meals Tsh5000-16,000; lunch & dinner Tue-Sun;) A comfortably casual spot with an enticing menu and by appointment you can cook for yourself over a charcoal stove at your table. Finish off the meal with baklava, Turkish coffee or sheesha.

Spices & Herbs ETHIOPIAN, EUROPEAN $$
(Simeon Rd; meals Tsh7500-14,500; lunch & dinner;) Unpretentious alfresco spot serving two menus; Ethiopian and continental.

Chinese Dragon CHINESE $$
(Kanisa Rd; meals Tsh7000-32,500; lunch & dinner) A long-time favourite in a new location, this place at the Gymkhana Club is in the same family as the wonderful Shanghai, detailed above.

Bay Leaf EUROPEAN $$$
(Vijana Rd; meals Tsh17,000-34,900; lunch & dinner;) Arusha's poshest menu features dishes such as spiced tandoori tofu curry

CULTURAL TOURISM PROGRAMS

Numerous villages outside Arusha (a sampling of which is described below) and elsewhere in the country (including Mto wa Mbu, Babati, Kondoa, the Usambara Mountains, Morogoro and Pangani) have organised 'Cultural Tourism Programs' that offer an alternative to the safari scene.

Although some have deviated from their initial founding purpose of serving as income generators for community projects (many now revolving around the enterprising individuals who run them) they nevertheless offer an excellent chance to experience Tanzania at the local level and they still provide employment for locals. Most have various 'modules' available, from half a day to several nights, and fees are generally reasonable, starting from Tsh15,000/30,000 per person for a half-/full-day program with lunch (usually cooked by the local women's group) and prices drop with bigger groups. Transportation, sometimes by dalla-dalla and sometimes by private vehicle, is extra. Overnight tours are either camping or homestays; though expect conditions to be basic. Payments should be made on site; always ask for a receipt.

All tours can be booked through the Tanzania Tourist Board (TTB) Tourist Information Centre (p125). Most should be booked a day in advance; but for Ng'iresi and other programs close to town, guides usually wait at the TTB office on stand-by each morning. If you have further questions, the **Cultural Tourism Program office** (☎027-205 0025; www.tanzaniaculturaltourism.com) in the back of the Natural History Museum in Arusha may (or may not) be able to assist.

Mkuru

The Maasai village of Mkuru, 14km off the Nairobi road north of Mt Meru and 60km out of Arusha, is the region's pioneering and largest camel camp (www.mkurucamelsafari.com). You can take a short camel ride around the village or safari as far away as Mt Kilimanjaro and Lake Natron. Rides can be combined with various cultural activities or a short (about two hours to the summit) climb up Ol Doinyo Landaree ('Mountain of Goats'). Most people spend the night at a simple tented camp in the village before riding off in to the savannah.

Monduli Juu

A well-rounded and well-regarded choice, with both natural and cultural activities on offer. Monduli Juu (Upper Monduli) comprises four small villages along the Monduli Mountains, northwest of Arusha in Maasai country. You can visit traditional doctors, see a school or eat a meaty meal in a bush 'orpul'. Many people come to trek along the escarpment for views over the Rift Valley plains and to the distant cone of Ol Doinyo Lengai. Bring plenty of water, sunscreen, a hat and long pants, as many of the trails are overgrown with thick, thorny brush. Most trips are one way and they'll arrange a car to pick you up at the end. Most activities begin in Emairete village (9km from Monduli town), where there are several simple spots to camp (bring everything with you from Arusha) and some Maasai *bomas* that take overnight guests.

Mulala

Set on the southern slope of Mt Meru about 30km northeast of Arusha; this is the only program completely implemented by women. Tours focus on farming and daily life and include visits to a women's cooperative, cheesemakers, and some short walks through the countryside.

Ng'iresi

One of the most popular programs, the primary tours at Ng'iresi village (about 7km northeast of Arusha on the slopes of Mt Meru) includes visits to Wa-arusha farms, houses and a school. There's also a traditional medicine tour, several waterfalls and a hike up a small volcano. There's no public transport here.

DON'T MISS

RIVER HOUSE

An off-shoot of the inspiring Shanga (p124) project, diners at **River House** (☎0689-759067; www.shanga.org/River_House.html; Dodoma Rd; per person US$20; ⊙lunch) are greeted with champagne and then served a huge and delicious four-course lunch in gorgeous gardens. Reservations are required.

and confit of organic duck leg on lentils plus a great wine list. Seating indoors and out.

Self-Catering

Shoprite (Dodoma Rd; ⊙8am-7pm Mon-Sat, 8am-4pm Sun) On the edge of the city centre, this is the largest grocery in Arusha.

Meat King (Goliondoi Rd) The best meat in town, plus cheeses and frozen pastas and spring rolls.

Drinking & Entertainment

Via Via CAFE

(Boma Rd) This cafe (see Eating) is a good spot for a drink and one of the best places to find out about upcoming cultural events. Thursday nights there's karaoke and a live band. Things get started at 9pm and admission is a steep Tsh7000.

Greek Club BAR

(Nyerere Rd; ⊙Tue, Wed & Fri 4.30pm-late, Sat & Sun 3pm-late; 📶) This sports bar is a popular expat hang-out, especially on weekends.

Masai Camp CLUB

(Old Moshi Rd; admission Tsh5000; ⊙9pm-dawn Fri & Sat) Arusha's loudest and brashest club is an institution on the Arusha party scene. The music is a mix of African and Western.

Shopping

The Clock Tower area, mainly Boma Rd and Joel Maeda St, is lined with craft vendors selling their wares. Hard bargaining is required so keep your wits about you. The enormous and unmissable **Cultural Heritage** (Dodoma Rd; ⊙9am-5pm Mon-Sat, 9am-2pm Sun) on the west edge of Arusha has all the same wares plus many other less common items. Shopping is hassle-free, but prices are higher.

The following offer something different.

Shanga HANDICRAFTS

(www.shanga.org; Dodoma Rd; ⊙10am-5pm) Shanga started out making beaded necklaces, but has branched into furniture, paper, clothing and many other products, mostly using recycled materials and made by disabled workers. It's on the Burka Coffee Estate and plantation tours can be arranged.

Maasai Women Fair Trade Centre HANDICRAFTS

(www.maasaiwomentanzania.org; Simeon Rd) A project of MWEDO (Maasai Women Development Organisation), this small shop raises money for education and other projects. Has expensive, but high-quality beadwork (and a few other crafts).

Kase BOOKS, MAPS

(Boma Rd & Joel Maeda St) Best bet for national park books and maps. If one shop doesn't have what you want, try the other.

ℹ Information

Immigration

Immigration office (East Africa Rd; ⊙7.30am-3.30pm Mon-Fri)

Internet Access

There are many internet cafes around the market and Clock Tower areas. The normal rate is Tsh1500 per hour.

Hot Bread Shop (Sokoine Rd; per hr Tsh2000; ⊙7am-6.30pm Mon-Sat, 7am-2.30pm Sun) Has computers and wi-fi.

L&D Internet Café (Somali Rd; per hr Tsh1500; ⊙8.30am-7.30pm Mon-Sat, 9am-5pm Sun)

New Safari Hotel (Boma Rd; per hr Tsh3000; ⊙24hr)

Garage

Fortes (☎027-250-6094; www.fortes-africa.com; Nairobi-Moshi Rd)

Meserani Snake Park (☎027-253 8282; www.meseranisnakepark.com) 25km west of town on the Dodoma Rd.

Medical Services

Arusha Lutheran Medical Centre (☎027-254 8030; http://selianlh.habari.co.tz) The best medical facility in the region, but for anything truly serious, get yourself to Nairobi.

Moona's Pharmacy (☎0754-309052; Sokoine Rd; ⊙8.45am-5.30pm Mon-Fri, to 2pm Sat)

Money

Forex bureaus are clustered along Joel Maeda St, India St, and Sokoine Rd near the Clock Tower.

Many change travellers cheques, but at a rate of around 15% less than cash. **Sanya Bureau de Change**, with several locations along Sokoine Rd, is open until 8pm Sundays and public holidays. Some expensive business-class hotels, like Impala and Kibo Palace, have bureaus open daily until late at night, but the rates are poor.

Banks with ATMs accepting both Visa and/or MasterCard are shown on the map.

Tourist Information

The bulletin boards at the Tourist Information Centre and Hot Bread Shop are good spots to find safari mates.

Ngorongoro Conservation Area Authority (NCAA) Information Office (☎027-254 4625; Boma Rd) Has free Ngorongoro booklets and a cool relief map of the Conservation Area.

Tanzania National Parks Headquarters (Tanapa; ☎027-250 3471; www.tanzaniaparks.com; Dodoma Rd) Just west of town.

Tanzania Tourist Board (TTB) Tourist Information Centre (☎027-250 3842/3; www.tanzaniatouristboard.com; Boma Rd; ⏰8am-4pm Mon-Fri, 8.30am-1pm Sat) Knowledgeable and helpful staff have information on Arusha, Northern Circuit parks and other area attractions. They can book cultural tourism program tours and provide a good free map of Arusha and Moshi. Also keeps a 'blacklist' of tour operators and a list of registered tour companies.

Travel Agencies

For listings of Arusha-based safari and trekking operators, see p120.

Skylink (☎0754-465321; www.skylinktanzania.com; Goliondoi Rd) Domestic and international flight bookings.

ℹ Getting There & Away

Air

There are daily flights to Dar es Salaam and Zanzibar (Coastal Aviation, Precision Air, Regional Air, Safari Plus, ZanAir), Nairobi (Fly540, Precision Air), Seronera and other airstrips in Serengeti National Park (Air Excel, Coastal Aviation, Regional Air, Safari Plus), Mwanza (Precision Air), Lake Manyara National Park (Air Excel, Coastal Aviation, Regional Air) and Tarangire National Park (Coastal). Kigali (RwandAir) is served four times a week. Some sample prices: Arusha–Dar (Tsh239,000 one way), Arusha–Mwanza (Tsh235,000) and Arusha–Seronera (US$175).

Most flights use Kilimanjaro International Airport (KIA), about halfway between Moshi and Arusha, while small planes, mostly to the national parks, leave from Arusha airport, 8km west of town along the Dodoma Rd. Verify the departure point when buying your ticket. Other than flights to Nairobi, international airlines using KIA include Ethiopian Air and KLM, the later has no office in Arusha.

Air Excel (☎0754-211227; www.airexcelonline.com; 2nd fl, Subzali (Exim Bank) Bldg, Goliondoi Rd)

Coastal Aviation (☎027-250 0343, www.coastal.cc; Arusha airport)

Ethiopian Airlines (☎027-250 4231; www.ethiopianairlines.com; Boma Rd)

Fly540 (☎0783-540540; www.fly540.com; India St, 2nd fl)

Precision Air (☎0784-471202; www.precisionairtz.com; Boma Rd) Also handles Kenya Airways bookings.

Regional Air (☎0784-285753; www.regionaltanzania.com; Great North Rd)

RwandAir (☎0732-978558; www.rwandair.com; Swahili St)

Safari Air (☎0716-360000; www.safariplus.co.tz; Arusha airport)

ZanAir (☎027-254 8877; www.zanair.com; Summit Centre, Sokoine Rd)

Bus

Arusha has two bus stations. The **central bus stand** near the market is the biggest while the **Makao Mapya bus stand** (aka Dar Express bus stand) a little to the northwest handles most of the luxury buses to Dar es Salaam. The central bus station is intimidatingly chaotic in the morning and both are popular haunts for flycatchers and touts. If you get overwhelmed head straight for a taxi, or, if arriving at the central station, duck into the lobbies of one of the hotels across the street, to get your bearings. If you want to avoid the bus stations altogether, most buses make a stop on the edge of town before going to the stations. Taxis will be waiting.

When leaving Arusha, the best thing to do is book your ticket the day before, so that in the morning when you arrive with your luggage you can get straight on your bus. For pre-dawn buses, take a taxi to the station and ask the driver to drop you directly at your bus.

Despite what you may hear, there are no luggage fees (unless you have an extraordinarily large pack).

DAR ES SALAAM

The best companies to/from Dar es Salaam (eight-10 hours) include the following. If you take an early departure, with luck you *might* be able to catch the last ferry to Zanzibar. Super luxury means there's a toilet on board.

Generally the best company, Dar Express has five luxury (Tsh25,000) and three full luxury (Tsh30,000) buses departing Makao Mapya bus stand 5.50am to 9am. Metro Express (luxury/full luxury Tsh25,000/32,000) and Ngorika (luxury 28,000) also have morning departures from Makao Mapya while Kilimanjaro Express

NORTHERN CIRCUIT SAFARI OPERATORS

Recommended operators focusing on the northern circuit include the following, although the list is not exclusive.

Access2Tanzania (☎0732-979903; www.access2tanzania.com; budget to midrange) Customised, community-focused itineraries.

Africa Travel Resource (ATR; ☎in UK 44-01306-880770; www.africatravelresrouce.com; midrange to top end) A web-based safari broker that matches your safari ideas with an operator and offers lots of background information on its website.

Base Camp Tanzania (☎027-250 0393, 0784-186422; www.basecamptanzania.com; 1st fl, Golden Rose Arcade Bldg, Col Middleton Rd; budget to midrange) Northern circuit safaris and treks.

Duma Explorer (☎0787-079127; www.dumaexplorer.com; Njiro Hill; budget to midrange) Northern Tanzania safaris, Kilimanjaro and Meru treks, northern Tanzania cultural tours and safari-coast combinations.

Firelight Expeditions (☎027-250 8773, 0784-266558; www.firelightexpeditions.com; top end) A high-end outfit with a handful of luxury and mobile camps, including in the Serengeti, Katavi and on Lake Tanganyika.

Hoopoe Safaris (☎027-250 7011; www.hoopoe.com; India St; upper midrange) Luxury camping and lodge safaris in the northern circuit, also with its own tented camps at Lake Manyara, West Kilimanjaro and mobile camps in the Serengeti. Combination itineraries with Kenya, Uganda, Rwanda and Sudan are also possible. Very good value for price.

IntoAfrica (☎in UK 44-114-255 5610; www.intoafrica.co.uk; midrange) Fair-traded cultural safaris and treks in northern Tanzania, including a seven-day wildlife-cultural safari in Maasai areas.

Lake Tanganyika Adventure Safaris (☎0766-789572; 0763-993166; www.safaritourtanzania.com; midrange) Adventure safaris focusing on Katavi and Mahale Mountains National Parks and Lake Tanganyika.

Maasai Wanderings (☎0755-984925; www.maasaiwanderings.com; midrange) Northern Tanzania safaris and treks.

Nature Discovery (☎0732-971859, 0754-400003; www.naturediscovery.com; midrange) Northern-circuit safaris, and treks on Kilimanjaro, Meru and in the Crater Highlands.

Ranger Safaris (www.rangersafaris.com; midrange to top end) A large company offering a full range of northern circuit safaris.

Roy Safaris (☎027-250 2115, 027-250 8010; www.roysafaris.com; Serengeti Rd; all budgets) Budget and semi-luxury camping safaris in the northern circuit, and competitively priced luxury lodge safaris and Kilimanjaro and Meru treks.

Safari Makers (☎0732-979195; www.safarimakers.com; budget) No-frills northern circuit camping and lodge safaris and treks, some incorporating cultural tourism program tours.

Shaw Safaris (☎0768-945735; www.shawsafaris.com; midrange) Northern circuit self-drive safaris.

Wayo Africa (☎0784-203000; www.wayoafrica.com; top end) Northern circuit active and vehicle safaris, including Serengeti walking safaris plus visits to Hadzabe areas.

has four buses, one luxury (Tsh28,000) from its own stand on Col Middleton Rd.

The last departure of the day to Dar es Salaam is the non-air-conditioned Akamba bus (Tsh25,000) that arrives from Nairobi around noon at its own office north of the centre.

MOSHI

Buses and minibuses run between Arusha and Moshi (about Tsh2500, 1½ hours) up to 8pm. It's pricier (US$10) but more comfortable to take one of the Arusha to Nairobi shuttles (p207).

LUSHOTO

Chikito and Fasaha buses (Tsh12,000 to Tsh13,000, six hours) depart daily at 6am and 6.45am respectively. However, it's more comfortable overall and often works out just as fast (although more expensively) to take an express bus heading for Dar as far as Mombo, and then get local transport from there to Lushoto.

TANGA

Frey's and other lines go from the central bus stand between 6am and noon (Tsh14,500, seven hours).

BABATI, KOLO & KONDOA

Mtei line buses depart the central bus station, but then stop at their own office on Kilobero Rd 300m north of Shoprite. They leave hourly to Babati (Tsh6000, three hours) between 6am and 4pm. Their 6am bus continues on to Kondoa (Tsh12,000, seven hours) via Kolo (Tsh11,500, 6½ hours).

MWANZA

Most buses to Mwanza (Tsh30,000 to Tsh35,000, 12 hours) leave the central bus stand (some use Makao Mapya), between 6am and 7.30am. Jordan is one of the best companies; all travel via Singida.

MUSOMA

Coast Line, Kimotco and Manko have buses to Musoma (Tsh28,000, 11 to 12 hours) at 6am, passing through Serengeti National Park and Ngorongoro Conservation Area. Foreigners must pay the park entry fees (US$100) to ride this route.

NAIROBI (KENYA) & KAMPALA (UGANDA)

For information on these routes see p207 and p209.

 Getting Around

To/From Kilimanjaro International Airport

Precision Air and Fly540 have shuttles (Tsh10,000) to KIA for their passengers (Precision doesn't offer this service for its Nairobi flight), departing from its offices two-three hours before the scheduled flight departure. In the other direction, look for them at the arrivals area.

The starting price for taxis from town to KIA is US$50, though some drivers will go for less. Others will only go for more.

To/From Arusha Airport

Taxis from town charge from Tsh15,000. Any dalla-dalla heading out along the Dodoma road can drop you at the junction, from where you'll have to walk almost 1.5km.

Car

A standard 4WD typically costs US$150 per day with unlimited kilometres. A smaller RAV4-style 4WD, which isn't ideal for wildlife viewing but can get to just about all attractions in and around the area's national parks (albeit at a slower pace) in the dry season can be had for US$600 per week and about 100km free per day. Drivers are included in the price. Book as early as possible because demand is high.

Reliable companies include:

Arusha Naaz (☎027-250 2087; www.arushanaaz.net; Sokoine St)

Fortes (☎027-250-6094; www.fortescarhire.com; Nairobi–Moshi Rd) Allows self-drive.

Rainbow (☎0754-204025; www.rainbowcarhire.com, India St)

Local Transport

Dalla-dallas (Tsh300) run along major roads from early until late. There are taxi stands all around the city centre and some park in front of most hotels, even many budget ones. A ride across town, from the Clock Tower to Makao Mapya bus stand, for example, shouldn't cost more than Tsh3000. Motorcycle taxi drivers will almost always tell you Tsh2000 for a ride in the city centre, but will go for Tsh1000 if you insist.

Arusha National Park

Arusha National Park is one Tanzania's smallest (322 sq km) but most beautiful and topographically varied northern circuit parks. It's dominated by **Mt Meru**, an almost perfect cone with a spectacular crater. Also notable is **Ngurdoto Crater** (often dubbed Little Ngorongoro) with its swamp filled floor.

The park's altitude, which varies from 1400m to more than 4500m, has a variety of vegetation zones but most of the park is forested. Animal life is nowhere near as abundant as in the other northern circuit parks and the dense vegetation reduces visibility; nevertheless you can be fairly certain of sighting zebras, giraffes, waterbucks, bushbucks, klipspringers, dik-diks, buffaloes and hippos. There are also elephant, leopard, red duiker and the amazing black-and-white colobus (most often sighted near the Ngurdoto Museum). There are no lions or rhinos due to poaching.

Walking safaris (US$20 per person per half-day) are popular. Several trails pass

Arusha National Park

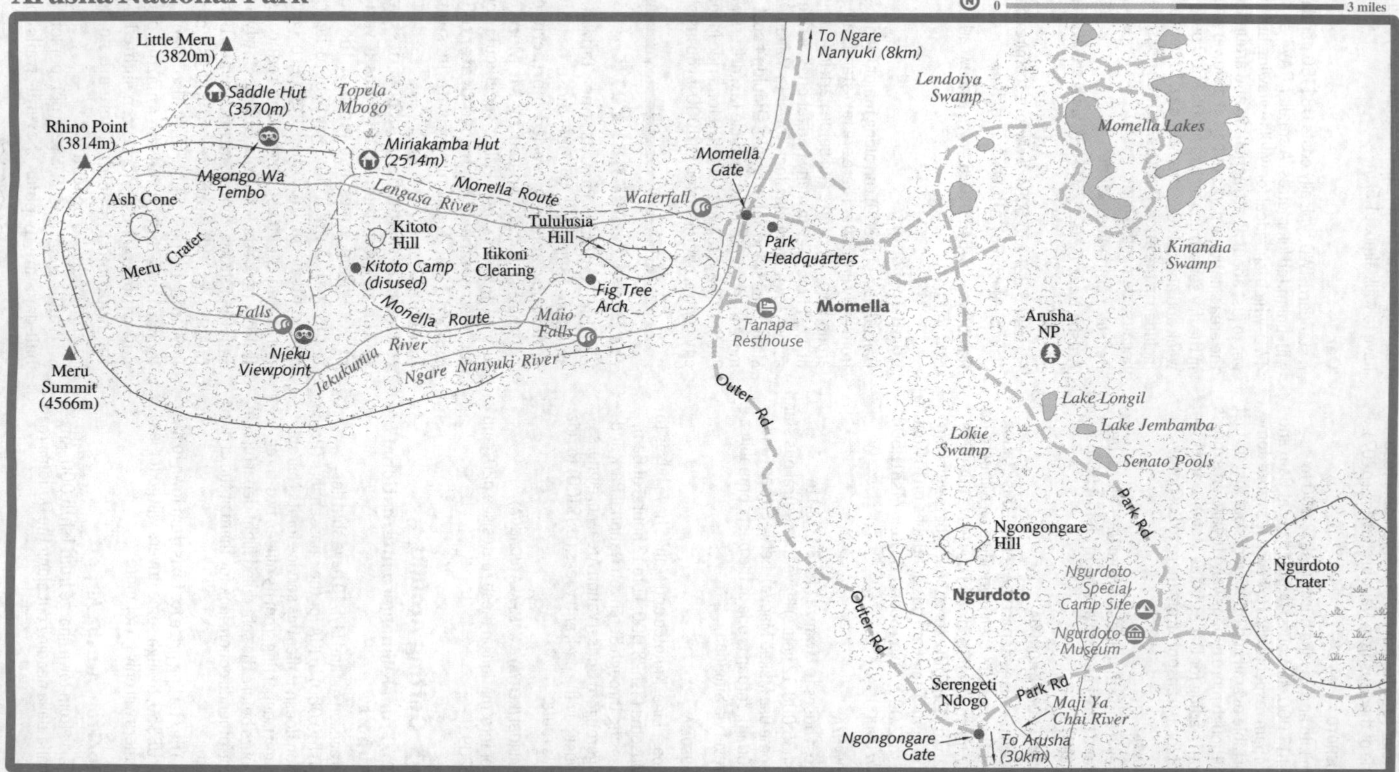
0 5 km
0 3 miles
Little Meru (3820m)
Saddle Hut (3570m)
Topela Mbogo
Rhino Point (3814m)
Miriakamba Hut (2514m)
Mgongo Wa Tembo
Ash Cone
Meru Crater
Lengasa River
Monella Route
Waterfall
Momella Gate
To Ngare Nanyuki (8km)
Lendoiya Swamp
Momella Lakes
Kinandia Swamp
Kitoto Hill
Kitoto Camp (disused)
Itikoni Clearing
Tululusia Hill
Fig Tree Arch
Park Headquarters
Momella
Tanapa Resthouse
Falls
Njeku Viewpoint
Monella Route
Maio Falls
Jekukumia River
Ngare Nanyuki River
Meru Summit (4566m)
Arusha NP
Outer Rd
Lake Longil
Lake Jembamba
Lokie Swamp
Senato Pools
Park Rd
Ngongongare Hill
Ngurdoto
Ngurdoto Special Camp Site
Ngurdoto Museum
Ngurdoto Crater
Serengeti Ndogo
Maji Ya Chai River
Ngongongare Gate
To Arusha (30km)

below Mt Meru and another follows Ngurdoto Crater rim trail (it's not permitted to descend into the crater). **Wayo Africa** (☎0784-203000; www.wayoafrica.com) offers half-day Momella Lake **canoe safaris** (US$55 per person plus a US$20 canoeing fee paid at the park gate).

Sleeping & Eating

The park has three **campsites** (per adult/child US$30/10) in the vicinity of Momella gate (including one with a shower), there's also a good **special campsite** (US$50/10) in the east near Ngurdoto and another near Fig Tree Arch.

Tanapa Resthouse GUESTHOUSE **$$**
(per person US$30) Has three decent carpeted rooms, a TV lounge and a kitchen (bring your own food) 3.5km south of Momella gate; turn at the 'Halali' sign.

OUTSIDE THE PARK

TOP CHOICE **Kiboko Lodge** LODGE **$$**
(☎0784-659809; www.wfkibokolodge.com; s half board US$63, dUS$106-126, ste US$186; P) Most employees at this non-profit, charity-run lodge are former street kids who received training at the Watoto Foundations' vocational training school. But, it's not just a feel-good project; it's a great place to stay. The spacious and attractive stone cottages have fireplaces, hot water and safes and the thatched-roof lounge is almost homey. It's 5km down a 4WD-only road east of Ngongongare gate.

Rivertrees Country Inn LODGE **$$$**
(☎027-255 3894; www.rivertrees.com; s/d/tr from US$180/220/290, 2-room River House US$950; P@) With a genteel old-world ambience and excellent cuisine served family-style around a large wooden dining table, Rivertrees is a perfect post-national park stop. A variety of rooms and cottages, some wheelchair accessible, are spread throughout vast natural gardens with huge trees along the Usa River. It's just east of Usa River village, set back off the Moshi Highway.

Meru View Lodge LODGE **$$**
(☎0784-419232; www.meru-view-lodge.de; s/d/tr US$90/130/180; P@) This unassuming place has a mix of large and small (all priced the same) cottages set in quiet grounds just 1km south of Ngongongare gate. The small rooms feel like childrens' playhouses, but the others are fine.

ARUSHA NATIONAL PARK

» **Why Go** Trekking on Mt Meru; canoe and walking safaris; fine birding.

» **When to Go** Year-round.

» **Practicalities** Drive in from Arusha or Moshi.

Information

Entry fees are adult/child US$35/10 per 24-hour period. There's a US$20 rescue fee per person per trip for treks on Mt Meru and the Meru huts also cost $20.

The main park entrance is at the southern Ngongongare gate. The northern Momella gate is 12km further north near **park headquarters** (☎027-255 3995; arusha@tanzaniaparks.com), which is the main contact for making campsite or resthouse reservations. Both gates are open 6.30am to 6.30pm.

Getting There & Away

Arusha National Park is 25km outside Arusha, and Ngongongare gate is 6.5km north of the Arusha–Moshi road. From the northern entrance, by Momella gate, it's possible to continue via a rough track that joins the main Nairobi highway near Lariboro.

Via public transport, there are four daily buses between Arusha and Ngare Nanyuki village (6km north of Momella gate) that depart Arusha from 1.30pm to 4pm and Ngare Nanyuki between 7am and 8am. The park has asked the drivers to wait at Ngongongare gate (Tsh3500, 1½ hours) while climbers pay all their fees, but if they don't (which is common) you may have to catch the next bus or perhaps one of the irregular dalla-dallas heading to Ngare Nanyuki from Usa River. Another option is to take any bus between Arusha and Moshi, get off at Usa River village and take a taxi to Momella gate for about Tsh30,000. A taxi direct from Arusha should cost about Tsh45,000.

If you're driving your own vehicle, officially the park prohibits parking during the climb, but unofficially it can be arranged with staff at headquarters; for a fee, of course.

Trekking Mt Meru

At 4566m, Mt Meru is Tanzania's second-highest mountain. Although completely overshadowed by Kilimanjaro in the eyes of trekkers, it's a spectacular volcanic cone with one of East Africa's most scenic and rewarding climbs since it involves a dramatic and exhilarating walk along the knife edge of the crater rim.

Costs

Trekking companies in both Arusha and Moshi organise treks on Mt Meru. Most charge from US$450 to US$700 for four days. That said, you can do things quite easily on your own: park entrance, hut, rescue and guide fees total US$280 for a four-day trek. You'll also need to add in the costs of food (which you should get in Arusha, as there's nowhere to stock up near the park), and of transport to and from the park.

TIPPING

Park rangers receive a fixed monthly salary for their work, and get no additional payment from the park for guiding; the fee of US$15 per day is paid to the national park rather than to the guides themselves, which means that tips are much appreciated. Generally the rangers and porters on Mt Meru are hard-working and reliable, but as the popularity of Meru has increased, so has their expectation of the big tips demanded by their counterparts on Kilimanjaro. Although rare, it's not unheard of for some poorly motivated rangers to ask you what their tip will be and if they're not satisfied they won't continue up the mountain. If this happens, work out an arrangement to keep going, and then report them to headquarters when you get down the mountain.

As a guideline, for a good guide who has completed the full trek with you, plan on a tip of about US$50 per group. Cook and porter tips should be around US$30 and US$20 respectively. Tip more with top-end companies.

Guides & Porters

A ranger-guide is mandatory and can be arranged at Momella gate. Unlike on Kilimanjaro, guides on Meru are regular park rangers whose purpose is to assist (and protect) you in case you meet some of the park's buffaloes or elephants, rather than to show you the way (which is why the park refers to 'ranger services' rather than guiding), although they do know the route. There has been a shortage of rangers, resulting in the need to trek in large groups (10 trekkers is normal and it could be as high as 20) sometimes. More hiring has been promised.

Optional porters are also available at Momella gate. The charge is US$10 per porter per day and this is paid directly to them at the end of the trek. They come from one of the nearby villages and are not park employees so you'll also need to pay their park entrance (Tsh1500 per day) and hut (Tsh800 per night) fees at Momella gate before starting to trek. Porters will carry rucksacks weighing up to 20kg (excluding their own food and clothing).

Maps

The only map is on the reverse of Maco's *Arusha National Park* map.

MOMELLA ROUTE

The Momella Route is the only route up Mt Meru. It starts at Momella gate on the eastern side of the mountain and goes to the summit along the northern arm of the horseshoe crater. The route can be done comfortably in four days (three nights). Some trekkers do it in three days by combining Stages 3 and 4 of the trek; but the park authorities now actively discourage this and even if you're in good shape it's so rushed it's hard to enjoy your last day on the mountain. Trekkers aren't allowed to begin after 3pm, which means that if you travel to the park by bus you'll almost certainly have to camp and wait until the next day to start climbing.

While Meru is small compared with Kilimanjaro, don't underestimate it: because of the steepness, many have found that Meru is almost as difficult a climb. And it's still high enough to make the effects of altitude felt, so don't try to rush up if you're not properly acclimatised.

Sleeping

The Momella Route has two blocks of four-bed bunkhouses ('huts') spaced for a four-day trek. Especially during the July–August and December–January high seasons, they're often full, so it's a good idea to carry a tent (though if you camp, you'll still need to pay hut fees). It's currently not possible for independent trekkers to book beds in the bunkhouses, which operate on a first-come, first-served basis. Each bunkhouse has a cooking and eating area; bring your own stove and fuel. There's a separate dorm for guides and porters.

STAGE 1: MOMELLA GATE TO MIRIAKAMBA HUT

(10km, 4-5hr, 1000m ascent)

There are two routes, one long and one short, at the start of the climb. Most people prefer taking the mostly forested long route up and the short route down so that's how the trek is described here. However, since the long route mostly follows a road, some people prefer the shorter route's wilderness feel for both ascent and descent. Either way, don't stray far from the ranger, there are many buffalo in this area.

From Momella gate, the road winds uphill for an hour to **Fig Tree Arch**, a parasitic wild fig that originally grew around two other trees, eventually strangling them. Now only the fig tree remains, with its distinctive arch large enough to drive a car through. After another hour the track crosses a large stream, just above Maio Falls and one hour further you'll reach Kitoto Camp, with excellent views over the Momella Lakes and out to Kilimanjaro in the distance. It's then one final hour to Miriakamba Hut (2514m). From Miriakamba you can walk to the **Meru Crater floor** (a two- to three-hour return trip) either in the afternoon of Stage 1, before Stage 2, or during Stage 4, but you need to let your guide know you want to do this before starting the climb. The path across the floor leads to Njeku Viewpoint on a high cliff overlooking a waterfall, with excellent views of the Ash Cone and the entire extent of the crater.

STAGE 2: MIRIAKAMBA HUT TO SADDLE HUT

(4km, 3-5hr, 1250m ascent)

From Miriakamba the path climbs steeply up through pleasant glades between the trees to reach **Topela Mbogo** (Buffalo Swamp) after 45 minutes and **Mgongo Wa Tembo** (Elephant Ridge) after another 30 minutes. From the top of Mgongo Wa Tembo there are great views down into the crater and up to the main cliffs below the summit. Continue through some open grassy clearings and over several stream beds (usually dry) to **Saddle Hut** (3570m).

From Saddle Hut a side trip to the summit of **Little Meru** (3820m) takes about an hour and gives impressive views of Meru's summit, the horseshoe crater, the top of the Ash Cone, and the sheer cliffs of the crater's inner wall. As the sun sets behind Meru, casting huge jagged shadows across the clouds, the snows on Kili turn orange and then pink as the light fades.

STAGE 3: SADDLE HUT TO MERU SUMMIT & RETURN

(5km, 4-5hr, 816m ascent, plus 5km, 2-3hr, 816m descent)

This stage, along a very narrow ridge between the outer slopes of the mountain and the sheer cliffs of the inner crater, is one of the most dramatic and exhilarating sections of trekking anywhere in East Africa. During the rainy season, ice and snow can occur on this section of the route, so take care. If there's no mist, the views from the summit are spectacular. You can see the volcanoes of Kitumbeini and Lengai along the Rift Valley Escarpment and also far across the plains of the Maasai Steppe beyond Arusha.

If you're looking forward to watching the sunrise behind Kilimanjaro, but you're not keen on attempting this section in the dark, the views at dawn are just as impressive from **Rhino Point** (3814m), about an hour from Saddle Hut, as they are from the summit. Perhaps even more so because you'll also see the main cliffs of the crater's inner wall being illuminated by the rising sun.

STAGE 4: SADDLE HUT TO MOMELLA GATE

(5km, 3-5hr, 2250m descent)

From Saddle Hut, retrace the Stage 2 route to Miriakamba (1½ to 2½ hours). From Miriakamba, the short path descends gradually down the ridge directly to Momella gate (1½ to 2½ hours). It goes through forest some of the way, then open grassland, where giraffes and zebras are often seen. Most companies will finish the day with a wildlife drive through the park.

Tarangire National Park

Beautiful baobab-studded Tarangire National Park stretches along its namesake river and covers 2850 sq km, though adjacent preserves help protect the extended ecosystem. It's usually assigned only a day-visit as part of a larger northern circuit safari, though longer visits are rewarding in the dry season when it has the second highest (after Serengeti) concentration of wildlife of any Tanzanian national park. Large herds of elephants, zebras, wildebeest, hartebeest, elands, oryx, waterbucks, lesser kudus, giraffes and buffaloes gather along the Tarangire River and several large permanent swamps until the short wet season allows them to disperse across the Maasai Steppe; over an area 10 times larger than the park. Lion, leopard and cheetah are also on offer, but these predators are harder to spot here than in Serengeti. With more than 450 species, including many rare ones, Tarangire is also an excellent birdwatching destination.

The best spot for **wildlife drives** is along the river in the northern end of the park. Three-hour **walking safaris** (US$20 per person plus US$20 per group) can be done from the park gate (though the armed

TARANGIRE NATIONAL PARK

» **Why Go** Excellent dry season wildlife watching, especially elephants; evocative baobab-studded landscapes.

» **When to Go** August through October is best for wildlife watching.

» **Practicalities** Drive or fly in from Arusha.

rangers are simply security and haven't had much training about wildlife). Walking and night drives are also available from most of the camps and lodges outside the park boundaries.

Sleeping

BEFORE THE PARK GATE

Maramboi Tented Lodge TENTED CAMP $$$
(☎0784-207727; www.tanganyikawildernesscamps.com; s/d/tr full board US$220/300/410; P@ 🛜🏊) Unlike any other lodge around Tarangire, Maramboi sits amid palms and savannah on Lake Manyara's southeastern shore, 17km from Tarangire's entrance. The 20 large, airy tents with wooden floors all have decks looking out towards the lake, Rift Valley Escarpment and sunset. The turn-off to the lodge is 6km south of Kigongoni.

Roika Tarangire Tented Lodge TENTED CAMP $$$
(☎0787-673338; www.tarangireroikatentedlodge.com; s/d US$197/325, camping US$30; P@🏊) Though it's set off from the park, 5km southwest of the gate, Roika sits in the bush and is visited by lots of wildlife, especially elephants. The 21 widely spaced tents sit on elevated platforms under thatched roofs and have bizarre concrete animal-shaped bathtubs. The common areas are full of carved wood and the lounge features a pool table and satellite TV. Maasai village visits and night drives are available. The campsite has hot showers and a kitchen is planned.

Zion Campsite CAMPGROUND $
(☎0754-460539; camping US$10; P) A bare and unkempt compound 6km before the park gate, but it's cheaper than camping inside the park, and the showers are warm. Bring your own food.

INSIDE THE PARK

There is a campsite a short drive into the park with a good bush location but simple cold-water facilities. Special campsites are spread around the park's northern half.

Tarangire Safari Lodge TENTED CAMP $$$
(☎027-254 4752; www.tarangiresafarilodge.com; s/d full board US$185/300; P🛜🏊) A large lodge, in a prime location on a bluff overlooking the Tarangire River. It's 10km inside the park gate and there's good wildlife watching and birding right at the lodge. Accommodation is in closely spaced tents or thatched bungalows. Simple, but good value.

Tarangire Sopa Lodge LODGE $$$
(☎027-250 0630; www.sopalodges.com; s/d full board US$335/580/740; P🛜🏊) This is a comfortable though rather functional place about 30km from the gate in a good area for wildlife drives. The 75 carpeted rooms are large and four are wheelchair accessible.

Tanapa Resthouse GUESTHOUSE $$
(per person US$30; P) Simple rooms near the headquarters. There's a kitchen and staff might be able to cook meals for you, but bring your own food to be safe.

IN THE TARANGIRE CONSERVATION AREA

Lodges in this remote region outside the park to the northeast, with access through the Boundary Hill gate, can all do night drives and walking safaris. There are animals aplenty from November to March, much less so other months. The main downside is that it's a long way from the wildlife viewing circuit inside the park.

Boundary Hill Lodge LODGE $$$
(☎0787-293727; www.tarangireconservation.com; s/d all-inclusive per person US$550; P🏊) Almost universally praised for its commitment to the environment and the Maasai community (it owns a 50% stake), Boundary Hill has eight large individually designed hilltop rooms with balconies peering out over Silale Swamp in the park.

Tarangire Treetops Lodge TENTED CAMP $$$
(☎027-250 0630; www.elewana.com; s/d all-inclusive US$1128/1690; P🛜🏊) Not your ordinary tented camp, this pampered place has 20 huge suites set on stilts or built tree-house-style around the baobabs. It's far outside the park.

Information

Entry fees are US$35/10 per adult/child, valid for multiple entries within 24 hours. For book-

ings, contact the **senior park warden** (☎027-253 1280/1; tnp@tanzaniaparks.com). The entry gate, open 6am to 6.30pm, and headquarters are near the northern tip of the park.

Getting There & Away

Tarangire is 130km from Arusha via Makuyuni (the last place for petrol and supplies). At Kigongoni village there's a signposted turn-off to the main park gate, which is 7km further down a good dirt access road. The only other entrance is Boundary Hill gate along the northeast border which provides access to some lodges located in the area. The park doesn't rent vehicles.

Coastal Aviation and Air Excel stop at Tarangire's Kuro Airstrip (one way US$120) on request on their flights between Arusha and Lake Manyara.

Lake Manyara National Park

Lake Manyara National Park is one of Tanzania's smallest and most underrated parks. The dramatic western escarpment of the Rift Valley forms the park's western border and to the east is the alkaline Lake Manyara, which covers one-third of the park's 648 sq kms but shrinks considerably in the dry season. During the rains the lake hosts millions of flamingos (best seen outside the park on the lake's east shore) and a diversity of other birdlife.

While Manyara lacks the raw drama and many of the particular animals of other northern circuit destinations its vegetation is diverse and it supports one of the high biomass densities of large mammals in the world. Elephants, hippos, zebras, giraffes, buffalo, wildebeest, waterbucks, klipspringers and dik-diks are often spotted. Leopards, hyena and the famous tree-climbing lions are here, but seldom seen.

Night drives are offered by **Wayo Africa** (p126; US$60 per person with a group of four plus park fees, which must be paid directly to the park before 5pm). Advanced booking is required. Lake Manyara Tree Lodge and Lemala Manyara also do night drives for their guests. The park also allows two- to three-hour **walking safaris** (US$20 per person and US$20 per group up to eight people) with an armed ranger. Reservations are required and the park has no vehicles to take hikers to the trailheads. Wayo leads walks down the escarpment from the Serena lodge and, if there's enough water (usually there's not), **canoe safaris** on the lake.

Sleeping & Eating

IN THE PARK

There are **public campsites** (adult/child US$30/5) with toilets and cold-water showers by the park gate and another near the Endabash River about an hour's drive into the park. There are nine **bandas** (per adult/child US$20/10) with hot water and a cooking area near the park gate and three **special campsites** (adult/child US$50/10) elsewhere in the park.

Lake Manyara Tree Lodge LODGE $$$
(☎028-262 1267; www.andbeyond.com; per person all-inclusive US$995; ⏲May-Mar; P🛜🏊) This lovely, luxurious place is the only permanent camp inside the park. The 10 oversized stilted tree-houses with private decks and views from the bathtubs and outdoor showers are set in a mahogany forest at the remote southern end of the park. The food is excellent and the rooms have butler service.

ATOP THE ESCARPMENT

TOP CHOICE **Panorama Safari Campsite** CAMPGROUND $
(☎0784-118514; camping Tsh10,000; P) The first accommodation you reach going up the hill is hot and dusty with rundown hot-water ablutions, but the price is great and the views are as wonderful as those at any of the luxury lodges up here. They have small no-frills tents right up against the cliff and sunset views are just a short walk away. They serve drinks, but no food. Dalla-dallas from Mto

MTO WA MBU

Mto wa Mbu is the busy gateway to Lake Manyara, which is fed by the town's eponymous 'River of Mosquitoes'. The busy **Cultural Tourism Program** (☎0784-606654; mtoculturalprogramme@hotmail.com; ⏲8am-6.30pm) offers tours to surrounding villages, with an emphasis on farming, and hiking along the escarpment. Prices start at US$28 per person (less if you have a group) for day trips and most can be done by mountain bike rather than walking. The office is in the back of the Red Banana Café on the main road near where buses stop.

LAKE MANYARA NATIONAL PARK

» **Why Go** Excellent birding; tree-climbing lions; dramatic Rift Valley Escarpment scenery.

» **When to Go** Year-round. June to October is best for large mammals, November to June is best for birds.

» **Practicalities** Drive or fly in from Arusha; bring binoculars to optimise wildlife watching over the lake.

wa Mbu heading to Karatu pass the entrance (Tsh500).

Kirurumu Manyara Lodge TENTED CAMP $$$
(☎027-250 7011, www.kirurumu.net; s/d/tr half board US$167/262/375; P) A genteel, unpretentious ambience, closeness to the natural surroundings and memorable cuisine are the hallmarks of this highly regarded camp. It's about 6km down a rough road from the main road, with views of Lake Manyara in the distance and a bush feel up close. The tents are well-spaced amid the vegetation, and there are several larger 'family suite' tents. Maasai-guided ethno-botanical and sunset walks are free and fly-camping can be organised.

Lake Manyara Serena Safari Lodge LODGE $$$
(☎027-254 5555; www.serenahotels.com; s/d full board US$290/460; P@) A large complex with shady grounds, the 67 well-appointed rooms are in appealing two-storey conical thatched bungalows. Nature walks and village visits are available, as is massage.

BELOW THE ESCARPMENT

These places are all east of Mto wa Mbu.

Migunga Tented Camp TENTED CAMP $$$
(☎0754-324193; www.moivaro.com; s/d/tr full board US$241/287/373, camping US$10; P@) The main attraction of this place is its setting in a grove of enormous fever trees (*migunga* in Swahili) that echoes with bird calls. The 21 tents ringing large, grassy grounds are small but quite adequate, and there's a great rustic dining room. The adjacent campsite has good hot water facilities. Village tours and mountain-bike hire are available. It's 2km south of the main road.

E Unoto Retreat LODGE $$$
(☎0787-622724; www.maasaivillage.com; s/d full board US$395/640; P) This classy Maasai-themed lodge has 25 spacious round bungalows nestled at the base of the Rift Valley Escarpment by Lake Miwaleni. There's rewarding birding in the area, as well as the chance for various cultural activities. It's 11km out of Mto wa Mbu, off the Lake Natron road.

Ol Mesera Tented Camp TENTED CAMP $$
(☎0784-428332; www.ol-mesera.com; s/d full board US$105/195; P) Run by a spritely Slovenian pensioner, this personalised place, in a placid deep bush setting amid baobab and euphorbia trees, has four straightforward safari tents and is an ideal spot to do cultural walks or just relax for a few days. Barbara's meals are served in a little grass-roofed dining hall between two giant baobabs. Student discounts available. It's 14km up the Lake Natron road. Public transport towards Engaruka or Lake Natron can drop you at the turn-off, from where it's an easy 1.5km walk.

IN MTO WA MBU

Maryland Resort GUESTHOUSE $
(☎0754-299320; camping Tsh10,000; s Tsh30,000, d Tsh40,000-50,000; d without bathroom Tsh20,000; P) Signposted off the main road just before the park gate, this bright peach building is meticulously maintained by the friendly owner who lives on-site. Most of the nine rooms are on the small side, but with hot water and cable TV they're priced right. Meals are available by request and there's a kitchen.

New Continental Luxury Lodge GUESTHOUSE $
(☎0784-712143; s/d Tsh20,000/30,000; P) Far from luxurious, but it's one of the best guesthouses in town. Rooms have hot water and cable TV.

Njake Jambo Lodge & Campsite BACKPACKERS $$
(☎027-250 1329; www.njake.com; Arusha–Karatu Rd; camping US$7, camping with tent & bedding rental US$25, s/d US$60, tw US$90; P) A base for both independent travellers and large overland trucks, there's a shaded and well-maintained grassy camping area, plus 16 good rooms in double-storey chalet blocks.

Twiga Campsite & Lodge BACKPACKERS $$
(☎0713-334287; www.twigacampsitelodge.com; Arusha–Karatu Rd; camping US$10, old r US$40, new r US$60-70; P@) A larger version of the

nearby Jambo with a less attractive though still decent camping area. The new rooms (with TV and mini-fridge) are far better than the old. Bike hire is available.

Camp Vision Lodge GUESTHOUSE $
(027-253 9159; d/tw Tsh4000/5000; P) No-frills rooms, and lots of them.

Information

The entry gate, also the site of the tourist information office and several display panels about Manyara's natural history, is at the northern tip of the park just west of Mto wa Mbu village. It's open 6am to 6pm. Entry fees are US$35/10 per adult/child, valid for multiple entries within 24 hours. Bookings can be made through the **park warden** (027-253 9112; lake.manyara@tanzaniaparks.com).

There's an ATM (by Twiga Campsite & Lodge) and a couple of slow internet cafes in Mto wa Mbu.

Getting There & Away

Air

Air Excel, Coastal Aviation and Regional Air offer daily flights between Arusha and Lake Manyara for about US$70 one way. The airstrip is atop the escarpment near the Serena.

Bus

Buses and dalla-dallas run all day from Arusha (Tsh5000 to Tsh6000, two hours) and Karatu (Tsh2000, one hour) to Mto wa Mbu. You can also come from Arusha on the minibuses that run to Karatu (p137). All vehicles stop along the main road in the town centre near Red Banana Café.

Car

Car hire (US$150 including fuel and driver) for trips to the park is available in Mto wa Mbu through the Cultural Tourism Program office and Twiga and Jambo campsites.

Lake Natron

Shimmering amid the sun-scorched Kenyan border northeast of Ngorongoro Conservation Area, this 58km-long but just 50cm-deep alkaline lake should be on every adventurer's itinerary. The drive from Mto wa Mbu is remote, with a desolate, otherworldly beauty and an incomparable feeling of space and ancientness. After the drive, the lake itself is secondary; except during the June-November breeding season when upwards of three million flamingos gather here. It's the most important flamingo breeding site in East Africa.

The base for visits is the small oasis of **Engaresero** (also spelled Ngare Sero) on the southwestern shore. The **Engarasero Association of Guides** (emolo88@yahoo.com; 8am-6.30pm) has an office at the village council, just north of town, for arranging guided walks, overnights in Maasai *boma* and climbs of Ol Doinyo Lengai (p140), 25km to the south (US$100 per group for a guide for up to four climbers, plus US$60 transport if you don't have your own vehicle).

Sleeping & Eating

Ngosek Guesthouse GUESTHOUSE $
(0754-287628; per person without bathroom US$20; P) Despite the higher than reasonable rate (you can usually negotiate it down) and lower than expected cleanliness in the ablutions block, we love this place in Engaresero for its lake, mountain, village and sunrise views.

Lake Natron Tented Camp CAMPGROUND $$
(0754-324193; www.moivaro.com; cottage/tent per person full board US$120/150, camping per person US$10; P) Near the village with a view of the lake. The tents and grass-roofed cottages are in shady grounds near the river. There's a large and sometimes busy campground with good facilities next door and campers can use all lodge facilities, including the restaurant (breakfast/lunch/dinner US$10/15/25) and swimming pool.

Getting There & Away

The road from Mto wa Mbu is part sandy, part rocky, all bad: 4WD is necessary. During the rainy season you may have to wait a few hours at some of the seasonal rivers before you can cross. The road past the lake to Loliondo and into the Serengeti is in better shape than the road from Mto wa Mbu because it's used far less. Those continuing this way should carry extra supplies of petrol since the last proper station is in Mto wa Mbu.

Chilia Tosha line has a rickety, crowded bus between Arusha and Loliondo that stops in Engaresero (Tsh20,000, nine hours from Arusha). It departs Arusha 6.30am Sunday and passes back through Engaresero on Thursday around 10am. Trucks run between Mto wa Mbu and Engaresero pretty much daily (including sometimes 4WDs operating as public transport) but it's not unheard of to have to wait two days to find a ride; especially in the rainy seasons.

The best way to come here is by camel from Mkuru (p123) village, a remote seven-day trip.

District fees (ie tourist taxes) must be paid at three gates along the way: Engaruka Chini, US$10; 7km before Engaresero US$10, and Engaresero, US$15.

Karatu

This charmless town 14km southeast of Lodoare gate makes a convenient base for visiting Ngorongoro if you want to economize on entry fees. There are ATMs plus a few internet cafés. There are also several mini-supermarkets, but it's better to stock up in Arusha.

Sleeping & Eating

IN KARATU

Octagon Safari Lodge & Irish Bar LODGE $$
(027-253 4525; www.octagonlodge.com; per person US$55; P @ wi-fi) This Irish-Tanzanian owned lodge is tops in town, but the unexpectedly lush and lovely grounds mean you'll soon feel far away from Karatu. The cottages are small but comfortable and by Karatu standards the rates are excellent. The restaurant and Irish bar (open to nonguests, but call before coming) round out the relaxing vibe. Cultural walks can be arranged, as can Ngorongoro safaris. It's 1km south of the main road on the west side of town.

Vera Inn GUESTHOUSE $
(0754-578145; Milano Rd, Bwani; s/d Tsh25,000/30,000; P) One of the best guesthouses in Karatu, rooms are small but sparkling clean and have hot water showers and cable TV.

Continental Guesthouse GUESTHOUSE $
(0754-781040; Bwani, d/tw with no bathroom Tsh5000/8000, d with bathroom Tsh10,000; P) Simple but clean with squat toilets and sometimes hot water showers.

Ngorongoro Camp & Lodge BACKPACKERS $$$
(027-253 4287; www.ngorongorocampandlodge.net; Arusha Rd; camping US$7, s/d/tr US$81/160/220; P @ pool) Also using the name Ngorongoro Safari Resort, this place behind a petrol station on the main road is always busy with overland trucks. Camping facilities are good and the rooms are too, though they should be half the price.

Bump's Café TANZANIAN, EUROPEAN $
(Arusha Rd; meals Tsh4000-8000; breakfast, lunch & dinner; wi-fi) A simple (but fancy by Karatu standards) American–Maasai-owned restaurant on the west end of town with a mix of local and Western meals. The menu is limited after lunchtime, and they close at

ENGARUKA

Halfway to Lake Natron, on the eastern edge of the Ngorongoro Conservation Area, are 300- to 500-year-old ruins of a farming town that developed a complex irrigation system with terraced stone housing sites. Archaeologists are unsure of their origin, though some speculate the town was built by ancestors of the Iraqw (Mbulu) people, who once populated the area and now live around Lake Eyasi, while others propose it was the Sonjo, a Bantu-speaking people. Though important among researchers, casual visitors will likely be more impressed with the up-close views of the escarpment than the vaguely house-shaped piles of rocks. Knowledgeable English-speaking guides (no set prices) can be found at Engaruka Ruins Campsite, or arranged in advance through the tourist information office in Arusha. The ruins are unsigned above the village of Engaruka Juu. Turn west at Engaruka Chini, a smaller village along the Lake Natron road, and follow the rough track 4.5km until you reach Engaruka Juu Primary Boarding School. Visiting costs Tsh5000, payable at the government office in Engaruka Juu.

Engaruka Ruins Campsite (camping US$10; P) in Engaruka Juu is dusty but shady with acceptable ablutions. You can use their tents for free and meals are available on request. Engaruka Chini has an unnamed/unsigned bucket-shower **guesthouse** (s/d without bathroom Tsh5000/10,000). It's the green-fronted building right near the entrance gate into town.

There's a daily bus to Arusha (Tsh7000, four to five hours) via Mto wa Mbu (Tsh4000, 1½ hours) leaving Engaruka at 6am and turning right around for the return trip shortly after arrival.

7pm. But it's an excellent spot to order lunch boxes and there's also an internet cafe.

AROUND KARATU

TOP CHOICE **Plantation Lodge** LODGE $$$
(☎0784-260799; www.plantation-lodge.com; s/d half board US$255/380, ste US$550-990; P@) A place that makes you feel special, this relaxing lodge fills a renovated colonial farmstead and the decor is unpretentiously gorgeous down to the last detail. The uniquely decorated rooms spaced around the gardens have large verandahs and crackling fireplaces to enhance the highland ambience. It's west of Karatu and about 2.5km north of the highway and signposted so poorly you'd think they don't want you to come. Once you've visited here, you know this couldn't be further from the truth.

Rhotia Valley Tented Lodge TENTED LODGE $$$
(☎0784-446579; www.rhotiavalley.com; s/d half board US$160/280; P@) Right up against the Ngorongoro Conservation Area, this refreshingly unpretentious hilltop lodge has 15 large tents (two are family sized) with either forest or valley views, the latter offering a peek at Lake Manyara. Cultural tours and nature walks are also available. Rates include a 20% donation to the school-orphanage the owners opened nearby. Rhotia Valley Tented Lodge is 10km northeast of Karatu; well signposted off the highway.

Ngorongoro Farm House LODGE $$$
(☎0784-207727; www.tanganyikawildernesscamps.com; s/d/tr full board US$220/300/410; P@) This atmospheric place, 4km from Lodoare gate, is set in the grounds of a 500-acre working farm that provides coffee, wheat and vegetables for this and the company's other lodges. The 50 well-appointed rooms, some a long walk from the restaurant and other public area, are huge. Farm tours and coffee demonstrations are available, as is massage.

Getting There & Away

There are several morning buses between Karatu and Arusha (Tsh5000, three hours); some continuing to Moshi (Tsh7500; 4½ hours). There are also more comfortable nine-seater minivans to/from Arusha (Tsh7000, three hours) that depart throughout the day. While Karatu awaits a new bus stand, transport departs from several spots along the main road.

NGORONGORO CONSERVATION AREA

» **Why Go** Amazing scenery, high wildlife density, good chance to see rhinos.

» **When to Go** Year-round.

» **Practicalities** Usually visited en route to Serengeti from Arusha via Karatu. It can get very cold on the crater rim, so come prepared.

Ngorongoro Conservation Area

Pick a superlative: amazing, incredible, breath taking…they all apply to the stunning ethereal blue-green vistas of the Ngorongoro Crater. But as wonderful as the views are from above, the real magic happens when you get down inside and drive amongst an unparalleled concentration of wildlife, including the highest density of both lions and overall predators in Africa. And this world-renowned natural wonder is just a single feature of the 8292 sq km Ngorongoro Conservation Area (NCA), a Unesco World Heritage Site. The Crater Highlands (to which Ngorongoro Crater belongs) warps along numerous extinct volcanoes, calderas (collapsed volcanoes), and the dramatic Rift Valley Escarpment on the park's eastern side while vast savannah stretches out across the west. Out here is the Oldupai (Olduvai) Gorge, where many important fossils have been unearthed.

Unlike national parks where human residents were evicted, the NCA remains part of the Maasai homeland and over 40,000 live here with grazing rights; though no permanent agriculture is allowed. You'll surely see them out tending their cattle and goats, as well as selling necklaces and knives alongside the road. Many children wait along the road to pose for photos, but note that most of them are skipping school or shirking their chores so it's best not to stop. There are cultural *bomas* too which charge US$50 per vehicle.

NGORONGORO CRATER

At 19km wide and with a surface of 264 sq km, Ngorongoro is one of the largest unbroken calderas in the world that isn't a lake. Its steep, unbroken walls soar 400m to 610m and provide the setting for an in-

Ngorongoro Conservation Area

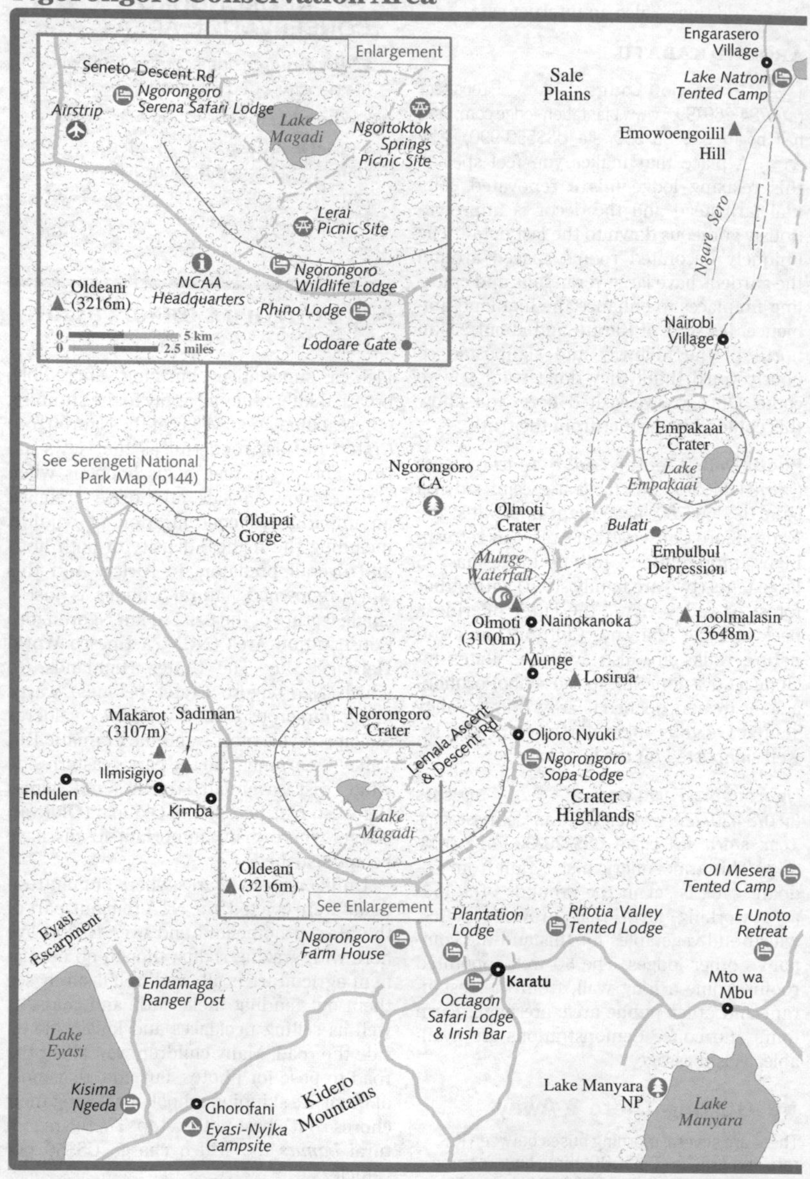

credible natural drama as lions, elephants, buffaloes, ostriches and plains herbivores such as wildebeest, elands, buffaloes, zebras, reedbucks graze and stalk their way around the grasslands, swamps and acacia woodland on the crater floor. Chances are good that you'll also see the critically endangered black rhino, and for many people this is one of the crater's main draws. There are plenty of hippos around Ngoitoktok Springs picnic site and Lake Magadi attracts flocks of flamingos to its shallows in the rainy season.

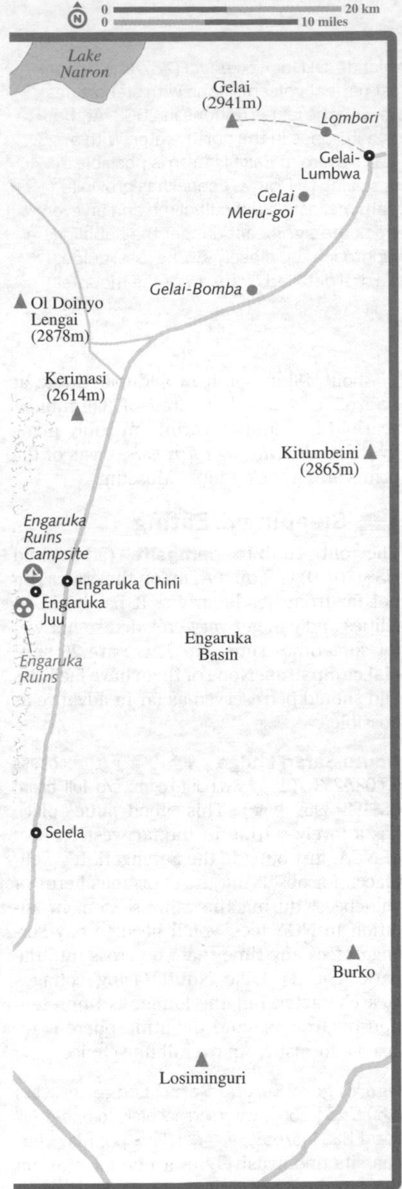

Early morning is the best wildlife watching time and if you depart at first light, you'll have some time in the crater before the masses arrive. Afternoons are less busy than mornings. The gates open at 6am and close for descent at 4pm; all vehicles must be out of the crater before 6pm.

Entering the crater costs US$200 per vehicle per entry and you're only allowed to stay for six hours. Even though the fee is per vehicle, the guards check the number of passengers against the permit so it's not possible to join up with people you meet at your campsite or lodge. Only 4WDs are allowed into the crater. The roads down are in good shape, though steep and thus somewhat difficult when wet. The main route in is the Seneto descent road, which enters the crater on its western side. To come out, use the Lerai ascent road, which starts south of Lake Magadi and leads to the rim near headquarters. The Lemala road is on the northeastern side of the crater near Ngorongoro Sopa Lodge and used for both ascent and descent. Self-drivers are supposed to hire a park ranger (US$20 per vehicle) for the crater, but are sometimes let in without one.

THE CRATER HIGHLANDS

The ruggedly beautiful Crater Highlands consist of an elevated range of volcanoes and calderas rising up along the Great Rift Valley on the NCA's eastern side. The peaks include Oldeani (3216m), Makarot (Lemagurut; 3107m), Olmoti (3100m), Loolmalasin (3648m), Empakaai (also spelled Embagai; 3262m), Ngorongoro (2200m) and the still-active Ol Doinyo Lengai ('Mountain of God' in Maasai; 2878m) which is just outside the NCA.

Trekking the Crater Highlands

The best way to explore the Crater Highlands is on foot, although because of the logistics and multiple fees involved, trekking here is expensive; from US$350 and up (less if you have a large group) for overnight trips. Treks range from short day jaunts to excursions of up to two weeks or more. For all routes, you'll need to be accompanied by a guide, and for anything except day hikes, most people use donkeys or vehicle support to carry water and supplies.

Nearly all visitors arrange treks through a tour company. Many Arusha-based companies can take you up Ol Doinyo Lengai (just outside the NCA boundaries), but for most trekking in this region you'll need to contact a specialist. For some recommendations, see the boxed text on p120.

There are no set routes, and the possibilities are numerous. Good day hikes from Ngorongoro Crater or Karatu include

OL DOINYO LENGAI

The northernmost mountain in the Crater Highlands, Ol Doinyo Lengai (2878m), 'Mountain of God' in the Maasai language, is an almost perfect volcanic cone with steep sides rising to a small flat-topped peak. It's still active with the last eruptions in 2008. At the peak, you can see hot steam vents and growing ash cones in the north crater. With a midnight start, a trek from the base village of Engaresero at Lake Natron is possible in one long day. Although the number of climbers scaling Ol Doinyo Lengai has grown in recent years, the loose ash along most of the path makes it a difficult climb and an even tougher, often painful, descent. And don't overlook the significant danger the bubbling lava in the north crater poses to trekkers who approach too closely. Some local guides no longer climb out of fear of another eruption. For a detailed overview of the mountain see www.oldoinyolengai.pbworks.com.

climbing Makarot or Oldeani, or walking along Empakaai or Olmoti Craters. Apart from transport costs, these involve only the US$50 NCA entry fee and US$20 per group guide fee. If you're trying to do things on your own through the NCA, rather than through a tour operator, the least complicated option is Oldeani, since the climb starts at headquarters. From Oldeani, it's possible to camp and continue on down to Lake Eyasi where there's public transport.

OLDUPAI GORGE

Slicing its way through up to 90m of rock and two million years of history, Oldupai (Olduvai) Gorge on the plains northwest of Ngorongoro Crater is a dusty, 48km-long ravine that has become one of the African continent's most important archaeological sites. Thanks to its unique geological history, in which layer upon layer of volcanic deposits were laid down in an orderly sequence up until 15,000 years ago, it provides remarkable documentation of ancient life, allowing us to begin turning the pages of history back to the days of our earliest ancestors.

Fossils of over 60 early hominids (human-like) have been unearthed here, including *Homo habilis, Homo erectus* and most famously a 1.8 million-year-old ape-like skull known as *Australopithecus boisei,* which was discovered by Mary Leakey in 1959. The skull is also often referred to as 'zinjanthropus', which means 'nutcracker man', referring to its large molars.

The small **Oldupai Museum** (adult/child Tsh3000/1500; ⌚8.30am-4.30pm) on the rim of the gorge documents its formation, fossil finds and the Leakeys' legacy. The museum is 5.5km off the road to Serengeti National Park.

About 45km south of Oldupai Gorge at **Laetoli** is a 27m-long trail of 3.6-million-year-old hominid footprint, probably made by *Australopithecus afarensis.* Casts of the prints are in the Oldupai Museum.

Sleeping & Eating

The only **public campsite** (adult/child US$/30/10) is Simba A, up on the crater rim not far from headquarters. It has basic facilities and can get very crowded so hot water sometimes runs out. There are 25 **special campsites**. None of them have facilities and should be reserved as far in advance as possible.

Ndutu Safari Lodge LODGE $$$
(☎027-253 7015; www.ndutu.com; s/d full board US$198/396; P@) This good-value place has a lovely setting in the far western part of NCA, just outside the Serengeti. It's well-placed for observing the enormous herds of wildebeest during the rainy season. In addition to NCA fees, you'll need to pay Serengeti fees any time that you cross into the park. The 34 Lake Ndutu-facing cottages lack character, but the lounge is unpretentiously attractive and the atmosphere is relaxed and rustic. An overall fine choice.

Ngorongoro Serena Safari Lodge LODGE $$$
(☎027-254 5555; www.serenahotels.com; s/d full board US$445/655; P@) The popular Serena sits unobtrusively in a fine location on the southwestern crater rim near the main descent route. It's comfortable and attractive with good service and views (from the upper-floor rooms), though it's also big and busy.

Rhino Lodge LODGE $$
(☎0762-359055; www.ngorongoro.cc; s/d full board US$125/220; P) Up on the crater rim, but

without a crater view, this small, friendly lodge, run in conjunction with the Maasai community, is the cheapest place in the NCA. The 24 rooms lack pizzazz and will be too rustic for some, but it's nice for the price. Wildlife often wanders through the grounds. Vehicle hire costs US$200 per day.

Ngorongoro Wildlife Lodge LODGE **$$$**
(☎027-254 4595; www.hotelsandlodges-tanzania.com; r per person US$460; Ⓟ@) If all other lodges on the rim are full, but you really want a room with a view, consider this large relic, which can only be recommended for its excellent setting.

Kitoi Guesthouse GUESTHOUSE **$**
(☎0754-334834; r without bathroom Tsh7000; Ⓟ) This unsigned place is the newest and best of four guesthouses in Kimba village, near the crater. The ablution block is out back; and so are awesome views of Oldeani. On request someone will cook food or heat water for bucket showers. Officials at the park gate may insist that you have to pay the camping fee upon entering the park, even if you plan to sleep in this village.

Information

The NCA is under the jurisdiction of the Ngorongoro Conservation Area Authority (NCAA), which has its **headquarters** (☎027-253 7006; www.ngorongorocrater.org; ⌚8am-4pm) at Park Village at Ngorongoro Crater. Entry costs US$50/10 per adult/child for single-entry lasting 24 hours. The vehicle fee is US$40/Tsh10,000 per foreign-/Tanzanian-registered vehicle per day.

All fees, including those for the crater and walks, are paid at **Lodoare gate** (⌚6am-6pm), just south of Ngorongoro Crater on the road from Arusha, or **Naabi Hill gate** on the border with Serengeti National Park. Should you wish to add days or activities to your visit, you can pay fees at the headquarters. There's an NBC ATM at headquarters that accepts Visa and MasterCard, but it sometimes goes offline.

Getting There & Around

If you aren't travelling on an organised safari and don't have your own vehicle, the easiest thing to do is hire in Karatu where most lodges charge about US$160 per day including fuel for a 4WD with a pop-up top. It's also possible, if arrangements are made in advance, to travel by bus (see Arusha or Musoma for details) to headquarters where staff informally hires vehicles for US$150 including fuel, but it's much easier to arrange things in Karatu.

Driving is not allowed before 6am or (officially, anyway) after 7pm. Petrol is sold at headquarters, but it's cheaper in Karatu.

Lake Eyasi

Uniquely beautiful Lake Eyasi lies at 1030m between the Eyasi Escarpment in the north and the Kidero Mountains in the south. Like Lake Natron way to the north-east, Eyasi makes a rewarding detour on an Ngorongoro trip for anyone looking for something remote and different, and prepared for the rough road trip from Karatu. It's a hot, dry area, around which live the Hadzabe (also known as Hadzapi or Tindiga) people who are believed to have lived here for nearly 10,000 years. Several hundred still follow ancient nomadic hunting and gathering traditions. Also in the area are the Iraqw (Mbulu), a people of Cushitic origin who arrived about 2000 years ago, and Datoga, noted metal smiths whose dress and culture is quite similar to the Maasai.

All foreigners must pay a US$5 village tax at the **Lake Eyasi Cultural Tourism Program office** (☎0782-175099; ⌚8am-6pm) at the entrance to Ghorofani. Here you can hire English-speaking guides (US$30 per group up to 10 people) to visit nearby Hadzabe (an extra US$20 per group) and Datoga communities or the lake.

Sleeping & Eating

Basic supplies are sold in Ghorofani, but it's better to stock up in Karatu.

Eyasi-Nyika Campsite CAMPGROUND **$**
(☎0762-766040; camping US$10; Ⓟ) Along with the more distant Kisima Ngeda, this is Eyasi's best campground. It's got seven widely spaced grassy sites, each under an acacia tree and you can cook for yourself using charcoal. It's in the bush, 3km outside Ghorofani, signposted only at the main road: after that, just stick to the most travelled roads and you'll get there.

Kisima Ngeda TENTED CAMP **$$$**
(☎027-254 8715; www.kisimangeda.com; s/d half board US$325/450; camping US$10; Ⓟ) This highly recommended spot on the lake has a location that will 'wow' you. Kisima Ngeda roughly translates as 'spring surrounded by trees', and there's a natural spring at the heart of the property creating an unexpectedly green and lush oasis of fever trees and doum palms. The six tents are plenty comfortable

and the cuisine is excellent. There's basic camping 2km past the main lodge (the only camping on the lakeshore) with a toilet and shower and the same awesome scenery. It's signposted 7.5km from Ghorofani.

Getting There & Away

Two daily buses connect Arusha to Barazani passing Ghorofani (Tsh10,000, 4½ to five hours) on the way. They leave Arusha about 5am and head back about 2pm and you can also catch them in Karatu (Tsh4000, 1½ hours to Ghorofani). There are also several passenger-carrying 4WDs to Karatu (Tsh5000; they park at Mbulu junction) departing Ghorofani and other lake towns during the morning and returning throughout the afternoon. At other times, hitching is usually possible.

Serengeti National Park

In the vast plains of the Serengeti, nature's mystery, power and beauty surround you. It's here that one of earth's most impressive natural cycles has played out for eons as hundreds of thousands of hoofed animals, driven by primeval rhythms of survival, move constantly in search of fresh grasslands. The most famous, and numerous, are the wildebeest (of which there are some 1.5 million) and their annual migration is the Serengeti's calling card. During the rainy months of January to March, the wildebeest are scattered over the southern section of the Serengeti and the western side of Ngorongoro Conservation Area. Most streams dry out quickly when the rains cease, nudging the wildebeest to concentrate on the few remaining green areas, and to form thousands-strong herds that by April begin to migrate northwest in search of food. The crossing of the crocodile-filled Grumeti River, which runs through the park's Western Corridor, usually takes place between late May and early July, and lasts only about a week. Usually in August they make an even more incredible river crossing while leaving the Serengeti to find water in the Masai Mara (just over the Kenyan border) before roaming back south in November in anticipation of the rains. Besides the migrating wildebeest, there are also resident populations in the park and you'll see these smaller but still impressive herds year-round. In February more than 8000 wildebeest calves are born per day, although about 40% of these die before reaching four months old.

The 14,763 sq km Serengeti National Park is also renowned for its predators, especially its lions. Hunting alongside the lions are cheetahs, leopards, hyenas, jackals and more. These feast on zebras (about 200,000), giraffes, buffaloes, Thomson's and Grant's gazelles, topis, elands, hartebeest, impalas, klipspringers, duikers and so many more.

Wayo Africa (☎0784-203000; www.wayoafrica.com) leads multiple-day walking safaris in the Moro Kopjes and Kogatende regions. A few lodges, mostly in the north, are allowed to lead short (under two hours) walks.

Sleeping

There are nine **public campsites** (adult/child US$30/5) in the Serengeti: six around Seronera, one at Lobo and one each at Ndabaka and Ikoma gates. All have flush toilets while Pimbi and Nyani have kitchens, showers and solar lighting. There are also dozens of **special campsites** (adult/child US$50/10), which should be booked well in advance.

If you don't want to cook yourself, there are two local **restaurants** (meals around Tsh5000) and three little **groceries** at staff quarters and anyone can dine at Twiga Resthouse.

CENTRAL & SOUTHERN SERENGETI

Central Serengeti is the most visited area of the park, and it's readily accessed from both Arusha and Mwanza. Park offices and many campsites are around Seronera, which has a good mix of habitats and year-round water in some places making wildlife especially abundant. southeast of Seronera is a prime base for wildlife watching during the December to April wet season, when it's full of wildebeest, though wildlife concentrations here are quite low in the dry season and this area has the fewest lions in the Serengeti. The more rugged southwest has many attractive hills and kopjes and is the best place to see predators, particularly lions and leopards.

Twiga Resthouse GUESTHOUSE **$$**
(☎028-262 1510; serengeti_tourism@yahoo.com; per person US$30; P) Simple but decent rooms with electricity and hot showers and satellite TV in the lounge. Guests can use the kitchen or meals can be cooked for you if you order way in advance. If Twiga is full, they might have room at the similar **Taj**

Resthouse, used mostly used by visiting park officials.

Serengeti Serena Safari Lodge LODGE **$$$**
(027-254 5555; www.serenahotels.com; s/d full board US$445/655;) Serena's two-storey Maasai-style bungalows each have three very comfortable and well-appointed rooms with lovely furnishings and views. The top-floor rooms are best. A good location for those who want to explore several parts of the park but not switch accommodation.

Serengeti Sopa Lodge LODGE **$$$**
(027-250 0630; www.sopalodges.com; s/d full board US$335/580;) The 73 rooms are uninspired but spacious, with small sitting rooms and two double beds, plus views. Good food too. It's 45 minutes south of Seronera on the edge of the Niaroboro Hills.

Robanda Safari Camp TENTED CAMP **$$$**
(0754-324193; www.moivaro.com; s full board US$70-195, d US$140-290;) A refreshingly small budget (by Serengeti standards) camp on the plains near Robanda village just outside Ikoma gate with ten no-frills tents: standard large ones and cheaper small ones with toilet outdoors. You can do guided walks and night drives here, if you have your own vehicle.

Seronera Wildlife Lodge LODGE **$$$**
(027-254 4595; www.hotelsandlodges-tanzania.com; r per person full board US$330/460;) Fantastic common areas built on and around the boulders (home to many rock hyrax), this large and crowded place has an ideal location. The rooms and service however, are overdue for improvement.

WESTERN SERENGETI

In addition to seasonal proximity to the migration (which generally passes through sometime between late May and early July), the Western Corridor offers resident herds of wildebeest and reliable year-round wildlife watching, particularly close to the forest-fringed Grumeti River with its hippos and giant crocodiles.

TOP CHOICE **Grumeti Serengeti Tented Camp** TENTED LODGE **$$$**
(028-262 1267; www.andbeyond.com; per person all-inclusive US$995; May-Mar;) Instead of taking to the hills for panoramic views, Grumeti gets down into the thick of the action along the Kanyanja River; a prime spot during the migration when you can watch crocs catch wildebeest as you lounge in the swimming pool. It mixes its wild bush location with a chic pan-Africa decor and the 10 tents are as luxe as can be; though only three have unobstructed river views.

Serengeti Stop-Over CAMPGROUND, BUNGALOWS **$$**
(0784-406996; www.serengetistopover.com; camping/banda per person US$10/35;) Just 1km from Ndabaka gate along the Mwanza-Musoma road, this sociable place has camping with hot showers and a cooking area, plus 14 simple (and overpriced, but it's the only option of its sort in the area) rondavels, and a restaurant-bar. Safari vehicle rental is available and Serengeti day trips are feasible. They also offer trips on Lake Victoria with local fishermen, visits to a traditional healer and other Sukuma cultural excursions.

Balili Mountain Resort TENTED LODGE **$$**
(0754-710113; eeedeco@yahoo.com; camping per person with own/hired tent US$15/20 s/d/tr US$40/60/75; day entry per person US$2;) Neither a mountain nor a resort, but no-frills tented lodge on a big rocky hill doesn't have the same ring to it. It's perfectly comfortable, but its main draws are the huge views of Lake Victoria and Serengeti. It's up above Bunda, north of Ndabaka gate, reached by a roller-coaster of a road. There's an office in town at the main junction, next to FINCA.

NORTHERN SERENGETI

The north receives relatively few visitors. It begins with acacia woodlands, where elephants congregate in the dry season, but north of Lobo is vast open plains. The migration passes through the western side

SERENGETI NATIONAL PARK

» **Why Go** Wildebeest migration; excellent chance of seeing predators; overall high wildlife density; fine birding; stunning savannah scenery.

» **When to Go** Year-round; July-August for wildebeest migration across Mara River; February for wildebeest calving; February-May for birding.

» **Practicalities** Drive in from Arusha or Mwanza, or fly-in. To avoid congestion, spend some time outside the central Serengeti/Seronera area.

Serengeti National Park

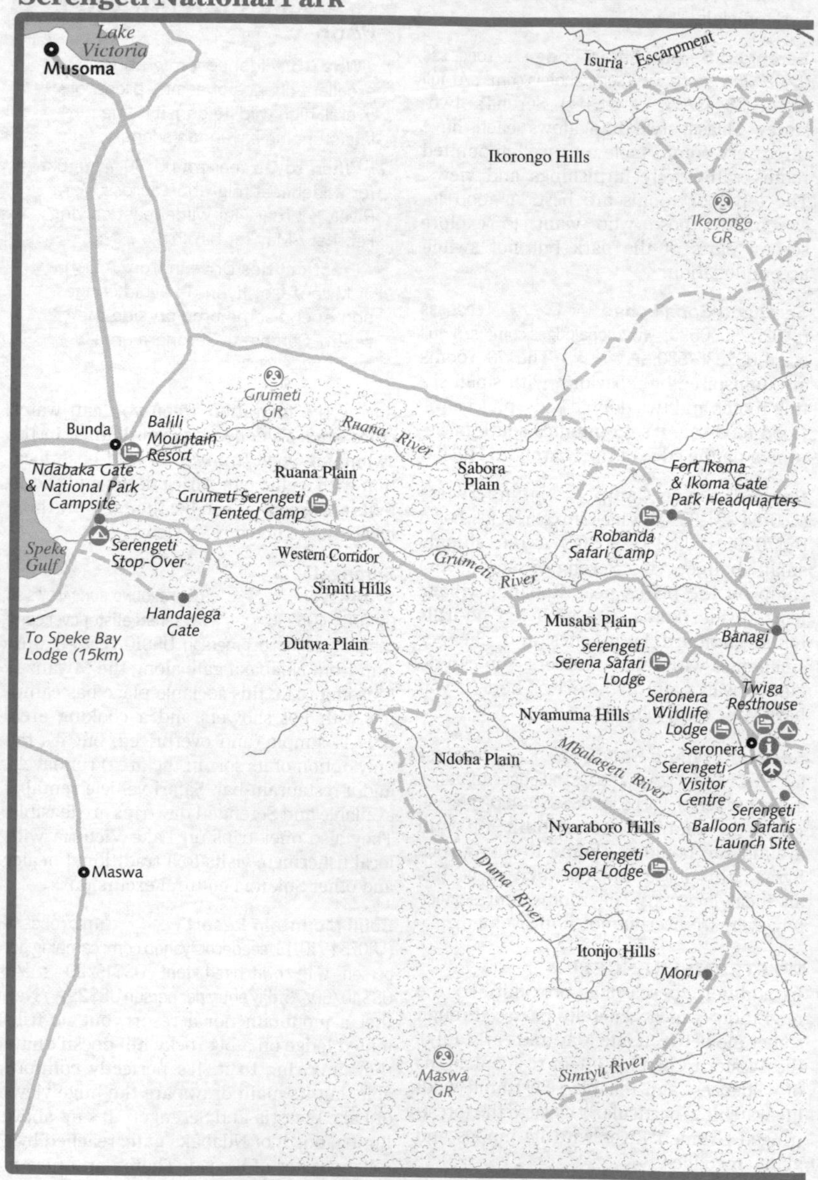

during August and September and comes down the eastern flank in November. Elephants concentrate in the area's acacia woodlands during the dry season. The Loliondo area, just outside the Serengeti's northeastern boundary, offers the chance for Maasai cultural activities, walking safaris, night drives and off-road drives.

Mbuzi Mawe TENTED CAMP **$$$**
(027-254 5555; www.serenahotels.com; s/d full board US$380/595; P@) A 16-tent camp built around a kopje, it's an excellent loca-

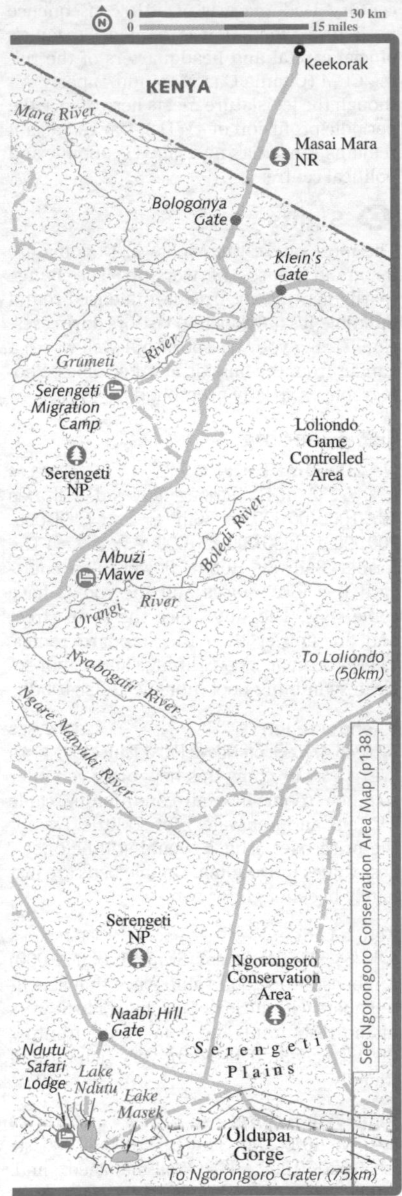

tion about 45km north of Seronera, convenient for both northern and Seronera wildlife drives. By northern Serengeti standards it's quite a simple spot, but it's also relatively good value.

Serengeti Migration Camp TENTED CAMP **$$$**
(027-250 0630; www.elewana.com; s/d full board US$1118/1490; P) One of the most highly regarded places in the Serengeti has 20 large tents with decks and a plush lounge around a kopje by the Grumeti River. Great views and front-row seats during the few weeks the migration passes through. Walks from the camp are possible.

MOBILE CAMPS

Mobile camps are a great idea, but something of a misnomer. They do move (though never when guests are in camp), following the wildebeest migration so as to try to always be in good wildlife watching territory. But with all the fancy amenities people expect on a luxury safari, relocating is a huge chore and most only move two or three times a year. They're perfect for some and too rustic (or, at least too rustic for the typically high prices) for others.

TOP CHOICE **Wayo Green Camp** CAMPGROUND, TENTED CAMP **$$$**
(0784-203000; www.wayoafrica.com; per person all-inclusive from US$285) These 'private mobile camps' combine the best aspects of both tented camps and budget camping safari and are the best way possible to get a deep bush experience in the Serengeti. They use 3m x 3m dome dents and actual mattresses and move from site to site every couple of days. Highly recommended.

Kirurumu Serengeti Camp TENTED CAMP **$$$**
(027-250 7011; www.kirurumu.net; per person full board US$400) A seven-tent camp from a company with a solid record of protecting the environment and working with local communities.

Information

Entry fees are US$50/10 per adult/child per 24-hour period. Leaving the park and re-entering (except at Naabi Hill gate) is currently allowed, though confirm this before your trip as the policy is under review.

The **Serengeti Visitor Centre** (0732-985761; serengeti_tourism@yahoo.com; 8am-5pm) at Seronera has an excellent self-guided walk through the Serengeti's history and ecosystems, and it's well worth spending time here before exploring the park. The gift shop here sells various booklets and maps, including the excellent MaCo map, and there's a coffee shop with snacks and cold drinks.

Getting There & Around

Air

Air Excel, Coastal Aviation, Regional Air and Safari Plus have daily flights from Arusha to the park's seven airstrips, including Seronera (US$150 per person one way) and Grumeti (US$225).

Bus

Although not ideal, shoestring travellers can do their wildlife watching through the window of the Arusha–Musoma buses that cross the park, but you'll need to pay US$100 in entrance fees for Serengeti and Ngorongoro. The buses stop at the staff village at Seronera, but you're not allowed to walk or hitchhike to the campsites or resthouses and the park has no vehicles for hire, so unless you've made some sort of prior arrangement for transportation it's nearly pointless to get off here.

Car

Access from Arusha is via the heavily used **Naabi Hill gate** (6am-6pm), 45km from Seronera. The Western Corridor's **Ndabaka gate** (6am-6pm), a 1½-hour drive from Mwanza, is 145km from Seronera. **Klein's gate** (6.30am-6pm) in the far northeast allows a loop trip combining Serengeti, Ngorongoro and Lake Natron, the latter just two to three hours from the park. The last entry at these gates is 4pm. **Bologonya gate** would be on the route to/from Kenya's Masai Mara National Reserve, but the border is closed and unlikely to open any time soon. Driving is not permitted in the park after 7pm, except in the visitor centre area where the cut-off is 9pm. Petrol is sold at Seronera.

CENTRAL TANZANIA

Although well off most tourist itineraries, central Tanzania has several attractions. Prime among these are the enigmatic Kolo Rock-Art Sites scattered across remote hills along the Rift Valley Escarpment. Dodoma, Tanzania's legislative capital, hosts interesting architecture and the region's best facilities.

Dodoma

POP 150,000

Arid Dodoma sits in not-so-splendid isolation in the geographic centre of the country, at a height of about 1100m. Although the town was located along the old caravan route connecting Lake Tanganyika and Central Africa with the sea, and the Central Line railway arrived just after the turn of the 20th century, Dodoma was of little consequence until 1973 when it was named Tanzania's official capital and headquarters of the ruling CCM (Chama Cha Mapinduzi) party. Although the legislature meets here (hence the periodic profusion of 4WDs), Dar es Salaam remains Tanzania's unrivalled economic and political centre.

Sights

The most interesting sights in Dodoma are its grand houses of worship. The Bunge (parliament) is an African-influenced round building. It's only open to visitors during sessions (bring your passport) but well worth a gander from the outside at other times. Photography is strictly prohibited.

Sleeping

New Dodoma Hotel HOTEL $$

(026-232 1641; Railway Rd; s/d with fan Tsh60,000/90,000, s with air-con Tsh90,000-200,000, d Tsh130,000-220,000; P) The former Railway Hotel's flower-filled courtyard is a lovely oasis and the rooms have some style. The suites face the main street and are noisier than the standard rooms. There's a gym, good dining, and a not-so-clean swimming pool (nonguests Tsh4000).

Kilondoma Inn GUESTHOUSE $

(0745-477399; off Ndovu Rd; d Tsh15,000; P) We're not sure how this new place can offer so much (rooms have air-conditioning, cable TV, fans and hot water) for so little. Even if the price rises a bit it would still be one of best values in Dodoma. Double beds are just barely big enough for two.

Kenya Lodge GUESTHOUSE $

(0764-538 6541; Seventh St; r Tsh15,000-22,000) A modest little good-value place that sets itself apart with little details, like fake flowers in the restaurant and a fake cliff fronting the terrace. Staff here are very helpful and friendly.

Kidia Vision Hotel HOTEL $

(0784-210766; 9th St; d Tsh25,000-40,000, ste Tsh60,000-70,000; P) Well-managed and, unlike most other hotels in its class, well-maintained, this is very solid choice at this level. Rooms are comfy and clean, though you don't get much extra as the price rises.

Yarabi Salama GUESTHOUSE $

(CDA St; d without bathroom Tsh8000) As good as any (and better than most) similarly priced guesthouses in the commercial centre.

Central Tanzania

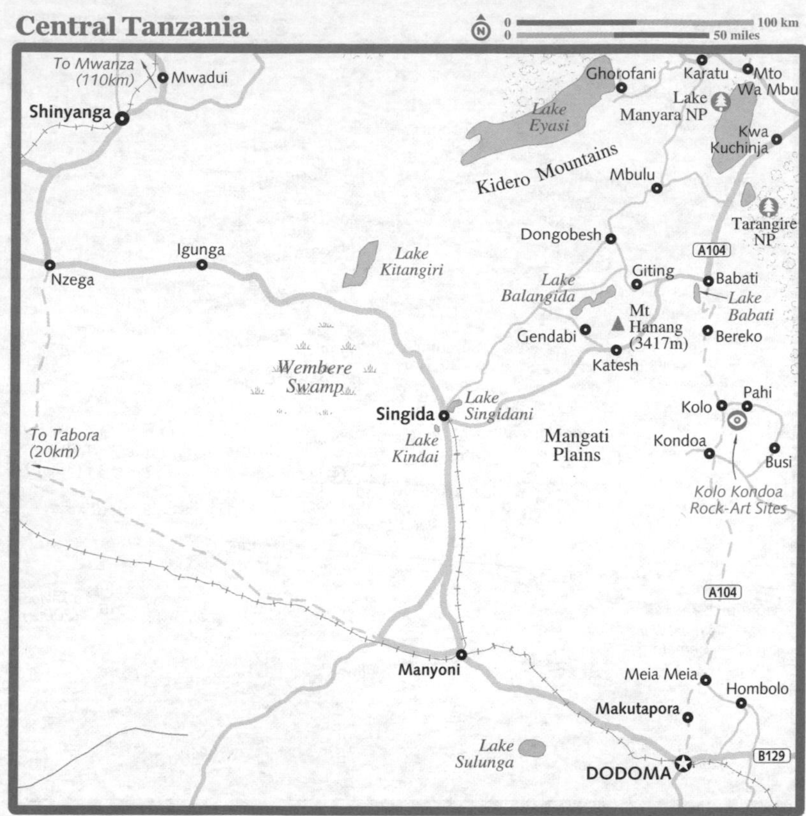

Eating

Leone l'Africano ITALIAN $$
(☎0788-629797; Mlimwa Rd; meals Tsh8500-12,000; ⌚lunch Sat & Sun, dinner Tue-Sun) Tasty Italian food, including one of Tanzania's better pizzas. Try local wines or play it safe with a European vintage. There's a playground and a 12-hole mini-golf course.

Aladdin's Cave SNACKS, EUROPEAN $
(CDA St; snacks from Tsh300, meals Tsh2000-8000; ⌚9.30am-1pm daily & 3.30-5.30pm Tue-Sat; ✍) Dodoma's version of an old-fashioned candy store and soda fountain. They also serve vegie burgers and pizzas.

New Dodoma Hotel INTERNATIONAL $$
(Railway Rd; meals Tsh5000-15,000; ⌚breakfast, lunch & dinner) The menu here goes global with choices such as pizza, fish and chips, dhal tadka and fajitas. The Indian and local dishes are the most reliable and the outdoor Barbeque Village grills up all kinds of meat at dinnertime. The Chinese-owned restaurant (meals Tsh4000 to Tsh12,000) within the hotel is a crapshoot since dishes can be both good and awful.

Rose's Café INDIAN $
(9th St; meals Tsh2000-6500; ⌚lunch Mon-Sat; ✍) Good, cheap Indian food, including a vegetarian *thali*.

Self-Catering

Yashna's (Nyerere St; ⌚9.30am-6.30pm Mon-Sat, 9.30am-2.30pm Sun), **Mama King** (Nyerere St; ⌚8.30am-9pm Mon-Sat, 2-9pm Sun), and **Two Sisters** (Hatibu St; ⌚9am-6pm Mon-Sat, 9am-1pm Sun) are three good minimarkets for self-caterers.

Information

Internet Access

Gracia Business Centre (Lindi St; per hr Tsh1500; ⌚7.30am-8pm Mon-Sat, 9am 6pm Sun) Fast connection. Can do Skype calls.

Dodoma

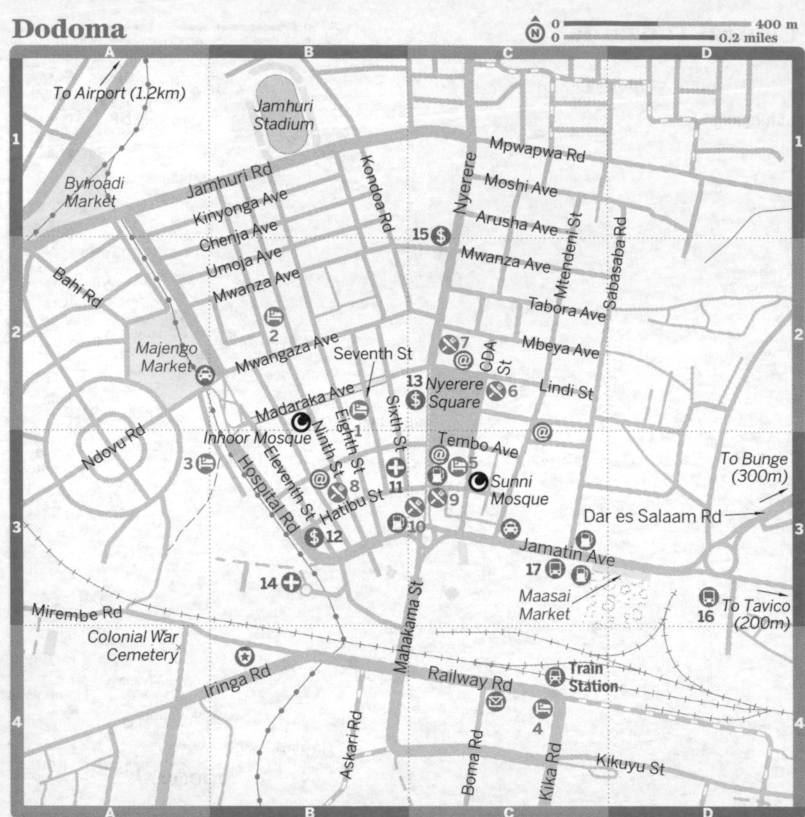

Internet Resources

Dodoma Guide (www.dodoma-guide.com)

Medical Services

Aga Khan Health Centre (☎026-232-1789; 6th St; ⌚8am-8pm Mon-Sat) First destination for illnesses. Has a good pharmacy.

Money

CRDB (Nyerere St) Has an ATM and changes dollars, Euro and pounds plus regional African currencies.

DTC Bureau de Change (Nyerere St) Next door to CRDB. Shorter lines, but not necessarily better rates.

ℹ Getting There & Away

Air

Coastal Aviation flies daily between Dodoma and Arusha (US$250). The airport is just north of the city centre; Tsh3000 in a taxi.

Bus

The best buses to Dar es Saalam (six to seven hours) are the 'full luxury' (meaning four-across seating and toilets; standard 'luxury' have no toilets) buses offered by Shabiby (Tsh20,000), who has its own terminal across the round-about from the main bus terminal. Other buses (Tsh10,000 to Tsh17,000) depart Dodoma frequently from 6am to 1pm plus buses that started their trip to Dar in Mwanza pass through in the afternoon and you can usually get a seat.

Buses to Mwanza (Tsh30,000, eight hours) via Singida (Tsh13,000, three hours) leave Dodoma between 6am and 7.30am and Mwanza-bound buses from Dar es Salaam pass through around midday. There are also three coastals to Singida leaving Dodoma at 8am, 10am and noon.

Buses to Kondoa (Tsh7000, three hours) depart 6am, 6.30am, 10.30am and noon: they use a section of the old Great North Rd connecting Cape Town and Cairo. If you take the morning

Dodoma

Sleeping

1	Kenya Lodge	B2
2	Kidia Vision Hotel	B2
3	Kilondoma Inn	A3
4	New Dodoma Hotel	C4
5	Yarabi Salama	C3

Eating

6	Aladdin's Cave	C2
7	Mama King	C2
	New Dodoma Hotel	(see 4)
8	Rose's Café	B3
9	Two Sisters	C3
10	Yashna's	C3

Information

11	Aga Khan Hospital	B3
12	Barclays Bank	B3
13	CRDB Bank & ATM	C2
14	General Hospital	B3
15	NBC & ATM	C1

Transport

16	Bus Stand	D3
17	Jamatini Dalla-Dalla Stand	C3

bus you *may* be able to get a connection to Babati the same day.

Buses direct to Arusha (Tsh28,000 to Tsh34,000, 11 to 12 hours) and Moshi (Tsh25,000 to Tsh32,000, 10 to 11 hours) all leave at 6am and take the route through Chalinze rather than the direct route to the north. Shabiby is the best.

Most buses to Iringa (Tsh22,000 to Tsh25,000, eight to nine hours) also travel via Chalinze, leaving Dodoma at 6 to 6.30am, but some take the direct route (Tsh15,000 to Tsh16,000, nine to 10 hours).

For local destinations, use the Jamatini dalla-dalla stand west of the bus stand.

Train

Dodoma lies on the Central Line between Kigoma and Dar es Salaam. See p214 for details. The spur line to Singida isn't operational.

Babati

The dusty market town of Babati, about 175km southwest of Arusha in a fertile spot along the edge of the Rift Valley Escarpment, is notable as a jumping-off point for climbs of Mt Hanang, 75km southwest.

Sleeping & Eating

Kahembe's Modern Guest House GUESTHOUSE $
(☎0784-397477; www.kahembeculturalsafaris.com; Sokoine Rd; s/d Tsh20,000/25,000) Home of Kahembe's Culture & Wildlife Safaris (p150), this friendly place just northwest of the bus stand has decent twin- and double-bedded rooms with TVs and reliable hot-water showers. It's 'Modern' not because of the building, but because of the full breakfast complete with sausages, cornflakes, fruit, toast and eggs included in the price.

White Rose Lodge GUESTHOUSE $
(☎0784-392577; Ziwani Rd; d Tsh20,000; P) A good-value spot set somewhat inconveniently (unless you're driving) off the Singida Rd south of town. Rooms are similar in standard to Kahembe's only much newer.

Ango Bar & Restaurant TANZANIAN $
(Arusha–Dodoma Rd; breakfast/lunch-dinner buffet Tsh5000/7000; ⊙breakfast, lunch & dinner) Behind a petrol station near the bus stand, this unexpectedly colourful place offers local fare, including always a few vegie dishes.

Information

There are internet connections at **Manyara Internet Café** (Mandela Rd; per hr Tsh2000; ⊙7.30am-7pm Mon-Sat & 10am-2pm Sun) and **Rainbow Communication** (Mandela Rd; per hr Tsh2000; ⊙8am-6.30pm Mon-Sat), two roads south of the bus station. **NBC** (Arusha–Dodoma Rd) bank nearby changes cash and travellers cheques and has an ATM.

Getting There & Away

Buses to/from Arusha (Tsh6000, three hours) are frequent. The first depart in both directions at 5.30am and the last leave at 4pm, though dalla-dallas go until 6pm. If you're heading to Mto wa Mbu, you can stop at Makuyuni and catch a connection. Going west the last vehicles out of Babati (which begin in Arusha) leave about 10am for Katesh (Tsh5000, 2½ hours), Singida (Tsh7000, four hours) and Mwanza (Tsh25,000 to Tsh30,000, 10 hours). Though you'll be sold a single ticket to Dodoma (Tsh14,000), there's no direct bus. You'll be shifted to another bus at Kondoa (Tsh7000, 3½ hours).

Kondoa Rock-Art Sites

The district of Kondoa, especially around the tiny village of Kolo, lies at the centre of one of the most impressive collections of

CULTURAL TOURISM IN CENTRAL TANZANIA

Babati and Kondoa districts are home to a colourful array of tribes, many of whom have changed their lifestyle little over the past century. The most famous (and most visited) tribe is the Barabaig, who still follow a traditional semi-nomadic lifestyle and are recognisable by the goatskin garments still worn daily by many women.

In Babati the reliable and knowledgeable **Kahembe's Culture & Wildlife Safaris** (☎0784-397477; www.kahembeculturalsafaris.com; Sokoine Rd) has been doing cultural tourism in the region since 1992. Besides village visits, it's the main operator organising Mt Hanang climbs. The Kondoa Rock-Art Sites are the bread and butter of the **Kondoa Irangi Cultural Tourism Program** (☎0784-948858; www.tanzaniaculturaltours.com) in Kondoa town, but director Moshi Changai also leads Barabaig, Sandawe and Irangi village visits by bicycle or car. Overnights in local homes are possible.

ancient rock art on the African continent; and one of the most overlooked attractions in Tanzania. If you can tolerate a bit of rugged travel, this is an intriguing and worthwhile detour.

Some experts maintain that the oldest paintings date back around 6000 years and were made by the Sandawe, who are distantly related linguistically to South Africa's San, a group also renowned for its rock art. Others are definitely more recent and were done from 800 up until probably 200 years ago by Bantu-speaking peoples who migrated into this area.

There are 186 known sites (and surely many more), of which only a portion have been properly documented. The most visited, though not the best, the Kolo sites (B1, B2 and B3), are 9km east of Kolo village and 4WD is required. You'll need to climb a steep hill at the end of the road to see them. The most varied, and thus best overall collection of paintings is at Thawi, about 15km northwest of Kolo and reachable only by 4WD. If you base yourself in Kolo or Kondoa you can comfortably see three of these places in a day, and all four if you really rush.

If you'll be in Arusha before visiting, stop by Warm Heart Art Gallery and talk with Seppo Hallavainio, director of the **Rock Art Project** (☎0754-672256; www.racctz.org), who has made it his mission to promote and protect the sites.

Sleeping

Amarula Campsite CAMPGROUND $

(☎0754-672256; www.racctz.org; camping with own/hired tent US$10/20) A venture of the Rock Art Project, this work in progress, 6km east of Kolo on the road to Pahi, has beautiful scenery and simple facilities. Rooms are planned.

New Planet GUESTHOUSE $

(☎0787-907915; s/d Tsh15,000/18,000; P) In Kondoa, about a five-minute walk north of the bus stand, this clean and quiet place is the best Kondoa has to offer. Rooms are fairly large and have fans and TV; buckets of hot water are available on request. Meals at the **restaurant** (Tsh2000-5000) hidden in the back are quite good and they plan to branch out into curries and pastas.

Information

The **Rock Art Project** (see p149) offers three-day trips out of Arusha from US$170 per person (in a group of four) that also include cultural activities in the village and **Kahembe's Culture & Wildlife Safaris** (p150; US$60 per person per day plus US$120 for transport) in Babati and the **Kondoa Irangi Cultural Tourism Program** (p150; US$60 per person, minimum two people) in Kondoa regularly bring people here.

It's also possible to do things yourself. Stop at the **Antiquities Department office** (☎0752-575096; ⏱7.30am-6pm) along Kolo's main road to arrange a permit (Tsh2500) and mandatory guide (free, but tips expected), some of whom speak English. Motorcycle hire can be arranged expensively through the Antiquities Department (Tsh20,000 just to the Kolo sites, for example) or with locals, or hire a vehicle in Kondoa, 25km south of Kolo, the nearest proper town to the rock art.

Kondoa has internet access, but no banking services for travellers. Catching a bus in Kondoa means you'll get a seat; wait for it to pass Kolo and you'll need to stand.

Getting There & Away

Kolo is 80km south of Babati. Buses to Kolo (Tsh6000, 3½ hours) depart Babati at 7am and 8.30am. From Arusha, Mtei and Dolphin buses to Kondoa, leaving at 6am, and Kilimanjaro and Ebenezer (they alternate departure days) buses to Busi leaving at 7.30am pass Kolo (Tsh11,500, 6½ hours). The last bus north from Kondoa leaves at 9am. There are only buses to Dodoma (Tsh7000, three hours) from Kondoa, not Kolo. They leave at 6am, 10am and 12.30pm.

It could be possible to visit as a day trip from Babati (or as a stop en route to Dodoma) using public transport if you're willing to hitchhike after visiting the Kolo sites; there are *usually* some trucks travelling this road in the afternoon.

LAKE VICTORIA

Tanzania's half of Africa's largest lake sees few visitors, but the region holds many attractions for those with a bent for the offbeat and a desire to immerse themselves in the rhythms of local life beyond the tourist trail. The cities of Musoma and Bukoba have a quiet waterside charm while most villagers on Ukerewe Island follow a subsistence lifestyle with little connection to the world beyond the shore.

Mwanza, Tanzania's second largest city, is appealing in its own way and it's the perfect launch pad for a Serengeti–Lake Natron-Ngorongoro loop. And adding the forest of idyllic Rubondo Island National Park, deep in the lake's southwest reaches, gives you a well-rounded safari experience.

Musoma

Little Musoma, capital of the Mara region, sits serenely on a Lake Victoria peninsula with both sunrise and sunset views over the water.

There are banks and internet cafes along and just off Mukendo Rd. The **Nyerere museum** (☎028-262 1338; www.museum.or.tz/nyerere.asp; adult/student Tsh6500/2,600; ⊙8am-

Lake Victoria

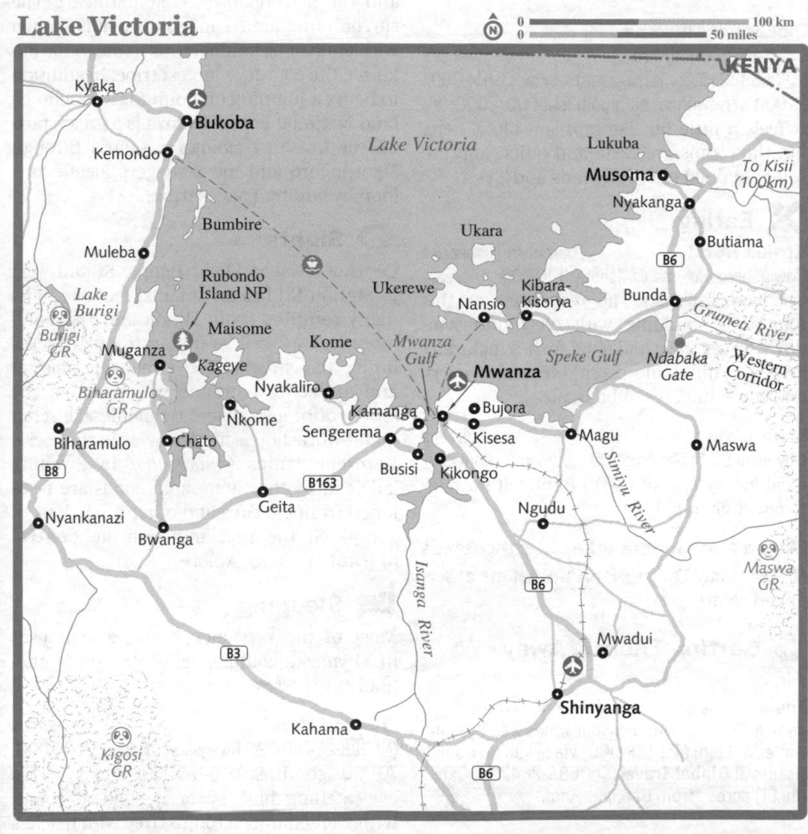

4pm), 45km southeast of Musoma in Butiama, documents the famous stateman's life.

Sleeping

Tembo Beach Hotel CAMPGROUND, GUESTHOUSE $
(☎028-262 2887; camping Tsh15,000, r Tsh45,000; P) With its new jacked-up prices, what used to be the best bargain in Musoma is now one of the worst, but the sunset-facing beachfront makes it worth considering…if you don't mind that noisy overland truck companies frequently camp here. Rooms (the ones upstairs have a loft bed) are clean and the restaurant prices (Tsh3000 to Tsh4000) are reasonable. Follow the signs north of town.

Matvilla Beach CAMPGROUND $
(per person Tsh10,000; P) Out at the tip of the peninsula, 1.5km from the centre, this is a gorgeous spot amid the rocks with hot showers; however, as the bar is the main business, it can be noisy at night.

Diocese of Musoma Conference Centre GUESTHOUSE $
(☎0688-124510; Kusaga Rd; s/tw Tsh14,000/16,000, s/tw without bathroom Tsh6000/8000; P) It feels a little bit like a prison block here, but the rooms are clean and quiet; and the self-contained ones have fans and TVs.

Eating

Afrilux Hotel TANZANIAN, EUROPEAN $
(Mwigobero Rd; meals Tsh5000-10,000; ⏰breakfast, lunch & dinner) The restaurant at this four-storey building with all round windows serves the usual hotel dishes including grilled tilapia (Nile perch), vegetable curry and something resembling pizza.

Mara Dishes BUFFET $
(Kivukani St; buffet Tsh5000; ⏰lunch & dinner) A local eatery east of CRDB Bank with a relatively large buffet.

Manga Mini Supermarket SELF-CATERING $
(Mukendo Rd) For stocking up before a Serengeti safari.

Getting There & Away

Air

The airport is a five-minute walk from the city centre. Precision Air flies four times weekly from Dar es Salaam (Tsh188,000) via Mwanza. Book tickets at **Global Travel** (☎0683-264294; Gandhi St) across from Barclays Bank.

Bus

The bus terminal is 6km out of town at Bweri, though booking offices remain in the town centre. Dalla-dallas (Tsh300, 20 minutes) go there frequently to/from the city centre and a taxi costs Tsh5000. Frequent buses connect Musoma and Mwanza (Tsh6000, three to four hours) via Bunda (Tsh3000, one hour) departing between 5.30am and 4pm. Mohammed Trans has good service and its morning bus departs from its ticket office east of CRDB bank. Between Coast Line, Kimotco and Manko there's a direct bus to Arusha (Tsh28,000, 11 to 12 hours) at 6am daily, passing through Serengeti National Park (using Ikoma gate) and Ngorongoro Conservation Area, but you'll need to pay $100 in total park fees to ride this route.

For transport to Kisii, Kenya, see p208.

Mwanza

POP 378,000

Mwanza is Tanzania's second-largest city, and the lake region's economic heart. The surrounding area – marked by hills strewn with enormous boulders – is home to the Sukuma, the country's largest tribe. In addition to being a jumping off point for Rubondo Island National Park, Mwanza is a great starting or finishing point for safaris through Ngorongoro and the Serengeti, ideally as a loop by adding Lake Natron.

Sights

Central Mwanza along Temple St and west to Station Rd has an Oriental feel due to its many **temples** (both Hindu and Sikh) and **mosques** as well as Indian trading houses lining the streets. The street-side market and ambience continue west through the **Makoroboi** area where the namesake scrap metal workshop is hidden away in the rocks. Kerosene lamps (*makoroboi* in Swahili), ladles and other household goods are fashioned from old cans and other trash. East of Temple St, the huge and confusing **central market** is fun to explore.

Sleeping

Most of the very inexpensive guesthouses in Mwanza's commercial centre are by-the-hour businesses.

Midland Hotel HOTEL $
(☎028-254 1509; Rwagasore Rd; r Tsh40,000-70,000, ste Tsh90,000-120,000; P❄📶) This eye-catching blue tower is solid all-round with well-equipped rooms (free wi-fi reaches

most), good service, a rooftop bar and a proper breakfast buffet. Best of all, they'll sometimes discount. There are no mosquito nets, but they spray daily. The only knock is that traffic noise drifts up to the rooms.

Treehouse B&B $$
(☎0756-682829; www.streetwise-africa.org/treehouse; s without bathroom US$30; s US$50-55, d US$55-60, 5-person family banda US$115; P) Ideal for socially conscious travellers, this homey place with spotless, comfortable rooms gives much of its earnings to support the affiliated Streetwise Africa charity. It's in the Isamilo area and though signposted, it's hard to find, so call ahead. Volunteer discounts available.

Isamilo Lodge HOTEL $$
(☎0756-771111; www.isamilolodge.com; r US$60-120; P❄@📶) This big complex with comfortable rooms is all about the views, though rooms are plenty comfortable. It's worth coming up for a meal or drink just for the scenery, but despite what their brochures claim, this isn't the spot where 'Speke first spied Lake Victoria in 1858'. They'll usually give travellers the lower resident rates.

Hotel Tilapia HOTEL $$
(☎028-250 0517; www.hoteltilapia.com; Capri Point; r US$90-140; P❄@📶🏊) The ever-popular Tilapia, on the city side of Capri Point, has a variety of rooms, most of which are dated but decent and look out at the lake. They also have smaller rooms on a historic boat. Nonguests (adult/child Tsh10,000/5000) can use the pool: bring your own towel.

Christmas Tree Hotel HOTEL $
(☎028-250 2001; off Karuta St; r Tsh16,000-18,000) The best hotel in the city centre in this price range (few others even come close), rooms are small but clean with good beds, TV and hot water. A few even squeeze out a lake view. Because it's in an alley it's quieter than other hotels in this neighbourhood.

Kishamapanda Guesthouse GUESTHOUSE $
(Uhuru St; s without bathroom Tsh8000, s/d Tsh10,000/12,000) This tidy little place down a tiny alley is one of the best cheapies in Mwanza; even the shared-bath rooms have ceiling fans and there are Western sit toilets.

Ryan's Bay HOTEL $$
(☎028-254 1702; www.ryansbay.com; Station Rd; s/d/ste US$90/120/180; P❄📶🏊) This new place with lake views has seized much of the holidaying miner and NGO worker business from the Tilapia. Though rooms are undeniably better, it's lacks the character of its competition.

Mwanza Yacht Club CAMPGROUND $
(☎0784-510441; Capri Point; per person Tsh10,000; P) Mwanza's stop on the overlander's trail, this has simple facilities but a great lakeside location and good food.

Tulale Guesthouse GUESTHOUSE $
(☎0782-464130; Shinyanga Rd; r Tsh15,000-20,000; P) This spic-and-span guesthouse directly across from Nyegezi bus station is a good choice for the night before a dawn departure.

Eating & Drinking

Kuleana Pizzeria INTERNATIONAL $
(Post St; meals Tsh2500-7500; ⏰breakfast, lunch & dinner; ✎) Simple good vegetarian meals (pizzas, omelettes, sandwiches and breads) and a good mix of locals and expats. The friendly owner feeds many street children.

Diners INDIAN, CHINESE $$
(Kenyatta Rd; meals Tsh5000-18,900; ⏰lunch & dinner; ❄✎) This odd, time-warp serves some of Mwanza's best Indian food, though Chinese decorations and menu items are hold-overs from its previous incarnation as Szechuan.

Yun Long CHINESE $$
(Nasser Dr; meals Tsh5000-17,000; ⏰lunch & dinner) The food is exceptionally ordinary (unless you can convince the Chinese chefs to cook you something authentic), but we love this place anyway because of its leafy lakeside garden overlooking Bismarck Rock.

Hotel Tilapia INTERNATIONAL $$
(Capri Point; meals Tsh8000-15,000; ⏰lunch & dinner; 📶) The hub of Mwanza's expat population has an attractive terrace overlooking the lake and a choice of everything from Japanese teppanyaki to Indian to continental. But give the pizzas a miss.

U-Turn SELF-CATERING $
(Nkrumah St) Mwanza's best stocked grocery.

Information

Internet Access

Karibu Corner (Kenyatta Rd; per hr Tsh1300; ⏰8am-7pm Mon-Sat, 10am-4pm Sun) Expensive, but fast.

Mwanza

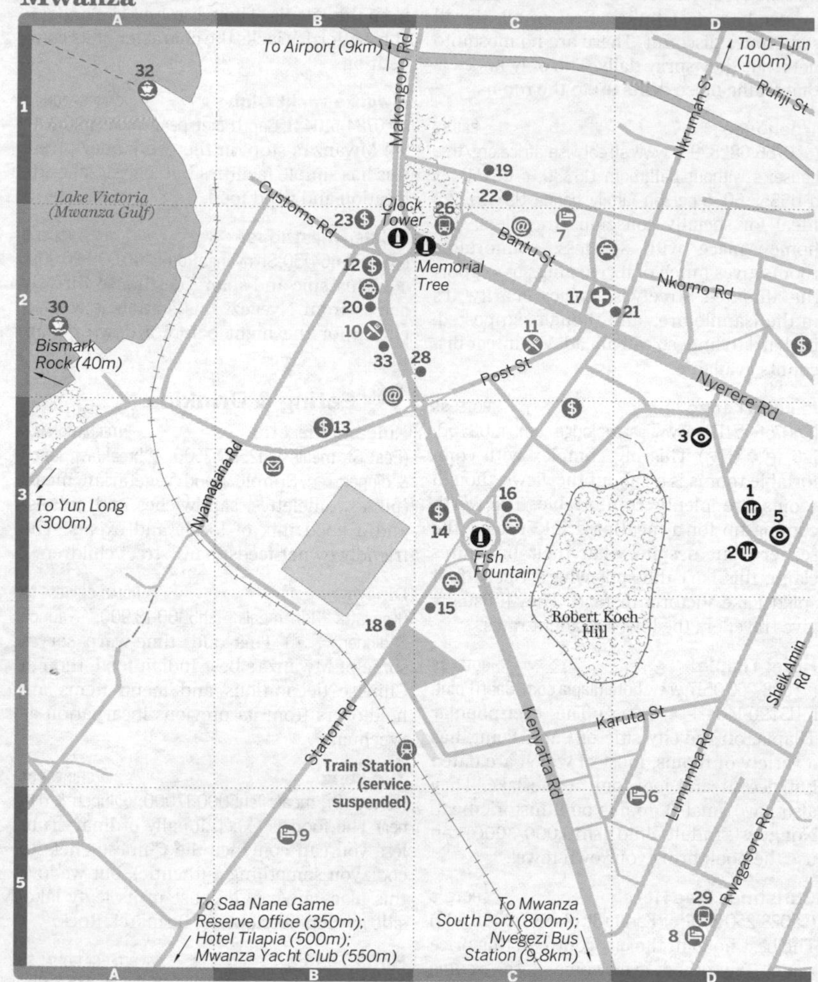

Internet Resources

Mwanza Guide (www.mwanza-guide.com)

Garage

Fortes Africa (☎028-250 0561; www.fortes-africa.com; Station Rd)

Medical Services

Aga Khan Health Centre (☎028-250 2474; Miti Mrefu St; ⏲24hr) For minor illnesses.

Bugando Hospital (Wurzburg Rd) The government hospital has a 24-hour casualty department.

Global Pharmacy (Bantu St; ⏲8am-10.30pm)

Money

All the major banks are here and most change cash.

DBK Bureau de Change (Post St) Inside Serengeti Services travel agency; the easiest place to change cash and best rate for travellers cheques.

Travel Agencies

The following hire 4WDs and can organise complete safaris to Serengeti and Rubondo Island national parks. None of Mwanza's operators are as on the ball as the best agencies in Arusha, but we're also unaware of any in town that will bla-

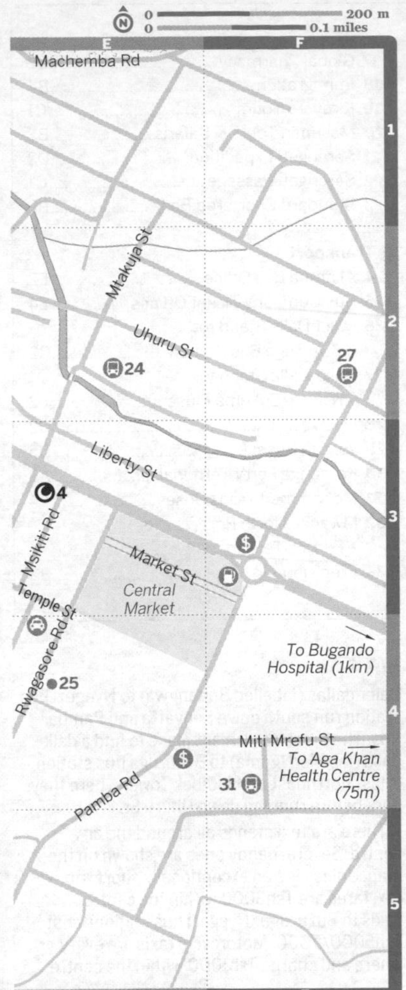

tantly rip you off. All-inclusive two-day Serengeti camping safaris can cost as little as US$600 for two people. It's not easy to meet other travellers in Mwanza, but you can ask the agencies whether they have other clients interested in combining groups to save money or try posting a notice at Kuleana Pizzeria.

Fortes Africa (☎028-250 0561; www.fortes-africa.com; Station Rd)

Fourways (☎0713 230620; www.fourwaystravel.net; Kenyatta Rd) Also books plane tickets.

Kiroyera Tours (☎0784-568276, www.kiroyeratours.com; Uhuru St) Bukoba's cultural tourism specialist (p160) now has a Mwanza branch.

Masumin Tours & Safaris (☎028-250 0192; www.masumintours.com; Kenyatta Rd) Also books plane tickets.

Serengeti Expedition (☎028-254 2222; www.serengetiexpedition.com; Nkrumah Rd) Usually the cheapest safari operator in Mwanza. Also books plane tickets.

Serengeti Passage (☎028-254 2065; www.serengeti-passage.com; Uhuru St) Another low-cost specialist.

Getting There & Away

Air

Precision Air (☎028-250 0819; www.precisionairtz.com; Kenyatta Rd) and **Fly540** (☎0767-540543; www.fly540.com; Kenyatta Rd) each fly three times daily to Dar es Salaam (Tsh161,000 one way). Precision also flies daily to/from Kilimanjaro International Airport (Tsh225,000), Bukoba (Tsh170,000) and Nairobi (Tsh238,000) and four days weekly to Kigoma (Tsh300,000). **Auric Air** (☎0783-233334; www.auricair.com; at the airport) also has a Bukoba flight.

Coastal Aviation (☎0875-502000; www.coastal.cc; at the airport) has a daily flight to Arusha airport (US$300) stopping at various Serengeti National Park airfields (Seronera US$180) on the way and also flies to Kigali (US$500).

Auric and Coastal both do charters.

Boat

Ferries connect Mwanza with Bukoba and Ukerewe Island. For details see p212 and p157 respectively.

Cargo boats to Uganda (p211) and Kenya (p210) depart from Mwanza South Port, about 1.5km south of the centre.

Bus

Nyegezi Bus Station, about 10km south of town, handles buses to all points east, south and west including Dar es Salaam (Tsh40,000, 14 hours). Mohammed Trans, departing for Dar at 6am and 8.30am, has good service (Bunda and Mombasa Raha have also been recommended) and their buses conveniently begin at their city centre ticket office before heading to the bus terminals. NBS and many other companies go to Tabora (Tsh14,000, six hours) during the morning.

Jordan has the best buses to Arusha (Tsh30,000, 12 hours). The buses leave their city centre office at 5am and the bus station at 6am and make their journey via Singida, as do all other Arusha-bound buses. Buses to Bukoba (Tsh20,000, six to seven hours), departing between 6am and 1pm, now mostly make use of

Mwanza

Sights

- **1** Hindu Temple D3
- **2** Hindu Temple D3
- **3** Makoroboi D3
- **4** Mosque E3
- **5** Sikh Temple D3

Sleeping

- **6** Christmas Tree Hotel D5
- **7** Kishamapanda Guesthouse C2
- **8** Midland Hotel D5
- **9** Ryan's Bay B5

Eating

- **10** Diners B2
- **11** Kuleana Pizzeria C2

Information

- **12** CRDB Bank B2
- **13** DBK Bureau de Change B3
- **14** Exim Bank C3
- **15** Fortes Africa C4
- **16** Fourways C3
- **17** Global Pharmacy C2
- **18** Immigration B4
- **19** Kiroyera Tours C1
- **20** Masumin Tours & Safaris B2
- **21** Serengeti Expedition D2
- **22** Serengeti Passage C1
- **23** Standard Chartered Bank B2

Transport

- **24** Akamba Bus Office E2
- **25** Bus Company Ticket Offices E4
- **26** Dalla-Dalla Stand for Buzuruga Bus Station C2
- **27** Dalla-Dalla Stand for Kisesa/Sukuma Museum F2
- **28** Fly540 .... C2
- **29** Jordan Buses D5
- **30** Kamanga Ferry Terminal A2
- **31** Mohammed Trans Buses F4
- **32** Mwanza North Port & Lake Ferries Terminal A1
- **33** Precision Air B2

the Busisi ferry, but if they're redirected to the Kamanga ferry in central Mwanza, you can meet them there.

Golden Inter-City is the best of four companies departing daily at 5.30am to Kigoma (Tsh25,000, 10 to 12 hours).

Buses for Musoma (Tsh6000, three to four hours, last bus 4pm) and other destinations along that road depart from **Buzuruga Bus Station** in Nyakato, 4km east of the centre.

There's no need to travel to the bus stations to buy tickets since numerous ticket agencies are stationed at the old city centre bus terminal (now a car park). They don't charge an official commission, but they will overcharge you if they can get away with it.

See p651 for travel details to Burundi, Kenya, Rwanda and Uganda.

Train

Mwanza is the terminus of a branch of the Central Line (p214), but service has been suspended.

Getting Around

To/From the Airport

Mwanza's airport is 10km north of town (Tsh10,000 in a taxi). Dalla-dallas to the airport (Tsh300) follow Kenyatta and Makongoro Rds.

Bus & Taxi

Dalla-dallas (labelled Buhongwa) to Nyegezi bus station run south down Kenyatta and Pamba Rds. The most convenient place to find a dalla-dalla (labelled Igoma) to Buzuruga bus station is just northeast of the Clock Tower where they park before running down Uhuru St.

There are taxi stands all around the city centre. Several handy ones are shown on the map. Unless it's an exceptionally short trip, taxi fares are Tsh3000 within the centre. Taxis to Buzuruga/Nyegezi bus stations cost Tsh5000/7000. Motorcycle taxis are everywhere and charge Tsh1000 within the centre.

Around Mwanza

SUKUMA MUSEUM

The **Sukuma Museum** (☎0756-376109; www.sukumamuseum.org; adult/student Tsh10,000/5000, camera/video Tsh1000/10,000; 🕗8am-6pm Mon-Sat, 10am-6pm Sun) in Bujora village is an open-air museum where, among other things, you'll see traditional Sukuma dwellings and the grass house of a traditional healer. Also on the grounds is the **royal drum pavilion**, built in the shape of a king's stool, holding a collection of royal drums that are still played at special events, and a **round church** with many traditional Sukuma stylings that was built in 1958 by David

Fumbuka Clement, the Québecois missionary priest who founded the museum.

Sleeping & Eating

The centre has no-frills **bandas** (per person Tsh5000) in the style of Sukuma traditional houses and a **campground** (per person Tsh5000). There's a little bar and meals are available with advance notice; or you can use the kitchen yourself.

Getting There & Away

Bujora is 18km east of Mwanza off the Musoma road. Take a dalla-dalla (Tsh500, 30 minutes) to Kisesa from Uhuru Rd north of the market in Mwanza. From Kisesa taxis/motorcycle taxis costs Tsh3000/1000. Or, walk a short way along the main road and turn left at the sign, following the small dirt road for 1.7km. A taxi from Mwanza, with waiting time, will cost Tsh45,000 to Tsh50,000.

En route from Mwanza, just past Igoma on the left-hand side of the road, is a graveyard for victims of the 1996 sinking of the Lake Victoria ferry MV *Bukoba*.

UKEREWE

With its simple lifestyle and rocky terrain broken by lake vistas and tiny patches of forest, Ukerewe Island, 50km north of Mwanza, makes an intriguing, offbeat diversion. Nansio, the main town, has no internationally linked ATMs. Shared taxis and dalla-dallas connect Ukerewe's few sizable villages and bikes can be hired at the bus stand.

La Bima Hotel (☎0732-515044; s Tsh12,000-15,000 tw Tsh18,000; Ⓟ) is Nansio's best lodging, despite cramped rooms (some with hot water) and peeling paint, this ok place. It's got the top restaurant too.

Getting There & Away

The passenger ferry MV *Clarius* sails daily from Mwanza North Port to Nansio (Tsh3600, 3½ hours) at 9am/10am weekdays/weekends; it returns at 2pm. Two other ferries (3rd-/1st-class/car Tsh4000/5000/7000, three hours) dock at Kirumba, north of Mwanza's centre near the giant Balimi ad. The MV *Nyehunge* departs Mwanza/Nansio at 9am/2pm and the MV *Samar III* departs Mwanza/Nansio at 2pm/8am.

It's also possible to reach Nansio from Bunda, a town on the Mwanza–Musoma road, which means that you can go from Mwanza to Ukerewe and then on towards Musoma or the Serengeti without backtracking. Via public transport, take an Mwanza–Musoma bus and disembark at Bunda. Here buses and sometimes dalla-dallas head to Nansio (Tsh4000, five to to six hours) daily at 10am and 1pm using the Kisorya ferry (passenger/car Tsh300/5000, 40 minutes), which crosses four times daily in each direction. In the reverse, vehicles to Bunda leave Nansio at 8am and 10am. After these buses depart there are no vehicles direct to Nansio, but you can take a dalla-dalla to Kisorya and catch another on the island. The last ferry to Ukerewe sails at 6.30pm. The last ferry leaving Ukerewe is at 5pm, but don't use it unless you have your own vehicle or are willing to try hitching part of the way to Bunda.

Rubondo Island National Park

Rubondo, alluring for its tranquillity and sublime lakeshore scenery, is one of Tanzania's best kept secrets. **Birdwatching**, brings the most visitors, but **walking safaris** (half-day walks US$10 per group), **bush camping** (adult/child US$50/5) and **sport fishing** per day (US$50) can also be rewarding. Elephants, giraffes, black and

CROSSING MWANZA GULF

Travelling west from Mwanza along the southern part of Lake Victoria entails crossing the Mwanza Gulf. There are two ferries, each with advantages.

The Kamanga ferry (passenger/vehicle Tsh800/6000) docks right in town. It departs Mwanza hourly between 7.30am and 6.30pm, except Sunday when departures are every two hours from 8am to 6pm. If you're travelling to Bukoba or anywhere along that highway, ask which ferry the bus will use; you may be able to save a trip to the bus station by boarding the bus here.

The government-run Busisi (aka Kigongo) ferry (passenger/vehicle Tsh300/8000), 30km south of Mwanza has the advantage of the road west being paved and it sails more often: every 30 minutes from 7am to 10pm. But, there are often delays since many trucks use this boat and also government officials sometimes call and tell the pilots to wait for them.

RUBONDO ISLAND NATIONAL PARK

» **Why Go** Tranquil setting and lovely lakeshore scenery; fine birding; chance to see sitatungas.

» **When to Go** June through early November.

» **Practicalities** Start from Bukoba or Mwanza, travel to the nearest port and continue by park boat. Alternatively, arrive by charter flight.

white colobus and chimpanzees were long ago introduced alongside the island's native hippo, bushbuck and sitatunga. Rubondo's chimps are not habituated, and even with concerted effort, there's little chance of spotting them. Though the beaches look inviting, there are enough crocodiles that swimming is prohibited.

Sleeping

Tanapa Campsite/ Bandas/Resthouse CAMPGROUND, BUNGALOWS **$$**
(camping per adult/child US$30/5, r per adult/child US$35/15) The nine total rooms facing the beach at Kageye on Rubondo's eastern shore are very good. Resthouse rooms are smaller (except for the VIP room) but have TVs. All rooms have electricity in the mornings and evenings and hot water all day. There are fully equipped kitchens for cooking, and staff can be hired to cook for you; a free meal for them should be payment enough. A tiny shop 10 minutes walk north of the *bandas* sells a few basics, like rice, eggs and potatoes and there's a cool little bar on the rocky shore right by the *bandas*.

Information

Park entry fees are US$20/5 per adult/child. Book accommodation and transportation through **park headquarters** (☎028-252 0720; rubondoisland@yahoo.co.uk). If the phones are down, staff at the Saa Nane/Tanapa office on Capri Point in Mwanza can help.

Getting There & Away

Air

Auric Air (☎0783-233334; www.auricair.com) will make a Rubondo (US$325 return) diversion on its Mwanza–Bukoba flights. This would require a two-night stay if flying return out of Mwanza since arrival would be in the late afternoon and departure in the early morning. A straight charter flight with Auric costs around US$3000.

Boat

There are two ways to reach Rubondo by boat (up to seven passengers); both should be arranged in advance. Because of a habit of scamming tourists, fishermen are now prohibited from delivering people to the island.

The park recommends using Kasenda, a small port about 5km from Muganza (Tsh1000 on a motorcycle taxi and Tsh3500 in a taxi), from where it's 20 to 30 minutes by boat to Rubondo Island and another 15 minutes by park vehicle to drive across the island to Kageye. This costs US$100 return per boat. Public transport to Muganza is fairly frequent; more so in the morning than the afternoon. All buses between Bukoba (Tsh10,000, two hours) and Mwanza (Tsh10,000, four hours) pass through as do Bukoba to Dar es Salaam buses. Dalla-dallas run to nearer destinations such as Biharamulo (Tsh5000, two hours).

The second option is Nkome, at the end of a rough road north of Geita, where the boat costs US$185 to Kageye and takes about one hour. Expect choppy water on this crossing. The warden's office, where you get the boat is outside Nkome, a Tsh500/2000 *boda-*/taxi-ride from where the final dalla-dalla stop. Two buses go direct from Mwanza to Nkome (Tsh5000, four to five hours). They leave Mwanza at 10am, but you can meet them at the Kamanga ferry. Alternatively, take a bus to Geita where dalla-dallas to Nkome (Tsh3500, two hours) are fairly frequent.

Bukoba

Bukoba is a bustling town with an attractive waterside setting and amenable small-town feel. The surrounding Kagera region is home of the Haya people, known for their powerful kingdoms.

Sleeping & Eating

TOP CHOICE **Balamaga Bed & Breakfast** B&B **$**
(☎0789-757289; www.balamagabb.com; s/d Tsh45,000/75,000, without bathroom Tsh40,000/70,000; P ᯤ) High up in the hills overlooking the lake this homey great-value place has four spacious, comfortable rooms (two self-contained and two sharing a bathroom) and a garden so gorgeous and full of birds you'll forget you're in Bukoba. Dinner must be ordered long in advance.

Bukoba

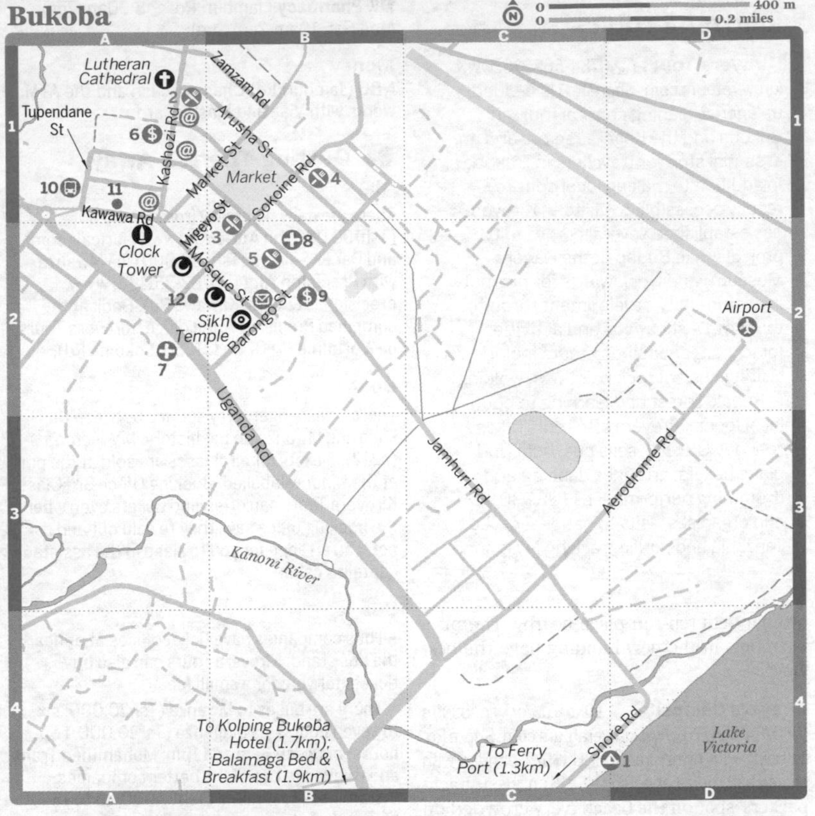

Bukoba

Sleeping
- 1 Kiroyera Campsite ... D4

Eating
- 2 Dolly's Cash & Carry ... A1
- 3 Fido Dido ... B2
- 4 Hussein Shop ... B1
- 5 New Rose Café ... B2

Information
- 6 CRDB Bank ... A1
- 7 Kagera Regional Hospital ... A2
- Kiroyera Tours ... (see 1)
- 8 MK Pharmacy ... B2
- 9 NBC ... B2

Transport
- 10 Bus Station ... A1
- 11 Precision Air ... A1
- 12 Worldlink ... A2

Bukoba Co-op Hotel HOTEL $
(☎028-222 1251; Shore Rd; s Tsh25,000 d Tsh30,000-40,000; P) The former Yaasila Top has slightly aged, but decent enough rooms with TVs, ceiling fans and mini-fridge, but the best feature is its location at the end of Bukoba Beach. Rooms on the second floor have limited lake views and the restaurant is one of Bukoba's best.

ELCT Bukoba Hotel HOTEL $
(☎0754-415404; www.elctbukobahotel.com; Aerodrome Rd; s/tw/ste Tsh30,000/35,000/50,000; P@) This Lutheran conference centre between the lake and the city centre is a good, long-standing place with comfortable rooms and pleasant grounds. The sign promises 'Tranquillity' and the hotel delivers.

Kolping Bukoba Hotel HOTEL $
(☎028-222 1236; r Tsh35,000-55,000, ste Tsh75,000; P@) If Balamaga is full, you can enjoy similar lake views from this otherwise

KIROYERA TOURS

Kiroyera Tours (☎0784-568276; www.kiroyeratours.com; Shore Rd) is a clued-up agency leading cultural tours in Bukoba and the Kagera region, and an essential stop for travellers in Bukoba. In addition to making local culture readily accessible to visitors, Kiroyera has established several community projects (like Budap at the Kagera Museum) and won awards for promoting community development through tourism. Destinations and activities for its half- and full-day tours include visiting ancient rock paintings, walking in Rubale Forest and learning to cook local foods. Kiroyera also rents bikes (per day US$10); sells bus, boat and plane tickets; arranges dancing and drumming performances (US$80); and organises visits to national parks in Tanzania and gorilla tracking in Uganda.

ordinary church-run place nearby. The pricier rooms in the new building have the best views.

Kiroyera Campsite BUNGALOW, CAMPGROUND **$**
(☎0784-568276; www.kiroyeratours.com; Shore Rd; camping with own/hired tent US$5/7, bandas with shared bathroom per person US$15) A great backpackers' spot on the beach (very crowded on weekends) with a simple restaurant and the most original rooms in Tanzania: three genuine Haya *msonge* (grass huts) with beds and electricity. It's expensive, but a fantastic idea.

New Rose Café TANZANIAN **$**
(Jamhuri Rd; meals Tsh2000-3000; ⏲breakfast, lunch & dinner Mon-Sat) An unassuming Bukoba institution for local meals and snacks.

Self-Catering

For Western grocery goods try **Fido Dido** (Jamhuri Rd), **Dolly's Cash & Carry** (Kashozi Rd) and the smaller but cheaper **Hussein Shop** (Arusha St).

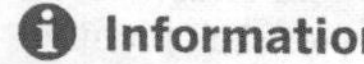

Information

Internet Access

4 Ways (Kashozi Rd; per hr Tsh1000; ⏲7am-6pm Mon-Sat, 10am-6pm Sun) In the little alley.

Medical Services

Kagera Regional Hospital (Uganda Rd)

MK Pharmacy (Jamhuri Rd; ⏲8.30am-7pm Mon-Sat, 10am-2pm Sun)

Money

NBC (Jamhuri Rd) Changes cash and the ATM works with Visa and MasterCard.

Getting There & Away

Air

There are daily flights to/from Mwanza (Tsh130,000) on **Auric Air** (www.auricair.com) and Dar es Salaam (Tsh289,000) via Mwanza with **Precision Air** (☎0782-351136; www.precisionairtz.com; Kawawa Rd). Book at the combined Precision-Auric office, Kiroyera Tours or **Worldlink** (☎0717-331666; Sokoine Rd).

Boat

There's passenger-ferry service between Bukoba and Mwanza on the historic MV *Victoria* (p212). Tickets for all classes are sold at the port at the window labelled 'Booking Office 3rd Class'. Kiroyera Tours can often find tickets even when the booking office says they're sold out and if not, can arrange for you to sleep in the assistant captain's cabin.

Bus

All bus companies have ticket offices at or near the bus stand. Kiroyera Tours can also buy tickets for you; for a small fee.

There are buses to Mwanza (Tsh20,000, six to seven hours) via Muganza (Tsh10,000, two hours) between 6am and 1pm; Mohammed Trans and Bunda are two of the better companies. Visram goes to Kigoma (Tsh27,000, 13 to 15 hours) three times a week at 6am; but when the road paving is finished service should increase to daily. All Dar es Salaam (Tsh52,000 to Tsh60,000, 21 hours) buses leave at or before 6am. The route goes through Muganza, Kahama, Singida and Dodoma and some buses continue to Dar in a single trip, including Mohammed Trans and Sumry, the two best companies, while others overnight in Morogoro to avoid reaching Dar in the wee hours. See p209 for details of buses to Uganda.

WESTERN TANZANIA

It's wildlife watching that brings most people to remote, rugged Western Tanzania: Gombe, Jane Goodall's former stomping grounds, and Mahale Mountains National Parks are two of the world's best places for chimpanzee encounters, while the vast floodplains of rarely visited Katavi National Park offer an almost primeval safari experience.

Western Tanzania

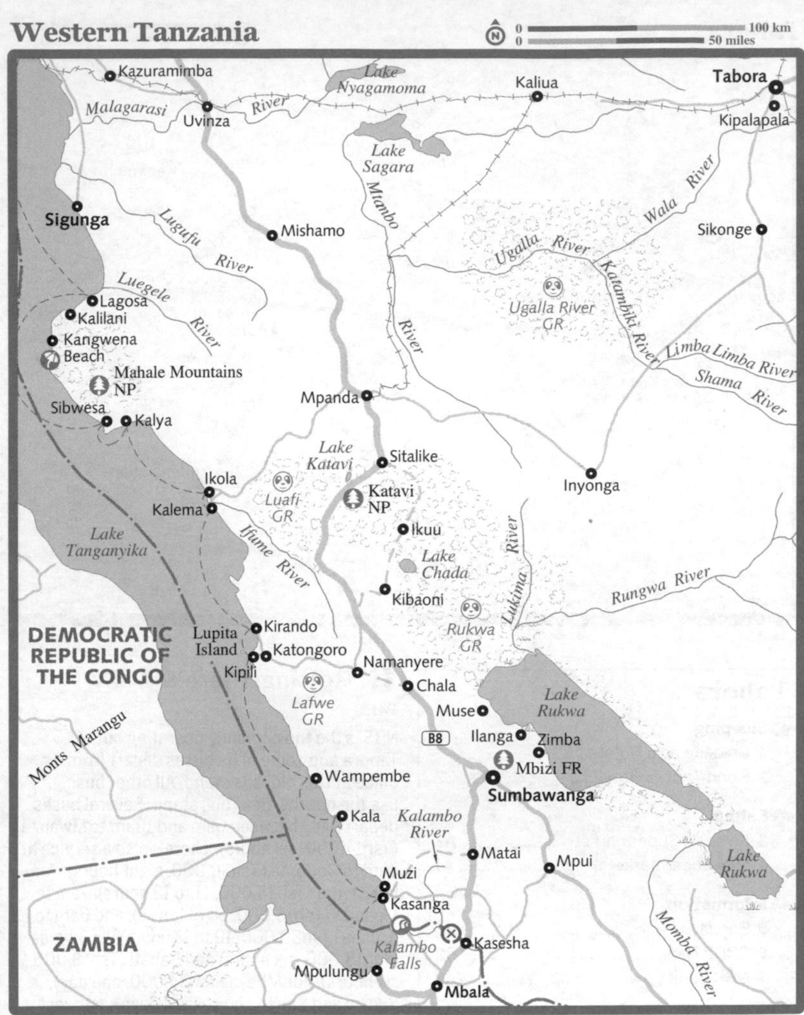

Tabora

Leafy Tabora was once the most important trading centre along the old caravan route connecting Lake Tanganyika with Bagamoyo and the sea. Today, it's primarily of interest to history buffs and rail fans, who'll have to wait here if taking a branch line to Mpanda or, assuming service resumes, Mwanza.

Sleeping & Eating

Orion Tabora Hotel HISTORIC HOTEL $
(026-260 4369; oriontbrhotel@yahoo.com; Station Rd; s/d Tsh50,000/65,000, ste s Tsh80,000-125,000, ste d Tsh95,000-150,000; P) The old railway hotel, originally built in 1914 by a German baron as a hunting lodge, has been nicely restored and provides an unexpected respite for anyone travelling in the region. There's also a good restaurant and a well-stocked bar. It's rather loud Friday to Sunday when the live band plays in the outdoor bar. Camping is allowed, but you'll have to negotiate a price with the manager.

Golden Eagle Hotel GUESTHOUSE $
(026-260 4623; Market St; tw without bathroom Tsh10,000, d Tsh10,000-20,000; P) Thanks to the friendly owner (plus the central location

Tabora

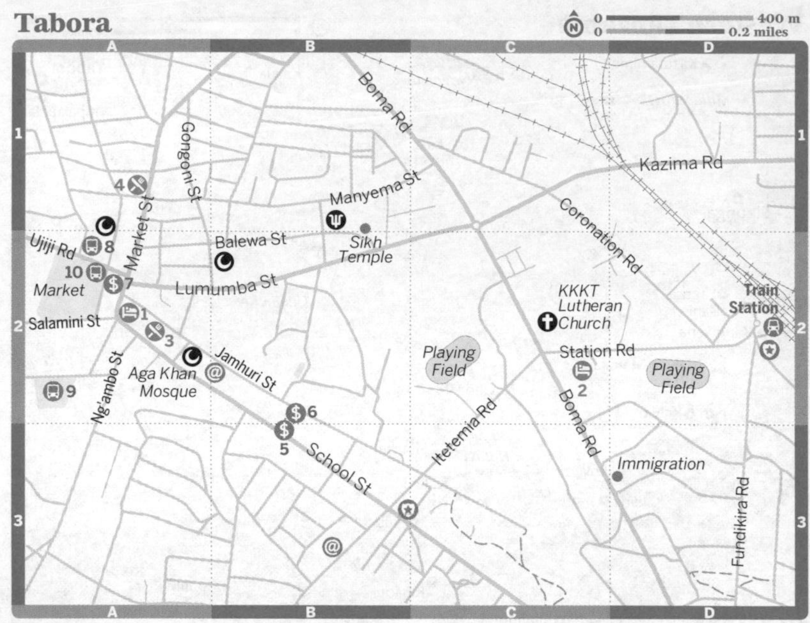

Tabora

Sleeping

1 Golden Eagle Hotel ... A2
2 Orion Tabora Hotel ... C2

Eating

3 Kaidee's Supermarket ... A2
4 Mini Supermarket ... A1

Information

5 Barclays Bank ... B3
6 CRDB Bank ... B2
7 NBC Bank ... A2

Transport

8 NBS Office ... A2
9 New Bus Stand ... A2
10 Old Bus Stand ... A2

and good, cheap restaurant), this 1st-storey place is the most traveller friendly spot in town. Rooms are old though tidy and have TVs, hot water and ceiling fans.

Self-Catering

Self-caterers can choose between the unsigned **Kaidee's Supermarket** (Jamhuri St) in the large brown and white building and the unnamed **mini supermarket** (Market St).

Getting There & Away

Bus

NBS is the top company operating out of Tabora and some of its buses depart from its office at the 'old' bus stand. All other buses use the nearby 'new' bus stand. Several buses depart daily between 6am and 10am to Mwanza (Tsh14,000, six hours). There's also a service at 6am to Dodoma (Tsh30,000, eight hours), 7am to Kigoma (Tsh25,000, 11 to 12 hours), 7am to Mpanda (Tsh18,000, eight hours), and 6am to Arusha (Tsh30,000, 10 to 11 hours) via Singida (Tsh18,000, six hours) and Babati (Tsh18,000, six hours). For Mbeya (Tsh34,000, one day), Sumry and Sabena go several days each week.

Train

See p214 for Central Line fare and schedule information.

Kigoma

The regional capital and only large Tanzanian port on Lake Tanganyika is a scrappy but agreeable town. It's also the end of the line of the Central Line train and a starting point for the MV *Liemba* and visits to Gombe National Park.

Sleeping & Eating

Aqua Lodge GUESTHOUSE $
(☎0764-980788; Katonga Rd; s/d Tsh10,000/15,000; P wi-fi) A fairly basic place now owned by the Catholic order Brothers of Charity. With large clean rooms (some have fans) on the beach, each with a screened porch and cheap wi-fi access, this is Kigoma's best value offering. There's no sign: it's across from the Tanesco generator. There are also no restaurants on site or nearby.

Kigoma Hilltop Hotel HOTEL $$
(☎028-280 4437; www.mbalimbali.com; s/d from US$90/110, ste US$150; P) The double and twin cottages here (half of which just got a thorough renovation) sit atop an escarpment overlooking the lake within a large walled compound roamed by zebra. Rooms have all the mod-cons they should at this price and the pool (nonguests Tsh10,000) is very large. Snorkelling, jet-skiing and fishing trips are available.

Poyongo Lodge GUESTHOUSE $
(Ujiji Rd; r Tsh 15,000, without bathroom Tsh10,000-12,000; P) By virtue of being one of the newest hotels in the Mwanga neighbourhood (convenient to the bus stand) Poyongo is one of the best.

Sun City TANZANIAN $
(Lumumba St; Tsh2500-4000; breakfast, lunch & dinner) A clean and almost artistic spot for *wali maharagwe* (rice and beans) and other local meals. There's also chicken *biryani* on Sunday.

There are several small shops around the market. **Khalfan** (Mlole Rd), **Supermarket** (off Mlole Rd) and **Kigoma Bakery** (Lumumba St) sell expensive imported goods.

Information

Consulates

Burundi (☎028-280 2865; 9am-3pm Mon-Fri)

Congo (Bangwe Rd; 9am-4pm Mon-Fri)

Immigration there are immigration offices at Ami Port and Kibirizi.

Internet Access

Baby Come & Call (Lumumba St; per hr Tsh2000; 8am-6pm Mon-Sat)

Mpenda Internet Café (off Mlole Rd; per hr Tsh1500; 9am-8pm Mon-Sat)

Medical Services

Kigoma International Health Clinic (☎0784-591995; Ujiji Rd; 24hr) For minor medical issues. It's 1km beyond Bera petrol station.

Mamboleo Pharmacy (Lumumba St; 8am-6pm Mon-Sat, 10.30am-2pm Sun)

Money

Both banks' ATMs accept MasterCard and Visa.

CRDB (Lumumba St) Changes dollars, Euros and pounds.

NBC (Lumumba St)

Tourist Information & Travel Agencies

Gombe/Mahale Visitors Information Centre (☎028-280 4009; gonapachimps@yahoo.com; Tanapa Rd; 9am-4pm) The staff know plenty about Gombe, but were very misinformed about Mahale. It's signposted off Ujiji Rd near the top of the hill: turn left at the T-junction.

Maji Makubwa (☎0755-662129; www.majimakubwa.com) For boat rental and fishing or scuba trips. Based at Aqua Lodge.

Mbali Mbali (☎028-280 4437; www.mbalimbali.com) Western Tanzania-focussed safari operation based at Kigoma Hilltop Hotel. They do boat and air charters.

Getting There & Away

Air

Precision Air (www.precisionairtz.com) flies daily to Dar es Salaam via Mwanza while **Air Africa International** (www.airafricainternational.com) flies direct on Monday, Wednesday and Friday. Both charge around Tsh300,000 one-way. Air travel to Kigoma is in a constant state of flux, so expect this information to change.

Global Travel Services (☎0759-896711; Lumumba St) Sells tickets for most airlines in Kigoma and elsewhere.

The airport is about 5km east of the town centre. A taxi costs Tsh5000.

Boat

FERRIES

For scheduling and price information for the MV *Liemba* between Kigoma and Mpulungu (Zambia) via Lagosa (for Mahale Mountains National Park) and other lake-shore towns, see p211. It departs from the Passenger Terminal, north of the Lake Tanganyika Hotel.

Cargo ships to Burundi and the DRC, which also take passengers, depart from Ami Port near the train station. See p210 for details.

LAKE TAXIS

Lake taxis are small, wooden motorised boats, piled high with people and produce that connect villages along the entire Tanzanian lakeshore. They're inexpensive, but offer no toilets or other

Kigoma

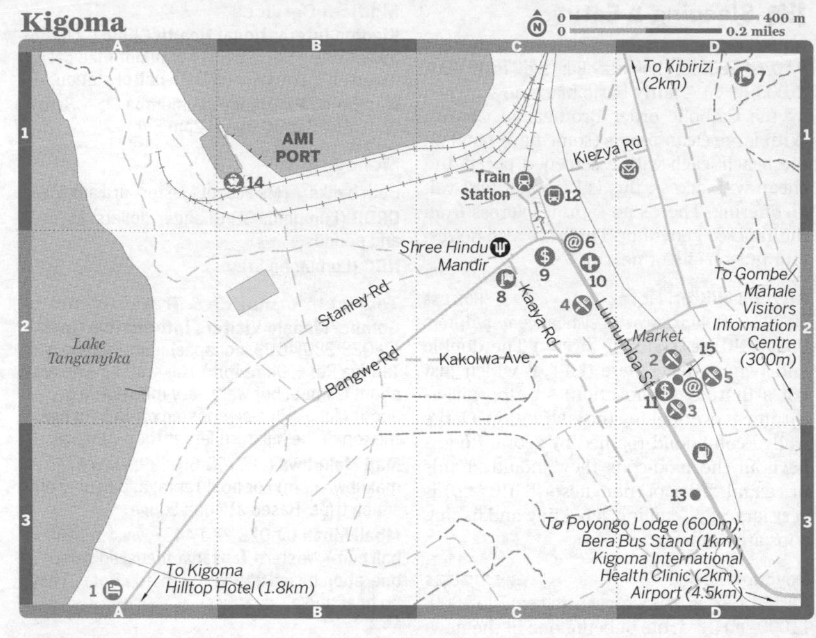

Kigoma

Sleeping
1 Aqua Lodge A3

Eating
2 Khalfan D2
3 Kigoma Bakery D2
4 Sun City C2
5 Supermarket D2

Information
6 Baby Come & Call C2
7 Burundi Consulate D1
8 Congo (DRC) Consulate C2
9 CRDB Bank & ATM C2
Maji Makubwa .... (see 1)
10 Mamboleo Pharmacy C2
11 NBC & ATM D2

Transport
12 Dalla-Dalla Stand C1
13 Global Travel Services D3
14 Passenger Terminal/MV Liemba ticket office B1
15 Precision Air D2

creature comforts, little if any shade, and can be dangerous when the lake get rough. Nights are very cold. Lake taxis going north depart Kibirizi. village, 2km north of Kigoma; you can walk here following the railway tracks or the road around the bay. Boats to the south, leave from Ujiji.

Bus

All buses depart from the streets behind the unsigned Bera petrol station. (Coming from Kigoma, look for the large, white petrol station with an NBC ATM.) But ticket offices are scattered around the Mwanga area just to the west.

There are four early morning buses daily to Mwanza (Tsh25,000, 10 to 12 hours) via Nyankanazi (Tsh20,000, seven hours); Golden Inter-City (aka Wenying) has the best service. Visram has three buses weekly to Bukoba (Tsh27,000, 13 to 15 hours) via Biharamulo (Tsh22,000, nine hours) departing at 5am. On other days you could take a Mwanza bus to Nyakanazi and continue in stages to Bukoba using shared taxis and dalla-dallas via Biharamulo and Muleba. NBS and Saratoga travel to Tabora (Tsh25,000, 11 to 12 hours) while NBS and Adventure swap days to Mpanda (Tsh20,000, eight to 10 hours). Buses to both depart at 6am and pass through Uvinza (Tsh5000, four hours). For travel to Burundi see p207.

Train

For schedule and price information on the Central Line train from Dar es Salaam, Dodoma or Tabora see p214.

Getting Around

Dalla-dallas (Tsh300) park in front of the train station and run along the main roads to Bera bus stand, Kibirizi, Katonga and Ujiji. Taxis between the town centre and Bera bus stand or Kibirizi charge Tsh2000 to Tsh3000. Don't pay more than Tsh1000 for a motorcycle taxi anywhere within the city.

Gombe National Park

With an area of only 52 sq km, Gombe is Tanzania's smallest national park, but its connection to Jane Goodall has given it world renown. Gombe's 100-plus chimps are well habituated and though it can be difficult, sweaty work traversing steep hills and valleys, if you head out early in the morning sightings are nearly guaranteed.

Sleeping & Eating

Tanapa Resthouse GUESTHOUSE **$**

(per person US$20) Next to the visitor centre at Kasekela this quite comfortable place has six simple rooms with electricity during morning and evening. Two overflow facilities have rooms of lesser quality and toilets out back. Camping costs the same as the rooms. Due to some very aggressive baboons, campers must eat and store food inside the kitchen. The restaurant's prices are high (breakfast/lunch/dinner US$10/15/15) but you can bring your own food and use the kitchen for free. Cold drinks are sold at more reasonable prices.

Information

Entry fees are US$100/20 adult/child per 24 hours. If you arrive late in the afternoon, park officials generously don't start the clock on your visit until the following morning, which means that for a two-night stay and one day of chimp tracking, you'll only be charged one 24-hour entry; if you leave for Kigoma early in the morning. While this policy has been in place for some time, it's always possible it will change, so confirm before you go. Children under 16 are not permitted to enter the forest, though they can stay at the resthouse.

All tourism activities are organised and paid for at Kasekela, on the beach near the centre of the park, and this is where lake taxis drop you.

GOMBE NATIONAL PARK

» **Why Go** Up-close encounters with chimpanzees.

» **When to Go** Year-round; June through October are the easiest (driest) months for chimpanzee tracking.

» **Practicalities** The only way here is by boat.

Getting There & Away

Gombe is 16km north of Kigoma, and the only way there is by boat. Tanapa boats travel to Kigoma three or four times per week and if they have space available you can ride for free. Inquire at park office in Kigoma.

At least one lake taxi (see p163) to the park (Tsh4000, 2½ to three hours) departs from Kibirizi Monday to Saturday around 2pm. Returning, it passes Kasekela as early as 7.30am.

You can also hire boats at Kibirizi; but don't believe the owners who tell you there are no lake taxis in an effort to get business. Hiring here requires hard bargaining, but the price will be cheaper than any of the charter options below. You may have to pay an advance for petrol, but don't pay the full amount until you've arrived back in Kigoma.

It's safer and more comfortable (in part because there will be a sun shade) to arrange a charter with one of the established companies. **Maji Makubwa** (p163) is the cheapest option with its little boat (holding three to four people, who will likely get wet) costing US$150 day-return and a regular boat costing US$250. The overnight charge is US$20/night. Other options are **Mkuzi Hotel** (☎0755-914231; US$300, no overnight charge) at Kibirizi, Lake Tanganyika Hotel (US$400, US$50 per night overnight charge) in Kigoma and Mbali Mbali (US$655, no overnight charge) in Kigoma. These boats take one-and-a-half to two hours. Mbali Mbali's speedboat (US$650) makes the trip in 45 minutes.

With a chartered boat day trips are possible, but leave very early because late starts reduce your chances of meeting the chimps.

Mahale Mountains National Park

It's difficult to imagine a more idyllic combination: clear, blue waters and white-sand beaches backed by lushly forested mountains soaring straight out of Lake Tanganyika and some of the continent's most intriguing wildlife watching. Like Gombe, Mahale is most notable as a chimpanzee sanctuary, and there are about 1700 of our primate relatives residing in and around the park, with leopard, blue duiker, black-and-white colobus, giant pangolin and many Rift Valley bird species not found elsewhere in Tanzania keeping them company. There are also hippo, crocs and otter in the lake and lions, elephants, buffaloes and giraffes roaming the savannah of the currently off-limits eastern half.

There are no roads in Mahale; walking and boating along the shoreline are the only ways to get around.

Sleeping

Mango Tree Bandas BUNGALOW **$$**
(per person US$30) Basic but quite decent park-run double *bandas* set about 100m in from the shore. While they lack the lake views of the private camps, their position in the forest means the night sounds are wonderful. No drinks are sold and you should bring your own food to cook in the kitchen, but usually you can buy expensive local meals from the staff.

Kungwe Beach Lodge TENTED CAMP **$$$**
(0713-620154; www.mbalimbali.com; per person all-inclusive except drinks US$550; mid-May–mid-Feb;) A lovely place with 10 spacious and widely spaced double tents and a comfy dining area-lounge. The price includes chimp tracking.

Information

Entry fees are US$80/30 per adult/child years. Children under seven years aren't permitted to enter the forest. Guide fees are US$20 per group (up to six people). Porters cost US$15 per day. Park headquarters, where all fees are paid, are at Bilenge in the park's northwestern corner, about 10 minutes by boat south of the airstrip and 20 minutes north of Kasiha, site of the park's *bandas* and guides' residences. As there's no phone service in the park, all advance arrangements are done online at sokwe@mahale.org or www.mahalepark.org.

Getting There & Away

Air

Safari Airlink (www.flysal.com; Monday & Thursday) and **Zantas Air** (www.zantasair.com; Tuesday & Friday) fly to Mahale twice-weekly, the former starting in Dar es Salaam and the later in Arusha, when there are enough passengers (usually four) to cover costs. Zantas continues to Kigoma, but doesn't fly in the other direction. Flycatcher, which operates a camp in the park, has Monday and Friday flights from Arusha during the July to October high season and will sell seats (US$625) if seats are available. All flights stop at Katavi National Park en route, and thus the parks are frequently visited as a combination package. Expect to pay approximately US$930 one way from Dar, US$825 one way from Arusha, and US$400 one way between Mahale and Katavi National Parks. A four-seater charter flight from Kigoma costs about US$850 per plane.

If you've booked with one of the lodges, a boat will meet your flight. Otherwise, arrange a boat in advance with park headquarters.

Boat

LAKE TAXI

Lake taxis (p163) head south from Ujili to Kalilani (Tsh10,000), 2km north of park headquarters, most days of the week around 5pm to 6pm. The trip often takes more than a day. Generally they depart from Kalilani around noon. Park staff know what's up with the boats, so they can advise you on days and times.

One option to make the journey more bearable is take a Saratoga bus from Kigoma to Sigunga (Tsh7000, 11am, six to seven hours) and wait for the lake taxi there. Sigunga to Kalilani usually takes seven to eight hours. You could also have the park boat pick you up in Sigunga; it's two hours to headquarters. Sigunga has a basic guesthouse.

There are also a couple of weekly boats heading north from Kalema (Tsh20,000) or nearby Ikola each evening for an even choppier journey than the one from Kigoma. It can take anywhere from 12 to 36 hours depending on the winds. They head south from Kalilani about 3pm.

MV LIEMBA

It's hard to beat the satisfyingly relaxing journey to Mahale via ferry. The MV *Liemba* stops at Lagosa (also called Mugambo) to the north of the park (1st/2nd/economy class US$28/26/16), about 10 hours from Kigoma. It's scheduled to reach Lagosa around 3am whether coming from the north (Thursday) or south (Sunday), but with the frequent delays, southern arrivals present a good chance of passing the park during daylight, which makes for a very beautiful trip.

You can arrange in advance for a park boat (holding eight people with luggage) to meet the *Liemba*. It's one hour from the *Liemba* to the *bandas*, including stopping to register and pay at headquarters. The cost depends on the price of petrol; but our last journey cost US$39. Chartering a fisherman's boat for the trip will cost less. It's also possible to take lake taxis from Lagosa to Kalilani (Tsh3000, two hours), a village about 2km north of the headquarters, but then you'll need to use the park boat for the final 10km to Kasiha. Lagosa has a basic guesthouse where you can wait for the *Liemba* after leaving the park.

TANAPA BOAT

With a bit of luck you can travel for free on the park boat. Park staff travel to Kigoma several times a month and if space is available they'll take passengers. This is usually only possible when leaving the park since on the return trip from Kigoma the boat will be carrying supplies. The Gombe/Mahale Visitors Information Centre (p163) in Kigoma knows when boats are travelling.

MAHALE MOUNTAINS NATIONAL PARK

» **Why Go** Up-close encounters with chimpanzees; stunning scenery with mountains rising up from the lakeshore.

» **When to Go** Open year-round, but March–mid-May is too wet to enjoy it. June through October are the easiest (driest) months for hiking up the steep slopes. In June and July the chimps often come down to feed around the lodges.

» **Practicalities** There are no roads to the park. Most visitors fly but a variety of boats, including the historic MV *Liemba*, goes from Kigoma, Kipili and other lakeshore towns.

Mpanda

This small and somewhat scruffy town is a major transit point. Historically it was a major trade hub and there are still many Arab businessmen living here.

The post office has reliable internet and the CRDB Bank has an internationally linked ATM.

New Super City Hotel (☎0783-309608; r Tsh12,000-17,000; P) has rooms with much wear and many quirks (like sinks without taps), but it's friendly, popular and the restaurant is probably the best in town. It's at the southern roundabout.

Getting There & Away

Bus

Mpanda's bus station is east of the Sumbawanga road, near the southern roundabout, but most companies have ticket offices near the half-built Moravian church in the town centre, and their buses actually start at them before going to the station.

Sumry serves Sumbawanga (Tsh14,000, five to six hours) via Sitalike (Tsh3000, 45 minutes) at 6am and noon; NBS goes to Tabora (Tsh18,000, eight hours) on Tuesday and Saturday at 6am; and together NBS and Adventure offer daily buses to Kigoma (Tsh20,000, eight to 10 hours) via Uvinza (Tsh15,000, four to five hours) at 6am.

Trucks to Kigoma pass the roundabout near the train station (go early and expect a long wait) while trucks heading south towards Sumbawanga and east to Tabora pass New Super City Hotel.

Train

A branch of the Central Line connects Mpanda with Tabora via Kaliua. For schedule and fare information, see p214). If you're heading to Kigoma from Mpanda, you'll need to spend at least one night in Tabora. You can wait for the Kigoma connection at Kaliua, but as there are only simple guesthouses and little to do, most travellers wait at Tabora.

Katavi National Park

Katavi, 35km southwest of Mpanda, is Tanzania's third-largest national park and one of its most unspoiled wilderness areas.

Katavi's predominant feature is the 425 sq km Katisunga Plain. Small rivers and large swamps that last all year support huge populations of hippos and crocodiles and Katavi has over 400 bird species. The park really comes to life in the dry season, when the floodplains dry up and herds of buffaloes, elephants, lions, zebras, giraffes, elands, topis, and many more gather at the remaining waters.

Marula Expeditions (☎0786-224078, 0784-946188; www.marulaexpedition.com) in Mpanda charges US$150 to US$200 per day depending on how much driving you want to do while the less-flexible Riverside Camp (see Sleeping) has two 4WDs with pop-up roofs for US$250 per day.

Walking safaris (short/long US$10/15 per group) with an armed ranger and **bush camping** (US$50 per person plus walking fee) are permitted.

Sleeping

There are two **public campsites** (adult/child US$30/5); one at Ikuu near Katisunga Plain and the other 2km south of Sitalike. Both get a lot of wildlife walking through. Bring all food and drink with you.

IN THE PARK

TOP CHOICE **Katavi Wildlife Camp** TENTED CAMP **$$$**
(0784-237422; www.tanzaniasafaris.info; s/d all inclusive except drinks US$525/850; Jun-Feb; P) This comfortable, well-run camp has a prime setting overlooking Katisunga making it the best sited for in-camp wildlife watching. The six tents have extra large porches with hammocks. Top-notch guides and good food round out the experience.

Katuma Bush Lodge TENTED CAMP **$$$**
(0713-620154; www.mbalimbali.com; per person all inclusive except drinks US$490; mid-May–mid-Feb; P) The 10 tents here are good, but the defining feature is the relaxing lounge fronted by a deck with a small swimming pool.

Flycatcher Camp TENTED CAMP **$$$**
(0732-979486; www.flycat.com; s/d/tr full board US$180/330/580, Jul-Oct; P) The tents here are a couple levels lower on the luxury meter than Katavi's other camps, but it's a great setting and price.

SITALIKE

Most backpackers stay at this little village on the northern edge of the park.

Riverside Camp BUNGALOW, CAMPGROUND **$**
(camping US$5, s/d US$20/35; P) Aimed at park visitors, hence the high prices, its best feature is the resident pod of hippos, but the *bandas* are decent enough. Discounts for students and volunteers.

KATAVI NATIONAL PARK

» **Why Go** Outstanding dry season wildlife watching. Rugged and remote wilderness ambience.

» **When to Go** August through October is best for seeing large herds of wildlife. February through May it's very wet.

» **Practicalities** Drive in or bus from Mpanda or Sumbawanga; fly in from Ruaha National Park or Arusha.

Park Bandas BUNGALOW **$$**
(r per person US$30; P) Two kilometres south of the village, within park boundaries (thus you need to pay park entry fees when staying here), these rooms are big, bright and surprisingly good. Zebra, giraffe and other animals are frequent visitors.

Information

Entry fees are US$20/5 per adult/child. All payments must be made at **park headquarters** (025-282 0213; katavinp@yahoo.com) located 1km south of Sitalike or the Ikuu Ranger Post near the main airstrip.

Getting There & Away

Air

Safari Airlink (www.flysal.com; one-way from Dar es Salaam US$775) and **Zantas Air** (www.zantasair.com; one-way/return from Arusha US$825/995) fly twice a week to Ikuu airstrip and the lodges will often let nonguests fly on their planes if space is available. All lodges provide free pick-up there for their guests. If you aren't staying at a lodge, arrange a vehicle or a ranger for walking *before* you arrive.

Bus

Buses and trucks between Mpanda and Sumbawanga can pick you up and drop you off in Sitalike or at park headquarters. Transport is pretty frequent in the mornings, but after lunch you may have to wait several hours for a vehicle to pass. Two dalla-dallas depart Sitalike for Mpanda (Tsh3000, 45 minutes) at dawn and return at noon and 4pm. If you're driving, the only petrol stations are in Mpanda and Sumbawanga.

Sumbawanga

While there's little reason to make the peppy and pleasant capital of the Rukwa region a destination in itself, anyone travelling through will find two ATMs on the main road and some internet cafes.

Moravian Conference Centre (025-280 2853; Nyerere Rd; s/d Tsh15,000/25,000, s/d/tr without bathroom or breakfast Tsh7000/14,000/20,000; P@) has spare but bright rooms, clean ablutions and inexpensive meals. It's 1km east of the bus station.

Sumry has three morning buses daily to Mbeya (Tsh15,000 to Tsh17,000, seven hours) via Tunduma. To Mpanda (Tsh14,000, five to six hours), Sumry departs daily at 8am and 2pm.

WORTH A TRIP

LAKE TANGANYIKA

Lake Tanganyika is the world's longest (660km), second-deepest (over 1436m) and second largest by volume freshwater lake. At somewhere between nine and 13 million years old, it's also one of the oldest. Thanks to its age and ecological isolation it's home to an exceptional number of endemic fish, including 98% of the 250-plus species of cichlids. Popular aquarium fish due to their bright colours, the cichlids make Tanganyika an outstanding snorkelling and diving destination.

Kipili

The old mission station of Kipili has hilltop ruins of an 1880s church, 3km north of town, that are very evocative and offer wonderful lake views. The only guesthouse here is just past the town at the lakeside **St Benedict Mission** (Tsh12,000; P) whose semi-scruffy rooms lack electricity and working showers. About 1.5km further is the universally praised **Lake Shore Lodge & Campsite** (0763-993166; www.safaritourtanzania.com; camping US$12, banda s/d full board US$120/170, chalet s full board US$415-495, d US$590-700; P) . It has chalets, cosy *bandas*, camping with spotless ablutions, and many activities: kayaking on the lake, quad biking, mountain biking, diving, village tours, island dinners and more. The lodge makes a great combination with Katavi and/or Mahale Mountains National Parks, and they can take you to both using their own trucks and boats.

Sumry has the only bus from Sumbawanga. Its destination is Kirando, so get off at Katongoro (Tsh10,000, 11am Monday to Saturday, five hours), 5km from Kipili, and either walk, wait for a passing vehicle or ride on the back of a bicycle. Lake Shore Lodge will pick up their guests here for free. From Mpanda, there's a daily Sumry bus to Namanyere (Tsh14,000, noon, four hours) where you can catch a passing vehicle heading to Kipili. North to Mpanda, the Namanyere bus departs at 10am, but if you miss it it's easy to catch an Mpanda-bound vehicle on the highway in Chala.

Most trucks, both large lorries and small 4WDs, depart from various points (just go and ask around) behind the three OILCOM petrol stations on the main road. You can also hire private 4WDs here. One exception is that trucks to Kasesha, on the Zambian border, park in front of Datoo Guesthouse.

SOUTHERN HIGHLANDS

Tanzania's Southern Highlands officially begin at Makambako Gap, about halfway between Iringa and Mbeya, and extend southwards into Malawi. Here, the term encompasses the entire region along the mountainous chain running between Morogoro in the east and Lake Nyasa and the Zambian border in the west.

The highlands are a major transit route for travellers to Malawi or Zambia. They are also wonderfully scenic and a delight to explore, with rolling hills, lively markets, jacaranda-lined streets, lovely lodges and plenty of wildlife.

Morogoro

POP 250,000

Morogoro would be a fairly scruffy town were it not for its verdant setting at the foot of the Uluguru Mountains, which brood over the landscape from the southeast. Hiking is one of the main attractions.

Sleeping

Hotel Oasis HOTEL $

(023-261 4178, 0754-377602; hoteloasistz@morogoro.net; Station St; s/d/tr US$45/50/70; P) The Oasis has faded but good-value rooms with fan, air-con, TV and fridge, plus grassy grounds and a popular restaurant serving Indian, Chinese and continental cuisine (including many vegetarian options). It's frequently fully booked.

Princess Plaza Lodge & Restaurant GUESTHOUSE $

(0754-319159; Mahenge St; r Tsh25,000;) This friendly lodge has clean, small no-frills rooms, all with double bed and hot water (no nets), plus helpful management and a restaurant downstairs. Room prices include

Morogoro

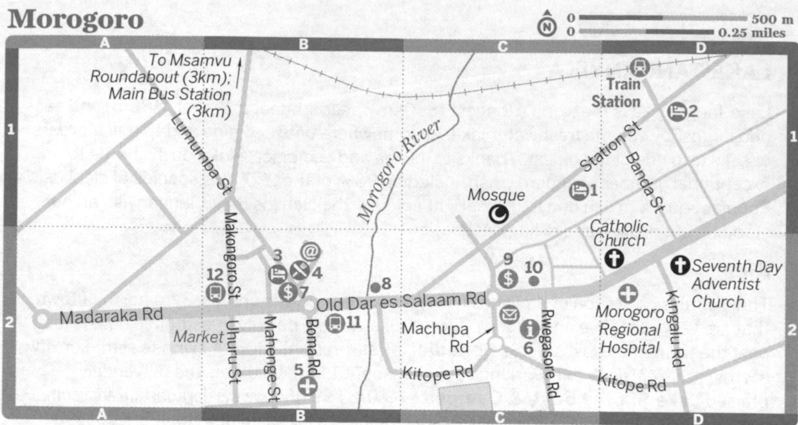

Morogoro

Sleeping

1 Hotel Oasis C1
2 New Savoy Hotel D1
3 Princess Plaza Lodge & Restaurant B2

Eating

4 Pira's Supermarket B2

Information

5 Aga Khan Health Centre B2
6 Chilunga Cultural Tourism C2
7 Exim Bank B2
8 Morogoro Medical Stores Pharmacy B2
9 NBC C2
10 Wildlife Conservation Society of Tanzania C2

Transport

11 Dalla-Dalla & Taxi Stand B2
12 Dalla-Dalla & Taxi Stand B2

free wi-fi access. It's one block in from the main road in the town centre.

New Savoy Hotel HOTEL $
(Station St; budget/standard r Tsh18,000/25,000) The atmospheric old railway hotel, directly opposite the train station, has spacious twin-bedded 'standard' rooms upstairs overlooking the garden with views to the hills. They're well worth the few extra shillings over the lower-floor budget rooms. There's a restaurant.

Pira's Supermarket SUPERMARKET $
(Lumumba Rd) For self-catering try this well-stocked supermarket.

Information

Internet Access

Internet Café (off Lumumba St; per hr Tsh2000; ⏲8am-10pm Sun-Fri, 7am-10pm Sat) Around the corner from Pira's Supermarket.

Money

Exim Bank (Lumumba St) ATM; opposite Pira's Supermarket.

NBC (Old Dar es Salaam Rd) ATM; changes cash.

Getting There & Away

Bus

The main bus station is 3km north of town on the main Dar es Salaam road, about 300m east of Msamvu roundabout (Tsh3000 in a taxi and Tsh300 in a dalla-dalla). No larger buses originate in Morogoro. Buses from Dar es Salaam going southwest towards Mikumi and Iringa begin passing Morogoro about 9am (Tsh5000, 3½ hours Dar to Morogoro). To Tanga, there's a direct bus daily (Tsh6000, five hours), departing by 8am.

The main dalla-dalla stand is in front of the market, where there is also a taxi rank. There's another dalla-dalla stop and taxi rank further east along Old Dar es Salaam Rd before the post office.

Train

Morogoro is on the Central Line (p214). Arrivals from Dar es Salaam are generally about 10pm.

Mikumi National Park

Mikumi is Tanzania's fourth-largest national park. It's also the most accessible from Dar es Salaam. With almost guaranteed wildlife sightings, it makes an ideal safari destination for those without much time. Mikumi hosts buffaloes, wildebeests, giraffes, elephants, lions, zebras, leopards, crocodiles and more, and chances are high that you'll see a respectable sampling of these within a short time of entering the park.

Sleeping & Eating

The park has four ordinary campsites. The two closest to the park headquarters have toilet facilities and one has a shower. There is a special campsite near Choga Wale in the north of the park.

Also see the accommodation options in Mikumi town (p171), 23km west.

Vuma Hills Tented Camp TENTED CAMP **$$$**
(☎0784-237422; www.tanzaniasafaris.info; s/d full board plus wildlife drives US$365/570; P ≋) The pleasant Vuma Hills is set on a rise about 7km south of the main road, with views over the plains in the distance. The 16 tented en suite cottages each have a double and a single bed, the mood is relaxed and the cuisine good. The turn-off is diagonally opposite the park entry gate.

Information

Entry fees are US$20/5 per adult/child, payable only with a Visa or MasterCard and your PIN. For camping fees see p202. For booking campsites and park *bandas*, contact the **senior park warden** (☎023-262 0498/87; mikumi@tanzania
parks.com). Driving hours inside the park (off the main highway) are 6.30am to 6.30pm.

MIKUMI NATIONAL PARK

» **Why Go** Easy access from Dar es Salaam; good wildlife watching and birding.

» **When to Go** Year-round.

» **Practicalities** Drive or bus from Dar es Salaam.

DON'T MISS

CHILUNGA CULTURAL TOURISM PROGRAM

Chilunga Cultural Tourism (☎023-261-3323, 0754-477582; www.chilunga.or.tz; YWCA Compound, Rwegasore Rd) offers day and overnight excursions around Morogoro, including village visits, hikes and Mikumi safaris. Prices average from Tsh25,000 per person per day plus village and admin fees (from about Tsh10,000/Tsh5000 per person per day, respectively). Mikumi safaris cost from US$250 for the vehicle, including guide and park entry fees.

Getting There & Around

Bus

There is no vehicle rental at the park, so you'll need to have your own car or arrange a rental in advance with one of the lodges. It's often possible to see animals along the roadside if you're passing through on a bus, but the buses move too fast for decent viewing. Good budget options for visiting the park include the safari packages offered by Chilunga Cultural Tourism in Morogoro, or hotels in Mikumi town.

Mikumi Town

Mikumi is the last of the lowland towns along the Dar es Salaam–Mbeya highway before it starts its climb through the Ruaha River gorge up into the hills of the Southern Highlands, and of interest almost exclusively as a transit point for visits to the Mikumi or Udzungwa Mountains National Parks.

Sleeping & Eating

Tan-Swiss Hotel & Restaurant LODGE **$$**
(☎0755-191827; www.tan-swiss.com; Main Rd; camping US$5, s/d/tw/tr US$45/50/50/65, d bungalow US$85; P) This Swiss- and Tanzanian-run establishment has a large camping area with hot-water ablutions, comfortable en suite rooms and several double and family bungalows. All are spacious, with fans and surrounding greenery, and there's a restaurant-bar. Vehicle rental to Mikumi/Udzungwa costs about US$190/130 per day.

Genesis Motel GUESTHOUSE **$**
(☎023 262 0461; camping US$5, r per person US$30, with half board US$45; P) This functional hotel is located on the main highway

Southern Highlands

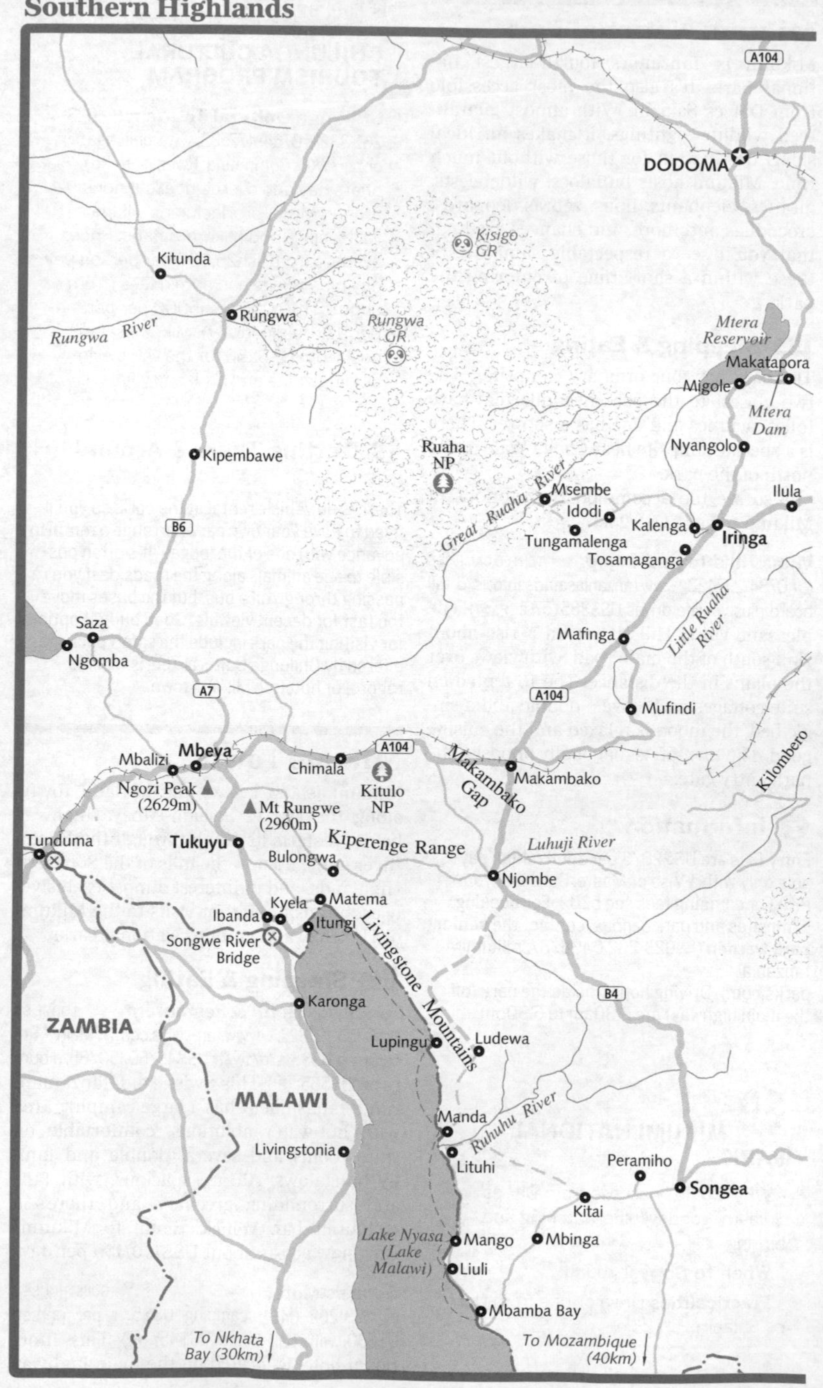

A104
DODOMA
Kisigo GR
Kitunda
Rungwa
Rungwa River
Rungwa GR
Mtera Reservoir
Makatapora
Migole
Mtera Dam
Nyangolo
Kipembawe
Ruaha NP
Msembe
Great Ruaha River
Ilula
Idodi
Kalenga
Iringa
B6
Tungamalenga
Tosamaganga
Little Ruaha River
Saza
Ngomba
Mafinga
A7
A104
Mufindi
Kilombero
Mbalizi
Mbeya
Chimala
A104
Makambako Gap
Makambako
Ngozi Peak (2629m)
Kitulo NP
Mt Rungwe (2960m)
Tunduma
Tukuyu
Kiperenge Range
Luhuji River
Bulongwa
Njombe
Matema
Kyela
Ibanda
Itungi
Livingstone Mountains
Songwe River Bridge
B4
Karonga
ZAMBIA
Lupingu
Ludewa
MALAWI
Manda
Ruhuhu River
Livingstonia
Lituhi
Peramiho
Songea
Kitai
Lake Nyasa (Lake Malawi)
Mango
Mbinga
Liuli
Mbamba Bay
To Nkhata Bay (30km)
To Mozambique (40km)

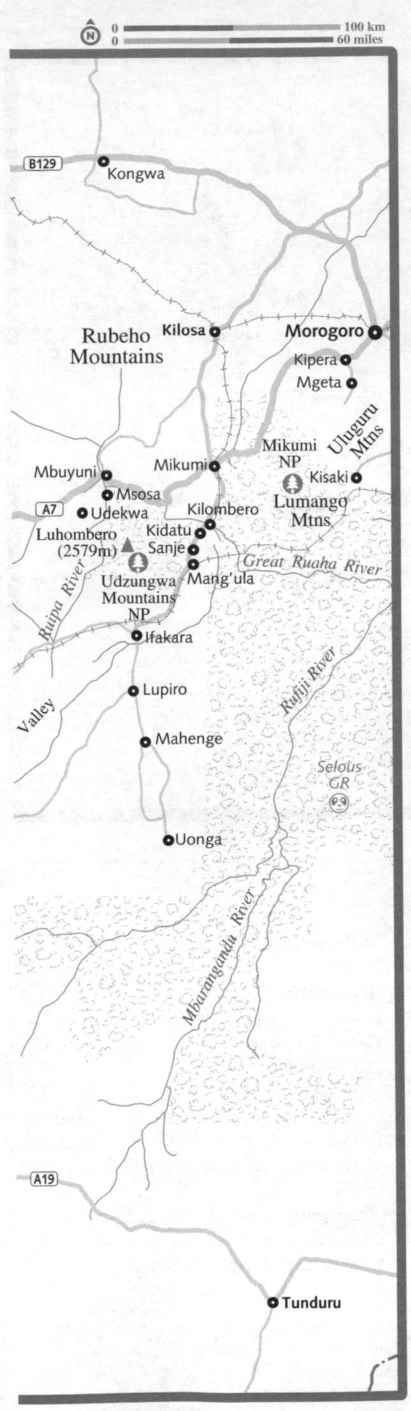

2.5km east of the Ifakara junction. Rooms are small, clean and closely spaced (ask for one of the newer ones) and there's a restaurant and an attached snake park (adult/child US$5/2). For campers, there are hot-water showers and a kitchen. Vehicle rental (with advance notice) for Mikumi costs from US$150 per vehicle per day.

Getting There & Away

Mikumi's bus stand is at the western end of town on the main highway.

Going west, buses from Dar es Salaam begin passing Mikumi en route to Iringa (Tsh5000, three hours), Mbeya and Songea from about 9.30am. Going east, there are large buses to Dar es Salaam (Tsh10,000, 4½ hours) departing at 6.30am and 7.30am.

Iringa

POP 110,000

Perched at a cool 1600m on a cliff overlooking the valley of the Little Ruaha River, Iringa was initially built up by the Germans at the turn of the 20th century as a bastion against the local Hehe people. Now it's a district capital, an important agricultural centre and the gateway for visiting Ruaha National Park. It's also a likeable place, with its bluff-top setting, healthy climate and highland feel, and well worth a stop.

Sights & Activities

Neema Crafts CRAFT WORKSHOP
(0786-431274; www.neemacrafts.com; Hakimu St; 8.30am-6.30pm Mon-Sat) This vocational training centre for young deaf and disabled people is operated by the Anglican church and sells beautiful crafts, handmade paper and cards, jewellery, quilts, clothing, batiks and more. Free tours of the workshops can be arranged. It's just southeast of the Clock Tower roundabout. Highly recommended. Volunteer opportunities are occasionally available.

Market Area MARKET
Iringa's market is piled high with fruits and vegetables, plus other wares, including large-weave, locally made Iringa baskets. On its southern edge, in front of the police station, is a **monument** honouring Africans who fell during the Maji Maji uprising between 1905 and 1907. West along this same street is the main trading area, dominated

Iringa

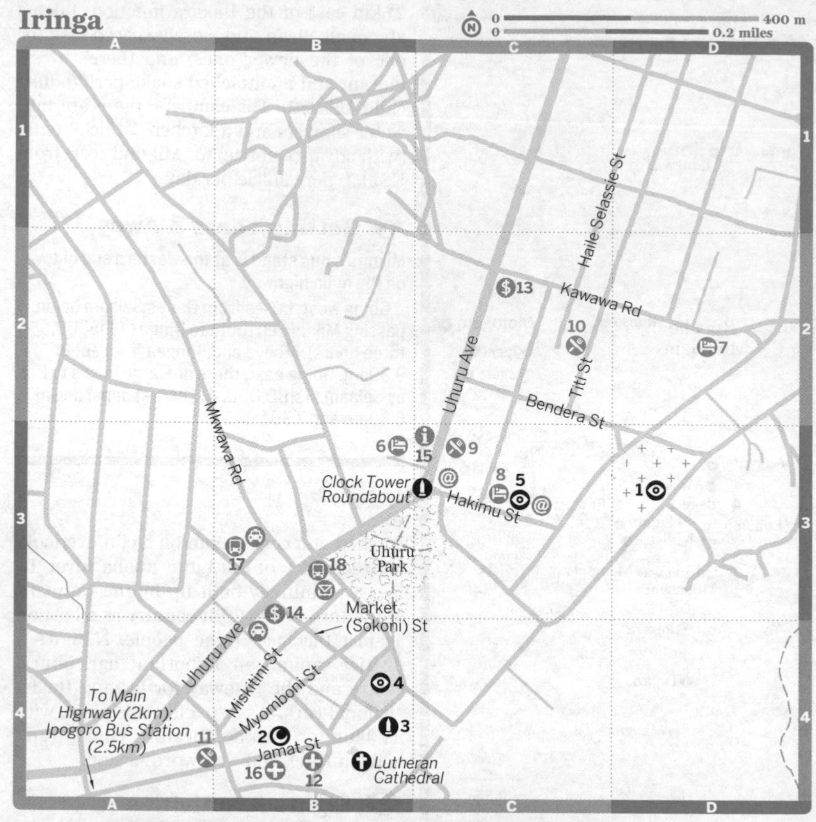

Iringa

Sights

1 Commonwealth War Graves Cemetary D3
2 Ismaili Mosque B4
3 Maji Maji Uprising Monument B4
4 Market B4
5 Neema Crafts C3

Sleeping

6 Central Lodge Hotel B3
7 Iringa Lutheran Centre D2
8 Neema Umaki Guest House C3

Eating

9 Hasty Tasty Too C3
10 Lulu's C2
Neema Crafts Centre Café .... (see 5)
11 Premji's Cash & Carry A4

Information

12 Aga Khan Health Centre B4
13 Barclay's Bank C2
14 CRDB Bank B3
15 Iringa Info C3
Iringa Info Bookstore .... (see 15)
16 Myomboni Pharmacy B4
Warthog Adventures Tanzania .... (see 15)

Transport

17 Bus Station B3
18 Myomboni Dalla-Dalla Stand B3

by the German-built **Ismaili Mosque** with its distinctive Clock Tower.

Commonwealth War Graves Cemetery CEMETERY
At the southeastern edge of town is this cemetery, with graves of the deceased from both world wars.

Sleeping

Rivervalley Campsite CAMPGROUND $
(026-270 1988, 0782-507017, 0787-111663; www.rivervalleycampsites.com; camping US$6, tented bandas per person US$15, d in wooden cottage US$40; P) Rivervalley Campsite (formerly Riverside Campsite) has a lovely setting on the banks of the Little Ruaha River, a large, shaded camping area, twin-bedded tents, wooden cottages (some with bathroom), hot-water showers and good buffet-style meals. It's good overall value for families and budget travellers. Tents are available for rent, and there are on-site Swahili language courses. It's 13km northeast of Iringa; take a dalla-dalla heading towards Ilula (ie go towards Dar es Salaam along the main road) and ask the driver to drop you at the signposted right-hand turn-off (Tsh1000), from where it's 1.5km further down an unpaved track. Taxis charge Tsh10,000 to Tsh15,000 from town. Staff can help you arrange car rentals and Ruaha safaris.

Iringa Lutheran Centre GUESTHOUSE $
(026-270 0722, 0755-517445; www.iringalutherancentre.com; Kawawa Rd; s/d/tr US$20/40/60; P) This long-standing place has been completely renovated, and now has clean, pleasant twin and double-bedded rooms with bathrooms and hot water, and a restaurant. Room prices include full breakfast. It's on the northeastern edge of town, about 700m southeast of the main road.

Neema Umaki Guest House GUESTHOUSE $
(026-270 2499, 0786-431274; www.neemacrafts.com; Hakimu St; dm Tsh15,000, s/d/f Tsh25,000/45,000/65,000; @) Located at Neema Crafts Centre, this good-value, centrally located guesthouse has an array of twins, doubles and family rooms, plus a three-bed dorm (breakfast Tsh3000 per person extra for the dorm beds) and a honeymoon suite. It's just off Uhuru Ave; turn east at the Clock Tower roundabout. Staff can help with information and guides for walking tours of town and excursions, including visits to a local family and homestays. Profits go to support the work of the craft centre.

Sai Villa GUESTHOUSE $$
(0786-757757; www.saivilla.net; off Kenyatta Dr, Gangilonga Area; r Tsh90,000-120,000; P) This private residence has 10 comfortable guest rooms and a perfectly decent restaurant. To get here, follow Kawawa Rd past the Lutheran Hostel for about 500m to Mama Siyovelwa pub. Then continue past Mama Siyovelwa pub for 300m and take the second right (you'll find it just after the road merges with Kenyatta Dr). Sai Villa is the first gate (white) on your right opening into a large private compound. There's no signboard.

Central Lodge Hotel GUESTHOUSE $
(Uhuru Ave; d Tsh15,000-20,000, tr Tsh30,000) Quiet, no-frills, centrally located rooms with bathrooms around a small garden. The front rooms facing the garden are spacious; smaller rooms are in the row behind. It's just behind Iringa Info, entered through the small alley lined with vendors.

Eating

Hasty Tasty Too TANZANIAN, EUROPEAN $
(026-270 2061; Uhuru Ave; snacks & meals from Tsh2000; 7.30am-8pm Mon-Sat, 10am-2pm Sun) This long-standing Iringa classic has good breakfasts, yoghurt, shakes and reasonably priced main dishes, plus an amenable mix of local and expat clientele. Another bonus is you can get delicious toasted sandwiches packed to go and arrange food for Ruaha camping safaris.

Neema Crafts Centre Café CAFE $
(026-270 2499; www.neemacrafts.com; Hakimu St; meals from Tsh5000; @) Located upstairs at Neema Crafts Centre, this cafe is justifiably popular, with local coffees and teas, milkshakes, homemade cookies, cakes, soups, light meals, sandwiches and ice cream. In one corner is a small library where you can read up on various development projects in the area.

Lulu's CHINESE $
(027-270 2122; Titi St; meals Tsh4000-6000; 8.30am-3pm & 6.30-9pm Mon-Sat) A quiet place with mostly Chinese and Asian dishes, plus soft-serve ice cream, milkshakes and an umbrella-shaded outdoor seating area. It's one block southeast of the main road, just off Kawawa Rd.

Premji's Cash & Carry SELF CATERRING $
(Jamat St) For self catering.

Information

Internet Access

Neema Crafts Centre Internet Café (Hakimu St; per hr Tsh1000; ⌚8.30am-6.30pm Mon-Sat) Also has wi-fi, and a small tourist information centre.

IringaNet (Uhuru Ave; per hr Tsh1000; ⌚8am-6pm Mon-Sat, 10am-1pm Sun) A few doors down from Hasty Tasty.

Medical Services

Aga Khan Health Centre (☎026-270 2277; Jamat St; ⌚8am-6pm Mon-Fri, 8am-2pm Sat & Sun) Next to the Lutheran cathedral and near the market.

Myomboni Pharmacy (☎026-270 2277/2617; ⌚7.30am-7.30pm) Just downhill from the Aga Khan Health Centre.

Money

CRDB (Uhuru Ave) ATM.

Barclays (Uhuru Ave) ATM.

Tourist Information

Iringa Info (☎026-270 1988; infoiringa@gmail.com; Uhuru Ave; ⌚9am-5pm Mon-Fri, 9am-3pm Sat) A good place to organise Ruaha safaris, reliable car rentals, town and village tours and excursions. They also have a cafe and a great little bookstore. It's opposite Hasty Tasty Too.

Warthog Adventures Tanzania (☎026-270 1988, 0688-322888, 0718-467742; www.warthogadventures.com; Uhuru Ave) Excellent, well-maintained vehicles for Ruaha safaris and travels to Mikumi and elsewhere. They also do transfers to/from Dar es Salaam.

Getting There & Away

Air

There are six flights weekly on Auric Air and Flightlink to Dar es Salaam (US$260 to US$300) and Mbeya (US$225 to US$250). Book at Iringa Info. Iringa's Nduli airfield is about 12km out of town along the Dodoma road.

Bus

To catch any bus not originating in Iringa, you'll need to go to the main bus station at Ipogoro, 3km southeast of town below the escarpment (Tsh5000 in a taxi from town), where the Morogoro–Mbeya highway bypasses Iringa. This is also where you'll get dropped off if you're arriving on a bus continuing towards Morogoro or Mbeya. Dalla-dallas to Ipogoro leave from the Myomboni dalla-dalla stand at the edge of Uhuru Park in town. All buses originating in Iringa start at the bus station in town and stop also at Ipogoro to pick up additional passengers.

Green Star Express and others go daily to Dar es Salaam, leaving from 7am onwards (Tsh15,000 to Tsh20,000, 7½ hours); book in advance at the bus offices at the bus station in town.

To Mbeya, Chaula Express departs daily at 7am (Tsh15,000, four to five hours). Otherwise, you can try to get a seat on one of the through buses from Dar es Salaam that pass Iringa (Ipogoro bus station) from about 1pm.

To Njombe (Tsh8000 to Tsh9000, 3½ hours) and Songea (Tsh17,000, eight hours), Super Feo departs at 6am from the town bus station, with a second bus to Njombe only departing at 10am.

To Dodoma, Kings Cross and Urafiki depart on alternate days at 8am (Tsh15,000 to Tsh16,000, nine to 10 hours), going via Nyangolo and Makatapora. Otherwise, all transport is via Morogoro, which is the route most travellers take (Tsh22,000 to Tsh25,000, eight to nine hours).

Getting Around

The main dalla-dalla stand ('Myomboni') is just down from the market and near the bus station. Taxi ranks are along the small road between the bus station and the market, in front of MR Hotel, and at the Ipogoro bus station. Fares from the town bus stand to central hotels start at Tsh3000.

Ruaha National Park

Ruaha National Park, together with neighbouring conservation areas, forms the core of a wild and extended ecosystem covering about 40,000 sq km and providing home to one of Tanzania's largest elephant populations. In addition to the elephants, which are estimated to number about 12,000, the park (Tanzania's largest, with an area of approximately 22,000 sq km) hosts large herds of buffaloes, as well as greater and lesser kudus, Grant's gazelles, wild dogs, ostriches, cheetahs, roan and sable antelopes, and more than 400 different types of birds. Bird life is especially prolific along the Great Ruaha River, which winds through the eastern side of the park, as are hippos and crocodiles.

Sleeping & Eating

INSIDE THE PARK

There are several ordinary campsites about 9km northwest of park headquarters, and about five special campsites well away from the Msembe area. The twin-bedded and poorly ventilated **old park bandas** (per person US$20) close to park headquarters, come with bedding and shared ablutions. The park sells soft drinks and a few basics; otherwise you'll need your own supplies or arrange to eat at the staff canteen. There are also the much nicer single, double and four- to five-person family **new park bandas** (per person US$50) with bedding and basic meals available. Park accommodation can be booked at the gate on arrival, or through Iringa Info in Iringa. Payment must be made at the park gate with Visa or MasterCard.

Mwagusi Safari Camp TENTED CAMP **$$$**
(in the UK 020-8846 9363; www.mwagusicamp.com; s/d all inclusive from US$635/1140; Jun-Mar; P) This highly regarded 16-bed owner-managed camp is set in a prime location for wildlife viewing on the Mwagusi Sand River about 20km inside the park gate. The atmosphere is intimate and the guiding is top-notch.

Ruaha River Lodge LODGE **$$$**
(0784-237422; www.tanzania safaris.info; s/d full board with wildlife drives US$405/650; P) This unpretentious, beautifully situated 28-room lodge about 15km inside the gate was the first in the park and is the only place on the river. Run by the Fox family, who have several decades of experience in Ruaha, it's centred on two separate sections, each with its own dining area, giving the feel of a smaller lodge. The stone cottages directly overlook the river, and there's a treetop-level bar-terrace with stunning riverine panoramas.

Mdonya Old River Camp TENTED CAMP **$$$**
(022-245 2005; www.adventurecamps.co.tz; s/d full board plus excursions US$415/700; Jun-Mar; P) The relaxed Mdonya Old River Camp, about 1½ hours drive from Msembe, has eight tents on the bank of the Mdonya Sand River, with the occasional elephant wandering through camp. It's run by Coastal Travels (p54), and if you take advantage of Coastal's specials, it offers fine value for a Ruaha safari.

Kwihala Tented Camp TENTED CAMP **$$$**
(022-245 2005; www.adventurecamps.co.tz; s/d full board plus excursions US$500/800; P) This is a new and highly regarded camp in a fine location near the Mwagusi Sand River, with top-notch guides. It's under the same management as Mdonya Old River Camp.

RUAHA NATIONAL PARK

» **Why Go** Outstanding dry season wildlife watching, especially known for its elephants and hippos; good birding; rugged scenery.

» **When to Go** June through October for wildlife; December through April for birding.

» **Practicalities** Drive in from Iringa; fly in from Arusha or Dar es Salaam.

OUTSIDE THE PARK

There are several places just outside the park boundaries along the Tungamalenga village road (take the left fork at the junction when coming from Iringa).

Tandala Tented Camp TENTED CAMP **$$$**
(www.tandalatentedcamp.com; per person full board US$175; Jun-Mar; P) A lovely spot just outside the park boundary about 12km from the park gate and shortly before the Tungamalenga road rejoins the main park access road. Accommodation is in raised tents scattered around shaded grounds with a bush feel (elephants and other animals are frequent visitors). The camp can organise vehicle rental to Ruaha and guided walks in park border areas.

Ruaha Hilltop Lodge LODGE **$$**
(026-270 1806, 0784-726709; www.ruahahilltoplodge.com; per person full board US$80; P) This friendly lodge has a fine hilltop perch about 1.5km off the Tungamalenga road, with wide views over the plains from the raised restaurant-bar area. Behind this are simple two-person cement *bandas*. During the dry season, it's common to see wildlife passing by down below. Cultural walks in the area can be arranged, as can vehicle rental for Ruaha safaris.

Tungamalenga Camp GUESTHOUSE **$**
(026-278 2196; camping US$10, r per person with breakfast/full board US$35/60; P) This long-standing place, about 35km from the park gate and close to the bus stand, has a small, crowded garden for camping, small rooms and a restaurant. Village tours can be arranged. Vehicle rental with advance arrangement only.

Information

Entry fees are US$20/5 per adult/child aged per 24-hour period, payable with Visa or MasterCard and PIN. For camping fees, see p202.

The main gate (open 7am to 6pm) is about 8km inside the park boundary on its eastern side, near the park's Msembe headquarters. Driving is permitted within the park from 6am to 6.30pm.

Ruaha can be visited at any time of year. The driest season is between June and November (August through October are peak), and this is when it's easiest to spot wildlife along the river beds.

From June to January, it's possible to organise two- to three-hour walks (US$25 per group park walking fee).

Getting There & Away

Air

There are airstrips at Msembe and Jongomero.

Coastal Aviation flies from Dar es Salaam and Zanzibar to Ruaha via Selous Game Reserve (US$350 one way, from Dar es Salaam or Zanzibar, and between Ruaha and Arusha (US$330). Safari Airlink has similarly priced flights to Dar es Salaam, Selous and Arusha, and also flies to Katavi and Mikumi.

Bus

There's a daily bus between Iringa and Tungamalenga village, departing Iringa at 1pm and Tungamalenga (from the village bus stand, just before Tungamalenga Camp) at 5am (Tsh5000, five to six hours). From Tungamalenga, there's no onward transport to the park, other than rental vehicles arranged in advance through the Tungamalenga road camps, and there's no vehicle rental once at Ruaha, except what you've arranged in advance with the lodges.

Warthog Adventures in Iringa (p176) offers day safaris from US$250 per vehicle per day, and is a good contact for finding other travellers interested in joining a group.

Car

Ruaha is 115km from Iringa along an unsealed road. About 58km before the park, the road forks; both sides go to Ruaha and the distance is about the same each way. To access Tungamalenga and accommodation outside the park, take the left fork. The closest petrol is in Iringa.

Makambako

Makambako (a stop on the Tazara railway line) is a windy highland town at the junction where the road from Songea and Njombe meets the Dar es Salaam–Mbeya highway.

Triple J Hotel (026-273 0475; Njombe Rd; s/d Tsh20,000/25,000; P) has clean, small rooms and a restaurant with meals from about Tsh4500. It's 800m south of the main junction along the Njombe road, 700m north of the bus stand and signposted.

The bus stand is about 1.5km south of the main junction along the Njombe road. The first bus to Mbeya (Tsh7000, three hours) leaves at 6am, with another bus at 7am. The first buses (all smaller Coastals) to Njombe (Tsh3000, one hour) and Songea (Tsh12,000, five hours) depart about 6.30am, and there's a larger bus departing at 6.30am for Iringa (Tsh7000) and Dar es Salaam.

Njombe

Njombe, about 60km south of Makambako and 235km north of Songea, is a district capital, regional agricultural centre and home of the Bena people.

Sleeping & Eating

Lutheran Centre Guest House & Annex HOSTEL $
(026-278 2118; Main Rd; dm Tsh4000, r without bathroom Tsh5000, s/d in annex Tsh12,000/15,000, new r Tsh30,000; P) The draughty, multistorey Lutheran Centre Annex, next to the Lutheran church, has spartan albeit spacious rooms. Diagonally behind (south), and one block off the main street is the Lutheran Centre, with spacious new rooms and some older, smaller, faded rooms plus a small dorm. Turn off the main road just south of the Lutheran Centre Annex. Both have meals on order.

Chani Motel HOTEL $
(026-278 2357; r Tsh15,000-20,000; P) This cosy place has modest twin- and double-bedded rooms, hot water (usually), small poinsettia-studded gardens and a restaurant with TV and filling meals. It's signposted at the northern end of town and is 600m west of the main road.

Duka la Maziwa DAIRY $
(Cefa Njombe Milk Factory; 026-278 2851; 7am-6pm Mon-Sat, 10am-2pm Sun) Fresh milk, yogurt and cheese. It's just off the main road: turn in by the TFA building and go down about two blocks. The shop is to the left.

Getting There & Away

The bus stand is on the west side of the main road, about 600m south of the large grey-water tank.

Buses go daily to Songea (Tsh10,000 to Tsh12,000, four hours), Makambako (Tsh2500, one hour), Iringa (Tsh8000 to Tsh9000) and Mbeya (Tsh8000 to Tsh9000, four hours), with the first departures at 6.30am.

Mbeya

POP 270,000

The thriving town of Mbeya sprawls at about 1700m in the shadow of Loleza Peak (2656m), in a gap between the verdant Mbeya mountain range to the north and the Poroto mountains to the southeast. Today, it's a major trade and transit junction between Tanzania, Zambia and Malawi. The surrounding area is lush, mountainous and scenic, with many nearby excursions.

Sleeping & Eating

Utengule Country Hotel LODGE $$

(025-256 0100, 0753-020901; www.riftvalley-zanzibar.com; camping US$10, bungalows per person US$45, s/d/ste/f from US$85/125/180/170; P) This lodge is set in expansive grounds on a working coffee plantation in the hills 20km west of Mbeya. Accommodation includes spacious standard rooms, two-storey king-size suites with balconies, a rustic family room and no-frills self-catering cottages in separate grounds. Take the Tunduma road west from Mbeya for 12km to Mbalizi, where there's a signposted turn-off to the right. Follow this road 8.5km, keeping left at the first fork. The lodge is signposted to the right. Via public transport, take any Tunduma-bound dalla-dalla to Mbalizi, from where sporadic pick-ups en route to Chunya will take you within about 2km of Utengule.

Mbeya Peak Hotel HOTEL $

(025-250 3473; Acacia St; d Tsh30,000; P) With a central, sunny setting and decent rooms, some with views over the hills, this is one of the better-value budget choices. There's one twin-bedded room; all the others have one large-ish bed. It's on a small side street about 300m east of the market. There's a restaurant.

Mbeya Hotel HOTEL $

(025-250 2224, 025-250 2575; mbeyahotel@hotmail.com; Kaunda Ave; s/d Tsh35,000/50,000; P) The former East African Railways & Harbours Hotel has straightforward, good-value rooms in separate bungalows near the main building, small gardens and a restaurant. It's opposite NBC bank.

Karibuni Centre HOSTEL $

(025-250 3035/4178; www.mec-tanzania.ch; camping Tsh5000, s/d Tsh18,000/30,000; P) You'll find this quiet mission-run place in a small, enclosed compound where you can

WORTH A TRIP

IRINGA TO MAKAMBAKO

About 50km southwest of Iringa and just off the highway is **Kisolanza: The Old Farm House** (0754-306144; www.kisolanza.com; camping with hot showers US$5, tw stables/chalets US$35/40, d/f cottages US$70/90, d/q luxury cottage with half board US$170/250, 'sheep's pen' US$60-90; P), a gracious 1930s farm homestead fringed by stands of pine and rolling hill country. It comes highly recommended both for its accommodation and for its cuisine. There are two camping grounds, one for overlanders and one for private vehicles, plus various styles of rooms and two 'luxury' cottages surrounded by gardens. All are spotless, impeccably furnished and excellent value. Buses will drop you at the Kisolanza turn-off, from where it's about a 1.5km walk in to the lodge.

Continuing southwestwards, about 45km further on at Mafinga is the turn-off to reach the forested highlands around **Mufindi**, which are laced with small streams and known for their tea estates and trout fishing. **Mufindi Highlands Lodge** (0784-237422; www.tanzaniasafaris.info; s/d full board US$210/300; P), set amid the hills and tea plantations around Mufindi, is another recommended place for those seeking cool highland air and a chance to recharge, with the cosy wooden cabins, family-style cuisine, landscaped gardens, expansive grounds with walking trails and small lakes for fishing, plus cycling and horse riding. The lodge is about 15km south of Mafinga. Pick-ups from Mafinga can be arranged.

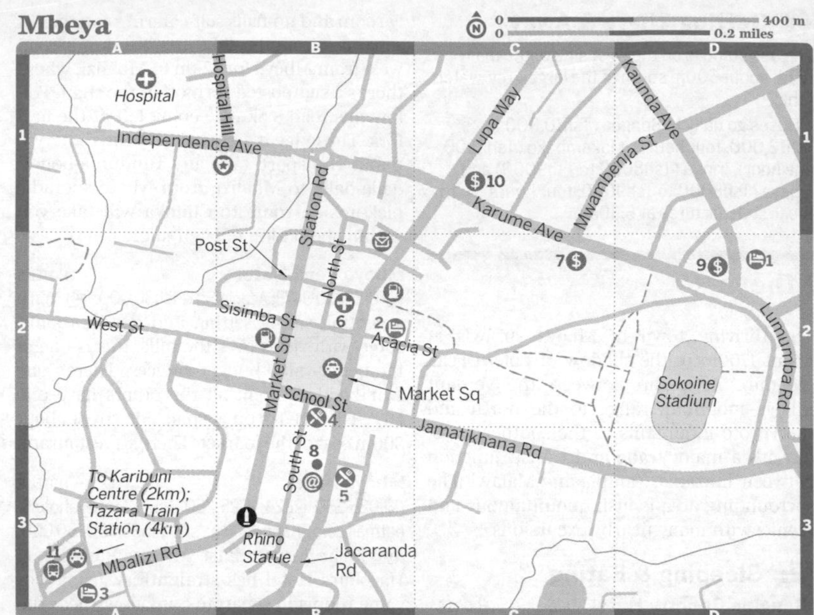

also pitch a tent. Most rooms have bathrooms, and there's a restaurant (closed Sunday). Karibuni is 3km southwest of the town centre and about 10 minutes on foot from the dalla-dalla stop for transport into town. As you approach, watch for the signpost along the north side of the main highway and about 500m west of the first junction coming from Dar es Salaam, from where it's 300m further.

New Millennium Inn GUESTHOUSE $
(☎025-250 0599; Mbalizi Rd; rm Tsh 16,000-17,000) This guesthouse is located in a noisy but convenient location directly opposite the bus stand, with good-value 'newer' rooms upstairs and separate from the main building, and smaller, darker rooms near the reception. If you're looking at the more expensive rooms, they have beds big enough for two, but be warned there's no same-gender sharing.

New Apricourt Restaurant TANZANIAN $
(Jacaranda Rd; meals from Tsh4000; 8am-5pm Mon, 8am-11pm Tue-Sat) Inexpensive meals, just opposite Gazelle Safaris.

Azra Supermarket SUPERMARKET $
(School St) Small but well-stocked; just up from Tanesco.

Mbeya

Sleeping
1 Mbeya Hotel D2
2 Mbeya Peak Hotel B2
3 New Millennium Inn A3

Eating
4 Azra Supermarket B2
5 New Apricourt Restaurant B3

Information
6 Aga Khan Medical Centre B2
7 CRDB C2
8 Gazelle Safaris B3
9 NBC Bank & ATM D2
10 Stanbic Bank C1

Transport
11 Bus Station A3

Information

Dangers & Annoyances

As a major transport junction, Mbeya attracts many transients, particularly in the area around the bus station. Watch your luggage, don't change money with anyone, only buy bus tickets in the bus company offices and avoid walking alone through the small valley behind the station. Also be very wary of anyone presenting themselves as a tourist guide and don't make tourist arrangements with anyone outside of an office. Bus ticketing scams abound, especially for cross-border connections. Ignore all touts, no matter how apparently legitimate, trying to sell you through-tickets to Malawi (especially) or Zambia. Pay the fare only to the border, and then arrange onward transport from there.

Internet Access

Gazelle Safaris Internet Café (Jacaranda Rd; per hr Tsh1000; ⌚8.30am-5.30pm Mon-Fri, 9am-2.30pm Sat) At Gazelle Safaris.

Medical Services

Aga Khan Medical Centre (☎025-250 2043; cnr North & Post Sts; ⌚8am-8pm Mon-Sat, 9am-2pm Sun) Just north of the market.

Money

CRDB (Karume Ave) ATM.

NBC (cnr Karume & Kaunda Aves) Changes cash; ATM.

Stanbic (Karume Ave) ATM; just up from CRDB.

Tourist Information

Gazelle Safaris (☎025-250 2482, 0784-666600; www.gazellesafaris.com; Jacaranda Rd) Guides and transport for day tours around Mbeya, excursions to Kitulo National Park, reliable car rental and southern circuit safaris. They also do domestic and international flight bookings.

 Getting There & Away

Air

Mbeya airfield, 5km south of town, handles six flights weekly to Iringa (US$225 to US$250, one way) and Dar es Salaam (US$300 to US$350, one way), currently on Auric Air and Flightlink. Book through Gazelle Safaris.

Bus

Green Star Express, Sumry and other lines depart daily from the main bus station to Dar es Salaam from 6am (Tsh30000 to Tsh35,000, 12 to 14 hours), going via Iringa (Tsh18,000 to Tsh20,000) and Morogoro.

To Njombe (Tsh9000, four hours) and Songea (Tsh18,000, eight hours), Super Feo departs daily at 6am, sometimes with a later departure as well.

To Tukuyu (Tsh2500, one to 1½ hours), Kyela (Tsh5000, two to 2½ hours) and the Malawi border (Tsh5000, two to 2½ hours; take the Kyela bus), there are several smaller Coastal buses daily. It's also possible to get to the Malawi border via dalla-dalla, but you'll need to change vehicles in Tukuyu. Note that there are no direct buses from Mbeya into Malawi, though touts at the Mbeya bus station may try to convince you otherwise.

To Matema, there is one direct bus daily via Kyela, departing Mbeya by about 1pm (Tsh7000).

To Tunduma, on the Zambian border, there are daily minibuses (Tsh3500, two hours). Once across, there's Zambian transport. There is no cross-border transport between Mbeya and Zambia.

To Sumbawanga, Sumry goes daily at 6am and 8am (Tsh15,000, seven hours). For Mpanda, you'll need to change vehicles in Sumbawanga. Plan on spending the night there, since most vehicles to Mpanda depart Sumbawanga in the morning, although sometimes in the dry season – and daily once the Sumbawanga road is fully rehabilitated – it's possible to get a direct connection without staying overnight in Sumbawanga.

To Tabora, there are a few vehicles weekly during the dry season. Some, which you can pick up at Mbalizi junction, take the western route via Saza and Makongolosi, while others – catch them along the main Tanzam highway just east of central Mbeya – go via Chunya.

To Moshi, Sumry departs daily at 5am (Tsh55,000, 18 gruelling hours).

Train

Book tickets at least several days in advance at **Tazara train station** (⌚8am-noon & 2-5pm Mon-Fri, 10am-1pm Sat). See p656 for schedules and fares between Mbeya and Dar es Salaam, and p209 for connections with Zambia.

 Getting Around

Taxis park at the bus station and near Market Square. Fares from the bus station to central hotels start at Tsh3000. The Tazara train station is 4km out of town on the Tanzania–Zambia highway (Tsh6000 in a taxi).

Tukuyu

The small, peppy town of Tukuyu is set in the heart of a beautiful area of hills and orchards near Lake Nyasa. There are many hikes and natural attractions nearby, and basic tourist infrastructure.

Hiking opportunities abound, with Rungwe Tea & Tours (see Information) the main option for organising something. Destinations include the 2960m Mt Rungwe, Ngozi Peak & Crater Lake and Daraja la Mungu (Bridge of God).

Around Mbeya

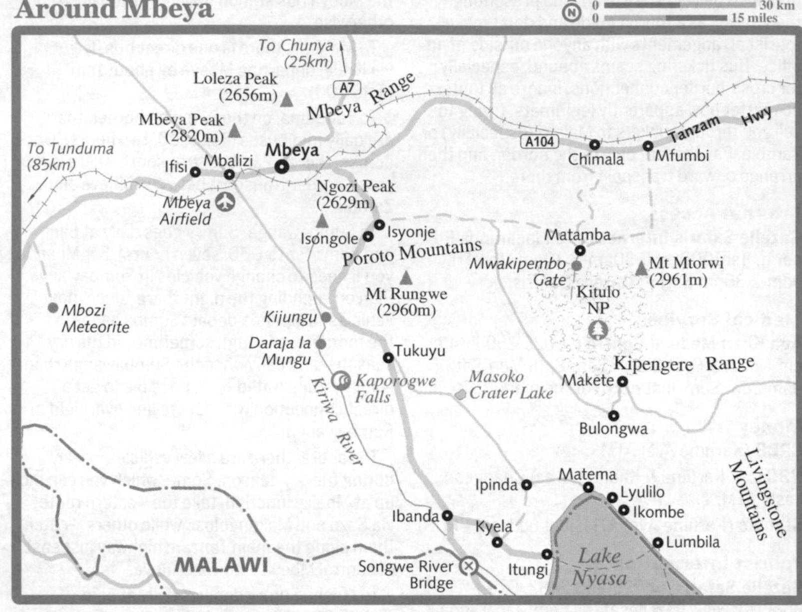

Sleeping & Eating

Landmark Hotel HOTEL $

(☎025-255 2400; camping per tent US$5, s/d Tsh30,000/40,000; P) Spacious, good-value rooms, all with TV and hot water, a small lawn where it's sometimes permitted to pitch a tent and a good restaurant. The doubles have two large beds, and the singles have one that's big enough for two people. It's the large multistorey building at the main junction just up from NBC bank.

DM Motel GUESTHOUSE $

(☎025-255 2332; s/d Tsh15,000/20,000, s without bathroom Tsh10,000; P) Clean en suite rooms with a large bed (no same-gender sharing permitted) and meals on request. It's just off the main road at the turn-off into Tukuyu town, and signposted.

Bongo Camping CAMPGROUND $

(☎0784-823610; www.facebook.com/bongocamping; camping with your/their tent Tsh6000/8000; P) A backpacker-friendly place with a large, grassy area to pitch your tent, basic cooking facilities, hot-bucket showers, tents for hire and meals on order. It's at Kibisi village, 3km north of Tukuyu, and 800m off the main road. English-speaking guides can be arranged for hikes and excursions.

Information

NBC in the town centre has an ATM, and you can get online at **Syaka Internet Café** (per hr Tsh1000), diagonally opposite the bank.

Rungwe Tea & Tours (☎025-255 2489, 0784-293042; rungweteatours@yahoo.com), next to the post office and just off the main road leading up to Landmark Hotel, can help you organise guides for hikes and excursions in the surrounding area. Prices start about Tsh20,000 per day including a guide and local community fee.

Getting There & Away

Minibuses run several times daily between Tukuyu and both Mbeya (Tsh3000, one to 1½ hours along a scenic, sealed road) and Kyela (Tsh1500, one hour).

Two roads connect Tukuyu with the northern end of Lake Nyasa. The main tarmac road heads southwest and splits at Ibanda, with the western fork going to Songwe River Bridge and into Malawi, and the eastern fork to Kyela and Itungi port. A secondary dirt road heads southeast from Tukuyu to Ipinda and then east towards Matema.

Lake Nyasa

Lake Nyasa (also known as Lake Malawi) is Africa's third-largest lake after Lake Victoria and Lake Tanganyika. It's more than

550km long, up to 75km wide and as deep as 700m in parts. It also has a high level of biodiversity, containing close to one-third of the world's known cichlid species. The Tanzanian side is rimmed to the east by the Livingstone Mountains, whose green, misty slopes form a stunning backdrop as they cascade down to the sandy shoreline.

MATEMA

This quiet lakeside settlement is the only spot on northern Lake Nyasa that has any sort of tourist infrastructure, and with its stunning beachside setting backed by the Livingstone Mountains, it makes an ideal spot to relax for a few days. There's nowhere in Matema to change money, so bring enough shillings with you.

Sleeping & Eating

Blue Canoe Safari CAMPGROUND, BUNGALOW **$**
(Crazy Crocodile Camp; ☎0783-575451; www.bluecanoelodge.com; camping Tsh6000, s/d bungalow without bathroom Tsh25,000/30,000, s/d ste with bathroom US$70/90; P@) This friendly backpackers has beachside camping, no-frills thatched bungalows sharing facilities, a good restaurant and a fully stocked bar. By the time this book is published, there should also be a handful of comfortable, waterfront bungalow suites with bathrooms and hot water. It's on a long beach 2km beyond Matema Lake Shore Resort. Free pick-ups can be arranged from Matema bus stand with advance notice, or it's a pleasant half-hour walk through the palm trees.

Matema Lake Shore Resort BUNGALOW **$**
(☎025-250 4178, 0754-487267; www.twiga.ch/TZ/matemaresort.htm; camping Tsh5000, d without bathroom Tsh20,000, d/tr/f Tsh50,000/40,000/50,000; P) Directly on the beach about 1km beyond Matema Beach View Lutheran Centre, this Swiss-built place has several clean, breezy en suite family chalets, each of which can accommodate up to five people in three beds downstairs and one double bed upstairs, plus several smaller, equally nice en suite double and triple cottages and a quad. Breakfast is not included in room prices, but there is a restaurant serving simple, reasonably priced meals.

Matema Beach View Lutheran Centre BUNGALOW **$**
(☎0787-275164; www.matemabeachview.com; camping Tsh3000, d/tr/q Tsh25,000/35,000/30,000, d/q without bathroom Tsh10,000/20,000; P) Rooms here – in brick *bandas* on or close to the beach – are no frills and rather faded these days, although the local ambience is amenable. Meals are available with advance order, and cooking is allowed for campers. Prices for rooms without bathrooms don't include breakfast. It's about 700m west of Matema hospital and the village centre.

Getting There & Away

BOAT

Schedules are highly variable these days, but there is usually at least one boat weekly – either the MV *Iringa* (p212) or the MV *Songea* – which stops at Matema on its way from Itungi port down the eastern lake shore to Mbamba Bay. The boat stop for Matema is actually at Lyulilo village, about 25 minutes on foot from the main Matema junction. Just follow the main 'road' going southeast from the junction, paralleling the lake shore, and ask for the 'bandari'.

BUS

From Tukuyu, pick-ups to Ipinda leave around 8am most mornings from the roundabout by NBC bank (Tsh2000, two hours). Although drivers sometimes say they are going all the way to Matema, generally they go only as far as Ipinda. Once in Ipinda, pick-ups run sporadically to Matema (Tsh2000, 35km), departing around 2pm, which means you'll need to wait around in Ipinda for a while. Returning from Matema, departures are in the morning. Chances are better on weekends for finding a lift between Matema and Ipinda with a private vehicle. If you get stuck in Ipinda, there are several basic guesthouses.

From Mbeya, a bus departs by about 1pm to Matema via Kyela (Tsh7000, five hours Mbeya to Matema). Departures from Matema direct to Mbeya are daily at 5am. All transport in Matema departs from the main junction near the hospital.

CAR & MOTORCYCLE

From Kyela, the signposted turn-off to Ipinda and Matema is about 3km north of Kyela town centre. From here, it's about 14km to Ipinda, and another 25km to Matema along a readily passable but rough road. Allow one to 1½ hours for the 40km stretch. There's also a shorter, scenic, slightly less rough, route directly from Tukuyu to Ipinda.

MBAMBA BAY

The relaxing outpost of Mbamba Bay is the southernmost Tanzanian port on Lake Nyasa. **St Benadetta Guest House** (www.chipolestagnes.org/mbambabay.htm; r Tsh12,000) near the water is the top of the lot in Mbamba Bay, with simple, clean rooms and meals.

There's one direct vehicle daily from Songea (see p185). Otherwise you will need to change vehicles at Mbinga.

For details of ferry services between Mbamba Bay and Itungi port, see p212. For ferry connections with Nkhata Bay, see p210.

Entering or leaving Tanzania via Mbamba Bay, you'll need to stop at the immigration office/police station near the boat landing to take care of passport formalities.

Songea

The sprawling town of Songea, just over 1000m in altitude, is capital of the surrounding Ruvuma region. The main tribal group here is the Ngoni. Songea takes its name from one of their greatest chiefs, who was killed following the Maji Maji rebellion (see p184) and is buried about 1km from town near the Maji Maji museum.

Sights & Activities

Maji Maji Museum MUSEUM
(admission Tsh6000; 8am-4pm) About 1km from the town centre, off the Njombe road, is this small museum commemorating the Maji Maji uprising. Behind it is Chief Songea's tomb. From town, take the first sealed road to the right after passing CRDB bank and continue about 200m. The museum entrance is on the left with a pale-blue archway.

Sleeping

Heritage Cottage HOTEL $$
(025-260 0888; www.heritage-cottage.com; Njombe Rd; s/d Tsh60,000/75,000; P) This place has modern, clean rooms with TV, a popular bar-restaurant, a large lawn area behind and a playground for children. It's about 3km north of town along the Njombe Rd.

Seed Farm Villa B&B $$
(025-260 2500; seedfarmvilla@yahoo.co.uk; s Tsh55,000-90,000, d Tsh65,000-100,000; P) This place has eight modern, quiet rooms with TV set in tranquil garden surroundings away from the town centre in the Seed Farm area. There's a sitting room with TV, and a restaurant (with advance order). Head out of town along the Tunduru Rd for 2.5km to the signposted turn-off, from where it's 200m further.

THE MAJI MAJI REBELLION

The Maji Maji rebellion, which was the strongest local revolt against the colonial government in German East Africa, is considered to contain some of the earliest seeds of Tanzanian nationalism. It began around the turn of the 20th century when colonial administrators set about establishing enormous cotton plantations in the southeast and along the railway line running from Dar es Salaam towards Morogoro. These plantations required large numbers of workers, most of whom were recruited as forced labour and required to work under miserable salary and living conditions. Anger at this harsh treatment and long-simmering resentment of the colonial government combined to ignite a powerful rebellion. The first outbreak was in 1905 in the area around Kilwa, on the coast. Soon all of southern Tanzania was involved. In addition to deaths on the battlefield, thousands died of hunger brought about by the Germans' scorched-earth policy, in which fields and grain silos in many villages were set on fire. Fatalities were undoubtedly exacerbated by a widespread belief among the Africans that enemy bullets would turn to water before reaching them, and so their warriors would not be harmed – hence the name Maji Maji (*maji* means 'water' in Swahili).

By 1907, when the rebellion was finally suppressed, close to 100,000 people had lost their lives. The Ngoni put up the strongest resistance to the Germans. Following the end of the rebellion, they continued to wage guerrilla-style war until 1908, when the last shreds of their military-based society were destroyed. In order to quell Ngoni resistance once and for all, German troops hanged their leaders and beheaded their most famous chief, Songea.

Among the effects of the Maji Maji uprising were a temporary liberalisation of colonial rule and replacement of the military administration with a civilian government. More significantly, the uprising promoted development of a national identity among many tribal groups and intensified anti-colonial sentiment, kindling the movement for independence.

OK Hotels 92 GUESTHOUSE $
(☎026-260 2640; d Tsh14,000-16,000) Small but decent rooms. From the bus stand, head uphill 400m past the market, take the second right (watch for the sign for the Lutheran church). After about 200m go right again, and look for the apricot-coloured house in a fenced compound to your left. Meals are available at Krista Park across the street.

Eating

Krista Park Fast Food TANZANIAN $
(meals Tsh4000) Snacks and local-style meals opposite OK Hotel Hotels 92. They also have a small bakery.

Information

NBC, on the street behind the market, changes cash, and both NBC and CRDB (at the beginning of the Njombe road) have ATMs (Visa and MasterCards). There's an internet connection at **Amani Internet Café** (per hr Tsh1000; 8.30am-6pm Mon-Sat), on a side street directly opposite the main market entrance. The immigration office (where you'll need to get your passport stamped if you are travelling to or from Mozambique), is at the beginning of the Tunduru Rd.

Getting There & Away

To Dar es Salaam, Super Feo and other buses depart daily from 5am (Tsh38,000 to Tsh40,000, 12 to 13 hours). Going as far as Iringa costs Tsh17,000.

To Mbeya, Super Feo departs daily at 6am in each direction (Tsh18,000, eight hours) via Njombe (Tsh8000, four hours). There are also departures to Njombe at 9.30am and 3pm.

For Mbamba Bay, there's one direct vehicle departing daily by 7am (Tsh9000, six to eight hours). Otherwise, you'll need to get transport to Mbinga (Tsh4500, four hours) and from there on to Mbamba Bay (Tsh5000).

To Tunduru, there's a daily bus departing by about 7am (Tsh15,000, seven to eight hours). There's also one bus daily direct to Masasi (Tsh25,000, 13 hours), departing by 6am.

Transport to Mozambique departs from the Majengo C area, southwest of the bus stand and about 600m in from the main road; ask locals to point out the way through the back streets. If you're driving, head west 18km from Songea along the Mbinga road to the signposted turnoff, from where it's 120km further on an unpaved but good road to the Mozambique border. See p208 for more information.

Tunduru

Tunduru, halfway between Masasi and Songea, is in the centre of an important gemstone-mining region. You'll likely need to spend the night here if travelling between Masasi and Songea.

Adela Guest House & Hotel (r Tsh15,000-20,000, without bathroom Tsh10,000) has small, clean, modern rooms, and meals with advance notice. It's one block north of the main road; coming from Songea and the bus stand, turn left just before reaching NMB bank (across the street). Go down one block and turn left again. Adela is on your right.

Getting There & Away

Bus

There's at least one bus daily between Tunduru and Masasi, departing by 6am (Tsh10,000, five hours) and a daily bus direct from Tunduru to Dar es Salaam (Tsh35,000). Between Tunduru and Songea, there's also daily transport in the dry season (Tsh15,000, seven to eight hours). In both directions from Tunduru, there is little en route, so bring food and water with you. Reserve a seat for onward travel when you arrive in Tunduru for rainy season travel, as vehicles fill up quickly.

Car & Motorcycle

The road from Tunduru in either direction is unpaved but easily passable in the dry season, somewhat more challenging (especially between Tunduru and Songea) during the rains. Heading east, the sealed road currently starts about 55km before Masasi, and large sections in both directions from Tunduru are being prepared for paving.

SOUTHEASTERN TANZANIA

Time seems to have stood still in Tanzania's sparsely populated southeast. It lacks the development and bustle of the north, tourists numbers are a relative trickle and Arusha's crush of Land Cruisers and safari companies is so far removed that it might as well be in another country. Yet, for adventurous travellers seeking to learn about traditional local life, for safari enthusiasts and for divers, the southeast makes an ideal destination.

Southeastern Tanzania

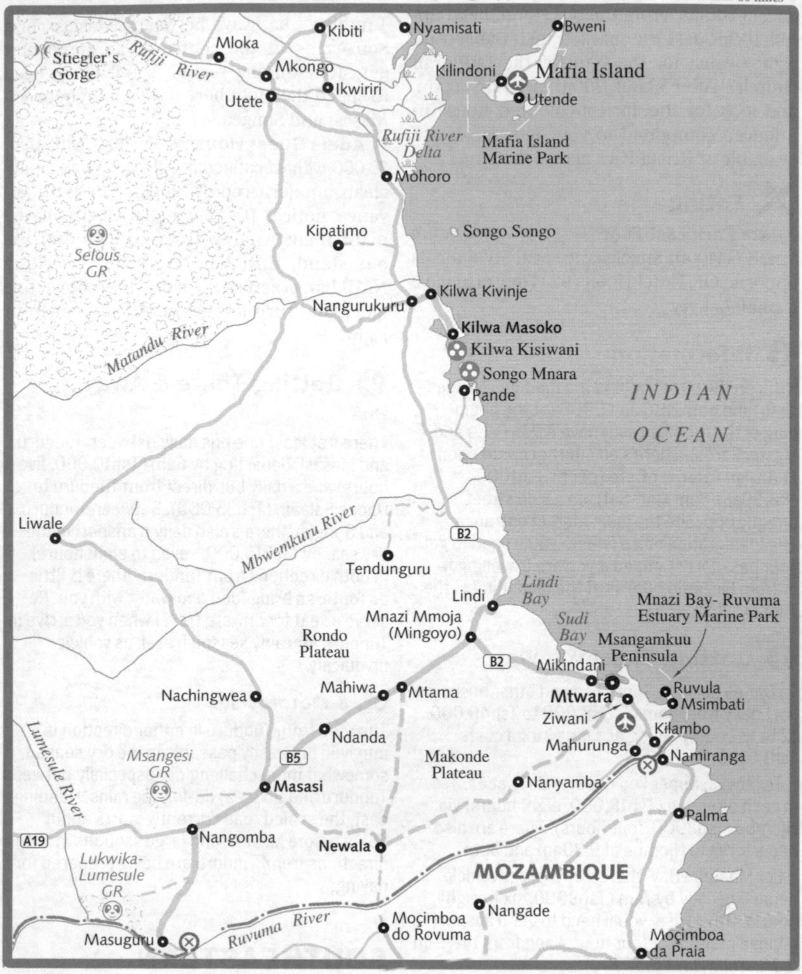

Mafia

Stroll along sandy lanes through the coconut palms. Explore a coastline alternating between dense mangrove stands and white-sand beaches. Get to know traditional Swahili culture. If these appeal, you're likely to love Mafia, which remains refreshingly free of the mass tourism that is overwhelming Zanzibar.

Sights & Activities

Chole Island HISTORIC SITE

(day visitors per person US$5) This is a good place to start exploring, especially around its crumbling but atmospheric ruins, which date from the 19th century.

Big Blu DIVING

(☎0784-918069; www.bigblumafia.com; Chole Bay) A friendly place on the beach just north of Mafia Island Lodge, and under the direction of Moez, a veteran diver with long experience on Mafia.

Mafia Island Lodge Seapoint Watersports Centre DIVING
(☎022-260 1530; www.mafialodge.com; Mafia Island Lodge, Chole Bay) At Mafia Island Lodge.

Sleeping & Eating

For all Chole Bay accommodation (including all budget hotels in Utende situated both before and after entering the park gate and accommodation on Chole Island), you'll need to pay daily marine park entry fees, whether you go diving or not. These fees are not included in accommodation rates.

Mafia Island Lodge LODGE **$$**
(☎022-260 1530, 0786-303049; www.mafialodge.com; Chole Bay; s/d with half board from US$114 /190; ⏲Jun-Apr; ❄@) This lodge – the former government hotel – is set on a long lawn sloping down to a small beach, and is a recommended choice, especially for families. There's a mix of 'standard' and 'superior' rooms and two spacious family suites. The main restaurant, under a soaring *makuti* (thatched) roof, overlooks Chole Bay. There's a beachside bar and a diving and watersports centre. Half board and full board options only.

Whale Shark Lodge GUESTHOUSE **$**
(Sunset Camp; ☎/fax 023-201 0201, 0755-696067; carpho2003@yahoo.co.uk; Kilindoni; bandas per person US$20) This backpacker-friendly place, in a quiet, cliff-top setting overlooking a prime whale-shark viewing area, is a good budget choice, with six simple, clean *bandas* with fans and several with private bathrooms. There's a gazebo with sunset views, and local-style meals on order. A short walk down the cliffside is a small beach with high-tide swimming. It's 1.5km from the town centre, behind the hospital and Tsh1500 in a *bajaji* (tuk-tuk).

Big Blu GUESTHOUSE **$**
(☎0784-918069; www.bigblumafia.org; Chole Bay; d US$40; ⏲Jul–mid-Apr; @) This dive outfitter on the beach next to Mafia Island Lodge has three good-value en suite rooms. It's primarily for divers with Big Blu, although anyone is welcome. Breakfast is included; a restaurant is planned.

Meremeta Guest House & Apartment GUESTHOUSE **$**
(☎0715-345460, 0787-345460; r US$50) On the main road about 800m before the marine park entry gate, with two simple but well-appointed budget rooms, and meals with advance order. Look for the pink building and local artwork display.

Information

Internet Access

Internet Café (Kilindoni; per hr Tsh600) At New Lizu Hotel at the main junction in Kilindoni.

Medical Services & Emergencies

For malaria tests, there's a village clinic on Chole Island. For treatment or anything serious, go to Dar es Salaam.

Money

National Microfinance Bank Just off the airport road, and near the main junction in Kilindoni; changes cash only (dollars, euros and pounds). There are no ATMs.

Getting There & Away

Air

Coastal Aviation (☎022-284 2700, 0767-404350, 0654-404350) flies daily between Dar es Salaam and Mafia (US$120), and between Mafia and Kilwa Masoko (US$156, minimum two passengers), both routes with connections to Zanzibar, Selous Game Reserve and Arusha. **Tropical Air** (☎024-223 2511; www.tropicalair.co.tz) has a similarly priced daily flight between Mafia and Dar es Salaam with connections to

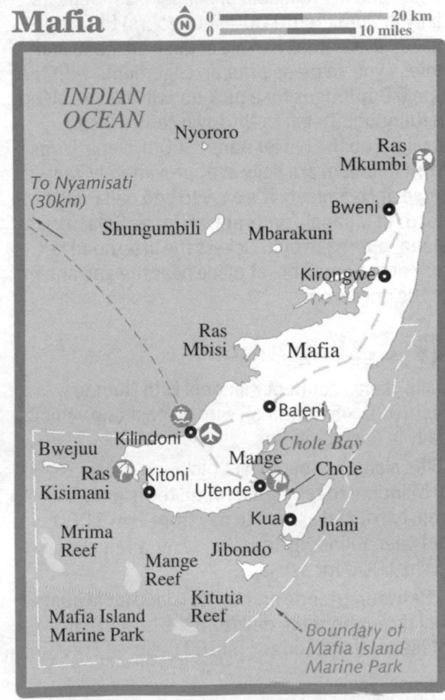

MAFIA ISLAND MARINE PARK

Mafia Island Marine Park – at around 822 sq km the largest marine protected area in the Indian Ocean – shelters a unique complex of estuarine, mangrove, coral reef and marine channel ecosystems. The main way to visit is on a diving excursion with one of the Chole Bay dive operators.

Entry fees (payable by everyone, whether you dive or not) are US$20/5 per adult/child per day. They are collected at a barrier gate across the main road about 1km before Utende, and can be paid in any major currency, cash only. Save your receipt, as it will be checked again when you leave. The **park office** (☎023-240 2690; www.marineparktz.com) is in Utende, just north of Pole Pole Bungalow Resort.

Zanzibar. Costs of a transfer from the airfield to Chole Bay range from US$15 to US$30 per person.

Boat

There's only one motorised boat daily in each direction between Mafia (Kilindoni port) and Nyamisati village on the mainland south of Dar es Salaam. While there's a trickle of budget travellers who reach Mafia this way, it's worth keeping in mind that there is no safety equipment on any of these boats. The vessels are often terribly crowded, and there is minimal shade. If you want to take your chances with this option, get a south-bound dalla-dalla (minibus) from Mbagala mwisho/Rangi Tatu (along the Kilwa road, and reached via dalla-dalla from Dar es Salaam's Posta) to Nyamisati (Tsh3000), from where the motorised MV *Kilindoni* or similar craft departs daily at 2pm (Tsh10,000; four hours) to Kilindoni. You'll eventually arrive at dusk on Mafia and, unless you've made prior arrangements with the Chole Bay lodges for a pick-up, will need to sleep in Kilindoni. To get to the town centre, head straight up the hill for about 300m. Departures from Kilindoni are daily at approximately 7am. Once at Nyamisati, it's easy to find dalla-dallas north to Mbagala and central Dar es Salaam. On Mafia, purchase boat tickets the afternoon before at the small ticket office near the entrance to the port area.

Getting Around

Dalla-dallas connect Kilindoni with Utende (Tsh1000, 45 minutes), with at least one vehicle daily in each direction.

It's also possible to hire pick-ups or *bajajis* in Kilindoni to take you around the island. Bargain hard, and expect to pay from Tsh15,000 between Kilindoni and Utende for a vehicle (Tsh10,000 for a *bajaji*).

Between Utende and Chole Island local boats sail throughout the day from the beach in front of Mafia Island Lodge (Tsh100).

Selous Game Reserve

At the heart of southern Tanzania is the Selous, a vast 48,000 sq km wilderness area stretching over more than 5% of mainland Tanzania. It is Africa's largest wildlife reserve, and Tanzania's most extensive protected area, although the extended ecosystems of Ruaha National Park and the Serengeti come close. It's also home to large herds of elephants, plus buffaloes, crocodiles, hippos, wild dogs, many bird species and some of Tanzania's last remaining black rhinos. Bisecting it is the Rufiji River, which winds its way more than 250km from its source in the highlands through the Selous to the sea, and boasts one of the largest water-catchment areas in East Africa. En route, it cuts a path past woodlands and grasslands and stands of borassus palm, and provides the chance for some unparalleled water-based wildlife watching.

Boat safaris down the Rufiji or on the reserve's lakes are offered by most of the camps and lodges. Most also organise walking safaris, usually three-hour hikes near the camps, or further afield, with the night spent at a fly camp.

Sleeping

INSIDE THE RESERVE BOUNDARIES

TOP CHOICE **Selous Impala Camp** TENTED CAMP $$$
(☎022-245 2005; www.adventurecamps.co.tz; s/d full board plus excursions US$625/1090; ⌚Jun-Mar; P) The well-located Impala is one of the smallest of the Selous camps, and good value if you take advantage of some of Coastal Travel's flight-accommodation deals. It has eight well-spaced, beautifully appointed tents in a prime setting on the river near Lake Mzizimia. The restaurant overlooks the river and has an adjoining bar area on a

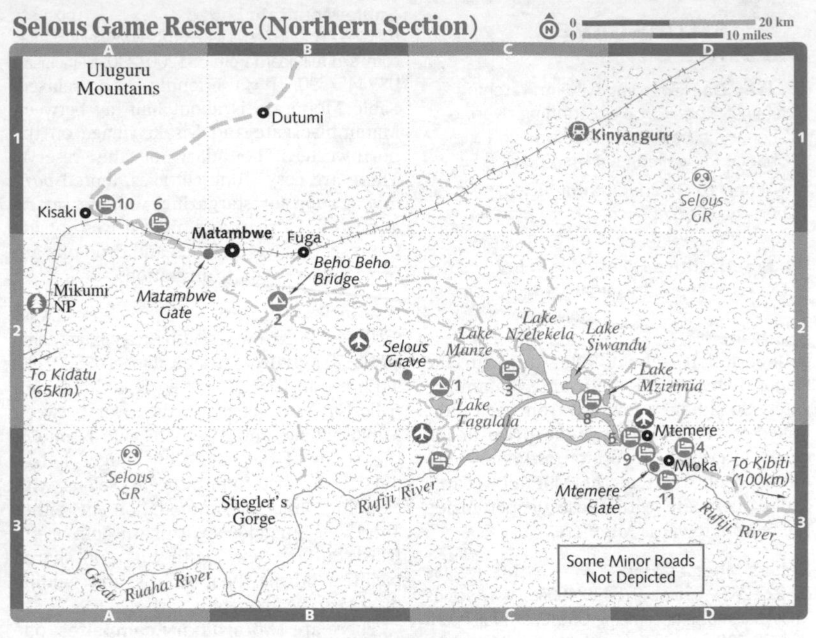

Selous Game Reserve (Northern Section)

Sleeping

1 Campsite ... C2
2 Campsite ... B2
3 Lake Manze Tented Camp ... C2
4 Ndoto Kidogo ... D3
5 Rufiji River Camp ... D3
6 Sable Mountain Lodge ... A1
7 Sand Rivers Selous ... C3
8 Selous Impala Camp ... C2
9 Selous Mbega Camp ... D3
10 Selous Mbega Kisaki Annex ... A1
11 Selous River Camp ... D3

deck jutting out towards the water, and the surrounding area is rich in wildlife.

Lake Manze Tented Camp TENTED CAMP **$$$**
(☎022-245 2005; www.adventurecamps.co.tz; s/d full board plus excursions US$435/740; ⏲Jun-Mar; P) Run by the same management that oversees the Selous Impala Camp, this place is more rustic than its sister camp but quite comfortable and favourably situated, with 12 well-outfitted tents in a good location along an arm of Lake Manze. Ask about flight-accommodation deals.

Rufiji River Camp TENTED CAMP **$$$**
(☎0784-237422; www.rufijirivercamp.com; per person all inclusive US$415/670; P) This long-standing and unpretentious camp, now run by the Fox family, has a fine location on a wide bend in the Rufiji River about 1km inside Mtemere gate. The tents all have river views and there's a sunset terrace. Activities include boat safaris, and walking safaris with the possibility of staying overnight at a fly camp.

Sand Rivers Selous LODGE **$$$**
(www.nomad-tanzania.com; per person all inclusive US$890; ⏲Jun–mid-Mar; P) Set splendidly on its own on the Rufij south of Lake Tagalala, this is one of the Selous' most exclusive options, with some of Tanzania's most renowned wildlife guides.

OUTSIDE THE RESERVE BOUNDARIES

Most lodges outside Mtemere gate arrange boat safaris on the Rufiji and walking tours outside the reserve, as well as wildlife drives inside Selous. Reserve fees are payable only for days you enter within the Selous'

SELOUS GAME RESERVE

» **Why Go** Rewarding wildlife watching against a backdrop of stunning riverine scenery; excellent boat safaris and the chance for walking safaris.

» **When to Go** June through December; many camps close from March through May.

» **Practicalities** Fly or drive in from Dar es Salaam; drive in from Morogoro.

boundaries. It's about 90km through the Selous between Mtemere and Matambwe gates. Spending a few days on each side, linked by a full-day's wildlife drive in between, is a rewarding option, although wildlife concentrations in the Matambwe area cannot compare with those deeper inside the reserve towards Mtemere.

Selous Mbega Camp TENTED CAMP **$$**
(☎022-265 0250, 0784-624664; www.selous-mbega-camp.com; camping US$10, s/d full board US$135/190, s/d full board 'backpackers' special US$85/120, for those arriving by public bus at Mloka, excursions extra; P) This laid-back, good value, family-friendly camp is located about 500m outside the eastern boundary of the Selous near Mtemere gate and about 3km from Mloka village. It has eight no-frills tents set in the foliage somewhat back from the river bank, each with three beds, a bathroom and verandah, and a camping ground (for which you'll need to be self-sufficient with food). Pick-ups and drop-offs to and from Mloka are free. Cash only. The same management also runs the similarly good-value and similarly outfitted **Selous Mbega Kisaki Annex** (camping US$10, s/d full board US$135/190, excursions extra; P), near Kisaki village and the train line, and 17km from Matambwe gate.

Ndoto Kidogo BUNGALOW **$$**
(☎0787-521808, 0782-416861; www.ndoto-kidogo-lodge.com; camping US$10, per person full board in backpacker/bungalow room US$50/120; P) This place just outside Mloka village has simple stone-and-thatch bungalows, plus a no-frills backpacker block with twin-bedded rooms sharing toilet and with its own eating area, plus a campsite. It's on the river, clean and good value.

Sable Mountain Lodge LODGE **$$$**
(☎022-211 0507, 0713-323318; www.selouslodge.com; s/d full board from US$200/290, all-inclusive US$445/590; P ✘) Friendly and relaxed, Sable Mountain is about halfway between Matambwe gate and Kisaki village on the northwestern boundary of the reserve. There are cosy stone cottages, tented *bandas*, a snug for stargazing, walking safaris and wildlife drives and night drives outside the reserve. Free pick-ups and drop-offs are provided to Kisaki train station.

Selous River Camp BUNGALOW **$$**
(☎0784-237525; www.selousrivercamp.com; camping US$10, s/d in tent sharing bathroom US$90/130, s/d in mud hut US$125/160; P) This simple, no-frills but cosy place on the river between Mloka village and Mtemere gate is one of the better of the clutch of 'budget' lodges outside the eastern entrance to Selous, with camping, and accommodation in either 'mud hut' bungalows with bathroom or no-frills standing tents with cots and shared facilities. Meals, boat safaris and wildlife drives can be arranged.

There are two **ordinary campsites**, one at Beho Beho bridge, about 12km southeast of Matambwe, and one at Lake Tagalala, roughly midway between Mtemere and Matambwe. Each has a pit toilet, but otherwise there are no facilities. For both, you will need to be self-sufficient, including with drinking water. **Special campsites** can be arranged in the area between Mtemere gate and Lake Manze (northeast of Lake Tagalala). All campsites can be arranged on arrival at the gates.

Information

The best times to visit are during the cooler, drier season from June to October, and into November, December and January. Much of the reserve is inaccessible between March and May as a result of heavy rains. Many camps close during this time, and boat safaris are difficult due to swollen river levels.

Both the Mtemere and Matambwe gates are open from 6am to 6pm daily. Reserve headquarters are at Matambwe on the Selous' northwestern edge.

Getting There & Away

Air

Coastal Aviation and ZanAir have daily flights linking Selous Game Reserve with Dar es Salaam (US$156 one way), Zanzibar (US$190) and (via Dar) Arusha, with connections to other northern circuit airstrips. Coastal also flies between Selous and Mafia, and Selous and Ruaha National Park. Flights into the Selous are generally suspended during the March to May wet season. All lodges provide airfield transfers.

Bus

There are two daily buses between Dar es Salaam's Temeke bus stand (Sudan Market area) and Mloka village, about 10km east of Mtemere gate (Tsh10,000, seven to nine hours). Departures in both directions are at 5am. From Mloka, you'll need to arrange a pick-up in advance with one of the camps. Hitching within the Selous isn't permitted, and there are no vehicles to rent in Mloka.

If you are continuing from the Selous southwards, there's a daily dalla-dalla to Kibiti, departing Mloka anywhere between 3am and 5am (three to four hours). Once at Kibiti, you'll need to flag down one of the passing buses coming from Dar es Salaam to take you to Nangurukuru junction (for Kilwa) or on to Lindi or Mtwara.

Coming from Morogoro, Madanganya Bus Line goes daily to/from Kisaki, departing in each direction by about 8am (Tsh11,000, seven hours).

Car & Motorcycle

You'll need a 4WD in the Selous. There's no vehicle rental at the reserve and motorcycles aren't permitted.

To get here via road, there are two options. The first: take the Dar es Salaam to Mkongo road, via Kibiti, and then on to Mtemere (250km). The road is in reasonable to good shape as far as Mkongo. From Mkongo to Mtemere (75km) is sometimes impassable during heavy rains. Allow about eight hours from Dar es Salaam.

Alternatively, you can go from Dar es Salaam to Kisaki via Morogoro and then on to Matambwe via a scenic but rough 350km route through the Uluguru Mountains. This route has improved considerably in recent times, but is still sometimes impassable during heavy rains and a 4WD is required at any time of the year.

From Dar es Salaam, the road is sealed as far as Morogoro. Once in Morogoro, take the Old Dar es Salaam road towards Bigwa. About 3km or 4km from the centre of town, past the Teachers' College Morogoro and before reaching Bigwa, you will come to a fork in the road, where you bear right. From here, the road becomes steep and scenic as it winds its way through the Uluguru Mountains onto a flat plain. Allow at least five to six five hours for the stretch from Morogoro to Matambwe, depending on the season.

If you are coming from Dar es Salaam and want to bypass Morogoro, take the an unsignposted left-hand turn-off via Mikese, about 25km east of town on the main Dar es Salaam road that meets up with the Kisaki road at Msumbisi.

Coming from Dar es Salaam, the last petrol station is at Kibiti (about 100km northeast of Mtemere gate), although supplies aren't reliable (otherwise try Ikwiriri – there is no fuel thereafter). Coming from the other direction, the last reliable petrol station is at Morogoro (about 160km from the Matambwe ranger post). Occasionally you may find diesel sold on the roadside at Matombo, 50km south of Morogoro. If you plan to drive around the Selous, bring sufficient petrol supplies with you as there is none available at any of the lodges, nor anywhere close to the reserve.

Train

All Tazara trains stop at Kisaki, which is about five to six hours from Dar es Salaam and the first stop for the express train, and ordinary trains stop at Kinyanguru and Fuga stations

SELOUS GAME RESERVE FEES

All fees are per 24-hour period and currently payable in US dollars cash, although a credit card only system (using Visa card and similar to that in the northern parks) is likely to be implemented within the lifetime of this book.

» **Admission** US$50/30/free per adult/child six to 16 years/child five and under

» **Conservation fee** US$25 per person (payable only by those staying at camps within the Selous' boundaries)

» **Vehicle fee** US$30

» **Camping at ordinary campsite** US$20/5/free per adult/child six to 15 years/child five and under

» **Camping at special campsite** US$40/10/free per adult/child six to 15 years/child five and under

» **Wildlife guard (mandatory in camping areas)** US$20

» **Guide** US$10 (US$15 outside normal working hours and US$20 on walking safaris)

(both of which are closer to the central camps) and at Matambwe (near Matambwe gate). All the lodges do pick-ups (usually combined with a wildlife drive) at varying prices. For schedules, see p214.

It works best to take the train from Dar es Salaam to Selous, though be sure you have a pick-up confirmed in advance, as there's no station, and the train usually arrives after nightfall. Going the other way around, be prepared for delays of up to 20 hours. The lodges can help you monitor the train's progress with their radios.

Kilwa Masoko

Kilwa Masoko (Kilwa of the Market) is a sleepy coastal town nestled amidst dense coastal vegetation and several fine stretches of beach about halfway between Dar es Salaam and Mtwara. It's the springboard for visiting the ruins of the 15th-century Arab settlements at Kilwa Kisiwani and Songo Mnara.

Sights & Activities

On the eastern edge of town is **Jimbizi Beach**, reached via a path that heads downhill by the Masoko Urban Health Centre.

Sleeping

Kilwa Seaview Resort LODGE $$
(☎023-201 3064, 0784-613335, 022-265 0250; www.kilwa.net; Jimbizi Beach; camping US$5; s/d/tr/q US$80/90/100/110; P) This family- and backpacker-friendly place has spacious, good-value A-frame cottages perched along a small escarpment at the eastern end of Jimbizi beach. Driving, the access turn-off is signposted from the main road. By foot, the quickest way to get here from the bus stand is to head south along the main road towards the port, then turn left near the police station, making your way past the police barracks and health clinic down the hill by Kilwa Ruins to Jimbizi Beach. At the north-eastern end of the beach is a small path leading up to the cottages.

Kimbilio Lodge LODGE $$
(☎0656-022166, 0785-991681, 0778-080147; www.kimbiliolodges.com; s/d/tr/q US$90/130/165/200; P) This pleasant Italian-run divers' base has a good beachside setting next door to Kilwa Ruins Lodge, a PADI-certified dive centre offering instruction and dives, and accommodation in six, spacious, tastefully decorated *makuti*-roofed rondavels. There's also good Italian cuisine.

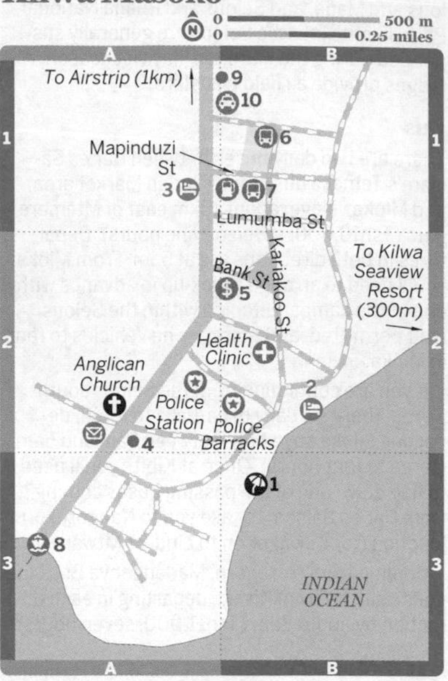

Kilwa Masoko

Sights
1 Jimbizi Beach B3

Sleeping
2 Kimbilio Lodge B2
3 New Mjaka Enterprises Guest House A1

Information
4 District Commissioner's Office A2
5 National Microfinance Bank B2

Transport
6 Buses to Dar es Salaam B1
7 Buses to Lindi B1
8 Jetty & Boats to Kilwa Kisiwani, Songo Mnara & Pande A3
9 Sudi Travel Agency & Coastal Aviation Booking Office B1
10 Transport to Kilwa Kivinje & Nangurukuru B1

New Mjaka Enterprises Guest House GUESTHOUSE $
(☎023-201 3071; Main rd; s without bathroom Tsh4000, s/d banda from Tsh15,000/20,000; P❄) This otherwise undistinguished place is the best of Kilwa's clutch of local guesthouses,

with a few basic rooms in the main building sharing facilities and somewhat better *bandas* next door.

Information

The **National Microfinance Bank** (Main Rd) changes cash. There's no ATM. There's an on again-off again internet connection at the market.

Getting There & Away

Air

Coastal Aviation flies daily between Dar es Salaam and Kilwa (US$260 one way) and between Kilwa and Mafia (US$200, minimum two passengers). Book through its Dar es Salaam office (p54), or in Kilwa through **Sudi Travel Agency** (☎023-201 3004, 0784-824144; Main Rd), north of the petrol station and just north of the transport stand. The airstrip is about 2km north of town along the main road.

Bus

To Nangurukuru (the junction with the Dar–Mtwara road, Tsh2000, one hour) and Kilwa Kivinje (Tsh2000, 45 minutes), shared taxis depart several times daily from the transport stand on the main road just north of the market. The transport stand is also the place to hire taxis or *bajajis* for local excursions.

To Dar es Salaam, there is at least one bus daily (stopping also in Kilwa Kivinje), departing in each direction by about 5.30am (Tsh11,000, seven hours). Buses from Kilwa depart from the eastern edge of the market area, and should be booked the day before. Departures in Dar es Salaam are from Mbagala (take a dalla-dalla to 'Mbagala Mwisho'), along the Kilwa road, which is also the end terminus for this bus on its run up from Kilwa.

Coming from Dar es Salaam it's also possible to get a bus heading to Lindi or Mtwara and get out at Nangurukuru junction, from where you can get local transport to Kilwa Kivinje (Tsh700, 11km) or Kilwa Masoko (Tsh2000, 35km), although you'll often need to pay the full Lindi or Mtwara fare. This doesn't work as well leaving Kilwa, as buses are often full when they pass Nangurukuru (from about 11am).

There are no direct connections to Mtwara; you'll need to transfer at Mingoyo junction.

Around Kilwa Masoko

KILWA KISIWANI

Today, Kilwa Kisiwani (Kilwa on the Island) is a quiet fishing village baking in the sun just offshore from Kilwa Masoko, but in its heyday it was the seat of sultans and centre of a vast trading network linking the old Shona kingdoms and the gold fields of Zimbabwe with Persia, India and China.

While these glory days are now well in the past, the ruins of the settlement are among the most significant groups of Swahili buildings on the East African coast and a Unesco World Heritage Site.

The Ruins

The ruins at Kilwa Kisiwani are in two groups. When approaching Kilwa Kisiwani, the first building you'll find is the Arabic **fort** *(gereza)*. It was built in the early 19th century by the Omani Arabs, on the site of a Portuguese fort dating from the early 16th century. To the southwest of the fort are the ruins of the beautiful **Great Mosque**, with its columns and graceful vaulted roofing, much of which has been impressively restored. In its day, this was the largest mosque on the East African coast. Further southwest and behind the Great Mosque is a smaller **mosque** dating from the early 15th century. To the west of the small mosque are the crumbling remains of the **Makutani**, a large, walled enclosure in the centre of which lived some of the sultans of Kilwa. It is estimated to date from the mid-18th century.

Almost 1.5km from the fort along the coast is **Husuni Kubwa**, once a massive complex of buildings covering almost a hectare and, together with nearby **Husuni Ndogo**, the oldest of Kilwa's ruins. Watch in particular for the octagonal bathing pool. To reach these ruins, you can walk along the beach at low tide or follow the slightly longer inland route.

Information

To visit the ruins, you will need to get a permit (per person Tsh1500) from the **District Commissioner's office** (Halmashauri ya Wilaya ya Kilwa; ⏲7.30am-3.30pm Mon-Fri) in Kilwa Masoko, diagonally opposite the post office. Ask for the Ofisi ya Mambo ya Kale (Antiquities Office); the permit is issued without fuss while you wait. To maximise your chances of finding the Antiquities Officer in, it's best to go in the morning. On weekends, Kilwa Seaview Hotel can help you track down the permit officer, who is usually quite gracious about issuing permits outside of working hours. You'll need to be accompanied by a guide to visit the island, arranged through the Antiquities Office or Kilwa Seaview Hotel.

There are no restaurants or hotels on the island.

Getting There & Away

Local boats go from the port at Kilwa Masoko to Kilwa Kisiwani (Tsh200) whenever there are enough passengers – usually only in the early morning, about 7am, which means you'll need to arrange your permit the day before. To charter your own boat costs Tsh2000 one way (from Tsh15,000 return for a boat with a motor). There is a Tsh300 port fee for tourists, payable in the small office just right of the entry gate. With a good wind, the trip takes about 20 minutes. Kilwa Seaview Hotel arranges excursions for US$30 per person (minimum two people), including guide, permit and boat costs.

Mtwara

POP 93,000

Sprawling Mtwara is southeastern Tanzania's major town. While it lacks the historical appeal of nearby Mikindani and other places along the coast, it has decent infrastructure, easy access and a relaxed pace, and is a convenient entry/exit point for travelling between Tanzania and Mozambique.

Mtwara is loosely located between a business and banking area to the northwest, near Uhuru and Aga Khan Rds, and the market and bus stand about 1.5km away to the southeast. The main north–south street is Tanu Rd. In the far northwest on the sea, and 30 to 40 minutes on foot from the bus stand, is the Shangani quarter, with a small beach. In Mtwara's far southeastern corner, just past the market, are the lively areas of Majengo and Chikon'gola, and St Paul's church, with beautiful paintings inside.

Sleeping & Eating

Drive-In Garden & Cliff Bar GUESTHOUSE $

(☎0784-503007; Shangani; camping Tsh5000, r Tsh20,000; P) This friendly place has a tiny area for camping with bucket baths and several simple, clean rooms, plus a restaurant. Breakfast is not included in the room price. It's just inland from the beach, but for swimming you'll need to walk up to the main Shangani beach near Shangani junction. Go left at the main Shangani junction and follow the road parallel to the beach for about 1.2km to the small signpost on your left. If you can't find it, ask at Safina Grocery Shop at the main Shangani junction.

VETA HOTEL $

(☎023-233 4094; Shangani; s Tsh35,000, ste Tsh60,000; P❄) This large compound has clean rooms, all with one large twin bed, fan, TV and views towards the water, plus a restaurant. It's in Shangani, about 200m back from the water (though there's no swimming beach here). From the T-junction in Shangani, go left and continue for about 3km. There's no public transport; taxis charge from Tsh5000 from town.

Southern Cross Hotel HOTEL $$

(Msemo; ☎023-233 3206; www.msemo.com; Shangani; garden/deluxe/bungalow r Tsh70,000/80,000/100,000; P) This popular and often full place has comfortable rooms with fan, TV and sea-facing windows. Choose between garden rooms (smaller and set slightly back from the water), larger waterfront rooms or spacious bungalows – the latter two all seafront. There's also a waterside restaurant. It's on a small, rocky outcrop overlooking the sea in Shangani, with Shangani swimming beach just a short walk away. Profits from the hotel are channelled into primary healthcare services in the Mtwara region. The hotel is signposted as 'Msemo'.

Mtwara Lutheran Centre HOSTEL $

(☎023-233 3294, 0784-621624; Mikindani Rd; dm Tsh6000, s/d with air-con Tsh30,000/35,000, d without bathroom/air-con Tsh10,000/Tsh15,000; P) Clean, no-frills rooms with fan, and meals with advance notice. It's on the south-

Mtwara

Sights

1 St Paul's Church C7

Sleeping

2 Mtwara Lutheran Centre A7
3 Southern Cross Hotel C1

Eating

4 Himo 2 Restaurant C5
5 Safina Grocery B1

Information

6 CRDB Bank B4
7 Exim Bank B4
8 NBC Bank & ATM C5

Transport

9 Bus & Taxi Stand C7
10 Dhow Port C3
11 Fly 540 .... C5
12 Pick-ups to Msimbati & Kilambo (for Mozambique) C7
13 Precision Air B4

Mtwara

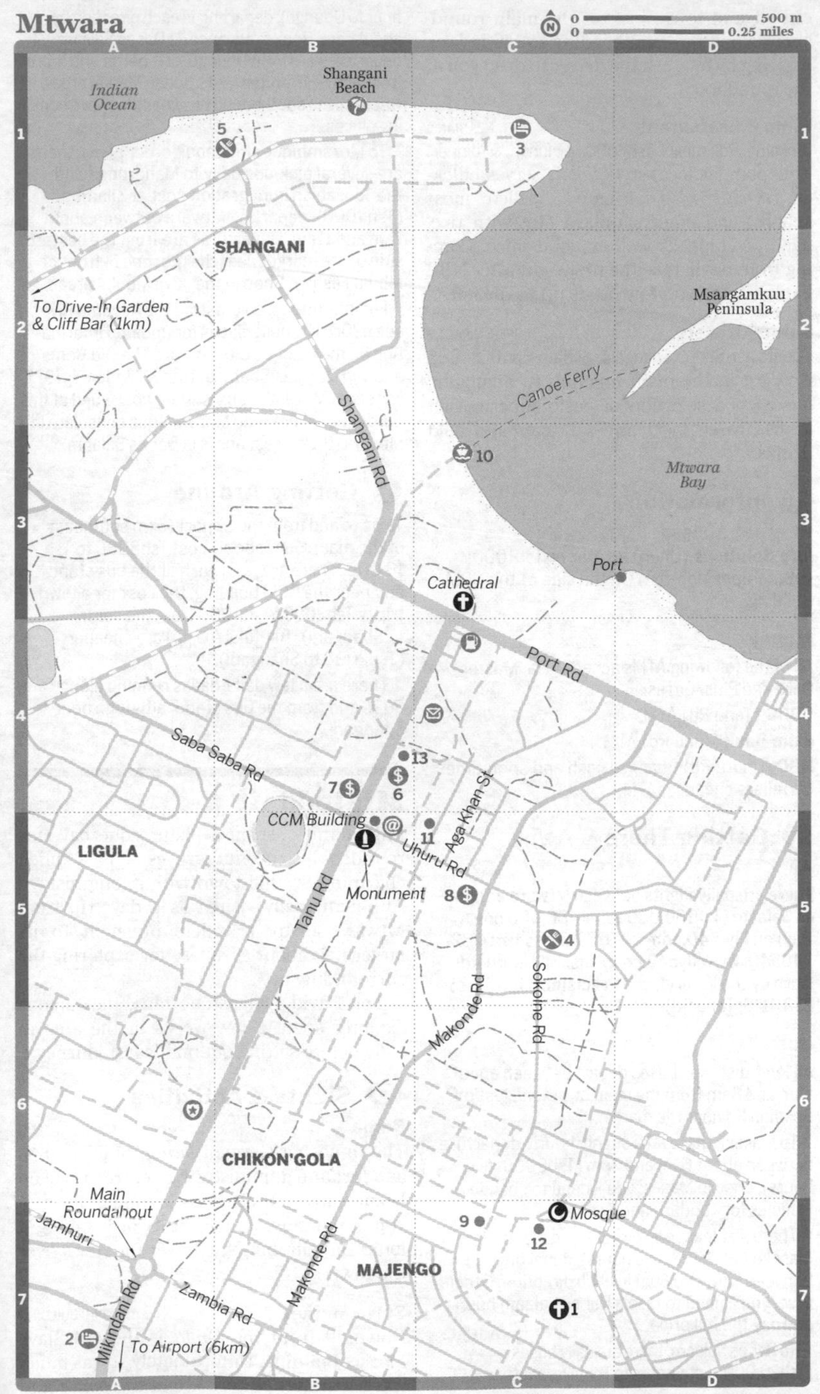

0 500 m
0 0.25 miles
A
B
C
D
1
2
3
4
5
6
7
Indian Ocean
Shangani Beach
5
3
SHANGANI
To Drive-In Garden & Cliff Bar (1km)
Msangamkuu Peninsula
Canoe Ferry
Shangani Rd
10
Mtwara Bay
Port
Cathedral
Port Rd
Saba Saba Rd
13
7
6
CCM Building
11
Aga Khan St
LIGULA
Uhuru Rd
Monument
8
Tanu Rd
4
Makonde Rd
Sokoine Rd
CHIKON'GOLA
Main Roundabout
Jamhuri
9
Mosque
12
Makonde Rd
MAJENGO
Mikindani Rd
Zambia Rd
2
1
To Airport (6km)

ern edge of town, just off the main roundabout along the road heading to Mikindani. Arriving by bus, ask the driver to drop you at the roundabout.

Himo 2 Restaurant TANZANIAN $

(Sokoine Rd; meals Tsh4000; ⏲lunch & dinner) This popular local-style *hoteli* serves chicken, *mishikaki* (marinated, grilled meat kebabs) and other standard fare with rice, ugali or chips, as well as good juice. Coming from town, take the first right after NBC bank. Himo 2 is a few doors up to the left.

Safina Grocery SUPERMARKET $

('Container Shop'; Shangani; ⏲8am-6pm) Safina Grocery, at the main junction in Shangani, has a good selection of basic supermarket items, frozen meat and sausages and cold drinks.

Information

Internet Access

Info Solutions (Uhuru Rd; per hr Tsh1000; ⏲8am-6pm Mon-Sat) On the side of the CCM Building.

Money

All of the following ATMs accept Visa, MasterCard and Plus/Cirrus.

CRDB (Tanu Rd) ATM.

Exim Bank (Tanu Rd) ATM.

NBC (Uhuru Rd) Changes cash and sometimes travellers cheques; ATM.

Getting There & Away

Air

There are daily flights between Mtwara and Dar es Salaam (Tsh100,000 to Tsh180,000 one way) on **Fly 540.com** (☎0779-000540, 0782-840540; www.fly540.com), just off Uhuru Rd (turn by the library), and **Precision Air** (☎023-233 4116; Tanu Rd).

Bus

All long-distance buses depart between about 5am and 8am from the main bus stand just off Sokoine Rd near the market.

To Masasi, there are roughly hourly departures between about 6am and 2pm (Tsh6000, five hours); once in Masasi you'll need to change vehicles for Tunduru and Songea.

There's at least one direct bus daily to Kilwa Masoko (Tsh7000, five hours), departing between 5am and 6am in each direction. Otherwise, you'll need to take a Dar es Salaam bus, and pay the full price.

To Dar es Salaam, there are daily buses (Tsh20,000, eight hours to Temeke, another hour to Ubungo), departing in each direction by about 6am. Book in advance. In Dar es Salaam, departures are from Ubungo, or – better and more frequently – from Temeke's Sudan Market area, where all the southbound bus lines also have booking offices.

To Mozambique (Kilambo border post), there are several pick-ups daily to Mahurunga and the Tanzanian immigration post at Kilambo (Tsh4000), departing Mtwara between about 7am and 11am. Departures are from the eastern side of the market near the mosque in front of Mbulu Fashion Shop in the 'kwa Mbulu' area.

For information on crossing the Ruvuma River, see p208. The best places for updated information on the Kilambo crossing are The Old Boma and Ten Degrees South, both in Mikindani (p197). Note that Mozambican visas are *not* issued at this border and there is no Mozambique consulate in Mtwara (the closest one is in Dar es Salaam).

Getting Around

Taxis to and from the airport (6km southeast of the main roundabout) cost Tsh8000 to Tsh 10,000. There are taxi ranks at the bus stand and near the CCM building; the cost for a town trip is Tsh2000 (Tsh4000 from the centre to Shangani). Tuk-tuks *(bajaji)* are cheaper (Tsh2000 to Shangani).

There are a few dalla-dallas running along Tanu Rd to and from the bus stand, although none to Shangani.

Mikindani

Mikindani – set on a picturesque bay surrounded by coconut groves – is a quiet, charming Swahili town with a long history. Although easily visited as a day trip from Mtwara, many travellers prefer it to its larger neighbour as a base for exploring the surrounding area.

For David Livingstone fans, the famous explorer spent a few weeks in the area in 1866 before setting out on his last journey.

Sights & Activities

Boma HISTORIC BUILDING

The imposing German *boma*, built in 1895 as a fort and administrative centre, has been beautifully renovated as a hotel. Even if you're not staying here, it's worth taking a look, and climbing the tower for views over the town.

Slave Market HISTORIC BUILDING

Downhill from the *boma* is the old Slave Market building. Unfortunately, it was much less accurately restored than the *boma* and lost much of its architectural interest when its open arches were filled in.

Prison Ruins RUINS

These ruins are opposite the jetty, and nearby is a large, hollow baobab tree that was once used to keep unruly prisoners in solitary confinement.

Sleeping & Eating

TOP CHOICE The Old Boma at Mikindani HOTEL $$
(☎023-233 3875, 0756-455978; www.mikindani.com; s Tsh100,000, r without/with balcony from Tsh160,000/230,000, tr ste Tsh300,000; P) This beautifully restored building, on a breezy hilltop overlooking town and Mikindani Bay, offers spacious, atmospheric, high-ceilinged doubles and the closest to top-end standards that you'll find in these parts. There's a sunset terrace overlooking the bay, a pool surrounded by bougainvillea bushes and lush gardens, and a restaurant. Rooms vary, so check out a few before choosing. It's run by Trade Aid (www.tradeaiduk.org), a non-profit group committed to improving employment and educational opportunities for the local community. A stay at the Old Boma supports their work; check out their website if you want to get involved.

Ten Degrees South Lodge LODGE $
(ECO2; ☎0784-855833; www.eco2tz.com; r without/with bathroom Tsh30,000/75,000; P) A good budget travellers' base, with four refurbished rooms – all with large beds, all sharing bathroom, plus bay views and deck chairs up on the roof. Next door are a handful of new, lovely, self-contained rooms, and there's a restaurant-bar (meals from Tsh12,000) under a shady, thatched *banda* with a TV. **ECO2** (www.eco2tz.com) is based here, and is the best contact for arranging diving in Mnazi Bay–Ruvuma Estuary Marine Park.

Information

The closest banking facilities are in Mtwara.

The Old Boma has a tourist information office and an internet connection. Walking tours of towns and local excursions can be organised here and at Ten Degrees South.

Getting There & Away

Mikindani is 10km from Mtwara along a sealed road. Minibuses (Tsh400) run between the two towns throughout the day. Taxis from Mtwara charge from about Ts10,000.

Masasi

Masasi, a scruffy district centre and birthplace of former Tanzanian President Benjamin Mkapa, stretches itself out along the main road off the edge of the Makonde Plateau against a backdrop of granite hills. It's a potentially useful stop if you are travelling to/from Mozambique via the Unity Bridge. If you're cash-strapped there's an NBC bank with an ATM on the main road at the eastern end of town.

Sleeping & Eating

Holiday Hotel GUESTHOUSE $
(Tunduru Rd; r Tsh30,000-40,000; P) Clean, straightforward rooms with fan in a convenient location opposite and about 100m east of the bus stand.

Mbalache Two Guest House GUESTHOUSE $
(Tunduru Rd; r Tsh8000) This guesthouse has basic rooms, all with fan, and is convenient to the bus stand – about 200m east along the main road opposite Masasi Inn and diagonally opposite Holiday Hotel. There's no food.

Getting There & Away

The bus stand is at the western edge of Masasi at the intersection of the Tunduru, Nachingwea and Newala roads.

To Mtwara, buses go approximately hourly between 6am and 2pm daily (Tsh4500, five hours).

To Newala (Tsh4000, 1½ hours) transport leaves several times daily.

UNDERSTAND TANZANIA

History

Tanzania's history begins with the dawn of humankind. Hominid (humanlike) footprints unearthed near Oldupai (Olduvai) Gorge, together with archaeological finds from Kenya and Ethiopia, show that our earliest ancestors were likely roaming the Tanzanian plains over three million years ago. For more on these and subsequent millennia, and an overview of colonial-era developments, see p572.

The Independence Struggle

The 1905 Maji Maji rebellion (see boxed text p184) contains the earliest seeds of Tanzanian independence. During the following decades, the nationalist movement in Tanganyika – which is what mainland Tanzania was then known – solidified. Farmers' cooperatives began to play an increasingly important political role, as did a relatively up-and-coming group known as the Tanganyika Africa Association (TAA). Soon the TAA came to dominate Tanganyika's political scene, serving as the central channel for grass-roots resentment against colonial policies.

In 1953 the TAA elected an eloquent young teacher named Julius Nyerere as its president. He quickly transformed the group into an effective political organisation. A new internal constitution was introduced on 7 July 1954 (now celebrated as Saba Saba Day) and the TAA became the Tanganyika African National Union (TANU), with the rallying cry of '*uhuru na umoja*' (freedom and unity).

Independence was the main item on TANU's agenda. In 1958 and 1959, TANU-supported candidates decisively won general legislative elections, and in 1959 Britain – which at the time held the reins in Tanganyika as governing 'caretaker' – agreed to the establishment of internal self-government. On 9 December 1961 Tanganyika became independent and on 9 December 1962 it was established as a republic, with Nyerere as president.

On the Zanzibar Archipelago, which had been a British protectorate ever since 1890, the predominant push for independence came from the radical Afro-Shirazi Party (ASP). Opposing the ASP were two minority parties, the Zanzibar and Pemba People's Party (ZPPP) and the sultanate-oriented Zanzibar Nationalist Party (ZNP). Both the ZPP and the ZNP parties were favoured by the British. As a result, at Zanzibari independence in December 1963, it was the two minority parties that formed the first government.

This new government did not last long. Within a month, a Ugandan immigrant named John Okello initiated a violent revolution against the ruling ZPPP–ZNP coalition, leading to the toppling of the government and the sultan, and the massacre or expulsion of most of the islands' Arab population. The sultan was replaced by an entity known as the Zanzibar Revolutionary Council, which comprised ASP members and was headed by Abeid Karume.

On 26 April 1964 Nyerere signed an act of union with Karume, thereby creating the United Republic of Tanganyika (renamed the United Republic of Tanzania the following October).

Formation of the union, which was resented by many Zanzibaris from the outset, was motivated in part by the then-prevailing spirit of pan-Africanism, and in part as a cold war response to the ASP's socialist program.

Karume's government lasted until 1972, when he was assassinated and succeeded by Aboud Jumbe. Shortly thereafter, in an effort to subdue the ongoing unrest resulting from the merger of the islands with the mainland, Nyerere authorised formation of a one-party state and combined TANU and the ASP into a new party known as Chama Cha Mapinduzi (CCM; Party of the Revolution). This merger, which was ratified in a new union constitution on 27 April 1977, marked the beginning of the CCM's dominance of Tanzanian politics, which endures to this day.

The Great Socialist Experiment

Nyerere took the helm of a country that was economically foundering and politically fragile, its stability plagued in particular by the mainland's lack of control over the Zanzibar Archipelago. Education had also been neglected, and at independence there were only a handful of university graduates in the entire country.

This inauspicious beginning eventually led to the Arusha Declaration of 1967, which committed Tanzania to a policy of socialism and self-reliance. The policy's cornerstone was the *ujamaa* (familyhood) village – an agricultural collective run along traditional African lines, with an emphasis on self-reliance. Basic goods and tools were to be held in common and shared among members, while each individual was obligated to work on the land.

Tanzania's experiment in socialism was acclaimed in the days following independence, and is credited with unifying the country and expanding education and health care. Economically, however, it was a failure. Per capita income plummeted, agricultural production stagnated and industry limped along at less than 50% of capacity. The decline was precipitated by a combination of factors, including steeply rising oil prices, the 1977 break-up of the East African Community (an economic and customs union between Tanzania, Kenya and Uganda) and sharp drops in the value of coffee and sisal exports.

Democracy

Nyerere was re-elected to a fifth term in 1980, amid continuing dissatisfaction with the great socialist experiment in the country. In 1985 he resigned from political office, handing over power to Zanzibari Ali Hassan Mwinyi. Mwinyi tried to distance himself from Nyerere and his policies, and instituted an economic recovery program. Yet the pace of change remained slow, and Mwinyi's presidency was rather unpopular. The collapse of European communism in the early 1990s, and pressure from Western donor nations, accelerated the move towards multiparty politics, and in 1992 the constitution was amended to legalise opposition parties.

The first elections took place in October 1995 in an atmosphere of chaos. On the mainland, the CCM, under Benjamin Mkapa, won 62% of the vote in relatively smooth balloting. On the Zanzibar Archipelago, voting for the Zanzibari presidency was universally denounced for its dishonesty. In the ensuing uproar, foreign development assistance was suspended and most expatriates who were working on the islands left.

In October 2000 the elections proceeded without incident on the mainland, with a decisive victory for incumbent Mkapa and the CCM. On Zanzibar the balloting was again highly controversial. The government declared the demonstrations illegal, but they were held anyway. On Pemba, a CUF stronghold where demonstrators greatly outnumbered the police, government security units responded with force, resulting in at least several dozen deaths and causing many Pembans to temporarily flee the island.

In the wake of the violence, the CCM and CUF initiated renewed their attempts to reach agreement through dialogue. An accord was signed aimed at ending the civil unrest on the archipelago and negotiating a long-term solution to the crisis. However, progress has been only modest at best in the current climate, and tensions continue to simmer.

Recent Developments

One of the effects that the introduction of multiparty politics had on Tanzanian life was the unmasking of underlying political, economic and religious frictions, especially between the mainland and the Zanzibar Archipelago. Yet – the volatile Zanzibar situation notwithstanding – Tanzania as a whole remains reasonably well integrated, with comparatively high levels of religious and ethnic tolerance, particularly on the mainland. Tanzanians have earned a name for themselves in the region for their moderation and balance, and most observers consider it highly unlikely that the country would disintegrate into the tribal conflicts that have plagued some of its neighbours.

On the political front, President Mkapa was constitutionally prevented from seeking another term in the 2005 presidential elections, which were won in a landslide victory by CCM's Jakaya Kikwete, the charismatic former Foreign Minister. In the 2010 national elections, Kikwete again won, although with a considerably smaller majority (62% of the vote) against opposition candidate Willibrod Slaa of the Party for Democracy and Progress, who garnered 27% of the vote.

Despite this, the CCM remains entrenched, and the opposition relatively splintered.

People

Tanzania is home to about 120 tribal groups, in addition to relatively small but economically significant numbers of Asians and Arabs, and a miniscule European community. Most tribes are very small; almost 100 of them combined account for only one-third of the total population. As a result, none has succeeded in dominating politically or culturally, although groups such as the Chagga and the Haya, who have a long tradition of education, are disproportionately well-represented in government and business circles.

About 95% of Tanzanians are of Bantu origin. These include the Sukuma (who live around Mwanza and southern Lake Victoria, and constitute approximately 13% of the overall population), the Nyamwezi (around Tabora), the Makonde (Southeastern Tanzania), the Haya (around Bukoba) and the Chagga (around

Mt Kilimanjaro). The Maasai and several smaller groups incorporating the Arusha and the Samburu (all in northern Tanzania) are of Nilo-Hamitic or Nilotic origin. The Iraqw, around Karatu and northwest of Lake Manyara, are Cushitic, as are the tiny northern-central tribes of Gorowa and Burungi. The Sandawe and, more distantly, the seminomadic Hadzabe (around Lake Eyasi), belong to the Khoisan ethnolinguistic family.

Tribal structures, however, range from weak to nonexistent – a legacy of Nyerere's abolishment of local chieftaincies following independence.

About 3% of Tanzania's total population live on the Zanzibar Archipelago, with about one-third of these on Pemba. Most African Zanzibaris belong to one of three groups: the Hadimu, the Tumbatu and the Pemba. Members of the non-African Zanzibari population are primarily Shirazi and consider themselves descendants of immigrants from Shiraz in Persia (Iran).

Religion

About 35% to 40% of Tanzanians are Muslim and between 40% and 45% are Christian. The remainder follow traditional religions. There are also small communities of Hindus, Sikhs and Ismailis. Muslims are traditionally found along the coast and in the inland towns that line the old caravan routes. The population of the Zanzibar Archipelago is almost exclusively Sunni Muslim, with tiny Christian and Hindu communities.

Music & Dance

The greatest influence on Tanzania's modern music scene has been the Congolese bands that began playing in Dar es Salaam in the early 1960s (see p632), and the late Remmy Ongala ('Dr Remmy'), who was born in the Democratic Republic of Congo (Zaïre), but gained his fame in Tanzania.

On Zanzibar, the music scene has long been dominated by *taarab* (see p73).

Visual Arts

Tanzania's Makonde, together with their Mozambican counterparts, are renowned throughout East Africa for their original and highly fanciful carvings. Although originally from the Southeast around the Makonde Plateau, commercial realities lured many Makonde north. Today, the country's main carving centre is at Mwenge in Dar es Salaam (p52), where blocks of hard African blackwood (*Dalbergia melanoxylon* or, in Swahili, *mpingo*) come to life under the hands of skilled artists. Also see the Makonde Woodcarvings boxed text on p633.

Environment & National Parks

At over 943,000 sq km (almost four times the size of the UK), Tanzania is East Africa's largest country. It is bordered to the east by the Indian Ocean. To the west are the deep lakes of the Western Rift Valley with mountains rising up from their shores. Much of central Tanzania is an arid highland plateau averaging 900m to 1800m in altitude and nestled between the eastern and western branches of the Great Rift Valley.

Tanzania's mountain ranges are grouped into a sharply rising northeastern section (Eastern Arc), and an open, rolling central and southern section (the Southern Highlands or Southern Arc). A range of volcanoes, the Crater Highlands, rises from the side of the Great Rift Valley in northern Tanzania.

The largest river is the Rufiji, which drains the Southern Highlands en route to the coast. The Ruvuma River forms the border with Mozambique.

Wildlife

ANIMALS

Tanzania's fauna is notable for its sheer numbers and its variety, with 430 species and subspecies among the country's more than four million wild animals. These include zebras, elephants, wildebeests, buffaloes, hippos, giraffes, antelopes, dik-diks, gazelles, elands and kudus. Tanzania is known for its predators, with Serengeti National Park one of the best places for spotting lions, cheetahs and leopards. There are also hyenas and wild dogs and, in Gombe and Mahale Mountains National Parks, chimpanzees. Complementing this are over 1000 bird species of birds, including many endemics.

PLANTS

Small patches of tropical rainforest in Tanzania's Eastern Arc mountains provide home to a rich assortment of plants, many found nowhere else in the world. These include the Usambara or African violet *(Saintpaulia)* and *Impatiens,* which are sold as house plants in grocery stores throughout the West. Similar forest patches – remnants of the much larger tropical forest that once extended across the continent – are also found in the Udzungwas, Ulugurus and several other areas. South and west of the Eastern Arc range are stands of baobab.

Away from the mountain ranges, much of the country is covered by miombo ('moist' woodland), where the main vegetation is various types of *Brachystegia* tree. Much of the dry central plateau is covered with savannah, bushland and thickets, while grasslands cover the Serengeti Plain and other areas that lack good drainage.

National Parks & Reserves

Tanzania has 15 mainland national parks (with one more, Saa Nane Game Reserve, on the way), 14 wildlife reserves, the Ngorongoro Conservation Area, three marine parks and several protected marine reserves.

NATIONAL PARKS

Tanzania's national parks are managed by the **Tanzania National Parks Authority** (Tanapa; www.tanzaniaparks.com; Dodoma Rd, Arusha). For park entry fees see the individual listings.

You'll also need to pay park concession fees (fees per visitor levied by Tanapa for those staying at hotels and lodges within the parks). These vary by hotel, but average US$10 per child per night, and US$30 to US$50 per adult per night. Most lodges include these fees in their accommodation rates, but confirm this when booking. Other costs include guide fees of US$10/15/20 per group per day/overnight/walking safari, plus vehicle fees (US$40/Tsh10,000 per foreign-/Tanzanian-registered car).

WILDLIFE RESERVES

Wildlife reserves are administered by the **Wildlife Division of the Ministry of Natural Resources & Tourism** (www.mnrt.go.tz; cnr Nyerere & Changombe Rds, Dar es Salaam). Fees currently must be paid in US dollars cash, although a credit card system (Visa card) is planned imminently for Selous Game Reserve. Selous is the only reserve with tourist infrastructure. Large areas of most others have been leased as hunting concessions, as has the southern Selous.

> Lonely Planet's *Tanzania* guidebook has full coverage of all of Tanzania's national parks, including Kitulo and Udzungwa Mountains National Parks for hikers, and Mkomazi National Park.

MARINE PARKS & RESERVES

Mafia Island Marine Park (p188) and the Dar es Salaam Marine Reserves (Mbudya, Bongoyo, Pangavini and Fungu Yasini Islands; p57) and Tanzania's other marine protected areas are under the jurisdiction of the Ministry of Natural Resources & Tourism's **Marine Parks & Reserves Unit** (www.marineparks.go.tz; Olympio St, Upanga, Dar es Salaam).

NGORONGORO CONSERVATION AREA

The Ngorongoro Conservation Area was established as a multiple-use area to protect wildlife and the pastoralist lifestyle of the Maasai, who had lost other large areas of their traditional territory with the formation of Serengeti National Park. It is administered by the **Ngorongoro Conservation Area Authority** (www.ngorongorocrater.org). For information and fees, see p141.

SURVIVAL GUIDE

Directory A–Z

Accommodation

» Most upmarket hotels consider July, August and the Christmas and New Year holidays to be high season. A peak-season surcharge is sometimes levied on top of regular high-season rates from late December through early January.

» During the March to early June low season, it's often possible to negotiate significant discounts (up to 50%) on room rates.

» A residents' permit entitles you to discounts at some hotels.

CAMPING

Carry a tent to save money and for flexibility off the beaten track. Note that camping in most national parks costs at least US$30 per person per night. All parks have campsites, designated as either 'public' ('ordinary') or 'special'. For most national park campsites, you'll need to bring everything in with you, including drinking water. Most parks also have simple huts or cottages ('*bandas*'), several have basic resthouses. Both the *bandas* and the resthouses have communal cooking facilities.

National Park Public Campsites These have toilets (usually pit latrines) and, sometimes, a water source.

National Park Special Campsites These are smaller, more remote and more expensive than public sites, with no facilities. The idea is that the area remains as close to pristine as possible. Advance booking required; once you make a booking, the special campsite is reserved exclusively for your group.

Elsewhere There are campsites situated in or near most major towns, near many of the national parks and in some scenic locations along a few of the main highways (ie Dar es Salaam–Mbeya, and Tanga–Moshi).

Camping away from established sites is generally not advisable. In rural areas, seek permission first from the village head or elders before pitching your tent.

Camping is not permitted on Zanzibar.

GUESTHOUSES

» In Tanzanian Swahili, *hotel* or *hoteli* refers to food and drink rather than accommodation. The better term if you're looking for somewhere to sleep is *nyumba ya kulala wageni* – or less formally, *pa kulala*.

» Water can be a problem during the dry season, and many of the cheapest places won't have running or hot water, though all will arrange a bucket if you ask.

HOTELS & LODGES

» En suite rooms are widely referred to in Tanzania as 'self-contained' or 'self-containers' rooms.

» There's a good selection of midrange and top-end accommodation in major towns, as well as beautiful luxury lodges on safari and along the coast.

Activities

BIRDING

Birding resources include the **Tanzania Bird Atlas** (www.tanzaniabirdatlas.com), the Tanzania Hotspots page on www.camacdonald.com/birding/africatanzania.htm and http://birds.intanzania.com.

CYCLING

Tanzania bicycling contacts include:

AfriRoots (www.afriroots.co.tz) Budget cycling trips.

International Bicycle Fund (www.ibike.org/bikeafrica) Highly recommended; organises cycling tours in Tanzania and provides information.

NATIONAL PARK FEES

In theory, entry fees and all other park fees must be paid electronically with a Visa card (MasterCard is also accepted at some northern parks) using your PIN number. However, if the park credit card machine is broken (a frequent occurrence), or not yet installed (as is the case in most parks outside the northern circuit), visitors are required to pay in US dollars cash. Some parks also accept Tanzanian shillings. It's also possible to pay using a 'smart card' available for purchase from CRDB and Exim banks.

Until Tanapa gets the kinks in its system sorted out, our advice is to bring both a Visa card and sufficient US dollars cash to cover payment of park entry fees, guide fees and Tanapa-run park accommodation.

ACCOMMODATION	US$ (16YR +)	US$ (5-15YR)
Public campsite	30 (Mt Kilimanjaro 50)	5
Special campsite	50	10
Hostel	10	-
Resthouse (Serengeti, Arusha, Ruaha, Katavi)	30 (Gombe 20)	-
Banda or hut	20-50	-

Summits Africa (www.summits-africa.com) Upmarket adventure cycling in the northern circuit.

Tanzanian Bike Safaris (www.tanzaniabiking.com) Multi-day rides in northern Tanzania.

Wayo Africa (www.wayoafrica.com) Upmarket rides around Arusha and in the Lake Manyara region.

HIKING & TREKKING

Except in the western Usambaras around Lushoto (where there's an informal guide organisation and a network of guesthouses) and in the Crater Highlands (where most hiking is organised through operators), you'll need to organise things yourself when hiking in Tanzania. In most areas it's required or recommended to go with a guide, which, apart from adding to the cost, can feel constraining if you're used to just setting off on your own. When formalising your arrangements, be sure you and the guide agree on how much territory will be covered each day, as local expectations about suitable daily sections on standard routes are often unsatisfyingly short if you're an experienced hiker. For trekking operator listings (for Mt Kilimanjaro and Mt Meru treks), see the Arusha, Moshi and Marangu sections; many of the safari operators listed on p126 also organise treks. All trekking requires local guides and (usually) porters.

HORSE RIDING

Riding safaris are possible in the West Kilimanjaro and Lake Natron areas. Contacts include Equestrian Safaris (www.safaririding.com), Makoa Farm (www.makoa-farm.com) and Ndarakwai (www.ndarakwai.com).

Customs Regulations

Exporting seashells, coral, ivory and turtle shells is illegal. You can export a maximum of Tsh2000 without declaration. There's no limit on the importation of foreign currency; amounts over US$10,000 must be declared.

Embassies & Consulates

Embassies and consulates in Dar es Salaam include the following.

Australia (www.embassy.gov.au) Contact the Canadian embassy.

Burundi (☎022-212 7008; Lugalo St, Upanga) Just up from the Italian embassy, and opposite the army compound. The consulate in Kigoma (p163) also issues single and multiple-entry visas.

Canada (Map p50; ☎022-216 3300; www.dfait-maeci.gc.ca/tanzania; Umoja House, cnr Mirambo St & Garden Ave)

Democratic Republic of the Congo Embassy (Formerly Zaïre) (Map p50; 435 Maliki Rd, Upanga) The consulate in Kigoma (p163) officially only issues visas to Tanzanian residents, but will give them to travellers if they provide a good reason for not getting one in their home country.

France (Map p50; ☎022-219 8800; www.ambafrance-tz.org; Ali Hassan Mwinyi Rd)

Germany (Map p50; ☎022-211 7409 to 7415; www.daressalam.diplo.de/en/Startseite.html; Umoja House, cnr Mirambo St & Garden Ave)

India (Map p50; ☎022-266 9040; www.hcindiatz.org; 82 Kinondoni Rd)

Ireland (Map p50; ☎022-260 2355/6; iremb@raha.com; Toure Dr) Opposite Golden Tulip Hotel.

Italy (Map p50; ☎022-211 5935; www.ambdaressalaam.esteri.it; 316 Lugalo Rd, Upanga)

Kenya (Map p50; ☎022-266 8285/6; www.kenyahighcomtz.org; cnr Ali Hassan Mwinyi Rd & Kaunda Dr, Oysterbay)

Malawi (Map p50; ☎022-213 6951; 1st fl, Zambia House, cnr Ohio St & Sokoine Dr)

Mozambique (Map p50; ☎022-211 6502; 25 Garden Ave)

Netherlands (Map p50; ☎022-211 0000; http://tanzania.nlembassy.org; Umoja House, cnr Mirambo St & Garden Ave)

Rwanda (Map p50; ☎022-212 0703, 213 0119; www.tanzania.embassy.gov.rw; 32 Ali Hassan Mwinyi Rd, Upanga)

Uganda (Map p50; ☎022-266 7009; 25 Msasani Rd, near Oyster Bay Primary School)

PRACTICALITIES

- **Currency** Tanzanian shilling.
- **Newspapers** *Guardian* and *Daily News* (dailies); *Business Times*, *Financial Times* and *East African* (weeklies).
- **Radio** Radio Tanzania (government-aligned); Radio One; Radio Free Africa; BBC World Service; Deutsche Welle.
- **Weights & Measures** Metric system.

UK (Map p50; ☎022-229 0000; http://ukintanzania.fco.gov.uk; Umoja House, cnr Mirambo St & Garden Ave)

USA (☎022-266 8001; http://tanzania.usembassy.gov; Old Bagamoyo & Kawawa Rds)

Zambia (Map p50; ☎022-212 5529; Ground fl, Zambia House, cnr Ohio St & Sokoine Dr)

Gay & Lesbian Travellers

Homosexuality is officially illegal in Tanzania, including Zanzibar, incurring penalties of up to 14 years imprisonment. Prosecutions are rare, but public displays of affection, whether between people of the same or opposite sex, are frowned upon, and homosexuality is culturally taboo.

Internet Access

If you will be in Tanzania for a while, consider buying a USB stick from one of the main mobile providers (US$50 to US$75), which you can then load with airtime (about Tsh15,000 for 1GB, valid for seven days) and plug into your laptop.

Language Courses

Institute of Swahili & Foreign Languages (Map p62; ☎024-223 0724, 223 3337; www.suza.ac.tz/Institues/IKFL.htm; Vuga Rd, Zanzibar Town)

KIU Ltd (☎022-285 1509; www.swahilicourses.com) At various locations in Dar es Salaam, plus branches in Iringa and Zanzibar.

Makoko Language School (☎028-264 2518; http://swahilimakoko.110mb.com) In Makoko neighbourhood, on the outskirts of Musoma.

MS Training Centre for Development Cooperation (☎027-254 1044/6; www.mstcdc.or.tz) About 15km outside Arusha, near Usa River.

Rivervalley Campsite (☎026-270 1988; www.rivervalleycampsites.com) Outside Iringa.

University of Dar es Salaam (☎022-241 0757; www.iks.udsm.ac.tz)

Legal Matters

Apart from traffic offences such as speeding and driving without a seatbelt (mandatory for driver and front-seat passengers), the main area to watch out for is drug use and possession. In Dar es Salaam, the typical scam is that you'll be approached by a couple of men who walk along with you, strike up a conversation and try to sell you drugs. Before you've had a chance to shake them loose, policemen (sometimes legitimate, sometimes not) suddenly appear and insist that you pay a huge fine for being involved in the purchase of illegal drugs. Protestations to the contrary are generally futile and there's often little you can do other than instantly hightailing it in the opposite direction if you smell this scam coming. If you are caught, insist on going to the nearest police station before paying anything and whittle the bribe down as far as you can. Initial demands may be as high as US$300, but savvy travellers should be able to get away with under US$50.

Maps

Good country maps include those published by Nelles and Harms IC, both available in Tanzania and elsewhere, and both also including Rwanda and Burundi. Harms-ic also publishes maps for Lake Manyara National Park, the Ngorongoro Conservation Area and Zanzibar.

MaCo (www.gtmaps.com) Hand-drawn maps by Giovanni Tombazzi, cover Zanzibar, Arusha and the northern parks. They're sold in bookshops in Dar es Salaam, Arusha and Zanzibar Town.

Surveys and Mapping Division's Map Sales Office (Map p50;cnr Kivukoni Front & Luthuli St, Dar es Salaam; ⏲8am-2pm Mon-Fri) Sells dated topographical maps (1:50,000) for mainland Tanzania.

Money

» Tanzania's currency is the Tanzanian shilling (Tsh). There are bills of Tsh10,000, 5000, 1000 and 500, and coins of Tsh200, 100, 50, 20, 10, five and one shilling(s) (the latter three coins are rarely used).

» Bill design has recently been changed for all amounts, with both the old and new styles currently accepted and in circulation. For exchange rates, see p43.

» Credit cards are not widely accepted. Where they are accepted, it's sometimes only with commissions. As a result, you will need to rely here rather heavily on cash and ATMs.

» A Visa or MasterCard is essential for accessing money from ATMs.

» Visa (some parks also take MasterCard) is required for paying entry fees at most national parks.

ATMS

» ATMs are widespread in major towns, and all are open 24 hours. But, they are often temporarily out of service or out of cash, so have back-up funds. All allow you to withdraw shillings with a Visa (most widely accepted) or MasterCard. Withdrawals are usually to a maximum of Tsh300,000 to Tsh400,000 per transaction (ATMs in small towns often have a limit of Tsh200,000 per transaction) with a daily limit of Tsh1.2 million.

CASH

US dollars, followed by euros, are the most convenient foreign currencies and get the best rates, although other major currencies are readily accepted in major centres. Bring a mix of large and small denominations, but note that US$50 and US$100 note bills get better rates of exchange than smaller denominations. Old-style (small head) US bills are not accepted anywhere, and many places only accept bills dated 2006 or later.

CREDIT CARDS

Credit cards, mainly Visa, are essential for withdrawing money at ATMs. And, a Visa (MasterCard is also sometimes accepted) together with your PIN is required for paying park fees at some national parks. For payment, some upmarket hotels and tour operators accept credit cards, often with a commission averaging from 5% to 10%, but confirm in advance.

EXCHANGING MONEY

» Change cash at banks or foreign exchange (forex) bureaus in major towns and cities; rates and commissions vary, so shop around.

» To reconvert Tanzanian shillings to hard currency, save at least some of your exchange receipts, although they are seldom checked. The easiest places to reconvert currency are at the airports in Dar es Salaam and Kilimanjaro, or try at forex shops or banks in major towns.

» For after-hours exchange and exchanging in small towns, as well as for reconverting back to dollars or euros, many Indian-owned businesses will change money, although often at bad rates.

» In theory, it's required for foreigners to pay for accommodation, park fees, organised tours, upscale hotels and the Zanzibar ferries in US dollars, though (with the exception of some parks, where Visa card or US dollars are required) shillings are accepted almost everywhere at the going rate.

TAXES

Tanzania has an 18% value-added tax (VAT) that's usually included in quoted prices.

TIPPING

» On treks and safaris, it's common practice to tip drivers, guides, porters and other staff. For guidelines, see p27 for safaris and p113 and p130 for treks.

TRAVELLERS CHEQUES

Travellers cheques can be cashed with difficulty and high commissions in Dar es Salaam, Arusha and Mwanza, but not at all or with even greater difficulty elsewhere. Most banks and forex bureaus that accept travellers cheques require you to show the original purchase receipt before exchanging the cheques. The bottom line is that travellers cheques are not much use in Tanzania.

Public Holidays

New Year's Day 1 January

Zanzibar Revolution Day 12 January

Easter March/April – Good Friday, Holy Saturday and Easter Monday

Union Day 26 April

Labour Day 1 May

Saba Saba (Peasants' Day) 7 July

Nane Nane (Farmers' Day) 8 August

Independence Day 9 December

Christmas Day 25 December

Boxing Day 26 December

Islamic holidays are also celebrated as public holidays; see p646.

Telephone

The major mobile companies are currently Vodacom, Airtel and (on Zanzibar) Zantel. To reach a mobile telephone number from outside Tanzania, dial the country code, then the mobile phone code without the initial 0, and then the six-digit number. From within Tanzania, keep the initial 0 and don't use any other area code. Dialling from your own mobile is generally the cheapest way to call internationally.

PHONE CODES

To make an international call, dial ☎000, followed by the country code, local area code (without the initial '0') and telephone number.

All land-line telephone numbers are seven digits. Area codes (included with all numbers in this chapter) must be used whenever you dial long-distance.

Time

Tanzania time is GMT/UTC plus three hours. There is no daylight saving.

Tourist Information

The **Tanzania Tourist Board** (TTB; www.tanzaniatouristboard.com) is the official tourism entity.

Visas

Almost everyone needs a visa, which costs US$50 for most nationalities (US$100 for citizens of the USA and of Ireland) for a single-entry visa valid for up to three months. It's best to get the visa in advance (and necessary if you want multiple entry), though visas are currently readily issued at Dar es Salaam and Kilimanjaro airports and at most border crossings (US dollars cash only, single-entry only).

VISA EXTENSIONS

One month is the normal visa validity and three months the maximum. For extensions within the three-month limit, there are immigration offices in all major towns; the process is free and straightforward. Extensions after three months are difficult; you usually need to leave the country and apply for a new visa.

Volunteering

Note that the Tanzanian government has recently drastically raised the cost of volunteer (Class C) resident permits to US$550 for three months. Tanzania-specific places to start your research are listed following; also see the Volunteering in Moshi boxed text on p105.

Indigenous Education Foundation of Tanzania (www.ieftz.org)

Kigamboni Community Centre (www.kccdar.com)

Trade Aid (www.tradeaiduk.org/volunteer.html)

Ujamaa Hostel (www.ujamaahostel.com)

Getting There & Away

For information on getting to East Africa from outside the region, see p650.

Entering the Country

» Visas are available at all major points of entry, and must be paid for in US dollars cash.
» Yellow fever vaccination is required if you are arriving from an endemic area (which includes many of Tanzania's neighbours).

Air

AIRPORTS

Julius Nyerere International Airport (DAR) Dar es Salaam; Tanzania's air hub.

Kilimanjaro International Airport (JRO) Between Arusha and Moshi, and the best option for itineraries in Arusha and the northern safari circuit. (Note: not to be confused with the smaller Arusha airport (ARK), 8km west of Arusha, which handles domestic flights only.)

Kigoma airport Occasional regional flights.

Mtwara airport (MYW) Regional flights.

Mwanza airport (MWZ) Regional fights.

Zanzibar International Airport (ZNZ) International and regional flights.

AIRLINES

Air Tanzania, the national airline, is currently not operating any flights. Regional carriers include the following (all servicing Dar es Salaam, except as noted). For international connections to/from Tanzania see the Transport in East Africa chapter (p650).

Airkenya (www.airkenya.com) Affiliated with Regional Air in Arusha.

Air Uganda (www.air-uganda.com)

Fly540 (www.fly540.com) Also serves KIA.

Kenya Airways (www.kenya-airways.com)

Precision Air (www.precisionairtz.com) In partnership with Kenya Airways; also serves KIA.

Land

» **Buses** cross Tanzania's borders with Kenya, Uganda, Rwanda and Burundi.
» At the border, you'll need to disembark on each side to take care of visa formalities, then reboard and continue on. Visa fees

aren't included in bus ticket prices for trans-border routes.

» For crossings with other countries, you'll need to take one vehicle to the border and board a different vehicle on the other side.

» To enter Tanzania with your **own vehicle** you'll need:

- *the vehicle's registration papers*
- *your driving licence*
- *temporary import permit (Tsh20,000 for one month, purchased at the border)*
- *third-party insurance (Tsh50,000 for one year, purchased at the border or at the local insurance headquarters in the nearest large town)*
- *one-time fuel levy (Tsh5000)*
- *carnet de passage en douane (see p654)*

BURUNDI

The main crossings are at Kobero Bridge between Ngara (Tanzania) and Muyinga (Burundi); and, at Manyovu (north of Kigoma).

» **For Kobero Bridge** From Dar es Salaam, the Spider Coach (aka Taqwa) has a bus departing Wednesdays at 6am from Dar es Salaam to Bujumbura (Tsh105,000, two days) via Dodoma, Singida, Kahama (where you'll overnight) and Nyakanazi. A better option is to start in Mwanza, from where the trip is done in stages. Zuberly and Nyehunge lines have buses daily at 5.30am to Ngara (Tsh16,000, seven to eight hours). Also, shared-taxis run all day from Nyakanazi to Ngara (Tsh9000, two hours). Once in Ngara, there is onward transport to the Tanzanian border post at Kabanga.

» **For Manyovu** Burugo Travel (its ticket office is at Kigoma's Bero bus stand) has a 'coastal' *(thelathini)* bus direct between Kigoma and Bujumbura (Burundi; Tsh13,000, five hours) at 7am Monday and Friday. Otherwise, take a dalla-dalla from Kigoma to Manyovu (Tsh4000, one hour), walk through immigration and find onward transport. There's always something going to Mabanda (Burundi), where you can find minibuses to Bujumbura, three to four hours away.

KENYA

The main route to/from Kenya is the good sealed road connecting Arusha (Tanzania) and Nairobi (Kenya) via Namanga border post (open 24 hours). There are also border crossings at Horohoro (Tanzania), north of Tanga; at Holili (Tanzania), east of Moshi; at Loitokitok (Kenya), northeast of Moshi; and, at Sirari (Tanzania), northeast of Musoma. With the exception of the Serengeti-Masai Mara crossing (which is currently closed), there is public transport across all Tanzania–Kenya border posts.

» **To/From Mombasa** Buses between Tanga and Mombasa depart daily in the morning in each direction (Tsh12,000 to Tsh15,000, four to five hours). There's nowhere official to change money at the border. Touts here charge extortionate rates, and it's difficult to get rid of Kenyan shillings once in Tanga, so plan accordingly. There are also direct buses daily between Dar es Salaam and Mombasa (Tsh24,000 to Tsh30,000).

» **To/From Nairobi** From Dar es Salaam, the best buses to Nairobi (16 to 17 hours) are Kampala Coach (Tsh45,000) and Dar Express (Tsh55,000); both depart about 6am. You can also board these lines in Moshi (Tsh25,000, six to seven hours to Nairobi) and Arusha (Tsh20,000 to Tsh22,000, five hours), if seats are available. The two companies also have Nairobi buses that begin in Arusha, leaving at 2pm and 3pm, respectively.

» The questionably named Perfect line has four ordinary buses from Arusha and Nairobi (Tsh14,000, five to seven hours), departing Arusha's central bus station daily between 7am and 11.30am.

» Comfortable nine-seater **minivans** (Tsh7000, two hours) and decrepit, overcrowded full-sized vans (which stop frequently along the way) go between Arusha's central bus station (they park at the northernmost end) and the Namanga border frequently throughout the day from 6am. At Namanga, you'll have to walk a few hundred metres across the border and then catch one of the frequent matatus (Kenyan minibuses) or shared taxis to Nairobi (KSh450). From Nairobi, the matatu and share-taxi depots are on Ronald Ngala St, near the River Rd junction.

» The most convenient and comfortable option between Moshi or Arusha and Nairobi are the **shuttle buses**. They depart daily from Arusha and Nairobi at 8am and 2pm (five hours) and from Moshi (seven hours) at 6am and 11am. The non-resident rate is US$25/30 one way from Arusha/Moshi, but with a little prodding it's usually possible to get the resident price

(Tsh25,000/30,000). Pick-ups and drop-offs are at their offices and centrally located hotels. Depending on the timing, they may pick you up or drop you off at Kilimanjaro International Airport. Confirm locations when booking.

The following companies are recommended.

» **Jamii** Arusha (☎0757-756110; www.jamiitours.com; old Mezza Luna Hotel, Simeon Rd); Moshi (☎0755-763836; THB House, Boma Rd); Nairobi (☎0734-868686; Rentford House, Muini Mbingu St)

» **Rainbow** Arusha (☎0754-204025; www.rainbowcarhire.com, India St); Moshi (☎0784-204025; THB House, Boma Rd); Nairobi (☎0712-508922; Parkside Hotel, Monrovia St)

» **Riverside** Arusha (☎027-250 2639; www.riverside-shuttle.com; Sokoine Rd); Moshi (☎027-275 0093; THB House, Boma Rd); Nairobi (☎0254-20-229618; Lagos House, Monrovia St)

To/From Voi Raqib Coach's daily 8.30am bus from Moshi to Mombasa travels via Voi (Tsh15,000, four hours). Also, dalla-dallas go frequently between Moshi and the border town of Holili (Tsh1500, one hour). At the **border** (⏲6am-8pm) you'll need to hire a *piki-piki* (motorbike; Tsh1000) or bicycle to cross 3km of no-man's-land before arriving at the Kenyan immigration post at Taveta. From Taveta, sporadic minibuses go to Voi along a rough road, where you can then find onward transport to Nairobi and Mombasa. If you're arriving/departing with a foreign-registered vehicle, the necessary paperwork is only done during working hours (8am to 1pm and 2pm to 5pm daily).

To/From Kisii Akamba passes Kisii on its daily runs between Mwanza and Nairobi (Tsh36,000, 15 hours, 1pm). It doesn't stop in Musoma, but you can catch it (if you have already booked a ticket) in nearby Nyakanga. Batco buses go daily from Mwanza to the Sirari–Isebania border post (Tsh10,000, four to five hours), where you can get Kenyan transport to Kisii. Also, several dalla-dallas go daily from Musoma to the border (Tsh5500, one hour).

MALAWI

The only crossing is at **Songwe River bridge** (⏲7am-7pm Tanzanian time, 6am-6pm Malawi time), southeast of Mbeya (Tanzania).

» **From Mbeya** There are daily minibuses and 30-seater buses (known as 'Coastals' or *thelathini*) to the border (Tsh5000, two hours). Once through the Tanzanian border post, there's a 300m walk to the Malawian side, and minibuses to Karonga. There's also one Malawian bus daily between the Malawi side of the border and Mzuzu (Malawi), departing the border by mid-afternoon and arriving by evening.

» Look for buses going to Kyela (these detour to the border) and verify that your vehicle is really going all the way to the border, as some that say they are actually stop at Tukuyu (40km north) or at Ibanda (7km before the border). Asking several passengers (rather than the minibus company touts) should get you the straight answer.

» Your chances of getting a direct vehicle are better in the larger *thelathini,* which depart from Mbeya two or three times daily and usually go where they say they are going.

» The border buses stop at the Songwe River transport stand, about a seven-minute walk from the actual border; there's no real need for the bicycle taxis that will approach you.

» There are currently no cross-border vehicles from Mbeya into Malawi, although touts at Mbeya bus station may try to convince you otherwise. Going in both directions, plan on overnighting in Mbeya; buses from Mbeya to Dar es Salaam depart between 6am and 7am.

MOZAMBIQUE

The main vehicle crossing is via Unity Bridge over the Ruvuma at Negomano, reached via Masasi. There is also the Unity 2 bridge across the Ruvuma at Mitomoni village, 120km south of Songea. It's possible to cross at Kilambo (south of Mtwara), but the river is bridged only by dugout canoes. For those travelling along the coast by boat, there are immigration officials at Msimbati (Tanzania) and at Palma and Moçimboa da Praia (Mozambique). Mozambique visas are not issued anywhere along the Tanzania border, so arrange one in advance.

Buses depart daily from Mtwara between 7am and 11am to the Kilambo border post (Tsh4000, one hour) and on to the Ruvuma, which is crossed via dugout canoe (Tsh3000, 10 minutes to over an hour, depending on water levels, and dangerous during heavy rains; it's common for boat captains to stop mid-river and demand higher fees from foreigners). On the Mozambique side, there are usually two pick-ups daily to the Mozambique border post (4km further) and on to

Moçimboa da Praia (US$10, four hours), with the last one departing by about noon. The Ruvuma crossing is notorious for pickpockets. Watch your belongings, especially when getting into and out of the boats, and keep up with the crowd when walking to/from the river bank.

Further west, one or two vehicles daily depart from Songea's Majengo C area by around 11am (Tsh10,000, three to four hours) to Mitomoni village and the Unity 2 bridge. Once across, you can get Mozambique transport on to Lichinga (Tsh25,000, five hours). It's best to pay in stages, rather than paying the entire Tsh34,000 Songea–Lichinga fare in Songea, as is sometimes requested. With an early departure, the entire Songea–Lichinga trip is very possible in one day via public transport.

The main **vehicle crossing** is via the Unity Bridge at Negomano, southwest of Kilambo, near the confluence of the Lugenda River. From Masasi, go about 35km southwest along the Tunduru road to Nangomba village, from where a 68km good-condition track leads southwest down to Masuguru village. The bridge is 10km further at Mtambaswala. On the other side, there is a decent 160km dirt road to Mueda. There are immigration facilities on both sides of the bridge (although you will need to get your Mozambique visa in advance). Entering Tanzania, take care of customs formalities for your vehicle in Mtwara.

The Unity 2 bridge south of Songea is another option; see the preceding Bus section. With a private vehicle the Songea to Lichinga stretch should not take more than about eight or nine hours.

There is no longer a vehicle ferry at Kilambo. However, local entrepreneurs strap dugout canoes together to take vehicles across. This is obviously risky, especially during the rains. And, it's potentially expensive; expect to pay from US$250 to US$400 for the crossing depending on your negotiating skills. In Mozambique, the road is unsealed, but in reasonable condition from the border to Palma, a mix of tarmac and good dirt from Palma to Moçimboa da Praia, and tarmac from there to Pemba.

RWANDA

» The main crossing is at Rusumu Falls, southwest of Bukoba (Tanzania).

» Four bus companies connect Mwanza to Kigali daily (Tsh25,000, 12 hours), leaving Mwanza at 5.30am. Golden Inter-City, with four-across seating, is the best of the bunch.

UGANDA

The main post is at Mutukula (Tanzania), northwest of Bukoba, with good sealed roads on both sides. There's another crossing further west at Nkurungu (Tanzania), but the road is bad and sparsely travelled. From Arusha or Moshi, travel to Uganda is via Kenya.

» **Bus** Kampala Coach's buses to Nairobi from both Dar es Salaam and Arusha continue to Kampala (Tsh95,000, 30 hours from Dar es Salaam to Kampala; Tsh60,000, 20 hours from Arusha to Kampala). The cost to Jinja is the same as Kampala. Akamba is another option, but its buses aren't air-conditioned and they cost as much as Kampala Coach's air-con buses.

» Several companies (Friends Safari is best) leave Bukoba at 7am for Kampala (Tsh10,000, five to six hours). Departures from Kampala are at 7am and usually again at 11am.

» From Mwanza, Akamba goes Wednesday, Friday and Sunday to/from Kampala (Tsh38,000, 16 hours), departing Mwanza at 7am.

ZAMBIA

The main border **crossing** (⌚7.30am-6pm Tanzania time, 6.30am-5pm Zambia time) is at Tunduma (Tanzania), southwest of Mbeya. There's also a crossing at Kasesya (Tanzania), between Sumbawanga (Tanzania) and Mbala (Zambia).

» **Minibuses** go several times daily between Mbeya and Tunduma (Tsh3500, two hours), where you walk across the border for Zambian transport to Lusaka (US$20, 18 hours).

» The Kasesya crossing is seldom travelled, and in the rainy season the road can be extremely bad. There's no direct transport; at least one truck daily goes to the border from each side. With luck you can make the full journey in a day, but since departures from both Sumbawanga and Mbala are in the afternoon, and departures from the borders are in the early morning, you'll likely need to sleep in one of the (rough) border villages.

» **Train** The **Tanzania–Zambia train line** (Tazara; www.tazarasite.com) links Dar es Salaam with Kapiri Mposhi in Zambia twice weekly via Mbeya and Tunduma. 'Express' service departs Dar es Salaam at 3.50pm Tuesday (1st/2nd/economy class Tsh75,000/60,000/45,000, about 40 hours). Ordinary service departs Dar es Salaam at 1.50pm on Friday (Tsh55,000/45,000/37,000, about 48 hours). Delays of up to 24 hours on both express and ordinary are the rule. Departures from Mbeya to Zambia (Tsh40,000/30,000/25,000 for express 1st/2nd/economy class) are at 1.30pm Wednesday and 2.40pm Saturday. Students with ID get a 50% discount. From Kapiri Mposhi to Lusaka, you'll need to continue by bus. Departures from New Kapiri Mposhi are at 4pm Tuesday (express) and 2pm Friday (ordinary). Visas are available at the border in both directions.

» **Car** If driving from Zambia into Tanzania, note that vehicle insurance isn't available at the Kasesya border, but must be purchased 120km further on in Sumbawanga.

Sea & Lake

There's a US$5 port tax for travel on all boats and ferries from Tanzanian ports.

BURUNDI

The regular passenger ferry service between Kigoma and Bujumbura is currently suspended. Inquire at the passenger port in Kigoma for an update. However, it's possible to travel on cargo ships between Kigoma and Bujumbura; inquire at Ami Port, and expect to hear that ships are sailing 'tomorrow' for several days in a row. Lake taxis (p163) go once or twice weekly from Kibirizi (just north of Kigoma) to Bujumbura, but are not recommended as they take a full day and are occasionally robbed. However, you could use the afternoon lake taxis to Kagunga (the Tanzanian border post, where there's a simple guesthouse), cross the border in the morning, take a motorcycle-taxi to Nyanza-Lac (Burundi) and then a minibus to Bujumbura.

DEMOCRATIC REPUBLIC OF THE CONGO (DRC; FORMERLY ZAÏRE)

Cargo boats go several times monthly from Kigoma's Ami Port to Kalemie (US$20, deck class only, seven hours) or Uvira. The MV *Liemba* (p211) also sometimes travels to Kalemie during its off week. Check with the Congolese embassy in Kigoma about sailing days and times. Bring food and drink with you, and something to spread on the deck for sleeping.

KENYA

» **Dhow** Dhows sail sporadically between Pemba, Tanga and Mombasa (Tsh15,000 to Tsh20,000 between Tanga and Mombasa); the journey can be long and rough. Ask at the ports in Tanga, or in Mkoani or Wete on Pemba for information on sailings. In Kenya, ask at the port in Mombasa, or better, at Shimoni.

» **Ferry** There's currently no passenger ferry service on Lake Victoria between Tanzania and Kenya, but cargo boats sail about twice weekly between Mwanza and Kisumu (occasionally stopping in Musoma) and are usually willing to take passengers. Inquire at the Mwanza South port about sailings. A passenger and vehicle ferry is scheduled to start service between Musoma and Kisumu by early 2012.

MALAWI

The MV *Songea* sails between Mbamba Bay and Nkhata Bay, in theory departing from Mbamba Bay on Friday morning and Nkhata Bay on Friday evening (1st/economy class US$12/5, four to five hours). The schedule is highly variable and sometimes cancelled completely.

MOZAMBIQUE

» **Dhow** Dhows between Mozambique and Tanzania (12 to 30 or more hours) are best arranged at Msimbati and Moçimboa da Praia (Mozambique).

» **Ferry** The official route between southwestern Tanzania and Mozambique is via Malawi on the MV *Songea* between Mbamba Bay and Nkhata Bay, and then from Nkhata Bay on to Likoma Island (Malawi), Cóbuè and Metangula (both in Mozambique) on the MV *Ilala*. Unofficially, there are small boats that sail along the eastern shore of Lake Nyasa between Tanzania and Mozambique. However, Lake Nyasa is notorious for its severe and sudden squalls, and going this way is risky and not recommended.

» The MV *Ilala* departs from Monkey Bay (Malawi) at 10am Friday, arriving in Metangula (Mozambique, via Chipoka and Nkhotakota in Malawi) at 6am Saturday, reaching Cóbuè around midday, Likoma Island at 1.30pm and Nkhata Bay at 1am Sunday morning.

» Southbound, departures are at 8pm Monday from Nkhata Bay and at 6.30am Tuesday from Likoma Island, reaching Cóbuè at 7am and Metangula at midday.

» The schedule changes frequently; get an update locally.
» Fares are about US$40/20 for 1st-class cabin/economy class between Nkhata Bay and Cóbuè.
» There's an immigration officer at Mbamba Bay, Mozambique immigration posts in Metangula and Cóbuè, and immigration officers on Likoma Island and in Nkhata Bay for Malawi.
» You can get a Mozambique visa at Cóbuè, but not at Metangula.

UGANDA

There's no passenger-ferry service, but it's relatively easy to arrange passage between Mwanza and Kampala's Port Bell on cargo ships (about 16 hours). Boats sail about three times weekly. On the Ugandan side, you'll need a letter of permission from the train station director (free). Ask for the managing director's office, on the 2nd floor of the building next to Kampala's train station. In Mwanza, a letter isn't required, but check in with the immigration officer at the South Port. Expect to pay about US$20, including port fees. Crew are often willing to rent out their cabins for a negotiable extra fee.

ZAMBIA

The venerable MV *Liemba* has been plying the waters of Lake Tanganyika for the better part of a century on one of Africa's classic adventure journeys. It connects Kigoma with Mpulungu in Zambia every other week (1st/2nd/economy class US$66/56/41, US dollars cash only, at least 40 hours; single/double VIP cabin US$264/330), stopping en route at various lake shore villages, including Lagosa (for Mahale Mountains National Park, US$28 for 1st class from Kigoma), Kalema (southwest of Mpanda, US$42), Kipili (US$48) and Kasanga (southwest of Sumbawanga, US$63). In theory, departures from Kigoma are on Wednesday at 4pm, reaching Mpulungu Friday morning. Departures from Mpulungu are (again, in theory) on Friday afternoon at about 2pm, arriving back in Kigoma on Sunday afternoon. Delays are common. Food, soft drink, beer and bottled water are sold on board, but it's a good idea to bring supplements. First class is surprisingly comfortable, with two clean bunks, a window and a fan. Second-class cabins (four bunks) are poorly ventilated and uncomfortable. There are seats for third (economy) class passengers, but it's more comfortable to find deck space for sleeping. Keep watch over your luggage. **Booking** (☎028-280 2811 for inquiries) early is advisable, but not always necessary, as 1st-class cabins are usually available.

There are docks at Kigoma, Kasanga and Mpulungu, but at all other stops you'll need to disembark in the middle of the lake, exiting from a door in the side of the boat into small boats that take you to shore. While it may sound adventurous, it can be rather nerve-wracking at night, and if the lake is rough.

Getting Around

Air

AIRLINES IN TANZANIA

The national airline, **Air Tanzania** (www.airtanzania.com) is currently not operating any flights. Following is a list of other airlines flying domestically:

Air Excel (☎027-254 8429, 027-250 1597; www.airexcelonline.com) Arusha, Serengeti National Park, Lake Manyara National Park, Dar es Salaam, Zanzibar.

Coastal Aviation (☎022-284 3293, 022-211 7959; www.coastal.cc) A recommended company, with flights to many parks and major towns, including Arusha, Dar es Salaam, Dodoma, Kilwa Masoko, Lake Manyara National Park, Mafia, Mwanza, Pemba, Ruaha National Park, Rubondo Island National Park, Saadani Game Reserve, Selous GR, Serengeti National Park, Tanga, Tarangire National Park and Zanzibar.

Fly540 (☎022-212 5912/3, 0752-540540, 0765-540540; www.fly540.com) Kilimanjaro, Arusha, Dar es Salaam, Zanzibar, Mtwara, and Mwanza.

Precision Air (☎022-216 8000, 022-213 0800, 0784-402002, 0787-888407; www.precisionairtz.com) Flights to many major towns, including Bukoba, Dar es Salaam, Kigoma, Kilimanjaro, Mtwara, Mwanza, Shinyanga, Tabora and Zanzibar.

Regional Air Services (☎027-250 4477/2541, 0784-285753; www.regionaltanzania.com) Arusha, Dar es Salaam, Kilimanjaro, Lake Manyara National Park, Ndutu, Serengeti National Park and Zanzibar.

Safari Airlink (☎0777-723274; www.safariaviation.info) Dar es Salaam, Arusha, Katavi National Park, Mahale Mountains NP, Mufindi, Ruaha National Park, Selous Game Reserve and Zanzibar.

Tropical Air (☎024-223 2511, 0777-412278; www.tropicalair.co.tz) Zanzibar, Dar es Salaam, Tanga, Pemba, Mafia and Arusha.

ZanAir (☎024-223 3670/8; www.zanair.com) Arusha, Dar es Salaam, Lake Manyara NP, Mafia, Pangani, Pemba, Saadani National Park, Selous Game Reserve, Serengeti National Park, Tarangire National Park and Zanzibar.

Zantas Air (☎022-213 0476, 0773-786016; www.zantasair.com) Arusha, Katavi National Park, Mahale Mountains National Park, Kigoma and Tabora

Bicycle

For more on cycling in Tanzania see p202.

Boat

DHOW

Main routes connect Zanzibar and Pemba with Dar es Salaam, Tanga, Bagamoyo and Mombasa; Kilwa Kivinje, Lindi, Mikindani, Mtwara and Msimbati with other coastal towns; and Mafia and the mainland. However, foreigners are officially prohibited on non-motorised dhows, and on any dhows between Zanzibar and Dar es Salaam; captains are subject to fines if they're caught, and may be unwilling to take you. A better option is to arrange a charter with a coastal hotel (many have their own dhows), or with Safari Blue (p66).

FERRY

Ferries operate on Lake Victoria, Lake Tanganyika and Lake Nyasa, and between Dar es Salaam, Zanzibar and Pemba. There's a US$5 port tax per trip. .

» **Lake Victoria** The MV *Victoria* departs from Mwanza at 9pm on Tuesday, Thursday and Sunday (1st class/2nd-class sleeping/2nd-class sitting/3rd class Tsh35,000/25,600/20,600/15,600, nine hours). Departures from Bukoba are at 9pm Monday, Wednesday and Friday. First class has two-bed cabins and 2nd-class sleeping has six-bed cabins. Second-class sitting isn't comfortable, so if you can't get a spot in 1st class or 2nd-class sleeping, the best bet is to buy a 3rd-class ticket. With luck, you may then be able to find a comfortable spot in the 1st-class lounge. First- and 2nd-class cabins fill up quickly in both directions, so book as soon as you know your plans. Food is available on board. Note that there's a risk of theft for all deck and seating passengers.

» **Lake Tanganyika** For the MV *Liemba* schedule between Kigoma and Mpulungu (Zambia) via various Tanzanian towns en route, see p211.

» **Lake Nyasa** In theory, the MV *Songea* departs from Itungi port about noon on Thursday and makes its way down the coast via Matema, Lupingu, Manda, Lundu, Mango and Liuli to Mbamba Bay (1st/economy class Tsh23,000/10,000, 18 to 24 hours). It continues to Nkhata Bay in Malawi, before turning around and doing the return trip, departing Mbamba Bay in theory on Saturday, and reaching Matema and Itungi port on Sunday.

» The smaller MV *Iringa*, which also services lakeside villages between Itungi and Manda (about halfway down the Tanzanian lake shore) was not operating at the time of research. When it is, it usually alternates with the *Songea*.

» Schedules for both boats change frequently. For an update, ask in Kyela, or at one of the Matema hotels.

Bus

» On major long-distance routes, there's a choice of express and ordinary buses; price is usually a good indicator of which is which. Express buses make fewer stops, are less crowded and depart on schedule. Some have toilets and air-conditioning, and the nicest ones are called 'luxury' buses. On secondary routes, the only option is ordinary buses, which are often packed to overflowing, stop often and run to a less rigorous schedule (and often not to any recognisable schedule at all).

» For popular routes, book in advance. You can sometimes get a place by arriving at the bus station an hour prior to departure. Each bus line has its own booking office, at or near the bus station.

» Prices are basically fixed, although overcharging happens. Buy your tickets at the office and not from the touts, and don't believe anyone who tries to tell you there's a luggage fee, unless you are carrying an excessively large pack.

» For short stretches along main routes, express buses will drop you on request, though you'll often need to pay the full fare to the next major destination.

» On long routes, expect to sleep either on the bus, pulled off to the side of the road, or at a grubby guesthouse.

Car & Motorcycle

Unless you have your own vehicle and are familiar with driving in East Africa, it's relatively unusual for travellers to tour mainland Tanzania by car. More common is to focus on a region and arrange local transport through a tour or safari operator. On Zanzibar, however, it's easy to hire a car or motorcycle for touring, and self-drive is permitted.

DRIVING LICENCE

On the mainland you'll need your home driving licence or (preferable) an International Driving Permit (IDP) along with your home licence. On Zanzibar you'll need an IDP plus your home licence, or a permit from Zanzibar (p75), Kenya, Uganda or South Africa.

FUEL & SPARE PARTS

Petrol and diesel cost about Tsh2200 per litre. Tank up whenever you get the opportunity. It is common, including at major roadside filling stations, for petrol or diesel to be diluted with kerosene or water. Check with local residents or business owners before tanking up. It's also common for car parts to be switched in garages (substituting inferior versions for the originals). Staying with your car while it's being repaired helps minimise this problem.

CAR HIRE

In Dar es Salaam, daily rates for 2WD start at about US$65, excluding fuel, plus US$20 to US$30 for insurance and tax. Prices for 4WDs are US$80 to US$200 per day plus insurance (US$30 to US$40 per day), fuel and driver (US$20 to US$40 per day). There's also a 20% value added tax.

Outside the city, most companies require 4WD. Also, most will not permit self-drive outside of Dar es Salaam, and few offer unlimited kilometres. Charges per-kilometre are US$0.50 to US$1. Clarify what the company's policy is in the event of a breakdown.

Elsewhere in Tanzania, you can hire 4WD vehicles in Arusha, Karatu, Mwanza, Mbeya, Zanzibar Town and other centres through travel agencies, tour operators and hotels. See the individual sections for hire agency listings. Except on Zanzibar, most come with a driver. Rates average US$80 to US$200 per day plus fuel, less on Zanzibar.

For motorcycle hire, try the Arusha-based **Dustbusters** (www.dustbusters-tz.com).

ROAD CONDITIONS & HAZARDS

Around one-third of Tanzania's road network is sealed. Secondary roads range from good to impassable, depending on the season. For most trips outside major towns you'll need 4WD. Also see p654.

> **PERILS OF THE ROAD**
>
> Road accidents are probably your biggest safety risk while travelling in Tanzania, with speeding buses being among the worst offenders. Road conditions are poor and driving standards leave much to be desired. Many vehicles have painted slogans such as *Mungu Atubariki* (God Bless Us) or 'In God we Trust' in the hope that a bit of extra help from above will see them safely through the day's runs.
>
> To maximise your chances of a safe arrival, avoid night travel, and ask locals for recommendations of reputable companies. If you have a choice, it's usually better to go with a full-sized bus than a minibus or 30-seater bus.

ROAD RULES

Unless otherwise posted, the speed limit is 80km per hour; on some routes, including Dar es Salaam to Arusha, police have radar. Tanzania has a seat-belt law for drivers and front-seat passengers. The traffic-fine penalty is Tsh20,000.

Motorcycles aren't permitted in national parks except for the section of the Dar es Salaam–Mbeya highway passing through Mikumi National Park and on the road between Sumbawanga and Mpanda via Katavi National Park. Also see p654.

Hitching

Hitching is generally slow going. It's prohibited inside national parks, and is usually fruitless around them. That said, in remote areas, hitching a lift with truck drivers may be your only option. Expect to pay about the same or a bit less than the bus fare for the same route, with a place in the cab costing about twice that for a place on top of the load. See also p655.

Minibus & Shared Taxi

For shorter trips away from the main routes, the choice is often between 30-seater buses ('Coastals' or *thelathini*) and dalla-dallas. Both options come complete with chickens on the roof, bags of produce under the seats, no leg room and schedules only in the most general sense of the word. Dalla-dallas, especially, are invariably filled to overflowing. Shared taxis are rare, except in northern Tanzania near Arusha and several other locations. Like ordinary buses, dalla-dallas and shared taxis leave when full, and are the least safe transport option.

Truck

In remote areas, such as much of Western Tanzania, trucks operate as buses (for a roughly similar fare) with passengers sitting or standing in the back. Even on routes that have daily bus service, many people still use trucks.

Local Transport

DALLA-DALLA

Local routes are serviced by dalla-dallas and, in rural areas, pick-up trucks or old 4WDs. Prices are fixed and cheap (Tsh100 to Tsh300 for town runs). The vehicles make many stops and are very crowded. Accidents are common, especially in minibuses. Many accidents occur when drivers race each other to an upcoming station to collect new passengers. Destinations are either posted on a board in the front window, or called out by the driver's assistant, who also collects fares.

TAXI

Taxis, which have white plates on the mainland and a *'gari la abiria'* (passenger vehicle) sign on Zanzibar, can be hired in all major towns. None have meters, so agree on the fare with the driver before getting in. Fares for short town trips start at Tsh2000. In major centres, many drivers have an 'official' price list, but rates shown (often calculated on the basis of Tsh1000 per 1km) are generally much higher than what is normally paid. Ask locals what the price should be and use this as a base for negotiations. For longer trips away from town, negotiate the fare based on distance, petrol costs and road conditions, plus a fair profit for the driver. Only use taxis from reliable hotels or established taxi stands. Avoid hailing taxis on the streets, and never get in a taxi that has a 'friend' of the driver or anyone else already in it.

Train

There are two lines: **Tazara** (off Map p50; ☎022-286 5137/2406, 022-286 0340/2033, 0713-225292; www.tazarasite.comz; cnr Nyerere & Nelson Mandela Rds, Dar es Salaam), linking Dar es Salaam with Kapiri Mposhi in Zambia via Mbeya and Tunduma; and Tanzanian Railway Corporation's rundown **Central Line** (Map p50; ☎022-211 7833; cnr Railway St & Sokoine Dr, Dar es Salaam), linking Dar es Salaam with Tabora and Kigoma. Central Line branches also link Tabora with Mpanda, and Dodoma with Singida. Central Line service to/from Mwanza has been suspended.

Tazara is considerably more comfortable and efficient, but on both lines, breakdowns and long delays (up to 24 hours or more) are common. If you want to try the train, consider shorter stretches, eg from Dar es Salaam into the Selous, or between Tabora and Kigoma. Food is available on both lines.

CLASSES

Tazara has three classes: 1st class (four-bed compartments); 2nd-class sitting and economy class (benches, usually very crowded). Some trains also have 2nd-class sleeping (six-bed compartments). Men and women can only travel together in the sleeping sections by booking the entire compartment. At night, secure your window with a stick, and don't leave luggage unattended. Central Line currently only has 1st class (four-bed compartments) and economy.

RESERVATIONS

Tickets for 1st and 2nd class should be reserved at least several days in advance, although occasionally you'll be able to get a seat on the day of travel. Economy-class tickets can be bought on the spot.

» Tazara runs two trains weekly between Dar es Salaam and Kapiri Mposhi in Zambia via Mbeya, departing Dar es Salaam at 3.50pm Tuesday (express) and 1.50pm Friday (ordinary). Express train fares between Dar es Salaam and Mbeya are Tsh35,000/29,800/22,000 for 1st/2nd/economy class (Tsh30,100/24,000/20,000 for ordinary train). Departures from Mbeya are at 2.30pm Wednesday (express) and 3pm Saturday (ordinary). For train information to/from Zambia see p209.

» Central Line trains depart Dar es Salaam for Kigoma at 5pm Tuesday and Friday (1st/economy Tsh60,600/19,100, approximately 40 hours). Departures from Kigoma are Sunday and Thursday.

» Trains between Tabora and Mpanda (economy class only Tsh15,600, about 14 hours) depart from Tabora at 9.30pm Monday and Saturday and Mpanda at 1pm Tuesday and Sunday.

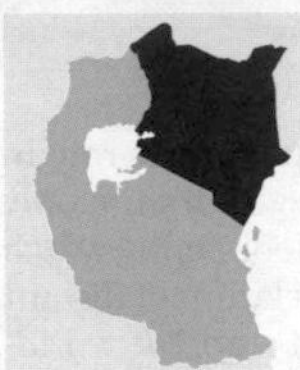

Kenya

Includes »

Nairobi 217
Amboseli National Park 240
Tsavo West National Park 243
Lake Nakuru National Park 256
Masai Mara National Reserve 261
Mt Elgon National Park 281
Mt Kenya National Park 291
Mombasa 320
Lamu 346

Best of Nature

- » Masai Mara National Reserve (p261)
- » Amboseli National Park (p240)
- » Tsavo West and Tsavo East National Parks (p243 and p247)

Best of Culture

- » Mombasa (p320)
- » Lion Guardians (p242)
- » Loyangalani (p316)
- » Lamu (p346)

Why Go?

Kenya is the Africa you always dreamed of: a land of vast savannah, immense herds of wildlife and peoples with proud traditions rooted in the soil where human beings emerged.

The Maasai, the Samburu, the Turkana, the Swahili, the Kikuyu: these are the peoples whose histories and daily struggles tell the story of a country and of a continent – the struggle to maintain traditions as the modern world crowds in, the daily fight for survival in some of the harshest environments on earth, the ancient tension between those who farm and those who roam.

Then, of course, there's the wildlife. From the Masai Mara to Tsavo, this is a country of vivid experiences – elephant families wallowing in swamps in the shadow of Mt Kilimanjaro, the massed millions of pink flamingos bathing elegantly in lake shallows, the landscape suddenly fallen silent and brought to attention by the arrival of an as-yet-unseen predator. There's nowhere better than Kenya to answer Africa's call to the wild.

When to Go

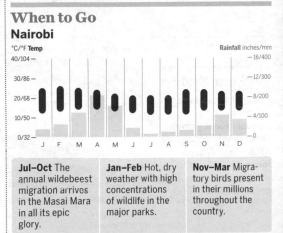

Nairobi

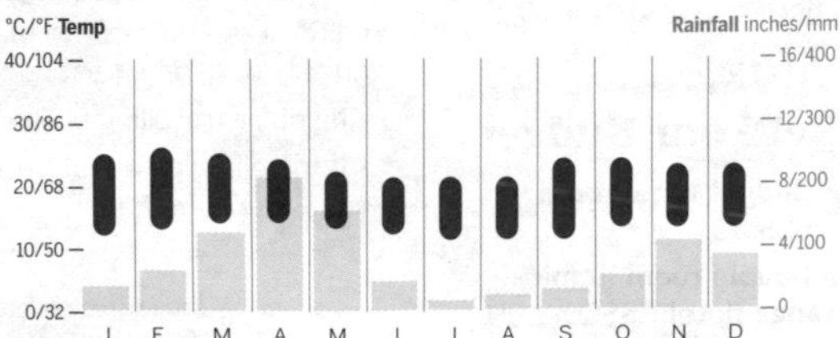

Jul–Oct The annual wildebeest migration arrives in the Masai Mara in all its epic glory.

Jan–Feb Hot, dry weather with high concentrations of wildlife in the major parks.

Nov–Mar Migratory birds present in their millions throughout the country.

AT A GLANCE

» **Currency** Kenyan shilling (KSh)

» **Languages** English and Swahili; other tribal languages also spoken

» **Money** ATMs in major towns; credit cards widely accepted

» **Mobile Phones** Local SIM cards widely available; mobile coverage extensive but patchy in wilderness areas

» **Visas** Issued on arrival at Nairobi's international airport; valid for three months

Fast Facts

» **Area** 580,367 sq km

» **Capital** Nairobi

» **Country code** ☎254

» **Population** 41.07 million

Exchange Rates

Australia	A$1	KSh88
Canada	C$1	KSh83
Euro Zone	€1	KSh109
Japan	¥100	KSh102
New Zealand	NZ$1	KSh67
UK	UK£1	KSh130
USA	US$1	KSh83

Set Your Budget

» **Budget hotel room** US$5–10

» **Double room in midrange hotel** US$50–200

» **Full board in safari lodge** US$200 and up

» **Independent safari with car rental** US$75–100 per day

Itineraries

One Week *Safari njema* – have a good trip! Kenya's rough-and-ready capital, Nairobi, is where you begin; it's the only capital city with a national park on its doorstep – watch lions, leopards and cheetahs against the backdrop of distant skyscrapers. This is just a taster for the next stop, the world-renowned Masai Mara National Reserve. Between July and October, the Mara hosts the annual wildebeest migration, an iconic slice of safari Africa and one of the greatest wildlife concentrations on earth.

Staying in Maasailand, head to Amboseli National Park, where you can get closer to elephants than almost anywhere else in Africa. The views of Mt Kilimanjaro, Africa's highest peak, are without rival.

Three Weeks Start your search for the 'Big Five' – elephant, lion, leopard, rhino and buffalo – at Lake Nakuru National Park, a stunning alkaline lake in the Rift Valley. Its population of many thousands of pink flamingos and pelicans is one of Kenya's signature images. This vitally important national park also protects the country's largest population of endangered black rhinos, as well as large herds of buffalo; sightings are almost guaranteed.

From Lake Nakuru, your next stop is the obligatory safari in Masai Mara National Reserve.

TRANSPORT IN KENYA

Kenya has a reasonably extensive and well-developed transport network. Things to remember:

» Transport options and road quality are excellent in central and western Kenya and along the coast, but take what you can get (and be prepared to shake and rattle) in the north.

» You'll need a private vehicle (usually a 4WD) for most safaris inside national parks.

» Distances in Kenya can be considerable and travel times invariably longer than you expect; consider flying to make the most of your time.

» If you decide to travel by train, do so to experience a colonial-era relic rather than to arrive comfortably or quickly or in any great comfort.

» If you're travelling by land, *never* do so by night.

» If travelling on a matatu, *never* sit next to the driver if you value your life.

Cultural Tips

» Linger over greetings; they play an important societal role.

» Learn a few words in Swahili.

» Don't eat or pass things with the left hand.

» If asked for a bribe, ask for ID from the official in question and a receipt.

NAIROBI

020 / POP 3.5 MILLION / AREA 680 SQ KM

Nairobi's reputation for crime is well known, but the horror stories obscure a vibrant and cosmopolitan city full of attractions. Primary among these is the world's only national park on the cusp of a capital city – a park packed with the free-roaming mega-fauna more associated with remote African plains. There's also an elephant orphanage and a brilliant park that has played a crucial role in saving the Rothschild's giraffe from extinction – a visit to both promises experiences that will rank alongside your favourite wildlife memories of your time in Kenya. Not far away, the former home of Karen Blixen (of *Out of Africa* fame), an outstanding museum and fantastic restaurants and hotels all add to the city's appeal. And those horror stories? Yes, many of them are true. But the majority of visitors to Kenya's capital never experience a problem. If you keep your wits about you, you're far more likely to leave with a lasting impression of Kenya's dynamism than tales of personal disaster.

Sights

CITY CENTRE

National Museum MUSEUM

(Map p220; www.museums.or.ke; Museum Hill Rd; adult/child KSh800/400, combined ticket with Snake Park KSh1200/600; 8.30am-5.30pm) Kenya's National Museum has a good range of cultural and natural history exhibits. Also check out the life-sized fibreglass model of pachyderm celebrity Ahmed, the massive elephant who, at the height of the 1980s poaching crisis, was placed under 24-hour guard by Jomo Kenyatta; he's in the inner courtyard next to the shop.

The museum's permanent collection is entered via the **Hall of Kenya**. In a room off this hall is the **Birds of East Africa** exhibit, a huge gallery of at least 900 stuffed specimens. In an adjacent room is the **Great Hall of Mammals**, with dozens of stuffed mammals, as well as a skeleton reproduction of Ahmed the elephant. Accessible off the mammals room is the **Cradle of Humankind** exhibition, the highlight of which is the **Hominid Skull Room** – an extraordinary collection of skulls that describes itself as 'the single most important collection of early human fossils in the world'; the information panels in this room are worth poring over.

Upstairs, the **Historia Ya Kenya** display is an engaging journey through Kenyan and East African history. It's well presented, well documented and offers a refreshingly Kenyan counterpoint to colonial historiographies. Also on the first floor, the **Cycles of Life** room is rich in ethnological artefacts from Kenya's various tribal groups.

Snake Park ZOO

(Map p220; www.museums.or.ke; Museum Hill Rd; adult/child KSh800/400, combined ticket with National Museum KSh1200/600; 8.30am-5.30pm) In the grounds of the National Museum, the zoo-like Snake Park has some impressive snake species, including the puff adder, black mamba, African rock python and the Gaboon viper (which rarely bares its 4cm-long fangs, the longest in the world). There are also local fish species, lizards, turtles and some sad-looking crocodiles.

Kenyatta Conference Centre LOOKOUT

(Map p224) Towering over City Square on City Hall Way, Nairobi's signature building was designed as a fusion of modern and traditional African styles. Staff will accompany you up to the **viewing platform** (adult/child KSh500/250; 9.30am-6pm) and helipad on the roof for wonderful views over Nairobi. You can take photographs from the viewing level but not elsewhere in the building.

Railway Museum MUSEUM

(Map p220; Station Rd; adult/child KSh400/100; 8am-5pm) The main collection at this interesting little museum is housed in an old railway building and consists of relics from the East African Railway. There are train and ship models, photographs, tableware and oddities from the history of the railway, such as the engine seat that allowed visiting dignitaries like Theodore Roosevelt to take potshots at unsuspecting wildlife from the front of the train. In the grounds are dozens of fading locomotives in various states of disrepair, dating from the steam days to independence. At the back of the compound is the steam train used in the movie *Out of Africa*.

The museum is reached by a long lane beside the train station.

Jamia Mosque MOSQUE

(Map p224; Banda St) Amid the clutter of downtown, Nairobi's main mosque is a lovely building in typical Arab-Muslim style, with all the domes, marble and Quranic inscriptions you'd expect from an important Islamic site, plus the traditional row of shops down one side to provide rental income for

Kenya Highlights

1. Experience expansive savannah, unmatched wildlife and the world's biggest wildlife traffic jam in **Masai Mara National Reserve** (p261)

2. Spot elephants and Kilimanjaro, two big bulks combined in Kenya's most famous picture-postcard views at **Amboseli National Park** (p240)

3. Plunge yourself into the ultimate Swahili cultural-immersion experience at **Lamu Archipelago** (p346) that makes Tanzania's Zanzibar blush with envy

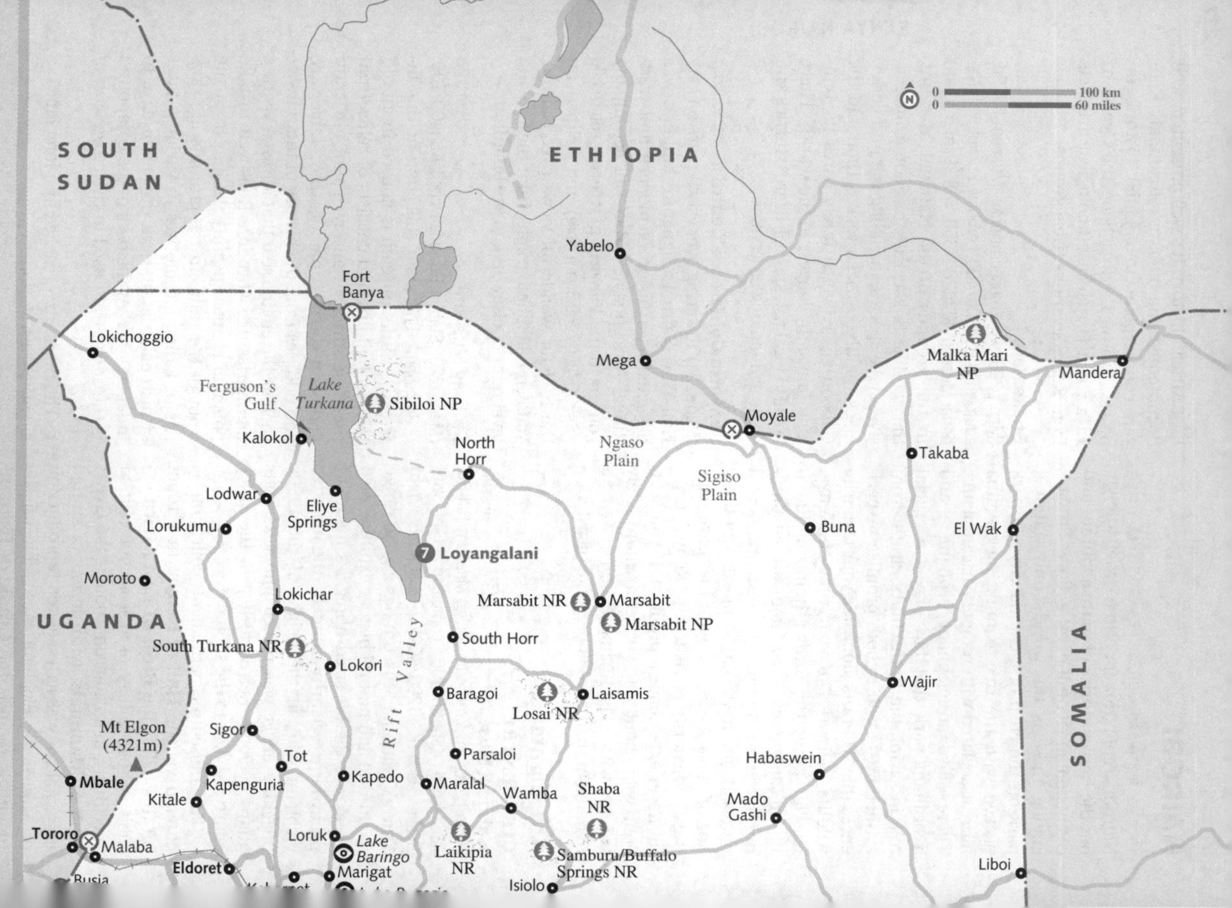

4 Go on tremendous treks and climb jagged peaks on **Mt Kenya** (p291) – this sacred mountain, Kenya's tallest and Africa's second-tallest

5 Cherish the rare chance to see the 'Big Five' in one day at **Tsavo West National Park** (p243)

6 Explore lush rainforest and fabulous birdwatching in **Kakamega Forest** (p274), Kenya's taste of central Africa

7 Discover the unforgettable tribes and the sublime Lake Turkana at **Loyangalani** (p316), the jade jewel at the end of a long quest

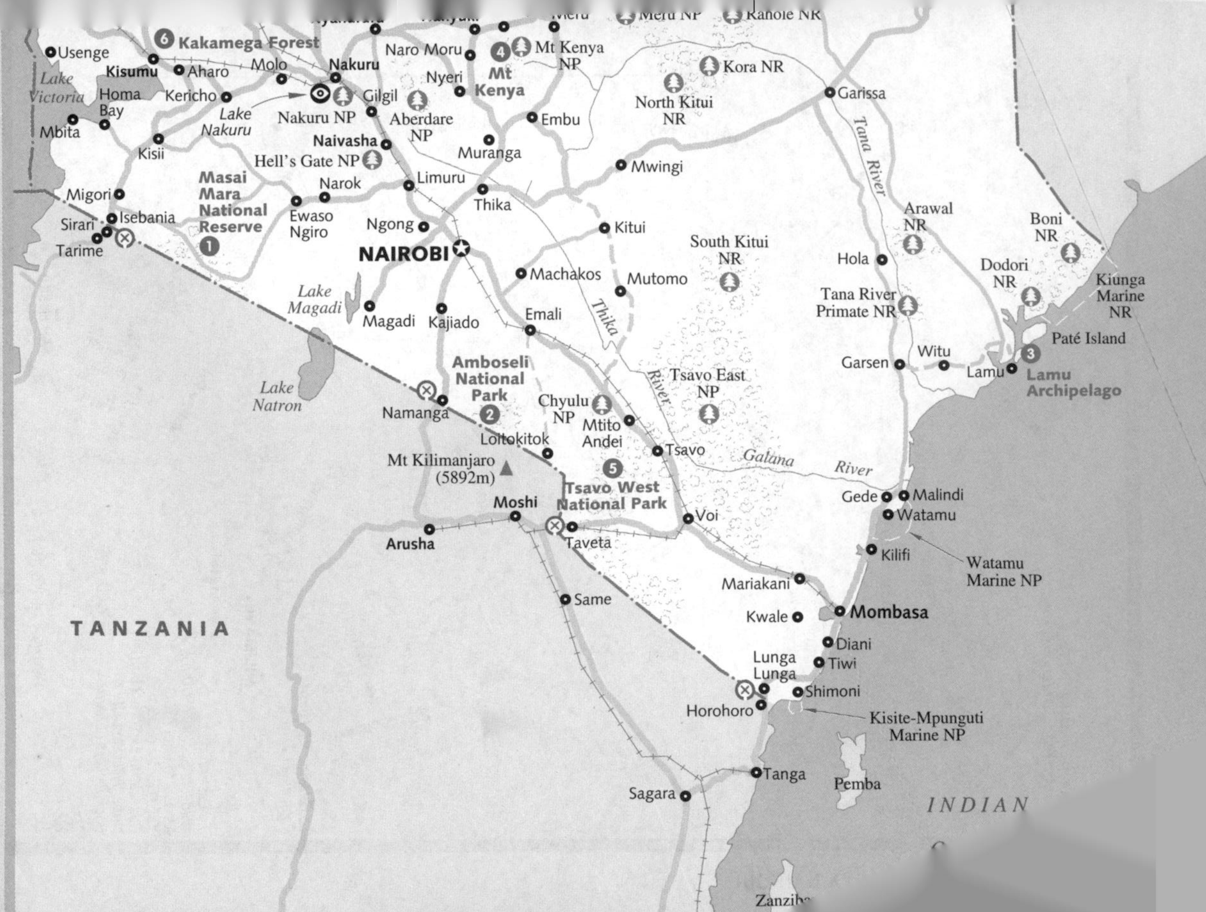

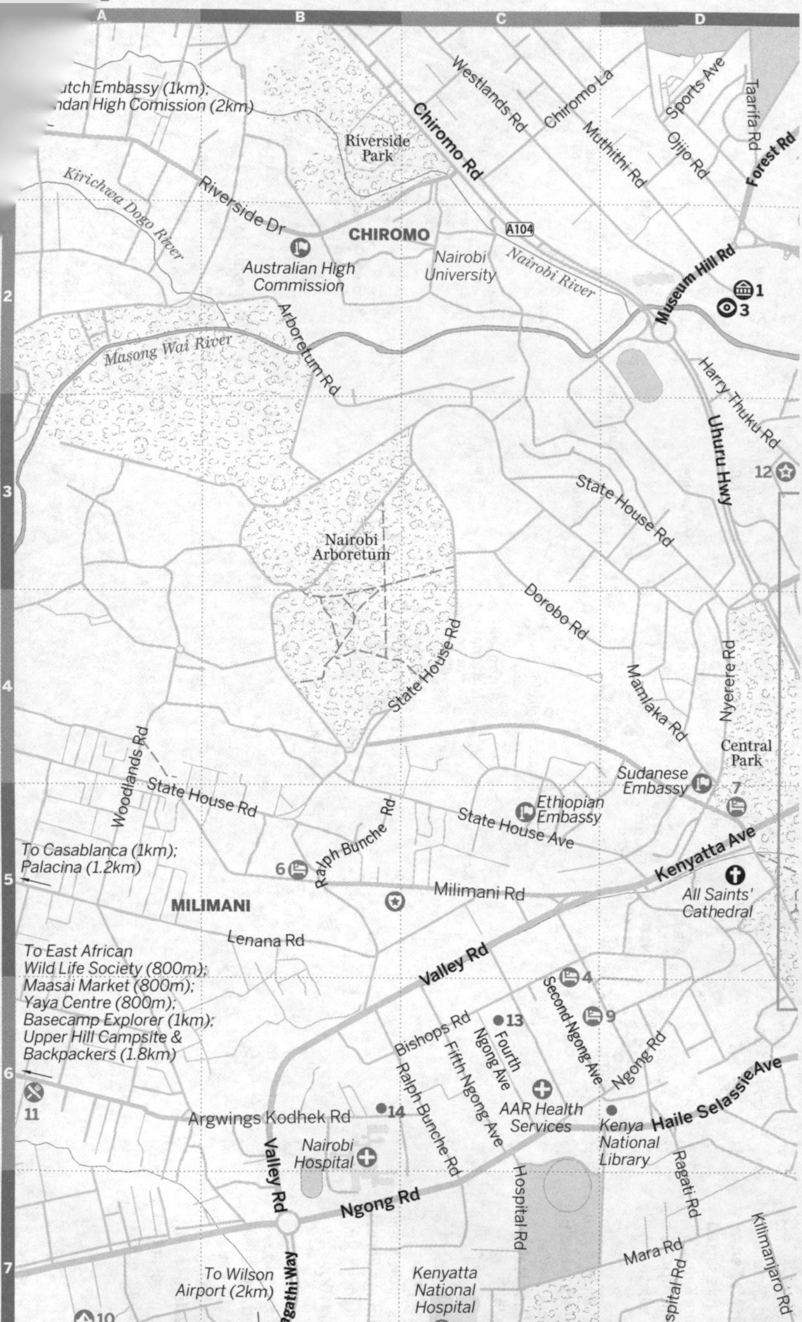

A B C D

...utch Embassy (1km);
...ndan High Comission (2km)

Riverside Park

Westlands Rd

Chiromo Rd

Chiromo La

Muthithi Rd

Sports Ave

Ojijo Rd

Taarifa Rd

Forest Rd

Kirichwa Dogo River

Riverside Dr

CHIROMO

A104

Australian High Commission

Nairobi University

Nairobi River

Museum Hill Rd

1

3

Arboretum Rd

Masong Wai River

Harry Thuku Rd

Uhuru Hwy

12

State House Rd

Nairobi Arboretum

Dorobo Rd

State House Rd

Mamlaka Rd

Nyerere Rd

Central Park

Woodlands Rd

State House Rd

Sudanese Embassy

7

Ralph Bunche Rd

Ethiopian Embassy

State House Ave

Kenyatta Ave

To Casablanca (1km);
Palacina (1.2km)

6

Milimani Rd

All Saints' Cathedral

MILIMANI

Lenana Rd

To East African
Wild Life Society (800m);
Maasai Market (800m);
Yaya Centre (800m);
Basecamp Explorer (1km);
Upper Hill Campsite &
Backpackers (1.8km)

Valley Rd

4

9

13

Second Ngong Ave

Bishops Rd

Fourth Ngong Ave

Fifth Ngong Ave

Ngong Rd

Ralph Bunche Rd

11

14

Argwings Kodhek Rd

AAR Health Services

Kenya National Library

Haile Selassie Ave

Nairobi Hospital

Valley Rd

Ngong Rd

Hospital Rd

Ragati Rd

Kilimanjaro Rd

Mara Rd

To Wilson
Airport (2km)

Mbagathi Way

Kenyatta National Hospital

Hospital Rd

10

A B C D

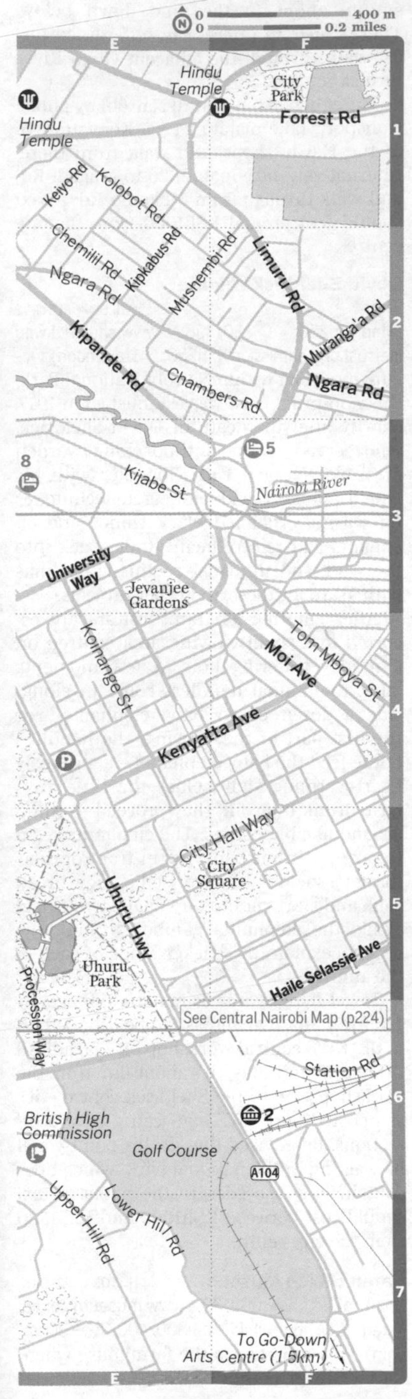

Nairobi

Sights

1 National Museum D2
2 Railway Museum F6
3 Snake Park D2

Sleeping

4 Fairview Hotel C5
5 Kahama Hotel F3
6 Milimani Backpackers & Safari Centre B5
7 Nairobi Serena Hotel D5
8 Norfolk Hotel E3
9 Upper Hill Country Lodge C6
10 Wildebeest Camp A7

Eating

11 Blue Nile Ethiopian Restaurant A6
Lord Delamere Terrace & Bar (see 8)
Savanna: The Coffee Lounge (see 1)

Entertainment

12 Kenya National Theatre D3

Shopping

African Heritage Design (see 1)

Information

13 ACK Language & Orientation School C6
14 Kenya Youth Voluntary Development Projects B6

its upkeep. Non-Muslims are very rarely allowed to enter, but the appealing exterior is visible from the street.

American Embassy Memorial Garden GARDEN

(Map p224; Moi Ave; admission KSh20; ⏲8am-6pm) This well-tended walled garden occupies the former site of the American embassy, which was destroyed by terrorist bombings in 1998. It's a lovely spot, despite being right between busy Moi and Haile Selassie Aves.

KAREN & LANGATA

Nairobi National Park PARK

(Map p230; www.kws.org/parks/parks_reserves/NANP.html; adult/child/student US$40/20/15; ⏲6am-sunset) Welcome to Kenya's most accessible yet incongruous safari experience. Set on the city's southern outskirts, Nairobi

National Park (at 117 sq km, it's one of Africa's smallest) has abundant wildlife which can, in places, be viewed against a backdrop of city skyscrapers and airliners coming in to land at the nearby airport. Remarkably, the animals seem utterly unperturbed by it all.

Nairobi National Park has acquired the nickname 'Kifaru Ark', a testament to its success as a rhinoceros (*kifaru* in Kiswahili) sanctuary. The park is home to the densest concentration of **black rhinoceros** (over 50) in the world. **Lions** and **hyenas** are also commonly sighted within the park. You'll need a bit of patience and a lot of luck to spot the park's resident **cheetahs** and **leopards**. Other regularly spotted species include **gazelle**, **warthog**, **zebra**, **giraffe**, **ostrich** and **buffalo**. The park's wetland areas also sustain approximately **400 bird species**, which is more than in the whole of the UK!

The park's main entrance and **KWS headquarters** is on Langata Rd. Other entrances are on Magadi Rd and the Athi River gate; the latter is handy if you're continuing on to Mombasa, Amboseli or the Tanzanian border. The roads in the park are passable with 2WDs, but travelling in a 4WD is never a bad idea, especially if the rains have been heavy.

Unless you already have your own vehicle, the cheapest way to see the park is on the **park shuttle** (adult/child US$20/5), a big KWS bus that leaves the main gate at 2pm on Sunday for a **2½-hour tour**. You'll need to book in person at the main gate by 1.30pm.

Giraffe Centre — WILDLIFE RESERVE

(Map p230; www.giraffecenter.org; Koitobos Rd; adult/child KSh700/250; ⌚9am-5.30pm) In 1979, Jock Leslie-Melville (the Kenyan grandson of a Scottish earl) and his wife Betty began raising a baby giraffe in their Langata home. At the time, when their African Fund for Endangered Wildlife (AFEW) was just getting off the ground, there were no more than 120 Rothschild's giraffes in the wild. Today, the population numbers more than 300, and the centre has successfully released these charismatic creatures into Lake Nakuru National Park (home to around 45 giraffes), Mwea National Reserve, Ruma National Park and Nasalot National Reserve. The centre combines serious conservation with enjoyable activities. You can observe, hand-feed or even kiss a Rothschild's giraffe from a raised wooden structure, while warthogs snuffle about in the mud down below. There's also an interesting self-guided forest walk through the adjacent Gogo River bird sanctuary.

To get here from central Nairobi by public transport, take matatu 24 via Kenyatta Ave to the Hardy shops, and walk from there. Alternatively, take matatu 26 to Magadi Rd, and walk through from Mukoma Rd. A taxi should cost around KSh1000 from the city centre.

David Sheldrick Wildlife Trust — WILDLIFE RESERVE

(Map p230; ☎2301396; www.sheldrickwildlifetrust.org; admission KSh500; ⌚11am-noon) Occupying a plot within Nairobi National Park, this non-profit trust was established in 1977, shortly after the death of David Sheldrick, who served as the anti-poaching warden of Tsavo National Park. Together with his wife Daphne, David pioneered techniques for raising orphaned black rhinos and elephants and reintroducing them back into the wild, and the trust retains close links with Tsavo for these and other projects.

After entering at 11am, visitors are escorted to a small viewing area centred on a muddy watering hole. A few moments later, the animal handlers come in alongside a dozen or so baby elephants. For the first part of the viewing, the handlers bottle-feed the baby elephants – a strangely heart-warming sight. Once the little guys have drunk their fill, they proceed to romp around like big babies. The elephants seem to take joy in misbehaving in front of their masters, so don't be surprised if a few break rank and start rubbing up against your leg! While the elephants gambol around, the keepers explain the backgrounds of each of the animals.

To get here by bus or matatu, take 125 or 126 from Moi Ave and ask to be dropped off at the KWS central workshop on Magadi Rd (KSh50, 50 minutes). It's about 1km from the workshop gate to the Sheldrick centre – it's signposted and KWS staff can give you directions. Be advised that at this point you'll be walking in the national park, which does contain lions, so stick to the paths. A taxi should cost between KSh1000 and KSh1500 from the city centre.

Karen Blixen Museum — HISTORIC BUILDING

(Map p230; ☎8002139; www.museums.or.ke; Karen Rd; adult/child KSh800/400; ⌚9.30am-6pm) This museum is the farmhouse where Karen Blixen, author of *Out of Africa*, lived between 1914 and 1931. She left after a series of personal tragedies, but the lovely colonial house, set in expansive gardens, has been preserved as a museum. The movie was actually shot at a nearby location, so don't be surprised if things don't look entirely right! Guides (non-mandatory, but useful) are included in the admission fee, but they do expect a tip.

The museum is about 2km from Langata Rd. The easiest way to get here by public transport is by matatu 24 via Kenyatta Ave, which passes right by the entrance. A taxi should cost between KSh1000 and KSh1500 from the city centre.

Bomas of Kenya CULTURAL CENTRE

(Map p230; ☎891801; www.bomasofkenya.co.ke; Langata Rd; adult/child KSh600/300; ⏲performances 2.30-4pm Mon-Fri, 3.30-5.15pm Sat & Sun) The talented resident artists at this cultural centre perform traditional dances and songs taken from the country's various tribal groups, including Arabic-influenced Swahili *taarab* music, Kalenjin warrior dances, Embu drumming and Kikuyu circumcision ceremonies. It's touristy, of course, but still a spectacular afternoon out.

The centre is at Langata, near Nairobi National Park's main gate. Bus or matatu 125 or 126 run here from Nairobi train station (KSh40, 30 minutes). Get off at Magadi Rd, from where it's about a 1km walk, clearly signposted on the right-hand side of the road. A taxi should set you back between KSh1000 and KSh1200.

Festivals & Events

Kenya Fashion Week FASHION

(Sarit Centre, Westlands) An expo-style fashion event held in June, bringing together designers and manufacturers from all over the country.

Kenya Music Festival MUSIC FESTIVAL

(Kenyatta Conference Centre) Kenya's longest-running music festival was established almost 80 years ago by the colonial regime. Held over 10 days in August.

Tusker Safari Sevens SPORT

(www.safarisevens.com; Nyayo National Stadium) A high-profile international seven-a-side rugby tournament. The Kenyan team reached the semi-finals in 2011. Held in October and November.

Sleeping

The heart and soul of Nairobi is the city centre, so if you want to go to bed and wake up in the centre of it all, look no further. Of the outlying areas, the eastern districts of Nairobi Hill and Milimani have the most promising selection, catering for all budgets. For a decidedly different take on Nairobi, consider heading right out into the 'burbs, namely Karen and Langata.

CITY CENTRE

TOP CHOICE **Kahama Hotel** HOTEL $

(Map p220; ☎3742210; www.kahamahotels.co.ke; Murang'a Rd; s/d from KSh3100/3700) Almost equidistant between the city centre and the National Museum, this place is a terrific choice. Its catch cry is 'Economy with Style' and it's safe to say it pretty much lives up to it, with pleasant rooms, comfy beds and free wireless access (no Yahoo! for some reason). The only downside? The new highway passes by the front door – ask for a room at the back.

TOP CHOICE **Norfolk Hotel** HOTEL $$$

(Map p220; ☎2265000; www.fairmont.com/norfolkhotel; Harry Thuku Rd; s/d from US$275/300; P❄☎≋) Built in 1904, Nairobi's oldest hotel was *the* place to stay during colonial days. The hotel remains the traditional starting point for elite safaris. Thanks to the leafy grounds, it has an almost rustic feel, and it's by far the best spot in town for those looking for a bit of historical authenticity.

Nairobi Serena Hotel HOTEL $$$

(Map p220; ☎2842000; www.serenahotels.com; Central Park, Procession Way; s/d from US$290/320; P❄☎≋) Consolidating its reputation as one of the best top-flight chains in East Africa, this entry in the Serena canon has a fine sense of individuality, with its international-class facilities displaying a touch of safari style. Given the choice, opt for one of the amazing garden suites, where you can take advantage of your own private patio garden.

Meridian Court Hotel HOTEL $$

(Map p224; ☎2220006; www.meridianhotelkenya.com; Muranga'a Rd; s/d from KSh7850/8950; P☎≋) The elaborate lobby here is rather more prepossessing than the grey concrete blocks above it, but it's hardly worth

Central Nairobi

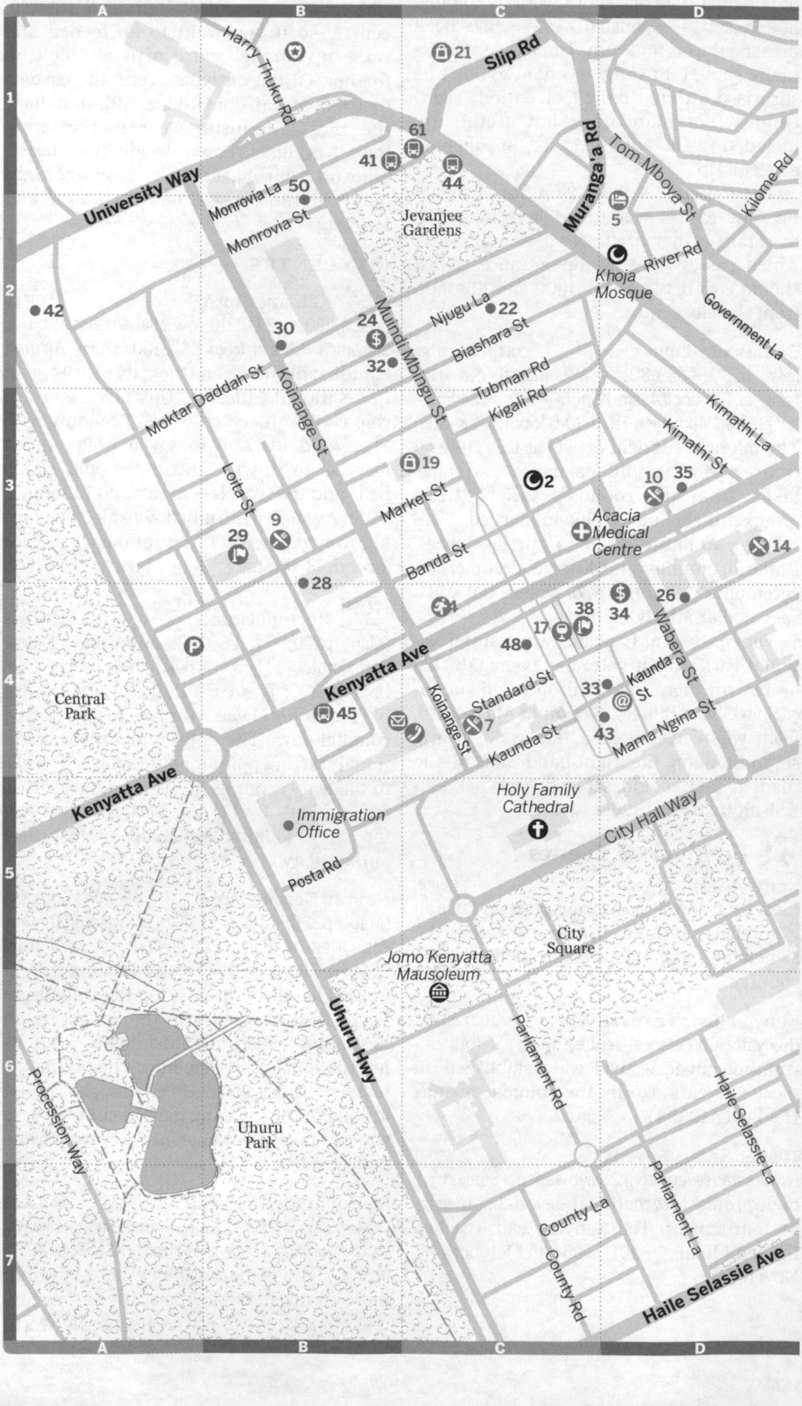

A B C D
1 2 3 4 5 6 7

Harry Thuku Rd
21
Slip Rd
61
41
44
University Way
Monrovia La
50
Monrovia St
Jevanjee Gardens
Muranga'a Rd
Tom Mboya St
Kilome Rd
5
Khoja Mosque
River Rd
Government La
42
30
24
Muindi Mbingu St
Njugu La
22
Biashara St
32
Moktar Daddah St
Koinange St
Tubman Rd
Kigali Rd
Kimathi La
Kimathi St
Loita St
19
2
10
35
Market St
9
29
Acacia Medical Centre
14
Banda St
28
4
26
34
38
17
Wabera St
48
Kenyatta Ave
Koinange St
Standard St
33
Kaunda St
Central Park
45
7
Kaunda St
43
Mama Ngina St
Kenyatta Ave
Holy Family Cathedral
Immigration Office
City Hall Way
Posta Rd
City Square
Jomo Kenyatta Mausoleum
Uhuru Hwy
Parliament Rd
Haile Selassie La
Procession Way
Uhuru Park
Parliament La
County La
County Rd
Haile Selassie Ave

A B C D

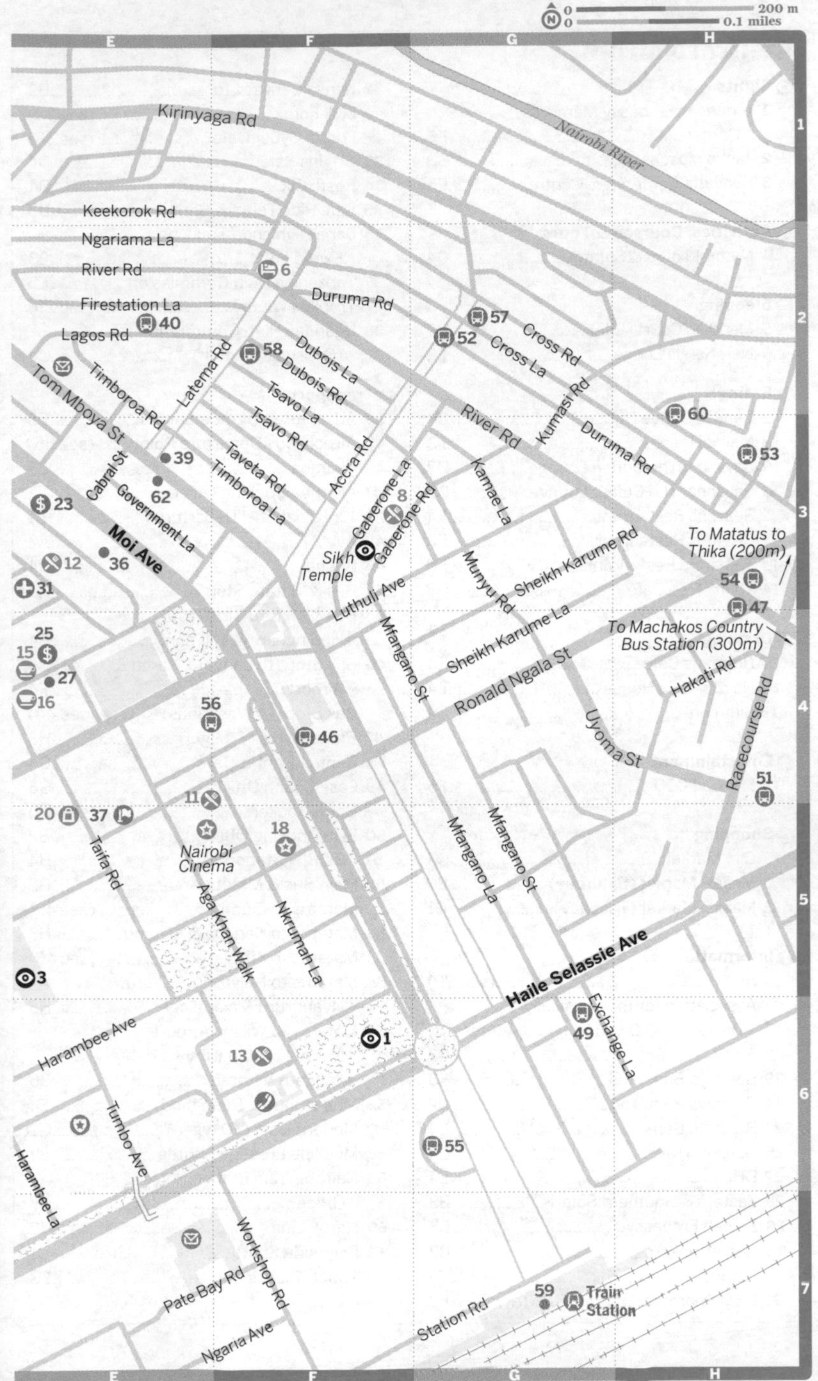
0 200 m
0 0.1 miles
Kirinyaga Rd
Nairobi River
Keekorok Rd
Ngariama La
River Rd
Firestation La
Lagos Rd
Duruma Rd
Dubois La
Dubois Rd
Tsavo La
Tsavo Rd
Taveta Rd
Timboroa La
Timboroa Rd
Laterna Rd
Tom Mboya St
Cabral St
Government La
Moi Ave
Accra Rd
Gaberone La
Gaberone Rd
Sikh Temple
Luthuli Ave
Cross Rd
Cross La
River Rd
Kumasi Rd
Duruma Rd
Kamae La
Munyu Rd
Sheikh Karume Rd
Sheikh Karume La
Mfangano St
Ronald Ngala St
To Matatus to Thika (200m)
To Machakos Country Bus Station (300m)
Hakati Rd
Uyoma St
Racecourse Rd
Nairobi Cinema
Taifa Rd
Aga Khan Walk
Nkrumah La
Mfangano La
Mfangano St
Haile Selassie Ave
Exchange La
Harambee Ave
Turnbo Ave
Harambee La
Workshop Rd
Pate Bay Rd
Ngaria Ave
Station Rd
Train Station

Central Nairobi

Sights

1 American Embassy Memorial Garden F6
2 Jamia Mosque C3
3 Kenyatta Conference Centre E5

Activities, Courses & Tours

4 Natural Tours & Safaris C4

Sleeping

5 Meridian Court Hotel D2
6 New Kenya Lodge F2

Eating

7 Beneve Coffee House C4
8 Malindi Dishes F3
9 Savanna: The Coffee Lounge B3
10 Savanna: The Coffee Lounge D3
11 Seasons Restaurant E4
12 Seasons Restaurant E3
13 Tamarind Restaurant F6
14 Thorn Tree Café D3

Drinking

15 Dormans Café E4
16 Nairobi Java House E4
17 Simmers C4

Entertainment

18 Florida 2000 .... F5

Shopping

19 City Market C3
20 Maasai Market (Saturday) E5
21 Maasai Market (Tuesday) C1

Information

AGX .... (see 29)
Association for the Physically Disabled (APDK) .... (see 40)
22 Atul's C2
23 Barclays Bank E3
24 Barclays Bank B2
25 Barclays Bank E4
26 Bunson Travel D4
27 DHL E4
28 Eastern & Southern Safaris B3
29 French Embassy B3
30 Gametrackers B2
Goldfield Forex .... (see 33)
31 KAM Pharmacy E3
32 Kenya Canvas Ltd B2
Link Forex .... (see 38)
Lucille Cyber Café .... (see 38)
33 Origins Safaris D4
34 Postbank D4
35 Safe Ride Tours & Safaris D3
36 Sana Highlands Trekking Expeditions E3
37 Tanzanian High Commission E5
Tropical Winds .... (see 29)
38 Ugandan High Commission (Consular Section) C4

Transport

39 Adventure Upgrade Safaris E3
Airport Bus Departure Point .... (see 56)
40 Akamba E2
41 Akamba Booking Office & International Departures B1
42 Avis A2
43 Budget D4
44 Bus & Matatu Stop C1
45 Bus & Matatu Stop (to Hurlingham & Milimani) B4
46 Bus Stop (to Langata, Karen & Airport) F4
Bus Stop (to Westlands) .... (see 44)
47 Buses to Kisii & Migori H3
48 Central Rent-a-Car C4
49 Easy Coach Office G6
Gametrackers .... (see 30)
50 KBS Booking Office B2
51 KBS Bus Station H4
52 Main Bus & Matatu Area G2
Matatus to Eldoret .... (see 49)
53 Matatus to Kericho & Kisumu H3
Matatus to Kibera .... (see 46)
54 Matatus to Naivasha, Nakuru, Nyahururu & Namanga H3
55 Matatus to Wilson Airport, Nairobi National Park, Langata & Karen G6
56 Metro Shuttle Bus Stand E4
57 Modern Coast (Oxygen) G2
58 Mololine Prestige Shuttle F2
59 Nairobi Train Station Booking Office G7
60 Narok Line H2
61 Riverside Shuttle C1
62 Tough Trucks Kenya E3

complaining when you're essentially getting a suite for the price of a standard room. There's no great luxury involved and some of the furnishings have seen better days, but the pool, bar and restaurants make it terrific value in this price range.

New Kenya Lodge HOTEL $
(Map p224; 2222202; www.nksafari.com; River Rd; dm/s/d with shared bathroom KSh600/700/1200) This classic long-standing shoestringer's haunt has seen better decades (some of the beds sag prodigiously), though it has an aged charm if you're not too fussy about things like, well, cleanliness. Staff here are friendly and there's hot water in the evening (or so they claim).

MILIMANI & NAIROBI HILL

TOP CHOICE **Upper Hill Country Lodge** HOTEL $$
(Map p220; 2881600; www.countrylodge.co.ke; Second Ngong Ave, Milimani; s/d from KSh11,400/15,600; P) The focus here is on affordable luxury for business travellers. Despite a recent price hike, it remains one of the best-value midrange options in Nairobi – its minimalist yet stylish living quarters can compete with the best of them.

TOP CHOICE **Palacina** BOUTIQUE HOTEL $$$
(off Map p220; 2715517; www.palacina.com; Kitale Lane, Milimani; ste 1-/2-person US$270/409, penthouses US$690; P) The fabulous collection of stylish suites – at what is possibly the first genuine boutique hotel in Kenya – is perfect for well-heeled sophisticates who still like the personal touch. Intimate rooms are awash with calming tones, boldly accented by rich teak woods, lavish furniture and private jacuzzis.

Wildebeest Camp BACKPACKERS $
(Map p220; 2720740; www.wildebeestcamp.com; Milimani Rd, Milimani; camping KSh1000, dm/s/d KSh1250/2500/3500, s/d garden tent from KSh3500/4500; P@) This fabulous place, next to the Royal Nairobi Golf Course west of Upper Hill, is another of Nairobi's outstanding budget options. The atmosphere is relaxed yet switched on, and the accommodation is spotless and great value however much you're paying. A great Nairobi base.

Upper Hill Campsite & Backpackers BACKPACKERS $
(off Map p220; 2500218; www.upperhillcampsite.com; Othaya Rd, Kileleshwa; camping KSh450, dm KSh700, d KSh3000 d without bathroom KSh2000; P@) An attractive, secure compound and an oasis from the mean city streets, Upper Hill offers a range of accommodation, attracting a loyal following of overland truck groups and an international mix of backpackers and budget travellers. It's centred on an elegant, restored colonial house on a sprawling estate in the embassy district of Kileleshwa. To get here, take matatu or bus 46 along Othaya Rd.

Milimani Backpackers & Safari Centre BACKPACKERS $
(Map p220; 2724827; www.milimanibackpackers.com; Milimani Rd, Milimani; camping KSh600, dm KSh750, s/d cabins KSh2200/2500, with shared bathroom KSh1500/2000; P@) This terrific place is one of the friendliest accommodation options in town, and whether you camp out back, cosy up in the dorms or splurge on your own cabin, you'll end up huddled around the fire at night, swapping travel stories and dining on home-cooked meals (KSh450) with fellow travellers. Take matatu 46 (KSh30) from the city centre.

Fairview Hotel HOTEL $$
(Map p220; 2711321; www.fairviewkenya.com; Bishops Rd, Milimani; s/d/ste from KSh14,800/17,300/24,000;) An excellent top-end choice that puts many of the more prestigious and pricier places in town to shame. The Fairview is nicely removed from the central hubbub and defined by its winding paths and green-filled grounds.

KAREN & LANGATA

TOP CHOICE **Karen Blixen Cottages** BOUTIQUE HOTEL $$$
(Map p230; 882130; www.karenblixencoffeegarden.com; 336 Karen Rd, Karen; s/d US$300/465; P) Located near the Karen Blixen Museum, this gorgeous clutch of spacious cottages is centred on a formal garden, and adjacent to a small coffee plantation and a country restaurant. It's sophisticated and supremely comfortable.

Giraffe Manor HISTORIC HOTEL $$$
(Map p230; 8891078; www.giraffemanor.com; Mukoma Rd, Karen; s/d full board US$660/960; P) Built in 1932 in the typical English style, this elegant manor is situated on 56 hectares, much of which is given over to the adjacent Giraffe Centre (p222). As a result, you may have a Rothschild's giraffe peering through your bedroom window first thing in

KENYAN SAFARI COMPANIES

The following companies can organise safaris to Kenya's major safari destinations. If, on the other hand, you prefer to organise it all yourself, check out the vehicle-hire options on p374.

» **Abercrombie & Kent** (Map p230; ☎020-6950000; www.abercrombiekent.com; Abercrombie & Kent House, Mombasa Rd, Nairobi) Luxury travel company with authentic safaris to match.

» **Basecamp Explorer** (off Map p220; ☎0733333709; www.basecampexplorer.com; off Ngong Rd, Nairobi) Scandinavian-owned ecotourism operator offering comprehensive camping itineraries.

» **Desert Rose** (www.desertrosekenya.com) Walking camel-train safaris (everything from bare bones to luxury) in northern Kenya.

» **Eastern & Southern Safaris** (Map p224; ☎020-2242828; www.essafari.co.ke; 6th fl, Finance House, Loita St, Nairobi) Classy and reliable outfit aiming at the midrange and upper end of the market.

» **Eco-Resorts** (☎0733618183; www.eco-resorts.com) Activity-based volunteer and cultural packages and customised safaris around Kenya.

» **Gametrackers** (Map p224; ☎020-2222703; www.gametrackersafaris.com; 5th fl, Nginyo Towers, cnr Koinange & Moktar Daddah Sts, Nairobi) Reliable company with camping and lodge safaris around Kenya; one of the best operators for Lake Turkana and the north.

» **IntoAfrica** (☎UK 0114-2555610; www.intoafrica.co.uk; 40 Huntingdon Cres, Sheffield, UK) Highly regarded company specialising in 'fair-traded' trips combining culture and wildlife viewing.

» **Natural Tours & Safaris** (www.naturaltoursandsafaris.com) Mombasa (☎041-2226715; Jeneby House, Moi Ave); Nairobi (Map p224; ☎020-2216830; 1st fl, Gilfillan House, Nairobi) Well-organised safaris visiting all the major parks.

» **Origins Safaris** (Map p224; ☎3312137; www.originsafaris.info; EcoBank Towers, Standard St, Nairobi) A natural history and cultural focus.

» **Pollman's Tours & Safaris** (Map p230; ☎020-3337234; www.pollmans.com; Pollman's House, Mombasa Rd, Nairobi) Kenyan-based operator with coastal and Tanzanian trips as well.

» **Safe Ride Tours & Safaris** (Map p224; ☎020-2229484; www.saferidesafaris.com; 2nd fl, Ave House, Kenyatta Ave, Nairobi) Relatively new budget operator recommended by readers for camping excursions.

» **Samburu Trails Trekking Safaris** (☎UK 0131-6256635; www.samburutrails.com) A range of foot excursions in some less-visited parts of the Rift Valley.

» **Southern Cross Safaris** (www.southerncrosssafaris.com) Mombasa (☎041-2434600; Kanstan Centre, Nyali Bridge, Malindi Rd); Nairobi (Map p230; ☎020-3884712; Symbion House, Karen Rd) A good choice for individually designed safaris.

the morning. And yet, the real appeal of the Giraffe Manor is that you're treated as a personal guest of the owners, which means you can use their chauffeur, sample their wines and dine in lavish excess.

Margarita House GUESTHOUSE **$$**
(Map p230; ☎2018421; www.themargaritahouse.com; Lower Plains Rd, Karen; s/d from US$85/125; P 📶 🏊) Tucked away on a quiet street on Karen's north side, this tranquil guesthouse is one of the few midrange options in the area, and thankfully it's a good one. Rooms are large and comfortable, contemporary artworks adorn the walls, and Elizabeth and Joel are welcoming hosts. The roads can be a little confusing around here – print out the detailed directions from the website.

Karen Camp CAMPGROUND **$**
(Map p230; ☎8833475; www.karencamp.com; Marula Lane, Karen; camping US$6, s/d walk-in tent US$20/30, r from US$40; P) You wouldn't expect to find a backpacker-friendly option

out here in affluent Karen, which is why we like this friendly little spot so much. The quiet location and smart facilities are reason enough to make the trek out to the shady campsites, spic-and-span dorms and permanent safari-style tents.

Eating

Nairobi is well stocked with places to eat, particularly in the city centre. For dinner it's worth heading out to the suburbs, where there are dozens of choices of cuisine from all over the world.

CITY CENTRE

TOP CHOICE **Savanna: The Coffee Lounge** CAFE $
(Map p220; Museum Hill Rd; snacks from KSh180, mains KSh440-590; ⌚7am-8pm Mon-Sat, 9am-6pm Sun); Central Nairobi (Map p224; Loita St); Central Nairobi (Map p224; Kenyatta Ave) This classy little chain has outposts across Nairobi, but we particularly like the tranquillity of the branch inside the grounds of the National Museum. Decor is safari chic without being overdone, service is friendly and unobtrusive, and dishes include pies, wraps, samosas, sandwiches, burgers, pasta, soup and salads.

TOP CHOICE **Lord Delamere Terrace & Bar** INTERNATIONAL $$$
(Map p220; ☎2265000; www.fairmont.com/norfolkhotel; Norfolk Hotel, Harry Thuku Rd; mains KSh1450-2575; ⌚lunch & dinner) This popular rendezvous spot at the Norfolk Hotel has existed as the unofficial starting and ending point for East African safaris since 1904. While the atmosphere may be a bit too colonial for some, there's no denying the palpable sense of history. Dishes include wonderful steaks, Lamu crab cakes, Indian Ocean lobster, crocodile kebabs and ostrich fillets.

Tamarind Restaurant SEAFOOD $$$
(Map p224; ☎2251811; www.tamarind.co.ke; off Harambee Ave; mains KSh1000-2500; ⌚lunch & dinner Mon-Sat) Kenya's most prestigious restaurant chain runs Nairobi's best seafood restaurant. Starters range from Kilifi oysters to red snapper in spicy harissa, though save room for the crustacean onslaught of flambéed lobster with cognac, sunset Pwani crab and tikka masala prawns. Smart dress is expected, and you'll need to budget at least KSh2500 for the full works – much more if you want wine or cocktails and lobster – though seafood gourmands agree that it's money well spent.

Thorn Tree Café INTERNATIONAL $$
(Map p224; ☎2757000; New Stanley Hotel, Kimathi St; mains KSh950-1950; ⌚lunch & dinner) The Stanley's legendary cafe still serves as a popular meeting place for travellers of all persuasions, and caters to most tastes with a good mix of food, from grilled giant prawns to Kenyan-style chicken stew. The original thorn-tree noticeboard in the

KIBERA

Home to an estimated one million residents, the shanty town of Kibera (off Map p220)is second in size only to Soweto in Johannesburg, South Africa. Kibera is a sprawling urban jungle of shanty town housing. The neighbourhood was thrust into the Western imagination when it featured prominently in the Fernando Meirelles film *The Constant Gardener*.

Although it's virtually impossible to collect accurate statistics on shanty towns, with the demographics changing almost daily, the rough estimates for Kibera are shocking enough: according to local aid workers, Kibera is home to one pit toilet for every 100 people; its inhabitants suffer an HIV/AIDS infection rate of more than 20%; and four out of every five people living here are unemployed.

Kibera covers 2.5 sq km in area and is home to somewhere between a quarter and a third of Nairobi's population with a density of an estimated 300,000 people per sq km. The railway line heading to Kisumu intersects Kibera, though the shanty town doesn't actually have a station.

A visit to Kibera is one way to look behind the headlines and touch on, albeit briefly, the daily struggles and triumphs of life in the town. Although you could visit on your own, security is an issue, and such visits aren't always appreciated by residents. One company we recommend is **Kibera Tours** (☎0723669218; www.kiberatours.com; per person KSh2500).

Nairobi National Park

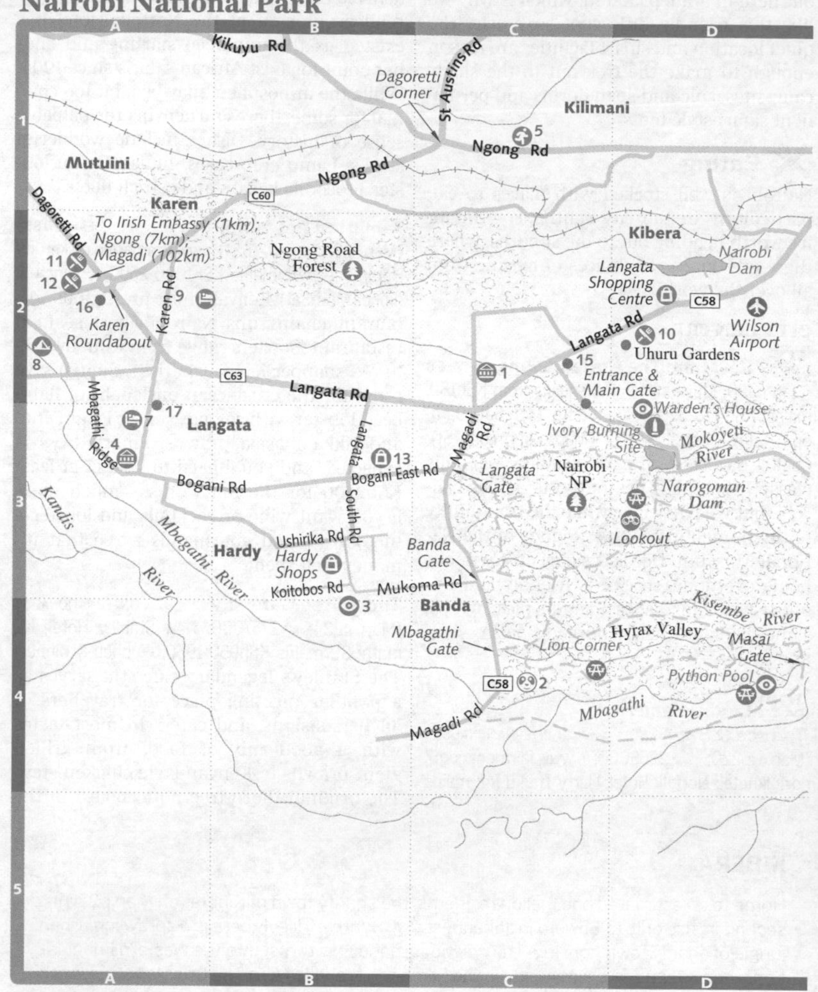

courtyard gave rise to the general expression, and inspired Lonely Planet's own online Thorn Tree Travel Forum. While the cafe is now on its third acacia and the noticeboard's not quite the paperfest it once was, a little nostalgia is *de rigueur,* even if only to pause and recognise an original landmark on the Cape to Cairo overland trail.

Beneve Coffee House KENYAN $
(Map p224; cnr Standard & Koinange Sts; mains KSh180-250; ⏲lunch & dinner Mon-Fri) This small self-service cafe has locals queuing outside in the mornings waiting for it to open. Food ranges from African- and Indian-influenced stews to curries, fish and chips, samosas, pasties and a host of other choices, all at low, low prices.

Malindi Dishes KENYAN $
(Map p224; Gaberone Rd; mains KSh80-250; ⏲lunch & dinner, closed Fri lunch) This small Swahili canteen serves great food from the coast, including pilau (curried rice with meat), birianis (spicy rice casseroles) and coconut fish, with side dishes such as ugali (maize- or cassava-based staple), naan and rice.

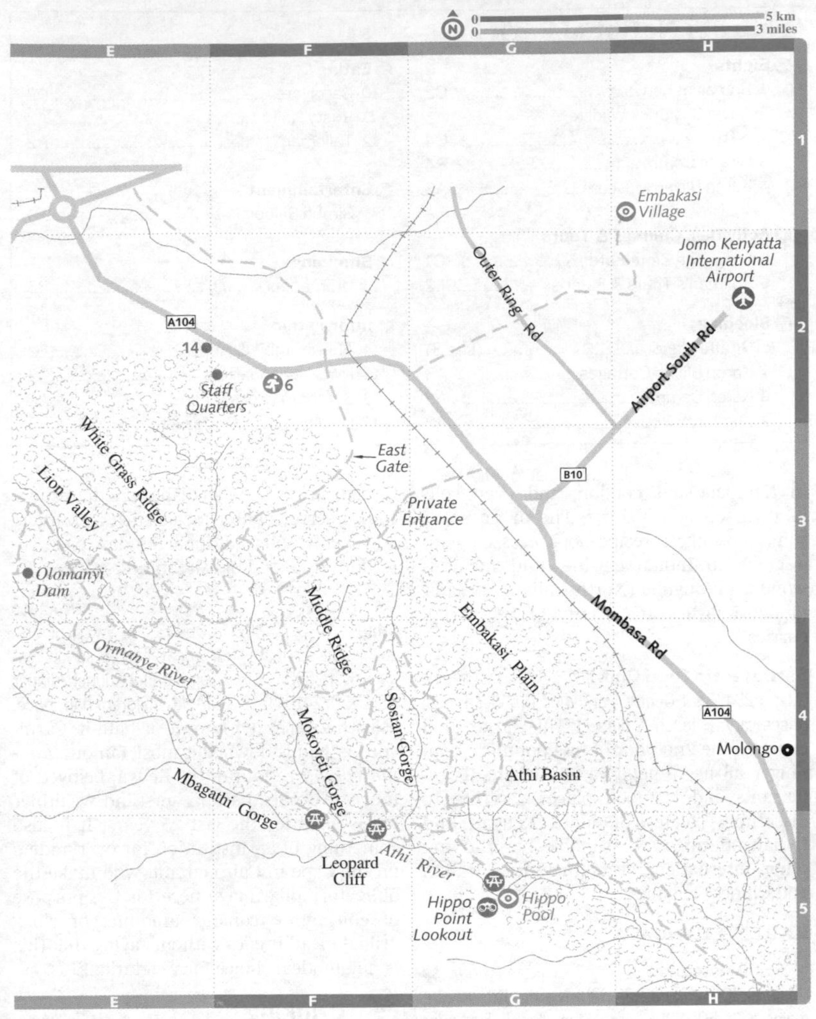

Seasons Restaurant KENYAN $
(Map p224; mains KSh390-500, buffets KSh500; ⏰lunch & dinner); Nairobi Cinema (Uchumi House, Aga Khan Walk); Kimathi St (Mutual Bldg) The cafeteria vats always brim with cheap Kenyan and Western favourites. It claims to open 24 hours, but we didn't pass by at 4am to check.

MILIMANI

TOP CHOICE **Blue Nile Ethiopian Restaurant** ETHIOPIAN $$
(Map p220; ☎2271851; bluenile@yahoo.com; Argwings Kodhek Rd, Hurlingham; mains KSh400-700; ⏰lunch & dinner) One of those rare places with a character all its own, Blue Nile's quirky lounge is painted with stories from Ethiopian mythology. The *yebeg key wot* (spiced goat meat sauce marinated in butter and spicy berebere) is a fine order.

WESTLANDS

TOP CHOICE **Haandi Restaurant** INDIAN $$
(Map p234; ☎4448294; The Mall Shopping Centre, Ring Rd, Westlands; mains KSh750-1500; ⏰lunch & dinner; ❄) This international award-winner is widely regarded as the best Indian restaurant in Kenya. Haandi has sister restaurants

Nairobi National Park

Sights
1 Bomas of Kenya C2
2 David Sheldrick Wildlife Trust C4
3 Giraffe Centre B4
4 Karen Blixen Museum A3

Activities, Courses & Tours
5 Language Center Ltd C1
6 Pollman's Tours & Safaris F2

Sleeping
Giraffe Manor .... (see 3)
7 Karen Blixen Cottages A3
8 Karen Camp A2
9 Margarita House A2

Eating
10 Carnivore D2
11 Rusty Nail A2
12 Talisman A2

Entertainment
Simba Saloon .... (see 10)

Shopping
13 Utamaduni B3

Information
14 Abercrombie & Kent E2
15 KWS Headquarters C2
16 Southern Cross Safaris A2
17 Uniglobe Let's Go Travel A3

in Kampala and London, and even sells its own souvenir T-shirts. The menu reads something like a recipe book crossed with a guide to Indian cuisine, and includes wonderful Mughlai (North Indian) spreads, tandoori dishes and plenty of vegetarian curries.

Sarit Centre Food Court FAST FOOD $
(Map p234; Sarit Centre, Parklands Rd, Westlands; prices vary; lunch & dinner) This large food court on the 2nd floor of this popular shopping mall has a good variety of small restaurants and fast-food places catering to discerning palates. Standard Kenyan and Indian offerings are available here, as are other international eats including Italian and Chinese cuisines.

KAREN & LANGATA

TOP CHOICE **Talisman** INTERNATIONAL $$
(Map p230; 3883213; 320 Ngong Rd, Karen; mains KSh950-1800; breakfast, lunch & dinner Tue-Sun) This classy cafe/bar/restaurant is incredibly fashionable with the Karen in-crowd, and rivals any of Kenya's top eateries for imaginative international food. The comfortable lounge-like rooms mix modern African and European styles and specials such as chilli coconut mangrove crab curry perk up the palate no end.

Rusty Nail INTERNATIONAL $$
(Map p230; 3882461; Dagoretti Rd, Karen; mains KSh950-1300; lunch & dinner) The relaxed atmosphere of this pavilion restaurant sits nicely with the wide range of food on offer. Lunch and dinner menus change weekly, although steaks and fish dishes are mainstays. It also serves lighter meals such as burgers and salads, and traditional Sunday roasts cater for nostalgic English foodies.

Carnivore KENYAN $$$
(Map p230; 020-605933; www.carnivore.co.ke; off Langata Rd; meat buffet lunch/dinner KSh2530/2835, veg buffet lunch/dinner KSh2150/2410, 5-12 year-old children half price; lunch & dinner; P) Love it or hate it, Carnivore is hands-down the most famous *nyama choma* restaurant in Kenya, beloved of tourists, expats, backpackers and wealthier locals alike for the last 25 years. It is also something of an institution for overlanders on the Cape to Cairo circuit, who make the obligatory pilgrimage here for the purpose of consuming copious amounts of chargrilled meat. It goes without saying that this is not an ideal choice for vegetarians.

Drinking

Western cafe culture has hit Nairobi, seized upon enthusiastically by local expats and residents pining for a decent cup of Kenyan coffee. This is the best place in the country for *real* coffee.

There are plenty of cheap but very rough-and-ready bars around Latema Rd and River Rd, although these places aren't recommended for female travellers, and even male drinkers should watch themselves. You can also head to Westlands and Karen, where the drinking scene brings in a lot more expats. Be aware that, even in the 'burbs, foreign women without a man in tow will draw attention.

CITY CENTRE

TOP CHOICE Simmers BAR

(Map p224; cnr Kenyatta Ave & Muindi Mbingu St; ⌚8am-1am) If you're tired of having your butt pinched to the strains of limp R&B in darkened discos, Simmers is the place to come to rediscover a bit of true African rhythm. With free-flowing Tusker, a separate shots bar and plenty of *nyama choma* to keep the lion from the door, it's no wonder the place always feels like a party.

Dormans Café CAFE

(Map p224; Mama Ngina St; coffee KSh110-340; ⌚6.30am-8.30pm Mon-Sat, 9am-7.30pm Sun) Established in the 1960s, this venerable firm has only recently branched out into the cafe business. The coffee's good (everything from cappuccino to iced coffee and hazelnut mocha), the selection of teas is impressive, and the food (main dishes and light meals) hits the spot.

Nairobi Java House CAFE

(Map p224; www.nairobijava.com; Mama Ngina St; coffee KSh120-280; ⌚6.30am-10pm Mon-Fri, 7am-9pm Sat, 8am-8pm Sun) This fantastic coffeehouse is rapidly turning itself into a major brand, and aficionados say the coffee's some of the best in Kenya. There are also plenty of cakes and other sweet and savoury treats (even New York cheesecake).

WESTLANDS

TOP CHOICE Gypsy's Bar BAR

(Map p234; Woodvale Grove; ⌚11am-4am) This is probably the most popular bar in Westlands, pulling in a large, mixed crowd of Kenyans, expats and prostitutes. Snacks are available, and there's decent Western and African music, with parties taking over the pavement in summer.

Klub House BAR

(Map p234; Parklands Rd; ⌚24hr) At the western end of Westlands, the Klub House is another old favourite. Music is predominantly Latin, Caribbean and home-grown Swahili, and every night has a different theme, from chill-out (Monday) and live jazz (8pm to 11pm Tuesday) to disco (Friday) and live bands (Saturday).

MILIMANI

TOP CHOICE Casablanca LOUNGE

(off Map p220; ☎2723173; Lenana Rd, Hurlingham; ⌚hours vary) This Moroccan-style lounge bar continues to be a hit with Nairobi's fastidious expat community, and you don't have to spend much time here to become a convert. Shisha pipes, wines and cocktails conspire to ease you into what's bound to end up a late night.

NAIROBI SAFETY

'Nairobbery', as it has been nicknamed by jaded residents and expats, is often regarded as the most dangerous city in Africa, beating stiff competition from Johannesburg and Lagos. Read the local newspapers and you'll quickly discover that carjacking, robbery and violence are daily occurrences. But it's worth remembering that the majority of problems happen in the shanty towns, far from the main tourist zones.

The downtown area, bound by Kenyatta Ave, Moi Ave, Haile Selassie Ave and Uhuru Hwy, is unthreatening and comparatively trouble-free as long as you use a bit of common sense. If you stay alert, walk with confidence, keep a hand on your wallet and avoid wearing anything too flashy, by day you should encounter nothing worse than a few persistent safari touts and the odd con artist. Once the shops in the CBD have shut, the streets empty rapidly. After sunset, mugging is a risk anywhere on the streets; you should always take a taxi, even if you're only going a few blocks.

Potential danger zones include the area around Latema and River Rds (east of Moi Ave), which is a hotspot for petty theft. Uhuru Park is a pleasant place during daylight hours, though it tends to accumulate all kinds of dodgy characters at night.

In the event that you are mugged, never, ever resist – simply give up your valuables and, more often than not, your assailant will flee the scene rapidly. Remember that a petty thief and a violent aggressor are very different kinds of people, so don't give your assailant any reason to do something rash.

Westlands

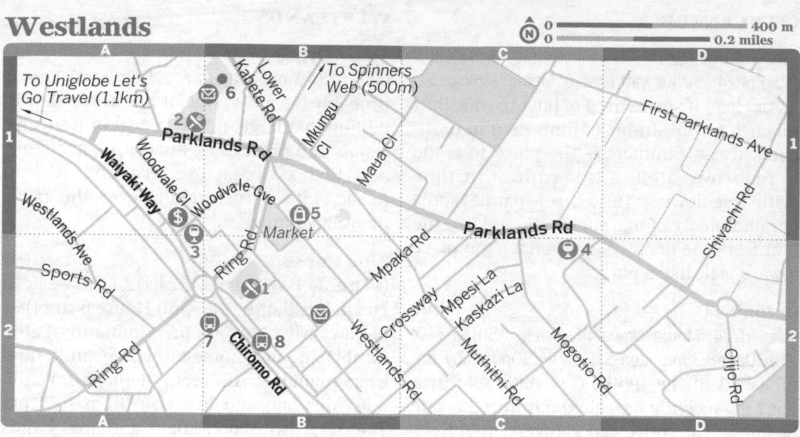

Westlands

Eating

1 Haandi Restaurant B2
2 Sarit Centre Food Court A1

Drinking

3 Gypsy's Bar A1
4 Klub House C2

Shopping

Banana Box .... (see 2)
5 Undugu Craft Shop B1

Information

AAR Health Services Clinic .... (see 2)
Automobile Association of Kenya. (see 2)
Barclays Bank .... (see 2)
EasySurf .... (see 2)
6 Savage Wilderness Safaris B1
Travellers Forex Bureau .... (see 1)

Transport

7 Bus & Matatu Stands B2
8 Bus & Matatu Stands B2

☆ Entertainment

For information on entertainment in Nairobi and for big music venues in the rest of the country, get hold of the *Saturday Nation,* which lists everything from cinema releases to live-music venues. Nightclubs usually open from 9pm until 6am.

Florida 2000 NIGHTCLUB

(Map p224; www.floridaclubskenya.com; Moi Ave; men/women KSh250/150) This big dancing den, known by everyone as F2, still works to the same formula of booze, beats and tightly packed bodies. As is typical in Nairobi, every night is a little different: Thursday is techno trance, Friday is rumba and so on.

Simba Saloon NIGHTCLUB

(Map p230; off Langata Rd; admission KSh200-300) Next door to Carnivore out on the road to Karen, this large bar and nightclub pulls in a huge crowd, particularly on Wednesday, Friday and Saturday. There are video screens, several bars, a bonfire and adventure playground in the garden, and unashamedly Western music on the dance floor, although you might get the occasional African superstar playing live. It's usually crammed with wealthy Kenyans, expat teenagers, travellers and NGO workers, plus a fair sprinkling of prostitutes.

Kenya National Theatre THEATRE

(Map p220; ☎2225174; Harry Thuku Rd; tickets from KSh250) This is the major theatre venue in Nairobi. As well as contemporary and classic plays, there are special events such as beauty pageants, which are less highbrow but still culturally interesting. Check out the *Daily Nation* to see what's on. It's opposite the Norfolk Hotel.

Shopping

TOP CHOICE **Utamaduni** HANDICRAFTS

(Map p230; www.utamaduni.com; Bogani East Rd, Karen; admission free; ⏲9am-6pm) Utamaduni is a large crafts emporium, with more than a dozen separate rooms selling all kinds of excellent African artworks and souvenirs. Prices start relatively high, but there's *none* of the hard sell you'd get in town.

Maasai Market Central Nairobi MARKET
(Map p224; off Slip Rd; ⌚Tue); Gigiri (Village Market, Limuru Rd; ⌚Fri); City Centre (Map p224; opposite Reinsurance Plaza, Taita Rd; ⌚Sat); Yaya Centre (off Map p220; Argwings Kodhek; ⌚Sun) These busy curio markets are held every Tuesday on the waste ground near Slip Rd in town, Friday in the rooftop car park at the Village Market shopping complex, Saturday in the city centre and Sunday next to the Yaya Centre. The markets are open from early morning to late afternoon.

African Heritage Design Company HANDICRAFTS
(Map p220; Museum Hill Rd; ⌚9am-6pm daily) With various outlets around town, including this one opposite the entrance to the National Museum, African Heritage Design Company has a classy range of statues, ceramics and textiles. Not all of the items are from Kenya, but the quality is good.

Banana Box HANDICRAFTS
(Map p234; www.bananaboxcrafts.com; Sarit Centre, Westlands; ⌚9.30am-6pm Mon-Sat, 10am-2pm Sun) Amid the rather less-altruistic commercialism of the Sarit Centre, Banana Box works in conjunction with community projects and refugee groups and offers modern uses for traditional objects. It's one of the better handicrafts stores around town.

Spinner's Web HANDICRAFTS
(off Map p234; www.spinnerswebkenya.com; Getathuru Gardens, off Peponi Rd, Spring Valley; ⌚9.30am-6.30pm Mon-Fri, 9.30am-5.30pm Sat & Sun) This place works with workshops and self-help groups around the country. Appealing items include carpets, wall-hangings, ceramics, wooden bowls, baskets and clothing.

Undugu Craft Shop HANDICRAFTS
(Map p234; www.undugukenya.org; Woodvale Grove, Westlands; ⌚8.30am-5.30pm Mon-Fri, 9am-2pm Sat) This nonprofit organisation supports community projects in Nairobi and has top-quality crafts including wood and soapstone carvings, basketwork and fair-trade food products.

City Market MARKET
(Map p224; Muindi Mbingu St; ⌚9am-5pm Mon-Fri, 9am-noon Sat) The city's souvenir business is concentrated in this covered market, which has literally dozens of stalls selling woodcarvings, drums, spears, shields, soapstone, Maasai jewellery and clothing. It's certainly a hectic place and you'll have to bargain hard (and we mean *hard*), but there's plenty of good merchandise on offer. It's an interesting place to wander around in its own right, though you generally need to be shopping to make the constant hassle worth the bother.

Information

Camping Equipment

Atul's (☎2225935; Biashara St; ⌚9am-1pm & 2-5pm Mon-Fri, 9am-4pm Sat) Hires out everything from sleeping bags to folding toilet seats.

Kenya Canvas Ltd (☎2223045; www.kenyacanvas.com; Muindi Mbingu St)

X-treme Outdoors (☎2722224; www.xtremeoutdoors.co.ke; Yaya Centre, Hurlingham)

Emergency

Aga Khan Hospital (☎3662020; Third Parklands Ave) A reliable hospital with 24-hour emergency services.

WORTH A TRIP

ACACIA CAMP

Just 36km from central Nairobi, just off the busy Nairobi–Mombasa Rd, **Acacia Camp** (Swara Plains; ☎2529500; www.swaraplains.com; full board s/d US$102/192; P Wi-Fi) is a wonderful escape from city life. The camp is extremely comfortable without being over the top, with well-appointed bungalows, good food and lovely gardens in the shade of acacias. The ranch itself spreads out over 20,000 acres and is home to giraffe, zebra, wildebeest, warthog, gazelle, antelope and more than 270 bird species (but not cheetah as advertised on its website); the only predator is a resident hyena. For additional charges, there are game drives and a visit to some captive (yet still rather wild) lions on the ranch's outer reaches.

Emergency services (☎999) The national emergency number to call for fire, police and ambulance assistance. A word of warning, though - don't rely on prompt arrival.

Police (☎2240000) Phone for less-urgent police business.

St John Ambulance (☎2210000)

Tourist helpline (☎604767; ⊙24hr)

Internet Access

There are hundreds of internet cafes in downtown Nairobi – most of them tucked away in anonymous office buildings in the town centre. It can be difficult to find any cyber cafe open in the downtown area on Sunday.

AGX (Barclays Plaza, Loita St; per min KSh1; ⊙8am-6pm Mon-Fri, 8am-3pm Sat) Best connections in town, with a choice of browsers.

EasySurf (Sarit Centre, Westlands; per hr KSh180; ⊙8.30am-8pm Mon-Fri, 10am-7.30pm Sat, 10.30am-3.30pm Sun)

Lucille Cyber Café (ground fl, Uganda House, Standard St; per hr KSh30; ⊙7am-8pm Mon-Fri, 9am-6pm Sat, 10am-4pm Sun)

Medical Services

AAR Health Services (Map p220; ☎2715319; Williamson House, Fourth Ngong Ave) Probably the best of a number of private ambulance and emergency air-evacuation companies. It also runs a private clinic in Westlands.

Acacia Medical Centre (Map p224; ☎2212200; ICEA Bldg, Kenyatta Ave; ⊙7am-7pm Mon-Fri, 7am-5pm Sat, 8am-5pm Sun)

KAM Pharmacy (Map p224; ☎2251700; IPS Bldg, Kimathi St; ⊙8.30am-6pm Mon-Fri, 8.30am-2pm Sat) A one-stop shop for medical treatment, with a pharmacy, doctor's surgery and laboratory.

Nairobi Hospital (Map p220; ☎2846000; www.nairobihospital.org; off Argwings Kodhek Rd; ⊙24hr)

Money

If you're looking to change money the minute you arrive (or while you wait for your bags), Jomo Kenyatta International Airport has several exchange counters in the baggage reclaim area and a **Barclays Bank** (⊙24hr) with an ATM outside in the arrivals hall.

There are Barclays branches with guarded ATMs on Mama Ngina St, Muindi Mbingu St and on the corner of Kenyatta and Moi Aves. There are also branches in the Sarit Centre and on Woodvale Grove in Westlands, and the Yaya Centre in Hurlingham.

Goldfield Forex (EcoBank Towers, Kaunda St; ⊙9am-5pm Mon-Thu, 9am-12.30pm & 2-5pm Fri, 9am-1pm Sat)

Link Forex (☎226212; ground fl, Uganda House, Standard St; ⊙9am-5pm Mon-Fri, 9am-1pm Sat)

Postbank (13 Kenyatta Ave) For Western Union money transfers.

Travellers Forex Bureau (The Mall Shopping Centre, Westlands; ⊙8.30am-5pm Mon-Fri, 9am-1pm Sat)

Post

Main post office (☎2243434; Kenyatta Ave; ⊙8am-6pm Mon-Fri, 9am-noon Sat)

Telephone

Telkom Kenya (☎2232000; Haile Selassie Ave; ⊙8am-6pm Mon-Fri, 9am-noon Sat) This place has dozens of payphones and you can buy phonecards.

BUSES FROM NAIROBI

TO	FARE (KSH)	DURATION (HR)	COMPANY
Eldoret	1050-1100	6-8	Akamba Easy Coach
Kakamega	1150-1300	7-9	Easy Coach
Kisumu	900-1250	5½-7	Akamba Easy Coach Modern Coast (Oxygen)
Mombasa	1100-1200	8-10	Akamba Easy Coach Modern Coast (Oxygen)
Malaba	1250	6-7	Easy Coach
Malindi	1500	10-13	Modern Coast (Oxygen)

Around Nairobi

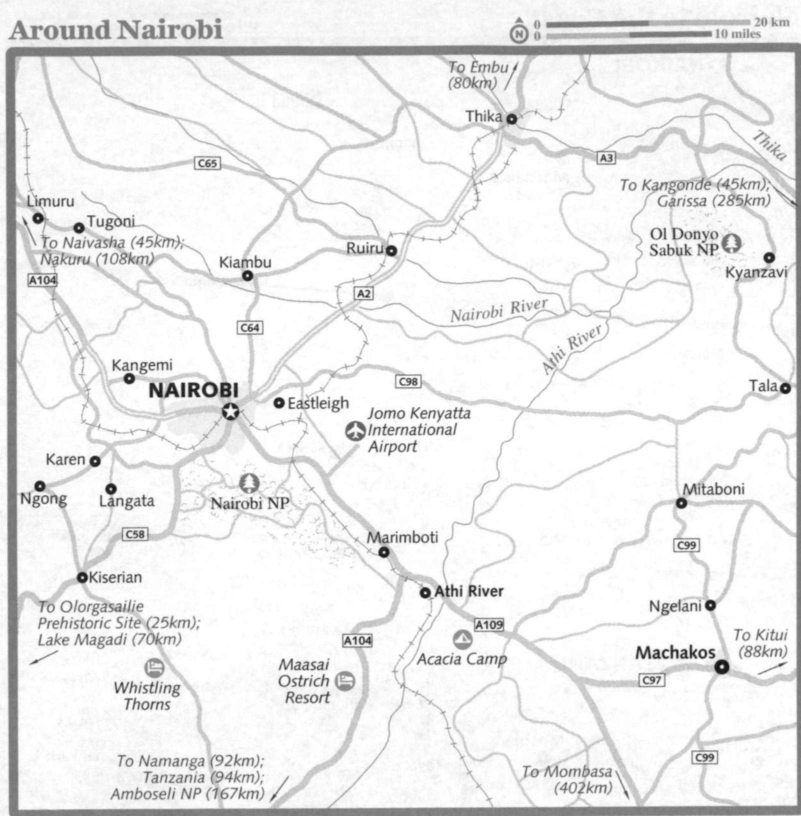

Travel Agencies

Bunson Travel (Map p224; ☎2248371; www.bunsontravel.com; Pan Africa Insurance Bldg, Standard St) A good upmarket operator selling air tickets and safaris.

Uniglobe Let's Go Travel Westlands (off Map p234; ☎4447151; ABC Pl, Waiyaki Way); Karen (Map p230; ☎3882505; Karen shopping centre, Langata Rd) This place is good for flights, safaris and pretty much anything else you might need.

Getting There & Away

Air

For information about international services to and from Nairobi, and domestic and international airlines that serve the city, see p370.

Nairobi has two airports:

Jomo Kenyatta International Airport (NBO; Map p230; ☎6611000; www.kenyaairports.co.ke) Most international flights to and from Nairobi arrive at this airport, 15km southeast of the city.

Wilson Airport (WIL; Map p230; ☎3603260; www.kenyaairports.co.ke) Six kilometres south of the city centre on Langata Rd; mostly domestic flights.

Bus

In Nairobi, most long-distance bus company offices are in the River Rd area, although some also have offices on Monrovia St for their international services. Prices vary from company to company, and there are many companies servicing these routes. You should always make your reservation up to 24 hours in advance and check (then double-check) the departure point from where the bus leaves.

The **Machakos Country Bus Station** (off Map p224; Landhies Rd) is a hectic, disorganised place with buses heading all over the country; it serves companies without their own departure point. However, if you can avoid coming here, do so as theft is rampant.

Nairobi to the Coast

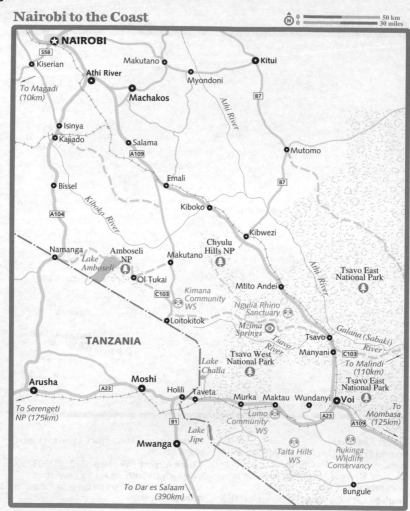

For international bus services from Nairobi, see p371.

Akamba (Map p224; ☎2365790; Lagos Rd) The biggest private bus company has an extensive network with a **booking office** (Map p224; Monrovia St) from where its international buses go to Uganda and Tanzania.

Easy Coach (Map p224; ☎2210711; Haile Selassie Ave) Another reliable company serving western Kenyan destinations as well as international buses to Uganda and Tanzania.

Modern Coast (Oxygen; Map p224; cnr Cross Lane & Accra Rd) Safer, more reliable and slightly more expensive buses to Mombasa, Malindi and Kisumu. They don't take phone bookings.

Riverside Shuttle (Map p224; ☎0722220176; Monrovia St) Mostly international services to Arusha and Moshi (Tanzania).

Matatu

Most matatus leave from the chaotic Latema, Accra, River and Cross Rds and fares are similar to the buses. Most companies are pretty much the same, although there are some that aim for higher standards than others. **Mololine Prestige Shuttle** (Map p224), which operates along the Nairobi–Naivasha–Nakuru–Eldoret route, is one such company, with others set to follow its example on other routes. Departure points are shown on the Central Nairobi map.

Train

Nairobi train station booking office (Map p224; Station Rd; ⏲9am-noon & 2-6.30pm) You need to come in person to book tickets a few days in advance of your intended departure. On the day of departure, arrive early.

For more information on train travel in Kenya, see p376.

ℹ Getting Around

To/From Jomo Kenyatta International Airport

Kenya's main **international airport** (Map p230; ☎6611000) is 15km out of town, off the road to Mombasa. We recommend that you take a taxi (KSh1200 to KSh1500, but you'll need to bargain hard) to get to/from the airport, especially after dark.

A far cheaper way to get into town is by city bus 34 (KSh30), but a lot of travellers get robbed on the bus or when they get off. Always hold onto valuables and have small change ready for the fare. Buses run from 5.45am to 9.30pm weekdays, 6.20am to 9.30pm Saturdays and 7.15am to 9.30pm Sundays, though the last few evening services may not operate. Heading to the airport, the main departure point is along Moi Ave, right outside the Hotel Ambassadeur Nairobi. Thereafter, buses travel west along Kenyatta Ave.

To/From Wilson Airport

To get to **Wilson airport** (Map p230; ☎3603260), the cheapest option is to take bus or matatu 15, 31, 34, 125 or 126 from Moi Ave (KSh25, 15 to 45 minutes depending on traffic). A taxi from the centre of town will cost you KSh750 to KSh1000, depending on the driver. In the other direction, you'll have to fight the driver down from KSh1250.

Car

See p373 for comprehensive information on car hire, road rules and conditions. Parking in the centre is by permit only (KSH140), available from the parking attendants who roam the streets in bright yellow jackets.

Matatu

Nairobi's horde of matatus follows the same routes as buses and displays the same route numbers. For Westlands, you can pick up 23 on Moi Ave or Latema Rd. Matatu 46 to the Yaya Centre stops in front of the main post office, and 125 and 126 to Langata leave from in front of the train station.

There are plans to phase out matatus and replace them with larger (and fewer) minibuses to reduce traffic congestion. No new matatu licences were being issued at the time of research, but don't expect to notice any difference in the short-term.

MAJOR MATATU ROUTES

TO	FARE (KSH)	DURATION (HR)	DEPARTURE POINT
Eldoret	700	6	Easy Coach Terminal
Kericho	650	3	Cross Rd
Kisumu	600-900	4	Cross Rd
Meru	550	3	Main Bus & Matatu Area
Naivasha	200-300	1½	cnr River Rd & Ronald Ngala St
Nakuru	400	3	cnr River Rd & Ronald Ngala St
Namanga	300-400	2	cnr River Rd & Ronald Ngala St
Nanyuki	400	3	Main Bus & Matatu Area
Narok	400	3	Cross Rd
Nyahururu	400	3½	cnr River Rd & Ronald Ngala St
Nyeri	350	2½	Latema Rd

TRAIN ROUTES

FROM	TO	1ST-CLASS FARE (KHS)	2ND-CLASS FARE (KHS)	DEPARTURE TIME	DURATION (HR)
Nairobi	Kisumu	2550	1400	6.30pm Mon, Wed & Fri	14½
Nairobi	Nakuru	1560	1560	6.30pm Mon, Wed & Fri	6½
Nairobi	Naivasha	1805	1255	6.30pm Mon, Wed & Fri	3
Nairobi	Mombasa	3660	2640	7pm Mon & Fri	15

Taxi

As people are compelled to use them due to Nairobi's endemic street crime, taxis here are overpriced and under-maintained, but you've little choice, particularly at night. You find them parked on every other street corner in the city centre – at night they're outside restaurants, bars and nightclubs.

Fares around town are negotiable. Any journey within the downtown area costs KSh400, from downtown to Milimani Rd costs KSh500, and for longer journeys such as Westlands or the Yaya Centre, fares range from KSh600 to KS700. From the city centre to Karen and Langata is around KSh1000 one way.

SOUTHERN KENYA

Southern Kenya is one of the premier safari destinations in Africa. Here you find a triumvirate of epic wildlife parks – Amboseli, Tsavo West and Tsavo East – that are home to the Big Five and much more. In short, this is Kenya at its wildest and yet most accessible.

Amboseli National Park

Amboseli (adult/child per day US$75/40) belongs in the elite of Kenya's national parks, and it's easy to see why. Its signature attraction is the sight of hundreds of big-tusked elephants set against the backdrop of Africa's best views of Mt Kilimanjaro (5895m); Africa's highest peak broods over the southern boundary of the park, and you'll be rewarded with stunning vistas when the weather clears, usually at dawn and dusk.

Sights & Activities

The Swamps LAKE

Amboseli's permanent swamps of **Enkongo Narok** and **Olokenya** create a marshy belt across the middle of the park and this is where you'll encounter the most wildlife. **Elephants** love to wallow around in the muddy waters, and you've also a good chance of seeing **hippos** around the edge, especially in Enkongo Narok. For *really* close-up elephant encounters, **Sinet Causeway**, which crosses Enkongo Narok near Observation Hill, is often good. The surrounding grasslands are home to grazing **antelope**, **zebras** and **wildebeest**, with **spotted hyenas** and **lions** sometimes lurking nearby. Birdlife is rich in these swamps; migrants arrive in November and stay until March.

Normatior (Observation Hill) LOOKOUT

Observation Hill provides an ideal lookout from which to orientate yourself to the plains, swamps and roads below. The views range south to Kilimanjaro or east across the swamps. Wildlife is generally a fair way off, but the views here put them in their context.

Sinet Delta PARK

From Observation Hill, the northern route runs across the Sinet Delta, which is an excellent place for birdwatching. Commonly sighted species include jacanas, herons, egrets, ibises, geese, plovers, storks, ducks, fish eagles and flamingos. The vegetation is thicker the further south you go, providing fodder for giraffes and also framing some of the park's best Kilimanjaro views.

Kimana Gate WILDLIFE RESERVE

If you're taking the road that runs east across the park to the Kimana gate, watch

Amboseli National Park

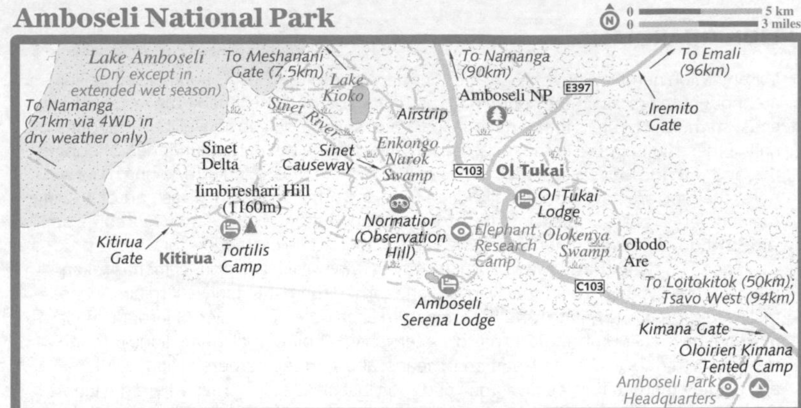

for Masai giraffes in the acacia woodlands; this is the best place inside the park for giraffe-spotting. There are numerous lodges and campsites just outside the gate, while the road (in poor condition) continues on to Tsavo West National Park.

Elephant Research Camp WILDLIFE RESERVE

(☎0710149131; www.elephanttrust.org; group of 10 or less US$500, group of more than 10 per person US$50; ⏱by prior appointment 3pm Mon-Sat) The elephants of Amboseli are among the most studied in the world, thanks largely to the work of Cynthia Moss, whose books include *The Amboseli Elephants* and *Elephant Memories;* she was also behind the famous documentary DVD *Echo of the Elephants.* The research camp remains in operation in the heart of the park, under the guidance of the **Amboseli Trust for Elephants** (www.elephanttrust.org). Although the camp is not open for casual visits, it is possible, with prior arrangement, to arrange a one-hour lecture at the camp, during which the researchers explain their work and other related issues of elephant conservation, with time for questions at the end. The visit doesn't come cheap, but this is one of the mother lodes for elephant research in Africa and a visit here is a rare opportunity to learn more about these soulful creatures.

Sleeping & Eating

Accommodation in Amboseli is either top end or budget simplicity, with not much else in between. All prices for the lodges (but not the campsites) given here are for full board.

TOP CHOICE **Ol Tukai Lodge** LODGE $$$

(☎020-4445514; www.oltukailodge.com; s/d US$308/385; P@≋) Lying at the heart of

AMBOSELI NATIONAL PARK

» **Why Go** To see big-tusked elephants, the best Mount Kilimanjaro views in Africa, lions, wildebeest and zebras, rich birdlife and elephant and lion conservation programs.

» **When to Go** Year-round. The dry season (May to October and January to March) is best for spotting wildlife, while November to March is the best time to see migratory birds.

» **Practicalities** Drive in from Nairobi or Mombasa; flying is also possible. There are three main gates; approaches to the park from the west (Kitirua and Meshanani gates) are in poor conditions. Iremito (northeast) or Kimana (southeast) gates are in better conditions. The park accessible in 2WD. Iremito is the only gate where you can top up your safaricard.

LION GUARDIANS

In Kenya, lion numbers have reached critical levels: less than 2000 adult breeding lions are thought to remain in the country. An estimated 60 of these inhabit the Amboseli ecosystem, which refers to the national park and surrounding Amboseli basin. Around half of these lions (more in the rainy season) live outside the park boundaries, sharing the land with the Maasai and their herds of livestock. In Maasai culture, young male warriors (the *morran*) have traditionally killed lions and other wild animals as part of proving their bravery and as an initiation rite into manhood. But one organisation has come up with an innovative way of honouring Maasai tradition while protecting lions in the process. The **Lion Guardians** (www.lionguardians.org, www.wildlifeguardians.com) has taken many of these young, traditional warriors and turned them into Lion Guardians, whose task is to protect the Maasai and the lions from each other. Each Lion Guardian, most of whom have killed lions before, patrols a territory, keeping track of the lions through radio transmitters and more traditional means, and warning herders of lion locations and helping them to find lost livestock and even lost children. In areas where the Lion Guardians operate, lion-killings (and livestock lost to lions) have fallen dramatically.

Visiting the Lion Guardians

Although the idea was still on the drawing board at the time of writing, there are plans to allow **guided visits** of the Lion Guardians program, which would include time spent talking with Lion Guardians and possibly even patrolling with them in search of lions. Check the website for a list of participating lodges through which the visits may be booked. The cost of visits is still being worked out, but it is likely to cost around US$250 to US$500 per person – expensive perhaps, but this is a fabulous opportunity to learn more about the Maasai and lions at the cutting edge of wildlife conservation.

Amboseli on the edge of a dense acacia forest, Ol Tukai is a splendidly refined lodge with soaring *makuti* (thatched palm-leaved roofs) and tranquil gardens defined by towering trees. Accommodation is in wooden chalets, which are brought to life with vibrant zebra prints, while the split-level bar has a sweeping view of Kili, and a pervading atmosphere of peace and luxury. This is an ideal place to unwind.

Tortilis Camp TENTED CAMP **$$$**
(☎045-622195; www.tortilis.com; s/d high season US$470/780, family tent US$1950; P wi-fi) This wonderfully conceived site is one of the most exclusive ecolodges in Kenya, commanding a superb elevated spot with perfect Kilimanjaro vistas. The luxurious canvas tents have recently been given a facelift; the family rooms have the biggest wow factor we found in southern Kenya. The lavish meals, which are based on North Italian traditional recipes from the owner's family cookbook, feature herbs and vegetables from the huge on-site organic garden.

Amboseli Serena Lodge LODGE **$$$**
(☎020-2842000; www.serenahotels.com; US$270/370; P wi-fi pool) A classically elegant property in Amboseli, the Serena is comprised of fiery-red adobe cottages, some of which overlook the wildlife-rich Enkongo Narok swamp and are fringed by lush tropical gardens of blooming flowers and manicured shrubs; there are no Kilimanjaro views from the lodge. Stay here and you won't have a care in the world; service is impeccable.

Oloirien Kimana Tented Camp CAMPGROUND **$**
(☎0720951500; per person tent/banda KSh1500/2000; P) Just outside the park boundaries, 2.8km south of the Kimana gate, this camp is bare and dusty but friendly with basic tents and simple bandas with cold showers. There's a kitchen for DIY cooking.

Information

Kenya Wildlife Service (☎045-622251; www.kws.org/parks/parks_reserves/AMNP.html; adult/child US$75/40, safaricard required)

Getting There & Away

Air

Airkenya (www.airkenya.com; one way from $101) Daily flights between Nairobi's Wilson airport and Amboseli.

Car & 4WD

Whichever route you take, allow around four hours from Nairobi.

VIA NAMANGA 180km sealed road, whereafter the 75km dirt road to the Meshanani gate is pretty rough but passable.

VIA EMALI 240km sealed road, then 18km graded but not sealed road to Irimeto gate.

Tsavo West National Park

Welcome to the wilderness. **Tsavo West** (adult/child per day US$60/30) is one of Kenya's larger national parks (9065 sq km), covering a huge variety of landscapes, from swamps, natural springs and rocky peaks to extinct volcanic cones, rolling plains and sharp outcrops dusted with greenery.

This is a park with a whiff of legend about it, first for its famous man-eating lions in the late 19th century and then for its devastating levels of poaching in the 1980s. Despite the latter, there's still plenty of wildlife here, although you'll have to work harder and be much more patient than in Amboseli or the Masai Mara to see them all. If possible, come here with some time to spare to make the most of it.

Sights & Activities

TOP CHOICE Ngulia Rhino Sanctuary WILDLIFE RESERVE

(4-6pm) At the base of Ngulia Hills and part of the Rhino Ark program, this recently expanded 90-sq-km area is surrounded by a 1m-high electric fence, and provides a measure of security for the park's last 50-odd highly endangered black rhinos. In the 1960s, Tsavo had Africa's largest population of black rhinos with between 6000 and 9000. There are driving tracks and waterholes, but the rhinos are mainly nocturnal and the chances of seeing one are slim. Thankfully these archaic creatures are breeding successfully and around 15 have been released elsewhere in Tsavo West National Park.

TOP CHOICE Rhino Valley PARK

This is one of our favourite areas for wildlife watching, with plenty of antelope species keeping a careful eye out for the resident lions, leopards and cheetah. You'll also see elephants, giraffes and, if you're lucky, black rhinos. Birdlife is also particularly diverse here. The signposted 'Rhino Valley Circuit' is a good place to start, while anywhere along the Mukui River's ponds and puddles is a place to watch and wait.

Ngulia Hills MOUNTAIN

Rising more than 600m above the valley floor and to a height over 1800m above sea level, this jagged ridgeline ranks among the prettiest of all Tsavo landforms, providing a backdrop to Rhino Valley. The peaks are a recognised flyway for migrating birds heading south from late September through to November.

TOP CHOICE Mzima Springs SPRING

Mzima Springs is an oasis of green in the west of the park and produces an incredible 250 million litres of fresh water a day. The springs, whose source rises in the Chyulu Hills, provides the bulk of Mombasa's fresh water. A walking trail leads along the shoreline. The drought in 2009 took a heavy toll on the springs' hippo population (around 20 remain); there are also crocodiles and a wide variety of birdlife. There's an underwater viewing chamber, which gives

TSAVO WEST NATIONAL PARK

» **Why Go** For the dramatic scenery, wilderness and good mix of predators (lion, leopard, cheetah and hyena), prey (lesser kudu, gazelle, impala) and other herbivores (elephant, rhino, zebra, oryx and giraffe).

» **When to Go** Year-round. The dry season (May to October and January to March) is best for spotting wildlife; November to March is the best time to see migratory birds.

» **Practicalities** Drive in from Kibwezi along the Nairobi–Mombasa Rd. There is a campsite close to the park entrance, and lodges throughout the park. The park works on the safaricard system (you can only add credit at Mtito Andei gate); gates open from sunrise to sunset.

Tsavo East & West National Parks

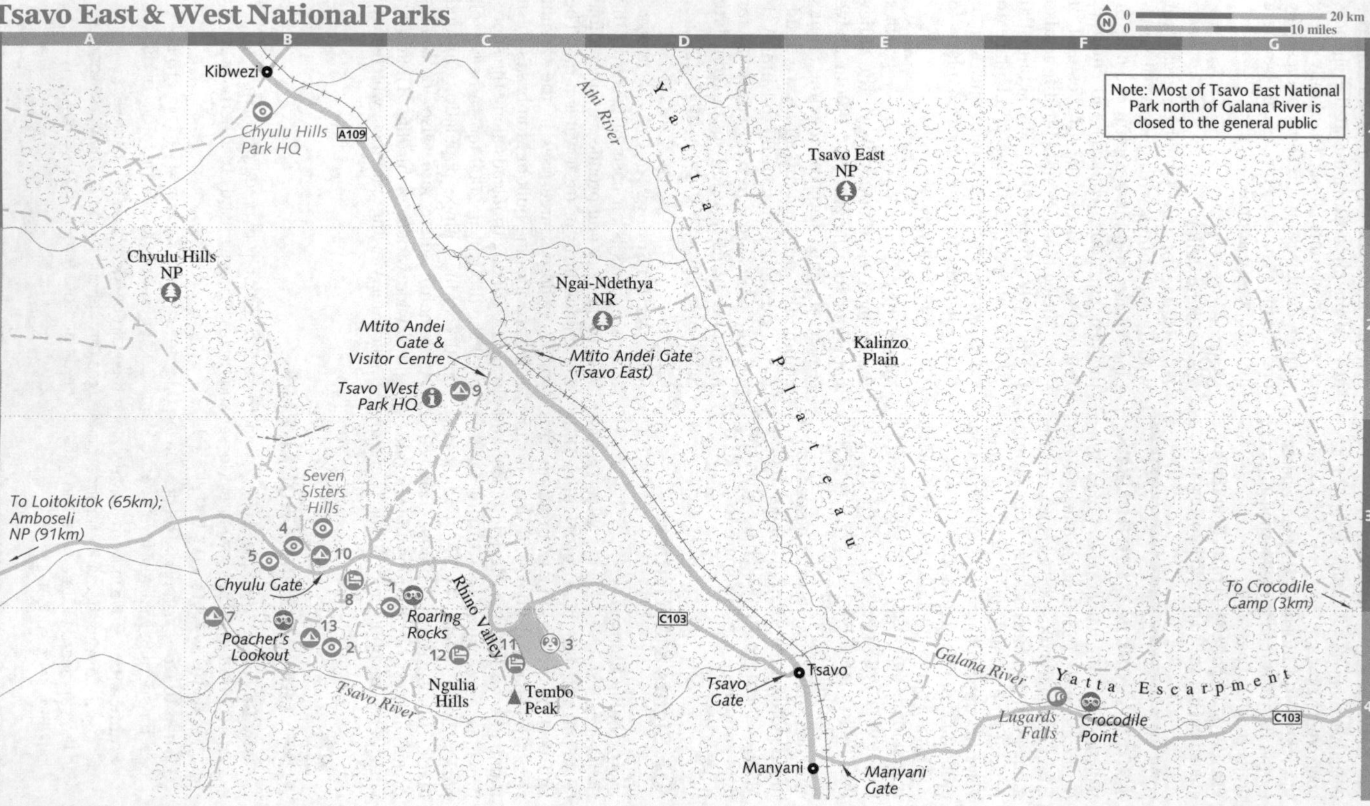

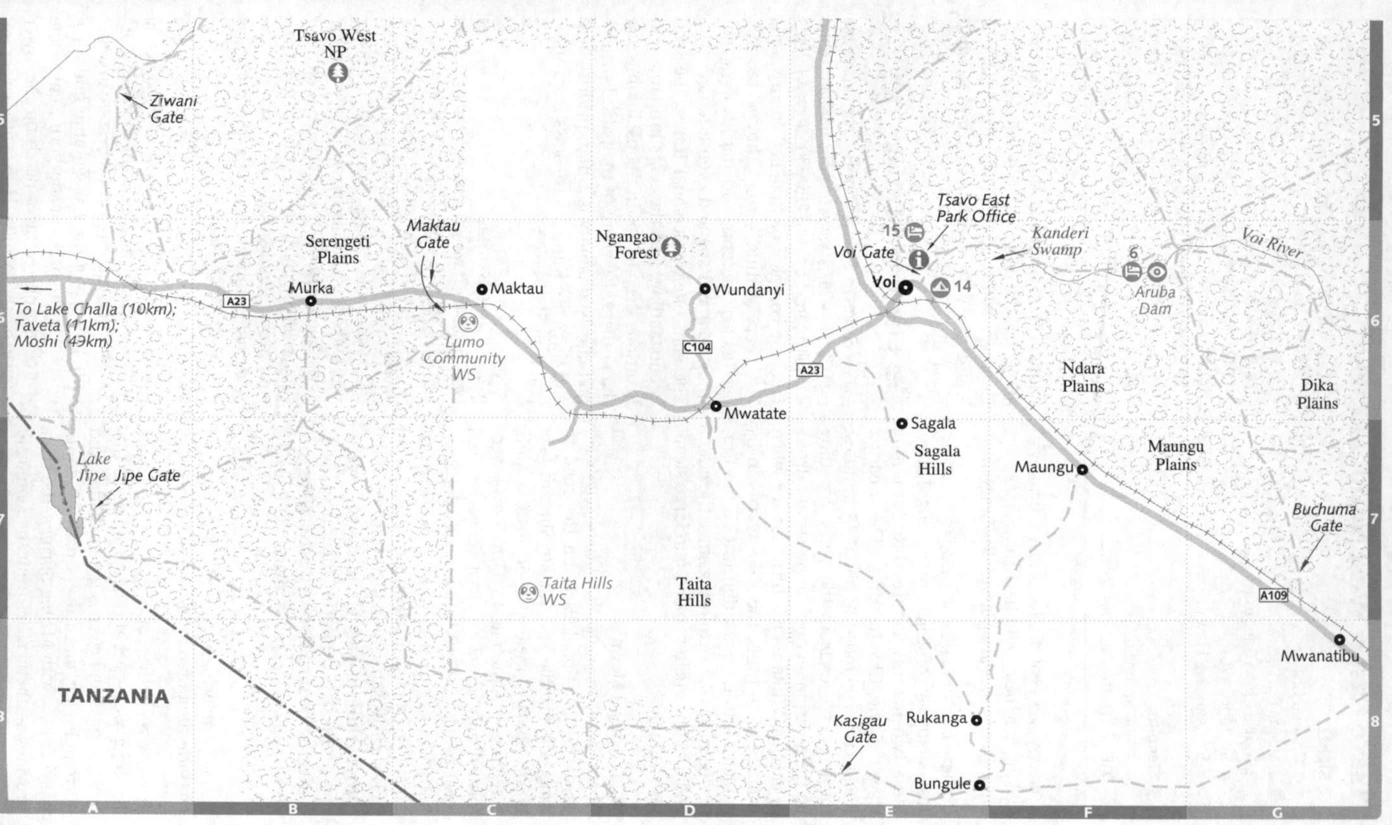
Tsavo West NP
Ziwani Gate
Serengeti Plains
Maktau Gate
Ngangao Forest
Tsavo East Park Office
15
Kanderi Swamp
Voi River
Voi Gate
6
Voi
14
Aruba Dam
Murka
Maktau
Wundanyi
A23
To Lake Challa (10km); Taveta (11km); Moshi (49km)
Lumo Community WS
C104
A23
Ndara Plains
Dika Plains
Mwatate
Sagala
Sagala Hills
Maungu
Maungu Plains
Lake Jipe
Jipe Gate
Buchuma Gate
Taita Hills WS
Taita Hills
A109
Mwanatibu
TANZANIA
Kasigau Gate
Rukanga
Bungule
A
B
C
D
E
F
G
5
6
7
8

Tsavo East & West National Parks

Sights

1 Chaimu Crater C3
2 Mzima Springs B4
3 Ngulia Rhino Sanctuary C4
4 Shetani Caves B3
5 Shetani Lava Flows B3

Sleeping

6 Ashnil Aruba Lodge F6
7 Finch Hatton's Safari Camp B4
8 Kilaguni Serena Lodge B3
Kitani Bandas .... (see 13)
9 KWS Campsite C2
10 KWS Campsite B3
11 Ngulia Safari Lodge C4
12 Rhino Valley Lodge C4
13 Severin Safari Camp B4
14 Tsavo Mashariki Camp E6
15 Voi Safari Lodge E6

a creepy view of thousands of primeval-looking fish. Be careful here though, as both hippos and crocs are potentially dangerous.

Chaimu Crater & Roaring Rocks LOOKOUT

Just southeast of Kilaguni Serena Lodge, these two natural features offer stunning views of the Chyulu Hills. The Roaring Rocks can be climbed in about 15 minutes; the name comes from the wind whistling up the escarpment and the persistent drone of cicadas. While there's little danger when walking these trails, the KWS warns in its guidebook to the park that in Chaimu Crater, 'be wary when exploring since the crater and lava may shelter snakes and large sleeping mammals'.

Shetani Lava Flows LOOKOUT

About 4km west of the Chyulu gate of Tsavo West National Park, on the road to Amboseli, are the spectacular Shetani lava flows; 'shetani' means 'devil' in Kiswahili, a reference to the fact that the flows were formed only a few hundred years ago and local peoples believed that it was the devil himself emerging from the earth. This vast expanse of folded black lava spreads for 50 sq km across the savannah at the foot of the Chyulu Hills, looking strangely as if Vesuvius dropped its comfort blanket here.

Nearby are the **Shetani Caves**, which are also a result of volcanic activity. You'll need a torch (flashlight) if you want to explore, but watch your footing on the razor-sharp rocks, and keep an eye out for the local fauna – hyenas are rumoured to inhabit the caves.

Tsavo River & the South RIVER

Running west–east through the park, this lovely year-round river is green-shaded and surrounded for much of its path by doum palms. Along with Mzima Springs, the river provides aesthetic relief from the semi-arid habitats that dominate the park. The trees all along the river are known to shelter leopards. South of the river, the foliage is less dense with cheetah sightings a small possibility.

Sleeping & Eating

TOP CHOICE **Severin Safari Camp** TENTED CAMP $$$

(☎020-2684247; www.severinsafaricamp.com; s/d full board from US$215/330; P wi-fi pool) This fantastic complex of thatched luxury tents just keeps getting better. They've recently overhauled the tents, added a luxury swimming pool and spa and even a tented gym. The staff offer a personal touch, the food is outstanding, and the tents are large and luxurious despite costing considerably less than others elsewhere in the park. Environmental sustainability is a high priority here and there are Kilimanjaro views from some points on the property.

TOP CHOICE **Kitani Bandas** BANDA $$

(☎020-2684247; www.severinsafaricamp.com; s/d bandas US$55/110, meals US$10-15; P wi-fi pool) Run by the same people as the top-end luxury Severin Safari Camp, Kitani is located next to a waterhole, about 2km past its sister site, and offers the cheapest Kili views in the park. These *bandas* (which have their own simple kitchens), have far more style than your average budget camp and you can use Severin's facilities (including the pool and free wi-fi). Great value.

Rhino Valley Lodge BANDA $$

(Ngulia Bandas; ☎0721328567; www.tsavocampsandlodges.com; s/d bandas from US$80/130; P) This hillside camp is Tsavo's best luxury bargain and one of the few genuine midrange choices in the parks of southern Kenya. The thatched stone cottages perch on the lower slopes of the Ngulia Hills with sweeping

POACHING IN TSAVO

As poaching reached epidemic proportions in Kenya in the 1980s, Tsavo was very much on the frontline. In a few short years, the elephant population dropped from 45,000 to just 5000, and rhinos were almost wiped out entirely; at the height of the crisis, an estimated 5000 elephants were being killed every year. Populations are slowly recovering, and there are close to 12,500 elephants in the two parks, but less than 100 rhinos, down from about 9000 in 1969. If you're used to the human-habituated elephants of Amboseli, who'll scarcely move when approached in a vehicle, Tsavo's elephants may come as a surprise – they're skittish, and prone to sudden retreats.

views of Rhino Valley. The decor is designer rustic with plenty of space and private terraces. The setting and standards outdo plenty of the more ambitious lodges. It's still signposted throughout the park under its old name, Ngulia Bandas.

Ngulia Safari Lodge LODGE **$$$**
(☎043-30000; www.safari-hotels.com; s/d US$140/200; P) Tsavo vantage points don't come any better than this – the surrounding Ngulia Hills attract loads of birds, there's a waterhole right by the restaurant (which attracts buffalo, elephants and hyena at night) and a leopard is fed right next to the restaurant every evening. Out the back there are sweeping views down off the escarpment. It's all enough to make you forget that the building itself is a monstrosity and the rooms (especially the bathrooms) are tired and in need of an overhaul.

Kilaguni Serena Lodge LODGE **$$$**
(☎045-622376; www.serenahotels.com; s/d US$225/320; P) As you'd expect from the upmarket Serena chain, this lodge is extremely comfortable, with semi-luxurious rooms, many of which have been recently renovated. The centrepiece here is a splendid bar and restaurant overlooking a busy illuminated waterhole; the best watering-hole views are in rooms 14 to 39.

KWS campsites CAMPGROUND **$**
(camping US$15; P) The public sites are at Komboyo, near the Mtito Andei gate, and at Chyulu, just outside the Chyulu gate. Facilities are basic, so be prepared to be self-sufficient.

Finch Hatton's Safari Camp TENTED CAMP **$$$**
(☎020-3518349; www.finchhattons.com; s/d US$360/560; P) This upmarket tented camp, which is distinguished by its signature bone china and gold shower taps (guests are requested to dress for dinner), was named after Denys Finch Hatton, the playboy hunter and lover of Karen Blixen, who died at Tsavo. The camp is situated among springs and hippo pools in the west of the park, in grounds so sprawling you have to take an escort at night to keep you safe from the animals.

Information

Kenya Wildlife Service (☎043-30049; www.kws.org/parks/parks_reserves/TWNP.html; adult/child US$60/30, safaricard required)

ENTRY Six gates, but safaricard can only be topped up at Mtito Andei gate

FUEL Generally available at Kilaguni Serena Lodge and Severin Safari Camp; fill up before entering park

MAPS *Tsavo West National Park* map and guidebook available from Mtito Andei gate

Getting There & Away

The main access to Tsavo West is through the Mtito Andei gate on the Mombasa–Nairobi road in the north of the park. Although security is much improved, vehicles for Amboseli travel in armed convoys from Kilaguni Serena Lodge; check at the lodge for departure times.

Tsavo East National Park

☎043

Kenya's largest national park has an undeniable wild and primordial charm and is a terrific wildlife-watching destination. Although the permanent greenery of the river and the endless grasses and thorn trees that characterise much of the park are visually arresting, the landscape here lacks the drama of Tsavo West. Tsavo East is markedly flatter and drier than its sister park. The flipside is that spotting wildlife is generally easier thanks to the thinly spread foliage.

Sights & Activities

TOP CHOICE Kanderi Swamp & Voi River RIVER

Around 10km from Voi gate, the lovely area of green known as Kanderi Swamp is home to a resident pride of lions, and elephants also congregate near here; this is one of only two water sources in the park during the dry season. The landscape here has a lovely backdrop of distant hills. A number of vehicle tracks also follow the contours of the Voi River; keep an eye on the overhanging branches for leopards.

TOP CHOICE Aruba Dam & the Southeast LAKE

Some 30km east of Voi gate is the Aruba Dam, which spans the Voi River. It attracts heavy concentrations of diverse wildlife; the park's other regularly spotted lion pride ranges around here. Away to the east and southeast, all the way down to the Buchuma gate, the open grasslands provide the perfect habitat for cheetahs and sightings are more common here than anywhere else in southeastern Kenya.

TOP CHOICE Galana River & Around RIVER

Running through the heart of the park and marking the northernmost point in the park that most visitors are allowed to visit, the **Galana River** cuts a green gash across the dusty plains. Surprisingly few visitors make it this far, and sightings of crocs, hippos, lesser kudus, waterbucks, dik-diks and, to a lesser extent, lions and leopards, are relatively common. Watch out also for the distinctive Somali ostrich. There are several places along the flat-topped escarpments lining the river where you can get out of your vehicle (with due caution, of course). Most scenic are **Lugards Falls**, a wonderful landscape of water-sculpted channels, and **Crocodile Point**.

The area north of the Galana River is dominated by the **Yatta Escarpment**, a vast prehistoric lava flow which is estimated by some to be the longest lava flow in the world at 300km. However, much of this area is off limits to travellers because of the ongoing campaign against poachers.

ONE OF THE WORLD'S RAREST ANTELOPES

Until their partial translocation to Tsavo East, the sole surviving population of **hirola antelope** was found near the Kenya–Somalia border in the south Tana River and Garissa districts. Intense poaching (for meat) and habitat destruction have reduced their numbers from an estimated 14,000 in 1976 to 450 today. At the time of writing, there were approximately 100 left within the park confines, mostly in the little visited southern reaches of the park.

Sleeping & Eating

INSIDE THE PARK

Voi Safari Lodge LODGE $$$

(Mombasa 041-471861; www.safari-hotels.com; s/d high season US$140/200; P) Just 4km from Voi gate, this is a long, low complex perched on the edge of an escarpment overlooking an incredible sweep of savannah. There's an attractive rock-cut swimming pool, as well as a natural waterhole that draws elephants, buffaloes and the occasional predator; a photographers' hide sits at the level of the waterhole. Rooms are attractive and many have superlative views.

Ashnil Aruba Lodge LODGE $$$

(020-4971008; www.ashnilhotels.com; s/d US$175/215; P@) A stone's throw from the wildlife-rich Aruba Dam, this lodge has attractively decorated rooms decked out in safari prints. In the heart of the park, it's an ideal starting point for most Tsavo East safaris. Wildlife wanders around the property's perimeter at regular intervals.

OUTSIDE THE PARK

TOP CHOICE Tsavo Mashariki Camp TENTED CAMP $$

(2031444; www.masharikicamp.com; per person bed & breakfast from KSh4500, full board from KSh7000; P) The closest camp to Voi gate just outside the park, this charming Italian-run place has some fine tents made out of all-natural local materials; the family tent is brilliant. Best of all, the prices here put many other tented camps to shame. Highly recommended.

Information

Kenya Wildlife Service (043-30049; www.kws.org/parks/parks_reserves/TENP.html; paradult/child nonresident US$60/30, smartcard required)

FUEL Available in Voi; fill up before the park.

MAPS *Tsavo East National Park* map and guidebook available from Voi gate.

TSAVO EAST NATIONAL PARK

» **Why Go** To see wilderness, red elephants; and maybe leopards, lions and cheetahs. The park also has close to 500 bird species.

» **When to Go** June to February. Wildlife concentrations are highest in the dry season (September to October and January to early March).

» **Practicalities** Drive in from Voi, Mandanyi or Tsavo gates along the Nairobi–Mombasa Rd. The Sala and Buchuma gates are good for Mombasa. There is a small number of lodges and camps throughout the park or close to Voi gate. The park works on the safaricard system (you can only add credit at Voi gate); gates open from sunrise to sunset.

Getting There & Away

TO/FROM NAIROBI OR TSAVO WEST Voi, Tsavo and Manyani gates.

TO/FROM MOMBASA Sala or Buchuma gates.

Voi

043

Voi is a key service town at the intersection of the Nairobi–Mombasa road, the road to Moshi in Tanzania and the access road to the main Voi gate of Tsavo East National Park. While there is little reason to spend any more time here than is needed to get directions, fill up on petrol, change money and buy some snacks for the road, you'll inevitably pass through here at some point.

Frequent buses and matatus run to/from Mombasa (KSh500, three hours), and buses to Nairobi (KSh800 to KSh 1000, six hours). There are at least daily matatus to Wundanyi (KSh250, one hour) and Taveta (KSh450, two hours), on the Tanzanian border.

THE RIFT VALLEY

Africa's Great Rift Valley is one of the continent's grand epics. Here in Kenya, the battle of geological forces that almost rent Africa in two has left the Rift Valley looking as if it were created by giants: the ribbon of steaming and bubbling soda lakes (inscribed on Unesco's World Heritage list in 2011) scars the valley like the footprints of a massive hippopotamus, and numerous dried-out volcanic cones stand to attention like amplified termite mounds.

The Rift Valley's dramatic landscapes are lent personality by some of central Kenya's most charismatic wildlife. Here, the massed colonies of flamingos turn the earth to pink, endangered rhinos snuffle by the lakeshore and Rothschild's giraffes stride gracefully across lacustrine plains. Lions laze under trees, and leopards lurk in the undergrowth.

The combination of stunning natural forms and soulful wildlife gives the Rift Valley its charm; it's all that's good about Kenya in microcosm.

Longonot National Park

One of the shapeliest peaks in all the Rift Valley, Mt Longonot (2776m) and its serrated crater rim offer fabulous views. The dormant volcano rises 1000m above the baking hot valley floor and was formed 400,000 years ago; it last erupted in the 1860s. The park itself covers only 52 sq km, and was set up to protect the volcano's ecosystem and little else.

Sights & Activities

Climbing Mount Longonot HIKING
(adult/child US$20/10; guide to crater rim/summit & back KSh1500/2500) The one to 1½-hour hike from the park gate up to the crater rim (2545m) is strenuous but, without question, worth the effort. There are two steep stretches that will challenge those not used to hiking. Your reward is to emerge at the lip of the crater rim for superb views of the 2km- to 3km-wide crater, a little lost world hosting an entirely different forest ecosystem. It takes between 1½ and 2½ hours to circumnavigate the crater; watch for occasional steam vents rising from the crater floor. Including time for pausing to take in the views, this 21km trek from the park gate and back should take about five to six hours.

Information

Kenya Wildlife Service (050-50407; www.kws.org/parks/parks_reserves/MLNP.html; park admission adult/child US$20/10, safaricard not valid)

Getting There & Away

Mt Longonot is 75km northwest of Nairobi on the Old Naivasha Rd. If you're without a vehicle, take a matatu from Naivasha to Longonot village, from where there's a path (ask locals) to the park's access road.

Lake Naivasha

050

The freshwater Lake Naivasha is the highest of the Rift Valley lakes (1884m above sea level) and is for many travellers the first port

Rift Valley

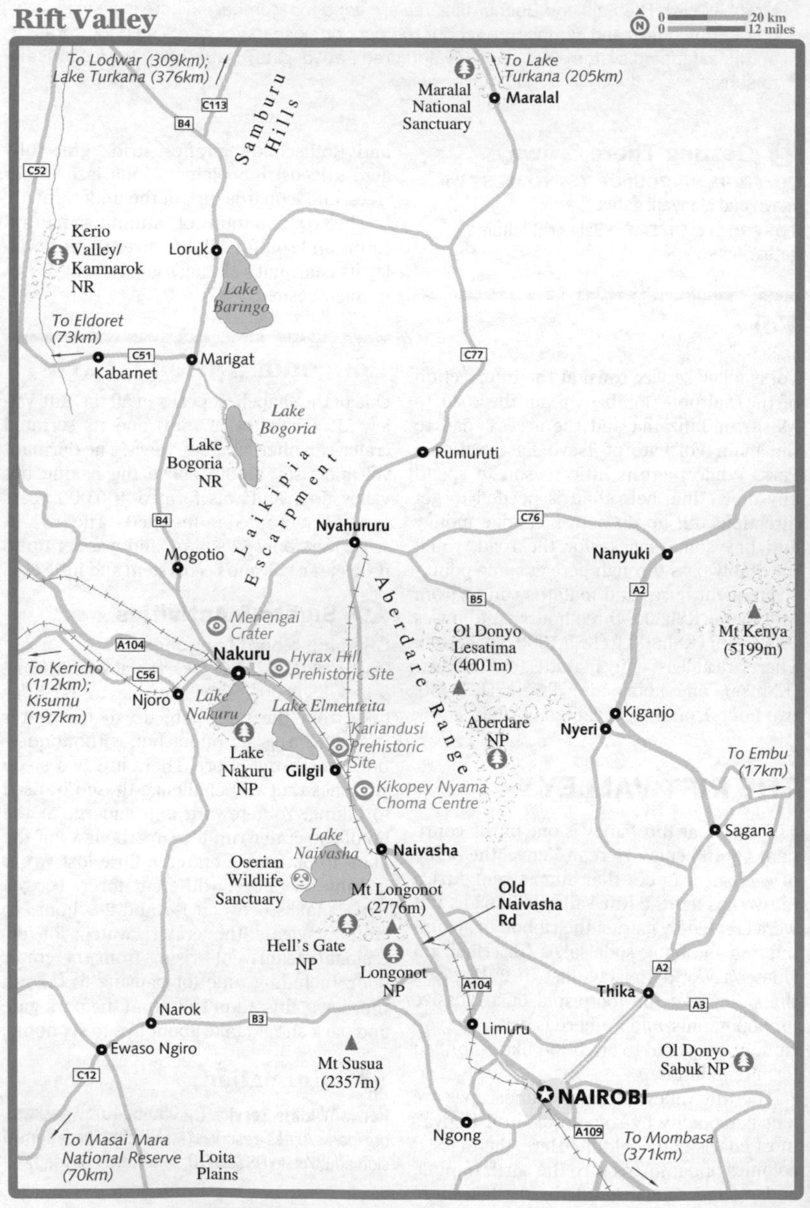

of call after Nairobi. With its shores fringed in papyrus and yellow-barked acacias, bulbous snorting hippos playing in the shallows, a cacophony of twittering birds and a gentle climate, there's no denying its appeal over the urban mayhem of Nairobi. If you're staying here, wander down to the water's edge early in the morning when a barely perceptible layer of fine mist hangs above the water's surface – this is when you'll most appreciate being here.

Lake Naivasha has one of the largest settler and expat communities in Kenya, and half of Nairobi seems to decamp here at weekends. It can have a resort-feel to it in high season, when it essentially becomes Kenya's earthier version of St Tropez, with Tusker beer rather than champagne.

Sights & Activities

TOP CHOICE Elsamere Conservation Centre WILDLIFE RESERVE
(2021055; www.elsamere.com; admission KSh800; 8am-6.30pm) This conservation centre is the former home of the late Joy Adamson of *Born Free* fame. Now a conservation centre focused on lake ecology and environmental awareness programs, the site is open to the public. Entry includes afternoon tea on the hippo-manicured lawns (with a chance to see eastern black-and-white colobus monkeys and over 200 bird species), a visit to the small museum dedicated to the Adamsons, and a showing of the weathered 40-minute *Joy Adamson Story*.

Boat Safaris BOAT TOUR
(per boat per hr KSh3000-6000) Most of the camps and lodges along Lake Naivasha's southern shore rent out boats; most boats have seven seats and come with pilot and lifejackets. Places where nonguests can organise a boat rental include Marina's Camp, Fisherman's Camp and the Elsamere Conservation Centre.

TOP CHOICE Crater Lake Game Sanctuary WILDLIFE RESERVE
(admission per person US$15, plus car KSh200) Surrounding a beautiful volcanic crater lake fringed with acacias, this small sanctuary has many trails, including one for hikers along the steep but diminutive crater rim. Besides the impressive 150 bird species recorded here, giraffes, zebras and other plains wildlife are also regular residents on the more open plains surrounding the crater; when we last visited, a lone hippo had taken up residence.

TOP CHOICE Lake Oloiden LAKE
(boat safaris per 30/60min KSh2000/4000) Lake Naivasha may be a freshwater lake, but the alkaline waters of its near neighbour Lake Oloiden draw small but impressive flocks of flamingos. Boat safaris are available here.

Crescent Island Wildlife Sanctuary WILDLIFE RESERVE
(adult/child US$25/12.50, plus car KSh200, horse-riding per hr KSh2000; sunrise to sunset) The curious form left by the protruding rim of a collapsed volcanic crater forms this island on the eastern side of Lake Naivasha. It's a private sanctuary, where you can walk beneath acacias in search of giraffes, zebra, wildebeest, Thomson's and Grant's gazelles, elands, waterbucks and countless bird species. Oh, and there are some rather gigantic pythons too!

Sleeping & Eating

Lake Naivasha has the Rift Valley's best range of accommodation.

MOI SOUTH LAKE ROAD

TOP CHOICE Dea's Gardens GUESTHOUSE $$
(2021015; www.deasgardens.com; per person half board €60; P) A place with an unusually personal feel along the southern lake shore, this charming guesthouse is run by the elegant Dea. The main house (with two rooms) is a gorgeous chalet of Swiss inspiration, while the two cottages in the lush grounds are large and comfortable. Meals are served in the main house with Dea as your host. Warmly recommended.

TOP CHOICE Marina's Camp TENTED CAMP $$
(0722728054; cottages per person KSh3500, full board KSh4000) The cottages here are nothing to write home about, but the semi-luxurious tents that were almost completed when we visited promise to be among the best places to stay around Lake Naivasha. Prices weren't yet available at the time of writing.

Connelley's Camp CAMPGROUND, BANDA $
(50004; camping KSh600, dm/tw KSh800/2500, old bandas from KSh6000, new bandas KSh6000-10,000) Camping here is excellent value, and even at weekends it remains slightly more tranquil than some of its neighbours. The

Lake Naivasha

Lake Naivasha

Sights

1 Crater Lake Game Sanctuary....A3
2 Crescent Island Wildlife Sanctuary....C3
3 Elsamere Conservation Centre....B4

Sleeping

4 Connelley's Camp....B4
5 Crayfish Camp....C4
6 Dea's Gardens....D3
Elsamere Conservation Centre.. (see 3)
7 Fisherman's Camp....B4
8 Lake Naivasha Sopa Resort....D3
9 Marina's Camp....D3
10 Olerai House....A2

accommodation varies, from old *bandas* (huts) that inhabit former shipping crates and basic twins to rather lovely new *bandas* closer to the water.

Lake Naivasha Sopa Resort LODGE $$$
(☎50358; www.sopalodges.com; s/d US$248/347; P 📶 🏊) This expansive, verdant property, with roaming gazelle and other wildlife, sweeps down to the lake's edge. The rooms have a slightly dated style but they're large and semi-luxurious. All look out onto the lawns where hippos range at night; an escort is required in the evening.

Fisherman's Camp CAMPGROUND, BANDA $
(☎50462, 0726870590; fishermanscamp@gmail.com; camping KSh400, tents from KSh500, bandas Sun-Thu per person KSh1300, Fri & Sat per banda KSh4000, 6-person cottage KSh8000) Spread along the grassy tree-laden southern shore, Fisherman's is a perennial favourite of campers, overland companies and backpackers. The site is huge, and weekends get busy, with a noisy party atmosphere; keep an eye on your belongings. Hippos lurk by the lakeshore (they're kept out by an electric fence). Nonguests are charged KSh100 admission.

Crayfish Camp CAMPGROUND $
(☎2020239; camping KSh500, r per person with shared bathroom KSh1700, s/d KSh4000/6000; @) Following Fisherman's lead, the Crayfish Camp can seem more like a beer garden than a campsite, but it's not a bad option. The rooms are simple but adequate (full- and half-board rates are available), but the real novelty is sleeping on a mattress crammed into a converted combivan, car or boat! Meals are available from KSh700.

MOI NORTH LAKE ROAD

TOP CHOICE **Olerai House** GUESTHOUSE $$$
(☎Nairobi 020-8048602; www.olerai.com; s/d full board US$390/600) Hidden under a blanket of tropical flowers, this beautiful house is like something from a fairy tale, where petals dust the beds and floors, zebras and vervet monkeys hang out with pet dogs, and your every whim is attended to. Perhaps best of all, the camp is owned by renowned elephant conservationists Iain and Oria Douglas-Hamilton – if they're at home, there are few more fascinating hosts in Kenya.

Getting There & Away

Frequent matatus (KSh100, one hour) run along Moi South Lake Rd between Naivasha town and Kongoni on the lake's western side, passing the turn-offs to Hell's Gate National Park and Fisherman's Camp (KSh70).

Getting Around

Most lodges and camps hire mountain bikes if you're heading for Hell's Gate National Park; costs start from KSh700 ... bikes carefully before pay...

Hell's Gate Natio...

Looking at animals from ... your car is all well and goo... honest – after a while wh... the urge to get out of the vel... and re-enter the food chain? This unique park actively encourages you to walk or, better still, cycle, through an African savannah-scape teeming with large animals. You'll find that your senses become heightened tenfold when a buffalo starts looking annoyed with you and wow, giraffes really are tall aren't they? It's largely a predator-free zone – a few leopards and hyenas roam the park but they're rarely seen.

Sights

Hell's Gate Gorge PARK
The gorge that runs through the heart of the park is a wide, deep valley hemmed in by sheer, rusty-hued rock walls. Marking its eastern entrance is **Fischer's Tower**, a 25m-high volcanic column named after Gustav Fischer, a German explorer who reached the gorge in 1882. Commissioned by the Hamburg Geographical Society to find a route from Mombasa to Lake Victoria, Fischer was stopped by territorial Maasai, who slaughtered almost his entire party. Even if you visit nowhere else in the park, this main valley is worth the entry fee (adult/child US$25/15).

Hell's Gate National Park

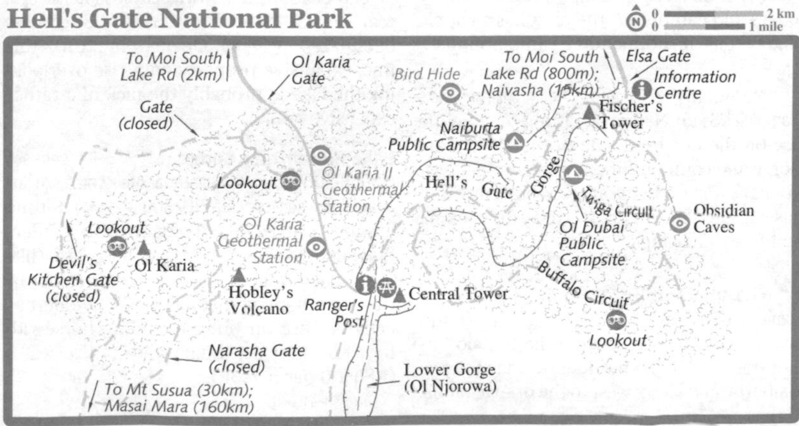

CANYON

...guide per hr KSh500) Rising from ...n gorge's southern end is the large ...ntral Tower, an unusual volcanic plug. A picnic site and ranger's post are close by, from where an excellent walk descends into the Lower Gorge (Ol Njorowa). This narrow sandstone ravine has been sculpted by water, and the incoming light casts marvellous shadows. In some places the riverbed is broad and dry, in others you'll find yourself wading through a shallow stream and scrambling down a steep and slippery descent. We recommend taking a guide.

Activities

If you intend to **walk** through the park, allow a full day and take plenty of supplies.

Cycling is our favourite way to explore the park, and the main Hell's Gate Gorge is relatively flat; it's around 7km from Elsa gate to the Lower Gorge. Mountain bikes can be rented at Elsa gate (per day KSh500), but test them out rigorously before handing over the money – dodgy brakes and gears are common problems.

The sheer rock walls of Hell's Gate are just made for **climbing** and, thankfully, the park has two resident climbers, **Simon Kiane and James Maina** (0720909718, 0727039388), who act as instructors and guides; they also have some basic equipment. They offer relatively easy 10 to 15-minute climbs of Fischer's Tower (US$10) and more challenging routes on the gorge's sheer red walls (US$100).

Sleeping

Most visitors sleep at Lake Naivasha's many lodges and camps, but the park has a couple of gorgeous, if rudimentary, campgrounds.

Naiburta CAMPGROUND $

(camping US$15) Naiburta, sitting on a gentle rise on the northern side of the Hell's Gate Gorge and commanding fine views west past Fischer's Tower, is the most scenic site, and has basic toilets, an open banda for cooking and freshwater taps.

Ol Dubai Public Campsite CAMPGROUND $

(camping US$15) Resting on the gorge's southern side and accessible from the Buffalo Circuit track, Ol Dubai has identical facilities to Naiburta, and views west to the orange bluffs.

Information

Kenya Wildlife Service (www.kws.org/parks/parks_reserves/HGNP.html; park admission adult/child US$25/15, safaricard not valid)

Information Centre (050-2020284; Elsa gate)

Getting There & Around

The usual access point to the park is through the main Elsa gate, 1km from Moi South Lake Rd. With the two gates on the northwest corner of the park closed, the only other gate is Ol Karia.

Lake Elmenteita

A major tourist attraction with passing water birds, though strangely less popular with passing humans.

Sights & Activities

Lake Elmenteita LAKE

(adult/child KSh500/200, car KSh200, guide KSh300) The lake itself has a beautiful soda shoreline that is often fringed in rainbow shades, thanks to hundreds of brilliant flamingos (when the water level's low), breeding pelicans and more than 400 other bird species.

Go Ballooning Kenya BALLOONING

(0715555777; www.goballooningkenya.com; per person 1hr US$420) Loved by children and adults alike, these hot-air balloon safaris promise the best possible Rift Valley views.

Sleeping

Elementaita Country Lodge LODGE $$$

(020-2220572; www.seasonshotelskenya.com; s/d full board from US$131/213, cottages US$191/294; P) Opened in 2010, this fine, expansive property on a rise overlooking the lake is probably the pick of a rather expensive bunch.

Lake Elmenteita Lodge LODGE $$$

(050-50648; www.jacarandahotels.com; s/d full board high season US$210/300; P) Sitting around a maze-like bougainvillea garden, the slightly dated cottages here are (like most such places) overpriced but nevertheless full on a regular basis. Numerous activities are on offer, including horse riding (KSh1800 per hour) and nature walks (KSh500 per person).

Nakuru

051 / POP 300,000

Despite being Kenya's fourth-largest city and despite its busy markets that crowd the downtown streets, Nakuru still feels like an overgrown country town. Its relaxed atmosphere, and proximity to the outstanding Lake Nakuru National Park make it a good base for a few days.

Sleeping

Merica Hotel HOTEL $$
(2216013; www.mericagrouphotels.com; Kenyatta Ave; s/d US$80/125;) This contemporary tower hosts Nakuru's best rooms. Ride the glass elevators up the sunlit atrium to well-appointed rooms large enough to host a wildebeest migration. The bathrooms could do with a little freshening up.

New Mount Sinai Hotel HOTEL $
(Bazaar Rd; s/tw with shared bathroom KSh500/600) Foreigners are considered 'special' and therefore get the posh and clean rooms right up on the roof (5th floor, no lift). The rooms are basic and stripped of anything that's not completely necessary (eg you'll have to be a porcelain jockey – the toilets lack seats), but most rooms have mosquito nets.

Carnation Hotel HOTEL $
(2215360; Mosque Rd; s/tw KSh1000/1550) Carnation Hotel is the town's prettiest budget rose. Rooms are simple but with their multicoloured tiled floors and kitsch bed sheets they have plenty of character, as well as hot showers.

Eating

TOP CHOICE **Ribbons Restaurant** KENYAN $
(Gusii Rd; mains KSh80-250; 24hr) One of the best restaurants for cheap Kenyan dishes, this 1st-floor restaurant has a balcony overlooking the street. In addition to whole tilapia with ugali, other local specialties include *githeri* (maize and beans) and *ndengu* (pea stew). Take the staircase signed as Care Guest House to get here.

TOP CHOICE **Hygienic Butchery** KENYAN $
(Tom Mboya Rd; mains KSh180-250; lunch & dinner) Great name, great place. The Kenyan tradition of *nyama choma* (barbecued meats) is alive and well here. Sidle up to the counter, try a piece of tender mutton or beef and order half a kilo (per person) of whichever takes your fancy, along with chapattis or ugali (no sauce!). The meat will then be brought to your table, carved up, and you dig in with your hands. Bliss!

Café Guava INTERNATIONAL $
(cnr Moi & Watali Rds; mains KSh350-500; breakfast, lunch & dinner Sun-Fri) This brilliant place serves great coffee and fruit juices, as well as snacks, breakfasts, cakes and a daily lunch choice; when we were there they were offering honey-and-chilli rump steaks. With free wi-fi, it's easily the most sophisticated place in town.

Information

Changing cash in Nakuru is easy, with numerous banks and foreign exchange bureaus. Barclays Bank's ATMs are the most reliable.

Aga Khan University Hospital (Nakuru Medical Centre; Kenyatta Ave) Various lab services including malaria tests.

Crater Travel (2215019; cratertravel@yahoo.com; off Kenyatta Ave) Good for air tickets and excursions into Lake Nakuru National Park.

Petmary Cyber Café (Kenyatta Ave; per hr KSh60; 8am-5.30pm Mon-Fri, to 1pm Sat) Nakuru's fastest connections.

Getting There & Away

PARKING Street parking in central Nakuru requires a ticket from the nearest warden; ask at your hotel for help.

SHUTTLE A cut above your average matatus, **Mololine Prestige Shuttle** (off Geoffrey

DON'T MISS

KIKOPEY NYAMA CHOMA CENTRE

This agglomeration of roadside barbecued-meat stalls 31km north of Naivasha is famous throughout Kenya. These places don't survive long if their meat isn't perfectly cooked. The restaurants closest to the road hassle new arrivals to try to draw you in. We tried **Acacia Restaurant**, a little back from the main road on a side road, and found it outstanding, but they're all good. You'll pay around KSh400 per kilo of meat.

Nakuru

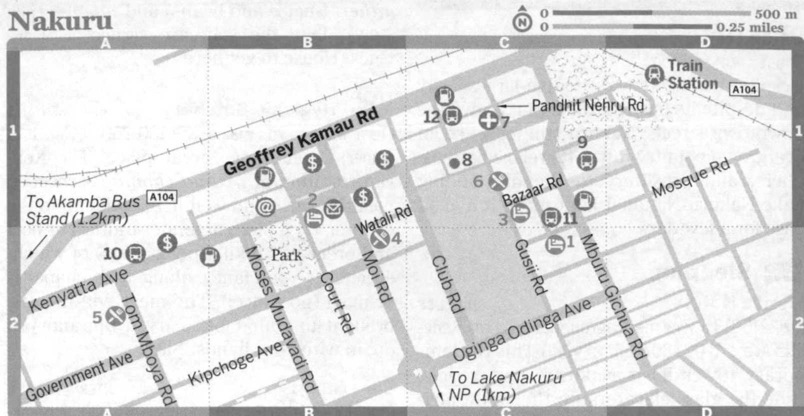

Nakuru

Sleeping

1	Carnation Hotel	C2
2	Merica Hotel	B1
3	New Mount Sinai Hotel	C1

Eating

4	Café Guava	B2
5	Hygienic Butchery	A2
6	Ribbons Restaurant	C1

Information

7	Aga Khan University Hospital (Nakuru Medical Centre)	C1
8	Crater Travel	C1

Transport

9	Bus & Matatu Station	C1
10	Easy Coach	A2
11	Matatus to Kampi ya Samaki & Marigat	C1
12	Mololine Prestige Shuttle	C1

Kamau Rd) has services to Nairobi (KSh400), Eldoret (KSh400) and Kisumu (KSh600).

MATATUS Most other matatus leave from the chaotic stands along Mburu Gichua Rd. Services include Naivasha (KSh150 to KSh200, 1¼ hours), Nyahururu (KSh175, 1¼ hours), Kericho (KSh350, two hours), Nyeri (KSh350, 2½ hours), Eldoret (KSh300, 2¾ hours), Nairobi (KSh400, three hours) and Kisumu (KSh500 to KSh600, 3½ hours).

LAKES BOGORIA & BARINGO Matatus for Lake Baringo (Kampi Ya Samaki, KSh250, 2½ hours) or Marigat (for Lake Bogoria, KSh150, two hours) leave from the southern end of Pandhit Nehru Rd.

BUS **Easy Coach** (Kenyatta Ave) is one of several bus companies offering services to Nairobi (KSh500, three hours), Eldoret (KSh650, 2¾ hours) and Kisumu (KSh750, 3½ hours).

Lake Nakuru National Park

Just a few kilometres from the hustle of central Nakuru, this is one of Kenya's finest national parks. Although the massive flamingo flocks that made the lake famous aren't always present, there are lions, leopards, endangered Rothschild's giraffes, buffaloes and zebra. Perhaps best of all, this is one of the premier places in Kenya to see black and white rhinos. The landscape is fringed with euphorbia trees, acacia forests, an escarpment or two and at least one lovely waterfall.

Sights

Lake Circuit PARK

The park's relatively small size (188 sq km) makes it easy to get around in a day. The forests anywhere in the park are good for **leopards**. If you're very, very lucky, you'll catch a glimpse of a rare **tree-climbing lion**. The park's **rhinos** (around 80 white and 60 black) tend to stick fairly close to the lakeshore and sightings are almost a given on the southern shore; the shy black rhinos, browsers by nature and much more aggressive, are more difficult to spot. Around the cliffs you may catch sight of **hyraxes** and **birds of prey** amid the countless **baboons**;

black-and-white colobus monkeys are present in small numbers in the forests near the eastern shore of the lake. A small herd of **hippos** generally frequents the lake's northern shore. Even if the flamingos aren't in residence, the thousands of breeding **pelicans** still put on a show.

To get the best view that takes in much of the park, head up to **Baboon Cliff**; it's at its best late afternoon as the sun casts a warm glow over the lake. The **Makalia Falls**, at the extreme southern end of the park, are really impressive (by Kenyan waterfall standards) after the rains.

Sleeping & Eating

TOP CHOICE **Sarova Lion Hill Lodge** LODGE $$$
(☎020-2315139; www.sarovahotels.com; s/d full board US$366/486; @≋) Sitting high up the lake's eastern slopes, this lodge offers first-class service and comfort. The views from the open-air restaurant-bar and from most rooms are great. Rooms are understated but pretty, while the flashy suites are large and absolutely stunning. On quiet days you may get the residents' rate, which is less than half that quoted here.

TOP CHOICE **Wildlife Club of Kenya Guesthouse** HOSTEL $
(☎0710579944; r with shared bathroom per person KSh1250) For atmosphere alone, this beats anywhere in Nakuru hands down. It's like staying in a secluded cottage in the countryside, but instead of a garden full of bunny rabbits it's full of rhinos and buffaloes! There are six simple rooms here, as well as an equipped kitchen and a nicely appointed dining room.

Makalia Falls Public Campsite CAMPGROUND $
(camping US$25) While it may be difficult to get to and have cruder facilities than Backpackers', this is the best place to camp in the park. It's picturesque and sits next to the seasonal Makalia Falls.

Backpackers' Campsite CAMPGROUND $
(camping US$25) This large public campsite just inside the main gate has the park's best camping facilities and is the easiest to reach. Baboons are particularly prevalent around here, so take care of your .

LAKE NAKURU NATIONAL PARK

» **Why Go** To see lions, leopards, Rothschild's giraffes, black and white rhinos, and sometimes flamingos, plus the pretty and varied landscape.

» **When to Go** June to March; November to March for birding.

» **Practicalities** Driving in from Nakuru there are three gates (Main, Lanet and Nderit); you can only top up your safaricard at the Main gate. The park is accessible in a 2WD.

Information

Kenya Wildlife Service (☎051-2217151; www.kws.org/parks/parks_reserves/LNNP.html; park admission adult/child US$75/40, safaricard required)

Getting There & Away

Crater Travel (Map p256; ☎051-2214896; cratertravel@yahoo.com; off Kenyata Ave, Nakuru; 5-hour car/jeep/minivan KSh5000/6000/11,000) is your best bet for exploring the park if you don't have your own wheels. Prices include driver, as well as park entry for the driver and vehicle.

Lake Bogoria National Reserve

In the late 1990s this reserve's shallow soda lake achieved fame as 'the new home of the flamingo', with a migrant population of up to two million birds. In 2000 it was designated a Ramsar site, establishing it as a wetland of international importance. Flamingos can be a fickle lot and may move on without notice, but for now the alkaline Lake Bogoria remains one of the best places in Kenya to see the massed flocks of blushing pink flamingos. The rare and rather impressive greater kudu also lurks in the undergrowth.

Sights & Activities

Lake Bogoria LAKE
(adult/child KSh2500/250, car KSh750, guide half-/full day KSh750/1500) Lake Bogoria is backed by the bleak Siracho Escarpment, and moss-green waves roll down its rocky, barren shores. A road that becomes a

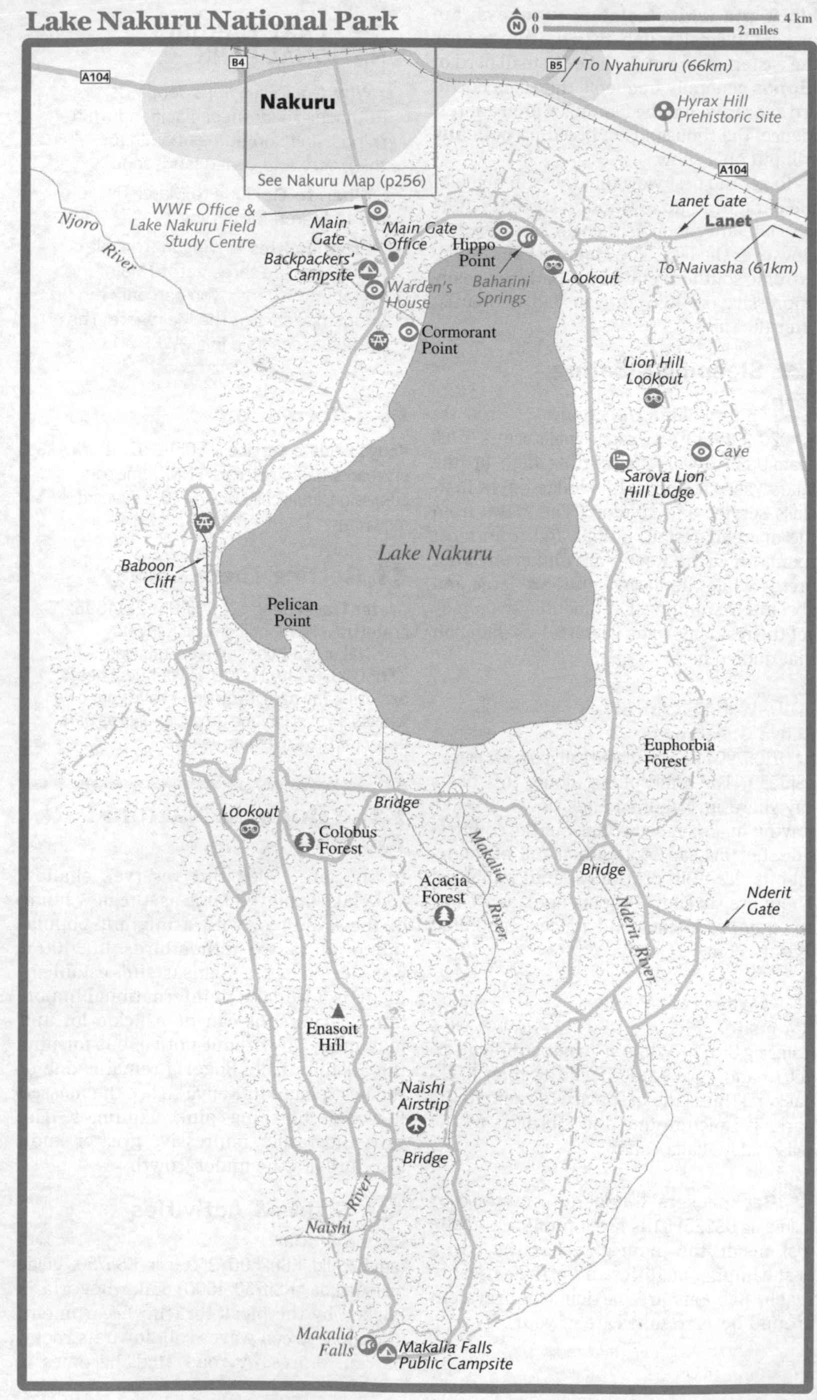
Lake Nakuru National Park
0 4 km
0 2 miles
B4
A104
B5
To Nyahururu (66km)
Nakuru
See Nakuru Map (p256)
Hyrax Hill
Prehistoric Site
A104
Lanet Gate
Lanet
To Naivasha (61km)
WWF Office &
Lake Nakuru Field
Study Centre
Njoro
River
Main
Gate
Main Gate
Office
Hippo
Point
Baharini
Springs
Lookout
Backpackers'
Campsite
Warden's
House
Cormorant
Point
Lion Hill
Lookout
Cave
Sarova Lion
Hill Lodge
Lake Nakuru
Baboon
Cliff
Pelican
Point
Euphorbia
Forest
Bridge
Lookout
Colobus
Forest
Makalia
River
Bridge
Acacia
Forest
Nderit River
Nderit
Gate
Enasoit
Hill
Naishi
Airstrip
Bridge
River
Naishi
Makalia
Falls
Makalia Falls
Public Campsite

LAKE NAKURU'S FLAMINGOS

Since the park's creation in 1961, the population of lesser and greater flamingos has risen and fallen with the soda lake's erratic water levels. When the lake dried up in 1962 (happy first birthday!), the population plummeted, as it later did in the 1970s, when heavy rainfall diluted the lake's salinity and affected the blue-green algae – the lesser flamingos' food source. Over much of the last decade healthy water levels have seen flamingo numbers blossom again. If future droughts or flooding make them fly the coop again, you'll probably find them at Lake Bogoria, with smaller populations at Lake Oloiden and Lake Magadi.

rough track (and then peters out entirely) runs along the lake's western shore, which is where flamingos gather. About halfway along the lake, **hot springs** and **geysers** spew boiling fluids from the earth's insides. If you're here early in the morning, you may have the place to yourself and that's when this other-worldly place feels totally unlike any other Rift Valley lake.

While the isolated wooded area at the lake's southern end is also home to leopards, klipspringers, gazelles, caracals and buffaloes, an increase in human activity means that the greater kudu is increasingly elusive.

Getting There & Away

GATES Entrances are at Loboi (north), Emsos (south) and Maji Moto (west); only Loboi is accessible by 2WD.

PETROL The nearest petrol is available in Marigat.

PUBLIC TRANSPORT Matatus run to Loboi gate from Marigat (KSh100, 30 minutes). Regular matatus serve Marigat from Nakuru (KSh250, two hours) and Kabarnet (KSh165, 1¼ hours).

Lake Baringo

051

This rare freshwater Rift Valley lake, encircled by mountains and with a surface dotted with picturesque islands and hippos batting their eyelids, is probably the most idyllic of the Rift Valley lakes, as well as the most remote. Topping the scenic surrounds is an amazing abundance of birdlife, with over 450 of the 1100 or so bird species native to Kenya present. This is serious birdwatching territory.

With some of the best value accommodation in the Kenyan interior and a go-slow vibe, the lake is easily one of the Rift Valley's highlights.

Sights & Activities

Boat Rides BOAT TOURS

The most popular activities around Lake Baringo are boat rides and this is far and away the best way to experience the lake. Literally anyone you talk to will claim to have access to a boat and be able to undercut anyone else's price. A speciality is a trip to see fish eagles feeding; the birds dive for fish at a whistle. The most reliable trips are organised by **Lake Baringo Boats Excursions** (0727856048; Kampi ya Samaki; per boat per hr KSh3000) and **Roberts' Camp** (0733207775; Kampi ya Samaki; per boat per hr KSh3000).

Bird & Nature Walks BIRDWATCHING

Even if you're not an avid twitcher, it's hard to resist setting off on a dawn or late afternoon bird walk – this is prime time when the birds are most active. Robert's Camp and Lake Baringo Boats Excursions lead excellent walks for between KSh400 and KSh600 per person; a night-time bird walk may also be an option for KSh700.

Sleeping

TOP CHOICE **Robert's Camp** BANDA, CAMPGROUND $

(0733207775; www.robertscamp.com; Kampi ya Samaki; camping KSh500, s/d bandas from KSh2000/3400, 4-person cottages KSh7500; P)

As one of our devoted readers gushed, 'This place keeps getting better and better', and we couldn't agree more. Robert's Camp is right on the lake shore and full of chirping birds, wallowing hippos and toothy crocodiles. There's a variety of accommodation options and it doesn't matter whether you opt for camping in your own tent, a beautifully furnished banda, or an extravagant cottage, what you get for your money here is, quite simply, superb value. Numerous excursions are organised here too.

Lake Baringo & Lake Bogoria National Reserve

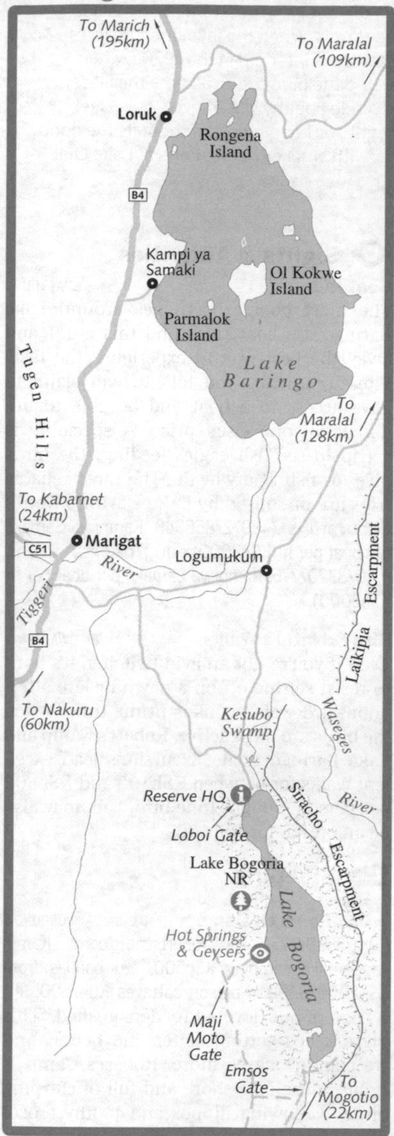

Lake Baringo Club LODGE $$
(☎020-4450636; www.sunafricahotels.com; Kampi ya Samaki; s/d full board US$160/180; P) Set amid lovely grounds that descend gently down to the lakeshore, this old-style hotel has a colonial air and reasonable if overpriced rooms. They offer a full if pricey array of bird walks and boat tours.

Weavers Lodge HOTEL $
(☎0721556153; Kampi ya Samaki; r KSh600; P) Down a rocky alley off the town's main drag, you'll find music-filled African fun at this simple lodging, which has clean rooms with attached bathrooms and solid mattresses. This is where the safari drivers stay, which is a good sign.

Eating & Drinking

TOP CHOICE Thirsty Goat INTERNATIONAL $$
(Roberts' Camp, Kampi ya Samaki; mains KSh450-650; ⊙breakfast, lunch & dinner) This lovely open-air restaurant and bar serves a welcome variety of foreign fare with hornbills regular visitors to your table. There's a range of dishes here from Moroccan meatballs or chicken curry to the spicy 'spitting cobra pizza'. Easily the best place to eat in town.

Bahari Lodge & Hotel KENYAN $
(Kampi ya Samaki; mains from KSh300; ⊙lunch & dinner) Of Kampi ya Samaki's few remaining local restaurants, this is the best place for cheap food, with fish, chicken and vegetables all on the menu. You'll need to order at least a couple of hours in advance.

Getting There & Away

Lake access is easiest from Kampi ya Samaki on the lake's western shore, some 15km north of Marigat.

BUS A 25-seater bus leaves for Nakuru each morning (KSh300) between 6.30am and 9.30am (it departs when full).

PICK-UPS Slightly more regular pick-up trucks head to Marigat (KSh100, 30 minutes) and catch more frequent matatus from there to Nakuru (KSh250, two hours) or Kabarnet (KSh200, 1¼ hours).

WESTERN KENYA

For most people, the magic of western Kenya is summed up in two poetic words: Masai Mara. Few places on earth support such high concentrations of animals, and the Mara's wildebeest-spotted savannahs are undeniably the region's star attraction. Drama unfolds here on a daily basis, be it a stealthy trap co-ordinated by a pride of lions, the infectious panic of a thousand wildebeest crossing a river or the playful pounce of a cheetah kitten on its sibling.

But there is much more to western Kenya than these plains of herbivores and carnivores. The dense forests of Kakamega are buzzing with weird and wonderful creatures, the rain-soaked hills of Kericho and their verdant tea gardens bring new meaning to the word 'green', and amid the boat-speckled waters of Lake Victoria lie a smattering of seldom-visited islands crying out for exploration.

Narok

050 / POP 24,000

Three hours west of Nairobi, this ramshackle provincial town is civilisation's last stand before the vast savannahs of the Masai Mara and the region's largest town. It's a friendly and surprisingly hassle-free place but few travellers have reason to stop. Most people roll on in, browse the curio shops while their driver refuels, then roll on out again.

Sleeping & Eating

Chambai Hotel HOTEL $

(22591; s/d from KSh1050/1250; P) The standard rooms out the back are simple, spotless and sport mosquito nets. The newer and pricier, 'super' rooms in the main building have inviting beds, balconies, large TVs and huge bathrooms.

Seasons Hotel HOTEL $$

(020-2220572; reservationseasonsnarok@gmail.com; B3 Hwy; camping KSh700, s/d from KSh3000/4000; P) While undeniably nicer than anything else around, the Seasons isn't that much better than the Chambai to warrant paying triple. Locally it is regarded as having the best restaurant in town although its buffet (KSh700, lunch and dinner) has seen better days – possibly some time ago.

Information

Barclays Bank (B3 Hwy) With a temperamental ATM.

Info Point Cyberdome (B3 Hwy; per hr KSh60) The last reasonably priced connection before entering the Mara.

Getting There & Away

Narok Line matatus run between Narok and Nairobi (KSh400, three hours) from the Shell petrol station on the B6 Hwy. All other matatus leave from the main matatu stand just around the corner in the centre of town. Destinations include: Naivasha (KSh350, 2½ hours), Kisii (KSh400, three hours), Kericho (KSh400, 2½ hours) and Nakuru (KSh400, two hours).

Public trucks also leave from the matatu stand to Sekenani and Talek gates for KSh300 to KSh400.

There are several petrol stations –fill up, it's much cheaper here than in the reserve.

Masai Mara National Reserve

The world-renowned Masai Mara needs little in the way of introduction; its tawny, wildlife-stuffed savannahs are familiar to everyone who owns a TV set and the scene for umpteen documentaries and movies (most recently Disney's *African Cats*).

The Masai Mara (or Mara, as locals refer to it) is the northern extension of Tanzania's equally famous Serengeti Plains and the whole ecosystem is greatly extended by the numerous privately and community owned conservancies and group ranches that surround the reserve. Most importantly, the Mara hosts some of Africa's greatest battles between herbivores in their millions and the predators who follow them.

Sights & Activities

TOP CHOICE **Wildlife Drives** DRIVING TOUR

Whether you're pursuing elephant silhouettes or parked next to a pride of lions and listening to their bellowed breaths, wildlife

MASAI MARA NATIONAL RESERVE

» **Why Go** For the spectacular Esoit Oloololo (Siria) Escarpment, astonishing amount of wildlife, including the highest lion densities in the world, and the 1510 sq km of open rolling grasslands.

» **When to Go**
Year-round, though the annual wildebeest migration is in July and August.

» **Practicalities** The Mara is very expensive during the annual migration; to share costs, join a group safari in Nairobi, scour the noticeboards at Nairobi backpackers or go to www.lonelyplanet.com/thorntree in search of travel companions.

drives are *the* highlight of a trip to the Mara. During the busy Christmas and migration seasons it can seem that there are as many minivans as animals.

Central Plains

The southeast area of the park, bordered by the Mara and Sand Rivers, is characterised by rolling grasslands and low, isolated hills. With the arrival of the migration,

Western Kenya

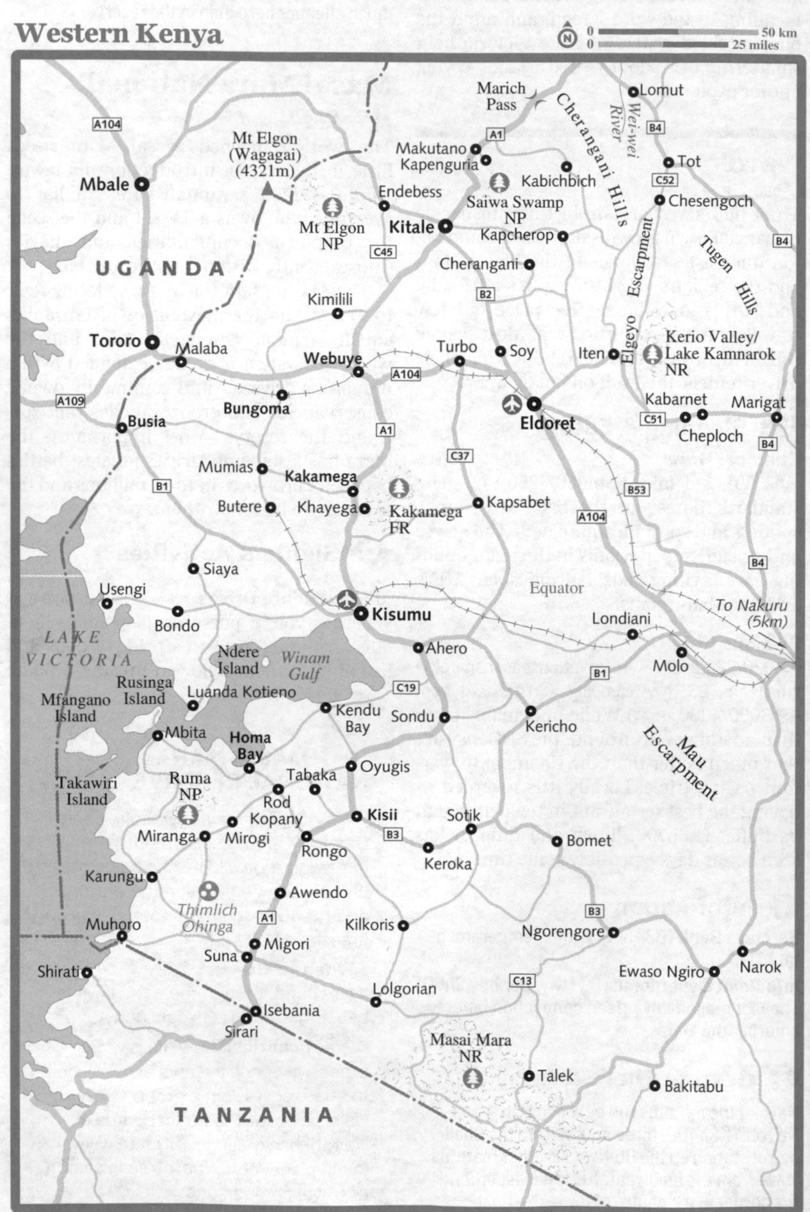

enormous herds of **wildebeest** and **zebra** interspersed with smaller herds of Thompson's and Grant's gazelles, topi and eland all graze here. The **riverine forests** that border the Mara and Talek Rivers are great places to spot **elephant**, **buffalo** and **bushbuck**. **Leopards** are sometimes seen near the Talek and Sand Rivers and around the Keekorok valleys.

Rhino Ridge & Paradise Plains

Rhino Ridge is a good area to see black-backed jackal, as they are known to use the old termitaria here for den sites. **Lookout Hill** is worth a detour as it offers phenomenal views over the seasonal Olpunyaia Swamp. You may also get lucky and spot one of the few **black rhinos** that inhabit the reserve anywhere between Lookout Hill and Rhino Ridge and in the vicinity of Roan Hill. For lions, the **Marsh Pride** near Musiara Swamp and the **Ridge Pride** near Rhino Ridge both starred in the BBC's *Big Cat Diary* and are fairly easy to find. **Cheetahs** are far more elusive but are sometimes found on the Paradise Plains hunting gazelles.

Mara River

Pods of **hippos** can be found in any of the major rivers with the largest and most permanent concentrations occurring in the Mara River. The river is also home to huge **Nile crocodiles**, and is the scene where wildebeest make their fateful crossings during the migration. The New Mara Bridge in the south is the only all-weather crossing point and another great place to see hippo.

Mara Triangle & Esoit Oloololo (Siria) Escarpment

Unlike the rest of the park, which is under the control of the Narok County Council, the northwest sector of the reserve is managed by the nonprofit Mara Conservancy. The only way to reach this part of the park is from either the Oloololo gate or via the New Mara Bridge. Consequently, this area is less visited than elsewhere despite having high game concentrations.

The **Oloololo Escarpment**, which forms the northwest boundary of the park, was once wooded but fire and elephant damage means that it is now mostly grasslands. Rock hyrax and klipspringer can be readily seen here.

Maasai Manyatta Visit VILLAGE

The Maasai are synonymous with the Masai Mara, and their slender frames, blood-red cloaks, ochre hairstyles and beaded jewellery make them instantly recognisable. Despite their reputation as fearsome warriors with somewhat lofty dispositions, many Maasai *manyattas* (villages) now welcome visitors, using the income to fund schools, buy medicine and expand their precious cattle herds. Admission is by negotiation but KSh1000 to KSh1500 per person is reasonable.

Ballooning SCENIC FLIGHTS

(flight per person US$450) Several companies operate dawn balloon safaris and there's no better way to start your day than soaring majestically over the rolling grasslands. Trips can be booked at most of the lodges or campsites.

Sleeping & Eating

In general, accommodation in the Masai Mara is insanely overpriced. Don't be at all surprised if you end up paying more for a lacklustre room or tent here than you would for a decent hotel room in a major Western European city.

Where available, we have listed accommodation-only rates, although all places also offer full-board options.

TOP CHOICE **Aruba Mara Camp** TENTED CAMP $

(0723997524; www.aruba-safaris.com; Talek gate; camping KSh600, unpowered/powered tent per person KSh2000/8000; P) With only five safari tents available, you'll have to fight tooth and nail to get one in high season, but it's a battle well worth fighting as this is one of the few lodges in Kenya where you actually feel as if you're getting value for money, especially if you book the full-board package, as this includes two game drives. The nearby campsite is decent with a kitchen area and reliable hot water in the shower block.

River Side Camp CABIN $

(0720218319; www.riversidecampmara.com; Talek gate; camping KSh400 plus KSh400 security fee, s/d KSh2250/4500; P) Occupying a prime bend on the Talek River, these basic, yet comfy self-contained rooms are a stone's throw from the river waters and, with patience, you could well spot the hippos and baboons that live along its banks. This is the

Masai Mara National Reserve

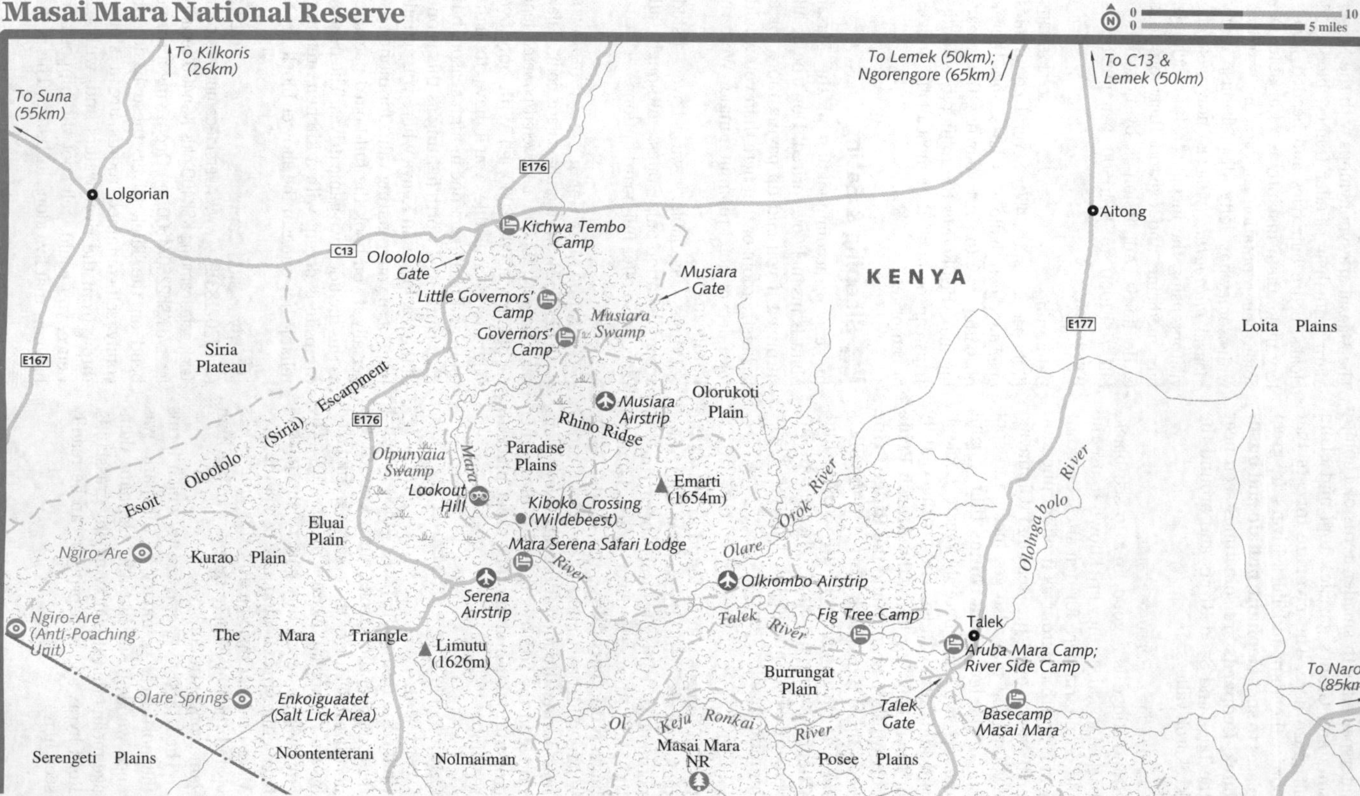

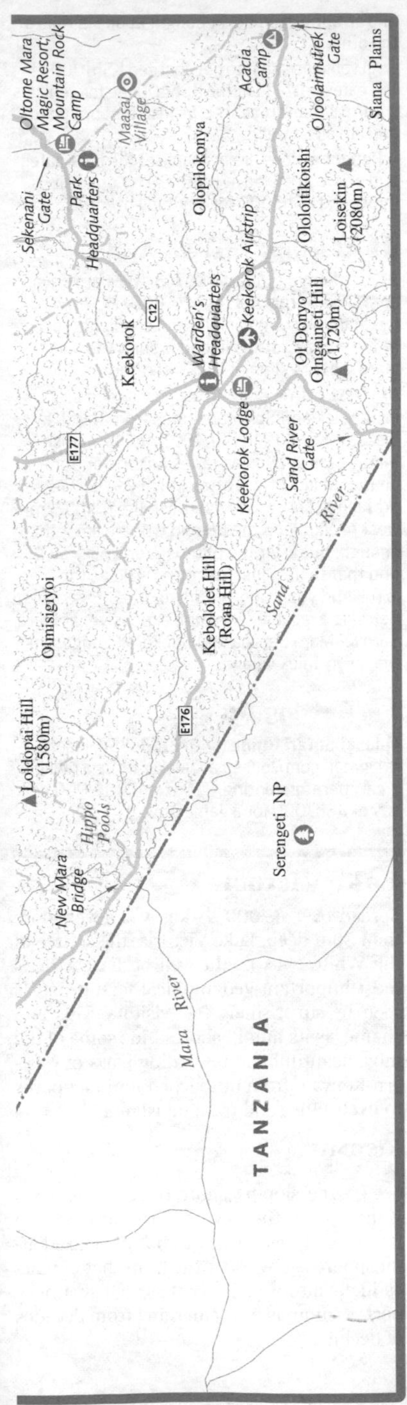

only Talek camp owned and run by the local Maasai community.

Governors' Camp TENTED CAMP **$$$**
(☎020-2734000; www.governorscamp.com; Musiara & Oloololo Gates; tent s/d full board US$544/872;) This camp, and **Little Governors' Camp** (tent s/d full board US$634/1014;) are widely regarded as the most magisterial camps in the Mara and offer great service, pleasing riverside locations and activities aplenty. The extraordinary rates include three wildlife drives and someone keen to wash your dirty clothes.

Fig Tree Camp LODGE **$$$**
(☎Nairobi 020-2500273, 0722202564; www.madahotels.com; Talek gate; tent s/d full board US$360/440; P) Vegetate on your tent's verandah, watching the Talek's waters gently flow pass this sumptuous camp with a colonial-days feel. The gardens are about the most luxurious you'll ever see and the bathrooms about the biggest and most inviting you'll find under canvas. To round things off, there's a small but scenic pool and a trendy treetop bar.

Basecamp Masai Mara LODGE **$$$**
(☎0733333909; www.basecampexplorer.com; Talek gate; tent s/d full board US$290/500; P) 'Eco' is a much-abused word in the tourism industry and sadly some so-called 'eco-friendly' establishments are often nothing of the sort. To see what an ecofriendly hotel really looks like come to this upmarket lodge. The safari tents fall squarely into the luxury bracket with open-air showers and stylish furnishings.

Keekorok Lodge LODGE **$$$**
(☎Nairobi 020-4450636; www.sunafricahotels.com; Masai Mara Reserve; s/d/tr fullboard US$320/490/630; P) This may be the oldest lodge in the Mara but thanks to a recent makeover the rooms are modern, bright and tastefully decorated with tribal chic. The bar and restaurant areas also incorporate tribal art to great effect and flow to manicured gardens and a wooden boardwalk that leads to a gazebo overlooking a hippo pool. Its website often lists great deals.

Mara Serena Safari Lodge LODGE **$$$**
(☎020-2842000; www.serenahotels.com; Masai Mara Reserve; s/d full board US$445/595;) Of all the lodges within the park, the Serena has the best view. Built on a small hill, most rooms have commanding views over

the Paradise Plains and the Mara River above not one, but two, migration crossing points. The rooms themselves are inspired by Maasai *manyatta* (don't worry, they're not made from dung and sticks) and are perfectly comfortable, although they're due for a makeover.

Mountain Rock Camp TENTED CAMP **$**
(020-2242133; www.mountainrockkenya.com; Sekenani gate; camping KSh350, tent s/d shared bathroom KSh2000/3000, tent s/d KSh 3000/5000; P) The simple safari tents here come in two categories; those with private bathrooms, cloth wardrobes and firm beds and those that are smaller and use a shared ablution block.

Kichwa Tembo Camp TENTED CAMP **$$$**
(020-3740920; www.kichwatembo.com, Musiara & Oloololo gates; tent full board per person US$375-475;) Just outside the northern boundary, Kichwa has permanent tents with grass-mat floors, stone bathrooms and tasteful furnishings. Hop in a hammock and take in spectacular savannah views. The camp has an excellent reputation for its food.

Oltome Mara Magic Resort TENTED CAMP **$$$**
(020-2498512, 0727267723; www.oltomemaramagic.com; Sekenani gate; tent s/tw full board US$145/260; P) This small camp has only seven semi-permanent tents so there's plenty of privacy and personalised service from the staff. Each tent is tastefully furnished and features stone floors, wooden verandahs and an attached modern bathroom.

Acacia Camp TENTED CAMP **$**
(0726089107; www.acaciacamp.com; Ololaimutiek gate; camping US$8, tent s/tw US$36/54; P) Thatched roofs shelter closely spaced, spartan semi-permanent tents in this quaint campground. There are numerous cooking areas, a bar, a campfire pit and a simple restaurant that serves meals for US$7 a pop. The communal bathrooms are clean and hot water flows in the evening. The only downside for campers is the lack of shade.

Information

Although the main **reserve** (www.maasaimara.com; park admission adult/child staying within the park US$70/40, adult/child staying outside the park US$80/45; 6am-7pm) is managed by the Narok County Council and the **Mara Triangle** (www.maratriangle.org) is managed by the Mara Conservancy, both charge the same and an admission ticket bought at one is valid at the other.

All vehicles seem to get charged KSh1000 at the gates, instead of the KSh400 fee for vehicles with less than six seats – be insistent but polite and all will be well.

Ranger guides are available at the park gates and prices are fixed at KSh1500 for up to six hours and KSh3000 for anything over this.

Getting There & Away

AIR Airkenya (020-605745; www.airkenya.com) and **Safarilink** (020-600777; www.flysafarilink.com) each have daily flights to any of the eight airstrips in and around the Masai Mara. Flights start at US$250 return.

MATATU, CAR & 4WD It's possible to access Talek and Sekenani gates from Narok by matatu (KSh300 to KSh400), and from Kisii a matatu will get you as far as Kilkoris or Suna on the main A1 Hwy, after which you'll have problems. For those who drive, the first 52km west of Narok on the B3 and C12 are smooth enough, but after the bitumen runs out you'll find that there's just as much rattle as there is roll and you'll soon come to dread this road. Petrol is available (although expensive) at Mara Sarova, Mara Serena and Keekorok Lodges, as well as in Talek village.

Getting Around

Maasai Safari Guide (0721633864, joseftira@gmail.com), based at Talek gate, is a reliable local operator, renting 4WDs for KSh12,000 per day or KSh7000 for a game drive.

Lake Victoria

Spread over 68,000 sq km, yet never more than 80m deep, Lake Victoria, the source of the White Nile, might well be East Africa's most important geographical feature but is seen by surprisingly few visitors. This is a shame, as its humid shores hide some of the most beautiful and rewarding parts of western Kenya – from untouched national parks to lively cities and tranquil islands.

KISUMU

057 / POP 322,700

Set on the sloping shore of Lake Victoria's Winam Gulf, the town of Kisumu might be the third largest in Kenya, but its relaxed atmosphere is a world away from that of places like Nairobi and Mombasa. Once a busy port, Kisumu is now emerging from decades of decline.

Kisumu

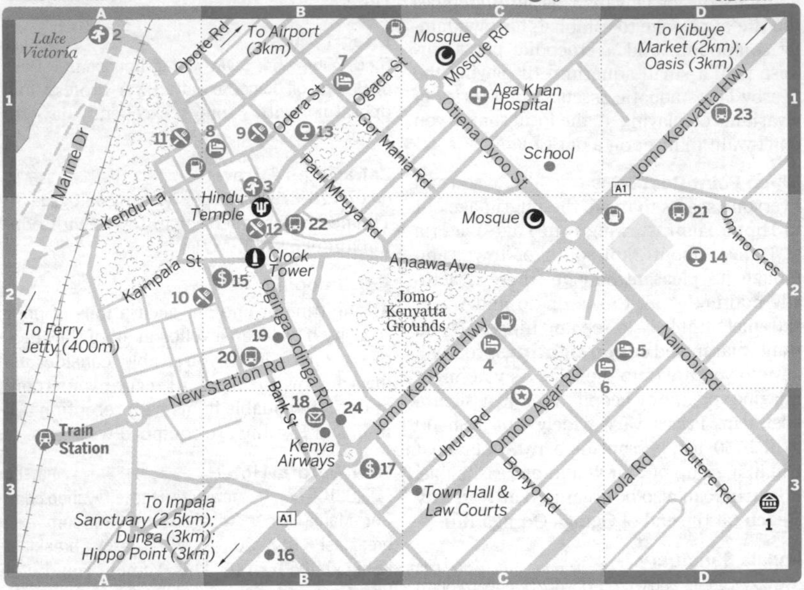

Kisumu

Sights

1 Kisumu Museum....................D3

Activities, Courses & Tours

Integri Tours....................(see 4)
2 Railway Beach Hippo Trips....................A1
3 Zaira Tours & Travel....................B1

Sleeping

4 Duke of Breeze....................C2
5 Hotel Palmers....................D2
6 New East View Hotel....................D2
7 New Victoria Hotel....................B1
8 Sooper Guest House....................B1

Eating

9 Green Garden Restaurant....................B1
Grill....................(see 11)
10 Juice Parlour....................B2
11 Laughing Buddha....................A1
12 Senorita....................B2
Tin-Shack Restaurants....................(see 2)

Drinking

13 Octopus Bottoms-Up Club....................B1
14 Social Centre....................D2

Information

15 Barclays Bank....................B2
Clinipath Laboratory....................(see 18)
16 Immigration Office....................B3
17 Kenya Commercial Bank....................B3
Moscom Cyber....................(see 18)
18 Post Office....................B3
19 Shiva Travels....................B2

Transport

20 Akamba....................B2
21 Bus & Matatu Station....................D2
22 Easy Coach....................B2
23 Easy Coach....................D1
24 Jet Link....................B3

Sights & Activities

Kisumu Museum MUSEUM

(Nairobi Rd; admission KSh500; ⌚8am-6pm) Set on sprawling grounds southwest of the town centre, this educational facility has three sections: a small museum about Western Kenya's three principal linguistic groups (the Luo, who were predominantly fishermen, the agricultural Bantu and the Kalenjin, famed for their animal husbandry);

a traditional Luo homestead depicting the fictitious life of Onyango as he undergoes the rite of passage to establish his own family compound; and a crocodile pit, a tortoise pen, a small aquarium displaying the nearby lake's aquatic assets, and a series of vivariums displaying all the local snakes you don't want to meet on a dark night.

Hippo Point Boat Trips BOAT TOUR

Everyone seems to make the pilgrimage out to Hippo Point, sticking into Lake Victoria at Dunga, about 3km south of town, and though it's pleasant enough, there is actually nothing at all to see or do and you're extremely unlikely to see any hippos. If you want guaranteed **hippo sightings**, you will have to venture onto the lake. As you might imagine, plenty of people offer just such a boat trip. Prices vary widely but KSh500 to Ksh750 per person for a two-hour boat trip in a group of four would be reasonable. Boat trips can also be organised at **Railway Beach** (at the end of Oginga Odinga Rd).

Impala Sanctuary PARK

(www.kws.go.ke; adult/child US$15/5; ⏲6am-6pm) On the road to Dunga, this 1-sq-km sanctuary is home to a small impala herd and provides important grazing grounds for local hippos.

Ndere Island National Park PARK

(www.kws.go.ke; adult/child US$20/10; ⏲6am-6pm) Gazetted as a national park back in 1986, tourism to this small 4.2-sq-km island has never taken off. It is forested and very beautiful, housing a variety of bird species, plus hippos, impalas (introduced) and spotted crocodiles – a lesser-known cousin of the larger Nile crocodile.

Although twice-daily matatus reach the shore just opposite the island, your only reliable option to get to Ndere is with chartered boats. Expect to pay around KSh2000 per hour, with typical return trips taking five hours (including three hours on shore).

Tours

It's quite feasible to see the sights of Kisumu on your own, but if you don't know your eagle from your snowy egret, or want to visit further afield with limited time, then consider hiring a guide.

Ibrahim Nandi NATURE

(☎0723083045; ibradingo@yahoo.com) A well-known and trusted tour guide to the many sights and sounds of the Kisumu region. He can be contacted through the New Victoria Hotel.

Integri Tours NATURE

(☎0720647864; www.integritour.com; Duke of Breeze, off Jomo Kenyatta Hwy) Professional operator with some excellent day-trip itineraries.

Zaira Tours & Travel SAFARIS

(☎0722788879; zairatours@yahoo.com; Ogada St) The best safari operator in town, with pop-top minivans and 4WDs.

Sleeping

At one time or another accusations of poor security have been levelled at all of the cheapies we list here. If you're able, consider using your own padlock to secure your room or deposit valuable items with reception. All rooms in Kisumu are equipped with fans.

New Victoria Hotel HOTEL $

(☎2021067; newvictoriahotel@yahoo.com; Gor Mahia Rd; s with shared bathroom excl breakfast KSh900, s/tw/tr excl breakfast KSh1450/1950/2700) This Yemeni-run hotel has character in abundance and is something of a focal point for the town's small Arab population. Rooms have fans, mosquito nets and comfy foam mattresses. The next-door mosque will rouse you at 5am.

Sooper Guest House BACKPACKERS $

(☎0725281733; kayamchatur@yahoo.com; Oginga Odinga Rd; s excl breakfast KSh1000-1200, d excl breakfast KSh 1200-1400, tw/tr excl breakfast KSh1200/1600) Sooper has become the defacto backpackers in town and you have a good chance of meeting other travellers here. The rooms aren't quite the bargain we once found them to be but still offer decent low cost digs. The rooms in the newer block are larger than those in the old block but cost KSh200 more and suffer from street noise.

Kiboko Bay Resort TENTED CAMP $$$

(☎2025510, 0724387738; www.kibokobay.com; Dunga; s/d/tr US$145/175/195; ❄🏊) At Kiboko, you will find nine Masai Mara-style safari tents huddled under the trees on the banks of the lake. Each has a hardwood floor, a huge bed, canopy mosquito nets and an attached permanent bathroom. Considering the price, we were surprised to find the pool more than a tinge green.

New East View Hotel HOTEL $
(☎0722556721; Omolo Agar Rd; s KSh1700-2300, d KSh2300-2800; P) One of the many family homes in the area that have been converted into a hotel. It retains just enough furniture and decoration to give the rooms a homely, pre-loved feel.

Duke of Breeze HOTEL $
(☎0717105444; reservations@thedukeofbreeze.com; off Jomo Kenyatta Hwy; s/d/tr KSh1900/2400/3000; wi-fi) Popular with Peace Corp volunteers, the Duke has large, fan-cooled rooms that have seen better days. The real attractions are the roof-top restaurant, free wi-fi (but the soft drinks here are twice the price as elsewhere) and the relaxed, chilled vibe.

Hotel Palmers HOTEL $
(☎2024867; hotel.palmers@yahoo.com Omolo Agar Rd; s/d/tw/tr KSh1500/2300/2800/3500; P) The doubles here are particularly nice, with large bay windows and enormous double beds. The singles, alas, are far more poky.

Eating

The fact that Kisumu sits on Lake Victoria certainly isn't lost on restaurants here, and fish is abundant on menus.

If you want an authentic local fish fry, there are no better places than the dozens of smoky **tin-shack restaurants** sitting on the lake's shore at Railway Beach at the end of Oginga Odinga Rd. Dive in between 7am and 6pm; a midsized fish served with ugali or rice is sufficient for two people and will set you back KSh400.

TOP CHOICE **Green Garden Restaurant** INTERNATIONAL $
(Odera St; mains KSh380-500; ⏰lunch & dinner) Surrounded by colourful murals and potted palms, the Green Garden remains an oasis of culinary delight set in an Italian-themed courtyard. As you would expect, it's an expat hot spot and the word is that the tilapia (fish) in a spinach and coconut sauce is the way to go.

The Laughing Buddha VEGETARIAN $
(Swan Centre, Accra St; mains KSh350-500; ⏰lunch & dinner, Tue-Sun; ✎) Guaranteed to smack a smile on your face, The Laughing Buddha rounds off its excellent vegetarian menu with treats like sizzling chocolate fudge brownies and Oreo milkshakes (greedy little monkeys take note: the second one is only KSh50). The curb-side dining is a novelty in these parts.

Juice Parlour CAFE $
(off New Station Rd; juice from KSh50; ⏰breakfast, lunch & dinner) You name it and they'll stick it in a blender and pulverise the bejesus out of it. The pumpkin and beetroot juice looked foul so we shared a very special moment with a mango and pineapple combo instead.

Grill INTERNATIONAL $
(Swan Centre, Accra St; mains KSh400; ⏰lunch & dinner) Right next door to The Laughing Buddha, The Grill is *the* place to come if you want to sink your teeth into some excellent steaks and chicken fillets. Steak treatments include mushroom, masala, Mexican and garlic sauces. Befitting its name, there's also a charcoal barbecue out front serving *nyama choma* (and smoke, if the wind is blowing unfavourably).

Senorita KENYAN $
(Oginga Odinga Rd; mains KSh150-250; ⏰lunch & dinner) This upmarket locals' restaurant has a great '50s feel and a menu that covers everything that involves chips and other fried food.

Drinking & Entertainment

Kisumu's nightlife has a reputation for being even livelier than Nairobi's. Check flyers and ask locals who are plugged into the scene. Be careful when leaving as muggings and worse are not unheard of. Solo women should take a chaperone – Ibrahim Nandi (p268) offers just such a service.

Oasis DANCE
(Kondele, Jomo Kenyatta Hwy; club entry KSh150-200) Well known locally, with live music most nights, this is the place to see Lingala music performed by Congolese bands. Be prepared for a fair bit of shaking and sweating.

Social Centre DANCE
(off Omino Cres; club entry KSh100) Tucked behind the main matatu stage, this club is big on *ohangla* (Luo traditional music) with the odd Kiswahali hip-hop tune thrown in for good measure.

Octopus Bottoms-Up Club DANCE
(Ogada St; bar free, club entry KSh100) This heavyweight bar and club rages all night, but be warned that the scene isn't that pretty.

Information

Aga Khan Hospital (☎2020005; Otiena Oyoo St) A large hospital with modern facilities and 24-hour emergency room.

Barclays Bank (Kampala St) With ATM.

Clinipath Laboratory (☎2022363; Mega Plaza, Oginga Odinga Rd; ⌚8am-5pm Mon-Fri, 8am-1pm Sat, 10am-noon Sun)

Kenya Commercial Bank (Jomo Kenyatta Hwy) With ATM (Visa only).

Moscom Cyber (Mega Plaza, Oginga Odinga Rd; per hr KSh60; ⌚8am-8.30pm) One of many Internet cafes around town although this one also has a licence to burn CDs (KSh100).

Police station (Uhuru Rd)

Post office (Oginga Odinga Rd)

Shiva Travels (☎2024331; Oginga Odinga Rd) Airline ticketing and hotel reservations.

Getting There & Away

AIR All three airlines here offer daily morning and afternoon flights to Nairobi (from KSh5500 one way, 50 minutes).

Fly540 (www.fly540.com) The 5.30pm flight to Nairobi is via Eldoret.

Jet Link (☎0714333377; www.jetlink.co.ke; Al-Imran Plaza, Oginga Odinga Rd)

Kenya Airways (☎2056000; www.kenya-airways.com; Alpha House, Oginga Odinga Rd)

BOAT Despite the reduced water hyacinth in the Winam Gulf, ferry services to Tanzania and Uganda haven't restarted. **Earthwise Ferries** (http://earthwiseferries.com) has plans (but then somebody always does) for a ferry to once again link Kisumu with Mwanza (Tanzania) and Kampala (Uganda).

BUS & MATATU Buses, matatus and Peugeots (shared taxis) battle it out at the large bus and matatu station just north of the main market. Peugeots cost about 25% more than matatus.

Akamba (off New Station Rd) Four daily buses to Nairobi (KSh1100, seven hours) via Nakuru (KSh800, 4½ hours); also a 1pm departure to Kigali (KSh2500, 20 hours) via Busia (KSh400, three hours) and Kampala (KSh1500, seven hours) and an 11pm departure to Mwanza (KSh1800, 12 hours).

Easy Coach (Jomo Kenyatta Hwy) serves similar domestic destinations, as well as Kakamega (KSh250, one hour), with some added comfort and cost.

TRAIN Trains have once again sprung (well, spluttered) into life between Kisumu and Nairobi (1st/2nd/3rd class KSh2550/1400/500, 13½ hours) via Nakuru (KSh1560/1125/280, seven hours) and Naivasha (KSh1805/1255/360, 11 hours). All going well, the train departs Kisumu at 6.30pm every Tuesday, Thursday and Sunday. It departs Nairobi at the same time on Monday, Wednesday and Friday.

Getting Around

BODA-BODA & TUK-TUK Both boda-boda (bicycle or motorbike-taxis) and tuk-tuks (motorised mini-taxis) are a great way to get around Kisumu. A trip to Hippo Point should be no more than KSh50/150 for a boda-boda/tuk-tuk.

MATATU Matatus 7 and 9 travel along Oginga Odinga Rd and Jomo Kenyatta Hwy and are handy for the main matatu station, main market and Kibuye Market.

TAXI A taxi around town costs between KSh100 and KSh200, while trips to Dunga range from KSh250 to KSh400, with heavy bargaining.

MATATUS FROM KISUMU

DESTINATION	FARE (KSH)	DURATION (HR)
Busia	300	2
Eldoret	400	2½
Homa Bay	350	3
Isebania	500	4
Kakamega	250	1¾
Kericho	300	2
Kisii	300	2
Kitale	450	4
Nairobi	900	5½
Nakuru	500	3½

HOMA BAY

059 / POP 42,600

Homa Bay has a slow, tropical, almost Central African vibe, and the near total absence of other tourists means it's extraordinarily and genuinely friendly. There's little to do other than trudge up and down the dusty, music-filled streets or wander down to the lake edge to watch the marabou storks pick through the trash as they wait for the fishermen and their morning catch. The town makes a great base from which to visit Ruma National Park.

Sleeping & Eating

TOP CHOICE Twin Towers Hotel HOTEL $

(0715032988; s/d/tw KSh1200/1500/2000) Just opened and seriously under-priced, the Twin Towers (slightly unfortunate name that) is easily the town's best-value digs. If all you require is a comfy bed and a bathroom that doesn't require a biohazard suit to enter, then look no further. The restaurant here offers decent, if unimaginative, mains for around KSh300.

Homa Bay Tourist Hotel HOTEL $$

(072711265; s/d/tw excl breakfast from KSh3000/6200/7500; P@) This lakeside 'resort' is the town's only operation aimed squarely at the tourist sector. The expansive lawns running down to the water's edge surround this ageing but still presentable complex, make it an ideal place to chill with a book.

Information

Barclays Bank (Moi Hwy) With ATM.

Fezza Online (per hr KSh60, closed Sat) Up the hill from Twin Towers Hotel.

KWS warden's office (22544) In the district commissioner's compound.

Getting There & Away

Akamba's office is just down the hill from the bus station and its buses serve Nairobi (KSh1200, nine hours, 7.30pm) via Kericho (KSh650, four hours) and Nakuru (KSh900, six hours). Several other companies and matatus (operating from the bus station) also ply these routes, as well as Mbita (KSh250, 1½ hours), Kisii (KSh250, 1½ 1½ hours) and Kisumu (KSh350, three hours).

RUMA NATIONAL PARK

Bordered by the dramatic **Kanyamaa Escarpment**, and home to Kenya's only population of **roans** (one of Africa's rarest and largest antelope), is the seldom-visited, 120-sq-km **Ruma National Park** (0717176709, www.kws.go.ke; adult/child US$20/10, plus vehicle from KSh300; 6am-6pm). Due to leopard and hyena predation, the roan population has fallen to a mere 31 individuals but there are plans to make a predator-free sanctuary within the park and possibly bolster the gene pool with roans brought in from Tanzania.

Besides roan, other rarities like **Bohor's reedbuck**, **Jackson's hartebeest**, the tiny **oribi** antelope and Kenya's largest concentration of the endangered **Rothschild's giraffe** can also be seen here. Birdlife is prolific, with 145 different bird species present, including the migratory blue swallow that arrives between June and August.

The best game viewing is near the new airstrip as both the giraffes and roans favour that area.

Tours

The park is set up for those with vehicles; otherwise, contact the **KWS rangers** (0717176709) at the park gates who may be able to send a local with a pop-top minivan to collect you from Homa Bay. At the time of research, a full-day **game drive** cost KSh5000 for the vehicle (plus entrance park fees), but as this is drastically out of kilter with higher charges elsewhere, it's almost certain to rise. The rangers can also accompany you on a **guided trek** (half-/full day KSh1500/3000).

Sleeping & Eating

Camping CAMPGROUND $

(camping US$15; P) There are two simple campsites near the main gate. Nyati special campsite is the more scenic.

Oribi Guesthouse CABIN $$

(0717176709; www.kws.go.ke; per cabin excl breakfast US$100; P) Your only other option is the KWS-run Oribi Guesthouse, which is extortionate if there are only two of you but quite good value for groups. It has dramatic views over the Lambwe Valley and is well equipped with solar power, hot showers and a fully functioning kitchen.

Getting There & Away

With your own vehicle, head a couple of kilometres south from Homa Bay and turn right onto the Mbita road. About 12km west is the main access road, and from there it's another 11km. The park's roads are in decent shape, but require a mega 4WD in the rainy season.

Kisii

☎058 / POP 59,300

Let's cut straight to the chase. Kisii is a noisy, polluted and congested mess, and most people (quite sensibly) roll right on through without even stopping.

Sleeping & Eating

Nile Restaurant, Fast Food & Guesthouse HOTEL $
(☎0710847277; Hospital Rd; s/d excl breakfast Ksh650/1000) Clean, cheap rooms and a central location make the Nile the best deal in town. The icing on the cake is that the 2nd-floor restaurant (mains Ksh200 to Ksh300) has a commanding view of the chaos below. Our hopes were high for the chicken tikka (which appears in the Italian section of the menu) but it turned out to be just chicken and chips.

Kisii Hotel HOTEL $
(☎30134; s/d/tw KSh1100/1500/1500; P) This is a relaxed place in what feels like an old school building off Moi Hwy. It boasts large gardens and sizeable rooms with decent bathrooms. This is great for those who need quiet surroundings in order to sleep soundly.

Information

Barclays Bank (Moi Hwy) With ATM.

Fast Web Computer Centre (Hospital Rd; per hr KSh30) Internet and CD/DVD burning facilities.

Post office (Moi Hwy) With cardphones.

Getting There & Away

All hell breaks lose daily at the congested Matatu terminal in the centre of town. Regular departures serve Homa Bay (KSh250, 1½ hours), Kisumu (KSh350, 2½ hours), Kericho (KSh300, two hours) and Isebania (KSh250, 1¾ hours) on the Tanzanian border.

Tabaka matatus (KSh100, 45 minutes) leave from Cemetery Rd. Returning, it is sometimes easier to catch a boda-boda (KSh70) to the 'Tabaka junction' and pick up a Kisii bound matatu there.

Akamba (Moi Hwy) has a daily bus to Nairobi (KSh1000, eight hours) via Nakuru (KSh700, 5½ hours) departing at 9pm – it's wise to book a day in advance. Its bus bound for Mwanza (Tanzania; KSh1600, four hours) from Nairobi calls in at the unseemly hour of 3.30am.

Kericho

☎052 / POP 82,100

The polar opposite of Kisii, Kericho is a haven of tranquillity. Its surrounds are blanketed by a thick patchwork of manicured tea plantations, each seemingly hemmed in by distant stands of evergreens. With a pleasant climate and a number of things to see and do, Kericho makes for a very calming couple of days.

Sights & Activities

Tea Plantation FARMS
This is the centre of the most important tea gardens in all of Africa, so you might expect tea plantation tours to be touted left, right and centre. Surprisingly, though, they are fairly few and far between. If you just want to take a stroll in the fields, then the easiest plantations to get to are those behind the Tea Hotel.

Otherwise take a **guided tour** with **Harman Kirui** (☎0721843980; kmtharman@yahoo.com; per person KSh200). Most tours involve walking around the fields and watching the picking in process (note that the pickers don't work on Sunday). If you want to actu-

KISII SOAPSTONE

While the feted Kisii soapstone obviously comes from this area, it's not on sale here. Quarrying and carving go on in the Gusii village of **Tabaka**, 23km northwest of Kisii. Soapstone is relatively soft and pliable (as far as rocks go) and with simple hand tools and scraps of sandpaper the sculptors carve chess sets, bowls, animals and the unmistakable abstract figures of embracing couples. Each artisan specialises in one design before passing it on to someone else to be smoothed with wet sandpaper and polished with wax. Most pieces are destined for the curio shops of Nairobi and Mombasa and trade-aid shops around the world. As you would expect, prices are cheaper here than elsewhere. If you are undaunted by adding a few heavy rocks to your backpack, you can save a packet.

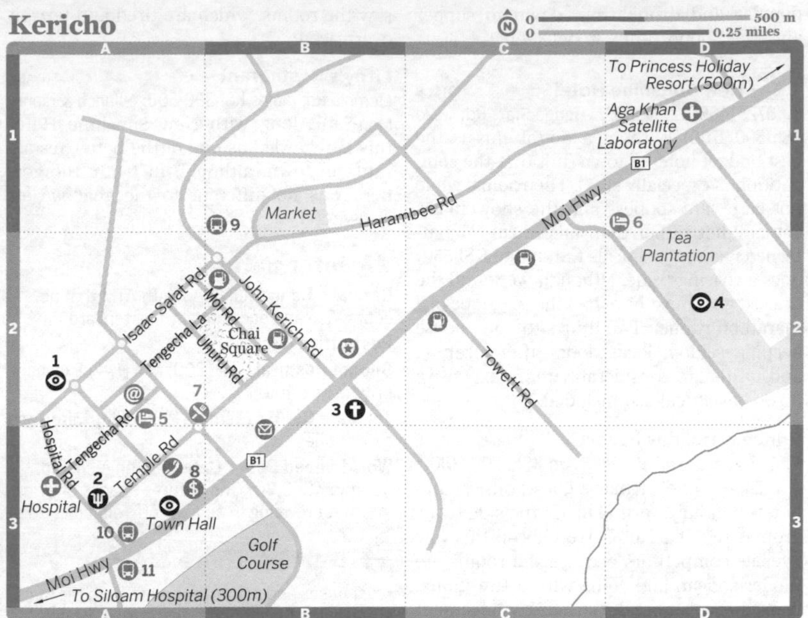

ally see the process through to the end and visit a factory, you should book at least four days in advance through the Tea Hotel or by emailing Harman directly. The factory most often visited is the **Momul Tea Factory** (per person/group KSh300/1000, ⏲Mon-Sat), 28km from Kericho (for those without transport, Harman can arrange a car for KSh2000). The factory has 64 collection sites servicing the area's small-scale farmers and processes a staggering 15 million kilos of green leaf a year.

Arboretum GARDENS
(B4 Hwy; ⏲closed when raining) Eight kilometres east of town, this tropical park is popular with weekend picnickers and colobus, vervet and red-tailed **monkeys** (best seen in the early morning). The main attraction here is the shade afforded by the tropical trees planted by estate owner Tom Grumbley in the 1940s.

Notable Buildings ARCHITECTURE
Theologically speaking, Kericho is well-represented, with the impressive, ivy-clad **Holy Trinity Church**, built in 1952; Africa's largest **Gurdwara** (Sikh place of worship); and a modest Hindu temple on Hospital Rd.

Kericho

Sights
1 Gurdwara ... A2
2 Hindu Temple ... A3
3 Holy Trinity Church ... B2
4 Tea Plantation ... D2

Sleeping
5 New Sunshine Hotel ... A2
6 Tea Hotel ... D1

Eating
7 Litny's Restaurant ... A2

Information
8 Barclays Bank ... A3

Transport
9 Bus & Matatu Stand ... B1
10 Buses (South & West) ... A3
11 Buses to Kisumu, Kisii & Homa Bay ... A3
Total Petrol Station ... (see 10)

Sleeping & Eating

Being a stronghold of the Kipsigis people, this is good place to try *kimyet* (maize-meal served with vegetables and beef) or *mursik* (soured milk). Naturally, tea is extremely popular and drunk from dawn to supper and every opportunity in between.

TOP CHOICE **New Sunshine Hotel** HOTEL $
(☎0725146601, 30037; Tengecha Rd; s/d KSh1500/1700) Without a doubt this is the best budget hotel in town (not that the competition is especially stiff). The rooms, while not large, are spotless and the showers are actually hot rather than lukewarm. The attached restaurant (meals KSh320 to KSh550) does a roaring trade, although we found the braised goat must have had the physique of a marathon runner. Two things to note: house keeping seldom locks doors after cleaning and tariffs are considerably more expensive if you have breakfast included.

Princess Holiday Resort GUESTHOUSE $
(☎0721254736; off Moi Hwy; s/d KSh2500/3000; P) This is one of many guesthouses-cum-hotels that have sprung up on the side roads around the Tea Hotel. We choose this one over its competitors because the rooms are modern, clean and come with a traditional cooked English breakfast. The management will bend over backwards to be helpful and if you give them a call, they will collect you from town.

Tea Hotel HOTEL $$
(☎020-2050790; teahotel@africaonline.co.ke; Moi Hwy; camping KSh700, s/d excl breakfast US$65/90; P) This grand property was built in the 1950s by the Brooke Bond company and still has a lot of period charm about it. We liked it in the same way you do a favourite teddy bear despite its missing eye and loose stuffing. The hotel's most notable features are the vast hallways and dining rooms full of mounted animal heads and its beautiful gardens with their tea-bush backdrops. Unfortunately any sentimentality that we found endearing about the communal spaces had worn thin by the time we saw the rooms, which are tired and terribly overpriced.

Litny's Restaurant KENYAN $
(Temple Rd; mains KSh300-500; ⏲lunch & dinner, Mon-Sat) Along with New Sunshine Hotel, this is regarded as one of the better restaurants in town, although in truth, the goat here was no different to the goat we ate elsewhere.

Information

Barclays Bank (Moi Hwy) With ATM that accepts Visa and occasionally MasterCard.
Post office (Moi Hwy)
Siloam Hospital (☎21200; Moi Hwy) Excellent private hospital.
Telecare Centre (Temple Rd) Calling cards and cardphones.
World Speed Cyber Cafe (off Tengecha Rd; per min KSh0.80) One of three shacks offering internet browsing in an alley off Tengecha Rd.

Getting There & Away

Most buses and matatus operate from the main stand in the town's northwest corner, while those heading south and west leave from the Total petrol station on Moi Hwy.

Buses to Nairobi (KSh600, 4½ hours) are quite frequent, as are matatus to Kisumu (KSh250, 1½ hours), Kisii (KSh300, two hours), Eldoret (KSh400 to KSh500, 3½ hours) and Nakuru (KSh300, two hours).

Kakamega Forest

☎056

Not so long ago much of western Kenya was hidden under a dark veil of jungle and formed a part of the mighty Guineo-Congolian forest ecosystem – even gorillas are rumoured to have once played in the mists here. However, the British soon did their best to turn all that lovely virgin

ANYONE FOR TEA?

Kenya is the world's third-largest tea exporter after India and Sri Lanka, with tea accounting for between 20% and 30% of the country's export income. It's unique in that its small landholders produce the bulk (60%) of the country's tea.

Tea-picking is a great source of employment around Kericho, with mature bushes picked every 17 days and the same worker continually picking the same patch. Good pickers collect their own body weight in tea each day!

Despite Kericho producing some of the planet's best black tea, you will have trouble finding a cup of the finest blends here – most of it's exported.

forest into tea estates. Now all that's left is this slab of tropical rainforest surrounding Kakamega.

Though seriously degraded, this forest is unique in Kenya and contains plants, animals and birds that occur nowhere else in the country. It's so wild here trees actually kill each other – seriously! Parasitic fig trees grow on top of unsuspecting trees and strangle their hosts to death.

Sights & Activities

Walking Trails HIKING

The best way, indeed the only real way, to appreciate the forest is to walk and trails radiate from Buyangu and Isecheno areas.

While guides are not compulsory, they are well worth the extra expense. Not only do they prevent you from getting lost, but most are walking encyclopaedias and will reel off both the Latin and common name of almost any plant or insect you care to point out, along with any of its medicinal properties. They are also able to recognise and imitate birdcalls so effectively that you wouldn't be surprised if they suddenly sprouted wings and flew off.

Buyangu Area

Rangers state that trails vary in length from 1km to 7km. Of the longer walks **Isiukhu Trail**, which connects Isecheno to the small **Isiukhu Falls**, is one of the most popular and takes a minimum of half a day. The 4km drive or walk to **Buyangu Hill** allows for uninterrupted views east to the Nandi Escarpment.

Isecheno Area

The five-hour return hike to **Lirhanda Hill** for sunrise or sunset is highly recommended as too are the night walks, which occasionally turn up slow-moving pottos (an insanely cute, furry primate). An interesting short walk (2.6km) to a 35m-high **watchtower** affords views over the forest canopy and small grassland.

Sleeping & Eating

BUYANGU AREA

If you're staying at either of the KWS-managed options, you will have to pay park entry fees for each night you're there.

Isikuti Guesthouse GUESTHOUSE $$

(☎30603, 0727415828; www.kws.go.ke; cottage US$50) Hidden in a pretty forest glade close to Udo's are four massive KWS cottages

Kakamega Forest

Kakamega Forest

Sleeping

1 De Brazza's Campsite........B1
2 Forest Rest House........B2
Isikuti Guesthouse........(see 4)
3 Rondo Retreat........B2
4 Udo's Bandas & Camping........B1

Information

Kakamega Forest Guide Association........(see 6)
5 Kakamega Forest Reserve Office........B2
Kakamega Rainforest Tour Guides........(see 5)
6 KWS Office........B1

(sleeping up to four), with equipped kitchens and bathrooms.

De Brazza's Campsite CAMPSITE $

(☎0721628343; camping KSh400, bandas per person KSh600) Just before the park gates, this simple campsite is as basic as basic gets. There's no electricity and the toilets are the kind where the long-drops aren't long enough.

Udo's Bandas & Camping BANDA $
(☎30603, 0727415828; www.kws.go.ke; camping US$15, bandas per person US$30) Named after Udo Savalli, a well-known ornithologist, this lovely KWS site is tidy, well maintained and has seven simple thatched *bandas*; nets are provided, but you will need your own sleeping bag and other supplies. There are long-drop toilets, bucket showers, and a communal cooking and dining shelter.

ISECHENO AREA

TOP CHOICE **Rondo Retreat** GUESTHOUSE $$
(☎056-30268; www.rondoretreat.com; full board adult/child KSh7400/5400) To arrive at the Rondo Retreat is to be whisked back to 1922 and the height of British rule. Consisting of a series of wooden bungalows filled with a family's clutter, this gorgeous and eccentric place is a wonderful retreat from modern Kenya. The gardens are stunning and dinner is a formal affair; dress smart (no shorts) and expect old-fashioned English meat-and-two-veg. Profits go to a Christian charity.

Forest Rest House HUT $
(☎0727486747; camping KSh650, r per person KSh500) The four rooms of this wooden house, perched on stilts 2m above the ground and with views straight onto a mass of impenetrable jungle, might be as basic as it gets (no electricity, no bedding and cold-water baths that look like they'd crash through the floor boards if you tried to fill one), but it's guaranteed to bring out the inner Tarzan in even the most obstinate city-slicker.

KAKAMEGA FOREST

» **Why Go** For the unique rainforest ecosystem with over 330 species of birds, 400 species of butterfly and seven different primate species (including the rare de Brazza's monkey).

» **When to Go** June, August and October, when many migrant bird species arrive; October also sees many wildflowers bloom.

» **Practicalities** As the northern section of the forest is managed by KWS and the southern section by the Forest Department, it's not possible to visit the whole park without paying both sets of admission charges.

Information

Kakamega Forest National Reserve (www.kws.go.ke; park admission adult/child US$20/10, vehicles KSh300) in the north is under the stewardship of KWS. Ranger guides cost the standard KSh1500 for up to six hours and can be arranged at the park gates. Alternatively, guides from the **Kakamega Forest Guide Association** (per person per hr KSh400) are also on hand to offer their services.

Kakamega Forest Reserve (park admission adult/child KSh600/150) in the southern Isecheno area is managed by the Forest Department, which maintains a small office with friendly staff next to the just as friendly **Kakamega Rainforest Tour Guides** (☎0729911386; kakamegaforestguides@yahoo.com; per person short/long walk KSh500/800).

Getting There & Away

Buyangu Area

Matatus heading north towards Kitale can drop you at the access road about 18km north of Kakamega town (KSh70). It is a well-signposted 2km walk from there to the park office and Udo's.

Isecheno Area

Regular matatus link Kakamega with Shinyalu (KSh70), but few go on to Isecheno. Shinyalu is also accessed by a rare matatu service from Khayega. From Shinyalu you'll probably need to take a boda-boda for KSh1000 to Isecheno.

Eldoret

☎053 / POP 167,000

The Maasai originally referred to this area as *eldore* (stony river) after the nearby Sosiani River, but this proved too linguistically challenging for the South African Voortrekkers who settled here in 1910 and they named their settlement Eldoret instead.

In 2008 Eldoret achieved notoriety when 35 people (mostly Kikuyus) were burnt alive in a church on the outskirts of town. This incident was the largest single loss of life during the 2007 post-election violence.

Today, Eldoret is a thriving service town straddling the Kenya–Uganda highway but, for the traveller, there is little to see, and even less to do. The highlight is a visit to the **Doinyo Lessos Creameries Cheese Factory** (Kenyatta St; ⏲8am-6pm) to stock up any one of 20 different varies of cheese.

Eldoret

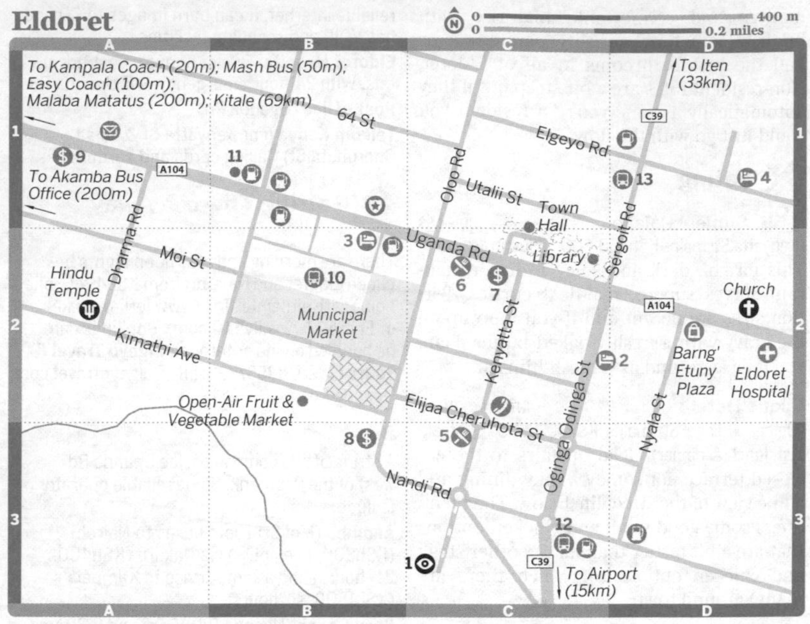

Eldoret

Sights

1 Doinyo Lessos Creameries Cheese Factory C3

Sleeping

2 Klique Hotel C2
3 White Castle Motel B2
4 White Highlands Inn D1

Eating

Klique Hotel .... (see 2)
5 Sunjeel Palace C3
6 Will's Pub & Restaurant C2

Information

7 Barclays Bank C2
Consani .... (see 6)
8 Postbank B3
9 Postbank A1

Transport

10 Bus & Matatu Stand B2
11 Elgeyo Travel & Tours B1
12 Local Matatus C3
13 Matatus to Iten & Kabarnet D1

Sleeping

White Castle Motel HOTEL $

(☎62773; whitecastle@deepafrica.com; Uganda Rd; s KSh1500-1800, tw KSh3000) While it has little in the way of frills or personality, the White Castle is a sound choice. It's centrally located, comparatively clean, the security is top-notch and the staff delightful. The street-level restaurant is similarly reliable and surprisingly, most things on its menu are actually available.

White Highlands Inn HOTEL $

(☎0734818955; Elgeyo St; s/d KSh1800/2500; P) In a quiet corner on the edge of town, this place offers good value. Its spacious rooms were so spotless we actually lay in the bathtub as opposed to just look at it wistfully. The whole complex is a bit rambling but retains a certain old-fashioned charm, and has a popular bar and less-popular restaurant.

Klique Hotel HOTEL $$

(☎0732060903; www.kliquehotel.com; Oginga Odinga St; s/d excl breakfast US$40/50) A modern and comfortable high-rise with brightly (sometimes garishly) painted rooms and the best bathrooms in all of Eldoret. Non-resident rates are a bit steep but if they automatically assume you're a resident you could just go with the flow...

Eating

TOP CHOICE **Sunjeel Palace** INDIAN $$
(Kenyatta St; mains KSh450-600; ⏲lunch & dinner) This formal, dark and spicy Indian restaurant serves superb, real-deal curries. Portion sizes are decent and if you mop up all the gravy with a freshly baked butter naan, you'll be as rotund as Ganesh himself.

Klique Hotel INTERNATIONAL $
(Oginga Odinga St; mains KSh400-500; ⏲breakfast, lunch & dinner) Head upstairs to the enclosed terrace, for some swanky dining and a fine view of the street life below. The menu offers some good steak and chicken options that are a bit tastier than all the other steak and chicken options (of which there are many) around town.

Will's Pub & Restaurant INTERNATIONAL $
(Uganda Rd; mains KSh300-450; ⏲breakfast, lunch & dinner) Looks and feels like an English pub, with similarly heavyweight food – salads, pasta, steak and fried breakfasts. The big-screen TV makes it a great place for a cold beer, and the low-key vibe makes it a safe spot for solo female travellers.

Information

Barclays Bank (Uganda Rd) With ATM.

Consani (Uganda Rd; per hr KSh60) Besides reliable internet, it can burn images to CD and has VOIP and scanning facilities.

Eldoret Hospital One of Kenya's best hospitals. With 24-hour emergency. Off Uganda Rd.

Post office (Uganda Rd)

Telkom Kenya (cnr Kenyatta St & Elijaa Cheruhota St) Calling cards and cardphones.

Getting There & Away

Air

There are morning and afternoon flights between Eldoret and Nairobi (from KSh4940, one hour) with either **Jetlink** (www.jetlink.co.ke) or **Fly540** (www.fly540.com). Bookings can be handled online or through **Elgeyo Travel & Tours** (☎20733557798; info@elgeyotravel.com; Uganda Rd).

Bus

A string of bus companies line Uganda Rd west of the Postbank. Some reliable operators include:

Akamba (Moi St) 10pm buses to Nairobi (KSh800, five hours) via Nakuru (KSh400, 2¾ hours) and a 1am service to Kampala (KSh1500, six hours).

Easy Coach (Uganda Rd) 10am and 9.30pm buses to Nairobi (KSh1100) via Nakuru (KSh600).

Kampala Coach (Uganda Rd) Noon and midnight buses to Kampala (KSh1800) and a 6pm coach to Kigali (KSh3300, 14 hours).

Mash Bus (Uganda Rd) Direct bus to Mombasa (KSh1600, 12 hours, 5pm).

Matatu

The main matatu stand is in the centre of town by the municipal market although some local matatus and more Kericho services leave from

MATUTUS FROM ELDORET

DESTINATION	FARE (KSH)	DURATION (HR)
Iten	100	1
Kabarnet	300	2
Kakamega	250	2
Kericho	350-400	3
Kisumu	350-400	3
Kitale	200	1¼
Nairobi	700	6
Nakuru	300	2¾
Nyahururu	450	3½

Nandi Rd. Irregular matatus to Iten and Kabarnet leave from Sergoit Rd. Further west on Uganda Rd, matatus leave for Malaba on the Uganda border.

Getting Around

A matatu to or from the airport costs KSh70, and a taxi will cost around KSh1000 to KSh1500.

Kitale

☎054 / POP 86,100

Agricultural Kitale is a small and friendly market town with a couple of interesting museums and a bustling market. If you're travelling further afield, it makes an ideal base for explorations of Mt Elgon and Saiwa Swamp National Parks. It also serves as the take-off point for a trip up to the western side of Lake Turkana.

Sights & Activities

Kitale Museum MUSEUM
(☎30996; A1 Hwy; adult/child KSh500/250; ⏰8am-6pm) Founded on the collection of butterflies, birds and ethnographic memorabilia left to the nation in 1967 by the late Lieutenant Colonel Stoneham, this museum has an interesting range of ethnographic displays of the Pokot, Akamba, Marakwet and Turkana peoples. There's also any number of stuffed dead things shot by various colonial types. The best thing here is the small **nature trail** that leads through some not-quite-virgin rainforest at the back of the museum.

FREE **Olof Palme Agroforestry Centre** GARDENS
(A1 Hwy; ⏰8am-5pm) The Olof Palme Agroforestry Centre is a Swedish-funded program aimed at educating local people about the protection and rehabilitation of the environment by integrating trees into farming systems. The project includes a small demonstration farm and agroforestry plot, an information centre and an arboretum.

Sleeping

Bongo Lodge HOTEL $
(☎32520593; Moi Ave; s/d/tw excl breakfast KSh800/800/900) Stop wasting time and come straight to Bongo Lodge if you want to get your hands on the best budget beds in town. All rooms have bathrooms and are scrupulously clean (well at least by Kenyan standards; by Swiss standards they're filthy).

Jehova Jireh Hotel HOTEL $$
(☎31752; s excl breakfast KSh1500, tw excl breakfast KSh2200-3500) A solid midrange choice that boasts twin rooms that are spacious, quiet and clean and, don't worry, it's not as God-fearing as it sounds. There's an excellent downstairs restaurant that serves food later than most.

Kahuruko Bar & Lodge HOTEL $
(☎0750107384; kahurukoh@yahoo.com; Mt Elgon Rd; s excl breakfast KSh600) These small but spiffy rooms are a bargain and well suited to solo travellers and feuding couples as they only have singles. You can sink your teeth into some decent dead cow at the *nyama choma* restaurant downstairs (half a kilo KSh260).

Eating & Drinking

TOP CHOICE **Coffee Shop** INTERNATIONAL $
(A1 Hwy; mains KSh200-400; ⏰breakfast & lunch) While it may not be the first choice for many locals, the Coffee Shop provides welcome relief from the chicken and chips menus found elsewhere. Some of the tempting treats include Mexican style fajitas and enchiladas, European desserts (including a warm chocolate brownie with ice cream), cheeseburgers, filtered coffee and sweet honey *lassis* (an Indian yoghurt drink).

Iroko Boulevard Restaurant KENYAN $
(Askari Rd; mains KSh170-250; ⏰breakfast, lunch & dinner) It's got style, it's got glamour, it's got big-city aspirations and it's totally unexpected in Kitale. With cheap dishes that include a different African special every day and an old Morris car hanging from the ceiling, this is the most popular place to eat in town.

Corner Café KENYAN $
(Kenyatta St; mains KSh110-180; ⏰breakfast & lunch) This cheap and cheerful local eatery is located inside an old colonial building and it's a magnet for a steady stream of locals after no nonsense African staples at low prices.

Information

Barclays Bank (Bank St) With ATM. Other banks are next door.

Cyber Cafe (Kenyatta St; internet per hr KSh60)

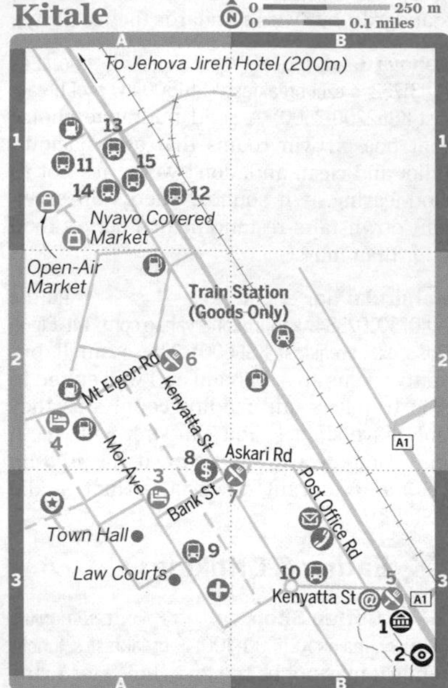

Kitale

Sights

1 Kitale Museum B3
2 Olof Palme Agroforestry Centre B3

Sleeping

3 Bongo Lodge A3
4 Kahuruko Bar & Lodge A2

Eating

5 Coffee Shop B3
6 Corner Café A2
7 Iroko Boulevard Restaurant B3

Information

8 Barclays Bank A3

Transport

9 Akamba A3
10 Easy Coach B3
11 Main Bus & Matatu Park A1
12 Matatus to Eldoret and Nairobi A1
13 Matatus to Kapenguria A1
14 Matatus to Kisumu & Kakamega A1
15 Matatus to Marich Pass A1

Post office (Post Office Rd)

Telkom Kenya (Post Office Rd) Calling cards and cardphones.

Getting There & Away

Matatus, buses and Peugeots are grouped by destination, and spread in and around the main bus and matatu park.

Regular matatus run to Endebess (KSh70, 45 minutes, change here for Mt Elgon National Park), Kapenguria (KSh120, 45 minutes, change here to continue north to Marich), Eldoret (KSh200 to KSh230, 1¼ hours), Kakamega (KSh250, 2½ hours) and Kisumu (KSh450, four hours).

Most bus companies have offices around the bus station and serve Eldoret (KSh200, one hour), Nakuru (KSh600, 3½ hours), Nairobi (KSh700, seven hours) and Lodwar (KSh800, 8½ hours) each day.

Akamba (Moi Ave) runs buses from outside its office to Nairobi at 8pm (KSh1000, seven hours).

Easy Coach (Kenyatta St) does the same (Nairobi, KSh1200) but there is also an 8.30am departure that calls into Nakuru (KSh900, 3½ hours).

Saiwa Swamp National Park

This small and rarely visited **park** (0717672121; www.kws.go.ke, saiwapark@kws.go.ke; adult/child US$20/10; 6am-6pm), north of Kitale, is a real treat. Originally set up to preserve the habitat of Kenya's only population of **sitatunga antelope**, the 15.5-sq-km reserve is also home to blue, vervet and de Brazza's monkeys and some 370 species of birds. The fluffy black-and-white colobus and the impressive crowned crane are both present, and you may see the Cape clawless and spot-throated otters. At the park headquarters, ask to be introduced to the diminutive antelope, Ippo, an orphaned Maxwell's duiker.

The park is only accessible on foot and walking trails skirt the swamp, duckboards go right across it, and there are some rickety **observation towers**.

Guides are not compulsory although your experience will be greatly enhanced by taking one. Ours, **Chesoli Lutah** (0726427040; lutahchesoli@yahoo.com), could rattle off the names and characteristics of any plant or bird we cared to ask about.

Sleeping

Public Campsite CAMPGROUND $
(www.kws.go.ke; camping US$15; P) A lovely site with flush toilets, lock boxes, showers and two covered cooking *bandas*.

Sitatunga Treetop House HUT $$
(www.kws.go.ke; tree house US$50; P) Perched on stilts overlooking the Saiwa swamp, this KWS tree house can sleep three in a double and single bed. It has electricity, bedding and mosquito nets.

Sirikwa Safaris GUESTHOUSE $$
(0737133170; sirikwabarnley@gmail.com; camping KSh500, tents excl breakfast from KSh1200, farmhouse with shared bathroom excl breakfast s/d KSh4000/5600) Owned and run by the family that started Saiwa, this beautiful old farmhouse is 11km from the swamp. You can chose between camping in the grounds, sleeping in a well-appointed safari tent or, best of all, opting for one of the two bedrooms full of *National Geographic* magazines, old ornaments and antique sinks. Wholesome, though fairly expensive, home-cooked food and excursions, including ornithological tours of the Cherangani Hills and Saiwa Swamp, can all be arranged here.

Getting There & Away

The park is 18km northeast of Kitale; take a matatu towards Kapenguria (KSh120, 30 minutes) and get out at the second signposted turn-off (KSh70, 15 minutes), from where it is a 5km walk or KSh70 *moto-taxi* (motorcycle taxi) ride.

Mt Elgon National Park

Straddling the Ugandan border and peaking with Koitoboss (4187m), Kenya's second-highest peak, and Uganda's Wagagai (4321m), the mist-shrouded slopes of Mt Elgon are a sight indeed. With rainforest at the base, the vegetation changes as you ascend to bamboo jungle and finally alpine moorland featuring the giant groundsel and giant lobelia plants.

Common animals include buffaloes, bushbucks (usually grazing on the airstrip near Cholim gate), olive baboons, giant forest hogs and duikers. The lower forests are the habitat of the black-and-white colobus, and blue and de Brazza's monkeys. There are more than 240 species of birds here, including red-fronted parrots, Ross's turacos and casqued hornbills. On the peaks you may even see a lammergeier raptor gliding through the thin air.

Sights & Activities

Elkony Caves CAVE
Four main lava tubes (caves) are open to visitors: **Kitum**, **Chepnyalil**, **Mackingeny** and **Rongai**. While rarely seen, **elephants** are known to 'mine' for salt from the walls of the caves. Kitum holds your best hope for glimpsing them (particularly before dawn in the dry season), but sadly the number of these saline-loving creatures has declined over the years, mainly due to incursions by Ugandan poachers. Nonetheless, a torch-light inspection will soon reveal their handiwork in the form of tusking – the groves and gouges made by their tusks during the digging process.

Mackingeny, with a **waterfall** cascading across the entrance, is the most spectacular of the caves and has colonies of large fruit **bats** and smaller horseshoe bats towards the rear. If you plan on visiting the bats, be sure to bring whatever kind of footwear you feel will cope well with 100 years of accumulated dusty bat shit.

The caves are a 6km drive or walk (one way) from Chorlim gate.

MT ELGON NATIONAL PARK

» **Why Go** For some superb overnight and half-day treks, some to caves occasionally visited by salt-loving elephants.

» **When to Go** It's extremely wet most of the year; serious trekkers should visit between December and February when it's at its driest.

» **Practicalities** The easiest section of the park to visit is the area accessed via Chorlim gate, from where you can walk or drive to the caves and surrounding forest. Waterproof gear and warm clothing is essential; altitude may also be a problem for some people. Check the security situation with **KWS headquarters** (kws@kws.org), **Nairobi** (020-600800) or **Mt Elgon National Park** (0538005393) before you plan anything. Crossing into Uganda wasn't permitted at the time of research.

Mt Elgon National Park

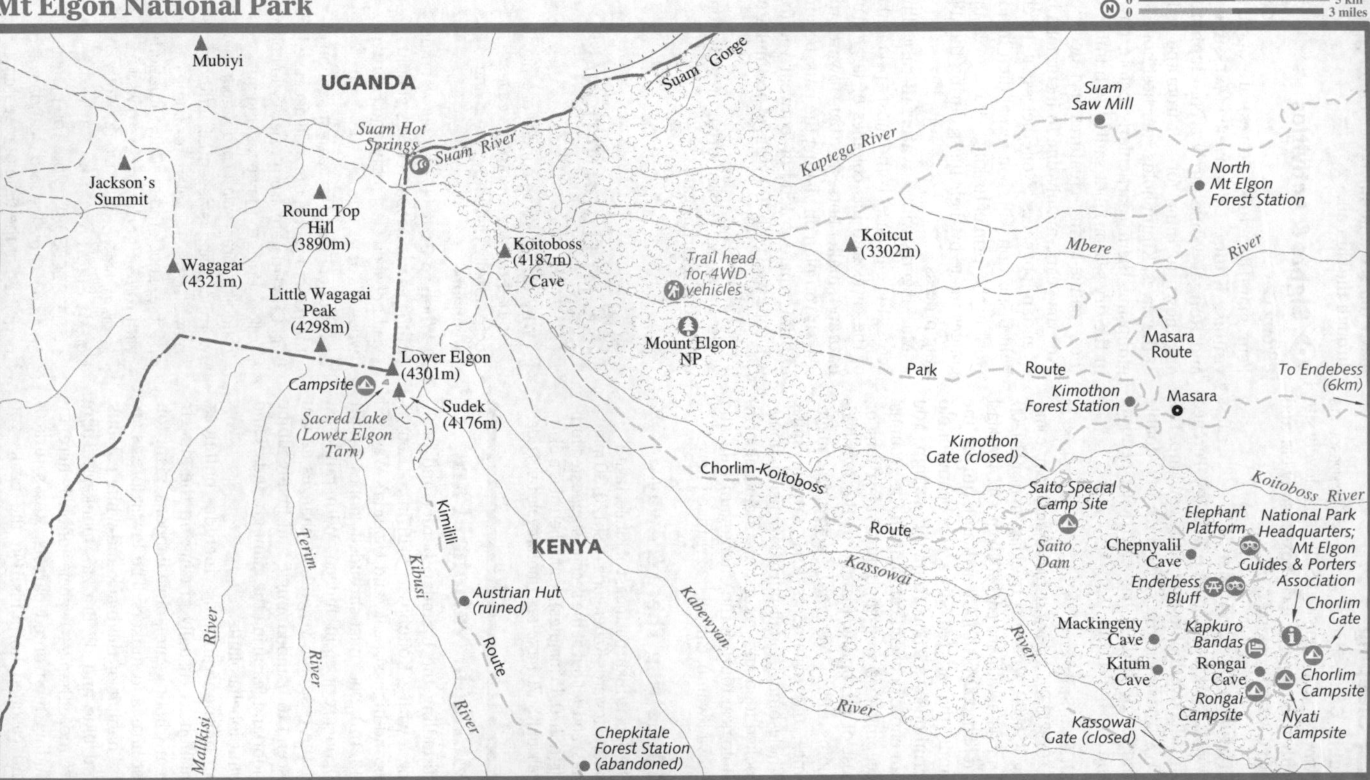
0 5 km
0 3 miles
Mubiyi
UGANDA
Suam Gorge
Suam Saw Mill
Suam Hot Springs
Suam River
Kaptega River
North Mt Elgon Forest Station
Jackson's Summit
Round Top Hill (3890m)
Koitoboss (4187m)
Cave
Trail head for 4WD vehicles
Koitcut (3302m)
Mbere River
Wagagai (4321m)
Little Wagagai Peak (4298m)
Mount Elgon NP
Masara Route
Park Route
To Endebess (6km)
Lower Elgon (4301m)
Campsite
Sudek (4176m)
Sacred Lake (Lower Elgon Tarn)
Kimothon Forest Station
Masara
Kimothon Gate (closed)
Chorlim-Koitoboss Route
Koitoboss River
Saito Special Camp Site
Saito Dam
Elephant Platform
National Park Headquarters; Mt Elgon Guides & Porters Association
Chepnyalil Cave
Enderbess Bluff
Chorlim Gate
KENYA
Kimilili Route
Kibusi River
Terim River
Mallkisi River
Kassowai River
Kabewyan River
Austrian Hut (ruined)
Mackingeny Cave
Kapkuro Bandas
Kitum Cave
Rongai Cave
Chorlim Campsite
Rongai Campsite
Nyati Campsite
Kassowai Gate (closed)
Chepkitale Forest Station (abandoned)

Koitoboss Trek HIKING

Allow at least four days for any round trips, and two or three days for any direct ascent of **Koitoboss** from the Chorlim gate. Once you reach the summit, there are a number of interesting options for the descent. You can descend northwest into the crater to **Suam Hot Springs**. Alternatively you could go east around the crater rim and descend the **Masara Route**, which leads to the small village of Masara on the eastern slopes of the mountain (about 25km) and then returns to Endebess. Or you can head southwest around the rim of the crater (some very hard walking) to **Lower Elgon Tarn**, where you can camp before ascending **Lower Elgon Peak** (4301m).

If all of this sounds too tiring, you'll be pleased to know that it's possible to get within 4km of the summit with a 4WD in decent weather.

Sleeping

Camping CAMPGROUND $

(www.kws.go.ke; camping US$15) If you're trekking, your only option is to camp. The fee is the same whether you drop tent in the official campsites (Chorlim, Nyati and Rongai) or on any old flat spot during your trek.

Kapkuro Bandas BANDA $

(www.kws.go.ke; per banda US$25; P) These excellent stone *bandas* can sleep three people in two beds and have simple bathrooms and small, fully equipped kitchen areas.

Information

Mt Elgon Guides & Porters Association (0733919347) is a cooperative of six guides and 10 porters based at the KWS headquarters. Their services (per day guide/porter/cook KSh1500/1000/700) can be booked through KWS.

Mt Elgon National Park (www.kws.go.ke; park admission adult/child US$25/15, vehicles from KSh300; 6am-6pm) It's possible to walk unescorted but due to the odd elephant and buffalo you will need to sign a waiver to do so. KWS produces a 1:35,000 map of the park that is sold at Chorlim gate.

Getting There & Away

From Kitale, catch an Endebess-bound matatu (KSh70, 45 minutes) to the park junction, from where it is a 15-minute motorbike taxi (KSh100) ride to the park gate. Be sure to grab your driver's phone number so you can contact him for a ride back to Endebess.

CENTRAL HIGHLANDS

The Central Highlands are the fertile, mist- and rain-fattened breadbasket of the nation and the green-girt, red-dirt spiritual heartland of Kenya's largest tribe, the Kikuyu. This is the land the Mau Mau fought for, the land the colonists coveted and the land whose natural, cyclical patterns define the lives of the country's largest rural population as they tend their *shambas* (small plots) in its valleys.

The prime attraction here is Kirinyaga, the Mountain of Mysteries (or Ostriches, depending on who's translating). Better known as Mt Kenya, this icy massif dominates the small towns scattered in its shadow and looms large near some of the nation's most stunning, and least visited, national parks.

Southwest of Mt Kenya, some of the oldest mountains on the continent, the Aberdare Range, help bolster the region's reputation as Kenya's premier trekking destination.

Nyeri & Around

061 / POP 98,910

Nyeri is sort of the epitome of a busy Kikuyu market town, and is as welcoming and bustling as the Central Highlands gets. With that said, there's not much reason to linger for more than a day or two unless you have a thing for chaotic open-air bazaars and the mad energy of Kikuyu and white Kenyans

WEST TO UGANDA

There are two main border crossing points into Uganda: **Malaba** and **Busia**. Both are generally pain-free as Ugandan (or Kenyan) visas are available on arrival (see p369 for further information on visa requirements).

Both towns have a couple of banks where you can exchange cash but unless you're a fan of bureaucracy, it is easier to use one of the numerous moneychangers prowling around. Just make sure you know the exchange rate beforehand and count your money carefully.

The Kenyan border is open 24 hours, but we've heard the Ugandan one runs to a somewhat more 'flexible' timetable, so try to arrive in daylight hours.

Central Highlands

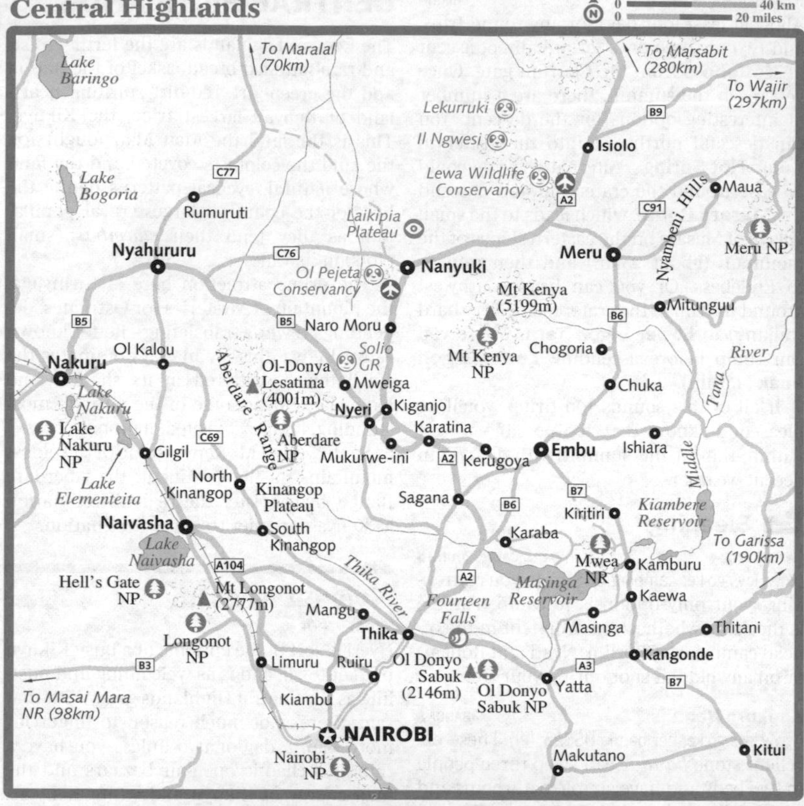

selling maize, bananas, arrowroot, coffee and macadamia nuts. Boy Scout founder Lord Baden-Powell, who died here in 1941, might beg to differ. He once wrote, 'The nearer to Nyeri, the nearer to bliss.'

Sights & Activities

TOP CHOICE Solio Game Reserve WILDLIFE RESERVE
(Map p288; ☎55271; B5 Hwy; adult/child/guide/vehicle KSh2000/1000/500/500) This family-run, private 17,000-acre reserve 22km north of Nyeri, is an important breeding centre for **black rhinos** and many of the horned beasts you see wandering national parks were actually born here. The physical contours of the park, which run between clumps of yellow-fever acacia, wide skies and wild marsh, are lovely in and of themselves. Self-drive safaris are permitted but you'll need to be accompanied by a Solio guide (KSh500).

Baden-Powell Museum MUSEUM
(admission KSh250; ⏲opened on request) Lord Baden-Powell, the founder of the Boy Scout Association, spent his last three years at Paxtu cottage in the Outspan Hotel. Paxtu is now a museum filled with scouting scarves and paraphernalia. The young woman next to Baden-Powell in the photographs isn't his granddaughter but his wife. Famed tiger-hunter Jim Corbett later occupied the grounds. The museum is a short (1km) walk west from the town centre, in the grounds of the Outspan Hotel.

Baden-Powell's Grave CEMETERY
(B5 Hwy; admission Ksh250; ⏲8.30am-5pm) The scoutmaster's grave is tucked behind **St Peter's Church,** facing Mt Kenya and marked with the Scouts trail sign for 'I have gone home'. His more famous Westminster Abbey tomb is empty.

Tours

Bongo Asili Travel TOURS
(☎0700391203; www.bongoasilitravel.com; Kanisa Rd; ⏰9am-5pm Mon-Sat) The only locally based tour operator, Bongo Asili can arrange safaris to Solio Game Reserve, Aberdare National Park and multiday excursions further abroad.

Sleeping

TOP CHOICE **Sandai Guesthouse** GUESTHOUSE $$$
(☎0721656699; www.africanfootprints.de; camping KSh500, s/d/tw full board US$130/220/220, cottages US$80; P) Fourteen kilometres northwest of town, Sandai is run by the effervescent Petra Allmendinger, whose enthusiasm and warm welcome make this a great weekend escape from Nairobi's bustle or for those looking for something a little more personal than what is on offer elsewhere. Accommodation is either in the extremely cosy lodge, where you will feel like part of the family, or in self-contained cottages that can accommodate up to six. Horse riding, nature walks (the guesthouse's guide, Sammy, is an excellent birder) and wildlife drives can all be organised here.

Green Hills Hotel HOTEL $$
(☎2030604; www.greenhills.co.ke; Bishop Gatimu Rd; s KSh4500-5600, d KSh6900-9100, ste KSh18,000; P) The best deal in town is actually a little way out of Nyeri. The small drive is worth it for the palm-lined, poolside ambience (nonguests KSh300) and general sense of serenity.

Ibis Hotel HOTEL $
(☎2034858; kihuria@ibishotel.co.ke; Kanisa Rd; s/d/tw excl breakfast KSh1000/1200/1600) Located in a building with a surprisingly grand facade (it's not that opulent on the inside), Ibis has comfortable and clean rooms with brilliant power-showers.

White Rhino Hotel HOTEL $$
(☎0726967315; www.whiterhinohotel.com; Kanisa Rd; s/d/tw KSh9600/10,800/14,000; P) The White Rhino had fallen into disrepair, but since its remodelling in 2011 now boasts smart rooms that are polished to an inch of their lives and swanky, tiled bathrooms. With three bars and two restaurants, this is the top hotel in the city centre.

Outspan Hotel HOTEL $$$
(☎2032424, Nairobi 020-4452095, www.aberdaresafarihotels.com; s full board US$220-275, d full board $299-432, cottages US$464; P) This rather gorgeous lodge was last decorated in the '50s, when wood panelling was the height of interior design. The dining room is a cross between Hogwarts and a colonial retreat. Nineteen of the 34 standard rooms have cosy fireplaces, and all have a whiff of historical class. A Kikuya cultural group performs here daily at 1.45pm (nonguests adult/child US$10/5).

Eating

Green Hills Hotel INTERNATIONAL $
(Bishop Gatimu Rd; mains/buffets KSh600/650; ⏰breakfast, lunch & dinner) As with accommodation, so with food: Green Hills dominates again. The full buffet (when numbers permit) is an impressive piece of work, with some tasty mixed-grill options done up in a satisfyingly fancy fashion. Steaks are tender and come sizzling on a platter with a good mix of vegies.

Rayjo's Café KENYAN $
(Kimathi Way; meals KSh50-140; ⏰lunch & dinner) This canteen is usually packed with customers, including bus and matatu drivers, notoriously good judges of cheap places to eat.

Raybells INTERNATIONAL $
(Kimathi Way; meals KSh120-400; ⏰breakfast, lunch & dinner) Pretty much anything you want to eat (well, anything Kenyan or Western), from pizza to *nyama choma*, is available and cooked passably well here. You may want to avoid the fresh juice as it has tap water added to it.

Drinking

Green Oaks PUB
(off Kimathi Way) The friendliest bar in town, usually with European football on the box, but like every other joint, it gets rowdy as the night wears on. Teetotallers will appreciate the balcony's fine view over the taxi stands and the warming chai on any of Nyeri's many rainy days.

Julie's Coffee Shop CAFE
(Kanisa Rd; snacks KSh35-80; ⏰breakfast & lunch;) The best (and by best, we mean only) place in town for genuine espresso coffee and free wi-fi.

Kifaru BAR
(White Rhino; Kenyatta Rd, ⏰11am-3am) The largest of White Rhino's three bars, Kifaru doubles as a spacious, open-air restaurant and late nightclub. The nightly DJ plays an eclectic mix of African and Western pop.

Nyeri

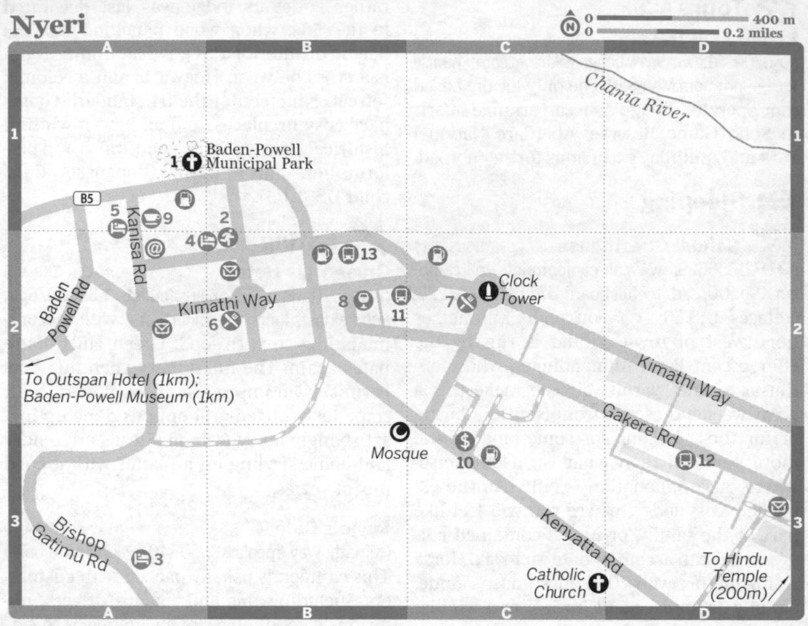

Nyeri

Sights

Baden-Powell's Grave .... (see 1)
1 St Peter's Church A1

Activities, Courses & Tours

2 Bongo Asili Travel B2

Sleeping

3 Green Hills Hotel A3
4 Ibis Hotel B2
5 White Rhino Hotel A1

Eating

Green Hills Hotel .... (see 3)
6 Raybells B2
7 Rayjo's Café C2

Drinking

8 Green Oaks B2
9 Julie's Coffee Shop A1
Kifaru .... (see 5)

Information

10 Barclays Bank C3

Transport

11 Local Matatus B2
12 Lower Bus Stand D3
13 Upper Bus Stand B2

Information

Barclays Bank (Kenyatta Rd) One of several banks around town with an ATM and which exchanges cash.

Villa Cyber (Kanisa Rd; per hr KSh30) Decent, fast connection.

Getting There & Away

The **upper bus stand** deals with sporadic buses and a plethora of matatus to destinations north and west of Nyeri including Nanyuki (KSh150, one hour), Nyahururu (KSh280, 1¼ hours) and Nakuru (KSh450, 2½ hours).

From the **lower bus stand** matatus head in all directions south and east including Thika (KSh250, two hours) and Nairobi (KSh350, 2½ hours).

Some **local matatus** are also found on Kimathi Way.

Aberdare National Park

While there's plenty of reason to wax rhapsodic over herds of wildlife thundering over an open African horizon, there's also something to be said for the soil-your-pants shock of seeing an elephant thunder out of bush that was, minutes before, just plants.

And that's why people love Aberdare National Park. Camera reflexes are tested as the abundant wildlife pops unexpectedly out of bushes, including elephants, buffaloes, black rhinos, spotted hyenas, bongo antelope, bush pigs, black servals and rare black leopards. And baboons. Lots and lots of baboons.

The park has two major environments: an eastern hedge of thick rainforest and waterfall-studded hills known as the Salient, and the Kinangop plateau, an open tableland of coarse moors that huddles under cold mountain breezes.

Ten years in the making and completed in 2009, a 400km-long electric fence now completely encircles the park. Powered by solar panels, the fence is designed to reduce human–animal conflict by keeping would-be poachers and cattle on one side and marauding wildlife on the other.

Sights & Activities

Trekking HIKING

To trek within the park requires advance permission from the warden at park headquarters, who may (depending on where you plan to walk) insist on providing an **armed ranger** (half-/full day KSh1500/3000) to guide and protect you against inquisitive wildlife.

Northern Moorland

The high moorland and four main peaks (all 3500m to 4000m) are excellent trekking spots; the tallest mountain in the park is **Ol Donyo Lesatima** (4000m), a popular bag for those on the East African mountain circuit. Between Honi Campsite and Elephant Ridge is the site of the **hideout** of Mau Mau leader Dedan Kimathi, who used these mountains as a base.

Kinangop Plateau

From the dirt track that connects the Ruhuruini and Mutubio West gates, it's possible to walk to the top of **Karura Falls** and watch Karura Stream slide over the rocky lip into the 272m abyss. Weather permitting, you may be able to make out the misty veil of Kenya's tallest cascade, the **Gura Falls** (305m), in the distance. Unfortunately there are no tracks to Gura Falls or the base of Karura Falls. You can, however, visit the far smaller **Chania Falls** further north.

Wildlife Drives DRIVING TOUR

The park is home to Kenya's second-largest population of black rhinos, but due to the dense forest, animal sightings are scarcer here than down on the open savannah. If you're lucky, you may spot one of the melanistic (black) leopards that are said to prowl the forest's shadowy depths. The Outspan Hotel (p285) runs two-hour wildlife drives here for US$45 per person (minimum of four).

Sleeping

Kiandongoro Fishing Lodge CABIN $$

(www.kws.go.ke; cottages US$180) Two large stone houses sleep seven people each and command a good view of the moors that sweep into the Gura River. There are two bathrooms in each house, along with gas-powered kitchens, paraffin cookers and fireplaces.

Tusk Camp CABIN $$

(www.kws.go.ke; cottages US$120) Two dark and cosy alpine cottages located near Ruhuruini gate sleep four people each. The lounge area is comfy, with great views (if the fog hasn't rolled in), and plenty of rhinos around to boot. Hot water, blankets, kerosene lamps, a gas cooker and some utensils are provided.

ABERDARE NATIONAL PARK

» **Why Go** Two interesting ecosystems to explore: a dense rainforest and high, Afro-alpine moorlands with great trekking possibilities and some spectacular waterfalls.

» **When to Go** The park is cooler and mistier than you would expect. The driest months are January to February and June to September.

» **Practicalities** During the rains, roads are impassable and the numbered navigation posts in the Salient are often difficult to follow. The most straightforward visit is to drive between the Ruhuruini and Mutubio West gates.

Aberdare National Park

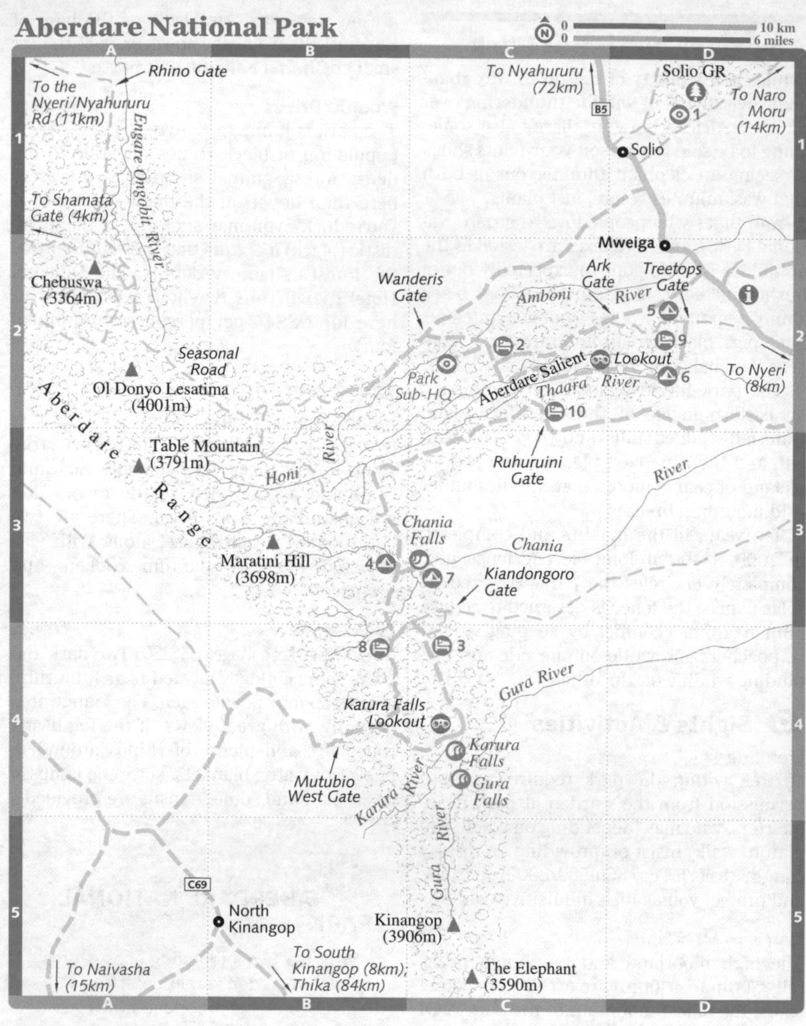

Aberdare National Park

Sights

1 Solio Game Reserve D1

Sleeping

2 Ark C2
3 Kiandongoro Fishing Lodge C4
4 Public Campsite B3
5 Public Campsite D2
6 Public Campsite D2
7 Public Campsite C3
8 Sapper Hut B4
9 Treetops D2
10 Tusk Camp C2

Ark HOTEL $$$

(☎in Nairobi 0737799990; www.arkkenya.com; s/d/tr US$210/288/340) The Ark is more modern (1960s as opposed to 1950s chic) and roomier than Treetops, and has a lounge that overlooks a waterhole. Watch buffalo as you sip wine in a moulded chair lifted from *Austin Powers* and you'll have an idea of the ambience. An excellent walkway leads over a particularly dense stretch of the Salient, and from here and the waterhole lounge you can spot elephants, rhinos, buffaloes and hyenas.

RIGHT ROYAL CONNECTIONS

Trivia for royal-philes: Treetops isn't actually the spot where Princess Elizabeth became Queen Elizabeth II. Yes, Liz was sleeping in Treetops when George VI died in 1952, but in 1954 Mau Mau guerrillas blew the original lodge to twigs; three years later, a much larger rendition was built on the opposite side of the waterhole. 'Every time like the first time', goes the Treetops slogan, and we agree: sleeping here feels like travelling back to the day that the 25-year-old Elizabeth went to bed a princess, and awoke a queen.

Fifty-eight years later, another young lady, this time a commoner, answered 'yes' to a question that will eventually see her crowned the Queen of the Commonwealth. On the verandah of a small log cabin, high on the flanks of Mt Kenya, Prince William asked Kate Middleton to be his wife. Under the guise of fishing on Lake Alice, William and Kate travelled to the remote Rutundu cabins where he popped the big question. And so it is, that while the fishing trip was a complete failure, Prince William still managed quite the catch.

Sapper Hut BANDA $
(www.kws.go.ke; bandas US$50) A simple *banda,* with an open fire, two beds and a hot-water boiler, overlooking a lovely waterfall on the Upper Magura River. It's best to bring your own gear.

Public Campsites CAMPGROUND $
(www.kws.go.ke; camping US$15) Basic sites with minimal facilities – some have water.

Treetops HISTORIC HOTEL $$$
(☎in Nairobi 020-4452095; www.aberdaresafarihotels.com; s/tw without bathroom full board US$328/415; @) Treetops is sold as part of a package with the Outspan Hotel in Nyeri. Rooms are small and decorated in mid-20th century wood panelling/floral linens chic, but there is excellent wildlife viewing and a sense of rusticity (and a little neglect) pervades. High rollers can splurge for the Queen Elizabeth 'suite', which has a picture of the monarch and – wait for it – a *double bed!*

Information

To enter the **park** (www.kws.go.ke; adult/child US$50/25) through the Treetops or Ark gates, ask permission at **national park headquarters** (☎061-2023/9409, Mweiga; ⏰6am-6pm). Excellent 1:25,000 maps are available at the gates.

Getting There & Away

Access roads from the B5 Hwy to the Wanderis, Ark, Treetops and Ruhuruini gates are in decent shape. Keep in mind that it takes a few hours to get from the Salient to the moorlands and vice versa.

Nyahururu (Thomson's Falls)

☎065 / POP 24,750

This unexpectedly attractive town leaps out of the northwest corner of the highlands and makes a decent base for exploring the western edge of the Aberdares. Its former namesake, Thomson's Falls, are beautiful in their own right and offer excellent trekking options on small forested tracks that lead to friendly, farming villages. At 2360m, this is Kenya's highest major town, with a cool and invigorating climate.

Sights & Activities

Thomson's Falls WATERFALL
(adult/child KSh200/100) Set back in an evergreen river valley and studded with sharp rocks and screaming baboons, the white cataracts that plummet over 72m are Nyahururu's undeniable main attraction. A fairly straight path approaches the falls over a series of stone steps and leads to the bottom of the ravine. The dramatic sight of looking up at the falls as baboons pad over the surrounding cliffs is worth the drenching you get from the fall's spray. There are some fantastic **walks** downstream through the forested valley of the Ewaso Narok River and upstream a couple of kilometres to one of the highest **hippo pools** in Kenya.

Don't sweat finding a guide; they will find you.

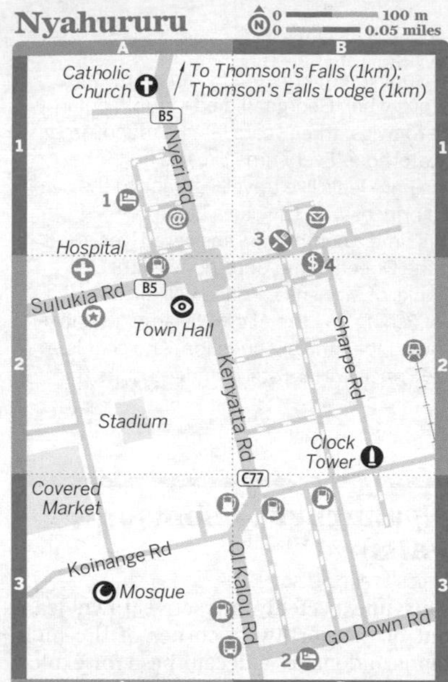

Nyahururu

Sleeping

1 Nyaki Hotel A1
2 Safari Lodge B3

Eating

Nyaki Hotel .... (see 1)
3 Savannah Green Hotel B1

Information

4 Barclays Bank B2

Sleeping

TOP CHOICE Safari Lodge HOTEL $
(☎2022334; Go Down Rd; s/d excl breakfast KSh500/1000; P) Clean toilets with *seats*; big, soft beds with couches in the rooms; a nice balcony; TV and a place to charge your phone – what did we do to deserve this luxury? Especially at this price, which makes Safari one of the best budget deals around.

Thomson's Falls Lodge HOTEL $$
(☎2022006; www.thomsonsfallslodge.com; off B5 Hwy; camping KSh500, s/d/tr KSh4100/5100/7700; P) The undisputed nicest splurge in the area sits right above the falls and does a great job of instilling that good old, 'I'm a colonial aristocrat on a hill country holiday' vibe. Rooms are spacious but cosy, thanks in no small part to the log fireplaces.

Nyaki Hotel HOTEL $
(☎2022313; off Nyeri Rd; s/tw excl breakfast KSh600/1800; P) This five-storey building hosts small but comfy singles and large, clean twins that have small separate lounges and reliable hot-water showers.

Eating & Drinking

It's best to eat early in Nyahururu; for reasons we couldn't fathom, most eateries were shutting shop by 7pm.

Thomson's Falls Lodge BUFFET $$
(off B5 Hwy; buffet breakfast/lunch/dinner KSh455/850/900; ⏲breakfast, lunch & dinner) This is the best (and only) place in town to go for a fancy feast. There's a set buffet for each of the day's three meals, and while they're pricey for this area, you'll walk away well stuffed and satisfied.

Savannah Green Hotel KENYAN $
(Sulukia Rd; mains KSh150-300; ⏲breakfast, lunch & dinner) There may not be any rooms at this 'hotel' but there's a decent restaurant with outdoor seating and a fine selection of all things fried or stewed. With huge portions and tempting, freshly squeezed juice, bring an appetite.

Nyaki Hotel KENYAN $
(off Nyeri Rd; mains KSh250-280; ⏲breakfast, lunch & dinner) Serves standard Kenyan fare in a standard Kenyan setting: bare bones, smiling service and about 100 watts away from being well lit.

Information

Barclays Bank (cnr Sulukia & Sharpe Rds) With ATM.

Clicks Cyber Cafe (Mimi Centre, Nyeri Rd; per hr KSh60)

Post office (Sulukia Rd)

Getting There & Away

Numerous matatus run to Nakuru (KSh150, 1¼ hours) and Nyeri (KSh280, 1¾ hours) until late afternoon. Less plentiful are services to Naivasha (KSh300, two hours), Nanyuki (KSh330, three hours) and Nairobi (KSh400, 3½ hours). The odd morning matatu reaches Maralal (KSh500, four hours).

Several early-morning buses also serve Nairobi (KsH350, three hours).

Mt Kenya National Park

Africa's second-highest mountain attracts spry trekkers, long, dramatic cloud cover and all the eccentricities of its mother continent in equal measure. Here, mere minutes from the equator, glaciers carve out the throne of Ngai, the old high god of the Kikuyu. To this day the tribe keeps its doors open to the face of the sacred mountain, and some still come to its lower slopes to offer prayers and the foreskins of their young men – this was the traditional place for holding circumcision ceremonies. Besides being venerated by the Kikuyu, Mt Kenya has the rare honour of being both a Unesco World Heritage Site and a Unesco Biosphere Reserve.

In the past, 12 glaciers wore Mt Kenya down to 5199m worth of dramatic remnants, but today it is the ice itself that is under threat, disappearing under increased temperatures and taking with them crystalline caves and snowy crevasses. That means the climb up the mountain is easier than it has ever been – but by no means does it mean the ascent is easy.

The highest peaks of Batian (5199m) and Nelion (5188m) can only be reached by mountaineers with technical skills, but Point Lenana (4985m), the third-highest peak, can be reached by trekkers and is the usual goal for most mortals. The views are awe-inspiring – when they're not hemmed in by opaque mist.

Environment

There are flora, fauna and ecosystems on the slopes of Mt Kenya that can't be found anywhere else in the country.

This extinct volcano accommodates, at various elevations, upland forest, bamboo forest (2500m), high-altitude equatorial heath (3000m to 3500m) and lower alpine moorland (3400m to 3800m), which includes several species of bright everlasting flowers. Some truly surreal plant life grows in the Afro-alpine zone (above 3500m) and the upper alpine zone (3800m to 4500m), including hairy carpets of tussock grass, the brushlike giant lobelias, or rosette plants, and the science-fiction-worthy *Senecio Brassica,* or giant groundsel, which looks like a bizarre cross between an aloe, a cactus and a dwarf. At the summit it's predominantly rock and ice, a landscape that possesses its own stark beauty, especially this close to the equator.

Unfortunately, there's more rock than ice these days. 'In 15 years I've seen all the glaciers move. I don't need crampons any more,' one guide told us. Warmer weather has led to disappearing glaciers, and ice climbing in Mt Kenya is largely finished. We've heard these conditions have led to drier rivers in the region, which makes sense as Mt Kenya is the country's most important permanent watershed.

In lower elevations large wildlife are around; you may need to clap and hoot as you trudge to stave off elephants and buffaloes. Rock hyraxes are common, as are, rather annoyingly, bees. Other animals, including Sykes's monkeys, Mackinder's eagle owls, waterbucks, leopards, hyenas and servals, tend to stay hidden in the thick brush of the lower forests.

Preparations

Safety

Many people ascend the mountain too quickly and suffer from headaches, nausea and other (sometimes more serious) effects of altitude sickness. By spending at least three nights on the ascent, you'll enjoy yourself more.

Unpredictable weather is another problem. The trek to Point Lenana isn't an easy hike and people die on the mountain every year.

MT KENYA NATIONAL PARK

» **Why Go** Awe-inspiring views from Africa's second-highest mountain, and with arguably better scenery than from Kilimanjaro.

» **When to Go** The climbing seasons are during the driest months: mid-January to late February, and late August to September.

» **Practicalities** Unless you're a seasoned trekker with high-altitude experience and a good knowledge of reading maps and using a compass, you'd be flirting with death by not taking a guide.

Mt Kenya National Park

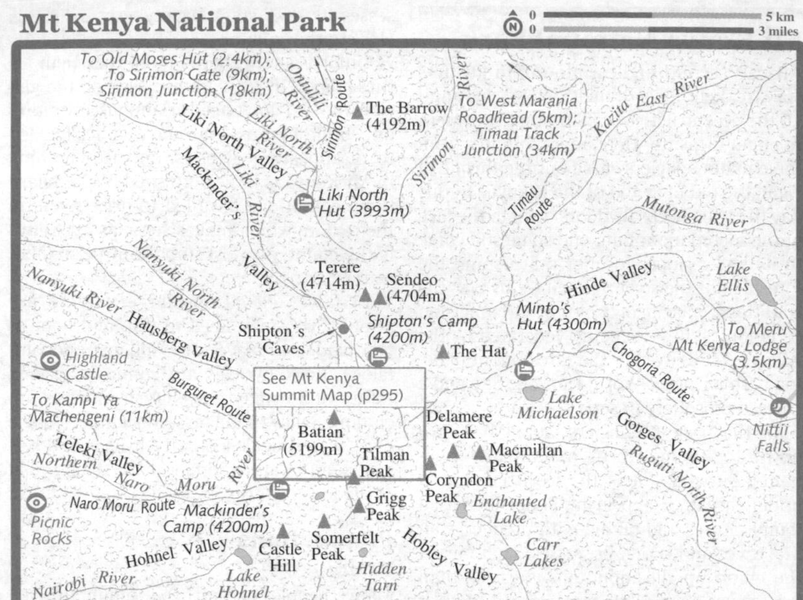

Clothing

Nightly temperatures near the summit often drop to below -10°C, so bring a good sleeping bag and a closed-cell foam mat or Therm-a-Rest if you're camping. A good set of warm clothes (wool or synthetics – never cotton, as it traps moisture) is equally important. As it can rain heavily any time of year, you'll need waterproof clothing (breathable fabric like Gore-Tex is best). A decent pair of boots and sandals or light shoes (for the evening when your boots get wet) are a great idea. At this altitude the sun can do some serious damage to your skin and eyes, so sunblock and sunglasses are also crucial items.

If a porter is carrying your backpack, always keep essential clothing (warm- and wet-weather gear) in your day pack because you may become separated for hours at a time.

Be wary of hypothermia and dehydration; fluids and warm clothing go a long way towards preventing both.

It's not a good idea to sleep in clothes you've worn during the day because the sweat your clothes absorbed keeps them moist at night, reducing their heat-retention capabilities.

Equipment

If you don't intend to stay in the huts along the way, you'll need a tent, stove, basic cooking equipment, utensils, a 3L water container (per person) and water-purifying tablets. Stove fuel in the form of petrol and kerosene (paraffin) is fairly easily found in towns, and methylated spirits is available in Nairobi, as are gas cartridges. Fires are prohibited in the open except in an emergency; in any case, there's no wood once you get beyond 3300m.

If you don't have your own equipment, items can be rented from the guiding associations listed in Organised Treks, p296. Prices vary but expect to pay in the vicinity of KSh500/200/150/300 for a two-person tent/sleeping bag/pair of boots/stove per day.

If you have a mobile phone, take it along; reception on the mountain's higher reaches is actually very good, and a link to the outside world is invaluable during emergencies.

Guides, Cooks & Porters

Having a porter for your gear is like travelling in a chauffeured Mercedes instead of a matatu. A good guide will help set a sustainable pace and hopefully dispense interesting information about Mt Kenya and its flora, fauna and wildlife. With both on your team, your appreciation of this mountain will be enhanced a hundredfold. If you hire a guide or porter who can also cook, you won't regret it.

The KWS now issues vouchers to all registered guides and porters, who should also hold identity cards; they won't be allowed into the park without them.

The cost of guides varies depending on the qualifications of the guide(s), whatever the last party paid and your own negotiating skills. You should expect to pay a minimum of US$20/18/15 per day for a guide/cook/porter.

These fees don't include park entry fees and tips, and the latter should only be paid for good service.

Food & Drink

In an attempt to reduce luggage, many trekkers exist entirely on canned and dried foods.

Increased altitude creates unique cooking conditions. The major consideration is that the boiling point of water is considerably reduced. At 4500m, for example, water boils at 85°C; this is too low to sufficiently cook rice or lentils (pasta is better) and you won't be able to brew a good cup of tea (instant coffee is the answer).

Take plenty of citrus fruits and/or citrus drinks as well as chocolate, sweets or dried fruit to keep your blood-sugar level up.

To avoid severe headaches caused by dehydration or altitude sickness, drink at least 3L of fluid per day and bring rehydration sachets. Water purification tablets, available at most chemists, aren't a bad idea either.

The Routes

There are at least seven different routes up Mt Kenya. Of those, we cover Naro Moru, the easiest and most popular, as well as Sirimon and Chogoria, which are excellent alternatives, and the exciting but demanding Summit Circuit, which circles Batian and Nelion, thus enabling you to mix and match ascending and descending routes.

As well as the sleeping options given for each route it is also possible to **camp** (www.kws.go.ke; camping US$15) anywhere on the mountain; the nightly fee is payable to KWS at any gate. Most people camp near the huts or bunk-houses, as there are often toilets and water nearby.

NARO MORU ROUTE

Although the least scenic, this is the most straightforward and popular route and is still spectacular.

Starting in Naro Moru town, the first part of the route takes you along a gravel road through farmlands for some 13km (all the junctions are signposted) to the start of the forest. Another 5km brings you to the park entry gate (2400m), from where it's 8km to the road head and the Met Station Hut (3000m), where you stay for the night and acclimatise.

On the second day, set off through the forest (at about 3200m) and Teleki Valley to the moorland around so-called **Vertical Bog**; expect the going here to be, well, boggy. At a ridge the route divides into two. You can either take the higher path, which gives better views but is often wet, or the lower, which crosses the Naro Moru River and continues gently up to Mackinder's Camp (4200m). This part of the trek should take about 4½ hours. Here you can stay in the dormitories or camp.

On the third day you can either rest at Mackinder's Camp to acclimatise or aim for **Point Lenana** (4895m). This stretch takes three to six hours, so it is common to leave around 2am to reach the summit in time for sunrise. From the bunk-house, continue past the ranger station to a fork. Keep right, and go across a swampy area, followed by a moraine, and then up a long scree slope – this is a long, hard slog. The KWS Austrian Hut (4790m) is three to four hours from Mackinder's and about one hour below the summit of Lenana, so it's a good place to rest before the final push.

The section of the trek from Austrian Hut up to Point Lenana takes you up a narrow rocky path that traverses the southwest ridge parallel to the Lewis Glacier, which has shrunk more than 100m since the 1960s. Be careful, as the shrinkage has created serious danger of slippage along the path. A final climb or scramble brings you up onto the peak. In good weather it's fairly straightforward, but in bad weather you shouldn't attempt the summit unless you're experienced in mountain conditions or have a guide.

Sleeping

There are three good bunk-houses along this route: **Met Station Hut** (Map p298; dm US$12) is at 3000m, **Mackinder's Camp** (Map p292; dm US$15) is at 4160m and **Austrian Hut** (Map p295; dm KSh500) is at 4790m. Beds in

Met Station and Mackinder's are harder to find, as they're booked through Naro Moru River Lodge (p297). If you're denied beds, you can still climb this route if you camp and carry all the appropriate equipment.

Those needing more luxury can doss in lovely, KWS-run **Batian Guest House** (Map p298; www.kws.go.ke; cottages US$180), which sleeps eight and is a kilometre from the Naro Moru gate.

SIRIMON ROUTE

A popular alternative to Naro Moru, Sirimon has better scenery, greater flexibility and a gentler rate of ascent but takes a day longer. It's well worth considering combining it with the Chogoria route for a six- to seven-day traverse that really brings out the best of Mt Kenya.

The trek begins at the Sirimon gate, 23km from Nanyuki, from where it's about a 9km walk through forest to Old Moses Hut (3300m), where you spend the first night.

On the second day you could head straight through the moorland for Shipton's Camp, but it is worth taking an extra acclimatisation day via **Liki North Hut** (Map p292; 3993m), a tiny place on the floor of a classic glacial valley. The actual hut is a complete wreck and meant for porters, but it's a good campsite with a toilet and stream nearby.

On the third day, head up the western side of Liki North Valley and over the ridge into Mackinder's Valley, joining the direct route about 1½ hours in. After crossing the Liki River, follow the path for another 30 minutes until you reach the bunk-house at Shipton's Camp (4200m), which is set in a fantastic location right below Batian and Nelion.

From Shipton's you can push straight for **Point Lenana** (4895m), a tough 3½- to five-hour slog via Harris Tarn and the tricky north-face approach, or take the Summit Circuit in either direction around the peaks to reach Austrian Hut (4790m), about one hour below the summit. The left-hand (east) route past Simba Col is shorter but steeper, while the right-hand (west) option takes you on the Harris Tarn trail nearer the main peaks.

From Austrian Hut take the standard southwest traverse up to Point Lenana; see p293. If you're spending the night here, it's worth having a wander around to catch the views up to Batian and down the Lewis Glacier into Teleki Valley.

Sleeping

Old Moses Hut (Map p298; dm US$12) at 3300m and **Shipton's Camp** (Map p292; dm US$12) at 4200m serve trekkers on this route. They're both booked through the Mountain Rock Lodge (p297).

Many trekkers acclimatise by camping at Liki North Hut. If you'd like a little more comfort, book into the excellent KWS **Sirimon Bandas** (Map p298; www.kws.go.ke; bandas US$80), which are located 9km from the Sirimon gate. Each *banda* sleeps four.

CHOGORIA ROUTE

This route crosses some of the most spectacular and varied scenery on Mt Kenya, and is often combined with the Sirimon route (usually as the descent). The main reason this route is more popular as a descent is the 29km bottom stage. While not overly steep, climbing up that distance is much harder than descending it.

The only disadvantage with this route is the long distance between Chogoria and the park gate. These days most people drive, although it's a beautiful walk through farmland, rainforest and bamboo to the park gate. Most people spend the first night here, either camping at the gate or staying nearby in Meru Mt Kenya Lodge (3000m).

On the second day, head up through the forest to the trailhead (camping is possible here). From here it's another 7km over rolling foothills to the Hall Tarns area and **Minto's Hut** (Map p292; 4300m). Like Liki North, this place is only intended for porters, but makes for a decent campsite. Don't use the tarns here to wash anything, as careless trekkers have already polluted them.

From here follow the trail alongside the stunning **Gorges Valley** (another possible descent for the adventurous) and scramble up steep ridges to meet the Summit Circuit. It is possible to go straight for the north face or southwest ridge of Point Lenana, but stopping at Austrian Hut or detouring to Shipton's Camp is probably a better idea and gives you more time to enjoy the scenery; see Sirimon and Naro Moru routes for details.

Allow at least five days for the Chogoria route, although a full week is better.

Sleeping

The only option besides camping on this route is **Meru Mt Kenya Lodge** (Map p298; per person KSh1500), a group of comfortable cabins administered by **Meru South County Council** (☎0729390686; Chuka). Ask your

Mt Kenya Summit

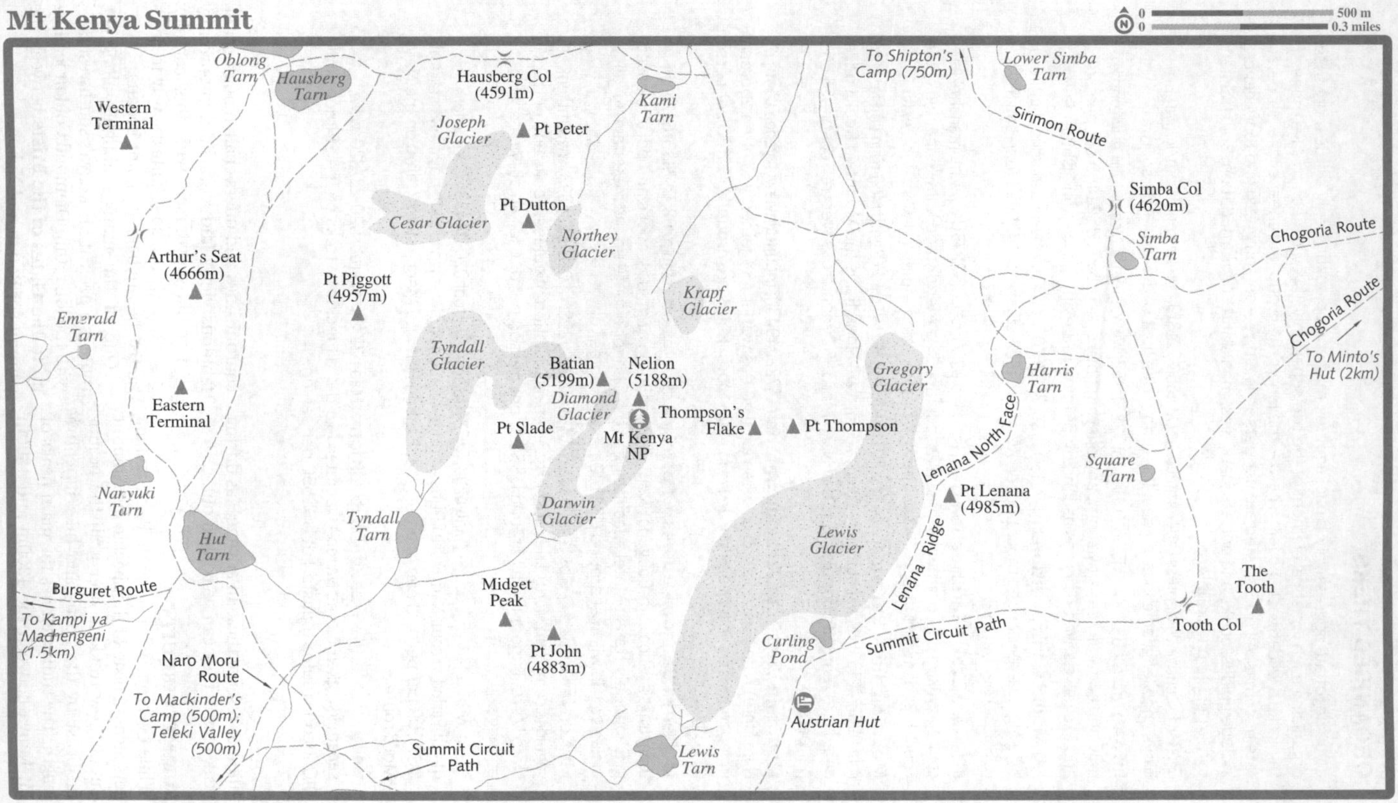

ORGANISED TREKS

If you negotiate aggressively, a package trek may end up costing only a little more than organising each logistical element of the trip separately. If you're keen to save money, think like a wildebeest and join a herd – the larger the group, the cheaper the per person rate becomes. All prices listed are per person in a three-person group and tours generally include guides, cooks and porters, park fees, meals and accommodation. Solo trekkers can expect to pay double.

EWP (Executive Wilderness Programmes; ☎UK 1550-721319; www.ewpnet.com/kenya) Employs knowledgeable local guides; three-day trips cost US$645 per person.

IntoAfrica (☎UK 0114-255 5610, Nairobi 722511752; www.intoafrica.co.uk) An environmentally and culturally sensitive company offering both scheduled (US$1495 per person) and exclusive seven-day trips ascending Sirimon route and descending Chogoria.

KG Mountain Expeditions (☎721604930, 722261028; www.kenyaexpeditions.com) Run by a highly experienced mountaineer, KG offers all-inclusive scheduled four-day treks (US$550 per person).

Montana Trek & Information Centre (Map p300; ☎062-32731; www.montanatrekks.com; Nanyuki) This community-based association has friendly and knowledgeable guides. Four-day trips start at US$440 per person but vary depending on where you exit.

Mountain Rock Safaris Resorts & Trekking Services (Bantu Mountain Lodge; ☎Nairobi 020-242133; www.mountainrockkenya.com; Naro Moru) Runs the Mountain Rock Lodge near Naro Moru. Its popular four-day Naro Moru–Sirimon crossover trek costs US$650 per person.

Mountain View Tour Trekking Safaris (☎722249439; mountainviewt@yahoo.com; Naro Moru) A new association of seven local guides working together who often approach independent travellers as they arrive in Naro Moru. Rates are around US$120 per person per day.

Mt Kenya Chogoria Guides & Porters Association (Map p298; ☎733676970; anthonytreks@yahoo.com; Chogoria) A small association of guides, cooks and porters based in Chogoria's Transit Motel specialising in the Chogoria route up the mountain. An all-inclusive trip will cost around US$120 per person per day.

Mt Kenya Guides & Porters Safari Club (Map p298; ☎020-3524393; www.mtkenyaguides.com; Naro Moru) The most organised association of guides, cooks and porters in Naro Moru. Expect to pay around US$120 per person per day for an all-inclusive package.

Naro Moru River Lodge (Map p298; ☎724082754, Nairobi 020-4443357; www.naromoruriverlodge.com; Naro Moru) Runs a range of all-inclusive trips (four-day treks start at US$609 per person) and operates Met Station Hut and Mackinder's Camp on the Naro Moru route.

Sana Highlands Trekking Expeditions (Map p224; ☎Nairobi 020-227820; www.sanatrekkingkenya.com; Nairobi) Operates five-day all-inclusive treks on the Sirimon and Chogoria routes that start at US$550 per person.

guide to reserve these in advance, as during peak season they can be booked out.

SUMMIT CIRCUIT

While everyone who summits Point Lenana gets a small taste of the spectacular Summit Circuit, few trekkers ever grab the beautiful beast by the horns and hike its entire length. The trail encircles the main peaks of Mt Kenya between the 4300m and 4800m contour lines and offers challenging terrain, fabulous views and a splendid opportunity to familiarise yourself with this complex mountain. It is also a fantastic way to acclimatise before bagging Point Lenana.

One of the many highlights along the route is a peek at Mt Kenya's southwest face, with the long, thin Diamond Couloir leading up to the **Gates of the Mists** between the summits of Batian and Nelion.

Depending on your level of fitness, this route can take between four and nine hours. Some fit souls can bag Point Lenana (from Austrian Hut or Shipton's Camp) and complete the Summit Circuit in the same day.

The trail can be deceptive at times, especially when fog rolls in, and some trekkers have become seriously lost between Tooth Col and Austrian Hut. It is imperative to take a guide.

Information

The daily fees for the **national park** (www.kws.go.ke; adult/child US$55/25, 3-day package adult/child US$150/70) are charged upon entry, so you must estimate the length of your stay. If you overstay, you pay the difference when leaving.

Technical climbers and mountaineers should get a copy of the *Guide to Mt Kenya & Kilimanjaro* by **Mountain Club of Kenya** (MCK; Nairobi 020-602330; www.mck.or.ke). MCK also has reasonably up-to-date mountain information posted on its website.

Naro Moru

062 / POP 9880

Naro Moru may be little more than a string of shops and houses, with a couple of very basic hotels and a market, but it's the most popular starting point for treks up Mt Kenya. There's a post office, and internet is available above Nice and Spice Cafe – the town's best local eatery (not that this is any endorsement). There are no banks.

Sights & Activities

In addition to gawking at Mt Kenya (best before 6.30am, after which it is obscured by clouds) and starting the Naro Moru route up to its summit, there are some interesting day excursions. Either of the guide associations listed in the boxed text, p296, can organise **nature walks** on Mt Kenya and hikes to the **Mau Mau caves**, which are impressive from both a physical and historical perspective. Mountain Rock Lodge and Naro Moru River Lodge also run similar trips, as well as offering **horse riding**, **fishing** and **wildlife drives** to Aberdare National Park, Solio Game Reserve or Ol Pejeta Conservancy.

Sleeping & Eating

TOP CHOICE **Naro Moru River Lodge** LODGE $$
(Map p298; 31047, 0724082754, in Nairobi 020-4443357; www.naromoruriverlodge.com; Naro Moru; camping/dm US$11/15, s full board US$142-201, d & tw full board US$204-309; P) A bit like a Swiss chalet, the River Lodge is a lovely collection of dark, cosy cottages and rooms embedded into a sloping hillside that overlooks the rushing Naro Moru River 3km from town. All three classes of room are lovely, but the middle-of-the-road 'superior' option seemed the best of the lot. The restaurants here are the best in town.

Mt Kenya Guides & Porters Safari Club BANDA $
(Map p298; 020-3524393; www.mtkenyaguides.com; per person incl breakfast KSh1500) Principally in the business of supplying guides and porters, this association has branched out with a couple of excellent value cottages with open fires. Meals can be arranged on request and obviously, organising a trek here is a breeze.

Mountain Rock Lodge HOTEL $$
(Bantu Mountain Lodge; Map p298; 020-8097157, in Nairobi 020-242133; www.mountainrockkenya.com; camping KSh550, s/d/tw full board US$95/140/140; P) This is one of the major bases for Mt Kenya climbers and the operators of Old Moses Hut and Shipton's Camp on the mountain. There are three classes of rooms and the prices quoted are for the better value, midrange 'superior' rooms. Like most hotels in this price bracket, the rooms are serviceable enough but in need of refurbishment. It's located 9km north of Naro Moru.

Timberland Hotel HOTEL $
(Naro Moru; s/d excl breakfast KSh350/500) It doesn't get much cheaper or more basic than this. If you don't mind squat toilets, the odd bug and a little late night noise, you can save a packet.

Getting There & Away

There are plenty of buses and matatus heading to Nanyuki (KSh50, 30 minutes), Nyeri (KSh120, 45 minutes) and Nairobi (KSh400, three hours) from either the northbound or southbound 'stages'.

Nanyuki

062 / POP 31,580

This small but bustling mountain town makes a living off sales, be it of treks to climbers, curios to soldiers of the British Army (which has a training facility nearby)

Around Mt Kenya

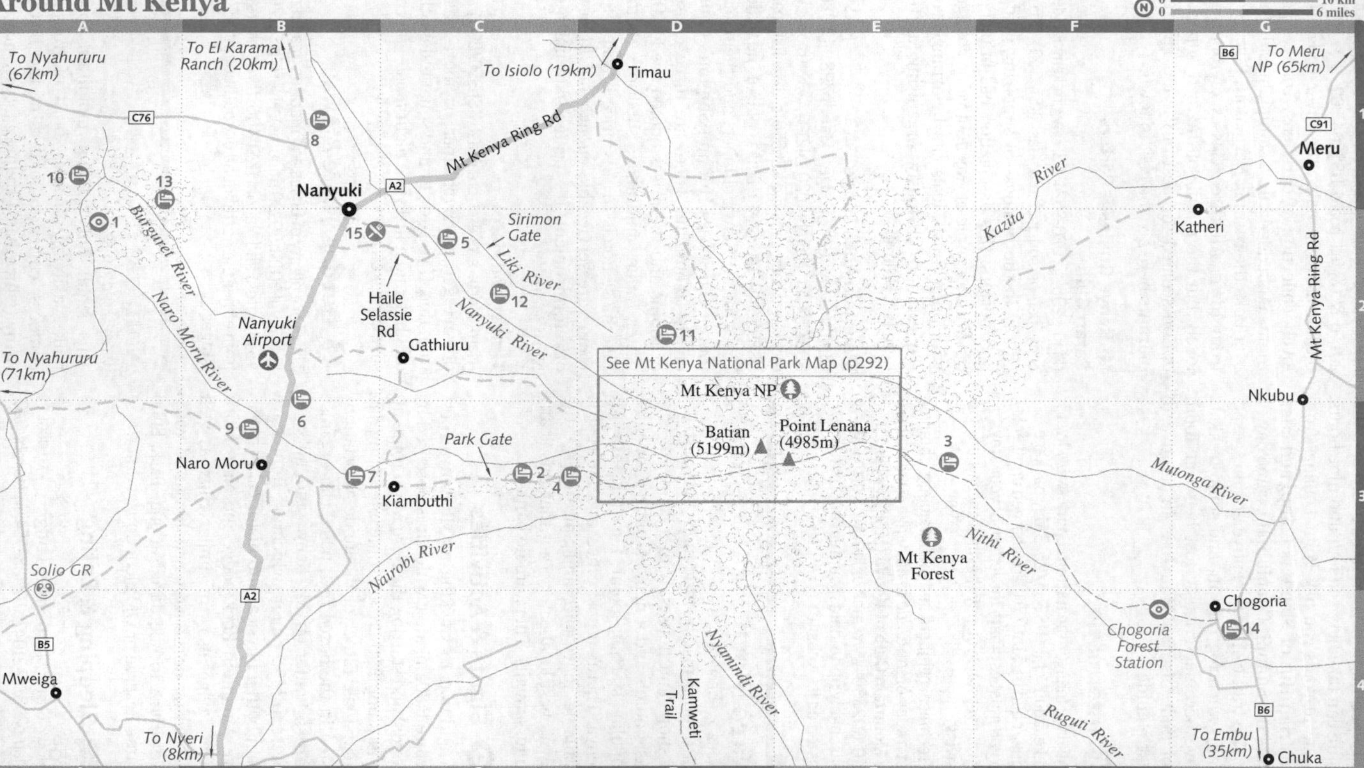

Around Mt Kenya

Sights
Mt Kenya Wildlife Conservancy Animal Orphange .... (see 7)
1 Ol Pejeta Conservancy A2

Activities, Courses & Tours
Mt Kenya Chogoria Guides & Porters Association .... (see 14)
Mt Kenya Guides & Porters Safari Club .... (see 6)
Naro Moru River Lodge .... (see 9)

Sleeping
2 Batian Guest House C3
3 Meru Mt Kenya Lodge E3
4 Met Station Hut C3
5 Mountain Rock Lodge C2
6 Mt Kenya Guides & Porters Safari Club B3
7 Mt Kenya Safari Club B3
8 Nanyuki River Camel Camp B1
9 Naro Moru River Lodge B3
10 Ol Pejeta House A1
11 Old Moses Hut D2
12 Sirimon Bandas C2
13 Sweetwaters Tented Camp A1
14 Transit Motel G4

Eating
15 Cape Chestnut B2
Mt Kenya Safari Club .... (see 7)

or drinks to pilots of the Kenyan Air Force (this is the site of its main airbase). For all that mercantilism, it's laid back for a market town. Nanyuki also serves as a gateway to the Laikipia plateau, one of Africa's most important wildlife conservation sites.

Sights & Activities

Besides tackling Mt Kenya's Sirimon or Burguret routes, you should stroll 3km south to the **equator** (there's a sign).

Mt Kenya Wildlife Conservancy Animal Orphanage ZOO
(Map p298; Mount Kenya Safari Club; per person KSh1500; 8am-12.30pm & 1.30-5.30pm) It may come off a little zoo-like at first but this orphanage is one of the few places in the world to have successfully bred the rare **mountain bongo**. Its success is such that there are now plans to release some of the captivate-bred antelope into the Mt Kenya forests to bolster the current population of around 70.

Sleeping

TOP CHOICE **Kirimara Springs Hotel** HOTEL $
(off Map p300; 0726370191; www.kirimaraspringshotel.com; Kenyatta Ave; s/d/tw incl breakfast KSh2300/3000/3500; P, wi-fi) While Kirimara isn't going to win any architecture awards, its friendly staff and spacious and bright rooms were cleaner and cheaper than others in this price bracket. The rooms on the western side of the building catch less traffic noise, while those on the east get glimpses of Mt Kenya.

TOP CHOICE **Mount Kenya SafariClub** LUXURY HOTEL $$$
(Map p298; in Nairobi 020-2265000; www.fairmont.com; d US$329-479; P, wi-fi, pool) For our money this is *the* top-end resort in the Central Highlands – it's the kind of place that makes you want to grow a moustache, kick back and smoke a pipe. The rooms are safari-*chic* and decorated to a sumptuous standard, all with their own open fires and exquisite bathrooms. The whole shebang overlooks the Mt Kenya Wildlife Conservancy and there are more facilities here than you can shake a Maasai throwing-stick at (including a heated pool, clay tennis court, topiary maze, wedding chapel and art gallery).

Ibis Hotel HOTEL $
(0714420888; nanyuki@ibishotels.co.ke; Willy Jimmy Rd; s/d/tw excl breakfast KSh1000/1200/1800; wi-fi) A little smarter than others nearby, the few extra shillings buy you a little more cheer and a slightly larger bathroom. This multilevel building encloses a covered courtyard restaurant which is better than most. Angle for a room with Mt Kenya views.

Kongoni Camp BANDA $
(702868888; www.kongonicamp.com; camping KSh600, bandas per person KSh3200, d KSh5400; P, wi-fi) Founded by a friendly local-turned-Londoner-turned-local-again, Kongoni boasts five, concrete circular *bandas*. Each contains a double and single bed. The large barn-like restaurant-cum-bar comes as a refreshing dash of hip after the many spartan

Nanyuki

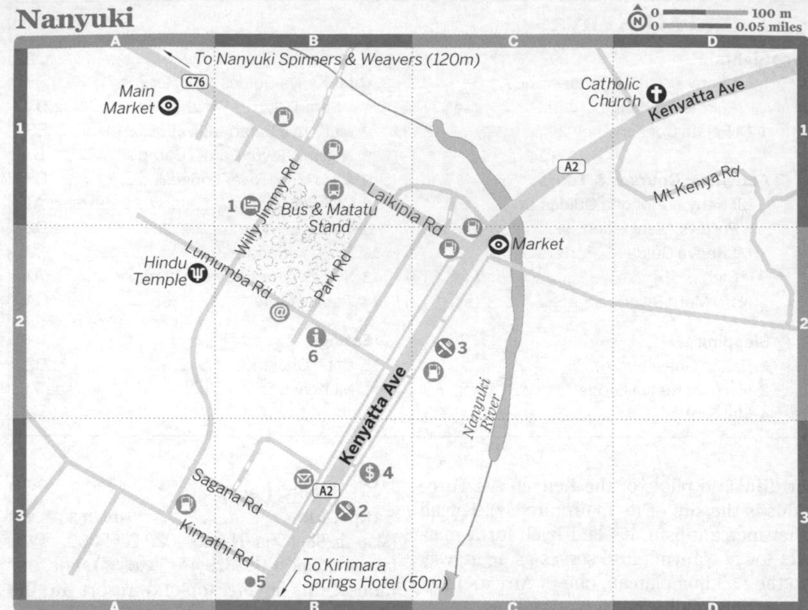

Nanyuki

Sleeping
1 Ibis Hotel B1

Eating
2 Marina Grill & Restaurant B3
3 Walkers Kikwetu C2

Information
4 Barclays Bank B3
5 Boma Holidays B3
6 Montana Trek & Information Centre B2

budget digs around town. Kongoni Camp is located just off the A2, 4km east of town.

Nanyuki River Camel Camp HUT $
(Map p298; 0722-361642; www.fieldoutdoor.com; camping KSh1000, huts without bathroom half/full board KSh4500) The most innovative sleep in town (well, 4km outside of it, off the C76 Hwy) is this ecocamp, set in a dry swab of scrub. The camp offers lodging in genuine Somali grass-and-camelskin huts imported from Mandera. Best known for its camel treks (half-/full day KSh3500/5000), it's a good idea to give them at least 48 hours advance notice as the camels are often grazed many kilometres away. Somalian food such as *nyiri nyiri* (fried camel jerky with cardamom) is a house speciality but also requires advance notice.

Eating

Mount Kenya Safari Club INTERNATIONAL, BUFFET $$$
(Map p298; meals KSh850-1000, buffets KSh4300; breakfast, lunch & dinner) If you're looking to splurge then this is the place to do it. Sink back into a sofa in the drawing room or saunter over to the pool and take in the vista. The buffet is only served at breakfast and lunch and includes all kinds of delectable yummies.

Marina Grill & Restaurant INTERNATIONAL $
(Map p300; Kenyatta Ave; mains KSh140-420; lunch & dinner) Popular with trekking groups, British soldiers and Kenyan Air Force officers (the odd cross-section that is Nanyuki), this place does good burgers and pizza and has a nice rooftop eating area for those needing fresh air.

Walkers Kikwetu BUFFET $
(Map p300; Kenyatta Ave; mains KSh200-350; breakfast, lunch & dinner, Mon-Sat) *Kikwetu* means 'ours' in Kikuyu and provides the inspiration behind the menu. Several African

dishes from various tribes are brought together and served buffet style (but charged according to the dishes you select). If you haven't tried *matoke* (cooked plantains), *pilau* (Swahili curried rice) or *mukimo* (mashed beans and vegetables), here's your big chance.

Cape Chestnut INTERNATIONAL $
(Map p298; off Kenyatta Ave; mains KSh350-550 ⏲breakfast, & lunch, Mon-Sat; 📶) This coffee garden caters mostly to white farmers and expats, although all are welcome. The blackboard menu changes daily but features mostly Western-style home-cooked fare. Tuesday night is tapas night (KSh600 to KSh800), and the only day it stays open late. It's off Kenyatta Ave, 1km south of town.

Information

Barclays Bank (Kenyatta Ave) Reliable ATMs.

Boma Holidays (☎020 269194; pamela@bomaadventures.com; 2nd fl, Nakumart Centre, Kenyatta Ave) Travel agency that can arrange airline ticketing, car hire, airport transfers, hotel reservations and local safaris.

Montana Trek & Information Centre (☎062-32731; www.montanatrekks.com; Nanyuki) As well as supplying guides for Mt Kenya treks, it's an excellent source of local information.

Peak Cyber (2nd fl, Bidhaa Bora Bldg, Lumumba Rd; per hr KSh60) Internet and CD burning services.

Post office (Kenyatta Ave)

Getting There & Away

Airkenya (☎020-3916000; www.airkenya.com) and **Safarilink** (☎020-600777; www.flysafarilink.com) fly daily from Wilson airport in Nairobi to Nanyuki. A return trip on Airkenya/Safarilink costs US$200/220.

Tropic Air (☎020-2033032; www.tropicairkenya.com) operates its charter-helicopter and light-aircraft services from here.

Nanyuki is well connected to all points north and south, as well as most major Rift Valley towns. Sample matatu fares include Nyeri (KSh150, one hour), Isiolo (KSh200, 1½ hours), Meru (KSh150, 1½ hours), Nakuru (KSh500, three hours) and Nairobi (KSh400, three hours).

Meru

☎064 / POP 126,430

Meru is the largest municipality in the Central Highlands and the epicentre of Kenyan production of *miraa*, a mild, leafy stimulant more widely known outside of Kenya as *khat*. The town itself is like a shot of the stuff: a briefly invigorating, slightly confusing head rush.

The obvious base for exploring Meru National Park, Meru is worth a day visit in its own right and is a focal point for the Meru people.

Sleeping

Hotel Westwind HOTEL $
(☎31890; westwindhotelmeru@gmail.com; Angaine Rd; s KSh1800-2500, d KSh2500-3000; P) Catering to the business elite, this is Meru's accommodation at its finest. Service here is friendly and comes from the heart; the decor, however, comes from the '80s. Some rooms are surprisingly small.

Pig & Whistle BANDA $
(☎31411; off Kenyatta Hwy; s/tw KSh1500/1800) There's a rambling sense of alpine chaos here, offset by friendly staff and truly comfortable cottages set around a sprawling rustic compound. The concrete huts may not look like much from the outside, but they are actually nicely self-contained slices of good-value sleeping pleasure.

Eating

Books First Sherlocks Den CAFE $
(Nakumart, Kenyatta Hwy; mains KSh350-700; ⏲breakfast, lunch & dinner) This Western-style diner could be lifted straight from an American mall. With a backdrop of easy-listening classics, you can take your pick from some pretty decent pizza, burgers, Tex-Mex standards, sandwiches and cakes. From 5pm to 7pm, the two-for-one pizza deal is the way to go.

Meru County Hotel INTERNATIONAL $
(Kenyatta Hwy; meals KSh300-600; ⏲breakfast, lunch & dinner) Thatched umbrellas hover over each table on this pretty *nyama choma* terrace. If you want to give the flaming flesh a rest, try the Western, Kenyan and Indian meals on offer.

Information

Barclays Bank (Tom Mboya St) Reliable ATM.

Books First Cyber Cafe (Nakumart, Kenyatta Hwy; per hr KSh120)

Post office (Kenyatta Hwy)

Getting There & Away

Kensilver (Mosque Hill Rd) and **Sunbird** (Mosque Hill Rd) have 15 daily departures

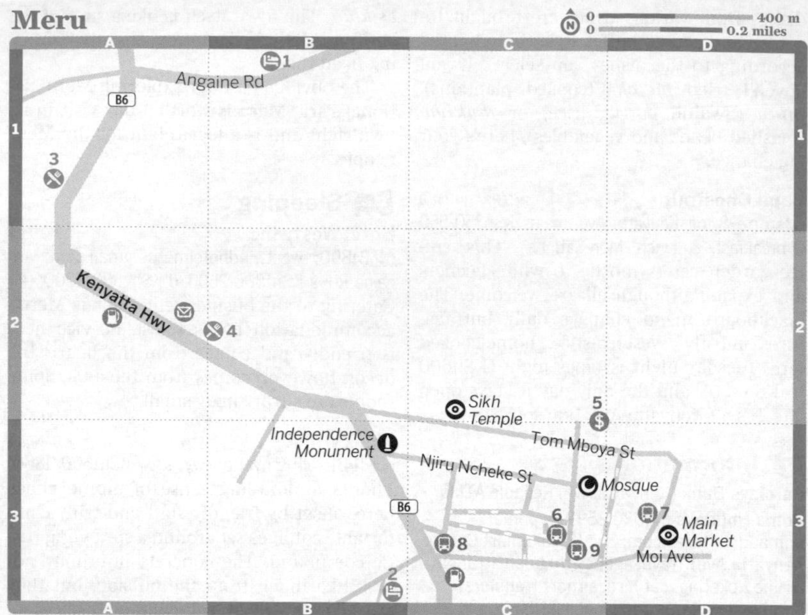

Meru

Sleeping
1 Hotel Westwind........B1
2 Pig & Whistle........B3

Eating
3 Books First Sherlocks Den........A1
4 Meru County Hotel........B2

Information
5 Barclays Bank........C2
Books First Cyber Cafe........(see 3)

Transport
6 Kensilver Buses........C3
7 Matatu Stand........D3
8 Matatu Stand........C3
9 Sunbird, Vanga & Combo Buses........C3

between them from 6.45am onwards, covering Embu (KSh300, two hours), Thika (KSh300, 3½ hours) and Nairobi (KSh400, five hours).

Vanga (Mosque Hill Rd) and **Combo** (Mosque Hill Rd) run daily buses at 6.30pm and 5.30pm to 5pm respectively to Mombasa (KSh1300, 12 hours). The Vanga bus is the more comfy.

Regular matatus also serve Nairobi (KSh650, four hours), Thika (KSh550, 3½ hours), Embu (KSh300, two hours), Nanyuki (KSh250, 1½ hours) and Isiolo (KSh200, 1½ hours).

Meru National Park

Marred by a decade of poaching in the 1980s and the subsequent murder of George Adamson (of *Born Free* fame) in 1989, Meru rather dramatically fell off the tourist map and has never quite managed to struggle back on despite recent massive investment by the KWS. This is a pity because with wildlife numbers on the rise, Hemingway-esque green hills and fast-flowing streams bordered by riverine forests, baobab trees and doum palms, Meru is one of Kenya's best-kept secrets.

Sights & Activities

Walking within the park is not permitted, so without your own 4WD you'll need to join an organised tour to see the **zebras**, **waterbucks**, **buffaloes**, **giraffes** and **elephants** the park is renowned for. Thanks to the cover afforded by the long grass and thickets of acacia bushes, animals are not seen as readily here as they are in the more open parks. Consequently, it is not uncommon to turn a corner and find yourself practically bumper-to-snout with some large and threatening herbivore.

WORTH A TRIP

LAIKIPIA PLATEAU

Set against the backdrop of Mt Kenya, the **Laikipia plateau** (www.laikipia.org) extends over 9500 sq km (roughly the size of Wales) of semi-arid plains, dramatic gouges and acacia thicket-covered hills. Conceived in 1992, this patchwork of privately owned ranches, wildlife conservancies and small-scale farms has become one of the most important areas for biodiversity in the country. It boasts wildlife densities second only to those found in the Masai Mara and is the last refuge of Kenya's **African wild dogs**. Indeed, these vast plains are home some of Kenya's highest populations of endangered species including half of the country's **black rhinos** and half of the world's **Grevy's zebras** and one of the last viable lion populations in Kenya.

Ol Pejeta Conservancy (Map p298; www.olpejetaconservancy.org; adult/child US$65/32, vehicle from KSh300; ⌚7am-7pm) was once one of the largest cattle ranches in Kenya, but is now a 90,000-acre, privately owned wildlife reserve. It possesses a full palette of African plains wildlife, including the Big Five, massive eland and a healthy population of rhinos (including a blind and tame orphan named Barrack). The on-site **chimpanzee sanctuary** (⌚9-10.30am & 3-4.30pm), is less inspiring, in no small part because many of the orphaned chimps show signs of psychological damage (presumably from before they were rescued and brought here). Accommodation options include **Sweetwaters Tented Camp** (Map p298; www.serenahotels.com) beside a floodlit waterhole and **Ol Pejeta House** (Map p298; www.serenahotels.com), a massive bush villa that was once home to Lord Delamere.

Visiting Laikipia

Even though Laikipia now boasts a brand new national park, the vast majority of protected lands are owned by private conservatories and their efforts have helped to create one of the country's foremost safari destinations.

Virtually all of the lodges and camps (now numbering over 40) fall squarely into the luxurious bracket and cater to the well-heeled who visit as part of prepackaged tours.

El Karama Ranch (☎0720386616; www.horsebackinkenya.com) Affordable horse-riding safaris.

Bobong Campsite (☎062-32718; olmaisor@africaonline.co.ke) Self-catering *bandas* and camping at a child-friendly farm.

Borana Lodge (www.borana.com) One of two lodges on the Borana Ranch – both overlooking waterholes.

Il Ngwesi Eco Lodge (☎020-2033122; www.ilngwesi.com) A Maasai-owned ecolodge with exceptional wildlife viewing.

Ol Malo (☎062-32715; www.olmalo.com) Posh rock and olive-wood cottages in an equally stunning setting.

Tassia Lodge (☎0725972923; www.tassiasafaris.com) Beautifully sited on the edge of a rocky bluff with sweeping views.

Tharua Safaris (☎0721638337; www.tharua-safaris.info) Affordable homestays and horse-riding safaris.

Most safaris enter the park at Murera gate and head for the **rhino sanctuary**, a fenced portion of the park that's home to both **black and white rhinos** reintroduced here from Lake Nakuru National Park after the disastrous poaching of the '80s.

The park's most significant waterway, **Rojewero River**, is a reliable place to view **hippos** and **crocodiles**. To the south you may want to check out **Elsa's Grave**, a stone memorial to the Adamson's star lioness.

Meru National Park

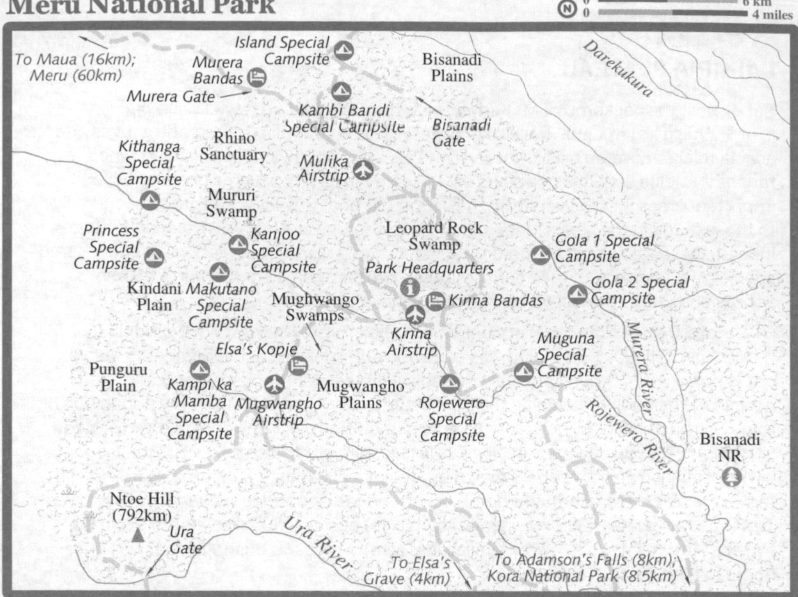

Access to the adjacent **Kora National Park** is via the bridge near **Adamson's Falls**.

Sleeping

Kinna Bandas BANDA **$$**

(www.kws.go.ke; bandas US$100;) These four *bandas* each sleep two and are stocked with kerosene lanterns that add the right romanticism to a star-studded bush night. Located in the heart of the park, you can't get closer to the wildlife without the risk of being eaten by it.

Elsa's Kopje BANDA **$$$**

(020-6003090; www.elsaskopje.com; d full board from US$1190;) Plenty of hotels claim to blend into their environment, but Elsa's did so in such a seamless manner that the bar on chic ecosuites was permanently raised. Carved into Mughwango Hill, these highly individualised 'three-walled' rooms open out onto views *The Lion King* animators would have killed for. Stone-hewn infinity pools plunge over the clifftops, while rock hyraxes play tag in your private garden.

Murera Bandas BANDA **$$**

(www.kws.go.ke; bandas US$50-$70) The Murera camp, overflowing with plain wooden cottages and huts, is a fine place to doss if everything is booked up. Each *banda* sleeps three.

Special Campsites CAMPGROUND **$**

(www.kws.go.ke; camping US$30, reservation fee KSh7500) There are about a dozen of these bush campsites (no facilities) located throughout the park. The gate will let you know which are currently open.

Information

Entrance to **Meru National Park** (020-2109508; www.kws.go.ke; adult/child US$60/30, vehicles from KSh300; 6am-7pm) also entitles you to enter the adjacent **Kora**

MERU NATIONAL PARK

» **Why Go** Meru is a pristine, seldom-visited park where you're guaranteed a 'congestion-free' experience.

» **When to Go** The park is accessible year-round with a 4WD.

» **Practicalities** There is no public transport within the park but self-drive safaris are possible.

National Park although visits into Kora must be prearranged with Meru's warden at the park headquarters.

The KWS *Meru National Park* map (KSh450), sold at the park gates, is essential if you want to find your way around. Even so you may want to hire a guide (six-hour/full-day tour KSh1500/3000).

Getting There & Away

J Kiirimi Safaris (☎0721683700; www.jkirimisafaris.com), a small safari operator, has a Land Rover based 31km from the main gate. A full-day safari, including pick-up and drop-off at Meru town, costs around US$135 for the whole 4WD.

Airkenya (www.airkenya.com) has daily flights connecting Meru to Nairobi (returnUS$449).

Chogoria

☎064 / POP 3021

This town shares its name with the most difficult route up Mt Kenya. It's a friendly enough place but, unless you're trekking, there's no reason to stop here.

You can probably arrange local accommodation with one of the many touts offering Mt Kenya climbs; otherwise, head to **Transit Motel** (Map p298; ☎0725609151; www.transitmotelchogoria.com; camping per tent KSh500, s/d/tr KSh1200/1900/2600), 2km south of town. This is a large, friendly lodge with pleasant rooms (some with small balconies) and a decent restaurant (meals KSh350 to KSh500). **Mt Kenya Chogoria Guides & Porters Association** (Map p298; ☎733676970; anthonytreks@yahoo.com; Chogoria) is also based here.

Chogoria is 3km off the main B6 drag to which it is connected by two roads that radiate out from it. Sample fares include Meru (KSh150, one hour), Embu (KSh220, 1½ hours) and Nairobi (KSh400, four hours).

NORTHERN KENYA

Calling all explorers! We dare you to challenge yourself against some of the most exciting wilderness in Africa. Step forward only if you're able to withstand appalling roads, searing heat, clouds of dust torn up by relentless winds, primitive food and accommodation, vast distances and more than a hint of danger (see p311).

The rewards include memories of va[illegible] shattered lava deserts, camel herders wa[illegible]ing their animals to lost oases, fog-shro[illegible] mountains full of mysterious creature[illegible] prehistoric islands crawling with massiv[illegible] reptiles and jokes shared with traditionally dressed warriors. Additional perks include camel trekking through piles of peachy dunes, elephant encounters in scrubby acacia woodlands and the chance to walk barefoot along the fabled shores of a sea of jade.

Isiolo to Ethiopia

For most people this route means two things: the wildlife riches of the Samburu ecosystem or the road to the cultural riches of Ethiopia. But in between and beyond, this area has much more to offer. You can drink tea and track game with the Samburu people, climb mist-shrouded volcanoes in the desert, blaze trails in untrammelled mountains and get so far off the beaten track you'll start to wonder whether you're still on the same planet.

ISIOLO

☎064

Isiolo is where anticipation and excitement first start to send your heart a-flutter. This vital pit stop on the long road north is a true frontier town, a place on the edge, torn between the cool, verdant highlands just to the south and the scorching badlands, home of nomads and explorers, to the north. On a more practical note it's also the last place with decent facilities until Maralal or Marsabit.

One of the first things you'll undoubtedly notice is the large Somali population (descendants of WWI veterans who settled here) and the striking faces of Boran, Samburu and Turkana people walking the streets. It's this mix of people, cultures and religions that is the most interesting thing about Isiolo. Nowhere is this mixture better illustrated than in the hectic market.

Sleeping

Range Land Hotel COTTAGES $$

(☎0721434353; A2 Hwy; camping KSh500, tw cottages KSh2500; P) About 8km south of to[illegible] this is a nice option for those wi[illegible] set of wheels. The sunn[illegible] ering weaver bi[illegible] as neat a[illegible] sh[illegible]

[illegible]ick- well [illegible] with hot [illegible] available and [illegible]KSh1200), a deli- [illegible]sine.

Northern Kenya

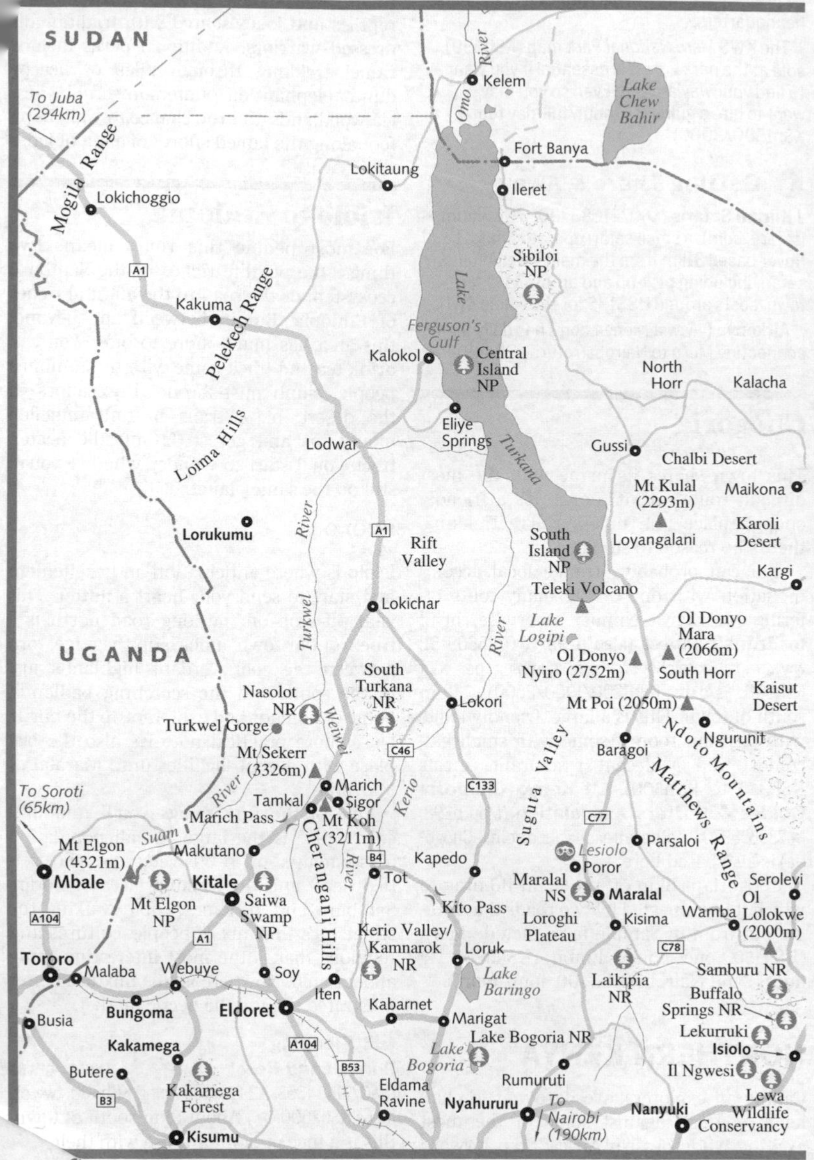

Jos...
(☎072...
Excellen... ...ouse HOTEL $
from tiny... breakfast KSh800-1500)
swing a bac... rooms that range ...e enough to ...ve hot showers and there's a decent in-house restaurant.

Gaddisa Lodge LODGE $$
(☎0724201115; www.gaddisa.com; camping KSh400; s/tw with breakfast KSh3000/4000; 🅿)

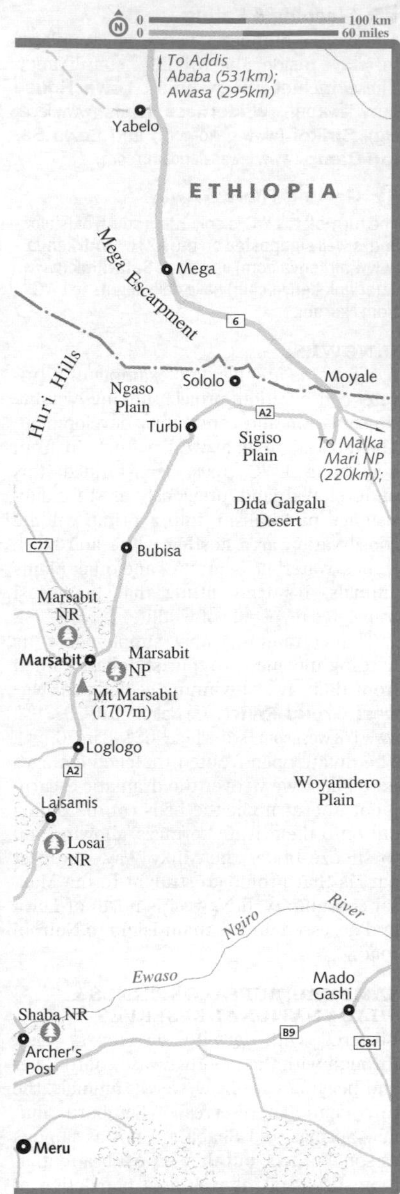

Around 3km northeast of town is this spotlessly clean Dutch-run lodge, where peaceful cottages overlook the fringes of the northern savannah country. There's an occasionally full pool to wallow like a hippo in.

Eating

There are numerous cheap eating establishments throughout the town, but in general the hotel restaurants tend to offer more variety as well as a more salubrious environment.

Northbound self-caterers should head to **101 Supermarket** (8am-6pm Mon-Sat) and the daily **market** near the mosque to purchase food and drink, as there's very little available beyond here.

Bomen Hotel KENYAN **$$**
(Meals KSh300-500; lunch & dinner) A rare place serving more than the local usuals, with fried tilapia, pepper steak, goulash and curries up for grabs.

Information

Barclays Bank (A2 Hwy) With an ATM. Banks are scarce in the north, so plan ahead.
District Hospital (Hospital Rd; 24hr)
Green Acres.com Cyber Cafe (per hr KSh60; 8am-9pm)
Isiolo Telephone Exchange (Hospital Rd) Calling cards and card phones.
Kenya Commercial Bank (A2 Hwy) With an ATM.
Post office (Hospital Rd)

Getting There & Away

A couple of bus companies serve Nairobi with most buses leaving between 6am and 6.30am (KSh600, 4½ hours) from the main road through town and also stopping at the matatu and bus stand just south of the market. Nightly buses operated by **Liban Buses** creep north to Marsabit (KSh700, six hours), where you can change for Moyale.

For Maralal take an early-morning matatu to Wamba (KSh350, 2½ hours), and then a Maralal-bound matatu (KSh400, 2½ hours) from there. Regular matatus leave from a chaotic stand around the market and also serve Archer's Post (KSh100, 25 minutes), Meru (KSh150, 1½ hours) and Nanyuki (KSh250, 1¾ hours).

LEWA WILDLIFE CONSERVANCY

Falling away from the Mount Kenya highlands is a vast region of open savannah grasslands that make up some of the most incredible wildlife viewing territory in Kenya.

TOP CHOICE **Lewa Wildlife Conservancy** WILDLIFE RESERVE
(LWC; 064-31405; www.lewa.org; admission US$90) While the massive 62,000-sq-acre reserve, just south of Isiolo, could boast about their

GETTING AROUND NORTHERN KENYA

Having your own 4WD gives you flexibility but comes with its own challenges, thanks to wide-ranging road conditions. For starters, you'll need a large 4WD with high ground clearance and a skid plate to protect the undercarriage. Do not underestimate how bad the roads are up here – during a month's research in the far north we ploughed through three large 4WDs. It's sensible to take an experienced driver and, if possible, travel in company with another 4WD.

There's regular public transport as far north as Kalokol and Lokichoggio on Turkana's west side, but it's more limited up the lake's east side, only reaching Maralal via Nyahururu or Isiolo.

A few organised safaris and overland trucks now go to Lake Turkana's west, but most still stick to the lake's east side. Average trips are seven to 10 days.

luxury lodges, stunning scenery, astounding wildlife activities and having hosted Prince William, they'd rather talk about their community and conservation projects. Founded in 1995, LWC is a nonprofit organisation that invests around 70% of its annual US$2.5 million-plus budget into healthcare, education and various community projects for surrounding villages, while the rest funds further conservation and security projects.

The conservation effort has been astounding and 20% of the world's Grevy's zebras, 12% of Kenya's black rhinos, a rare population of aquatic sitatunga antelope (though many of these have recently been eaten by lions!) and sizeable populations of white rhinos, elephants and buffaloes call the reserve home. Of the predators there are small, but growing, populations of leopards, lions and cheetahs. All of this makes Lewa not just a flagship model for private conservation but one of the finest wildlife viewing areas in all of Kenya – and there's no minibus circus to contend with.

Visiting this Kenyan Garden of Eden doesn't come easily – nor cheaply. Wildlife drives in private vehicles aren't permitted; only guests of the LWC's lodges are allowed into the conservancy, and the accommodation is only for the very well-heeled.

Sleeping & Eating

There are a number of very exclusive places to stay inside the wildlife conservancy. These include the beautiful **Lewa House** (www.lewa.org), **Wilderness Trails** (www.lewa.org), **Sirikoi** (www.sirikoi.com) and **Lewa Safari Camp** (www.lewasafaricamp.com).

Getting There & Away

The turn-off to LWC is only 12km south of Isiolo and is well signposted on the A2 Hwy. **Airkenya** (www.airkenya.com) as well as **Safarilink** (www.safarilink-kenya.com) have daily flights to LWC from Nairobi.

IL NGWESI

Il Ngwesi is another fine example of a private conservation project linking wildlife conservation and community development. The Maasai of Il Ngwesi, with help from neighbour LWC, have transformed this undeveloped land, previously used for subsistence pastoralism, into a prime wildlife conservation area hosting white and black rhinos, waterbucks, giraffes and other plains animals. It's truly fitting that Il Ngwesi translates to 'people of wildlife'.

The community now supplements its herding income with tourist dollars gained from their award-winning ecolodge, **Il Ngwesi Group Ranch** (Nairobi 020-2033122; www.ilngwesi.com; s/d all incl US$485/770;). The divine open-fronted thatched cottages here boast views over the dramatic escarpment and at night the beds can be pulled out onto the private 'terraces' allowing you to snooze under the Milky Way. The best part is that profits go straight to the Maasai community. Il Ngwesi is north of Lewa and accessed off the main Isiolo to Nairobi road.

SAMBURU, BUFFALO SPRINGS & SHABA NATIONAL RESERVES

Blistered with termite skyscrapers, shot through with the muddy Ewaso Ngiro River and heaving with heavyweight animals, the three national reserves of Samburu, Buffalo Springs and Shaba are not as famous as some others, but they have a beauty that is unsurpassed, as well as a population of creatures that occur in no other major Kenyan park. These include the blue-legged Somali ostrich, super-stripy Grevy's zebras, unicorn-like beisa oryxes, ravishing reticulated giraffes and the gerenuk – a gazelle that dearly wishes to be a giraffe. Despite comprising just 300 sq km, the variety of vegetation and landscapes here is amazing.

Shaba, with its great rocky *kopjes* (isolated hills), natural springs and doum palms, is the most physically beautiful, as well as the least visited (but it often has a lot less wildlife than the other two reserves). Meanwhile the open savannahs, scrub desert and verdant river foliage in Samburu and Buffalo Springs virtually guarantee close encounters with elephants and all the others.

Sleeping & Eating

BUFFALO SPRINGS NATIONAL RESERVE

The five **public campsites** (camping US$10) close to Gare Mara gate are overgrown, hard to find and have absolutely no facilities or water. For toilets, showers and less solitude, camp in Samburu.

SAMBURU NATIONAL RESERVE

TOP CHOICE **Elephant Watch Camp** TENTED CAMP **$$$**
(Nairobi 020-8048602; www.elephantwatchsafaris.com; s/d full board incl guided walks US$800/1360 plus US$25 per person service charge; closed Apr & Nov) Undoubtedly the most unique and memorable place to stay in Samburu. Massive thatched roofs cling to crooked acacia branches and tower over cosy, palatial, eight-sided tents and large grass-mat-clad terraces. Natural materials dominate and the bathrooms are stunning. Owners Iain and Oria Douglas-Hamilton are renowned elephant experts.

Beach Camp TENTED CAMP **$**
(0721252737, 0711565156; per person KSh1500) On the banks of the Ewaso Ngiro River's northern bank, the scrappy (and hot) dark canvas safari tents here might not climb as high in the luxury stakes as some of the big boy lodges but, let's face it, this is much more authentic Africa. Meals can be prepared on request. Vervet monkeys and baboons can be a menace though.

Samburu Intrepids Club TENTED CAMP **$$$**
(020-446651 Nairobi; full board s/d KSh12,450/16,800; @) Owned by Kenya's very own 'Royal Family', the Kenyattas, the 28 tightly packed tents here are sited along a gorgeous stretch of river, but the dark decor makes it all feel a little gloomy. Despite this it's one of the cheaper, and better value luxury options in the reserve. Game drives US$55 per person.

SHABA NATIONAL RESERVE

TOP CHOICE **Joy's Camp** TENTED CAMP **$$$**
(Nairobi 020-6003090; www.joyscamp.com; s/d full board US$700/1180;) Once the home of Joy Adamson, this is now an outrageously luxurious camp in the remotest corner of Shaba. The accommodation here is in 'tents', but we use the word in the loosest possible

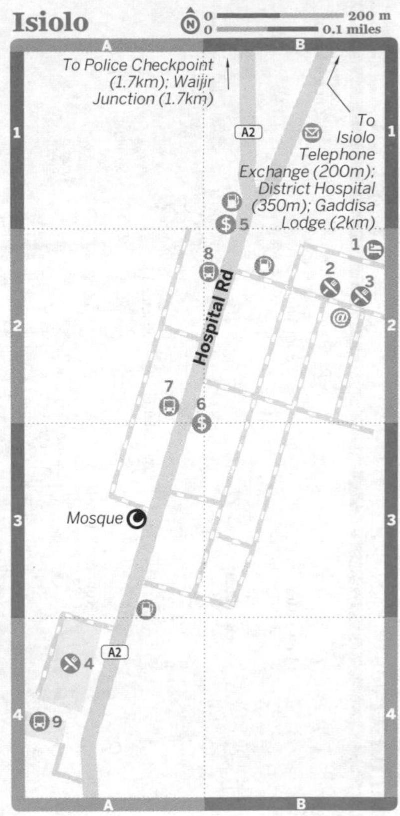

Isiolo

Sleeping
1 Josera Guest House B2

Eating
2 101 Supermarket B2
3 Bomen Hotel B2
4 Market A4

Information
5 Barclays Bank B1
6 Kenya Commercial Bank A2

Transport
7 Bus Offices for Nairobi A2
8 Liban Buses B2
9 Matatu & Bus Stand A4

Samburu & Buffalo Springs National Reserves

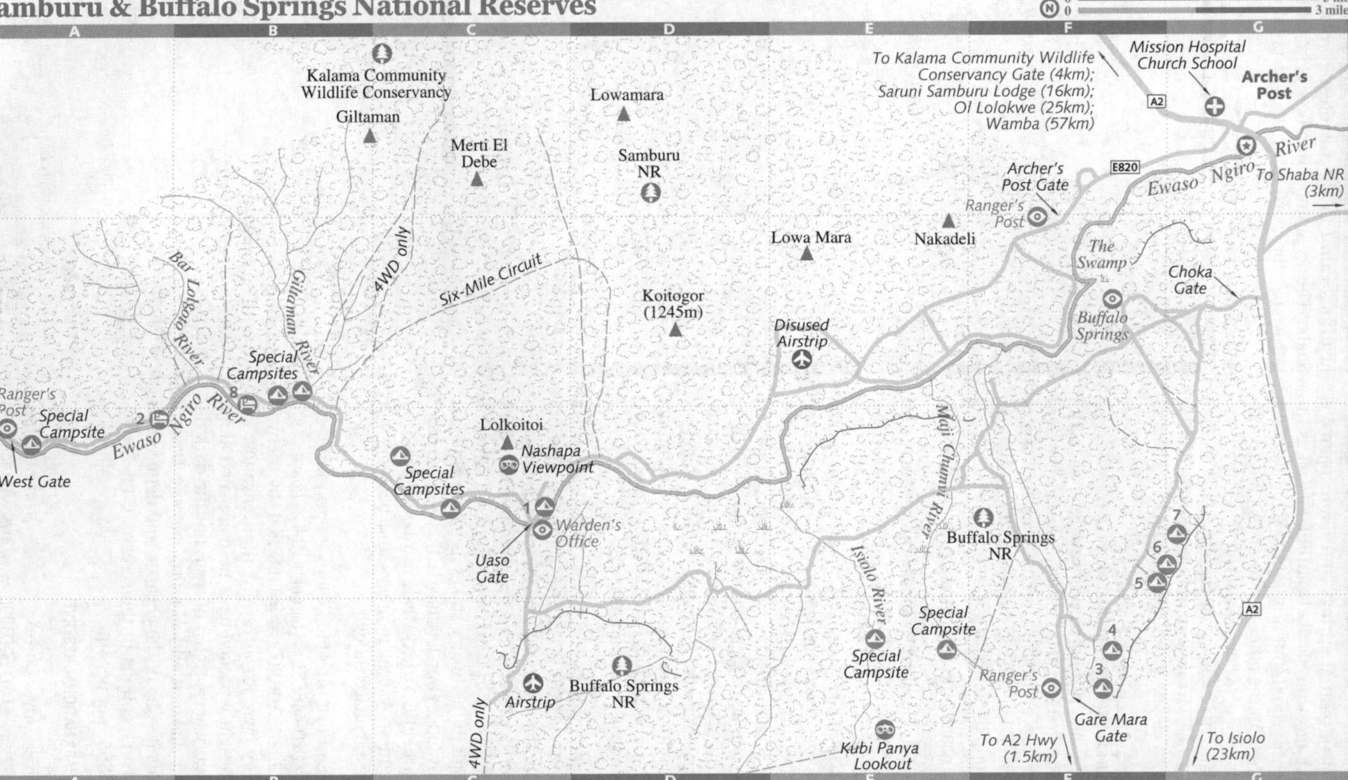
0 5 km
0 3 miles
Kalama Community Wildlife Conservancy
Giltaman
Lowamara
Merti El Debe
Samburu NR
To Kalama Community Wildlife Conservancy Gate (4km); Saruni Samburu Lodge (16km); Ol Lolokwe (25km); Wamba (57km)
Mission Hospital
Church School
Archer's Post
A2
E820
River
Ewaso Ngiro
To Shaba NR (3km)
Archer's Post Gate
Ranger's Post
Nakadeli
Lowa Mara
The Swamp
Choka Gate
Buffalo Springs
Koitogor (1245m)
Disused Airstrip
Six-Mile Circuit
4WD only
Bar Lolgoto River
Giltaman River
Special Campsites
Ranger's Post
Special Campsite
West Gate
Ewaso Ngiro River
Lolkoitoi
Nashapa Viewpoint
Special Campsites
Warden's Office
Uaso Gate
Maji Chumvi River
Buffalo Springs NR
Isiolo River
Special Campsite
Special Campsite
Ranger's Post
Gare Mara Gate
Airstrip
Buffalo Springs NR
4WD only
Kubi Panya Lookout
To A2 Hwy (1.5km)
To Isiolo (23km)
A2

Samburu & Buffalo Springs National Reserves

Sleeping

1 Beach Camp C3
2 Elephant Watch Camp A3
3 Public Campsite 1 .... F4
4 Public Campsite 2 .... F4
5 Public Campsite 3 .... F3
6 Public Campsite 4 .... F3
7 Public Campsite 5 .... G3
8 Samburu Intrepids Club B2

way. These tents come with underfloor lighting, lots of stained glass and giant, walk-in rain showers. Oh, you can also throw in a swamp filled with wallowing buffalo overlooked by an infinity pool full of wallowing guests.

Special campsites CAMPGROUND $
(camping US$15) Of the several sites (no facilities), Funan, set in Shaba's core, takes the cake. Shaded by acacias, it's next to a semi-permanent spring, which provides water for visitors and wildlife. A ranger must accompany you to these sites; the cost is included in the fee but a tip is appropriate.

Information

Buffalo Springs, **Shaba** and **Samburu** (admission adult/child US$70/20) entries are interchangeable, so you only pay once, even if you're visiting all three in one day.

Getting There & Away

The vehicle-less can wrangle a 4WD and driver in Archer's Post for about US$100 per half-day. **Airkenya** (www.airkenya.com) and **Safarilink** (www.safarilink-kenya.com) have frequent flights from Nairobi to Samburu and Shaba.

MARSABIT

☎069

Marsabit is a long way from anywhere. The road from Isiolo is now smooth tarmac for about half the distance (and it's likely that during the lifetime of this book the road will be surfaced all the way) but even so for hour after scorching hour you'll pass an almost unchanging monoscape of scrubby bush, where encounters with wildlife are common and elegant Samburu walk their herds of camels and goats. As the afternoon heats up, and your brain starts to cook, you'll find the world around you sliding in and out of focus, as

WARNING

Unfortunately, the strong warrior traditions of northern Kenya's nomadic peoples have led to security problems plaguing the region for years. With an influx of cheap guns from conflict zones surrounding Kenya, minor conflicts stemming from grazing rights and cattle rustling have quickly escalated into ongoing gun battles that the authorities struggle to contain.

While travellers, who rarely witness any intertribal conflict, may consider the issue exaggerated, the scale of the problem is enormous and growing. Over the past decade hundreds of people are thought to have been killed and more than 160,000 been displaced by intertribal conflicts. The serious drought of the past few years has dramatically reduced grazing land, dried up water supplies and had a huge impact on traditional nomadic social structures. This has led in turn to a major escalation in intertribal fighting and cattle rustling. Fortunately, security on the main routes in the north, and anywhere a tourist is likely to be, is generally good (though a group of tourists was attacked in 2011 on the Moyale to Isiolo road and, for a few days in October 2011, the Isiolo to Samburu National Reserve road was cut due to tribal violence). For the moment, though, convoys and armed guards are no longer used between Marich and Lodwar or between Isiolo and Moyale, on the Ethiopian border.

Sadly, bloody conflict continues in large parts of the north. The whole northeastern region around Garsen, Wajir and Mandera is still unstable and you should avoid travelling here. And anywhere even remotely close to the Somali border is definitely off-limits. And wherever you're travelling in the north, you should always seek local advice about the latest developments before travelling, and never take unnecessary risks.

SAMBURU, BUFFALO SPRINGS & SHABA NATIONAL RESERVES

» **Why Go** To see the unusual dry country and northern versions of all the animals you've seen elsewhere in Kenya, as well as for fantastic bird-watching.

» **When to Go** Year-round, but between November and March animals congregate near the Ewaso Ngiro River.

» **Practicalities** Isiolo is the main gateway town. Tickets are valid for all three parks but you must buy your ticket at the gate to the park in which you're staying.

mirages flicker on the horizon. Then, as evening comes, one final mirage appears: a massive wall of forested mountains providing an unlikely home to mammoth tusked elephants. But this is no mirage, this is Marsabit.

The small town sits on the side of a 6300-sq-km shield volcano, whose surface is peppered with 180 cinder cones and 22 volcanic craters (*gofs* or *maars*), many of which house lakes – at least they did until recently. The drought which began in 2009 has hit Marsabit hard. At the time of research, the area, which just a couple of years earlier had been relatively lush and green, was utterly parched and covered in dust.

Sleeping

Water is a very scarce commodity in Marsabit and all the guesthouses have to truck it in. Use it sparingly.

JeyJey Centre HOTEL $

(☎0717383883; A2 Hwy; s/tw with shared bathroom KSh400/600, r with bathroom KSh750) This mud-brick castle bedecked in flowers is something of a travellers' centre and is always bursting with road-hardened souls. Basic rooms with mosquito nets surround a courtyard, and bathrooms (even shared ones) sport on-demand hot water. There's also an unattractive campsite (per person KSh250).

Nomads Trail Hotel HOTEL $

(☎0722259699; A2 Hwy; r incl breakfast KSh1200-1500) The smartest accommodation in town, though not necessarily the best value, are the prim and proper rooms on offer here. All rooms have attached bathrooms that come with, wait for it, real hot water from a real shower!

Henry's Camp CAMPGROUND $

(☎0717766145; camping per person KSH300, dm KSh500) The only real option for campers is this sun-blasted campsite a couple of kilometres out of town. There's a barbecue, fire pit, shady dining area and, for those who've had enough of camping, a mud-walled cabin with six dorm beds.

Eating & Drinking

Five Steers Hotel KENYAN $

(A2 Hwy; meals KSh70-130; ⊙lunch & dinner) With a wooden fenced-off terrace, this place is the height of Marsabit style. The '½Federation' meal (a bulging pile of rice, spaghetti, beef, vegetables and chapatti) is filling and tasty. The owner is a good source of information on onward transport.

WORTH A TRIP

NDOTO MOUNTAINS

Climbing from the Korante Plain's sands are the magnificent rusty bluffs and ridges of the Ndoto Mountains. Kept a virtual secret from the travelling world by their remote location, the Ndotos abound with hiking, climbing and bouldering potential. **Mt Poi** (2050m), which resembles the world's largest bread loaf from some angles, is a technical climber's dream, its sheer 800m north face begging to be bagged. If you're fit and have a whole day to spare, it's a great hike to the summit and the views are extraordinary.

The tiny village of **Ngurunit** is the best base for your adventures and is interesting in its own right, with captivating, traditionally dressed Samburu people living in simple, yet elegantly woven, grass huts.

Al-Subra Modern Hotel KENYAN, ETHIOPIAN $
(meals KSh70-150; ⏲lunch & dinner) As well as all the Kenyan staples, this place presents the first flavours of Ethiopia with its *injera* (Ethiopian sour pancake-like staple) and *wat* (spicy stew). It has two TVs, one blasting out Kenyan programs, the other Ethiopian, making either impossible to watch.

Information

Kenya Commercial Bank (off Post Office Rd) With ATM.

Cyber Wireless Internet World (per hr KSh60; ⏲8am-7pm Mon-Sat, until 5pm Sun) Opening hours aren't always what they're supposed to be.

Medical clinic (Post Office Rd; ⏲8am-7pm Mon-Sat, noon-7pm Sun)

Post office (Post Office Rd)

Getting There & Away

Get the latest security and Ethiopian border information from locals and the police station before leaving town.

4WD The road to Moyale is still a rutted, dusty, car-destroying mess. The only fuel north is in Moyale, so stock up in Marsabit.

BUS **Moyale Raha Buses** connect Marsabit to Moyale daily at 8.30am (KSh1000, 8½ hours). Calling it a bus is something of a misnomer: instead try to picture the offspring of a truck that slept with a bus! Heading south **Liban Buses** run boringly normal buses to Isiolo (KSh700, six hours) at 8am. Journey times will fall as the sealed road grows.

MARSABIT NATIONAL PARK

Within the larger national reserve, this small **park** (adult/child US$20/10), nestled on Mt Marsabit's upper slopes, is coated in thick forests and contains lions, leopards, elephants (some with huge tusks) and buffaloes. The dense forest makes spotting wildlife very difficult but help is at hand in the form of a couple of natural clearings, where animal sightings are almost guaranteed.

It used to be possible to walk in the park but at the time of writing this had been suspended due to a shortage of rangers and widespread encroachment by local herders with animals to feed.

Sleeping & Eating

Lake Paradise Special Campsite CAMPGROUND $
(camping US$30, plus set-up fee KSh5000) Although there's nothing except a dried-up lake bed and firewood, this picturesque site is easily the best place to stay in the park.

Marsabit National Park

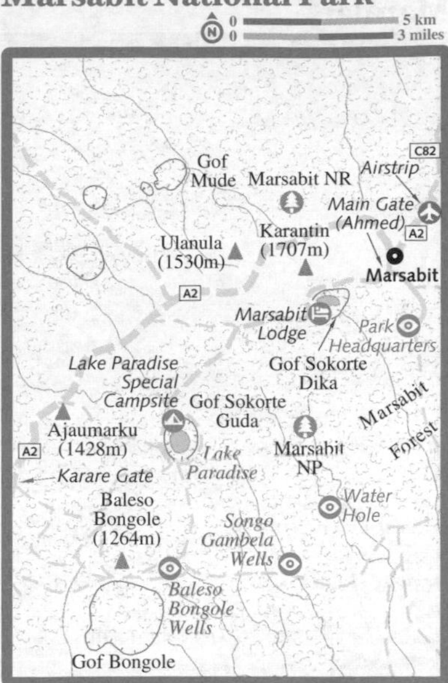

Due to roaming buffalo and elephants, a ranger must be present when you camp here.

Marsabit Lodge LODGE $$
(☎Nairobi 020-604781; www.marsabitlodge.com; s/tw incl breakfast US$83/106) Judging by the drab 1970's deco, mouldy bathrooms and not quite as clean as you'd like surfaces you'd never know that this place has been recently renovated. Still, the location, on the edge of the (now largely dry) lake occupying Gof Sokorte Dika, is spectacular and it's about as cheap a national park lodge as you'll find.

Maralal to Turkana's Eastern Shore

Journeying to a sea of jade shouldn't be something that is easy to do and this route, the ultimate Kenyan adventure, is certainly not easy. But for the battering you'll take you'll be rewarded a thousand times over with memories of vibrant tribes, camel caravans running into a red sunset, mesmerising volcanic landscapes and, of course, the north's greatest jewel – the Jade Sea, Lake Turkana.

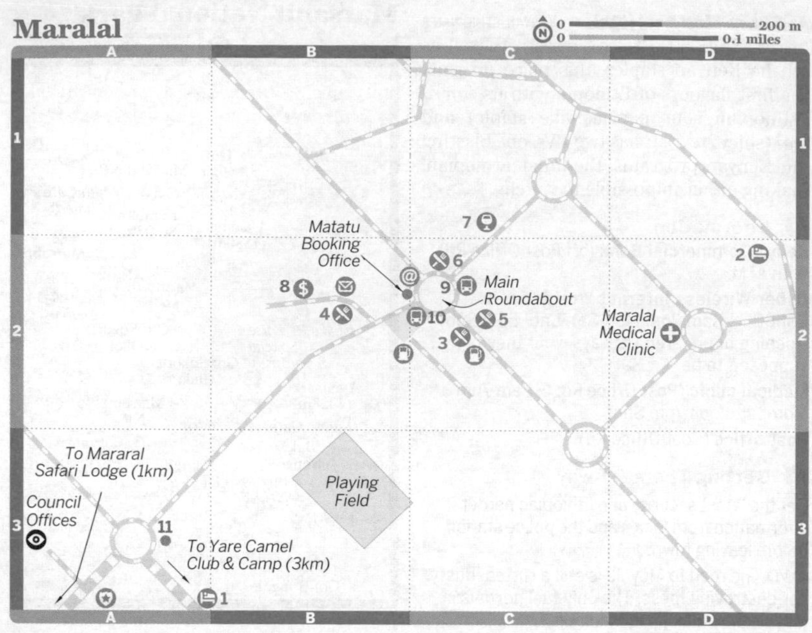

Maralal

Sleeping

1 Samburu Guest House A3
2 Sunbird Guest House D2

Eating

3 Hard Rock Café C2
4 Market B2
5 Pop Inn Hotel C2
Samburu Guest House .... (see 1)
Sunbird Guest House .... (see 2)
6 Sunguia Supermarket C2

Drinking

7 Buffalo House Hotel C1

Information

8 Kenya Commercial Bank B2

Transport

9 4WD Matatus & Land Rover Taxis C2
BP Petrol Station .... (see 11)
10 Matatus C2
11 Truck Pick-up Area A3

MARALAL

☎065

Walking down Maralal's dusty streets, you can imagine Clint Eastwood emerging from a bar and proclaiming the town not big enough for the two of you. With its swinging cowboy doors and camels tied up outside colourful wooden shopfronts, it's impossible not to think that you've somehow been transported to the Wild West.

Maralal has gained an international reputation for its fantastically frenetic **International Camel Derby** and a visit over its duration is truly unforgettable. Less crazy, but almost as memorable, are the year-round camel safaris and treks that are offered here.

Sadly, most visitors don't delve into Maralal, stopping only for a night en route to Lake Turkana. The opposite is true for independent travellers, who often end up spending more time here than planned, simply because transport north is erratic at best. Take it in your stride, though. After all, the town's most famous former resident was one of the greatest explorers of the 20th century, Wilfred Thesiger, and if he decided that Maralal was the perfect place for retirement, then it must be doing something right.

Sights & Activities

Trekking WALKING

The **Loroghi Hills Circuit**, which takes in one of Kenya's most astounding vistas, Lesiolo, is a rewarding five days and 78km. This trek is detailed in Lonely Planet's *Trekking in East Africa*. Somewhat less lengthy walks are possible by just strolling aimlessly around the high country and down the paths linking *shambas* that surround the town.

Yare Camel Club & Camp CAMEL SAFARI

(☎62295, Nairobi 020-2101137) Organises guides and camels for independent camel safaris in the region. Self-catered day/overnight trips cost US$15/30 per person.

FREE **Maralal National Sanctuary** WILDLIFE RESERVE

Surrounding the town is this sanctuary, home to zebras, impalas, hyenas and elephants. There's no entry fee and you'll probably have the place much to yourself. One of the best ways to take in the animals is with a cold beverage in hand at Maralal Safari Lodge's bar, which also attracts animals after a thirst-quencher from the waterhole just in front.

Sleeping

TOP CHOICE **Sunbird Guest House** GUESTHOUSE $

(☎0720654567; s/d KSh700/1000; P) This shiny and very friendly place has quiet, clean and comfortable rooms with nice linen, mosquito nets, sparkling bathrooms, 24-hour hot water and good security. The courtyard has a sunny, garden vibe and there's a pleasant attached restaurant.

Samburu Guest House HOTEL $

(☎0729733435; s/d KSh700/1300; P) Only a month old at the time of our visit this large pink cube of a building has spacious rooms that still retain their sparkling just-out-of-the-wrapper look – of course whether it manages to maintain these lofty standards remains to be seen. It's a bit of a walk into the town centre.

Maralal Safari Lodge LODGE $$

(☎0727373406, in Nairobi 020-211124; www.angelfire.com/jazz/maralal; camping KSh500, s/d/tw with breakfast Ksh4950/7000/7000; P) The wooden cottages are starting to show their age, but the low lighting helps hide the worst of it and, as discounts are as common as impala at the waterhole right outside your window, you can't really moan. The open fireplaces in each room and the views over animal-filled plains provide a romantic atmosphere.

Yare Camel Club & Camp CAMPGROUND $

(☎62295, in Nairobi 020-2101137; www.yaresafaris.co.ke; camping KSh300, s/tw/tr US$32/48/55; @) This longstanding favourite, 3km south of town, is under new management and although the dreary cabins, which have seen price hikes, are now laughably poor value it's still a good spot for overlanders thanks to grassy lawns perfect for camping on.

Eating

Unless you've got the ugali (a staple made from maize or cassava flour, or both) or *nyama choma* itch, few of your taste buds will be scratched here. That said, check out the restaurants of the **Sunbird** and **Samburu Guest Houses**. Stock up at the **market** or

DON'T MISS

MARALAL INTERNATIONAL CAMEL DERBY

Inaugurated by Yare Safaris in 1990, the annual Maralal International Camel Derby held in early August is one of the biggest events in Kenya, attracting riders and spectators from around the world. The races are open to anyone, and the extended after-parties at Yare Camel Club & Camp are notorious – you're likely to bump into some genuine characters here.

Not interested in parties and just want some fast-moving camel action? Then the derby's first race has your name written all over it – it's for amateur camel riders. Pony up KSh1000 for your entry and another KSh3000 for your slobbering steed and get racing! It's a butt-jarring 11km journey. Don't even start feeling sorry for your backside – the professional riders cover 42km.

For further information contact **Yare Safaris** (☎Maralal 020-2101137; www.yaresafaris.co.ke) or Yare Camel Club & Camp in Maralal.

the **Sunguia Supermarket** if you're heading north.

Hard Rock Café KENYAN $
(meals KSh60-170; ⏲lunch & dinner) While the Hard Rock Café chain would cringe at the use of their name, this Somali-run restaurant is the town centre's best, and pinkest, restaurant. If you eat here you will of course partake in the KK, the house special, which is a heavy mash of rice, chapatti and spaghetti with some token vegetables.

Pop Inn Hotel KENYAN $
(meals KSh80-150; ⏲lunch & dinner) This zebra-striped building has decent Kenyan staples but its claim to have the 'best food south of the Sahara' might be pushing it a tad – south of the roundabout seems more realistic.

Drinking

The **Buffalo House Hotel** used to be a legendary drinking and partying spot but not so much these days. Even so the sight of a Samburu Moran in full regalia propping up the bar isn't something you'll forget in a hurry.

Information

Kenya Commercial Bank Behind the market, with an ATM (the last one going north).
Links Cyber Café (per hr KSh120; ⏲8am-8pm Mon-Sat & 2-8pm Sun)
Maralal Medical Clinic (⏲Mon-Sat)
Post office Next to the market.

Getting There & Away

Matatus serve Nyahururu (KSh500, three to four hours), Rumuruti (KSh500, 2½ hours), Wamba (KSh400, 3½ hours). For Nairobi you need to change in Nyahururu. Reaching Isiolo involves overnighting in Wamba to catch the early-morning southbound matatu.

During the dry season a few 4WD matatus (KSh500, five hours) and Land Rover taxis head north each week along a diabolical road to Baragoi (KSh600, five hours). If you're intending to head to Loyangalani and Lake Turkana, you'll have to wait a few days to a week for a truck (KSh1000 to KSh1500, nine to 12 hours). After rain you can expect prices of all transport to rise.

Most transport leaves from the main roundabout, while trucks usually pick up passengers at the former BP station.

BARAGOI

The long descent off the Loroghi Plateau towards Baragoi serves up some sweet vistas and for mile after gorgeous mile you'll literally see nothing but tree-studded grasslands alive with wildlife. Reaching Baragoi is a bit of an anticlimax though, as the dusty, diminutive town is clearly outdone by its surroundings.

The **Star Station Filling** sells pricey petrol and the bougainvillea-dressed **Morning Star Guest House** (r with shared bathroom KSh300) provides for a night's kip – though they don't supply the peg you'll need to place over your nose before entering the communal toilets.

Getting There & Away

The dirt track from Maralal to Baragoi is very rocky in places. The drive takes a minimum of four or five hours.

APPROACHING THE LAKE

The road between Baragoi and South Horr, the next town along, is in reasonable shape and consists of compacted sand and bumpy rocky sections. Almost 23km north of South Horr, when the valley opens to the northern plains, you'll see massive Mt Kulal (2293m) in the distance and Devil's Hand, a large rock outcrop resembling a fist, to your immediate right. Just north is the eastern turn-off to Marsabit via Kargi, so if you're heading for Turkana keep left. If you get mixed up, just remember that Mt Kulal on your right is good and that Mt Kulal on your left is very, very bad (unless, of course, you're heading to Marsabit!).

Further north, the scrub desert scatters and you'll be greeted by vast volcanic armies of shimmering bowling-ball-sized boulders, cinder cones and reddish-purple hues – Mt Kulal's shattered lava fields. If this arresting and barren Martian landscape doesn't take your breath away, the first sight of the sparkling Jade Sea a few kilometres north certainly will.

As you descend to the lake, South Island stands proudly before you, while Teleki Volcano's geometrically perfect cone lurks on Turkana's southern shore. Before you jump in the water, remember that Turkana has the world's largest crocodile population.

LOYANGALANI

Standing in utter contrast to the dour desert shades surrounding it, tiny Loyangalani assaults all your senses in one crazy explosion of clashing colours, feather headdresses and blood-red robes. Overlooking Lake Turkana and surrounded by small ridges of pillow lava (evidence that this area used to be underwater), the sandy streets of this one-camel town are a meeting point of the great northern tribes, Turkana and Samburu, Gabbra and El Molo. It's easily the most exotic corner of Kenya and a fitting reward after the hard journey here.

Sights & Activities

South Island National Park WILDLIFE RESERVE
(adult/child US$20/10) Opened as a public reserve in 1983 and made a World Heritage Site by Unesco in 1997, this tiny 39-sq-km purplish volcanic island is completely barren and uninhabited, apart from large populations of crocodiles, poisonous snakes and feral goats. Spending the night at a **special campsite** (camping US$15) makes for an even eerier trip.

In calm weather a speedboat can reach the island in 30 minutes and circumnavigate it in another hour. As speed boats are somewhat limited in number, you'll probably end up in something much more sedate: reckon on a six-hour return trip, for which you'll pay about KSh4000 per hour. Ask at either the KWS office in town or the Oasis Lodge about hiring boats.

Mt Kulal MOUNTAIN
Mt Kulal dominates Lake Turkana's eastern horizon, and its forested volcanic flanks offer up some serious hiking possibilities. This fertile lost world in the middle of the desert is home to some unique creatures, including the Mt Kulal Chameleon, a beautiful lizard first recorded in only 2003. No matter what the local guides tell you, trekking up to the summit (2293m) from Loyangalani in a day isn't feasible. Plan on several days for a return trip; guides (KSh1000 per day) and donkeys (KSh500 per day) to carry your gear can be hired in Loyangalani, or you can part with substantial sums of cash (KSh8000 to KSh12,000) for a lift up Mt Kulal to the villages of **Arapal** or **Gatab**. From there you can head for the summit and spend a long day (eight to 10 hours) hiking back down to the base of the mountain.

El Molo Villages VILLAGE
The El Molo tribe (see p584), which is one of Africa's smallest, lives on the lake shore just north of here in the villages of **Layeni** and **Komote**. Although outwardly similar to the Turkana, the El Molo are linguistically linked to the Somali and Rendille people. Unfortunately, the last speaker of their traditional language died before the turn of the millennium. Visiting their villages (per person KSh700 to KSh1000) is something of a circus.

Sleeping & Eating

Let's face it; you came north for adventure, not comfort.

TOP CHOICE **Palm Shade Camp** BANDA $
(0726714768; camping KSh500, s/tw bandas with shared bathroom KSh750/1500) Drop your tent on the grass beneath acacias and doum palms or crash in the tidy domed rondavels. The huts have simple wood beds with foam mattresses and unique walls with meshed cut-outs that let light and heavenly evening breezes in. Throw in the town's best toilets and showers, a cooking shelter and electricity until 10pm and your decision is an easy one.

Cold Drink Hotel KENYAN $
(meals KSh100-150; lunch & dinner) Not just cold drinks but also, according to locals, the finest eating experience in all of Turkana country. Well, OK, maybe in Loyagalani.

Getting There & Away

Trucks, loaded with fish (and soon-to-be-smelly passengers) leave Loyangalani for Maralal (KSh1000 to KSh1500, nine to 12 hours) around once or twice a week at best. Trucks heading in any other direction are even rarer.

If you're travelling in your own vehicle, you have two options to reach Marsabit: continue northeast from Loyangalani across the dark stones of the Chalbi Desert towards North Horr, or head 67km south towards South Horr and take the eastern turn-off via Kargai. The 270km Chalbi route (10 to 12 hours) is hard in the dry season and impossible after rain. It's also wise to ask for directions every chance you get, otherwise it's easy to take the wrong track and not realise until hours later. The 241km southern route (six to seven hours) via the Karoli Desert and Kargi is composed of compacted sands and is marginally less difficult in the rainy season.

Marich to Turkana's Western Shore

Despite boasting some of northern Kenya's greatest attributes, such as copious kilometres of Jade Sea shoreline, striking volcanic landscapes, ample wildlife and vivid Turkana tribes, this remote corner of the country has seen relatively few visitors. With fairly reliable public transport this is definitely the easier side of the lake in which to grab a taste of the northern badlands.

MARICH TO LODWAR

The spectacular descent from Marich Pass through the lush, cultivated Cherangani Hills leads to arid surroundings, with sisal plants, cactus trees and acacias lining both the road and the chocolate-brown Morun River. Just north, the minuscule village of Marich marks your entrance into northern Kenya.

Sights & Activities

Trekking WALKING

Although the northern plains may beckon, it's worth heading into the hills for some trekking action. **Mt Sekerr** (3326m) is a few kilometres northwest of Marich and can be climbed comfortably in a three-day round trip via the agricultural plots of the Pokot tribe, passing through forest and open moors.

The **Cherangani Hills**, the green and lush chalk next to the northern desert's baked cheese, sit immediately south and are also ripe with superb trekking options. In fact, many people consider these intensely farmed and deeply forested hills to be one of the most beautiful corners of the country. Reaching the dome of **Mt Koh** (3211m), which soars some 1524m above the adjacent plains, is a hard but rewarding two-day slog. A more horizontally endowed (13km one way) and vertically challenged (only 300m elevation gain) trek is possible up the **Weiwei Valley** from **Sigor** to **Tamkal**.

The Marich Pass Field Studies Centre offers English-speaking Pokot and Turkana guides for half-day (KSh550), full-day (KSh750) and overnight (KSh1000) treks.

Sleeping & Eating

Marich Pass Field Studies Centre CAMPGROUND, BANDA $

(www.gg.rhul.ac.uk/MarichPass; camping KSh360, dm KSh420, s/tw with private bathroom KSh1450/1950, with shared bathroom KSh900/1240) Just north of Marich village, this is basically a residential facility for visiting student groups, but it also makes a great base for independent travellers. The centre occupies a beautiful site alongside the misty Morun River and is surrounded by dense bush and woodland. Facilities include a secure campsite with drinking water, toilets, showers and firewood, as well as a tatty dorm and simple, comfortable *bandas*.

Getting There & Away

The road from Kitale via Makutano is the oh-so-scenic A1 Hwy, often described as 'Kenya's most spectacular tarmac road'. The buses plying the A1 between Kitale and Lodwar can drop you anywhere along the route. You may be asked to pay the full fare to Lodwar (KSh1000), but a smile and some patient negotiating should reduce the cost.

DON'T MISS

SIBILOI NATIONAL PARK

A Unesco World Heritage Site and probably Kenya's most remote national park, **Sibiloi** (www.sibiloi.com; adult/child US$20/10) is located up the eastern shore of Lake Turkana and covers 1570 sq km. It was here that Dr Richard Leakey discovered the skull of a *Homo habilis* believed to be 2½ million years old, and where others have unearthed evidence of *Homo erectus*. Despite the area's fascinating prehistory, fossil sites and wonderful arid ecosystem, the difficulties involved in getting this far north tend to discourage visitors, which is a shame. It seems slightly ironic that the so-called 'Cradle of Mankind' is now almost entirely unpopulated.

The National Museums of Kenya (NMK) maintain a small museum and **Koobi Fora** (www.kfrp.com), a research base. It's usually possible to sleep in one of the base's **bandas** (per person KSh1000) or to pitch a tent in one of the **campsites** (camping per person KSh200). At the time of research a member of the Leakey family was in the process of constructing a lodge here.

Contact the **KWS** (kws@kws.org) and **NMK** (☎Nairobi 020-3742131; www.museums.or.ke) before venturing in this direction.

In the dry season it's a tricky seven-hour drive north from Loyangalani to Sibiloi. You'll need a guide from the KWS. Hiring a jeep in Loyangalani will work out at around KSh15,000 per day. It's also possible to hire a boat (KSh22,000 to KSh30,000 return with an overnight stop) from Fergusons Gulf (see p320) on the western side of the lake.

DON'T MISS

CENTRAL ISLAND NATIONAL PARK

Bursting from the depths of Lake Turkana and home to thousands of living dinosaurs is the Jurassic world of Central Island Volcano, last seen belching molten sulphur and steam just over three decades ago. It's one of the most otherworldly places in Kenya.

Both a **national park** (adult/child US$20/10) and Unesco World Heritage Site, Central Island is an intriguing place to visit, and budding Crocodile Dundee types will love the 14,000 or so Nile crocodiles, some of which are massive in proportion, who flock here at certain times of year (May is the most crocodile-friendly month, but there are some crocs here year-round). The most northerly crater lake, which is saline, attracts blushing pink flocks of flamingos.

Camping (adult/child US$15/10) is possible and, unlike South Island National Park, there are trees to tie your tent to. But there's no water or any other facilities, so come prepared.

Hiring a boat from Ferguson's Gulf is the only option to get here. Depending on what you drive up in, locals can ask anywhere from KSh8000 to KSh20,000 for the trip. A fair price is KSh8000 to KSh9000 for a motorboat. You should also visit the KWS office, a couple of kilometres out of Kalokol towards Ferguson's Gulf, to pay your entrance fees and get the latest lowdown on the island.

Between Marich and Lokichar the A1 is a bumpy mess of corrugated dirt and lonely islands of tarmac. The opposite is true for the remaining 60km to Lodwar, where patches outnumber potholes and driving is straightforward.

The security situation is in a constant state of flux in this area. At the time of research convoys were not required, but there had been numerous incidents of cattle rustling as well as tribal clashes. This is most prevalent in the area between Marich and Lokichar.

LODWAR

054

Besides Lokichoggio near the South Sudan border, Lodwar is the only town of any size in the northwest. Volcanic hills skirted by traditional Turkana dwellings sit north of town and make for fine sunrise spots. If you're visiting Lake Turkana, you'll find it convenient to stay here for at least one night.

Sleeping

Nawoitorong Guest House HOTEL $
(0722938814; camping KSh300, s/tw with shared bathroom KSh500/800, cottages KSh800 – 2000) Built entirely out of local materials and run by a local women's group, Nawoitorong is an excellent option, and the only one for campers. Thatched roofs alleviate the need for fans and all rooms have mosquito nets.

Lodwar Lodge HOTEL $
(0728007512; r with breakfast KSh850-1350; P) Smart concrete cottages that are quiet and secure. The best of several town centre options.

Eating

Nawoitorong Guest House KENYAN $
(meals KSh150-225; lunch & dinner) Burgers and toasted sandwiches join local curries and various meaty fries on the menu. It offers the most pleasant dining experience in the region but give them time – lots of it – to prepare dinner!

Salama Hotel KENYAN $
(meals KSh80-150; lunch & dinner) The most popular place in the town centre. The culinary highlight of the Salama has to be its giant bowl of *pilau* (KSh100). There's always a crowd of people here waiting for buses to depart.

Information

Kenya Commercial Bank Has ATM and changes cash and travellers cheques.

Maxtech Computer Solutions and Cyber Café (per hr KSh60; 7am-7pm Mon-Sun)

Getting There & Away

Fly540 (www.fly540.com) runs daily flights from Nairobi to Lodwar via Kitale for around US$150.

A couple of different bus companies operate along the route to Kitale (KSh1000, 8½ hours). Most depart nightly at 5.30 to 6pm from outside the Salama Hotel.

ELIYE SPRINGS

Spring water percolates out of crumbling bluffs and oodles of palms bring a taste of the tropics to the remote sandy shores of

Lake Turkana. Down on the slippery shore children play in the lake's warm waters, while Central Island lurks magically on the distant horizon.

Besides the spring water there are no facilities, bar the skeleton of an old resort which locals may allow you to camp in.

Getting There & Away

The turn-off for Eliye Springs is signposted a short way along the Lodwar–Kalokol road. The gravel is easy to follow until it suddenly peters out and you're faced with a fork in the road – stay left. The rest of the way is a mix of gravel, deep sand and even deeper sand, which can turn into a muddy nightmare in the wet season. If you don't have your own vehicle, you can usually arrange a car and driver in Lodwar for about KSh5000 including waiting time.

FERGUSON'S GULF

Ferguson's Gulf, while more accessible than Eliye Springs, has none of its southern neighbour's charm. Fishing boats in various states of disrepair litter its grubby western beach and a definite feeling of bleakness pervades.

If you're planning on visiting Central Island National Park (p319) or Sibiloi National Park (p318), this is the best place to arrange a boat.

If you want to stay the nearby village of **Kalokol** contains the **Starehe Lodge** (s/d Ksh250/400) which claims to offer the 'best accommodation in town'; it's also the only accommodation in town.

Getting There & Away

Few people in Lodwar have heard of Ferguson's Gulf so you need to ask around for transport to nearby Kalokol, which is 75km along a good stretch of sealed road. Ferguson's Gulf is only a few kilometres from there. Matatus to Kalokol cost KSh250 or a taxi direct to Ferguson's Gulf will be around KSh4000 to KSh5000 with waiting time.

THE COAST

There's something in the air here. It's the smell of salt and spice on the streets of Mombasa (*Kisiwa Cha Mvita* in Swahili – the Island of War). It's muttered chants echoing over the flagstones of a Jain temple, and the ecstatic passion of the call to prayer. It's the sun's glint off coral castles, it's ribbons of white sand, it's the teal break of a vanishing wave and it's the sight of a Zanzibar-bound dhow slipping over the horizon.

Thanks to the long interplay of Africa, India and Arabia, the coast feels wildly different to the rest of Kenya. Its people, the Swahili, have created a distinctive Indian Ocean society – built on the scent of trade with distant shores – that lends real romance to the coast's sugar-white beaches and to a city the poets have embraced for as long as ivory has been traded for iron.

Mombasa

041 / POP 939,000

Mombasa, like the coast it dominates, is both quintessentially African and somehow...not.

If your idea of Africa is roasted meat, toasted maize, beer and cattle, and farms and friendliness, those things are here (well, maybe not the cows). But it's all interwoven into the humid peel of plaster from Hindu warehouses, filigreed porches that lost their way in a Moroccan *riad* (traditional town house), spice markets that escaped India's Keralan coast, sailors chewing *miraa* (shoots chewed as a stimulant) next to boats bound for Yemen, and a giant coral castle built by invading Portuguese sailors. Thus, while the city sits perfectly at home in Africa, it could be plopped anywhere on the coast of the Indian Ocean without too many moving pains.

Therein lies Mombasa's considerable charm. But said seduction doesn't hide this town's warts, which include a sleazy underbelly, bad traffic and tribal tension. Overlaying everything is the sweating, tropical lunacy you tend to get in the world's hot zones (and it gets *hot* here).

Perhaps it's best to let the Swahili people themselves describe their city in their native tongue with an old line of poetry and proverb: *Kongowea nda mvumo, maji maangavu. Male!* ('Mombasa is famous, but its waters are dangerously deep. Beware!')

Sights & Activities

Fort Jesus FORTRESS
(Map p322; adult/child KSh800/400; 8am-6pm), All along the coast you'll spot castles and mosques carved out of coral, but the exemplar of the genre, as it were, is Fort Jesus: Mombasa's most visited site, Unesco World Heritage Site, anchor of Old Town and dominant structure of the city's harbour. The metre-thick walls, frescoed interiors, traces of European graffiti, Arabic inscriptions and

The Coast

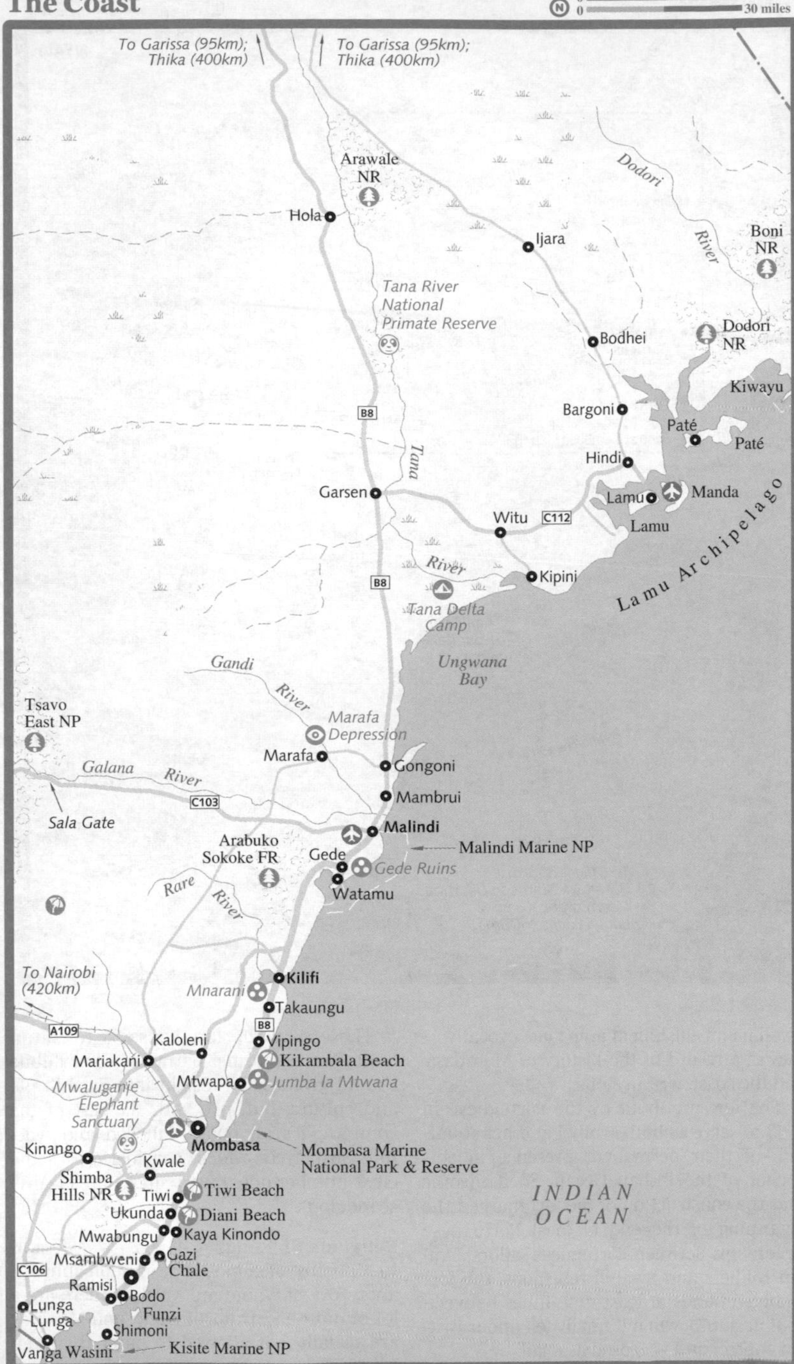
0 50 km
0 30 miles
To Garissa (95km); Thika (400km)
To Garissa (95km); Thika (400km)
Arawale NR
Hola
Dodori
River
Ijara
Boni NR
Tana River National Primate Reserve
Bodhei
Dodori NR
Kiwayu
B8
Bargoni
Paté
Paté
Hindi
Tana
Garsen
Lamu
Manda
Witu
C112
Lamu
Lamu Archipelago
River
Kipini
B8
Tana Delta Camp
Ungwana Bay
Gandi
River
Tsavo East NP
Marafa Depression
Marafa
Gongoni
Galana
River
Mambrui
C103
Sala Gate
Malindi
Arabuko Sokoke FR
Malindi Marine NP
Gede
Gede Ruins
Watamu
Rare
River
To Nairobi (420km)
Kilifi
Mnarani
Takaungu
A109
B8
Vipingo
Kaloleni
Mariakani
Kikambala Beach
Mtwapa
Jumba la Mtwana
Mwaluganje Elephant Sanctuary
Mombasa
Mombasa Marine National Park & Reserve
Kinango
Kwale
Shimba Hills NR
Tiwi
Tiwi Beach
Ukunda
Diani Beach
INDIAN OCEAN
Mwabungu
Kaya Kinondo
Msambweni
Gazi
Chale
C106
Ramisi
Bodo
Lunga Lunga
Funzi
Shimoni
Vanga
Wasini
Kisite Marine NP

Mombasa

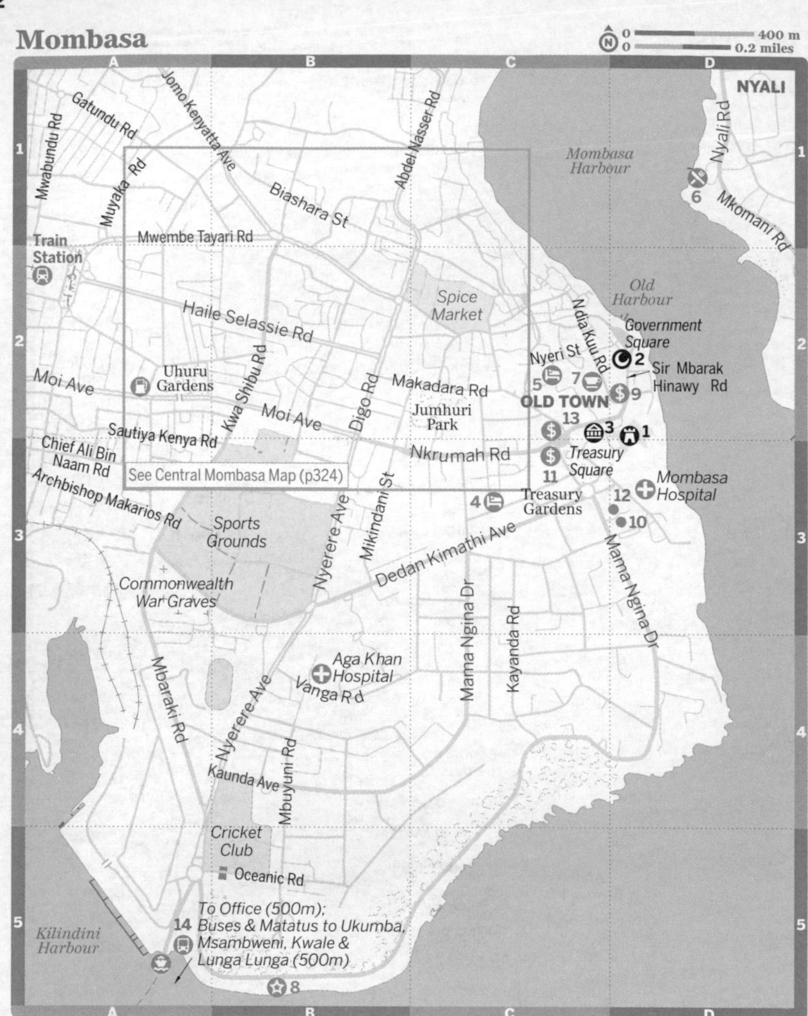

Swahili embellishment aren't just evocative – they're a record of the history of Mombasa, and the coast, writ in stone.

The fort was built by the Portuguese in 1593 to serve as both symbol and headquarters of their permanent presence in this corner of the Indian Ocean. So it's ironic that the construction of the fort marked the beginning of the end of local Portuguese hegemony. Between Portuguese sailors, Omani soldiers and Swahili rebellions, the fort changed hands at least nine times between 1631 and 1875, when it finally fell under British control and was used as a jail.

These days the fort houses a **museum** built over the former barracks. The exhibits should give a good insight into Swahili life and culture, but, like with the rest of the complex, it's all poorly labelled and woefully displayed, which, considering it's the city's number-one tourist attraction, is fairly scandalous.

Religious Buildings RELIGIOUS

In this city of almost one million inhabitants, 70% of whom are Muslim, there are a lot of mosques. Unfortunately, non-Muslims are usually not allowed to enter them, al-

Mombasa

Sights
1 Fort Jesus ... D2
2 Mandhry Mosque ... D2
3 Old Law Courts ... C2

Activities, Courses & Tours
Tamarind Dhow ... (see 6)

Sleeping
4 Lotus Hotel ... C3
5 Royal Palace Hotel ... C2
Tamarind Village ... (see 6)

Eating
6 Tamarind Restaurant ... D1

Drinking
7 Jahazi Coffee House ... C2

Entertainment
8 New Florida Nightclub ... B5

Information
9 Fort Jesus Forex Bureau ... D2
10 Immigration Office ... D3
11 Kenya Commercial Bank ... C3
12 KWS Office ... D3
13 Standard Chartered Bank ... C2

Transport
14 Local Bus & Matatu Stand ... A5

though you can have a look from the outside. **Mandhry Mosque** (Map p322; Sir Mbarak Hinawy Rd) in Old Town is an excellent example of Swahili architecture, which combines the elegant flourishes of Arabic style with the comforting, geometric patterns of African design; note, for example, the gently rounded minaret.

Mombasa's large Hindu (and smaller Jain) population doesn't lack for places of worship. The enormous **Lord Shiva Temple** (Map p324; Mwinyi Ab Rd) is airy, open and set off by an interesting sculpture garden, while the **Swaminarayan Temple** (Map p324; Haile Selassie Rd) is stuffed with highlighter-bright murals that'll make you feel as if you've been transported to Mumbai. For even more esoteric design, there's a **Sikh Temple** (Map p324; Mwembe Tayari Rd), a **Hare Krishna Temple** (Map p324; Sautiya Kenya Rd) and a lovely **Jain Temple** (Map p324; Langoni Rd).

Of the Christian churches, worth seeing is the **Holy Ghost Cathedral** (Map p324; Nyerere Ave), a very European hunk of neo-Gothic buttressed architecture, with massive fans in the walls to cool its former colonial congregations.

Spice market MARKET
(Map p324; Langoni Rd; ⌚to sunset) This market, which stretches along Nehru and Langoni Rds west of Old Town, is an evocative, sensory overload; expect lots of jostling, yelling, wheeling, dealing and of course the exotic scent of stall upon stall of cardamom, pepper, turmeric, curry powders and everything else that makes eating enjoyable.

FREE **Old Law Courts** ART GALLERY
(Map p322; Nkrumah Rd; ⌚8am-6pm) Dating from 1902, the old law courts on Nkrumah Rd have been converted into an informal gallery, with regularly changing displays of local art, Kenyan crafts, school competition pieces and votive objects from various tribal groups.

Harbour Cruises BOAT TOUR
Luxury dhow cruises around the harbour are popular in Mombasa and, notwithstanding the price, they are an excellent way to see the harbour, the Old Town and Fort Jesus, and get a slap-up meal at the end of it.

Tamarind Dhow (Map p322; ☎474600; www.tamarinddhow.com; lunch/dinner cruise per person US$40/70) is run by the posh Tamarind restaurant chain. The cruise embarks from the jetty below Tamarind restaurant in Nyali, and includes a harbour tour and fantastic meal. The lunch cruise leaves at 1pm and dinner cruise at 6pm. Prices include a complimentary cocktail and transport to and from your hotel, and the dhow itself is a beautiful piece of work.

Jahazi Marine (☎2111800; adult/child from €60/30) also offers a range of dhow trips.

Festivals & Events

Mombasa Triathlon TRIATHLON
(www.kenyatriathlon.com) An open competition with men's, women's and children's races, held in November.

Sleeping

Many people choose to skip Mombasa and head straight for the beaches to the south and north, but we'd suggest spending at least

Central Mombasa

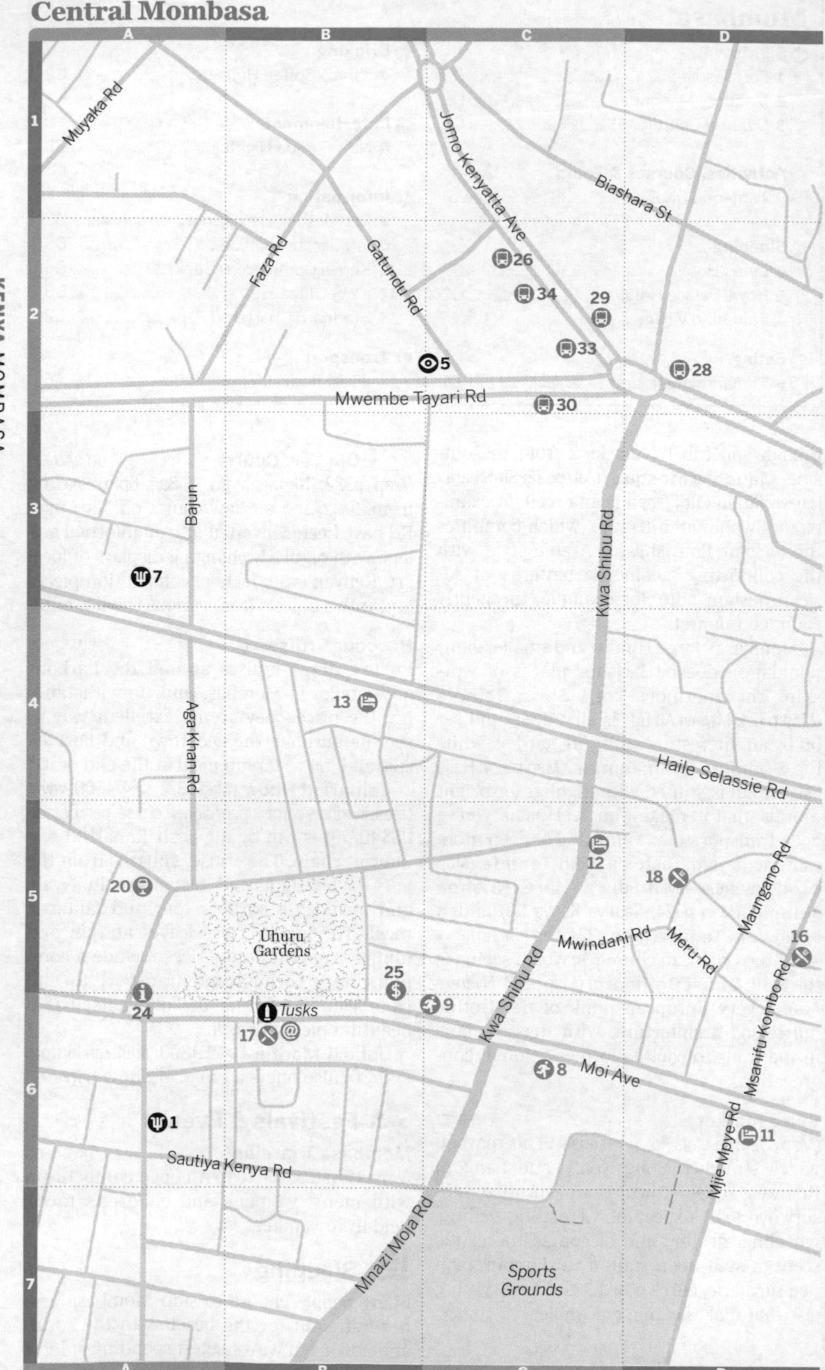

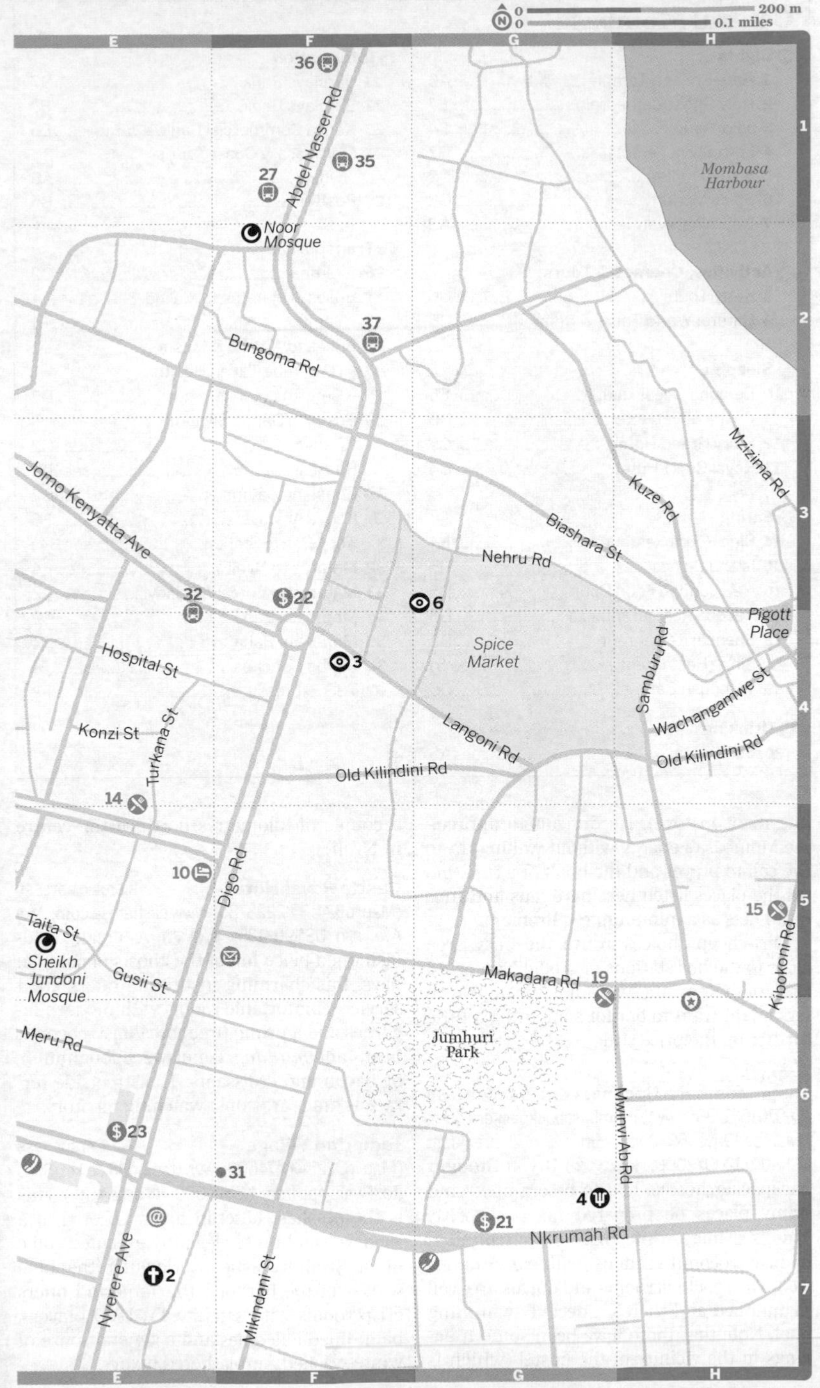
0 200 m
0 0.1 miles
E
F
G
H
1
2
3
4
5
6
7
36
35
27
Abdel Nasser Rd
Mombasa Harbour
Noor Mosque
37
Bungoma Rd
Mzizima Rd
Kuze Rd
Jomo Kenyatta Ave
Biashara St
Nehru Rd
32
22
6
Pigott Place
Spice Market
3
Hospital St
Samburu Rd
Wachangamwe St
Turkana St
Konzi St
Langoni Rd
Old Kilindini Rd
Old Kilindini Rd
14
10
Digo Rd
15
Taita St
Sheikh Jundoni Mosque
Gusii St
Makadara Rd
19
Kiboroni Rd
Meru Rd
Jumhuri Park
Mwinyi Ab Rd
23
31
4
21
Nkrumah Rd
Nyerere Ave
2
Mikindani St

Central Mombasa

Sights

1 Hare Krishna Temple ... A6
2 Holy Ghost Cathedral ... E7
3 Jain Temple ... F4
4 Lord Shiva Temple ... G7
5 Sikh Temple ... C2
6 Spice Market ... G3
7 Swaminarayan Temple ... A3

Activities, Courses & Tours

8 Ketty Tours ... C6
9 Natural World Tours & Safaris ... C6

Sleeping

10 Beracha Guest House ... E5
11 Castle Royal Hotel ... D6
12 Glory Grand Hotel ... C5
13 Royal Court Hotel ... B4

Eating

14 Blue Room Restaurant ... E4
15 Island Dishes ... H5
16 New Jundan Food Court ... D5
17 Recoda Restaurant ... B6
18 Shehnai Restaurant ... D5
Singh Restaurant ... (see 5)
19 Tarboush Cafe ... G5

Drinking

20 Bella Vista ... A5

Information

21 Barclays Bank ... G7
22 Barclays Bank ... F3
23 Kenya Commercial Bank ... E6
24 Mombasa & Coast Tourist Office ... A6
25 Postbank ... B5

Transport

26 Akamba ... C2
27 Buses & Matatus to Malindi & Lamu ... F1
28 Buses to Arusha & Moshi (Mwembe Tayari Health Centre) ... D2
29 Buses to Dar es Salaam & Tanga ... C2
Busscar ... (see 35)
30 Coastline Safaris ... C2
31 Kenya Airways ... F6
Kobil Petrol Station ... (see 34)
32 Matatus to Nyali ... E4
33 Matatus to Voi & Wundanyi ... C2
34 Mombasa Raha ... C2
35 Mombasa Raha ... F1
36 Simba Coaches ... F1
37 TSS Express ... F2

one night in town. It's difficult to appreciate Mombasa's energy without waking up to the call to prayer and the honk of a *tuk-tuk*. All the places listed here have fans and mos quito nets as a minimum requirement.

Dirt-cheap choices are in the busy area close to the bus stations on Abdel Nasser Rd and Jomo Kenyatta Ave. Lone female travellers might want to opt for something a little further up the price scale.

TOP CHOICE **Mombasa Backpackers** BACKPACKERS **$**
(☎0701561233; www.mombasabackpackers.com; Mwamba Drive 69, Nyali; dm/s/d excl breakfast KSh800/1200/2000; ❄@☜≋) If you thought backpacker hostels had to be cramped and grimy places be prepared for a surprise. This is a huge white mansion surrounded by lush, coconut gardens (with camping areas). The spacious rooms and dorms are well maintained and there's a decent swimming pool. Note that there have been some muggings in the vicinity of the hostel (which is a couple of kilometres north of the centre in Nyali).

Castle Royal Hotel HISTORIC HOTEL **$$**
(Map p324; ☎2228780; www.castlemsa.com; Moi Ave; s/d US$90/125; ❄@☜) A creaky, old-fashioned place full of the ghosts of colonial days, this charming institution offers great service, comfortable rooms with modern facilities and a primo (free) breakfast: coconut beans and *mandazi* (semisweet doughnuts), or bacon and croissants. The streetside terrace is grade A people-watching territory.

Tamarind Village RESORT **$$$**
(Map p322; ☎474600; www.tamarind.co.ke; Silos Rd, Nyali; apt from KSh13,000; P❄@☜≋) This is the plushest hotel in town. Located in a modern (and quite elegantly executed) take on a Swahili castle overlooking the blue waters of the harbour, the Tamarind offers crisp rooms with satellite TV, DVD players, palm-lined balconies and a general sense of white-washed, sun-lathered luxury.

TOURS & SAFARIS FROM MOMBASA

A number of tour companies offer standard tours of the Old Town and Fort Jesus (per person from US$45), plus safaris to Shimba Hills National Reserve and Tsavo East and Tsavo West National Parks. Most safaris are expensive lodge-based affairs, but there are a few camping safaris to Tsavo East and West.

The most popular safari is an overnight tour to Tsavo, but be warned that a typical two-day, one-night safari barely gives you time to get there and back and that your animal-spotting time will be very limited. It's much better to add in at least one extra night.

We receive a constant stream of emails from travellers who feel that their promised safari has not lived up to expectations, but the following two companies have received positive feedback.

Ketty Tours (Map p324; ☎2315178; www.kettysafari.com; Ketty Plaza, Moi Ave) Organised and reliable.

Natural World Tours & Safaris (Map p324; ☎2226715; www.naturaltoursandsafaris.com; Jeneby House, Moi Ave) A reputation for delivering what it promises.

Glory Grand Hotel BUSINESS HOTEL **$**
(Map p324; ☎2228202; Kwa Shibu Rd; s/d from KSh2500/3500) The recently renovated Glory offers top notch value for money. The rooms are cool, quiet and pleasantly furnished, and all up it's a great retreat from the noise and heat of the big city outside.

Beracha Guest House HOTEL **$**
(Map p324; ☎0725006228; Haile Selassie Rd; s/d excl breakfast KSh1200/1350) This popular central choice is located in the heart of Mombasa's best eat-streets. It has variable but clean rooms in a range of unusual shapes. It's probably the most backpacker-friendly option in the city centre.

Royal Palace Hotel HISTORIC HOTEL **$**
(Map p322; ☎0717620602; cnr Old Kilindini Rd & Kibokoni Rd; s/d from KSh1300/2500) This is an interesting new budget hotel, and the only place to stay within the exotic tangled streets of the Old Town. The rooms are so colourful it looks rather like a group of children have gone on a rampage with tins of paint. Our favourite is the 'Honeymoon' room, covered in hundreds of bright red hearts! Sadly, despite being fairly new, it was already starting to look a little rundown when we visited.

Royal Court Hotel BUSINESS HOTEL **$$**
(Map p324; ☎223379; www.royalcourtmombasa.co.ke; Haile Selassie Rd; s/d KSh5350/6550; ❄@🛜≋) The swish lobby is the highlight of this stylish business hotel. Still, service and facilities are good, disabled access is a breeze, and you get great views and great food at the Tawa Terrace restaurant on the roof, which also has a pool. It wins points for charging tourists and residents (expatriates) the same, but loses points for charging KSh1100 to use the wi-fi.

Eating

If an endless parade of chicken, chips, meat and corn roasted beyond palatability, and starch that tastes like...well, nothing, doesn't do it for you, well here comes the coast. Flavours! Fresh seafood! Spice! Anything but more ugali (maize- or cassava-based staple)!

Mombasa's good for street food: stalls sell cassava, samosas, bhajis, kebabs and the local take on pizza (meat and onions wrapped in soft dough and fried). A few dish out stew and ugali. For dessert, vendors ply you with *haluwa* (an Omani version of Turkish delight), fried taro root, sweet baobab seeds and sugared doughnuts.

TOP CHOICE **Shehnai Restaurant** INDIAN **$$**
(Map p324; ☎222847; Fatemi House, Maungano Rd; mains from KSh300; ⏱noon-2pm & 7.30-10.30pm Tue-Sun) Mombasa's classiest curry-house specialises in tandoori and rich *mughlai* (North Indian) cuisine complemented by nice decor that's been copied from Indian restaurants the world over (pumped-in sitar music thrown in for free). It's very popular with well-heeled Indian families, probably because the food is authentic and very good. Add 25% in various taxes to all prices.

TOP CHOICE **New Jundan Food Court** KENYAN **$**
(Map p324; Gussi St; mains KSh100-200; ⏱lunch) You'll need to kick and shove your way through crowds of locals to get to this

excellent 2nd-floor restaurant that backs onto the Sheikh Jundoni Mosque. It's Swahili food through and through and the special is a stunning pilau.

Tamarind Restaurant KENYAN $$$
(Map p322; ☎471600; Silos Rd, Nyali; mains KSh1100-1800) If you're entertaining an 'I'm a Swahili sultan overlooking my coastal kingdom with a giant plate of chilli-crab' fantasy, can we recommend the Tamarind? Big Moorish- palace exterior, big jewellery-box dining room, big keyboard music (ugh) and a big menu that concentrates on seafood (but does everything well) equals big satisfaction (and, yeah, a big bill). If you're staying elsewhere they'll collect you from your hotel.

Tarboush Cafe INTERNATIONAL $
(Map p324; Makadara Rd; mains KSh70-250) Most people come to this open-air, park-side restaurant for the chicken tikka and rightfully so. Eat it with lovely soft naan bread, rice or chips. There's also a good range of Swahili staples and some curries.

Recoda Restaurant KENYAN $
(Map p324; Moi Ave; mains around KSh120; ⊙lunch & dinner) This Muslim eatery is packed in the evenings with locals clamouring for the local take on kebabs, which are grilled to fat-dripping perfection. Service is a bit sharp, but take it with a spoonful of sugar, because the food is worth your patience.

Island Dishes KENYAN $
(Map p324; Kibokoni Rd; mains KSh80-220) Once your eyes have adjusted to the dazzling strip-lights, feast them on the tasty menu at this very popular Swahili restaurant. *Mishikaki* (marinated, grilled meat kebabs), chicken tikka, fish, fresh juices and all the usual favourites are on offer to eat in or take away, though the *biryani* (rice with meat or seafood) is only available at lunchtime.

Singh Restaurant INDIAN $
(Map p324; Mwembe Tayari Rd; mains KSh250-320) This used to be a very simple cafeteria, but it has received an extensive makeover and now looks like your standard, dark-wood and Mughal painting–bedecked classy Indian restaurant. With that said, the food is excellent and, thanks to the nearby Sikh temple, this spot serves vegetarians, and well.

Blue Room Restaurant INTERNATIONAL $
(Map p324; Haile Selassie Rd; mains KSh170-380; ⊙lunch & dinner) It's not blue but between the steaks, pizzas, curries and...internet access (no, really), the Blue Room has basically been constructed to serve the needs of every traveller anywhere.

Drinking

There are plenty of good drinking holes in Mombasa, and many restaurants cater primarily to drinkers in the evening.

Jahazi Coffee House CAFE
(Map p324; Ndia Kuu Rd; ⊙8am-8pm) Bringing a touch of cosmopolitan style to Mombasa Old Town, this stylish Swahili boutique cafe is a superb place to wile away a few hours playing cards over a steaming pot of tea in the front room or lounging like Persian royalty on the pompous cushions with a fruit juice or snack in the backroom. A percentage of profits goes toward local development projects.

Office BAR
(off Map p322; Shelly Beach Rd, Likoni; ⊙11am until late) Perched above the Likoni ferry jetty and matatu stand, the entirely unaptly named Office is a real locals' hang-out, with regular massive reggae and dub nights shaking the thatched rafters. Any business that goes on here is definitely not the executive kind.

Bella Vista BAR
(Map p324; west of Uhuru Gardens; ⊙midday until late) This two-storey beer-o-fest is plenty of fun for those who feel the need to kick back with a cold one, some sports on the tube, a few rounds of pool and a great view of Mombasa's nightlife action unfolding in all it's storied, slightly sleazy, glory.

☆ Entertainment

New Florida Nightclub CLUB
(off Map p322; Mama Ngina Dr; ⊙6pm-6am; entry KSh500;) This vast seafront complex houses Mombasa's liveliest nightclub, which boasts its own open-air swimming pool. It's owned by the same people as the infamous Florida clubs in Nairobi and offers the same atmosphere, clientele and Las Vegas-style floorshows, with the bonus of outdoor bars, table football and German *Currywurst* (curry sausage)! Friday, Saturday and Sunday are the big party nights. A taxi fare here from central Mombasa is around KSh500.

Shopping

Biashara St, west of its Digo Rd intersection (just north of the spice market), is Kenya's main centre for *kikoi* (brightly coloured woven sarongs for men) and *kangas* (printed wraps worn by women). *Kangas* come as a pair, one for the top half of the body and one for the bottom, and are marked with Swahili proverbs. You may need to bargain, but what you get is generally what you pay for; bank on about KSh500 for a pair of cheap *kangas* or a *kikoi*. *Kofia*, the handmade caps worn by Muslim men, are also crafted here; a really excellent one can run you up to KSh2500.

Bombolulu Workshops & Cultural Centre ARTS & CRAFTS
(www.apdkbombolulu.org; adult/child KSh360/180; ⌚8am-6pm Mon-Sat, 10am-3pm Sun) This non-profit organisation produces crafts of a high standard and gives vocational training to physically disabled people. Visit the workshops and showroom for free to buy jewellery, clothes, carvings and other crafts. The turn-off for the centre is on the left about 3km north of Nyali Bridge.

Akamba Handicraft Industry Cooperative Society HANDICRAFTS
(off Map p322; www.akambahandicraftcoop.com; Port Reitz Rd; ⌚8am-5pm Mon-Fri, to noon Sun) This cooperative employs an incredible 10,000 people from the local area. It's also a non-profit organisation and produces fine woodcarvings. Kwa Hola/Magongo matatus run right past the gates from the Kobil petrol station on Jomo Kenyatta Ave. Many coach tours from Mombasa also stop here.

Information

Dangers & Annoyances

Mombasa isn't Nairobi, but the streets still clear pretty rapidly after dark so it's a good idea to take taxis rather than walk alone at night. The Likoni ferry is a bag-snatching hotspot.

Emergency

AAR Health Services (Lulu Centre, Machakos St, off Moi Ave; ⌚24hr)

Central Police Station (Map p322; ☎999; Makadara Rd)

Internet Access

All of the following charge KSh60 per hour.

Blue Room Cyber Café (Haile Selassie Rd; ⌚9am-10pm)

Cyber Dome (Moi Ave; ⌚8am-9pm Mon-Sat, 9am-6pm Sun)

FOTech (☎225123; Ambalal House, Nkrumah Rd)

Internet Resources

MombasaInfo.com (www.mombasainfo.com) Descriptive tourist information.

Mombasa North Coast (www.mombasanorthcoast.com) More tourist-info goodness.

TOMASI Holidays Africa (www.hotelsmombasa.com) Good for booking online and checking current contact details.

Medical Services

Aga Khan Hospital (Map p322; ☎2227710; www.agakhanhospitals.org; Vanga Rd)

Mombasa Hospital (Map p322; ☎2312191, 2312099, 2228010; www.mombasahosptial.com; off Mama Ngina Dr)

Money

Barclays Bank Nkrumah Rd (Map p324); Digo Rd (Map p324) All with ATMs.

Fort Jesus Forex Bureau (Map p322; Ndia Kuu Rd)

Kenya Commercial Bank Nkrumah Rd (Map p322); Moi Ave (Map p324) All with ATM's.

Postbank (Map p324; Moi Ave) Western Union money transfers.

Standard Chartered Bank (Map p322; Treasury Sq, Nkrumah Rd) With ATM.

Tourist Information

Mombasa & Coast Tourist Office (Map p324; Moi Ave; ⌚8am- 4.30pm) Provides information and can organise accommodation, tours, guides and transport.

Getting There & Away

Air

Airkenya (☎0727131977; Moi International Airport; www.airkenya.com) Flies between Nairobi and Diani Beach (45 minutes away) once a day (one way US$152, one hour).

Kenya Airways (Map p324; ☎2125000; www.kenya-airways.com; TSS Towers, Nkrumah Rd) Flies between Nairobi and Mombasa at least 10 times daily (one way US$200, one hour).

Mombasa Air Safari (☎0734400400; www.mombasaairsafari.com; Moi International Airport) Flies to Amboseli (US$315, one hour), Tsavo (US$315, 1¾ hours) and Masai Mara (US$305, 2¾ hours) national parks amongst other destinations.

Fly540 (☎3434821; www.fly540.com; Moi International Airport) Flies between Nairobi and Mombasa at least five times daily (one way from US$69, one hour) as well as Malindi (one way from US$40, 20 minutes), Lamu (one way from US$55, 45 minutes) and Zanzibar (one way from US$80, 40 minutes).

Bus & Matatu

Most bus offices are on either Jomo Kenyatta Ave or Abdel Nasser Rd. Services to Malindi and Lamu leave from Abdel Nasser Rd, while buses to destinations in Tanzania leave from the junction of Jomo Kenyatta Ave and Mwembe Tayari Rd.

For buses and matatus to the beaches and towns south of Mombasa, you first need to get off the island via the Likoni ferry. Frequent matatus run from Nyerere Ave to the transport stand by the ferry terminal.

NAIROBI Dozens of daily departures in both directions.

Akamba (Map p324; ☎490269; Jomo Kenyatta Ave)

Busscar (Map p324; ☎222854; Abdel Nasser Rd)

Coastline Safaris (Map p324; ☎220158; Mwembe Tayari St)

Mombasa Raha (Map p324; ☎225716) Offices on Abdel Nasser Rd and Jomo Kenyatta Ave.

Simba Coaches (Map p324; Abdel Nasser Rd)

Daytime services take at least six hours, and overnight trips eight to 10 hours and include a meal/smoking break about halfway. Fares vary from KSh800 to KSh1300.

All buses to Nairobi travel via Voi (KSh300 to KSh500), which is also served by frequent matatus from the Kobil petrol station on Jomo Kenyatta Ave (KSh200).

HEADING NORTH There are numerous daily buses and matatus up the coast to Malindi, leaving from in front of the Noor Mosque on Abdel Nasser Rd. Buses take up to 2½ hours (around KSh300), matatus about two hours (KSh350 rising to KSh600 during holidays and very busy periods).

Tawakal, Simba, Mombasa Raha and **TSS Express** have buses to Lamu, most leaving at around 7am (report 30 minutes early) from their offices on Abdel Nasser Rd. Buses take around seven hours to reach the Lamu ferry at Mokoke (KSh600 to KSh800) and travel via Malindi.

HEADING SOUTH Regular buses and matatus leave from the Likoni ferry terminal and travel along the southern coast.

For Tanzania, Simba and a handful of other companies have daily departures to Dar es Salaam (KSh1200 to KSh1600, eight hours) via Tanga from their offices on Jomo Kenyatta Ave, near the junction with Mwembe Tayari Rd. Dubious-looking buses to Moshi and Arusha leave from in front of the Mwembe Tayari Health Centre in the morning or evening.

Train

Currently the 'iron snake' departs Mombasa **train station** (Map p322; ⏲booking office 8am-5pm) at 7pm on Tuesday, Thursday and Sunday, arriving in Nairobi the next day somewhere between 8.30am and 11am. Fares are US$65 1st class, US$55 2nd class, including bed and breakfast (you get dinner with 1st class); reserve as far in advance as possible.

ℹ Getting Around

To/From the Airport

There is currently no public transport to or from the airport. The taxi fare to central Mombasa is around KSh1200.

Boat

The two Likoni ferries connect Mombasa island with the southern mainland. There's a crossing roughly every 20 minutes between 5am and 12.30am, less frequently outside these times. It's free for pedestrians, KSh75 per small car and KSh165 for a safari jeep.

Matatu, Taxi & Tuk-tuk

Matatus charge between KSh20 and KSh30 for short trips. Mombasa taxis are as expensive as those in Nairobi, and harder to find; a good place to look is in front of Express Travel on Nkrumah Rd. Assume it'll cost KSh250 to KSh400 from the train station to the city centre. There are also plenty of three-wheeled *tuk-tuks* about, which run to about KSh70 to KSh150 for a bit of open-air transit.

Shimba Hills National Reserve

If you're in need of traditional African landscapes of the rolling hills variety, this 320-sq-km **reserve** (adult/child US$20/10; ⏲6am-6pm) is just 30km from Mombasa, directly inland from Diani Beach. This is one of the most underrated parks in the country, as well as one of the easiest to visit. The park's gentle grassy hills are interspersed with patches of forest which together provide a home to elephants, leopards, warthogs, buffaloes, baboons, a variety of antelope species and a small population of masai giraffes (which have been introduced), but the park is best known for its population of magnificent sable antelope, which occur in no other Kenyan park. The sable antelope have made a stunning recovery after their numbers dropped to less than 120 in 1970.

In 2005, the elephant population reached an amazing 600 – far too many for this tiny space. Instead of culling the herds, Kenya Wildlife Service (KWS) organised an unprecedented US$3.2 million translocation operation to reduce the pressure on the habitat, capturing no fewer than 400 elephants and moving them to Tsavo East National Park.

More than 150km of 4WD tracks crisscross the reserve; Marere Dam and the forest of Mwele Mdogo Hill are good spots for seeing birdlife. Excellent free guided forest walks are run by the KWS from the Sheldrick Falls ranger post. Walks normally take place at 10am and 2pm. A tip is appropriate.

Sleeping

The **public campsite** (per person KSh300) and **bandas** (per person US$25) are basic and have cold-water-only bathrooms, but they're superbly located on the edge of an escarpment close to the main gate. Monkeys sit in the trees around the camp, birds sing in the mornings and a camp fire can be lit at night. You must be self-sufficient.

Kwale Golden Guest House HOTEL $
(☎0722326758; Kwale town; r KSh600-1200) In the regional 'capital' of Kwale and just a couple of kilometres from the park entrance this typical small town boarding house has two classes of room: one with hot showers and sit-down toilets and the other with cold showers and squat toilets.

Getting There & Away

You'll need a 4WD to enter the reserve. From Likoni, small lorry-buses to Kwale pass the main gate (KSh80).

SHIMBA HILLS NATIONAL RESERVE

» **Why Go** It's an easy day trip from the coast, has excellent elephant spotting, and is the only Kenyan home of the sable antelope.

» **When to Go** Year-round, but the dry season between November to March is best.

» **Practicalities** Diani Beach, 45 minutes away, is a popular base; numerous safari companies and hotels there offer safaris to Shimba Hills.

Tiwi Beach

☎040

The sleepy sister to manic Diani is a string of blissed-out resorts, accessible by dirt tracks, about 20km south of Likoni. It's good for a quiet, cottage-style escape. One of the best features of Tiwi is Diani reef (which, funnily enough, isn't as evident in Diani), creating a pool-like area between the shore and the coral that's great for swimming.

Sleeping & Eating

All of these places are located off the unnamed dirt track that runs parallel to the main highway and the beach.

TOP CHOICE **Sand Island Beach Cottages** COTTAGE $$
(☎0722395005; www.sandislandbeach.com; cottages from KSh6000) A bunch of friendly dogs greet you as you enter this gardenlike strip of lovely cottages, fronting a beach that the owners claim is the 'best beach in East Africa'. Now that is a mighty big claim, but when you see for yourself how sublime this patch of paradise is, with its shimmering white desert island poking out of a turquoise lagoon, you probably won't argue.

Coral Cove Cottages COTTAGE $$
(☎3300010; www.coralcove.tiwibeach.com; cottages from KSh4800) When Dr Doolittle goes on vacation, he looks no further than this top beachfront option. There are dogs, roosters, monkeys, geese, ducks and other fluffy denizens scattered throughout, and they're all tame. The self-catering cottages are as full of colour and character as the rest of the place.

Twiga Lodge HOTEL $
(☎0721577614; twigakenya@gmail.com; camping KSh300, s/d KSh1500/2500, new wing s/d KSh3000/4800) Twiga is great fun when there's a crowd staying, with the palpable sense of isolation alleviated by the sheer tropical exuberance of the place. The older rooms are set off from the beach and are slightly grotty, while the newer wing is crisper. The on-site restaurant is OK, but having a drink under thatch while stars spill over the sea is as perfect as moments come.

Getting There & Away

Buses and matatus on the Likoni–Ukunda road can drop you at the start of either track down to Tiwi (KSh50) – keep an eye out for the signs to Capricho Beach Cottages or Tiwi Beach Resort. The southern turn-off, known locally as Tiwi 'spot', is much easier to find.

Although it's only 3.5km to the beach, both access roads are notorious for muggings so take a taxi or hang around for a lift.

Diani Beach

☎040

Diani, the biggest resort town on the Kenyan coast, is a mixed bag. It's an undeniably stunning swath of white-sand perfection, and if you're looking to party, you're in the right spot. On the other hand, it's rife with the sort of uniform uber-resorts that could be plopped anywhere in the world. We've tried to review the more distinctive places. There's a lot beyond the stale blocks of hotel overdevelopment. You can visit coral mosques with archways that overlook the open ocean and sky; go to sacred forests where guides hug trees that speak in their ancestors' voices; and (well, why not) head to a monkey sanctuary – these are all good ways of experiencing more of the coast than the considerable charms of sun and sand.

Sights & Activities

Package-holiday tat seems ubiquitous in Diani, but there's far more waiting to be discovered by independent travellers.

All the big resorts either have their own dive schools or work with a local operator. Rates run around €75 to €90 for a reef dive. Most dive sites are under 29m, including the purposely sunk 15m-MFV *Alpha Funguo*, at 28m.

If you prefer to be above water than below it then Diani, with its near-constant trade winds, is rapidly gaining a name for itself as a kitesurfing hotspot.

TOP CHOICE Colobus Trust WILDLIFE RESERVE

(☎0711479453; www.colobustrust.org; Diani Beach Rd; tours KSh500; ⏲8am-5pm Mon-Sat) Notice the monkeys clambering on rope ladders over the road? The ladders are the work of the Colobus Trust, which aims to protect the Angolan black-and-white colobus monkey *(Colobus angolensis palliatus)*, a once-common species now restricted to a few isolated pockets of forest south of Mombasa. The trust runs superb tours of its headquarters where you'll likely get to see a few orphaned or injured colobus and other monkeys in the process of rehabilitation to the wild. With advance notice it can organise **forest walks** (per person KSh1000) in search of wilder primates and other creatures.

Kongo Mosque MOSQUE

At the far northern end of the beach road (turn right at the three-way intersection where the sealed road ends) is the 16th-century Kongo Mosque – Diani's last surviv-

DON'T MISS

BEST BEACHES

- » **Tiwi Beach** (p331)
- » **Diani Beach** (p332)
- » **Takaungu** (p339)
- » **Manda Island** (p354)
- » **Shela Beach** (p353)
- » **Watamu** (p339)

Tiwi & Diani Beaches

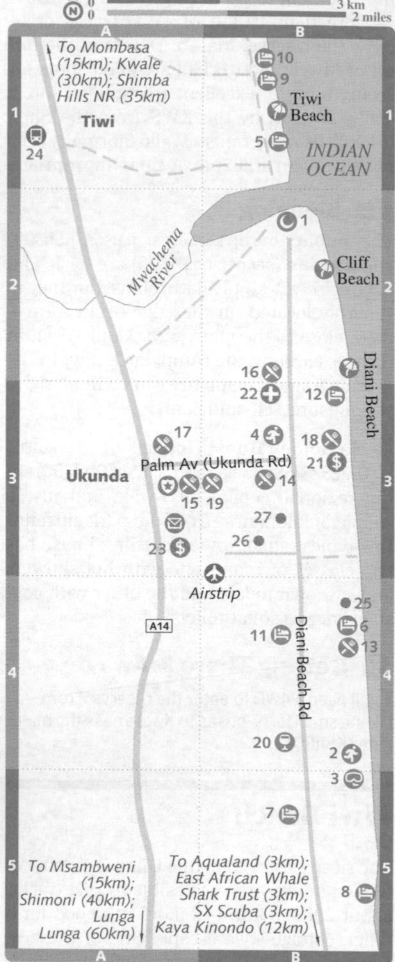

Tiwi & Diani Beaches

Sights
1 Kongo Mosque ... B2

Activities, Courses & Tours
2 Charlie Claw's ... B4
Diani Marine ... (see 6)
3 Diving the Crab ... B5
H^2O Extreme ... (see 6)
H^2O Extreme ... (see 3)
4 Pilli Pipa ... B3

Sleeping
5 Coral Cove Cottages ... A3
6 Diani Marine Village ... B4
7 Forest Dream Cottages ... B5
8 Kenyaways Kite Village ... B5
9 Maweni & Capricho Beach Cottages ... B1
10 Sand Island Beach Cottages ... B1
11 Stilts Eco-Lodge ... B4
12 Warandale Cottages ... B3

Eating
13 Ali Barbour's Cave Restaurant ... B4
Aniello's ... (see 4)
14 Coast Dishes ... B3
15 Rongai Fast Food ... A3
16 Shan-e-Punjab Restaurant ... B2
17 Swahili Pot Restaurant/African Pot Restaurant ... B3
18 Swahili Pot Restaurant/African Pot Restaurant ... B3
19 Swahili Pot Restaurant/African Pot Restaurant ... A3

Drinking
Forty Thieves Beach Bar ... (see 13)
20 Shakatak ... B4

Information
Baba's Bistro & Cyber Cafe ... (see 13)
21 Barclays Bank ... B3
22 Diani Beach Hospital ... B3
23 Kenya Commercial Bank ... A3

Transport
24 Bus Stop ... A1
25 Fredlink Tours ... B4
26 Glory Car Hire ... B3
27 Ketty Tours ... B3

ing relic of the ancient Swahili civilisations that once controlled the coast, and one of a tiny handful of coral mosques still in use in Kenya.

Diani Marine DIVING
(☎3202367; www.dianimarine.com; Diani Marine Village) This German-run centre provides its own accommodation. Open-water diving courses cost €495.

Diving the Crab DIVING
(☎0723108108; www.divingthecrab.com; Sands at Nomad) The most popular outfit used by the big hotels. Open-water courses cost €480.

H_2O Extreme KITESURFING
(☎0721495876; www.h2o-extreme.com) The best regarded kitesurfing outfit in Diani offers half-day beginner courses for €100.

SX Scuba DIVING
(☎3202720, 0734601221; www.southerncrossscuba.com; Aqualand) Does open-water diving courses for €470.

Sleeping

Diani is largely known for its 20-odd high-end resorts, strung out all along the beach. Those listed here are among the best of the bunch, but don't expect a particularly 'authentic Africa' experience. Note that many of these places close for renovation between May and June, and most increase rates during the Christmas holiday up to mid-January.

TOP CHOICE **Kenyaways Kite Village** BOUTIQUE HOTEL $$
(☎0728886821; www.thekenyaway.com; Diani Beach Rd; s/d from UK£30/50; wi-fi) This small and casual beachside hotel has a handful of brightly painted and funkily decorated rooms that come with a dollop of bohemian surf attitude. It's primarily a kitesurfers camp (it's the main base for H_20 Extreme), but it's open to anyone. Easily one of the better value places in Diani.

DON'T MISS

MWALUGANJE ELEPHANT SANCTUARY

This **sanctuary** (☎040-41121; adult/child US$15/2, vehicles KSh150-500; ⊙6am-6pm) is a good example of community-based conservation with local people acting as stakeholders in the project. It was opened in October 1995 to create a corridor along an elephant migration route between Shimba Hills and Mwaluganje Forest Reserve, and comprises 2400 hectares of rugged, beautiful country along the valley of the Cha Shimba River.

Other than the 150 or so elephants, the big-ticket wildlife can be a little limited. However, you're likely to have the place to yourself, the scenery is almost a cliché of what East Africa should look like, and there's plenty of little stuff to see.

Mwaluganje Elephant Camp (☎Mombasa 011-5486121; s/d US$160/225) is a rather fine place to stay, with very plush safari tents overlooking a waterhole. If you can't afford the fancy-pants tents then camping in your own tent is possible at the **campsite** (per person KSh300), located near the main gate. The setting is sublime (though the rock surface makes things tricky for tent pegs!). It's as genuine an African wilderness experience as you can ask for.

The main entrance to the sanctuary is about 13km northeast of Shimba Hills National Reserve, on the road to Kinango. A shorter route runs from Kwale to the Golini gate, passing the Mwaluganje ticket office. It's only 5km but the track is 4WD only. The roads inside the park are pretty rough and a 4WD is the way to go.

TOP CHOICE Diani Marine Village BOUTIQUE HOTEL **$$**
(☎3202367; www.dianimarine.com; Diani Beach Rd; s/d from €49/78; 🛜🏊) The huge guest rooms at this dive resort are more than just a little bit appealing; with stone floors, a modern Swahili style and a beautiful pool and gardens this place represents superb value for money. The included breakfast is fit for a king.

Stilts Eco-Lodge HUTS **$**
(☎0722523278; www.stiltsdiani.com; Diani Beach Rd; s/d KSh1500/2400) The only dedicated backpacker lodgings at the time of research, Stilts offers seven charming stilted tree houses set back in a sandy swathe of coastal forest, across the street from Forty Thieves. It attracts a young, fun-seeking crowd, has its own thatched lounge/bar area and is all-round enjoyable. Book ahead.

Forest Dream Cottages COTTAGES **$$**
(☎3300220; www.forestdreamkenya.com; Diani Beach Rd; cottages from €89; ❄🏊) This fantastic choice is set in an actual forest reserve. The thatched cottages are slightly kooky but always plush, and the little open-air rooftop lounge areas are great. Fish ponds, jacuzzis and fully fitted kitchens round out this secluded, tree-clad escape.

Warandale Cottages COTTAGES **$$**
(☎3202186; www.warandale.com; cottages from KSh7000; 🏊) These excellent cottages are strung along a pleasant gardenlike retreat that is utterly Edenesque. The rooms are tastefully done in an understated Swahili style, with the right amount of dark wood and white walls to evoke Africa without a steaming surfeit of safari tat.

Eating

All of the top-end hotels have on-site restaurants that tend to be pricey and fairly dull. Otherwise, you're spoilt for choice.

Swahili Pot Restaurant KENYAN **$**
(☎3203890; Coral Beach Cottages; mains KSh150-230; ⊙lunch & dinner) This place and its culinary siblings (there are two other branches, one about halfway down the beach access road and another at Ukunda junction) does excellent traditional African and Swahili dishes. The title comes from the gimmick of selecting a meat and having it cooked in a variety of sauces and marinades, all of which are highly rated. Note that the three branches are also trading under their old name of African Pot Restaurant.

Coast Dishes KENYAN **$**
(Palm Ave, Ukunda; mains KSh300) Want to give the overpriced tourist restaurants a miss? Want to eat where the locals eat? Coast Dishes ticks both of these criteria and if you're sensible you'll opt for a steaming great bowl of *biryani*, the house special.

Shan-e-Punjab Restaurant INDIAN $
(☎3202116; Diani Complex; mains KSh350-800; ⏲lunch & dinner) One of the only dedicated Indian options in town could easily hold its own against any high-class curry house in the world. The food is well spiced, rich and delicious. It often closes in the low season.

Ali Barbour's Cave Restaurant SEAFOOD $$
(☎3202033; Diani Beach Rd; mains KSh550-1200; ⏲from 7pm) Well, they've got coral mosques and palaces on the coast – why not a restaurant set in a coral cave? The focus here is seafood, cooked up poshly and generally quite tasty. It's served under the stars, jagged rocks and fairy lights.

Rongai Fast Food KENYAN $
(Palm Ave, Ukunda; mains KSh200; ⏲lunch & dinner) This rowdy joint is a pretty popular place for *nyama choma;* if you've been missing your roast meat and boiled maize, Rongai's here for you.

Drinking & Entertainment

Be aware that there are many prostitutes and gigolos in Diani's bars.

Forty Thieves Beach Bar BAR $
Of all the phrases you'll hear in Diani, 'Meet you at Forty's?' is probably the most common, and the most welcome – this is easily the best bar on the strip. It has movie nights and live bands, there's a pub quiz at least once a week and it's open until the last guest leaves.

Shakatak CLUB $
(Diani Beach Rd) The only full-on nightclub in Diani not attached to a hotel is Shakatak. It's quite hilariously seedy, but can be fun once you know what to expect. Like most big Kenyan clubs, food is served at all hours.

Information

Dangers & Annoyances

Take taxis at night and try not to be on the beach by yourself after dark. Souvenir sellers are an everyday nuisance, sex tourism is pretty evident and beach boys are a hassle; you will hear a lot of, 'Hey, one love one love' Rasta-speak spouted by guys trying to sell you drugs or scam you into supporting fake charities for 'local schools'. Yes, very 'one love'.

Emergency

Diani Beach Hospital (☎3202435; www.dianibeachhospital.com; Diani Beach Rd; ⏲24hr)
Police (☎3202229; Ukunda)

Internet Access

Baba's Bistro & Cyber Cafe (Forty Thieves Beach Bar; per hr KSh60; ⏲9am-late)

Internet Resources

Diani Beach (www.dianibeach.com) Includes information on Tiwi and Funzi Island.

Money

Barclays Bank (Barclays Centre) With ATM.
Kenya Commercial Bank (Ukunda) With ATM.

Post

Diani Beach post office (Diani Beach Rd)
Ukunda post office

Tourist Information

i-Point (Barclays Centre; ⏲8.30am-6pm Mon-Fri, 9am-4pm Sat) Private information office with plenty of brochures.

WORTH A TRIP

IT'S A SAILOR'S LIFE

The salty breeze and the high seas, it's a sailor's life for you and I. There's no more romantic a way to explore the Kenyan coast than sailing by dhow (a traditional sailing boat that has been used here for centuries) past slivers of sand, offshore coral islands and reefs bubbling with colourful fish. Several companies offer dhow trips down the coast. **Pilli Pipa** (☎3203559; www.pillipipa.com; Colliers Centre, Diani Beach Rd, per person US$130) is probably the best known, but there are several other operators in Diani.

The **East African Whale Shark Trust** (☎0720293156; www.giantsharks.org; Aqualand) is an excellent conservation body monitoring populations of the worlds largest fish – the harmless, plankton-feeding whale shark. In February and March (the busiest time for whale sharks) it occasionally opens survey and shark-tagging expeditions to paying guests. Trip costs vary depending on how much sponsorship money has been raised but averages US$150 per person, with a minimum of six people needed for a trip. Its offices are located in the Aqualand centre, about 4km south of Diani.

DON'T MISS

ENTERING THE SACRED FOREST

Entering the *kaya* (sacred forests) of the Mijikenda can be one of the crowning experiences of a visit to the coast. Visiting these groves has elements of nature walk, historical journey and cultural experience. Currently, the most visited and accessible *kaya* is **Kaya Kinondo** (www.kaya-kinondo-kenya.com; admission KSh700), near Diani Beach.

Before entering the Kaya Kinondo you have to remove headwear, promise not to kiss anyone inside the grove, wrap a black *kaniki* (sarong) around your waist and go with a guide; ours was Juma Harry, a local *askari* (security guard) and member of the Digo tribe.

The Mijikenda (Nine Homesteads) are actually nine subtribes united, to a degree, by culture, history and language. Yet each of the tribes – Chonyi, Digo, Duruma, Giriama, Jibana, Kambe, Kauma, Rabai and Ribe – remains distinct and speaks its own dialect of the Mijikenda language. Still, there is a binding similarity between the Nine Homesteads, and between the modern Mijikenda and their ancestors: their shared veneration of the *kaya*.

This historical connection becomes concrete when you enter the woods and realise – and there's no other word that fits here – they simply feel *old*.

Many trees are 600 years old, which corresponds to the arrival of the first Mijikenda from Singwaya, their semi-legendary homeland in southern Somalia. Cutting vegetation within the *kaya* is strictly prohibited, to the degree that visitors may not even take a stray twig or leaf from the forest.

Harry explains: 'When we are near the trees, we feel close to our ancestors. I know my father, and my grandfather, and his grandfather and so on, all cared for this tree.' Here Harry, who is a tough-looking character (and decidedly not a hippie), hugs a tree so large his arms cannot encircle it.

'We feel if the tree is old, it is talking. If you hold it and hear the wind,' and there is a pause for breezy effect, 'you can hear it talking.'

The main purpose of the *kaya* was to house the villages of the Mijikenda, which were located in a large central clearing. Entering the centre of a *kaya* required ritual knowledge to proceed through concentric circles of sacredness surrounding the node of the village; sacred talismans and spells were supposed to cause hallucinations that disoriented enemies who attacked the forest.

The *kaya* were largely abandoned in the 1940s, and conservative strains of Islam and Christianity have denigrated their value to the Mijikenda, but a resurgence of interest in the forests will hopefully preserve them for future visitors – 11 of the forests were inscribed together as Kenya's fourth World Heritage Site in July 2008.

The *kaya* have lasted 600 years; with luck, the wind will speak through their branches for much longer.

Getting There & Around

Bus & Matatu

Numerous matatus run south from the Likoni ferry directly to Ukunda (KSh70, 30 minutes) and onwards to Msambweni and Lunga Lunga. From the Diani junction in Ukunda, matatus run down to the beach all day for KSh40.

Car & Motorcycle

Motorcycles can be hired from **Fredlink Tours** (☎3300253; www.motorbike-safari.com; Diani Plaza). A full motorcycle licence, passport and credit card or cash deposit are required for rental.

You can rent cars from **Glory Car Hire** (☎3203076; Diani Beach shopping centre) and **Ketty Tours** (☎23203582; www.kettysafari.com; Diani Beach Rd).

Taxi

Taxis hang around Ukunda junction and all the main shopping centres; most hotels and restaurants will also have a couple waiting at night. Fares should be between KSh150 and KSh800, depending on the distance.

Shimoni & Wasini Island

☎040

The final pearls in the tropical beach necklace that stretches south of Mombasa are the mainland village of Shimoni and the idyllic island of Wasini, located about 76km south of Likoni.

Although you wouldn't know it by looking at the group tours, this is a fairly conservative Muslim area, and women travelling independently may want to cover up their legs and shoulders.

SHIMONI

The mainland village of Shimoni is the departure point for boats to Wasini, and can be a bit of a circus when the tour buses rock up. But after sunset, when the day trippers go home, a tranquil Swahili vibe returns.

Sights & Activities

Slave Caves HISTORICAL SITE

(KSh400; ⌚8.30-10.30am & 1.30-6pm) These caves, where slaves were supposedly kept before being loaded onto boats, are the main attraction in Shimoni. A custodian takes you around the dank caverns to illustrate this little-discussed part of East African history. Actual evidence that slaves were kept here is a little thin, but as piles of empty votive rosewater bottles indicate, the site definitely has significance to believing locals.

Shimoni Reef FISHING

(☎041-4473969; www.shimonireeflodge.com; Shimoni; trips per day from US$700) The Pemba Channel is famous for deep-sea fishing, and Shimoni Reef can arrange a variety of different offshore fishing trips.

WASINI ISLAND

Wasini Island is a slowly decaying delight of coral houses and sticky alleyways. There are no roads or running water, and the only electricity comes from generators. Long ago Lamu and Zanzibar must have felt a little like this. It's worth poking about the ancient **Swahili ruins** and the **coral gardens** (KSh200), a bizarre landscape of exposed coral reefs with a boardwalk for viewing, on the edge of Wasini village.

Sights & Activities

Kisite Marine National Park WILDLIFE RESERVE

(adult/child US$20/10) Off the south coast of Wasini, this marine park, which also incorporates the Mpunguti Marine National Reserve, is one of the best in Kenya. The park covers 28 sq km of pristine coral reefs and offers excellent diving and snorkelling. You have a reasonable chance of seeing dolphins in the Shimoni Channel, and humpback whales are sometimes spotted between August and October.

It's easy to organise your own boat trip with a local captain – the going rate is KSh2500 per person for a group (or KSh10,000 per boat), including lunch and a walk in the coral gardens on Wasini Island. Masks and snorkels can be hired for KSh200 (fins are discouraged as they may damage the reef).

During the monsoon season you can snorkel over the **coral gardens** (adult/child US$5/3) just opposite the pier in Wasini. Although the marine life can't compare with that of the national park, it's completely sheltered from the worst of the monsoon weather.

Mkwiro Village VILLAGE

Mkwiro is a small village on the unvisited end of Wasini Island. There are few facilities here and not a lot to do, but there are some wonderful, calm swimming spots around the village, and the gorgeous hour-long walk from Wasini village, through woodlands, past tiny hamlets and along the edge of mangrove forests, is more than reason enough to visit.

The Mkwiro Youth Group can help you dig a little deeper into village life by organising village tours and cooking classes. It's all a

WASINI TOURS

Various companies offer organised dhow tours for snorkelling, and there are loads of private operators hanging out around the piers at either Shimoni or Wasini. Hotels can normally recommend someone reliable as well. Tours generally follow the same pattern: leave Shimoni pier at 9am, travel through Kisite Marine National Park, stop for snorkelling and beach time, head for Wasini for a seafood lunch, visit the coral gardens and return to Shimoni around 3pm or 4pm.

Charlie Claw's (Map p332; ☎040-3203154, 0722410599; www.wasini.com; office Jadini Beach Hotel, Diani Beach) and **Pilli Pipa** (Map p332; ☎040-3203559; www.pillipipa.com; office Colliers Centre, Diani Beach) are good outfits offering well-managed dhow trips. Trips cost around US$130 to US$150 per person.

little vague and prices are highly flexible but the man you need to speak to about organising these is **Shafii Vuyaa** (☎0728741098).

You can arrange homestays in Mkwiro for roughly KSh650, which should include a nice home-cooked coastal dinner.

Sleeping & Eating

Mpunguti Lodge HOTEL $
(☎0710562494; Wasini Island; r without/with bathroom per person KSh950/1850) The rooms here, which overlook the delicious turquoise ocean, are uncomplicated, with mosquito nets and small verandahs. Running water is collected in rain barrels and doesn't always look pleasant! The food is excellent (ask for the seagrass starter – possibly the nicest thing we ate on the Kenyan coast), and it's a common lunch-stop for boat trips. On the edge of Wasini village.

Shimoni Reef LODGE $$$
(☎041-4473969, 020-2327669; www.shimonireeflodge.com; Shimoni; s/d US$180/300;) This waterfront fishing camp has a pleasant series of white-washed cottages, but considering the price we'd have hoped for more of a 'wow' factor. Fortunately, walk-in guests are normally assumed to be residents and thus are offered massive discounts which make it much more worthwhile.

KWS Bandas & Camping BANDA $
(☎0728854118; Shimoni; per person camping KSh200, bandas per person US$25) The reasonably well-maintained *bandas* are set in a hunk of monkey-infested forest on the edge of the KWS grounds. Great if you're in a group; it'd be a bit spooky staying here alone.

Getting There & Around

There are matatus every hour or so between Likoni and Shimoni (KSh300, 1½hrs) until about 6pm. It's best to be at Likoni by 6.30am if you want to get to Shimoni in time to catch one of the dhow sailings.

Getting to Wasini island is easy enough. 'Matatu' boats charge KSh50 per person although frankly the only way you'd ever get to pay this is if you get yourself reincarnated as a Kenyan. Otherwise you're looking at KSh300 for the crossing.

Kilifi

☎041

Like Mtwapa to its south, Kilifi is a gorgeous river estuary with effortlessly picture-perfect views from its massive road bridge. Many Kenyans have yachts moored in the creek and there are numerous beach houses belonging to artists, writers and adventurers from around the globe.

The main reasons that most travellers come here are to stay at one of the pleasant beach resorts at the mouth of the creek or to visit the ruins of Mnarani, high on a bluff on the south bank of the creek.

DON'T MISS

JUMBA LA MTWANA

These Swahili **ruins** (adult/child KSh500/100; ⊙8am-6pm), just north of Mtwapa Creek, are easily comparable in terms of archaeological grandeur to the more-famous Gede (p342), but unlike those, you're likely to have Jumba la Mtwana largely to yourself. In the dying evening light, let your imagination run riot with thoughts of lost treasures, ghosts, pirates and abandoned cities. The remains of buildings, with their exposed foundations for mangrove beam poles; ablution tanks; floors caked with millipedes and swarms of safari ants; and the twisting arms of 600-year-old trees, leftover from what may have been a nearby *kaya*; are quite magical.

Jumba la Mtwana means 'Big House of Slaves', and while there is no hard historical evidence to back the theory, locals believe the town was once an important slave port.

While here, keep your eyes peeled for the upper-wall holes that mark where mangrove support beams were affixed; the **House of Many Doors**, which is believed to have been a guesthouse (no breakfast included); and dried out, 40m-deep wells. You'd be remiss to miss the **Mosque by the Sea**, which overlooks a crystal-sharp vista of the Indian Ocean (and don't forget your swimmers for a splash in the empty waters here).

The custodian gives excellent tours for a small gratuity. Regular matatus and buses run from Mtwapa to Mombasa (KSh50) and Malindi (KSh80).

WORTH A TRIP

TAKAUNGU

If you want breathtaking Indian Ocean beaches and utter tranquillity, Takaungu fits the bill. The creek here, with its luxurious blue waters framed by an explosion of greenery and pockets of golden cove beaches, will do the aforementioned breath stealing. And for seclusion, the exposed ocean-facing beaches (1km east of the village) are unlikely to contain a single other footprint.

The village of Takaungu is a real Swahili fishing village, absolutely untouched by tourism. This of course means there are no facilities whatsoever, but it's easy to find a very basic room in someone's house for around KSh1000, including meals.

Takaungu is just south of Kilifi and any bus or matatu between there and Mombasa can drop you at the junction from which it's a pleasant (but hot) 3km walk to the village or you can grab a ride on the back of a motorbike.

Sights

Mnarani RUINS

(adult/child KSh500/250; 7am-6pm) The partly excavated, atmospheric and deliciously peaceful ruins of the Swahili city of Mnarani are high on a bluff just west of the old ferry landing-stage on the southern bank of Kilifi Creek. The site was occupied from the end of the 14th century to around the first half of the 17th century, when it was abandoned following sieges by Galla tribespeople from Somalia and the failure of the water supply.

The best-preserved ruin is the **Great Mosque**, with its finely carved inscription around the mihrab (prayer niche showing the direction of Mecca). Under the minaret lies the skeleton of the supposed founder of the town. A group of **carved tombs** (including a restored pillar tomb), a **small mosque** dating back to the 16th century and parts of the **town wall** are also preserved.

Don't miss the monstrous old **baobab trees** just beyond the walls of the main complex. The largest, a right royal 900-year-old beauty, is the site of frequent religious offerings by the local (Muslim) community – a throw back to pre-Islamic times.

Sleeping & Eating

Dhows Inn HOTEL $

(0722375214; dhowsinn_kilifi@yahoo.com; Malindi Rd; s/d KSh1200/1800) On the main road south of Kilifi Creek, this small, well-maintained hostelry is a real travellers' institution. It has simple but comfortable and immaculate rooms around a garden, and offers exceptional value for the coast. The Mnarani ruins are within walking distance, and it has a popular bar and restaurant.

Kilifi Bay Beach Resort RESORT $$$

(522511; www.madahotels.com; s/d full board €135/190;) About 5km north of Kilifi on the coast road, this small resort has a Swahili palace exterior and rooms that are just as swanky. There are lots of facilities, although at high-tide the beach almost disappears under the waves.

Kilifi Members Club KENYAN

(mains KSh150-400) This is a fantastic spot to watch the sunset, perched on the northern cliff edge with breathtaking views over the creek to the Mediterranean-like beaches lining the opposite bank (and the Hollywood-like houses beyond). There's a good menu with lots of *nyama choma*, seafood and beer. Despite the name you don't have to be a member.

Getting There & Away

All buses and matatus travelling between Mombasa (KSh100 to KSh130, up to 1½ hours) and Malindi (KSh100 to KSh150, 1¼ hours,) stop at Kilifi.

Watamu

042

This fishing village has evolved into a small expat colony, a string of high-end resorts and a good base for exploring a glut of ruins, national parks and eco-sites that are within an easily accessible radius. The main attraction is 7km of pristine beach and a cosy scene that caters to peace, quiet and/or big-game fishing (although there's still some bad behaviour and beach boys).

DON'T MISS

DIVING, FISHING & WINDSURFING

There are plenty of waterborne activities on offer at Watamu, including diving, deep-sea fishing and windsurfing.

Aqua Ventures (☎32420/0703628102; www.diveinkenya.com), at Ocean Sports resort, offers guided dives in the marine park for €32 and a PADI course for €320; they're also good for diving expeditions around Malindi.

Tunda Tours (☎0733952383; www.tundatourssafaris.com; Beach Way Rd) runs fishing safaris (half/full day UK£250/350).

Ocean Sports (☎2332288; www.oceansports.net) based inside the hotel of the same name, offers windsurfing courses from €20, which is about as cheap as you'll find in Kenya.

Sights & Activities

TOP CHOICE Bio Ken Snake Farm & Laboratory ZOO

(www.bio-ken.com; adult/child KSh750/250; ⏲10am-noon & 2-5pm) Of some 126 snake species in Kenya, 93 don't pose a threat to humans. The rats and similar species that snakes prey on are much more of a health threat than the reptiles themselves. Learn this and other lessons on this excellent research centre and farm, which is by far the best reptile park on the coast. If the snakes here have got you slithering with excitement, you might also be interested in the **snake safaris** (per person from US$70), run under the guidance of expert herpetologists.

Watamu Marine National Park DIVING, SNORKELLING

(adult/child US$15/10) The southern part of Malindi Marine National Reserve, this park includes some magnificent coral reefs, abundant fish life and sea turtles. To get here you'll need a boat, which is easy enough to hire at the **KWS office** at the end of the coast road, where you pay the park fees. Boat operators ask anywhere from KSh2500 to KSh3000 for two people for two hours, excluding park fees; it's all negotiable.

Watamu Turtle Watch WILDLIFE WATCHING

(www.watamuturtles.com; ⏲2.30-4pm Mon, 9.30am-12pm & 2.30-4pm Tue-Fri, 9.30am-12pm Sat) Watamu Turtle Watch provides a service protecting the marine turtles that come here to lay eggs on the beach. You can get up close and personal with various cutesy turtles at the trust's rehabilitation centre.

Sleeping

Mwamba Field Study Centre GUESTHOUSE $

(☎Nairobi 020-2335865; www.arocha.org; Watamu Beach; r full board per person KSh3000) This lovely guesthouse/study centre is run by A Rocha, a Christian conservation society. The beach is 50m away, and when you're done relaxing you have the option of giving something back to Watamu – Mwamba runs myriad community and environmental programs. All power is solar generated.

Turtle Bay Beach Club RESORT $$$

(☎32003; www.turtlebaykenya.com; s/d full board US$113/226; ❄@📶🏊) This is easily one of the best top-end resorts in Watamu: an eco-minded hotel that uses managed tree-cover to hide its environmental imprint, runs enough ecotourism ventures to fill a book (including birdwatching safaris and turtle protection programs), contributes to local charities and all sorts of other do-gooder stuff. On top of that, it's a pretty plush resort with beautiful marine-themed rooms.

Villa Veronika GUESTHOUSE $

(☎0728155613; Beach Way Rd; r KSh800-1000) Colourful walls, flowery murals and well-maintained rooms (they were even renovating some rooms when we went past) set around a shady courtyard garden make this cheapie hard to beat.

Eating

For local cuisine, try the several tiny stalls lining Beach Way Rd, selling kebabs, chicken, chips, samosas, chapattis and the like.

Bistro Coffee Shop CAFE $

(⏲until 5pm) Quick, run away from Africa! Sometimes you just need to escape to a relaxed Western-style cafe and this is the place in Watamu to do so. Great juices, tea, coffee and homemade cakes – lemon tart or apple pie?

Savannah INTERNATIONAL **$$**
(KSh550-700; ⌚dinner Tue-Sat, lunch & dinner Sun) This pleasant garden restaurant doesn't have the world's most imaginative menu, but its burgers and pasta are decent enough and it's a great place for an evening beer. It's signed down a dirt track just off the main road into town.

ℹ Information

KCB (Beach Way Rd) Has an ATM.
Post office (Gede Rd)

ℹ Getting There & Around

There are matatus between Malindi and Watamu throughout the day (KSh80 to KSh100, one hour). All matatus pass the turn-off to the Gede ruins (KSh40). For Mombasa (KSh250), the easiest option is to take a matatu to Gede and flag down a bus or matatu. A handful of motorised rickshaws ply the village and beach road; a ride to the KWS office should cost around KSh200.

Bicycles can be hired from most hotels or guesthouses for around KSh100 per hour.

Arabuko Sokoke Forest Reserve

Elephants are such an indelibly African image, but what about the elephant shrew? Specifically, the golden-rumped elephant shrew, which is about the size of a rabbit and cute as a kitten?

They're only found here, in **Arabuko Sokoke Forest Reserve** (adult/child US$20/10; ⌚6am-6pm), the largest tract of indigenous coastal forest remaining in East Africa. But with 240 bird species, forest elephants, baboons, Syke's monkey and 260 species of butterfly, there's a lot more to Arabuko Sokoke than just shrews.

The **Arabuko Sokoke Visitor Centre** (Malindi Rd; ⌚8am-4pm) is very helpful; it's at Gede Forest Station, with displays on the various species found here.

From the visitors centre, nature trails and 4WD paths cut through the forest. There are more bird trails at **Whistling Duck Pools**, **Kararacha Pools** and **Spinetail Way**, located 16km further south. Near Kararacha is **Singwaya Cultural Centre**, where you can arrange to see traditional dance performances.

DON'T MISS

MIDA CREEK

Mida Creek is a different world from that of the all-inclusive tourist resorts of nearby Watamu and Malindi. It's a quiet, gentle place hugged by silver-tinged mudflats flowing with ghost crabs and long tides, it's a place where the creeping marriage of land and water is epitomised by a mangrove forest and the salty fresh scent of wind over an estuary. Mida Creek saves its real appeal for evening, when the stars (no exaggeration) simply rain down on you.

There's no shortage of activities on offer either. Excellent Giriama guides will take you through the water-laced landscape of the creek and through the mangroves on a rickety **walkway** (adult/child KSh250/150, guides per hr KSh300). At the end of the walkway a bird hide looks out over the surrounding wetlands. Of all the mangrove walkways on the Kenyan coast this one is by far the best and has the most knowledgeable guides. You can also organise three-hour **canoe trips** (KSh700) from here. Best of all, as this is a community project, visiting here helps the local Giriama people.

If you want to savour the peace a little longer (and you will) the **Mida Ecocamp** (☎0729213042; www.midaecocamp.com; huts per person KSh800-1400, camping KSh200), located just off the coast highway (B8) about 6km south of Watamu, has three lovely huts for rent. There's also a laid-back **restaurant** (meals KSh650) with tasty local meals, a wind-conditioned *makuli*-topped bar and the opportunity to venture into nearby villages on culture tours (your money goes to local schools).

Any bus travelling between Mombasa and Malindi can drop you on the main road near Mida Creek, from where it's a pleasant 20-minute walk to the camp.

There are basic **campsites** (adult/child US$15/10) close to the visitors centre and further south near Spinetail Way.

The forest is just off the main Malindi–Mombasa road. The main gate to the forest and visitors centre is about 1.5km west of the turn-off to Gede and Watamu, while the Mida entrance is about 3km further south. Buses and matatus between Mombasa and Malindi can drop you at either entrance. From Watamu, matatus to Malindi can drop you at the main junction.

Gede Ruins

If you thought Kenya was all about nature, you're missing an important component of her charm: lost cities. The remains of medieval Swahili towns dot the coast, with perhaps the most impressive of the bunch being the **Gede ruins** (adult/child KSh500/250; 7am-6pm).

This series of coral palaces, mosques and townhouses lies quietly in the jungle's green grip, but excavation has unearthed many structures. Within Gede archaeologists found evidence of the modern nature of Swahili society: silver necklaces with Maria Teresa coins (from Europe) and Arabic calligraphy (from the Middle East), vermicelli makers from Asia, Persian sabres, Arab coffeepots, Indian lamps, Egyptian or Syrian cobalt glass, Spanish scissors and Ming porcelain.

Gede, which reached its peak in the 15th century, was inexplicably abandoned in the 17th or 18th century. Some theories point to disease and famine; others blame guerrilla attacks by Somalian Gallas and cannibalistic Zimba from near Malawi, or punitive expeditions from Mombasa. Or Gede ran out of water – at some stage the water table here dropped rapidly and the 40m wells dried up.

Getting There & Away

The ruins lie off the main highway on the access road to Watamu. The easiest way here is via any matatu plying the main highway between Mombasa and Malindi. Get off at the village of Gede and follow the well-signposted dirt road from there – it's about a 10-minute walk.

Malindi

042

Malindi is lot nicer than its detractors realise, and probably not quite as nice as its advocates insist. It's easy to bash the place as an Italian beach resort – which it is. But you can't deny it's got a *bella spiaggia* (beautiful beach) and all those Italians have brought some high gastronomic standards with them. Did we mention a fascinating history that speaks to the great narrative of exploration, Malindi Marine Park and the twisty warren of thatch and whitewash that is Old Town? Throw it all together and you get a lot more character than the beach bums let on.

Sights & Activities

Malindi Marine National Park WILDLIFE RESERVE

(off Map p344; adult/child US$15/10; 7am-7pm) The oldest marine park in Kenya covers 213 sq km of rainbow clouds of powder-blue fish, organ-pipe coral, green sea-turtles and beds of *Thalassia* seagrass. If you're extremely lucky, you may spot mako and whale sharks. Unfortunately, these reefs have suffered (and continue to suffer) extensive damage, evidenced by the piles of seashells on sale in Malindi. Note that silt from the Galana River reduces underwater visibility between March and June and the monsoon generated waves can make visibility very low from June to September.

You're likely to come here on a snorkelling or glass-bottom boat tour, which can be arranged at the **KWS office** on the coast road south of Malindi. Boats only go out at low tide, so it's a good idea to call in advance to check times (your hotel can help with this). The going rate is around KSh5000 per boat (five to 10 people) for a two-hour trip.

Most hotels offer diving excursions. Or try **Blue-Fin-Diving** (www.bluefindiving.com), which operates out of several Malindi resorts. Charges €95 for a Discover Scuba course and €360 for the PADI Open Water course.

Malindi Historic Circuit HISTORIC BUILDINGS

National Museums of Kenya has smartly put the three major cultural sites of Malindi under the one general ticket of this **circuit** (adult/child KSh500/250; 8am-6pm).

The most compelling attraction covered in the Malindi Historic Circuit is the **House of Columns** (Mama Ngina Rd). The structure itself is a good example of traditional Swahili architecture and, more pertinently, contains great exhibits of all sorts of archaeological finds dug up around the coast. The **Vasco da Gama pillar** is admittedly more impressive for what it represents (the genesis of the Age of Exploration) than the edifice it-

DON'T MISS

MARAFA

Away from the hedonistic delights of sun and sand one of the more intriguing sights along the north Kenyan coast is the **Marafa Depression** (Map p321), also known as Hell's Kitchen or Nyari ('the place broken by itself'). It's an eroded sandstone gorge where jungle, red rock and cliffs upheave themselves into a single stunning Marscape.

About 30km northeast of Malindi, the Depression is currently managed as a local tourism concern by **Marafa village**. It costs (a steep) KSh600 (that goes into village programs) to walk around the lip of the gorge, and KSh400 for a guide who can walk you into the sandstone heart of the ridges and tell Hell's Kitchen's story. Which goes like so: a rich family was so careless with their wealth that they bathed themselves in the valuable milk of their cattle. God became angry with this excess and sunk the family homestead into the earth. The white and red walls of the Depression mark the milk and blood of the family painted over the gorge walls. The more mundane explanation? The Depression is a chunk of sandstone that is geologically distinct from the surrounding rock and more susceptible to wind and rain erosion.

Most people visit here on organised tours, with a self-drive car or by taxi (KSh7000). Alternatively, there are one or two morning matatus from Mombasa Rd in Malindi to Marafa village (KSh150, three hours) and from there it's a 20-minute walk to Hell's Kitchen. There are two very basic places to stay if needed.

self. Erected by da Gama as a navigational aid in 1498, the coral column is topped by a cross made of Lisbon stone, which almost certainly dates from the explorer's time. The tiny thatched **Portuguese church** (Mama Ngina Rd) is so called because Vasco da Gama is reputed to have erected it, and two of his crew are supposedly buried here. It's certainly true that St Francis Xavier visited on his way to India.

Sleeping

Note that most of the top-end places close or scale down operations between April and June or July.

TOP CHOICE **Scorpio Villas** RESORT $$

(☎20194; www.scorpio-villas.com; Mnarani Rd; s/d KSh4800/7600; ❄@🛜🏊) Every once in a while Kenya throws a hotel at you that is so much better value than anything else in its class that it leaves you wondering if you misheard the price. The Italian-run Scorpio Villas is one such place. Its 40-odd rooms are whitewashed and art bedecked with wooden roof beams. Step into the bathroom and you'll find huge walk-in rain showers. When you're feeling sleepy, dive into the giant four-poster beds. Throw in gardens heavy with foliage, a fantastic pool complex and a restaurant with excellent Italian food (four course evening meal KSh1200) and it's hard to beat.

Jardin Lorna GUESTHOUSE $$

(☎30658; harry@swiftmalindi.com; Mtangani Rd; s with/without bathroom KSh2500/1500, d with/without bathroom KSh5000/3000; ❄🏊) Lorna is very unpretentious, providing accommodation mainly for students of the Hospitality Training and Management Institute. Rooms are endearingly quirky with zebra rugs and local art punctuating the interior. Outside are some very peaceful gardens.

African Pearl Hotel HOTEL $

(☎0725131956; www.africanpearlhotel.com; Lamu Rd; d/tw from KSh2500/3500; 🛜❄🏊) This complex is done up with Africana accents, dark-wood sculptures, safari-themed souvenirs and a (murky) pool and lounge area that connects the scattered corners of this large resort.

Driftwood Beach Club RESORT $$$

(☎20155; www.driftwoodclub.com; Mama Ngina Rd; s/d with breakfast KSh10,560/15,070; ❄🛜🏊) One of the best-known resorts in Malindi and a key expat and Anglo-Kenyan hangout, Driftwood prides itself on an informal atmosphere and attracts a more independent clientele than many of its peers. The ambience is closer to palm-breezed serenity than the party atmosphere at similar hotels.

Ozi's Guest House HOTEL $

(☎20218; ozi@swiftmalindi.com; Mama Ngina Rd; s/d KSh900/1800) Popular with backpackers,

Malindi

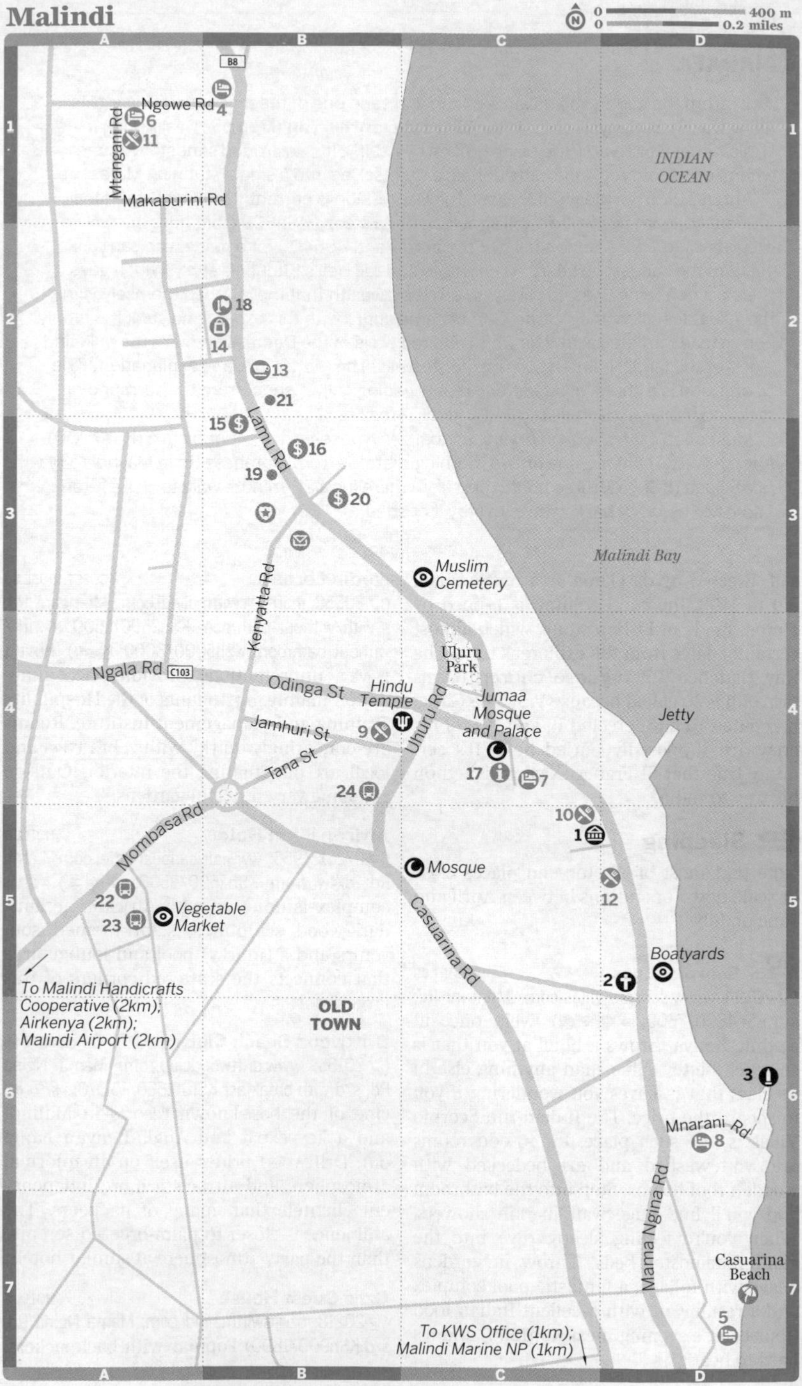

0 400 m
0 0.2 miles

A B C D
1 2 3 4 5 6 7

B8
Ngowe Rd
4
6
11
Mtangani Rd
Makaburini Rd
INDIAN OCEAN
18
14
13
21
15
16
Lamu Rd
19
20
Malindi Bay
Kenyatta Rd
Muslim Cemetery
Uluru Park
Ngala Rd
C103
Odinga St
Hindu Temple
Uhuru Rd
Jumaa Mosque and Palace
Jetty
Jamhuri St
9
Tana St
17
7
24
Mombasa Rd
10
1
Mosque
12
22
Vegetable Market
23
Casuarina Rd
Boatyards
2
To Malindi Handicrafts Cooperative (2km); Airkenya (2km); Malindi Airport (2km)
OLD TOWN
3
Mnarani Rd
8
Mama Ngina Rd
Casuarina Beach
5
To KWS Office (1km); Malindi Marine NP (1km)

Malindi

Sights

1 Malindi Museum/House of Columns ... C5
2 Portuguese Church ... D5
3 Vasco da Gama Pillar ... D6

Sleeping

4 African Pearl Hotel ... B1
5 Driftwood Beach Club ... D7
6 Jardin Lorna ... A1
7 Ozi's Guest House ... C4
8 Scorpio Villas ... D6

Eating

9 Barani Dishes ... B4
10 I Love Pizza ... C5
11 La Malindina ... A1
12 Old Man and the Sea ... D5

Drinking

Fermento Piano Bar ... (see 13)
13 Karen Blixen Restaurant & Coffee Shop ... B2

Shopping

14 Malindi Centre ... B2

Information

15 Barclays Bank ... B3
16 Dollar Forex Bureau ... B3
17 Immigration Office ... C4
18 Italian Consulate ... B2
19 North Coast Travel Services ... B3
20 Standard Chartered Bank ... B3
Tourist Office ... (see 14)

Transport

Buses to Lamu ... (see 24)
21 Kenya Airways ... B2
22 Matatus to Mombasa & Nairobi ... A5
23 New Malindi Bus Station ... A5
Southern Sky Safaris ... (see 14)
24 Starways Express ... B4

probably because it perches on the attractive edge of Old Town (next to a mosque – a very noisy mosque), Ozi's runs good tours and has friendly service that knows the needs of independent travellers. Rooms share bathrooms.

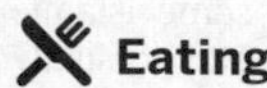

Eating

Many cheaper Swahili places close during the month of Ramadan. Of the hotel restaurants open to nonguests those of the **Scorpio Villas** and the **Driftwood** offer the best meals.

La Malindina ITALIAN $$$
(☎31449; Mtangani Rd; meals around KSh2000-2500; ⏰late-Jul–mid-Apr dinner only) This extremely upmarket Italian seafood place serves locally caught, fantastically fresh seafood and is regarded by all and sundry as the best place in town to eat.

I Love Pizza ITALIAN $
(☎20672; Mama Ngina Rd; pizzas around KSh900, pastas around KSh400-600) We do too, and the pizza is done really well here – way better than you might expect this far from Naples. No matter how good the pizza, many people come instead for the seafood and pastas. The porch-front and Mediterranean atmosphere tops off this excellent place.

Old Man and the Sea SEAFOOD $$
(☎31106; Mama Ngina Rd; mains KSh400-750, seafood KSh550-1100) This Old Man's been serving elegant, excellent seafood using a combination of local ingredients and fresh recipes for years. The classy waitstaff and wicker-chic ambience all combine for some nice colonial-style, candlelit meals under the stars. The menu also contains a small selection of vegetarian options.

Barani Dishes KENYAN $
(Jamhuri St; meals KSh80-220) If you ask a local where they think the best cheap local food comes from then chances are they'll point you towards this packed town centre place. It's clean, bright and has all the Kenyan staples you must surely be missing so much!

Drinking

Karen Blixen Restaurant & Coffee Shop CAFE $
(Lamu Rd; coffee KSh90-400, snacks KSh500-900) Despite being outrageously pretentious, this Italian-style pavement cafe is a fine place to escape the hubbub of the street outside. As befits an Italian cafe, it's Italian coffees and snacks all the way and lots and lots of Italians who think they're in Milan. It's open for breakfast as well.

Fermento Piano Bar LOUNGE $
(☎31780; Galana Centre, Lamu Rd; admission KSh200; ⊙from 10pm Wed, Fri & Sat; ❄) Fermento has the town's hippest dance floor, apparently once frequented by Naomi Campbell. It's young and trendy, so try to look so if you show up here.

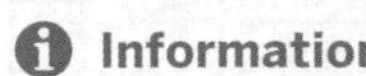

Information

Dangers & Annoyances

Being on the beach alone at night is asking for trouble as is walking along any quiet beach back roads at night. Also, avoid the far northern end of the beach or any deserted patches of sand as muggings are common. There are lots of guys selling drugs and sales of drugs often turn into stings; remember, everything from marijuana on up is illegal. There's also a lot of prostitution here.

Emergency

Ambulance (☎30575, 041-3432411, 999)

Police (☎20485, 999; Kenyatta Rd)

Money

Barclays Bank (Lamu Rd) With ATM.

Dollar Forex Bureau (Lamu Rd)

Standard Chartered Bank (Stanchart Arcade, Lamu Rd) With ATM.

Tourist Information

Italian Consulate (☎20502; Sabaki Centre, Lamu Rd)

Tourist office (☎20689; Malindi Complex, Lamu Rd; ⊙8am-12.30pm & 2-4.30pm Mon-Fri)

Travel Agencies

North Coast Travel Services (☎20370; Lamu Rd) Agent for Fly540.

Southern Sky Safaris (☎20493; www.southernskysafaris.com; Lamu Rd) Has a good reputation.

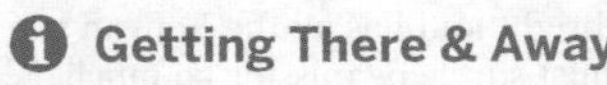

Getting There & Away

Air

Airkenya (☎30646; Malindi airport) has daily afternoon/evening flights to Nairobi (US$100, two hours). **Kenya Airways** (☎20237; Lamu Rd) flies the same route at least once a day (US$134).

Bus & Matatu

MOMBASA There are numerous daily buses and matatus (bus/matatu from KSh300/350, two hours). Bus company offices are found opposite the old market in the centre of Malindi.

NAIROBI All the main bus companies have daily departures to Nairobi at around 7am and/or 7pm (KSh110 to KSh1200, 10 to 12 hours), via Mombasa. **Starways Express** is one of the bigger operators.

WATAMU Matatus (KSh80 to KSh100, one hour) leave from the not very new **New Malindi Bus Station** on the edge of town.

LAMU Usually at least six daily buses (from KSh600, four to five hours). Most leave around 9am.

Getting Around

You can rent bicycles from most hotels or the KWS for KSh200 to KSh500 per day. Cycling at night is not permitted. *Tuk-tuks* are ubiquitous – a trip from town to the KWS office should cost around KSh150 to KSh200. A taxi to the airport is at least KSh150 and a *tuk-tuk* is KSh50; you'll need the gift of the gab to actually bargain them down to this.

Lamu

☎042

Lamu town has that excellent destination quality of immediately standing out as you approach it from the water (and let's face facts – everything is better when approached from water). The shop fronts and mosques, faded under the relentless kiss of the salt wind, creep out from behind a forest of dhow masts. Then you take to the streets, or more accurately, the labyrinth: donkey-wide alleyways, from which children grin; women whispering by in full-length bui-bui (black cover-all worn by some Islamic women outside the home); cats casually ruling the rooftops; blue smoke from meat grilling over open fires; and the organic, biting scent of the cured wooden shutters on houses built of stone and coral. Many visitors call this town – the oldest living town in East Africa, Unesco World Heritage Site and arguably the most complete Swahili town in existence – the highlight of their trip to Kenya. Residents call it Kiwa Ndeo – The Vain Island – and, to be completely fair, there's plenty for them to be vain about. We find no argument for humility.

Sights

Lamu is one of those places where the real attraction is just the overall feel of the place and there actually aren't all that many 'sights' to tick off. Having said that there are a couple of museums; all of which are open from 8am to 6pm daily. Admission to each is a much overpriced KSh500 for a nonresident adult, KSh250 for a child.

Lamu Museum MUSEUM
(Harambee Ave) The best museum in town is housed in a grand Swahili warehouse on the waterfront. This is as good a gateway as you'll get into Swahili culture and that of the archipelago in particular. There are exhibits dedicated to artefacts from Swahili ruins, the bric-a-brac of local tribes and the nautical heritage of the coast (including the *mtepe,* a traditional coir-sewn boat meant to resemble the Prophet Mohammed's camel – hence the nickname: 'camels of the sea'). Guides are available to show you around.

Lamu Fort FORTRESS
(Kenyatta Rd) This squat castle was built by the sultan of Paté in 1810 and completed in 1823. From 1910 right up to 1984 it was used as a prison. It now houses the island's library, which holds one of the best collections of Swahili poetry and Lamu reference work in Kenya. Entrance is free with a ticket to the Lamu Museum.

Swahili House Museum MUSEUM
This preserved Swahili house, tucked away to the side of Yumbe House hotel, is beautiful, but the KSh500 entry fee is very hard to justify, especially as half the hotels in Lamu are as well preserved as this small house.

German Post Office Museum MUSEUM
(Kenyatta Rd) In the late 1800s, before the British decided to nip German expansion into Tanganyika in the bud, the Germans regarded Lamu as an ideal base from which to exploit the interior. As part of their efforts, the German East Africa Company set up a post office, and the old building is now a museum exhibiting photographs and memorabilia from that fleeting period when Lamu had the chance of being spelt with umlauts.

FREE **Donkey Sanctuary** ZOO
(Harambee Ave; 9am-1pm Mon-Fri) With around 3000 donkeys active on Lamu, *Equus asinus* is the main form of transport

SAFETY ON LAMU

In September 2011 an English couple staying on the island of Kiwayu, north of Lamu, was attacked by Somali pirates/militants. The husband died and the wife was kidnapped and taken to Somalia. It was widely thought that this was a one-off attack and that Lamu itself was not at risk. However, just over two weeks later another attack occurred. This time a French woman was kidnapped from her home on Manda Island and taken to Somalia (where she later died); with Manda being almost within swimming distance of Lamu it suddenly seemed as if anywhere within the archipelago was at risk. Because of this, at the time of writing most Western governments were advising against all but essential travel to coastal areas within 150km of the Somalia border, which includes the entire Lamu archipelago. In addition, at the time of writing, the Kenyan government had announced that all fishing boats and their crews along the entire Kenyan coast were to report to police before and after each fishing trip, and that all boats were to be inspected. Fishing was banned altogether in the waters between Kiwayu Island and the Somali border.

Such statements mean that most tour operators will pull out of Lamu and the effects on the local tourist industry are likely to be enormous. Many locals and tourists will see such warnings as being unnecessarily cautious. Even so, as long as the government travel warnings remain in force many insurance companies will not cover you for trips to Lamu. This means that if, for example, you were hospitalised in Lamu then your insurance company is not obliged to pay out.

In October 2011 the Kenyan military invaded southern Somalia in an effort to push militants and criminal gangs away from the common border. In response, al-Shahab threatened to launch attacks on Kenya. Once again Lamu, with its combination of western tourists, a US naval base, the construction of a huge oil pipeline to South Sudan and ease of access via sea or land from Somalia, will be a prime target for terrorist attacks. Sadly this is a threat that is unlikely to decrease until the conflicts of Somalia are solved.

The above information is likely to change within the lifetime of this book and we would urge you to check the latest on the security situation before venturing to Lamu.

Lamu

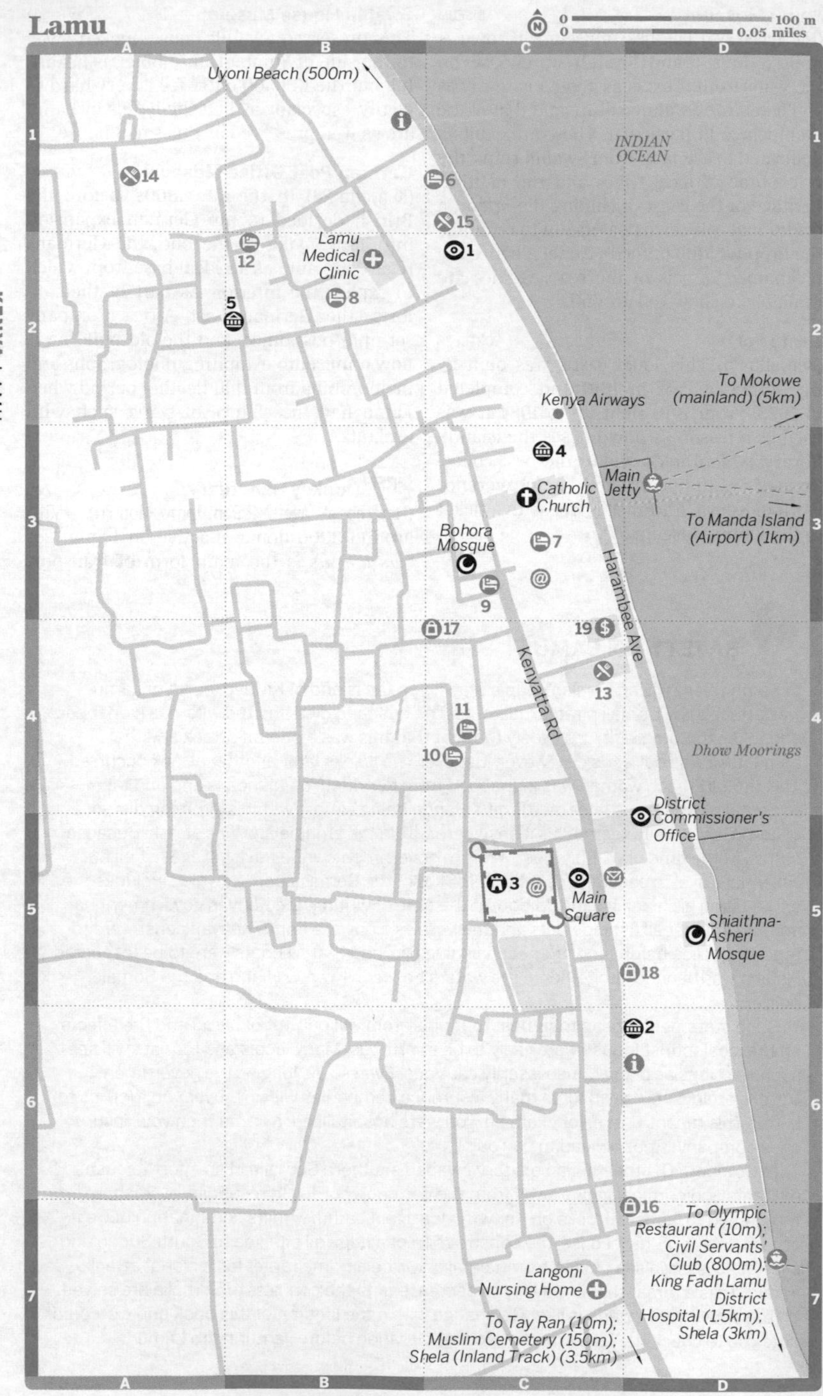

0 100 m
0 0.05 miles
A
B
C
D
1
2
3
4
5
6
7
Uyoni Beach (500m)
INDIAN OCEAN
14
6
15
1
12
Lamu Medical Clinic
8
5
Kenya Airways
To Mokowe (mainland) (5km)
4
Main Jetty
Catholic Church
To Manda Island (Airport) (1km)
Bohora Mosque
7
9
Harambee Ave
17
19
Kenyatta Rd
13
11
10
Dhow Moorings
District Commissioner's Office
3
Main Square
Shiaithna-Asheri Mosque
18
2
16
To Olympic Restaurant (10m); Civil Servants' Club (800m); King Fadh Lamu District Hospital (1.5km); Shela (3km)
Langoni Nursing Home
To Tay Ran (10m); Muslim Cemetery (150m); Shela (Inland Track) (3.5km)

Lamu

Sights
1 Donkey Sanctuary ... C2
2 German Post Office Museum ... D6
3 Lamu Fort ... C5
4 Lamu Museum ... C3
5 Swahili House Museum ... B2

Sleeping
6 Lamu House ... C1
7 Petley's Inn ... C3
8 Stone House Hotel ... B2
9 Sultan Palace Hotel ... C3
10 Wildebeeste 1 ... C4
11 Wildebeeste 2 ... C4
12 Yumbe House ... B2

Eating
13 Bush Gardens Restaurant ... C4
14 Bustani Café ... A1
Lamu House ... (see 6)
15 Mwana Arafa Restaurant Gardens ... C1
Stone House Hotel ... (see 8)

Shopping
16 Baraka Gallery ... D7
17 Black & White Gallery ... C4
Lamu Museum Shop ... (see 4)
18 Mani Books & Stationers ... D5

Information
19 Kenya Commercial Bank ... C4

Transport
Airkenya ... (see 16)

here. This sanctuary was established by the International Donkey Protection Trust of Sidmouth, UK, to improve the lot of the island's hard-working beasts of burden. Donations appreciated.

Festivals & Events

Maulidi Festival ISLAMIC
The Maulidi Festival celebrates the birth of the Prophet Mohammed. Its date shifts according to the Muslim calendar; during the lifetime of this book it will fall in January or February. The festival has been celebrated on the island for over 100 years and much singing, dancing and general jollity takes place around this time. On the final day a procession heads down to the tomb of the man who started it all, Ali Habib Swaleh.

Lamu Cultural Festival CULTURAL FESTIVAL
The Lamu Cultural Festival is another colourful carnival, exact dates vary each year but in 2011 it was held in November.

Sleeping

The alleyways of Lamu are absolutely rammed with places to stay and competition means that prices are often lower than in other parts of Kenya. There's always scope for price negotiation, especially if you plan to stay for over a day or two. Touts will invariably try to accompany you to get commission; the best way to avoid this is to book at least one night in advance, so you know what you'll be paying.

TOP CHOICE **Stone House Hotel** BOUTIQUE HOTEL **$$**
(☎633544; www.stonehousehotellamu.com; s/d with breakfast from US$40/60) This Swahili mansion is set into a tourist-free back street and is notable for its fine, whitewashed walls and fantastic rooftop, which includes a superb restaurant (no alcohol) with excellent views over the town and waterfront. The rooms are spacious and nicely decorated and it's easily one of the better value midrange options in town.

TOP CHOICE **Lamu House** BOUTIQUE HOTEL **$$$**
(☎633491; www.lamuhouse.com; Harambee Ave; s/d €190/235;) In a city where every building wants to top the preservation stakes, Lamu House stands out as the leader of the pack. It looks like an old Swahili villa, but it feels like a contemporarily decked-out boutique hotel, where they've blended the pale, breezy romance of the Greek islands into an African palace, with predictably awesome results.

Jambo House BOUTIQUE HOTEL **$**
(☎0713411714; www.jambohouse.com; s/d KSh2100/2500, without bathroom KSh1800/2200, ;) The new star on the Lamu hotel scene, this highly regarded budget hotel has small, but immaculate rooms in terracotta colours with electric blue bathrooms. There's a

DON'T MISS

DHOW TRIPS

More than the bustle of markets or the call to prayer, the pitch of, 'We take dhow trip, see mangroves, eat fish and coconut rice', is the unyielding chorus Lamu's voices offer up when you first arrive. With that said, taking a dhow trip (and seeing the mangroves and eating fish and coconut rice) is almost obligatory and generally fun besides, although this depends to a large degree on your captain.

Incompetent crews will lead you on a dreary day of nonstop tacking up Manda Channel and give you disastrously false information about local sites. Good ones are competent seamen and knowledgeable of the area. And the good is, frankly, great. There's a real joy to kicking it on the boards under the sunny sky, with the mangroves drifting by in island time while snacking on spiced fish.

Prices vary depending on where you want to go and how long you go for; with bargaining you could pay around KSh1000 per person in a group of four or five people. Make sure you know exactly how much you'll be paying and what that will include. Don't hand over any money until the day of departure, except perhaps a small advance for food. On long trips, it's best to organise your own drinks. A hat and sunscreen are essential.

fantastic rooftop terrace and a breakfast to rave about, but it's the owner, Arnold, who really makes the place stand out.

Yumbe House BOUTIQUE HOTEL $
(☎633101; lamuoldtown@africaonline.co.ke; s/d KSh2200/3000) As coral castles go, Yumbe's pretty good. (Yes, it's a coral castle!) With spacious rooms decorated with pleasant Swahili accents, verandahs that are open to the stars and the breeze, and a ridiculously romantic top-floor suite that's perfect for couples needing a palace tower retreat, Yumbe's a well-priced winner in a field of standouts.

Petley's Inn HOTEL $
(☎0726275438; Harambee Ave; r KSh3500) With the prime waterfront location and views to kill for, you might well expect Petley's too be vastly overpriced, but its spacious rooms are some of the better value ones in town. It had just been taken over by new management when we last passed by, so expect some changes to have taken place by the time you get there (including even the name).

Sultan Palace Hotel APARTMENT $
(☎0723593292; Kenyatta Rd; apt per person KSh3000) Central lodging house with a handful of impressive apartment-style rooms in sunny Mediterranean colours and with creaky Swahili four-poster beds. It's a good value option for single travellers; overpriced for couples.

Wildebeeste 1 & 2 APARTMENTS $
(☎0712851499; apt KSh2500-3000) Well it's certainly the most memorable place to stay in Lamu, but depending on your mood it will either come across as dusty and neglected or eccentric and arty. The truth lies somewhere in-between (though it probably leans more towards the former). The compound is divided into apartments, which sleep from two to six people.

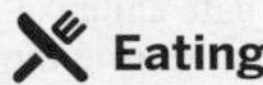

Eating

It's important to know that all the cheap places to eat, and many of the more expensive restaurants, are closed until after sunset during Ramadan.

The fruit juices, which almost every restaurant sells, are worth drawing attention to. They're good. They're really, really good.

As well as the restaurants listed here it's worth checking out the very up-market dining on offer at **Lamu House** or the slightly less-refined rooftop restaurant inside the **Stone House Hotel**.

TOP CHOICE **Mwana Arafa Restaurant Gardens** SEAFOOD $$
(Harambee Ave; meals KSh350-800; ⏲lunch & dinner) One of the more upmarket restaurants in Lamu; it has a perfect combination of garden seating and views over the dhows bobbing about under the moonlight. With barbecued giant prawns, grilled calamari, lobster or a seafood platter we guess you'll be eating the fruits of the sea tonight.

START LAMU MAIN JETTY
FINISH SHIAITHNA-ASHERI MOSQUE
DISTANCE ABOUT 1KM
DURATION 45 MINUTES TO ONE HOUR

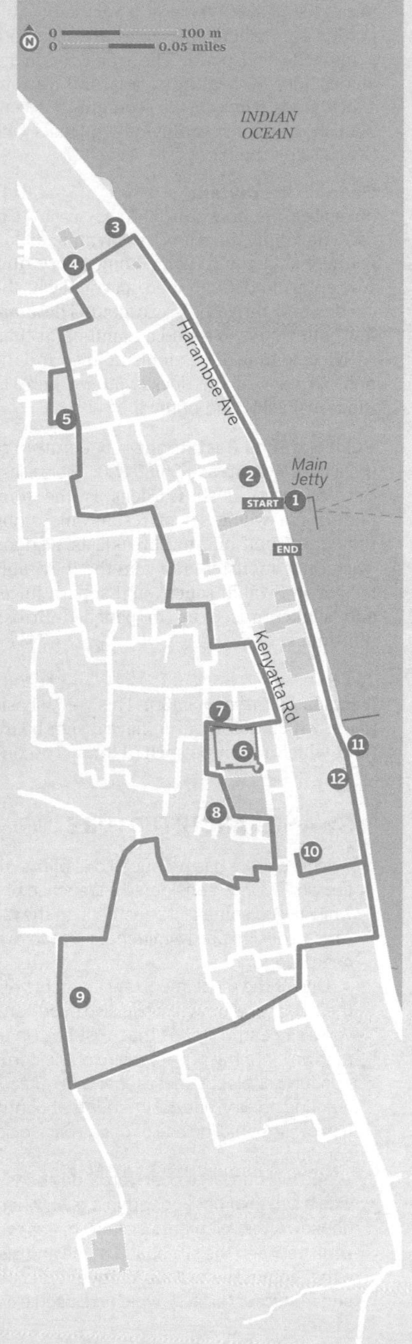

Walking Tour
Lamu Town

The best, indeed only, way to see Lamu town is on foot. Few experiences compare with exploring the far back streets, where you can wander amid wafts of cardamom and carbolic and watch the town's agile cats scaling the coral walls. There are so many wonderful Swahili houses that it's pointless for us to recommend specific examples – keep your eyes open wherever you go, and don't forget to look up.

Starting at the 1 **main jetty**, head north past the 2 **Lamu Museum** and along the waterfront until you reach the 3 **door-carving workshops**. From here head onto Kenyatta Rd, passing an original Swahili 4 **well**, and into the alleys towards the 5 **Swahili House Museum**. Once you've had your fill of domestic insights, take any route back towards the main street.

Once you've hit the main square and the 6 **fort**, take a right to see the crumbled remains of the 14th-century 7 **Pwani Mosque**, one of Lamu's oldest buildings – an Arabic inscription is still visible on the wall. From here you can head round and browse the covered 8 **market**, then negotiate your way towards the bright Saudi-funded 9 **Riyadha Mosque**, the centre of Lamu's religious scene.

Now you can take as long or as short a route as you like back to the waterfront. Stroll along the promenade, diverting for the 10 **German Post Office Museum** if you haven't already seen it – the door is another amazing example of Swahili carving. If you're feeling the pace, take a rest and shoot the breeze on the 11 **baraza ya wazee** ('old men's bench') outside the stucco minarets of the 12 **Shiaithna-Asheri Mosque**.

Carrying on up Harambee Ave will bring you back to the main jetty.

Bustani Café CAFE $

(meals KSh120-300) This is a very enjoyable garden cafe where the tables are set about a lily-bedecked pond. The small menu includes lots of healthy salads and various snack foods. The cafe also contains a decent bookshop and an evening-only internet cafe (KSh240 per hour).

Olympic Restaurant KENYAN $

(Harambee Ave; mains KSh250-700; ⊙lunch & dinner) The family that runs the Olympic makes you feel as if you've come home every time you enter, and their food, particularly the curries and biriyani, is excellent. There are few better ways to spend a Lamu night than with a cold mug of passionfruit juice and the noir-ish view of the docks you get here, at the ramshackle end of town.

Bush Gardens Restaurant INTERNATIONAL $$

(Harambee Ave; mains KSh180-800; ⊙breakfast, lunch & dinner) Bush Gardens is the template for a whole set of restaurants along the waterfront, offering breakfasts, seafood (including 'monster crab' and the inevitable lobster in Swahili sauce), and superb juices and shakes mixed up in panelled British pint-mugs.

Tay Ran KENYAN $

(Kenyatta Rd; mains KSh100) This very basic place, which doesn't even have a sign board (and which might be spelt Tehran – no one behind the counter seemed to know or care) serves dirt-cheap meals of fish, beans done in several ways (the best is *maharagwe ya chumvi* – with coconut milk) and chapattis. It's consistently packed with locals.

Drinking & Entertainment

As a Muslim town, Lamu has few options for drinkers and local sensibilities should be respected. Full moon parties sometimes take place in season over on Manda Island. The local beach boys should be able to advise.

Civil Servants' Club CLUB

(admission KSh100) Even bureaucrats need to let their hair down and the Civil Servants Club, along the waterfront towards Shela village, is virtually the only reliable spot for a drink and a dance on weekends. It's small, loud and rowdy. Lone women should run for cover, lone men should expect working-girl attention and the harbour wall outside is a potential death-trap after a few Tuskers.

Shopping

Baraka Gallery CRAFT

(Kenyatta Rd) For upmarket Africana, Baraka Gallery has a fine selection, but stratospheric prices.

Black & White Gallery CRAFT

Spanish-run art shop with some beautiful tribal-inspired crafts and paintings.

SWAHILI ARCHITECTURE

Swahili culture has produced one of the most distinctive architectures in Africa, if not the world. Once considered a stepchild of Arabic building styles, Swahili architecture, while owing some of its aesthetic to the Middle East, is more accurately a reflection of African design partly influenced by the Arab (and Persian, Indian and even Mediterranean) world.

One of the most important concepts of Swahili space is marking the line between the public and private while also occasionally blurring those borders. So, for example, you'll see Lamu stoops that exist both in the pubic arena of the street yet serve as a pathway into the private realm of the home. The use of stoops as a place for conversation further blends these inner and outer worlds. Inside the home, the emphasis is on creating an airy, natural interior that contrasts with the exterior constricting network of narrow streets. The use of open space also facilitates breezes that serve as natural air-conditioning.

You will find large courtyards, day beds placed on balconies and porches that all provide a sense of horizon within a town where the streets can only accommodate a single donkey. Other elements include: *dakas* (verandahs), which again sit in the transitional zone between the street and home and also provide open areas; *vidaka*, wall niches that either contain a small decorative curio or serve a decorative purpose in their own right; and *mambrui* (pillars), which are used extensively in Swahili mosques.

Lamu Museum Shop BOOKS
(Harambee Ave) Specialists in Lamu and Swahili cultural books.

Mani Books & Stationers BOOKS
(Kenyatta Rd) A very meagre collection of novels and other books.

Information

Dangers & Annoyances

Most Western governments were advising against all travel to Lamu and the remainder of the archipelago at the time of writing.

When times are normal the biggest real issue is the beach boys. They'll come at you the minute you step off the boat, offering drugs, tours and hotel bookings.

Lamu has long been popular for its relaxed, tolerant atmosphere, but it does have Muslim views of what is acceptable behaviour. In 1999, a gay couple who planned a public wedding here had to be evacuated under police custody. Whatever your sexuality, it's best to keep public displays of affection to a minimum and respect local attitudes to modesty.

Internet Access

Cyberwings (per hr KSh40; across from Petley's Inn; ⌚8am-8pm)

Real Tyme Cyber Cafe (per min KSh1; ⌚8am-10pm) Inside Lamu Fort.

Medical Services

King Fadh Lamu District Hospital (☎633075) One of the most modern and well-equipped hospitals on the coast.

Lamu Medical Clinic (Kenyatta Rd; ⌚8am-9pm)

Langoni Nursing Home (☎633349; Kenyatta Rd; ⌚24hr) Offers clinic services.

Money

Kenya Commercial Bank (Harambee Ave) The only bank on Lamu has an ATM (Visa only).

Post

Post office (Harambee Ave)

Tourist Information

Tourist information office (☎633132; Harambee Ave; lamu@tourism.go.ke; ⌚9am-1pm & 2-4pm)

Getting There & Away

Air

The airport at Lamu is on Manda Island, and the ferry across the channel to Lamu costs KSh150.

Airkenya (☎633445; www.airkenya.com; Baraka House, Kenyatta Rd) Daily flights between Lamu and Nairobi's Wilson airport (US$195, 1¾ hours).

Fly540 (☎632054; www.fly540.com) Flies twice daily to Malindi (around US$45) and Nairobi (around US$170).

Safarilink (www.flysafarilink.com) Daily flights to Nairobi Wilson airport (around US$185).

Bus

There are booking offices for several bus companies on Kenyatta Rd. The going rate for a trip to Mombasa (six hours) is KSh600 to KSh700 and to Malindi (four hours) it's KSh500; most buses leave between 7am and 8am, so you'll need to be at the jetty at 6.30am to catch the boat to the mainland. Book early.

Getting Around

There are ferries (KSh50) between Lamu and the bus station on the mainland (near Mokowe). Boats leave when the buses arrive at Mokowe; in the reverse direction, they leave at around 6.30am to meet the departing buses. Private charters cost KSh1500. Ferries between the airstrip on Manda Island and Lamu cost KSh150 and leave about half an hour before the flights leave (yes, in case you're wondering, all the airline companies are aware of this and so that's sufficient time).

Between Lamu village and Shela there are plenty of motorised dhows throughout the day until around sunset; these cost about KSh150 per person and leave when full.

Shela

Shela has undergone a severe case of gentrification and you could say it's a little bit like Lamu put through a high-end wringer. Overall it's cleaner, more sterile, has less character and there seems to be a lot more expats hovering about. On the plus side, there's a long, lovely stretch of beach and a link to a specific slice of coast culture – the locals speak a distinct dialect, of which they're rather proud.

Sights & Activities

Beach BEACH
Most people are here for the beach – a 12km-long sweep of sand where you're guaranteed an isolated spot. But as locals say, *Yana vuta kwa kasi* – 'There is a violent current there'. And no lifeguards. Tourists drown every year, so don't swim out too far. It should be pointed out that, beautiful as Shela beach is, it's more of a wild, windy and empty kind of beauty rather than an intimate palm tree-backed tropical beauty.

Water Sports WATER SPORTS
There's reasonable **windsurfing** in the channel between Shela and Manda Island.

The **water-sports centre** at Peponi Hotel runs all kinds of activities of the damp sort, including diving, snorkelling, windsurfing and kayaking.

Sleeping

All room rates include breakfast. You can negotiate all these prices when business is slow. As so many houses in Shela are owned by expats who only live here part time, there's a huge amount of accommodation available. **Lamu Retreats** (www.lamuretreats.com) can help you into 11 posh houses situated between Shela and Lamu town.

TOP CHOICE **Stopover Guest House** GUESTHOUSE $
(☎0720127222; s/d KSh4500-5000) The first place you come to on the waterfront is this simply beautiful guesthouse of pure white unfussy lines. Rooms are spacious, airy, bright and crisp, and a salt wind through your carved window-shutters is the best alarm clock we can think of. It's above the popular restaurant of the same name.

Kijani House Hotel BOUTIQUE HOTEL $$$
(☎Nairobi 020-243700; www.kijani-lamu.com; s/d €125-180; closed May & Jun; @) This villa complex is enormous, yet the design is elegantly understated, achieving a sort of Zen or Swahili aesthetic even as it spoils you with luxuriant tropical gardens, the nicest pool in Lamu and palatial-sized, and equally palatially decorated, rooms. It's one of the best top-end deals on the island.

White House HOTEL $
(☎0734183500; www.shelalamu.com; d from KSh3500) With rooms that look like they could fit in a Swahili cultural museum, a great roof lounge and breeze-laced views, this is one of the better deals in Shela. It's located a little way north of Peponi.

Peponi Hotel HOTEL $$$
(☎Nairobi 020-2435033; www.peponi-lamu.com; s/d from €175/215; closed May & Jun; @) If there were a capital of Shela it would be located here: this top-end resort has a grip on everything in this village, from tours to water sports to whatever else you can imagine. Sleeping-wise it's a winner, but then for the price they're charging you'd hope so!

Eating & Drinking

TOP CHOICE **Stopover Restaurant** SEAFOOD $$
(Stopover Guesthouse; mains KSh350-1200) There are waterfront restaurants all over the place, but the Stopover's friendly staff and excellent grub (of the spicy Swahili seafood sort) make it a cut above the competition. Oh, and it's a big call, but its fruit juices might just be the best around.

Rangaleni Café KENYAN $
(meals KSh60-100) Hidden away in the alleys behind the shorefront mosque is this tiny greeny-turquoise cafe, which does the usual stews and ugali (staple made from maize or cassava flour or both).

Peponi's Bar BAR
(Peponi's Hotel) Naturally, the bar at a Swiss-owned Kenyan hotel with an Italian name has to resemble an English pub. Pretty much everyone on Shela comes to this terrace for a (ridiculously expensive) sundowner as evening sets in.

Getting There & Away

You can take a motorised dhow here from the moorings in Lamu for KSh150 per person. Boat captains, for all their 'brother, we are one' prattle, will rip you off if you want a ride back at night.

Islands Around Lamu

The Lamu archipelago has plenty to offer outside Lamu itself. The easiest to get to is **Manda Island**, just across the channel, where most visitors go on dhow trips for snorkelling and to visit the Takwa ruins. The tiny **Manda Toto Island**, on the other side of Manda, has perhaps the best reefs on the coast.

Further northeast, **Paté Island** was the main power centre in the region before Lamu came to prominence, but is rarely visited now, preserving an uncomplicated traditional lifestyle as much by necessity as by choice. A regular motor launch shuttles between the towns of Mtangawanda, Siyu, Faza and Kizingitini.

UNDERSTAND KENYA

History

The early history of Kenya, from prehistory up until independence, is covered in the History chapter (p572).

Mau Mau Rebellion

Despite plenty of overt pressure on Kenya's colonial authorities, the real independence movement was underground. Tribal groups of Kikuyu, Maasai and Luo took secret oaths, which bound participants to kill Europeans and their African collaborators. The most famous of these movements was Mau Mau, formed in 1952 by disenchanted Kikuyu people, which aimed to drive the white settlers from Kenya forever.

The first blow was struck early with the killing of a white farmer's entire herd of cattle, followed a few weeks later by the massacre of 21 Kikuyu loyal to the colonial government. The Mau Mau rebellion had started.

Within a month, Jomo Kenyatta and several other Kenyan African Movement (KAU) leaders were jailed on spurious evidence, charged with 'masterminding' the plot. The various Mau Mau sects came together under the umbrella of the Kenya Land Freedom Army, led by Dedan Kimathi, and staged frequent attacks against white farms and government outposts. By the time the rebels were defeated in 1956, the death toll stood at more than 13,500 Africans (guerrillas, civilians and troops) and just more than 100 Europeans.

Upon his release in 1959 Kenyatta resumed his campaign for independence. Soon even white Kenyans began to feel the winds of change, and in 1960 the British government officially announced their plan to transfer power to a democratically elected African government. Independence was scheduled for December 1963, accompanied by grants and loans of US$100 million to enable the Kenyan assembly to buy out European farmers in the highlands and restore the land to the tribes.

Independence

With independence scheduled for 1963, the political handover began in earnest in 1962, with the centralist Kenya African National Union (KANU) and the federalist Kenya African Democratic Union (KADU) forming a coalition government.

The run-up to independence was surprisingly smooth, although the redistribution of land wasn't a great success; Kenyans regarded it as too little, too late, while white farmers feared the trickle would become a flood. The immediate effect was to cause a significant decline in agricultural production, from which Kenya has never fully recovered.

The coalition government was abandoned after the first elections in May 1963 and Kikuyu leader, Jomo Kenyatta (formerly of the KANU), became Kenya's first president on 12 December, ruling until his death in 1978. Under Kenyatta's presidency, Kenya developed into one of Africa's most stable and prosperous nations.

While Kenyatta is still seen as one of the few success stories of Britain's withdrawal from empire, he wasn't without his faults. Biggest among these were his excessive bias in favour of his own tribe and escalating paranoia about dissent. Corruption soon became a problem at all levels of the power structure and the political arena contracted.

The 1980s

Kenyatta was succeeded in 1978 by his vice-president, Daniel arap Moi. A Kalenjin, Moi was regarded by establishment power brokers as a suitable frontman for their interests, as his tribe was relatively small and in thrall to the Kikuyu. Moi went on to become one of the most enduring 'Big Men' in Africa, ruling in virtual autocracy for nearly 25 years.

On assumption of power, Moi sought to consolidate his regime by marginalising those who had campaigned to stop him from succeeding Kenyatta. Lacking a capital base of his own, and faced with shrinking economic opportunities, Moi resorted to the politics of exclusion. He reconfigured the financial, legal, political and administrative institutions. For instance, a constitutional amendment in 1982 made Kenya a de jure one-party state, while another in 1986 removed the security of tenure for the attorney-general, comptroller, auditor general and High Court judges, making all these positions personally beholden to the president. These developments had the effect of transforming Kenya from an 'imperial state' under Kenyatta to a 'personal state' under Moi.

Winds of Change

By the late 1980s, most Kenyans had had enough. Following the widely contested 1988 elections, Charles Rubia and Kenneth

Matiba joined forces to call for the freedom to form alternative political parties and stated their plan to hold a political rally in Nairobi on 7 July without a licence. Though the duo was detained prior to their intended meeting, people turned out anyway, only to be met with brutal police retaliation. Twenty people were killed and police arrested a slew of politicians, human-rights activists and journalists.

Things came to a head on 7 July 1990 when the military and police raided an opposition demonstration in Nairobi, killing 20 and arresting politicians, human-rights activists and journalists. The rally, known thereafter as Saba Saba ('seven seven' in Swahili), was a pivotal event in the push for a multiparty Kenya. The resulting pressure led to a change in the constitution that allowed opposition parties to register for the first time.

Faced with a foreign debt of nearly US$9 billion and blanket suspension of foreign aid, Moi was pressured into holding flawed multiparty elections in early 1992. To make matters worse, about 2000 people were killed during tribal clashes in the Rift Valley. Moi was overwhelmingly re-elected.

The 1997 election, too, was accompanied by violence and rioting. European and North American tour companies cancelled their bookings and around 60,000 Kenyans lost their jobs. Moi was able to set himself up as peacemaker, calming the warring factions and gaining 50.4% of the seats for KANU. After the elections, KANU was forced to bow to mounting pressure and initiate some changes: some Draconian colonial laws were repealed, as well as the requirement for licences to hold political rallies.

But Kenya was about to enter a difficult period. On 7 August 1998, Islamic extremists bombed the US embassies in Nairobi and Dar es Salaam in Tanzania, killing more than 200 people and bringing al-Qaeda and Osama bin Laden to international attention for the first time. The effect on the Kenyan economy was devastating. It would take four years to rebuild the shattered tourism industry.

Democratic Kenya

Having been beaten twice in the 1992 and 1997 elections, 12 opposition groups united to form the National Alliance Rainbow Coalition (NARC). With Moi's presidency due to end in 2002, many feared that he would alter the constitution again to retain his position. This time, though, he announced his intention to retire.

Moi put his weight firmly behind Uhuru Kenyatta, the son of Jomo Kenyatta, as his successor, but the support garnered by NARC ensured a resounding victory for the party, with 62% of the vote. Mwai Kibaki was inaugurated as Kenya's third president on 30 December 2002.

When Kibaki assumed office in January 2003, donors were highly supportive of the new government. During its honeymoon period, the Kibaki administration won praise for a number of policy initiatives, especially a crackdown on corruption. In 2003-04, donors, contributed billions of dollars to the fight against corruption, including support for the office of a newly appointed anticorruption 'czar', and the International Monetary Fund resumed lending in November 2003.

Corruption Continues

Despite initially positive signs, it became clear by mid-2004 that large-scale corruption was still a considerable problem in Kenya. Western diplomats alleged that corruption had cost the treasury US$1 billion since Kibaki took office. In February 2005, the British High Commissioner Sir Edward Clay denounced the 'massive looting' of state resources by senior government politicians, including sitting cabinet ministers. Within days, Kibaki's anticorruption 'czar', John Githongo, resigned and went into exile amid rumours of death threats related to his investigation of high-level politicians. The UK, the US and Germany rapidly suspended their anticorruption lending. With Githongo's release of a damning detailed dossier on corruption in the Kibaki regime in February 2006, Kibaki was forced to relieve three ministers of their cabinet positions.

But it hasn't all been bad news. The Kibaki government has succeeded in making primary and secondary education more accessible for ordinary Kenyans, while state-control over the economy has been loosened.

Things Fall Apart

On 27 December 2007, Kenya held presidential, parliamentary and local elections. While the parliamentary and local government elections were largely considered credible, the presidential elections were marred by serious irregularities, reported by both

Kenyan and international election monitors, and by independent nongovernmental observers. Nonetheless, the Electoral Commission declared Mwai Kibaki the winner, triggering a wave of violence across the country. The Rift Valley, Western Highlands, Nyanza Province and Mombasa – areas afflicted by years of political machination, previous election violence and large-scale displacement – exploded in ugly tribal confrontations. The violence left more than 1000 people dead and over 600,000 people homeless. Fearing the stability of the most stable linchpin of East Africa, former UN Secretary-General Kofi Annan and a panel of 'Eminent African Persons' flew to Kenya to mediate talks. A power-sharing agreement was finally signed on 28 February 2008 between President Kibaki and Raila Odinga, the leader of the ODM opposition. The coalition provided for the establishment of a prime ministerial position (to be filled by Raila Odinga), as well as a division of cabinet posts according to the parties' representation in parliament.

Rebuilding Confidence

Despite some difficult moments, the fragile coalition government has stood the test of time, thereby going some way towards reassuring Kenyans and the international community that the violence was a one-off, rather than a vision of Kenya's future. The government has also begun the complex (and long-overdue) task of long-term reform. Arguably its most important success has been the 2010 constitution, which was passed in a referendum by 67% of Kenya's voters. Among the key elements of this new constitution are the devolution of powers to Kenya's regions, the introduction of a bill of rights and the separation of judicial, executive and legislative powers.

Kenya Today

Kenya is holding its breath in advance of the 2012 poll. The surprising stability with which the government of erstwhile foes President Mwai Kibaki (who will be standing down after two terms) and Prime Minister Raila Odinga (a leading candidate for the presidency) has ruled Kenya – since being forced into a marriage of convenience – has restored considerable faith in the country's democratic institutions. Cynicism, however, remains high among ordinary Kenyans when it comes to their political class. More than that, the underlying suspicions between various tribal groupings, poverty, and the increasing competition for scarce resources which lay behind the violence remain unresolved.

Kenya's economy, however, is booming, and neither natural disasters, post-election violence or war with Somalia can shake the country's confidence that Kenya is on the up. There's just one problem: only a small percentage of Kenyans see the benefits of the growing prosperity. Unemployment sits at around 40%, a staggering 50% of Kenyans live below the poverty line and the prices of basic foodstuffs are soaring. By one estimate, Kenya would require an annual growth rate of 11% for the prosperity gains to even begin to trickle down to poorer sectors of Kenyan society.

In October 2011, for the first time in its independent history, Kenya went to war. The spark for such a drastic move was a series of cross-border raids allegedly carried out by al-Shabaab, an al-Qaeda–affiliated Somali group accused of kidnapping foreign-aid workers and tourists from inside Kenya. Aware that its lucrative tourism industry could be at risk, Kenya's military launched a large-scale invasion of Somalia, claiming that it was acting in self defence; most Western governments agreed.

Daily Life

Traditional cultures are what hold Kenya together. Respect for one's elders, firmly held religious beliefs, traditional gender roles and the tradition of *ujamaa* ('familyhood') create a well-defined social structure with stiff moral mores at its core.

Historically, the majority of Kenyans were either farmers or cattle herders with family clans based in small interconnected villages. Even today, as traditional rural life gives way to a frenetic urban pace, this strong sense of community remains and the importance of social interactions such as greetings should never be underestimated.

Kenya is home to over 40 tribal groups. Although most tribal groups have coexisted quite peacefully since independence, the ethnocentric bias of government and civil service appointments has led to escalating unrest and disaffection. During the hotly contested elections of 1992, 1997 and 2007, clashes between two major tribes, the Kikuyu and Luo, bolstered by allegiances with other smaller tribes like the Kalenjin, resulted in death and mass displacement. This has led to an increasing anxiety among the middle and upper classes that the country may be riven along tribal lines if something isn't done to address major inequalities. Local analysts point out that election violence is more to do with economic inequality than with tribalism – they insist that there are only two tribes in Kenya: the rich and the poor.

Religion

As a result of intense missionary activity, the majority of Kenyans outside the coastal and eastern provinces are Christians (including some home-grown African Christian groups that do not owe any allegiance to the major Western groups). Street preachers are common throughout the country, and their fire-and-brimstone sermons normally attract a large crowd. Hard-core evangelism has made some significant inroads and many TV-style groups from the US have a strong following.

In the country's east, the majority of Kenyans are Sunni Muslims. They make up about 10% of the population.

Arts

Music

With its diversity of indigenous languages and culture, Kenya has a rich and exciting music scene. Influences, most notably from the nearby Democratic Republic of Congo and Tanzania, have helped to diversify the sounds. More recently, reggae and hip hop have permeated the pop scene.

Benga is the contemporary dance music of Kenya. It refers to the dominant style of Luo pop music, which originated in western Kenya, and spread throughout the country in the 1960s being taken up by Akamba and Kikuyu musicians. The music is characterised by clear electric guitar licks and a bounding bass rhythm. Contemporary Kikuyu music often borrows from *benga*.

Taarab, the music of the East African coast, originally only played at Swahili weddings and other special occasions, has been given a new lease of life by coastal pop singer Malika.

Popular bands today are heavily influenced by *benga, soukous* and also Western music, with lyrics generally in Kiswahili. These include bands such as Them Mushrooms (now reinvented as Uyoya) and Safari Sound. For upbeat dance tunes, Ogopa DJs, Nameless, Redsan and Deux Vultures are recommended acts. Other names to keep an eye or ear out for include Prezzo (Kenya's king of bling), Nonini (a controversial women-and-booze rapper), Nazizi (female MC from Necessary Noize) and Mercy Myra (Kenya's biggest female R&B artist).

Literature

Ngũgĩ wa Thiong'o (b 1938), Kenya's best-known writer, is uncompromisingly radical, and his harrowing criticism of the neocolonialist politics of the Kenyan establishment landed him in jail for a year (described in his *Detained: A Prison Writer's Diary*), lost him his job at Nairobi University and forced him into exile. His works include *Petals of Blood, Matigari, The River Between, A Grain of Wheat, Devil on the Cross* and *Wizard of the Crow,* which was short-listed for the 2007 Commonwealth Writers' Prize. His latest work is the 2010 memoir *Dreams in a Time of War*. All offer insightful portraits of Kenyan life and will give you an understanding of the daily concerns of modern Kenyans. Ngũgĩ has also written extensively in his native language, Gikuyu.

Another important Kenyan writer is Meja Mwangi, who sticks more to social issues and urban dislocation but has a mischievous sense of humour, while Binyavanga Wainaina is one of Kenya's rising stars. Highly regarded female writers include Grace Ogot, Margaret Atieno Ogola, Marjorie Magoye and Hilary Ngweno.

To stay up to date with the contemporary scene, look out for *Kwani?* (http://kwani.org), Kenya's first literary journal, established by Wainaina in 2003. It hosts an annual literary festival that attracts a growing number of international names.

Environment

The Land

Kenya straddles the equator and covers an area of some 583,000 sq km, including around 13,600 sq km of Lake Victoria. It is bordered to the north by the arid bushlands of Ethiopia and Sudan, to the east by the Indian Ocean and the deserts of Somalia, to the west by Uganda and Lake Victoria, and to the south by Tanzania.

KENYA PLAYLIST

» *Amigo* – classic Swahili rumba from one of Kenya's most influential bands, Les Wanyika

» *Guitar Paradise of East Africa* – ranges through Kenya's musical styles including the classic hit 'Shauri Yako'

» *Journey* – Jabali Afrika's stirring acoustic sounds complete with drums, congas, shakers and bells

» *Kenyan: The First Chapter* – Kenya's home-grown blend of African lyrics with R&B, house, reggae and dancehall genres

» *Mama Africa* – Suzanna Owiyo, the Tracy Chapman of Kenya, with acoustic Afropop

» *Nuting but de Stone* – phenomenally popular compilation combining African lyrics with American urban sounds and Caribbean *ragga*

» *Rumba is Rumba* – infectious Congolese *soukous* with Swahili lyrics

» *Nairobi Beat: Kenyan Pop Music Today* – regional sounds including Luo, Kikuyu, Kamba, Luhya, Swahili and Congolese

» *Virunga Volcano* – from Orchestre Virunga, with samba, with sublime guitar licks, a bubbling bass and rich vocals

Kenya is dominated by the Rift Valley, a vast range of valleys that follows a 5000km-long crack in the earth's crust. Within the Rift are numerous 'swells' (raised escarpments) and 'troughs' (deep valleys, often containing lakes), and there are some huge volcanoes, including Mt Kenya, Mt Elgon and Mt Kilimanjaro (across the border in Tanzania).

The Rift Valley divides the flat plains of the coast from the hills along the lakeshore. Nairobi, the capital, sits in the Central Highlands, which are on the eastern edge of the Rift Valley. Kenya can roughly be divided into four zones: the coastal plains; the Rift Valley and Central Highlands; the lakeshore; and the wastelands of northern Kenya.

The main rivers in Kenya are the Athi/Galana River, which empties into the Indian Ocean near Malindi, and the Tana River, which hits the coast midway between Malindi and Lamu. Aside from Lake Victoria, Kenya has numerous small volcanic lakes and mighty Lake Turkana, which straddles the Ethiopian border.

Within volcanic craters, and on the Rift Valley floor, are several soda lakes, rich in sodium bicarbonate, created by the filtering of water through mineral-rich volcanic rock and subsequent evaporation.

Wildlife

Kenya is home to all of the charismatic mega-fauna that draws so many visitors to Africa and the daily battle between predators and prey brings so much personality to the Kenyan wilds. The 'Big Five' – lion, buffalo, elephant, leopard and rhino – are relatively easy to spot in at least two of the major parks. The birdlife here is equally diverse – Kenya is home to over 1100 species with millions of migratory birds arriving or passing through the country from November to October.

Endangered Species

Many of Kenya's major predators and herbivores have become endangered because of the continuous destruction of their natural habitat and merciless poaching for ivory, skins, horn and bush meat.

The **black rhino** is probably Kenya's most endangered species, due to poaching for its horn. Faced with relentless poaching by heavily armed gangs in the 1980s, the wild rhino population plummeted from 20,000 in 1969 to just 630 (one-sixth of Africa's total) today. **Rhino Ark** (☎020-2136010; www.rhinoark.org) raises funds to create rhino sanctuaries in the parks, complete with electric fencing and guards, and donations are always appreciated. Sanctuaries already in existence include the Ngulia Rhino Sanctuary in Tsavo West National Park, the privately run Solio Game Reserve and Ol Peteja Conservancy. Lake Nakuru National Park and the Aberdares National Park also have viable populations of black rhinos. While the **elephant** is not technically endangered, it is still the target of poachers, and a large number are killed every year, especially in the area around Tsavo East National Park. Elephant numbers in Kenya dropped to an estimated 5400 in 1988, but numbers have recovered to around 35,000.

Lions are also considered endangered in Kenya with fewer than 2000 thought to survive, although this is feared to be an over-estimate. The only viable lion populations in the long-term are those in Laikipia, Meru National Park and Maasailand (which stretches across southern Kenya from the Masai Mara National Reserve to Tsavo East National Park).

Other endangered species include the **hirola antelope** (found in Tsavo East National Park), **Grevy's zebra** (found only in the Lewa Wildlife Conservancy, Ol Pejeta Conservancy and the Samburu, Buffalo Springs and Shaba National Reserves) and the **Rothschild's giraffe** (which still roams Lake Nakuru and Ruma National Parks).

National Parks & Reserves

Kenya's national parks and reserves rate among the best in Africa, and around 10% of the country's land area is protected by law – that means, at least in theory, no human habitation, no grazing and no hunting within park boundaries. These parks range from the 15.5-sq-km Saiwa Swamp National Park to the massive, almost 21,000-sq-km Tsavo East and West National Parks, and together they embrace a wide range of habitats and ecosystems, and contain an extraordinary repository of Africa's wildlife. Quite apart from anything else, these parks are home to some of the most beautiful corners of Africa.

Park & Reserve Entry

Entry fees to national parks are controlled by the **KWS** (Kenya Wildlife Service; ☎020-6000800; www.kws.org; Nairobi National Park) and admission to parks in Kenya is being converted to a **safaricard** system for payment of fees. The cards must be charged

PARK ENTRY FEES

CATEGORY	PARK	ADULT/CHILD (US$) JAN-MAR, JUL-OCT	ADULT/CHILD (US$) REST OF YEAR	CAMPING ADULT/ CHILD (US$)
Masai Mara	Masai Mara	70-80/40-45	70-80/40-45	30-40
Premium	Amboseli, Lake Nakuru	70/40	60/30	25/20
Wilderness	Meru, Tsavo East & Tsavo West	60/30	50/25	15/10
Aberdare	Aberdare	50/25	50/25	15/10
Urban Safari	Nairobi	40/20	40/20	15/10
Mountain Climbing	Mt Kenya day trip	55/25	55/25	15/10
Mt Kenya (3-day package)	Mt Kenya	150/70	150/70	15/10
Scenic & Special Interest 1	Hell's Gate & Mt Elgon	25/15	25/15	15/10
Scenic & Special Interest 2	Chyulu, Marsabit, Arabuko Sokoke, Kakamega, Shimba Hills & all other parks	20/10	20/10	15/10
Marine Parks	Kisite & Mpunguti	20/10	20/10	N/A
Other Marine Parks	Kiunga, Malindi, Mombasa & Watamu	15/10	15/10	N/A

with credit in advance and can be topped up at certain locations (usually the parks' main gates only, which can be inconvenient). Remaining credit is not refundable.

At the time of writing the safaricard system was in use at Nairobi, Lake Nakuru, Aberdare, Amboseli and Tsavo National Parks. The other parks still work on a cash system.

At the time of writing, safaricards are only available at the KWS headquarters in Nairobi and Mombasa, at the main gates of the participating parks, and at the Malindi Marine National Park office.

What to do if you don't have a safaricard? It is still possible to purchase a temporary entry card at the main gates of most national parks, although we recommend purchasing a safaricard in advance where possible.

In the Park Entry Fees table you'll find the various entry fees for nonresidents during high season (January to March and July to October) and 'normal' season (April to June, November and December) and year-round camping fees for nonresidents. Rates for Kenyan citizens and residents are available from the KWS website.

Although the changes had not yet come into effect at the time of writing, there are plans to raise the entry for Premium parks to US$80 per adult regardless of the season.

Further costs in the land-based parks and reserves include KSh300 for vehicles with fewer than six seats and KSh1000 for vehicles seating six to 12.

Environmental Issues

Kenya faces a daunting slew of environmental issues, among them deforestation, desertification, threats to endangered species and the impacts of tourism. The ongoing debate over whether conservation should be in public or private hands is also a hot topic in Kenya.

Deforestation

Forest destruction continues on a large scale in parts of Kenya – today, less than 3% of the country's original forest cover remains. Land grabbing, charcoal burning, agricultural encroachment, the spiralling use of firewood and illegal logging, have all taken their toll over the years. However, millions of Kenyans (and the majority of hotels, lodges and restaurants) still rely on wood and charcoal for cooking fuel, so travellers to the country will almost certainly contribute to this deforestation, whether they like it or not.

WHICH CURRENCY?

Note that Kenya Wildlife Service (KWS) now accepts euros and UK pounds, but you're still better off paying in Kenyan shillings or US dollars as KWS exchange rates are punitive.

The degazetting of protected forests is another contentious issue, sparking widespread protests and preservation campaigns. On the flipside, locals in forest areas can find themselves homeless if the government does enforce protection orders.

Desertification

Northern and eastern Kenya are home to some of the most marginal lands in East Africa. Pastoralists have eked out a similarly marginal existence here for centuries, but recurring droughts have seriously degraded the land, making it increasingly susceptible to creeping desertification and erosion. As a consequence, the UN estimates that the livelihoods of around 3.5 million herders may be under medium- to long-term threat.

Private vs Public Conservation

KENYA WILDLIFE SERVICE (KWS)

Conservation in Kenya has, for over two decades, been in the hands of the government-run **Kenya Wildlife Service** (www.kws.org) and few would dispute that they've done a pretty impressive job. In the dark years of the 1970s and '80s when poaching was rampant, a staggering number of Kenya's rhinos and elephants were slaughtered and many KWS officers were in league with poachers. It all changed after the famous palaeontologist Dr Richard Leakey cleaned up the organisation in the 1980s and '90s. A core part of his policy was arming KWS rangers with modern weapons and high-speed vehicles and allowing them to shoot poachers on sight, which seems to have dramatically reduced the problem. However, there have been several raids on elephant and rhino populations over the past decade and KWS rangers continue to lose their lives every year in battles with poachers.

PRIVATE CONSERVATION

An estimated 75% of Kenya's wildlife lives outside the country's national parks and reserves, to the extent that the future of conservation in Kenya lies in private hands. Private wildlife reserves often have the resources to work more intensively on specific conservation issues than national parks and reserves can.

Lewa Wildlife Conservancy (p307), near Isiolo, is probably the best known, and most successful, private reserve. The private conservancies of the Laikipia Plateau (see the boxed text, p303) have also produced some startling results – without a single national park or reserve in the area, Laikipia has become a major safari destination, and is proving to be a particularly important area for viable populations of endangered black rhinos, Grevy's zebras, African wild dogs and lions.

Other private game ranches and conservation areas (some of which we've covered throughout the chapter) can be found across the country, particularly close to Tsavo (East and West, though mainly West) and Amboseli National Parks, and the Masai Mara National Reserve.

Tourism

The tourist industry is at once the saviour of Kenya's animals and the cause of some pretty major environmental problems, most notably the heavy use of firewood by tourist lodges and erosion caused by safari minibuses.

As a visitor, the best way to help combat these problems is to be selective about who you do business with and very vocal about the kind of standards you expect. The more that tourists insist on responsible practices, the more safari operators and hotels will take notice, and, while you may end up paying more for an ecofriendly trip, in the long term you'll be investing in a sustainable tourist industry and the preservation of Kenya's delicate environment.

SURVIVAL GUIDE

Directory A–Z

Accommodation

Kenya has a wide range of accommodation options, from basic cubicle hotels overlooking city bus-stands to luxury tented camps hidden away in remote corners of national parks. There are also all kinds of campsites, budget tented camps, *bandas* (thatched-roof, wood or stone huts) and cottages scattered around the parks and rural areas.

High-season prices usually run from June to October, from January until early March, and include Easter and Christmas. Low season usually covers the rest of the year, although some lodges and top-end hotels also have intermediate shoulder seasons.

On the coast, peak times tend to be July to August and December to March, and a range of lower rates can apply for the rest of the year.

Kenya operates on a dual pricing system – nonresidents pay significantly more (often double or triple the price) than Kenyan (or other East African) residents. When things are quiet, you may be able to get the residents' rate if you ask, but don't count on it. Prices quoted throughout this book are nonresident rates, unless otherwise stated. We also quote prices in the currency preferred by the place in question (usually US$ or KSh), but in most cases you can pay in dollars, shillings, euros and (sometimes) other foreign currencies.

The website of **Uniglobe Let's Go Travel** (www.uniglobeletsgotravel.com) displays almost all the major hotels and lodges in Kenya, giving price ranges and descriptions.

PRACTICALITIES

» **Newspapers & Magazines** The *Daily Nation*, the *East African Standard*, the *East African*, the *Weekly Review* and the *New African*.

» **TV** KBC and NTV, formerly KTN, are the main national TV stations. CNN, Sky and BBC networks are also widely available on satellite or cable (DSTV).

» **Radio** KBC Radio broadcasts across the country on various FM frequencies. BBC World Service is easily accessible.

» **Weights & Measures** Metric

» **Smoking** Banned in restaurants, bars and public areas, with expensive fines for breaches.

BANDAS

These are Kenyan-style huts and cottages, usually with some kind of kitchen and bathroom, which offer excellent value. There are Kenya Wildlife Service (KWS) *bandas* at some national parks. Facilities range from basic dorms and squat toilets to kitchens and hot water provided by wood-burning stoves. In such places, you'll need to bring all your own food, drinking water, bedding and firewood.

CAMPING

There are many opportunities for camping in Kenya and, although gear can be hired in Nairobi and around Mt Kenya, it's worth considering bringing a tent with you. There are KWS campsites in just about every national park or reserve. These are usually very basic, with a toilet block with a couple of pit toilets, a water tap, perhaps public showers and very little else. They cost US$25/20 per adult/child in Amboseli and Lake Nakuru National Parks, US$30 to US$40 in Masai Mara National Reserve and US$15/10 in all other parks.

As well as these permanent campsites, KWS also runs so-called 'special' campsites in most national parks. These sites move every year and have even fewer facilities than the standard camps, but cost more because of their wilder locations and set-up costs. They cost US$40/20 per adult/child in Amboseli and Lake Nakuru, US$30/15 elsewhere; a reservation fee of KSh7500 per week is payable on top of the relevant camping fee.

All camping prices in this book are per person unless otherwise specified.

HOSTELS

The only youth hostel affiliated with Hostelling International (HI) is in Nairobi. It has good basic facilities and is a pleasant enough place to stay, but there are plenty of other cheaper choices that are just as good. Other places that call themselves 'youth hostels' are not members of HI, and standards are variable.

HOTELS & GUEST HOUSES

Real bottom-end hotels (often known as 'board and lodgings' to distinguish them from *hotelis,* which are often only restaurants) are widely used as brothels, and tend to be very rundown; security at these places is virtually nonexistent.

Proper hotels and guesthouses come in many different shapes and sizes. As well as the top-end Western companies, there are a number of small Kenyan chains offering reliable standards across a handful of properties in particular towns or regions, and also plenty of private family-run establishments.

Self-catering options are common on the coast, where they're often the only mid-priced alternative to the top-end resorts, but not so much in other parts of the country.

Terms you will come across in Kenya include 'self-contained', which just means a room with its own private bathroom, and 'all-inclusive' (called 'full board' in this book), which generally means all meals, certain drinks and possibly some activities should be included. 'Half board' generally means breakfast and dinner or lunch are included.

PRICE RANGES

Throughout this guidebook, the order of accommodation listings is by author preference, and each place is accompanied by one of the following budget-category symbols (the price relates to a high-season double room with private bathroom and, unless stated otherwise, includes breakfast):

- » **$** less than US$50
- » **$$** US$50 to US$150
- » **$$$** more than US$150

SAFARI LODGES

Hidden away inside or on the edges of national parks are some fantastic safari lodges. These are usually visited as part of organised safaris, and you'll pay much more if you just turn up and ask for a room. Some of the older places trade heavily on their more glorious past, but the best places feature five-star rooms, soaring *makuti*-roofed bars (with a thatched roof of palm leaves) and restaurants overlooking waterholes full of wildlife. Rates tend to fall significantly in the low season.

TENTED CAMPS

As well as lodges, many parks contain some fantastic luxury tented camps. These places tend to occupy wonderfully remote settings, usually by rivers or other natural locations, and feature large, comfortable, semipermanent safari tents with beds, furniture, bathrooms (usually with hot running water) and often some kind of external roof thatch to keep the rain out; you sleep surrounded by the sounds of the African bush. Most of the camps are very upmarket and the tents are pretty much hotel rooms under canvas.

Activities

Kenya has a long list of activities that are at once terrific ways to explore Kenya's varied terrain and fabulous experiences in their own right. These include:

Ballooning Usually includes a 1½-hour flight champagne breakfast and wildlife drive for around US$500 per person.

Cycling & Mountain-Biking Bike Treks (020-2141757; www.biketreks.co.ke) offers specialised trips for around US$120 per day; many places to stay (particularly campgrounds) can arrange bicycle hire for KSh500 to KSh700 per day, but always check the quality of the bike as standards vary wildly.

Diving & Snorkelling If you aren't certified to dive, almost every hotel and resort on the coast can arrange an open-water diving course. They're not much cheaper (if at all) than anywhere else in the world – a five-day PADI certification course will cost between US$400 and US$500. Trips for certified divers including two dives go for around US$100. October to March is the best time, but during June, July and August it's often impossible to dive due to the poor visibility caused by heavy silt flow from some rivers. That said, some divers have taken the plunge in July and found visibility to be a very respectable 7m to 10m, although 4m is more common.

Trekking & Climbing Kenya has some of the best trekking trails in East Africa, ranging from strenuous mountain ascents to rolling hill country and forests. It is, of course, always worth checking out the prevailing security situation in the area you wish to trek, not to mention the prevalence of any wild animals you might encounter along the trail. In some instances, it may be advisable to take a local guide, either from the Kenyan Wildlife Service (KWS) if they operate in the area, or a local village guide. The Mountain Club of Kenya (MCK; www.mck.or.ke) in Nairobi meets at 8pm every Tuesday at the clubhouse at Wilson airport (Map p230). Members organise frequent climbing and trekking weekends around the country.

Water Sports Conditions on Kenya's coast are ideal for windsurfing – the country's offshore reefs protect the waters, and the winds are usually reasonably strong and constant. Most resort hotels south and north of Mombasa have sailboards for hire.

White-Water Rafting The most exciting times for white-water rafting trips are late October to mid-January and early April to late July, when water levels are highest. The people to talk to are Savage Wilderness Safaris (Map p234; 020-521590; www.whitewaterkenya.com; Sarit Centre, Westlands, Nairobi), run by the charismatic Mark Savage.

Business Hours

Reviews won't list business hours unless they differ significantly from the following standards:

Banks 9am-3pm Monday to Friday; 9-11am Saturday

Post offices 8.30am-5pm Monday to Friday, 9am-noon Saturday

Restaurants 11am-2pm, 5-9pm

Shop: 9am-3pm Monday to Friday; 9-11am Saturday

Supermarkets 8.30am-8.30pm Monday to Saturday; 10am-8pm Saturday

Customs Regulations

There are strict laws about taking wildlife products out of Kenya. The export of products made from elephant, rhino and sea turtle are prohibited. The collection of coral is also not allowed. Ostrich eggs will also be confiscated unless you can prove you bought them from a certified ostrich farm. Always check to see what permits are required, especially for the export of any plants, insects and shells.

You are allowed to take up to KSh100,000 out of the country.

Otherwise, allowable quantities which you can bring into Kenya include the following:

Cigars 50

Cigarettes 200

Alcohol 1L

Perfume 250ml

Embassies & Consulates

Missions are located in Nairobi (area code 020) unless otherwise stated.

Australia High Commission (Map p220; 4277100; www.kenya.embassy.gov.au; Riverside Dr, off Chiromo Rd)

KENYA'S BEST TREKKING

Mountain Trekking

» **Mt Kenya** (5199m; p291)

» **Mt Elgon National Park** (4187m; p281)

» **Mt Longonot** (2776m; p249)

» **Cherangani Hills** (p318)

» **Loroghi Hills** (p315)

» **Aberdare** (p287)

» **Ndoto Mountains** (see the boxed text, p312)

Forest Trekking

» **Kakamega Forest** (p274)

» **Arabuko Sokoke Forest Reserve** (p341)

Canada High Commission (off Map p220; ☎3663000; www.canadainternational.gc.ca/kenya/index.aspx; Limuru Rd, Gigiri)

Ethiopia (Map p220; ☎2732050; off State House Rd)

France (Map p224; ☎2778000; www.ambafrance-ke.org; Barclays Plaza Bldg, Loita St)

Germany (off Map p220; ☎4262100; www.nairobi.diplo.de; 113 Riverside Dr)

Netherlands (off Map p220; ☎4288000; http://kenia.nlembassy.org; Riverside Lane)

South Sudan (Map p220; ☎2356542; gossmissionkenya.org; 6th fl Bishops Gate House, 5th Ngong Ave)

Tanzania High Commission (Map p224; ☎2311948; 9th fl, Reinsurance Plaza, Aga Khan Walk)

Uganda High Commission (off Map p220; ☎4445420; Riverside Paddocks); **Consular section** (Map p224; ☎2217447; 1st fl, Uganda House, Kenyatta Ave)

UK High Commission (Map p220; ☎2844000; ukinkenya.fco.gov.uk/en; Upper Hill Rd)

USA (off Map p220; ☎3636000; http://nairobi.usembassy.gov; United Nations Ave)

Gay & Lesbian Travellers

Negativity towards homosexuality is still widespread in Kenya and recent events ensure that it's a brave gay or lesbian Kenyan who comes out of the closet. In a 2007 poll, 96% of Kenyans surveyed stated that homosexuality should be rejected by society. In early 2010, mob violence rocked a health centre where suspected homosexuals were targeted. In November 2010, Prime Minister Raila Odinga described homosexuality as 'unnatural' and called for gays and lesbians to be arrested. And when British PM David Cameron threatened in November 2011 to withdraw aid to some African countries if they did not improve their record on gay and lesbian rights, there was a vociferous public outcry in Kenya. Underlying all of this is a penal code which states that homosexual behaviour is punishable by up to 14 years in prison.

Of course, people do live homosexual lifestyles covertly, particularly along the coast. There are very few prosecutions under the law, but it's certainly better to be extremely discreet – some local con artists do a good line in blackmail, picking up foreigners then threatening to expose them to the police.

USEFUL RESOURCES

Gay Kenya (www.gaykenya.com) Organises discreet gay events.

Global Gayz (www.globalgayz.com) Links to country-by-country gay issues, including Kenya.

Purple Roofs (www.purpleroofs.com/africa/kenyata.html) Lists a number of gay or gay-friendly tour companies in Kenya that may be able to help you plan your trip.

Internet Access

Internet cafes Common in large and medium-sized Kenyan towns; connection speeds fluctuate wildly; prices range from KSh1 to KSh10 per minute.

Post offices At almost every main post office in the country; prepaid cards with PIN valid at any branch around Kenya.

Wireless Increasingly common in midrange and top-end hotels; often available in upmarket safari lodges.

Local networks Both Safari.com and Airtel have dongles/modems that you plug into your laptop, giving you wireless access anywhere that there's mobile coverage. Rates start at KSh1999 for the dongle; credit costs extra and you top up using scratch cards.

Language Courses

Taking a language course (or any course) entitles you to a Pupil's Pass, an immigration permit allowing continuous stays of up to 12 months. For more information, see p369.

ACK Language & Orientation School (Map p220; ☎020-2721893; www.ackenya.org/institutions/language_school.html; Bishops Rd, Upper Hill, Nairobi) The Anglican Church runs full-time courses of varying levels lasting 14 weeks and taking up to five hours a day.

Language Center Ltd (Map p230; ☎020-3870610; www.language-cntr.com/welcome.shtml; Ndemi Close, off Ngong Rd, Nairobi) Another good centre offering a variety of study options ranging from private hourly lessons to daily group courses.

Legal Matters

All drugs except *miraa* (a leafy shoot chewed as a stimulant) are illegal in Kenya. Marijuana (commonly called *bhang*) is widely available but illegal; possession carries a penalty of up to 10 years in prison. Dealers are common on the beaches north and south of Mombasa and frequently set up travellers for sting operations for real or phoney cops to extort money.

African prisons are unbelievably harsh places – don't take the risk! Note that *miraa* is illegal in Tanzania, so if you do develop a taste for the stuff in Kenya you should leave it behind when heading south.

Maps

The *Tourist Map of Kenya* gives good detail, as does the *Kenya Route Map;* both cost around KSh250. Otherwise, Marco Polo's 1:1,000,000 *Shell Euro Karte Kenya,* Geocenter's *Kenya* (1:1,000,000) and IGN's *Carte Touristique: Kenya* (1:1,000,000) are useful overview maps that are widely available in Europe.

Most maps to Kenya's national parks might look a bit flimsy on detail (you won't get much in the way of topographical detail), but they include the numbered junctions in the national parks.

Macmillan publishes a series of maps to the wildlife parks that are not bad value at around KSh250 each (three are available in Europe: *Amboseli, Masai Mara* and *Tsavo East & West*). Tourist Maps also publishes a national park series for roughly the same price. The maps by the KWS are similar.

Money

The unit of currency is the Kenyan shilling (KSh), which is made up of 100 cents. Notes in circulation are KSh1000, 500, 200, 100, 50 and 20, and there are also coins of KSh40, 20, 10, five and one in circulation.

The most convenient way to bring your money is in a mixture of cash and a debit or credit card. You'll find information on exchange rates and costs on p216.

ATMS

Virtually all banks in Kenya now have ATMs at most branches, but their usefulness to travellers varies widely. Barclays Bank has easily the most reliable machines for international withdrawals, with a large network of ATMs covering most major Kenyan towns. They support MasterCard, Visa, Plus and Cirrus international networks.

Standard Chartered and Kenya Commercial Bank ATMs also accept Visa but not the other major providers, and are more likely to decline transactions. Whichever bank you use, the international data link still goes down occasionally, so don't rely on being able to withdraw money whenever you need it.

CASH

While most major currencies are accepted in Nairobi and Mombasa, once away from these two centres you'll run into problems with currencies other than US dollars, pounds sterling and euros.

CREDIT CARDS

Credit cards are becoming increasingly popular, although the connections fail with tedious regularity. Visa and MasterCard are now widely accepted in midrange and top-end hotels, top-end restaurants and some shops.

MONEYCHANGERS

The best places to change money are foreign exchange or 'forex' bureaus, which can be found everywhere and usually don't charge commission. The rates for the main bureaus in Nairobi are published in the *Daily Nation* newspaper. Watch out for differing small bill (US$10) and large bill (US$100) rates; the larger bills usually get the better rates.

INTERNATIONAL TRANSFERS

Postbank, a branch of the Kenyan Post Office, is the regional agent for Western Union, the global money-transfer company. Using its service is an easy way (if the phones are working) of receiving money in Kenya.

Handily, the sender pays all the charges and there's a Postbank in most towns, often in the post office or close by. Senders should contact **Western Union** (www.westernunion.com) **Australia** (☎1800-501500); **New Zealand** (☎0800-270000); **UK** (☎0800-833833); and **USA** (☎1800-3256000) to find the location of their nearest agency.

TIPPING

Tipping is not common practice among Kenyans, but there's no harm in rounding up the bill by a few shillings if you're pleased with the service.

Hotel porters Tips expected in upmarket hotels.

Restaurants A service charge of 10% is often added to the bill along with the 16% VAT and 2% catering levy.

Taxi drivers No need to tip unless they provide you with exceptional service.

Tour guides, safari drivers & cooks Will expect some kind of gratuity at the end of your tour or trip.

Post

The Kenyan postal system is run by the government **Posta** (www.posta.co.ke). Letters sent from Kenya rarely go astray but can take up to two weeks to reach Australia or the USA. If sent by surface mail, parcels take three to six months to reach Europe, while airmail parcels take around a week.

Most things arrive eventually, although there is still a problem with theft within the system. Curios, clothes and textiles will be OK, but if your parcel contains anything of obvious value, send it by courier. Posta has its own courier service, EMS, which is considerably cheaper than the big international courier companies. The best place to send parcels from is the main post office in Nairobi.

Public Holidays

In addition to the following, Muslim festivals are significant events along the coast. See p646 for dates.

1 January New Year's Day

March/April Good Friday and Easter Monday

1 May Labour Day

1 June Madaraka Day

10 October Moi Day

20 October Kenyatta Day

12 December Independence Day

25 December Christmas Day

26 December Boxing Day

Safe Travel

While Kenya is a comparatively safe African destination, there are still plenty of pitfalls for the unwary or inexperienced traveller, from everydayirritations to more serious threats.

BANDITRY

The ongoing conflict in Somalia has had an effect on the stability and safety of northern and northeastern Kenya. AK-47s have been flowing into the country for many years, and the newspapers are filled with stories of hold-ups, shoot-outs, cattle rustling and general lawlessness. Bandits and poachers infiltrating from Somalia have made the northeast of the country particularly dangerous. In 2011, tourists and aid workers were kidnapped close to the Somali border, prompting Kenya to briefly invade their neighbour.

Security has improved considerably in previously high-risk areas such as the Isiolo–Marsabit, Marsabit–Moyale and Malindi–Lamu routes. However, you should check the situation locally before taking these roads, or travelling between Garsen and Garissa or Thika.

The areas along the Sudanese and Ethiopian borders are risky, so please enquire about the latest security situations if you're heading overland.

CRIME

Even the staunchest Kenyan patriot will readily admit that the country's biggest problem is crime. It ranges from petty snatch theft and mugging to violent armed robbery, carjacking and, of course, white-collar crime and corruption. As a visitor you needn't feel paranoid, but you should always keep your wits about you, particularly at night.

Perhaps the best advice for when you're walking around cities and towns is not to carry anything valuable with you – that includes jewellery, watches, cameras, bumbags, day-packs and money. Most hotels provide a safe or secure place for valuables, although you should also be cautious of the security at some budget places.

While pickpocketing and bag-snatching are the most common crimes, armed muggings do occur in Nairobi and on the coast.

Always take taxis after dark. Conversely, snatch-and-run crimes happen more in crowds. If you suddenly feel there are too many people around you, or think you are being followed, dive straight into a shop and ask for help.

Luggage is an obvious signal to criminals that you've just arrived. When arriving anywhere by bus, it's sensible to take a 'ship-to-shore' approach, getting a taxi directly from the bus station to your hotel. You'll have plenty of time to explore once you've safely stowed your belongings. Also, don't read this guidebook or look at maps on the street – it attracts unwanted attention.

In the event of a crime, you should report it to the police, but this can be a real procedure. You'll need to get a police report if you intend to make an insurance claim.

Although crime is a fact of life in Kenya, it needn't spoil your trip. Above all, don't make the mistake of distrusting every Kenyan just because of a few bad apples – the honest souls you meet will far outnumber any crooks who cross your path.

SCAMS

At some point in Kenya you'll almost certainly come across people who play on the emotions and gullibility of foreigners. Nairobi is a particular hot spot, with 'friendly' approaches a daily, if not hourly, occurrence. People with tales about being refugees or having sick relatives can sound very convincing, but they all end up asking for cash. It's OK to talk to these people if they're not actively hassling you, but you should ignore any requests for money.

Be sceptical of strangers who claim to recognise you in the street, especially if they're vague about exactly where they know you from – it's unlikely that any ordinary person is going to be *this* excited by seeing you twice. Anyone who makes a big show of inviting you into the hospitality of their home also probably has ulterior motives. The usual trick is to bestow some kind of gift upon the delighted traveller, who is then emotionally blackmailed into reciprocating.

Tourists with cars also face potential rip-offs. Don't trust people who gesticulate wildly to indicate that your front wheels are wobbling; if you stop, you'll probably be relieved of your valuables. Another trick is to splash oil on your wheels, then tell you the wheel bearings, differential or something else has failed, and direct you to a nearby garage where their friends will 'fix' the problem – for a substantial fee, of course.

Telephone

International call rates from Kenya are relatively expensive, though you can save serious cash by using VOIP programs like Skype. If you're calling internationally using a mobile with a local SIM card, rates are likely to be considerably cheaper (as little as KSh3 per minute) than from fixed-line phones.

Calls made through a hotel operator from your room will cost an extra 25% to 50%, so check before making a call.

MOBILE PHONES

More than two-thirds of all calls in Kenya are now made on mobile phones, and coverage is good in all but the furthest rural areas. Kenya uses the GSM 900 system, which is compatible with Europe and Australia but not with the North American GSM 1900 system. If you have a GSM phone, check with your service provider about using it in Kenya, and beware of high roaming charges.

Alternatively, if your phone isn't locked into a network, you can pick up a prepaid starter pack from one of the Kenyan mobile-phone companies: **Safaricom** (www.safaricom.co.ke) or **Airtel** (africa.airtel.com/kenya/). A SIM card costs about KSh100, and you can then buy top-up 'scratch cards' from shops and booths across the country.

You can easily buy a handset anywhere in Kenya, generally unlocked and with a SIM card. Prices start at around KSh2500 for a very basic model.

PHONE CODES

Kenya's regions have area codes which must be dialled, followed by the local number. These area codes are listed throughout this book under the name of each town or region.

The international dialling code for Kenya is ☎254.

PHONECARDS

With Telkom Kenya phonecards, any phone can be used for prepaid calls – you just have to dial the **access number** (☎0844) and enter in the number and passcode on the card. There are booths selling the cards all over the country. Cards come in denominations of KSh200, KSh500, KSh1000 and KSh2000.

Time

Kenya time is GMT/UTC plus two hours. There is no daylight saving.

Tourist Information

LOCAL TOURIST OFFICES

Incredibly, there is still no tourist office in Nairobi. There are a handful of information offices elsewhere in the country, ranging from helpful private concerns to underfunded government offices.

Diani Beach i-point (Map p332; ☎040-3202234; Barclays Centre)

Lamu (Map p348; ☎042-633449; off Kenyatta Rd)

Malindi (Map p344; ☎042-20689; Malindi Centre, Lamu Rd)

Mombasa & Coast Tourist Office (Map p324; ☎041-225428; Moi Ave)

TOURIST OFFICES ABROAD

The **Ministry of Tourism** (www.tourism.go.ke) maintains a number of overseas offices, including in the UK, USA, Canada and Italy. Most only provide information by telephone, post or email. Visit the ministry website; click on 'Contact Us' for contact details around the world.

Travellers with Disabilities

In Nairobi, only the ex-London taxi cabs are spacious enough to accommodate a wheelchair, but many safari companies are accustomed to taking disabled people out on safari.

The travel agency **Travel Scene Services** (☎020-2431699; www.travelsceneafrica.com) has lots of experience with disabled travellers.

Many of the top-end beach resorts on the coast have facilities for the disabled, whether it's a few token ramps or fully equipped rooms with handrails and bathtubs.

Out on safari, other places may have varying degrees of disabled access, but in **Amboseli National Park**, **Ol Tukai Lodge** (p241) has two disabled-friendly cottages.

For more general advice for travellers with disabilities, see p647.

Visas

Tourist visas can be obtained on arrival in Kenya at Nairobi's Jomo Kenyatta International Airport, and the country's land borders with Uganda and Tanzania. This applies to Europeans, Australians, New Zealanders, Americans and Canadians, although citizens from a few smaller Commonwealth countries are exempt. Visas cost US$50/€40/UK£30 and are valid for three months from the date of entry.

Under the East African partnership system, visiting Tanzania or Uganda and returning to Kenya does not invalidate a single-entry Kenyan visa, so there's no need to get a multiple-entry visa unless you plan to go further afield. Always check the latest entry requirements with embassies before travel.

PUPIL'S PASS

If you're enrolled in a language course (see p366) that extends beyond the period of your three-month visa, you are usually entitled to a visa extension. The fee for a Pupil's Pass varies. A charge will be levied by your school for sorting out the paperwork, so expect to pay a minimum of KSh3500 for a one-year pass. A deposit of KSh5000 or a letter of guarantee by an approved body registered in Kenya (your language school) is usually required along with two photographs and a copy of your passport.

VISA EXTENSIONS

Visas can be renewed at immigration offices during normal office hours, and extensions are usually issued on a same-day basis. Staff are generally friendly and helpful, but the process takes a while. You'll need two passport photos for a three-month extension, and prices tend to vary depending on the office and the whims of the immigration officials. Immigration offices are only open Monday to Friday; note that the smaller offices may sometimes refer travellers back to Nairobi or Mombasa for visa extensions.

Local immigration offices include the following:

Kisumu (Map p267; Nyanza Bldg, cnr Jomo Kenyatta Hwy & Wuor Otiende Rd)

Lamu (Map p348; ☎042-633032; off Kenyatta Rd) Travellers are sometimes referred to Mombasa.

Malindi (Map p344; ☎042-20149; Mama Ngina Rd)

Mombasa (Map p322; ☎041-311745; Uhuru ni Kari Bldg, Mama Ngina Dr)

Nairobi (Map p224; ☎020-222022; Nyayo House, cnr Kenyatta Ave & Uhuru Hwy; ⌚8.30am-12.30pm & 2-3.30pm Mon-Fri)

VISAS FOR ONWARD TRAVEL

Most embassies will want you to pay visa fees in US dollars, and most open for visa applications from 9am to noon, with visa pick-ups around 3pm or 4pm.

Three-month, single-entry visas can be obtained for South Sudan, Tanzania and Uganda, but the Ethiopian embassy was not issuing tourist visas at the time of writing, putting a major dent in the overland travel plans of many.

Volunteering

A Rocha Operates the Mwamba Field Study Centre (p340) at Watamu Beach.

Kenya Youth Voluntary Development Projects (Map p220; ☎020-2726011; www.kvcdp.org; Nairobi International Youth Hostel, Ralph Bunche Rd, Nairobi) Excellent local organisation that runs a variety of three- to four-week projects, including road building, health education and clinic construction.

Volunteer Kenya (Inter-Community Development Involvement; www.volunteerkenya.org) Offers a number of longer community projects focusing on health issues such as AIDS awareness, agriculture and conservation in Western Kenya.

Watamu Turtle Watch (p370) Helps protect the marine turtles that come to Watamu to lay eggs on the beach.

Getting There & Away

Nairobi is a major African hub with numerous African and international airlines connecting Kenya to the world. By African standards, flights between Kenya and the rest of Africa or further afield are common and relatively cheap, and flying is by far the most convenient way to get to Kenya.

Kenya is also a popular and relatively easy waystation for those travelling overland between Southern Africa and Egypt. Finding your way here can be tricky – with several war zones in the vicinity – and such journeys should only be considered after serious planning and preparation. But they're certainly possible, and it's rarely Kenya that causes problems.

Flights, tours and rail tickets can be booked online at lonelyplanet.com/travel_services.

Entering the Country

Entering Kenya is generally pleasingly straightforward, particularly at the international airports. Visas are typically available on arrival at Mombasa and Nairobi international airports and Kenya's land borders with Uganda and Tanzania – for more information see p369.

Air

AIRPORTS

Kenya has three international airports; check out the website www.kenyaairports.co.ke for further information:

Jomo Kenyatta International Airport (NBO; ☎020-6611000) Most international flights to and from Nairobi arrive at this airport, 15km southeast of the city. There are two international terminals and a smaller domestic terminal; you can walk easily between the terminals.

Moi International Airport (MBA; ☎041-3433211) In Mombasa, 9km west of the centre, and Kenya's second-busiest international airport. Apart from flights to Zanzibar, this is mainly used by charter airlines and domestic flights.

Wilson Airport (WIL; ☎020-3603260) Located 6km south of Nairobi's city centre on Langata Rd; some flights between Nairobi and Kilimanjaro International Airport or Mwanza in Tanzania, as well as some domestic flights.

AIRLINES

The following airlines fly to/from Kenya. Kenya Airways is the main national carrier, and has a generally good safety record, with just one fatal incident since 1977.

African Express Airways (www.africanexpress.co.ke)

Air India (www.airindia.com)

Air Madagascar (www.airmadagascar.mg)

Air Malawi (www.airmalawi.com)

Air Mauritius (www.airmauritius.com)

Airkenya (www.airkenya.com)

British Airways (www.britishairways.com)

Daallo Airlines (www.daallo.com)

Egypt Air (www.egyptair.com.eg)

Emirates (www.emirates.com)

Ethiopian Airlines (www.ethiopianairlines.com)

Fly540 (www.fly540.com)

Gulf Air (www.gulfairco.com)

Jetlink Express (www.jetlink.co.ke)

Kenya Airways (www.kenya-airways.com)

KLM (www.klm.com)

Monarch (www.monarch.co.uk)

Precision Air (www.precisionairtz.com)

Qatar Airways (www.qatarairways.com)

Rwandair (www.rwandair.com)

Safarilink (www.flysafarilink.com)

SN Brussels Airlines (www.brusselsairlines.com)

South African Airways (www.flysaa.com)

Swiss International Airlines (www.swiss.com)

Thomson Airways (flights.thomson.co.uk)

Virgin Atlantic Airways (www.virgin-atlantic.com)

Land

Kenya's borders with Somalia and Sudan remain closed at the time of writing.

ETHIOPIA

With ongoing problems in Sudan and Somalia, Ethiopia offers the only viable overland route into Kenya from the north. The security situation around the main entry point at Moyale is changeable – the border is usually open, but security problems often force its closure. Check the security situation carefully before attempting this crossing.

If you're heading in the other direction, remember that Ethiopian visas were not being issued in Nairobi at the time of research.

Public Transport There were no cross-border services at the time of writing. If you don't have your own transport from Moyale, lifts can be arranged with the trucks from the border to Isiolo for around KSh1500 (or KSh1000 to Marsabit). From immigration on the Ethiopian side of town it's a 2km walk to the Ethiopian and Kenyan customs posts. A yellow-fever vaccination is required to cross either border at Moyale. A cholera vaccination may also be required.

Car & Motorcycle Those coming to Kenya with their own vehicle could also enter at Fort Banya, on the northeastern tip of Lake Turkana, but it's a risky route with few fuel stops. There's no border post; you must already possess a Kenyan visa and get it stamped on arrival in Nairobi. Immigration is quite used to this, but not having an Ethiopian exit stamp can be a problem if you want to re-enter Ethiopia.

TANZANIA

The main land borders between Kenya and Tanzania are at Namanga, Taveta, Isebania and Lunga Lunga, and can be reached by public transport. There is also a crossing from the Serengeti to the Masai Mara, which can only be undertaken with your own vehicle.

Although all of the routes may be done in stages using a combination of buses and local matatus, there are six main land routes to/from Tanzania:

Mombasa–Tanga/Dar es Salaam

Mombasa–Arusha/Moshi

Nairobi–Arusha/Moshi

Nairobi–Dar es Salaam

Serengeti–Masai Mara

Nairobi–Mwanza

Following are the main bus companies serving Tanzania:

Akamba (☎0722203753; www.akambabus.com)

Easy Coach (☎020-3210711)

Riverside Shuttle (☎020-3229618; www.riverside-shuttle.com)

Simba Coaches (Abdel Nasser Rd, Mombasa)

All of the bus routes mentioned here are easily accomplished in your own vehicle. It's also possible to cross between Serengeti National Park and Masai Mara National Reserve with your own vehicle, but you'll need the appropriate vehicle documentation (including insurance and entry permit).

UGANDA

The main border post for overland travellers is Malaba, with Busia an alternative if you're travelling via Kisumu. For more details on crossing the frontier, see the boxed text, p283.

Numerous bus companies run between Nairobi and Kampala. From Nairobi – and at the top end of the market – **Easy Coach** (Map p224; ☎2210711; Haile Selassie Ave) and **Akamba** (☎0722203753; www.akambabus.com) have buses at least once daily, ranging from ordinary buses at around KSh1200 to full-blown 'luxury' services with drinks and movies, hovering around the KSh2400 mark. All buses take about 10 to 12 hours and prices include a meal at the halfway point.

Various other companies have cheaper, basic services, which depart from the Accra Rd area in Nairobi.

If you want to do the journey in stages, Akamba has morning and evening buses from Nairobi to Malaba and a daily direct bus from there to Kampala. There are also regular matatus to Malaba from Cross Rd.

The Ugandan and Kenyan border posts at Malaba are about 1km apart, so you can walk or take a boda-boda (bicycle taxi). Once you get across the border, there are frequent matatus until the late afternoon to Kampala, Jinja and Tororo.

Buses and matatus also run from Nairobi or Kisumu to Busia, from where there are regular connections to Kampala and Jinja.

Sea & Lake

At the time of writing there were no ferries operating on Lake Victoria, although there's been talk for years of services restarting.

It's theoretically possible to travel by dhow between Mombasa and the Tanzanian islands of Pemba and Zanzibar, but first of all you'll have to find a captain who's making the journey and then you'll have to bargain hard. Perhaps the best place to ask about sailings is at Shimoni (p337).

Getting Around

Air

AIRLINES IN KENYA

Including the national carrier, Kenya Airways, five main domestic operators of varying sizes run scheduled flights within Kenya. Destinations served are predominantly around the coast and the popular national parks.

With all these airlines, be sure to book well in advance. You should also remember to reconfirm your return flights 72 hours before departure. Otherwise, you may find that your seat has been reallocated.

The following airlines fly domestically, mostly from Nairobi:

Airkenya (☎020-3916000; www.airkenya.com) Amboseli, Diani, Lamu, Masai Mara, Malindi, Meru, Mombasa, Nanyuki and Samburu

Fly540 (www.fly540.com) Eldoret, Kisumu, Kitale, Lamu, Lodwar, Malindi, Masai Mara and Mombasa

Jetlink Express (☎020-3827531; www.jetlink.co.ke) Mombasa, Kisumu and Eldoret

Kenya Airways (☎020-6422560; www.kenya-airways.com) Kisumu, Malindi and Mombasa

Mombasa Air Safari (☎0734400400; www.mombasaairsafari.com) Amboseli, Diani Beach, Lamu, Malindi, Masai Mara, Meru, Mombasa, Samburu and Tsavo West

Safarilink (☎020-6000777; www.flysafarilink.com) Amboseli, Diani Beach, Kiwayu, Lamu, Lewa Downs, Masai Mara, Naivasha, Nanyuki, Samburu, Shaba and Tsavo West

Bicycle

Loads of Kenyans get around by bicycle, and while it can be tough for those who are not used to the roads or climate, plenty of hardy visiting cyclists do tour the country every year. But whatever you do, if you intend to cycle here, do as the locals do and get off the road whenever you hear a car coming. No matter how experienced you are, it would be tantamount to suicide to attempt the road from Nairobi to Mombasa, or from Nairobi to Nakuru, on a bicycle.

Many local people operate boda-bodas, so repair shops are quite common along the roadside. Be wary of cycling on dirt roads as punctures from thorn trees are a major problem.

It's possible to hire road and mountain bikes in an increasing number of places, usually for KSh500 to KSh700 per day. Few places require a deposit, unless their machines are particularly new or sophisticated.

Boat

Motorised canoes run to Mfangano Island from Mbita Point, near Homa Bay, while an occasional ferry service also runs between Kisumu and Homa Bay.

Dhows (traditional Swahili sailing boats) are commonly used to get around the islands in the Lamu archipelago and the mangrove islands south of Mombasa. For the most part, these trips operate more like dhow safaris than public transport. Although some trips are luxurious, the trips out of Lamu are more basic. When night comes you simply bed down wherever there is space. Seafood is freshly caught and cooked on board on

MAJOR BUS ROUTES

FROM	TO	PRICE (US$)	DURATION (HRS)	COMPANY
Mombasa	Tanga	9	4	Simba Coaches
Mombasa	Dar es Salaam	12-16	5-8	Simba Coaches
Nairobi	Moshi	35-40	7½	Riverside Shuttle Akamba
Nairobi	Arusha	25-30	5½	Riverside Shuttle Akamba
Nairobi	Dar es Salaam	34	16-18	Akamba
Nairobi	Mwanza	21	13½	Akamba

charcoal burners, or else barbecued on the beach on surrounding islands.

Bus

Kenya has an extensive network of long- and short-haul bus routes, with particularly good coverage of the areas around Nairobi, the coast and the western regions. Services thin out the further away from the capital you get, particularly in the north, and there are still plenty of places where you'll be reliant on matatus.

In general, if you travel during daylight hours, buses are a fairly safe way to get around and you'll certainly be safer in a bus than in a matatu. The best coaches are saved for long-haul and international routes and offer DVD movies, drinks, toilets and reclining airline-style seats. On the shorter local routes, however, you may find yourself on something resembling a battered school bus.

Whatever kind of conveyance you find yourself in, don't sit at the back (you'll be thrown around like a rag doll on Kenyan roads), or right at the front (you'll be the first to die in a head-on collision, plus you'll be able to see the oncoming traffic, which is usually a terrifying experience).

There are a few security considerations to think about when taking a bus in Kenya. Some routes, most notably the roads from Malindi to Lamu and Isiolo to Marsabit, have been prone to attacks by *shiftas* (bandits) in the past; check things out locally before you travel. Another possible risk is drugged food and drink: it is best to politely refuse any offers of drinks or snacks from strangers.

The following are the main bus companies operating in Kenya; all have offices in Nairobi and/or Mombasa.

Akamba (☎0722203753; www.akambabus.com) Rift Valley, Western Kenya, Mombasa and Namanga

Busways (☎020-2227650) Western Kenya and the coast

Coastline Safaris (☎020-217592) Western and Southern Kenya, Mombasa

Easy Coach (☎020-3210711) Rift Valley and Western Kenya

Eldoret Express (☎020-6766886) Western Kenya and Rift Valley

Kenya Bus Services (KBS; Map p224; ☎020-2341250) Rift Valley, Western Kenya and Mombasa

Mombasa Metropolitan Bus Services (☎041-2496008) Coast

RESERVATIONS

Most bus companies have offices or ticket agents at important stops along their routes, where you can book a seat. For short trips between towns reservations aren't generally necessary, but for popular longer routes, especially the Nairobi–Kisumu, Nairobi–Mombasa and Mombasa–Lamu routes, we recommend buying your ticket at least a day in advance.

Car & Motorcycle

For information on the documents you may need for bringing your own vehicle into the region, see p654.

AUTOMOBILE ASSOCIATIONS

Automobile Association of Kenya (Map p234; ☎020-4449676; www.aakenya.co.ke, Sarit Centre, Westlands)

BRIBES

Although things have improved markedly in recent years, police will still stop you and will most likely ask you for a small 'donation'. To prevent being taken advantage of, always ask for an official receipt – this goes a long way in stopping corruption. Also, always ask for their police number and check it against their ID card as there are plenty of con artists running about.

DRIVING LICENCE

An international driving licence is not necessary in Kenya, but can be useful. If you have a British photo card licence, be sure to bring the counterfoil, as the date you passed your driving test (something car-hire companies may want to know) isn't printed on the card itself.

FUEL & SPARE PARTS

Fuel prices are generally lower outside the capital, but can creep up to frighteningly high prices in remote areas, where petrol stations are scarce and you may end up buying dodgy supplies out of barrels from roadside vendors. Petrol, spare parts and repair shops are readily available at all border towns, though if you're coming from Ethiopia you should plan your supplies carefully, as stops are few and far between on the rough northern roads.

CAR HIRE

Unless you're just planning on travelling on the main routes between towns, you'll need a 4WD vehicle. Few of the car-hire companies will let you drive 2WD vehicles on dirt roads, including those in the national parks.

A minimum age of between 23 and 25 years usually applies for hirers. Some require you to have been driving for at least two years.

Hiring a vehicle to tour Kenya (or at least the national parks) is an expensive way of seeing the country. Starting rates for hire almost always sound very reasonable, but once you factor in mileage and the various types of insurance you'll be lucky to pay less than KSh7500 per day for a saloon car, or KSh10,000 per day for a small 4WD; make sure this includes insurance against collision damage and theft. Ask also how much excess you're likely to pay in the event of an accident, and how much it costs to remove the excess entirely.

As a final sting in the tail, you'll be charged 16% value added tax (VAT) on top of the total cost of hiring the vehicle.

While hiring a 'chauffeur' may sound like a luxury, it can actually be a very good idea in Kenya for financial, practical and safety reasons. Most companies will provide a driver for a few thousand shillings per day – the big advantage of this is that the car is covered by the company's insurance, so you don't have to pay any of the various waivers and won't be liable for any excess in the case of an accident (though tyres, windows etc remain your responsibility).

We recommend the following local and international hire companies:

Adventure Upgrade Safaris (Map p224; ☎0722529228; www.adventureupgradesafaris.co.ke) An excellent local company.

Avis (Map p224; ☎020-2533610; www.avis.co.ke)

Budget (Map p224; ☎020-2223581; www.budget.co.ke)

Central Rent-a-Car (Map p224; ☎020-2222888; www.carhirekenya.com) Another highly recommended local company.

Tough Trucks Kenya (Map p224; ☎020-2228725; www.toughtruckskenya.com)

Uniglobe Let's Go Travel (Map p230; ☎020-4447151; www.uniglobeletsgotravel.com)

ROAD CONDITIONS

Road conditions vary widely in Kenya, from flat smooth highways to dirt tracks and steep rocky pathways. The roads in the north and east of the country are particularly poor. The main Mombasa–Nairobi–Malaba road (A104) is badly worn due to the constant flow of traffic, but has improved in recent years. The never-ending stream of trucks along this main route through the country will slow travel times considerably.

Roads in national parks are all made of *murram* (dirt) and many have eroded into bone-shaking corrugations through overuse by safari vehicles.

ROAD HAZARDS

The biggest hazard on Kenyan roads is simply the other vehicles on them, and driving defensively is essential. Ironically, the most dangerous roads in Kenya are probably the well-maintained ones, which allow drivers to go fast enough to do really serious damage in a crash. On the worse roads, potholes can be a problem.

On all roads, be very careful of pedestrians and cyclists – you don't want to contribute any more to the death toll on Kenya's roads. Animals are another major hazard in rural areas, be it monkeys, herds of goats and cattle or lone chickens with a death wish.

Certain routes have a reputation for banditry, particularly the Garsen–Garissa–Thika road, which is still essentially off limits to travellers. The roads from Isiolo to Marsabit and Moyale and from Malindi to Lamu have improved considerably security-wise in the last few years, but you're still advised to seek local advice before using any of these routes.

ROAD RULES

Driving practices here are some of the worst in the world and all are carried out at breakneck speed. Never drive at night unless you absolutely have to. Drunk driving is also very common.

Kenyans drive on the left – at least in theory. Kenyans habitually drive on the wrong side of the road whenever they see a pothole, an animal or simply a break in the traffic – flashing your lights at the vehicle hurtling towards you should be enough to persuade the driver to get back into their own lane.

Indicators, lights, horns and hand signals can mean anything from 'I'm about to overtake' to 'Hello *mzungu* (white person)!' or 'Let's play chicken with that elephant', and should never be taken at face value.

Hitching

Hitchhiking is never entirely safe in any country, and we don't recommend it. Travellers who hitch should understand they are taking a small but potentially serious risk; it's safer to travel in pairs and let someone know where you are planning to go. Also beware of drunken drivers.

The traditional thumb signal will probably be understood, but locals use a palm-downwards wave to get cars to stop. Many Kenyan drivers expect a contribution towards petrol or some kind of gift from foreign passengers, so make it clear from the outset if you are expecting a free ride.

If you're hoping to hitch into the national parks, dream on! You'll get further asking around for travel companions in Nairobi or any of the gateway towns.

Local Transport

BOAT

The only local boat service in regular use is the Likoni ferry between the mainland and Mombasa island, which runs throughout the day and night and is free for foot passengers (vehicles pay a small toll).

BODA-BODA

Boda-bodas (bicycle or motorcycle taxis) are common in areas where standard taxis are harder to find, and also operate in smaller towns and cities such as Nakuru or Kisumu. There's a particular proliferation on the coast, where the bicycle boys also double as touts, guides and drug dealers in tourist areas. A short ride should cost around KSh50 or so.

MATATU

Local matatus are the main means of getting around for local people, and any reasonably sized city or town will have plenty of services covering every major road and suburb. Fares start at around KSh20 and may reach KSh100 for longer routes in Nairobi.

For inter-city transport, apart from in the remote northern areas, where you'll rely on occasional buses or paid lifts on trucks, you can almost always find a matatu going to the next town or further afield.

Matatus leave when full and the fares are fixed. It's unlikely you will be charged more than other passengers.

Despite a briefly successful government drive to regulate the matatu industry, matatus are once again notorious for dangerous driving, overcrowding and general shady business. Under no circumstances should you sit in the 'death seat' next to the matatu driver. Play it safe and sit in the middle seats away from the window.

SHARED TAXI (PEUGEOT)

Shared Peugeot taxis are a good alternative to matatus. The vehicles are usually Peugeot 505 station wagons that take seven to nine passengers and leave when full.

Peugeots take less time to reach their destinations than matatus as they fill quicker and go from point to point without stopping, and so are slightly more expensive.

TAXI

Even the smallest Kenyan towns generally have at least one banged-up old taxi for easy access to outlying areas or even remoter villages, and you'll find cabs on virtually every corner in the larger cities, especially in Nairobi and Mombasa, where taking a taxi at night is virtually mandatory. Fares are invariably negotiable and start around KSh250 to KSh400 for short journeys.

Since few taxis in Kenya actually have functioning meters (or drivers who adhere to them), it's advisable that you agree on the fare prior to setting out.

TUK-TUK

They're an incongruous sight outside southeast Asia, but several Kenyan towns and cities have these distinctive motorised mini-taxis. The highest concentration is in Malindi, but they're also in Nairobi, Mombasa, Nakuru, Machakos and Diani Beach; Watamu has a handful of less-sophisticated motorised rickshaws. Fares are negotiable, but should be at least KSh100 less than the equivalent taxi rate.

Train

The Uganda Railway was once the main trade artery in East Africa, but these days the network has dwindled to two main routes, Nairobi–Kisumu (via Nakuru and Naivasha) and Nairobi–Mombasa.

For a list of destinations, fares and journey times, see p240.

CLASSES

There are three classes on Kenyan trains, but only 1st and 2nd class can be recommended. First class consists of two-berth compartments with a washbasin, wardrobe, drinking water and a drinks service. Second class consists of plainer, four-berth compartments with a washbasin and drinking water. No compartment can be locked from the outside, so remember not to leave any valuables lying around if you leave it for any reason. You might want to padlock your rucksack to something during dinner and breakfast. Always lock your compartment from the inside before you go to sleep. Third class is seats only and security can be a real problem. Note that passengers are divided up by gender.

Passengers in 1st class on the Mombasa line are treated to a meal typically consisting of stews, curries or roast chicken served with rice and vegetables. Tea and coffee is included; sodas (soft drinks), bottled water and alcoholic drinks are not. Cold beer is available at all times in the dining car and can be delivered to your compartment.

RESERVATIONS

There are booking offices at the train stations in Nairobi and Mombasa, and it's recommended that you show up in person rather than trying to call. You must book in advance for 1st and 2nd class, otherwise there'll probably be no berths available. Two to three days is usually sufficient, but remember that these services run just three times weekly in either direction. Note that compartment and berth numbers are posted up about 30 minutes prior to departure.

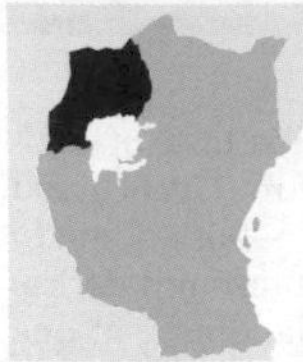

Uganda

Includes »

Kampala....379
Entebbe....398
Rwenzori Mountains National Park....428
Queen Elizabeth National Park....432
Bwindi Impenetrable National Park....437
Lake Bunyonyi....445
Mgahinga Gorilla National Park....450
Ssese Islands....455
Murchison Falls National Park....460
Kidepo Valley National Park....469

Best of Nature

» Tracking gorillas (p437)

» Source of the Nile River (p403)

» 'Big Five' wildlife watching at Murchison Falls National Park (p460) and Ziwa Rhino Sanctuary (p457)

Best of Culture

» Coffee tours at Sipi Falls (p415)

» Forest walks with the Twa (Batwa) people (p439 & p451)

Why Go?

Emerging from the shadows of its dark history, a new dawn of tourism has risen in Uganda, polishing a glint back into the 'pearl of Africa'. Travellers are streaming in to explore what is basically the best of everything the continent has to offer.

For a relatively small country, there's a lot that's big about the place. It's home to the tallest mountain range in Africa, the world's longest river and the continent's largest lake. And with half the remaining mountain gorillas residing here, and the Big Five to be ticked off, wildlife watching is huge.

While anti-gay sentiments have cast a shadow on the otherwise positive tourism picture, and tensions continue to simmer with the Karamojong in the northeast, Uganda remains one of the safest destinations in Africa. Other than watching out for the odd hippo at your campsite, there's no more to worry about here than in most other countries.

When To Go

Kampala

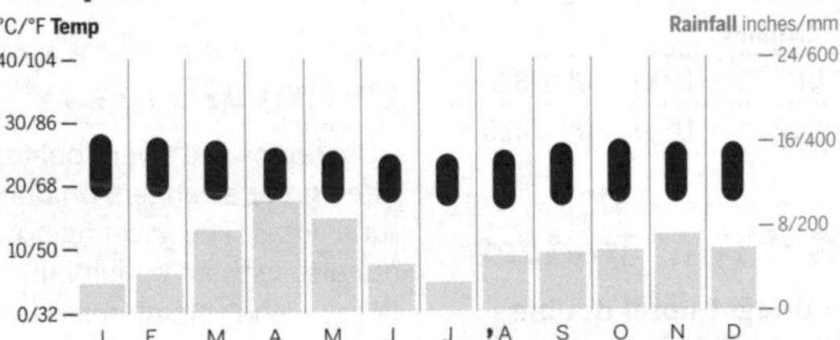

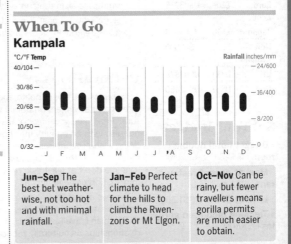

Jun–Sep The best bet weather-wise, not too hot and with minimal rainfall.

Jan–Feb Perfect climate to head for the hills to climb the Rwenzoris or Mt Elgon.

Oct–Nov Can be rainy, but fewer travellers means gorilla permits are much easier to obtain.

AT A GLANCE

» **Currency** Uganda Shilling (USh)

» **Languages** English (official), Luganda and Swahili most widely understood

» **Money** ATMs abundant, US dollars widely accepted (bills dating pre-2006 are not), credit cards rarely accepted

» **Visas** single-entry tourist visas (US$50), see p488

Fast Facts

» **Area** 241,038 sq km

» **Capital** Kampala

» **Country code** ☎256

» **Emergency number** ☎999 from landline or ☎112 from mobile phone

» **Population** 34.6 million

Exchange Rates

Australia	A$1	USh2603
Canada	C$1	USh2466
Euro Zone	€1	USh3235
Japan	¥100	USh3032
New Zealand	NZ$1	USh2006
UK	UK£1	USh3871
USA	US$1	USh2460

Set Your Budget

» **Budget hotel double room** US$20

» **Meal at decent restaurant** US$5 to US$15

» **Litre of petrol** US$1.50

» **Tracking mountain gorillas** US$500

Itineraries

One Week Fly into Entebbe and get your first taste of wildlife at the Uganda Wildlife Education Centre (UWEC) and the Ngamba Island Chimpanzee Sanctuary – both home to injured or orphaned animals rescued from around Africa. Spend the next day sightseeing in Kampala, dining at one of its cosmopolitan restaurants, before a boozy night on the town. Cure your hangover the next day by being flung into the Nile while white-water rafting in Jinja, 80km east of Kampala. Then it's time to head west for some serious wildlife watching. Begin with the unforgettable experience of gorilla tracking in Bwindi Impenetrable National Park. Then it's further north to Queen Elizabeth National Park for tree-climbing lions, hippos and elephants to finish your one week visit.

Two Weeks A more realistic timeframe, which allows you to take in the above activities plus a few days chilling out on scenic Lake Bunyonyi, and Murchison Falls National Park for more animals and thundering waterfalls. Finish up by ticking off the Big Five at Ziwa Rhino Sanctuary on the way back to Kampala.

TRANSPORT IN UGANDA

» Hiring a 4WD is the best way to get around Uganda.

» Most people hire a driver, but it's becoming more common for tourists to get around the national parks on their own, especially those experienced at bush driving and self-sufficient with repairs.

» Potholes are common, although roads are generally in good condition, but be warned things can get very messy come rainy season.

» Uganda is well connected by public transport and you're likely to take a string of buses, minivans, boda-bodas (motorcycle taxis), ferries and shared cars – sometimes all in the same day.

» Night travel is best avoided due to a high number of accidents and a risk of banditry.

Cultural Tips

» Ugandans are a very polite and friendly people, and will often greet strangers on public transport or while walking in rural areas. The greeting comes not just with a simple 'hello' but also with an enquiry into how you and your family are doing – and the interest is genuine. In fact, you risk offending someone (though Ugandans would likely never show it) if you don't at least ask 'How are you?' before asking for information or beginning a conversation.

» Displays of public affection are generally frowned upon, so it's best to avoid this. This is especially the case for gay and lesbian travellers, with Ugandans generally viewing such relationships as culturally taboo.

KAMPALA

☎ 0414 / POP 1.5 MILLION

Unlike what Nairobi's unfortunate reputation does for Kenya, Kampala makes a good introduction to Uganda. It's a dynamic and engaging city, with few of the hassles of its eastern neighbour and several worthy attractions to keep you occupied for a couple of days. Best of all, it's safe to walk around virtually everywhere in the daytime and downtown doesn't shut down until well into the evening.

Today's forward-looking capital is vastly different from the battered city to which it was reduced in the 1980s. In the period since Museveni's victory, Kampala has been transformed from a looted shell to a thriving, modern place.

There are several faces to Kampala. From the impossibly chaotic jam of central Kampala, with streets thronging with shoppers, hawkers, two of the most mind-boggling taxi parks you're ever likely to see and the city's bus parks, it's no surprise that even boda-bodas get trapped in traffic here. Heading up Nakasero Hill you quickly hit Kampala's most expensive hotels as the urban core fades into something of a garden city. Here you'll find many of the embassies and government buildings, as well as some fairly exclusive residential zones, home to swanky restaurants and bars, popular with expats.

Dangers & Annoyances

Kampala is a very hassle-free city and safe as far as Africa's capitals go. Take care in and around the taxi parks, bus parks and market, as pickpockets operate there. Bigger incidents can and sometimes do happen, like anywhere else in the world, so follow the ordinary big-city precautions. As per elsewhere in Africa, thieves who are caught red-handed will often face a mob-justice beating, but the Kampala twist is that they'll also be stripped down to their 'Adam suits' before being sent off. See boxed text, p396 for info on Kampala's notorious traffic jams.

Sights & Activities

While what's on offer in Kampala is fairly limited compared to the amazing attractions elsewhere in the country, there's enough to keep you busy here for a day or two. Quite a few activities beyond the city can be easily done as day trips, including everything in the Around Kampala (p398) section as well as all the activities in and around Jinja (p403).

Kampala remains the heartland of the Buganda kingdom, and within the capital are a number of administrative centres and royal buildings. It's worth having a read over the **Buganda Home Page** (www.buganda.com) to get some background on the kingdom's history, culture and language.

Uganda Museum MUSEUM

(Map p382; Kira Rd; adult/child USh3000/1500; ⏲10am-5.30pm) One of the best museums in East Africa, there's plenty to catch your interest here. There's a varied and well-captioned collection covering hunting, agriculture, war, religion and recreation (get the lowdown on banana beer here), as well as archaeological and natural history displays. The most popular feature is a collection of traditional musical instruments, some of which you can play. There's a fantastic fossil display including the remains of a Napak rhino, a species that became extinct 8 million years ago. There are also some more unexpected items, such as entertaining Olympic Game memorabilia and a Model T Ford. Out back are replicas of the traditional homes of the various tribes of Uganda.

Kasubi Tombs CULTURAL SITE

(Map p382; www.kasubitombs.org; adult/child incl guide USh10,000/1000; ⏲8am-6pm) Of great significance to the Buganda kingdom, the huge thatched-roof palace of the Unesco World Heritage–listed Kasubi Tombs was tragically destroyed in an arson attack in March 2010. Fortunately construction had begun at the time of research to restore it. Built in 1882 as the palace of the King Mutesa I, it was converted into his tomb following his death two years later. Subsequently, the next three *kabaka* (kings) – Mwanga; Daudi Chwa II; and Edward Mutesa II, father of the current *kabaka,* Ronald Mutebi II (known also by his Baganda name, Muwenda) – broke with tradition and chose to be buried here instead of in their own palaces. Outside, forming a ring around the main section of the compound are homes (fortunately not damaged by the fire) of the families of the widows of former *kabaka*. Royal family members are buried amid the trees out the back, and it has the distinct feel of a small rural village. Minibuses don't come here directly, so you'll need to alight at Kasubi Trading Centre at the junction of Hoima and Masiro Rds. From there it's 500m uphill.

Uganda Highlights

1. Jaunt through the jungle to marvel at mountain gorillas in **Bwindi Impenetrable National Park** (p437)
2. Take on the wild waters of the **Nile River** (p405), some of the best white-water in the world
3. Check out the world's most powerful waterfall on a wildlife-watching bonanza of a boat ride up the Victoria Nile at **Murchison Falls** (p461)
4. Chill out at the most beautiful lake in Uganda at **Lake Bunyonyi** (p445)
5. Explore unvarnished Africa at its wild and colourful best in **Kidepo Valley National Park** (p469)
6. Tackle the ice-capped **Rwenzori Mountains** (p428), evocatively known as the 'Mountains of the Moon'
7. Laze in a hammock on a powdery white-sand beach in the middle of Lake Victoria on the **Ssese Islands** (p455)

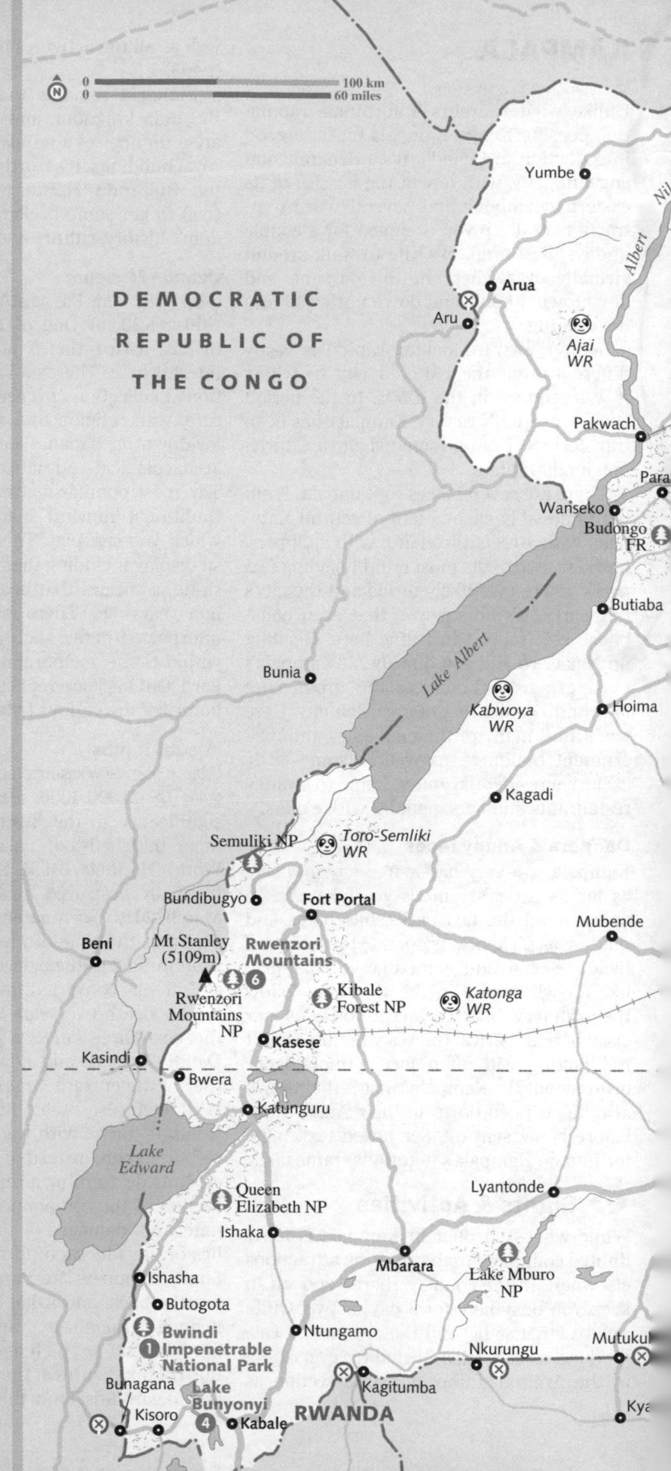

SUDAN
Mt Kinyeti (3187m)
Moyo
Nimule
5 Kidepo Valley National Park
Karenga
Kaabong
Rom
Koputh
KENYA
Atiak
Kitgum
Acholibur
Kotido
Gulu
Patongo
Waiwer
Bokora-Matheniko WR
Moroto
Ogur
Murchison Falls
3
Murchison Falls NP
Karuma
Lira
Aloi
2 Nile River
Pian-Upe WR
Masindi
Soroti
Namasale
Lake Kyoga
Kumi
Sipi Falls
Ziwa Rhino Sanctuary
Mt Elgon NP
Suam
Mt Elgon (4321m)
Bale
Mbale
Kiboga
Victoria Nile
Luwero
Tororo
Malaba
Iganga
Busunju
To Nairobi (300km)
Busia
Jinja
KAMPALA
Port Bell
Lake Wamala
Mpanga FR
Entebbe
Equator
Mabamba Swamp
Bulago Island
Kkome Island
Kisumu
Ngamba Island
Bukakata
Masaka
Kalangala
Buggala Island
7 Ssese Islands
LAKE VICTORIA
KENYA
TANZANIA

Kampala

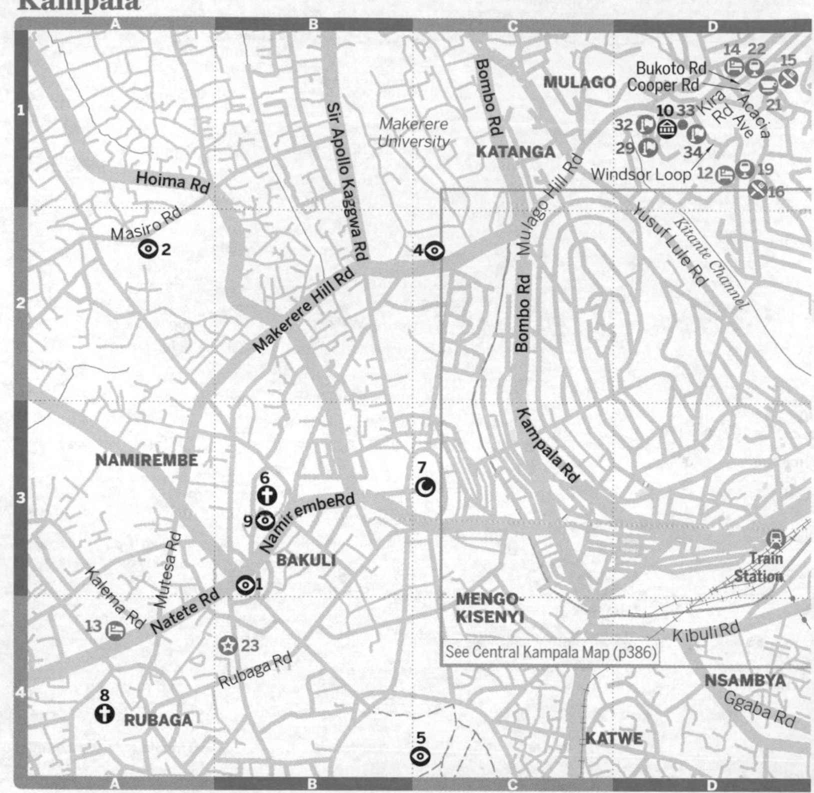

Kasubi Tombs is also the place to arrange a guide to the more low-key Buganda royal sights of **Wamala Tombs** (Map p398; adult/child incl guide USh5000/2000; ⏲8am-5pm), 11km north of Kasubi and the less interesting **Tomb of Nnamasole Kanyange** (Map p398; adult/child incl guide USh5000/2000; ⏲10am-6pm), 4km from the Wamala Tombs.

Buganda Parliament NOTABLE BUILDING
(Map p382; Kabakanjagala Rd; admission incl guide USh10,000; ⏲8am-5pm) A great place to learn about the history and culture of the Buganda Kingdom, guided tours here take you inside the parliament building, and provide interesting stories and details about the 56 different clans. Parliament is held twice a month on Monday mornings – though it's all conducted in Lugandan. Buy your ticket at the adjacent **Buganda Tourism Centre** (☎0414-271166) which also sells bark-cloth clothing and books on Buganda culture.

Mengo Palace PALACE
(Twekobe; Map p382; admission incl guide USh10,000) At the other end of a ceremonial drive leading from parliament, Mengo Palace was built in 1922 and is the former home of the Buganda king. But it has remained empty since 1966 when the then prime minister Milton Obote ordered a dramatic attack to oust King Mutesa II (then president of Uganda). Led by the forces of Idi Amin, soldiers stormed the palace and, after several days of fighting, Mutesa was forced to flee and live in exile in the UK (where he died three years later). The building was duly converted to army barracks, while an adjacent site became a notorious underground prison and torture-execution chamber built by Idi Amin in the 1970s. Guides will lead you to this terrifying site, a dark concrete tunnel with numerous dark, damp cells separated by an electrified passage of water to prevent escape. You'll see some original

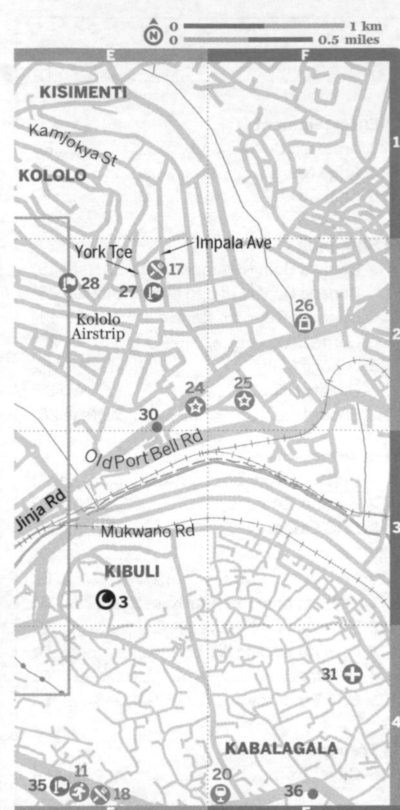

charcoal messages written by former prisoners on the walls: one reads 'Obote, you have killed me, but what about my children!'

Rebuilt in 1999, the palace itself is an attractive building, but inside remains out of bounds to tourists Also here are the scrap metal remains of Mutesa's Rolls Royce destroyed by Idi Amin. Tickets are purchased down the road at the Buganda Tourism Centre.

Parliament House NOTABLE BUILDING
(Map p386; Parliament Ave; ⌚8.30am-4.30pm Mon-Fri) Open to the public, a visit to parliament is an interesting way to spend an hour or two. You can either tour the building, or see the government in action – parliament sits from 2.30pm Tuesday to Thursday and is conducted in English. You need to visit the public relations department (Room 114) to arrange a visit, and make a written request to see question time. Usually you can arrange a visit on the spot. You'll need to bring an identification card and be decently dressed. In the main lobby look out for the huge wooden cultural map of Uganda featuring the country's flora and fauna.

Uganda Martyrs' Shrine HISTORIC SITE
(Map p398; www.ugandamartyrsshrine.org.ug) Located in Namugongo, this Catholic shrine marks the spot where Kabaka Mwanga II ordered the execution of 14 people who refused to denounce their faith. This included church leader Charles Lwanga, who was burnt alive on or around 3 June 1886 – which is now celebrated as Martyrs' Day. The shrine represents an African hut but looks more like something built by NASA rather than the Catholic church. One and a half kilometres up the road, where 25 of Lwanga's followers met a similar fate that same day, is an older Anglican church; this site costs USh2000 and someone will show you around and tell you the whole story of the Martyrs. Both sites have statues of the gruesome events. The shrine is just outside Kampala off Jinja Rd. To get here, you'll need to take a minibus from Kampala's Old Taxi Park.

Namirembe Cathedral CHURCH
(Map p382) The huge domed Anglican cathedral, finished in 1919, has a distinct Mediterranean feel. In years past the congregation was called to worship by the beating of enormous drums, which can still be seen in a little hut located alongside the church.

Katereke Prison HISTORIC SITE
(Map p398; adult/child incl guide USh3000/1000; ⌚8am-5pm) Located on the outskirts of town, the prison ditch here is where royal prisoners were starved during the upheavals of 1888–89. Kabaka Kalema killed 30 of his brothers and sisters here in 1889 in his quest to keep control of his throne. It's not much more than just a deep, circular trench, but it's a very evocative site and worth the trip if you have time. The unmarked turnoff is opposite the police post in Nsangi and the prison is 1.7km north. A boda-boda from Kampala should cost USh1000.

National Mosque MOSQUE
(Map p382; Old Kampala Rd) The prominent National Mosque was begun by Idi Amin in 1972 and finished in 2007 by Colonel Gadaffi. For a small donation (USh2000 should suffice) someone will show you around the simple but striking interior.

Kampala

Sights

1	Buganda Parliament	B3
2	Kasubi Tombs	A2
3	Kibuli Mosque	E3
4	Makerere University Art Gallery	C2
5	Mengo Palace	C4
6	Namirembe Cathedral	B3
7	National Mosque	C3
8	Rubaga Cathedral	A4
9	Sanyu Babies Home	B3
10	Uganda Museum	D1

Activities, Courses & Tours

11	Great Lakes Safaris	E4
	Matoke Tours	(see 22)

Sleeping

12	Athina Club House	D1
13	Backpackers Hostel	A4
14	Kampala Inn	D1

Eating

15	Crocodile Café & Bar	D1
16	Khana Khazana	D1
17	Lawns	E2
18	Le Chateau	E4

Drinking

19	Bubbles O'Learys	D1
20	Café Cheri	F4
21	Endiro	D1
22	Iguana	D1

Entertainment

23	Amakula Culture Club	B4
24	Ange Noir	E2
25	Club Silk	F2

Shopping

	Banana Boat (Kisimenti)	(see 15)
	Banana Boat (Lugogo Mall)	(see 26)
	Buganda Tourism Centre	(see 1)
	Game	(see 26)
26	Lugogo Mall	F2
	Quality Hill	(see 18)
	Shoprite	(see 26)

Information

	Buganda Tourism Centre	(see 1)
27	Burundi Embassy	E2
28	DRC Embassy	E2
29	Ethiopian Embassy	D1
30	Immigration Office	E2
31	International Hospital Kampala	F4
32	Rwandan Embassy	D1
33	Uganda Wildlife Authority	D1
34	UK Embassy	D1
35	USA Embassy	E4

Transport

36	City Cars	F4

Kibuli Mosque MOSQUE

(Map p382) Less overwhelming in terms of size but more attractive, the gleaming white Kibuli Mosque, dominating Kibuli Hill southeast of the centre was the previous principal mosque in Kampala. If you want to be further impressed, for another donation someone will take you up the minaret for superb city views.

Rubaga Cathedral CHURCH

(Map p382) The twin-towered Roman Catholic cathedral is just as enormous as Namirembe, but not nearly as spectacular. Nevertheless, it has great historical significance: in the transept is a memorial to the Uganda Martyrs (dozens of Ugandan Christians burnt or hacked to death by Kabaka Mwanga II in 1885 and 1886 for refusing to renounce the white man's religion); 22 Catholic victims, later declared saints, are enshrined in the stained-glass windows.

Kampala Hindu Temple TEMPLE

(Map p386; Snay Bin Amir Rise; 4-7.30pm) Right in the city centre, with elaborate towers and a swastika-emblazed gate. Peek inside to see the unexpected dome.

Tours

TOP CHOICE **Uganda Bicycle** CYCLING

(0787-016688; www.ugandabicycle.com; per person USh100,000) Popular bicycle tours explore some less visited parts on the outskirts of Kampala, including schools and local villages. Tours depart daily, meeting at Cassia Lodge at 8am, and last around five hours. Otherwise if you want to go solo it rents bikes for USh25,000 per day.

Coffee Safari CULTURAL TOUR

(0772-505619; www.1000cupscoffee.com; per person US$100; 7.30am Fri) You can trace back your coffee from the cup to the farm on day tours run by 1000 Cups Coffee House (p392). Book before noon on Thursday.

Slum Tour CULTURAL TOUR
(☎0755-149932; per person USh20,000) Led by locals who grew up in the area, these guided walks serve up a dose of reality, taking you through one of Kampala's poorest districts in Bwaise-Kawempe. The tours include visits to schools, meetings with youth sex workers and trips to water sources. It's organised by **Action for Fundamental Change and Development** (AFFCAD; www.affcad.org), and 100% of funds go back to the community.

Festivals & Events

LaBa! Street Art Festival ART
(www.goethe.de/ins/ug/kam/kue/laba/enindex.htm; Mackinnon Rd) An open-air art space where artists sell their works along with music and dance performances. Sponsored in part by the Ugandan German Cultural Society, it takes place the first weekend of June.

Royal Ascot Goat Races SOCIAL EVENT
(www.thegoatraces.com) The biggest event on the *muzungu* (white person) social calendar, this charity event is held around September at the enormous and gorgeous Speke Resort and Conference Centre on Lake Victoria. Goats really do race, but that's largely beside the point. People come here to eat, drink and wear funny hats.

Amakula Kampala International Film Festival FILM FESTIVAL
☎0414-273532; www.amakula.com) Taking place at the National Theatre and smaller halls around town, this festival celebrates cinema from around the world, with an African focus. Screening dates seem to change, but it's generally held in the latter months of the year.

Sleeping

Kampala has good accommodation in all price brackets. Most budget travellers choose to stay at Backpackers Hostel or Red Chilli Hideaway (both excellent places if that's your sort of vibe), and these are the best places to meet other travellers. Those who don't want such an insulated experience have some good options in the heart of the city. Meanwhile there are some superb, beautiful hotels at the upper end of the midrange, though most are well outside the centre.

Red Chilli Hideaway HOSTEL $
(Map p398; ☎0414-223903; www.redchillihideaway.com; 17 Gangaram Rd; camping US$5, dm US$8, s/d excl breakfast $30, without bathroom from US$15/20, cottage from US$50; @🛜🏊) Red Chilli is very popular with long-term and return guests, and it gets most of the overland truck business. The cottages with lounge, bathroom and kitchen facilities are in the former managers' quarters of an old soap factory. Recreation options include playing billiards or cooling off in the world's smallest pool. There's food available, with a pizza oven and lively bar. Equally popular is the free internet access. Check out the reliable travel information here before moving on and take a look at its bargain three-day Murchison Falls (p461) trips. Located off the road to Port Bell, about 6km out of the city centre; to get here take a minibus from the eastern end of Kampala Rd to Bugolobi for USh1000, get off at the Gaz petrol station and take the road up the hill, following signs from there. Take note that Red Chilli is planning to move location to a new site in Butabika, a few kilometres from its current spot – expected to happen early 2013.

Villa Kololo BOUTIQUE HOTEL $$
(Map p386; ☎0414-500533; info@villakololo.com; 31 Acacia Ave; r incl full breakfast from US$120; 🛜) While still under construction at the time of research, the rooms that were finished were stunning and great value. Tastefully decorated with a blend of North African and Rajasthani motif, rooms have decadent touches such as four-poster beds, spa baths, zebra-skin rugs, rustic wooden furniture and even antique rocking horses. Wooden slat windows open up to nice views of the hills and Moroccan lampshades cast atmospheric light patterns on the walls. Downstairs is the popular Mediterraneo Italian restaurant.

Backpackers Hostel HOSTEL $
(Map p382; ☎0772-430587; www.backpackers.co.ug; Natete Rd, Lunguja; camping USh12,000, dm USh16,000-18,000 s/d excl breakfast without bathroom USh26,000/48,000, banda s/d USh45,000/60,000; @🛜) The first budget hostel to open its doors in Kampala and still going strong. Set in lush gardens with lots of shade, it's an escape from the bustle of the city. The building itself is of historic note, being the former residence of the Baganda Katikiro (prime minister), Michael Kawalya Kagwa, who was killed during

Central Kampala

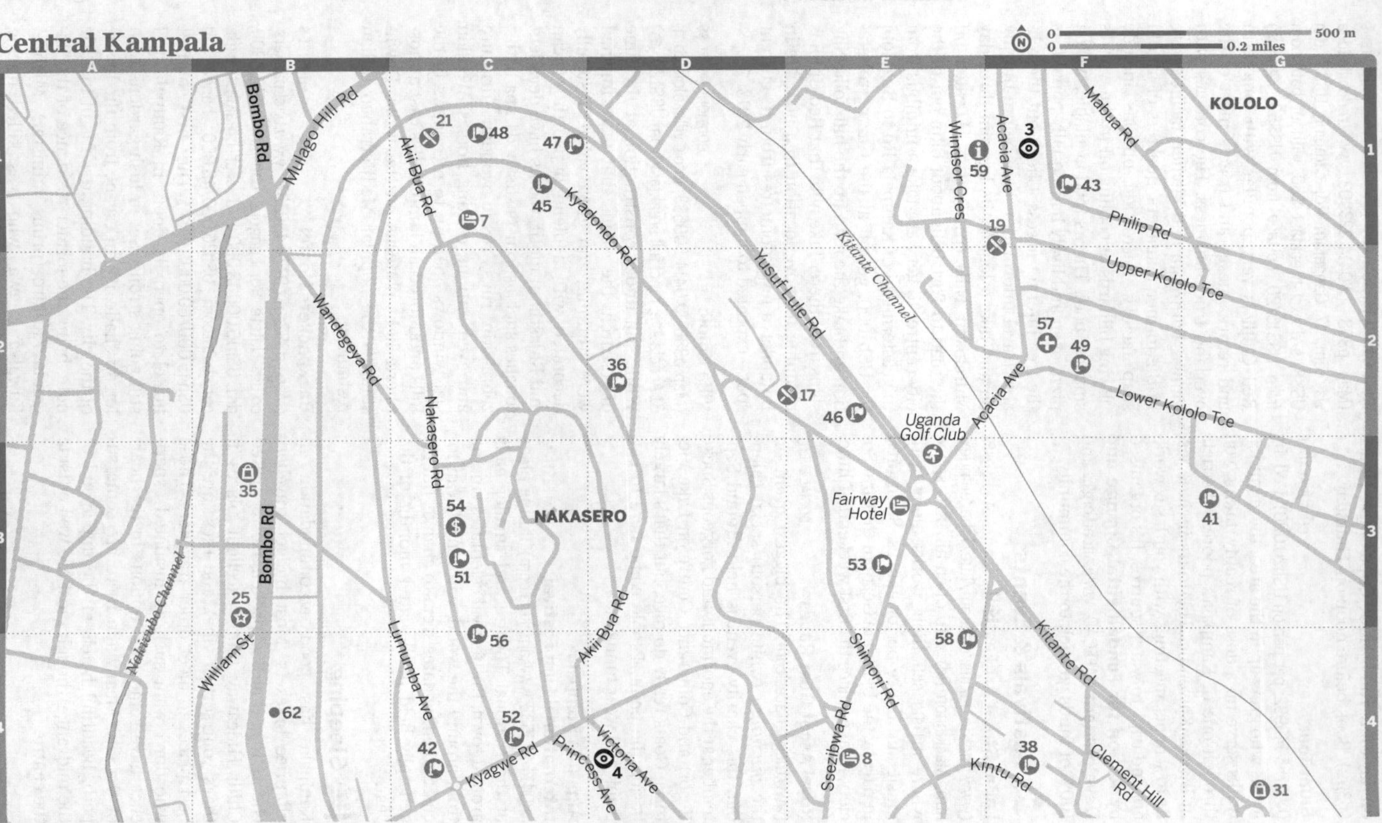

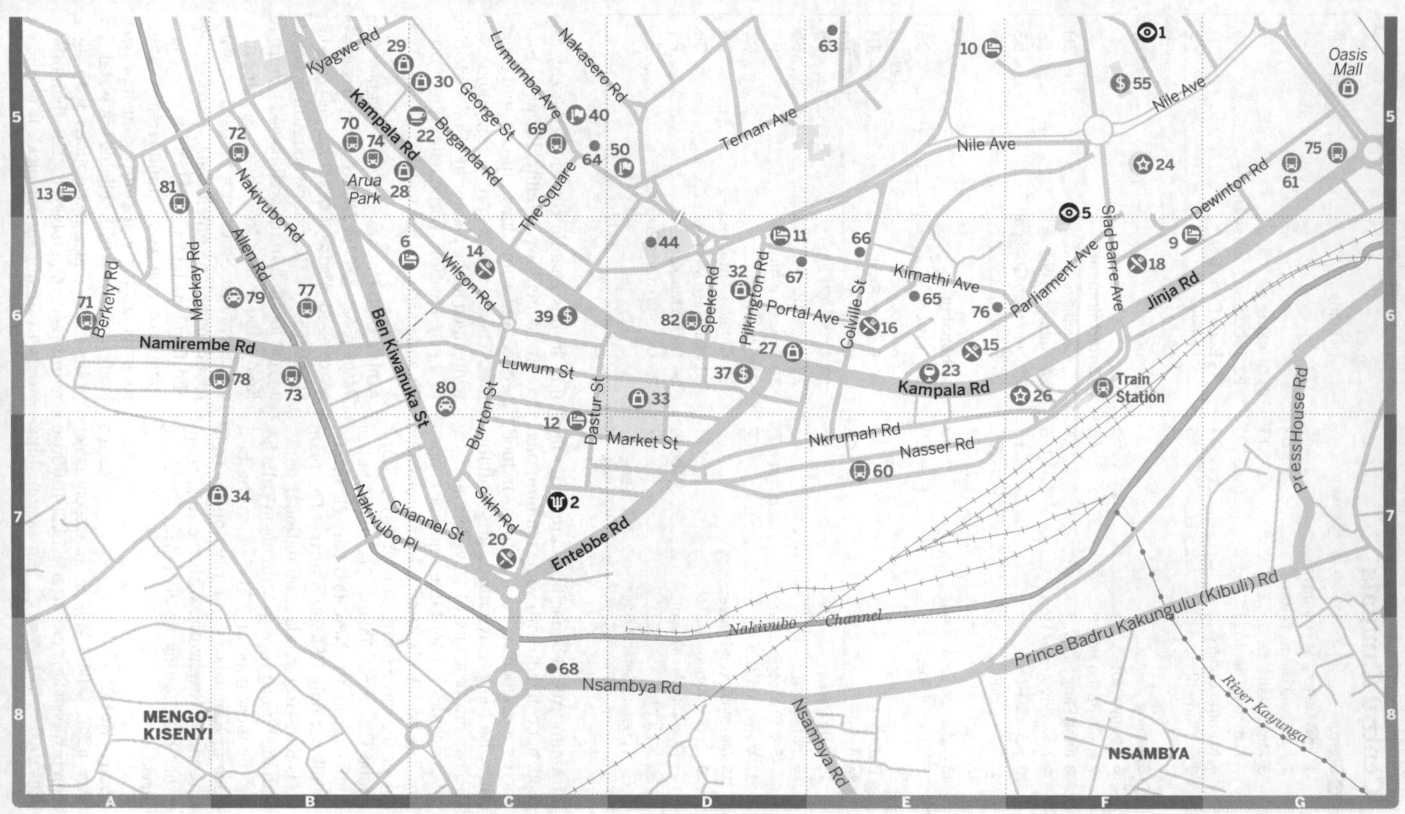
Kyagwe Rd
Kampala Rd
George St
Buganda Rd
Lumumba Ave
Nakasero Rd
The Square
Arua Park
Ternan Ave
Nile Ave
Nile Ave
Oasis Mall
Dewinton Rd
Nakivubo Rd
Allen Rd
Mackay Rd
Berkely Rd
Wilson Rd
Siad Barre Ave
Parliament Ave
Kimathi Ave
Speke Rd
Pilkington Rd
Portal Ave
Colville St
Jinja Rd
Namirembe Rd
Ben Kiwanuka St
Luwum St
Burton St
Dastur St
Market St
Kampala Rd
Train Station
Nkrumah Rd
Nasser Rd
Press House Rd
Sikh Rd
Channel St
Nakivubo Pl
Entebbe Rd
Nakivubo Channel
Prince Badru Kakungulu (Kibuli) Rd
Nsambya Rd
Nsambya Rd
River Kayunga
MENGO-KISENYI
NSAMBYA

Central Kampala

Sights

1 AKA Gallery at Tulifanya F5
2 Kampala Hindu Temple C7
3 MishMash F1
National Theatre .... (see 24)
4 Nommo Gallery D4
5 Parliament House F5

Sleeping

6 Aponye Hotel B6
7 Emin Pasha Hotel C1
8 Fang Fang Hotel E4
9 New City Annex Hotel F6
10 Serena Hotel E5
11 Speke Hotel D6
12 Tourist Hotel C7
13 Tuhende Safari Lodge A5
Villa Kololo .... (see 19)

Eating

14 Antonio's C6
15 Café Pap E6
16 Fang Fang E6
Fez Brasserie .... (see 7)
17 Mama Ashanti E2
18 Masala Chaat House F6
19 Mediterraneo F1
New City Annex Hotel .... (see 9)
20 Shoprite C7
Tuhende Safari Lodge .... (see 13)
Uchumi .... (see 31)
21 Yuj C1

Drinking

22 1000 Cups Coffee House C5
Boda Boda Bar .... (see 31)
23 Mateo's E6
MishMash .... (see 3)
Rock Garden .... (see 11)

Entertainment

Cineplex .... (see 31)
24 National Theatre F5
25 New Club Obbligato B3
26 Rouge F6

Shopping

27 Aristoc D6
Aristoc .... (see 31)
Banana Boat .... (see 31)
Bookend .... (see 57)
28 Colour Chrome B5
29 Craft Africa B5
30 Exposure Africa C5
31 Garden City G4
32 Gerald's Antiques D6
33 Nakasero Market D6
34 Owino Market B7
35 Uganda Crafts 2000 .... B3

Idi Amin's rule. The facilities are generally good, but could do with some maintenance. There's a kitchen to cook your own food, otherwise inexpensive meals are available. The bar draws a mix of travellers and expats, includes a pool table and stays open late. The hostel is a 10-minute minibus ride out of the city centre, not far from Namirembe Cathedral. Take a Natete/Wakaliga minibus from the New Taxi Park (USh1500 uphill, but only USh500 return!). The team leads tours to Uganda's top national parks, with the budget trips to Murchison Falls being the most popular. This is also the best place in Kampala for information on trekking in the Rwenzoris, with the Australian owner here setting up Rwenzori Trekking Services.

Aponye Hotel HOTEL **$**
(Map p386; ☎0414-349239; www.aponyehotel.com; 17 William St; s excl breakfast USh40,000, d USh45,000-60,000; ❄@🛜) An astonishing find in this chaotic corner of the city, the comfy rooms have satellite TV, wi-fi, room service and some have air-con and balconies. There's also secure parking and even white linen in the restaurant. Downsides are its noisy location, perpetually out-of-order lift and unreliable hot water.

Athina Club House GUESTHOUSE **$$**
(Map p382; ☎0414-341428; maryroussos@yahoo.com; 30 Windsor Cr; s/d incl full breakfast $US60/65) The Cypriot-owned Athina boasts a great location in the well-heeled suburb of Kololo and is one of the city's best value midrange options. Stuck in a 1950s time warp, rooms have lime green walls, retro fittings and floral curtains; it feels a bit like you're staying over at your grandparents' house. Its beds are big and comfy, and have spacious bathrooms with reliable hot water. Try to have a look at a few options, with some rooms being much better value than others (room 1 is definitely our pick). It also has a

Information		**Transport**	
36 Australian Consulate	D2	Air Uganda	(see 76)
37 Barclays Bank	D6	**60** Airport Bus	E7
Belgian Embassy	(see 64)	**61** Akamba Buses	G5
38 Burundi Embassy	F4	**62** Alpha Car Rentals	B4
Canadian Consulate	(see 76)	**63** British Airways	E5
39 Crane Bank	C6	**64** Brussels Airlines	C5
40 Danish Embassy	C5	**65** Eagle Air	E6
41 Finnish Consulate	G3	**66** Emirates	E6
42 French Embassy	C4	**67** Ethiopian Airlines	D6
43 German Embassy	F1	**68** Europcar	C8
44 Global Interlink	D6	**69** Falcon	C5
45 Indian Embassy	C1	**70** Gateway	B5
46 Irish Embassy	E2	Hertz	(see 16)
47 Italian Embassy	C1	**71** Horizon	A6
48 Japanese Embassy	C1	**72** Jaguar Executive Coaches	B5
49 Kenya High Commission	F2	**73** Kalita Transport	B6
Let's Go Travel	(see 31)	**74** Kampala Coach (Arua Park)	B5
50 Netherlands Embassy	D5	**75** Kampala Coach (Jinja Rd)	G5
51 Nigerian High Commission	C3	**76** Kenya Airways	E6
52 South African High Commission	C4	KLM	(see 76)
53 Southern Sudan Embassy	E3	**77** Main Bus Park	B6
54 Stanbic ATM	C3	**78** New Bus Park	B6
55 Stanbic Bank Main Branch	F5	**79** New Taxi Park	B6
56 Sudanese Embassy	C4	**80** Old Taxi Park	C6
57 Surgery	F2	**81** Onatracom	A5
58 Tanzanian High Commission	E4	**82** Post Bus	D6
59 Uganda Tourism Board	E1	Precision Air	(see 76)
		Rwandair Express	(see 64)
		Simba	(see 69)

Greek restaurant and beer garden, though many items on the menu often aren't available. On weekends it can be noisy from rowdy Bubbles O'Learys pub (which it backs on to), but otherwise it's conveniently located near a number of excellent restaurants and nightspots.

Speke Hotel HOTEL **$$**
(Map p386; ☎0414-259221; www.spekehotel.com; Nile Ave; r incl full breakfast US$138; ❄@📶) One of Kampala's oldest hotels, this characterful, refurbished address adds creature comforts to age and grace. All rooms are rather simple, but have wooden floors and many have balconies. It's a great central location and the terrace bar is a popular meeting place. All up it's an excellent deal if you're sharing a room. There's also a good Italian restaurant (Mammamia) but the heaving Rock Garden (p392) bar is right next door so take a room in the back.

Emin Pasha Hotel LUXURY HOTEL **$$$**
(Map p386; ☎0414-236977; www.eminpasha.com; 27 Akii Bua Rd; s/d excl breakfast from US$260/290; ❄@🏊) Kampala's first boutique hotel is beautifully housed in an elegant old colonial property. Rooms blend atmosphere and luxury, and more expensive suites feature such touches as claw-foot bathtubs. All have classic writing desks. Respected Fez Brasserie (p391) restaurant shares the grounds, as does the Spa if you want to pamper yourself some more.

Serena Hotel LUXURY HOTEL **$$$**
(Map p386; ☎0414-309000; www.serenahotels.com; Kintu Rd; r incl full breakfast from US$321; ❄@📶🏊) Setting the standard in large, luxurious hotels, the stunning Serena is the result of a massive multimillion dollar renovation of the former Nile Hotel – a hotel notorious as one of Idi Amin's interrogation chambers. It's now the classiest address in Kampala. Set in 17-acre grounds

full of streams and ponds while the building itself is full of flair-like mosaic pillars and wrought iron fixtures. Both the public areas and the 152 fully fitted rooms, each with a large balcony, feature art from across the continent, and fresh flowers greet you in the hallways. Facilities include a top-notch spa, enormous pool, gym and great dining.

New City Annex Hotel HOTEL $
(Map p386; ☎0414-254132; 7 Dewinton Rd; s/d excl breakfast from USh60,000/80,000, s without bathroom USh18,000-25,000, d without bathroom USh40,000-60,000) A convenient city location opposite the National Theatre, this is one of the best downtown budget options. Rooms range from spotless shared-bath ones to larger self-contained units with TVs. Walls in the cheapest rooms are thin, but the tiled floors give the place a hint of distinction and the restaurant downstairs is excellent.

Tuhende Safari Lodge HOSTEL $
(Map p386; ☎0772-468360; www.tuhendesafarilodge.com; 8 Martin Rd, Old Kampala; dm USh15,000, r excl breakfast USh60,000) Not many travellers stay in Old Kampala, but this place on the east side of Kampala Hill has become a favourite with Peace Corps volunteers and other aid workers due to its large comfortable rooms (no bunks here) and good food.

Kampala Inn GUESTHOUSE $
(Map p382; ☎0782-399358; akolkumi@yahoo.com; 92 Kira Rd; s/d USh60,000/80,000) A great budget choice that gets you a spacious, homely room with plenty of natural light, and a clean en suite bathroom. It's on a busy main road, but its location is very convenient to a host of museums, galleries, restaurants and bars.

Tourist Hotel HOTEL $
(Map p386; ☎0414-251471; www.touristhotel.net; Dastur St; s excl breakfast USh63,000-74,000, d USh92,000-123,000; @🛜) This large, older hotel overlooking Nakasero Market does a good job on the high standards-to-low-prices ratio. Rooms are fitted with keycard entry, satellite TV and telephones. The vibrant art on the walls also adds to its appeal. The restaurant serves local, Indian and Chinese food.

Le Bougainviller BOUTIQUE HOTEL $$
(Map p398; ☎0414-220966; www.bougainviller.com; Port Bell Rd, Bugolobi; r incl full breakfast US$96-126; ❄@🛜🏊) A little slice of the Mediterranean in Africa, Le Bougainviller's 24 sleek rooms are split across two buildings. The nicest ones have plush four-poster beds and plasma TVs, and face a flower-filled garden, while the apartments feature lofts, kitchens and bathtubs. There's also a sauna. A French restaurant rounds out the experience. Traffic noise is a bit of a nuisance.

Cassia Lodge HOTEL $$
(Map p398; ☎0755-777002; www.cassialodge.com; Buziga Hill; s/d excl breakfast from US$120/140; ❄@🛜🏊) This quiet spot boasts sweeping vistas of Lake Victoria and hills that seem to never end. The rooms, all facing the lake with balconies and patios for taking it all in, are simple but tasteful and feature minibars and wi-fi. There's a good stock of Uganda books and DVDs for sale. It's a long way from the centre, signposted 2.3km off Ggaba Rd. Perfect for if you have to be in Kampala, but don't want to be.

Fang Fang Hotel HOTEL $$
(Map p386; ☎0414-235828; www.fangfang.co.ug; 9 Ssezibwa Rd; s incl full breakfast US$40-110, d US$99-130; ❄@🛜) Just beyond the city centre, this old-timer warrants consideration less on its own merits than the outlandish prices of most of its neighbours. Although Fang Fang could use a renovation, rooms are perfectly adequate, most featuring bathtubs and pot plants. The cheaper (US$40) rooms at the back are very good value. Also has an attached Chinese restaurant, not to be confused with its flagship, eponymous one in Colville St.

Eating

Kampala is packed with quality restaurants, and the international population brings considerable variety to the dining scene.

There are plenty of large supermarkets that are ideal for stocking up before heading up-country, including **Shoprite** Clock Tower Roundabout (Map p386; Ben Kiwanuka St); Lugogo Mall (Map p382; Jinja Rd) and **Uchumi** (Map p386; Garden City).

Mediterraneo ITALIAN $$
(Map p386; ☎0414-500533; 31 Acacia Ave; mains USh20,00-59,000; ⏰10.30am-10.30pm; 🛜) Classy open-air Italian restaurant in atmospheric surrounds of raised polished-wood decking, umbrellas and sumptuous curtains. At night it's lit with kerosene lamps. The Italian chef does fantastic, authentic dishes, such as thin-crust pizzas and

handmade pastas (think: pappardelle funghi with porcini imported from Italy). Also serves up steaks and such gourmet dishes as grilled rock lobster. Reservations are recommended.

Mama Ashanti WEST AFRICAN **$**

(Map p386; 20 Kyadondo Rd; mains USh11,000-20,000; 9am-11pm Mon-Sat) One of our favourite Kampala restaurants, Mama Ashanti has moved to a new location set out among a lovely spacious garden. It specialises in delicious and authentic Ghanaian and Nigerian dishes such as *egusi* (minced spinach, pumpkin seed and groundnut) with pounded yam, or egg and goat stew. It imports its yams from across the continent.

Fez Brasserie INTERNATIONAL **$$$**

(Map p386; 27 Akii Bua Rd; mains USh30,000-38,000; 12.30-3pm & 6.30-11pm) One of Kampala's most renowned restaurants, this gorgeous spot looking out over the leafy grounds of the Emin Pasha Hotel does not coast by on its reputation. The ever-evolving fusion menu, which respects vegetarians, unites flavours from five continents. Typical options include cashew and coriander chicken, grilled vegetable tartlet and the ever-popular chargrilled beef fillet. And, how about homemade ice cream or baked mango cardamom cheesecake for dessert? Or, just come for the comfy couches in the wine bar.

Crocodile Café & Bar CAFE, BAR **$$**

(Map p382; www.thecrocodilekampala.com; Cooper Rd; sandwiches & salads USh6000-14,000, mains USh10,000-20,000; 9am-11pm Mon-Sat) A Kampala classic, this atmospheric cafe-bar manages to pull off something of an old Parisian vibe. The menu is a tempting mix of salads, sandwiches, pastas and heartier meat dishes. The avocado and smoked Nile perch sandwich is a good lunch selection.

Khana Khazana INDIAN **$$**

(Map p382; 0414-233049; Acacia Ave; mains USh12,500-40,000; noon-3.30pm & 7-11.30pm Mon-Sat) Regarded by many as the best Indian in town, classy Khazana is a great place to treat yourself. It features lovely Rajasthani inspired decor, crisp white tablecloths, ultraprofessional waiters and an attractive water feature. All spices are imported from India, and it does wonderful tandoori dishes and creamy north Indian curries. Also home delivers.

Antonio's UGANDAN **$**

(Map p386; Kampala Rd; mains USh3500-7500; 6.30am-4.30pm) A pretty good greasy spoon serving Ugandan, Kenyan and western favourites. The menu claims burritos, but you won't recognise them as such.

Masala Chaat House INDIAN **$**

(Map p386; 3 Dewinton Rd; mains USh8000-12,000; 9.30am-10pm) A winning combination of authentic flavours (both south and north Indian) and affordable prices has kept this local institution going strong over the years. It offers plenty to keep both vegetarians and carnivores smiling for the night, and anyone who's been to South India will be pleased to see masala dosa on the menu.

Lawns AFRICAN **$$**

(Map p382; www.thelawns.co.ug; 34 Impala Ave; mains USh15,000-45,000; 1pm-midnight;) Carnivores wanting to sample something different will want to try this garden restaurant in upmarket Kololo, with choices including Ostrich burgers, wildebeest steaks with black pepper sauce or crocodile in garlic wine sauce. If you're really into the idea, you can preorder an entire 1.5kg croc tail that feeds up to four. All exotic meats are imported from South Africa. There's occasionally live music.

Tuhende Safari Lodge BARBECUE **$**

(Map p386; 8 Martin Rd, Old Kampala; mains USh7500-9900; 4pm-midnight) A mix of simple snacks and meals during the day, but the chargrilled steaks and fish in the evenings are the speciality. The vegetable stew is pretty good too.

Fang Fang CHINESE **$$**

(Map p386; Colville St; mains USh9900-56,000; 11am-midnight;) Although there's much more competition these days, Fang Fang remains Kampala's best Chinese restaurant. The interior is lovely, typical of a pricey Chinese restaurant anywhere, and there's a large, quiet outdoor terrace with a full selection of Chinese classics. Specialities include fried crispy prawns with ginger and garlic.

Café Pap CAFE **$$**

(Map p386; www.cafepap.com; 13 Parliament Ave; mains USh12,000-32,000; 7.30am-11pm Mon-Sat, 9.30am-11pm Sun;) This stylish, busy cafe might be the place to meet some movers and shakers. There's good coffee from the slopes of Mt Elgon, and a mouthwatering cake selection to match. There's also a full menu with fresh juices, breakfasts, sandwiches, salads, fajitas and pastas.

Le Chateau BELGIAN $$
(Map p382; Ggaba Rd; lunch USh9500-22,000, dinner USh22,500-42,800; ⏲7am-11pm Mon-Sat, 7am-10pm Sun; 📶) Popular for serious steaks, Le Chateau shares a home with the Quality Cuts Butchery, guaranteeing top meat. The extensive Belgian menu, served under an enormous thatched roof, includes steak tartare and frogs' legs, so if you're looking to indulge, this is a good place to do it. The simpler lunch menu features salads, burgers and croquettes.

New City Annex Hotel UGANDAN $
(Map p386; 7 Dewinton Rd; mains USh5000-15,000) The menu has all the expected meat and fish dishes, but also features more vegie choices than usual, including *firinda,* a simple but tasty bean sauce. Many locals eat here.

Yuj JAPANESE $$
(Map p386; Kyadondo Rd; mains USh12,000-40,000; ⏲9am-11pm Mon-Sat) New Japanese restaurant opening next door to the Japanese embassy means big things are expected. Has a pleasant hillside setting with a good sushi selection.

Quality Hill DELI $$
(Map p382; Ggaba Rd) To pack a gourmet picnic, visit this fashionable foodie enclave, home to Quality Cuts Butchery for meat and cheese, the superb La Patisserie bakery and the Cellar wine shop.

Abalimi Market MARKET $
(Map p398; 11 Neptune Ave; ⏲9am-2pm Sat) A farmers market open Saturdays that sells fresh produce including cheeses, meats, stone-baked breads and Ugandan vegetables.

Drinking

Nightlife in Kampala is something to relish these days, with a host of decent bars and clubs throughout the city. There's generally something happening in the city on most nights, although Friday is the biggest bash. Meanwhile caffeine lovers have plenty of choice to find a decent cup of coffee.

Be warned that pickpockets are prevalent, and it's not advisable to carry any valuables, especially phones. The presence of prostitutes is another tedious reality in many of Kampala's nightspots.

MishMash CAFE
(Map p386; www.mishmashuganda.com; 28 Acacia Ave; ⏲11am-late) Just opening its doors at the time of research, this art gallery-cafe-bar promises great things. Art adorns the walls to admire (or buy) while sipping on a coffee or a cold beer on its comfy couches, otherwise there's outdoor seating on the grass. Also does breakfast, brunch and tapas. Monthly art shows, live music and outdoor cinema were all on the cards.

Cayenne BAR, CLUB
(Map p398; Kira Rd; ⏲noon-late Mon-Sat; 📶) Attractive outdoor set-up with a luxurious pool (but no swimming allowed) and stage with live music, this is one of Kampala's best nightspots. There's also a dancefloor, a popular restaurant and a chillout area too. Dress is smart casual (no shorts or flipflops), and there's a small cover charge on weekends.

1000 Cups Coffee House CAFE $
(Map p386; www.1000cupscoffee.com; 18 Buganda Rd; ⏲8am-9pm Mon-Sat, 8am-7pm Sun) For a coffee kick, caffeine cravers should head here; there's a good range of beans from across East Africa, and also a menu of light bites and ice cream. It's a good place to hang out and catch up with the rest of the world, as there's a large selection of international newspapers and magazines.

Bubbles O'Learys PUB
(Map p382; 19 Acacia Ave; ⏲noon-late; 📶) Kampala's contribution to Irish-themed pubs, its bar and furnishings were shipped in from an old Irish pub back on the Emerald Isle. The food's not so great and the 'Guinness' isn't the real thing, but it's a surprisingly buzzing spot drawing a fun expat and local crowd. There are movies on Tuesday, live music on Wednesday, quiz night on Thursday, and DJs at weekends; mind the cheeky USh5000 cover charge on big nights. A great beer garden here too.

Iguana BAR
(Map p382; ⏲5pm-late) Popular with expats and locals alike, boozy Iguana is a contender for most popular bar in town. Upstairs on Wednesday nights and weekends is pumping.

Rock Garden BAR
(Map p386; Nile Ave) One of the definitive stops on the Kampala nightshift, this cool place located at the Speke Hotel has a covered bar and a huge outdoor area with small dancefloor, often heaving with people as early as 9pm.

Al's Bar BAR
(Map p398; Ggaba Rd) A legend in Kampala, this is the most famous bar in Uganda, although notorious might be a better word! This is the one place in Kampala that never sleeps. It gets very busy at weekends, and attracts a regular crowd of expats and Ugandans. It's theoretically open 24 hours, but doesn't really get kicking till well after midnight. One of the few places that plays decent rock music.

Boda Boda Bar BAR
(Map p386; www.bodaboda.co.ug; Garden City; ⌚11am-late; 📶) Popular and stylish rooftop bar in Garden City, with an attractive outdoor area that looks out to the greenery of the golf course. Has a good cocktail list, and there's occasional live music. Also has a swish restaurant.

Endiro CAFE
(Map p382; www.endirocoffee.com; 23 Cooper Rd; ⌚7am-10pm; 📶) Full of expats plugged into their laptops, this pleasant outdoor cafe has free wi-fi to go with its great coffee, breakfast and sandwiches.

Mateo's PUB
(Map p386; Parliament Ave) This pub-like place is a relaxing spot for an evening tipple, unless a big football match is on or the DJ is spinning on weekend nights.

Café Cheri BAR
(Map p382; Muyenga Rd) This is a smaller, less raucous spot than other notorious Kabalagala spots. Monday nights are popular for its live music.

☆ Entertainment

Nightclubs

Ange Noir CLUB
(Map p382; 1st St; ⌚9pm-5am Thu-Sun) The 'black angel' is pronounced locally as 'Angenoa', a pretty fair rendition of the French. Despite the dour exterior and industrial location, it has long held Kampala's most popular dance floor. When you're this cool you don't have to flaunt it.

Club Silk CLUB
(Map p382; www.clubsilk.co.ug; 1st St; ⌚9pm-5am Thu-Sat) On the same street as Ange Noir, this is an identikit club that's usually full of university students. Most people will tell you that Silk Royale has the best music of all the rooms.

Rouge CLUB
(Map p386; Kampala Rd; ⌚9pm-5am Tue-Sun) Kampala's first lounge club, the uberhip Rouge wouldn't be out of place in a Euro-capital. Wednesday is rock night and local pop stars make appearances on Friday.

Live Performance

TOP CHOICE **National Theatre** LIVE MUSIC
(Map p386; ☎0414-254567; www.ugandanationalculturalcentre.org; Siad Barre Ave) There's a quality program of music, film, dance and drama performances in the theatre itself, but most tourists are here for the popular, free weeknightly outdoor events. Grab a beer and a chair and catch an informal open-stage jam on Monday evenings, infectious Afro-fusion grooves on Tuesdays, underground hip-hop on Wednesdays or comedy night (USh10,000) at 8pm on Thursdays, where the merriment comes in a mix of English and Luganda.

Ndere Centre DANCE
(Map p398; ☎0414-597704; www.ndere.com; Kisaasi Rd) If you're interested in traditional dance and music, try to catch a dinner-theatre performance of the Ndere Troupe. It showcases dances from many of Uganda's tribal groups. The troupe has a lovely base way out in Ntinda, which includes a 700-seat amphitheatre, a restaurant-bar and a guesthouse. The high-energy show takes place every Sunday from 6pm to 9pm, while Wednesday has storytelling and Fridays afro-jazz from 7pm to 9pm. It also offers traditional drumming and dance classes from USh20,000 per hour.

New Club Obbligato LIVE MUSIC
(Map p386; Bombo Rd; ⌚Mon-Sat 9pm-late) Once a top joint for Ugandan musicians, Obbligato has a new location, but is still home to the popular Afrigo Band, which plays here every weekend (10.30pm, USh10,000).

Cinemas

Cineplex CINEMA
(Map p386; www.cineplexuganda.com; Garden City) Screens a mix of Hollywood and Bollywood fare. Also has another complex at nearby Oasis Mall.

FREE **Amakula Culture Club** CINEMA
(Map p382; 0414-273532; www.amakula.com; 266 Kivebulaya Rd) Local film screenings every Tuesday at 7pm.

FREE **National Theatre** CINEMA
(discussion 2-6.30pm, film 7pm) See some Ugandan-born movies on the last Tuesday of the month at **Film Chat** at the National Theatre.

Shopping

Kampala is a good place to do your craft shopping since items from all regions of the country are available, though much of the merchandise comes from neighbouring Kenya, despite what the sellers claim. Note the airport also has a good bookstore and handicraft store, convenient for last-minute souvenirs.

Banana Boat ARTS & CRAFTS
(Map p382; www.bananaboat.co.ug; Cooper Rd, Kisimenti; 9.30am-7pm Mon-Sat, 10am-4pm Sun) This sophisticated craft shop has three branches. The original has smart local items such as excellent batiks plus stuff from all over Africa, including Congolese carvings. There's a similar branch at Garden City (Map p386), plus an outlet with an emphasis on homes and interiors in Lugogo Mall (Map p382).

Uganda Crafts 2000 ARTS & CRAFTS
(Map p386; www.ugandacrafts2000ltd.org; Bombo Rd) A small nonprofit, fair-trade shop selling the usual crafts and trinkets; these are made mostly by widows and the disabled. It sells bark-cloth clothing, and takes custom-made orders too. There are also some interesting sustainable paper products.

Exposure Africa ARTS & CRAFTS
(Map p386; 13 Buganda Rd) The largest of the city's craft 'villages', stocking woodcarvings, drums, sandals, batiks, basketry, beaded jewellery and '*muzungu*' t-shirts. Some items have price tags, but everything is negotiable.

Craft Africa ARTS & CRAFTS
(Map p386; Buganda Rd) Right next door to Exposure Africa, with similar items and one standout stall with some great Congolese and Sudanese carvings.

Quality Hill ARTS & CRAFTS
(Map p382; Ggaba Rd) A guy with a great selection of Congolese carvings lays out his wares at this complex.

Gerald's Antiques ANTIQUES
(Map p386; Pilkington Rd) Has stamps and money from the past and present (including notes with Idi Amin's face), plus tribal artefacts that may or may not be old.

Game SHOPPING CENTRE
(Map p382; Lugogo Mall) A great place to buy all your camping needs, including tents (two-person from USh100,000), sleeping bags, chairs and ice coolers.

Aristoc BOOKS
(Map p386; www.aristocbooklex.com; Kampala Rd; 8.30am-5.30pm Mon-Fri, 9am-4.30pm Sat) The best place for English-language publications, with a great selection of books on Uganda, as well as novels. Prices are very reasonable for imported books, so stock up here for reading material before a long road trip. There's also a branch at **Garden City** (Map p386; Yusuf Lule Rd 9am-7pm Mon-Sat, 10am-2pm Sun).

Bookend BOOKS
(Map p386; Acacia Ave; 10.30am-3.30pm Mon-Fri, 10am-12.30pm Sat) Best place for secondhand books with a good selection of novels. All books are sold for USh6000 and bought for USh3000. Located on the grounds of the Surgery.

Colour Chrome PHOTOGRAPHY
(Map p386; 0441-230556; www.colour-chrome.com; 54 Kampala Rd; 8am-7pm Mon-Sat). The best camera shop in Uganda stocks an impressive selection of film, including black and white and 400-speed slide film (for gorilla photos). This is the only place to reliably develop film.

Markets

If Kampala's taxi parks make you agoraphobic, then you'll definitely want to stay out of the markets.

Owino Market MARKET
(St Balikuddembe Market; Map p386) Sprawling around Nakivubo Stadium, Owino has everything from traditional medicines to televisions. It's most famous for its secondhand clothing, but you can also buy some material and let one of the army of tailors sew you something new. You're bound to spend a lot of time here: not only because it's so much fun, but also because once you're inside it's really difficult to find your way out.

KAMPALA ART

With a number of decent galleries opening up over the years, Kampala is home to a healthy and dynamic contemporary art scene. While it still lacks a museum dedicated to art, all the commercial galleries listed here have monthly art shows, and a few have permanent exhibitions. Keep an eye out for the LaBa! Streetart Festival (see p385), as well as art initiatives run by **Goethe-Zentrum** (www.goethe.de/ins/ug/kam/enindex.htm), **Alliance Française** (www.afkampala.org) or the **British Council** (www.britishcouncil.org). While **START** (www.startjournal.org) is an excellent online art journal that provides good info on Kampala's art scene.

» **MishMash** (Map p386; www.mishmashuganda.com; 28 Acacia Ave) A relative newcomer to Kampala's art scene, the English–Australian run MishMash has been doing great things with its monthly art shows featuring Ugandan artists. Hosted in a garden, it's become a big feature on the social calendar, with live music, dance performances, food and plenty of booze. At the time of research it was opening a bar/cafe (p392) in the upmarket suburb of Kololo, which promises to be an excellent addition to Kampala's art scene. Check its website for the latest, as well as its catalogue of artists.

» **Afriart Gallery** (Map p398; www.afriartgallery.org; 56 Kenneth Dale Dr; ⊙9am-6pm Mon-Sat) Just off Kira Rd, this classy little gallery features work by serious local artists. Downstairs has changing monthly exhibits, while upstairs is a permanent collection, but everything is for sale.

» **AKA Gallery at Tulifanya** (Afrique Kontemporary Art Gallery; Map p386; www.tulifanyagallery.com; 28 Hannington Rd; ⊙10am-5pm Tue-Fri, 10am-4pm Sat). Formerly known as Tulifanya, this well-established gallery has knowledgeable owners who can inform you about artists who matter. It features a notable Geoffrey Mukasa collection.

» **Isha's Hidden Treasures** (Map p398; 44 Kenneth Dale Dr; ⊙10am-11pm Mon-Fri & 10am-4pm Sat & Sun) Next door to AfriArt, this stylish outdoor bar/gallery has attractive wall hangings and features East African artists. It's a wonderful place to pop in for an afternoon beer.

» **Nommo Gallery** (Map p386; Princess Ave; ⊙8am-6pm Mon-Fri & 10am-4pm Sat & Sun) Established by the Ugandan Culture Centre in 1964, Nommo is a reliable spot for quality artwork.

» **Makerere University Art Gallery** (Map p382; ⊙9am-5pm Mon-Sat) Small, but worthwhile with fascinating monthly exhibitions. There's also some cool sculpture on the grounds.

Nakasero Market MARKET
(Map p386) The partially covered and hectic Nakasero Market near the junction of Kampala and Entebbe Rds, is all about fresh food.

 Information

Emergency

Police or ambulance (☎999) You can also dial ☎112 from mobile phones.

Internet Access

You can't walk far in Kampala without passing an internet cafe. Prices usually cost USh2000 to USh3000 per hour.

Wi-fi hotspots are becoming more common in hotels, restaurants, bars and cafes.

Medical Services

International Hospital Kampala (Map p382; ☎0772-200400 emergency; St Barnabus Rd; ⊙24hr) This should be your destination if you suffer serious trauma.

Surgery (Map p386; ☎0414-256003, emergency 0752-756003; www.thesurgeryuganda.org; 2 Acacia Ave; ⊙8am-6pm Mon-Sat, emergency 24hr) A highly-respected clinic run by Dr Dick Stockley, an expat British GP. Stocks self-test malaria kits.

Money

Stanbic Bank (Map p386; 17 Hannington Rd, Crested Towers Bldg) and **Barclays Bank** (Map p386; Kampala Rd & Lugogo Mall) are the most useful banks in Kampala. Both accept international cards, but Stanbic is the only bank that takes MasterCard. There are plenty of ATMs about town; Stanbic is particularly abundant. Near the UWA office, the suburb of Kisimenti has all the banks, which is convenient for when you're paying your gorilla permit.

Most main bank branches and foreign exchange bureaus are along or near Kampala Rd. The Speke Hotel (p389) changes money 24 hours a day at competitive rates.

See p486 for more information about money matters.

Post

Main Post Office (Kampala Rd; ⏲8am-6pm Mon-Fri, 9am-2pm Sat) Offers postal and telecom services. The reliable poste restante service is at counter 14.

Tourist Information

See p482 for information on booking gorilla permits in Kampala.

The Eye Free, bi-monthly listings magazine, available from selected hotels and restaurants.

Muzungus in Uganda A Facebook page primarily for expats but has some good info on local events and happenings.

Uganda Tourism Board (UTB; Map p386; ☎0414-342196; www.visituganda.com; 42 Windsor Crescent; ⏲8.30am-5pm Mon-Fri, 9am-1pm Sat) Staff will try to answer your questions, but are frequently unable to.

Travel Agencies

The following are reliable places to buy plane tickets. For information on tours and safari companies in Uganda, see p25.

Global Interlink (Map p386; ☎0414-235233; www.global-interlink.org; Grand Imperial Hotel) Hidden away in the mall behind the hotel.

Let's Go Travel (Map p386; ☎0414-346667; www.ugandaletsgotravel.com; Garden City) Part of the Uniglobe empire and also a representative for STA Travel.

Getting There & Away

Air

See p489 for domestic and international flight details.

Boat

For cargo ships sailing between Kampala's Port Bell and Mwanza, Tanzania, see p211.

A new company, **EarthWise** (www.earthwiseventures.com) were about to launch a speedy ferry service to Ssese Islands from Kampala's Port Bell. Boats (economy/first-class USh30,000/70,000) were scheduled to depart at 8am, arriving at Kalangala on Buggala Island at noon. Also plans to run a service to Mwanza in Tanzania. Check its website for the latest info.

Bus

Destinations are posted in the front windows and buses generally follow the times they tell you, though the later it is in the day, the more likely there are to be delays. Buses leave early if they're full. See the appropriate town listing for prices and travel times.

Main Bus Park (Map p386; off Namirembe Rd) Aka the old bus park, for most departures.

DESTINATION	FARE (USH)	DURATION (HR)
Arua	30,000	7
Fort Portal	20,000	5
Gulu	20,000	5
Hoima	15,000	5
Jinja	10,000	2
Kabale	30,000	8
Kasese	25,000	7
Kisoro	30,000	8
Kitgum	30,000	7
Kutunguru	25,000	8
Masaka	13,000	3

TRAFFIC JAM NIGHTMARES

Traffic jams are a major headache in Kampala, so no matter where you're going in the city, plan ahead if you need to get there at an appointed time. Rush hour is particularly bad, usually from 7.30am to 9.30am, 1pm to 2.30pm and 4.30pm to 7.30pm; on Friday it seems to last all day.

It all comes to a head in central Kampala, where you get snared among the chaos of two taxi parks, two bus parks and a bustling market, all within 1 sq km of each other. It's not uncommon for the last few kilometre crawl of your journey to take an hour, which can be demoralising after returning to town from a long journey. If your luggage is handy, jump off and grab a boda-boda to clear the mess, otherwise if it's in the luggage storage compartment, you have no choice but to wait it out.

DESTINATION	FARE (USH)	DURATION (HR)
Masindi	15,000	4
Mbale	15,000	5
Soroti	20,000	7

New Bus Park (Map p386; off Namirembe Rd) Has buses to Kisoro, Kabale, Gulu and Kihihi (USh30,000, 12 hours).

POST BUS

Main Post Office (Map p386; Kampala Rd) For mail-delivery buses (take a little longer but safer than normal buses) departing around 7.30am to 8am Monday to Saturday. Information and day-before reservations in building next to post office, or turn up around 7am. From originating provincial towns to Kampala, they depart from the post offices earlier in the morning, around 6am to 7am.

DESTINATION	FARE (USH)	DURATION (HR)
Kabale	25,000	8
Mbarara	15,000	5
Fort Portal	15,000	5
Hoima	12,000	6½
Masindi	10,000	5
Gulu	20,000	6
Soroti	16,000	7
Tororo	10,000	4
Mbale	12,000	6

INTERNATIONAL BUSES

Numerous bus companies offer direct daily links from Kampala to Kenya, Tanzania, Rwanda, Sudan, the DRC and even Burundi. See p489 for details and prices.

Minibus

Kampala has two main taxi parks for minibuses, and both serve destinations around the country as well as within Kampala itself. Although packed, there's a degree of organisation. Buses to Entebbe leave from both parks.

Old Taxi Park (Map p386) The busier of the two and serves towns in eastern Uganda.

New Taxi Park (Map p386) Services western and northern destinations.

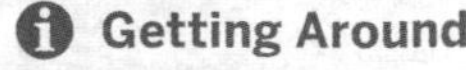

Getting Around

To/From the Airport

The international airport is at Entebbe (p398), 40km from Kampala.

AIRPORT BUS The cheapest and most direct option is to take the green bus that heads to the airport (USh2500, one hour) from Nasser Rd (off Nkrumah Rd) in Central Kampala, which depart on the hour from 8am to 6pm – leave plenty of time to get to Entebbe.

MINIBUS Another option is to take a minibus between Kampala (from either taxi park) and Entebbe (USh2500, 45 minutes), and then a taxi from Entebbe's taxi park (USh10,000).

SPECIAL-HIRE A special-hire is obviously the least stressful option, and costs around USh60,000. Try **CAB Transport** (☎0772-465378).

HOTEL TRANSFER Most of the upmarket hotels and some midrange ones offer airport pick-up services, but it usually costs more than getting your own special-hire.

Boda-Bodas

Motorbike taxis are the fastest way to get around Kampala since they can weave in and out of the traffic jams.

Drivers have imposed an unofficial minimum fare of USh1500 around the city centre and are pretty good about sticking to it. The fare from the centre out to the UWA office or museum is likely to be USh3000. Boda-bodas can also be hired by the hour or day, but prices will depend on how big a swath of the city you plan to tackle. If you go this route, buy them a newspaper to read while they wait and you'll have a new best friend.

Minibus

The ubiquitous white and blue minibus taxis fan out from the city centre to virtually every point in Kampala. Many start in the taxi parks (for most destinations you can use either park), but it's quicker to flag one down on Kampala Rd as they don't need to navigate the nightmare tailbacks around the taxi parks.

BODA BODAS

While boda-bodas (motorcycle taxis) are perfect for getting through heavy traffic, they're are also notorious for their high rate of accidents. Most incidents occur as a result of reckless young drivers: the *New Vision* newspaper has reported that on average there are five deaths daily as a result of boda-boda accidents. So if you decide to use their services, if possible try to get a recommendation from your hotel for a reliable, safe driver. It's also *very* wise to find a driver with a helmet you can borrow, and insist they drive slowly. Boda-bodas are best avoided at night.

Special-Hire Taxi

Most 'special-hire' taxis are unmarked to avoid licensing and taxes, but if you see a car with its door open or with the driver sitting behind the wheel while parked, it's probably a special-hire. They're always found outside hotels (except for the cheapest), near busy shopping areas and at the taxi and bus parks. At night they wait in great numbers outside popular bars and clubs.

A standard short-distance fare is around USh5000. You'll be looking at USh10,000 from the city centre to the UWA office or Kisimenti, and USh15,000 to the Kabalagala/Ggaba Rd area. Waiting time is around USh6000 per hour. Prices will be higher at night and during rush hour.

AROUND KAMPALA

There are some pretty nice places to visit around Kampala; and if you have the time, most can be reached by public transport.

Entebbe

☎ 0414 / POP 76,500

Entebbe is an attractive, verdant town that served duty as the capital city during the early years of the British protectorate; though it's the relaxed pace of life and natural attractions rather than any notable colonial relics that give the city its charm.

Unless you have reason to rush into Kampala, Entebbe makes a nice, relaxing introduction to Uganda. It's also the ideal place to end your trip if you're stuck with one of the many early morning flights out of Uganda's only international airport.

Sights & Activities

There's enough to do here to factor in a day or two of sightseeing, especially for day trips to visit Ngamba Island Chimpanzee Sanctuary (p401) and Mabamba Swamp Wetlands (p402).

Uganda Wildlife Education Centre ZOO

(UWEC; ☎0414-322169; www.uweczoo.org; 56-57 Johnstone St; adult/child USh30,000/15,000; ⏲9am-6.30pm) While it functions primarily as a zoo, this centre is actually a world-class animal refuge that has benefited from international assistance in recent years. Most of the animals on display were once injured or were recovered from poachers and traffickers. Star attractions include white rhinos, lions, leopard, chimpanzees and shoebill storks. If you want to get closer to the animals, there's a variety of programs on offer that can range from a behind the scenes look ($75) to acting zookeeper for the day

Around Kampala

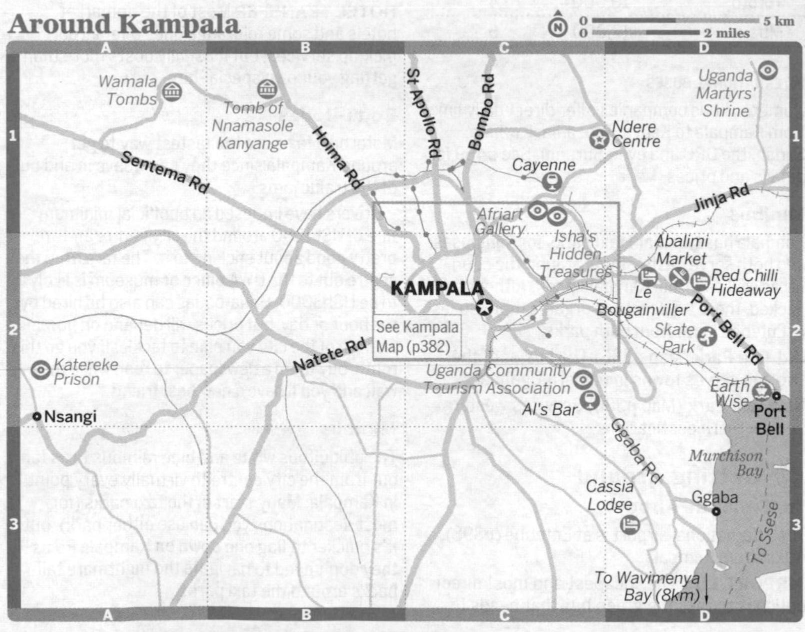

($150) to long-term volunteering opportunities ($2500 per month); book directly through UWEC for discounts. There's decent lodging here too.

Entebbe Botanical Gardens GARDENS
(adult/child USh2000/1000; ⌚9am-7pm) Laid out in 1898, these peaceful gardens are perfect for a leisurely stroll or a picnic on the lake. There are some interesting, unusual trees (although most have their labels missing) and shrubs making it worth a wander. And, if you're a birdwatcher, then it's a must for the often unobstructed viewing. The trail through the garden's thick rainforest centre (where locals claim some of the Johnny Weissmuller *Tarzan* films were made) is known as the 'spider walk', and if you look carefully you might see some rather large examples. There's a little restaurant and picnic area down by the lake.

Beaches BEACH
Entebbe has several inviting beaches on the shores of Lake Victoria, most with white powdery sand. All are part of resorts comprising hotels, restaurants and bars, and get very crowded at weekends, but are nearly empty on weekdays. The most popular are **Imperial Resort Beach Hotel** and **Lido Beach**. Like elsewhere in Lake Victoria, swimming is a no-no due to risks of bilharzia. Those wanting to swim can try the swimming pool (USh10,000) at Lake Victoria Hotel (p401), with a diving platform, deckchairs and bar.

Sleeping

Entebbe has a very good selection of accommodation options. Most places, except the cheapest, offer free airport transfers.

TOP CHOICE **Airport Guesthouse** GUESTHOUSE $$
(☎0414-370932; www.gorillatours.com; 17 Mugula Rd; s/d/tr incl full breakfast US$45/55/75; @📶) One of the best value options in town, this guesthouse's newly renovated rooms find a great balance between style and homeliness. Beds are comfy, huge and laden with pillows, and rooms feature verandahs looking out to the peaceful garden and lawn – home to a roaming flock of guinea fowl. The delicious four-course dinners (USh25,000) are worth hanging around for.

Entebbe Backpackers BACKPACKERS $
(☎0414-320432; www.entebbebackpackers.com; 33-35 Church Rd; camping with/without tent USh8000/12,000, dm USh14,000, s/d excl breakfast USh30,000-60,000, without bathroom USh20,000/25,000 📶) This popular, colourful, spic-and-span backpackers has spacious rooms with clean shared facilities. The helpful owners can suggest things to do around town and beyond. It's often full, so book ahead.

Boma BOUTIQUE HOTEL $$
(☎0772-467929; www.boma.co.ug; 20A Julia Sebutinde Rd; s/d/tr incl full breakfast US$100/130/180; @📶) Entebbe's answer to the upmarket B&B, this little luxurious guesthouse has grown to 12 rooms, but hasn't lost its intimate atmosphere – thanks to lovely 1940s decor and a flower-filled yard. The food gets rave reviews.

New Haven Guesthouse GUESTHOUSE $
(☎0782-803248; vine_entebbe@yahoo.com; 16 Julie Sebutinde Rd; r incl full breakfast USh80,000-100,000; 📶) The leafy neighbourhood, heavy security doors opening up to the compound-like grounds and a Spanish-style villa all suggest this place will exceed the budgets of many travellers. So it's a surprise to find this is actually an affordable option. Its homely lounge and lack of front desk reception make it feel like you're in a private residence, while the garden is well kept and features a lovely avocado tree.

Uganda Wildlife Education Centre BANDA $
(☎0414-322169; www.uwec.ug; 56-57 Johnstone St; camping US$10, dm US$10, r without bathroom US$20, bandas US$35) The choices here are decent for the price, especially the *bandas* (thatched roof huts) that back onto the giraffe enclosure. But the top highlight is the nightly lions' roars and hyenas' howls. Plus, your money helps fund the centre's rescue activities.

Imperial Resort Beach Hotel HOTEL $$$
(☎0414-303000; www.imperialhotels.co.ug; Mpigi Rd; r incl full breakfast from US$177; ❄@📶🏊) Imposing blue building shaped like a wave, Entebbe's only five-star hotel has gaudy rooms and is in need of some refurbishment, but remains decent value. Has a great beach on the lake, with a bar, several restaurants and swimming pool. Discounts available.

Kidepo Guest House GUESTHOUSE $
(☎0414-322722; www.kidepoguesthouse.com; Moroto St; s/d incl full breakfast USh50,000/60,000) A few rough edges, but the basic rooms here are clean and make for a fine budget choice. Bathrooms sparkle and staff are friendly.

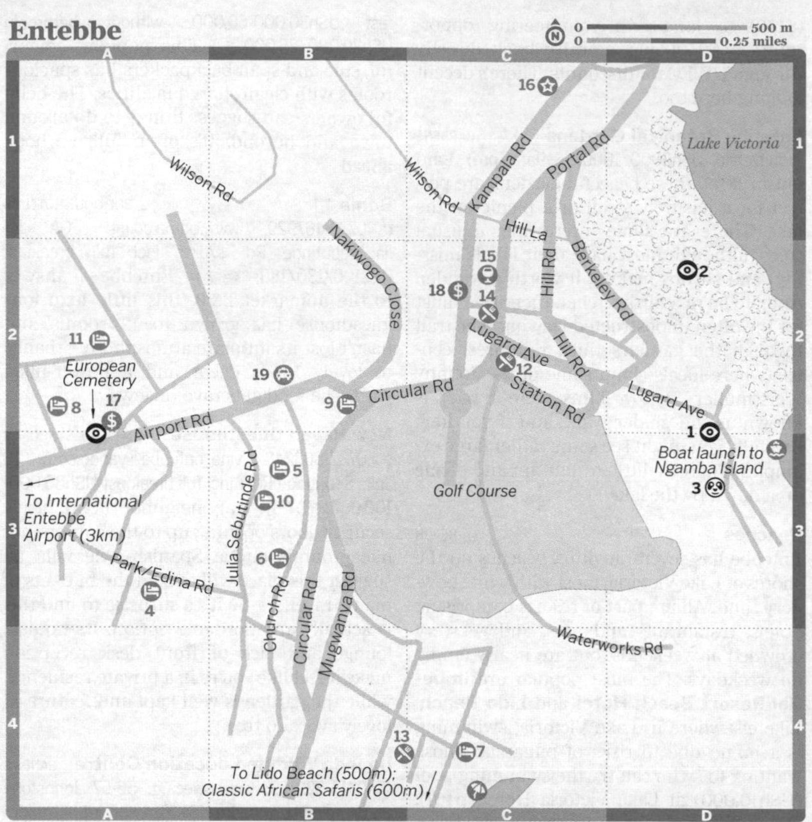

Entebbe

Sights

1 Chimpanzee Sanctuary & Wildlife Conservation Trust ... D2
2 Entebbe Botanical Gardens ... D2
3 Uganda Wildlife Education Centre ... D3

Sleeping

4 Airport Guesthouse ... A3
5 Boma ... B3
6 Entebbe Backpackers ... B3
7 Imperial Resort Beach Hotel ... C4
8 Kidepo Guest House ... A2
9 Lake Victoria Hotel ... B2
10 New Haven Guesthouse ... B3
11 Shade Guesthouse ... A2
Uganda Wildlife Education Centre ... (see 3)

Eating

12 Anna's Corner ... C2
13 Ciao Bella ... B4
14 Gately Inn Entebbe ... C2
Imperial Resort Beach Hotel ... (see 7)

Drinking

15 Four Turkeys ... C2

Entertainment

16 Club Knight Riders ... C1

Information

17 Barclays Bank ATM ... A2
18 Stanbic Bank ... C2

Transport

19 Taxi Park ... B2

Lake Victoria Hotel HOTEL $$$
(0414-351600; www.laico-lakevictoria.com; Circular Rd; s/d incl full breakfast from US$180/230;) Feels like a conference centre, but rooms are well-appointed and make for a reliable choice. Has a very popular swimming pool. Keep an eye out for the tortoises in the garden.

Shade Guesthouse GUESTHOUSE $
(0414-321715; Kiwafu Close; r incl full breakfast USh20,000-22,000) The pick of the bottom-end places around the taxi park. Rooms are clean and not cramped. Bathrooms are shared and cold water only.

Pineapple Bay Resort RESORT $$$
(0414-251182; www.wildplacesafrica.com/bulago-island) Yet to open at the time of research, this luxury resort on Bulago Island is the latest offering from Wildplaces, and one to keep your eye on. It's a very pricey 30-minute boat ride from Entebbe (US$200 for the boat!), but those who can afford it will enjoy its wonderful location with 6km of sandy beaches, and activities such as waterskiing, horseriding and fishing.

Eating & Drinking

When it comes to food in Entebbe, most people end up eating at their hotel, but there are some good choices if you want to go out.

The standard night out in Entebbe involves meeting for some good pub grub and beers at friendly **Four Turkeys** (Kampala Rd) and then heading up the road to dance at **Club Knight Riders** (Kampala Rd; 9pm-late Wed & Fri-Sun).

Gately Inn Entebbe INTERNATIONAL $$
(www.gatelyinn.com/dining.html; Portal Rd; mains USh11,000-20,000; 7am-10pm;) A sister spot to Jinja's Gately on Nile, this version serves the exact same menu in an open-air restaurant surrounded by an attractive garden. Dishes range from healthy salads, pita wraps and meze plates, to Elvis-esque peanut butter smoothies and three-cheese schnitzel. There are lovely rooms here, but the traffic noise is way too loud for us to recommend them.

Imperial Resort Beach Hotel INTERNATIONAL $$
(Mpigi Rd, mains USh15,000-45,000) Good place for fish and chips on the beach (but watch out for scavenging maribou stork), or a choice of meat dishes or pizza. Alternatively there are garden tables, or those with jetlag can hit the 24-hour restaurant inside the hotel.

Ciao Bella ITALIAN $$
(0794-213141; Alice Reef Rd; mains USh15,000-27,000; noon-10.30pm Tue-Sun) Italian owned restaurant for authentic pizzas in an open-air African hut set in the garden. Does home delivery.

Anna's Corner CAFE $
(1 Station Rd; coffee USh5000, pizzas USh14,000-20,000;) Affiliated with 1000 Cups Coffee House in Kampala, this pleasant garden cafe has the best coffee in town. Also does decent pizza and has internet access.

Information

There are payphones and a couple of internet cafes (USh2000 per hour) along Kampala Rd in the centre of town, plus more internet access at Anna's Corner or the airport.

Exchange rates at the banks in town are better than those at the airport, but lower than Kampala. **Stanbic Bank** (Kampala Rd) has an ATM and changes money.

Getting There & Away

BUS Minibuses run between Entebbe and either taxi park in Kampala (USh2500, one hour) throughout the day. There are also green buses that run directly from the airport to Kampala (USh2500, one hour) every hour from 8am to 6pm arriving in Central Kampala. A special-hire from the airport to Kampala will cost you anywhere from USh60,000 to USh80,000.

TAXI Shared car taxis run very infrequently to the airport (USh1500) from the taxi park in Entebbe, so most people use a special-hire (USh10,000 to USh20,000).

FERRY For details on the Ssese Islands ferry, which leaves from near Entebbe, see p456.

Ngamba Island Chimpanzee Sanctuary

'Chimp Island', 23km from Entebbe, is home to over 40 orphaned or rescued chimpanzees who are unable to return to the wild. Humans are confined to about one of the 40 hectares while the chimps wander freely through the rest, emerging from the forest twice a day for feeding at 11am and 2pm. This coincides with visitor arrival times to the island, with viewings of the chimps via a raised platform. The chimps return in the evening to sleep in their compound. While it can't compare to the experience of seeing chimps in the wild, especially due to the large electrified fence that separates chimp from human, it still makes for a very worthwhile excursion to observe the animals' remarkable behaviour. Guides here are informative, and there are individual profiles for each chimp, detailing both their distinct personalities and history on where they were rescued from. There are also big monitor lizards in residence as well as abundant birdlife.

The island is a project of the **Chimpanzee Sanctuary & Wildlife Conservation Trust** (CSWCT; 0414-320662; www.ngambaisland.org; 24 Lugard Ave), which arranges bookings for day trips and accommodation.

Wild Frontiers (☎0772-502155 www.wildfrontiers.co.ug; Plot 3 Nsamizi Close, Entebbe), which was the main operator until recently, is also a reputable company that can arrange trips out here. Both companies charge US$88 for a minimum of 4 people departing twice daily in the morning (8.45am to 1pm) and afternoon (12.45pm to 5pm). If you don't have a group of four, it will sign you up to share the boat with others. Otherwise prices will increase from what's quoted here. Boats that fit six people can also be hired for day trips for US$250, plus $US35 per person for admission.

The CSWCT also offer the overnight experience (singles/doubles including full board US$296/400) where you can spend two days on the island and one night in a self-contained, solar-powered safari tent. Note the rates don't include the boat trip and entry. Recommended add-ons (for those aged 18 to 65) include a one-hour forest walk (US$400 per person) with the chimps, who'll climb all over you, and the caregiver experience (US$200 per person) where you spend a day behind the scenes – this requires passing a long health checklist (www.ngambaisland.com/html_pages/vaccinations.html).

Mabamba Swamp Wetlands

A popular destination for birdwatchers, Mabamba Swamp, 15km west of Entebbe, is one of the best places in Uganda to spot the highly sought-after shoebill. Regularly featured on tourism brochures, these appealingly grotesque birds look like they've crawled straight out of the swamp, with their out-of-proportion features and massive dirty-yellow bill that resembles an old battered shoe. Birdwatching is via canoe, where you'll navigate waterways comprising lily pads and papyrus swamp. Among the 260 species in the region, other notable birds include the papyrus yellow warbler, pallid harrier and blue swallow.

To get here catch a minibus taxi to Kasanje, then a boda-boda to the Mabamba jetty. Otherwise a private car will cost around USh80,000 return. Guides can be arranged from UWEC (p398) in Entebbe for around USh10,000.

Wavimenya Bay

Only a 25-minute boat ride from Kampala proper, Wavimenya Bay on Lake Victoria makes for a great antidote to the city's traffic jams and pollution. It's a lovely laid-back location with peaceful village life that feels miles from Kampala. It's best accessed by boat from Ggaba in southeast Kampala and, while it's fun to explore by bicycle, most come here to do nothing. There are some nice sandy beaches but, like elsewhere in Lake Victoria, swimming isn't recommended due to risks of bilharzia.

Sleeping

Lagoon Resort RESORT **$$**
(☎0775-787291; www.ug-lagoonresort.com; camping $US10, s/d incl full board $US140/240;) A popular weekend getaway for European expats, this wonderfully low-key resort makes for a magnificent choice. Rooms comprise mainly thatched-roof tented bungalows that are each on a raised platform with balcony looking out to the trees. The resort is set among a tropical garden with plenty of lawn and an attractive beach. Unfortunately, there's no swimming allowed in the lake, but you can cool off in the resort's sparkling swimming pool. The restaurant has a classy interior design with plenty of art on the walls. Boat transfers are complimentary, as is use of mountain-bikes and kayaks to explore the island. It can also arrange fishing trips.

Andrews Farm FARMHOUSE **$$**
(☎0750-462646; www.andrewslakefarm; house US$150) Charming two-bedroom farmhouse that's a half-timber, half mudbrick *banda,* and set amid a quaint English garden overlooking the lake. There's abundant birdlife and a pleasant, private sand-pebble

beach. You'll need to bring all your food and drink, which can be cooked in the fantastic country-house kitchen with huge window looking out to the pretty garden. Also has a wonderfully rustic bathroom with a wooden-cased bathtub. It's perfect for either families or as a romantic getaway. There's no TV, but plenty of board games. Tents are provided for larger groups. As it's essentially a house rental, prebooking is essential; boat transfers are inclusive.

Along Masaka Road

MPANGA FOREST RESERVE

About 35km out of Kampala, the 453-hectare **Mpanga Forest Reserve** (0776-949226; admission USh5000) is a decent option if you want to escape the chaos of Kampala for a day or two. It hasn't nearly the diversity or density of fauna as Uganda's larger, more famous reserves, but it's one of the most accessible, and is best known for its 181 species of butterfly. Red-tailed monkeys can be seen during the day and bushbabies during guided night walks (USh5000 per person). Most visit on a day trip, but there's decent **accommodation** (camping Ush10,000, s/d Ush16,000/30,000, cottage Ush40,000) if you want to spend the night.

Take a minibus from the New Taxi Park in Kampala to Mpigi (US3500, 45 minutes) and then a boda-boda on to Mpanga for USh2500. Alternatively, take a Masaka minibus (USh4000, one hour) and get off at Mpanga, walking the last 800m.

THE EQUATOR

The equator crosses the Kampala–Masaka road at a point 65km southwest of the capital, and here you'll find the expected monument of the sort that spring up in equator-hopping destinations. Two cement circles mark the spot, though if you have a GPS you could get your photo taken on the real equator, about 30m to the south; but it's not nearly as photogenic.

Drop in to the excellent **Equation Café** (www.aidchild.org/equation.asp) for a coffee and to browse some artwork, where all profits fund activities to assist HIV/AIDS orphans. Kampala's **AKA Gallery** has an outlet here too.

To get here from Kampala, jump on a Masaka bus or minibus and expect to pay around USh5000.

Along Jinja Road

MABIRA FOREST RESERVE

This 306-sq-km **forest reserve** (admission ½ days USh6000/10,000) has a well-established trail system and though no guide is needed, they don't charge much (prices are negotiable) so consider bringing one along to tell you about the surprisingly diverse forest life: 218 species of butterfly, 312 species of tree and 315 species of bird. The trails are open to bikes and these can be rented here for USh20,000.

The **Mabira Forest Ecotourism Centre** (0712-487173; camping USh3000, dm USh5000) is a decent place to stay, but it does suffer highway noise. It's best to bring your own food. Otherwise there's **Griffin Falls Community Campsite** (0752-634926; camping USh5000, banda USh25,000), 10km from Lugazi at Wasswa (a boda-boda here will cost around Ush4000). There's also the luxurious **Rainforest Lodge** (0414-4258273; www.geolodgesafrica.com/the_rainforest_lodge.htm; s/d incl full board US$175/300;) with very private cabins 2½km south of the highway.

To get here, jump on a minibus travelling between Kampala and Jinja and get off at Najjembe (from Jinja, USh2000), 20km west of Jinja. The visitor centre is a short walk to the north.

EASTERN UGANDA

Eastern Uganda, where the mighty Nile begins its epic journey north, is becoming a must on any East African sojourn thanks to an intoxicating blend of adrenaline adventures and superb scenery. White-water rafting on the Nile River undoubtedly leads the way as the biggest drawcard, but superb trekking at Mt Elgon, and stunning Sipi Falls are also beautiful spots to soak up the scenery. If you're the adventurous sort, consider the overland assault through the heartland of the Karamojong people, a tough tribe of cattle herders, where the route leads to the seldom visited Kidepo Valley National Park.

Jinja

0434 / POP 87,400

Famous as the source of the Nile River, Jinja has emerged as the adrenaline capital

Eastern Uganda

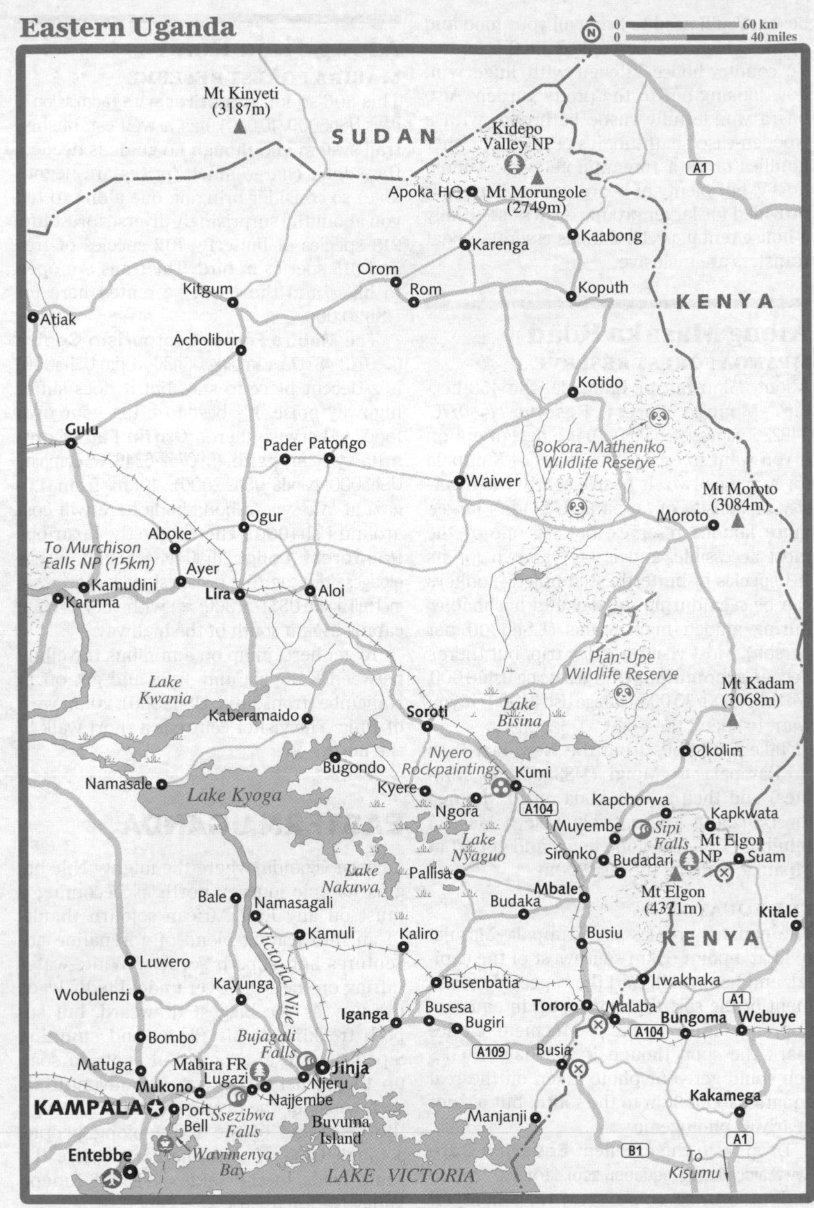

of East Africa. Here you can get your fix of white-water rafting, kayaking, quad biking, mountain biking, horseback riding and bungee jumping. The town has a lush location and is the major market centre for eastern Uganda. It's a buzzing little place with much Indian-influenced architecture.

Coming from Kampala, the Owen Falls Dam forms a spectacular gateway to the town, but don't take pictures, as people have been arrested for doing so, even though there are no signs informing people of this law.

Sights

Source of the Nile River RIVER
(admission per person/car/motorcycle USh10,000/2000/500; admission charged 7am-7pm, open 24hr) The birthplace of the mighty Nile river, here at the source the water spills out of Lake Victoria on its journey to the Mediterranean flowing fast from the get-go. It's estimated no more than 5% of water here will end up in Egypt. Despite being touted as one of Jinja's premier drawcards, don't come here expecting to be awestruck as, on the Jinja side of the river, there really isn't much to see. There's a landmark identifying the source and a few restaurants and bars, which can make for a nice place for a sunset beer, but it's all a bit commercialised. It's more pleasant across the river from Jinja on the western bank with the **Source of the Nile Gardens** and **Speke Monument** – a pillar commemorating the British explorer's visit. Exploring the source by boat (p406) is another popular option.

Bujagali Falls WATERFALL
(admission/car USh3000/1000; 24hr) Situated about 10km from central Jinja, Bujagali is not an actual waterfall, but rather a widespread series of large rapids, and was once one of Uganda's outstanding natural beauty spots. The controversial and long-delayed Bujagali Dam is almost completed, though exactly how much of the roar will be lost is still unclear.

A boda-boda ride to/from Jinja should cost about USh3000 and a special-hire about USh10,000; prices go up late at night.

Activities

Those planning on hanging around to do a few activities, should look into the combos offered by the two main adventure operators – Adrift and Nile River Explorers – which can bring decent discounts. Both companies also offer free transport from Kampala.

White-Water Rafting RAFTING
The upper stretch of the Nile, a long, rollicking string of grade IV and V rapids, is one of the world's most spectacular white-water rafting destinations, and for many people rafting here is the highlight of their visit to Uganda. Despite the intensity of some of the rapids, most people who venture here are first-time rafters; it's the perfect opportunity to get out of your comfort zone and give something different a go.

While the almost-complete Bujagali Dam has changed things slightly in that a few favourite rapids have disappeared, there's still no shortage of grade-V adrenaline and adventure. Trips now start at a new launching point 10km further downstream.

Adrift (0312-237438; www.adrift.ug) and **Nile River Explorers** (NRE; 0434-120236; www.raftafrica.com) are both professional outfits with an outstanding emphasis on safety. Both charge US$115/125/250 for a half-/full-/two-day trip and offer a second day of rafting at half-price for repeat offenders. They will also shuttle you out from Kampala for free, picking up punters from popular hostels and hotels, and back again in the evening if you just want to make it a day trip, and they'll give you a free night's accommodation in a dormitory if you want to stick around. Both also offer pick-ups from hotels in Jinja. **Nalubale Rafting** (0782-638938; ww.nalubalerafting.com) is another reputable company, with similar prices and packages to the others.

Safety standards are impeccable, with all rafting trips accompanied by a fleet of rescue kayaks and a safety boat you can retreat to if you find things a bit too hairy for your liking.

Besides the standard big water runs, there's also less extreme options for those who don't want to be flung into the raging water. Family float trips are offered by both companies, which bypass the big waves and are guaranteed to garner squeals of delight from young kids. A full-day family float with NRE and Nalubale Rafting costs

GANDHI IN UGANDA?

A surprising find at the source of the Nile is a shrine to Mahatma Gandhi. As per his wishes, on his death in 1948 his ashes were divided up to be scattered in several of the world's great rivers, including the Nile in Uganda. This bronze bust, donated by the Indian government, commemorates the act. So, Gandhi was rafting the Nile long before the Adrift team came to town.

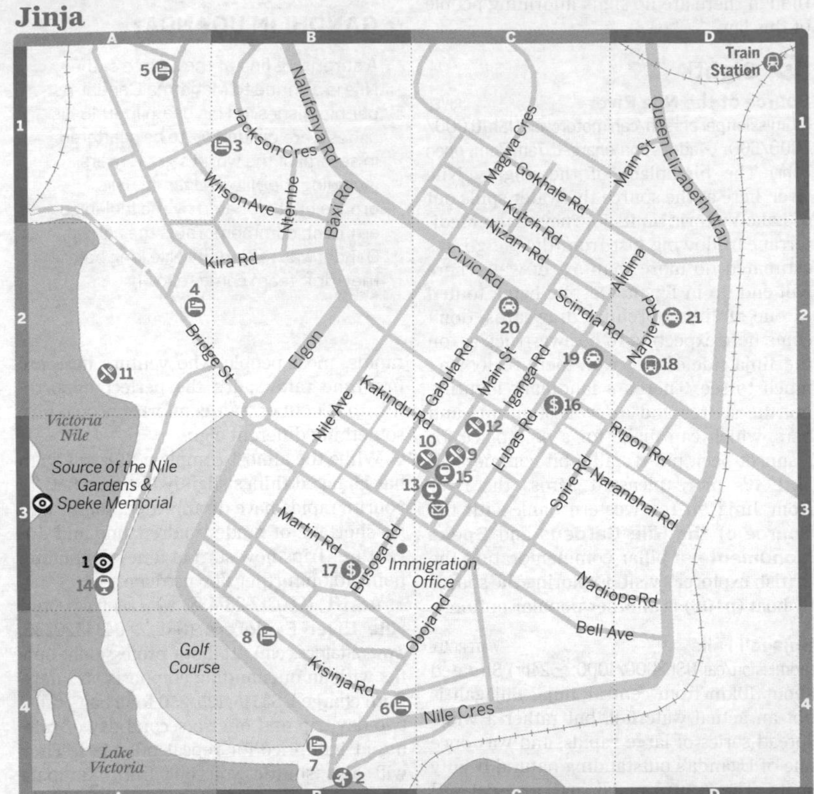

US$30/20 adult/child while Adrift charges US$50/30.

Kayak the Nile KAYAKING
(☎0772-880322; www.kayakthenile.com) An alternative to rafting is to go solo and kayak through the raging river with a variety of paddling courses, starting with a one-day introduction at US$115. Tandem trips (US$140) give you all the fun without the effort. Several locals it has trained as staff have gone on to compete on the world stage. It also offers some quieter trips in sit-on-top kayaks.

Boat Cruises BOAT TOUR
Those who prefer to take in the river at a more leisurely pace have plenty of options. The most popular choices are **sunset canoe cruises** (US$50) with Kayak the Nile, or a **booze cruise** (per person incl snacks & drinks $US45; ⏲5-7pm) that can be arranged through Nile River Explorers.

One of the newest activities is a two-hour cruise on the steam-powered **African Queen** (☎0776-237438; $US85), which is supposedly the restored vessel that appeared in the film starring Humphrey Bogart and Katherine Hepburn. Based at Wildwaters Lodge, trips go along the Kalagala Falls stretch of the Nile and include champagne and snacks.

Another option is to arrange a boat at **Ripon Landing Boat Hire**, next to the defunct Jinja Sailing Club, where you'll find several guys hanging about the leisure centre offering rides. From here, a half-hour ride to the source of the Nile and back costs USh40,000 while longer trips, which could include visiting Samuka Island for birdwatching, or a fishing village or seeing hippos and crocodiles, are also available. It's a much better option than pricier boats offered at the source of the Nile River.

Jinja

Sights

1 Source of the Nile River A3

Activities, Courses & Tours

2 Ripon Landing Boat Hire B4

Sleeping

3 2 Friends Guesthouse B1
4 Bridgeway Guesthouse A2
5 Explorers Backpackers A1
6 Gately on Nile B4
7 Hotel Triangle B4
8 Surjio's B4

Eating

9 Flavours C3
Gately on Nile .... (see 6)
10 Leoz C3
11 Mezzanine A2
12 Source Café C3

Drinking

13 Babez C3
14 Rumours A3
15 Spot 6 .... C3

Information

16 Crane Bank C2
First African Bicycle Information Office .... (see 10)
17 Stanbic Bank B3

Transport

18 Bus Station D2
19 Night-time Taxi Park for Bujagali C2
20 Night-time Taxi Park for Kampala C2
21 Taxi Park D2

Jet Boating BOATING

Bringing a high octane thrill to the Nile, Adrift's **Wild Nile Jet** (adult/child US$75/50) is an exhilarating 90km/h speedboat trip over the rapids with plenty of thrills, 360-degree spins, jumps and near misses. At the time of research Nile River Explorer had just launched its **Gorilla Jet**, which is the same price and also lasts 30 minutes.

Zen Tubing WATERSPORTS

(☎0778-732199; zentubing@gmail.com; two hours/full day $US30/75) Yet another alternative to navigating the rapids, this involves being hurled around in a rubber tube. You don't take on any grade V rapids, but you'll still get thrown about.

All Terrain Adventures ADVENTURE SPORTS

(☎0772-377185; www.atadventures.com/ata/index.html) Quad biking along the beautiful banks of the Victoria Nile is a real blast. After a little spin on the practice circuit, it's time to explore the paths and trails criss-crossing the nearby countryside; kid-sized rides are available. There are several possible circuits, including a one-hour safari (US$45) and the 3½-hour twilight safari (US$80) that includes dinner in a village. It also offers overnight trips. All Terrain Adventures also makes contributions to local communities in the area, ensuring a warm welcome on the way. It's located at Bujagali Falls.

Explorers Mountain Biking MOUNTAIN BIKING

(☎0772-422373; www.raftafrica.com; US$45 incl lunch) Offers a range of guided rides including through the villages between Bujagali Falls and Jinja, which finishes off with a boat ride to the source of the Nile River. There's also more hardcore trips through Mabira Forest Reserve, and it can tailor-make other trips. Also rents mountain bikes: $15 (half day) or $25 (full day).

Nile Horseback Safaris HORSE RIDING

(☎0774-101196; www.nilehorsebacksafaris.com; one-/two-/three-hour rides $US30/50/70) Yet another way to explore the area is on horseback, taking you along the hills above the Nile River and through local villages. There are longer rides for experienced riders. Reservations are a good idea because it's often booked days in advance. Riders need to wear long trousers, closed shoes and there's a 90kg weight limit. Trips depart at 10am and 2pm daily. To get here, cross the bridge over Owen Falls dam and take a right at Kayunga Rd, from where it's 5km; a boda-boda from Jinga will cost around Ush8000.

Bungee Jumping EXTREME SPORTS

(☎0772-286433; www.adrift.ug; US$95) Nearer to Jinja, but more in tune with Bujagali's vibe, Uganda's only bungee jump is a 44m plunge to the Nile River from the Adrift rafting company's Nile High Camp.

Community Walks WALKING TOUR
(US$5 per person) Offers walks that help fund projects in area villages. You'll visit farms and a health clinic, eat local food and sample village beers on the three-hour tour. Eden Rock Resort at Bujagali Falls has a similar program on offer.

Nile River Fishing FISHING
Those wanting to land a Nile River perch can arrange it through Haven or at Mezzanine restaurant. Another option is fly-fishing clinics ($US150 per day) arranged through Nile River Camp (p410).

Kilombera Workshop HANDICRAFTS
(☎0772-824206; ⏲8.30am-5pm Mon-Fri, 9am-1pm Sat) The colourful cotton textiles (place mats, table runners, bedspreads) for sale in spots around Jinja are made on hand-operated looms at the Nile-side workshop. Visitors are welcome to stop by to watch the process. There's a showroom here with items for sale. It's signposted 200m off the road, halfway between Jinja and the falls.

Sleeping

Jinja has some nice choices in its leafy suburbs away from the dusty city centre. And there's some stunning options further down-river or near Bujagali Falls, around 5km from Jinja.

Surjio's BOUTIQUE HOTEL $$
(☎0772-500400; www.surjios.com; 24 Kisinja Rd; s/d incl full breakfast US$65/110;) Formerly the Palm Tree Guest House, relaxed Surjio's makes for a top midrange choice with a pleasant garden away from town near the edge of the Nile. Pricier rooms are spacious with polished blonde-wood floors, large beds and lovely bathrooms. Go for an upstairs room, which get a glimpse of the Nile. Staff are friendly and there's a popular wood-fire pizzeria.

Explorers Backpackers BACKPACKERS $
(☎0434-120236; www.raftafrica.com/site/accommodation.html; 41 Wilson Ave; camping US$5, dm US$7, d excl breakfast US$25; @) Jinja's original crash pad is still the most popular budget choice in Jinja itself. It has a buzzing bar plus free internet, a pool table and a satellite TV. Dorms are decent and there's one double room available. Overland trucks pop in now and then, but this is a much quieter spot than Bujagali.

Gately on Nile BOUTIQUE HOTEL $$
(☎0434-122400; www.gately-on-nile.com; 34 Kisinja Rd; annex incl full breakfast s/d US$60/80, house s/d US$100/140, cottages s/d US$120/160; @) Set in a grand old colonial house with sumptuous grounds, it offers a selection of thoughtfully decorated rooms, some with fine views, and boasts communal areas that have a great atmosphere for relaxing. Bungalows in the garden include Balinese-style open bathrooms and even the no-frills annex is homey. The restaurant is one of the best in town.

2 Friends Guesthouse GUESTHOUSE $$
(☎0772-984821; www.2friends.info; 5 Jackson Cres; s/d incl full breakfast from $US70/85; @) Rooms boast stone and tile floors and some plush decor with more of a log cabin than an African village feel. The pool-side rooms are the best, but it's very nice and relaxing all around, and has a popular pizzeria.

Bridgeway Guesthouse GUESTHOUSE $
(☎0772-480142; bridgewayguesthouse@yahoo.com; 34 Bridge St; s/d incl full breakfast from USh36,000/41,000) Boasting rates that are 'not just affordable, but also adorable', this simple, quiet place is good for those who want a little extra comfort, but don't want to break the bank.

Hotel Triangle HOTEL $
(Brisk Recreation; ☎0434-122099; www.briskhoteltriangle.co.ug; Nile Cres; s/d incl full breakfast from USh62,000/82,000, ste Ush132,000; @) Occupying a commanding ridge above Lake Victoria, the Triangle has a great location and every room looks out over the lake and the fishers working it. Ask to be upstairs to get the best views. The building itself is rundown and has an institutional feel but, with these views, the rooms are right for the price. There's a pool area, a gym and a sauna.

AROUND JINJA

TOP CHOICE **Wildwaters Lodge** LODGE $$$
(☎0772-237400; www.wild-uganda.com; s/d incl full board US$550/700; @) One of the best luxury hotels in the country, Wildwaters lives up to its name by overlooking a raging stretch of the Nile from its stunning island location. Accommodation here comprises private thatched-roof suites, which are accessed via a boardwalk running through forest teeming with birdlife and butterflies. Bedrooms have canvas walls that lend a sa-

fari feel, mixed with a palatial interior of gleaming polished floorboards, four-poster beds and sumptuous sofas. All open up to a balcony that features a decadent outdoor clawfoot bath looking out to unhindered Nile views. You can choose between a room on a peaceful point of the river or otherwise, with the drama of hardcore rapids right on your doorstep!. The lovely restaurant, natural-style swimming pool and lounge deck are also perched right on the river, and it's a good spot for lunch even if you're not staying here. It's located on the west bank of the Nile along Kayunga Rd (turn off near the Nile Brewery), about 20km from Jinja.

Nile High Camp BACKPACKERS, CAMPGROUND $
(☎0772-286433; www.adrift.ug; Kimaka Rd; camping US$5, dm US$10, safari tent US$50, chalet US$60) Located a short way off the road to Bujagali Falls, 4km north of Jinja, Adrift's base for bungee jumping offers fine views of the Nile. The cramped dorm beds are stacked four-high, and while the wooden cottages are very nice and have big river views, they don't have their own bathrooms. It's also a popular place for overland truck tour groups. The restaurant and bar is perched on a riverside cliff and offers wood-fired pizzas, steak and chicken dishes. To get here from Jinja, expect to pay around USh3000 for a boda-boda.

Haven BANDA $$
(☎0702-905959; www.thehaven-uganda.com; camping US$12-35, bandas s/d US$125/190, s/d without bathroom US$85/130;) Located right near the new starting point for white-water rafting, 15km along Kayunga Rd from Jinja, this small lodge is powered by solar panels and uses rainwater through a clever catchment system. Kudos for the ecofriendly design, of course, but the prime selling point here are the wide waterfall views, far more beautiful than Bujagali Falls, and that's some tough competition. The top-notch food is another draw. There's a swimming spot in the river, and boat and fishing trips are available, but the main leisure activity is time in the strategically placed hammocks. You can visit just for a meal (US$15/20/25 for set-menu breakfast/lunch/dinner) but, as with lodging, you must make a reservation. A boda-boda from Jinja will cost around Ush15,000.

Hairy Lemon BANDA $$
(☎0752-828338; www.hairylemonuganda.com; camping US$22, dm excl breakfast US$26, bandas s/d/q incl full board from US$48/84/120) Another 15km downstream from the starting point for rafting, Hairy Lemon is isolated on a small island that makes it the perfect getaway retreat. Perch on a rock on a riverbank and you can have a little world all to yourself. Three hearty meals are served a day, including vegie options if requested in advance. Volleyball, swimming and birdwatching are all possible, and a short paddle away is Nile Special, a world-class hole for those with their own kayak and plenty of experience. It's essential to book ahead. To get here, take a minibus from Jinja to Nazigo (USh3000, one hour) and then a boda-boda (USh2000) for the last 9km to the Hairy Lemon. A special-hire should be USh40,000. There's a wheel hub here to bang on to alert the boatdriver to come and pick you up. You need to arrive here before 6pm.

Nile River Explorers Campsite BACKPACKERS, CAMPGROUND $
(☎0782-320552; www.raftafrica.com/site/accommodation.html; camping US$5, dm US$7, r excl breakfast US$25; @) Nile River Explorers runs the most popular place to stay at Bujagali; it's full with overland trucks and backpackers. Thoughtful terracing means some brilliant views for those in *bandas* (which are due for a much needed renovation) and tents, while the showers look out over the river, which can make a scrub a whole lot more interesting than usual. The restaurant and beer garden are packed to the rafters come evening, so pitch your tent far enough away if you plan a quiet one. If not, just join the party.

Nile Porch LODGE $$
(☎0782-321541; www.nileporch.com; safari tent s/d/tr incl full breakfast US$75/95/120, cottages US$120; @) Sitting tight against Explorers Campsite, but a world away in style and standards, the Nile Porch brings the lodge experience to Bujagali; and the roar of the river drowns out all sounds from the campsite. The eight luxurious tents are superbly set on a cliff above the river, and include elegant furnishings and hammocks on the porches. There's a swimming pool for guests and some family units (minus the views) available for those travelling in numbers.

Nile River Camp CAMPGROUND, BACKPACKERS **$**
(☎0776-900450; www.camponthenile.com; camping US$5, dm excl breakfast US$10;) Great new spot for those on a budget with a scenic river location, good restaurant, bar and hammocks strung about the place.

Samuka Island Retreat BANDA **$$**
(☎0772-401508; www.samukaisland.com; s/d incl full breakfast US$100/140;) Set alone out on rugged Samuka Island, this breeding ground for egrets and cormorants is one purely for the birders: on the 10-acre island, over 50 bird species have been sighted here. Bandas are comfortable but overpriced. It's a 10-minute speedboat trip from Jinja, which costs a pricey US$40 from Rumours bar, so it's best to get a boat from Ripon Landing Boat Hire for USh40,000.

Eating & Drinking

Given its sizeable expat and Non-Government Organisation (NGO) community, Jinja has some fine restaurants and cafes in town. There are also some stunning options north along the Nile.

Most travellers aren't here for the nightlife in Jinja, though Main St offers a suitable strip for a bar crawl. **Spot 6** (Main St) and **Babez** (Main St), a few doors down from each other are the liveliest.

Black Lantern INTERNATIONAL **$$**
(mains USh10,000-22,000) Bujagali's premier dining destination, Black Lantern, part of the Nile Porch, is set under a traditional thatched roof looking through trees at the river. The extensive menu offers several stops around the world, including Mexican, Spanish, Indian and Chinese. Spare ribs are a speciality and the portions are enormous.

Gately on Nile INTERNATIONAL **$$**
(www.gately-on-nile.com; 34 Kisinja Rd; mains USh8000-15,000; ⏲7am-9.30pm) The restaurant on the back porch of Jinja's popular boutique hotel is a must for lovers of fine food. The fusion menu blends the best of local produce with international flair, and includes memorable tastes such as grilled tilapia with pesto.

Mezzanine TAPAS **$$**
(Bridge Close; tapas from USh9000; ⏲noon-10pm) Offering great river views, this basic African-hut restaurant does a great tapas menu. It's pricey, but if you like the sound of chilli salt squid with wasabi mayonnaise or mini pork schnitzels with oyster mushroom and white-wine sauce, you'll be happy to splash out. The fried tilapia with salsa verde is amazing, and it does good wood-fired pizzas too (USh14,000). Enquire about its fishing and wakeboarding trips.

Leoz INDIAN **$**
(11 Main St; mains USh5000-10,000; ⏲9am-10.20pm Wed-Mon) This is the kind of unassuming place you'd normally just walk right on by, but it's the first place locals will recommend for Indian food.

Source Café CAFE **$**
(www.source.co.ug; 20 Main St; mains USh3500-7500; ⏲7.30am-6.30pm Mon-Fri, 8am-6pm Sat; @) The superb bakery and coffee at this church-affiliated place makes the Source a *muzungu* magnet. More substantial meals, such as lemon-pepper grilled fish and pita pizzas, are priced right.

Flavours CAFE **$**
(www.enjoyflavours.com; 12 Main St; coffee USh4500, sandwiches USh11,500; ⏲9am-11pm Tue-Sun) Funky cafe to remind *muzungus* of back home, with good coffee, baguettes and plenty of artwork on the walls. Also has a beer garden out back.

Information

You can get online at tons of places along Main St, otherwise wi-fi is available at many hotels or restaurants. Main St also has many banks with ATMs.

The **Immigration Office** (Busoga Rd) can arrange visa extensions, and makes for a less hectic alternative to Kampala.

Getting There & Away

MINIVAN TAXIS The road between Jinja and Kampala (USh5000) takes around two hours by minivan taxis, depending on the traffic. At about 7pm these minivan taxis to Kampala move out to Clive Rd.

BUS There are also frequent minibuses from Jinja to Kampala (USh4000, two hours), Mbale (USh10,000, three hours), Soroti (USh15,000, four hours) or Busia (USh10,000, two hours) on the Kenyan border. There's no need to travel to Nairobi in stages since you can book tickets on the big buses coming from Kampala.

CAR If you're driving yourself, the best route is the longer but faster and almost completely truck-free road north through Kayunga.

Getting Around

The centre of Jinja is compact enough to wander about on foot; elsewhere you'll want a boda-boda; a few longish trips in town will cost USh3000.

The **First African Bicycle Information Office** (FABIO; 0434-121255; www.fabio.or.ug; 9 Main St; 9am-5pm Mon-Fri) rents simple, but well-maintained bikes for USh10,000 per day. Explorers Backpackers has high-end rides for US$25 per day including helmet and map if you want to explore further.

Mbale

0454 / POP 89,000

A bustling provincial city, Mbale is a place you'll pass through if planning an assault on Mt Elgon or en route to Sipi Falls, otherwise there's no real reason to hang around here. It has a scenic backdrop and is notable for the Abayudaya, native Baganda Jews, who live in and around town.

Sleeping

New Mt Elgon View Hotel HOTEL $

(0772-445562; 5 Cathedral Ave; r from USh36,000, s without bathroom USh15,000, d without bathroom USh20,000-26,000, annex r USh75,000) This Indian-owned hotel offers good-value rooms that are all well looked after, though singles are tiny. Room 11 has splendid mountain views, but the spacious self-contained rooms in the annex across the street are the nicest rooms. Downstairs is the excellent Nurali's Café. Note the 9am checkout time.

Landmark Inn HOTEL $

(0777-283352; Wanale Rd; r USh40,000) Set in a grand old house that's slightly rundown, but in a very charismatic way, the three huge rooms have high ceilings and bathrooms. Also has an excellent Indian restaurant downstairs.

Mt Elgon Hotel HOTEL $$

(0454-433454; www.mountelgonhotel.com; 30 Masaba Rd; s USh107,000-147,000, d USh132,000-172,000, ste s/d USh162,000/187,000;) After a major makeover that tacked on some modern flair, such as grooved doors, you wouldn't ever guess this is a colonial-era stalwart. Rooms are spacious and quite plush at the top of the price range. It's in a quiet part outside the city, surrounded by its own verdant grounds, and has minigolf. The restaurant is good and the bar is a lively gathering place for guests, aid workers and government officials.

Eating & Drinking

Nurali's Café INDIAN $

(5 Cathedral Ave; mains USh7500-14,000) Nurali's, located beneath the New Mt Elgon View Hotel, is a fine Indian restaurant that dishes out delicious flavours from the tandoori grill, and a great biriyani selection, plus some less reliable Chinese, a few Ugandan greatest hits and creative Italian. (How about steak-and-kidney or sausage-and-apple pizzas?). Its bar is the closest thing to a proper pub in Mbale.

Wimpy FAST FOOD

(Cathedral Ave; mains USh3500-8000; 9am-midnight) Far more Ugandan than a real Wimpy, it's still got the same greasy burgers you love to hate.

ABAYUDAYA JEWS OF MBALE

An unexpected find in this neck of the woods, the Jewish Abayudaya community near Mbale dates back to the early part of last century. Its founder was former military leader Semei Kakungulu who, in 1913, started a sect that featured elements of Judaism, Christianity and a disbelief in Western medicine that led to his falling out with the British rulers. In 1919 it was consolidated into full Judaism, with further knowledge acquired the following year with the arrival of a Jewish foreigner who educated the community on the religion. During the 20th century the group withstood widespread persecution, including under Idi Amin who outlawed Judaism and destroyed synagogues. Many converted to Christianity or Islam, while a small core group continued the religion in secrecy. Today there are estimated to be over 1000 followers in the region.

Those interested in learning more about the Abayudaya can visit the Moses Synagogue outside Mbale on Nabugoye Hill, which has Friday night and Saturday morning services in Hebrew and English.

Club Oasis CLUB
(Cathedral Ave) Next to Nurali's, the top club in town has karaoke on Saturday and DJs other nights, plus the occasional live band.

Information

All the big banks are concentrated on the southwest end of Republic St, a few hundred metres from the clocktower. Internet cafes are spread throughout the centre, including **PC Service** (North Rd; per hr USh1000; 6.30am-9.30pm).

Mt Elgon National Park Headquarters (0454-433170; 19 Masaba Rd; 8am-6pm Mon-Fri, 8am-3pm Sat & Sun) Organise your Mt Elgon visit here; about 1km from town.

Getting There & Away

MINIBUS There are frequent minibuses to Kampala (USh13,000, four hours), Jinja (USh10,000, three hours), Kumi (USh4000, one hour) and Soroti (USh7000, two hours) from the main taxi park off Manafa Rd. Behind it is the bus stand, with less-frequent transport to Jinja, Kampala, and Soroti. Prices are similar to minibus prices.

TAXI For Sipi Falls (USh7000, one hour), Kapchorwa (USh7000, one hour) and Budadari (USh4000, 45 minutes), head to the Kumi Rd taxi park northeast of town. Services are infrequent to these smaller places so it's best to travel in the morning.

BUS Both **Akamba** (www.akambabus.com; Naboa Rd) and **Gateway** (0414-234090; Cathedral Rd) have once-a-day services from Mbale to Nairobi departing from their own offices rather than the bus station. Akamba charges USh35,000 and Gateway USh28,000, and journey takes around 12 hours.

Mt Elgon National Park

Mt Elgon is a good alternative to climbing Uganda's Rwenzori Mountains or Mt Kilimanjaro in Tanzania since it offers a milder climate, lower elevation and much more reasonable prices. Also, it's arguably a more scenic climb than the latter. The park encompasses the upper regions of Mt Elgon to the Kenyan border and this is said to be one of the largest surface areas of any extinct volcano in the world.

Elgon, whose name is derived from the Maasai name, Ol Doinyo Ilgoon ('Breast Mountain'), has five major peaks with the highest, Wagagai (4321m), rising on the Ugandan side. It's the second tallest mountain in Uganda (after Mt Stanley at 5109m) and the eighth in Africa, though millions of years ago it was the continent's tallest. The mountain is peppered with cliffs, caves, gorges and waterfalls, and the views from the higher reaches stretch way across eastern Uganda's wide plains.

The lower slopes are clothed in tropical montane forest with extensive stands of bamboo. Above 3000m the forest fades into heath and then afro-alpine moorland, which blankets the caldera, a collapsed crater covering some 40 sq km. The moorland is studded with rare plant species, such as giant groundsel and endemic *Lobelia elgonensis,* and you'll often see duiker bounding through the long grass and endangered lammergeier vultures overhead. In September it's decorated with wildflowers. You'll probably see a few primates and lots of birds, including the rare Jackson's francolin, alpine chat and white-starred forest robin, but you'll be lucky to spot one of the leopard, hyena, buffalo, elephant or other big mammals.

See p281 for information on Kenya's smaller Mt Elgon National Park.

Activities

Trekking on Mt Elgon

Mt Elgon may be a relatively easy climb, but this is still a big, wild mountain. Rain, hail and thick mists aren't uncommon, even in the dry season, and night-time temperatures frequently drop below freezing. Pack adequate clothing and at least one day's extra food, just in case. Altitude sickness is rarely a problem, but heed the warning signs (p661). It's also wise to check the latest security situation, with occasional incidents along the Kenyan border, but an armed escort is provided.

The best time to climb is from June to August or December to March, but the seasons are unpredictable and it can rain at any time. You can get information and organise your trek at the **Mt Elgon National Park Headquarters** (0454-433170; www.ugandawildlife.org/national-parks/mt-elgon-national-park; 19 Masaba Rd; 8am-6pm Mon-Fri, 8am-3pm Sat & Sun) in Mbale or at the visitor centres at each of the trailheads, all open in theory the same hours as the HQ.

Even as the number of visitors on Mt Elgon increases, tourism remains relatively underdeveloped and no more than 250 people reach the caldera in the busiest months. It's possible to hike for days without seeing another climber; an impossible dream on Kilimanjaro. The climb is nontechnical and relatively easy, as far as 4000-plus metre ascents go.

Trekking on Mt Elgon costs US$90 per person per day, which covers park entry fees and a ranger-guide. Guides are mandatory whether heading to the summit or just doing a day trip. Camping fees are USh15,000 more per night and porters, who are highly recommended, charge USh15,000 per day for carrying 18kg. Tents, trekking boots, sleeping bags and mats can be hired from either Rose's Last Chance in Budadari for USh10,000, USh10,000, USh3000 and USh3000 per night respectively, or from UWA also in Budadari (not at HQ in Mbale) but for a higher price. Also, factor in tips, which are highly appreciated, to your grand total.

Mbale supermarkets (there are several in town) don't have nearly the selection of those in Kampala or Jinja, but you can pick up indulgences such as biscuits or pasta. For simple staples it's best to buy from locals at the trailheads with assistance from the guides. Porters can make campfires for cooking but, for environmental reasons, the park requests that you bring a campstove if you have one.

Trails

There are three routes up the mountain. Many people combine different routes going up and down for maximum variety. We've given the normal travel times for the various routes, but if you're up to the challenge these can all be shortened by a day or two. On the other hand, you may want to add an extra day to further explore the caldera or visit the Suam Gorge, or let the guides take you to waterfalls and caves. If summiting at Wagagai, it only takes an extra hour to hit Jackson's Summit (4165m) via Jackson's Pool, a little crater lake. You must use designated campsites, all of which have tent pads, latrines, rubbish pits and nearby water sources.

The **Sasa Trail** is the original route to Wagagai, and still the busiest since it can be easily be reached by public transport from Mbale. It's a four-day roundtrip to the summit with a 1650m ascent on first day. From Budadari, which is considered the trailhead, a road leads 5km to Bumasola, and you can take a car up this leg if you want, then it's a short walk to the forest. Almost as soon as you enter the forest, you reach Mudangi Cliffs, which are scaled via ladders and then it's 2½ hours of pure bamboo forest. The

MT ELGON NATIONAL PARK

Why Go Uganda's second-highest peak, Wagagai (4321m); trekking routes into Kenya or Sipi Falls.

When to Go Year-round, but generally less rain in June to August and December to March; September to October has wildflowers.

Practicalities Decent trekking equipment can be rented at Rose's Last Chance in Budadari. The park is best accessed via Mbale, a three hour's drive from Kampala. Kenya is best accessed from Kapchorwa, where there are minivans to the Kenyan border at Suam.

second day is an easier walk. On summit day, it's four hours from your campsite to Wagagai.

The **Sipi Trail**, which begins at the Forest Exploration Centre in Kapkwai, has become a popular return route since it lets you chill out at Sipi Falls following your trip to the top. It's a longer journey, taking seven days roundtrip. Also, note that it's an easier hike if you choose to descend via the Sasa Trail because the Sipi Trail starts at a higher elevation. On the first day you can camp inside the huge Tutum Cave, which has a small waterfall over its entrance and once attracted elephants to dig salt out of the rock like some more famous caves on the Kenyan side still do.

Also starting high, the **Piswa Trail** has an even gentler ascent than the Sipi Trail. It's the best wildlife watching route since it doesn't pass through bamboo stands, and it also offers the longest pass through the other-worldly moorland in the caldera. It's a six-day journey when returning by the Sasa Trail and seven days when coming back via the Sipi Trail. Piswa Trail is less used because it begins in the difficult to reach village of Kapkwata.

There's also the rarely used **Suam Trail** which is another five-day route starting at a higher elevation than the Sasa Trail and climbing through the Suam Gorge right along the Kenyan border.

Climbers have the option of continuing their trek into Kenya. Park staff at the headquarters will take you to the immigration office in Mbale for the requisite paperwork and then hand you off to the Kenya Wildlife

Service at the hot springs in the caldera. It's a two day hike down the Kenyan side.

There are also numerous options for **day hikes**, with the most popular a trio of short loops around the Forest Exploration Centre at the start of the Sipi Trail.

Sleeping & Eating

TOP CHOICE **Rose's Last Chance** GUESTHOUSE $
(☎0772-623206; mananarose@gmail.com; camping incl full breakfast USh10,000, dm USh15,000, s/d incl full board USh22,000/44,000) Those climbing the Sasa Trail can sleep in Mbale before the trek, but for many people a night with Rose is part of the Mt Elgon experience. Located near the trailhead in Budadari, this is a basic but fun and friendly place that brings guests closer to the local scene. Testing local brews is a favourite activity and Rose sometimes brings in musicians and dancers at night. She began with one bed and her hospitality has led to the construction of this new lodge. The dining room has good vibes and bedrooms are cosy and inviting. It's worth staying here even if you aren't trekking, and Rose can direct you to caves and waterfalls in the area. Camping gear can be hired and there's a car if you want to explore the area. It's located a few doors down from the UWA office.

Forest Exploration Centre GUESTHOUSE $
(camping USh15,000, dm excl breakfast USh15,000, s USh30,000, d USh50,000) This lovely, spread-out set-up is right at the Sipi trailhead. Run by UWA, the cottages with attached bathroom are tasteful, and there are also safari tents for the same price as the cottages, but you have to walk to the toilets. There's a little restaurant too.

Kapkwata Guesthouse GUESTHOUSE $
(camping per tent USh15,000, r excl breakfast USh35,000) This simple (cold-water only) UWA-run place is right at the trailhead and if you bring food, staff can cook it for you.

Wirr Community Campsite CAMPGROUND $
(camping excl breakfast USh10,000) Just outside the park gate next to the Forest Education Centre, but the community seem to have given up on it. Sipi Falls is a better bet if you'd rather not pay the park fee the first night.

Getting There & Away

MINIBUS There are regular, if infrequent, minibuses from Mbale to Budadari (USh3000, 45 minutes).

Sipi Trail

There's no regular transport to the Forest Exploration Centre, but minibuses between Mbale and Kapchorwa (USh7000, 1½ hours) pass the signposted turn-off to Kapkwai, 6km up from Sipi, from where it's a 6km walk to the centre; there's little chance of catching a ride. A boda-boda from Sipi should cost USh10,000 to USh15,000 depending on how dry the road is; a fair special-hire price is around USh80,000. A more interesting way to get to the centre is to hire a guide at Sipi to walk you through the villages, about a 90-minute trip.

Piswa Trail

Getting to the Piswa trailhead in Kapkwata takes a little more effort. The excellent paved road ends at Kapchorwa. From here you'll have to take another minivan taxi to Kapkwata (USh10,000, one hour) for the often rough 33km trip. They run until around 3pm, so it's possible to make it from Mbale in a day.

Suam Trail

From Kapchorwa there are minivans to the Kenya border at Suam (USh20,000, three hours) via a lower route with a better road. Otherwise there are trucks here from Kapkwata via a terrible road. You reach the border by early afternoon and should have little problem moving straight on to Kitale by matatu. There's basic lodging if you can't.

Sipi Falls

Sipi Falls, in the foothills of Mt Elgon, is a stunner; arguably the most beautiful waterfall in all of Uganda. There are three levels, and though the upper two are beautiful, it's the 95m main drop that attracts the crowds, and most of Sipi's lodging looks out over it. Not only are the falls spectacular, so too are the views of the wide plains disappearing into the distance below. It's well worth spending a night or two in this peaceful and pretty place.

Sights & Activities

Walks to Sipi Falls WATERFALL, WALKING
There are some excellent walks on a network of well-maintained (though often muddy) local trails and beautiful scenery in every direction. It's easy enough to just ramble off on your own, but a guide is highly recommended since you'll cross much private property (without a guide you'll need to pay at several points) and also will be pestered by children asking for money (either to be your guide or just because). All

the lodges can arrange guides and prices are pretty similar. Figure on about USh6000 to USh10,000 to get to the bottom of the main drop and USh15,000 to USh20,000 per person for the four-hour, 8km walk to all three. The most popular walk is to the bottom of the falls, which during the rainy season is an awe-inspiring sight. It's a steep climb down through villages and crops, and a sweaty, exhausting climb back up.

There's a cave behind the easy to reach second falls, and though most people end up deleting the top falls from their itinerary due to exhaustion, it's really worth the climb; if you have a clear day (which happens a couple of times each week) you can literally see halfway across Uganda from the ridge at the top.

There are also village walks and the forest walking trails at Mt Elgon National Park's Forest Exploration Centre nearby, though you have to pay the national park fees to hike there.

Mise Cave CAVE
(admission USh1000) There's not much to see at this cave, next to the little waterfall at the bend in the road just above the village, but the caretaker will tell you a few tales about how the Sabiny people used to live.

TOP CHOICE **Coffee Tours** ECOTOUR
(per person approx USh 25,000) Other than visiting the falls themselves, a highlight to visiting Sipi is a coffee tour that takes you through the whole process: from picking the coffee berries, to deshelling them, grinding them with a traditional mortar and pestle, before roasting them on an open fire and – of course – finishing with a fine cup of strong Arabic coffee. Most tours are in mud-brick villages with small coffee plantations, and it's possible to arrange overnight stays. All lodges here can arrange the tours.

Rob's Rolling Rock ADVENTURE SPORTS
(☎0776-963078; www.rollingrocksipifalls.wordpress.com, robsrollingrock@yahoo.com) A reliable local outfit offering climbing and abseiling around Sipi Falls. Its mainstay is a 100m abseil (US$50) alongside the main falls. It also has several rocks bolted in for climbing (US$40), with options for both beginners and experts. All equipment is provided.

Sleeping & Eating

Sipi has a good range of tasteful lodges; all good in their own way. A word of warning that food takes a very long time to cook, so it's best to preorder.

Sipi Falls Resort LODGE $$
(☎0753-153000; sipiresort@yahoo.com; camping USh25,000, s/d/tr incl full breakfast USh105,000/121,000/150,000) It may no longer be up to the standard of when it was run by Volcanoes Safaris, but it also no longer costs in excess of US$200. The *bandas* are well-appointed and have lovely outdoor private bathrooms. It has a lovely grassy sitting area that looks out to the main waterfall. The old house here was used as a residence by the last British governor of Uganda, but those rooms are overpriced and lack atmosphere.

Sipi River Lodge LODGE $$
(☎0751-796109; www.sipiriver.com; dm US$50, banda s/d full board US$85/105, cottage d/q full board US$170/290; @) A tranquil setting among a lovely flower garden, bubbling river and even a small waterfall in the backdrop. The cottages are the best pick here, in particular the one that opens right up to the small fall, while the *bandas* are a tad overpriced. A nightly set menu (USh30,000 for drop-in diners), with many of the ingredients coming from its small vegetable garden, is served around a fireplace. It's also a great spot for lunch and can organise a range of activities including fly fishing for trout.

Moses' Campsite GUESTHOUSE $
(☎0752-208302; camping USh6000, bandas per person excl breakfast USh12,000) Sipi's original backpacker destination, this small, laid-back operation is arguably the best, situated with a good look at the falls from its wonderful rickety terrace and unhindered views of the plains below from a rocky cliff (which you can abseil down for US$50). The *bandas* are decent, the staff friendly and colobus monkeys often hang around here.

Crow's Nest GUESTHOUSE $
(☎0772-687924; thecrowsnets@yahoo.com; camping USh6500, dm excl breakfast USh13,000, cabins USh31,000) Crow's Nest was set up by Peace Corps volunteers and the cabins are Scandinavian-style with private baths and views of all three waterfalls from their terraces. It can arrange cultural walks (USh15,000) that cover everything from throwing spears to learning how to ward off evil spirits. Yes, someone really did make a mess of the email address: crowsnets, not nest!

Lacam Lodge LODGE $$
(☎0752-292554; www.lacamlodge.co.uk; camping USh45,000, dm excl breakfast 60,000, r without bathroom s/d USh70,000/120,000, bandas s/d/tr USh130,000/220,000/270,000) This attractive lodge is the closest to the big waterfall, and from the viewing area you can see the water crash land. Accommodation here, from the three-bed dorms to the large *bandas,* is very comfy and the service is good. Accommodation is full board; except during the July to August and Christmas-time high season (when all prices rise USh10,000 to USh20,000 per night), when half-board rates are also available.

Getting There & Away

MINIBUSES Route is between Mbale and Sipi Falls (USh6000, one hour), but minibuses can take a long time to fill up. Drivers will drop you right at your lodge. Expect to pay around USh40,000.

For the return trip, most minibuses start at Kapchorwa and are often full when they pass through Sipi, so you may end up waiting a while. Ask at your lodge if they know when any minibuses will start the trip in Sipi.

SPECIAL-HIRE TAXI Those travelling in a group should consider a special-hire if it's late in the day.

Nyero Rockpaintings

Of the many ancient rock art sites scattered around eastern Uganda, this is one of the easiest to reach; and one of the few worth the effort to do so. The main site, known as **Nyero 2**, is a big white wall covered in groups of red circles, boats and some vaguely human and animal forms. Archaeologists have yet to unravel the significance of the designs, who painted them and even when they did so. If the caretaker is around, he'll charge USh5000 for an informative tour, otherwise local kids will show you around. **Nyero 1**, with a few more circles, lies just below the main site while **Nyero 3**, where you probably won't notice the modest painting unless someone shows you, is a few hundred metres north. The surrounding countryside is littered with similar bouldery peaks and cacti that gives it a Wild West feel.

Nyero is an easy day-trip from Mbale, Sipi, Soroti or even Jinja, but Kumi has you covered if you need to say the night. The spotless rooms at **Axsa Inn** (☎0773-920912; 29 Ngora Rd, Kumi; r USh31,000) makes a big leap over the nearby cheapies. It has a restaurant and bar with a pool table. There's an internet cafe and a Stanbic Bank with an ATM on this same block.

Getting There & Away

The Nyero rockpaintings are 9km west of Kumi, just past Nyero village. Look for the small, white signpost.

SHARED CAR-TAXIS Departing from the taxi park just north of the Kumi city centre to Ngora, these shared vehicles can drop you at the site (USh3000, 20 minutes), but departures are infrequent in the morning and rare in the afternoon.

BODA-BODA A roundtrip by boda-boda, with some time to explore, will cost USh4000.

MINIBUSES Running between Mbale (USh4000, one hour) and Soroti (USh4000, one hour) are frequent and stop along the highway.

SOUTHWESTERN UGANDA

If Uganda is the 'pearl of Africa', then southwestern Uganda is the mother of pearl. Easily the most beautiful part of the country, it's a lush region of lakes, islands and mountains. And whether you're here for adventure or respite, the southwest's got you covered in spades.

There are top-notch treks all along the western Rift Valley, whether it be taking in the three-nation vistas from atop the Virunga volcanoes or making a weeklong slog though the otherworldly moorlands on the snowcapped Rwenzoris. After the mountains, head to the water for an all out R&R assault on Lake Bunyonyi or the Ssese Islands.

With most of Africa's national parks, the southwest is Uganda's top wildlife-watching region too; and one of the world's best for primates. There are, of course, the mountain gorillas, living *la vida* languorous on the steep slopes of Bwindi Impenetrable National Park and Mgahinga Gorilla National Parks. Kibale Forest National Park has what's often described as the greatest variety of primates on the planet, and this is just one of the places where you can track a habituated troop of chimpanzees as they groove through the treetops. The famous tree-climbing lions steal the show at Queen Elizabeth National Park, but the area's largest and most diverse park is full of other big wildlife and is one place certain to satisfy your safari urge.

As in the rest of the country, it can take a long time to get from place to place. And it's tough to properly explore most of the national parks without your own set of wheels, but as this is the most popular part of Uganda it's usually not too tough to team up with other travellers to share the costs.

Fort Portal

☎ 0483 / POP 46,300

The fort may be gone, but this city is definitely a portal to places that offer sublime scenery, abundant nature and genuine adventure. Explore the beautiful Crater Lakes, track the chimps in Kibale Forest National Park or Toro-Semliki Wildlife Reserve, and drop into Semuliki National Park with its hot springs and central African wildlife.

Fort Portal is the heartland of a verdant tea-growing area and an important commercial centre, but the town itself is not an overly appealing place. Still, its pleasant cool climate mixed with a central location make it a very convenient base to explore the area, so many people end up staying here for a few days.

Sights & Activities

Tooro Palace PALACE

(admission incl guide USh5000; ⊙9am-6pm) Looking down over the town from its highest hill, the palace is worth a visit purely for its 360-degree panoramic views. It's the residence of King Oyo, when he's in town, who ascended the throne in 1995 at age three. The circular structure was built in 1963, fell into ruins after the abolition of the royal kingdoms by Idi Amin, and was restored in 2001 after Colonel Gadaffi met the king and donated the money for repairs. A guide will give you a quick history of the kingdom and explain the ceremonies that take place on the hill, but you can't go inside.

Karambi Royal Tombs CEMETERY

(Kasese Rd; admission USh5000; ⊙8am-6pm) While not an essential visit, the royal tombs 4km south out of town make for a peaceful excursion. From outside it's not much to look at, but if you can find the caretaker he'll let you in to look inside the tombs, which house some drums, spears and other personal effects of several of the Toro kings who are buried here. The cemetery outside is the resting place for various other royal family members.

Tooro Botanical Gardens GARDENS

(www.toorobotanicalgardens.org; Km 2 Kampala Rd; admission USh5000; ⊙8am-5pm) Making for an enjoyable visit, this organic farming project grows herbs, flowers, trees, natural dyes, vegetables and medicinal plants. Admission includes a tour through the extensive grounds where you can ask about the various plants.

Mugusu Market MARKET

(Kasese Rd) The Wednesday market, 11km south of Fort Portal, is the largest market in the west and attracts traders from all over, including many from the DRC.

CA Bikes Uganda CYCLING

(☎0382-280357; www.cabikesuganda.com) This NGO rents out bicycles, which are good way to explore the surrounding countryside. All money goes to providing free bicycles to the disadvantaged and to schooling orphans.

Tours

Kabarole Tours TOUR

(☎0483-422183; www.kabaroletours.com, rtooro@yahoo.com; 1 Moledina St; ⊙8am-6pm Mon-Sat, 10am-4pm Sun) The best way to enjoy Fort Portal and its surrounds is to stop by the reputable Kabarole Tours – it can take you anywhere in Uganda but focuses on its little corner of the country, including day trips to the Crater Lakes, tours of Queen Elizabeth and Kibale national parks and trekking trips into the foothills of the Rwenzoris. The company hires cars ($100/70 for sedan/4WD with driver per day) and mountain bikes (USh20,000 per day) and can give you some rough maps of the area, or send a guide with you. It can also arrange gorilla permits for a fee for both Uganda (US$30) and Rwanda ($US50).

Sleeping

The best accommodation is found in the scenic outskirts of Fort Portal at Boma or the nearby Crater Lakes, but there's a few decent options in the town itself.

TOWN CENTRE

Golf Course View Guesthouse GUESTHOUSE $

(☎0772-485602; golfcourse71@gmail.com; Rwenzori Rd; s/d incl full breakfast from USh30,000/60,000) Probably the best value in town with spacious comfortable rooms, huge bathrooms featuring bathtubs with piping hot

Southwestern Uganda

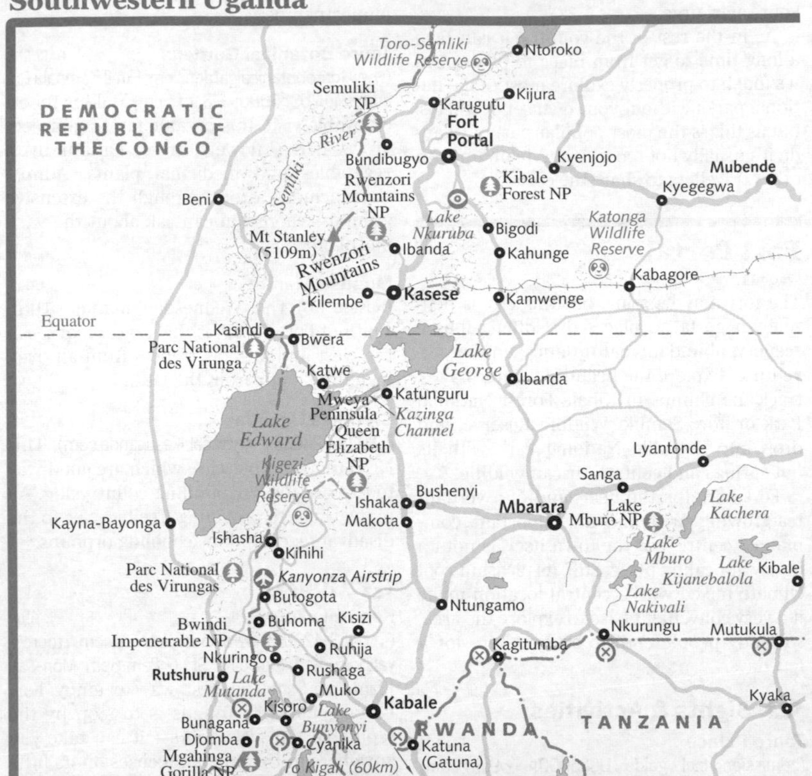

water. There's a restaurant, bar and a kitchen that guests are free to use. While there are no views of the golf course (it's situated across the road from it), on a clear day you can sneak views of the Rwenzoris.

Rwenzori Travellers Inn HOTEL $
(☎0483-422075; www.rwenzoritravellersinn.com; 16 Kyebambe Rd; s excl breakfast USh36,000, d USh52,000-87,000; @) This two-storey hotel with a range of rooms is still a popular choice, though it seems to be coasting on its reputation these days. Prices are high and they've fallen behind in minor maintenance: look at a couple of rooms before taking the keys. Still, you could do much worse and, with a good restaurant, two bars, an internet cafe, and craft shop on site, it's certainly a convenient stop.

Continental Hotel HOTEL $
(☎0772-484842; Lugard Rd; s USh25,000, with shared bathroom USh15,000) Far from the friendliest place in town, this centrally located spot is also not the scruffiest. And, since the rooms have TV and hot water showers, it's the pick of the budget options.

AROUND FORT PORTAL

The leafy and peaceful suburb of Boma just north of town has good mountain views and Fort Portal's best lodging. It's made even more appealing by the fact that downtown Fort Portal is one of Uganda's noisiest places.

TOP CHOICE **Kyaninga Lodge** RESORT $$$
(☎0772-999750; www.kyaningalodge.com; s/d incl full board $US270/390;) A long time in the making, the stunning Kyaninga Lodge has been worth the wait. Eight beautifully designed thatched-roof log cottages soar high upon stilts, and are adjoined by a wooden walking platform that makes for a spectacular sight – as do its views over Kyaninga Lake. The log cabins are spacious, private

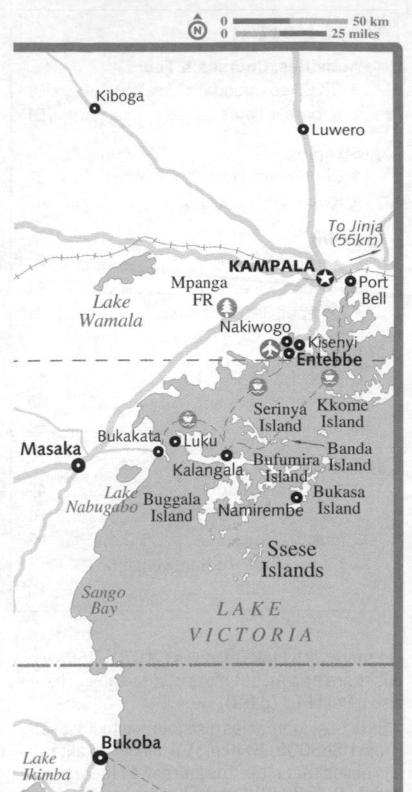

and comfortable, with shining wooden floors, and bathrooms with classy touches, such as clawfoot baths and marble countertop basins. The restaurant also has amazing views; you can dine on the outdoor decking or inside the heavy wooden interior that resembles a cosy Nepali teahouse complete with fireplace. There's a swimming pool and sundeck for when the sun beats down during the day. It's located 12km northeast from Fort Portal, and is a pleasant place to walk or cycle to for lunch here. Otherwise it's about Ush5000 by boda-boda.

RuwenZori View Guesthouse GUESTHOUSE **$$**
(☎0483-422102; www.ruwenzoriview.com; Lower Kakiiza Rd; s/d excl breakfast USh74,000/99,000, without bathroom 45,000/70,000;) A blissful little guesthouse run by a Dutch–Anglo couple, it feels refreshingly rural and has a lovely homely atmosphere. The rooms with attached bathrooms have their own patios overlooking the lovely garden. Rates include a hearty breakfast, while dinners (USh25,000) are served around the family table.

Y.E.S. Hostel BACKPACKERS **$**
(☎0772-780350; www.caroladamsministry.com/yes_hostel.html; Lower Kakiiza Rd; camping USh7000, dm USh10,000, s/d USh15,000/20,000; @) The hostel at this Christian charity, which supports orphans, is simple but remarkably tidy and offers a nice pastoral setting. There's a large kitchen, solar hot-water showers and internet access; and with 50 beds (four to six per room) but relatively few guests (unless a large group is there), you usually get a room to yourself. It's 3km from the centre; a boda-boda costs USh1500. There are some long-term volunteer opportunities available, and the staff can also connect people to schools and hospitals in the area for those with less time to volunteer.

Mpora Rural Family HOMESTAY **$**
(☎0752-555732; www.ugandahomestay.com; camping incl full board €10, banda excl bathroom per person €20) Morence Mpora has long been offering accommodation at his orphanage in an effort to help finance it, as well as the two schools he runs. Visitors are welcome to volunteer or just enjoy the friendly, rural setting; either way, it's a rewarding experience. Many people end up sticking around for a long time. It also hires mountain bikes (per day €10). Minibus drivers can drop you off at the Kichwamba–Kihondo Trading Centre (USh2000, 45 minutes) 15km from Fort Portal on the road to Bundibugyo. Then it's a little over 1km to walk: turn left at the Kisanga Valley School and start asking directions soon after.

Mountains of the Moon Hotel HOTEL **$$**
(☎0483-423200; www.mountainsofthemoon.co.ug; Nyaika Ave; s/d incl full breakfast from $US85/110; @) This colonial-era gem reopened in 2007 following an extensive makeover that added lots of eclectic little touches. All rooms have terraces and guests have use of a gym, a sauna and a business centre. Prices are high, but so are the standards. There's an excellent restaurant here with a good selection of international dishes (mains USh8000 to USh10,000).

Eating & Drinking

TOP CHOICE **Gluepot Bar & Pizzeria** PIZZERIA **$**
(☎0701-367711; www.gluepotpizzeria.com; Kahoyo Rd; pizzas USh8000-21,000; ⌚8.30am-midnight

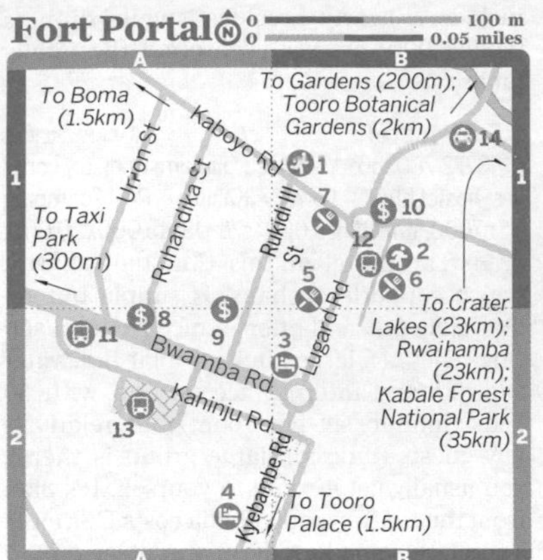

Fort Portal

Activities, Courses & Tours
1 CA Bikes Uganda ... B1
2 Kabarole Tours ... B1

Sleeping
3 Continental Hotel ... B2
4 Rwenzori Travellers Inn ... A2

Eating
5 Andrew & Brothers ... B1
6 Exotic Lodge ... B1
7 Gluepot Bar & Pizzeria ... B1

Information
8 Barclays Bank ... A2
9 Centenary Bank ... A2
10 Stanbic Bank ... B1

Transport
11 Coaster to Hoima ... A2
12 Kalita Transport Office ... B1
13 Link Coaches ... A2
14 Shared-Taxis to Kamwenge & Rwaihamba ... B1

Tue-Sun) Just off the main road, Gluepot does wonderful thin-crust pizzas, and is always busy with foreigners and locals – either here for food or to watch football in its rowdy upstairs bar. Home delivery costs an additional USh1000.

Gardens AFRICAN, INTERNATIONAL $
(Lugard Rd; mains USh3000-11,000; 7am-11pm) Pulling in much of the safari traffic passing through Fort Portal, this busy spot has a lively menu of foreign and local dishes including vegetable curry, fish stew, pizza, *firinda* (mashed skinless beans) and lots of *mochomo* (barbecued meat). There's also a good liquor list and a large African lunch buffet.

Exotic Lodge UGANDAN $
(Moledina St; mains USh3000-5000) A solid choice to try some Ugandan staples. Many locals lunch here.

Andrew & Brothers SUPERMARKET
(Lugard Rd) For those needing to buy their own provisions, this is the best of several supermarkets in town.

Information

Lugard Rd, Fort's main drag, has just about everything travellers may need including craft shops, internet cafes, post office and banks, including **Stanbic Bank** (Lugard Rd) and **Barclays Bank** (Babitha Rd).

Getting There & Away

BUS There's daily buses to Kampala (USh15,000, four hours) with **Kalita Transport** (Map p386; 0702-316155) but you can also get there with **Link Coaches** (0701-966181); buses are pricier, but more comfortable. There's also a Post Bus (p491).

Both bus companies also journey to Kasese (from USh5000, 1½ hours), while only Kalita has buses that make the journey all the way to Kabale (USh20,000, eight hours), via Katunguru (USh8000, 1½ hours) for Queen Elizabeth National Park, from the Kalita bus park opposite the taxi park. Tickets can be purchased from Kalita Transport Office on Lugard Rd. It also has a bus to Kamwenge (USh7000, one hour) for Kibale Forest National Park.

The easiest way to Hoima (USh25,000, six hours) is the coaster that goes at 7am every other day from in front of the Bata shoe store, but you can also do the trip by minibus in two stages: first to Kagadi (USh10,000, three hours) and then to Hoima (USh13,000, four hours).

TAXI Regularish departures from the **Taxi Park** (Malibo Rd) to Kampala (USh16,000, four hours), Ntoroko (USh5000, three hours) and Bundibugyo (USh7000, three hours); often in the backs of pick-up trucks for the latter two.

Minibuses and shared-car taxis to Mbarara (USh17,000, 3½ hours), Kamwenge (for Kibale Forest National Park; USh8000, 45 minutes) and Rwaihamba (for Lake Nkuruba; USh4000, 30 minutes) leave from the intersection near where the main road crosses the river.

SPECIAL-HIRE Drivers hang around the vacant lot by the Continental Hotel and charge from

USh100,000 per day if you aren't travelling too far. Kabarole Tours has 4WDs with driver for US$70 per day.

Around Fort Portal

CRATER LAKES

The landscape south of Fort Portal is dotted with picturesque crater lakes (some over 400m deep), all of which are ringed with improbably steep hills. It's a great spot to settle in for a few days to explore the footpaths or cycle the seldom-used roads. Much of the land is cultivated, but there are still plenty of primates and birds at the lake shores. Accommodation caters for all budgets and it's increasingly popular for visitors to stay at the lakes before continuing on to Kibale Forest National Park.

Most lodges and guesthouses organise walks through the local villages or to other area attractions (which have entrance fees if you go without a guide) such as **Top of the World** (admission USh5000) viewpoint on the highest hill behind Lake Nyamirima where you can see up to five lakes (depending on the air clarity) and **Mahoma Waterfall** (admission USh5000); small but attractive and a great spot for a natural power-shower.

The common wisdom is that the lakes are bilharzia-free, but we wouldn't risk it. Also be aware that a lone hippo roams between Nyamirima, Nyinabulitwa, Nyamikere and, according to some, Nkuruba, so check with locals before plunging into the waters.

LAKE NKURUBA

Probably the winner among the contenders for title of most beautiful crater lake, Nkuruba is one of the few still surrounded by forest. Many monkeys, including black-and-white and red colobus, frolic here. If you want to stay here, supplies are available in the village of Rwaihamba, 2km away.

There are two competing places for accommodation here: we can only recommend one; for further information about the other, ask locals from around the backpacker hostels in Kampala or people involved in the tourism industry in the Fort Portal area. As the blue and yellow sign at the entrance gate says, **Lake Nkuruba Nature Reserve Community Campsite** (☎0773-266067; camping USh6000, tent hire USh6000, dm USh16,000, lakeside cottage USh30,000, banda USh50,000) is the original. It's owned by the Catholic Church and the funds go towards community projects. The camp is set on a hill with some nice views and there's easy access to the lake. The *bandas* are clean and comfortable: some have private bathroom and others function as dorms (two to four beds). The cottage is down on the lakeshore for more privacy. Meals will set you back USh7000 to USh13,000. Guides lead walks all around the area. It's USh10,000 per person for a quick village tour, and you can add Top of the World to this for another USh10,000. There's plenty of birds here; keep your eye out for the great blue turaco. There are also black-and-white colobus monkeys, and is possible to do night tours to spot bushbabies. Bicycles (USh10,000 to USh15,000 per day) and motorcycles (USh40,000) are available for exploring the area on your own.

Minibuses and shared-car taxis from Fort Portal to Rwaihamba pass Lake Nkuruba (USh4000, 45 minutes), as do the trucks going to Kasenda, but they're not frequent, even on market days (Monday and Thursday). A special-hire will set you back about USh30,000, and a boda-boda USh15,000.

LAKE NYINABULITWA

Yet another beautiful and tranquil spot, the mid-sized 'Mother of Lakes', set back a bit off the road to Kibale Forest National Park, is home to the expensive (ask about discounts) but attractive **Nyinabulitwa Country Resort** (☎0712-984929; www.nyinabulitwaresort.com; camping incl full breakfast US$15, s US$70-80, d US$120-140, tr US$180-210), an intimate little place on the lake's south shore with five *bandas* and an excellent camping ground. With a beautiful garden setting, it's the perfect place to catch up on your journal. It does boat trips (US$10 per person) around the lake and can deliver you to a treehouse for bird- and primate-watching, otherwise you can paddle around yourself for free. It's 20km from Fort Portal, 1.5km off the main road just before Rweetera Trading Centre.

LAKE NYABIKERE

The 'Lake of Frogs' (you'll hear how it got its name at night!) lies just off the road to Kibale Forest National Park, 12km northwest of Kanyanchu visitor centre or 21km from Fort Portal. A recommended footpath circles the lake.

Facilities at the longest running Crater Lakes accommodation, **CVK Lakeside Resort** (☎0772-906549; info@kibaleforestcvklakesideresort.com; camping per tent US$10, dm excl breakfast USh20,000, s USh35,000, r USh70,000; 📶) are fairly basic, but the prices are right.

Meals from the restaurant-bar cost USh5000 to USh19,000 for a buffet. The resort can rustle up a canoe (USh10,000) if you fancy a paddle. It's just past Rweetera Trading Centre. Any minibus (USh5000) heading south from Fort Portal can drop you right at the entrance.

Not actually on the lake, but near enough to snatch some views of it, **Chimpanzee Forest Guesthouse** (0772-486415; www.chimpanzeeforestguesthouse.com; camping US$8, s/d incl full breakfast US$50/70, s/d cottages US$60/90) is ambitiously priced based on the quality of the accommodation (two of the rooms even share a shower) but people love the gardens, its valley views and the warm welcome. Meals, mostly local with some international touches cost USh20,000 to USh30,000, and it grows some of its own vegetables. The entrance is 300m south of the Kibale Forest National Park office on the Fort Portal Rd.

LAKE NYINAMBUGA

Emblazoned on Uganda's USh20,000 note, picturesque Lake Nyinambuga is home to the luxurious **Ndali Lodge** (0772-221309; www.ndalilodge.com; s/d incl full board US$240/340; @) with its stunning location on a ridge above the lake. The restaurant looks out this way, while the elegant cottages face west towards Mwamba and Rukwanzi lakes with the Rwenzori Mountains looming on the horizon. It makes for a lovely stopover for lunch with homely toasted sandwiches served on its tranquil porch.

LAKE KIFURUKA

Probably the least interesting of the crater lakes, but pleasant nevertheless, here you can stay at the **Lake Kifuruka Eco-Camp** (0772-562513; lakelyantonde@yahoo.com; camping USh5000, bandas s/d excl breakfast USh15,000/30,000), 2km southwest of Rwaihamba. Its log cabin *bandas* are very basic, but it remains a work in progress and proceeds go to funding local schools. It's a good spot for those wanting to do a stint of volunteer teaching. Here's also the place to arrange walks to Mahoma Falls (guide USh10,000), a three-hour return trip. Staff are friendly and meals are available from USh5000.

LAKE KASENDA

Little Lake Kasenda isn't at the end of the road, but it sure feels like it. **Ruigo Planet Beach** (0701-370674; camping USh10,000, s/d/tr excl breakfast USh20,000/50,000/100,000) sits right down on its shore looking up at the steep hills on the other side. Considering how few people come here it's rather surprising how well maintained the three self-contained *bandas* are. The 'treehouse' is secluded on the other side of the lake, and great for those who want solitude. The beer is cold, but it sometimes runs out: a good reason to call ahead. Despite the name, there's no actual beach, but you can relax by the lake on its pleasant lawn. There's plenty of thick forest for walking and you can easily wander over to nearby lakes Mulusi and Murigamire. Birdwatching and forest walks can be arranged for USh10,000. Day entry for non-guests is USh5000 and meals are a pricey USh15,000 to USh20,000.

Ruigo Beach is 35km south of Fort Portal and 11km south of Rwaihamba, from where a boda-boda will cost USh5000. You can drive here in about one hour: call to ask if the road is still in good enough shape for a car to make it. A special-hire from Fort Portal should cost around USh80,000, but drivers are unlikely to know where it is.

KIHINGAMI WETLAND

This **eco-tourism site** (0779-775790; 8am-5pm), set up with the help of Fort Portal's Kabarole Tours, preserves an attractive 15-sq-km valley that otherwise would have been gobbled up by the surrounding tea plantations. Despite its small size, a remarkable 384 bird species have been spotted here, including Jameson's wattle-eye and white-spotted flufftail. There's also a good chance of seeing red colobus monkeys and spotted-necked otters. Local guides lead forest walks (USh20,000 per person) and birdwatching walks (USh20,000 per person), and for an extra USh5000 you can plant a tree. You can also tour a fair-trade tea factory (US$45 per group of 10 people) at 9am and 2pm.

Kihingami is 15km east of Fort Portal, just before the Sebitoli section of Kibale Forest National Park. Take any minibus (USh2000, 30 minutes) heading east.

AMABEERE CAVE

The water dripping from the roof of this small **cave** (admission USh5000; 8am-6pm) is milky white, hence the name Amabeere ('Breasts'). Most of the rock formations are broken, but it's fun to walk behind the waterfall covering it and past the wall of vines along the adjacent ridge.

It's 8km northwest of Fort Portal, signposted 1.5km off the Bundibugyo road. It's a nice walking destination; Kabarole Tours (p417) in Fort Portal can set you off in the right direction, though it's probably easier to minibus (USh2500, 30 minutes) there and walk back.

Kibale Forest National Park

☎ 0483

Kibale is a lush tropical rainforest, believed to have the highest density of primates in Africa. This 795-sq-km **national park** (☎0483-425335; adult/child US$35/20; ⊙8am-5pm) is home to 13 primate species, including the rare red colobus and L'Hoest's monkey. The stars of the show are the chimpanzees, three groups of which have been habituated to human contact.

Larger but rarely seen residents include bushbuck, sitatunga, buffaloes, leopard and quite a few forest elephants. While on the smaller side, Kibale also has a great birdlist (over 375 species), but keen birdwatchers may want to bypass it and concentrate their time in Bigodi Wetland Sanctuary and Kihingami Wetland where open-canopy and wetland species can be seen alongside most of the same forest species living in the national park. There are also an incredible 250 species of butterfly that live here.

The park visitor centre is at Kanyanchu, 35km southeast of Fort Portal.

KIBALE FOREST NATIONAL PARK

Why Go The best place to track chimpanzees in the wild in Uganda; excellent birdwatching in nearby Bigodi Wetland Sanctuary.

When to Go Year-round.

Practicalities Regular minibuses to Kamwenge from Fort Portal. Prebooking permits in Kampala recommended.

Activities

Chimpanzee Tracking WILDLIFE WATCHING
(US$150 per person; ⊙8am & 2pm) With around a 90% chance of finding them on any particular day, Kibale Forest National Park is undoubtedly the most popular place to track chimpanzees in Uganda. It's also the most expensive, costing US$150 per person (though keep in mind the price includes park permit). While you've a good chance of being issued a chimp permit at the park, it occasionally gets booked out (particularly during the holiday season), so if you've really got your heart set on seeing the chimps, reservations at the UWA office in Kampala (see p482) are a very good idea. Chimp tracking takes place twice per day, in the morning and afternoon, and while there are plenty of hills along the trails, the walking isn't difficult if you're in shape. Children aged 12 and under aren't permitted. Regular trackers get just one hour with the playful primates, but those on the **Chimpanzee Habituation Experience** (1-/2-/3-days US$220/440/660) can spend the whole day with them. If you want to join the experience, you must the spend night before at Kanyanchu, since you head out to the nests around 5.30am.

Nature Walks WILDLIFE WATCHING
(US$15) You'll be very lucky to see chimps on a nature walk but, since nearly 1500 dwell here, you never know your luck, and there's a good chance you'll hear some scamper off through the treetops. Nature walks are also offered at the seldom-visited Sebitoli sector, 12km east of Fort Portal. This is the place to come if you want to see blue monkeys and some chimpanzees are in the process of habituation here. With frequent sightings of owls, civets and the 12cm-long Demidoff's dwarf galago, **night walks** (US$30 per person; ⊙7.30pm) can be very rewarding.

Bigodi Wetland Sanctuary BIRDWATCHING
(☎0772-886865; www.bigodi-tourism.org; ⊙7.30 am-5pm) Located 6km south of the Kibale Forest National Park visitor centre at Kanyanchu (so no park permit is required), Bigodi was established by the local development organisation Kibale Association for Rural and Environment Development (KAFRED) to protect the 4-sq-km **Magombe Swamp**. It's home to around 200 species of birds, as well as butterflies and eight different species of primates, including grey-cheeked mangabey. Three-hour guided walks (USh30,000 per person, including binoculars and gumboots) depart from the visitor centre on demand and some of the guides are birding specialists who can help you find papyrus gonolek, white-winged warbler and great blue turaco.

Other activities available from the visitor centre include **village walks** (USh20,000 per person), Saturday-afternoon **basket weaving demonstrations**, **dance** and **drama**

performances, and fun **interpretive meals** (USh10,000 per person; book in advance) where your hosts share the stories behind the local food they serve you. Volunteer opportunities are also available.

Any shared taxis (USh6000, 45 minutes) between Fort Portal and Kamwenge can drop you there.

Sleeping & Eating

Besides the following places, you can easily visit Kibale while spending the night in Fort Portal or at the Crater Lakes.

TOP CHOICE **Chimps' Nest** LODGE $$
(☎0774-669107; www.chimpsnest.com; camping US$5, dm US$8, cottages incl full breakfast s/d US$60/80, treehouse s/d US$120/150) This stunner of a lodge straddles Kibale Forest and Magombe Swamp, and there's lots of wildlife around, including a profusion of birds, and sometimes elephants and chimps. The lodge covers all options: peaceful camping ground, basic dorms and lovely cottages. But take the treehouse if you can. It's perched up in the canopy among the birds and monkeys, with great 360-degree treetop views right from the bed. The sun powers everything, so there's no generator rattle to ruin the mood. Add US$25 per day if you want full board. Chimps' Nest is 4km down a rough road from Nkingo. A boda-boda from Bigodi costs USh3000, or, with advance notice, the lodge owners might pick you up.

Primate Lodge LODGE $$
(☎0414-267153; www.ugandalodges.com; camping excl breakfast USh15,000, treehouse USh50,000, cottages s/d incl full board US$110/150, safari tents s/d incl full board US$190/330) Right in the thick of the forest at Kanyanchu, this renovated lodge operated by Great Lakes Safaris has a good choice of accommodation. The lovely cottages, with stone floors and verandahs, are a better bet than the nice but overpriced safari tents, but, if you don't mind roughing it a little, take the treehouse (secluded in the forest 800m from the lodge), which overlooks an elephant wallow; if you're very lucky you might see one. The lounge area surrounds two fire pits and has a well-regarded restaurant. The lodge also manages the camping ground and serves an à la carte menu (mains USh15,000 to USh20,000) next to the visitor centre.

Tinka's Homestay GUESTHOUSE $
(☎0772-468113; per person incl full board USh30,000) A wonderful budget option that's perfect for those seeking more of a homestay experience. It's located 6km from the park HQ, right near the visitor centre of Bigodi Wetland Sanctuary, convenient if you're here to see birds as well as chimps.

Sebitoli Forest Camp LODGE $
(☎0782-761512; camping USh15,000, s/d excl breakfast USh30,000/40,000) Up in the northern end of the park, this budget lodge has a relaxing location surrounded by trees with black-and-white colobus monkeys. The camp is seldom visited, but as it's in the process of habituating chimps in this area, it will eventually become very popular. Staff are friendly and you can arrange chimpanzee permits here, as well as nature walks (US$15).

Getting There & Away

MINIBUS The minibuses to Kamwenge from Fort Portal pass the park visitor centre (USh7000, one hour). For Sebitoli, take any minibus (USh2000, 30 minutes) heading east from Fort Portal.

Semuliki National Park

The Semliki Valley is a little corner of Congo poking into Uganda. The only tropical lowland rainforest in East Africa is a continuation of the huge Ituri Forest in the DRC and forms a link between the heights of East Africa and the vast, steaming jungles of central Africa. The views on the descent into the valley from Fort Portal are breathtaking. The **national park** (☎0382-276424; adult/child US$25/15) covers 220 sq km of the valley floor and harbours some intriguing wildlife, though sightings are difficult due to the thick vegetation.

Birdwatchers come for the central African species, such as the Congo serpent eagle, residing at their eastern limits. At least 133 of the 144 Guinea–Congo forest species have been recorded here and nearly 50 species are found nowhere else in East Africa. There are nine primate species, including De Brazza's monkey, and many mammals not found elsewhere in Uganda, such as Zenker's flying mice. Both the resident elephant and buffalo are the forest variety, smaller than their savannah brethren.

SEMULIKI NATIONAL PARK

Why Go Sulphur hot springs, primate walks.

When to Go Year-round.

Practicalities Minibuses and pick-ups head from Fort Portal to Bundibugyo, near park headquarters. There's only basic accommodation here, so day trips are a popular way to see the park.

Sights & Activities

Semuliki Hot Springs NATURAL SITE

(per person incl guide US$15) Most people are here to see the steamy sulphur **hot springs**, which, while not on the same scale as Rotorua (New Zealand) and Iceland, make for an impressive and unexpected sight nevertheless. There are two hot springs, and admission is the same price whether you visit one or both. The 'female' hot spring is the more accessible of the two, and was where women from the Bamaga clan would make sacrifices to the gods before bathing naked in the natural springs. Its steamy, soupy atmosphere has a distinct prehistoric feel, and features a small burbling geyser. Your guide can demonstrate the water's temperatures by boiling an egg – available from the information centre for USh500 each; though with the stench of sulphur it's probably the last thing you feel like eating. The 'male' spring, a half-hour's walk, is where the men carried out their sacrificial rituals, and is accessed via a muddy forest trail with plenty of primates and birdlife along the way. It leads to a verdant clearing of swamp where a boardwalk passes through sweeping grass and squawking frogs to the hot spring located in a 12m pool.

Twa (Batwa) Village CULTURAL SITE

(per person USh35,000) Located outside the park in Bundimusoli, the Twa people were relocated here when the park was established and, with no other choice, have since adopted agriculture, but they're keeping hold of their traditions as best as possible. The park allows them to collect rattan, leaves, mushrooms, medicines and other forest products and even practise limited hunting. Village visits are arranged at the **Office of the King of Batwa** (☎0781-553853) in Ntandi, 5km past the Sempaya Gate; the village is another 2km away. Tours include singing and dancing. As with many Twa settlements, living conditions here are extremely poor; see p446 for more information about visiting the Twa in this region.

Walking Trails HIKING

Walking options include the 11km **Kirimia Trail**, which is a full-day romp through the heart of the forest and the favoured destination of birdwatchers; and the somewhat shorter but hillier **Red Monkey Trail**. Both end at the Semliki River, which forms the border between Uganda and the DRC.

Sleeping & Eating

Bumaga Campsite CAMPGROUND $

(camping USh15,000, r excl breakfast USh30,000) Pleasant grassy campsite on the edge of the forest with several *bandas,* and a campsite with showers and latrines. There's a lovely elevated dining area, but you may need to bring your own food. You'll need to arrange accommodation at the UWA office at the Sempaya gate. The campsite is located 2km past the gate.

Getting There & Away

CAR The park is just 52km from Fort Portal, but plan on two hours to reach it by car in the dry season.

MINIBUS There are regular minibuses and pick-ups between Fort Portal and Bundibugyo that pass the park (USh10,000, three hours). The last one heads to Fort Portal around 4pm, so if you leave early and hustle on the trails, you can see the hot springs and hike the Red Monkey Trail as a day trip.

BUS You can also catch Kalita Transport's Kampala–Bundibugyo bus in Fort Portal departing at approximately 5pm for USh10,000; it returns to Fort Portal around 5am.

Toro-Semliki Wildlife Reserve

The **Toro-Semliki Wildlife Reserve** (☎0772-649880; adult/child US$25/15) is the oldest protected natural area in Uganda, having first been set aside in 1926. Once one of the best-stocked and most popular wildlife parks in East Africa, it suffered significantly during the civil war years and, after the war with Tanzania, the Tanzanian soldiers went home with truckloads of dead bush-meat.

Wildlife is recovering and you may encounter waterbuck, reedbucks, bushbuck, buffaloes, leopard, elephants and hyenas. A number of lions has also recently returned to the reserve, most likely refugees from the conflict in the DRC.

Activities

Chimpanzee Tracking WILDLIFE WATCHING
(per person $US30) Likely the best wildlife experience in the park is the morning chimp tracking (which the park prefers to call a primate walk). The hiking is more difficult than in Kibale and you're a little less likely to encounter chimps, but, when you do, the thinner forest means your views are superior. These are rare 'dry-habitat chimps' that spend considerable time in the savannah and so walk upright more often than the others.

Safari Drives WILDLIFE WATCHING
With a line of mountains behind it, the savannah scenery from the main road is often superb, but the wildlife viewing along it isn't: Ugandan kob and baboons are the only sure things. Best to get a ranger (US$20) from the park headquarters to lead you down other tracks. You don't need to be a guest of Semliki Safari Lodge to join its spotlit night drives (US$50 per vehicle).

Nature Walks WALKING
(per person US$15) Rangers also lead nature walks in various places around the park, including **Nyaburogo Gorge** behind the headquarters (which has lots of primates, butterflies and snakes), along the shore of **Lake Albert** and – via the steep climb to great views atop the mountains – on the southeastern edge of the park. Some people arrange for a driver to take them to the top of the mountain (via Fort Portal) and then walk down to the lodge.

Boat Trips WILDLIFE WATCHING
A **Lake Albert boat trip** will likely reveal hippo and crocodiles, but it's mostly undertaken by birdwatchers for the near-guaranteed **shoebill stork** sightings. Semliki Safari Lodge charges US$180 for a half-day on the water. You could also arrange the trip with fishers in Ntoroko village for about half the price: in a boat about half the size.

Sleeping & Eating

Ntoroko has some basic guesthouses but are not recommended and attract some shady characters; so if you try them, don't leave any valuables behind in your room.

UWA Campsites CAMPGROUND $
(camping USh15,000, bandas excl breakfast per person USh20,000) The small UWA campsite at Ntoroko is on the shores of Lake Albert, meaning you often have hippos joining you in the evening. There are three *bandas* without bathrooms here and you can either cook your own food or head into the village for meals. There's a brand new campsite (no *bandas* yet, but they're planned) at the headquarters, a more convenient but less attractive location; bring your own food.

Semliki Safari Lodge TENTED LODGE $$$
(☎0414-251182; www.wildplacesafrica.com; s/d incl full board US$570/810;) One of the first luxury lodges in Uganda, here there are eight luxury tents set under thatched *bandas,* and all with Persian carpets and four-poster beds. The lounge and dining room feature a huge eaved thatch roof, with plush furnishings, Congolese crafts and plenty of room to relax. While it's well overpriced for what you get, the prices include all food, alcohol and park activities.

Getting There & Away

CAR Head west toward Bundibugyo and then fork right at Karugutu, 27km from Fort Portal; the headquarters is 3km further on. A car can handle travel inside the reserve, but ask about conditions between Fort Portal and Karugutu as the road can be quite poor.

MINIBUS & TRUCK Connecting Fort Portal to Ntoroko (USh10,000, three hours), minibuses and trucks can drop you at the park headquarters. You could also get one of the more frequent Bundibugyo-bound vehicles and get off at Karugutu (USh5000, 1½ hours), to continue on from there.

Katonga Wildlife Reserve

Sights & Activities

The small, seldom-visited **Katonga Wildlife Reserve** (☎0772-365713; admission US$25) is certainly one of the best places to spy the elusive sitatunga antelope, known for its curious webbed feet. If you start your guided nature walk (US$15 per person) at 6am or 7pm you have an excellent chance of an encounter with its residents. Black-and-white colobus monkeys, red and blue duiker, reedbuck, a few elephant and loads of waterbuck can also be seen in the savannah. The southern side of the reserve is papyrus swamp.

Sleeping & Eating

There's a decent **dormitory** (per person USh10,000) with showers and electricity and a very basic **campsite** (per person USh15,000). Both sit on a hill way back from the road, but the park staff will drive you there from the headquarters at the reserve entrance; and if you didn't bring your own food to have cooked by the ranger, staff may go into the nearby village of Kabagore (2km from the headquarters) and bring back dinner (USh2000 to USh3000) for you. **Bush camping** (per person USh30,000) is also possible if you have your own gear.

Getting There & Away

The reserve is 40km south of Kyegegwa on the road between Fort Portal and Kampala.

MINIBUS A minibus to Kabagore (USh25,000, five hours) leaves Kampala's New Taxi Park around midday (it goes when it's full) and returns early the next day sometime between 3am and 5am. Another minibus connects Kabagore to Kyegegwa (USh10,000, 1½ hours) at 10am the next day, returning in the afternoon. If coming from Fort Portal, you'll have to change vehicles at Kyegegwa (USh5000, two hours). You can also get from Kabagore to Mbarara (USh10,000, three hours) on a 7am coaster, which turns around and comes back right away. Hitching from the reserve in either direction is pretty easy.

Kasese

☎ 0483 / POP 71,700

The long-closed Kilembe Copper Mines once brought great prosperity to this drab and dusty town, and the also-defunct train line from Kampala used to deposit a steady stream of visitors here. But now Kasese seems to have passed its use-by date and the only reason travellers come here is to organise an assault on the Rwenzori Mountains.

If you have to spend some time here, nearby Kilembe, in the foothills of the Rwenzoris, is an interesting town to walk through with all the old mining equipment and company housing.

Sleeping & Eating

There are some fairly well-stocked supermarkets for those heading up to the mountains, including **Titi's** (Rwenzori Rd), **ASWT** (Margarita St) and **City Top** (Rwenzori Rd).

See also the Sleeping & Eating section in the Rwenzori Mountains, which has the best budget options and the added convenience of being right near the trailhead.

TOP CHOICE **Rwenzori The Gardens** HOTEL $
(☎0772-466461; www.rwenzori-hotel.webs.com; Bukonjo Rd; r/cottage/ste incl full breakfast from USh50,000/70,000/100,000; ❄📶) With big heavy security gates, stone paved driveway, manicured lawn, water features and a stately white building, it feels like you've arrived at a Beverly Hills mansion. Standard rooms are excellent value – being squeaky clean, with air-con and big beds; though dainty touches like floral bedsheets won't be to everyone's taste. It has a lovely garden restaurant at the back, which would be splendid for a tea party. It's tucked away in the outskirts of Kasese, off the road to Kilembe.

White House Hotel GUESTHOUSE $
(☎0782-536263; whitehse_hotel@yahoo.co.uk; 46 Henry Bwambale Rd; s/d excl breakfast without bathroom USh15,000/28,000, r USh35,000; @📶) A mix of cleanliness and good prices makes White House one of Kasese's most popular hotels. The restaurant is pretty good too (meals from USh4500).

Hotel Margherita HOTEL $$
(☎0483-444015; www.hotel-margherita.com; s/d/ste/apt incl full breakfast from US$70/95/140/190; ❄@📶) Though it's still the fanciest option in town, Hotel Margherita's long silent corridors and dated '70s decor makes you feel like you're stepping onto the film set of *The Shining*. If that doesn't spook you, it has a delightful setting looking out towards the Rwenzoris, and some rooms feature amazing views. A few more shillings will get you air-con and a fridge, but rooms here are ultimately overpriced. It has a good restaurant that does everything from American burgers, BBQ goat ribs, cassava fries to roast duck with a Grand Marnier orange glaze! It's located 3km out of town on the road up to Kilembe.

Information

Stanbic Bank (Stanley St) and **Barclays** (cnr Margherita St & Rwenzori Rd) both have branches here. You can get online at **Friends' Café** (Stanley St; per hr USh1800; ⏰8am-9pm Mon-Sat, 10am-8pm Sun) or **White House Hotel**

Getting There & Away

BUS The quickest connection to Kampala (USh20,000, five hours) is the bus via Fort Portal (USh4000, one hour).

See p432 for information on how to get to the trailheads in the Rwenzoris.

Getting to Queen Elizabeth National Park is straightforward. Catch any Mbarara-bound vehicle and ask for the national park entrance (USh3000, one hour), which is signposted on the left just before the village of Katunguru.

Rwenzori Mountains National Park

The legendary, mist-covered Rwenzori Mountains are presumed to be the Mountains of the Moon, described in AD 350 by Ptolemy, who proclaimed them the source of the Nile River. Because of both its beauty and biodiversity, Unesco named the Rwenzoris a World Heritage Site. It's the tallest mountain range in Africa and several of the peaks are permanently (at least until global warming finishes the job – it has already started up here) covered by ice and glaciers. The three highest peaks in the range are Margherita (5109m), Alexandria (5083m) and Albert (5087m), all on Mt Stanley, the third highest mountain in Africa.

The mountain range, which isn't volcanic, stretches for about 110km by 50km wide and is a haven for an extraordinary number of rare plants and animals, and new examples of both are still being discovered. Two mammals are endemic to the range, the Rwenzori climbing mouse and the Rwenzori red duiker, as are 19 of the 241 known bird species. There's thick tropical rainforest on the lower slopes transitioning to the bizarre afro-alpine moorland on higher reaches.

Activities

Trekking

Back in Uganda's heyday, the Rwenzoris were as popular with travellers as Mt Kilimanjaro and Mt Kenya, but this is definitely a more demanding expedition. The Rwenzoris have a well-deserved reputation for being very wet and muddy, with trails that are often slippery and steep. There are treks available to suit all levels and needs, from one-day jaunts in the forest to 10-day treks with technical climbs. The six-day treks are about the standard.

There are now two companies who look after trekking in the Rwenzoris, with a

Rwenzori National Park

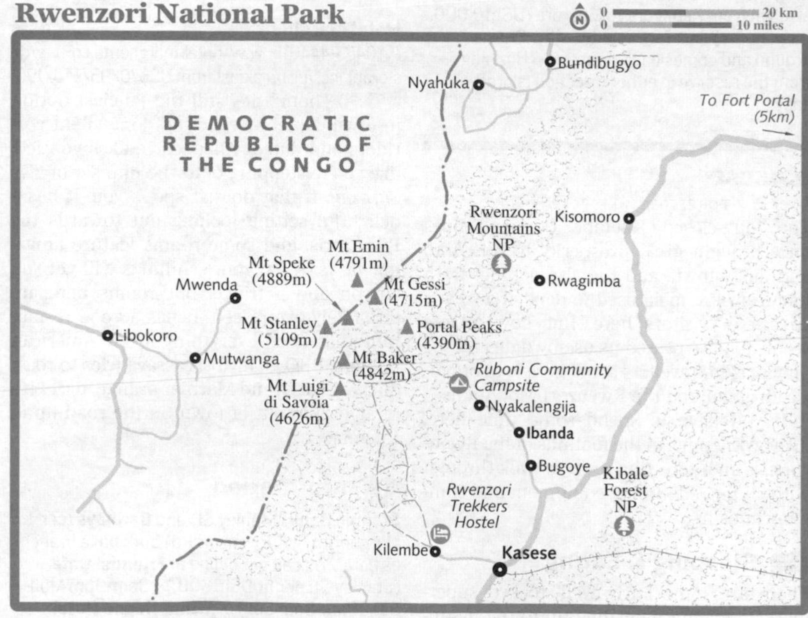

concession recently handed to the popular **Rwenzori Trekking Services** (RTS; ☎0774-199022; www.rwenzoritrekking.com), which looks after the Kilembe Trail, joining the long-established and community-owned **Rwenzori Mountaineering Services** (RMS; ☎0483-444936; www.rwenzorimountaineeringservices.com) based in Kasese, which arranges treks from Nyakalengija.

The best times to trek are from late December to mid-March and from mid-June to mid-August, when there's less rain. Even at these times, the higher reaches are often enveloped in mist, though this generally clears for a short time each day. April and October are the wettest months.

Guides, who are compulsory, even if you've conquered the seven summits, are on perpetual standby so you can book in the morning and leave the same day.

Walking trails and huts are in pretty good shape, particularly on the Kilembe trail, where huts use polynum insulation to make life more comfortable. There are wooden pathways over the bogs and bridges over the larger rivers; all this lessens the impact of walkers on the fragile environment.

EQUIPMENT

The routes to the peaks on Mt Stanley require the use of ice-axes, ropes and crampons (depending on conditions you may have to rope in for Mts Baker and Speke), but you don't need mountaineering experience to reach the summits if your guide is experienced – the catch is that not all of them are. From all reports, the guides from RTS are the most reliable. No special equipment is required for a trek if you don't go onto the ice or snow (and if you do, this gear can be hired at the trailhead), but bring clothing that's warm (temperatures often drop below zero) and waterproof. You'll also want a good sleeping bag. The most important item is a good, broken-in pair of trekking boots to get you over the slippery rock slabs, which can be quite treacherous at times. Gaiters are also highly recommended for the bogs. A small day pack is useful since your porters will travel at their own pace.

Do beware of the dangers of Acute Mountain Sickness (AMS, altitude sickness). In extreme cases it can be fatal. See p661 for more information.

Before attempting a trek in the Rwenzoris get a copy of the *Guide to the Rwenzori* (2006) by Henry Osmaston, which covers routes, natural history and all other aspects of the mountains. A good companion to Osmaston's opus is *Rwenzori Map & Guide,* an excellent large-scale contour map by Andrew Wielochowski.

RWENZORI MOUNTAINS NATIONAL PARK

Why Go Trekking along Africa's tallest mountain range, often through snow.

When to Go Year-round, but late December to mid-March & mid-June to mid-August are less muddy.

Practicalities Treks are booked at the park through Rwenzori Trekking Services (for the Kilembe Trail) and Rwenzori Mountaineering Services (for the Nyakalengija Trail). Kasese is best accessed either from Fort Portal or Queen Elizabeth National Park.

Sleeping & Eating

Rwenzori Trekkers Hostel BACKPACKERS **$**
(Rwenzori Backpackers; ☎0774-199022; www.backpackers.co.ug/rwenzoribackpack.html; camping USh7000, dm USh15,000, s/d USh20,000/35,000) Run by Rwenzori Trekking Services (who run Backpackers in Kampala), this scenic and peaceful option is located in Kyanjiki near Kilembe, 12km outside Kasese, a perfect starting point if you plan on tackling this side of the Rwenzori. Rooms are in restored miners' housing and slightly run-down with peeling linoleum floors, but fine for the price. The **restaurant** (meals USh4000-16,000) has a great trekking menu comprising T-bone steaks, Aussie meat pies, pizzas and a good vegetarian selection. It does some excellent work in the community, and also offers village walks and cultural performances, including drumming lessons.

Ruboni Community Campsite BANDA **$**
(☎0752-503445; www.rubonicamp.com; camping US$3, r with shared bathroom per person US$20, bandas per person US$25) This community-run place down the road from Nyakalengija is at the base of the hill just outside the park boundary, with an attractive setting and comfortable lodging. All profits go towards a health centre, tree planting projects and more. It also offers guided walks into the hills outside the park, drumming lessons and traditional dance performances The

TREKKING IN THE RWENZORIS

The peaks can now be accessed via two routes, with the **Kilembe Trail** opening up recently as an alternative to the long-standing **Central Circuit** that starts from Nyakalengija village.

From Kilembe

Opening up in late 2009, the new Kilembe Trail is proving a hit among trekkers. Organised through **Rwenzori Trekking Services** (RTS; ☎0774-199022; www.rwenzoritrekking.com), and run by John Hunwick of Backpackers Hostel in Kampala, this new company has both lifted the standards and breathed new energy into trekking in the Rwenzoris. While treks to the main peaks are further away compared with the Nyakalengija route, it receives glowing reviews for its professional guides, quality equipment and safety measures, as well as comfortable mountain huts that are being set up along this route.

For groups of one to two people, prices per person start at US$35 for one-day treks, US$240 for three days, US$630 for six days and US$1030 for nine-day treks to Margherita Peak. Prices include guides, porters, equipment, food and accommodation. Note that the price does not include park entry, which is an additional US$30 per day. Prices are slightly lower for groups of three or more trekkers.

A range of tailormade treks are offered, from technical climbs to leisurely strolls in the forested foothills. The most popular is the six-day trek to Weismann's Peak (outlined below), which is at times steep and strenuous; there are no ropes or climbing equipment involved. During April to May and September to October, it's common to experience snowfalls.

DAY 1

Starting from Rwenzori Trekkers Hostel in Kilembe, day one involves a five- to six-hour trek that passes through untouched montane forest that's home to abundant birdlife. Continuing through several river crossings and ridge climbs, keep an eye and ear out for chimps, before you reach the bamboo forest that leads to the first overnight stop at Samalira Camp (3170m).

DAY 2

The next day, a four- to five-hour trek takes you through a series of climbs and descents that lead through valleys of moss-covered rocks, magnificent cliff faces and misty forests before spending the night at Kiharo Camp (3380m).

DAY 3

Another five-hour day, continuing through scenic valleys where peaks loom above, and the reward of reaching camp with amazing views of the nine glacier lakes in Namusangi valley.

DAY 4

Offers more amazing views of Namusangi valley while taking a steep climb to a ridge en route to the summit of Weismann's Peak (4620m) and nearby Stella Peak (4635m), the highest point of the trek, before returning to Camp Three for the evening. It's about a three- to four-hour trek.

DAY 5

Prepare to get muddy as you trudge through boggy moorland, passing waterfalls and views of Mutinda Peak. Continue down the valley to reach the massive Mutinda Rock Shelter, a lovely natural site where tents await and can shelter up to 80 people. A four- to six-hour trek.

DAY 6

The last and the longest day of the trek, which covers 16.7km (ranging from six to 10 hours), beginning with a descent through a rocky valley with flowing streams, leading to a valley of colourful Lobelia plants. The final stretch takes you through more bamboo and montane forest, arriving back at Kilembe mid-afternoon.

From Nyakalengija

The Central Circuit that starts from Nyakalengija village is arranged through **Rwenzori Mountaineering Services** (RMS; www.rwenzorimountaineeringservices.com) Kasese (☎0772-572810; Rwenzori Rd, Kasese; ⏰8am-7pm); Nyakalengija (☎0782-586304; ⏰8.30am-5pm); Kampala (☎0772-523208; UWA compound; ⏰8am-5pm Mon-Fri, 9am-noon Sat). Long-established, and until recently the only company that you could trek with, RMS gets some negative feedback for dodgy equipment and huts that are in dire need of maintenance.

The standard Central Circuit trek costs $US600 per person for the seven days/six night trek, and includes park entrance, rescue fees, guides, porters, accommodation, heating fuel and Value-Added Tax (VAT). It's $US780 if you want to add a Margherita Peak summit. Extra days cost US$120 and extra peaks are US$150. The fee includes two porters per person, who can carry a total of 25kg; additional porters cost US$70. You can either arrange your own food or pay US$140 for RMS to buy it. Gas cookers can be hired for US$50, or you can get a cook for US$10 per day. Unlike RTS, prices do not include equipment, but have the following for hire at USh20,000 a pop: climbing boots, crampons, harnesses, ice-axes, ropes, rubber boots and sleeping bags.

The Central Trail loops back between the peaks of Mts Baker and Stanley taking six days.

DAY 1

Nyakalengija (1646m) to Nyabitaba Hut (2650m) is a fairly easy walk, taking about five hours. There are many primates and some forest elephant around.

DAY 2

The trail drops to cross the Bujuku River and then begins a long ascent on a rough, muddy path that eventually enters the amazing afro-alpine zone just before arriving at John Mate Hut (3505m). This is the longest day's walk (at least seven hours) and the most difficult.

DAY 3

You slog, often knee-deep, through Lower and Upper Bigo Bogs (there's a boardwalk on part of this path) before things dry out and you reach lovely Lake Bujuku, plopped between Mts Baker, Stanley and Speke. After more mud you reach Bujuku Hut (3962m), the base for climbing Mt Speke. This is a three- to five-hour day, depending on how wet things are, so there's usually time to check out the Irene Lakes or, if you want a more alpine experience, continue for three more difficult hours and sleep at Elena Hut (4430m), the primary starting point for ascending Mt Stanley.

DAY 4

The trail cuts through a profusion of giant groundsel before crossing Scott Elliot Pass (4372m), the highest point on the Central Circuit. There's great views of Margherita Peak and Elena and Savoia glaciers. The circuit weaves though boulders at the foot of Mt Baker and passes the twin Kitandara lakes before reaching lakeside Kitandara Hut (4023m).

DAY 5

Begin with a long climb to Freshfield Pass (4282m) and then it's all downhill to the scenically set Guy Yeoman Hut (3505m). On the descent, you pass through a bog to the attractive Kabamba rock shelter and waterfall. Count on at least five hours, but as this is another muddy, slippery stage, it often takes longer.

DAY 6

The start of the trail descends very steeply (which is why almost everyone travels the circuit anti-clockwise) and follows the Mubuku River down for five hours to Nyabitaba Hut. It's possible to spend the night here but by this point almost everyone is ready for a warm shower and a cold beer and continues the last two to three hours back to the bottom. Keep in mind that about an hour from Guy Yeoman Hut there's an unbridged river crossing, and when the river is high it can be dangerous. Your guides will surely want to get over it as fast as possible, but if you have any reservations about this, wait for the river level to fall.

restaurant (mains USh10,000-22,000) here (and another in Nyakalengija village) serves local food and international snacks. It's a great place to stay before or after your trek, but the pastoral setting makes it a great place to visit even if you won't be heading to the park.

Getting There & Away

Nyakalengija is 25km from Kasese, though minibuses only run as far as Ibanda (USh4000, one hour). From here you can take a boda-boda to Nyakalengija (USh4000) or Ruboni Community Camp (USh3500). Chartering a special-hire taxi from Kasese will set you back USh50,000.

For Kilembe (USh2000, 30 minutes), take one of the frequent shared-car taxis from near the Shell petrol station on Kilembe Rd. A special-hire will cost around USh10,000.

Queen Elizabeth National Park

Covering 1978 sq km, **Queen Elizabeth National Park** (☎0782-387805; www.queenelizabethnationalpark.com; adult/child US$35/20; ⏲booking office 6.30am-7pm, park gates 7am-7pm) is one of the most popular in Uganda.

Though the number of animals remains lower than the top Tanzanian and Kenyan parks, few reserves in the world can boast such a high biodiversity rating. With landscape varying from savannah, bushland, wetlands to lush forests, the park is inhabited by 96 species of mammals, including healthy numbers of hippos, elephants, lions and leopard as well as chimps and hyena. The remote Ishasha sector, in the far south of the park, is famous for its tree-climbing lions. There's also an amazing 611 bird species here; more than found in all of Great Britain.

Back in the 1970s, with its great herds of elephants, buffaloes, kob, waterbuck, hippos and topis, Queen Elizabeth was one of the premier safari parks in Africa. But during the troubled 1980s, Ugandan and Tanzanian troops (which occupied the country after Amin's demise) did their ivory-grabbing, trophy-hunting best. Thankfully, animal populations are recovering.

Besides the usual wildlife drives, the park is well worth a visit for a boat trip on the Kazinga Channel and a walk through beautiful Kyambura (Chambura) Gorge, a little Eden brimming with chimpanzees and other primates.

ISHASHA TREE-CLIMBING LIONS

Somewhat off the beaten track in the far southern sector of the park, Ishasha is famous for its population of tree-climbing lions. It's one of the few places in Africa where lions are known to hang out in trees, often found lazing on the sprawling limbs of fig trees during the heat of the day. You stand a reasonable chance of finding them in the morning (before 10am, ideally), unless it's wet, when the lions won't climb trees.

Sights & Activities

Kazinga Channel Launch Trip WILDLIFE WATCHING

(2hr trips $US25; ⏲9am, 11am, 3pm & 5pm) Almost every visitor takes a launch trip up the Kazinga Channel to see the thousands of hippos and pink-backed pelicans, plus plenty of crocodiles, buffaloes and fish eagles. With a little luck, it's also possible to catch sight of one of the elephant herds and – very occasionally – see a lion or a leopard. If numbers are low you may have to chip in to cover the boat's minimum USh300,000 charge. The boat docks below Mweya Safari Lodge, but you buy tickets at the UWA visitor centre next door. The lodge also has its own channel trips at 9am, 11am, 3pm and 4.15pm. It charges $24, or US$35 with drinks and fruit.

Wildlife Drives WILDLIFE WATCHING

(guides US$20) Most of the wildlife-viewing traffic is in the northeast of the park in **Kasenyi**, which offers the best chance to see lions, as well as elephants, waterbuck and kob. It's also one the most scenic sections of any park in Uganda, particularly in the morning when its savannah landscape shines golden and is dotted with cactus-like candelabra trees.

There's also a small network of trails between Mweya Peninsula and Katunguru gate that usually reveal waterbuck and kob, elephants and occasionally leopard.

As well as being famous for its tree-climbing lions, **Ishasha** in the south of the Queen

Queen Elizabeth National Park

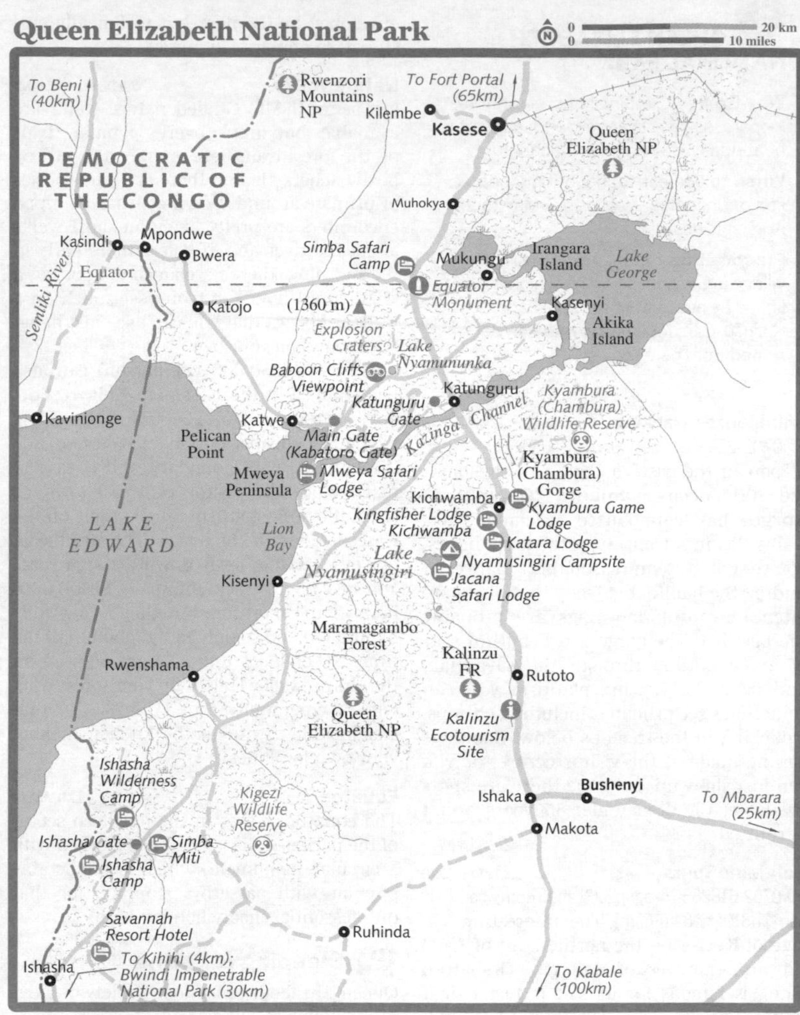

Elizabeth National Park is the only place to see topis and sitatunga.

Three salt lakes in the Kyambura (Chambura) Wildlife Reserve, behind Kyambura (Chambura) Gorge, sometimes attract huge numbers of flamingos, but they only nest at Lake Maseche north of Mweya on the road to Katwe. The 'explosion craters' in this area make for a beautiful drive, but there's not much wildlife to scrutinise. Baboon Cliffs gives excellent views over the surrounding area.

You can get just about everywhere by car if it isn't raining, though having a 4WD is a good idea in Ishasha year-round. If you don't have your own vehicle you can get special-hires from Katunguru. Count on paying US$50/70 for a half-/full day, including fuel and drivers' admission. Otherwise Kabarole Tours (see p417) is a reliable company that can arrange open-top 4WDs. Taking a UWA ranger-guide along for your drive is always a good idea, but more so in Ishasha than anywhere else because they know every fig tree in the area: the lions' preferred perches.

QUEEN ELIZABETH NATIONAL PARK

Why Go Tree-climbing lions, elephants, leopard, scenic savannah landscapes, boat rides along Kazinga Channel.

When to Go Year-round, but dry season of December to March & May to August is best.

Practicalities Katunguru is the main village in the park's centre, which is linked by buses from Kampala and Kasese. Cars for safari drives can be rented from here too.

Chimpanzee tracking WILDLIFE WATCHING
(0702-228292; per person US$50; 8am & 2pm) In the eastern region of the park, the 100m-deep **Kyambura (Chambura) Gorge**, has chimpanzee tracking, with walks lasting from two to four hours. You've got a semi-reasonable chance of finding the habituated troop, but visits are often unfruitful; mornings are probably the best bet. The gorge is a beautiful scar of green cutting through the savannah, and from the viewing platform you can sometimes see primates, including chimps, frolicking in the treetops below. Bookings can be made at the visitor centre, or you can just show up and hope there are spots available. Children under 15 years aren't permitted.

Salt Mine Tours CULTURAL TOUR
(0752-618265; nkagongo@yahoo.com; per person $US10; 8am-6pm) The interesting village of **Katwe** on the north shore of Lake Edward, 4km west of Main gate (Kabatoro gate), is famous for its salt industry. Salt mining on the crater lake behind the village goes back to at least the 15th century, and today some 3000 people still use the same traditional methods. Women pull salt from evaporation ponds when it's dry enough (generally December to March and July to September) while men dig rock salt year-round. Tours are booked at the Katwe Tourism Information Centre on the west side of the village, across from a defunct salt factory. Guides here will also take you birdwatching, give you a **fishing industry tour** (USh50,000 for 5 people; 8am-10am) and accompany you to the Kasindi Market (Tuesday and Friday) in the DRC. Katwe is enveloped by the park but technically outside it, so no park fees apply.

Nature Walks WILDLIFE WATCHING
(per person US$15) Guided nature walks are available, but aren't overly popular. Trips on the forest trails here are taken mostly by birdwatchers, though there are nine species of primate around. Down at Ishasha, hippo encounters are pretty likely on short walks along the river and, if you're there early in the morning, there's a chance of spotting a giant forest hog. You won't see much on a walk at Mweya that you can't see just hanging around on your own.

Walks (USh50,000 per person) can also be arranged in the 147-sq-km **Kalinzu Forest Reserve** (0751-360073; 7am-5pm), which is a cheaper option, as it lies outside the national park boundary, and is easy to reach since the visitor centre, known as the Kalinzu Ecotourism Site, is right on the Kasese–Mbarara highway. The trailhead, however, is 3km away down a rough road. You can try to track chimps (USh100,000) here in the morning, but they're not fully habituated and so only found about half the time. No children under 15 are allowed on the chimp walks. Follow-up your forest walk with a community tour (USh25,000) that can include a turn in the kitchen making your own local meal.

Equator LANDMARK
The equator crosses in the northern sector of the park near Kasenyi and is marked with a circular monument, which is predictably popular with passerbys stopping for that quintessential cheesy holiday snap.

Sleeping & Eating

Queen Elizabeth has a good variety of lodging available to suit all budgets.

MWEYA PENINSULA

The best variety of places to stay is on the Mweya Peninsula. A lot of wildlife roams through here, so you genuinely need to be careful at night; especially if you're walking to/from the Mweya campsite. You can also spot lots of wildlife along the river down below, so it's a great place to pop in for lunch during the day.

Mweya Safari Lodge LODGE $$$
(0312-260260; www.mweyalodge.com; s excl breakfast US$135, d US$240-280, ste US$305, cottages US$520-775;) This large, sophisticated outfit has excellent views over

Lake Edward and the Kazinga Channel, showcased through its huge window in the stunning lobby. The rooms have nice furniture and most have views of water. It's good value by national park lodge standards. Sitting on the terrace with a cold drink at sunset is perfect and the swimming pool (US$10 for nonguests) has an enviable setting. À la carte lunches (meals USh15,000 to USh25,000) and set-menu or buffet dinners (USh50,000) are available at the classy restaurant (open 7am to 11am, 1pm to 3pm and 7pm to 10pm). Book ahead during peak season as the lodge gets very busy.

Campgrounds CAMPGROUND **$**
(camping USh15,000) Although the facilities are rustic, the settings are superb, making Mweya a great place to pitch a tent. The main Mweya Campsite 3 has little shade but is set off from the other development on the peninsula and looks out over the channel. Much more isolated are Campsites 1 and 2, located 3.5km and 4.5km east of the visitor centre respectively. They have nothing but pit toilets and good channel views, especially Campsite 2. Expect a lot of animal sightings and sounds. Book all camping at the visitor centre in Mweya before setting up your tent.

Mweya Hostel HOSTEL **$**
(☎0414-373050; s/d/f without bathroom & incl full breakfast USh57,000/84,000/252,500) Still basic, but not with a capital B like the Students' Camp (a nearby budget lodging that occasionally accepts guests), this is the more reliable option for finding a cheap bed. It's frequently full in the July to August and December to January high seasons, so book ahead. The family cottage sleeps six.

Tembo Canteen INTERNATIONAL **$**
(meals USh4000-8000; ⏲7.30am-10.30pm) Overlooking the channel near the Students' Camp, this is where the safari drivers hang out during the day and park staff kicks back at night. There's a pool table and satellite TV.

Simba Canteen SELF-CATERING
(⏲8am-noon & 5-8pm Tue-Sun) Not far from Tembo, this is a small grocery store. There are also a few smaller shops just to the south inside the workers' village.

KIKORONGO

Simba Safari Camp LODGE, CAMPGROUND **$**
(☎0701-426368; www.ugandalodges.com; Bwera Rd; camping USh10,000, dm US$10, s/d/tr incl full breakfast US$45/60/90, cottage US$125; wi-fi) Located just outside the park on the edge of its northern border, Simba makes for an excellent addition to Queen Elizabeth's budget options. Popular with tour groups from Red Chilli, it's often got a youthful clientele and is the most social option in the park. Rooms are clean and excellent value, with plenty of space, canopy beds and stone-floor showers. If you're not up for camping, there are bunk-bed dorms, while its cottage sleeps five. It has a convenient location for early morning game drives in Kasenyi, and 45-minutes from boat trips in Mweya. To get here from Kampala, jump on a bus heading to Bwera and ask to be dropped off at Simba.

KATUNGURU

Rwenzori Salaama Hotel & Lodging LODGE **$**
(☎0782-156015; s excl breakfast without bathroom USh10,000, s/d Ush30,000/50,000) If you get stuck in Katunguru, this basic lodge has the cheapest and cleanest rooms.

KYAMBURA

There's talk of UWA opening up a campsite in Kyambura, so campers wanting to stay this side of the park should make enquiries.

TOP CHOICE **Kyambura Game Lodge** LODGE **$$$**
(☎0414-322789; www.kyamburalodge.com; low season s/d incl full breakfast US$90/150, high season s/d $US130/220; pool) Of the park's luxury lodges, this is hands-down the best value and a wonderful choice for those wanting to slow things down to enjoy a bit of relaxation. Set on the edge of a grassy escarpment it looks out to stunning panoramic views of Queen Elizabeth, where you've a good chance to see grazing elephants below. The rooms are massive and strike the perfect balance between deluxe and safari, with canvas walls and natural objects incorporated into their design. Each has a rustic wooden balcony with comfy sofas looking to stunning views. Bathrooms are delightful and feature inviting square bathtubs, while the swimming pool also has the views, with hammocks and lounges draped with Maasai blankets on the decking. The restaurant is tastefully decorated with Congo art, and has a great range of dishes. Keep an eye out for the resident family of mongoose, and also a leopard that hangs around. Its only downside is that you see traffic passing through the park in the distance. Low season rates are available from mid-March to mid-June

and November to mid-December, which are great value.

KICHWAMBA ESCAPMENT

This ridgetop spot along the Kasese–Mbarara highway, outside the park's eastern boundary, has some of the best views in Uganda. It looks over the Maramagambo Forest and a wide sweep of savannah out to Lake Edward and the Rwenzori Mountains. It's a 15 minute drive to chimp tracking at Kyambura (Chambura) Gorge and 45 minutes to wildlife drives at Kasenyi.

Katara Lodge LODGE **$$$**
(0773-011648; www.kataralodge.com; s/d incl full board US$180/300;) One of the best places to splash out, the five wood, thatch-and-canvas cottages were made for the stunning views: the sides roll up, the bed rolls out to the deck if you want to sleep under the stars and even the clawfoot tubs looks out over the valley.

Kingfisher Lodge Kichwamba LODGE **$$$**
(0774-159579; www.kingfisher-uganda.net/en/kichwamba-en; s/d/tr incl half-board US$90/185/230;) This little compound of white-washed and thatched-roof towers is as lovely as it is unique. Rooms are a bit small but still good and come with their own little covered porches. The pool also has amazing views.

MARAMAGAMBO FOREST

Jacana Safari Lodge LODGE **$$$**
(0414-4258273; www.geolodgesafrica.com/jacana_safari_lodge.htm; s/d incl full board US$160/280;) Jacana's 11 large and luxurious cottages sit widely spaced in the forest and all look out over Lake Nyamusingiri. Relax at the pool, in the sauna or on the lake with a kayak (US$15 per hour), and then dine lakeside or on a pontoon boat. It's competitively priced compared to most other safari camps in Uganda, but it sits a long way from the best wildlife drive locales.

ISHASHA

Ishasha Camp CAMPGROUND **$**
(0200-901560; camping USh15,000, banda excl breakfast USh40,000) This basic and blissfully remote set-up has two *bandas* and you can also pitch a tent. There's a canteen serving local meals (USh10,000). If you aren't pitching a tent, call ahead because the beds are often full. The site shares a location with an army camp, so most uniforms here aren't UWA officers. There are also two lovely campsites on the Ishasha River, which forms the border with the DRC.

Ishasha Wilderness Camp LODGE **$$$**
(0414-321479; www.ugandaexclusivecamps.com/ishasha.html; s/d incl full board US$390/580;) Another tented camp that's not as luxurious as it should be at these prices. Rather, it's all about the location: right on the river and perfectly poised for wildlife watching. The 10 tents look out over the forest-lined Ntungwe River; elephants wander down here like clockwork at lunch time. Rates drop by around $US100 during low season (April, May and November).

Simba Miti LODGE, CAMPGROUND **$$**
(0772-722688) Still under construction when we visited, but the riverside Simba Mita aims to fill a much-needed void for an affordable, comfortable lodge in Ishasha. It's just outside the park, 3km from Ishasha gate, and will have both camping and rooms.

KIHIHI

For more affordable accommodation you can consider staying in Kihihi, 16km from Ishasha gate – but you'll miss out on the whole wildlife experience. It can also make a handy base for those with a gorilla permit for Buhoma in Bwindi, 40km south.

Savannah Resort Hotel HOTEL **$$**
(0777-076086; www.savannahresorthotel.com; s/d/tr incl full breakfast US$75/115/140) Located 4km outside Kihihi, a 30-minute drive from Ishasha, this pleasant hotel has a mix of comfortable rooms and *bandas* in a peaceful location surrounded by greenery. Also has a good restaurant with a mix of international and African dishes (USh16,000 to USh25,000).

Rest Inn Gardens GUESTHOUSE **$**
(0772-565247; Kihihi; r excl breakfast USh 30,000-40,000; without bathroom USh20,000) Basic accommodation, which is clean and comfortable, and friendly staff.

Information

Internet access is available at the **Queens Pavilion** (per min USh200; 8am-6pm) UWA information centre. It also sells good maps and coffee from Mt Elgon.

Getting There & Away

CAR The majority of people visit the park either as part of an organised tour or by renting their own car. If you're driving, take care of animals crossing the road along the high-speed tarmac section, particularly at night. Petrol is available at Mweya, but it's pricier than in towns.

PUBLIC TRANSPORT There's a direct bus to Katunguru (USh25,000, eight hours) from Kampala's main bus park at 9am. Otherwise regular minibuses between Kasese (USh4000, one hour) and Mbarara (USh10,000, three hours) stop at Katunguru. Once in the park, you can either hitch or arrange a special-hire taxi in Katunguru.

The road from Katunguru to the village of Ishasha cuts through the park and passes Ishasha gate. Although no park entry fees are needed to travel this road, you'll be fined US$150 if you're caught venturing off it and into the park. The Ishasha sector is 100km from Mweya down a pretty good road (due to oil exploration in the area) in the far south of the park. During the rainy season the bridge is occasionally washed away, making the road unpassable, which results in a very, very long detour that'll lead up through Ishaka on the Mbarara–Kasese Rd.

From Ishasha, you can head south for Butogota and Bwindi Impenetrable National Park in about two hours in the dry season.

Tours

All tour operators can put together a short safari to Queen Elizabeth National Park. Kampala-based **Great Lakes Safaris** has fantastically priced three-day trips (from US$210 per person with six people) departing every Wednesday and Friday, while **Red Chilli Hideaway** has four-day safaris from $US340 per person. **Amagara Tours** also has great rates at US$170 per person (with six people) for its three-day tours. See p483 for further information on these operators.

Bwindi Impenetrable National Park

Home to almost half of the world's surviving mountain gorillas, the World Heritage-listed **Bwindi Impenetrable National Park** (0486-424121; adult/child US$35/25; park office 7.45am-5pm) is one of Africa's most famous national parks. Set over 331 sq km of improbably steep mountain rainforest, the park is home to an estimated 360 gorillas: undoubtedly Uganda's biggest tourist drawcard.

The Impenetrable Forest, as it's also known, is one of Africa's most ancient habitats, since it thrived right through the last Ice Age (12,000 to 18,000 years ago) when most of Africa's other forests disappeared. Along with the altitude span (1160m to 2607m) this antiquity has resulted in an incredible diversity of flora and fauna, even by normal rainforest standards. And we do mean rainforest; up to 2.5 metres of rain falls here annually.

Its 120 species of mammal is more than any of Uganda's other national parks, though sightings are less common because of the dense forest. Lucky visitors might see forest elephants, 11 species of primate (including chimpanzees and L'Hoest's monkeys), duiker, bushbuck, African golden cats and the rare giant forest hog, as well as a host of bird and insect species. For birdwatchers it's one of the most exciting destinations in the country, with almost 360 species, including 23 of the 24 endemic to the Albertine Rift and several endangered species, including the African green broadbill. With a good guide, sighting daily totals of over 150 species is possible. On the greener side of the aisle, Bwindi harbours eight endemic plants.

BWINDI IMPENETRABLE NATIONAL PARK

Why Go Tracking mountain gorillas, forest walks with Twa people.

When to Go December to March and June to September have the least rain, but permits are easier to obtain at other times.

Practicalities Best accessed via Kabale but, depending on the region for your permit, also Kisoro and Ishasha in Queen Elizabeth National Park. Take note the rainy season often brings delays due to landslides, so be sure to leave enough time to get there.

Activities

Gorilla Tracking

A genuine once-in-a-lifetime experience, hanging out with mountain gorillas is one of the most thrilling wildlife encounters in the world, and Bwindi Impenetrable National Park is one of the best places to see them.

There are theoretically 64 daily permits available to track gorillas in Bwindi. Permits cost US$500 (including park entry) and are booked through the UWA office (p482) in Kampala.

Trips leave (from the park office nearest the group you'll be tracking) at 8.30am daily, but you should report to park headquarters by 7.45am. For those who are based in Kisoro or Kabale and plan on leaving early in the morning be mindful that during rainy season there are potential delays, such as landslides or being bogged.

Once you finally join a tracking group, the chances of finding the gorillas are almost guaranteed. But, since the terrain in Bwindi Impenetrable National Park is mountainous and heavily forested, if the gorillas are a fair distance away it can be quite a challenge to get close. The path is often steep and slippery, and can take anywhere from 30 minutes to five hours to reach them, so you'll need to be in reasonable enough shape. If you think you're going to struggle it's strongly advised you hire a porter who can lend a hand getting up and down the hill. Walking sticks are also a very good idea and provided by UWA.

Of the 28 gorilla groups living in Bwindi Impenetrable National Park (varying from families of five to 27), nine have been habituated to be visited by tourists with permits issued for the following regions:

BUHOMA

Nestled in the northwest corner of the park, Buhoma has three groups of gorillas that range in size from families of five to 19. As the first section of the park to open for gorilla tracking, Buhoma is by far the most developed in terms of tourist infrastructure, and with the most permits available it's also the most popular. Gorillas are probably the most accessible here too, sometimes as little as a 30-minute trek away.

RUHIJA

Also located in the north of the park, Ruhija has two groups (Bitukura: 13 gorillas and Oruzogo: 23), as well a habituated group that's visited by researchers only. There's a good range of accommodation sprouting up here but otherwise it's easily accessible from Kasese or Buhoma, a two hour drive either direction.

NKURINGO

While there's only one group in Nkuringo, a family of 16 that includes two silverbacks, it's regarded as one of the most entertaining and relaxed of the gorilla groups. Nkuringo is spectacularly set in the southwest of the park on a ridge opposite the wall of green that is Bwindi. From various spots you can spy Lake Edward, the Rwenzoris, all of the Virungas and even Nyiragongo Volcano by Goma, the DRC.

RUSHAGA

Located in the southeast of the park, Rushaga is the newest place that's opened up for gorilla tracking, with three groups including Nshongi, Mishaya and Kahungye (who are the largest habituated group with 28 gorillas). This lovely thick tract of forest is also home to elephants.

Forest Walks

Even if you can't afford gorilla tracking, Bwindi is a rewarding park to visit just for a chance to explore the lush virgin rainforest. Several three- to four-hour nature walks penetrate the Impenetrable Forest around Buhoma. The walks begin at 9am and 2.15pm and cost US$10.

The **Waterfall Trail** includes, surprise, surprise, a 33m waterfall on the Munyaga

BWINDI GORILLA PERMITS

Demand for gorilla permits exceeds supply for most of the year in Bwindi. During the 'low seasons' of April to May and October to November (the rainiest months), you may be able to confirm a space a week or two in advance of your trip. During the rest of the year it's not unheard of for permits to be booked up months in advance. If nothing is available that fits your schedule, check at the backpacker places in Kampala and Jinja, where the safari companies advertise excess permits they want to sell. It's no problem to buy these, even when someone else's name is on them. Cancellations and no-shows are rare, but you can get on the list at the park office: it's first-come, first-served. If you haven't prearranged a gorilla permit, this should be your number one priority upon arrival in Kampala.

At the time of research UWA were offering discount permits during the low season months for $US350. The permits were for tracking newly habituated groups of gorillas, so it remains to be seen whether this initiative is a promotional or permanent move.

LOCAL KNOWLEDGE

AUGUSTINE MUHANGI: UWA RANGER

Augustine, 33, has worked as a ranger-guide in Bwindi Impenetrable National Park for over eight years, and is experienced with many gorilla groups in the park.

What does your daily job involve? I'll get to the visitor centre at 7.30am and brief the visitors on the requirements for tracking gorillas, including all the 'dos and do nots' involved. The trackers have already left an hour beforehand, and will radio me when they've found the gorillas. The trackers find them by starting at the point we saw them the day prior, looking out for broken vegetation to let us know what direction to follow. When we find their nest, which they make in a different location each night, we follow the trail to where they are feeding.

Have you worked with habituating the gorillas in the park? Yes, I participated with the Nshongi group (in Rushaga), who at the time were the largest gorilla group with 36 members [the group has since split into two familles]. The process is to firstly identify a family and visit them for a short time on a daily basis. There's only four of us, and it's essential for the first six months for it to be the same people each day at the same time. After this initial period, we can have different people and we stay for a few hours longer each day, where we pretend to eat the same food as they do at the same time – and this brings us closer. We also imitate their noise and beat our chests when they do. This goes on for two to three years. In the first week, they're very aggressive and charge regularly. It's only after a year they become more relaxed.

Having worked with many gorilla groups in Bwindi, do you have a favourite family? The Nkuringo group. Members are very friendly and relaxed with us, and they're easy to find too.

What's your favourite memory in Bwindi? In Nkuringo when the gorillas are feeding, sometimes the trees are too soft and won't support larger gorillas, so I see them send up the babies to pick the food for them. When I see these animals do this, I think they're just like us human beings. I also like it when I see them hug and kiss each other.

River, but just as worthwhile is the magnificently rich forest it passes through. This is the best trail for spotting both orchids and primates. Weather permitting, the **Muzabijiro Loop Trail** and **Rushura Hill Trail** offer excellent views south to the Virunga volcanoes and the Western Rift Valley in the DRC. The latter, which is a more difficult climb, also serves up views of Lake Edward and, on an exceptionally clear day, the Rwenzoris.

A longer but much easier trek is along the **River Ivi Trail**, which follows the path of a planned-but-never-built road between Buhoma and Nkuringo. It's 14km through the forest and then another 6km uphill along a road to Nkuringo village; you might be able to hitch this last part. **Nkuringo Walking Safaris** (0774-805580; www.nkuringowalkingsafaris.com) can arrange the walk with porters for US$64, but doesn't include park or forest walk fees.

Community Projects

Proceeds from all of these activities are ploughed back into the community for projects such as supporting schools and teaching adult literacy. All five groups can arrange volunteer opportunities if you contact them in advance.

Batwa Experience CULTURAL TOUR

(0392-888700; www.batwaexperience.com; $US70) The Twa (Batwa) people were displaced from their forest habitat when Bwindi became a national park. The 'Batwa Experience' does an excellent job in preserving their indigenous culture by allowing you to both meet the Twa and see how they lived in the forest. The five-hour tours include joining a mock hunting party with bow and arrows, stories from Twa legend, song and dance and a traditional meal. All proceeds go to helping Twa communities in the region.

Buhoma Village Tourist Walk CULTURAL TOUR, WALKING
(per person US$15; ⌚9am & 2pm) Offered by the Buhoma Community Rest Camp, these walks are very popular. Depending on who's home during your three- to four-hour walk through the surrounding countryside, you'll visit a local healer and a school, watch a Twa song-and-dance show, and witness the none-too-appetising production of banana wine and gin (the bananas are mashed by foot).

Ride 4 A Woman CYCLING
(☎0785-999112; www.ride4awoman.org; bicycle rental per hour/day US$20/50, tours US$25) Arranges guided mountain-bike tours through the forest or village. Also rents out bikes if you want to go exploring yourself. Proceeds go to helping women in the community.

Nyundo Community Eco-Trails CULTURAL TOUR, WALKING
(☎0414-501866; www.pearlsofuganda.org; per person USh20,000) Another group based at Buhoma, offering a wide variety of village walks including several with a farming focus and others that go to caves and waterfalls. Traditional dances can also be arranged. It has an information office by Buhoma gate, but the walks all begin an inconvenient 6km away.

Nkuringo Community Walk CULTURAL TOUR, WALKING
(☎0774-805580; www.nkuringowalkingsafaris.com; US$10; ⌚8.30am-5pm) Similar cultural tours as in Buhoma, but in Nkuringo in the park's far southwestern corner. The walks start at the Nkuringo Community Development Foundation office across from the park office.

Sleeping & Eating

BUHOMA

Given that there are only 24 gorilla permits per day available at Buhoma, there are a lot of lodges competing for your business. The set-up is touristy, yet Buhoma simply offers the worst overall value in the country when it comes to sleeping and eating. There are some more budget options in Buhoma town, or otherwise further north in Butogota.

Buhoma Lodge LODGE $$$
(☎0414-321479; www.ugandaexclusivecamps/buhoma.html, reservations@wildfrontiers.com; s/d incl full board US$330/500) Of the many luxury lodges in Buhoma, this is one of the best and perfect for those wanting to make their 'gorilla experience' that bit more memorable. Spacious rooms have a rustic touch mixed with polished-wood floors and plenty of natural light. Each has a private porch with fantastic views of the dense forest, and a stone bathtub with seats. There's also a classy restaurant and bar.

Buhoma Community Rest Camp BANDA $
(☎0772-384965; www.buhomacommunity.com; camping US$10, dm excl breakfast US$20, r US$60, with shared bathroom US$50) This is the most popular budget option simply as a result of a lack of alternatives. While the camp's standards continue to plummet, and prices inexplicably rise, it does have a beautiful location near the park headquarters looking out to the forest. *Bandas* and safari tents are spaced out on a hill heading down the valley, and the best are at the bottom, which puts you right near the jungle; gorillas sometimes pass by the clearing here. Breakfast is US$10 and a set dinner and lunch is US$15. Some of the profits go towards funding community-development projects.

Silverback Lodge LODGE $$$
(☎0414-258273; www.geolodgesafrica.com/silverback_lodge.htm; s/d incl full board US$250/380) If you can walk up to this hilltop place you should be fine on your gorilla trek. The isolated location earns you the best Bwindi views, and they're especially evocative with clouds floating between the peaks: that whole gorillas in the mist thing. The seven rooms are small but stylish and have some fine decorative touches, such as carved wooden headboards and artistic lampshades.

Jungle View Lodge GUESTHOUSE $
(☎0787-836969; s/d excl breakfast without bathroom USh25,000/50,000) A great option for those watching their wallets, Jungle View is where many safari drivers stay. Rooms are simple and bathrooms are shared, but cleanliness comes standard.

NKURINGO

While many shoestring travellers opt to stay in Kisoro or Kabale, and get an early start to see the gorillas as a day trip, if you can stretch your budget, Nkuringo is a wonderfully scenic place that's great to soak up the atmosphere before your trek. Also bear in mind that in the rainy season the roads here are notorious for delays. Alternatively there's the more affordable Nshongi Camp in nearby Rushaga.

TOP CHOICE **Nkuringo Gorilla Camp** LODGE $$
(☎0774-805580; www.gorillacamp.com; camping excl breakfast incl tent s/d US$30/45, r without bathroom s/d US$67/84, cottages incl full board s/d US$210/290; 📶) A wonderful set-up among nature and with views looking out to the misty Virungas, the Nkuringo Gorilla Camp is one of the best places to stay in Bwindi. It's only a short walk from the trailhead, and is run by a passionate Englishman, Robert, who is a wealth of knowledge on the region. Accommodation spans most budgets, from comfortable hotel-style rooms to boutique cottages with safari canvas walls and porches, to 'lazy camping' with pre-pitched tents and comfortable mattresses. Little touches like hot-water bottles and thermos with teabags outside your door in the morning go a long way. The fantastically simple restaurant has an open kitchen, and in the evenings is lit by paraffin lanterns, and a bucket of glowing coals are provided for warmth. It serves tasty homestyle dishes, and there's strong brewed coffee for breakfast. An extra US$33 will cover all your meals. There's also a generator to charge your camera batteries. Book donations are appreciated here for the Nkuringo village library.

Clouds Lodge LODGE $$$
(☎0414-251182; www.wildplacesafrica.com; s/d incl full board US$700/940; @) No, those prices aren't a typo. Built as a project between the Uganda Safari Company, African Wildlife Foundation, International Gorilla Conservation Programme and the local community, this lodge offers a subtle sort of luxury, but if you can afford it you'll enjoy it. The large stone cottages have big windows, original art and double-sided fireplaces, plus you get a butler during your stay.

RUSHAGA

The newest addition to Bwindi's gorilla tracking, Rushaga has a few new places that have opened here, both surrounded by delightful nature.

Nshongi Camp BANDA $
(☎0774-231913; www.nshongicamp.altervista.org; camping excl breakfast USh10,000, banda incl full board USh85,000 per person) A truly delightful spot with simple mud-brick *bandas* in among a lovely garden and forest. An occasional elephant wanders through, evidenced by the spore seen here. The owner, Silver, is a local, and very friendly and helpful. It's only a short walk up to the trailhead. There's no generator here, so be sure your camera batteries are fully charged.

Gorilla Safari Lodge LODGE $$$
(☎0414-345742; www.gorillasafarilodge.com; s/d incl full board from US$230/360) Suave solar-powered lodge with eight cottages with own fireplaces. Conveniently located, it's only a five minute walk from the trailhead.

RUHIJA

Several new places have opened up here, both luxury and community-camp style, so there should no longer be the need for an early morning drive or day trip from Buhoma to visit these gorillas. Though many accommodation options lack the views of Bwindi Impenetrable National Park, most are around a 30-minute walk from the briefing centre.

Ruhija Gorilla Friends Resort & Campsite GUESTHOUSE $
(☎0772-480885; bitarihorobert@gmail.com; camping excl breakfast without/with tent US$7/10 per person, s without bathroom US$15-25, d without bathroom US$30-50) Undoubtedly the best value for budget travellers, where you can pitch a tent, use one of theirs, or go for a room or tented room. Proceeds go to the community.

Ruhija Gorilla Lodge LODGE $$
(☎0414-503065; www.gorillasafari.travel; s excl breakfast US$61-176, d US$66-286) Good mix of rooms from simple, affordable options to upmarket timber cottages that look over rolling pastoral views. Its lovely open-air restaurant has a real lodge feel to it. Staff are exceptionally friendly.

Gorilla Mist Camp TENTED CAMP $$
(☎0756-563577; www.gorillamistcamp.com; s/d incl full board US$130/180) Newish option with four excellent-value thatched-roof cottages with balconies offering nice views of hilly surrounds, some have bathtubs.

ℹ Information

In Buhoma, you can check your email at **Tent Internet Cafe** (per hour USh2000; ⏰9.30am-6pm Mon-Sat, 2-6pm Sun) situated in the Buhoma Community Hospital Centre, 3km from the park gate.

The *Mgahinga Gorilla National Park & Bwindi Impenetrable National Park* (1998) booklet available at the park or UWA headquarters in Kampala is dated, but still informative about the park's environment.

Getting There & Away

Buhoma

Whether you have your own vehicle or not, getting to Buhoma can be complicated. A special-hire vehicle is the way to go, particularly if you can muster up a group to share the costs. The four-hour trip from Kabale to Buhoma costs around USh200,000/300,000 one-way/return.

By public transport, there are several options involving uncomfortable and often hair-raising truck journeys. If you're lucky you'll get a pick-up truck direct to Buhoma (USh15,000, four to six hours) from Kabale on Tuesday or Friday at around 10am. Otherwise you can try your luck with a truck from Kabale to Kihihi (departing daily other than Sunday), and disembark at Kanyantorogo (USh10,000, three hours). From here you'll need to get either another pick-up to Butogota (USh4000, 30 minutes) or wait for the Gateway bus from Kampala to pass (as early as 3pm, but usually later). Butogota is 17km northeast from Buhoma, so for the last leg of the trip, you have the option of an infrequent pick-up to Buhoma (USh2000, one hour), hitch a ride, or a special-hire for USh50,000 or boda-boda for about half that.

The other option from Kabale is to take a truck to Butogota (USh10,000, 4½ hours), which theoretically depart daily at 11am – but were not running at the time of research.

If you're heading to Buhoma from Kampala, there's a daily bus to Butogota (USh25,000, 10 to 12 hours), departing Kampala's New Bus Park at around 6am; it departs in the other direction from Butogota at 3am. It's actually usually much faster from Kampala to take a bus (several companies make the trip in each direction early each morning, including **Gateway** (Map p386; ☎0722-069349; Wilson Rd, Kampala) and Perfect Coach) to Kihihi (USh35,000, 10 hours) and change there for a pick-up or shared-car taxi (USh5000, 1½ hours) or special-hire (USh100,000) to Buhoma, 40km away.

If you're driving from Kabale to Buhoma, the best route is the long way through Kanungu (which can be done in a car if you're an experienced driver) rather than the totally rough road through Ruhija.

It's also possible to access Buhoma via walking through Bwindi Impenetrable National Park to Nkuringo, a lovely 12km stretch that takes five to seven hours.

If you're in a rush, charter flights can get you to the Kanyonza Airstrip, 19km from Buhoma. If you're not in a rush, consider going by canoe and foot, a trip described under Nkuringo.

If you're coming from Queen Elizabeth National Park, Butogota is best accessed from Ishasha (three hours), but is problematic if you don't have your own car, in which case special-hire is the most realistic option, costing around USh180,000.

Nkuringo

From Kabale there's a truck departing Tuesday and Saturday afternoon (USh8000, four hours). Otherwise try a boda-boda (USh35,000, 2½ hours) or special-hire (one-way/return USh180,000/120,000, 2½ hours).

From Kisoro a truck travels to Nkuringo (USh8000, three hours) on Monday and Thursdays. It leaves Nkuringo around 8am and returns about 3pm. In Kisoro it parks at 'Kanyaruju's House', about 50m north of junction on road to Nkuringo. Other times you can try to hitch, but there's not much traffic going all the way to Nkuringo, and the UWA trucks that sometimes come to town are usually too full to take passengers.

Because Nkuringo lodging falls squarely in the budget and luxury extremes, many visitors sleep in Kisoro and make the early morning drive for their gorilla trek; this usually takes 1½ hours. A special-hire costs around USh100,000/150,000 one-way/return. A boda-boda driver will charge you USh30,000, but it's a long, bottom-shaking ride. Once again be aware of the risks during rainy season when there can lengthy delays due to the poor condition of the road.

The best way to travel from Nkuringo (you can also do it uphill from Kisoro) is to leave the road behind. **Nkuringo Walking Safaris** (☎0774-805580; www.nkuringowalkingsafaris.com; US$143 for two people incl guide & porters) will lead you on an 18km trek to Lake Mutanda (this can be shortened to 10km with some driving) and then a 2½-hour paddle (lifejackets provided) in a dugout canoe. From here it's another 4km on foot to Kisoro, but you may want to just chill out at Mutanda Eco-Community Centre (p450) that night instead. There's also the option to divide this trip into two days, and is cheaper if you opt for no guide or porter.

You can also slip through the forest to/from Buhoma along the River Ivi Trail. The Walking Safaris team will accompany you on this walk too, if you want, but there's no need since a park ranger guide is required regardless of who else is with you.

Rushaga

Located 54km from Kabale, Rushaga can be reached via a special-hire taxi (USh100,000/160,000 one-way/return from Kabale) and takes two hours, while a boda-boda is around USh30,000 one-way.

Otherwise it's 32km from Kisoro, and costs USh60,000/90,000 one-way/return by special-hire taxi (one hour) or USh15,000 by boda-boda one-way. Trucks (USh3500, two hours) depart in the afternoon on Monday and Thursday, and 10am on Friday.

Ruhija

Ruhija is about 50km (up to two hours) from Buhoma gate, and 52km from Kasese. A special-hire will cost about USh140,000 return. If you're chancing your luck with public transport there are pick-up trucks that leave Kabale on Tuesday, Wednesday and Thursday, but there's no set departure time, leaving when they get enough passengers, usually in mid-afternoon.

Kabale

☎ 0486 / POP 44,000

While Kabale itself is nothing to write home about, it's a handy base from which to explore some superb hiking country, as the area is honeycombed with tracks and paths, trading centres and farms. It's also the gateway to Lake Bunyonyi, the number one spot for serious rest and relaxation in Uganda, and a good staging post for trips to see the gorillas at Bwindi Impenetrable National Park.

Sights & Activities

Home of Edirisa MUSEUM
(www.edirisa.org; Muhumuza Rd; adult/child USh5000/2000; ⏲8.30am-11pm) This interesting little museum houses a replica traditional homestead, built of sticks and papyrus, showing how the local Bakiga people lived a century ago. Besides the museum, you'll find a little travellers' village tucked away inside the attention-grabbing polka-dotted building. There's accommodation, food, a good gift shop (local basketry and Congolese masks) and internet access.

Edirisa also leads canoe trekking trips on Lake Bunyonyi, and if you're interesting in volunteering in the area, apply on its website (click Smiles) before you arrive.

Sleeping

Cepha's Inn BOUTIQUE HOTEL $$
(☎0486-422097; www.cephasinn.com; Archer Rd; s/d excl breakfast USh50,000/90,000, ste USh150,000; @) Set over two colourful buildings in a peaceful location near the golf course on the hill above town, this boutique hotel probably has the best rooms in town. Rooms have plush lounge chairs and oblong bathtubs, while other facilities include a sauna and steam bath. Book ahead as it's often full.

Home of Edirisa BACKPACKERS $
(☎0752-558222; www.edirisa.org; Muhumuza Rd; dm excl breakfast USh7000, d USh25,000, s/d without bathroom USh10,000/20,000; @) What is this place? It's a hostel, it's a museum, it's a restaurant, it's a cultural centre, it's a fair-trade craft shop: and it's a great place to hang out no matter which of these components tickles your fancy. The rooms are priced right for the budget traveller and the staff are friendly. Its chilled-out rooftop restaurant is a beautiful spot to relax for a bit and unwind after a hard day on the road. Internet is free for guests or those eating in the restaurant, and films are shown nightly. Book ahead to avoid disappointment.

Kabale Backpackers BACKPACKERS $
(Amagara Guesthouse; ☎0772-959667; Muhumuza Rd; s excl breakfast USh17,000, r USh22,000-32,000; @) The people behind Byoona Amagara on Lake Bunyonyi also run this little spot in town. There's no island vibe here, just simple, meticulously clean rooms. Many locals drink here at night, so it's a good place to break out of that backpacker shell. All but two rooms have a private bathroom but there's no discount if you end up sharing the bath with your neighbour. There's one larger, snazzier room. It also books budget tours, which are excellent value (see p483).

White Horse Inn HOTEL $$
(☎0772-459859; Rwamafa Rd; s/d incl full breakfast USh92,000/122,000, ste USh202,000; @) Set on 5 acres of lawn, White Horse has a lovely location, and built in 1937 it exudes the character of a faded upmarket hotel. The bar-restaurant has a roaring fireplace.

Eating

You can eat well at the Home of Edirisa and Kabale Backpackers, which have a mix of local and international favourites in the USh3000 to USh10,000 range. Both make a pretty good pizza. For something more Ugandan, the side-by-side **Skyline Hotel** and **Skyblue Motel**, out at the main junction, have good lunch and dinner buffets for USh6000.

Little Ritz INTERNATIONAL $
(Rugabo Rd; mains USh9000-12,000; ⏲7am-midnight) Located above the popular Hot Loaf Bakery (which does mini pizzas, croissants and pastries), this is the leading restaurant in town, both for the food and atmosphere. The eclectic menu of Western, Indian, Chinese and African dishes can be enjoyed outside on the balcony or inside by the fireplace and with international news programs on

Kabale

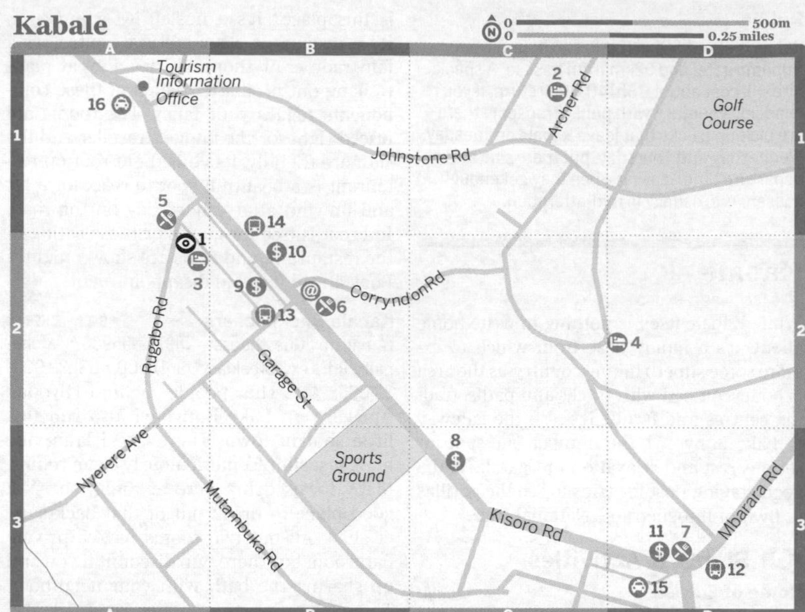

the TV. There's also a pool table for passing the night.

Royal Supermarket SUPERMARKET
(Kisoro Rd) Anyone planning to do a bit of self-catering at Bwindi or Lake Bunyonyi should hit the Royal, the best-stocked supermarket in town.

Information

Pick up a copy of the free *Gorilla Highlands* (www.gorillahighlands.com) guide with information and history on the area, available at the Home of Edirisa.

The Home of Edirisa has free internet for guests and restaurant patrons while Kabale Backpackers has internet access for USh40 per minute; the former also offers wi-fi, when it's functioning. There are several more internet cafes in town.

There's all the usual banks in town with ATMs. Exchange rates are very good by provincial standards

The **Tourism Information Centre** (☎0772-661854; Kisoro Rd; ⊙8.30am-8.30pm) is privately owned, and essentially a tour operator, but is a good source of information on the area, including Bwindi Impenetrable and Mgahinga Gorilla National Parks, with a noticeboard and brochures, as well as books and binoculars for sale.

Getting There & Away

For all the difficult details on getting from Kabale to Bwindi Impenetrable National Park, see p442. For travel to Lake Bunyonyi, see p448.

Transport to the Rwandan border at Katuna (Gatuna) and on to Kigali is frequent. See p490 for full details.

BUS There are numerous daily buses to Kampala (USh25,000, eight hours). Some of the companies have offices in town, and you can begin your journey there, but all buses (including those coming from Rwanda) also pick up passengers in front of the Skyblue Motel at the main junction.

Many of the buses from Kampala, including **Horizon** (Map p386) and **Gateway** (Map p386), continue on to Kisoro (USh13,000, two hours). You can catch these either at the main junction or in front of the Highland Hotel on the northwest side of town.

For Port Fortal (Ush25,000, eight hours) via Queen Elizabeth National Park and Kasese (Ush20,000, seven hours), there are two daily departures available, leaving at 7pm.

MINIBUS Minibuses to Mbarara (USh15,000, 2½ hours) also park near the Skyblue Motel, but in the morning you're better off using the buses. There are a few Kisoro minibuses from the taxi park.

TAXI Shared-car taxis park near the Highland Hotel.

Kabale

Sights
1 Home of Edirisa A2

Activities, Courses & Tours
Amagara Tours .... (see 3)

Sleeping
2 Cepha's Inn C1
Home of Edirisa .... (see 1)
3 Kabale Backpackers A2
Skyblue Motel .... (see 7)
4 White Horse Inn D2

Eating
5 Hot Loaf Bakery A1
Little Ritz .... (see 5)
6 Royal Supermarket B2
7 Skyline Hotel D3

Information
8 Barclays Bank C3
9 Centenary Bank B2
10 Stanbic Bank B2
11 Stanbic Bank D3

Transport
12 Gateway Buses D3
13 Horizon Coaches B2
14 Kibungo Coaches B1
15 Taxi Park D3
16 Taxis to Kisoro A1

Lake Bunyonyi

Lake Bunyonyi ('place of many little birds') is undoubtedly the loveliest lake in Uganda. Its contorted shore encircles 29 islands, and the steep surrounding hillsides are intensively terraced, almost like parts of Nepal. A magical place, especially with a morning mist rising off the placid waters, it has supplanted the Ssese Islands as *the* place for travellers to chill out on their way through Uganda.

Sights & Activities

All guesthouses can arrange boat trips on the lake, either in motorboats or dugout canoes, which is still how most locals get about. And it's one of the few places in Uganda where you can swim, with no crocodiles, hippos or bilharzia, so go ahead and jump in.

Akampeine Island HISTORIC SITE

Translating to Punishment Island, this tiny island was so named because it was once the place where unmarried pregnant women were dumped to die. Their only rescue from drowning or starvation was if a man who was too poor to pay a bride-price would come over to claim the banished woman as his wife. There's nothing to see here, with just one spindly tree in its centre.

Bwama & Njuyeera (Sharp's) Islands HISTORIC SITE

Many boat drivers will also take you to these islands, where British missionary Dr Leonard Sharp founded a leper colony and settled in 1921, but the story is more interesting than the sights. The colony on Bwama shut down in the 1980s (there are two schools on the island now) and nearly all history was stripped from Sharp's home on Njuyeera when it was converted into a (not recommendable) hotel.

Canoe Trekking CANOEING

(☎0752-558222; www.edirisa.org; half-/one-/two-/three-day trek per person US$35/65/105/135) The best way to get intimate with Bunyonyi is by canoeing its peaceful waters. Excellent tours, offered by the Home of Edirisa in Kabale, range from five hours to its flagship three-day tours. The longer tours have the benefit of allowing you to get a very up-close look at local life with village homestays and visits to the Twa (Batwa). Otherwise you can grab a dugout canoe on your own for a leisurely paddle; but practise for a while before paddling off on an ambitious trip, since many tourists end up going round in circles, doing what's known locally as the *muzungu* corkscrew. Keep an eye out for otters, particularly along the shore during early morning and late afternoon.

Twa (Batwa) Villages CULTURAL TOUR

There are a few Twa villages near the lake's south end, around Kyevu, which has a mildly interesting (mostly because nearly everybody arrives by dugout canoe) Wednesday and Saturday market. **Rotobo Village** is an hour by motorboat and then an hour on foot and boat owners at Rutinda will take you there for USh150,000, a quarter of which should go to the Twa people; otherwise if you get to Byoona Amagara lodge, it can arrange much cheaper transport to Rutinda. See boxed text, p446 for more information about visiting the Twa people.

Guided Walks CULTURAL TOURS

The guesthouses can also set you up for village walks to see, among other things, local

TWA (BATWA) TOURS: TO GO OR NOT TO GO...

The Twa (Batwa) people have almost all been forced out of their ancestral forest homes, where they lived as nomadic hunters and gatherers, because either the forest has been cleared for agriculture by neighbouring tribes or it's now part of a national park. One of Africa's most ancient tribal groups, the Twa are faced with a similar plight to many indigenous people: they are a marginalised sector of the Ugandan community, often living in squalid conditions.

Many Ugandans view the Twa with disdain and will tell you they're lazy. But the Twa are uninterested in living in modern agro-industrial society. Life in the forest was anything but easy, but this is the only life the older generation know, and even those who are making an effort to adopt farming have found it very hard to adapt to modern life.

In many of the places where the Twa now live, particularly near Lake Bunyonyi and Mgahinga, Bwindi and Semuliki national parks, guides will offer to take you to visit one of their villages. The visits invariably involve a song-and-dance demonstration, and once the music begins you can't help but notice that they project a genuine pride.

Most Twa today still rely on handouts, and so they're only too happy for a chance to cash in on their culture (your guide should be giving a good chuck of change to the village chairperson for the performance, and basketry is usually offered for sale) but, ironically, in some ways it's only this commercialisation process that ensures the survival of the Twa as a distinct tribal group within Uganda.

Despite this, visits can still end up taking on a 'human safari' feel, which is pretty unfortunate for everyone involved. The best way to visit the Twa is through new initiatives in Bwindi and Mgahinga national parks that allow you to explore the forest with Twa guides, receiving demonstrations on hunting and cultural performances. While it's not cheap (US$70 per person), all money goes to helping local Twa communities and ultimately preserving their indigenous culture.

blacksmiths (*abahesi*) who have replaced locally mined iron ore with scrap metal, but otherwise use traditional methods. But if you just want an easygoing amble along the lakeshore, it's straightforward enough to find your own way around.

Sleeping & Eating

The lake has a good choice of accommodation, both on the mainland and on several islands; and more places were under construction when we last visited. All have restaurants and bars (and surely you know the drill by now; order well in advance) and swimming piers. Most feature 'crayfish' on the menu, which is caught fresh from the lake, but these are tiny in size and more resemble shrimp.

MAINLAND

TOP CHOICE Arcadia Cottages LODGE $$
(☎0782-424232; www.arcadiacottages.net; camping per tent USh30,000, cottages incl full breakfast s/d USh142,000/182,000) Wow! Built not on the lake but high on a hill, Arcadia has some intoxicating views over dozens of islands way down below and the Virunga volcanoes off in the distance. The lower row of cottages are the pick of the rooms, boasting unhindered views, private porches and comfortable, spacious rooms. The back rooms are nice, but less atmospheric and the views not quite as good. Even if you won't be sleeping here, stop by for a meal or a drink in the **restaurant** (mains USh15,000-25,000), either at a table outside on the grass, or inside, with both having sweeping panoramic views. On chilly nights a brazier of hot coals is provided, which makes things nice and cosy. It sits 2km uphill off the main road to the lake.

Kalebas Camp GUESTHOUSE $
(☎0312-294894; camping USh10,000, safari tent s/d excl breakfast USh30,000/40,000, r s/d USh40,000/50,000) The original lakeside lodging and its lovely garden have gone through several owners over the years, but its present incarnation is now one of Bunyonyi's best. The accommodation comprises stilted tents to basic rooms. The restaurant has lovely lake views and makes a good wood-fired pizza. There's a laptop you can borrow to check your email (USh5000 per half hour).

Bunyonyi Overland Resort BACKPACKERS $
(☎0486-426016; www.bunyonyioverland.com; camping US$6, furnished safari tent s/d excl breakfast US$20/25, s/d US$30/40, without bathroom US$23/30, family cottage US$100; @) If you've seen Backpackers or Red Chilli in Kampala, then you already know the drill; only the sculpted gardens and lakeside setting make Bunyonyi Overland much more attractive. It's just as noisy though, since the wide range of accommodation, food (USh6000 to USh25,000) and leisure facilities (from badminton to satellite TV) ensure it's extremely popular with travellers and overland companies. It runs a shuttle (USh5000) from the Highland Inn in Kabale at 9.30am and 4.30pm.

Birdnest@Bunyoni Resort RESORT $$
(☎0754-252560; www.birdnestatbunyonyi.com; s/d incl full breakfast US$100/110;) A sophisticated new spot right on the lake, the Belgian-owned Birdnest is the most upmarket choice in Bunyonyi, but remains excellent value. Open-plan rooms have vibrant decor with lovely private balconies looking out to the lake, while the outside terrace decking has a swimming pool with huge hammocks to lounge about. Restaurant is suave with a quality European menu and a good wine list.

ISLANDS

Secure parking is available by the Rutinda landing for those driving here.

TOP CHOICE **Byoona Amagara** LODGE $
(☎0752-652788; www.lakebunyonyi.net; Itambira Island; camping USh9000, dm excl breakfast USh14,000-18,000, geodome per person USh25,000-33,000, cabin per person USh33,000, cottage USh150,000; @) Byoona Amagara bills itself as a backpacker's paradise, and it's hard to disagree. There's a great choice of rooms, most built of natural materials and all very reasonably priced. (Private rooms have a two-person minimum from June to September, December to January, and during Easter and a 50% single supplement at other times; and they stick to this, even if you're the only person on the island.) The stars of the show are the open-faced geodome huts – birds and lizards can come in, but so do unencumbered views – with their comfortable beds with mosquito nets. And all power comes from the sun, so there's no irritating generator rumble at night. The originality doesn't take a break in the kitchen, which turns out some yummy, creative dishes (USh4500 to USh12,500), such as crayfish avocado and *matoke* chips. A motorboat out here from Rutinda costs USh15,000 (USh20,000 after dark); and while the dugout *to* the island is free, it costs USh3000 per person for the return.

Bushara Island Camp BUNGALOW $
(☎0772-464585; www.busharaislandcamp.com; Bushara Island; camping US$6, safari tents s/d excl breakfast US$25/30, cottages US$50) This camp is run by the Church of Uganda to raise funds for community development projects. It offers a choice of cottages and safari tents (bathrooms out back), all widely spaced through the eucalyptus forest. The 'treehouse' cottage (US$38) set on stilts is wonderfully rustic and features a great balcony and memorable outdoor shower. With top service (breakfast delivered to your door), it's no surprise that there are many return visitors. The well-regarded **restaurant** (USh4000-35,000) serves pizza, crayfish dishes and tasty desserts, such as caramelised bananas and crêpes, and has a roaring fireplace. There's also an outdoor BBQ, volleyball court and playground for kids, and canoes for hire (per hour US$1). A motorboat transfer from Rutinda is free unless you're camping, in which case it costs USh15,000.

Nature's Prime Island BUNGALOW $$
(☎0772-423215; www.naturesprimeisland.com; Akarwa Island; safari tents & cabins per person incl full board US$50/100) Nature's Prime occupies a lovely little wooded island right near Rutinda. Scandinavian-style rustic log cabins and safari tents set on raised platforms are spread out over the island so views vary, but all see at least some of the lake from the front porches. Use of canoes is complimentary as is the boat transfer here.

Bunyoni Wildlife Resort COTTAGES $$
(☎0312-114581; www.bunyonyiwildliferesort.com; Kyahugye Island; camping per person USh20,000, cottages s/d incl full board US$100/150) The latest addition to Bunyonyi's island lodges, this resort on Kyahugye lives up to its name, being home to a small population of kob, impala and bushbuck, which were recently introduced here. Its wooden thatched cottages all have lake views and are terrific value. It can arrange a number of tours in the area, ranging from nature walks to canoe trips.

Getting There & Away

There are many pick-ups (USh2000) and shared-car taxis (USh2500) travelling from Kabale's main market on Monday and Friday to Rutinda, where most of the lodging and the main jetty is. It's 9km from Kabale. On other days, you can check at the taxi park, but transport is rare so you'll probably have to choose between a special-hire (USh20,000) or a boda-boda (USh6000).

Kisoro

0486 / POP 12,700

While Kisoro itself may not be much to look at – a gritty town with a frontier atmosphere – its verdant surrounds are undeniably beautiful. On a clear day the backdrop of the Virunga chain of volcanoes are stunning. Kisoro serves as a popular base for tourists, here primarily for nearby Mgahinga Gorilla National Park to see mountain gorillas (if they're this side of the border at the time, that is), track golden monkeys or to climb volcanos. It's also a convenient base for those with gorilla permits in the southern sector of Bwindi Impenetrable National Park or even Parc National des Virungas (p497) at Djomba, just over the border in the DRC. If you're en route to/from Rwanda it makes a pleasant place to spend the night.

Sights

There's not much to see and do in Kisoro itself, with Mgahinga Gorilla National Park and Lake Mutanda the real attractions just outside of town. It won't be long before would-be guides will approach you about a variety of trips they can lead you on. Not all of these guys are reliable, so get a recommendation from a fellow traveller or the UWA office.

If you're interested in visiting a Twa (Batwa) village, drop into the **United Organisation for Batwa Development in Uganda** (UOBDU; 0772-660810; Muahba Rd; 8am-5.30pm) to ensure that your trip will be culturally sensitive, and, thus, ultimately rewarding. There's a craft shop here too. Otherwise there are Twa forest tours in Mgahinga Gorilla National Park. See boxed text p446 for more information about visiting the Twa people.

Kisoro's Monday and Thursday **markets** are large, colourful affairs, well worth some of your time.

Cold winds blow through town, so pack that jacket.

Sleeping & Eating

There are also some good chilled-out sleeping options at Mgahinga Gorilla National Park and Lake Mutanda. There's not a great deal of eating choices in town, so most visitors usually end up eating at their hotel.

Travellers Rest Hotel HOTEL $$
(0772-533029; Mahuabura Rd; www.gorillatours.com/gorilla-tours/travellers-rest-hotel-kisoro.html; s/d/tr incl full breakfast US$65/75/95, ste US$85; @) This is a hotel with a history. It was once run by the so-called father of gorilla tourism, Walter Baumgärtel, and Dian Fossey called it her 'second home'. Through various thoughtful touches, this otherwise simple place has become a lovely little oasis. The suite room is easily the best pick. The garden has lots of shade and the dining room/bar areas are full of Congolese crafts (all for sale). It also has the best menu in Kisoro, a well-stocked bar and a fireplace.

Kisoro Tourist Hotel HOTEL $$
(0712-540527; www.kisorotouristhotel.net; Bunagana Rd; s/d excl breakfast US$50/65; @) Lacking the charm and history of Travellers Rest, but more reasonably priced, it has the added bonus of rooms looking out at splendid views of Mt Muhavura when the weather is clear.

Countryside Guesthouse GUESTHOUSE $
(0782-412741; countrysideguesthouse@yahoo.com; Bunagana Rd; s/d excl breakfast without bathroom USh15,000/20,000, r USh45,000) Another friendly place with well-priced rooms. The manager is good for advice on the surrounding area.

Hotel Virunga BACKPACKERS $
(0486-430109; camping USh14,000, s/d excl breakfast without bathroom USh20,000/30,000, r Ush50,000) The busiest backpacker place in Kisoro, with a buzzing little restaurant that rocks on as a bar when the overland trucks are in town. Those considering gorilla treks in the DRC can arrange tours here.

Golden Monkey Guesthouse BACKPACKERS $
(0772-435148; shebahanyurwa@hotmail.com; dm US$6, s/d excl breakfast without bathroom US$10/15, r US$22-25) It's overpriced, but this warm and friendly guesthouse remains popular with NGOs and return visitors. Also

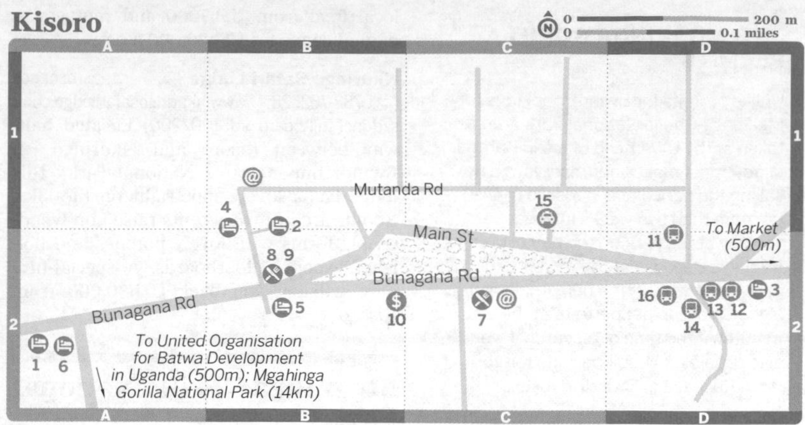

has Virunga Adventure Tours, which can arrange trips across Uganda.

Graceland Motel GUESTHOUSE $
(☎0382-276964; Kabale Rd; s excl breakfast USh15,000, d USh20,000-30,000) There's not much hip-shaking going on here, but what Graceland does have is quality rooms with private bathrooms, good food and exemplary service.

Coffee Masters CAFE $
(Bunagana Rd; cappuccino USh2000, mains USh3000-5000; ⏲7am-10pm) Worth popping into to get a locally grown coffee or fruit smoothies, plus a small selection of simple meals.

Coffee Pot Café CAFE $
(Bunagana Rd, espresso USh2000; ⏲9am-6.30pm Mon-Sat) Smart German-owned cafe with so-so coffee, light snacks and secondhand books for sale. Also has a good crafts store next door.

Information

There are several banks with ATMs. There's also a few internet places along the main road.

Mgahinga Gorilla National Park Office
(☎0414-680793; Main St; ⏲8am-5pm) The place to book your gorilla permits. Staff here are very friendly and have information about everything in and around Kisoro.

Getting There & Away

BUS Several bus companies, all departing from the east side of the city between 5am and 7am, make the long run to Kampala (USh30,000 to USh35,000, eight to 10 hours). Night travel is not recommended, due to increased chances of accidents and banditry.

MINIBUS Between Kisoro and Kabale (USh10,000, two hours) there are frequent daily minibuses, which wait outside the taxi park. On market days (Monday and Thursday) minibuses also run to Bunagana (USh4500, 45 minutes) on the DRC border from the same place.

Kisoro

Sleeping
1 Countryside Guesthouse A2
2 Golden Monkey Guesthouse B1
3 Graceland Motel D2
4 Hotel Virunga B1
5 Kisoro Tourist Hotel B2
6 Travellers Rest Hotel A2

Eating
7 Coffee Masters C2
8 Coffee Pot Café B2
Travellers Rest Hotel .... (see 6)

Information
9 Mgahinga Gorilla National Park Office B2
10 Stanbic Bank B2

Transport
Bismarkan Bus .... (see 12)
11 Gateway Buses D2
12 Horizon Coaches D2
13 Jaguar Coaches D2
14 Kampala Coaches D2
15 Taxi Park C1
16 Ubumwe Coaches D2

MGAHINGA GORILLA PERMITS

Unlike permits for Bwindi, bookings for Mgahinga Gorilla National Park aren't taken at the UWA head office in Kampala. You must make your reservation by calling the park office in Kisoro (p449) no more than two weeks in advance. You pay at the park on the day of your tracking. Because of this system, tour operators rarely come here, making it a good place to get permits at the last minute. At the time of research it was also possible to book permits for gorillas in Rushaga at Bwindi in Kisoro.

For details on how to get to Mgahinga Gorilla National Park, see p452.

The Rwandan border south of Kisoro at Cyanika is open 7am to 7pm and it's a pretty simple and quick trip to Musanze (Ruhengeri). See p490 for full details.

Lake Mutanda

This scenic lake lies just north of Kisoro and makes for a relaxing spot to hang out for a day or two. With a misty Virunga backdrop and a lake ringed by papyrus swamp it's a pretty spot, and worth the stroll out here. There's also dugout canoes for hire if you fancy a paddle; you don't need to worry about hippos, crocodiles or bilharzia here.

From Kisoro, the easiest, though not most direct, route, is to head west to the hospital and then ask someone to show you which gap in the hills to cross. A boda-boda or special-hire should cost USh5000 and USh20,000 respectively.

Lake Mutanda is also the starting point for eight-hour treks into Bwindi Impenetrable National Park with **Nkuringo Walking Safaris** (www.nkuringowalkingsafaris.com).

Sleeping

Mutanda Eco-Community Centre BUNGALOW $
(☎0772-435148; www.mcdoa.org/MECC.aspx; camping per tent USh15,000, cottage excl breakfast USh45,000) Comprising one simple log cabin (with excellent views across the lake from the porch) and a grassy camping ground, this is another good reason to come out to the lake. Deals can be made for volunteer swimming teachers to stay free. It will cook local food from USh7000 and rent you a dugout canoe for USh20,000 a day.

Nkuringo Safari Lodge LODGE $$$
(☎0782-762528; www.nkuringosafarilodge.com; s/d incl full board $US100/200) Located halfway between Kisoro and Nkuringo (in Bwindi Impenetrable National Park), this lodge has a lovely spot right on the lake. Rooms are in luxury tents raised on wooden platforms with lovely porches and polished wooden floorboards. A special-hire here will set you back USh30,000 from Kisoro.

Mgahinga Gorilla National Park

Although it's the smallest of Uganda's national parks at just 34 sq km, **Mgahinga Gorilla National Park** (☎0486-430098; adult/child US$35/20) punches well above its weight. Tucked away in the far southwest corner of the country, the tropical rainforest cloaks three dramatic extinct volcanoes and, along with the contiguous Parc National des Volcans (p519) in Rwanda and Parc National des Virungas (p497) in the DRC (which together with Mgahinga form the 434-sq-km Virunga Conservation Area), this is the home of half the world's mountain gorilla population. Elephants, buffaloes and serval are rarely seen, but they're also out there, and 115 species of bird flutter through the forests, including Rwenzori turaco and mountain black boo boo.

Gorilla tracking is still the main attraction here, but it's less popular than Bwindi Impenetrable National Park, due to the one habituated family having a tendency to duck across the mountains into Rwanda or the DRC. But there's much more on offer here than just gorillas. Mgahinga also serves up some challenging but rewarding treks and an interesting cave, plus golden monkey tracking is almost as fun as hanging out with the big boys.

All the following activities are booked through UWA in Kisoro, or otherwise its office in Mgahinga.

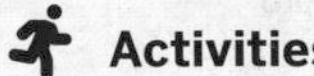

Activities

Gorilla Tracking WILDLIFE WATCHING
(☎0414-680793, 0775-906400; Main St, Kisoro; permits US$500; ⏲8am-5pm) If you plan on heading here specifically for gorillas, the first step is to check they're on this side of

the border. When the gorillas are living on Ugandan soil, which is about half the time, eight people can visit per day. The cost is US$500, including the entrance fee, a ranger-guide and armed guards. Trips depart from park headquarters at 8.30am, but try to check in at the office in Kisoro the day before your trip to confirm your arrival.

It usually takes longer to reach the gorillas here than at Bwindi, but the going is much easier than in the Impenetrable Forest. And photography is usually better because the gorillas are often found out in the open.

For more information on the mountain gorillas, including a list of tracking rules, see p32.

Volcano Trekking HIKING
(US$60 incl park fee & guide) The park has three dormant volcanoes that can be climbed, which, while strenuous (you just have to look at the mountains to know there's no point in trying if you aren't in good shape), require no mountaineering experience. There are some stunning views and the treks lead you into the otherworldly afro-alpine moorland, home of bizarre plants such as giant groundsel and lobelias.

The crater lake at the summit of **Mt Muhavura** (4127m) is almost too perfect to be true, and the views up here reach all the way to the Rwenzori Mountains. It's a 12km (at least seven hours) return trip. But the most popular climb is **Mt Sabyinyo** (3669m), which involves some breathtaking walks along gorges and a few ladder ascents. Not to mention the reward of getting to the third and final peak when you'll be standing in Uganda, Rwanda and the DRC at once. This is the longest (many would say most fun) climb, at 14km (eight hours). It's only 8km (five hours) to the swamp that was once a lake at the top of **Mt Gahinga** (3474m).

Two less taxing treks (US$10 per person), both about 10km long and great for birdwatchers, are the **Border Trail**, which starts out up Sabyinyo but then cuts back south along the Congolese border, and the **Gorge Trail**, which heads to a small waterfall in a gorge halfway up Sabyinyo. You could combine these into one longer trek.

Golden Monkey Tracking WILDLIFE WATCHING
(US$50 incl park entry & guide) When the gorillas are hanging out on the other sides of the mountains, golden monkeys (a very rare subspecies of the rare blue monkey) become the top lure to Mgahinga. You spend an hour with these beautiful creatures who live in large groups and are quite playful. Tracking starts at 8.30am, and the guides can find the habituated troop 85% of the time.

Batwa Trail CULTURAL TOUR
(US$80 incl guide) A new initiative, with forest tours led by Twa (Batwa) guides who explain how the Twa people used to live in the forest before they were forcibly removed from Mgahinga when it was turned into a national park. The 3½-hour tours include tales from Twa legend, demonstrations of day-to-day practices like hunting, firelighting and also a visit to the 342-m long **Garama Cave**, a historic residing spot of the Twa, where you'll get a song-and-dance performance. While at times it feels a bit contrived, the tour provides a much better insight to the Twa people than the often depressing village visits.

Sleeping & Eating

Most people sleep in Kisoro, but there are two choices just outside the park gate. Despite premium views of the Virunga volcanoes, this area just doesn't get many guests due to its out-of-the-way location; but for some people the peace and quiet is a bonus.

Amajambere Iwacu Community Campground BANDA $
(☎0382-278464; camping USh10,000, dm excl breakfast USh15,000, banda USh60,000, without bathroom USh45,000) A friendly place that's a community initiative with a variety of rooms and a nice verandah for relaxing. Local meals (USh5500 to USh8500) are available,

MGAHINGA GORILLA NATIONAL PARK

Why Go Mountain gorillas, golden monkeys, trekking in the stunning Virungas.

When to Go Year-round, but be sure to check the gorillas are here, as they often hangout on the Rwanda side.

Practicalities Most travellers spend the night in Kisoro, a short drive from the park headquarters. Otherwise, there are some good sleeping options at the park.

but only if you order early. It leads walks in the area and, if you contact in advance, can hook you up with some volunteer opportunities. Proceeds fund school projects in the area.

Mt Gahinga Lodge LODGE $$$
(☎0414-346464; www.volcanoessafaris.com; s/d incl full board US$400/800) The facilities are lovely but, at these prices, perhaps not lovely enough. Although alcohol is included in the rates.

Getting There & Away

There's no scheduled transport along the rough 14km track between Kisoro and park headquarters. You can try to hitch, although traffic is light so it's best to arrange a ride the night before.

SPECIAL-HIRE The most straightforward way to get out to the park. Should cost USh40,000; probably more in the wet season.

BODA-BODA Drivers will take you there for around USh15,000, but be prepared for a *very* rough ride.

Mbarara

☎ 0485 / POP 82,000

Mbarara is a prosperous town, a fact that brings many Ugandan business travellers here. But there's no reason for others to stop unless you want a well-stocked place to break your journey between Kampala and the far southwest.

LONG-HORNED ANKOLE

Overshadowed by gorillas and the Big Five, one exotic animal that you don't need to pay money to see in southwestern Uganda is the remarkable long-horned Ankole cow. It's pretty much your ordinary cow except for one notable feature –extreme horns that reach out as long as 2m, with some estimates up to 3.7m! Revered among many pastoralist indigenous groups as a status symbol, animal numbers are unfortunately on the decline, as farmers continue to abandon them in favour of more commercial breeds that yield more milk and meat.

Sights

Igongo Cultural Centre MUSEUM
(www.igongomuseum.co.ug; 16km Mbarara-Masaka Rd; adult/child USh20,000/3000; ⏰7.30-10pm) Located 10km from Mbarara on the road to Kampala, this new cultural village is set on the grounds of a former palace of the Ankole king, with the main highlight being its museum that explores the peoples of southwestern Uganda, particularly the Ankole. There's an outdoor restaurant with tables set on the lawn serving traditional Ankole dishes, such as smoked Ankole cow milk and boiled meats. There's a great bookstore with an interesting selection of Ugandan reading material, and it also sells handicrafts.

Sleeping & Eating

Hotel Westland HOTEL $
(☎0772-586769; Bananuka Dr; s/d/tr USh20,000/40,000/45,000. s/d without bathroom from USh10,000/13,000) A construction project that just never ends, this labyrinth place is a little rough around the edges, but it has a big array of good-value rooms available throughout: the top tier has satellite TV.

Lake View Resort Hotel HOTEL $$
(☎0772-367972; www.lakeviewresorthotel.co.ug; s/d excl breakfast from US$60/70; @🛜🏊) On the outskirts of town off the road to Kasese, this modern hotel sits in front of a tiny lake and has long been the place to be in Mbarara. The 100 rooms (all with balconies) aren't as flash as the public areas, but are still easily the best option. Facilities include a swimming pool, a sauna, tennis courts and a garden restaurant.

Getting There & Away

BUS & MINIBUS There are frequent buses and minibuses, departing from side-by-side parks, to Kampala (USh15,000, 4½ hours), Masaka (USh8,000, 2½ hours), Kabale (USh15,000, 3½ hours) and Kasese (USh12,000, three hours). You can also catch the Kigali-bound buses that begin in Kampala.

POST BUS The Post Bus (p491) to Kabale stops in Mbarara, leaving for Kampala about 9.30am.

Getting to Lake Mburo and Queen Elizabeth national parks (p432) is pretty straightforward.

Lake Mburo National Park

The 370-sq-km **Lake Mburo National Park** (☎0392-711346; adult/child US$35/20; ⏰7am-6.30pm) is an increasingly common stop on the safari circuit since it's the only place in southern Uganda to see zebra. It's also the only park in the country with impala, slender mongoose and giant bush rat, and is a great place to look for leopard, topi and eland. Furthermore, some excellent news is that a family of lions has retuned to the park after being absent for more than a decade. Some of the 325 species of bird include martial eagle and red-faced barbet in the acacia-wooded savannah and papyrus yellow warbler and African finfoot in the wetlands.

Animals are most abundant in the south in the dry season (as this is where the permanent water is) and the northeast in the wet season. Night drives (US$20 per person) are allowed. You can also take a **boat trip** (per person US$10; ⏰8am, 10am, noon, 2pm, 4pm & 5.30pm) on Lake Mburo, the largest of five lakes in the park, for something a bit more up close and personal with the hippos, crocodiles and waterbirds. Take note that if there's fewer than four people, then prices rise to US$40 per person.

Lake Mburo has some good nature walks, particularly the early morning **hyena walk** (per person U$10) at 6.30am. The other popular pedestrian destination is an observation blind overlooking a salt lick. Both walks take two hours. Birdwatchers should enquire about the Rubanga forest, which has a closed canopy in some places and you may find birds not yet recorded on the park's official list.

A more novel way of exploring the park is on **horseback safari** (one-hr/four-hr/overnight US$40/100/395), booked through Mihingo Lodge. Without the engine noise of a 4WD it's a peaceful way to get around the park to see wildlife and the park's lakes.

Fishing permits (US$15) are also available, but you'll need to bring your own equipment.

Adjacent to the park are the ranches of people of the Bahima tribe, who herd the famed long-horned Ankole cattle, which are a common sight here (all too often inside as well as outside the park).

LAKE MBURO NATIONAL PARK

Why Go The best place for zebras; healthy population of hippos and crocodiles; lions have made a comeback; the most accessible park to Kampala.

When to Go Year-round.

Practicalities A 3½-hour drive from Kampala. Reservations for boat trips are recommended June to August and December.

Sleeping & Eating

TOP CHOICE **Mihingo Lodge** LODGE $$$
(☎0752-410509; www.mihingolodge.com; s/d incl full board from US$155/240; 🏊) The most sumptuous and stylish lodging lies just outside the park's eastern border. The long, winding uphill drive fills you with anticipation and the facilities do not disappoint. The tent-cottage combos are spread out along the ridge (if you have a tough time walking, be sure to tell them when you book a room) and a watering hole busy with zebra, impala and waterhog among others is visible from the pool and some of the rooms. The best views are not of the park, but behind, looking out over Lake Kachera. Another highlight of the lodge is its family of habituated bushbabies who are regular visitors at night.

UWA Campsites CAMPGROUND $
(camping per person USh15,000) The park has three campsites, but most opt for the attractive Lakeside Camp 2, located 1¼km from the park headquarters. It has the scenic **Lakeside Restaurant** (mains USh12,000; ⏰7.30am-9.30pm), which is pretty good if you can spare a long time to wait for your food. If you have your own vehicle, consider Kingfisher Campsite 3, which is more rustic, but the whole site is first-come, first-served. At all these places you need to be mindful of wildlife encounters, particularly hippos.

Rwonyo Rest Camp BANDA, CAMPGROUND $
(banda s/d/f excl breakfast without bathroom USh35,000/40,000/60,000, safari tents s/d USh30,000/40,000) Located at park headquarters, the rest camp has camping, simple *bandas* and safari tents on wooden platforms, all with shared bathroom facilities. Overall, it's a very nice set-up with a classic

park feel. There's a small canteen selling beers and drinks, but the closest food is 1¼km away at the Lakeside Restaurant or upmarket Arcadia Cottages; due to an abundance of wildlife roaming the area, walking is not recommended, and UWA can arrange a boda-boda.

Arcadia Cottages LODGE $$$
(☎0486-26231; www.arcadiacottages.net/mburo; s/d incl full board US$150/220) Near but not right on the lake, this camp features bright, attractive cottages that are a melange of concrete, canvas, wood and thatch. The small daily menu (USh20,000) always has something Italian on it; non-guests are welcome to dine here.

Kimbla-Mantana Lake Mburo Camp LODGE $$$
(☎0392-967368; www.kimbla-mantana.com/permanent_camps_lodges.htm; s/d incl full board US$290/400) This luxury tented camp sits on a hill with commanding views of Lake Mburo (and sunsets behind the hills) available right from the hammocks on the big porches.

Getting There & Away

There are two possible ways into the park from the main Masaka–Mbarara road.

CAR If you're driving your own vehicle, it's better to use the Nshara gate, 13km after Lyantonde because you'll see much more wildlife on the drive in.

SPECIAL-HIRE, BODA-BODA & MINIBUS If you're hoping to hitch in or arrange a special-hire (USh70,000) or boda-boda (USh15,000) it's best to use the route from the Sanga gate, 27km after Lyantonde and 40km from Mbarara. Minibuses to Sanga cost USh5000 from Mbarara (45 minutes) and USh8000 from Masaka (two hours). It's about a 25km drive to Rwonyo from either gate.

If you're really rushed for time, Lake Mburo can be done as a day trip from Kampala. It's about a 3½-hour drive each way. A bus to Kampala is USh15,000.

Masaka

☎0481 / POP 73,000

In 1979 Masaka was trashed by the Tanzanian army during the war that ousted Idi Amin, and, unlike Mbarara, which suffered a similar fate, the scars remain very visible. There's a lot of construction going on these days, so perhaps Masaka has finally turned the corner. For most travellers, it's just a quick vehicle-swapping stop en route to the Ssese Islands or Tanzania.

Just out of Masaka on the way to Mbarara is the **Sitatunga Corner Observatory** (☎0772-306444; eanhs@imul.com), which offers excellent opportunities to spy two of Uganda's most elusive animals: the shoebill stork and the sitatunga.

All the usual banks are in town. For internet, try **Masaka Internet Services** (Kampala Rd; per hr USh2000; ⊙8am-9pm Mon-Fri, 8am-7pm Sat) where all proceeds support children's education.

Sleeping & Eating

Hotel Zebra HOTEL $
(☎0782-863725; s excl breakfast USh40,000, d USh80,000-100,000, tr USh120,000; @) All in all, when you combine price, facilities and location (not to mention the staff's snazzy striped uniforms) we think this is the top place to stay in town. All rooms have a satellite TV and a balcony with surprisingly nice views over town, plus there's a little garden for dining under the stars.

Masaka Tourist Cottage & Campsite BACKPACKERS $
(☎0752-619389; www.traveluganda.co.ug/touristcottageandcampsite; camping USh9000, dm excl breakfast USh15,000, s/d USh20,000/35,000) Formerly Masaka Backpackers, this fun, friendly place 4.5km south of town has a nice rural feel and a helpful owner. Meals (USh6000 to USh8000) are available. To get here from Masaka, a boda-boda will cost USh1500 and special-hire USh10,000. It can arrange visits to Sitatunga Corner Observatory and village tours.

TOP CHOICE **Aidchild's 10 Tables** INTERNATIONAL $
(☎0772-982509; www.aidchild.org/ten_tables.asp; Victoria St; lunch USh7000, dinner USh20,000; ⊙9.30am-11pm) One of Uganda's most surprising finds, this little pocket of sophistication (white linens and candlelight) puts all proceeds towards supporting AIDS orphans. Lunch comprises snacks and local food while the three-course set dinners alternate daily from mains such as fajitas or garlic-marinated tilapia. The titular 10 tables are downstairs while up above is a comfy lounge and a balcony with some sunset views. It also screen movies (USh5000) nightly at 6.30pm and 8.30pm.

Getting There & Away

MINIBUS, BUS & BODA-BODA Most minibuses pick up and drop-off passengers at the Shell petrol stations on Kampala Rd. Most buses, on the other hand, use the bypass rather than coming into town, so it's usually quickest to take a boda-boda (USh1000) to nearby Nyendo for eastbound services and Kyabakuza for westbound services. Service is frequent to Kampala (USh10,000, two hours) and Mbarara (USh10,000, 2½ hours), and less so to Kabale (USh20,000, five hours).

If you're crossing into Tanzania and onto Bukoba, either take a morning minibus to Kyotera (USh4000, one hour) and then another to the border at Mutukula (USh5000, one hour) where you can catch a third ride to Bukoba (Tsh4000, 1½ hours); or hop on the direct buses from Kampala out at the junction.

For Ssese Island transport information see p456.

Ssese Islands

If you're looking for a place to slow it right down, Ssese's lush archipelago of 84 islands along Lake Victoria's northwestern shore boasts some stunning white-sand beaches. The early 1990s saw their popularity peak, but the suspension of the ferry service largely took them off the *muzungu* map until 2006 when a ferry began running from Entebbe. At the time of research, the new ferry company EarthWise commenced a service from Port Bell in Kampala – which is likely to reaffirm the Sseses' rightful place on the tourist radar.

Early in the 20th century, sleeping sickness hit the islands (Ssese = Tsetse), which saw most of the original Bassese inhabitants flee. People slowly drifted back beginning about a decade and a half later, but it wasn't until the 1980s that serious settlement took place again. There are very few Bassese anymore and their Lussese language has all but died.

The lack of settlement left the islands largely unspoiled, though things have changed dramatically in the recent past. Massive scars of deforestation are visible on many of the islands, especially Buggala, and overfishing is another issue.

There's not much to do on Ssese other than grab a good book and relax. There are canoes for hire, but swimming is unadvisable due to risks of bilharzia, while some outlaying islands have the occasional hippo and crocodile. Most guesthouses on the beach have nightly bonfires, which is a great way to relax with a few drinks after enjoying one of Ssese's famous sunsets.

Few people venture far beyond Buggala Island's Lutoboka Bay, where the ferry lands and almost all accommodation sits, but if you make a little effort there are some good exploration opportunities. The biggest islands, including Buggala, Bufumira and Bukasa, are hilly and many spots afford beautiful views across to other islands, most of which are still ringed by virgin rainforest.

Sleeping & Eating

Almost all visitors limit themselves to Buggala Island, though the two other islands with accommodation are perfect if you want that added seclusion.

BUGGALA ISLAND

Most of the lodging is centred on attractive Lutoboka Bay, right where the ferry drops you off, and most hotels will pick you up for free. All hotels have restaurants, with decent food but expect a very long wait. Always ask for a discount if things look slow; you'll often get one.

TOP CHOICE Mirembe Resort GUESTHOUSE $
(☎0392-772703; www.mirembereresort.com; camping per tent USh15,000, safari tent per person USh20,000, s/d/tr excl breakfast USh65,000/90,000/135,000; @) In Luganda, 'mirembe' means peace, and by walking (about 1½km following the road) out to the last resort on this stunning stretch of beach you'll get more of it than at any of the other lodges on this side of the bay. There's a variety of rooms available, but the exterior ones, which have their own porches with lake views, are the best bet. There's a good choice of food (USh7000 to USh10,000) here, but give the pizzas a miss.

Islands Club GUESTHOUSE $
(☎0772-641376; sseseclub@yahoo.com; s/d incl full breakfast USh50,000/100,000) Located next door to Mirembe and one of the first lodgings on the island, its dark wooden bungalows have a real beachy feel to them, which is perfect considering they're right on a blinding stretch of white sand. Its spiced, fried tilapia is absolutely delicious and staff are extremely friendly and helpful.

Ssese Islands Beach Hotel HOTEL $
(☎0414-220065; www.sseseislandsbeachhotel.com; camping USh15,000, dm USh35,000, s incl

full breakfast USh65,000-80,000, d USh110,000-130,000; @) Its concrete rooms and golf course may not necessarily suit what the Sseses are about, but its deluxe rooms are right on the beach with great views from their private porches. The dorms and 'apartment' rooms are less attractive, namely because they're set back from the beach.

Hornbill Camp BACKPACKERS **$**
(☎0775-880200; camping USh10,000, dm excl breakfast USh15,000, r USh20,000, bungalows USh40,000) With its psychedelic murals, thatched bungalows, hammocks and lovely beach, Hornbill has a vibe reminiscent of Goa c 1990s (minus the full-moon parties). It gets mixed reviews from travellers, with your experience basically depending on how you get along with its hippie owners.

Panorama Cottages GUESTHOUSE **$**
(☎0782-310629; camping USh5000, tent hire USh10,000, bandas s excl breakfast USh30,000-50,000, bandas d USh35,000-55,000) Situated inland with a five minute walk to the beach, there are no views on offer, but it's laid-back with large, clean *bandas,* surrounded by plenty of trees and flowers.

Ssese Palm Beach RESORT **$$**
(☎0414-530731) Located alone out on a sandy headland, Palm Beach was under renovation at the time of research and with new management appears to transform itself into Ssese's only resort.

OTHER ISLANDS

You'll have no problems persuading fishermen to take you out on their boats, but try to get a group together first, as prices are very high.

Banda Island Resort GUESTHOUSE **$**
(☎0772-222777; banda.island@gmail.com; Banda Island; dm excl breakfast USh50,000, r USh150,000) Once legendary among backpackers, few people head to Banda Island anymore now that it's so much easier to get to Buggala, but Banda is much more peaceful, which is what an island escape should be. This ever-evolving Gilligan's Island–like place sits on a big beach and a little peninsula. The accommodation is comfortable (all prices include 'very full board' and you can pay for five days, stay for seven), the food is good. There's unlimited ground coffee for guests, but, due to lack of power, no cold drinks. Guests can walk around the island, paddle around Lake Vic in canoes and kayaks or just perform some quality control on the hammocks. It's now under German management after its popular owner, Dom, sadly passed away.

There's also Father Christopher's Guesthouse and some other basic sleeping options on **Bukasa Island**, out at the far end of the archipelago. Bukassa is the second largest of the Sseses and has several spots worth exploring, including lovely little Musenyi Beach, a small waterfall and a shrine to Wammena (a spirit associated with physical handicaps).

ℹ Information

The only full-on town is Kalangala on Buggala Island. There's a post office and a Stanbic Bank, which changes cash, but currently has no ATM. At the time of research, Ssese Islands Beach Hotel was the only place with an internet connection. The electricity supply on the island is also erratic, though most lodges have generators.

ℹ Getting There & Away

Boat & Ferry

With new company **EarthWise** (www.earthwise.com) recently launching a ferry service from Port Bell in Kampala on the *MV Armani*, getting to Ssese has got a lot easier. Boats from Kampala depart Port Bell at 8am, arriving at Kalangala on Buggala Island at noon. Departure times from Buggala are at 1.30pm, arriving at Port Bell by 6pm. Fares are USh30,000/70,000 for economy/first class; you'll need to arrive 30 minutes before departure.

FROM NAKIWOGO Visitors can get to Buggala Island on the MV *Kalangala* ferry from Nakiwogo near Entebbe. It departs the mainland at 2pm daily and leaves the island at 8am. The trip usually takes 3½ hours. First-class seating costs USh14,000 and second-class USh10,000, but there's little difference between the two. Vehicles cost USh50,000. At weekends and holidays the boat can be crowded, so show up early to claim a seat or you may have to stand on the deck.

FROM KASENYI To get to Banda Island there are small wooden boats departing from Kasenyi, a fishing village just before Entebbe (a 30-minute minibus ride from Kampala's Old Taxi Park; USh3000), but these aren't the safest way to go as winds on Lake Victoria can whip up some really big waves. Insist on wearing a lifejacket. Also note that schedules and prices are very fickle, so try to confirm things before heading out to the landing.

Boats to Banda Island (USh35,000, 3¼ hours) leave daily at 1pm, stopping via Kitobo Island. Otherwise there's a direct boat on Tuesdays at noon (USh20,000). There's also a weekly boat on Fridays to Bukasa Island (USh10,000, four hours).

FROM BUKAKATA From the west, a free car ferry (though when running low on fuel they often request money from drivers) links Bukakata (36km east of Masaka) on the mainland with Luku on Buggala Island. The ferry sails either direction every few hours from early in the morning to late afternoon. There are no morning trips on Sunday. The schedule changes often, so call one of the resorts on Buggala Island to get the current times. If you miss the free boat, there's frequent wooden fishing boats that run to Luku (USh5000), but they're often overcrowded and a bit leaky, so it's wise to ask for a lifejacket.

Taxi

On Buggala Island, there are shared taxis that run from Kalangala to Luku (USh5000, one hour), while coming from the mainland there are taxis that run from Nyendo (3km east of Masaka) to Bukakata (USh5000, one hour). Taxis in both directions run to coincide with the car ferry schedule, and neither is a fun trip as they're usually insanely overpacked with 15 passengers somehow squeezing into a five-seat car!

Getting Around

On Buggala Island, Kalangala trading centre is 2km uphill from the pier; a boda-boda costs USh2000.

A special-hire boat from Buggala Island to Banda Island is $US70. To get to the other islands is very pricey with rising fuel costs, so island hopping is not really a popular activity.

NORTHWESTERN UGANDA

For decades, the Lord's Resistance Army (LRA) and its war on civilians put most of northwestern Uganda effectively off limits. But now that the LRA has fled Uganda, this vast region is once again on the traveller's map. As before, Murchison Falls National Park remains the region's saving grace. The best all-round protected area in the country for wildlife and attractions, Murchison has large populations of lions, leopard, buffaloes, elephants, giraffes, hippos and chimpanzees, plus its namesake waterfall is world-class. Ziwa Rhino Sanctuary is also a popular stopover to see white rhinos.

Ziwa Rhino Sanctuary

The Big Five are back. In 2005, Rhino Fund Uganda opened this private 70-sq-km **reserve** (0772-713410; www.rhinofund.org; admission adult/child US$30/15, guide fee US$15; 7.30am-6pm; last tracking starts at 5pm), 170km northwest of Kampala, about 30 years after poachers shot the nation's last wild rhino. Ten southern white rhinos (the northern white rhino once found in Uganda is so close to extinction there's little hope of its survival) roam the savannah and wetland, four of which were born in the wild in Uganda. The long-term goal is for these magnificent beasts to be reintroduced to Murchison Falls and Kidepo Valley national parks.

A guide will lead you on an up-close encounter, either in your vehicle (a car is alright in the dry season, but you'll need a 4WD in the wet) or theirs (US$20). Once you reach the rhinos you finish your visit on foot. While tracking rhinos on foot sounds a bit foolhardy, the fact that they're in the company of anti-poacher rangers 24 hours, means they're well and truly used to human presence.

Reservations are rarely needed, but a good idea. Other animals living inside the 6ft-tall electric fence include leopard, hippos, crocodiles, bushbuck and oribis. There is discussion of introducing zebras to the park. It's also home to 239 species of bird including giant kingfisher and shoebill stork. There's occasionally volunteer opportunities, so enquire via its website.

While most visit as a day trip en route to Murchison from Kampala, there are two good sleeping options in the park. In the centre of the reserve there's budget **accommodation** (camping per tent US$5, r US$15, cottage incl full breakfast US$40), and there's a big thatched-roof **restaurant** (meals adult/child US$8/5). Otherwise deeper in the park there's the new **Amuka Lodge** (www.amukalodgeuganda.com; bandas incl full board per person US$180;) with upmarket, family tented *bandas* and lovely decking with a swimming pool, a bar and a firepit.

All buses from Kampala heading to Gulu or Masindi pass nearby. Get off at little Nakitoma (USh13,000, three hours) and take a boda-boda 7km to the sanctuary gate for USh7000.

Masindi

☎ 0465 / POP 43,000

Masindi is a quiet provincial headquarters, the last town of any substance on the road to Murchison Falls National Park. It's a good place to base yourself for the night, and stock up on provisions.

Sights & Activities

Kigaju Forest WILDLIFE WATCHING

(☎0702-389359; musinguzimathew@yahoo.co.uk) About 5km out of town, this privately owned 60-hectare swathe of forest is home to chimpanzees, baboons, black-and-white colobus monkeys and lots of butterflies. The owners had intended to clear the forest because of crop damage caused by baboons that live here, but were convinced to save it, at least for now. The chimps aren't yet habituated, and the forest is far from pristine, but sightings are quite common, especially around 6am and 5pm. A guided walk is US$20, and reservations mandatory – they'll pick you up in town. There's a small campsite. Note that you can't visit by yourself; it's essential to make reservations and meet the guides in town.

Walking Trail of Masindi Town WALKING TOUR

A group of Voluntary Service Overseas (VSO) volunteers has produced a brochure pointing out various historical sites. While the stories are better than the sights, it can still make for a few fun hours. Pick up a copy at the New Court View Hotel or Travellers' Corner.

Sleeping & Eating

TOP CHOICE **Masindi Hotel** HOTEL $$

(☎0465-420023; www.masindihotel.com; Hoima Rd; camping USh15,000, s/d incl full breakfast USh112,000/137,000; @☜) Up the road from New Court View Hotel, this lovely lodge, built in 1923 by East Africa Railways and

Northwestern Uganda

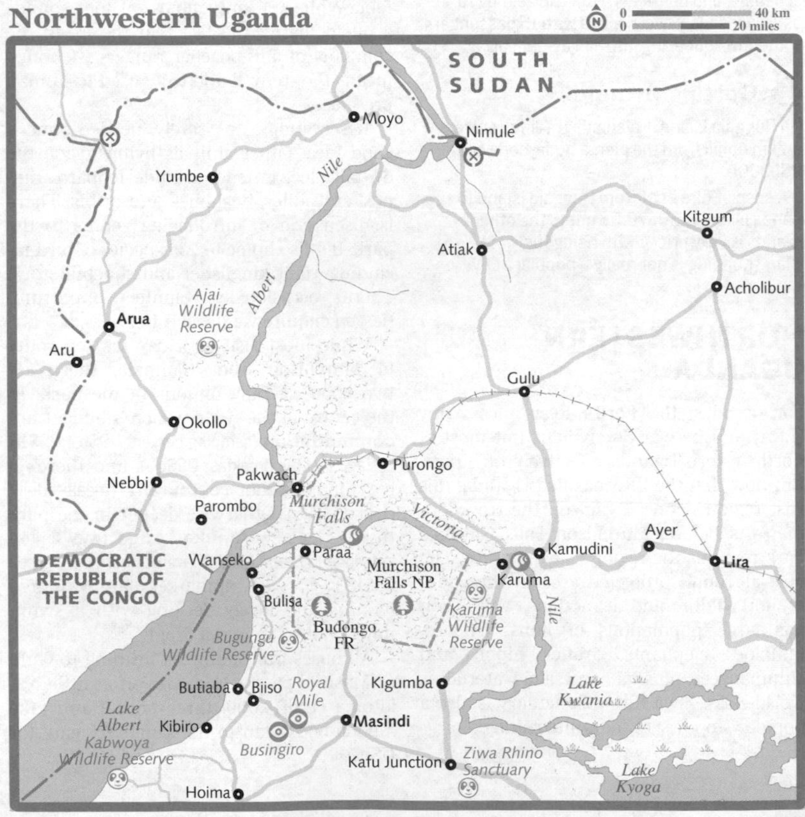

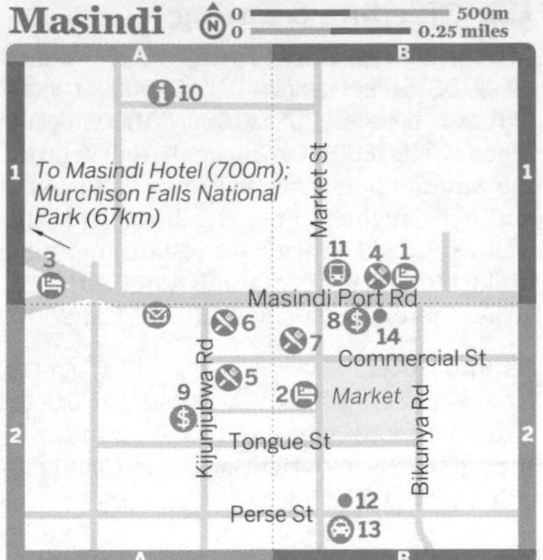

Harbours Company, is reportedly Uganda's oldest hotel and has hosted Ernest Hemingway (Room 6, where he recuperated from injuries sustained during a plane crash; see boxed text p463), Katharine Hepburn (Room 5) and Humphrey Bogart (Room 6). A 2005 renovation brought out the historic character. The **restaurant** (mains USh15,000-18,000) and the 'Hemingway' bar are popular.

New Court View Hotel BANDA $
(☎0752-446463; www.newcourtviewhotel.com; Hoima Rd; camping USh10,000, s/d excl breakfast USh51,000/60,000) This great little hotel has large, comfy *bandas* and smiling staff. The food in the **restaurant** (mains USh10,000-15,000) is some of the best in town and served promptly, which helps you overlook the high prices. There's also a book exchange.

Karibuni Guesthouse GUESTHOUSE $
(☎0787-203884; Market St; s/d excl breakfast USh20,000/30,000) Hidden behind an unlikely shopfront are comfy, newly renovated rooms with lots of greenery in between. Excellent value.

Alinda Guesthouse GUESTHOUSE $
(☎0772-520382; alindamasindi@yahoo.co.uk; 86 Masindi Port Rd; d excl breakfast USh40,000, s/d without bathroom USh15,000/25,000) You can't help notice that the ever popular Alinda, with big clean rooms and right on the main road from Kampala, is a bit tattered these days, but the mix of dead plants and plastic flowers almost gives it an unintended shabby-chic feel. Rooms in the nearby annex lack hot water. The restaurant under the tent is

Masindi

Sleeping

1 Alinda Guesthouse B1
2 Karibuni Guesthouse B2
3 New Court View Hotel A1

Eating

4 Alinda B1
5 Lucky 7 .... A2
6 Travellers' Corner Restaurant A2
7 Wat General Agencies B2

Information

8 Barclays Bank B2
9 Stanbic Bank A2
10 UWA Masindi Information Office A1

Transport

11 Buses to Kampala B1
12 Enyange B2
13 Taxi Park B2
14 Yebo Tours B2

popular and features a good value all-you-can-eat dinner buffet.

Travellers' Corner Restaurant INTERNATIONAL $
(Masindi Port Rd; mains USh4000-6000; @) With the same owners as New Court View Hotel, this is a popular gathering spot for locals and tourists alike. The food is cheaper than at the hotel, though the menu is much more limited: no Indian or Chinese choices here, but there are petite pizzas. It's more of a bar than restaurant at night and the pool table is always in use.

If you forget to pack anything in Kampala, there are three small supermarkets with some imported goods: **Alinda** (Masindi Port Rd), **Lucky 7** (Commercial St) and **Wat General Agencies** (Commercial St).

Information

There are a few internet cafes on Masindi Port Rd. **Stanbic Bank** (Kijunjubwa Rd) and **Barclays** (Masindi Port Rd have ATMs.

The **UWA Masindi Information Office** (☎0465-420428; ⏰7am-12.30pm & 2-6.30pm), down a dirt road north of the post office, has national park information.

Getting There & Away

See p465 for details of getting to Murchison Falls National Park from Masindi.

Minibuses from Masindi to Kampala (USh13,000, four hours) and Hoima (USh7000, two hours) travel throughout the day. **Link** (☎0465-421073) has buses to Kampala (USh13,000, 3½ hours) which leave from Masindi Port Rd between 7.30am and 4.30pm. The Post Bus (see p491) stops here on its way to and from Hoima.

Minibuses to Gulu (USh15,000, four hours) are infrequent, so it's usually quicker to go to Kafu Junction on the main highway and catch a northbound bus there. There are also departures to Butiaba (USh10,000, three hours), Bulisa (USh12,000, three hours) and Wanseko (USh12,000 three hours).

As a gateway town to Murchison Fall National Park, Masindi is a good place to arrange transport hire into the park. Two recommended companies are **Yebo Tours** (Map p460; ☎0772-637493; yebotours2002@yahoo.com; Masindi Port Rd), which hires 4WDs for US$80 per day (including one tank of fuel) and **Enyange** (☎0772-657404), which charges USh200,000 per day.

Hoima

POP 40,000

Hoima is the hub of the Bunyoro Kingdom, the oldest in East Africa. It's a useful starting point for a back route into Murchison Falls National Park via Lake Albert.

Sights

Karuziika Palace PALACE
(☎0782-128229; Main St) If you call his private secretary in advance you can visit the part-time home of the Bunyoro king, to see the throne room, which is draped with leopard and lion skins and filled with drums, spears, crowns and other traditional items.

Mparo Tombs HISTORIC SITE
(admission USh10,000) On the other side of town, 2km down the Masindi Rd (4km out of Hoima), is the final resting place of the renowned Bunyoro king Omukama ('King') Chwa II Kabalega and his son. Kabalega was a thorn in the side of the British for much of his reign until he was exiled to the Seychelles in 1899. Inside are his spears, bowls, throne and other personal effects on display above the actual resting place. A wedding-cake-shaped monument in the front memorialises the 1877 meeting of Kabalega and German naturalist/explorer/diplomat Emin Pasha.

Sleeping & Eating

African Village Guest Farm BANDA **$**
(☎0772-335115; camping USh12,000, bandas s/d excl breakfast USh30,000/60,000, deluxe banda USh100,000) On a small dairy farm, the *bandas* here have balconies, and Betty and her daughters are great hosts. Has the well-regarded Guinea Fowl restaurant and a funky little art gallery (admission USh1000). To get there, a boda-boda will cost USh2000.

Nsamo Hotel HOTEL **$**
(☎0754-134557; s/d excl breakfast USh20,000/30,000) A more convenient location in town, the ageing Nsamo, right near the Classic, is still a very good choice.

Information

Barclays Bank (Main St) West of the centre and most useful bank in town; has an ATM and exchanges cash.

Ugaprivi (per hr USh1500; ⏲7am-9.30pm) For internet access, opposite Barclays and located down a dirt road by the mobile phone tower in the centre of town.

Getting There & Away

Minibuses to Kampala (USh12,000, three hours) run all day while buses (USh10,000, 2½ hours) depart from their own spot next to the taxi park and run less frequently, finishing up at 2pm. The Post Bus (see p491) goes via Masindi.

A few minibuses to Masindi (USh6000, two hours) use the main taxi park, but most depart from the Petro Uganda station on Kampala Rd.

For Fort Portal it takes two minibuses with a change in Kagadi. The total price is USh23,000 and it usually takes seven hours. There's also a coaster (USh26,000, six hours) leaving Fort Portal and Kagadi on alternate days that make the run directly.

Minibuses also run to Butiaba (USh7000, two hours) in the morning plus Bulisa (USh12,000, three hours) and Wanseko (USh12,000, 3¼ hours) all day long.

Murchison Falls National Park

Uganda's largest **national park** (☎0392-881348; adult/child US$35/20; ⏲park gates 7am-7pm) and one of its very best; animals here are in plentiful supply and the raging Murchison Falls a sight to behold. Sir Samuel Baker named Murchison Falls in honour of a president of the Royal Geographical Society, and the park was subsequently named after the falls. The Victoria Nile River flows through the park on its way to Lake Albert.

During the 1960s, Murchison (3893 sq km; 5081 sq km with the adjoining Bugungu and Karuma wildlife reserves) was one of Africa's most famous parks; as many as 12 launches filled with eager tourists would buzz up the river to the falls each day. The park also had some of the largest concentrations of wildlife in Africa, including as many as 15,000 elephants. Unfortunately, poachers and troops wiped out practically all wildlife, except the more numerous (or less sought-after) herd species. While its rhino population was entirely killed off and remains absent from the park, other wildlife is recovering fast and you can find good numbers of elephants, Rothschild giraffes, lion, Ugandan kob (antelopes), waterbuck, buffaloes, hippos and crocodiles these days. Sitatunga, leopard and spotted hyenas might also be seen. Birdlife consists of some 460 species, including quite a few shoebill stork.

Despite this new beginning, don't come to Murchison expecting a scene from the Serengeti. Still, we've never heard of anybody going away disappointed in their visit. And, even if there were no animals, the awesome power of Murchison Falls would make this park worth visiting.

For more information on the park, pick up a copy of *Murchison Falls Conservation Area Guidebook* (2002) by Shaun Mann at the park office.

Sights & Activities

See p466 for information on chimpanzee tracking in Budongo Forest Reserve, which is officially part of the park but is operated separately.

Launch Trip to the Falls — BOAT TOUR

(US$25) The three-hour launch trip from Paraa (park headquarters) up to the base of the falls is the highlight of the park for most visitors. There are abundant hippos, crocodiles and buffaloes; thousands of birds, including many fish eagles; and usually elephants along this 17km stretch of the Nile. In the rainy season even shoebills might make an appearance. The animals are there all day long, but the best photos of the falls come on the afternoon trip. The halfway mark takes you 500m from the base of the falls, which provides splendid views, but to get a true sense of its power and might you'll have to head to the Top of the Falls walk. Nearby is the site where Ernest Hemingway's plane crashed (see boxed text, p463). The **UWA boats** sail daily at 9am and 2pm if there's enough demand, and costs US$25 per person if there are 10 or more people. You may have to cough up extra if there are fewer, though if tour company clients are on board, the boat will go regardless of the numbers.

Similar trips are also run by **Paraa Safari Lodge** (www.paraalodge.com) at roughly the same price and schedule to UWA, while **Wild Frontiers** (www.wildfrontiers.com) is slightly pricier but its boats are in better condition – it also runs more upmarket cheese-and-wine cruises (US$50 per couple); otherwise its standard trips have cold beers available.

Wildlife Drives — WILDLIFE WATCHING

Pretty much all wildlife-watching on land happens in the Buligi area, on the point between the Albert and Victoria Niles. Just about all the park's resident species might be seen in the savannah on the Albert, Queen and Victoria tracks, and the chances of spotting lions and leopard are quite good. There's very little wildlife south of the river, and driving in from Masindi you'll probably only see baboons and warthogs, though various antelope sometimes come out to play.

Drives can't begin before 7am and you'll want to budget a minimum of four hours to get out there and back. On the off-chance you haven't organised a vehicle, Paraa Safari Lodge offers game drives from US$200/300 for guests/nonguests. Budget travellers sometimes have luck hanging out at the ferry and finding space in someone's vehicle. Those with their own vehicle should definitely take a UWA ranger-guide (US$20) to boost their chances of close encounters.

MURCHISON FALLS NATIONAL PARK

Why Go Excellent wildlife watching from boat or car; Rothschild giraffe; lion; sheer power and fury of Murchison Falls; chimpanzee tracking in Budongo Forest Reserve.

When to Go Year-round.

Practicalities No public transport into park, but various hostels offer popular tours for budget travellers; try to tack on Ziwa Rhino Sanctuary en route to Kampala.

Murchison Falls National Park

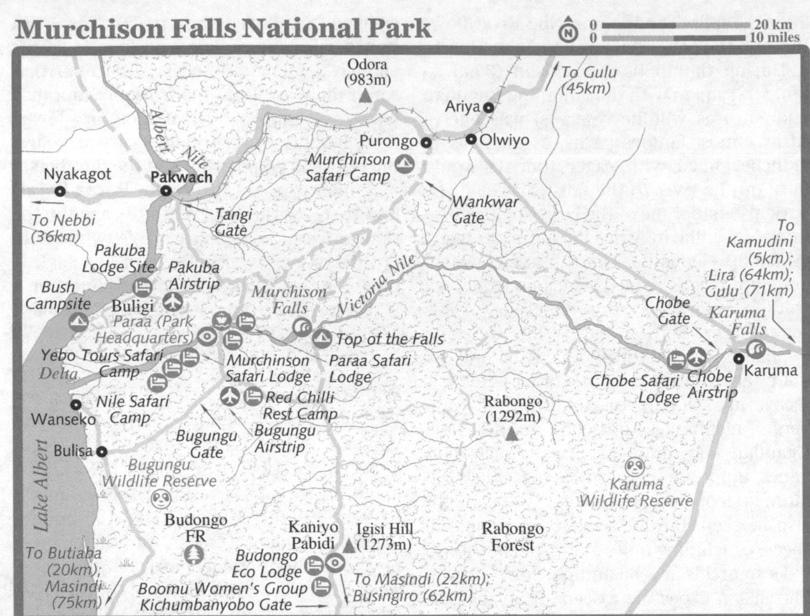

Top of the Falls WATERFALL

Once described as the most spectacular thing to happen to the Nile along its 6700km length, the 50m river is squeezed through a 6m gap in the rock and crashes through this narrow gorge with unbelievable power. The 45m waterfall was featured in the Katherine Hepburn and Humphrey Bogart film *The African Queen*. Murchison was even stronger back then, but in 1962 massive floods cut a second channel creating the smaller Uhuru Falls 200m to the north.

There's a beautiful **walking trail** from the top down to the river, and the upper stretch of this path offers views of Uhuru Falls, which the boat is not able to get close enough to appreciate, so the trail will give you the complete Murchison experience. A ranger (US$10 per person) is required on this walk. If you take the launch trip, the captain will let you off at the trailhead and a ranger will meet you there. The boat can then pick you up later *if* there's an afternoon launch. This is also a good way for backpackers to get to the campsite at the top of the falls before returning to Paraa the next morning. The hike takes about 45 minutes from the bottom, and some people find it difficult as there's no shade on the steepest parts.

Nile Cruises BOAT TOUR

(US$150; ⏲departs 7am) The five-hour Nile Delta boat trip is run by UWA and heads downstream to the papyrus-filled delta where the Nile empties into Lake Albert. While it's less popular than the trip upstream to the falls, wildlife-watching is still very good, though perhaps not as reliable. You may see leopard lounging in trees and shoebill sightings are very common. Tour companies often book the boat so you should be able to join for a fraction of the whole cost. Otherwise you could try **Nile Navigation** (☎0782-169474; www.nilenavigation.com) which charge US$330 for a 20-seater boat (excluding park entry fees).

Nature Walks WALKING, BIRDWATCHING

(per person US$10) The 1½km guided nature walk along the north bank of the Nile by Paraa Safari Lodge is popular with birdwatchers, but you're not likely to see many other animals.

Sport Fishing FISHING

(permits 1 day/4 days US$50/150) Murchison is a popular place to fish for the gargantuan tilapia (Nile perch), though from all reports fish numbers are in sharp decline. The normal catch ranges from 20kg to 60kg, but the record haul is 108kg. You can fish from the shore or get a boat, but be mindful of crocodiles and hippos. Wild Frontiers offer full-day fishing trips from US$180 per person for groups of three, not including permits or equipment. For more information, check out **Fishing Murchison** (www.fishingmurchison.com).

Sleeping & Eating

Most of Murchison's lodges are located within the vicinity of the Paraa park headquarters, a convenient choice for wildlife drives and the falls. There's also more remote options in the far west, north and south sectors, providing a more peaceful experience.

PARAA

TOP CHOICE **Red Chilli Rest Camp** BACKPACKERS $
(☎0772-509150; www.redchillihideaway.com; camping US$5, safari tent d excl breakfast US$20, banda d/f US$40/70, without bathroom US$25) The popular Red Chilli team from Kampala easily brings the best budget option to Murchison. The rooms here are great value, particularly the *bandas,* so it's strongly advised to book well in advance. Staff are personable and helpful.

The restaurant–bar is set under a huge thatched roof, and serves sandwiches (USh6000) for lunch and set dinners (from USh8500) at night plus the signature hippo breakfast that's so popular in Kampala. Speaking of hippos, they regularly graze here at night, so bring a torch in order to give them a very wide berth.

Paraa Safari Lodge LODGE $$
(☎0312-260260; www.paraalodge.com; s/d/ste incl full board US$165/265/335; @≋) On the northern bank of the river, this hotel-style lodge has a great location and views, as well as excellent facilities such as a swim-up bar. From across the river it looks rather like a POW camp, but up close it's lovely and the rooms are pretty much four-star standard. The business centre has the only internet access (USh6000 per 30 minutes) this side of the park.

THE MISADVENTURES OF HEMINGWAY IN UGANDA

Despite Ernest Hemingway's well-documented love of Africa, having based several novels and short stories here, he certainly could be forgiven for not looking back fondly upon his time spent in Uganda. Having the misfortune of experiencing two plane crashes within a week, in short, his time here was a total disaster.

As a Christmas present to his fourth wife Mary Welsh in 1954, Hemingway arranged a scenic flight from Nairobi to the Congo, which en route took in spectacular aerial views of the Nile around Lake Albert. While circling Murchison Falls at a low altitude, the small plane clipped a telegraph wire that led to them crashing into the dense forest. With relatively minor, yet painful injuries including broken ribs and a dislocated shoulder, they emerged from the wreck to face a night stranded near the falls.

Anyone who's done the Murchison Falls launch trip can attest to its abundance of wildlife, and a night spent out in the open with crocodiles, hippos, elephants and leopard is far from ideal. After an evening spent shooing off animals, they were fortuitously picked up the next day by a boat (allegedly the one filmed in the Humphrey Bogart and Audrey Hepburn classic, *The African Queen),* which was hosting a wedding anniversary party heading to Butiaba.

Undeterred by the shock of surviving a plane crash and in need of medical attention, Hemingway and Welsh decided to charter another flight to take them to Entebbe. But in a terrible stroke of bad luck, the plane crashed again! This time in a ball of flames upon take-off, and injuries sustained were far more serious, particularly for Hemingway who fractured his skull while headbutting his way out, ruptured his liver, suffered a collapsed intestine, two broken vertebrae, and a burnt scalp among other injuries. It was widely reported in the international media that he'd died in the crash, and during time spent recovering in Nairobi, Hemingway was able to read over his obituaries.

The severity of his injuries prevented Hemingway from accepting his Nobel Prize in Literature 10 months later, and many believed he never physically or mentally recovered from the accidents. Hemingway wrote about the incident for *Look* magazine in 1954 in an article with the innocuous sounding title: 'The Christmas Gift'.

HITCHING A RIDE TO MURCHISON

An issue for budget travellers who aren't in Murchison Falls National Park on a tour is the lack of public transport into the park. One option is to try chatting with other tourists to see if they're willing to split the costs to give you a ride in. **Travellers' Corner Restaurant** (during lunch), **New Court View Hotel** and **Masindi Hotel** (at night) are good spots in Masindi, which are popular rest stops for tourists.

Getting out of the park is much easier as you can find out where vehicles are heading to and arrange a ride in advance.

Besides hitching, the cheapest way into Murchison Falls National Park is to get to Bulisa or Wanseko, an interesting fishing village where the Nile empties into Lake Albert. Minibuses run to these neighbouring towns daily from Hoima and Masindi for USh12,000. Either go as far as Bulisa, from where you can negotiate for a boda-boda to take you to Paraa for around USh40,000 (boda-boda drivers are required to pay park admission of USh15,000 but often don't, so negotiate a fee without the admission costs and you might get lucky) or continue the 6km to Wanseko and then negotiate with the minibus drivers to continue to Paraa as a special-hire (perhaps as low as USh80,000).

ELSEWHERE IN THE PARK

It's worth keeping an eye out to see whether the old Pakuba Lodge has been renovated, since it has a stunning location on the Albert Nile. For sleeping options at Kaniyo Pabidi, near Kichumbanyobo gate, see p466.

TOP CHOICE Chobe Safari Lodge LODGE $$$
(☎0312-259390 www.chobelodgeuganda.com; s/d/ste incl full board US$180/325/380; @⛱) One of the first lodges to open in the park in the 1950s, Chobe has just reopened its doors after being abandoned for decades. Isolated on the far eastern reaches of the park, a few kilometres from the Chobe gate, renovations here have returned it to its former splendour, with a gorgeous river location that's teeming with honking hippos. The upstairs standard rooms are the best pick. They have great views, lovely decor and balconies. Otherwise there are comfortable tented rooms away from the main building, spread out along the river. Views can be enjoyed from its classy outdoors restaurant with decking and big umbrellas, or its three-tiered swimming pool. The place has the feel of a celebrity hideaway, and even has its own airstrip – though it's more popular with grazing buffaloes. It offers wildlife drives for US$200 for four people.

Top of the Falls Campsite CAMPGROUND $
(camping USh15,000) This simple spot has a very nice position right on the river, and a close walk to the falls. You'll need to be self-sufficient, as, for the time being, the only facilities are a pit toilet. At dusk you can watch a mass exodus of bats from a nearby cave, and it's popular with grazing hippos, which, obviously, you'll need to be careful of.

Bush Campsite CAMPGROUND $
(camping US$40 per person) Adventurous souls can have an unforgettable night in the wild (and an early start on your morning wildlife-viewing), sleeping out at Delta Point overlooking Lake Albert near the Buligi section of the park. The park has no tents, so the armed guard (compulsory) who accompanies you will probably want to sleep in your vehicle. Book the trip at the park office, but take note it's considerably more pricey than your normal camping.

OUTSIDE THE PARK

BULIGI

Nile Safari Camp LODGE $$$
(☎0414-258273; www.geolodgesafrica.com/nile_safari_lodge.htm; camping US$10, s/d incl full board US$160/280; ⛱) This fantastic lodge is high up on the south bank of the Victoria Nile River, with lovely views over the water and tons of monkeys and birds in the trees below. Accommodation is in comfortable permanent tents and wooden cottages, each with a river-view balcony. There's also an atmospheric bar and dining area (set-menu three-course lunch and dinner USh28,000), as well as a swimming pool with a view. Ask for directions to get here because the unmarked shortcut from

Paraa is more convenient than the main entrance.

Murchison Safari Lodge BANDA $$$
(☎0714-000085; www.murchisonriverlodge.com; camping US$10, safari tents s/d excl breakfast $US64/130,without bathroom US$45/90, cottage US$100 per person) A long time in the making, this luxury lodge on the Victoria Nile was on the verge of opening at the time of research, and certainly one to keep an eye on. It's located between Nile Safari Camp and Paraa. Prices are full board, other than for camping.

Yebo Tours Safari Camp BANDA $
(☎0465-420029; camping USh20,000, bandas excl breakfast USh30,000 per person) If Red Chilli's full, Yebo is the next best budget option with basic mud-wall *bandas*. But its site lacks shade and atmosphere. Local dishes are USh15,000.

WANKWAR GATE

Murchison Safari Camp BACKPACKERS $
(☎0776-799899; camping incl full breakfast USh20,000, safari tent 30,000, dm USh40,000, banda USh80,000 without bathroom) A new budget option – run by the team from Backpackers Hostel of Kampala – is located in the northern sector just outside the Wankwar gate. Accommodation is basic but well-priced, and while there's not an abundance of big wildlife out this way, it's a very peaceful spot, and you may hear the occasional lion roar at night. Most people who stay here are on a safari with Backpackers Hostel.

Getting There & Away

Road

The park headquarters at Paraa is on the southern bank of the Victoria Nile. From Masindi there's the choice of the direct route through the Kichumbanyobo gate or the longer but more scenic route, which heads west to Lake Albert and then enters the park via the western Bugungu gate. A round-trip might be best for those with a vehicle, entering via one route and leaving by the other. Both routes go through Budongo Forest Reserve, a recommended stopover.

With security now restored to northern Uganda, the northern gates, Chobe (near Karuma Falls on the Gulu Rd), Tangi (reached from Pakwach), Wankwar (from Purongo), are now viable options again; and are perhaps the best choices because your wildlife-watching will begin the moment you enter the park.

Getting from Masindi directly to Paraa by public transport isn't possible. With a bit of bargaining you can charter a special-hire taxi for around USh200,000 including fuel and the driver's park fees. The UWA office (p459) and all the hotels can help you find a driver. Rounding out the day with a wildlife-viewing drive will bump the price up to at least USh180,000. See p459 for some recommended car hire companies.

Tours

There's also, of course, the option of joining an organised safari from Kampala.

The three-day budget trips offered by Red Chilli Hideaway (p385) in Kampala leave at least thrice weekly in the high season, and include transport, park entrance fees, a launch trip, a wildlife drive and accommodation for US$210 per person, making it one of the best deals in East Africa. Backpackers Hostel (p385) has similar but slightly broader Murchison three-day trips for US$350 that include a walk to the bottom of Karuma Falls, boat trips, nature walks, wildlife viewing and chimp tracking, and all meals and accommodation – another great deal.

Getting Around

Boat

A vehicle ferry crosses the river at Paraa. The crossings take just a few minutes and are scheduled at least every two hours between 7am and 7pm. The ferry holds just eight vehicles, but will make as many crossings as necessary to get everyone over. The one-day fare is USh2000 for passengers and USh20,000 for cars. Unscheduled crossings cost USh100,000. Ferry fees are payable at a small booth near the landing.

Car

Tracks within the park are generally well maintained, and though 4WD is highly recommended, cars should have little trouble getting to the main places (except Nile Safari Lodge). However, some tracks, especially in the Buligi area, where most wildlife drives are done, can be treacherous in the wet season.

Fuel is available on the northern side of the Victoria Nile River at Paraa, but it costs about 10% more than in Masindi.

Budongo Forest Reserve

The Budongo Forest Reserve is a large (825 sq km) tract of virgin tropical forest on the southern fringes of Murchison Falls National Park. Its main attractions are chimpanzees and birds (366 species), but the huge mahogany trees are also worth a look. It's a great add-on to your Murchison Falls National Park visit.

KANIYO PABIDI

Kaniyo Pabidi Tourist Site is on the main park road, 29km north of Masindi and inside the southern boundary of Murchison Falls National Park. It's regarded as one of the more reliable places to track chimpanzees in Uganda, after Kibale National Park, with an estimated 70% chance of finding them. You have to pay the park entry fee on top of the site fees. This was the first place in Uganda to employ a female ranger, and Sauda still works here.

Kaniyo Pabidi isn't served by public transport, but it's possible to arrange a charter from Masindi for about USh60,000 or take a boda-boda for about USh25,000 (more if the guards make the driver pay admission fees).

Sights & Activities

The following activities are organised through Budongo Eco Lodge and while they can be booked at the lodge itself, it's safer to prebook permits through its website (www.ugandalodges.com/budongo) or via Great Lake Safaris (p483). Low season runs from March until mid-June.

Chimpanzee Tracking WILDLIFE WATCHING
(low/high season $55/65) Trips takes place daily and you'll have a good chance of finding the chimps, though not always. The walking is easy as the terrain is level, and walks last from two to four hours. Trekkers must be over 15 years old. Once you find the chimps, you get to spend an hour with them; two lucky visitors (October through June only) are allowed to spend a whole day for US$150 per person.

Forest Walks
(1½-/4hr US$15/20) Also worthwhile are the forest walks that pass through East Africa's last remaining mahogany forest. The largest specimens are 60m tall and 300 years old. Black-and-white colobus monkeys and duiker are commonly seen. The four-hour walks climb Pabidi Hill from which you can see most of the park and Lake Albert.

Birdwatching Walks BIRDWATCHING
(half-/full-day US$15/20) Those here for birdwatching usually seek Puvel's Illadopsis, which isn't known anywhere else in East Africa. Other highly sought species are the rufous-sided broadbill and white-naped pigeon.

Sleeping

Budongo Eco Lodge LODGE $$
(☎0414-267153; www.ugandalodges.com/budongo; dm incl full breakfast US$20, s/d/tr US$60/100/115) Excellent prices for a national park lodge. Cabins here are comfortable and surrounded by forest, and have hot water, solar power and eco-toilets. There's a good menu with a range of meat and vegetarian curries (USh15,000 to USh 21,000) and sandwiches (USh7000) for lunch. It sells greeting cards that are made from materials obtained from animal snares removed from the forest, with proceeds funding further removal.

Boomu Women's Group GUESTHOUSE $
(☎0772-448950; www.boomuwomensgroup.org; camping USh7000, s/d excl breakfast without bathroom USh20,000/40,000) Just before the Kichumbanyobo gate, this small set-up offers a chance to learn how rural Ugandans live, and your money funds a preschool. The five *bandas*, a mix of concrete and traditional (ie mud), are great for the price. Even if you don't plan to sleep here, you should make some time for a visit. Local meals cost USh10,000, and if you call before leaving Masindi there'll be breakfast waiting for you. If you have more time, its fascinating cooking tour (USh10,000) lets you follow the preparation of your meal, starting in the farm field. Call from Masindi and it'll send a boda-boda to pick you up for USh7000. For another USh7000 it'll deliver you to Kaniyo Pabidi.

BUSINGIRO

Busingiro Tourist Site, 40km west of Masindi on the Bulisa Rd, is for the birdwatchers. It's a great place to add yellow-footed flycatcher and African pitta to your spotting list. There used to be chimp tracking here too, but when the chimps lost their fear of humans they started raiding local farms, forcing an end to the program. The chimps are still here though, so you may get lucky and meet them.

The **Royal Mile** (half-/full-day US$15/20) is regarded by many to offer the best **birdwatching** in the whole country, both because there are some rare species but mostly because sightings are so easy. The bird list exceeds 350 species, including several types of flycatcher, sunbird, kingfisher, hornbill and eagle. At dusk it's possible to view bat hawks. Guided walks cost the same as at Kaniyo Pabidi, but Busingiro and the Royal

Mile lie outside the national park so there are no additional fees.

Lodging options here are poor. Busingiro Tourism Site has an overpriced but peaceful campsite (US$10 per person; bring your own food)

Busingiro is on the route used by minibuses heading for Bulisa from Masindi (see p464). The trip costs USh6000 and can take about an hour. You'll need your own vehicle to get to the Royal Mile. The first turn-off is 25km from Masindi, marked by the Nyabyeya Forestry College signpost, and there's another, also with a college sign, closer to Busingiro.

Lake Albert

Lake Albert, part of the Rift Valley system extending from the Middle East to Mozambique, runs for 160km (by 35km wide) along the border between Uganda and the DRC. The first European to spot the lake was the British explorer Sir Samuel Baker in 1864, who named it after Albert, prince consort of Queen Victoria. Oil has been found below its surface and pumping has recently begun. The region sees very few visitors, but Kabwoya Wildlife Reserve is an emerging tourist destination and can make a good stopover between Murchison and Queen Elizabeth national parks.

KABWOYA WILDLIFE RESERVE

This beautiful reserve offers an entirely different Lake Albert experience. It protects a large chunk of the Rift Valley's last ecologically intact savannah between Murchison Falls National Park and Toro-Semliki Wildlife Reserve. While the tide has been turned against poachers and cattle grazers, it remains very much a work in progress, particularly due to its proximity to where the government are drilling for oil. Wildlife watching is on the rise, given the healthy population of buffaloes, Jackson's hartebeests, waterbuck, chimpanzees and leopard, while the birdlist stands at an impressive 460 species.

Kabwoya probably wouldn't be worth a detour right now if it weren't for the superb **Lake Albert Safari Lodge** (0772-221003; www.lakealbertlodge.com; camping US$20, cottages s/d incl full board US$145/230;), whose owner, Bruce Martin (with funding from the United States Agency for International Development; USAID) is almost singlehand-edly

the r

cious

value

simila

locally

dining

the bu

quick

from h

ing tra

villages

The

near Ka

if you're

and Fort Po... it's an ideal journey-break. Check its website for detailed directions.

NORTHEASTERN UGANDA

Gulu

0471 / POP 150,000

Unless you're here volunteering or en route to Kidepo Valley National Park, there's no real reason to visit Gulu. It's the largest town in northern Uganda and one of the hardest hit during the LRA conflict. It's a town in transit and, in a sure sign of optimism, seemingly half the city is now under construction, store shelves are full and people are arriving from elsewhere in the country hoping to cash in on the coming boom. There's no shortage of *muzungus* about, explained by the abundance of NGOs in town. There's always need for volunteers here; see p488 for more information.

Sleeping

Gulu has a reasonable number of good hotels, but because of all the aid workers passing through, prices are usually higher than they should be.

Bomah Hotel HOTEL **$$**
(0471-432479; bomahhotelltd@yahoo.com; Eden Rd; s/d/ste incl full breakfast from USh82,000/182,000/502,000;) Located in a leafy pocket of town, the Bomah is a great place to escape from the dusty city centre. Having received extensive renovations, it's easily the smartest option in town, with sparkling new rooms in a hotel block over many levels. There's also a steam bath and a sauna, and its restaurant is the most popular

Sh11,000 to

HOTEL $$

ique@yahoo.com; Odongo ast from USh51,000/61,000) and good-value choice with ns, some with bathtubs. Pricier worth it, with tons more space. a restaurant and bar with live music weekends.

Happy Nest Hotel HOTEL $
(☎0782-791038; Coronation Rd; s/d excl breakfast without bathroom USh28,000/33,000) Great new budget hotel with bright sunny rooms. Located a few blocks west of the bus station.

Eating & Drinking

Coffee Hut CAFE $
(Awich Rd; coffee USh4200; wi-fi) Across from the bus park, this buzzing cafe is full of laptop users; they're here for excellent coffee and free wi-fi internet. Also does great breakfasts, including wraps with bacon, scrambled eggs and guacamole salsa (USh7500).

Country Bakeries BAKERY $
(Awich Rd; pies Ush2000) Next door to Coffee Hut, does wonderful freshly baked pies, including a vegetarian and chicken option.

Sankofa Cafe CAFE $$
(☎0776-712198; mains USh5000-12,000; wi-fi) Stylish cafe with a reputation for the best pizzas in town. Also does great sandwiches, and home delivers if you're feeling lazy. Wi-fi is USh1000 per 30 minutes.

Hotel Binen AFRICAN $
(☎0772-405038; Coronation Rd; mains USh3000-5000) A good place to try northern Ugandan food such as *malakwang* (a sour, leafy green vegetable) and *lapena* (pigeon peas). Also has decent **budget lodging** (s/d USh 12,000/15,000).

BJz PUB $
(Eden Rd; 6.30pm-late) Gulu's most popular drinking spot for locals and expats alike, with plenty of seating areas and live music on weekends.

Information

All major banks have branches here.
Internet cafes common, especially in the lower half of downtown near Hotel Kakanyero.

Getting There & Away

Gulu has a busy taxi/bus park right in the centre of town. Buses and minibuses go between Kampala and Gulu (USh20,000, five hours) all day long. Much of this road is new and in excellent shape. There's also a Gulu–Kampala Post Bus (p491).

Those heading to Kidepo can get a bus to Kitgum (USh10,000, three hours). Minibuses to Masindi (USh15,000, four hours) are infrequent, so it may be quicker to take a minibus to Kigumba (USh10,000, 2½ hours), and transfer to Masindi (USh5000, 1½ hours). There's also buses to Arua (USh12,000, four hours).

Buses to Juba (USh40,000, 10 hours) in South Sudan also depart from here.

Kitgum

POP 57,000

Those en route to Kidepo Valley National Park are likely to have to overnight in Kitgum, particularly those taking public transport. It suffered badly under the LRA's reign of terror but it's a surprisingly bustling little town, with a sizeable NGO population.

UWA (☎0777-328886) has an office here. Those without transport could enquire whether it has a car heading onwards to Kidepo – but it's unlikely. During rainy season you'll need to enquire about the state of the road and whether it's passable.

There are several banks with ATMs.

Sleeping & Eating

Fugly's GUESTHOUSE $$
(☎0757-760760; dm excl breakfast USh50,000, s USh80,000-150,000, d USh160,000-180,000; wi-fi, pool) South African-owned Fugly's is popular with NGOs and diplomats for its good range of rooms, plenty of lawn, small pool and BBQs in the evening. If this is full, try the similarly priced Bomah Hotel up the road.

Acholi Pride GUESTHOUSE $
(☎0772-687793; r excl breakfast 26,000, with shared bathroom USh13,000) Next door to UWA, this is by far the best cheapie, with simple and clean rooms.

Getting There & Away

BUS Many coach lines have buses straight from Kampala (USh25,000, seven hours) to Kitgum.

See p470, for information on how to get to Kidepo Valley National Park from Kitgum.

Kidepo Valley National Park

This lost valley in the extreme northeast, along the Sudanese border, has the most stunning scenery of any protected area in Uganda. The rolling, short-grass savannah of the 1442-sq-km **Kidepo Valley National Park** (adult/child US$35/20) is ringed by mountains and cut by rocky ridges.

Kidepo is most notable for harbouring a number of animals found nowhere else in Uganda, including cheetahs, bat-eared foxes, aardwolves, caracal, greater and lesser kudus. There are also large concentrations of elephants, zebras, buffaloes, bushbuck, giraffes, lions, jackals, leopard, hyenas and Nile crocodiles.

Amazingly, most of these animals, including even the occasional lion, are content to graze and lounge right near the park's accommodation, so you can see a whole lot without going very far: it's a safari from a lounge chair (or in Apoka Safari Lodge's case – from a bathtub!). One particular elephant, named Bull-bull by park staff, has taken a liking to the local brew and is sure to be seen up close and personal. But don't get foolishly close; he seems tame, but we've seen him charge people.

The bird checklist is fast approaching 500 species (second among the national parks only to the larger Queen Elizabeth National Park) and there are many 'Kidepo specials': birds such as ostrich, kori bustard, pygmy falcon, secretary bird, Karamoja apalis and Abyssinian ground hornbill that are found in no other Ugandan national park.

Activities

Wildlife-Watching WILDLIFE WATCHING

(per km USh4000) Kidepo is the only park in Uganda where UWA has a vehicle for wildlife-watching drives but it's not always available. When it is, a top target is the Narus Valley, where the lions began climbing trees around 2005. Also popular are the borassus palm forest and Kanangorok hot springs by the usually dry Kidepo River. If you want to see ostriches, you'll have to head to the northern sector of the park.

Nature Walk WALKING

(per person US$15) Another great option for wildlife viewing is on foot, accompanied by armed rangers. There's also hiking at Mt Morungole ($US15), arranged through UWA.

KIDEPO VALLEY NATIONAL PARK

Why Go Stunning scenery; best variety of wildlife in Uganda including zebra, cheetah and ostrich to go with lion, giraffe and elephant; the chance to visit a Karamojong village

When to Go November to January, when you might see some of the biggest buffalo herds in Africa, are the best months to visit. The rainy season (August to September) has long grass that impedes viewing, and it can also be problematic accessing the park on muddy roads. But you're sure to see lots of animals at any time.

Practicalities Can be reached in a day from Kampala if you have your own car, otherwise public transport takes a few days – with a night in Kitgum or Gulu.

Cultural Tours CULTURAL TOUR

(US$20) UWA can also organise visits to Karamojong and Ik villages, both memorable experiences that allows you to interact with these northeast tribal groups.

Sleeping & Eating

TOP CHOICE **Apoka Safari Lodge** TENTED CAMP $$$

(☎0414-251182, 0776-707004; http://www.wildplacesafrica.com/apoka-lodge; s/d incl full board US$450/810;) If you want something really special, you want Apoka Safari Lodge. It has 10 large and very private thatched-roof, canvas walled cottages that all look out to wildlife grazing right on your doorstep. Each features a porch outdoor tub (watch buffalo graze while you have a bubblebath), stone showers, perfect views and a writing desk that would suit Hemingway to a tee. It has a lovely swimming pool (US$25 nonguests) with a rocky bottom and sweeping savannah views. The dining area has the same great outlook and there's a tower where you can arrange for a romantic, private dinner. As everything is flown in from Kampala, there are no walk-ins for meals or drinks, but if you call ahead to its office in Kampala you may be able to arrange to eat here. The price includes meals, alcohol, wildlife-watching drives, walking safaris and, for an additional US$20, it can arrange Karamojong village tours. Reception displays the depressing sight of the skull of Kidepo's last rhino – shot by poachers in the early 1980s.

Apoka Hostel BANDA $
(☎0392-899500; camping USh15,000; s/d excl breakfast USh60,000/70,000, without bathroom USh40,000/50,000) Probably the best of UWA's park lodges, Apoka Hostel has 21 comfortable *bandas* with private bathrooms. There's plenty of wildlife about, so be sure to keep your distance, particularly at night, when there's a good chance you'll hear lions roaring. There's a small restaurant with a very limited menu (meals USh6000), and cheap, cold beer. Otherwise you can bring your own food to cook (USh10,000).

Nga'Moru Wilderness Camp TENTED CAMP $$
(☎0754-500555; brentait@gmail.com; s/d full board US$150/300) Run by the owners of Fugly's in Kitgum, this lovely new spot has a peaceful location just outside the edge of the park's border. Accommodation comprises luxury camping (meaning half tent, half room) with bush showers. Lions occasionally hang out here. Rates include food, most of which is cooked on the camp's kettle BBQ, and alcohol. It also has a small vegie patch.

Campsites CAMPGROUND $
(camping USh15,000) If you want to be in the thick of the action, the park also maintains two isolated campsites with latrines and water. You'll be accompanied by an armed guard who can arrange firewood for cooking.

Grand Katurum Lodge HOTEL $$
(☎0781-053118; issagem@yahoo.com; r US$100-400;) Perched on a huge rock bluff, this hotel is finally being rebuilt after opening during Idi Amin's regime, but closing soon after. At the time of research it was near completion, and with 53 rooms it'll provide the park's only midrange accommodation option. All rooms have great views of the grassy savannah, and there's a swimming pool too.

Getting There & Away

There are no longer scheduled flights to Kidepo, so the only way to get here is overland.

Undoubtedly the best bet is to rent a car, in which case you can make it in one day from Kampala to Kidepo if you get a very early start. Getting here by public transport is certainly possible too, but takes some effort, and you'll need to overnight in Kitgum or Kotido, depending what route you take.

There are two possible routes. Both are long and at times difficult journeys, but this is one place where travel is its own reward.

Via Kitgum

The vast majority of visitors take the route through to Kitgum (USh25,000, seven hours) via Gulu, which is the shortest, easiest and safest route; and currently the only one to consider if you're driving. You'll have to overnight in Kitgum, as getting to the park still requires a bit more travel.

From Kitgum, your best bet is to jump on a truck heading to Karenga (USh25,000, three hours), the gateway town for the park; these depart Kitgum around 7am till midday. From Karenga, you can either arrange to be picked up by the UWA vehicle (for a pricey USh4000 per km), or otherwise a boda-boda (USh30,000 including vehicle entry) for the 24km journey to the park's headquarters and lodging area. Make sure you pay for 24km, not 48km. Otherwise you can try your luck hitching a ride with other travellers heading into the park – try Fugly's, Bomah Hotel or the UWA office.

Via Karamojaland

The other option for getting to Kidepo from Kampala is via eastern Uganda through the wilds of Karamojaland, where many of the Karamojong people still wear traditional dress (similar to the Maasai) and AK-47s are as common as walking sticks. Due to volatile security in the region this route is more for adventure travellers, and you'll need to make enquiries on the security situation before heading out.

The two- or three-day journey takes you though some of the most stunning scenery in Uganda, crossing great plains peppered with tall peaks, and good wildlife-watching begins before you even reach the park gate. This trip involves heading to **Kotido**, a small but fast-growing town three hours north of Moroto. Be sure to stop by the **UWA Office** (☎0777-478856; ⏲7am-8pm Mon-Fri & most weekends), next to the central roundabout, where you can you can get onward travel advice. Try the **Skyline Hotel** (☎0774-802159; r USh21,000, without bathroom USh11,000), just down the road past the UWA office, which has small but clean rooms and friendly staff.

Gateway (Map p386; ☎0722-069349; Wilson Rd, Kampala) has daily buses to Kotido (USh35,000, 15 hours), departing Kampala's New Bus Park at 5.30am.

From Kotido there are frequent trucks and pick-ups to Kaabong (USh6500, two to three hours), a rough 'wild east' town. From there, jump on the less frequent trucks to Karenga (USh8000, two to three hours). See the Via Kitgum section to see how to get to the park from Karenga.

WARNING: SECURITY IN KARAMOJALAND

Despite a heavy military presence, Karamojaland in the northeast has a deserved reputation as a dangerous destination. In the past, groups of local cattle herders, the Karamojong, have been known to ambush highway travellers: sometimes to steal food or money, sometimes for vengeance and sometimes just for fun. There's also occasional fighting between the Karamojong and the army and among the Karamojong themselves. And, to make matters more complicated, large numbers of armed Turkana people from Kenya often cross the border looking to steal cattle. With that said, at the time of research, things had improved markedly on the years prior.

Aid workers and government officials travel with a military escort and, for the time being, driving your own vehicle would be foolish. It has long been considered safe to travel on the Gateway bus, but you'll want to check on this following two bus shootings, with one death and a dozen injuries, in August 2008. These appear to have been for revenge after a child was struck and killed by a bus, so they will probably prove nothing more than isolated incidents. The trucks that carry goods and locals between towns are *almost* never attacked.

We don't have statistics to back this up, and it flies in the face of conventional wisdom, but we feel that if you travel by public means, coming here is pretty safe; probably safer than riding a boda-boda in Kampala. Still, it's of paramount importance to check on security before setting out (national park staff will have the latest details) and again at every step of the way. Things can change very fast out here. One final note: when inquiring about the current situation, don't just ask locals 'is it safe?'. Invariably the answer will be yes: ask specifics about when the last ambushes happened so you can make an informed decision about whether you want to take the risk.

UNDERSTAND UGANDA

History

For the story on Uganda's history in the years before independence, see p572.

Independence

Unlike Kenya and, to a lesser extent, Tanzania, Uganda never experienced a large influx of European colonisers and the associated expropriation of land. Instead, farmers were encouraged to grow cash crops for export through their own cooperative groups. Consequently, Ugandan nationalist organisations sprouted much later than those in neighbouring countries, and, when they did, it happened along tribal lines. So exclusive were some of these that when Ugandan independence was discussed, the Baganda people (p583) considered secession.

By the mid-1950s, however, a Lango schoolteacher Dr Milton Obote managed to put together a loose coalition headed by the Uganda People's Congress (UPC), which led Uganda to independence in 1962 on the promise that the Buganda kingdom would have autonomy. The *kabaka* (king), Edward Mutesa II, became the president of the new nation, and Milton Obote became Uganda's first prime minister.

It wasn't a particularly favourable time for Uganda to come to grips with independence. Civil wars were raging in neighbouring Sudan, the DRC and Rwanda, and refugees streamed into Uganda, adding to its problems. Also, it soon became obvious that Obote had no intention of sharing power with the *kabaka*. A confrontation loomed.

Obote moved in 1966, arresting several cabinet ministers and ordering his army chief of staff, Idi Amin, to storm the *kabaka*'s palace in Kampala. The raid resulted in the flight of the *kabaka* and his exile in London, where he died in 1969. Following this coup, Obote proclaimed himself president, and the Buganda monarchy was abolished, along with those of the Bunyoro, Ankole, Toro and Busoga kingdoms. Meanwhile, Idi Amin's star was on the rise.

The Amin Years

Under Obote's watch, events began to spiral out of control. Obote ordered his attorney general, Godfrey Binaisa, to rewrite the constitution to consolidate virtually all powers in the presidency and then moved to nationalise foreign assets.

In 1969 a scandal broke out over US$5 million in funds and weapons allocated to the Ministry of Defence that couldn't be accounted for. An explanation was demanded of Amin. When it wasn't forthcoming, his deputy, Colonel Okoya, and some junior officers demanded his resignation. Shortly afterwards Okoya and his wife were shot dead in their Gulu home, and rumours began to circulate about Amin's imminent arrest. It never came. Instead, when Obote left for Singapore in January 1971 to attend the Commonwealth Heads of Government Meeting (CHOGM), Amin staged a coup. Uganda's former colonial masters, the British, who had probably suffered most from Obote's nationalisation program, were among the first to recognise the new regime. Obote went into exile in Tanzania.

So began Uganda's first reign of terror. All political activities were quickly suspended and the army was empowered to shoot on sight anyone suspected of opposition to the regime. Over the next eight years an estimated 300,000 Ugandans lost their lives, often in such horrific ways as being bludgeoned to death with sledgehammers and iron bars. Prime targets of Amin's death squads were the Acholi and Lango people, who were decimated in waves of massacres; whole villages were wiped out. Next Amin turned on the professional classes. University professors, doctors, cabinet ministers, lawyers, businesspeople and even military officers who might have posed a threat to Amin were dragged from their offices and shot or simply never seen again.

Also targeted was the 70,000-strong Asian community. In 1972 they were given 90 days to leave the country. Amin and his cronies grabbed the billion dollar booty the evictees were forced to leave behind and quickly squandered it on 'new toys for the boys' and personal excess. Amin then turned on the British, nationalising US$500 million worth of investments in tea plantations and other industries without compensation.

Meanwhile the economy collapsed, industrial activity ground to a halt, hospitals and rural health clinics closed, roads cracked and became riddled with potholes, cities became garbage dumps and utilities fell apart. The prolific wildlife was machine-gunned by soldiers for meat, ivory and skins, and the tourism industry evaporated. The stream of refugees across the border became a flood.

Faced with chaos and an inflation rate that hit 1000%, Amin was forced to delegate more and more powers to the provincial governors, who became virtual warlords in their areas. Towards the end of the Amin era, the treasury was so bereft of funds it was unable to pay the soldiers. One of the few supporters of Amin at the end of the 1970s was Colonel Gadaffi, who bailed out the Ugandan economy in the name of Islamic brotherhood (Amin had conveniently become a Muslim by this stage) and began an intensive drive to equip the Ugandan forces with sophisticated weapons.

The rot had spread too far, however, and was beyond the point where a few million dollars in Libyan largesse could help. Faced with a restless army beset with intertribal fighting, Amin looked for a diversion. He chose a war with Tanzania, ostensibly to teach that country a lesson for supporting anti-Amin dissidents. It was his last major act of recklessness, and in it lay his downfall.

War with Tanzania

On 30 October 1978 the Ugandan army rolled across northwestern Tanzania virtually unopposed and annexed more than 1200 sq km of territory. Meanwhile, the airforce bombed the Lake Victoria ports of Bukoba and Musoma.

Tanzanian President Julius Nyerere ordered a full-scale counterattack, but it took months to mobilise his ill-equipped and poorly trained forces. But by early 1979 he had managed to scrape together a 50,000-strong people's militia, composed mainly of illiterate youngsters from the bush. This militia joined with the many exiled Ugandan liberation groups – united only in their determination to rid Uganda of Amin. The two armies met. East Africa's supposedly best-equipped and best-trained army threw down its weapons and fled, and the Tanzanians pushed on into the heart of Uganda. Kampala fell without a fight, and by April 1979 organised resistance had effectively ceased.

Amin eventually ended up in Saudi Arabia where he died in 2003, never having faced justice.

Post-Amin Chaos

The Tanzanian action was criticised, somewhat half-heartedly, by the Organisation for African Unity (OAU, now called the African Union), but most African countries breathed

OPERATION ENTEBBE: 1976 HOSTAGE RESCUE

The site of one of the most well-known hostage-rescue missions, Uganda's international airport in Entebbe was where the hijacked Air France flight landed on 27 June 1976. Carrying 248 passengers, the flight from Tel Aviv en route to Paris was hijacked by Palestinian and German terrorists and diverted to Libya, before eventually being given permission to land in Entebbe by Idi Amin, a pro-Palestine supporter. Demanding the release of 53 Palestine Liberation Organization (PLO) prisoners in return for the release of the hostages, terrorists held passengers in the main hall of the airport building (now the old terminal building, and a popular site for Israeli tourists) for over a week. Eventually all non-Jewish passengers were released, leaving around 105 hostages onboard.

In what's considered one of the most daring and dramatic hostage operations to ever take place, the covert operation comprised an Israeli taskforce of around 100 commandos touching down in Entebbe at 11pm in a C-130 Hercules cargo plane. Several Mercedes rolled off the plane to give the appearance of being part of Idi Amin's entourage, from where Israeli commandos emerged to storm the terminal. Within 30 minutes, seven terrorists and around 40 Ugandan soldiers were killed, while three Israeli hostages also died in the crossfire. The freed hostages were loaded on to the plane while Ugandan soldiers fired away, resulting in one Israeli soldier being killed: the brother of Israeli prime minister, Benjamin Netanyahu. In the meantime more than half of Uganda's airforce planes were destroyed by the Israelis to prevent retaliatory airstrikes upon Israel. In response Amin ordered the killing of 75 year-old Dora Bloch, a British-Jewish hostage who remained in Kampala recovering in hospital following the ordeal.

a sigh of relief to see Amin finally brought to heel. All the same, Tanzania was forced to foot the entire bill for the war, estimated at US$500 million, a crushing blow for an already desperately poor country.

The rejoicing in Uganda was short-lived. The Tanzanian soldiers, who remained in the country, supposedly to assist with reconstruction and to maintain law and order, turned on the Ugandans when their pay did not arrive. They took what they wanted from shops at gunpoint, hijacked trucks arriving from Kenya with international relief aid and slaughtered more wildlife.

Once again, the country slid into chaos and gangs of armed bandits roamed the cities, killing and looting. Food supplies ran out and hospitals could no longer function. Nevertheless, thousands of exiled Ugandans began to answer the call to return home and help with reconstruction.

Yusuf Lule, a modest and unambitious man, was installed as president with Nyerere's blessing. But when he began speaking out against Nyerere, he was replaced by Godfrey Binaisa, sparking riots supporting Lule in Kampala. Meanwhile, Obote bided his time in Dar es Salaam.

Binaisa quickly came under pressure to set a date for a general election and a return to civilian rule. Obote eventually returned from exile to an enthusiastic welcome in many parts of the country and swept to power in what is widely regarded as a rigged vote.

It was 1981 and the honeymoon with Obote proved short. Like Amin, Obote favoured certain tribes. Large numbers of civil servants and army and police commanders belonging to the tribes of the south were replaced with Obote supporters belonging to the tribes of the north. The State Research Bureau, a euphemism for the secret police, was re-established and the prisons began to fill once more. Obote was on course to complete the destruction that Amin had begun. More and more reports of atrocities and killings leaked out of the country. Mass graves unrelated to the Amin era were unearthed. The press was muzzled and Western journalists were expelled. It appeared that Obote was once again attempting to achieve absolute power. Intertribal tension was on the rise, and in mid-1985 Obote was overthrown in a coup staged by the army under the command of Tito Okello.

The NRA Takeover

Okello was not the only opponent of Obote. Shortly after Obote became president for the second time, a guerrilla army opposed to his tribally biased government was formed

AMIN: 'THE BUTCHER OF UGANDA'

Regarded as one of Africa's most notorious and ruthless dictators, the name Idi Amin continues to be synonymous with Uganda despite it being nearly four decades since he was ousted as president. Following his defeat in the Uganda–Tanzania war in 1979, Amin fled the country never to return, heading to Libya and Iraq before living in exile in Saudi Arabia, where he died from kidney failure in 2003, aged 78. He never faced justice for the atrocities committed, with an estimated 300,000 losing their lives under his rule. President from 1971 to 1979, Amin will be remembered not only for executions, human-rights violations and ethnic persecution, but for his corruption and transformation of the once prosperous Ugandan economy into financial ruin.

Early Days

Born in 1925, near Koboko in northwestern Uganda, Amin was a member of the Kakwa tribal group and received his military training under the British with the King's African Rifles. He rose through the ranks and in 1962 was in charge of an operation to control cattle stealing by Karamojong tribesman, which resulted in an overzealous approach that became known as the Turkana Massacre. Bodies were unearthed from pits, many displaying evidence of torture.

Amin escaped court martial, but was later promoted to chief of staff by prime minister Milton Obote. He served as somewhat of a muscleman to Obote, and together they orchestrated an attack on the *kabaka's* palace to oust King Mutesa II. Amin launched shell attacks and set up a notorious prison and interrogation centre in the palace grounds.

In 1971, while Obote was at a Commonwealth Head of States meeting in Singapore, Amin led a coup to displace Obote, declaring himself president with a catchy title that would evolve to: "His Excellency President for Life, Field Marshal Al Hadji Doctor Idi Amin, VC, DSO, MC, Lord of All the Beasts of the Earth and Fishes of the Sea, and Conqueror of the British Empire in Africa in General and Uganda in Particular".

President of Uganda

Amin's first step as president was to immediately round up all Obote supporters. They were imprisoned, executed or simply disappeared. He also targeted Acholi and Lango tribal groups, who he believed to be supporters of Obote. Appointing his military buddies to top government posts, Amin formed killer squads that went under the euphemisms of the State Research Bureau and Public Safety Unit, and the Nile Mansions Hotel (now Serena Hotel) was set up as their headquarters and used for interrogation and torture.

In 1972, Amin ordered the deportation of Uganda's sizeable Asian population (most were of Indian and Pakistani origin) and he seized their property and valuables. Following a meeting with Gaddafi (who influenced his decision to expel Asians from Uganda) his allegiance swung from the West to Libya, USSR and East Germany, and Amin became staunchly anti-Israel. In 1972 the US withdrew a $3 million loan after a pro-Hitler rant by Amin in a telegraph to the UN secretary and prime minister of Israeli. The British severed diplomatic ties in the same year, following Amin's support for the Palestine terrorists in the hijacked Air France plane that he permitted to land in Entebbe.

Amin was a highly charismatic leader who had the ability to charm everyone he met. Physically imposing at 1.91m and with a broad build, Amin was a champion boxer who held Uganda's light heavyweight boxing championship from 1951 to 1960.

To many Africans. Amin was (and, to many, remains) highly respected for his fierce nationalism and courage to stand up to colonial powers. On the flipside, he was also known for his wild moodswings and paranoia. Henry Kyemba, one of Amin's most trusted ministers at the time, states in his autobiography *State of Blood* that Amin dabbled with cannibalism and blood rituals. Persisting rumours from exiled Ugandans also suggest that he kept the heads of his most prized enemies in a freezer, which he would take out on occasions to lecture them on their evil ways.

in western Uganda under the leadership of Yoweri Museveni.

A group of 27 soon swelled to a guerrilla force of about 20,000, many of them orphaned teenagers. In the early days few gave the guerrillas, known as the National Resistance Army (NRA), much of a chance, but the NRA had a very different ethos to the armies of Amin and Obote. New recruits were indoctrinated in the bush by political commissars and taught they had to be servants of the people, not oppressors. Discipline was tough. Anyone who got badly out of line was executed. Museveni was determined that the army would never again disgrace Uganda. A central thrust of the NRA was to win the hearts and minds of the people, who learnt to identify with the persecuted Baganda in the infamous Luwero Triangle, where people suffered more than most under Obote's iron fist.

By the time Obote was ousted and Okello had taken over, the NRA controlled a large slice of western Uganda and was a power to be reckoned with. Museveni wanted a clean sweep of the administration, the army and the police. He wanted corruption stamped out and those who had been involved in atrocities during the Amin and Obote regimes brought to trial.

The fighting continued in earnest, and by January 1986 it was obvious that Okello's days were numbered. The surrender of 1600 government soldiers holed up in their barracks in the southern town of Mbarara brought the NRA to the outskirts of Kampala itself. With the morale of the government troops low, the NRA launched an all-out offensive to take the capital. Okello's troops fled, almost without a fight, though not before looting whatever remained and carting it away in commandeered buses. It was a typical parting gesture, as was the gratuitous shooting-up of many Kampala high-rise offices.

During the following weeks, Okello's rabble were pursued and finally pushed north over the border into Sudan. The long nightmare was finally over.

Rebuilding

Despite Museveni's Marxist leanings, he proved to be a pragmatist after taking control. He appointed several arch conservatives to his cabinet and made an effort to reassure the country's large Catholic community.

In the late 1980s, peace agreements were negotiated with most of the guerrilla factions who had fought for Okello or Obote and were still active in the north and northeast. Under an amnesty offered to the rebels, as many as 40,000 had surrendered by 1988, and many were given jobs in the NRA. In the northwest of the country, almost 300,000 Ugandans returned home from Sudan.

With peace came optimism: services were restored, factories that had lain idle for years were again productive, agriculture was back online, the main roads were resurfaced, and the national parks' infrastructure was restored and revitalised.

The 1990s

The stability and rebuilding that came with President Museveni's coming to power in 1986 was followed in the 1990s with economic prosperity and unprecedented growth. For much of the decade Uganda was the fastest-growing economy in Africa, becoming a favourite among investors. One of the keys to the success was the bold decision to invite back the Asians who, as in Kenya, had held a virtual monopoly on business and commerce. Not surprisingly, they were very hesitant about returning, but assurances were given and kept, and property was returned.

The darkness didn't end for northern Uganda, however, due to the Lord's Resistance Army (LRA), the last remaining rebel group founded during the time of the NRA rebellion. Its leader, Joseph Kony, grew increasingly delusional and paranoid and shifted his focus from attacking soldiers to attacking civilians in an attempt to found a government based on the Biblical Ten Commandments.

His vicious tactics included torture, mutilation (slicing off lips, noses and ears), rape and abducting children to use as soldiers and sex slaves. Eventually over one million northerners fled their homes to Internally Displaced Persons (IDP) camps and tens of thousands of children became 'night commuters', walking from their villages each evening to sleep in schools and churches or on the streets of large and (sometimes) safer towns. In their half-hearted fight against the LRA, government forces reportedly committed their own atrocities too.

In 1993, a new draft constitution was adopted by the National Resistance Council (NRC). One surprising recommendation in the draft was that the country should adopt a system of 'no-party' politics. Given the potential for intertribal rivalry within a pluralist system, it was a sensible policy. Under the draft constitution, a Constituent Assembly was formed, and in 1994 elections for the assembly showed overwhelming support for the government. Also in 1993 the monarchies were restored, but with no actual political power.

Democratic 'no-party' elections were called for May 1996. The main candidates were President Museveni and Paul Ssemogerere, who had resigned as foreign minister in order to campaign. Museveni won a resounding victory, capturing almost 75% of the vote. The only area where Ssemogerere had any real support was in the anti-National Resistance Movement (NRM) north.

Museveni's election carried with it great hope for the future, as many believed Uganda's success story could only continue with a genuine endorsement at the ballot box. But Museveni's period as a democratically elected leader has been far less comfortable than his leadership period prior to the elections. At home, one corruption scandal after another has blighted the administration, though Museveni has so far stayed clean. Museveni can't seem to keep his focus on the homefront and has played a heavy hand with events in the DRC and Rwanda. Despite this, Museveni remained popular for the stability he brought to the lives of average Ugandans and he was re-elected in 2001.

Uganda Today

Eventually Museveni shifted his position on political parties, and in July 2005 a referendum was held that overwhelmingly endorsed the change. This political shift was of much less concern to the average Ugandan than the other that occurred the same month; parliament approving a constitutional amendment scrapping presidential term limits. Museveni himself had put the two-term limit in place, but had regrets as the end of his tenure drew closer. It was alleged that MPs were bullied and bribed into voting for the change. International criticism was strong and even many Ugandans who back Museveni remain angry at his move. The 'Big Man' school of African politics is better known to Ugandans than most, and plenty of people are worried he is setting himself to be president for life. Some even draw unflattering comparisons with Robert Mugabe.

Despite all this, Museveni convincingly won his fourth election in 2011 with 68.4% of the vote to make it 25 years in power. One of the more smoothly run elections, there were still some of the usual shenanigans along the way, with considerable amounts of the government budget allegedly used for his electoral campaign. Once again the main challenger was opposition leader, Kizza Besigye of the Forum for Democratic Change (FDC), who had also been the runner up in 2001 and 2006. In the lead-up to the 2006 elections, Besigye was imprisoned and accused of everything from treason to rape (he was subsequently cleared of all charges). He was arrested again in April 2011 after a walk to work protest over high fuel and food prices, which then sparked riots against Museveni in Kampala resulting in two deaths and 360 arrests. There's little doubt Museveni will run again in 2015, and though he continues to lose popularity, no credible opposition has arisen.

By early in the 2000's the LRA's campaign of terror had ebbed, though certainly not ceased. In 2002 the LRA lost its Sudanese support and the Ugandan military launched Operation Iron Fist, attacking the LRA's bases across the northern border. The mission failed and an angered Kony not only increased attacks in Uganda but expanded his targets to areas like Soroti that had not previously been affected. In the years that followed there were various ceasefires and nominal peace talks, but little progress until 2005 when the LRA fled to Garamba National Park in the DRC. The following year the Juba Peace Talks commenced and, though things progressed slowly, they showed genuine promise. Museveni guaranteed Kony amnesty (a move supported in Uganda as practical) and a legitimate ceasefire began in September. After on-again, off-again talks a peace deal was reached in February 2008, though Kony then broke his promise to sign it and the LRA began abducting more child soldiers and even attacked a Sudanese army base. Although the LRA hasn't threatened Uganda since 2007, most northern Ugandans remain too terrified to return to their homes. In October 2011, it was announced that around 100 US troops would be deployed in Uganda to help train local military forces to tackle the LRA in Central Africa Republic (where Kony is believed to be hiding), the DRC and Sudan.

In July 2010 Kampala was rocked by a deadly terrorist attack, with coordinated bombings across the city that left 74 dead and 70 badly injured. The most damage were twin bombs that exploded in a venue packed with people watching the 2010 World Cup final. The attack was claimed by the Somalian militia group, al-Shabab, and it's believed to be a reprisal for Uganda providing peacekeeping troops in Somalia. It was the first attack by the group outside Somalia, and hopefully remains an isolated incident.

The Culture

The National Psyche

Despite the years of terror and bloodshed, Ugandans are a remarkably positive and spirited people, and no one comes away from the country without a measure of admiration and affection for them. Most Ugandans are keen debaters, discussing politics

THE ANTI-GAY BILL

Uganda made world headlines from 2009 to 2012 with its controversial bill proposing the death penalty and life sentences for homosexual behaviour. The bill (known widely in the media as 'Kill the Gays bill') was drafted by David Bahati, a right-wing MP who's leading a one-man anti-homosexual crusade, and states the death sentence would apply to those convicted of 'aggravated homosexuality'. This would include homosexuals convicted of rape, sex with a minor or knowingly spreading HIV. It would also include those who are 'serial offenders', a ruling which remains vague. Furthermore, if the bill is passed, anyone who fails to report homosexual behaviour can also be imprisoned for up to three years.

The bill was predictably met with strong condemnation from the international community. US President Barack Obama described it as 'odious', several European governments threatened to withdraw foreign aid, while human-rights groups vowed to fight it. Despite the Ugandan government publically distancing itself from the bill, it does have local support – most notably from Uganda's first lady, and now MP, Janet Museveni. According to WikiLeaks, the US ambassador has stated that Ms Museveni is firmly behind the bill.

While the bill has been rejected on the occasions it's been debated in parliament (on the basis that homosexuality is already criminalised in Uganda), the bill has been shelved rather than outright defeated. But in Februrary 2012 Bahati announced his intention to rewrite the bill to remove the death penalty. A life prison sentence would remain under the proposed legislation.

Though homosexuality has officially been illegal in Uganda since the British introduced these laws in the 19th century, and subsequently retained by Uganda following independence, it is rarely, if ever, policed. It's widely accepted that visiting US evangelistic church groups preaching anti-gay beliefs have played a hand in whipping up anti-gay sentiment that are said to have influenced the anti-homosexuality bill.

Things escalated in October 2010 when the short-lived tabloid newspaper *Rolling Stone* (not to be confused with the music magazine) ran a front cover story that published the names and addresses of 100 gay Ugandans – which led to several attacks. This included the death of David Kato in February 2011, a notable gay activist, who was widely believed to be a victim of a hate crime.

So what does all this mean to gay, lesbian, bisexual and transgender travellers to Uganda, and is it safe to travel there? Unfortunately, homosexuality is banned in around 80 countries in the world (37 of which are African nations). There's no doubt Ugandan cultural is generally homophobic, so similarly when travelling in places like East Africa, Jamaica or the Middle East, discretion is vital. If travellers follow the lead of the local and expat gay community, who have to remain very much underground, there shouldn't be any threat. Also keep in mind that displays of public affection, whether couples are heterosexual or gay, are largely considered socially taboo.

and personality in equal measure. They are opinionated and eloquent during disagreements, yet unfailingly polite and engagingly warm.

They are also worried. Many Ugandans fear a fractured future. The country has had a remarkable run since 1986 when Museveni saved the nation, but nationalism has never taken hold. Tribe comes first. In fact, many Baganda still desire independence. This tribal divide has always manifested itself in politics, but the re-emergence of political parties is exacerbating the problem. Recently, even opposition to a vital land reform bill fell largely along tribal not economic lines.

There is also a serious north–south divide, and it doesn't appear to be closing with the advent of peace. Without Joseph Kony around to blame any more, northerners seem to be turning their resentment for the lack of prosperity and education opportunities towards the south; and not without some justification. During the war, many military officers used their power to swipe land, and today many of the new businesses in the north are owned and new jobs taken by carpetbaggers. Even most of the students in the vast new Gulu University, opened in 2002, come from the south.

Daily Life

Life in Uganda has been one long series of upheavals for the older generations, while the younger generations have benefited from the newfound stability. Society has changed completely in urban areas in the past couple of decades, but in the countryside it's often business as usual.

Uganda has been heavily affected by HIV/AIDS. One of the first countries to be struck by an outbreak of epidemic proportions, Uganda acted swiftly in promoting AIDS awareness and safe sex. This was very effective in radically reducing infection rates throughout the country, and Uganda went from experiencing an infection rate of around 25% in the late 1980s to one that dropped as low as 4% in 2003.

But things have changed. Due in large part to pressure from the country's growing evangelical Christian population, led on this issue by Museveni's outspoken wife (though the president himself has taken her lead), Uganda has reversed its policy on promoting condoms and made abstinence the focus of fighting the disease. The result is no surprise; the infection rate has since risen to 6.5%.

Education has been a real priority in Uganda and President Museveni has been keen to promote free primary education for all. It's a noble goal, but Uganda lacks the resources to realise it, and one-third of the population is illiterate. Sure, more pupils are attending class, but often the classes are hopelessly overcrowded and many teachers lack experience.

Agriculture remains the single most important component of the Ugandan economy, and it employs 75% of the workforce. The main export crops include coffee, sugar, cotton, tea and fish. Crops grown for local consumption include maize, millet, rice, cassava, potatoes and beans.

Population

Uganda's population is estimated at 34.6 million, and its annual growth rate of 3.6% is one of the world's highest, leading to some serious deforestation, erosion and other environmental problems, which will only get worse with time. The median age is 15, with a life expectancy of 53.2 years.

Uganda is made up of a complex and diverse range of tribes. Lake Kyoga forms the northern boundary for the Bantu-speaking peoples, who dominate much of east, central and southern Africa and, in Uganda, include the Baganda (17%) and several other tribes, such as the Banyankole (9.5%), Basoga (8.4%) and Bagisu (4.6%). In the north are the Lango (6%) near Lake Kyoga and the Acholi (4.7%) towards the Sudanese border, who speak Nilotic languages. To the east are the Iteso (6.4%) and Karamojong (2%), who are related to the Maasai, and also speak Nilotic languages. Small numbers of Twa (Batwa) people live in the forests of the southwest. Non-Africans, including a sizeable community of Asians, compose about 1% of the population.

Sport

The most popular sport in Uganda, as in most of Africa, is football (soccer) and it's possible to watch occasional international game at the Nelson Mandela Stadium on the outskirts of Kampala. There's also a domestic league (October to July), but few people follow it.

Cricket is also growing in popularity (tests are held at Lugogo Cricket Ground), while boxing has lost much of its popularity in recent years, though past world champions include John 'The Beast' Mugabi and Kassim 'The Dream' Ouma, a former child soldier.

Religion

Eighty-five percent of the population is Christian, split evenly between Catholics and Protestants, including a growing number of born-agains. Muslims, mostly northerners, compose about 12% of the population. The Abayudaya are a small but devout group of native Jewish Ugandans living around Mbale, see boxed text p411.

Arts

Cinema

Hollywood put Uganda on the movie map with a big screen version of *The Last King of Scotland* (2006) starring Forest Whitaker as the 'Big Daddy'. While not set in Uganda, much of the Hollywood classic *The African Queen* starring Humphrey Bogart and Katharine Hepburn was shot near Murchison Falls.

The conflict in the north has spawned many harrowing documentaries including *Invisible Children* (2006), *The Other Side Of The Country* (2007), and *Uganda Rising* (2006). In a different vein is the Oscar-nominated *War/Dance* (2006), an inspiring tale of northern refugee schoolchildren competing in Uganda's National Primary and Secondary School Music and Dance Competition.

The local film industry, known as Kina-Uganda or Ugawood, is in its infancy but growing. You can sometimes catch a local film at the National Theatre in Kampala and you'll surely have a chance during the Amakula Kampala International Film Festival (p385), held in the latter months of the year.

Books

Literature

Most of the interesting reading coming out of Uganda revolves around the country's darkest hours. Aristoc (p394) in Kampala stocks a good selection of local writers.

Giles Foden's *The Last King of Scotland* (1998) chronicles the fictional account of Idi Amin's personal doctor as he slowly finds himself becoming confidant to the dictator. This bestselling novel weaves gruesome historical fact into its Heart of Darkness-esque tale.

The highly regarded and somewhat autobiographical *Abyssinian Chronicles* (2001) is the best known work by Moses Isegawa. It tells the story of a young Ugandan coming of age during the turbulent years of Idi Amin and offers some fascinating insights into life in Uganda.

Waiting (2007), the fourth novel by Goretti Kyomuhendo, one of Uganda's pioneering female writers (and founder of Femrite: the Ugandan Women Writers' Association and publishing house), was published in the United States. It looks in on a rural family's daily life (and daily fear) as they await the expected arrival of marauding soldiers during the fall of Idi Amin. Femwrite titles include *A Woman's Voice* (1998) and *Words From a Granary* (2001), two collections of short stories.

Song of Lawino (1989) is a highly-regarded poem (originally written in Acholi) by Okot p'Bitek about how colonialism led to a loss of culture.

Fong & the Indians (1968) by Paul Theroux is set in a fictional East African country that bears a remarkable likeness to Uganda, where he taught English for four years in the 1960s. It's set in pre-civil war days, and is at times both funny and bizarre as it details the life of a Chinese immigrant and his dealings with the Asians who control commerce in the country.

Non Fiction

WILDLIFE

Keen birdwatchers will be best served by *The Birds of East Africa* (2006) by Terry Stevenson and John Fanshawe, with *The Bird Atlas of Uganda* (2005) making a good secondary source. Also available is *Butterflies of Uganda* (2004) by Nancy Carder et al.

The Uganda Wildlife Authority has published informative books on the natural history of some of the most popular national parks. They can be bought at the UWA office (p482) in Kampala, and occasionally at the parks themselves, although you may have to request them. Andrew Roberts' *Uganda's Great Rift Valley* (2006) is an entertaining study of the natural and human history of western Uganda.

For information on books about East African wildlife see p627.

HISTORY & POLITICS
Uganda: From the Pages of Drum (1994) is a lively compilation of articles that originally appeared in the now-defunct *Drum* magazine. These chronicle the rise of Idi Amin and the atrocities he committed, as well as President Museveni's bush war and his coming to power. It forms a powerful record of what the country experienced.

Ugandan Society Observed (2008) is another recommended collection of essays, these by expat Kevin O'Connor that originally appeared in the *Daily Monitor* newspaper.

The Man with the Key has Gone! (1993) by Dr Ian Clarke is an autobiographical account of the time spent in Uganda's Luwero Triangle district by a British doctor and his family. It's a lively read and the title refers to a problem travellers may encounter in provincial Uganda.

Widely available in Uganda, Henry Kyemba's *State of Blood* (1977) is an inside story of the horrors committed by Idi Amin, with insight only one of his former ministers could provide.

Aboke Girls (2001) by Els de Temmerman is a heart-wrenching account of female child soldiers and an Italian nun's attempt to rescue them during LRA's decade-long reign of terror in northern Uganda.

Music & Dance

Kampala is the best place to experience live music and several local bands play at nightclubs each weekend. Try to catch the Afrigo Band at New Club Obbligato (p393) and Maurice Kirya at Rouge (p393) every last Tuesday of the month, plus the weeknightly events at the National Theatre (p393).

To listen to Ugandan music, from hip-hop to northern-style thumb piano playing, log on to www.musicuganda.com.

The most famous dancers in the country are the Ndere Troupe (p393). Made up from a kaleidoscope of Ugandan tribes, they perform traditional dances from all regions of the country.

Handicrafts

Uganda's most distinctive craft is bark-cloth, made by pounding the bark of a fig tree. Originally used for clothing and in burial and other ceremonies, these days it's turned into a multitude of items for sale to tourists including hats, bags, wall hangings, pillows and picture frames.

Ugandans also produce some really good raffia and banana stem basketry, particularly the Toro of the west who have the most intricate designs and still use natural dyes. Traditional products are easy to find, but the old methods have been also adopted to make new items such as table mats and handbags for sale to tourists.

Baganda drum-makers are well known: the best place to buy is at Mpambire, along the Masaka Rd. Uganda also has interesting pottery, though all the soapstone carving comes from Kenya and almost all the interesting woodwork is Congolese.

Environment

Uganda suffers the same environmental problems as the rest of the region: poaching, deforestation and overpopulation. See p595 for more details.

Currently the biggest threat to Uganda's national parks and other protected areas comes from the oil industry. Significant oil finds in the Kabwoya Wildlife Reserve on Lake Albert have spurred invasive searches for more black gold in the Ishasha sector of Queen Elizabeth National Park and the delta area at Murchison Falls National Park. Providing the drilling companies explore and extract responsibly, then there may be hope for a sustainable marriage of interests; but conservationists are sceptical.

The Land

Uganda has an area of 236,040 sq km, small by African standards, but a similar area in size to Britain. Lake Victoria and the Victoria Nile River, which cuts through the heart of the country, combine to create one of the most fecund areas in Africa. Most of Uganda is a blizzard of greens, a lush landscape of rolling hills blanketed with fertile fields, where almost anything will grow if you stick it in the soil. The climate is drier in the north and some of the lands of the far northeast are semi-desert.

The tropical heat is tempered by the altitude, which averages more than 1000m in much of the country and is even higher in the cooler southwest. The highest peak is Mt Stanley (5109m) in the Rwenzori Mountains on the border with the DRC.

Wildlife

Uganda can't compete with Kenya or Tanzania for sheer density of wildlife, but with

500 species of mammal it has amazing diversity; and with the opening of the Ziwa Rhino Sanctuary (p457), the Big Five are all here again. Uganda is also home to more than half the world's mountain gorillas, and viewing them in their natural environment is one of the main attractions for visitors. On top of this, Uganda has a good number of chimpanzees and there are several places where you can track them. With well over 1000 species recorded inside its small borders, Uganda is one of the best birdwatching destinations in the world.

There are four national parks in Uganda that offer the opportunity for wildlife drives: Murchison Falls, Queen Elizabeth, Kidepo Valley and Lake Mburo. With more mammal and bird species than any park in Uganda, Queen Elizabeth offers the greatest variety; but Murchison Falls offers the larger mammals in greater concentration and also giraffes, which aren't found at Queen Elizabeth. At both parks you're very likely to spot elephants, buffaloes, hippos, bushbuck and kob; and, although it's not so easy to spot predators, with a bit of luck you'll also see lions and leopard.

Wildlife drives at Lake Mburo are very popular because it's the only place in the south with zebras and eland. These beauties can also be found in seldom-visited Kidepo Valley, which offers the chance to see cheetahs, ostriches, kudus, bat-eared foxes and many other animals found in no other part of Uganda. Wildlife drives are available in Toro-Semliki Wildlife Reserve too, although most people come here for chimpanzees.

Regardless of where you drive and what you're seeking, taking a UWA ranger-guide will almost guarantee more and better encounters. It must be stated again that Uganda doesn't have the mammalian bounty of Kenya and Tanzania, but it also doesn't have the masses. In Uganda, two trucks watching the same scene is a crowd.

Advantages to driving include covering more ground and getting closer to the animals, but nothing beats stalking animals on foot, and you can do this in the company of an armed ranger-guide in all parks mentioned above except Murchison Falls. Of course, birdwatching and gorilla and chimp tracking take place on foot too.

Gorilla Tracking

Gorilla tracking is one of the major draws for travellers in Uganda. These gentle giants live in two national parks: Bwindi Impenetrable and Mgahinga Gorilla. For more information on gorilla tracking see p32.

Chimpanzee Tracking

Chimpanzee tracking is a very popular activity in Uganda and there are several places where it's possible. The main ones are Kibale Forest National Park, Budongo Forest Reserve in Murchison Falls National Park and Kyambura Gorge in Queen Elizabeth National Park. While the little-known Toro-Semliki Wildlife Reserve is another good option, with a thinner forest often offering the best viewing. And, because there's plenty of savannah around, the little guys are a little more likely to be seen walking upright.

As with tracking the gorillas, you get to spend one hour with humans' closest living relatives; although they move much further and faster, so the chance of actually finding them is a little less certain.

Although golden monkeys lack the cache of chimpanzees, tracking this very rare primate in Mgahinga Gorilla National Park (p451) is also rewarding.

Birdwatching

Uganda is one of the world's best birdwatching destinations, a twitcher's fantasy offering 1041 species; that's almost half the total found in all of Africa. Even non-birdwatchers will be enthralled by the diversity of beauty among Uganda's birdlife.

The country's unique geographical position, where eastern, western, northern and southern ranges merge, allows visitors to view the 24 Albertine rift endemics (such as African green broadbill and handsome francolin) in Semuliki National Park on the same trip as dry-season eastern specials (karamoja apalis and red-billed oxpecker) in Kidepo Valley National Park.

A good starting point is **Uganda Birding** (www.birding-uganda.com), an excellent online resource with all there is to know – from birding hotspots, recommended tour operators, to info on the birds themselves. **Bird Uganda** (www.birduganda.com) also has plenty of good info. The country's top guides are members of the **Uganda Bird Guides Club** (www.ugandabirdguides.org).

Visiting birdwatchers may wish to contact the **Young Birders Club** (☎0777-912938; youngbirders@birduganda.com) to see about joining the kids (most aged seven to 12), on one of its outings in the Kampala area.

National Parks & Reserves

Uganda has an excellent collection of national parks and reserves. Twenty percent of your admission fees benefit local communities for things like construction of schools and health clinics, so you earn a warm fuzzy for every park you visit.

The **Uganda Wildlife Authority** (UWA; Map p382; ☎0414-355000; www.ugandawildlife.org; 7 Kira Rd, Kampala; ⊙8am-5pm Mon-Fri, 9am-1pm Sat) administers all Uganda's protected areas. It's the place to make bookings to see the gorillas in Bwindi Impenetrable National Park, and should be the first port of call for those needing to book permits. It's also the place to reserve *banda* accommodation in the parks that offer it. Some other activities, such as chimpanzee tracking, the launch trips in Murchison Falls and Queen Elizabeth national parks in Kibale can also be reserved here, though activities such as nature walks are arranged at the parks. Payments are accepted in shillings, dollars, euros and pounds in cash or Amex travellers cheques (1% commission). Staff are well versed on activities within the parks, but less so on getting to them, for those without transport. The UWA brochures about each of the parks are very informative: if there are none on the shelf, ask.

Most national parks charge US$35 (US$20 for children aged five to 15) and admission is valid for 24 hours. At the time of research UWA no longer offered 25% discount for students, but it's worth bringing your student ID in case this changes. Other charges, which can add up quite fast, include vehicle entry (USh10,000/20,000/30,000 per motorcycle/car/4WD) for locally registered vehicles. If you're coming in with a foreign registered vehicle, the prices are very expensive (US$30/50/150 per motorcycle/car/4WD). Nature walks cost US$10 per person and rangers for wildlife-watching

PRIMATE HABITUTATION

When it comes to tracking mountain gorillas in the wild, one common question is how it's possible to safely get mere metres from these beautiful, yet intimidating beasts that can weigh in excess of 200kg and have the strength to rip your arms out of their sockets. The simple answer lies in whether the gorilla group is habituated or not. Habituation is the process by which a group of primates (or other animals) are slowly exposed to human presence to the point where they regard us neutrally. While habituated and non-habituated gorillas are both considered wild, the latter are *truly* wild in the sense they're unaccustomed to human presence, in which they're either likely to flee into the forest or be downright dangerous and aggressive. Thankfully neither of these are the case when tracking gorillas in Bwindi – even though you might get the odd mock charge from a grumpy silverback.

The process of habituating gorillas is a long and patient affair that takes around two to three years. It's even longer for chimpanzees – normally around seven years before they're fully habituated. It involves spending time with a group every day and eventually winning over their trust, which is done by mimicking their behaviour: pretending to eat the same food as they do at the same time, grunting and even beating one's chest when they do. With gorillas, the first few weeks are fraught with danger for the human habitué, with repeated charges commonplace.

Habituation took place well before someone had the bright idea of charging tourists $US500 a pop to see the gorillas. It's a vital process for research that allows primatogilists to observe behavioural patterns of gorillas, chimps, golden monkeys, baboons etc. Some hold the view that the process of habituation is unethical: subjecting the creatures to our presence each day interferes with nature by changing their behavioural pattern. One example of things going wrong occurred in Busingiro on the edge of Murchison Falls National Park, where chimp tracking had to be abandoned when chimps lost their fear of humans and started raiding local farms. It also puts primates at risk of contagious ailments and disease while making them more susceptible to attacks from poachers or non-habituated 'wild' groups. But, pure and simple, had there not been habituation of gorillas (and the tourist trade to go with it), there's every chance the species would've been wiped out by poachers decades ago.

drives are US$20. Most prices are lower for Ugandan residents and much lower again for Ugandan citizens. Prices quoted in this book are valid until June 2013, so after that it's worth checking the UWA website.

If you're pressed for time, or money is no issue, you can charter flights to most of the parks.

Safari Operators

By far the most convenient way to visit the parks is on an organised safari, with a good range of options that cover most budgets.

In addition to the operators listed below, both Red Chilli Hideaway (p385) and Backpackers Hostel (p385) in Kampala offer popular and great value three- to four-day safaris to Murchison and Queen Elizabeth national parks.

Great Lakes Safaris (Map p382; ☎0414-267153; www.safari-uganda.com; Suzie House, Ggaba Rd, Kampala) One of the better all-round safari companies in Uganda, it offers a wide variety of safaris at prices for every pocket. Besides the usual wildlife trips, Great Lakes offers cultural encounters, and it will customise a blend of both experiences in any proportion that you wish. All budgets.

Matoke Tours (Map p382;☎0782-374667; www.travel-uganda.net; 8 Bukoto St, Kampala) The Matoke team focuses on the underserved midrange bracket. Besides excellent and enthusiastic service, it also stands out as one of the few quality companies that will take you to Kidepo Valley National Park overland. All budgets.

Classic Africa Safaris Entebbe (☎0414-320121; www.classicuganda.com; 77 Erica Magala Rd); USA (☎304- 724-8235) One of the best luxury companies in Uganda, Classic offers excellent service both in trip planning and in the parks. Top end.

Gorilla Tours (☎0414-200221; www.gorillatours.com, Kampala) Gorillas are the specialty, but it has itineraries covering all the major parks of southwest Uganda. The trips offer very good value, and it manages some of the country's best midrange hotels, including Travellers Rest Hotel in Kisoro and Airport Guesthouse in Entebbe. All budgets.

Amagara Tours (Map p444; ☎0752-197826; www.amagaratours.com; Kabale) Based out of Kabale Backpackers, which also manages the wonderful Byoona Amagara on Lake Bunyonyi, this newish company has great packages for all the national parks in the southwest, and a great option for the gorillas too. Budget.

Bird Uganda Safaris (☎0777-912938; www.birduganda.com; Kampala) Run by Herbert Byaruhanga, one of Uganda's pioneering birdwatchers, who leads most of the trips himself but also gets local guides at all of the sites to ensure top spotting. Birdwatching is the bread and butter, of course, but gorilla tracking and other wildlife encounters can be added to the mix. Herbert offers excellent value and has earned a multitude of rave reviews. Midrange to top end.

Food & Drink

Local food is much the same as elsewhere in the region, except in Uganda ugali (food staple usually made from maize flour or, rarely, cassava) is called *posho,* and is far less popular than *matoke* (cooked plantains). Rice, cassava and potatoes are also common starches and vegetarians travelling beyond the main tourist destinations will end up eating any of these with beans quite often, although Western, Indian and Chinese food is available at most hotels frequented by tourists. Kampala, Jinja and Entebbe (as well as the top hotels in many provincial towns) offer other international flavours such as Italian, Greek, Japanese and Mexican. One uniquely Ugandan food is the *rolex,* a chapatti rolled around an omelette. Grasshoppers are very popular during April and November and are sold by many street vendors. For more info on local cuisine, see p634.

Like all East Africans, Ugandans love their beer. Uganda Breweries and Nile Breweries are the two main local brewers, and they produce some drinkable lagers such as Nile, Club and Bell.

Waragi is the local millet-based alcohol and is relatively safe, although it can knock you around and give you a horrible hangover. It's a little like gin and goes down well with a splash of tonic. In its undistilled form it's known as *kasezi bong* and would probably send you blind if you drank enough of it.

Imported wines are quite expensive and not common beyond the tourist trail. Imported spirits are relatively cheaper, although, like wine, availability is somewhat restricted.

SURVIVAL GUIDE

This section covers information specific to Uganda. For general information applicable to the region, see p640.

Directory A–Z

Accommodation

CAMPING

Almost every popular destination in Uganda offers camping, so it's worth carrying a tent if you're on a budget. In provincial towns, many fancy hotels allow camping on their grounds, including use of swimming pools and other facilities. See p394 for information on buying camping equipment.

HOTELS

Hotels range from fleapit to five-star, and even in many smaller towns there's plenty of choice. You can even count on very small towns having at least one basic (and perhaps clean) lodge. There are few genuine upmarket hotels outside Kampala, Entebbe and some national parks, but all sizeable cities have something at about three-star quality.

Uganda does not offer exceptional value accommodation when compared with some other parts of Africa, and in Kampala there's currently a lot of price gouging going on. Outside the capital, the cheapest single/double rooms are available from around USh15000/20,000, rooms with bathroom usually start at USh20,000/25,000 and for another USh5000 to USh10,000 breakfast will be included. Modern, comfortable rooms with satellite TV (although often only the same channel that's turned on in the restaurant/bar) can be found from single/double USh50,000/70,000. Even most budget places, except at the very bottom of the price range, have hot water and attached restaurants. In Kampala a few hotels offer in-room wireless, but this is still uncommon. Top-end hotels and lodges start at around US$150 and can go much higher.

NATIONAL PARKS & RESERVES

The main national parks have a wide range of accommodation available, including luxury lodges and tented camps with outlandish prices. Always ask for discounts at these top-end places. The less-popular parks have simple campsites and basic *bandas*.

Camping in national parks costs USh15,000 per person per night (and in some parks US$40 for wilderness camping, which includes a guard), and tents are sometimes available for hire (the quality is usually low) for an additional USh10,000. *Bandas* are also common in the budget lodgings, starting from around USh20,000/30,000 for singles/doubles with shared facilities.

Activities

By far the most popular activity involves **wildlife viewing**, whether tracking mountain gorillas or on safari in one of Uganda's many national parks. But Uganda has always had a strong attraction among the dedicated **trekking** fraternity, mainly for the opportunities presented by the Rwenzori Mountains (p428) and Mt Elgon (p412). It's also possible to walk up the three volcanoes at Mgahinga Gorilla National Park (p450).

White-water rafting is another big attraction, with the Nile River offering world-class Grade Five rapids near Jinja, p405.

Business Hours

Government offices and businesses in Uganda are generally open between 8.30am and 5pm, often with a short break for lunch sometime between noon and 2pm. Most shops and banks don't break for lunch, but most banks

PRACTICALITIES

» Uganda uses the metric system.

» Electricity in Uganda is 240V, 50 cycles, and British three-pin plugs are used.

» Local newspapers include the government-owned daily the *New Vision* and the more independent *Daily Monitor*. International magazines, such as *Time* and *The Economist*, are readily available in Kampala.

» The state-run UBC and the private WBS are the main stations available on broadcast TV, but most hotels and bars have satellite TV for international news and sport.

» BBC World Service broadcasts on 101.3MHz and the phenomenally popular Capital FM can be found at 91.3MHz.

COMMUNITY PROJECTS

A visit to Uganda proves definitively that travel can make a positive impact. Near all the national parks and in many towns where tourists tend to go, there are a variety of community-run programs where a significant amount of the profit goes towards schools, health clinics and other projects that benefit local residents. The community-run Bigodi Wetland Sanctuary (p423), for example, is the main reason Bigodi is one of the few villages in Uganda where nearly everyone lives above the poverty line.

Many of these projects are set up and supported by the **Uganda Community Tourism Association** (UCOTA; Map p398; ☎0414-501866; www.ucota.or.ug; 3rd fl Aqua House, Ggaba Rd, Kansanga, Kampala) and the newly established **Pearls of Uganda** (www.pearlsofuganda.org). Both offer a range of initiatives that provide some memorable cultural experiences, from creative cooking tours offered by Boomu Women's Group (p466) to mock hunting parties with the Twa (Batwa) people in the forest. There's also the nearly ubiquitous village walks to dance groups, which are often worth checking out.

There are also some superb places to sleep, such as Ruboni Community Campsite (p429). Not all are small-scale. The residents of Nkuringo village are part owners of Clouds Lodge (p441) at Bwindi Impenetrable National Park, which charges a whopping US$940 per night.

close at 3pm. Few banks are open on Saturday, but more and more shops are adding weekend hours, usually closing about 1pm.

Local restaurant hours are 7am to 9pm or 10pm, while international-type restaurants are likely to be open 11.30am to 2.30pm and 5.30pm to 10.30pm.

Children

Although there are some risks and challenges to travelling the region with kids (see p36), with some great national parks and lots of water-based activities, Uganda can be a lot of fun for children. On the city side of things, Kampala isn't exactly bursting with activities for young people, but Entebbe and Jinja have plenty on offer.

Embassies & Consulates

For Ugandan embassies in Kenya, Rwanda and Tanzania, see the relevant section in those chapters.

EMBASSIES & CONSULATES IN UGANDA

The following are located in Kampala. Most close for an hour during lunch, and many close earlier on Fridays.

Australia (Map p386; ☎0312-515865; 15 Akii Bua Rd) Opposite from Nakasero Hospital.

Belgium (Map p386; ☎0414-349559; www.diplomatie.be/kampala; Rwenzori House, Lumumba Ave)

Burundi (Map p386; ☎0414-235850; 12a York Tce) A one-month single-entry visa costs US$90, requires two passport photos and takes two days to process. They're also issued at land borders and the airport.

Canada (Map p386; ☎0414-258141; kampala@canadaconsulate.ca; 14 Parliament Ave)

Denmark (Map p386; ☎0312-263211; www.uganda.um.dk; Lumumba Ave)

DRC (Map p382; ☎0414-250099; 20 Philip Rd) One-month single-entry visa costs US$60, requiring two passport photos and inconveniently takes one week to process. You can also get a seven-day visa at the border for US$50.

Ethiopia (Map p382; ☎0414-348340; Nakayima Rd)

Finland (Map p386; ☎0414-500969; 24a Golf Course Rd; ⏲9am-3pm Mon-Fri)

France (Map p386; ☎0414-304500; 16 Lumumba Ave; ⏲9am-noon Mon-Fri)

Germany (Map p386; ☎0414-501111; www.kampala.diplo.de; 15 Philip Rd; ⏲9am-11.30am)

India (Map p386; ☎0414-344631; 11 Kyadondo Rd; ⏲9.30am-12.30pm)

Ireland (Map p386; ☎0417-713000; 25 Yusuf Lule Rd)

Italy (Map p386; ☎0414-341786; www.ambkampala.esteri.it; 11 Lourdel Rd, Nakasero; ⏲10am-1pm Tue, Wed & Thu)

Japan (Map p386; ☎0414-349542; www.ug.emb-japan.go.jp; 8 Kyadondo Rd)

Kenya (Map p386; ☎0414-258235; www.kenyamission.or.ug; 4 Lower Kololo Tce) A single-entry visa costs US$50 and one passport photo is required. It will be ready the next day between 11am and 12.30pm. It's easier to get it on arrival.

Netherlands (Map p386; ☎0414-346000; 4th fl, Rwenzori Courts, Lumumba Ave)

Nigeria (Map p386; ☎0414-233691; 33 Nakasero Rd)

Rwanda (Map p382; ☎0414-344045; 2 Nakayima Rd; ⊙9.30am-noon Mon-Fri) Visas cost USh110,000 (for those who need them; see p554 for details), require one passport photo and will take around 72 hours to process. They're also available on arrival at the airport and at borders.

South Africa (Map p386; ☎0414-343543; 15A Nakasero Rd; ⊙8am-4pm Mon-Thu, 8am-1pm Fri)

Southern Sudan (Map p386; ☎0414-230272; 2 Ssezibwa Rd) Single/multiple entry visas cost US$80/100 and you'll need two passport photos. It takes one to two days to process. Visas weren't available at the border at time of research.

Sudan (Map p386; ☎0414-230001; 21 Nakasero Rd; ⊙10am-3pm Mon-Fri) A single-entry visa costs USh125,000 and you need two passport photos. Takes 24 hours to process.

Tanzania (Map p386; ☎0414-256272; 6 Kagera Rd) Visas are valid for three months, require two passport photos and take 24 hours to issue. Costs vary according to your country of origin. Single-entry visas are also available on entry.

UK (Map p382; ☎0312-312000; www.ukinuganda.fco.gov.uk/en; Windsor Loop)

USA (Map p382; ☎0414-259791; www.kampala.usembassy.gov; Ggaba Rd)

Gay & Lesbian Travellers

As with other East African nations, homosexuality is illegal in Uganda and in theory can result in a sentence of up to 14 years in prison. A controversial bill drafted in 2009 proposed the death penalty, receiving international condemnation from governments and human-rights groups. It's still being debated in parliament; see boxed text, p477.

The gay community here remains very much underground. For safe travel, it's urged that gay, lesbian, bisexual or transgender tourists likewise keep things discreet.

Internet Access

Internet cafes, charging around USh2000 per hour, are ubiquitous in Kampala, and wi-fi hotspots are getting more common. Elsewhere in the country, even most small towns have access for about the same price, albeit usually pretty slow.

Laptop users can easily get online by purchasing a wireless USB internet (or dongle) for around US$30, with the best networks being MTN and Orange, which have reliable access for most parts of the country.

Language Courses

The **City Language Centre** (CLC; ☎0772-501 679; www.clckampala.com; off Entebbe Rd, Bunamwaya) offers private lessons in Luganda, Luo and Swahili. It's located 6km south of Kampala and you can catch a Zana-bound taxi from the Old Taxi Park.

Maps

The Uganda maps by ITMB (1:800,000) and Nelles (1:700,000) will get you where you need to go. Only the latter is available in Uganda.

Being both beautiful and useful, Uganda Maps national park maps, available at Aristoc bookstore, UWA, safari lodges and tour companies, are a great buy if you're headed to any of the national parks.

The best available map of the city of Kampala is the *Kampala A-Z* street atlas, but Macmillan's *Kampala Traveller's Map* (1:8500) is good enough for most visitors. Both are available in bookshops and hotels around Kampala.

Money

The Ugandan shilling (USh) is a relatively stable currency that floats freely on international markets. Most tour operators and up-scale hotels quote in US dollars (a few in euros) but you can always pay with shillings.

Notes in circulation are USh1000, USh5000, USh10,000, USh20,000 and USh50,000, and commonly used coins are USh50, USh100, USh200 and USh500.

ATMS

The biggest banks (Barclays, Stanbic, Centenary, Crane, Orient, and Standard Chartered) have ATMs that accept international cards. Even many remote small towns will have at least one of these banks, though try not to let your cash run out in the assumption that you can easily get more, since the system sometimes goes down and machines sometimes run out of cash. You'll also notice tents and benches outside ATMs, which tells you how long the lines can get.

CASH

The Ugandan shilling trades at whatever it's worth against other major currencies, and there's usually little fluctuation from day to day. US dollars are the most useful hard currency, especially in small towns, though euros and pounds sterling are also widely accepted.

If you're using dollars, try to avoid bills printed before 2006, as often they're not accepted (due to a higher risk of them being counterfeit notes). If exchanging dollars, small denominations *always* get a much lower rate than US$50 and US$100 notes.

The best exchange rates by far are offered in Kampala. Forex bureaus offer slightly better rates than banks plus much faster service and longer hours; but they're rare outside Kampala.

Note that UWA offers fair exchange rates for park fees and accepts dollars, pounds and euros and either cash or travellers cheques.

CREDIT CARDS

Very few places other than top-end hotels and tour companies accept cards for payment; and there's usually a surcharge of 5% to 8%. Visa is the most widely accepted card, while MasterCard is pretty much nonexistent in Uganda.

TIPPING & BARGAINING

Tipping isn't expected in Uganda but, as wages are very low by Western standards, it will always be appreciated. The size of a given tip is up to the individual, but as a guideline USh1000 to USh1500 is enough in ordinary restaurants, while USh5000 to USh10,000 is reasonable for ranger-guides in national parks.

You'll usually need to bargain with boda-bodas and special-hires, though there are still many honest drivers out there. For bargaining tips while shopping, see p642.

TRAVELLERS CHEQUES

Try not to rely on travellers cheques as anything other than emergency back-up. Few banks or foreign exchange bureaus in or outside Kampala handle them, and they get lower rates than cash; often dramatically so.

Post

Sending a postcard costs USh1800 to Europe and USh2500 to the US or Australia. Kampala's post office (p396) is slow but reliable, while there's a chance things will go missing at provincial branches.

CASH AT THE AIRPORT

There are no banks, ATMs or forex bureaus before immigration, but, if you're in a pinch, an officer will hold your passport while you go get money from the ATM just beyond airport customs.

Public Holidays

New Year's Day 1 January

Liberation Day 26 January

International Women's Day 8 March

Easter (Good Friday, Holy Saturday and Easter Monday) March/April

Labour Day 1 May

Martyrs' Day 3 June

Heroes' Day 9 June

Independence Day 9 October

Christmas Day 25 December

Boxing Day 26 December

Banks and government offices also close on the major Muslim holidays. See p646 for the list.

Safe Travel

Despite a disarmament program, banditry remains rife in the Karamojong area of the far northeast (though not within Kidepo Valley National Park), and the border areas in the far northwest have their own problems. Various rebel groups hang out in the far eastern DRC and they occasionally slip across the porous border to make havoc and, even with additional Ugandan troops in the area, the chances of this happening again can not be completely discounted. Finally, there are smugglers and Kenyan rebels on and around Mt Elgon, though the risk to visitors is small.

Telephone

The country code for Uganda is ☎256. To make an international call from Uganda, dial ☎000 or, on a mobile, the + button. If you're calling Uganda from outside the country, drop the ☎0 at the start of the phone number.

Mobile (cell) phones are very popular as the service is better than landlines, though it's not one hundred percent reliable. All mobile numbers start with ☎07. Mobile-phone companies sell SIM cards for USh2000 and then you buy airtime vouchers for topping up credit from street vendors. Simple phones are available for USh45,000 in all sizeable towns and also at the airport. MTN and Orange currently have the best coverage across the country.

Landline telephone connections, both domestic and international, are pretty good, although not always so reliable in the provincial areas. The cheapest and easiest way to make a local call is from a payphone, which in Uganda is a person with a phone sitting in a kiosk or at a little table along the street. For international calls, many internet cafes in Kampala, Jinja and a few other towns offer rates ranging from USh200 to USh450 per minute depending on the country and whether you're calling a landline or mobile number.

Visas

Most non-African passport holders visiting Uganda require visas, including Americans, Australians, Canadians and almost all Europeans. Single-entry tourist visas valid for up to 90 days (but unless you ask for 90, you'll probably be given 30 or 60) cost US$50. It's easiest just to rock up at the airport or border and arrange one there; no photos needed. A yellow fever certificate is required if arriving from an affected area, but is rarely requested. At the time of research, multiple-entry visas weren't available on arrival, but it was possible for embassies abroad to issue them (US$100 for six months).

For visa requirements to neighbouring countries, see p485. Kampala is a good place for picking up visas to other countries, as there are rarely queues at the various embassies.

VISA EXTENSIONS

In Kampala, the **Immigration Office** (Map p382; ☎0414-595945; Jinja Rd; ⌚9am-1pm & 2-5pm) is just east of the centre. Regardless of how many days you were given on your original tourist visa, you can apply for a free two-month extension. Submit a letter explaining the reason for your request, stating where you're staying and detailing when and how you'll be leaving the country. Attach a copy of your passport and plane ticket, if you have one. It takes seven days to process, but extensions are much quicker at immigration offices outside the capital, and these exist in most large towns, including Jinja and Fort Portal.

Volunteering

Uganda has more volunteering opportunities than many African countries, thanks to a number of good grassroots organisations. The **Uganda Community Tourism Association** and **Pearl of Uganda** (see boxed text, p439) are in touch with many communities around the country and can connect you to a variety of projects, including tree-planting and teaching.

Also see the volunteering section in the regional directory (p648).

KAMPALA

Sanyu Babies Home (Map p382; www.sanyubabies.com) Receives and raises abandoned babies, many who have been left to die in ditches or latrines. Has a craft shop and a hostel popular with those volunteering here.

Skate Park (Map p398; ☎0752-397100) East Africa's only skate park in Kitintale, sometimes has volunteer opportunities. Jack, the local director, can tell you how to get there from wherever you are. Kids skate all weekend and after 4pm weekdays.

JINJA

Soft Power Education (www.softpowereducation.com) Has a number of projects to upgrade schools and improve education in the area, and around Murchison Falls National Park. Short and long-term volunteering options.

Soft Power Health (www.softpowerhealth.com) Also happy to accept volunteers to assist with their Malaria Education and Family Planning Outreach programmes. No medical training is necessary.

FORT PORTAL

Y.E.S. Hostel (www.caroladamsministry.com/yes_hostel.html) Voluntary work with children, see p419.

Mpora Rural Family (www.ugandahomestay.com) See p419.

GULU

THARCE-Gulu (www.tharcegulu.org) Does a range of work involving rehabilitating those who suffered during the LRA, including child soldiers. Occasionally looking for skilled volunteers.

St Jude Children's Home (☎0782-896897) Orphanage welcoming volunteers to teach or play with the children even if only for a day. It's 3km west of town.

LAKE BUNYONYI

Heart of Edirisa (www.edirisa.org) For volunteer opportunities in area schools or teaching swimming lessons.

MBALE

Foundation for Development of Needy Communities (FDNC; www.fdncuganda.org) Runs a host of community development programs in the area.

Getting There & Away

For information on getting to Uganda from outside East Africa, see p650.

Air

Located about 40km south of the capital, **Entebbe International Airport** (EBB) is the only aerial gateway to Uganda.

Uganda is well linked to its East African neighbours with daily flights to Kenya, Tanzania, Rwanda, Burundi and Sudan. For international flights, see p650.

AIRLINES IN UGANDA

Air Uganda (U7; ☎0414-258262; www.air-uganda.com; hub Entebbe) Regular flights to all the East African capital cities, as well as Mombasa and Zanzibar.

Fly540 (5H; ☎0414-346915; www.fly540.com; hub Nairobi) Flies to Nairobi.

Kenya Airways (KQ; Map p386; ☎0312-360000; www.kenya-airways.com; hub Nairobi) Flies to most East Africa cities via Nairobi.

Precision Air (PW; Map p386; ☎0312-360113; www.precisionairtz.com; hub Dar es Salaam)

RwandAir Express (WB; Map p386; ☎0414-344851; www.rwandair.com; hub Kigali) Flies to both Kigali and Bujumbura.

Land

Uganda shares land border crossings with Kenya, Rwanda, Tanzania, Sudan and the DRC. Direct bus services connect the major cities in each country, and local transport from towns nearer the border is available for those wanting to break their journey along the way. See relevant sections for prices.

KENYA

The busiest border crossing is at Busia on the direct route to Nairobi through Kisumu. Frequent minibuses link Jinja to Busia (USh7000, 2½ hours), and then again between Busia and Kisumu or Nairobi. The border crossing is straightforward, though there are a number of shady moneychangers: check everything twice.

The other busy border crossing to Kenya is through Malaba, a bit north of Busia and just east of Tororo. Though finding onward transport from here to Nairobi is less frequent than at Busia.

To visit Mt Elgon National Park or Sipi Falls, the seldom-used Suam border crossing, beyond which lies the Kenyan city of Kitale, may be convenient, but this is a pretty rough route. Trekkers in either the Ugandan or Kenyan national parks on Mt Elgon also have the option of walking over the border. See the Mt Elgon National Park section, p414 for information on both of these crossings.

Most travellers avoid local transport altogether and opt for the direct buses running between Kampala and Nairobi, which range from luxurious to basic. You can also pick up these buses (or get dropped off on your way into Uganda) in Jinja. The journey takes about 12 hours. See p654 for information on bus safety. All prices listed below are one-way.

Akamba Buses (Map p386; ☎0414-250412; www.akambabus.com; 28 Dewinton Rd, Kampala) Operates two classes daily: 'executive' class buses (USh60,000) depart at 7am, 3pm, 4pm and 7pm; the 7am daily 'royal' service is more comfortable, with huge, comfy seats, only three per row! It also heads to Mombasa (USh87,000, 20 hours) at 7am.

Kampala Coach (Map p386; ☎0784-573867; www.kampalacoach.com; Jinja Rd, Kampala) Uses spiffy new air-con buses showing movies. Departures for Kenya at 4pm (from Jinja Rd office), and 6am, 3pm, 7pm and 8pm (from Arua Park). The price is USh60,000.

There are also cheaper, but older buses to Nairobi (all depart at 3pm and cost USh45,000):

Kalita Transport (Map p386; ☎0772-522471; Namirembe Rd, Kampala).

Simba (Map p386; ☎0772-576196; Lumumba Ave).

Gateway (Map p386; ☎0722-069349; Wilson Rd, Kampala)

RWANDA

There are two main border crossing points: between Kabale and Kigali via Katuna (Gatuna on the Rwandan side), and between Kisoro and Musanze (Ruhengeri) via Cyanika. The Kagitumba border isn't very practical for most people, but there is public transport on both sides.

The busiest crossing by far is at Katuna/Gatuna, and it can take over an hour to get through immigration stations on both sides. From Kabale there are lots of shared-car taxis to the border, and a few minibuses each morning (except Sunday) direct to Kigali. You can also wait at the main junction in the morning for the Kigali-bound buses from Kampala to pass through and hope they have free seats. On the Rwandan side there are minibuses travelling to Kigali (RFr1300, two hours) throughout the day.

From Kisoro to Cyanika there's no public transport, so you'll need to get a special-hire (USh50,000) or a boda-boda (USh7000). Transport on the Rwandan side to Musanze (Ruhengeri) is frequent and the road in good condition; altogether it only takes about 1½ hours to travel between Kisoro and Musanze (Ruhengeri). The border is open 7am to 7pm.

There's also the option of taking a direct bus between Kampala and Kigali, a seven- to eight-hour journey including a slow border crossing.

Akamba Buses (Map p386; ☎0414-250412; www.akambabus.com; 28 Dewinton Rd, Kampala) Two daily buses to Kigali (USh40,000) at 9am and 11pm.

Horizon (Map p386; ☎0772-504565; 2 Berkely Rd, Kampala) Several daily buses to Kigali (USh35,000).

Jaguar Executive Coaches (Map p386; ☎0782-417512; Namirembe Rd, Kampala) Reliable company with daily services to Kigali at 7am, 9am, 8pm and 9pm. Also has a 'VIP' option with more comfortable seats.

Kampala Coach (Map p386; ☎0785-027465; Arua Park, Kampala) Good, modern buses, departing 11pm to Kigali (USh35,000).

Onatracom (Map p386; ☎0784-280500; Mackay Rd, Kampala) Older buses depart to Kigali (USh25,000) at 8pm and 9pm.

SOUTH SUDAN

With the advent of peace in northern Uganda and South Sudan, tenuous as it may be, travel has picked up dramatically. The principal, and shortest, route from Kampala to Juba is the 15-hour (much longer if it rains) trip via Gulu, crossing at Nimule.

Although the border to South Sudan is open (you'll need to arrange your visa in Kampala, and not the border), arranging permission to travel by land between South Sudan and Sudan is nearly impossible, so Juba is effectively a dead-end. And, because of the surfeit of aid workers and business people there, it's a very expensive one.

Kampala Coach (☎0785-027465; one-way USh80,000; ⏲depart midnight) Heads to Juba each evening with big, modern air-conditioned buses that's definitely worth the extra cash.

Gateway (one-way USh50,000; ⏲10pm) Located next door to Kampala Coach in Arua Park.

TANZANIA

The most commonly used direct route between Uganda and Tanzania is on the west side of Lake Victoria between Bukoba and Kampala, and goes via Masaka and the border crossing at Mutukula. Road conditions are good and the journey takes about six hours by bus from Kampala. Companies making this run include Ariazi Tours (USh17,000, 10.30am daily) and Gateway (USh20,000, 11am daily). You can also catch these buses in Masaka or travel from Masaka in stages; see p455 for details.

There's another border crossing located at Nkurungu, west of Mutukula, but the road is bad and little transport passes this way.

For the journey to Dar es Salaam taking a day and a half via Nairobi there's Akamba (USh140,000) at 3pm, Kampala Coach (USh150,000) at 1pm, while **Falcon** (Map p386) also makes the run to Dar es Salaam (USh150,000) at 1pm on less comfortable buses. These companies also stop in Arusha for two-thirds the price of the trip to 'Dar'.

Akamba also links Kampala direct to Mwanza (USh60,000, 22 hours), Moshi (USh90,000 20 hours) departing at 3pm.

THE DRC

As things stand at press time, it would be very unwise to visit the DRC. Assuming the fighting stops again, with the exception of the Bunagana border post (west of Kisoro) for mountain gorilla visits in Parc National des Virungas (p497), it will surely still be inadvisable to visit the DRC due to civil instability. Check, check and check again in Kampala and Kisoro about the current security situation before risking a crossing. See the Kisoro (p449) text for information on transport.

Lake

The passenger service on Lake Victoria to Mwanza (Tanzania) appears likely to be resurrected with the arrival of **EarthWise** (www.earthwiseventures.com; Port Bell, Kampala), a US-owned company that ambitiously aims to reduce the 17-hour trip to six to 10 hours. While at the time of research the service to Mwanza was still a bit away from commencing, instead focussing on launching a service to Ssese Islands, it appears likely it will go ahead, and possibly a service to Kenya too.

In the meantime, intrepid travellers can book passage on the MV *Umoja* cargo ferry that goes from Kampala's Port Bell. Typically these sail two or three days a week, but departures depend on demand. Check the schedule at the Marine Services offices on the second floor of the train station in downtown Kampala. Enter through the eastern gate. Pay your USh5000 port fee in the office in the green shipping container and then USh40,000 direct to the captain. The trip takes 16 to 17 hours and it's usually possible to make a deal with one of the crew for their bunk.

Getting Around

Air

Eagle Air (Map p386; ☎0414-344292; www.flyeagleuganda.com) and **Kampala Aeroclub** (☎077-706107; www.flyuganda.com) operate charter flights, which let you get to the national parks in comfort, but cost a fortune. Eagle Air has scheduled flights to Arua most days of the week, but is likely to have little interest for tourists. At the time of research **Air Uganda** (www.air-uganda.com) had announced plans to introduce domestic flights; check its website for details.

Boat

Boat travel in Uganda is limited to reaching the Ssese Islands, either by ferry from Port Bell, Nakiwogo (right by Entebbe) or Bukakata (east of Masaka) or with the less safe small boats operating from Kasenyi (also near Entebbe).

Bus

Standard buses and sometimes half-sized 'coasters' connect major towns on a daily basis and the longer your journey is, the more likely it will be on a bus rather than a minibus. Fares are usually a little less than minibuses and buses stop far less frequently, which saves time. Buses generally leave Kampala at fixed departure times; however, returning from provincial destinations, they usually wait until full. There are many reckless drivers, but buses are safer than minibuses. Night travel is simply best avoided.

In addition to the normal private buses, there are also Post Buses.

MINIBUS

Uganda is the land of shared minibuses (called taxis, or occasionally matatus), and there's never any shortage of these blue-and-white minivans. Except for long distances, these are the most common vehicles between towns. There are official fares (you can check at the taxi park offices if you want) but in reality the conductor charges whatever they think they can get, and not just for a *muzungu* but for locals as well. Ask fellow passengers the right price.

Minibuses leave when full; and 'full' means exactly that! As soon as you're a fair distance away from towns, where police spot-checks are less likely, more passengers will be crammed in. As is clearly painted on their doors, minibuses are licensed to carry 14 passengers, but travelling with less than 18 is rare, and the number often well exceeds 20. For all but the shortest journeys, you're better off taking a bus since they stop less frequently and are safer due to their size. Many minibus and bus drivers go much too fast to leave any leeway for emergencies. Crash stories are regular features in the newspapers. Most crashes are head-on, so sit at the back for maximum safety.

Way out-of-the-way places use shared-car taxis rather than minibuses, and similarly these are insanely overloaded with passengers. If the roads are exceptionally bad, then the only choice is to sit with bags of maize and charcoal, empty jerry cans and other cargo in the backs of trucks.

Car & Motorcycle

There's a pretty good system of sealed roads between most major population centres. Keep your wits about you when driving; cyclists, cows and large potholes often appear from nowhere.

The quality of dirt roads varies depending on whether it's the wet or dry season. In the dry, dirt roads are very dusty and you'll end up choking behind trucks and minibuses while everything along the road gets covered in a fine layer of orange-brown dust. In the wet season, a number of the dirt roads become muddy mires, almost carrot soup, and may be passable only in a 4WD vehicle. If you're travelling around Uganda in the wet seasons, always ask about the latest road conditions before setting off on a journey.

As with other transport, avoid travelling at night due to higher risks of accidents or banditry. Also take care in the national parks where there's a $US500 fine for hitting animals and US$150 for off-track driving.

Road signs are rare in Uganda so it's possible to get hopelessly lost. Don't hesitate to ask directions frequently along the way.

DRIVING LICENCE

If you have an International Driving Permit, you should bring it, although you really only need your local driving licence from home.

FUEL & SPARE PARTS

In Kampala petrol costs about USh3900 per litre while diesel is about USh3500 per litre. Prices rise as you move out into provincial areas. Like everywhere in the world, petrol prices are highly volatile.

Filling and repair stations are found even in some small towns, but don't let the tank run too low or you may end up paying around USh5000 per litre to fuel up from a jerry can in some really remote place.

HIRE

Due to high taxes and bad roads, car hire prices tend to be expensive compared to other parts of the world. Add fuel costs and there will be some real shock at the total price if you're considering driving around the country. Also remember that if you're going to national parks, you'll have to pay the driver's fees as well as your own.

The big international operators are **Europcar** (Map p386; ☎0414-237211; www.europcar.com; Nsambya Rd, Kampala), and **Hertz** (Map p386; ☎0772-450460; www.hertz.com; Colville St, Kampala), each with offices in downtown Kampala and at the airport in Entebbe. Daily rates are nearly US$100 for a small car with insurance and US$175 and up for 4WDs. This doesn't include excess kilometres, which are charged at US$0.30 above the paltry 100km allowance.

In virtually all instances it's better to deal with one of the local companies, though shop around. Quoted prices for a small car with driver can range from US$50 to US$150. The highest prices are just rip-offs by companies who hope *muzungu* don't know any better, but with the others, the difference is in the details. Always ask about the number of free kilometres (and the price for exceeding them) and driver costs for food and lodging. Try negotiating with special-hire drivers, but generally speaking they aren't as reliable.

Alpha Car Rentals (Map p386; ☎0772-411232; www.alpharentals.co.ug; 3/5 Bombo Rd, EMKA House, Kampala) Car with driver costs USh100,000 for the day around Kampala. Small 4WD with driver is US$90 (his food and lodging inclusive if you head upcountry). Both with unlimited mileage.

Wemtec (☎0772-221113; wemtec@source.co.ug) Well-known company based in Jinja but delivers country-wide. Hires a variety of Land Rovers with driver from USh180,000 to USh220,000. Prices all-inclusive (minus fuel), with no limits on mileage.

City Cars (Map p382; ☎0772-412001; www.driveuganda.com; Tank Hill Rd, Kampala) Expensive but reliable. Charges from US$100 per day including insurance for a self-drive small car. Beefy Land Rovers begin at US$120. Offers 150 free kilometres per day and charges US$0.40 for each extra kilometre. Also has camping gear (US$10 per day).

Hitching

Without your own transport, hitching is virtually obligatory in some situations, such as getting into national parks. Most of the lifts will be on delivery trucks, usually on top of the load at the back, which can be a very pleasant way to travel, though sun protection is a must. There's virtually always a charge for these rides.

See p655 for more on hitching in the region, including safety.

Local Transport

Kampala has a local minibus network, as well as special-hire taxis for private trips. Elsewhere you'll have to rely solely on two-wheel taxis, known as boda-bodas as they originally shuttled people between border posts: from 'boda to boda'. Most are now motorcycles, but you get the occasional bicycle in the smaller towns. Never hesitate to tell a driver to slow down if you feel uncomfortable with his driving skills, or lack thereof. Outside Kampala, there are few trips within any town that should cost more than USh3000.

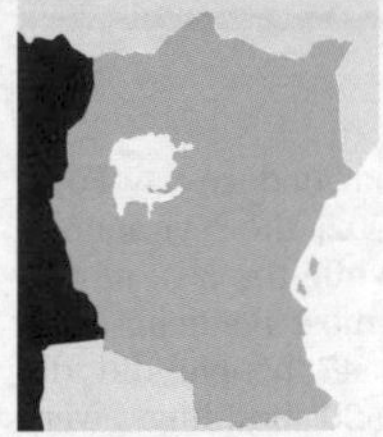

Detour: Democratic Republic of the Congo

Includes »

Goma 494
Parc National Des Virungas 497
Understand the DRC 500
History 500
Survival Guide 501
Directory A–Z 501
Getting There & Away .. 502

Best of Nature

» Nyiragongo Volcano (p498)
» Gorilla tracking (p498)
» Chimpanzee tracking (p499)

Best of Culture

» Twa (Batwa) community visit (p495)
» Eating *sambasa* (little fish fritters; p495)

Why Go?

The haunting yet unforgettable setting of Joseph Conrad's classic novel *Heart of Darkness,* the Democratic Republic of the Congo (DRC; formerly Zaïre) occupies a vast swathe of land in the centre of the African continent. The same size as Western Europe, most of the DRC falls outside of East Africa and this detour chapter only delves into the Nord-Kivu (North Kivu) province and its capital Goma.

After years of civil war, the Parc National des Virungas is once again open for business, and hard-core travellers are returning with stories of close encounters with critically endangered gorillas and tales of nights spent camped on the rim of a smouldering volcano, the night sky lit up by a witch's cauldron of molten lava below.

It's true, visiting the DRC isn't for everyone. The peace is young and fragile, but with a modicum of common sense, you could be blazing the trail that future generations of travellers will follow.

When to Go

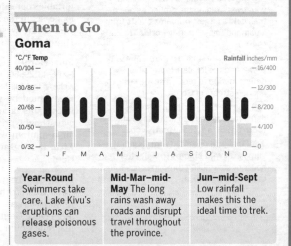

Goma

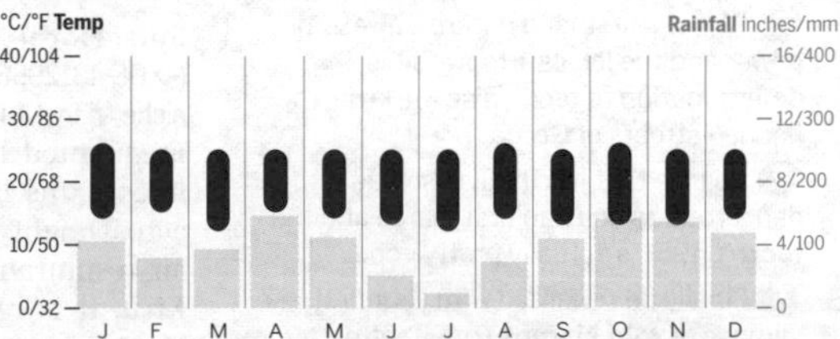

Year-Round Swimmers take care. Lake Kivu's eruptions can release poisonous gases.

Mid-Mar–mid-May The long rains wash away roads and disrupt travel throughout the province.

Jun–mid-Sept Low rainfall makes this the ideal time to trek.

Democratic Republic of Conga Highlights

1. Wipe the sweat from your brow, while staring slaw-jawed into the fiery bowels of the world's largest lava lake, **Nyiragongo Volcano** (p498)
2. Squat with your head bowed and your eyes fixed on the ground as one of the world's largest primates bursts from a bamboo thicket during **gorilla tracking** (p498)
3. Witness firsthand nature's awesome power and the locals' irrepressible determination to recolonise the lava-flooded streets of **Goma** (p494)
4. Realise that North Kivu isn't as dangerous as you had first feared and the **food** (p495) is actually pretty good
5. Finally be rewarded with your first glimpse of **wild chimps** (p499) after hours of scrambling through dense forest in the heart of Africa.

Goma

☎06

Goma is something of a modern-day Pompeii. On 17 January 2002, the Nyiragongo Volcano blew its top. While the lava moved slowly enough to give most residents time to evacuate (although 47 people did die from asphyxiation), 4500 buildings were destroyed, 120,000 people left homeless and much of the city, including the north end of the airport's runway, left buried under two metres of molten mess. Since then locals have been jackhammering their way through the lumpy rock, breaking it into manageable pieces and rebuilding their homes.

All tour companies listed on p497 can organise city tours, which incorporate some of the most badly affected areas and give you a rundown on how the disaster unfolded.

Sleeping

La Brise Guesthouse HOTEL $
(☎09 94403000; labriseguesthouse@yahoo.fr; Ave la Corniche; r US$30-50; P 📶) Large rooms, tight security, semi-reliable hot water and a quiet lakeside location make this one of Goma's best-kept secrets (although the restaurant is insanely overpriced). Of the three room categories available, you'll want to shell out for a US$40 or $50 room; the cheaper US$30 rooms don't have windows.

Stella Matutina Lodge BOUTIQUE HOTEL $$
(☎08 11510760; stellamatutina@yahoo.fr; Himbi; r excl breakfast $65-100; ❄ 📶) The most comfortable rooms in town are at this luxurious lodge, set in the spacious grounds of a grand villa to the west of the town centre in the Himbi district.

Ihusi Hotel HOTEL $$$
(☎08 13129560; www.ihusi-hotel.net; Ave la Corniche; r incl full breakfast US$75-200; P ❄ 📶 🏊) Frequented by visiting dignitaries and politicos, this large hotel offers smart rooms across eight price categories and an open-air restaurant with sweeping views of Lake Kivu. It is regarded at *the* place to stay in Goma.

Hotel des Grands Lacs HOTEL $
(☎09 97097959; hotelgrandslacs@gmail.com; Blvd Kanya Muhanga; r $US60, excl breakfast US$40; P 📶) Once Goma's grandest hotel, this colonial relic would struggle to earn just one star

these days, though it's atmospheric enough for a cheapie.

Hotel Nyira HOTEL **$$**
(☎09 93643112; nono.fabier@yahoo.fr; Blvd Kanya Muhanga; r US$50-60; P) Nyira's reputation has slipped over the years but could soon rebound thanks to new management keen to make the most of its central location, large rooms and lush green gardens.

Guesthouse Shushu HOTEL **$**
(☎09 91347578; Ave Grevilleas; r excl breakfast, shared bathroom US$15-20) Each room contains a small double bed, chair and mosquito net. The shared showers are cold and would benefit from a decent scrub.

Eating

Regional specialities and tasty snacks include *sambasa* (little fish fritters), local cheese and a local spiced sausage. *Foufou* (a starchy meal made from maize or cassava flour) on the other hand, while loved by the Congolese, we found it to taste a lot like dirt.

TOP CHOICE **Le Petit Bruxelles** EUROPEAN **$$**
(Ave du Rond Point; mains US$7-13; ⊙lunch & dinner, closed Sun) In the evenings, this Belgian-owned, open-air restaurant fires up its courtyard BBQ and serves tasty seared steaks and cold beer. The lunch menu is more limited, but the burgers are some of the best in town.

TOP CHOICE **Le Chalet** EUROPEAN, PIZZERIA **$$**
(Ave du Lac, Himbi 1; mains US$12-16; ⊙breakfast, lunch & dinner; 📶) Ten minutes north of the city centre by *moto-taxi* (motorcycle), Le Chalet is a tranquil oasis of tropical gardens and calm, lakeside dining. When you're done scoffing pizza and sipping vino on the patio, roll down to the lawn for a spot of sunbathing and swimming.

Village Fatimata BARBEQUE **$$**
(Ave Bougenvillier; mains US$15; ⊙lunch & dinner) Locals who come here for the grilled chicken, fish and goat ribs assure us it tastes better when washed down with a big bottle of local Primus (beer). We agree.

Kivu Market SUPERMARKET **$**
(Blvd Virunga; ⊙8am-10pm Mon-Sat, 10am-8pm Sun) The best stocked supermarket in town.

Drinking

If there is anything that the Congolese do well, it is partying!

Coco Jambo BAR
(Blvd Kanya Muhanga; ⊙6pm-late) Coco Jambo attracts a rowdy mix of locals and expats alike when the large garden bar takes on a nightclub vibe. From 6pm the resident DJ plays an upbeat mix of Congolese and Western hip-hop, pop and R&B. The place gets very busy on the weekends.

B-club BAR
(Ave Bougenvillier; ⊙6pm-late, closed Tue) Practically across the street from Coco Jambo, this large club is the other popular hangout for Goma's expat partygoers. The empty swimming pool, red lighting and flat-screen TVs help make the whole place feel like a cross between a dilapidated hotel and a bar from a *Mad Max* film.

WORTH A TRIP

VISITING THE TWA

Like much about the Twa (Batwa) people, opinions are divided about the effects tourism has on these fragile communities. The Twa were forcibly evicted from their forest homes in 1975 and have since been living on the fringes of society, the poorest of the poor. Some say that besides satisfying the voyeuristic curiosities of tourists, little is to be gained by parading Twa families, no matter how willing, in front of camera-touting tourists.

Others disagree, maintaining that tourism is one of the few avenues through which Twa can earn money and achieve a small measure of independence from the aid they rely on.

Travellers who do want to visit the Twa can call on the community living at Mubambiro Village near Goma. You will need to be taken by a tour operator who will phone ahead to get prior approval. Solo travellers are typically charged around US$50 to visit, while large groups can expect to pay at least US$100.

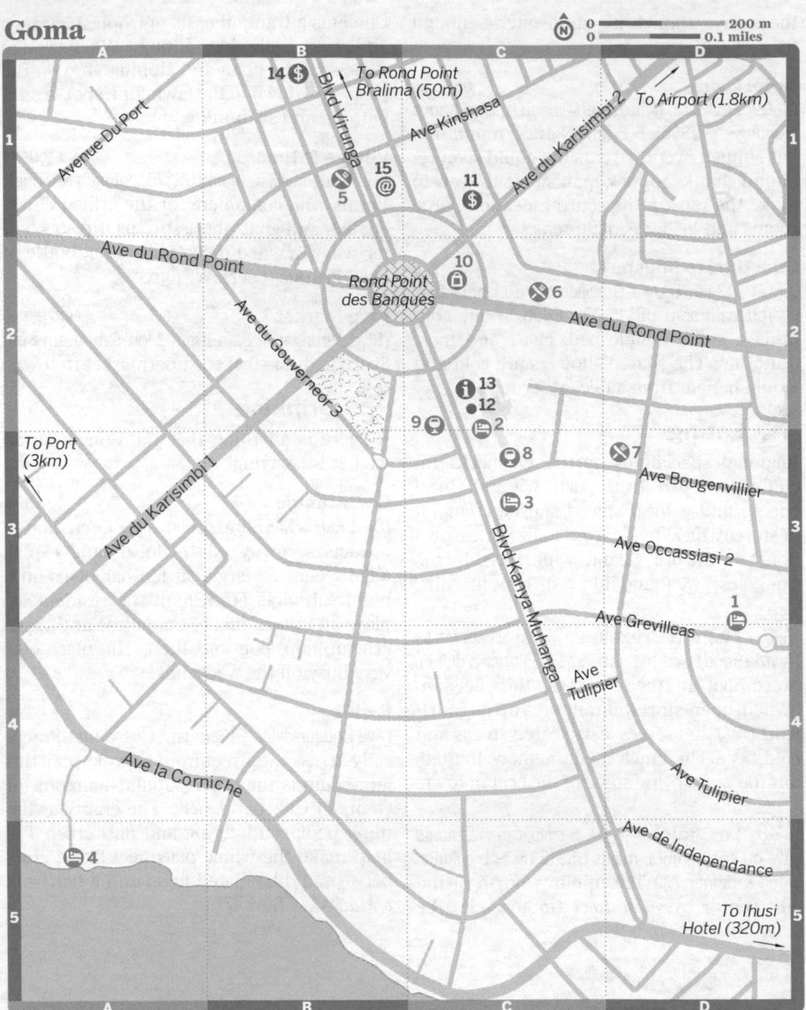

Shopping

The greater Congo area (Congo, the DRC and Gabon) is widely regarded as having some of the most potent art in Africa, and the quality and breadth of creative expression far exceeds that of the other countries found in this guide.

Traditional art was closely linked to spiritual beliefs although decorations were also applied to practical, everyday items. These days carvings are rarely strictly traditional, more a mixture of long-established motifs, imagination and commercial tastes.

Village des Artistes HANDICRAFTS
(Ave du Rond Point; ⌚7am-7pm) The Village des Artistes has a large and dusty selection of carved sculptures, wooden masks, ancestor figures, pots, drums, musical instruments and storage boxes. Don't be afraid to haggle.

Information

Internet Access

Tech Plus Internet Cafe (Blvd Virunga; per hr CFr1000; ⌚8am-8pm)

Money

Banque Internationale pour l'Afrique de Congo (BIAC; off Rond Point des Banques) In

Goma

Sleeping

1 Guesthouse Shushu D3
2 Hotel des Grands Lacs C2
3 Hotel Nyira C3
4 La Brise Guesthouse A5

Eating

5 Kivu Market B1
6 Le Petit Bruxelles C2
7 Village Fatimata D3

Drinking

8 B-club C3
9 Coco Jambo C2

Shopping

10 Village des Artistes C2

Information

11 BIAC Bank C1
12 GB Travel C2
13 ICCN C2
14 Raw Bank B1
15 Tech Plus Internet Cafe B1

addition to the downtown branch, there is also a BIAC ATM dispensing US dollars at the Ihusi Hotel.

Raw Bank (Blvd Virunga) Reliable ATM that accepts Visa and MasterCard.

Tourist Information

Institut Congolais pour la Conservation de la Nature (ICCN, the Congolese Wildlife Authority; ☎09 91715401; www.visitvirunga.org, www.gorillacd.org; Blvd Kanya Muhanga); Goma (⏲8.30am-5pm Mon-Fri, 8.30am-12pm Sat) Although ICCN is primarily concerned with Parc National des Virungas activities, it is also the de facto tourist office and your best source of advice.

Travel Agencies

GB Travel (☎09 92182250; Blvd Kanya Muhanga) Reliable airline ticketing office.

Tour Operators

Emmanuel Munganga Rufubya (☎09 94328077; www.gorillastracking.com, emmanuelrufubya@yahoo.fr) A one-man band, Emmanuel has a lot of experience guiding tourists and a vast network of contacts. You can expect a high degree of friendly, personal service and sound advice from him, although some of his drivers are unfamiliar with the roads outside of Goma and drive dangerously.

Go Congo (☎09 94379733; www.gocongo.com) A large Kinshasa based company specialising in boat tours on the Congo River between Kisangani and Kinshasa. It also has a representative in Goma.

Kivu Travel (☎in Belgium + 32 495 586 807; www.kivutravel.com) A Belgium/Congolese run company with a sound reputation.

Mapendano Voyages (☎in Rwanda +250 55106520; www.mapendanovoyages.com) An East African tour specialist with some experience in the DRC.

Okapi Tours & Travel Company (☎09 9432877; www.okapitoursandtravel.com) Reliable operators with Rwandan and eastern DRC experience.

Getting There & Away

Air

Compagnie Africaine d'Aviation (CAA; www.caacongo.com) Has daily flights to Kinshasa (one way, US$355) and Kisangani (one way, US$205), as well as less frequent flights to Lubumbashi (one way, US$395), Beni (one way, US$185) and Entebbe in Uganda (one way, US$300). All passengers are subject to a US$10 departure tax.

Road

Until civil unrest ends, it remains too dangerous to travel deeper into the DRC from Goma. For information on travelling overland to either Rwanda or Uganda, see p502.

Boat

Fast (two hours, US$50) and slow (eight hours, 1st/2nd/3rd class US$25/15/12) boats leave every morning (between 7am and 8am) and afternoon (usually between 2pm and 4pm) for Bukavu. The fast boats are enclosed speedboats, while the slow boats are the same grand old ferries that have been plying these waters for years.

Parc National Des Virungas

Established in 1925 by the Belgian colonial government as Albert National Park, Parc National des Virungas is the continent's oldest protected area, and arguably one of its most vital. Befitting such a vast country as the DRC, Virungas is, quite simply, enormous. To put things into perspective, Virungas is contiguous with five different national parks in Uganda, and protects an incredible range of endangered animals, from forest elephants and okapis to chimpanzees and mountain gorillas.

The park lies at the centre of a war-torn region, and has been threatened by poaching, land invasions, charcoal producers

CHUKUDU

If necessity is the mother of invention, then the *chukudu* is its most ungainly child. Something like a cross between an over-sized scooter, bicycle and wheelbarrow, *chukudus* are North Kivu's answer to the bumpy, lava-covered roads and something of a regional icon (there's a statue of one at Rond Point Bralima). Made entirely from wood – including the wheels – the whole thing is steered by handles carved from a branch in the shape of an inverted 'Y'. These contraptions first made an appearance in the 1970s and have been enabling the poor to make a living hauling goods and produce ever since. In case you need a hand with your luggage, current rates are: US$3 for around 2km, US$10 for 10km.

and rebel factions. The park reopened in 2008 and has been going from strength to strength ever since. The park and all park activities are run by the ICCN.

Sights & Activities

TOP CHOICE Nyiragongo Volcano VOLCANO

(www.visitvirunga.org, www.gorillacd.org; per person US$200) Beautiful and brooding, locals in Goma fear and respect the power of Nyiragongo Volcano. Having destroyed half the city in 2002, the volcano certainly deserves its reputation, though this isn't to say you shouldn't climb it if you're feeling fit. Those who do undertake the five-hour climb are rewarded with views into the earth's smouldering heart and the world's largest **lava lake** from the crater's rim. Wrapped in a sleeping bag, watching the fiery glow of the lava light up the night sky is a wickedly surreal, if slightly unnerving, experience.

Preparation

As the summit stands at 3468m, with a short but impressively steep section near the top, you will need to be moderately fit to tackle this beast. Guides and armed security are included with your permit, but consider hiring your own porter (US$12 per day, maximum weight carried 15kg) and cook (US$15 per day) at the small ranger post at the start of the climb.

While it is possible to make a round trip in one day, by doing so you'll miss the lava at its spectacular nighttime best. Most people opt to spend the night in one of the eight A-frame cabanas built on the crater's rim (no additional charge). Each cabana has two bunks, each bed with a mattress and pillow but nothing else. You will need to bring your own food, water, sleeping bag (these can be rented from ICCN for US$5), stove, cooking utensils, sunscreen, toilet paper, torch and warm clothing. The latter is essential; nights are extremely cold on the summit and gloves, hats, windbreakers and sweaters will go a long way towards making your experience more enjoyable.

Gorilla Tracking WILDLIFE ENCOUNTER

(www.visitvirunga.org, www.gorillacd.org; per person US$400) There are few experiences in the world more memorable than coming face to face with a wild eastern mountain gorilla.

There are six habituated families in Parc National des Virungas and you will be assigned a group to visit by the rangers based on how many people are tracking and their current locations. The largest family is Kabirizi with 32 individuals and offers excellent opportunities to see infants and rambunctious youngsters. The Humba and Mapuwa groups are also sizeable families, each with 16 individuals. Humba is a ranger favourite because of the easy-going nature of the dominant silverback. The smaller groups, Rugendo, Munyaga and Lulengo, have about eight members each and are only visited when there are four or fewer trackers. Despite it's smaller size, Munyaga has the distinction of having three silverbacks (one of which is bald) within the family.

No matter which family you are assigned, you can expect a magical encounter, although this will differ from day to day, group to group and the mood of the silverback. The ideal time to meet a gorilla family is from 10am to 11am (which means a 5.30am departure from Goma) when they will have finished foraging and are settling for a mid-morning rest. Youngsters are typically lively at this time, bounding over older siblings, climbing trees and generally annoying their parents as they relax. Older gorillas can often be seen grooming one another, sucking ants off twigs and climbing trees. The silverback will be doing whatever he damn well pleases.

The Trek

An entourage of armed rangers, trackers and a guide accompanies each group. The trackers leave at daybreak, locating the gorillas and radioing in their position so you won't have to climb every volcano in the Virunga massif in search of them. The machine gun–totting rangers are there for your protection and are standard practice in the park today.

All treks leave from one of three patrol posts, the most popular and the only one with accommodation is Bukima, the closest to Goma. If you arrive from the Ugandan border, you will most likely trek from either Jomba or Bikenge.

The treks can range from a 30-minute, sunny stroll to a five-hour ordeal up steep hills covered in dense forest in freezing cold rain. You need to be prepared for both. See the gorilla tracking section under Rwanda's Parc National des Volcans (p519) on what to bring.

The Encounter

Because gorillas are so genetically akin to humans, ICCN has imposed a number of strict rules to help minimise the chance of a disease jumping the species barrier and infecting the apes. Just like in Rwanda and Uganda, you will not be able to visit the gorillas if you are sick, nor will you be able to go to the toilet, eat, cough or blow your nose in their presence. But unlike in Rwanda and Uganda, you will also be required to wear a facemask to further reduce the potential for unwittingly transmitting a disease.

Visits are restricted to one hour and flash photography is banned. Your guide will tell you how to act while around the gorillas. Do exactly what they say, including the part about squatting low, eyes downcast in the face of a charge. Once you see the size of an adult silverback you will realise how difficult this will be. For further information on gorilla tracking in East Africa, see p32.

Senkwekwe Gorilla Orphanage WILDLIFE RESERVE

Provided you make it back from your gorilla track in a timely fashion, it should be possible to visit the world's only mountain gorilla orphanage at ICCN park headquarters in Rumangabo on the way back to Goma.

Named after the silverback who died defending the Rugendo group against gunmen in the infamous 2007 massacre, the orphanage is home to four gorillas including Ndakasi and Ndeze, both massacre survivors. Ndakasi was found clinging to her dead mother (who had been shot in the back of the head), and although Ndeze had been rescued by her brother, she was reliant on breast milk and had to be brought here.

Chimpanzee Tracking WILDLIFE ENCOUNTER

(www.visitvirunga.org; per person US$100) By the time this guidebook is published, ICCN hope to once again offer chimp tracking in Tongo, a unique 'forest island' cut off from the rest of the park by ancient lava flows. The Tongo chimps were first habituated way back in 1987, but civil war and lingering security concerns meant that the area has been off limits since 1992. Throughout this time, rangers have protected the chimps and now, with increased stability in the region, the area is once again safe to visit.

The Trek

The small forest block is home to 36 chimps, and although encounters are never guaranteed, you should have an excellent chance of seeing chimps here. Expect a 7am start and a challenging two-hour hike through primary and secondary forest over jagged and slippery, moss-covered lava flows. Unlike gorillas, chimps are fast moving, love to climb high into the canopy and are more wary of humans. This means you won't get as close to a wild chimp as you will to a mountain gorilla, but don't let this deter you. This is a rare chance to meet our closet evolutionary cousins.

Sleeping

Mikeno Lodge LODGE $$$

(☎0991715401; www.mikenolodge.com; s/d & tw incl meals US$450/700; P) Run by ICCN and based at Rumangabo (next to the gorilla orphanage), Mikeno Lodge brings a new level of comfort to the wilds of the Congo jungle. Each of the 12 luxurious bungalows is made of dark volcanic stone, rich mahogany and beautifully crafted thatched roofs. Inside they are divided between an open-plan room featuring a cosy lounge, open fire and sleeping area and a bathroom with a stone-lined shower. Meals are taken at the equally impressive main lodge where an enormous terrace allows you to look directly into a forest canopy alive with colobus and blue monkeys.

Bukima Camp CAMPGROUND $
(www.visitvirunga.org; camping half-board per person US$40, camping US$20, camping own tent US$15) This magical spot is also the departure point for many of the gorilla-tracking excursions, which means you'll be able to sleep later by staying here. The campsite consists of eight two-person tents made of heavy canvas, a large communal dining shelter and a shared toilet block with cold-water shower. The jungle backdrop, surrounding agricultural gardens and distant volcanoes make this one of the most beautiful campsites in East Africa.

Tongo Campsite CAMPGROUND $
(www.theforgottenparks.org; camping per person US$10) To coincide with the launch of chimpanzee tracking, the Frankfurt Zoological Society has been working to establish a small community-run campsite at Tongo Village with five tents. All profits will be returned to the community or used to develop community conservation initiatives. Congolese food and ample opportunities to mix with the local community make this a great option for anyone seeking a dash of cultural insight to go with their primate appreciation.

Information

The **Institut Congolais pour la Conservation de la Nature** (ICCN, the Congolese Wildlife Authority; 0991715401; www.visitvirunga.org, www.gorillacd.org; Blvd Kanya Muhanga, Goma; 8.30am-5pm Mon-Fri, 8.30am-noon Sat) should be your first point of contact when arranging a trip to the DRC. All park activities (as well as transport, accommodation and visas) can be booked directly through the ICCN website.

Getting There & Away

Bukima Post is about 52km (three hours) from Goma. The main road is in reasonable condition, but the 15km access road is appalling. Consisting of series of interconnected potholes, you'll need a serious – and we mean serious – 4WD to get here.

The road from the Ugandan border at Bunagana is little better and, again, a 4WD is required to get to the trekking trailheads of Jomba (45 minutes) or Bikenge (45 minutes).

Transport can be booked on the ICCN website when you purchase your permits. ICCN currently provides return transport from Goma to Bukima (US$60 per person, 5.30am departure), Tongo (US$80 per person) and the trailhead for the Nyiragongo Volcano (US$20 per person).

From Bunagana, ICCN arranges return transport to Jomba (US$30 per person), Bikenge (US$30 per person), Bukima (US$60 per person) and the Nyiragongo trailhead (US$80 per person).

UNDERSTAND THE DRC

History

While colonialism is fundamentally an exploitative force, there are few examples as harsh and severe as that of the Congo Free State (1877–1908). King Leopold of Belgium, who essentially ran the country like his own private colony for nearly three decades, increased his personal wealth through subjecting the Congolese population to forced labour on his massive rubber plantations. Leopold eventually transferred power to his own parliament, though the colony was run under equally undemocratic means until 1960.

Parliamentary elections in the newly dubbed 'Democratic Republic of the Congo' did initially have a measure of democracy, producing nationalist Patrice Lumumba as prime minister and pro-Western Joseph Kasavubu as president. However, it wasn't long before power struggles in the DRC launched a proxy war between the US and the Soviet Union. As in other corners of the globe that played host to the Cold War, the struggle between capitalism and communism severely limited the country's growth. With the aid of the US government and CIA, and the Belgian government, Kasavubu and his 'loyal' colonel Joseph Mobutu assassinated Lumumba, ushering in five years of political infighting and civil unrest.

In 1965, Mobutu seized control in a bloodless coup, declaring himself President Mobutu Sese Seko Kuku Ngbendu Waza Banga, or 'the fearless warrior who will go from strength to strength leaving fire in his wake.' Despite the lofty title, President Mobutu is remembered for using state coffers to fund Concorde charters to Paris for extravagant shopping trips. He created a new form of government along the way: kleptocracy, or governance by theft.

The country was officially known as the 'Republic of Zaïre' from October 1971 to May 1997, which coincided with much of the reign of President Mobutu Sese Seko.

When Mobutu fled the country in 1997, Kabila seized Kinshasa without a fight, consolidated power and changed the country's name back to the Democratic Republic of the Congo.

The Great War of Africa

Mobutu was eventually deposed in 1997, though the massive black hole that followed resulted in the 'Great War of Africa.' At its height, the war sucked in as many as nine countries, and led to the deaths of an estimated three to five million people, largely from disease and starvation, and became the world's deadliest conflict since World War II. Add to the mess the Interahamwe (Those Who Kill Together), responsible for the Rwandan genocide, and the Mai Mai, who wear sink plugs around their necks, and believe that holy water protects them from bullets. The Mai Mai were community-based militia groups that banded together to defend their territory against other armed groups including Rwandan forces and Rwandan-affiliated Congolese rebel groups.

Formal peace treaties were signed in 2002 and a Transitional Government saw the DRC through its first multiparty elections. A little unsurprisingly, allegations of electoral fraud saw fighting break out until it was eventually quelled by UN peacekeepers and a new election held. On 6 December 2006 the Transitional Government came to an end as Joseph Kabila was sworn in as President.

Since then the government has struggled to maintain the tenuous peace and galvanise the progress made in the 2002 peace accords. On 28 November 2011, the country returned to the polls in its second multiparty elections since independence. The lead-up to the election was characterised by intimidation and human rights abuses but the incumbent, Joseph Kabila, won the presidential elections and parties aligned with Kabila took 260 seats in the 500-seat National Assembly.

International observers described the process as deeply flawed and opponent Etienne Tshisekedi, citing massive electoral fraud and voter intimidation, proclaimed himself the victor and attempted to organise his own inauguration ceremony.

The uncertainty surrounding the election process has done nothing to calm the pre-election tensions, and discontent – both in the civilian population and the military – remains widespread.

Of course, it remains to be seen whether or not Kabila can bring stability to an enormous landmass that has been plagued by ill governance since its original demarcation.

In summary: it's not that democratic, it's barely a republic, but it is the Congo.

SURVIVAL GUIDE

Directory A–Z

Money

The US dollar is widely used although you may be given change in Congolese francs (CFr). Cash (US$ bank notes 2006 and younger) can be safely exchanged on the border or withdrawn from internationally equipped ATM machines in Goma.

Safe Travel

So, just how safe is the DRC? The unfortunate reality is that nobody really knows. The DRC's greatest blessing – and its inescapable curse – has always been its abundance of natural resources. As a direct consequence, the country is still something of a volatile powder keg, and armed struggles to control these riches could ignite the fuse at a moment's notice.

The situation at the time of research was uncertain. Despite the Second Congo War ending in 2003 and the demise of the Kivu

THE 2011 ELECTION IN NUMBERS

When a country the size of Europe goes to the polls, the election becomes a logistical nightmare. When the political landscape is as complex as that of the DRC, it becomes a US billion-dollar operation.

» 11 – the number of presidential candidates

» 56 – the number of pages per ballot

» 147 – the number of political parties in the DRC

» 18,000 – the number of parliamentary candidates

» 62,000 – the number of polling stations

conflict in 2009, eastern areas are still prone to outbreaks of violence including murder, rape and car-jackings.

What we can say is that in late 2011 it was perfectly safe to stay in Goma, visit the gorillas and climb Nyiragongo, but there is no substitute for your own careful research, as inevitably the situation will continue to change. Two reliable sources of information are the websites of the UN Mission in Congo (www.monuc.org) and the Parc National des Virungas (www.visitvirunga.org, www.gorilla.cd).

GOMA

The UN maintain several bases within the city and you will see more foreigners here than across the border in Gisenyi (Rwanda), although few of them will be travellers. We found it safe to travel by foot, car and *moto-taxi* around town. *Moto-taxis* were plentiful but taxis scarce, so get a driver's number if you rely on this form of transport. Most NGOs impose a strict 'no driving after dark' policy on their staff for good reason. We would go a step further and advise against bringing your own vehicle at all.

PARC NATIONAL DES VIRUNGAS

Park authorities have more than 300 rangers operating within the park and are well placed to recognise potential threats to their clients. Armed rangers escort all trips to the gorillas and Nyiragongo, and the Goma–Rumangabo, Bunagana–Rumangabo and Rumangabo–Bukima (site of gorillas) roads are relatively safe.

That said, rangers are regularly killed in gun battles and various rebel factions hold considerable sway deep inside the park. These areas are far from those currently open to travellers but illustrate how precarious the situation still is.

FURTHER AFIELD

While the vast remainder of the DRC is outside the extents covered in this book, it's worth mentioning that heading overland through the bush is definitely a no-no.

To the south, Bukavu (accessed by boat) is on the rise, though there are still scars from the thrashing it took in summer 2004 at the hands of a dissident pro-Rwandan faction. Nearby Parc National Kahuzi-Biéga is once again open for lowland gorilla viewing, though be sure you get the latest reports as there are still security risks in the area.

Telephone

Few people use landlines, most relying on mobiles with prefixes of ☎9 or ☎8. The country code for the DRC is ☎243.

Visas

Up until 2011, obtaining a visa for the DRC was a hot and complex issue, one that involved a US$285 payment (US$250 of this was used to line official pockets), a tour operator to meet you at the border and possibly a notarised invitation letter.

These days things are considerably more straightforward and visas (US$50, 14 days, single entry) are now available online from the ICCN (www.visitvirunga.org) website. These can only be brought in conjunction with a park activity and are only good for the entry at the Gisenyi (Rwanda) and Bunagana (Uganda) borders. It is hoped that this will eventually be extended to include entry via the Bukavu post (although it is possible to exit at Bukavu). The visa takes seven days to process.

If you need to stay longer, organise your visa in *your* country of residence (although visas are sometimes issued in East African embassies, unless you're an East African national, it is unlikely that officials at the borders will recognise it).

Getting There & Away

Land

Most people enter the DRC's North Kivu province at the Bunagana–Uganda or Goma–Gisenyi (Rwanda) borders. Provided you have your paperwork in place (including a yellow fever certificate), your border crossing should be hassle-free. Of the two possible crossing points that separate Goma and Gisenyi, the 'small' barrier is the one most commonly used by travellers.

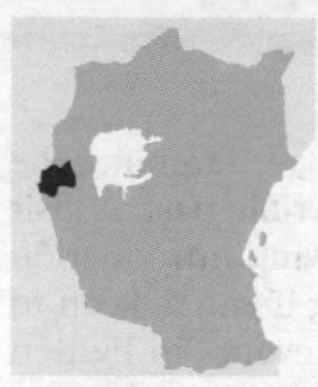

Rwanda

Includes »

Kigali ... 505
Musanze (Ruhengeri) ... 515
Parc National des Volcans ... 519
Gisenyi ... 525
Huye (Butare) ... 530
Around Huye ... 533
Nyanza (Nyabisindu) ... 534
Nyungwe Forest National Park ... 535
Cyangugu ... 540
Kibuye ... 540
Parc National de l'Akagera ... 542

Best of Nature

» Parc National des Volcans (p519)

» Nyungwe Forest National Park (535)

» Parc National de l'Akagera (p542)

Best of Culture

» National Museum of Rwanda (p532)

» Gorilla Naming Ceremony (p523)

» Rukari Ancient History Museum (p534)

Why Go?

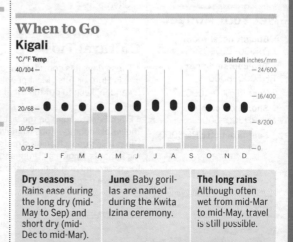

Mention Rwanda to anyone with a small measure of geopolitical conscience, and they'll no doubt recall images of the horrific genocide that brutalised this tiny country in 1994. But since those dark days a miraculous transformation has been wrought and today the country is one of tribal unity, political stability and a promising future.

Tourism is once again a key contributor to the economy and the industry's brightest star is the chance to track rare mountain gorillas through bamboo forests in the shadow of the Virunga volcanoes. These conical mountains are shrouded in equatorial jungles and helped earn Rwanda the well-deserved moniker of 'Le Pays des Mille Collines' (Land of a Thousand Hills).

So, while Rwanda's scars may run deep, now is the time to help the country look to its future and embrace its newfound optimism.

When to Go

Kigali

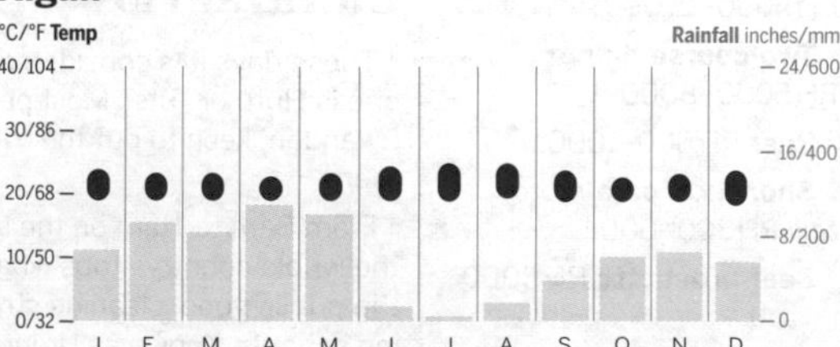

Dry seasons Rains ease during the long dry (mid-May to Sep) and short dry (mid-Dec to mid-Mar).

June Baby gorillas are named during the Kwita Izina ceremony.

The long rains Although often wet from mid-Mar to mid-May, travel is still possible.

AT A GLANCE

» **Currency** Rwandan franc (RFr)

» **Language** Kinyarwanda, English, French

» **Money** Some banks now equipped with international ATMs

» **Visa** If required, must be applied for in advance at www.migration.gov.rw

Fast Facts

» **Area** 26,338 sq km

» **Capital** Kigali

» **Country code** ☎250

» **Emergency** ☎112

Exchange Rates

Australia	A$1	RFr636
Canada	C$1	RFr602
Euro Zone	€1	RFr790
Japan	¥100	RFr741
New Zealand	NZ$1	RFr490
UK	UK£1	RFr946
USA	US$1	RFr601

Set Your Budget

» **Budget hotel room** RFr5000–15,000

» **Two-course dinner** RFr5000–8000

» **Beer** RFr600–1000

» **Short hop on a** ***moto-taxi*** RFr300–600

» **Beef brochette** RFr3000

Itineraries

Five Days Spend your first few days in Kigali sampling the country's finest food and learning of its terrible past. A visit to the Kigali Memorial Centre is a harrowing introduction to the 1994 genocide but essential viewing if you're keen to gain a little understanding of this tragic event. To lighten your mood, head north to Musanze (Ruhengeri) and spend the following day with a mountain gorilla family before returning to the capital.

Twelve Days With another week, spend a few days relaxing by Lake Kivu, only a short hop from Musanze, before heading back to Kigali. To round out your Rwanda experience, check out the country's southwestern corner, including chimpanzee tracking at Nyungwe Forest National Park and a day taking in the National Museum of Rwanda in the university town of Huye (Butare).

TRANSPORT IN RWANDA

» Rwanda has a reasonable road system, due mostly to its small size and a large dose of foreign assistance.

» The only major unsealed roads are those running along the shore of Lake Kivu and some smaller stretches around the country.

» The privately run buses and minibuses are more organised than elsewhere in East Africa, with scheduled (and usually hourly) departures.

» Bus tickets are available at bus offices prior to travelling and every passenger is guaranteed a seat.

» Most towns are small enough to negotiate by foot, but as Kigali sprawls over several hills you'll need to catch a minibus or taxi to get around the capital.

» Taxis are plentiful in Kigali although *moto-taxis* (motorcycle taxis) are a cheaper, if slightly hair-raising, alternative.

Cultural Tips

» These days it is considered inappropriate to ask if someone is Hutu or Tutsi. Most people identify themselves as Rwandan, keen to put the tribal divisions of the past behind them.

» From 8am to 11am on the last Saturday of every month, the whole country stops whatever it is doing and works for the public good, cleaning streets, repairing roads and building schools. Known as Umuganda Day, you'll find it difficult to get around at this time although some tour operators may have dispensation to travel during these hours.

KIGALI

POP 965,500

Spanning several ridges and valleys, the Rwandan capital of Kigali is an attractive city of lush hillsides, flowering trees, winding boulevards and bustling streets. Compared to the choking congestion of Kampala (Uganda) and the sinister edge of Nairobi (Kenya), Kigali is more akin to a tranquil mountain hamlet, perched on the edge of an intensively cultivated and terraced countryside.

Rwanda Highlights

1 Hike the forested slopes of the Virungas in search of silverback gorillas and golden monkeys in **Parc National des Volcans** (p519)

2 Trek through steamy rainforests in search of colobus monkeys and chimpanzees in the **Nyungwe Forest National Park** (p535)

3 Watch an Intore dance performance at the **National Museum of Rwanda** (p532), the finest museum in the country, in Huye (Butare)

4 Confront the horrors of the genocide at the haunting **Kigali Memorial Centre** (p506) on the outskirts of the capital

5 Kick back with a locally brewed Bralirwa on the sandy shores of Lake Kivu at **Gisenyi** (p525) or the equally beautiful **Kibuye** (p540) further south

6 Take a Rwandan-style safari in the up-and-coming **Parc National de l'Akagera** (p542)

AN UPHILL BATTLE

In Kigali it's a sorry child indeed who's given a bicycle as a gift. The city sprawls over several hills, and two points that appear relatively close on a map may be separated by a valley in reality. Our tip: unless you have the inclination of a goat and the thighs of a mountain gorilla, jump on the back of a *moto-taxi* (motorcycle taxi) and whiz to your destination in breezy comfort – just hang on tight during gear changes.

It wasn't always like this. Kigali exists as a testament to the peace and order that has defined Rwanda's trajectory for more than two decades, though it bore the brunt of the genocide in 1994. When the Rwandan Patriotic Front (RPF) finally captured Kigali after 100 days of systematic slaughter, dead and decaying bodies littered the streets. Dogs were shot en masse as they had developed a taste for human flesh.

In recent years, a massive amount of rehabilitation work has restored the city to its former graces, while increasing waves of foreign investment have sparked a number of ambitious building projects. Indeed, the rebirth of the capital has seen a surprising measure of cosmopolitanism take hold, and today Kigali is arguably one of the most pleasant cities in the whole of East Africa.

History

Kigali was founded in 1907 by German colonisers, but did not become the capital until Rwandan independence in 1962. Although Rwandan power was traditionally centred in Huye (Butare), Kigali was chosen because of its central location. Walking Kigali's streets today, it is hard to imagine the horrors that unfolded here during those 100 days of madness in 1994. Roadblocks, manned by Interahamwe militia, were set up at strategic points throughout the city and thousands upon thousands of Rwandans were bludgeoned or hacked to death. People swarmed to the churches in search of sanctuary, but the killers followed them there and showed a complete lack of mercy or compassion.

While all of this horror took place for days and nights on end, the UN Assistance Mission for Rwanda (UNAMIR) stood by and watched, held back by the bureaucrats and politicians who failed to grasp the magnitude of what was unfolding. In its defence, UNAMIR was bound by a restrictive mandate that prevented it from taking preliminary action, though it has been argued that the tragedy is that more deliberate action could have saved untold lives.

After 10 Belgian peacekeepers were murdered at the start of the genocide, the Belgian government withdrew its contingent, leaving UNAMIR to fend for itself with a minimal mandate and no muscle. There was little the 250 troops that remained could do but watch, and rescue or protect the few that they could.

Even more unbelievable is the fact that a contingent of the RPF was holed up in the parliamentary compound throughout this period, a legacy of the Arusha 'peace' process. Like the UNAMIR troops, there was little they could do to stop such widespread killing, though they did mount some spectacular rescue missions from churches and civic buildings around the city.

Throughout the massacre, the Hotel des Mille Collines became a refuge for those fleeing the violence, and thousands of people were holed up there, living in the direst of conditions. The Academy Award–winning film *Hotel Rwanda* tells the story of manager Paul Rusesabagina, who risked his life and the life of his family to selflessly help so many others.

When the RPF finally swept the genocidaires from power in early July 1994, Kigali was wrecked, much of the city's buildings were destroyed, and what little of the population remained alive were traumatised. As the Kigali Memorial Centre so aptly puts it, Rwanda was dead.

Remarkably, there are few visible signs of this carnage today. Kigali is now a dynamic and forward-looking city, the local economy is booming, investment is a buzzword, and buildings are springing up like mushrooms.

Sights

FREE **Kigali Memorial Centre** MEMORIAL

(www.kigalimemorialcentre.org, www.genocidearchiverwanda.org.rw; 8am-4pm, closed public holidays) In the span of 100 days, an estimated one million Tutsis and moderate Hutus were systematically butchered by the Interahamwe in one of the most savage genocides in history. This memorial honours the 250,000 people buried here in mass graves and tries to explain how it was that the world watched as the genocide unfolded in this tiny, landlocked country.

The informative audio tour (US$15) includes background on the divisive colonial experience in Rwanda and as the visit progresses, the exhibits become steadily more powerful, as you are confronted with the crimes that took place here and moving video testimony from survivors. If you have remained impassionate until this point, you'll find that it will all catch up with you at the section that remembers the children who fell victim to the killers' machetes. Life-size photos are accompanied by intimate details about their favourite toys, their last words and the manner in which they were killed.

The memorial concludes with sections on the refugee crisis in the aftermath of the genocide and the search for justice through the international tribunal in Arusha as well as the local *gacaca* courts (traditional tribunals headed by village elders). For more on the search for justice, see p548.

Upstairs is a moving section dedicated to informing visitors about other genocides that have taken place around the world and helps set Rwanda's nightmare in a historical context. The Kigali Memorial Centre is located in the northern Kisozi district of the capital, which is a short taxi ride from the centre (RFr4000). You can also come here as part of an RDB City Tour (p508).

FREE Camp Kigali Memorial MEMORIAL

(Rue de l'Hopital; ⏲7am-noon) The 10 stone columns you find here mark the spot where 10 Belgian UN peacekeepers were murdered on the first day of the genocide. Originally deployed to protect the home of moderate prime minister Agatha Uwilingimana, the soldiers were captured, disarmed and brought here by the Presidential Guard before being killed. Each stone column represents one of the soldiers and the horizontal cuts in it represent the soldier's age.

Museum of Natural History MUSEUM

(www.museum.gov.rw; off Ave de la Justice; adult/child incl guide RFr6000/3000; ⏲8am-5pm) This small museum houses a few simple exhibits (predominately captioned in German) on Rwanda's geology, fauna and flora. More interesting is the fact that this was the 1907 residence of explorer Richard Kandt and reputably the first building in Kigali. The view from the garden is sensational and looking over the urban sprawl, it's hard to imagine that it all started with this rather modest home.

State House Museum MUSEUM

(www.museum.gov.rw; Kanombe; adult/child incl guide RFr6000/3000; ⏲8am-5pm) This former presidential palace on the eastern outskirts of the city is slowly being restored and while it has few exhibits it's interesting to explore, with 'secret' rooms and an odd presidential nightclub. Wreckage from Juvenal Habyarimana's presidential plane can still be seen where it was shot down – just over his garden wall. The perpetrators were never caught but this act proved to be a rallying call for Hutu extremists and helped trigger the genocide. To get here, catch a Kanombe-bound minibus to the military hospital from where it's a short walk.

Hotel des Mille Collines HISTORIC BUILDING

(☎252-576530; www.millecollines.net; Ave de la République) The inspiration for the film *Hotel Rwanda,* this luxury hotel in the centre of Kigali was owned by the Belgian airline Sabena in 1994. At the time of the genocide, the hotel's European managers were evacuated, and control of the Mille Collines was given to Paul Rusesabagina, manager of the smaller Hotel des Diplomates.

As the situation in Kigali reached its boiling point, Paul opened the floodgates and allowed fleeing Tutsis and moderate Hutus to take refuge in the hotel, bribing the Interahamwe with money and alcohol in exchange for food and water. His heroic story is one of self-sacrifice in the most dire of situations.

Paul, his family and a few lucky survivors were eventually evacuated in a UN convoy as the Interahamwe seized the hotel. Today, Paul lives in Brussels and owns a small trucking company; he is an outspoken humanitarian and public hero.

FREE Nyanza Genocide Memorial MEMORIAL

(Kicukiro; ⏲8am-5pm Mon-Fri) Located in Kicukiro, a suburb southeast of the city centre towards the airport, there is little to see at this memorial other than the tiled tops of four mass graves believed to contain the remains of the 5000 Tutsis who took refuge in the Ecole Technique Officielle (ETO) grounds. Following the assassination of 10 Belgian soldiers at Camp Kigali and the subsequent withdrawal of Belgian troops, the Tutsis here were left unprotected and ultimately taken to Nyanza and massacred. If arriving by *moto-taxi* (RFr1000 from town), tell the driver you're heading to '*urwibutso rwa Nyanza ya Kicukiro*'.

Kigali

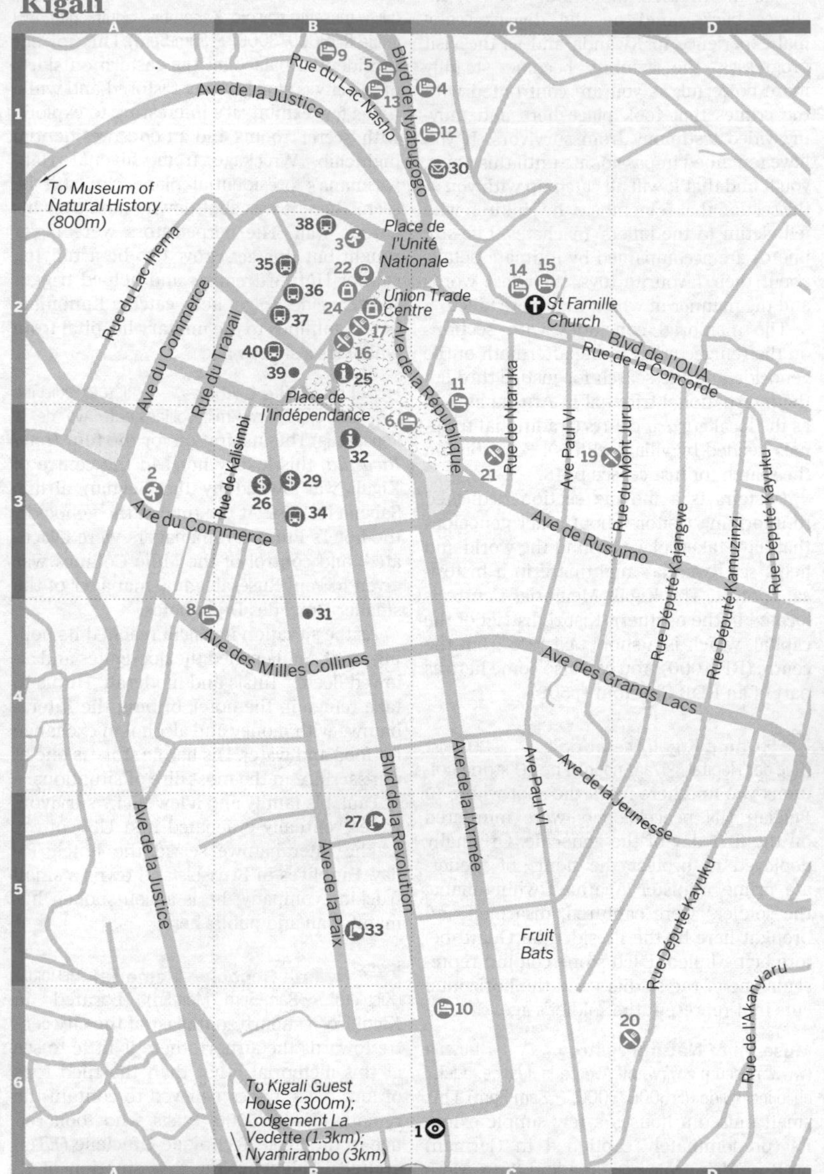

☞ Tours

RDB City Tour HISTORY

(Rwanda Development Board; ☎252-502350; www.rwandatourism.com; www.rdb.rw; tour US$20; ⊙departs at 8am or 2pm daily) This three-hour tour includes the Kigali Memorial Centre, as well as a few other prominent buildings around town. It's not amazing value given the memorial currently has no entry charge, but the guides are very knowledgeable and can give a local's perspective on the capital. Departs with a minimum of two people.

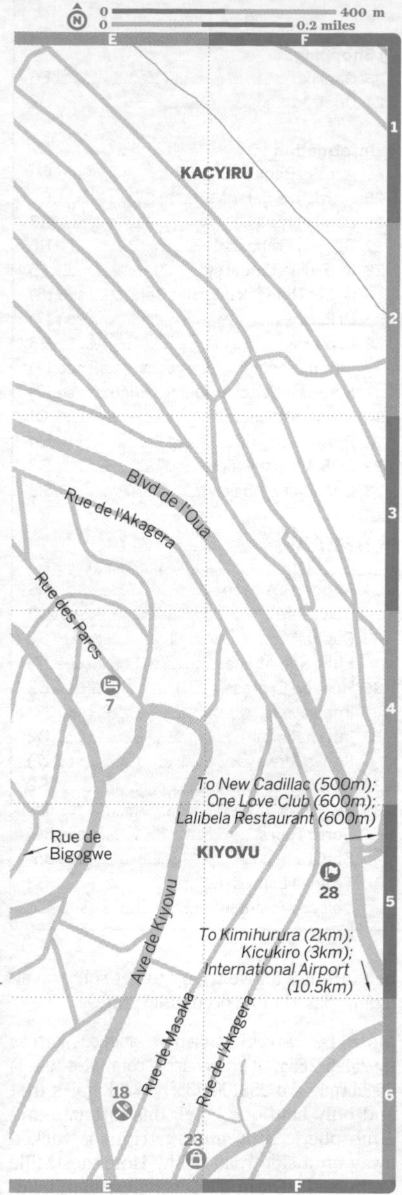

Sleeping

In the years since the genocide, Kigali has played host to legions of international aid workers, diplomats, bureaucrats, travellers and investors, all of whom have played their own small part in driving up the city's hotel prices.

The best budget options are found in Nyamirambo (a RFr500/150 *moto-taxi*/minibus ride from the city centre). As the price gap between budget and the lower end of the midrange options is not great, this is one time where it may be worth splashing out for a smarter room.

There's only a few genuine international four- or five-star hotels in Kigali (and indeed the whole country for that matter) but construction was well underway on the New Century Hotel when we passed through.

CITY CENTRE

TOP CHOICE **Hôtel Isimbi** HOTEL $
(252-75109; hotelisimbi@hotmail.com; Rue de Kalisimbi; s/d excl breakfast US$30/35) The most central of all the budget hotels, Isimbi is a good option for those who don't fancy walking up and down Kigali's endless hills. While the functional rooms here are somewhat lacking in atmosphere, they constitute a real bargain by Kigali standards and you may need to book ahead. If given a choice, opt for any room other than those that face the noisy street.

Dream Inn Hotel HOTEL $$
(252-503988; dreaminn7@yahoo.fr; Blvd de Nyabugogo; d US$40-60; P) Fair prices, spacious rooms and a handy central location means that this hotel is often full. The double beds are huge – large enough for a whole family of mountain gorillas.

Procure d'Accueil Religieux HOSTEL $
(072-8527974; off Blvd de l'OUA; tw excl breakfast with shared bathroom RFr8000, s with bathroom RFr10,000) This small lodging can be found tucked behind the St Famille Church next to the Gemera petrol station, in the heart of town. The problem is it's nearly always full with volunteers who book out these spotlessly clean rooms for months at a time. You can also try around the corner at **St Paul's Church** (252-576371; cnpsaintpaul@yahoo.fr), which has similar rooms for identical prices, but again, there is often 'no room at the inn'.

Kigali Serena Hotel LUXURY HOTEL $$$
(078-884500; www.serenahotels.com; Blvd de la Revolution; s/d from US$347/400, d ste from US$550; P) The capital's first and currently only five-star hotel, the Kigali Serena is certainly the smartest address in town. Formerly the Diplomates, and later the

Kigali

Sights

1	Camp Kigali Memorial	C6
	Hôtel des Milles Collines	(see 6)
	Volcanoes Safari	(see 6)

Activities, Courses & Tours

2	Bizidanny Tours & Safaris	A3
3	Kigali Safaris	B2

Sleeping

4	Auberge La Caverne	C1
5	Dream Inn Hotel	B1
6	Hôtel des Milles Collines	B3
7	Hotel Gorillas	E4
8	Hôtel Isimbi	A4
9	Impala Hotel	B1
10	Kigali Serena Hotel	C6
11	Motel Le Garni du Centre	C2
12	Muhima Motel	C1
13	Okapi Hotel	B1
14	Procure d'Accueil Religieux	C2
15	St Paul's Church	C2

Eating

16	Blues Café	B2
17	Bourbon Coffee Shop	B2
18	Chez John	E6
19	Heaven Restaurant & Bar	C3
	Le Panorama	(see 6)
	Nakumatt	(see 17)
20	New Cactus	D6
21	Shokola	C3

Drinking

	Hôtel des Milles Collines	(see 6)
22	Juicilicious	B2

Shopping

23	Caplaki	E6
24	Cootrac	B2

Information

	Access Bank	(see 17)
25	Attractive Safaris	B2
26	Bank of Kigali	B3
27	Belgian Embassy	B5
28	Canadian Embassy	F5
	Cyber Net Link Internet Café	(see 16)
	DHL	(see 17)
29	Ecobank	B3
	International Travel Agency	(see 17)
	Kampala Coach Booking Office	(see 17)
30	Main Post Office	C1
31	Primate Safaris	B4
32	RDB Tourist Office	B3
33	Ugandan Embassy	B5

Transport

	Air Uganda	(see 17)
34	Airport Bus Stop	B3
	Belvèdéré	(see 22)
35	Capital	B2
	Ethiopian Airlines	(see 17)
36	Horizon Express	B2
	Impala	(see 37)
37	International	B2
	Kenya Airways	(see 17)
38	New Yahoo Express	B2
39	RwandAir	B2
	Sorta Tours	(see 35)
	Stella	(see 35)
40	Virunga Express	B2
	Volcano Express	(see 40)

Intercontinental, the Kigali Serena was born after the Aga Khan Foundation pumped some serious style (and money) into this property in a bid to reel in Kigali's high-flying diplomats and business people. The result is the swishest spot in all of Rwanda, although you're going to need to peel some serious bills out of your bankroll if you want to bed-down with the country's movers and shakers.

Auberge La Caverne HOTEL $
(☎078-5833285; aubecav@yahoo.fr; Blvd de Nyabugogo; s US$20-30, d US$30-40) This little hotel has just 15 basic but clean rooms of varying sizes and shapes arranged around a nondescript courtyard. The boys who work here are not above trying to get solo travellers to pay 'double occupancy' rates.

Motel Le Garni du Centre BOUTIQUE HOTEL $$
(☎252-572654; garni@rwanda1.com; Ave de la République; s/d US$100/135;) Kigali's first and only boutique hotel, this intimate and atmospheric little *auberge* (inn) is tucked away on a side road below Hotel des Mille Collines. Le Garni du Centre boasts individually decorated rooms that are built around an inviting swimming pool. The tariffs get cheaper with every night you stay.

Okapi Hotel HOTEL $$
(☎078-8359877; hotelokapi@hotmail.com; Rue du Lac Nasho; s US$30-60, d US$40-80; P) A well-established midrange option that at-

tracts a loyal following, the Okapi benefits from a decent location that's within easy walking distance of the city centre. The rooms come in four levels of comfort. The bottom category has tiny, cell-like rooms with shared bathrooms and at US$40 a double is a complete rip-off. The middle two categories are another thing entirely, with satellite TV, comfy beds and balconies with wide views.

Hotel Gorillas HOTEL **$$$**
(☎252-501717; www.hotelgorillas.com; Rue des Parcs; standard s/d/tw excl breakfast US$110/130/140; P❄📶) A slick little hotel in the upmarket Kiyovu area of the city, this place is winning over a lot of customers thanks to its spacious rooms and friendly staff. The highlight of the property is Le Dos Argente (The Silverback Restaurant; mains RFr4200 to RFr7000), which is an open-air bistro serving an eclectic offering of Rwandan and continental classics.

Impala Hotel HOTEL **$$**
(☎078-3109636; emileha@yahoo.fr; Rue du Lac Nasho; s/d US$70/90; P📶) The most memorable thing about Impala (and its near neighbour – the Okapi Hotel) is the incredible views its ridge-top position allows, especially from the balconies. The rooms themselves are clean and smart and too small for the huge beds they contain. Like most in this price bracket, they were at their best about 10 years ago.

Muhima Motel HOTEL **$**
(☎078-5833285; Blvd de Nyabugogo; s/d/tw RFr10,000/15,000/18,000) Hard to spot (look for the small Heineken sign), this place is owned by, and just up from, the Auberge La Caverne. The rooms here are essentially the same as its sister's, but with more peeling paint and cracked tiles. Despite advertising hot showers, the boiler is seldom turned on long enough to produce anything other than tepid water. If you need to speak to a staff member and none are around, check at La Caverne where they spend most of their time.

Hotel des Mille Collines HISTORIC HOTEL **$$$**
(☎252-576539; www.millecollines.net; Ave de la République; s/d excl breakfast from US$233/255, d ste from US$435; P❄📶🏊) Welcome to the *Hotel Rwanda*. With the international success of the movie, the 'Hotel of a Thousand Hills' got a major renovation in 2009. While a South African hotel double was used for the movie, the real deal here in Kigali is a bit more of a cement and glass construction than the colonial compound that appeared in the film. The foyer and pool area are spacious and elegant and four-star quality all the way, but the lemon-yellow colour scheme used in the rooms still smacks of the '80s.

OUTER SUBURBS

One Love Club HOTEL **$$**
(☎072-2594118; onelove@rwanda1.com; Ave des Poids Lourds; camping RFr5000, s/d/tr excl breakfast RFr20,000/25,000/30,000; P📶) If it's the spirit of peace and harmony you're after, then this little retreat is the place for you. Since 1997, profits from this small guesthouse have been ploughed back into helping the disabled community in Rwanda. You can support this noble cause, which has so far supplied artificial limbs to more than 5000 Rwandans at no cost, by either pitching a tent in the shady campsite or bedding down in the simple but absolutely spotless rooms. Set in a tranquil, manicured garden on a valley floor, it's a short 1km *moto-taxi* ride up to town. On Fridays the restaurant has live reggae and *lumba* bands.

Kigali Guest House HOTEL **$**
(☎078-8499506; kigaliguesth@yahoo.com; Ave de la Nyabarongo, Biryogo; s/d/tw RFr7000/9000/10,000) A good bang-for-your-buck choice, the Kigali Guest House has large rooms that are thoroughly sanitised with en suite bathrooms featuring cold showers. The big drawback is it's quite a way from the action, tucked away behind the mosque on the road to Nyamirambo.

Lodgement La Vedette HOTEL **$**
(☎078-8429985; Ave de la Nyabarongo, Nyamirambo; r RFr6000-8000, with shared bathroom RFr5000-6000) On the same road as the Kigali Guest House, but another kilometre out from the centre, this small establishment has rooms with shared bathrooms in the main 'lodge' and better rooms with their own bathrooms in the house next door.

Eating

The dining scene in Kigali is increasingly sophisticated with each passing year, especially since the city's resident expats have been known to spend serious sums of cash in search of gourmet cuisine. Furthermore, the country's French roots shine through in its rich cuisine, which means (ubiquitous lunchtime buffets aside) you can generally expect a higher standard (and a pricier bill) here than in other East African capitals.

After much selfless sampling of fine food, we've narrowed our favourites down to the list following. *Bon appétit!*

TOP CHOICE Shokola MEDITERRANEAN, MEXICAN **$$**
(Rue de Ntaruka; mains RFr3500-7000; ⏲lunch & dinner; 📶) Step inside a walled garden to find an oasis of tranquillity that has become a firm favourite among expats in the relatively short time it's been open. Guests can sequester themselves beneath trees on comfy outdoor couches, in the book-lined drawing room or in one of the private Arabic-style tents in the garden. There is a hint of the Mediterranean about the menu, which ranges from delicately spiced Moroccan tagines to Turkish hummus. A Mexican-inspired buffet brunch (RFr7000) is served between 10am and 4pm every Sunday.

TOP CHOICE New Cactus ITALIAN **$$**
(Rue Député Kayuku; mains RFr4400-7000; ⏲lunch & dinner; 📶) Outrageously popular with the well-to-do, this Spanish-style hacienda is set on a ridge where you can soak up the sparkling lights of Kigali by night or get a bird's-eye appreciation of the city during the day. It boasts a broad menu of Italian favourites, including rich fondues and tasty pastas, but it's the wood-fired pizzas (RFr4400 to RFr5500) that are arguably the most popular meal here.

Blues Café AMERICAN **$**
(Ave de la Paix; light meals RFr2500-4500; ⏲breakfast, lunch & dinner) This American-style diner is great if you're in the heart of town and want something relatively familiar. Our cheeseburger had slabs of cheese on it so thick, forget clogging the arteries, it could have dammed the Nile. Salads, sandwiches, soups and spaghetti were also on the menu. The lunchtime buffet is excellent value at RFr2500.

Flamingo CHINESE **$$**
(Kimihurura; mains RFr5000-7000; ⏲lunch & dinner; 🖉) Something of a Kigali institution, the Flamingo (now located in the leafy Kimihurura sector of town) remains the best Chinese restaurant in the country and has all the accoutrements you'd expect in a successful Asian restaurant – the ubiquitous red-and-black colour scheme, the compulsory bamboo water feature, and juices served with swizzle sticks.

Bourbon Coffee Shop AMERICAN **$**
(Union Trade Centre, Ave de la Paix; mains RFr3500-5000; ⏲breakfast, lunch & dinner; 📶) While Rwanda produces some of the finest coffee beans in the world, the vast majority are marked for export, leaving behind only instant coffee. However, if you don't like your morning blend served in a packet, head to this popular spot where locals and expats alike queue up for the real stuff. You can follow your frothy cappuccino with a burger, light meal or continental pastry. The free wi-fi is switched off during the lunchtime rush hour.

Heaven Restaurant & Bar EUROPEAN **$$$**
(Rue du Mont Juru; mains RFr5000-9000; ⏲dinner) Another highlight of the burgeoning Kigali restaurant scene, Heaven has a relaxed, open-air deck bistro with a wide-ranging menu drawing from a variety of international influences. Saturday night is movie night (with popcorn/buffet RFr2500/7500), during which a relatively recent Hollywood movie is screened at 7.30pm.

Le Panorama EUROPEAN **$$$**
(☎252-576530; www.millecollines.net; Hotel des Mille Collines, Ave de la République; mains RFr7000-13,000; ⏲dinner) Proudly perched on the top floor of the Hotel des Mille Collines, Kigali's most famous restaurant attracts its fair share of international scenesters, who flock here for formal banquets with panoramic views. Although dining here can be a decidedly stuffy experience, the food is of very high quality and the views really do make it worth your while.

Chez John AFRICAN **$**
(Rue de Masaka; buffet RFr3000; ⏲lunch & dinner) A popular local haunt, Chez John serves up authentic, country-style Rwandan standards – namely meat and maize – in upmarket surrounds. The lunch buffet is extremely popular and offers a great opportunity to try a number of local dishes in one sitting. If you don't like them here, it's going to be a long trip around the rest of Rwanda.

Nakumatt SUPERMARKET **$**
(Union Trade Centre, Place de l'Unite Nationale; ⏲24hr) By far the best option for self-caterers, this huge supermarket in the Union Trade Centre has pretty much everything you'll need.

DON'T MISS

NYAMATA & NTARAMA GENOCIDE MEMORIALS

During the genocide, victims fled to churches seeking refuge, only to find that some of the clergy was providing information to the Interahamwe. As a result of this lack of compassion, some of the most horrific massacres took place inside the holy sanctums of churches throughout Rwanda.

Two of the most powerful genocide memorials are churches located on the outskirts of Kigali. **Nyamata**, about 30km south of Kigali, is a deeply disturbing memorial where skulls and bones of the many victims are on display. While the visual remains of the deceased are a visceral sight, their inclusion here is to provide firm evidence to would-be genocide deniers.

The nearby church at **Ntarama**, about 25km south of Kigali, is more understated but no less powerful. The church has not been touched since the bodies were removed more than a decade ago, and there are many bits of clothing scraps still on the floor.

Both of these memorials can be visited on a day trip from Kigali. Sotra Tours (p515) runs buses every half hour to Nyamata (RFr700, 45 minutes) from Kigali and the memorial is a 1km walk from the Nyamata bus station. Ntarama can easily be reached from Nyamata by *moto-taxi* (RFr1500). To return to Kigali, head back to the main road and catch a passing bus.

Drinking & Entertainment

The good folk of Kigali take their drinking and partying pretty seriously, and there are a number of good bars around town, some of which turn into clubs as the night wears on.

TOP CHOICE New Cadillac CLUB
(off Ave des Poids Lourds; admission from RFr2000; ⌚10pm-late Fri & Sat) This club is just holding off newcomers to remain the most popular place in town. Located in Kimikurure, this large, partly open-air venue plays a mixture of East African pop, Congolese *soukous* (dance music) and Western hits. It doesn't really pick up until after midnight, but once it does, it rocks well into the early morning.

Hotel des Mille Collines BAR
(Ave de la République) The swimming pool at the Hotel des Mille Collines serves as the city's most popular daytime bar at weekends, with expats coming here to relax by the water and partake of the Sunday brunch. The Thursday happy hour (6pm to 7.30pm) is also extraordinarily popular with everybody who is anybody (although those bodies who are nobodies are just as welcome).

Juicilicious JUICE BAR $
(Ave de la Paix; juice RFr1500-2000; ⌚breakfast & lunch; 📶) Perfect for those who like their fruit and vegies served with a straw, Juicilicious specialises in creative mixes like 'virgin sun' – a juice cocktail of orange, pineapple, lime and almond. Sheesha pipes (RFr3500) are also on hand to offset any healthy side effects the juice may have had.

Planet Club CLUB
(Kigali Business Centre, Ave du Lac Muhazi; admission RFr3500; ⌚6pm-late) This trendy nightclub is often called KBC by locals due to its location in the Kigali Business Centre, well out of the city centre. Drinks are pricey but from about 11pm onwards on a Friday and Saturday the place is jumping – literally.

Shopping

Rwanda produces some attractive handicrafts. Look for finely woven *nyiramabuno* (basketry), *iayansi* (flasks once used to store milk), batiks, drums and the striking symmetrical paintings called *imigongo*.

Sellers claim many items are 'antiques' and price their goods accordingly; the reality is most are modern replicas and you should bargain prices down to something more sensible.

Caplaki ARTS & CRAFTS
(Ave de Kiyovu; ⌚8am-6pm) This association of 38 stalls have banded together to market themselves collectively as Caplaki although each stall is an independent business. As you would expect, there is a great selection of Rwandan handicrafts on sale here but you'll also find lots of carvings and masks from across the border in the DRC, banana-fibre products from Uganda, and carvings and soapstone items from Kenya.

Cootrac ARTS & CRAFTS
(Ave de la Paix; ⌚8am-7pm) Modelled along the same lines as Caplaki, this smaller association of 22 stalls can be found in an old warehouse behind Belvèderé buses.

Information

Emergency

Police (☎112)

SAMU Ambulance Service (☎912)

Internet Access

Internet access is widespread and very cheap in Kigali. A large number of hotels and cafes offer free wi-fi, so if you're travelling with your laptop chances are you need not pay for a connection while in Kigali at all. Look out for the wi-fi symbol in reviews.

Cyber Net Link Internet Café (Ave de la Paix; per hr RFr600) Also has printing and scanning services. Next to Blues Café.

Iposita Cybercafé (off Blvd de Nyabugogo; per hr RFr400) Part of the post office complex.

Maps

Eye Magazine (www.theeye.co.rw) A free monthly magazine with several maps and a directory of businesses within the service industry.

Medical Services

Some embassies also have medical attachés who offer services through private practices. Serious surgical cases are usually medically evacuated to Nairobi (Kenya) or Pretoria (South Africa).

Adventist Dental Clinic (☎078-8675136) Near the Umubano Hotel about 3.5km from the centre of town in Kacyiru district, this place is run by an international dentist based in Kigali.

Netcare King Faycal Hospital (☎078-8309002) Also near the Umubano Hotel, this South African–operated hospital is the best in Kigali. Prices are high but so are standards.

Money

Euros and US dollars can be changed at any of the numerous banks in town or at any of the foreign exchange bureaus near the Bank of Kigali. Most exchange bureaus give better rates than the banks although the one at the airport is an exception.

Access Bank (2fl, Union Trade Centre, Ave de la Paix) Over-the-counter cash advances on MasterCard.

Bank of Kigali (Ave du Commerce) Has an ATM (Visa only), over-the-counter cash advances on MasterCard, and Western Union services.

Ecobank (Ave de la Paix) Besides the ATM (Visa only) here, there's also an unreliable machine at the airport.

Post

DHL (Union Trade Centre, Ave de la Paix) A 2kg parcel to US/UK/Australia costs RFr73,200/61,800/106,200. Ouch!

Main post office (www.i-posita.rw; off Blvd de Nyabugogo; ⌚7am-5pm Mon-Fri, 7am-1pm Sat)

Tourist Information

RDB (Rwanda Development Board; ☎252-502350, 252-573396; www.rwandatourism.com, www.rdb.rw; 1 Blvd de la Revolution; ⌚7am-5pm Mon-Fri, 7am-noon Sat & Sun) Formerly known as ORTPN (pronounced 'or-ti-pen'), the national tourism office has friendly staff who help promote tourism to the increasing streams of foreign visitors. Independent travellers can make reservations to track the mountain gorillas in Parc National des Volcans, we recommend you book several months in advance as permits are extremely difficult to attain in high season. There are rumours that this office will move as the great 'Kigali make-over' continues.

Travel Agencies

International Travel Agency (ITA; ☎252-572113; Union Trade Centre, Ave de la Paix) Reliable place to purchase airline tickets.

Getting There & Away

Air

For contact details of the international airlines flying in and out of Gregoire Kayibanda International Airport, see p554.

RwandAir (☎252-503687; www.rwandair.com; Union Trade Centre, Ave de la Paix) Has domestic flights to Gisenyi (US$177 return) and Kamembe (US$177 return).

Bus

Several bus companies operate services to major towns, which are less crowded and safer than local minibuses. Most companies have offices in town as well as at the Nyabugogo bus terminal, about 2km north of the city centre in the valley and easily reached by minibuses heading down Blvd de Nyabugogo. Buses usually depart from the office you bought your ticket at. See p554 for international coaches to neighbouring countries.

Belvèderé (Nyabugogo bus terminal & Ave de la Paix) Runs buses from 7.30am hourly to Gisenyi (RFr3100, three hours) via Musanze (Ruhengeri; RFr1800, 1½ hours).

Capital (Nyabugogo bus terminal & off Ave du Commerce) Hourly departures for Kibuye (Rfr2700, 2½ hours) via Gitarama (RFr900, one hour).

Horizon Express (Nyabugogo bus terminal & off Ave du Commerce) To Nyanza (RFr1800, 1¾ hours) and Huye (Butare; RFr2600, 2½ hours).

Impala (off Ave du Commerce) Runs buses west to Kibuye (RFr2700, 2½ hours) and Cyangugu (RFr5300, six hours).

International (Nyabugogo bus terminal & off Ave du Commerce) Heads east including Kayonza (RFr1500, 1½ hours) and Rusumo (RFr3000, three hours).

Kigali Safaris (Nyabugogo bus terminal & Ave du Commerce) To Musanze (Ruhengeri; RFr1800, two hours).

Omega (Nyabugogo bus terminal) To Cyangugu (RFr5300, six hours).

Onatracom Express (Nyabugogo bus terminal) Has large, old and uncomfortable 45-seat buses running to Musanze (Ruhengeri; two hours) and Gisenyi (three hours), plus Huye (Butare; 2½ hours) and Cyangugu (six hours).

Sotra Tours (Nyabugogo bus terminal & off Ave du Commerce) To Nymata (RFr700, 45 minutes), Rusumo (RFr3000, three hours) and Huye (Butare; RFr2500, 2½ hours).

Stella (off Ave du Commerce) To Kayonza (RFr1500, 1½ hours) and Rusumo (RFr3000, three hours).

Virunga Express (Nyabugogo bus terminal & off Ave du Commerce) To Musanze (Ruhengeri; RFr1800, two hours) and Gisenyi (RFr3100, three hours).

Volcano Express (off Ave du Commerce) Reliable operator for Huye (Butare; RFr2600, 2½ hours) and Nyanza (RFr1800, 1¾ hours).

Minibus

Local minibuses depart from the Nyabugogo bus terminal for towns all around Rwanda, including Huye (Butare; RFr2400, two hours), Katuna (RFr1600, 1½ hours), Kibuye (RFr2000, two hours), Musanze (Ruhengeri; RFr2500, two hours) and Gisenyi (RFr3000, four hours). These minibuses leave when full throughout the day, except at weekends when they tend to dry up after 3pm. Accepted practice for foreigners is to turn up, wander around for bit, eventually tell someone where you're going and then be directed to the appropriate minibus.

Getting Around

To/From the Airport

Gregoire Kayibanda International Airport is at Kanombe, 10km east of the city centre. A taxi/*moto-taxi* costs RFr10,000/1500, but a KBS, International or Sotra Tours bus is cheaper (RFr250) and can be caught from outside the airport gates. In town you can catch one opposite the Bank of Kigali.

Minibus

Minibuses cruise the streets looking for passengers. All advertise their destination in the front window and run to districts throughout the city. Costs are very cheap, from RFr100 to RFr300.

Moto-Taxi

These small Japanese trail bikes can be a swift way to get around Kigali, although it can be quite scary as the drivers really hit the throttle. Short hops are just RFr300 to RFr500, while trips out to the suburbs cost RFr700 to RFr1000.

Taxi

Taxis are not metered but a fare within the city centre costs, on average, RFr3000 to RFr4000, double that out to the suburbs or later at night.

NORTHWESTERN RWANDA

A formidable natural border between Rwanda, Uganda and the DRC, the Virunga volcanoes are where Rwanda really earns its nickname as the Land of a Thousand Hills. Home to their share of the last mountain gorillas on the planet, the Rwandan Virungas are protected by Parc National des Volcans, the undisputed highlight of the country. The region is also home to the tranquil town of Gisenyi on the sandy shores of Lake Kivu, Rwanda's top spot for a 'beach' holiday.

Musanze (Ruhengeri)

POP 115,000

For most travellers, Musanze (Ruhengeri) is the preferred staging post on their way to the magnificent Parc National des Volcans, one of the best places in East Africa to track the rare mountain gorilla. Since permit holders are required to check in at the park headquarters in nearby Kinigi at 7am on the day of tracking, staying in Musanze is a much safer option than leaving from Kigali at the crack of dawn.

Musanze is a pleasant enough town to explore on foot, and it's situated near a number of interesting natural sights, with the mighty Virunga volcanoes looming to the north and west.

Sights & Activities

Muko VILLAGE

Muko village is 5km southwest of Musanze and home to the **Ndufatanye Momahoro Association**, a collective of seven women

Musanze (Ruhengeri)

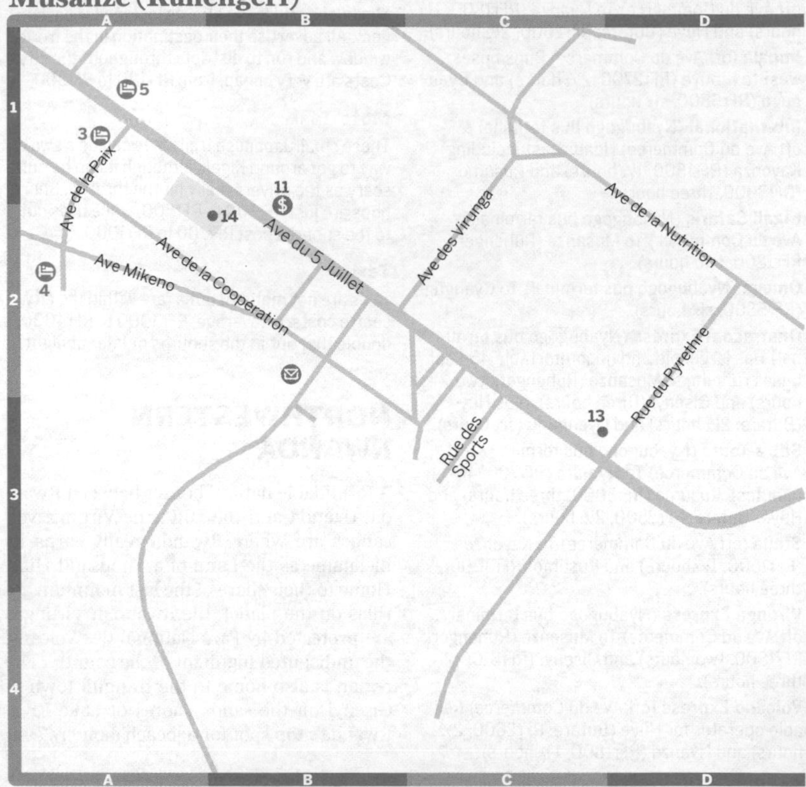

who show travellers how baskets are woven and banana beer fermented (RFr15,000 for a group of two). There is no charge for the basket-weaving demonstration but it is expected that you buy a basket (RFr3000 to RFr6000) in lieu of a fee. None of the women are proficient in English so it's worth bringing a guide (RFr5000 from Amahoro Tours) to show you the way and translate for you.

Musanze Cave CAVE

There are plans to open this huge cave complex to tourists but despite years of rumours and several internationally funded speleological projects, there has been little progress in this endeavour. The caves are just 2km from the town centre and were created when different lava flows joined to create the Albertine Rift Valley. Bat roosts are a significant feature of Musanze Cave, as are huge roof collapses that create vast arrays of coloured light shafts. Keen spelunkers may want to inquire at the RDB office to see if the cave is at last, open for tourism.

Lakes Ruhondo & Burera LAKES

The outskirts of Musanze are home to two large lakes, which are dotted with small villages and accessed via a network of undeveloped dirt roads. The scenery here is breathtaking as the shores of the lakes are heavily terraced and cultivated with crops, and the Virunga volcanoes loom ominously in the distance. While Ruhondo and Burera are not officially set up for tourism, you can easily have a do-it-yourself adventure here, especially if you have your own transport and are able to arrange a lake trip with a local fisherman.

Tours

Most tour operators who visit Muzanse and Parc National des Volcans are based in Kigali. See p556 for details.

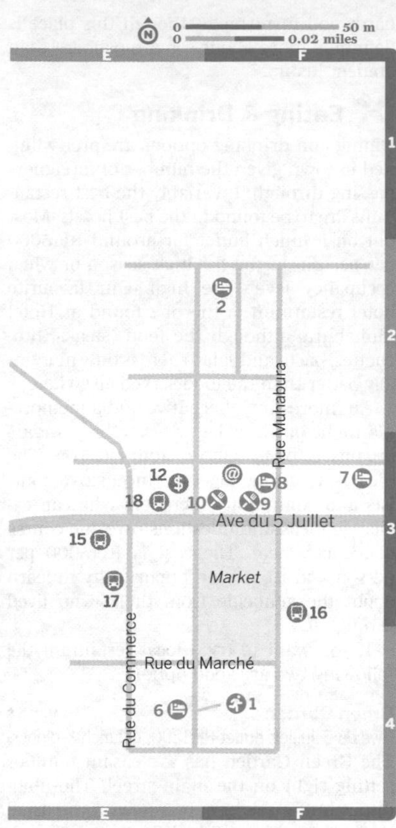

Musanze (Ruhengeri)

Activities, Courses & Tours

1 Amahoro Tours F4

Sleeping

2 Amahoro Guesthouse F2
3 Gorillas Volcanoes Hotel A1
4 Home Inn A2
5 Hôtel Muhabura A1
6 Hôtel Urumuri E4
7 St Anne Hotel F3
8 Tourist Rest House F3

Eating

9 Green Garden F3
10 Silverback F3

Information

11 Bank of Kigali B1
12 Ecobank E3
13 Hillywood Travel C3
14 RDB Office B2

Transport

15 Belvèdéré E3
16 Horizon F3
17 Jaguar Coaches E3
18 Virunga Express E3

Amahoro Tours TOURS
(☎078-8687448; www.amahoro-tours.com) A small, locally run operator that can help arrange gorilla tracking permits, cultural activities and homestays in the surrounding area at reasonable prices. The office is unsigned and down a small dirt alleyway next to the brick 'COODAT' building, near the central market.

Sleeping

As the main jumping-off point for Parc National des Volcans, there are quite a number of accommodation options in Musanze.

TOWN CENTRE

TOP CHOICE **Amahoro Guesthouse** GUESTHOUSE $
(☎078-5402928; www.amahoro-guesthouse.com; per person with shared bathroom RFr12,000, d RFr18,000; P) A little difficult to find as it doesn't have a sign, Amahoro Guesthouse is tucked behind a green gate in a house with a green roof. Although the rooms here have two or three beds in each, they are not dorms and each group is given their own room. Each share a series of common bathrooms. This may sound like a drawback, but the bathrooms are spacious, clean and modern, making the rooms a better bet than others with their own facilities.

Hotel Muhabura HOTEL $
(☎078-8364774; muhabura12@yahoo.fr; Ave du 5 Juillet; s/d/apt excl breakfast RFr20,000/25,000/25,000; P@) Long-time favourite Muhabura was once the town's leading hotel and although it has been superseded by a whole slew of midrange options it straddles the niche between midrange and budget options nicely. The doubles and 'apartments' are particularly good value as they cost only a fraction more than the singles. Even if you're not staying here, stop by for dinner as the hotel arguably has the best restaurant in town.

Home Inn HOTEL $
(☎078-8343127; www.homeinnhotel.com; Ave de la Paix; d/tw US$70/90; P) Painted an alarming shade of apricot, the Home Inn only

opened in 2011, with 12 fresh and bright rooms. The tiled bathrooms are spotless and each room has its own balcony that catches a refreshing breeze.

Gorillas Volcanoes Hotel HOTEL $$$
(☎252-546700; www.hotelgorillas.com; Ave de la Paix; s/d/ste US$90/110/180; P 📶 ❄) Part of the Gorilla group and one of the smartest hotels in Musanze town, this establishment caters mostly to package tours here to see the apes. Facilities include a restaurant cum bar and a massage/sauna room.

Ste Anne Hotel HOTEL $
(☎078-8777455; www.sainteannehotel.com; off Ave du 5 Juillet; s/d/tw RFr25,000/30,000/35,000) These rooms may be a step down in quality from other midrange options but they're a good choice if you want to save some money without scraping the bottom of the barrel. You still get satellite TV and a clean bathroom, it's all just a little tired. Prices are negotiable if you don't take the breakfast.

Hôtel Urumuri HOTEL $
(☎078-4423980; r excl breakfast RFr1000) Tucked away on a side street off Rue du Marché, this is a friendly enough spot assuming you're not too fussy about the lack of hot water and the somewhat dilapidated rooms. There is an annexe across the street that's a better option than the main hotel itself because it's considerably quieter.

Tourist Rest House HOTEL $
(☎252-546635; Rue Muhabura; s/d/tw excl breakfast RFr8000/10,000/20,000) The good news is that the Tourist Rest House doesn't charge much. The bad news is that they believe guests should get what they pay for. The rooms here are small, a little grimy and the concrete walls have that aged patina that suggests dampness. The bathrooms do have hot water but the light bulbs were so dim they appeared to be powered by little more than wishful thinking.

LAKES RUHONDO & BURERA

Virunga Lodge LUXURY HOTEL $$$
(☎252-502452; www.volcanoessafaris.com; s/d full board US$720/1200) One of the most stunningly situated camps in the region, the Virunga Lodge is nestled on a ridge above Lake Burera, offers incredible views across to the Virunga volcanoes, and is widely regarded as the finest lodge in all of Rwanda. Accommodation is in individual stone chalets that are decorated with local crafts and hardwood furnishings, though this place is definitely more about eco-atmosphere than opulent luxury.

Eating & Drinking

Dining and drinking options are pretty limited in town given the number of foreigners passing through. Invariably the best restaurants are to be found in the best hotels. Most put on a lunch buffet for around RFr5000 per person during the high season or when occupancy levels are high. Our favourite hotel restaurant is the one found at Hotel Muhabura, although the food (steaks, brochettes, pasta and salad) here is only marginally better than the food served elsewhere.

An interesting alternative and a memorable night out are the **'storytelling' meals** organised by Amahoro Tours (p517). The idea is to bring together inquisitive tourists and community members who can exchange ideas and questions over the course of a local meal. The cost is RFr5000 per person and it's a good opportunity to learn about the genocide from those who lived through it.

If you want to try a local restaurant the following two are good options.

Green Garden RWANDAN $
(Ave du 5 Juillet; buffet RFr1200; ⏰lunch & dinner) The Green Garden has a pleasant outdoor setting right on the main street. The ubiquitous buffet reigns supreme with the usual line-up of beef stew, chicken stew, rice, ugali (a staple made from maize or cassava flour, or both), *matoke* (cooked plantains), *isombe* (cassava leaves), chips and pasta.

Silverback RWANDAN $
(Ave du 5 Juillet; buffet RFr1200; ⏰lunch & dinner) Offering much the same meat and vegetable buffet as the Green Garden, the Silverback was the other eatery enjoying local popularity at the time of research.

Information

Bank of Kigali (Ave du 5 Juillet) Has an ATM (Visa) and can exchange US dollars and euros.

Cafe Internet (off Ave du 5 Juillet; per hr RFr300) Internet access; can also burn a CD of all your gorilla pics (RFr1000).

Ecobank (off Ave du 5 Juillet) Has an ATM (Visa) and can exchange US dollars and euros.

Hillywood Travel (☎078-4424480; Ishema Hotel, Ave du 5 Juillet) Travel agency good for airline ticketing and little else.

Post office (⌚8am-noon & 2-4pm Mon-Fri) Basic telephone and postal services.

RDB (Rwanda Development Board; ☎078-8519727; www.rwandatourism.com, www.rdb.rw; Ave du 5 Juillet; ⌚7am-5pm) Located in the prefecture headquarters, this RDB office is a small administrative branch. If you already have a gorilla permit, there's no reason to stop by here. If you don't have a gorilla permit, the warden on duty can phone the Kigali office, where gorilla tracking is coordinated, and enquire about any last-minute cancellations. Good luck with that.

Getting There & Away

Numerous bus companies offer scheduled hourly services between Musanze and Kigali (RFr1800, two hours) and between Musanze and Gisenyi (RFr1200, 1½ hours). The two most reliable are **Belvèdéré** (Ave du 5 Juillet) and **Virunga Express** (Ave du 5 Juillet).

Minibuses also travel these routes for much the same price but they stop frequently to let passengers on and off, fill up with petrol and buy bananas.

Virunga Express (and an armada of minibuses) also travels to Cyanika (RFr500, 45 minutes), on the Rwanda–Uganda border. Both **Horizon** (Rue Muhabura) and **Jaguar Coaches** (Rue du Commerce) have overnight buses to Kampala (RFr8000, 12½ hours) at 4pm.

See p525 for information on travelling to Kinigi, the location of the park headquarters for Parc National des Volcans and the meeting point for gorilla tracking.

Getting Around

There are few taxis in Musanze, but plenty of boda-bodas (bicycle taxis) and *moto-taxis* for those needing a rest. A typical fare from the town centre to the Hotel Muhabura is around RFr300 on a *moto-taxi*.

Parc National des Volcans

Volcanoes National Park, which runs along the border with the DRC and Uganda, is home to the Rwandan section of the Virungas. Comprising five volcanoes – Karisimbi (the highest at 4507m), Bisoke (Visoke), Sabinyo, Gahinga (Mgahinga) and Muhabura (Muhavura) – the Virungas are one of the most beautiful sights in both Rwanda and the whole of Africa. As if this wasn't enough of a drawcard, the park is also home to the endangered eastern mountain gorilla, first studied in depth by primatologist George Schaller, and later thrust into the international spotlight during the life of Dian Fossey.

> **PARC NATIONAL DES VOLCANS**
>
> **Why Go** Five bamboo- and rainforest-covered volcanoes that are sanctuaries to exceedingly rare mountain gorillas and endangered golden monkeys.
>
> **When to Go** The long dry season from June to September is the ideal time to track mountain gorillas as it is, well… drier.
>
> **Practicalities** Reservations are sold out months in advance, so make your booking as early as possible. Access to the park is via Musanze (Ruhengeri), although all trekkers need to report to the park headquarters in Kinigi (12km north of Musanze) at 7am on the day of their trek. The park does not provide transport to the trailheads.

Prior to 1999, the entire national park was out of bounds to tourists due to heavy poaching, armed conflict and the genocide and its aftermath. Since then, however, the park has emerged as the definitive location to track the captivating mountain gorilla.

While most tourists to the park are understandably driven by the desire to have a face-to-face encounter with real gorillas in the mist, there is good reason to stay in the area once you've finished tracking: the gorillas share the park with a troop of rare golden monkeys, which are slowly being habituated to human contact. The Virungas, which tower over Rwanda, Uganda and the DRC, also present a variety of rewarding climbing and trekking options.

History

Belgian colonists, who intended to protect the mountain gorillas on Karisimbi, Bisoke and Mikeno in Rwanda and the Belgian Congo from poachers, first gazetted the Virungas as a national park in 1925. At the time, this small conservation triangle was the very first protected area to be created on the continent of Africa. Four years later, the borders were extended further to form Parc National Albert (Albert National Park), a massive area that encompassed more than 8000 sq km.

Following the independence of the Congo in 1960 and Rwanda in 1962, Albert

National Park was split into two entities, the Rwanda portion being assigned the name Parc National des Volcans. During the early years of Rwanda's fragile independence, it wasn't poaching or fighting that harmed the gorillas most, but rather a small daisy-like flower known as pyrethrum. Due to a large grant by the European Community (EC), the 1960s saw the conversion of half of Parc National des Volcans into commercial farms for pyrethrum, which can be processed into a natural insecticide.

By the early 1970s, poachers were making inroads on both sides of the Rwanda–Congo border as the demand for stuffed gorilla heads and hands (which were depressingly used as ashtrays) began to burgeon. Thankfully, the plight of the mountain gorilla became an international issue following the work of the late Dian Fossey (p521).

Gorilla tracking in Rwanda was first launched in 1979 by Amy Vedder and Bill Webber, who marketed the charismatic creatures to tourists on overland trips. By the late 1980s, the sale of gorilla permits was the country's third-largest revenue earner, which was enough to convince ordinary Rwandans that these great apes were indeed a valuable natural resource worth protecting.

In 1991, Rwanda was plunged into civil war, and Parc National des Volcans became a battlefield. By the time the perpetrators of the genocide swept across Rwanda in 1994, the park had long been heavily land-mined and then abandoned as refugees fled into the neighbouring DRC.

It wasn't until 1999 that Parc National des Volcans was once again reopened to tourism.

Sights & Activities

Gorilla Tracking

An encounter with these charismatic creatures is the highlight of a trip to Africa for many visitors. An encounter with a silverback male gorilla at close quarters can be a hair-raising experience, especially if you've only ever seen large wild animals behind the bars of a cage or from the safety of a car. Yet despite their intimidating size, gorillas are remarkably nonaggressive animals, entirely vegetarian, and usually quite safe to be around.

GORILLA FAMILIES

There are 10 habituated gorilla groups in Parc National des Volcans, including the **Susa group**, which has 32 members and a set of twins born in 2011. Although nearly everyone who shows up at the park headquarters is most likely gunning to track the Susa group, the rangers usually select the most able-bodied and all-round fit individuals. Even though it's the largest group in the park, it's also the hardest to reach – you need to trek for three to four hours up the slopes of Karisimbi at an altitude of more than 3000m.

The **Sabinyo group** (12 members) is a good choice for anyone who doesn't want a strenuous tracking experience as it can usually be found in less than 30 minutes. **Agashya** (27 members) and **Amahura** (18 members) are also popular with visitors, although no matter which group you end up tracking, you're most likely going to have a memorable experience.

THE TREK

Make no mistake about it – gorilla tracking is no joyride. The guides can generally find the gorillas within one to four hours of starting out, but this often involves a lot of strenuous effort scrambling through dense vegetation up steep, muddy hillsides, sometimes to altitudes of more than 3000m. At higher altitudes, you'll also have to contend with the thick overgrowth of stinging nettles, which can easily penetrate light clothing. As if fiery skin rashes weren't enough of a deterrent, it also rains a lot in this area, so the going can certainly get tough (and muddy) in parts. At this altitude the air can thin out quickly, so descend to lower altitudes if you develop an intense headache.

THE ENCOUNTER

Visits to the gorillas are restricted to one hour and flash photography is banned. While you are visiting the gorillas, do not eat, drink, smoke or go to the bathroom in their presence. If you have any potential airborne illness, do not go tracking as gorillas are extremely susceptible to human diseases.

In theory, visitors are requested to remain more than 5m from the gorillas at all times, though in practice the guides (and the gorillas) tend to flaunt this rule. Although no tourists have ever been harmed by the gorillas, you should give them the respect and wide berth you would any wild animal.

Upon sighting the gorillas, the guides will make their presence known through a series of loud calls and grunts. This is an impor-

THE LIFE OF DIAN FOSSEY

> When you realise the value of all life, you dwell less on what is past and concentrate more on the preservation of the future.
>
> *Dr Dian Fossey, zoologist (1932–85)*

Dian Fossey was an American zoologist who spent the better part of her life at a remote camp high up on the slopes of the Virungas studying the mountain gorillas. Without her tenacious efforts to have poaching stamped out, and the work of committed locals since her violent murder, there possibly wouldn't be any of the great apes remaining in Rwanda.

Although trained in occupational therapy, in 1963 Fossey took out a loan and travelled to Tanzania where she met Dr Louis and Mary Leakey. At the time, she learned about the pioneering work of Jane Goodall with chimpanzees and George Schaller's groundbreaking studies on gorillas.

By 1966 Fossey had secured the funding and support of the Leakey family, and began conducting field research of her own. However, political unrest caused her to abandon her efforts the following year at Kabara (in the Democratic Republic of the Congo), and establish the Karisoke Research Center, a remote camp on Bisoke in the more politically stable Rwandan Virungas.

Fossey was catapulted to international stardom when her photograph was snapped by Bob Campbell in 1970 and splashed across the cover of *National Geographic*. Seizing her newfound celebrity status, Fossey embarked on a massive publicity campaign aimed at saving the mountain gorillas from impending extinction.

Tragically, Fossey was brutally murdered on 26 December 1985. Her skull was split open by a *panga*, a type of machete used by local poachers to cut the heads and hands off gorillas. This bloody crime scene caused the media to speculate that poachers, who were angered by her conservationist stance, murdered her in a fit of rage.

While this may have been the case, a good measure of mystery still surrounds Fossey's murder and despite the 1986 conviction of a former student, many people believe the murderer's true identity was never credibly established and her former student was merely a convenient scapegoat.

Following her death, Fossey was buried in the Virungas next to her favourite gorilla, Digit, who had previously been killed by poachers. Throughout her life Dian Fossey was a proponent of 'active conservation', the belief that endangered species are best protected through rigorous anti-poaching measures and habitat protection. As a result, she strongly opposed the promotion of tourism in the Virunga range, though the Dian Fossey Gorilla Fund International has changed its position on the issue since her untimely death.

Today, Fossey is best known for her book *Gorillas in the Mist*, which is both a description of her scientific research and an insightful memoir detailing her time in Rwanda.

Parts of her life story were later adapted in the film *Gorillas in the Mist: The Story of Dian Fossey*, starring Sigourney Weaver. The movie was criticised for several fictitious scenes in which Fossey aggressively harasses local poachers, as well as its stylised portrayal of her affair with photographer Bob Campbell. It does, however, serve as a good introduction to the ongoing plight of the endangered eastern mountain gorilla.

tant part of the habituation process, and also helps to alert the gorillas to the presence and whereabouts of their visitors.

For a compare and contrast look at the competing mountain gorilla experiences in Rwanda, Uganda and the DRC, see p32.

RESERVATIONS

Fees are now a hefty US$750 per person for a gorilla visit, which includes park entry, compulsory guides and guards. Numbers of people allowed to visit each of the groups are limited to a maximum of eight people per day, limiting the total number of daily permits to an absolute maximum of 80. Children under 15 are not allowed to visit the gorillas.

Bookings for gorilla permits can be made through the RDB tourist office in Kigali (p514) or a Rwandan tour company (p556). Those visiting on a tour package will have

Parc National des Volcans

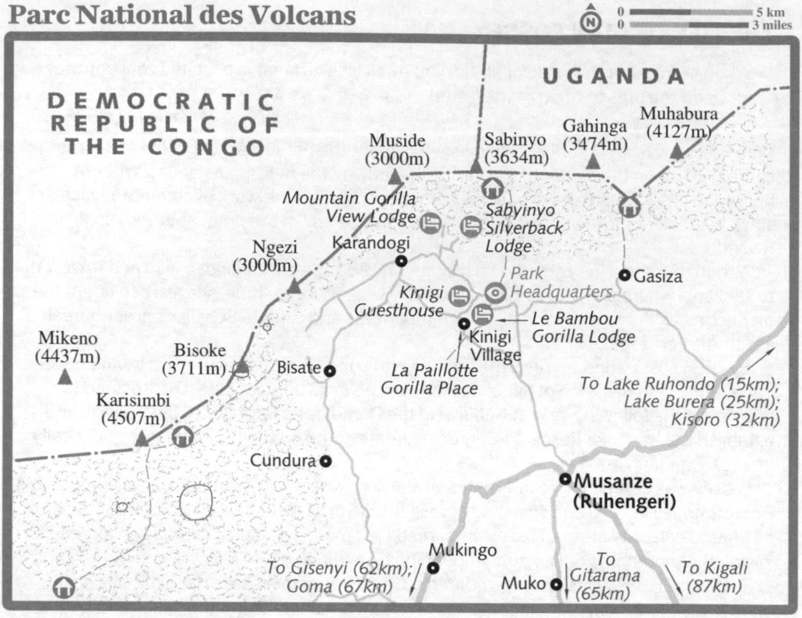

everything arranged for them, while independent travellers can secure permits if they make reservations early on. Frustratingly, it's not always easy to deal with the RDB by phone or email from overseas, so it's sometimes easier to book a permit through a Rwandan tour operator.

With demand exceeding supply you'll need to book well in advance if you want to be assured of a spot, especially during the peak seasons of December–January and July–August. Bookings are secured with a US$100 deposit (via bank transfer), and full payment must be made upon your arrival in Kigali.

Independent travellers who have only decided to visit the gorillas in Rwanda once in the East Africa region can turn up at the RDB office in Kigali and try to secure a booking at the earliest available date. During the high season waits of several days to more than a week are not uncommon. If you are desperate, cross the border to the Democratic Republic of the Congo (DRC), where permits are more readily available.

You'll need to present yourself at 7am on the day that your permit is valid at the park headquarters in Kinigi. It's worth emphasising that if you are late, your designated slot will be forfeited, and your money will not be refunded.

WHAT TO BRING

You need to be prepared for a potentially long, wet and cold trek through equatorial rainforest. A sturdy pair of hiking shoes is a must, as is plenty of warm and waterproof clothing. The stinging nettles at higher elevations can really put a damper on the experience, so consider wearing pants and long-sleeve shirts with a bit of thickness.

Despite the potential for high altitudes and cold temperatures, you also need to be prepared for the strong sun. Floppy hats, bandanas, sunglasses and lots of sunscreen are a good idea, as are plenty of cold water and hydrating fluids. Sugary snacks are also good for a quick energy boost.

When you check in at the park headquarters, you may be asked for identification by the park rangers. To avoid any potential hassles, carry your passport with you at all times in addition to your gorilla tracking permit.

Porters (US$10) are available for the trek, though they're not absolutely necessary. The guides, guards, drivers and any porters will expect a tip – the amount is entirely up to you, and ultimately depends on the quality of the service. However, keep in mind that

KWITA IZINA: THE GORILLA NAMING CEREMONY

In traditional Rwandan culture, the birth of a child is a momentous event that is celebrated with a tremendous amount of fanfare. The birth is marked by the presentation of the new infant to the general public, who then proceed to suggest round after round of possible names. After careful consideration, the proud parents select one for their newborn, and celebrate the naming with copious amounts of dining, drinking and dancing.

Gorillas in Rwanda are often awarded the same level of respect and admiration as humans, which is why it's only fitting they should be named in a similar manner. Since June 2005, the annual Kwita Izina (Gorilla Naming Ceremony) has been a countrywide event that is increasingly drawing a larger share of the spotlight. From local community events in Musanze (Ruhengeri) to gala balls in Kigali and Gisenyi, Kwita Izina is well on its way to becoming a global brand.

The event has even attracted a number of celebrities and conservationists, including Natalie Portman and Jack Hanna, testament to the growing appeal of the event and the future potential for Rwandan tourism. For more information on Kwita Izina, check out the official website: www.kwitizina.org.

the locals know you're paying US$750 for the privilege of gorilla tracking, so try not to be too stingy.

Golden Monkey Tracking

Golden monkey tracking (per person US$100) is a relative newcomer on the wildlife scene of East Africa, but is rapidly rising in popularity both in Parc National des Volcans and across the border at Mgahinga Gorilla National Park (p450) in Uganda. More like chimp-viewing than a gorilla encounter, these beautiful and active monkeys bound about the branches of bigger trees. If you're looking for a reason to spend an extra day in the park, don't miss the chance to track these rare animals.

Golden monkeys, which are a subspecies of the wider-spread blue monkey, are endemic to the Albertine Rift Valley and are distinguished by their gold body colouration, which contrasts sharply with black patches on their extremities. Classified as an endangered species, golden monkeys can only be seen in the Virungas, as deforestation and population growth in the Great Lakes region has greatly affected their home range.

Permits to track the golden monkeys are easy to get hold of – simply enquire at the RDB office in Kigali or Musanze, or at the park headquarters in Kinigi.

Climbing & Trekking the Volcanoes

Dian Fossey once declared: 'In the heart of Central Africa, so high up that you shiver more than you sweat, are great, old volcanoes towering up almost 15,000ft, and nearly covered with rich, green rainforest – the Virungas.'

Indeed, these stunning volcanoes serve as an evocative backdrop for a guided climb or trek. As you make your way along the ascents, you'll pass through some remarkable changes of vegetation, ranging from thick forests of bamboo, giant lobelia or hagenia on to alpine meadows. And there's further rewards in store: if the weather is favourable, you can enjoy spectacular views over the mountain chain.

There are several possibilities for climbing up to the summits of one or more of the volcanoes in the park, with treks ranging in length from several hours to two days. A guide is compulsory and is included in your trekking fee; additional porters are optional (US$20 per day). Note that it is forbidden to cut down trees or otherwise damage vegetation in the park, and you are only allowed to make fires in the designated camping areas.

One of the best parts of climbing and trekking the volcanoes is that you will be awarded ample opportunities to view wildlife (sans gorillas and golden monkeys, of course). The most common herbivores in the park are bushbucks and black-fronted duikers; buffaloes, bush pigs and giant forest hogs are infrequently spotted. Also, be sure to inspect the hollows of trees for hyraxes, genets, dormice, squirrels and forest pouched rats. The richest birdwatching zone is in the hagenia forests, where you can expect to see turaco, francolins, sunbirds, waxbills, crimson-wings and various hawks and buzzards.

KARISIMBI

Climbing Karisimbi (4507m), the highest summit in the Virungas, takes two long and taxing days. The track follows the saddle between Bisoke and Karisimbi, and then ascends the northwestern flank of the latter. Some five hours after beginning the trek, there is a metal shelter under which you can pitch your tent. The rocky and sometimes snow-covered summit is a further two to four hours walk through alpine vegetation.

To do this trek, take plenty of warm clothing, your own food, a sturdy tent and a very good sleeping bag. It gets very cold, especially at the metal shelter, which is on a bleak shoulder of the mountain at 3660m. The wind whips through here, frequently with fog, so there is little warmth from the sun.

The two-day climb up Karisimbi costs US$400 for a solo climber or US$300 per person for groups of two or more, including park fees and a guide.

BISOKE

The return trip up Bisoke (3711m) takes six to seven hours from Parking Bisoke. The ascent takes you up the steep southwestern flanks of the volcano to the summit, where you can see the crater lake. The descent follows a track on the northwestern side, from where there are magnificent views over the Parc National des Virungas. This climb costs US$75 per person, including park fees and a guide.

DIAN FOSSEY'S GRAVE

A popular trek is to the site of the former Karisoke Research Center, where Dian Fossey is buried alongside many of her primate subjects, including the famous Digit. From the park headquarters it's about a 30-minute drive to the trailhead, followed by a two- to three-hour hike to the ruins of the camp. This excursion costs US$75 per person, including park fees and a guide (though you are responsible for your own transportation to/from the trailhead).

NGEZI

The return walk to Ngezi (about 3000m) takes three to four hours from Parking Bisoke. This is one of the easiest of the treks, and at the right time of the day it is possible to see a variety of animals coming down from the hills to drink at streams and springs. This trek is slightly cheaper than the others at US$55 per person including a guide.

GAHINGA & MUHABURA

Climbing Gahinga (3474m; in Uganda) and Muhabura (4127m) is a two-day trip from Gasiza (US$200 per person including guide). The summit of the first volcano is reached after a climb of about four hours along a track that passes through a swampy saddle between the two mountains. The trip to the summit of Muhabura takes about four hours from the saddle. It is also possible to climb these volcanoes separately. The trekking fee is US$100 for Muhabura and US$75 for Gahinga, including a guide.

Sleeping & Eating

All of the hotels listed following (except La Paillotte Gorilla Place) rely on generators to supply electricity. These are usually turned on from 5am until 8am and then again in the evenings from 6pm to 10pm.

TOP CHOICE **Kinigi Guesthouse** HOTEL **$**

(☎078-8533606; kinigi2020@yahoo.fr; camping US$12, dm US$10, s/d from US$40/50; P Wi-Fi) Once again this locally run guesthouse, located within walking distance of the park headquarters, gets our pick for being the best-value option in the vicinity of the national park. All profits from the lodge are ploughed back into the Association de Solidarité des Femmes Rwandaises, which assists vulnerable Rwandan women of all backgrounds and ages. Accommodation is in a small clutch of wooden bungalows that are set in lush gardens with views of the towering Virungas. The dorms are simpler affairs containing four beds in each room.

Sabyinyo Silverback Lodge LUXURY HOTEL **$$$**

(☎078-8382030; www.governorscamp.com; d full board US$1358; P Wi-Fi) Boasting a hefty price tag of US$1.2 million, the Sabyinyo Silverback Lodge is a joint partnership between the Sabyinyo Community Lodge Association (SACOLA) and the highly exclusive Governors' Camp. With only 18 beds on the property, hotel guests are treated as friends of the management, which results in a highly personalised level of service. Accommodation is in Venetian plaster cottages with Rwandese-style terracotta-tile roofs, spacious sitting areas, individual fireplaces, stylish en suite bathrooms and sheltered verandahs. SACOLA gets US$58 per bed per night in addition to 7.5% of all quarterly profits. To date, these revenues have been used to implement several community projects, including the erection of a 74km fence to protect local crops from hungry buffalo.

La Paillotte Gorilla Place HOTEL **$**
(☎078-5523561; www.lapaillottegorillaplace.com; s/d excl breakfast RFr15,000/20,000) Right in Kinigi village, not far from the market and bus stand, this small hotel has six clean rooms (with hot showers) set around a garden restaurant.

Mountain Gorilla View Lodge HOTEL **$$$**
(☎078-8305708; www.3bhotels.com; s/d half board US$200/250; P) These 25 rock cottages with impressive views down the volcano range are more functional than comfortable and some may find the stone floors a little cold (ask the staff for a hot-water bottle). A cultural show featuring traditional dancers is held here at 4.30pm every evening during the high season.

Le Bambou Gorilla Lodge HOTEL **$$$**
(☎078-8586515; www.lebambougorillalodge.com; camping US$10, s/d with shared bathroom US$50/60, s/d/tw full board US$150/250/250; P) The grounds here aren't in the same league as the other midrange options but the stone cottages themselves are smart with large beds and small fireplaces. The 'budget' accommodation was still being built when we passed through but looked promising.

Information

Park Headquarters

RDB (Rwanda Development Board; ☎078-8771633; www.rwandatourism.com, www.rdb.rw; 6am-4pm) You are required to register at this office near the village of Kinigi at 7am on the day of your scheduled gorilla tracking. If you are late, your designated slot will be forfeited. This is also the place to arrange permits for golden monkey tracking, as well as climbs and treks in the Virunga volcanos.

Wildlife Conservation

There are a number of high-profile international nonprofit organisations that are involved in wildlife conservation in the Virungas.

Dian Fossey Gorilla Fund International (www.gorillafund.org) Founded by the late Dian Fossey in 1978, this fund is dedicated to the protection of gorillas and their habitats through active conservation measures.

International Gorilla Conservation Programme (www.igcp.org) Formed in 1991 through the joint efforts of the African Wildlife Foundation (AWF), Fauna & Flora International (FFI) and the World Wide Fund (WWF).

Mountain Gorilla Veterinary Project (http://gorilladoctors.org) Since 1986 this organisation has provided free-ranging veterinary care to mountain gorillas.

Getting There & Away

The main access point for Parc National des Volcans is the nearby town of Musanze (Ruhengeri); for information on getting there from other points in Rwanda, see p519.

The park headquarters is located near the village of Kinigi, approximately 12km north of Musanze. The condition of this road has been greatly improved over recent years and Virunga District Service runs buses every 30 minutes between Musanze and Kinigi (first departure 6am, RFr300, 35 minutes). From Kinigi it's a further 4km to the park headquarters (RFr700 to RFr1000 by *moto-taxi*).

It's also necessary to arrange transport from the park headquarters to the point where you start climbing up to where the gorillas are situated. Some solo travellers opt to hitch a ride with other tourists although this may be seen as freeloading and even if you offer to contribute your share towards the vehicle there's always the chance you'll be refused.

If you want the assurance of your own wheels and the peace of mind in knowing that you'll meet the critical 7am meeting time, the best option is to join a group in Musanze. Two places to ask around at are Amahoro Tours (p517) or Hotel Muhabura (p517). The cost of hiring a vehicle and driver is US$80 at either of these places.

Gisenyi

POP 113,000

Landlocked Rwanda may be a long way from the ocean, but that doesn't mean you can't have a beach holiday here. On the contrary, if you take another look at the map, you'll quickly realise that Rwanda's eastern border with the DRC runs along the entire length of Lake Kivu. One of the Great Lakes in the Albertine Rift Valley, Lake Kivu has a maximum depth of nearly 500m and is one of the 20 deepest and most voluminous lakes in the world.

Of course, most travellers in Gisenyi are perfectly content to stick to the shores, especially since they're surprisingly sandy and fringed with all manner of tropical vegetation. While much of the Lake Kivu frontage is lined with landscaped villas, plush hotels and private clubs, the town itself projects a languid air of some forgotten upcountry backwater. But this is precisely the low-key charm that lures an eclectic mix of rich

Rwandans, expat escapees and independent travellers.

In fact, the biggest obstacle in the way of Gisenyi assuming a full-on resort status is simply its ongoing image problem. The town is unfortunately remembered as the location of a major flashpoint during the Rwandan Civil War, the 1994 genocide and the First and Second Congo Wars. Indeed, sharing a border with the DRC hasn't done wonders for the town's reputation although it does allow it to serve as a staging post for trips to Goma; see p493 for the rundown on side trips to this fascinating, albeit unstable, country.

Gisenyi is roughly divided into upper and lower towns, with most tourist services clustered around the lower end along the shores of Lake Kivu.

History

The first European to visit Lake Kivu was the German count Adolf von Götzen in 1894, although it was the early accounts of the Duke of Mecklenburg that are credited with fixing the lake in the European imagination. In 1907 the Duke declared that Kivu was 'the most beautiful of all the Central African lakes, framed by banks which fall back steeply from the rugged masses of rock and at the rear the stately summits of eight Virunga volcanoes'.

Of course, the lake's history stretches back eons before the age of European colonisation. A shallow lake was most likely formed here approximately two million years ago by the very same tectonic activity that wrenched open the Albertine Rift Valley. However, the lake in its present shape formed about 20,000 years ago when lava flows from the Virungas created a natural dam, separating Kivu from Lake Edward and substantially increasing its water levels.

Lake Kivu gained notoriety as a place where many of the victims of the Rwandan genocide were dumped, their bodies washing up on the shores of the DRC.

Sights

Rubona Peninsula HARBOUR

Roughly 7km outside of town, along a lovely lakeshore road, the Rubona peninsula is home to both Gisenyi's **main harbour** and

LIMNIC ERUPTIONS

Interestingly enough, Lake Kivu is one of only three known 'exploding lakes' (the other two are Lakes Nyos and Monoun in Cameroon), which experience violent lake overturns dubbed 'limnic eruptions'. This rare type of natural disaster results when carbon dioxide (CO2) suddenly erupts from deep lake water, suffocating wildlife, livestock and humans, and causing violent tsunamis.

To date, only two limnic eruptions have been observed; on both occasions the consequences were deadly. In 1984, 37 people were asphyxiated following a limnic eruption at Lake Monoun. Two years later, an even deadlier eruption occurred at neighbouring Lake Nyos, releasing over 80 million cubic metres of CO2 and killing between 1700 and 1800 people.

A major limnic eruption has never been recorded at Kivu, though the deepwater lake contains massive amounts of dissolved CO2 as well as methane. In fact, sample sediments taken by Professor Robert Hecky from the University of Michigan indicate that living creatures in the lake tend to go extinct approximately every thousand years or so.

While not as catastrophic as a full-scale eruption, in the absence of a strong wind, toxic gases can also collect on the surface of the water, and quite a few people have been asphyxiated as a result. Moral of the story: watch where local people swim, and make sure you're doing the same.

If an eruption does occur, the exploding underwater methane is likely to push a huge cloud of carbon dioxide above the surface of the lake, as well as triggering a series of tsunamis along the shoreline. Since CO2 is denser than air, it sinks quickly to the ground, pushing breathable air up into the sky. At this point, there is little you can really do to survive, and it's only a matter of time before you succumb to CO2 poisoning, suffocation, drowning or a dastardly combination of all three. To make matters worse, the last thing you will probably smell will be the warm vapour of the combusting methane, which is somewhat reminiscent of a giant, earthy fart.

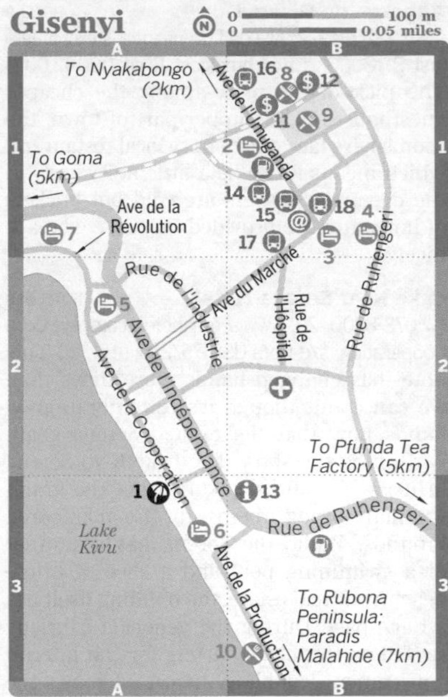

Gisenyi

Sights
1 Public Beach A3

Sleeping
2 Auberge de Gisenyi B1
3 Centre d'Accueil de l'Église Presbytérienne B1
4 City Lodge B1
5 Gorillas Lake Kivu Hotel A2
6 Lake Kivu Serena Hotel A3
7 Stipp Hotel A1

Eating
8 Boulangerie de Gisenyi B1
9 Main Market B1
10 New Tam-Tam Bikini Bar & Restaurant B3

Shopping
African Work Art Exposition ...... (see 13)

Information
11 Bank of Kigali B1
12 Ecobank B1
13 RDB Office B3

Transport
Atraco Express .... (see 18)
14 Belvèdéré B1
Jaguar Coaches .... (see 18)
15 Kampala Coach B1
16 Kigali Safaris B1
17 Main Bus Station B1
18 Okapi Car B1
Virunga Express .... (see 18)

the **Bralirwa Brewery**. Interestingly, the boilers at the brewery are largely powered by methane gas extracted from Lake Kivu. The project is something of a litmus test to determine whether or not large-scale extraction of methane is possible. In theory this could increase Rwanda's energy generation capability by as much as 2000%, enabling the country to sell electricity to its neighbours.

The peninsula is Lake Kivu at it's finest. Hills rise steeply from the lake foreshore and are a patchwork of garden plots and small homesteads. The shore itself is often rocky although there are enough sandy spots and places suitable for swimming should you become hot. The road between town and the port is often filled with laughing children, old men and shy women with baskets balanced on their heads.

Rubona is also home to some natural **hot springs**, which are reported by locals to cure a variety of ailments and are great for boiling potatoes. You'll have to ask around if you want to find them, but it's certainly worth the effort.

Public Beach BEACH

The wide strip of sand beneath the main town is one of the finest lake beaches in East Africa and is a justifiably popular place to take a dip. That said, some travellers, imagining Caribbean-like palms and sugary white sand, are disappointed to discover the waters are more grey-green than aqua blue and the sand, in typical lake fashion, is coarse and yellowish. There is, however, plenty of it and after days on the road Lake Kivu represents a welcome opportunity to throw down a beach towel or spread a picnic blanket under one of the many shade trees.

For those with money to burn, there are a variety of water sports and boat trips available at the upmarket hotels. However, far-reaching boat trips out on Lake Kivu are discouraged given the general climate of lawlessness in the neighbouring DRC.

Pfunda Tea Factory FACTORY

(admission US$10; 8am-5pm) During the rainy season, at the height of production, the Pfunda Tea Factory processes 60 tonnes of tea from the surrounding plantations daily. Guided tours follow the tea production from arrival of the green leaf, through to the withering, cutting, drying and sorting stages, before it is packaged for shipment to Mombasa (Kenya). The factory is about 5km from town and most easily reached by *moto-taxi* (RFr1000).

Sleeping

TOP CHOICE Centre d'Accueil de l'Église Presbytérienne HOSTEL $
(078-5730113; eprcagisenyi@yahoo.fr; Ave du Marché; dm RFr2000-3000, s/d/tr excl breakfast RFr8000/10,000/12,000) This church-run hostel has the cheapest beds in town – dorms come with varying numbers of beds, while the double rooms are spick and span with en suite facilities. Basic meals are served in a small restaurant, and there's a craft shop selling banana-leaf cards and stuffed toys to raise money for local women's groups.

TOP CHOICE Paradis Malahide HOTEL $$
(078-8648650; parmalahide@yahoo.fr; Rubona peninsula; d RFr40,000) Located along the shores of the Rubona peninsula just south of Gisenyi, this lodge continues to get wonderful reviews from loyal guests. Accommodation is in stone bungalows scattered around a small bar and restaurant, but the highlight of the property is clearly the stunning lakeside location. To reach Paradis Malahide, follow the road towards Rubona and turn right onto the lakeshore road just before you reach the brewery; the lodge will be on your left-hand side.

Stipp Hotel BOUTIQUE HOTEL $$
(252-540060; www.stipphotelrwanda.com; Ave de la Révolution; s/d excl breakfast from US$90/110; P) Gisenyi's first true boutique hotel rose from the ashes of a neglected colonial building and is now one of the classiest places to bed-down along the shores of Lake Kivu. Preferring intimacy to opulence, the Stipp is home to a small assortment of individually decorated rooms, striking an ideal blend of colonial elegance and modern convenience. Whether you're soaking in the enormous bathtubs, strolling around the lush garden or dining in one of the town's best restaurants, you're sure to have a relaxing stay here.

Auberge de Gisenyi HOTEL $
(078-2094922; Ave de l'Umuganda; s excl breakfast RFr8000, d excl breakfast RFr10,000-12,000) The pick of the pack among the cheaper guesthouses in the upper part of town, the rooms here face onto a busy local restaurant, which means it can be a little noisy early in the evening. Showers are cold but buckets of hot water are provided for those who ask nicely.

Lake Kivu Serena Hotel HOTEL $$$
(078-8200429; www.serenahotels.com; Ave de la Coopération; s/d from US$175/225; P) This hotel has changed hands more times than we can count though it's certainly in good hands now that the exalted Serena chain is running the show. The Lake Kivu Serena brims with refined luxury from the grand colonial dining rooms to the manicured grounds. While the Serena has a stunner of a swimming pool and a slice of prime beachfront real estate, the building itself has a dark past. During the genocide it briefly served as the headquarters for the interim government, enabling them to flee into the DRC when things got too hot.

City Lodge HOTEL $
(078-2686210; Rue de Ruhengeri; r excl breakfast, shared bathroom RFr8000) This reasonably clean town cheapie has had a spruce-up under the new management.

Gorillas Lake Kivu Hotel HOTEL $$
(252-540600; gorillashotel@rwanda1.com; Ave de l'Independance; s/d/tw/ste US$90/110/110/240; P) Part of the successful Gorilla chain, this hotel has more of resort feel than its sisters, largely thanks to the large freeform pool (RFr3000 nonguests).

Eating & Drinking

There are several simple restaurants on the main road in the upper part of town serving cheap meals and buffet lunches for around RFr2000, although the price varies depending on how much meat you take. One of the best is the small courtyard restaurant in the Auberge de Gisenyi.

If you like something more upmarket with a little more ambience, then head to one of the bigger hotels down by the lake.

TOP CHOICE Paradis Malahide EUROPEAN $$
(Rubona peninsula; mains RFr3000-6000; breakfast, lunch & dinner) Out on the Rubona peninsula, the Paradis Malahide is *the* place to

WORTH A TRIP

THE CONGO NILE TRAIL

It's possible to walk from Gisenyi at the northern end of Lake Kivu to Cyangugu at the lake's southern extremity. It's a 10-day hike of 227km in a country renowned for its hills, so you'd have to be extremely fit and possibly slightly insane to tackle the trail in its entirety without prior training. It is possible to walk a portion of the trail and the Gisenyi to Kibuye section can be covered in four days if you're prepared to walk from 7am to 5pm each day, averaging 18km a day.

You'll need to carry a tent and food for breakfast and lunch, but it's possible to get local families to cook for you in the evenings. Trekkers should contact the **RDB** (Rwanda Development Board; ☎252-540057; www.rwandatourism.com, www.rdb.rw) for the latest information; maps can be downloaded from its website. Amahoro Tours (p517) in Musanze can arrange guides for US$50 per day.

unwind and soak up the views. The outdoor seating and open-air restaurant make the most of the lush hibiscus- and bougainvillea-filled gardens. Service can be slow but the steak is second to none and worth the wait.

Stipp Hotel FRENCH **$$**
(Ave de la Révolution; mains RFr4000-7000; ⏲breakfast, lunch & dinner) Currently the Stipp Hotel has the best restaurant in town and draws a large crowd most nights. The menu is predominantly French and makes the most of the locally grown vegetables and fruit.

New Tam-Tam Bikini Bar & Restaurant BEER GARDEN **$**
(Ave de la Production; mains RFr1500-6000; ⏲lunch & dinner) While we don't know who came up with the name, we can vouch for the great beachfront location. The menu is limited but it's a smart spot for a beer and gets busy on the weekends when the drinking crowd rolls in.

Lake Kivu Serena Hotel EUROPEAN **$$$**
(Ave de la Coopération; mains RFr6000-8000; ⏲breakfast, lunch & dinner) The restaurant at the Lake Kivu Serena is also highly regarded, and serves a wide assortment of continental cuisine including pizza and other Western favourites. When occupancy permits, the hotel also puts on an impressive buffet (US$26 per person).

Main Market MARKET **$**
The best (and possibly only) place to stock up on fruit and vegetables.

Boulangerie de Gisenyi SUPERMARKET **$**
(off Ave de l'Umuganda) Another one for the self-caterers, this mini-supermarket has cheese, meats, yoghurts and fresh bread.

Shopping

African Work Art Exposition ARTS & CRAFTS
(Ave de la Independance) This small curio store has a varied and colourful collection of handicrafts from the DRC, Uganda and Rwanda, including lots of Congolese masks and other wooden items.

Information

Bank of Kigali (Ave de l'Umuganda & Ave de l'Independance) Of the bank's two branches, only the office up the hill has an ATM that will accept foreign Visa cards.

Cyber Café la Confiance (Ave du Marché; per 15min RFr100; ⏲8am-7pm Mon-Sat, 2-7pm Sun) If you ask nicely, the manager will transfer your photos to CD for RFr1200 on his laptop.

Ecobank (off Ave de l'Umuganda) Currency exchange, Western Union and an ATM (Visa only).

RDB (Rwanda Development Board; ☎078-8400042; www.rwandatourism.com, www.rdb.rw; Ave de l'Independance; ⏲7am-5pm Mon-Fri, 8am-2pm Sat & Sun) This office can direct you to the hotel that is currently offering boat trips and book national park activities.

Getting There & Away

AIR **RwandAir** (www.rwandair.com) flies six times a week between Kigali and Gisenyi (US$177 return).

BOAT Currently there are no passenger ferries across Lake Kivu to other Rwandan ports although it's sometimes possible to arrange passage to Kibuye on one of the cargo boats at the dock next to the Bralirwa Brewery.

BUS & MINIBUS It's a beautiful journey from Musanze (Ruhengeri) through rural farms and villages and there are panoramic views of Lake Kivu as the road descends into Gisenyi.

Kigali Safaris (off Ave de l'Umuganda), **Virunga Express** (Ave de l'Umuganda), **Belvèdéré** (off Ave de l'Umuganda) and **Jaguar Coaches**

WORTH A TRIP

FROM GISENYI TO KIBUYE BY BUS

The ride between Gisenyi and Kibuye is one of the most scenic in the country, skirting velvet-green tea plantations and tracing the ridges of tree-lined valleys. Unfortunately, the buses that travel this route are old and excruciatingly slow, with passengers packed in like fishes in a can.

Assuming you're setting out from Gisenyi, sit on the left side of the bus for wonderful views of the terraced gardens and mist-shrouded slopes as you crawl around the frequent hairpin bends.

When we last travelled this road, the Gisiza Bridge could no longer be trusted to bear the weight of a bus and we had to disembark and wait for an onward connection to Kibuye. Unlike other parts of Rwanda, the *mzungu* effect is alive and well and white skin has the power to draw a sizeable crowd of children.

The new bus for the onward journey to Kibuye was considerably larger than the one we had just unloaded from, but passenger numbers had magically swelled and when it came to securing a seat it was every man, woman and small child for themselves.

From Gisiza, sit on the right side of the bus for views of the banana and sugar-cane plantations and the first glimpse of Lake Kivu. As we rolled towards town, a church group broke into song and within moments the entire bus had joined in with levels of enthusiasm seldom seen outside of children's birthday parties.

In total the trip took us 6¼ hours but you may experience a lengthy delay at Gisiza. The first leg from Gisenyi to Gisiza costs RFr2000 and then it's a further RFr1500 from Gisiza to Kibuye.

(Ave de l'Umuganda) all operate buses between Gisenyi and Kigali (RFr3100, three hours) via Musanze (Ruhengeri; RFr1200, 1½ hours). Departures are hourly from 7am until 4pm.

There is a twice-daily service between Gisenyi and Kibuye departing at 7am and sometime around 1pm from Nyakabongo, 2km northwest of town.

Local minibuses for outlying villages gather at the main bus station on Ave du Marché. Follow the sounds of honking horns and racing engines.

Kampala Coach (off Ave de l'Umuganda) has a 3pm bus to Kampala (RFr12,000, 14 hours).

For the low-down on crossing the border into the DRC, see p554.

Getting Around

If you need wheels, *moto-taxis* swarm everywhere. From town to the DRC border should cost around RFr300. It's a RFr800 blast out to the Rubona peninsula.

SOUTHWESTERN RWANDA

The endless mountains and valleys don't stop as you head south towards the border with Burundi. While the gorillas in Parc National des Volcans tend to garner almost everybody's attention, southwestern Rwanda is home to East Africa's largest montane forest, Nyungwe Forest National Park, one of the most primate-rich areas in the world. The region is also home to the historic colonial and intellectual centre of Huye (Butare), which plays hosts to one of East Africa's best ethnographic museums.

Huye (Butare)

POP 107,000

Huye (Butare) is one of the most distinguished towns in Rwanda, having served as the country's most prominent intellectual centre since the colonial era. Home to the National University of Rwanda, the National Institute of Scientific Research and the excellent National Museum of Rwanda, Huye may be a step down in size after the capital, but it's certainly no lightweight on the Rwandan stage.

Historically speaking, Huye has always played a prominent role in regional affairs. During the era of Belgian occupation, the town was the colonial administrative headquarters of the northern half of Ruanda-Urundi. While Huye may have lost a bit of ground to Kigali after independence, today it still manages to maintain its political relevance, especially since it's ruled by legions of Rwanda's academic elite.

While Huye isn't a tourist destination in the traditional sense, it's nevertheless an interesting stopover on the way out to Nyungwe Forest National Park and the heavy concentration of liberal college students roaming the streets makes for an interesting atmosphere.

Note that in 2006, the name of the town was changed from Butare to Huye following an administrative reorganisation of Rwanda's 12 former provinces.

History

The tradition of Butare as an academic centre dates back to 1900 when it hosted the first Catholic mission in present-day Rwanda. As prominent intellectuals and religious figures were drawn to the area, Butare grew in favour among the Belgian occupiers. Following the death of Queen Astrid, the Swedish wife of King Leopold III, the town was renamed Astrida in 1935.

After independence in 1962, the town's name was changed back to Butare as it launched a strong bid to serve as the capital of Rwanda. Although Kigali was eventually chosen, due to its central location, Butare was selected to host the country's first university, which opened its doors to students in 1963.

In the early days of the 1994 genocide, Tutsis and moderate Hutus fled to Butare in the hope that its intellectual tradition would reign over the ensuing madness. For a short while, the Tutsi prefect of Butare, Jean Baptiste-Habyarimana, managed to maintain peace and order in the town.

Sadly, however, Habyarimana was quickly murdered by the Interahamwe and replaced by Colonel Tharchisse Muvunyi. Under his tenure, Butare was the site of horrific massacres that claimed the lives of nearly a quarter of a million people. Although Muvunyi

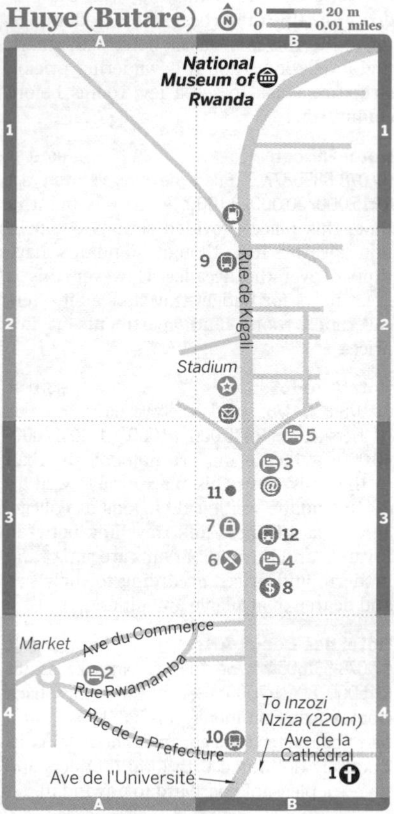

Huye (Butare)

Top Sights

National Museum of Rwanda B1

Sights

1 Cathedral B4

Activities, Courses & Tours

Sorta Tours .... (see 3)

Sleeping

2 Hôtel des Beaux-Arts A4
3 Hotel Faucon B3
4 Hotel Ibis B3
5 Hotel Ineza B3

Eating

6 Cheers Coffee & Fast Food B3
Hotel Ibis Restaurant .... (see 4)

Shopping

7 Expo Vente B3

Information

8 Bank of Kigali B3

Transport

Belvèdéré .... (see 11)
9 Bus/Minibus Stand B2
10 Horizon B4
11 New Yahoo Car B3
12 Volcano Express B3

fled to Britain after the genocide, he was eventually arrested and convicted.

Sights & Activities

National Museum of Rwanda MUSEUM

(www.museum.gov.rw; Rue de Kigali; adult/child RFr6000/3000; ⏲7am-7pm Mon-Fri, 8am-7pm Sat & Sun) This outstanding museum was given to the city as a gift from Belgium in 1989 to commemorate 25 years of independence. While the building itself is certainly one of the most beautiful structures in the city, the museum wins top marks for having one of the best ethnological and archaeological collections in the entire region.

While you certainly don't need more than an hour or two to stroll through the seven exhibition halls, take your time as there are some very interesting items on display; the first hall contains the museum shop. The second hall has geological displays including a large relief map that depicts the topography of Rwanda as something akin to a crumbled piece of paper. The middle halls exhibit items used in agriculture, hunting, animal husbandry, weaving, pottery and woodwork. The *kagondo* hut forms the centrepiece of an exhibit on housing and living compounds in pre-colonial times. The sixth hall features traditional clothing, including an *isinde* (wicker raincoat), pounded bark garments and goat-skin capes, while the final hall has information on Rwandan prehistory, including an interesting section on divination.

The museum is also the venue where the Intore dancers and drummers perform. Ask at reception about arranging a performance and see p533 for further information on this traditional Rwandan dance troupe. The museum is about 1km north of the centre, past the minibus stand. You can either walk or jump on a boda-boda for around RFr300.

National University of Rwanda GARDEN

Rwanda's finest institution of learning suffered terribly during the 1994 genocide, though today there are visible signs that it's turning towards the future with hope and optimism. Strolling through its campus is a pleasant diversion, especially if you find yourself at the **Arboretum de Ruhande**. Started by the Belgians in 1934, this attractive and peaceful arboretum is a great place to learn about African flora while indulging in a bit of leafy shade.

Cathedral CHURCH

Huye is also home to Rwanda's largest cathedral, which was constructed in the 1930s to commemorate the life of Princess Astrid. The red-brick building is still used for religious worship, so stop by if you happen to hear the sounds of gospel.

Sleeping

Hotel Ineza HOTEL $

(☎078-8953533; off Rue de Kigali; r excl breakfast RFr5000-6000) The rooms aren't very big but they're bright and clean, so if you're a solo traveller and after something cheap, then look no further. Double rooms here have only three-quarter-sized double beds that might struggle to fit two *mzungu*-sized bodies.

Hotel Ibis HOTEL $$

(☎252-530335; campionibis@hotmail.com; Rue de Kigali; s RFr15,000-26,000, d RFr19,000-35,000, all excl breakfast; P, wi-fi) Competing with the Credo for the title of the best accommodation in town, the Ibis is a classic hotel with smart, mid-level rooms and a bewildering pricing structure – ask to see a few rooms before committing.

Hotel Faucon HOTEL $$

(☎078-8890877; Rue de Kigali; s/d/apt RFr15,000/20,000/30,000; P) At one point in time, this place provided serious competition for the Ibis, though standards have slipped over the decades. However, this is great news for budget travellers as it offers cavernous rooms and apartments at low prices.

Hotel Credo HOTEL $$

(☎078-8504176; credohotel@yahoo.fr; Ave de l'Université; s RFr15,000-40,000, d RFr17,000-40,000; P, wi-fi, pool) A modern hotel on the road to the university, this place draws well-to-do Rwandans visiting their kids at college, as well as business folk travelling between Rwanda and Burundi. Rooms are smart and modern, and priced according to their size and degree of available amenities.

Hôtel des Beaux-Arts HOTEL $

(☎078-5316034; Ave du Commerce; s/d/tw RFr5000/8000/7000) Set a little way back from Ave du Commerce, this hotel has quite a bit of character for a cheapie. The hotel is attractively decorated with local products and there's a pleasant courtyard to unwind in.

Eating & Drinking

Like many towns in Rwanda, Huye is another place where most visitors tend to eat at the hotel they stay in. For something more traditional there are a number of local eateries offering brochettes and lunch buffets for around RFr2000 per person. As usual they involve mounds of carbs and a dollop of protein.

Chez Venant CHINESE **$$**
(Rue Rwamamba; mains RFr3500-7000; ⌚lunch & dinner) One of the few recommended restaurants in town, this place brings the taste of China to Huye. All the usual suspects turn up on the menu, including spring rolls and beef in black bean sauce, but there are also a few local dishes for good measure. Meals are large, and one main with a side of rice or noodles is enough for two. Unless you want to eat your dinner for breakfast, order well in advance as service is slow.

Cheers Coffee & Fast Food AMERICAN **$**
(Rue de Kigali; mains RFr2000-4000; ⌚breakfast, lunch & dinner Mon-Sat) Modelled on an American diner cum fast-food outlet, Cheers has a menu that's all about Western classics like pizza, burgers, sandwiches, waffles and pancakes, although it can be a bit hit and miss in terms of authenticity. It's located inside the Matar Supermarket, which is a great place for self-caterers.

Hotel Ibis Restaurant INTERNATIONAL **$$**
(Rue de Kigali; meals RFr2500-6000; ⌚breakfast, lunch & dinner) This hotel restaurant serves delicious food including a selection of meats, fish, pizzas, pastas and a wholesome range of salads. The pleasantly faded dining room brings a good measure of atmosphere to your dinner with its ivy-clad stonewalls.

Inzozi Nziza ICE CREAM **$**
(Ave de l'Université; ice cream RFr700; ⌚lunch) Three words: cookies, coffee and ice cream. Need we say more?

Entertainment

Traditional Rwandan Dance Troupe TRADITIONAL DANCE
(National Museum of Rwanda; 1-5 people RFr50,000, 6-10 people RFR60,000) There is a traditional Rwandan dance troupe based near Huye, and their show is spectacular. The Intore dance originated in Burundi and involves elaborate costumes and superb drumming routines. Performances can be organised through the National Museum and the larger the group size, the cheaper it will be per person. Photographers will need to pay an additional RFr2000 and note that prices substantially increase on weekends and during the evening.

Shopping

Expo Vente ARTS & CRAFTS
(Rue de Kigali) This large handicrafts shop exhibits local products made by cooperatives in villages around Huye. Prices are fixed and reasonable.

Information

Bank of Kigali (Rue de Kigali) Western Union, long queues and cash advances on Visa card.
Peace Cyber Cafe (Rue de Kigali; per hr RFr600) One of several internet cafes in town.
Post office (Rue de Kigali)

Getting There & Away

There are several bus companies found on Rue de Kigali that operate between Huye and Kigali (RFr2600, 2½ hours); some of these also have services to Nyamagabe (RFr600, 30 minutes), Nyanza (RFr700, 45 minutes), Cyangugu (RFr4000 to RFr5300, four hours) and Bujumbura (Burundi; RFr6000, four hours).

Belvèdéré (Rue de Kigali) The daily Bujumbura-bound bus from Kigali calls in at 10.30am.
Horizon (cnr Rue de la Prefecture & Rue de Kigali) Frequent departures for Kigali and Nyamagabe.
New Yahoo Car (Rue de Kigali) 8.30am, 10.30am and occasional 1pm bus to Bujumbura.
Sotra Tours (Rue de Kigali) Half-hourly departures for Kigali via Gitarama and six buses a day to Cyangugu.
Volcano Express (Rue de Kigali) A reliable operator with hourly buses to Kigali and Nyanza.

The local minibus stand is just a patch of dirt about 1km north of the town centre, by the stadium. Arriving buses often drop passengers here first before continuing to the centre of town.

The road from Huye to Kamembe (for Cyangugu) passes through the Nyungwe Forest National Park and some spectacular virgin rainforest.

Around Huye

MURAMBI GENOCIDE MEMORIAL

Nyamagabe (formerly called Gikongoro) and the satellite town of Murambi on its outskirts would be fairly forgettable places if it were not for the unforgettable horrors that took place here during the genocide. Refugees flocked to Murambi, the location of a well-known technical college before the war, in the hopes of seeking protection from their killers. As in Huye, the Interahamwe could not be stopped, and in a matter of days, thousands of people were brutally murdered.

This is by far the most graphic of the many **genocide memorials** (⏲8am-5pm, closed public holidays) in Rwanda, as hundreds of bodies have been exhumed, preserved with powdered lime and appear as they did when the killers struck. Wandering through the rooms at this former institute of learning, the scene becomes more and more macabre, beginning with the contorted corpses of adults, and finishing with a room full of toddlers and babies, fractures in their skulls from the machetes still visible on the shrivelled bodies.

As you can imagine from this description, Murambi can be overwhelming, and not everyone can stomach it for more than a few minutes. It is, however, another poignant reminder to us all of what came to pass here, and why it must never be allowed to happen again.

Nyamagabe is 28km west of Huye, and there are regular Horizon buses running between the two (RFr600, 30 minutes). The memorial is 2km beyond the town at Murambi. *Moto-taxis* can run you there for RFr500 if you don't fancy the walk.

Nyanza (Nyabisindu)

POP 55,000

In the 2006 provincial reshuffle, Nyanza – and not, as everyone assumed, Huye – ended up as the capital of the South Province. The most plausible explanation lies in the town's past. In 1899, Mwami Musinga Yuhi V established Rwanda's first permanent royal capital here. Until then, the royals had divided their time between 50 or so homes scattered throughout their kingdom.

Today his traditional palace (well, actually a very good replica of it) and the first home built by his son and successor Mutara III Rudahigwa has been restored and form the Rukari Ancient History Museum.

After visiting Belgium and seeing the stately homes there, Mutara concluded his own home wasn't up to scratch and had a second, and altogether grander, palace built on nearby Rwesero Hill, which today is the Rwesero Art Museum.

Most people visit the Nyanza museums as a day trip from either Kigali or Huye (Butare).

Sights

Keep hold of your ticket, as admission to one museum entitles you to entry to the other.

Rukari Ancient History Museum MUSEUM
(www.museum.gov.rw; adult/student RFr6000/3000; ⏲8am-5pm) Situated on a hill 2km from town, this museum is less about ancient history and more about royal residences. First up is a replica **'palace'** of the type that Mwami Musinga Yuhi V would have been born in. This large thatched hut has different areas for women and men and an exceptionally large bed. Inclusive in the ticket price is a guided tour in either French or English that helps explains some of the architectural idiosyncrasies inside the **royal compound**, including why the royal beer brewer's hut had an entrance without a lip, and why the woman who looked after the king's milk was never able to marry. Behind the royal compound are the **inyambo** (sacred cows) with their super-sized horns. In some, the span between horn tip and horn tip exceeds 2.5m.

Royal Residence of King Mutara III Rudahigwa

Crowning the hill itself is the royal residence of King Mutara III Rudahigwa, built by Belgium in 1931. This colonial-style home served as the royal palace until he died. Unfortunately much of the furniture and gifts he received from visiting dignitaries were stolen during the genocide, but it's still an interesting home to wander through with it's own peculiarities including three sitting rooms, the best of which was reserved for receiving white people. Mutara was the first *mwami* (king) to convert to Catholicism and in the beginning was so enthralled by the Belgian rulers that he once thanked 'Christ-the-King to have given Rwanda the divine light of Belgian colonial administration along with its science of good government'. He may have jumped to the wrong conclusion on that one.

Rwesero Art Museum MUSEUM
(www.museum.gov.rw; adult/student RFr6000/3000; ⏲8am-5pm) Unfortunately King Mutara III Rudahigwa died (in somewhat mysteri-

ous circumstances after a routine vaccination went wrong) before he saw his second home completed. Today it serves as an art museum housing mostly contemporary paintings and stylistic sculptures on themes dealing with the genocide, unity and brotherhood.

Sleeping & Eating

Boomerang Hotel HOTEL $
(078-8526617; s/d/tw RFr10,000/12,000/15,000; P) On the slopes of Rwesero Hill below the art museum, this popular local hotel and restaurant has presentable rooms, semi-reliable hot water and friendly staff.

Dayenu Hotel HOTEL $$
(078-3401791; s/d RFr18,000/30,000; P) This is a notch up from the Boomerang in terms of both quality and price, with rooms that are smarter and newer (although no cleaner). You'll find this multistorey hotel in the centre of town.

Getting There & Around

Any of the minibuses or buses that ply the main road between Kigali and Huye (Butare) can drop you at the turn-off for Nyanza. From here you can catch a *moto-taxi* to town (5km, RFr600). Better still, catch a Volcano Express or Horizon bus directly to Nyanza from either Kigali (RFr1800, 1¾ hours) or Huye (RFr700, 45 minutes).

The museums are a further 2km from town and can be reached on foot or by *moto-taxi* (RFr400).

Nyungwe Forest National Park

Quite simply, Nyungwe Forest National Park (formerly Parc National de Nyungwe) is Rwanda's most important area of biodiversity and has been rated the highest priority for forest conservation in Africa. While Nyungwe is the newest of Rwanda's parks to receive national park status, its protected area covers one of the oldest rainforests in Africa.

Despite rivalling Uganda's Kibale Forest National Park in virtually every comparison, Nyungwe is little known outside of East Africa and is largely undeveloped for tourism. Given its recent successes in promoting gorilla tourism to the international market, the Rwandan government is presently mounting a strong campaign to swing the tourist circuit southwest to Nyungwe.

Nyungwe's strongest drawcard is the chance to track chimpanzees, which have been habituated over the years to human visits. Hiking through equatorial rainforest in search of our closest genetic cousin is an unparalleled experience on par with gorilla tracking. Little can prepare you for the experience of watching chimpanzees tumbling down from the canopy and racing along the forest floor, all the while being mesmerised by the sounds of their distinctive 'pant-hoot'.

While chimps tend to garner most of the spotlight in Nyungwe, the park's second billing is a habituated troop of around 400 Angolan colobus monkeys, the largest group of arboreal primates in all of Africa. The lush, green valleys of the rainforest also offer outstanding hiking across more than 20km of well-maintained trails, passing through enormous stands of hardwoods, under waterfalls and through large marshes.

History

Part of the Albertine Rift Valley, Nyungwe is virgin equatorial rainforest that survived the last ice age. As a result, it's one of the oldest green expanses on the African continent, and is something of a 'Lost World' for rare and endangered species. It also spans several altitudinal bands, which facilitates its largely unparalleled biodiversity of both flora and fauna.

One of the largest protected montane rainforests in Africa, Nyungwe covers 970 sq km, and extends across the border to Parc National de la Kibira in Burundi. It also serves as a watershed for Africa's two largest rivers, the Nile and the Congo, and contains several springs that are believed to feed the headwaters of the Albertine Nile.

As stunning as Nyungwe is in its present manifestation, it is sadly nothing but a poor shadow of its former grandeur. Today, the outskirts of Nyungwe are heavily cultivated with rolling tea plantations and lush banana plantations. Beautiful though they may be, agriculture to feed the burgeoning masses of the Great Lakes region is largely to blame for the past deforestation.

In the past 100 years, the rainforests of the Albertine Rift Valley have been felled with little regard for the biodiversity they harboured. While Nyungwe received official protection under the Belgian colonial government as early as 1933, it lost 15% of its original size in the 1960s and 1970s to encroaching farms.

Fortunately, the Peace Corps, the World Conservation Society and the Rwandan government targeted Nyungwe for increased conservation in the 1980s. The original project aims were to promote tourism in an ecologically sound way, while also studying the forest and educating local people about its value.

Although tourism in the region was brought to a standstill during the tragic events of the 1990s, Nyungwe Forest is once again firmly on the tourist map. Having received official national park status in 2004, Nyungwe Forest National Park is now setting its sights on becoming one of East Africa's leading ecotourism destinations.

Sights & Activities

Chimpanzee Tracking

They may pale in size when compared to the hulking masses that are the eastern mountain gorillas, but there is no denying the incredible affinity that we humans have for chimpanzees. Sharing an estimated 94% of our genetic material, chimps display an incredible range of human-like behaviours ranging from tool use and waging war to face-to-face sex and possibly even rudimentary language.

Chimps are highly sociable creatures, and one of the few primates to form complex communities ranging upwards of 100 individuals. During the day these communities break down into smaller units that forage for food, a behaviour that has been dubbed by anthropologists as 'fission-fusion'. Since they cover a greater daily distance than the relatively docile gorilla, **chimpanzee tracking** (per person US$90) is a much more uncertain enterprise.

Chimpanzee habituation in Nyungwe is still very much a work in progress, and there are no guarantees you'll come face-to-face with one in the wild. However, you'll certainly be aware of their presence – they're very sensitive to territorial intrusions – especially since their distinctive 'pant-hoot' is one of the most distinctive sounds of the Central African rainforest.

If you are lucky and happen to come across a group of chimps on the move, you need to be quick with the camera. Chimps have a tendency to quickly disappear in the underbrush or climb up into the canopy and out of sight.

Much like gorilla tracking, you need to be prepared for lengthy and taxing hikes that can take up to several hours. Chimpanzees have large day ranges, which means that you need to enquire with the rangers as to their general whereabouts. In the rainy season you have a good chance of successfully tracking the chimps on the coloured trails, though in the dry season they have a tendency to head for higher elevations. Given their mobility, having a car is something of a necessity for chimp tracking as you'll need to arrange transportation for you and your guide to the trailhead.

Currently there are two habituated groups with a third that is expected to be ready sometime in 2013 or 2014. The **Uwinka group** is the largest with around 65 individuals and usually found within 12km of the Uwinka Reception Centre, often off roads that are only drivable in sturdy 4WDs.

The second group, the **Cyamudongo group**, is named after the Cyamudongo forest, a protected annexe of Nyungwe Forest National Park located approximately 45 minutes west of Gisakura on the road out to Cyangungu. Again, you need to have your own 4WD in order to get to this tiny forest.

Colobus Monkey Tracking

A subspecies of the widespread black-and-white colobus, the Angolan colobus is an arboreal Old World monkey that is distinguished by its black fur and long, silky white locks of hair. Weighing 10kg to 20kg, and possessing a dextrous tail that can reach lengths of 75cm, Angolan colobi are perfectly suited to a life up in the canopy.

Colobi are distributed throughout the rainforests of equatorial Africa, though they reach epic numbers in Nyungwe Forest National Park. While they may not be as a charismatic as chimps, colobi are extremely social primates that form enormous group sizes – the semi-habituated troop in Nyungwe numbers no less than 400 individuals, and is by far the largest primate aggregation on the continent.

As you might imagine, finding yourself in the presence of literally hundreds of primates bounding through the treetops can be a mesmerising experience. Curious animals by nature, colobi in Nyungwe seem to almost revel in their playful interactions with human visitors.

Troops of Angolan colobi maintain fairly regimented territories, which is good news for those planning a **colobus track** (per person US$70) as the semi-habituated group in Nyungwe tends to stick to the coloured

NYUNGWE FOREST NATIONAL PARK

Why Go Nyungwe Forest National Park enjoys some of the richest biodiversity in all of Africa, with no less than 1000 plant species, 13 species of primates, 75 species of mammals, at least 275 species of birds and an astounding 120 species of butterflies. The park's star activities are tracking chimpanzee and the world's largest troop of colobus monkey (around 400). Both species have been habituated to humans.

When to Go Nyungwe can be visited year-round and the chimps often descend from the higher elevations (and are therefore easier to find) during the wet season. No matter when you visit, expect rain and plenty of it. Nyungwe is equatorial rainforest and receives more than 2m of rainfall annually.

Practicalities Trails can get extremely wet and muddy, so make sure you have good hiking shoes, waterproof trousers, a solid raincoat and perhaps even a floppy hat or bandana. All activities begin at the Uwinka Reception Centre or at the Gisakura Booking Office.

While public transport does pass by the park, your ability to move around the park will be greatly restricted without access to a private vehicle. This is especially true if you want to see the chimps, as tracking can sometimes begin in the most seemingly random of locations.

trails. While watching wildlife is never a certainty, generally speaking, the rangers can find the colobus monkey troop in an hour or so.

There is a smaller, and often more accessible troop, of around 70 individuals near the Gisakura Tea Plantation. Be sure to ask which troop you'll be tracking when you make your reservation.

Trekking

In addition to tracking primates, Nyungwe Forest National Park has a number of walking trails that begin at either the Uwinka Reception Centre or the Gisakura Booking Office.

It's not possible to walk in the park without a guide and one is included when you pay your trek fees. What isn't advertised in park literature is if you pay for one trail, you can actually do any other trail in the same category that day at no further cost. It's therefore possible to do three 5km walks in one day, but only pay the US$40 fee once. To trek on trails that are 5km or less costs US$40 per person per day and to walk on any of the 5km to 10km trails costs US$50 per person, per day. Rates for subsequent days decrease thereafter.

Walks begin at set times; the first departures are around 9am, with further departures around 11am and 2pm.

COLOURED TRAILS

This system of colour-coded trails was constructed in the late 1980s in an attempt to open up Nyungwe to tourists. While tourism in the national park remains relatively low-key, these seven trails are nevertheless reasonably well maintained. Hikers can choose from the 2km-long **Buhoro Trail**, a proverbial walk in the woods, up to the 10km-long **Imbaraga Trail**, which winds steeply up forested slopes.

In 2010 a further effort was made to draw tourists south with the construction of a 160m-long and at times 60m-high **canopy walkway** (per person US$60). You won't encounter any wildlife while on the suspension bridge but you'll certainly appreciate the jungle anew from this unique monkey's-eye perspective. The canopy walkway is located on the **Igishigishigi Trail**.

Although you need to specifically request to engage in either chimpanzee or colobus tracking, in theory you could run across either primate while hiking the coloured trails. Even if you don't come across these two star billings, you're likely to spot any of Nyungwe's other 11 primates, as well as a whole slew of birdlife, and possibly even the odd mammal or two.

All coloured trails originate from the Uwinka Reception Centre.

WATERFALL TRAIL

While not as popular as the coloured trails, the **Waterfall Trail** (per person US$50) is a stunner of a hike and one of the highlights of Nyungwe. It's one of the few treks that start from the Gisakura side of the park and takes three to six hours to complete depending on your fitness level. The trail winds through a variety of landscapes from tea plantations to deep forest and its highlight (quite obviously) is a remote waterfall, where you can take a shallow dip and refresh your body after the hot and humid hike.

KAMIRANZOVU TRAIL

If you have your own wheels, the **Kamiranzovu Trail** (per person US$40) starts somewhere between Uwinka and Gisakura, and runs for about 4km to Kamiranzovu Swamp. Sadly, the last elephant was shot here in 1999, though the swamplands are still your best bet for spotting other large mammals. Even if you don't come across any other fauna, this trail is particularly famous for its rare species of orchids.

Birdwatching

There are four specialist **birding guides** (per person US$70) based in Nyungwe that need to be booked in advance if you require their particular services (email the tourist warden directly; p539). There are more than 25 endemics in the park including Rwenzori turacos as well as other large forest specialties including African crowned eagles and various hornbills. Depending on what you hope to see, the guide will choose a trail that maximises your chances of spotting your quarry.

If you're unsure of what to ask for, opt for the dirt **Rangiro Rd** that starts 1.5km east of Uwinka. Thanks to the frequent changes in elevation along this route you have increased chances of spotting a good number of Nyungwe's fine-feathered friends.

WATCHING WILDLIFE IN NYUNGWE FOREST NATIONAL PARK

Nyungwe Forest National Park is an outstanding island of biodiversity, and a veritable monkey forest. At least 20% of the total primate species in Africa are found within the confines of Nyungwe, an impressive statistic that is only equalled by Kibale Forest National Park in Uganda.

While they're more difficult to track than slow-moving gorillas, communities of chimpanzees on the move will certainly make their presence known to you. Habituated troops of monkeys – Angolan colobus (troops of which number up to 400), Dent's monkey (a local race of blue monkey) and grey-cheeked mangabeys (the last two often seen together) – are virtually guaranteed on guided walks.

Other monkey possibilities include l'Hoest's and diademed monkeys, which sometimes associate with colobus and blue monkeys. Olive baboons and vervet monkeys loiter near the park's eastern edge, while owl-faced monkeys and possibly golden monkeys live in the extensive bamboo stands in the southeastern part of the reserve. Nocturnal prosimian attractions include needle-clawed and greater galagos as well as the potto.

In addition to primates, you also have a fairly good chance of spotting mammals, particularly in and around Kamiranzovu Marsh. Marsh mongooses and Congo clawless otters stick to the water's edge, while giant forest hogs, bush pigs and duikers are sometimes startled along the trails. Rainforest squirrels are also commonly spotted, and include giant forest, montane sun and Boehm's bush squirrels.

Hyraxes are easily heard after dark, though you're going to have to look inside the hollows of trees if you want to spot one. Nocturnal mammals are a bit tricky to spot, but you do have a chance of running across jackals, civets and genets.

Nyungwe has something of a legendary status among birdwatchers in East Africa, and is by far the country's top spot for birdwatching. Even if you're not a hardcore birder, it's pretty easy to get excited by Nyungwe's 275-plus species, which include no less than 25 Albertine Rift Valley endemics.

The dirt road leading to Rangiro, and the Imbaraga, Umugote and Kamiranzovu Trails, are all highly recommended for birdwatching. The paved road through the park permits viewing at all levels of the forest: expect mountain buzzards and cinnamon-chested bee-eaters perched along here, plus numerous sunbirds, wagtails and flocks of waxbills. Other commonly sighted birds include francolins, turacos, African crowned eagles, hornbills and even Congo bay owls.

Sleeping & Eating

UWINKA

Uwinka Camp Site CAMPGROUND $
(camping excl breakfast US$30) The campsite at RDB's Reception Centre is currently the only option at Uwinka now that the small guesthouse has been leased long-term by researchers. There are several choice spots, many with impressive views overlooking the forest and one under a shelter with a tin roof that's a godsend in the likely event of rain. There's also a small canteen where you can get basic meals, clean toilets and a simple shower block (the rangers will bring you a bucket of hot water). Although there are no kitchen facilities, one of the rangers will light a campfire that you can cook on if you wish. You no longer need to be as self-sufficient as you once did to stay here; tents (RFr10,000) can be hired and the staff can usually rustle up an extremely thin sleeping mat and sleeping bag for those who haven't brought their own. There is little point in staying here unless you also plan to do an activity, as campers who visit but do not sign up for any activity are charged US$50 per person per night as opposed to the standard US$30 per night.

GISAKURA

The big problem with Gisakura is location, location, location – it's a long haul to Uwinka for those without transport.

Nyungwe Forest Lodge LODGE $$$
(☎252-504330; www.nyungweforestlodge.com; r per person incl meals US$175-250; P 📶 🏊) When you compare the prices here to other five-star lodges (like those in Parc National des Volcans which charge US$600 per person) this place is a bargain and a good option if you fancy a splurge. Built on the outskirts of a tea plantation with a stunning jungle backdrop, it is very easy to forget where you are as you lounge in the heated infinity pool or sip cocktails on the terrace. As you would expect, the rooms have all the bells and whistles, including fireplaces, flat-screen satellite TVs, lounging areas and beautifully decorated bedrooms. Massages are available in the treatment room and fitness freaks can do their thing in the small gym (as if bush-whacking your way through dense jungle in search of chimps wasn't enough).

Gisakura Guest House GUESTHOUSE $$
(ORTPN Resthouse; ☎078-8675051; www.gisakuraguesthouse.com; s/d/tr with shared bathroom US$43/64/85) A more sophisticated option for those without a tent, this guesthouse offers accommodation in simple but functional rooms that share communal showers and toilets and are set in a beautiful garden. Virtually no English is spoken here, which is surprising considering they rely on international tourists for much of their income. It's near the RDB booking office and still known locally as the ORTPN Resthouse – its pre-privatisation name.

Information

Nyungwe Forest National Park is sliced in two by the Huye–Cyangugu road. Visitors can access the park through either the Uwinka Reception Centre or the Gisakura Booking Office, both of which lie along this road. For information online, see www.nyungwepark.com and www.rwandatourism.com.

Uwinka Reception Centre (☎tourist warden for bookings 078-8436763; kambogoi@yahoo.fr) The park headquarters is a little over half way to Cyangugu from Huye (Butare). It got a revamp in 2010 and there is now a small but informative display on the ecology of the park, a new toilet block and an outdoor terrace area. From here you can get a good overview of the trails, arrange guides, book activities and pay fees.

Gisakura Booking Office (☎078-8841079) A second booking office can be found in Gisakura (near the Gisakura Guest House), where you can also pay fees and organise chimpanzee tracking.

Getting There & Away

Nyungwe Forest National Park lies between Huye and Cyangugu. Impala Express and Sotra Tours buses travel between Huye (RFr4000 to RFr5300, two hours, 90km) and Kamembe (for Cyangugu; one hour, 55km) throughout the day. Any one of these buses can drop you at either Uwinka Reception Centre or at the Gisakura Tea Plantation.

The trouble is that having arrived, your ability to move around the park is severely limited if you don't have a car. If you're sticking to the coloured trails and don't have your own transport, consider camping at Uwinka where the walks begin.

Leaving is more problematic as many of the passing buses are full and you may have to wait some time before one will stop. The rangers on duty at either of the booking centres can phone Impala Express on your behalf and secure a seat but you'll have to pay the full Cyangugu to Kigali fare (RFr5300) even if you only plan to travel as far as Huye. Once the ranger has made the booking he'll hold your fare as in the past some travellers go on to find lifts with other tourists and then refuse to pay for the empty seat that is being held for them.

Cyangugu

POP 69,000

Clinging to the southern tip of Lake Kivu, and looking across to Bukavu in the DRC, Cyangugu is an attractively situated town on the lake's shore.

The town has two distinct settlements: **Kamembe**, a few kilometres above the lake, is the main town and an important location for the processing of tea and cotton. This is the commercial heart of Cyangugu and you'll need to come here to change money and catch onward transport.

Most of the better hotels are down below in Cyangugu proper, which is far prettier, far quieter and right next to the DRC border.

Sleeping & Eating

All the hotels mentioned here have attached restaurants that are as good as the food is going to get in this town.

KAMEMBE

Motel Rubavu HOTEL $
(☎252-537093; motel_rubavu@yahoo.com; r RFr 7000-12,000) While the Rubavu is not going to win any style awards any time soon, the RFr10,000 rooms have beds large enough for two, hot water and a handy location near the bus ticketing offices.

Ten to Ten Paradise Hotel HOTEL $
(☎078-3197006; tentotenp@yahoo.fr; r excl breakfast RFr10,000-35,000; P) This hotel has rooms for all budgets and depending on how much you pay, breakfast may or may not be included. As you would expect, the RFr10,000 cheapies are little more than a box with a bed while the more upmarket options have hot-water showers and satellite TVs.

CYANGUGU

Hotel des Chutes HOTEL $
(☎078-441353; r RFr12,000-20,000; P) Hotel des Chutes offers well-equipped rooms with spacious balconies that boast fine views across the narrow strip of water to Bukavu. There's also a smart terrace restaurant that enjoys the same DRC views and the shade of a jacaranda tree. Understandably, this pretty setting is popular with locals.

Hotel du Lac HOTEL $
(☎078-8300518; hotel.dulac@yahoo.fr; r excl breakfast RFr8,000-25,000; P ≋) So close to the border it's almost in the DRC, this local landmark has a good mix of rooms, even though some of them have aged less than gracefully over the years. The swimming pool is open to nonguests for a small fee, and the lively terrace bar and restaurant is the place to be at night.

Information

You'll find all the banks and most other essential services (including internet cafes) in Kamembe. At the time of research the Bank of Kigali and Ecobank could give cash advances on Visa and were in the process of installing international-card-compatible ATMs while Access Bank was the only one that could give cash advances on MasterCard.

Moneychangers near the border in Cyangugu will change Rwandan francs to DRC francs although US dollars are widely accepted in the DRC.

Getting There & Away

Minibuses/*moto-taxis* for the short hop between Cyangugu and Kamembe cost RFr200/500.

Impala Express and Sotra Tours have several daily departures between them to Kigali (six hours) via Uwinka (two hours) and Huye (Butare; four hours). Regardless of where you leave the bus, you could well be charged the full Kigali RFr5300 fare.

This road is incredibly spectacular in parts and passes through the superb Nyungwe rainforest, where it is possible to see troops of Angolan colobus monkeys playing by the roadside.

Gasabo has an on-again, off-again, 6.30am bus to Kibuye (RFr4000, seven hours).

Cyangugu is literally a stone's throw away from the DRC and, providing you have all your paperwork in place, you can walk across the bridge and into the Congo. It's also possible to reach Bujumbura (Burundi) from here. See p554 for further information on international routes.

Kibuye

POP 50,000

Although it has a stunning location, spread across a series of tongues jutting into Lake Kivu, Kibuye has not caught on as a tourist destination for sun and sand in the same way that Gisenyi has, but for our money – and there are plenty who will disagree – this is the better of the two. True, on this part of the lake good beaches are a lot less common but the steep hills that fall into the deep green waters and the indented shoreline with a smattering of islands nearby make it extremely picturesque. Furthermore, accommodation is far more affordable and even budget rooms have million-dollar views. And, unlike Gisenyi, you can swim here without fear of drowning and asphyxiating in the event of an unforeseen limnic eruption.

One of the best ways to get accustomed to the town is to follow the ring road around the shores of the lake. There are some amazing views to be had along the way, and you're likely to find a few sandy patches where you can pause to take a cooling dip.

Perhaps what's holding Kibuye back is the chilling fact that this sleepy backwater hosted the largest wholesale slaughter of Tutsis during the dark days of the genocide.

History

During the 100 days of madness in 1994, Kibuye hosted some of the most horrific and despicable mass killings in all of Rwanda. Prior to the outbreak of the genocide, more than 20% of the local population was Tutsi; in 1994 the Interahamwe killed an estimated nine out of every 10 Tutsi. While these scars still run deep, today the residents of Kibuye are working together as a community to embrace the prospect of future tourism. A couple of memorials to the slain victims ensure that the past is not forgotten, while the frames of new buildings are signs of a brighter future.

Sights

Genocide Memorial Church MEMORIAL

While a good number of memorials in Rwanda are stark reminders of the past atrocities, the Genocide Memorial Church is a beautiful and evocative testament to the strength of the human spirit. The interior is adorned with colourful mosaics and vivid stained-glass windows while outside a rock memorial displays a few skulls from some of the 11,000 people who were killed by a drunken mob here.

Hill of Resistance MEMORIAL

The uphill road from Kibuye leads to the small village of **Bisesero**, which is home to an equally significant memorial. During the early days of the genocide, more than 50,000 Tutsis fled here in the hope of evading the Interahamwe. For more than a month, these brave individuals were able to fend off their aggressors with little more than basic farming implements.

On 13 May, a reinforced regiment of soldiers and militia descended on Bisesero, slaughtering more than half of the refugees. By the time the French arrived on the scene in June, there were less than 1300 Tutsis remaining. However, these individuals overcame insurmountable odds, and their stories reflect humanity's incredible will to survive.

Les Chutes de Ndaba WATERFALL

When returning on the road to Kigali, keep an eye out for the 100m-high waterfall. It's 20km from Kibuye, and buses usually slow down and helpful locals are quick to point it out.

Activities

Not surprisingly, most activities in Kibuye revolve around Lake Kivu. Most guests are content to simply sun themselves for days on end, occasionally taking breaks to go **swimming**. The other popular activity is **boating** to any of the small offshore islands. Boats for charter can be found at the water's edge beneath Hotel Centre Béthanie and Hotel Golf Eden Rock. Rates aren't fixed and will depend on how far you wish to venture and for how long you wish to go.

Sleeping & Eating

Backpackers rejoice! Rooms here are a lot more affordable than those in Gisenyi, making this an ideal spot to chill for a few days. Just bear in mind that Kibuye is a leading conference venue and it pays to ring ahead.

There are some local eateries in town (including two by the bus ticketing offices) but the best food can be found at the hotels.

TOP CHOICE **Hotel Centre Béthanie** GUESTHOUSE $

(252-568235; eprbethanie@yahoo.com; r RFr15,000-35,000; P) This popular guesthouse occupies a charming location on a wooded peninsula jutting into the lake. The small but cosy private rooms are kept spick and span and many have amazing views to the islands. Some rooms include breakfast for one in the excellent restaurant that also boasts free wi-fi.

Hôme St Jean GUESTHOUSE $

(078-8823135; r RFr10,000-15,000, s/tw with shared bathroom RFr6000/8000; P) Sitting on its own hillside with stunning 270-degree views across Lake Kivu, this church-run pad has some of the cheapest digs in town. The double beds in the self-contained rooms are smaller than your average double bed so better suited to solo travellers or those who are really into snuggling.

Hotel Golf Eden Rock HOTEL $
(☎252-568524; golfedenhotel@yahoo.fr; r RFr14,000-20,000; P 📶) This large and looming hotel is open to the public once more, having housed the Chinese road-construction crew working on the Kigali road for many years. The location is not quite as nice as Béthanie, but the rooms are slightly smarter. The most expensive quarters come equipped with private balconies and sweeping views over Lake Kivu. The restaurant has a large terrace with similarly impressive views and is *the* perfect spot for a sundowner.

Information

There is a post office near Guest House Kibuye, a Bank of Kigali (no ATM), plenty of MTN phones and an internet cafe in the centre of town.

Getting There & Away

The road linking Kibuye with Kigali is endlessly winding but in excellent shape, making Kibuye very accessible from the capital. Impala Express and Capital Express run the most comfortable buses to Kigali (RFr2700, 2½ hours) via Gitarama (RFr2000, 1½ hours). Bus services start around 6am and continue hourly until 5.30pm.

A 7am bus leaves for Gisenyi every morning (and a less reliable one may leave in the afternoon). This is one of the most spectacular roads in the country (see the boxed text, p530).

On the map Cyangugu (RFr4000, seven hours) looks like a promising onward destination but this road is in a dire state and only a few Gasabo buses now travel this route and those that do have a flexible view on departure times. Many people now backtrack to Gitarama and pick up a Cyangugu connection there with Impala Express.

At the time of writing, there were no regularly scheduled ferry services in operation on Lake Kivu. However, it is sometimes possible to arrange a boat trip to Gisenyi or Cyangugu if there's enough demand.

Getting Around

Moto-taxis wait for arriving buses in the centre of town. It's a RFr500/400/400 hop from here to Hotel Centre Béthanie/Hotel Golf Eden Rock/Hôme St Jean.

EASTERN RWANDA

While much of Rwanda is characterised by equatorial rainforest and richly cultivated farmland, eastern Rwanda is something else entirely. Contiguous with the dry and flat savannah lands of Tanzania, this region is more reminiscent of the classic images of East African landscapes. While sights are scarce in this part of the country, Parc National de l'Akagera is one of Rwanda's highlights, especially if you're looking to get your safari fix.

Parc National de l'Akagera

Created in 1934 to protect the lands surrounding the Kagera River, this national park once protected nearly 10% of Rwanda and was considered to be one of the finest wildlife reserves in the whole of Africa. However, due to the massive numbers of refugees who returned to Rwanda in the late 1990s, as much as two-thirds of the park was degazetted and resettled with new villages. Increased human presence took an incredible toll on the national park. Human encroachment facilitated poaching and environmental degradation, and Akagera's wildlife was very nearly decimated.

For more than a decade, Akagera was something of a vegetarian safari, given that most animals on four legs were taking an extended holiday in neighbouring Tanzania. However, the Rwandan government has recently implemented strict conservation laws (which are certainly complementary to their increased push for tourism in Rwanda) aimed at protecting Akagera. Furthermore, the once decrepit Akagera Game Lodge has been rehabilitated by South African investors and now stands as testament to the future potential of this once great safari park.

There are three distinct environments in the park: standard savannah as seen in much of the region; an immense swampy area along the border with Tanzania that contains six lakes and numerous islands, some of which are covered with forest; and a chain of low mountains on the flanks of the park with variable vegetation, ranging from short grasses on the summits to wooded savannah and dense thickets of forest.

Truth be told, Akagera is still a shadow of its former self, and you will be extremely disappointed if you come here expecting concentrations of wildlife on par with Kenya and Tanzania. While the once grand herds that characterised Akagera are a mere fraction of their original numbers, populations are noticeably on the rise. And, even if you don't come across too many wild animals, it's very likely that you won't come across too many other wildlife-viewing drivers. Indeed, the tourist trail has yet to fully incorporate Akagera, which means you can soak up the park's splendid nature in relative peace and isolation.

History

While the Belgians certainly didn't do Rwanda too many favours, they are credited with recognising the environmental significance of Akagera. In 1934, the colonial government gazetted 2500 sq km as protected lands, including a buffer zone where human activities were strictly prohibited. Following independence in 1962, the Rwandan government largely upheld its commitment to protect the sanctity of the national park. In fact, prior to the start of the civil war, Akagera, together with the country's other national parks, was Rwanda's third-largest revenue earner.

As history would have it, in 1997 Akagera was reduced to a mere 1085 sq km due to increased population pressures brought on by returning refugees. In an effort to resettle landless Rwandans, the government slashed the park's borders by two-thirds, devastating this once pristine ecosystem.

In response to substantial habitat loss, as well as depleted water supplies resulting from increased farming and ranching, Akagera's wildlife fled to Tanzania. Poachers, who carried out their illegal activities with virtual impunity, quickly decimated the animal herds that chose to stay put. In more recent years, the Rwandan government has changed its tune on Akagera, though it's going to take several more years before wildlife populations in the park can stabilise.

While human and wildlife conflicts are never a clear-cut issue, it's worth pointing out that Akagera is a vital part of Rwanda's push for a viable tourism industry. At present, the vast majority of tourists in Rwanda leave the country quickly after tracking gorillas, which is a trend the government would like to change. If people can be persuaded to spend a bit of extra time in Rwanda, then Akagera, along with Nyungwe Forest National Park, needs to be preserved.

On that note, consider extending your stay in Rwanda, and be sure to visit Akagera – this up-and-coming national park could certainly use your support.

PARC NATIONAL DE L'AKAGERA

Why Go While wildlife populations are still recovering, Akagera's strongest drawcard is its unique ecology; a mix of woodland habitats, swampy wetlands and jagged mountains.

When to Go The best time to visit is during the dry season (mid-May to September). November and April are the wettest months.

Practicalities Tsetse flies and mosquitoes can be bad in the north and east, so bring a good insect repellent.

While in theory it is possible to reach the park by public transport, you really do need a private vehicle in order to move around the park. Akagera can also be visited as a day trip from Kigali.

Sights & Activities

Wildlife Drives DRIVING TOUR

(adult/student/child one day US$30/25/20, two day US$50/40/30, three day US$70/50/40, vehicle from US$10) It's not possible to organise a safari on the spot and most people arrive with transport arranged in Kigali. Ranger guides are provided by the park authorities at no extra charge although a tip is expected. One option is to enter the park at the main gate, pick up your guide and spend the day making your way to the park's northern Nyungwe gate where you could drop your guide (with a *moto-taxi* fare to get him back to park headquarters) before returning to Kigali.

Lake Ihema Boat Trips BOAT TOUR

(1hr tour per person US$30, 2½hr tour per person US$50) Park authorities can arrange trips on Lake Ihema to see the hippo pods and some of the huge Nile crocodiles that are otherwise difficult to observe. This is also the best way to view the park's abundant waterbirds including breeding colonies of noisy and smelly cormorants and open-bill storks.

Birdwatching BIRDWATCHING

(birding guide incl park entry fee US$70) If you're a birdwatcher, you'll be happy to know that Akagera has Rwanda's greatest concentration of birds outside of Nyungwe Forest

WATCHING WILDLIFE IN PARC NATIONAL DE L'AKAGERA

Carnivores in Akagera include lions, leopards, spotted hyenas, genets, servals and jackals. There are even a few specialties, including the rare roan antelope. The national park also lies on the great Nile Valley bird migration route, which means that you could potentially spot up to 525 species of birds including several endemics and more than 40 different kinds of raptors.

Again, it's worth pointing out that while Akagera supports a full complement of East African wildlife, don't come here expecting your quintessential East Africa safari experience.

So how much wildlife is actually left in the park? That's the real question, though nobody truly knows the answer with any degree of certainty. There may only be one or two dozen lions left in the park, though hyenas, jackals and leopards are still active at night, and small cats such as the genet and serval are well represented. Since Akagera is contiguous with western Tanzania, there is hope that predatory cats will increase their ranges and move into Rwanda.

Akagera was once defined by its massive aggregates of herd animals and there is reason to believe that these densities will arise once more. There are no less than 11 different species of antelopes in the park, which includes the common safari staple that is the impala, as well as the majestic but rare roan antelope. Buffalo and zebra are also very well-represented animals, while Maasai giraffes and elephants are making a slow but steady comeback.

The national park is also something of a hippo paradise, especially given that much of the environment is swampland. There are at least a thousand of the lumbering giants in and around the shores of the lake, as well as a large enough population of crocodiles to keep you from the temptation of taking a cooling dip.

In the 1950s, Akagera was the first national park in Africa to receive translocated black rhinos, which were flown in from neighbouring Tanzania. These animals thrived in the dense brush of the park, but poachers quickly decimated their numbers during the 1980s.

National Park. The many kilometres of waterside habitat support African eagles, kingfishers, herons, ibises, storks, egrets, crakes, rails, cormorants, darts and pelicans. Seasonal visitors include large flocks of ducks, bee-eaters and terns, and the woodlands areas are particularly good places for barbets, shrikes, orioles and weavers.

Sleeping

Akagera Game Lodge HOTEL **$$**
(☎252-567805, 078-5201206; www.akageralodge.co.rw; s/d US$65/160, ste from US$245; ❄) Great news for those on an upmarket safari in the region, the Akagera Game Lodge offers four-star comfort for park visitors. Fully renovated by a South African group, this is really more of an upscale hotel than a luxury wildlife lodge, though it's still an excellent base for properly exploring Akagera. Full-board deals are available, a wise choice given there are no restaurants in the park; day trippers should head here for lunch.

Camping CAMPGROUND **$**
(camping US$30) Camping is possible at the park headquarters on the shores of Lake Ihema, but more attractive is the second, basic campsite at Lake Shakani, a few kilometres north. At either place facilities are so minimal as to be verging on nonexistent, although firewood is provided. If you don't partake of any of the park activities the per person rate is raised to US$50 per night.

Information

Parc National de l'Akagera (☎078-3359076; www.rwandatourism.com) The park headquarters is on the shore of Lake Ihema, 4km from the main gate and the Akagera Game Lodge. The only other park entrance is at the other end of the park at the northern Nyungwe gate. Park charges vary depending on the activity; see the listings in the Sights & Activities section for the respective fees.

Getting There & Away

Akagera is really only accessible for those with their own transport. Safari and tour companies in Kigali can arrange a vehicle (see p556), or you can negotiate with private taxis around Kigali.

UNDERSTAND RWANDA

History

For information on Rwanda's history prior to independence in 1962, see p572.

Decolonisation & Independence

Rwanda and neighbouring Burundi were colonised by Germany and later Belgium, both of whom played on ethnic differences to divide and conquer the population. Power was concentrated in the hands of the minority Tutsi, with the Tutsi *mwami* (king) playing the central role in political and legislative decision-making.

In 1956, Mwami Rudahigwa called for independence from Belgium, which influenced Rwanda's colonial occupiers to switch allegiance to the Hutu majority. The Tutsis favoured fast-track independence, while the Hutus wanted the introduction of democracy followed later by independence.

After the death of Rudahigwa in 1959, tribal tensions flared as the 'Hutu Revolution' resulted in the deaths of an estimated 20,000 to 100,000 Tutsis. Another 150,000 Tutsis were driven from the country, and forced to resettle as refugees in Uganda, Kenya and Tanzania.

Following independence in 1962, the Hutu majority came to power under Prime Minister Gregoire Kayibanda, who introduced quotas for Tutsis that limited their opportunities for education and work. In the fresh round of bloodshed that followed, thousands more Tutsis were killed, and tens of thousands fled across the borders.

Intertribal tensions erupted once again in 1972 when tens of thousands of Hutu were massacred in Burundi by the Tutsi-dominated government in reprisal for a coup attempt. The slaughter reignited old hatreds in Rwanda, which prompted Major General Juvenal Habyarimana to oust Kayibanda in 1973.

During the early years of his regime, Habyarimana made progress towards healing tribal divisions, and the country enjoyed relative economic prosperity. However, events unfolding in Uganda in the 1980s were to have a profound impact on the future of Rwanda.

In 1986, Yoweri Museveni became president of Uganda after his National Resistance Army (NRA) fought a brutal bush war to remove General Tito Okello from power. One of Museveni's key lieutenants was the current Rwandan president Paul Kagame, who capitalised on the victory by joining together with other exiled Tutsis to form the Rwandan Patriotic Front (RPF).

The Civil War Erupts

On 1 October 1990, 5000 well-armed soldiers of the RPF invaded Rwanda. All hell broke loose. Two days later at Habyarimana's request, France, Belgium and the DRC flew in troops to help the Rwandan army repel the invasion.

With foreign support assured, the Rwandan army went on a rampage against the Tutsis, as well as any Hutu suspected of having collaborated with the RPF. Thousands of people were shot or hacked to death, and countless others indiscriminately arrested, herded into football stadiums or police stations and left there without food or water for days.

Many died. Congolese Hutu troops joined in the carnage. Once again thousands of Tutsi refugees fled to Uganda. However, the initial setback for the RPF was only temporary as President Museveni was keen to see the repatriation of the now 250,000 Tutsi refugees living in western Uganda.

While he fervently denied such allegations, Museveni allegedly helped to reorganise and re-equip the RPF. In 1991, Kagame's forces invaded Rwanda for a second time, and by 1993 were garrisoned only 25km outside of Kigali.

With Habyarimana backed into a corner, the warring parties were brought to the negotiating table in Arusha, Tanzania. Negotiations stalled, hostilities were renewed, and French troops were flown in to protect foreign nationals in Kigali, though they were accused by the RPF of assisting the Rwandan army. A report released in 2008 by the Rwandan government accused the French government of committing war crimes, though all allegations were fervently denied by the present administration.

Meanwhile, with morale in the Rwandan army fading fast, the RPF launched an all-out offensive on the capital. Once again backed into a corner, Habyarimana invited the RPF to attend a conference of regional presidents. Power-sharing was on the agenda.

Tragically, on 6 April 1994, the airplane carrying Habyarimana and Cyprien Ntaryamira, the president of Burundi, was shot down by a surface-to-air missile while on approach to Kigali airport. It will probably never be known who fired the missile, although most observers believe it was Hutu extremists who had been espousing ethnic cleansing over the airwaves of Radio Télévision Libre des Mille Collines.

Regardless of who was responsible, the event unleashed one of the 20th century's worst explosions of bloodletting.

The Genocide

In the 100 days that followed, extremists among Habyarimana's Hutu political and military supporters embarked on a well-planned 'final solution' to the Tutsi 'problem'. One of the principle architects of the genocide was the cabinet chief of the Ministry of Defence, Colonel Theoneste Bagosora, who had been in charge of training the Interahamwe ('those who stand together') militia for more than a year.

One of Bagosora's first acts was to direct the army to kill the 'moderate' Hutu prime minister, Agathe Uwilingiyimana, as well as 10 Belgian UN peacekeepers. The killing of the UN peacekeepers prompted Belgium to withdraw all of its troops – precisely what Bagosora had calculated – which paved the way for the genocide to begin in earnest.

Rwandan army and Interahamwe death squads ranged at will over the countryside, killing, looting and burning, and roadblocks were set up in every town and city to prevent Tutsis from escaping. Every day, thousands of Tutsi and any Hutu suspected of sympathising with them or their plight were butchered on the spot. The streets of Kigali were littered with dismembered corpses, and the stench of rotting flesh was everywhere.

Those who attempted to take refuge in religious missions or churches did so in vain. In some cases, it was the nuns and priests themselves who betrayed the fugitives to the death squads. Any mission that refused the death squads access was simply blown apart.

Perhaps the most shocking part of the tragedy was the willingness with which ordinary Hutu – men, women and even children as young as 10 years old – joined in the carnage. The perpetrators of the massacre were caught up in a tide of blind hatred, fear and mob mentality, which was inspired, controlled and promoted under the direction of their political and military leaders.

The UN Assistance Mission for Rwanda (UNAMIR) was in Rwanda throughout the genocide, but was powerless to prevent the killing due to an ineffective mandate. Although UN Force Commander Lieutenant General Romeo Dallaire had been warning senior UN staff and diplomats about the coming bloodshed, his warnings went unheeded.

The international community left Rwanda to face its fate. While the RPF eventually succeeded in pushing the Rwandan army and the Interahamwe into the DRC and Burundi, more than one million people were killed, while another two million were huddled in refugee camps across the border.

UNAMIR was finally reinforced and given a more open mandate in July, but it was in the words of Dallaire, 'too much, too late'. The genocide was already over – the RPF had taken control of Kigali.

The Aftermath

Of course, that is far from the end of the story. Within a year of the RPF victory, a legal commission was set up in Arusha, Tanzania, to try those accused of involvement in the genocide. However, many of the main perpetrators – the Interahamwe and former senior army officers – fled into exile out of the reach of the RPF.

Some went to Kenya, where they enjoyed the protection of President Moi, who long refused to hand them over. Others – including Colonel Theoneste Bagosora, the principle architect of the genocide, and Ferdinand Nahimana, the director of the notorious Radio Télévision Libre des Mille Collines, which actively encouraged Hutus to butcher Tutsis – fled to Cameroon where they enjoyed the protection of that country's security boss, John Fochive. However, when Fochive was sacked by the newly elected president of Cameroon, Paul Biya, the Rwandan exiles were arrested.

Of greater importance were the activities of the Interahamwe and former army personnel in the refugee camps of the DRC and Tanzania. Determined to continue their fight against the RPF, they spread fear among the refugees that if they returned to Rwanda, they would be killed. When Rwanda began to demand the repatriation of the refugees, the grip of the Interahamwe on the camps was so complete that few dared move.

What was of most concern to the RPF was that the Interahamwe was using the refugee camps as staging posts for raids into Rwanda, with the complicity of the Congolese army. By 1996, Rwanda was openly warning the DRC that if these raids did not stop, the consequences would be dire.

The raids continued, and the RPF held true to its threat by mounting a lightning strike two-day campaign into the DRC, targeting one of the main refugee camps north of Goma. The Interahamwe fled deep into the jungles of the Congo, which allowed hundreds of thousands of refugees to return home to Rwanda.

Events changed in October 1996 when a guerrilla movement known as the Alliance of Democratic Forces for the Liberation of Congo-Zaïre, led by Laurent Kabila, emerged with the secret support of Rwanda and Uganda. The rebels, ably supported by Rwandan and Ugandan regulars, swept through the eastern DRC, and by December were in control of every town and city in the region.

The Congolese army, alongside the Interahamwe and former Rwandan army personnel, retreated west in disarray towards Kisangani, looting and pillaging as they went. However, the grip the Interahamwe had on the refugee camps was finally broken, which allowed the remaining refugees to stream back into Rwanda, not only from the DRC, but also from Tanzania.

Faced with a huge refugee resettlement task, the government began to build new villages throughout the country. Huge tracts of Parc National de l'Akagera were de-gazetted as a national park and given over to this 'villagisation' program, along with much of the northwest region, which had previously hosted some of the most intense battles of the civil war.

The Healing Begins

Rwanda has done a remarkable job healing its wounds, and has achieved an astonishing level of safety and security in a remarkably short space of time – albeit with considerable help from a guilty international community that ignored the country in its darkest hour. Visiting Kigali today, it is hard to believe the horror that swept across this land in 1994, though the scars are much more visible in the countryside.

On the international front, however, things have been rather less remarkable. In 1998, Rwanda and Uganda joined forces to oust their former ally Laurent Kabila. What ensued was Africa's first great war, sucking in as many as nine neighbours at its height, and costing an estimated three to five million deaths, mostly from disease and starvation.

Rwanda and Uganda soon fell out, squabbling over the rich resources that were there for the plunder in the DRC. Rwanda backed the Rally for Congolese Democracy, Uganda the Movement for the Liberation of the Congo, and the two countries fought out a brutal and prolonged proxy war.

Peace treaties were signed in 2002, and foreign forces were withdrawn from the DRC, though if and when an international inquiry is launched, Rwanda may find itself facing accusations of war crimes. Rwanda's motives for entering the fray were to wipe out remnants of the Interahamwe militia and former soldiers responsible for the genocide, but somewhere along the line, elements in the army may have lost sight of the mission.

Back on the domestic front, Paul Kagame assumed the presidency in 2000, and was overwhelmingly endorsed at the ballot box in presidential elections in 2003 and 2010 that saw him take 93% of the vote.

Meanwhile, the search for justice continues at home and abroad (see the boxed text, p548).

An Optimistic Future

Looking at the bigger picture, Rwanda remains the home of two tribes, the Hutu and the Tutsi. The Hutu presently outnumber the Tutsi by more than four to one, and while the RPF government is one of national unity with a number of Hutu representatives, it's viewed in some quarters as a Tutsi government ruling over a predominantly Hutu population.

However, the RPF government has done an impressive job of promoting reconciliation and restoring trust between the two communities. This is no small achievement after the horrors that were inflicted on the Tutsi community during the genocide of 1994, especially since it would have been all too easy for the RPF to embark on a campaign of revenge and reprisal.

On the contrary, Kagame and his government are attempting to build a society with a place for everyone, regardless of tribe. There are no more Tutsis, no more Hutus, only Rwandans. Idealistic perhaps, but it is realistically the best hope for the future.

The Culture

The National Psyche

Tribal conflict has torn Rwanda apart during much of the independence period, culminating in the horrific genocide that unfolded in 1994. With that said, there are basically two schools of thought when it comes to looking at Rwandan identity.

The colonial approach of the Belgians was to divide and rule, issuing ID cards that divvied up the population along strict tribal lines. They tapped the Tutsis as leaders to help control the Hutu majority, building on the foundations of pre-colonial society in which the Tutsi were considered more dominant. Later, as independence approached, they switched sides, pitting Hutu against Tutsi in a new conflict, which simmered on and off until the 1990s when it exploded onto the world stage.

In the new Rwanda, the opposite is true. Tribal identities have been systematically eliminated, and everyone is now treated as a Rwandan. The new government is at pains to present a singular identity, and blames the Belgians for categorising the country along tribal lines that set the stage for the savagery that followed. Rwanda was a peaceful place beforehand: Hutu and Tutsi lived side by side for generations, and intermarriage was common – or so the story goes.

The truth, as always, is probably somewhere in between. Rwanda was no oasis before the colonial powers arrived, but it was a sophisticated state compared to many others in Africa at the time. However, Tutsis probably had a better time of it than Hutus, something that the Belgians were able to exploit as they sought control.

But, it is true to say that there was no history of major bloodshed between the two peoples before 1959, and the foundations of this violence were laid by the Belgian insistence on ethnic identity and their cynical political manipulation. The leaders of the genocide merely took this policy to its extreme, first promoting tribal differences, and then playing on them to manipulate a malleable population.

Paul Kagame is trying to put the past behind, and create a new Rwanda for Rwan-

THE SLOW HAND OF JUSTICE

Following a slow and shaky start, the **International Criminal Tribunal for Rwanda** (ICTR; www.ictr.org) has managed to net most of the major suspects wanted for involvement in the 1994 genocide.

The tribunal was established in Arusha, Tanzania, in 1995, but was initially impeded in its quest for justice by the willingness of several African countries to protect suspects. Countries such as Cameroon, the DRC and Kenya long harboured Kigali's most wanted, frustrating the Rwandan authorities in their attempts to seek justice. However, due to changes in their attitude or government, many of the former ministers (including the former prime minister, Jean Kambanda) of the interim cabinet that presided over the country during the genocide have now been arrested.

While the architects of the tragedy are tried at the ICTR, Rwanda's judicial system suddenly found itself facing a backlog that would take a century to clear. With too many cases (in excess of 120,000) and too few jails to humanely detain such a large percentage of the population, an age-old solution was revived.

Across the country thousands of *gacaca* courts were set up and hundreds of thousands of judges appointed. Modelled on traditional hearings that were headed by village elders, these tribunals are empowered to identify and categorise suspects. Category 1 suspects who are thought to have organised, encouraged or instigated the genocide are remanded for processing in the formal judicial system. The *gacaca* court tries category 2 and 3 suspects, those accused of murder, bodily injury or causing property damage. Each court must contain a minimum of 15 community-elected judges and be witnessed by 100 citizens. It is hoped that these small courts will not only find the guilty but provide closure for the families of their victims and help relieve the burden the larger courts face.

dans. Forget the past? No. But do learn from it, and move on to create a new spirit of national unity.

All this of course will take time, maybe a generation or more, but what has been achieved in just over a decade is astonishing. Rwandans are taking pride in their country once more, investment is on the boil, and people are optimistic about their future. The real challenge, however, is to make sure the countryside comes along for the ride.

Daily Life

Urban Rwanda is a very sophisticated place – people follow a Mediterranean pattern of starting early before breaking off for a siesta or a long and boozy lunch. Late dinners inevitably lead into drinking and socialising that sometimes doesn't wind down until the early morning.

The rhythm of rural life is very different and follows the sun. People work long hours from dawn until dusk, but also take a break during the hottest part of the day. However, it is a hard life for women in the countryside, who seem burdened with the lion's share of the work, while many menfolk sit around drinking and discussing.

Faith is an important rock in the lives of many Rwandan people, with Christianity firmly rooted as the dominant religion. Churches from different denominations in Rwanda were tainted by their association with the genocide in 1994, though that doesn't seem to have dampened people's devotion to the faith.

Like many countries in Africa, Rwanda actively promotes universal primary education. Despite suffering terribly during the genocide, the education system continues to improve and the literacy rate now stands at around 71%, up from 58% in 1991.

Economy

Rwanda's economy was decimated during the genocide – production ground to a halt, and foreign investors pulled out all together. However, the current government has done a commendable job of stimulating the economy, which is now fairly stable and boasts steady growth and low inflation. Foreign investors are once again doing business in Kigali, and there are building projects springing up all over the capital. Tourism too has rebounded and is again the country's leading foreign exchange earner.

The agricultural sector is the principle employer and a major export earner, contributing around 42% of Rwanda's GDP. Coffee is by far the largest export, accounting for about 75% of export income, while tea and pyrethrum (a natural insecticide) are also important crops. However, the vast majority of farmers live subsistence lives, growing plantain, sweet potato, beans, cassava, sorghum and maize.

Population

The population exceeded 11 million in 2011, which gives Rwanda one of the highest population densities of any country in Africa. While tribal identities are very much a taboo subject in Rwanda, the population is believed to be about 85% Hutu, 15% Tutsi and 1% Twa. The Twa is a Central Africa indigenous group that has suffered from discrimination over the generations, though is slowly gaining a political and cultural foothold.

Sport

Football is Rwanda's national obsession and the Wasps, as the national team are known, are a growing force in the sport. In 2004 they qualified for the African Nations Cup for the first time.

Religion

About 65% of the population are Christians of various sects (Catholicism is predominant), a further 25% follow tribal religions, often with a dash of Christianity, and the remaining 10% are Muslim.

Arts

Dance

Rwanda's most famous dancers are the Intore troupe – their warrior-like displays are accompanied by a trance-like drumbeat similar to that of the famous Tambourinaires in Burundi (see p562).

Film

Hotel Rwanda put Rwanda on the map for movie-goers the world over. Although it was shot in South Africa, it tells the story of Hotel des Mille Collines (p507) manager Paul Rusesabagina, played by Don Cheadle, turning this luxury hotel into a temporary haven for thousands fleeing the erupting genocide. *100 Days* and the HBO miniseries *Sometimes in April* also convey the story of the Rwandan genocide through stark yet powerful narratives.

Gorillas in the Mist is based on the autobiography of Dian Fossey (p521), who worked with the rare mountain gorillas in Parc National des Volcans. This is essential viewing for anyone visiting the gorillas.

Environment

The Land

In the 'Land of a Thousand Hills', it is hardly surprising to find that endless mountains stretch into the infinite horizon. Rwanda's 26,338 sq km of land is one of the most densely populated places on earth, and almost every available piece of land is under cultivation (except the national parks). Since most of the country is mountainous, this involves a good deal of terracing, and the banded hillsides are similar to those seen in Nepal or the High Atlas of Morocco. Coffee and tea plantations take up considerable areas of land.

National Parks & Reserves

Due to its small size and high demand for cultivatable land, Rwanda only has a small network of national parks. The most popular protected area (and the focus of most visits to Rwanda) is Parc National des Volcans (p519), a string of brooding volcanoes that provides a home for the rare mountain gorilla. Nyungwe Forest National Park (p535), Rwanda's newest national park, is a tropical montane forest that is one of the richest primate destinations in the region. Parc National de l'Akagera (p542) is the third of Rwanda's parks, but is sadly a shadow of its former self due to habitat destruction during the civil war as well as postwar 'villagisation'. That said, Akagera has staged an impressive comeback in recent years, and wildlife populations are stabilising and flourishing again.

Environmental Issues

Soil erosion, resulting from the overuse of land, is the most serious problem confronting Rwanda today. The terracing system in the country is fairly anarchic, and unlike much of Southeast Asia, the lack of coordinated water management has wiped out much of the topsoil on the slopes. This is potentially catastrophic for a country with too many people in too small a space, as it points to a food-scarcity problem in the future.

Population density has also had a detrimental effect on the country's national park system, reducing Parc National des Volcans by half in 1969 and Parc National de l'Akagera by two-thirds in 1998.

Food & Drink

In the rural areas of Rwanda, food is very similar to that in other East African countries. Popular meats include tilapia (Nile perch), goat, chicken and beef brochettes (kebabs), though the bulk of most meals are centred on ugali (maize meal), *matoke* (cooked plantains) and 'Irish' potatoes. In the cities, however, Rwanda's French roots are evident in the *plat du jour* (plate of the day), which is usually excellently prepared and presented continental-inspired cuisine.

Drinking tap water is not recommended in Rwanda, though bottled water is cheap and widely available. Soft drinks (sodas) and the local beers, Primus (720mL) and Mulzig (330mL and 660mL), are available everywhere, as is the local firewater, *konyagi*. Wines (both South African and European) are generally only available in upmarket restaurants and hotels, though they can be quite expensive. A pleasant, nonalcoholic alternative is the purplish juice from the tree tomato (tamarillo), which is a sweet and tasty concoction that somewhat defies explanation – give it a try!

SURVIVAL GUIDE

Directory A–Z

Accommodation

The only fully functioning campsites in the country are at Nyungwe Forest National Park and Parc National de l'Akagera. At both, facilities are next to non-existent, which means that you will need to bring everything with you and be entirely self-sufficient.

Generally, budget accommodation in Rwanda is more expensive than elsewhere in East Africa, and it can be a real challenge to find somewhere that is both cheap and central to stay in Kigali.

Cheap hotels are often noisy – largely due to the fact that most have attached bars and unless you find the sound of bar banter soothing, it can be difficult to sleep. However, they are essentially clean, if characterised by missing toilet seats and lukewarm (if not completely cold) showers that tend to drench the entire bathroom. For reasons that defy explanation, shower curtains have failed to catch on in Rwanda.

Mission- and church-run hostels are quieter and cleaner than most other forms of budget accommodation as they seem to attract an exceptionally conscientious type of manager who takes the old adage 'cleanliness is next to godliness' fairly seriously.

Top-end hotels and ecolodges are found mostly found in Kigali, Gisenyi and near Musanze (Ruhengeri) on the edge of Parc National des Volcans and are modern with professional service.

Activities

BIRDWATCHING

Birdwatching in Rwanda may not be in the same league as the rest of East Africa, but there are some good opportunities for ornithologists in Nyungwe Forest National Park, where a host of Albertine Rift endemics can be seen. Another decent spot is Parc National de l'Akagera, in the east of the country, which offers an alternative range of savannah birds.

HIKING & TREKKING

Trekking is beginning to take off again in Rwanda. As the waiting list for gorilla permits grows longer in peak season, more and more travellers are taking the opportunity to climb and trek the volcanoes in Parc National des Volcans. There is also an excellent network of walking trails at Nyungwe Forest National Park, the largest tropical montane forest in East Africa.

PRIMATE TRACKING

Without a doubt, this forms the number-one attraction for all visitors to Rwanda: an encounter with the enigmatic mountain gorillas is simply magical. It's possible to track the mountain gorillas in Parc National des Volcans throughout the year. For more information on tracking the gorillas in East Africa, see p32.

PRACTICALITIES

» Rwanda uses the metric system (distances are in kilometres).

» Electricity in Rwanda is 240V, 50 cycles, and plugs are mainly two-pin.

» The English-language *New Times* is published several times a week, plus the Ugandan *New Vision* and *Monitor* are also available.

» Radio Rwanda is the government-run station, broadcasting in Kinyarwanda, French, Swahili and English.

» TV Rwandaise (TVR) is the state-owned broadcaster.

While not as popular as the gorillas, endangered golden monkeys can also be tracked in Parc National des Volcans.

Chimpanzee tracking is beginning to take off at Nyungwe, though sightings are not as common as in Uganda as habituation is still ongoing. There are also huge troops of colobus monkeys in Nyungwe that are easy to spot from the well-marked walking trails that cut through the forest.

WILDLIFE WATCHING

The only opportunity for wildlife drives is in Parc National de l'Akagera, though with wildlife numbers still recovering from years of conflict, it is not quite the Kenya or Tanzania experience yet.

Festivals & Events

For information on Kwita Izina, the gorilla naming ceremony, see the boxed text on p523.

Internet Access

Internet access is widely available in Kigali, as well as on a more limited basis in Gisenyi, Huye (Butare), Cyangugu, Kibuye and Musanze (Ruhengeri). It generally costs between RFr500 and RFr1000 per hour. An increasing number of hotels and restaurants offer free wi-fi.

If you're travelling with a laptop or tablet computer and require mobile internet access, an MTN modem stick costs RFr18,000 and data bundles cost RFr1500/6000/10,000 for 50/250/500MB.

Maps

It's difficult to get hold of decent maps of Rwanda before arriving in the country. The best map currently is *Rwanda & Burundi – International Travel Map* by **ITMB Publishing** (www.itmb.ca) at a scale of 1:300,000. Once in Kigali, track down a copy of the free **Eye Magazine** (www.theeye.co.rw), which has several maps and a directory of tourism-related businesses. You may also find it useful to get hold of the *Tanzania – Rwanda – Burundi Map* by Nelles.

Money

The unit of currency is the Rwandan franc (RFr). It is divided into 100 centimes. Notes come in RFr100, RFr500, RFr1000, RFr5000 and RFr10,000 denominations. Coins come in RFr10, RFr20 and RFr50.

ATMS

Banks in Kigali have a network of ATMs, but most are not yet wired up for international transactions (despite Visa signs at some). The notable exceptions are the **Bank of Kigali** (www.bk.rw) and **Ecobank** (www.ecobank.com), which both have ATMs that will accept international Visa cards. Unfortunately, the only things ATMs were giving out with MasterCards were headaches.

WHAT'S IN A NAME?

In 2006, following an administrative reorganisation of Rwanda's 12 former provinces, maps were redrawn on the more neutral divisions: North, South, East, West and Kigali. It was deemed that prior provincial boundaries were too closely associated with tribal divisions and inheritably stained with the atrocities of the genocide.

During this process, smaller districts within these provinces were also created and, along with their capitals, renamed. Since then confusion has reigned. On the ground most people are happy to promote the new titles but ambiguity arises when some governmental maps are still published using the superseded designations. In this guide we've used the newer names with the former names written in parentheses.

CASH

Banks throughout the country can exchange US dollars or euros, although they can be very slow to do so. Most people use the foreign exchange bureaus in Kigali instead and this is quite safe.

Rwanda, like other African countries, is very particular on which notes it will or will not accept. Anything older than 2006 or deemed too dirty, crinkled or tatty will be meet with scorn, and your pleas to have it changed, with indifference.

CREDIT CARDS

Credit cards are generally only accepted in relatively expensive hotels and restaurants in Kigali, Gisenyi and Musanze (Ruhengeri). It is possible to make cash withdrawals against credit cards at some banks in the capital (both Visa and MasterCard), though you can expect to pay a hefty commission (around 3.5%) and lose a lot of time waiting for the privilege.

TIPPING

Tipping is common in the cities these days due to the large international presence. Rwandan salaries are low and a tip of about 10% will be appreciated.

TRAVELLERS CHEQUES

Despite what your travel agent may have told you, travellers cheques are not accepted in Rwanda.

Post

Postal rates for postcards going overseas are around RFr275 to Europe and Africa, RFr450 to everywhere else.

Public Holidays

New Year's Day 1 January

Democracy Day 8 January

Easter (Good Friday, Holy Saturday and Easter Monday) March/April

Labour Day 1 May

Ascension Thursday May

Whit Monday May

National Day 1 July

Peace & National Unity Day 5 July

Harvest Festival 1 August

Assumption 15 August

Culture Day 8 September

Kamarampaka Day 25 September

A NEW LANGUAGE

In 2008, teachers woke to a shock. A curt government decree required that public school teachers throughout Rwanda were to instruct their students in English – a tongue that few spoke with proficiency. Prior to this, early grades had been taught in Kinyarwanda and senior classes in French. From 2011 all classes at primary (from fourth grade onwards), secondary and university levels have been conducted in English, whether or not the students – or their teachers – were prepared.

Officially, the reason cited for dropping French as the national language was based on economics. English is the international language of commerce, and since Rwanda is surrounded by anglophone neighbours, a switch to English is hoped to attract foreign investment and open up future opportunities for generations to come.

Others feel the abrupt move reflects a cooling of the close relations Rwanda once had with France. Leading up to the genocide, Rwanda's Hutu-supremacist leader Juvenal Habyarimana received aid and arms from the French. (An error of judgement not easily forgotten by the Uganda-bred English-speaking rebels led by current president Paul Kagame.)

So while the French are out, the English are in and not just linguistically. On 29 November 2009, Rwanda, although it lacks any British colonial ties, joined the Commonwealth.

Armed Forces Day 26 October

All Saints' Day 1 November

Christmas Day 25 December

Safe Travel

Mention Rwanda to most people and they think of it as a highly dangerous place. However, the reality today is very different, and stability has returned to all parts of the country.

That said, it is worth checking security conditions before entering Rwanda as this is still an unstable region of the world. There is always the remote possibility of Interahamwe rebels re-entering the country, or problems spilling over from the neighbouring DRC or Burundi.

Urban Rwanda is undoubtedly one of the safer places to be in this region, and Kigali is a genuine contender for the safest capital in Africa. However, like in any big city the world over, take care at night.

Never take photographs of anything connected with the government or the military (post offices, banks, bridges, border crossings, barracks, prisons and dams) – cameras can and will be confiscated. In fact, take care of where you point your camera anywhere in the country, as most Rwandans are very sensitive to who or what you are snapping.

Telephone

There are three main operators in Rwanda: MTN, Tigo and Rwandatel.

In 2009 all old six-digital numbers were extended by adding the prefix ☎252 to landline numbers, ☎078 and ☎072 to mobile numbers, and ☎255 to CDMA numbers. There are currently no area codes in Rwanda. The international country code is ☎250.

For calls within Rwanda, the easiest option is to use one of the street kiosks. The call will be metered and you pay the attendant when finished. International calls can be made from Kigali's main post office.

An MTN (which has the better network) SIM card costs RFr1000 and includes RFr500 worth of call-time credit. Pre-pay top-up cards are sold everywhere from street vendors to MTN branded stores and start from as little as RFr500. Mobile phone calls cost about RFr1 per second although rates vary depending on when you call.

Time

If you're crossing borders, be advised that Rwanda (and Burundi) is one hour behind the rest of East Africa.

Tourist Information

In line with the government's decision to drop French as a national language, the Office Rwandais du Tourisme et des Parcs Nationaux (ORTPN) has been rebranded as the Rwanda Development Board (RDB). Currently it has two offices, one in Kigali (p514) and another in Gisenyi (p529). Neither is particularly well resourced.

Visas

Visas are required by everyone except nationals of Germany, South Africa, Sweden, the UK, the USA and other East African countries. Everyone else needs to apply for a visa in their country of residence at a Rwandan embassy or high commission. These visas (called class T2) cost US$50, are valid for 90 days and are good for multiple entries within that time.

If Rwanda isn't represented in your country then you need to register online at **Rwanda Immigration** (www.migration.gov.rw) before you travel. The website is a little confusing (the exact page you're after is www.migration.gov.rw/singleform.php), but once you've submitted the online form you'll receive your letter of entitlement within three days. Present this letter at the border along with the US$30 fee to obtain a single-entry, 30-day visa (called a V1 visa). It is no longer possible to obtain a visa on arrival without first obtaining the aforementioned letter of entitlement.

Two points to note: first, although the online form asks you to attach a letter of invitation this is not a compulsory prerequisite and it's fine to skip this section; second, if things go awry you'll have a devil of a time trying to make contact with Rwanda Immigration – if you need to follow up with them, it's best done through Facebook (search Rwanda migration).

VISA EXTENSIONS

If you've arrived on a V1 visa and need to extend it or apply for a multi-entry visa you must do so at **Rwanda Immigration** (☎078-8152222; www.migration.gov.rw; Blvd de l'Umuganda; ⏲application submission 7-11.30am Mon-Wed & Fri, visa collection 1-4.30pm Mon-Wed & Fri, 1-3.30pm Thu) in Kigali's Kacyiru district, about 7km northeast of the city centre near the American Embassy. Bring the appropriate form (available online), a passport-sized photo, your passport, a letter of introduction or a letter addressed to the Director of Immigration explaining why you require a visa, and RFr30,000. Extensions take five days to issue.

Work

With all the international money sloshing around Rwanda, one might be forgiven for thinking it would be easy to pick up some work here. However, most international organisations tend to recruit professionals from home and in the local community. Anyone considering looking for work must secure a work permit from a Rwandan embassy before entering the country.

Getting There & Away

For information on getting to Rwanda from outside East Africa, see p650.

Entering the Country

Yellow-fever vaccination certificates are in theory compulsory for entry or exit, but in reality are rarely requested.

Air

Gregoire Kayibanda International Airport is located at Kanombe, 10km east of Kigali's city centre. Note that most of the discounted air fares available in Europe and North America use Nairobi (Kenya) as the gateway to East Africa. Air tickets bought in Rwanda for international flights are expensive, and compare poorly with what is on offer in Nairobi or Kampala (Uganda).

AIRLINES

Air Uganda (Map p508; ☎252-577928; www.air-uganda.com; Union Trade Centre, Ave de la Paix) Connects Kigali with Entebbe International Airport near Kampala (Uganda).

Kenya Airways (Map p508; ☎252-501652, 072-7555000; www.kenya-airways.com; Union Trade Centre, Ave de la Paix) Connects Kigali with Bujumbura (Burundi) and Nairobi (Kenya).

RwandAir (Map p508; ☎252-503687; www.rwandair.com; Union Trade Centre, Ave de la Paix) Rwanda's national airline has flights to Libreville (Gabon), Brazzaville (the DRC), Kampala (Uganda), Nairobi (Kenya), Mombasa (Kenya), Johannesburg (South Africa), Bujumbura (Burundi), Dubai (United Arab Emirates), Addis Ababa (Ethiopia), Dar es Salaam (Tanzania), Kilimanjaro (Tanzania) and Brussels (Belgium).

Land

Rwanda shares land borders with Burundi, the DRC, Tanzania and Uganda.

BURUNDI

The main border crossing between Rwanda and Burundi is via Huye (Butare) and Kayanza, on the Kigali–Bujumbura road, which is sealed pretty much all the way. The border post is called Kayanza Haut and Burundian transit visas are available on arrival. The safest way of reaching Bujumbura is to take a bus from Rwanda directly to the capital. It is certainly unsafe to linger in outlying towns.

There is also a direct road between Cyangugu and Bujumbura. There are no direct buses between the two although you can catch a bus from Cyangugu to Rugombo (RFr1500, one hour), from where a minibus can take you to Bujumbura (you may have to change in Cibitoke).

TANZANIA

Four bus companies connect Kigali to Mwanza daily (RFr8000 to RFr9000, 12 hours). It's also possible to go in stages. International, Sotra and Stella buses go from Kigali to Rusumo (RFr3000, three hours), where you'll need to walk across the Kagera river bridge. Once across, there are pick-up taxis to the tiny town (and former refugee camp) of Benako (marked as Kasulo on some maps), about 20km southeast, from where there are onward connections towards Lake Victoria.

THE DRC

There are two crossings between Rwanda and the DRC, both are on the shores of Lake Kivu. To the north is the crossing between Gisenyi and Goma; this is considered safer than the southern border between Cyangugu and Bukavu. Providing that the DRC remains stable and you have prearranged visas, the crossings are relatively straightforward.

UGANDA

There are two main crossing points for foreigners: between Kigali and Kabale via Gatuna/Katuna (called Gatuna on the Rwandan side, Katuna on the Ugandan side), and between Musanze (Ruhengeri) and Kisoro via Cyanika.

There are lots of minibuses running between Kigali and the border at Gatuna (RFr1300, 1½ hours) throughout the day. There are also plenty of shared taxis (USh4000) and special-hire taxis (USh20,000 for the whole car) travelling back and forth between Katuna and Kabale.

From Musanze (Ruhengeri) to Kisoro via Cyanika the road is in excellent shape on the Rwandan side and in rather poor condition on the Ugandan side. Minibuses link either side of the border with Musanze (RFr1000, 25km).

LEAVE YOUR PLASTIC BAGS AT HOME

In an effort to preserve the natural beauty of Rwanda, the government enforces a strict ban on plastic bags throughout the country. Police are particularly vigilant at border crossings, and you will be searched and possibly fined if contraband is found.

Getting Around

Air

RwandAir (Map p508; ☎252-503687; www.rwandair.com; Union Trade Centre, Ave de la Paix) recently introduced domestic flights between Kigali and Gisenyi.

Bus & Minibus

Rwanda has efficient and reliable public transport. Privately run buses cover the entire country, and with scheduled departure times you won't find yourself waiting for hours while the driver scouts for more passengers. Tickets are bought in advance from a ticket office which is usually (although not always) the point of departure.

You will also find plenty of well-maintained, modern minibuses serving all the main routes. Head to the bus stand in any town between dawn and about 3pm and it is quite easy to find one heading to Kigali and nearby towns. Destinations are displayed in the front window and the fares are fixed (you can ask other passengers to be sure). However, anyone who gets stuck somewhere late in the afternoon is going to have to pay top price for the privilege of getting out. Minibuses leave when full. Neither buses nor minibuses charge extra for baggage.

The only major unsealed roads are those running along the shore of Lake Kivu and some secondary roads in remoter parts of the country.

Car & Motorcycle

Cars are suitable for most of the country's main roads, but those planning to explore Parc National de l'Akagera or follow the shores of Lake Kivu might be better off with a 4WD.

Car hire isn't well established in Rwanda, but most travel agents and tour operators in Kigali can organise something.

INTERNATIONAL BUSES

Belvèderé (Map p508; Nyabugogo bus terminal & Ave de la Paix, Kigali) Operates an 8am and 10am service to Bujumbura (Burundi) from Kigali (RFr6000, six hours) that also collects passengers in Huye (Butare; RFr6000, four hours).

Horizon Coaches (horizon@ymail.com) Gisenyi (Market); Kigali (Map p508; Nyabugogo bus terminal) Has a daily 4.30pm service to Kampala (Uganda) from Gisenyi (RFr8000, 12½ hours) and more frequent services from Kigali to Kampala (RFr6000, six hours) and Bujumbura (Rfr6000, four hours) via Huye (Butare).

International (Map p508; Nyabugogo bus terminal & off Ave du Commerce, Kigali) Has buses to Rusumo (RFr3000, three hours) on the border with Tanzania.

Kampala Coach (Map p508; www.kampalacoach.com; Nyabugogo bus terminal, Kigali) There is also a booking office in the Union Trade Centre in Kigali but buses leave from the depot opposite the Nyabugogo minibus station next to the Kobil petrol station. Morning and evening buses run to Kampala (RFr8000, eight hours), Jinja (RFr10,000, 11 hours) and on to Nairobi (RFr23,000, 24 hours) via Nakuru (RFr23,000, 20 hours) or Eldoret (RFr23,000, 16½ hours). If you're travelling to Arusha (RFr30,000, 28 hours), Moshi (RFr35,000, 30 hours) or Dar es Salaam (RFr45,000, two days) in Tanzania, you will change buses in Kampala. There is also a Wednesday and Saturday service to Bujumbura (RFr5000, six hours).

New Yahoo Express (Map p508; off Ave du Commerce, Kigali) Has 6.30am, 8am and 9am buses to Bujumbura (RFr6000, six hours).

Sotra Tours (Map p508; Nyabugogo bus terminal & off Ave du Commerce, Kigali) Has buses to Rusumo (RFr3000, three hours) on the border with Tanzania.

Stella (Map p508; off Ave du Commerce, Kigali) Also heads east to Rusumo (RFr3000, three hours).

Ferry

Before the civil war, there were ferries on Lake Kivu that connected the Rwandan ports of Cyangugu, Kibuye and Gisenyi, but services have not been resumed. Speedboat charters are currently the only option between these ports, but they are prohibitively expensive.

Local Transport

TAXI

Taxis are only really necessary in Kigali. It's also possible to find the odd taxi in most other major towns.

MOTO-TAXI

Most towns are compact enough to walk around but otherwise the *moto-taxi* is a good bet. It's just a motorcycle, but the driver can usually sling a pack across the petrol tank. They're generally fast but safe and there's usually a helmet for the passenger.

Tours

Most of the country's tour operators are based in Kigali, and while they specialise in multiday excursions and gorilla tracking – the mainstay of Rwanda's tourism – they can arrange any number of day trips on request.

Following are some trustworthy operators, but for a more extensive list than we have space for here, visit the website of **Rwanda Tours and Travel Association** (www.rttarwanda.org) or **The Eye Magazine** (www.theeye.co.rw).

Attractive Safaris (Map p508; ☎078-8487682; www.attractivesafaris.com; Place de l'Unité Nationale roundabout, La Bonne Adresse House, Kigali) A small local operator.

Bizidanny Tours & Safaris (Map p508; ☎078-8501461; www.bizidanny.com; Ave du Commerce, Kigali) This small operator runs individually customised tours throughout the country.

Primate Safaris (Map p508; ☎252-503428; www.primatesafaris-rwanda.com; Ave de la Paix, Kigali) Organises all-inclusive safaris to Rwandan and Ugandan national parks.

Volcanoes Safaris (Map p508; ☎252-502452; www.volcanoessafaris.com; Hotel des Mille Collines, Ave de la République, Kigali) Probably the most professional operator in Rwanda, Volcanoes Safaris runs customised trips and owns the exclusive Virunga Lodge in Parc National des Volcans.

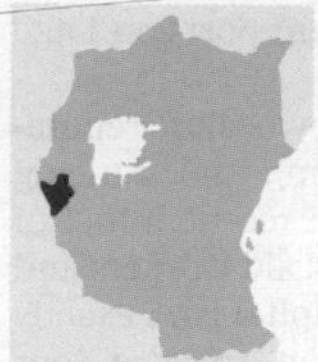

Burundi

Includes »

Bujumbura 558
Around Bujumbura 564
Understand Burundi 564
History 564
The Culture.................... 565
Economy 566
Environment................. 566
Survival Guide 566
Directory A–Z 566
Getting There & Away .. 567
Getting Around............ 568

Best of Nature

- Saga Beach (p559)
- Chutes de la Karera (p564)
- Source du Nil (p564)

Best of Culture

- Les Tambourinaires drummers (p562)
- Bujumbura Central Market (p559)
- Musée National de Gitega (p564)

Why Go?

Tiny Burundi is an incongruous mix of soaring mountains, languid lakeside communities and a tragic past blighted by ethnic conflict.

When civil war broke out in 1993, the economy was shattered and the tourist industry succumbed to a quick death. Since then, many of the upcountry attractions have been off limits, including the southernmost source of the Nile and the ancient forest of Parc National de la Kibira.

Now the word is out that the war is over, Burundi is receiving a trickle of travellers and the country is safer now than it has been for years. Its steamy capital, Bujumbura, has a lovely location on the shores of Lake Tanganyika, and just outside the city are some of the finest inland beaches on the continent. Burundians also have an irrepressible joie de vivre, and their smiles are as infections as a rhythm laid down by a Les Tambourinaires drummer.

When to Go

Bujumbura

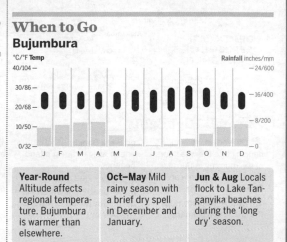

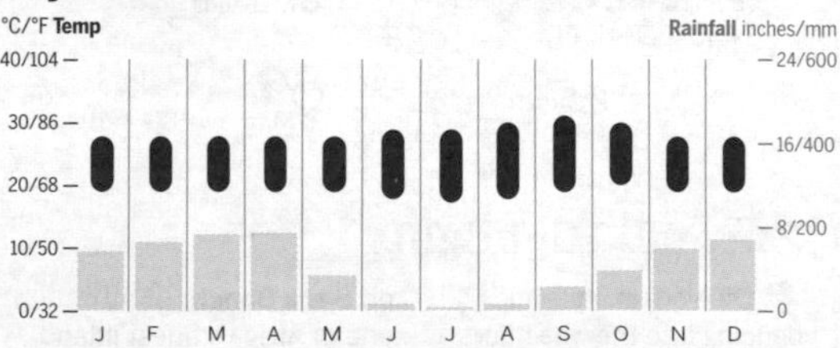

Year-Round Altitude affects regional temperature. Bujumbura is warmer than elsewhere.

Oct–May Mild rainy season with a brief dry spell in December and January.

Jun & Aug Locals flock to Lake Tanganyika beaches during the 'long dry' season.

BUJUMBURA

Frozen in time, thanks to more than a decade of conflict, there has been almost no development in Burundi's capital since the 1980s, a stark contrast to the changes in Kigali (Rwanda) and Kampala (Uganda) to the north. Indeed, Bujumbura retains much of its grandiose colonial town planning, with wide boulevards and imposing public buildings, and continues to function as one of the most important ports on Lake Tanganyika.

'Buj' has earned a freewheelin' reputation for its dining, drinking and dancing scene, especially given the recent influx of international peacekeepers, aid workers and foreign officials. But the capital isn't exactly the safest city in the region, so keep your wits about you; especially once the sun goes down.

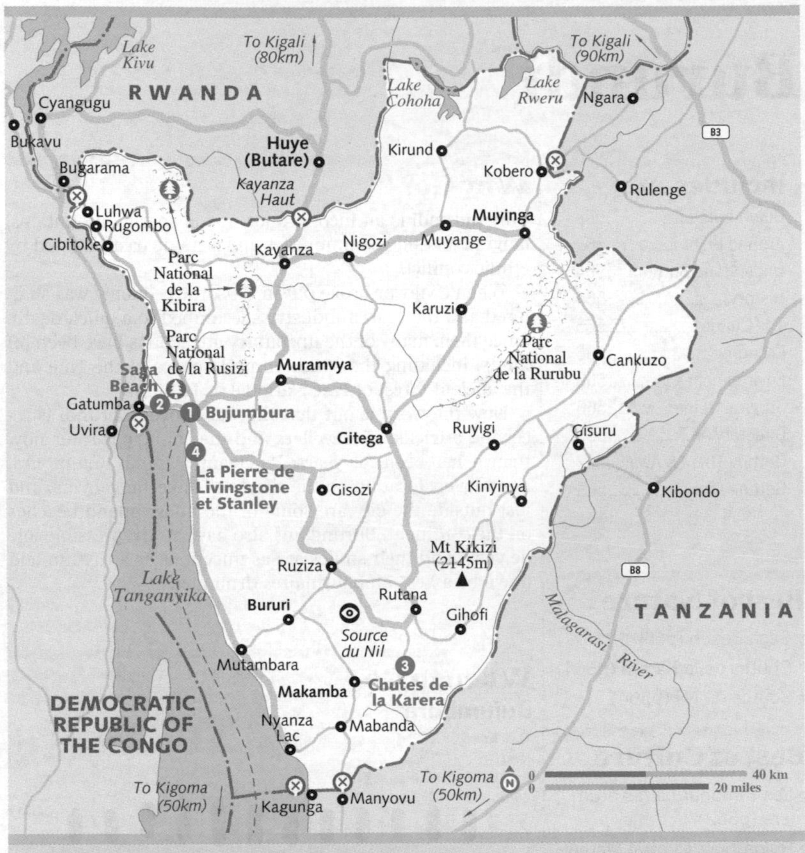

Burundi Highlights

1. Dine out in style and dancing into the wee hours of the morning in Burundi's surprisingly vibrant capital **Bujumbura** (p558)

2. Down a cold one under the shade of a palm tree on **Saga Beach** (p559), one of Africa's finest inland beaches

3. Take a cold shower under one of four waterfalls at the **Chutes de la Karera** (p564)

4. Travel to Burundi's very own pyramid, a memorial marking a small stream in Kasumo, the southernmost **Source du Nil** (p564)

Sights & Activities

The so-called sights of Bujumbura aren't really up to much. The biggest drawcards are the beaches.

Saga Beach BEACH

Bujumbura's Lake Tanganyika beaches are some of the best of any landlocked country in Africa and comparable with those in Malawi to the southeast. The sand is white and powdery, and the waves should keep the bilharzia at bay. The stretch of beach that lies about 5km northwest of the capital is the most beautiful and used to be known as Plage des Cocotiers (Coconut Beach). However, a number of resorts are located along the road and most locals now call it **Saga Plage** (pronounced Sagga), in honour of the most popular restaurant and bar here.

FREE **La Pierre de Livingstoneet Stanley** HISTORIC SITE

Locals claim that this large rock is the spot where the infamous 'Dr Livingstone, I presume?' encounter between missionary cum explorer David Livingstone and journalist Henry Morton Stanley took place. However, that exchange actually occurred in Ujiji, across Lake Tanganyika in Tanzania. Instead, this is where Livingston and Stanley camped for two nights from 25 to the 27 November 1871 as guests of Chief Mukamba during their joint exploration of the lake. The rock is at Mugere, 11km south of the capital. La Pierre de Livingstone et Stanley is easily visited by taxi or *moto-taxi*.

Central Market MARKET

(Ave de l'Enseignement) This covered market is the largest in Burundi and is an interesting place to poke around in with its maze-like corridors and closet-sized stalls. The market is organised into sections from the colourful fresh produce stores to shops selling nothing but secondhand clothing donated from the West. The tiny fish that smell so badly when fresh are a local delicacy when dried (*mukeke*).

Musée Vivant ZOO

(Ave du 13 Octobre; admission BFr5000; 7.30am-6.30pm) After years of neglect, this small zoo is attempting to regain the innovative 'living museum' reputation it enjoyed before things turned ugly during the civil war. We say 'attempting' because presently it houses a chimp, a leopard, several crocodiles, various snakes and some antelopes in cramped, dirty and exposed cages. The guinea pigs for sale at the reception (BFr5000 each) are food for the carnivores, and if you buy one, you'll get a graphic demonstration of the food chain in action.

All that remains of the cultural exhibits is a mildly interesting reconstructed **traditional Burundian hut** and living compound.

Tours

Given the time restraints imposed by the three-day visa and lingering concerns over security, it can make sense to hire a local tour operator.

Burundi Access CULTURAL TOUR

(78283273; www.burundiaccess.com, augustine@burundiacess.com; Ave du Lac) Augustin Ndikuriyo at Burundi Access is passionate about promoting Burundi to the world and has a wealth of local knowledge that he happily shares. He can take care of everything from airport transfers to day tours to every corner of the country.

Sleeping

Hotel prices in Bujumbura have shot up with the arrival of the UN (some would say to the point of hilarity) and pickings are now slim at the budget end of the spectrum. If you have no pressing need to be in the city centre, consider staying at the beaches on Lake Tanganyika, 5km northwest of town.

TOWN CENTRE

TOP CHOICE **Hôtel de l'Amitié** HOTEL $

(22226195; hotamitie@cbinf.com; Rue de l'Amitié; r incl breakfast US$25-50; P wi-fi) One of the best budget places in town, particularly for couples as all rooms contain either twin or large double beds (although you will have to shell out for an additional breakfast as only one is included in the rates quoted above). The free wi-fi and cheap(ish) laundry service are added bonuses, and thanks to a generator, you'll still have power when the electricity cuts out.

Hotel Amahoro HOTEL $$

(22247550; www.hotelamahoro.com; Rue de l'Industrie; s incl breakfast US$47, d & tw incl breakfast US$71-94; air-con wi-fi) One of the better midrange hotels in town, the Amahoro has established a name for itself as a comfortable, centrally located place to stay with a good range of amenities. More expensive rooms

Bujumbura

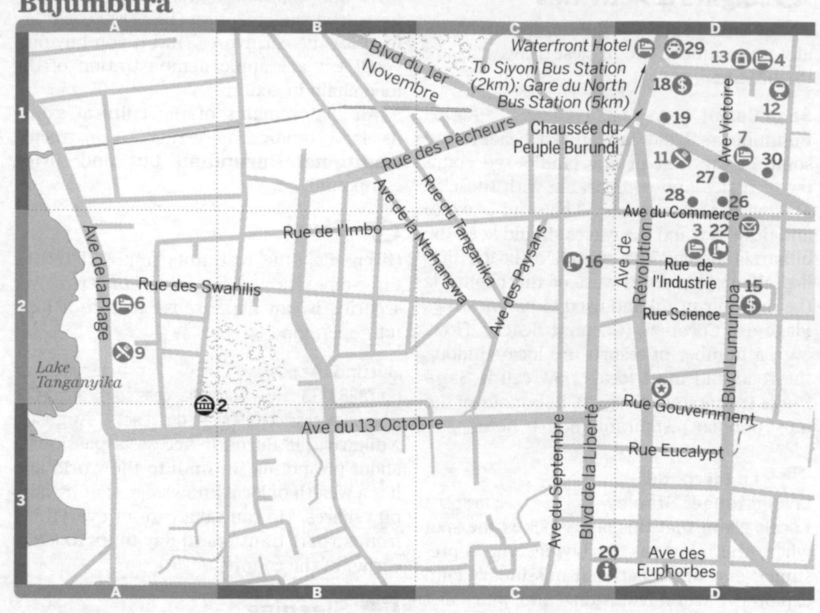

Bujumbura

Sights
1 Central Market E2
2 Musée Vivant A3

Sleeping
3 Hotel Amahoro D2
4 Hotel Botanika D1
5 Hôtel de l'Amitié E1
6 Hôtel Ubuntu Residence A2
7 Saga Residence Hotel D1
8 Shammah Hotel E1

Eating
Botanika .... (see 4)
9 Chinese Restaurant Club A2
10 Geny's Cafe E2
Kibiko Grill .... (see 6)
11 Tropicana Net Cafe D1

Drinking
12 Havana Club D1

Shopping
13 Burundi Tourisme D1
14 La Legumiere E2

Information
Alpha Cyber .... (see 11)
15 Banque du Crédit de Bujumbura D2
16 Belgian Embassy C2
17 DRC Embassy E2
18 Interbank Burundi D1
19 Manaf D1
20 Office National du Tourisme C3
21 Rwandan Embassy E1
22 Tanzanian Embassy D2
23 US Embassy E2

Transport
24 Belvèdere E2
25 Central Ville Bus Station E2
26 Kenya Airways D1
27 New Yahoo Express D1
28 Rwandair D1
29 Taxis D1
30 Yahoo Car Express D1

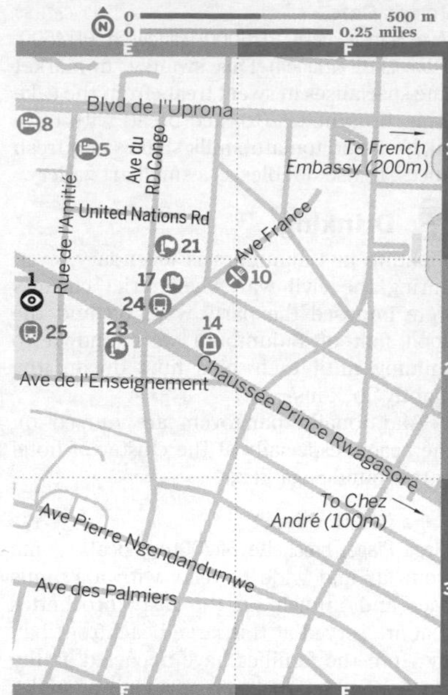

include air-con, but all have satellite TV, fridge and hot water in the bathroom.

Shammah Hotel HOTEL **$$**
(☎22275760; shammahhotel2006@yahoo.fr; Blvd de l'Uprona; s/d incl breakfast US$45/55; ❄📶) This well-run enterprise has spotless rooms with satellite TV, small balconies and reliable hot water. Its central location and helpful staff are other major draws.

Hôtel Ubuntu Residence HOTEL **$$**
(☎22244064; www.ubunturesidence.com; Ave de la Plage; r incl breakfast US$100-145; P❄📶🏊) All but the cheapest apartments here have small kitchens, balconies and upstairs bedrooms and bathrooms. Most rooms face the garden, which has some resident cranes, a turtle and the excellent Kibiko Grill restaurant. For some reason this place also appeals to mosquitoes.

Hotel Botanika BOUTIQUE HOTEL **$$**
(☎22226792; www.hotelbotanika.com; Blvd de l'Uprona; r incl breakfast US$90; ❄📶) Bujumbura's very own boutique hotel, the seven-room Botanika is a charming retreat from the rigours of life in Burundi. The only drawback is that on Friday and Saturday nights, the noise produced by the neighbouring bars would wake the dead. The breakfast here is top-notch.

Saga Residence Hotel HOTEL **$**
(☎22242225; Chaussée Prince Rwagasore; r US$25-45) Saga Residence is safe, secure and affordable with basic rooms in three price categories. All have huge beds, cold-water showers and temperamental plumbing. The big drawback – at least for those trying to sleep – is the popular and extremely noisy bar.

LAKE TANGANYIKA

Hotel Club du Lac Tanganyika HOTEL **$$$**
(☎22250220; www.hotelclubdulac; s/d incl breakfast US$150/190, ste incl breakfast US$240-400; P❄📶🏊) Occupying a slice of prime lakeside real estate, the Hotel Club du Lac Tanganyika is the only four-star hotel in Bujumbura (and by extension, Burundi) with a huge swimming pool (nonguests BFr6000), tennis court, on-call masseur, satellite TV, two restaurants and a sauna. Not all of these facilities are as well maintained as the pool and some rooms need a little sprucing up to be truly four-star material but, by and large, the hotel creates an excellent, resort-style ambience in a country where you'd least expect it.

Saga Beach Resort HOTEL **$$**
(☎75826514; sagaplage@yahoo.fr; r incl breakfast US$50-100; P❄📶) The Saga Beach resorts consists of the older Hotel Keza, which is set back from the beach with its block of comfortable if dated rooms, and the newer Hotel Urugo. Rooms here are right in the thick of the beach action and the only thing preventing beach goers wandering onto your private deck is the stick fence that runs around the hotel complex. The bar and restaurant here are extremely popular on the weekends.

Eating

The beachside places listed in the drinking section also do tasty meals. If you're looking for a cheap, no-frills buffet (usually lunch only), rather than the somewhat more Euro-centric selection below, you'll find no shortage of them around town. Most serve identical fare for identical prices. Expect a big helping of carbohydrates in the form of cassava, potatoes, rice and beans and some meat or fish in a stew-like sauce.

Tropicana Net Cafe AMERICAN **$**
(Chaussée Prince Rwagasore; mains BFr5000-9000; ⏰breakfast, lunch & dinner) This trendy

internet cafe does decent light meals (toasted sandwiches, burgers and steaks), salads and soups in air-conditioned, classic Starbucks-esque comfort. And if the thought of yet another omelette for breakfast is too much to bear, head here for some juice and croissants.

Chez André FRENCH **$$$**
(Chaussée Prince Rwagasore; mains BFr7500-20,000; ⏲lunch & dinner) Housed in a huge villa on the eastern extreme of Chaussée Prince Rwagasore, this French- and Belgian-inspired institution is one of the best restaurants in the city, with a flamboyant menu that wouldn't look out of place in Brussels or Paris.

Kibiko Grill INTERNATIONAL **$$**
(Ave de la Plage; mains BFr9000-14,000; ⏲dinner; 📶) Slap on some insect repellent and head here for tasty brochettes (kebabs), excellent pizza (half price on Tuesdays and Thursdays) and fresh fish straight from the lake. Kibiko Grill is inside the Hôtel Ubuntu Residence.

Chinese Restaurant Club CHINESE **$$**
(Ave de la Plage; meals BFr7000-12,000; ⏲dinner) Proving the theory that every capital city in the world has a Chinese restaurant, the 'Club' brings the reasonably authentic flavours of the Far East to Bujumbura.

Botanika FRENCH **$$$**
(Blvd de l'Uprona; mains BFr10,000-16,000; ⏲breakfast, lunch & dinner; 📶) Located in the Hotel Botanika, this excellent restaurant has an intimate courtyard setting and some of the most expressive French cuisine in the city.

Geny's Cafe CAFE **$$**
(Ave France; cake BFr6000, sandwich BFr4500; ⏲breakfast & lunch) This swanky, upmarket cafe specialises in sweet treats from the cake table, bruschettas (toasted bread with olive oil, basil and tomato), milk shakes and fresh juices. It also doubles as a small art gallery.

Drinking

Nightlife in Bujumbura is legendary; even during the civil war when strict curfews were imposed the party went on and the good folk of Bujumbura were known to shimmy until their hips hurt during the nightly 'lock-ins'.

Traditionally, hangovers are nursed on the beach, especially at the cluster of hotel bars around Saga Plage.

Saga Beach Resort BAR
(Saga Plage; brochette Bfr7000) Locals come from far and wide to relax with a Primus beer and munch on the tasty brochettes that are served at this large beachfront bar. By 11pm the families have departed as the whole complex rocks on as a club by night. Sundays draw a huge family, and if you time your visit for around 4pm, you'll likely catch a free Les Tambourinaires drummers performance (photography BFr5000) down on the beach.

Bora Bora BAR
(Saga Plage; meals BFr10,000-18,000; 📶🏊) The whitewashed weatherboards, palm-studded beach, blue-and-white nautical-inspired decor and a huge terrace-fronted villa make this the most popular of all the beachside bars with the expat community. The big draw here is the free pool and the chilled Caribbean vibe. On Saturday and Sunday

LES TAMBOURINAIRES DRUMMERS

Les Tambourinaires du Burundi is the country's most famous troupe and has performed in cities such as Berlin and New York. Its recitals are a high-adrenaline mix of drumming and dancing that drowns the audience in waves of sound and movement. Unfortunately, without a national theatre or any other such venue, you'll have to be content with a smaller beachside performance or an impromptu practice session.

From around 4.30pm on Sundays, drummers run through a series of routines at Saga Beach. There is no charge but tips are appreciated and you'll be charged (BFr5000) if you take photos.

Occasionally you will also find Les Tambourinaires drummers practicing at the Office National du Tourisme (usually between 3pm and 4pm on Fridays) or at Musée Vivant (usually on Thursdays and Sundays from 4pm to 5pm; p559), but once they notice a tourist snooping around, they'll only continue playing for a cash incentive.

nights the laid-back reggae and Cuban jazz give way to a mix of African and Western house and pop spun by a local DJ.

Havana Club BAR, DANCE
(Blvd de l'Uprona; meals BFr9000-15,000) Out the front is the trendy Balneo Lounge Bar with comfy leather chairs, mood lighting and private nooks. The whole place oozes the slightly worn sophistication of a bygone era. Most people are happy to drink and chill, but the food here is also recommended and the pizzas are half price from 9am to 7pm. The Havana Club itself is out back and doesn't open until 9pm on Fridays and Saturdays. It is one of the city's most popular nightspots, drawing a mixed crowd of locals and internationals. The party starts late (at around 11pm) and goes until sunrise.

Shopping

If you are looking for souvenirs you could try the small *object d'art* shop **La Legumiere** (Chaussée Prince Rwagasore) near the American embassy or the government-run **Burundi Tourisme** (Blvd de l'Uprona) next door to Hotel Botanika. Both stock masks, spears, woven baskets and wooden carvings.

Burundian coffee is another popular memento and can be bought at any of the small supermarkets around town.

Information

Emergency

The official emergency number for police is ☎17, though it's unlikely anyone will answer should you call. It's best to make contact with your embassy in the event of an emergency. If your country doesn't have an embassy in Burundi, then either Kenya (p364) or Tanzania (p203) are your best bets.

Internet Access

Bujumbura has a healthy sprinkling of internet cafes and provided there isn't a power outage, you'll have no trouble getting a good connection. Many cafes offer free wi-fi.

Alpha Cyber (Chaussée Prince Rwagasore; per min BFr10) This cheapie is tucked down an alley next to its upmarket competitor, Tropicana Net Cafe. It's four times cheaper than Tropicana, but unlike Tropicana, lacks the technology to transfer photos from camera to CD.

Medical Services

In the event of a medical emergency, it is best to get out of Burundi to somewhere with first-class medical facilities, such as Nairobi in Kenya.

Money

Banque du Crédit de Bujumbura (Rue Science) Offers credit card cash advances.

Interbank Burundi (Blvd de l'Uprona) Has several branches around town and represents Western Union if you need an urgent transfer. The branch marked on the Bujumbura map has an ATM that accepts foreign Visa and MasterCard.

Post

Main post office (cnr Blvd Lumumba & Ave du Commerce; ⏲8am-noon & 2-4pm Mon-Fri, 8-11am Sat)

Tourist Information

Office National du Tourisme (☎22224208; Ave des Euphorbes; ⏲7.30am-noon & 2-4pm Mon-Fri) Not many tourists in Burundi equals not much information in the tourist office.

Travel Agency

Manaf (Chaussée Prince Rwagasore; ☎22252244; manaftourandtravel@yahoo.fr) Reliable airline ticketing office.

> **SAFE TRAVEL IN BUJUMBURA**
>
> It is generally safe to wander about on foot during the day, though the streets empty at night – it is imperative to use a taxi or private vehicle once the sun goes down. Street crime is prevalent in Bujumbura, and foreigners are especially vulnerable given their perceived wealth. It's best to leave your camera behind any time you go out as locals often don't care to be photographed and *les petits bandits* have sticky fingers.
>
> These days the curfews (*couvret feu* in French) have gone, although roadblocks are erected nightly so that traffic can be controlled should the need arise.

Getting There & Away

International buses and minibuses leave from the **Siyoni bus station** at the Buyenzi Market, which is 2km north of the city centre, while those bound for Gitega leave from the **Gare du North bus station**, which is 5km north of the city centre.

For more information on getting to and from Burundi, see p567.

SATURDAY COMMUNITY WORK

From 8am to 10am every Saturday the country comes to a grinding halt. The reason? *Ibikorwa rusangi* – a time for obligatory community work. During these hours the populace is required to lend a hand on community projects for the greater good of their country. Shops, taxis, buses and restaurants are closed and instead trash gathered, grass cut and drains dug. One of the few exceptions is the international buses that have special dispensation to operate.

Getting Around

Taxi fares range from BFr1000 for short hops in the centre to BFr5000 out to the beaches. *Moto-taxis* (BFr1500) will also get you to the beaches or where you need to go if you're not scared by Bujumbura's racing traffic.

Minibuses to Gatumba can drop you off at Saga Beach and charge BFr300. These, along with minibuses to all places around Bujumbura (including Siyoni and Gare du North bus stations where the long-distance buses leave from), can be caught at the **Central Ville bus station** at Bujumbura's Central Market.

AROUND BUJUMBURA

As Burundi is so small, it is feasible (some would say, advisable) to visit these sights during the day and return to Bujumbura before nightfall.

SOURCE DU NIL

It is not quite as obvious and impressive as Jinja in Uganda, but this insignificant-looking little spring at Kasumo, 115km southeast of Bujumbura, may well be the southernmost **source du Nil** (source of the Nile; admission BFr5000). In a nice touch, a stone pyramid marks the site, but unless you have your own transport it is almost impossible to reach. If you fancy a swim there are some **hot springs** a further 10km south.

GITEGA

Gitega is the second-largest town in Burundi and home to the **Musée National de Gitega** (admission BFr3000; ⌚7.30am-3.30pm, closed Sat), which, although unlikely to enthral you, is the best museum Burundi has to offer. The one-room hall has a dusty collection of traditional household items including cow-horn snuffboxes, bark clothing, medicinal instruments and jewellery. There are also some interesting photos including our favourite, an 1896 shot of Bujumbura when the capital was little more than a few tents and a tree.

Minibuses (BFr5000) and shared taxis (BFr7000) from Bujumbura's Gare du North bus station make the run to Gitega throughout the day (two hours). Once in Gitega, the museum is a short walk or BFr500 bicycle-taxi hop out of town.

CHUTES DE LA KARERA

The **Chutes de la Karera** (admission incl guide BFr5000, vehicle BFr1000) is the collective name for the four beautiful waterfalls near Rutana. The prettiest is the cascade **Nyakai I** where you park your car. Upstream from this is the smallest of the four falls, **Nyakai II**, an ideal spot for an impromptu shower. This watercourse is joined by that of **Mwaro Falls** before creating the namesake and tallest waterfall in the area, **Karera Falls**.

As you would expect, the falls are at their best during the wet season (especially from October to January). The falls are 64km south of Gitega, but as there's no public transport, you'll have to charter a vehicle in Bujumbura to get here.

UNDERSTAND BURUNDI

History

For information on Burundian and East African history prior to independence, see p572.

A Fragile Independence

Burundi, like Rwanda, was colonised first by Germany and later by Belgium, and like its northern neighbour, the Europeans played on ethnic differences to divide and conquer the population. Power was traditionally concentrated in the hands of the minority Tutsi, though Hutus began to challenge the concentration of power following independence in 1962.

In the 1964 elections, Tutsi leader Mwami Mwambutsa refused to appoint a Hutu prime minister, even though Hutu candidates attracted the majority of votes. Hutu frustration soon boiled over, and Hutu military officers and political figures staged an attempted coup. Although it failed, Mwambutsa was exiled to Switzerland, and replaced by a Tutsi military junta.

A wholesale purge of Hutu from the army and bureaucracy followed, and in 1972 another large-scale Hutu revolt resulted in more than 1000 Tutsi being killed. The Tutsi military junta responded with the selective genocide of elite Hutu; after just three months, 200,000 Hutu had been killed and another 100,000 had fled into neighbouring countries.

In 1976, Jean-Baptiste Bagaza came to power in a bloodless coup, and three years later he formed the Union pour le Progrès National (Uprona). His so-called democratisation program was largely considered to be a failure, and in 1987 his cousin Major Pierre Buyoya toppled him in another coup.

The new regime attempted to address the causes of intertribal tensions by gradually bringing Hutu representatives back into positions of power. However, there was a renewed outbreak of intertribal violence in northern Burundi during the summer of 1988; thousands were massacred and many more fled into neighbouring Rwanda.

A Bloody Civil War

Buyoya finally bowed to international pressure, and multiparty elections were held in June 1993. These brought a Hutu-dominated government to power, led by Melchior Ndadaye, himself a Hutu. However, a dissident army faction, led by a Tutsi, Colonel Sylvestre Ningaba, staged yet another coup in late October the same year, and assassinated president Ndadaye. The coup eventually failed, though thousands were massacred in intertribal fighting, and almost half a million refugees fled across the border into Rwanda.

In April 1994 Cyprien Ntaryamira, the new Hutu president, was killed in the same plane crash that killed Rwanda's president Juvenal Habyarimana, and ignited the subsequent genocide over there. In Burundi, Sylvestre Ntibantunganya was immediately appointed interim president, though both Hutu militias and the Tutsi-dominated army went on the offensive. No war was actually declared, but at least 100,000 people were killed in clashes between mid-1994 and mid-1996.

In July 1996 former president Major Pierre Buyoya again carried out a successful coup, and took over as the country's president with the support of the army. However, intertribal fighting continued between Hutu rebels and the Tutsi-dominated government and Tutsi militia. Hundreds of thousands of political opponents, mostly Hutus, were herded into 'regroupment camps', and bombings, murders and other horrific activities continued throughout the country.

A Fragile Peace

At the end of 2002, the Forces for the Defence of Democracy (FDD), the largest rebel group, signed a peace deal. In April 2003, prominent Hutu Domitien Ndayizeye succeeded Buyoya as president, and a road map to elections was hammered out.

In 2004, the UN began operations in Burundi, sending more than 5000 troops to enforce the peace. Parliamentary elections were successfully held in 2005, and the former rebels, the FDD, emerged victorious. Pierre Nkurunziza, leader of the FDD, was sworn in as president in August. The 2010 elections were marred by violence and allegations of fraud and corruption. Despite international observers recognising the local elections as mainly free and fair, a growing mistrust between the incumbent's commitments to democracy, saw all opposition withdraw their candidacy and Nkurunziza was re-elected unopposed.

As of 2011, the situation remains tense. Since the elections, there have been no official talks between the government and opposition parties including the Hutu-led National Liberation Forces (NLF) who have since gone underground. What remains to be seen is whether this political impasse has the power to reverse the last decade's progress and push the country back into chaos.

The Culture

Like Rwanda to the north, Burundi has been torn apart by tribal animosities, and the conflict between Hutus and Tutsis has claimed hundreds of thousands of lives since independence. However, like most conflicts, it is more about politics than people, and it is the people who end up as victims of political manipulation. The Belgians masterminded the art of divide and rule, using the minority Tutsis to control the majority Hutus. Generations of intermarriage and cooperation went out the window, as the population was forced into choosing sides, Hutu or Tutsi. The pattern continued into independence as the minority Tutsis clung to power to protect their privileges, and marginalised the Hutu majority. Only with the advent of peaceful elections does it look like this cycle may come to an end.

Economy

The UN's 2010 *Human Development Report* listed Burundi as the fourth poorest country in the world. Civil wars, corruption, landlocked geography, poor education, AIDS and a lack of economic freedom have all but economically crippled the country and today it is largely dependent on foreign aid.

Burundi's largest industry is agriculture and it's largest source of revenue is coffee.

Environment

Taking up a mere 27,835 sq km, most of the country is made up of mountains that vanish into the horizon. Sadly, however, most of the national parks have been closed for more than a decade.

Assuming the situation improves with the coming of peace, it may be possible to visit Parc National de la Kibira, essentially a continuation of Parc National Nyungwe Forest in southwestern Rwanda and the largest rainforest in Burundi, home to colobus monkeys and chimpanzees, and Parc National de la Rurubu, the largest protected area in the country, with wonderful hiking and views.

The most accessible national park – and the only one currently open – is Parc National de la Rusizi, just 15km from Bujumbura. It's a wetland environment and provides a habitat for hippos, sitatungas and a wide variety of birds. The park is best visited on an organised tour (p559) as these often include a boat excursion which allows for better wildlife viewing. Alternatively, various minibuses leaving from the Central Market can drop you at the park gates.

SURVIVAL GUIDE

Directory A–Z

Accommodation

The choice of accommodation is reasonable in Bujumbura but fairly limited elsewhere in the country. The arrival of the UN in Burundi has inflated the prices.

Business Hours

Businesses tend to close for a couple of hours at lunch, approximately midday to 2pm. Most eateries are open from 7am to about 9pm.

Embassies & Consulates

Foreign embassies in Bujumbura include the following:

Belgium (☎22226781; www.diplomatie.be/bujumbura; Blvd de la Liberté)

Democratic Republic of the Congo (DRC; ☎22226916; Ave du RD Congo)

France (☎22222854; 60 Blvd de l'Uprona)

Rwanda (☎22226865; Ave du RD Congo)

Tanzania (☎248636; Blvd Lumumba)

US (☎223454; Chaussée Prince Rwagasore)

Money

The unit of currency is the Burundi franc (BFr). This is a cash economy and the US dollar is not only king, it's a tyrant. Interbank in Bujumbura has an ATM (Visa and MasterCard accepted) on the international network and cash advances on credit cards are possible at other major banks. There's an open black market in Bujumbura for changing money and you will find plenty of currency exchange bureaus (*forex bureaus*) around the Central Market and along Chaussée Prince Rwagasore. Travellers cheques are next to useless here.

Public Holidays

Unity Day 5 February

Labour Day 1 May

Independence Day 1 July

Assumption 15 August

Victory of Uprona Day 18 September

Anniversary of Rwagasore's Assassination 13 October

Anniversary of Ndadaye's Assassination 21 October

All Saints' Day 1 November

Safe Travel

At long last, Burundi's civil war has ended, though the country is still far from stable and despite recent peace accords, violence could flare up at any time. Quite simply, Burundi remains a potentially unstable country in a potentially unstable region of Africa and its best to stay informed of the current situation.

At the time of research, travel to the capital Bujumbura was reasonably safe, as was the main road north to Rwanda, though greater caution needs to be exerted while travelling in the countryside.

Unfortunately street crime is prevalent in Bujumbura, and foreigners are an especially easy target, so be particularly aware of your surroundings, especially once the sun goes down.

Telephone

There are no telephone area codes within the country. The country code for Burundi is ☎257.

Visas

One-month tourist visas cost US$90 and are available on arrival at the international airport in Bujumbura. For those arriving overland and haven't obtained a visa from an embassy elsewhere, your only option is to get a three-day transit visa (US$40) at the border and have it extended in Bujumbura.

VISA EXTENSIONS

Visa extensions are fairly straightforward although at first glance it seems all hell is breaking loose when you spot the disorderly queues at the **Bureau de l'immigration** (near Police de l'Air et Frontières in Ngagara; ⏲7.30am-noon & 2-4pm, Mon-Fri). Besides your passport, you need a photocopy of your passport ID page and the page containing your border-entry stamp, a passport-sized photo and US$20. If you apply for a visa extension in the morning, you can collect your passport that afternoon or the following day.

Getting There & Away

Air

Bujumbura International Airport (BJM) is located about 12km north of the city centre. Thanks to the protracted war, very few international airlines still serve Burundi, and Air Burundi itself, the national airline, has suspended operations and now functions only as a travel agency.

Kenya Airways (KQ; www.kenya-airways.com; Blvd Lumumba) Hub: Nairobi.

RwandAir (WB; www.rwandair.com; Ave du Commerce) Hub: Kigali.

For information on flying directly to Burundi from outside of East Africa, see p650.

Land

Burundi shares land borders with the DRC, Rwanda and Tanzania.

RWANDA

The main crossing point is between Kayanza (Burundi) and Huye (also known as Butare; Rwanda) on the main road linking Bujumbura and Kigali. The safest and quickest option for travel between Bujumbura and Kigali is to use one of the scheduled bus services listed following (six hours, BFr12,000), which pass through Huye (four hours, BFr10,000). All buses depart at 7am and 10am daily from the Siyoni bus station, although some have booking offices in the centre of town

Assuming all is still safe, it's possible to travel to Cyangugu at the southern tip of Lake Kivu in Rwanda. Catch a minibus or shared taxi from the bus stop opposite Waterfront Hotel Bujumbura (Chaussee du Peuple Burundi) to Rugombo (two hours, BFr6000) just past Cibitoke and then a motorbike or taxi to the Luhwa border. From there, it's a small hop to Cyangugu in a connecting vehicle (one hour, RFr1500).

Belvèdéré (booking office Ave France)

Horizon Coaches Has frequent services to Kigali and onward connections to Kampala (RFr6000, six hours).

Kampala Coach Has a comfortable Wednesday and Saturday service to Kigali.

New Yahoo Express (booking office Chaussée Prince Rwagasore)

Yahoo Car Express (booking office Chaussée Prince Rwagasore)

For more information, see the Getting There & Away section of the Rwanda chapter (p554).

TANZANIA

For Kobero, the trip is done in stages via Ngara (Tanzania). There are daily buses between Mwanza (Tanzania) and Ngara, from where there is onward transport to the border. From Kigoma (Tanzania), take a bus to Nyakanazi (Tanzania) and get onward transport to Ngara from there.

For the Manyovu crossing, there's a twice-weekly small bus (BFr10,000, five hours) that goes direct between Kigoma and Bujumbura, departing Kigoma from behind the Bero petrol station. The trip can also be done in stages. Once through the Tanzanian side of the border, you'll need to take one of the many waiting vehicles on to Makamba, where the Burundian immigration post is located. From there, get another vehicle to Bujumbura.

For more information, see the Getting There & Away section of the Tanzania chapter (p206).

THE DRC

The main crossing between Burundi and the DRC is at Gatumba on the road between Bujumbura and Uvira (the DRC), about 15km west of the capital. Unfortunately, this crossing is of little use to travellers as onward travel to Bukavu (the DRC) is risky and the areas south of Bukavu are prone to lawlessness. It would be wiser to stay on the Burundi side of the border and travel to Cyangugu in Rwanda and cross to Bukavu from there.

Getting Around

Air

There are no internal domestic flights in Burundi.

Road

Travelling around the countryside is not as dangerous as it once was, though things change quickly (for better or for worse) in this part of the world.

As in Rwanda, most major roads in Burundi are sealed. Public transport mostly consists of modern Japanese minibuses, which are cheaper than shared taxis and not overcrowded. Destinations are displayed in the front window, and minibuses depart when full. You can usually find a minibus or shared taxi heading in your direction any day between early morning and early afternoon at the *gare routière* (bus station) in any town.

Understand East Africa

EAST AFRICA TODAY 570
Fifty years after the region gained independence, many challenges remain, but there are bright spots, too.

HISTORY 572
From humankind's earliest days through migrations, colonialism and independence, East Africa's modern face reflects many influences.

LIFE IN EAST AFRICA 578
Daily life moves to its own pace, with hospitality, community solidarity and spirituality major themes.

TRIBAL CULTURES 583
Over 300 different groups are at home in East Africa, with fascinating and colourful traditions.

ENVIRONMENT 591
Diverse landscapes and fragile ecosystems host a wealth of plants, birds and wildlife.

WILDLIFE & HABITAT 597
Read the definitive full-colour guide to Tanzania's wildlife by renowned expert David Lukas.

NATIONAL PARKS & RESERVES 621
East Africa's parks range from open savannah lands to dense mountain forests, all packed with wildlife.

PRIMATES 627
Close-up encounters with chimpanzees and mountain gorillas are a regional highlight.

THE ARTS 631
Discover East Africa's lively arts scene, from Swahili-style architecture to Congolese dance bands.

A TASTE OF EAST AFRICA 634
Learn about everything from ugali to etiquette in this guide to dining East African style.

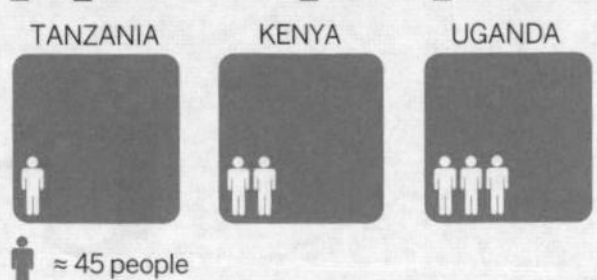

East Africa Today

Legendary Allure

East Africa's allure is legendary, with its charming old Swahili towns, wildlife-packed safari parks, the world's last remaining mountain gorillas, magical archipelagos and a vibrant kaleidoscope of cultures. Its cities pulse with energy as glitzy high-rises appear practically over night, the young and not-so-young wait in line at crowded internet cafes, and overflowing matatus (minibuses) careen wildly through the streets. Crowds pack churches on Sunday mornings and mosques at midday on Fridays; sidewalk vendors hawk everything from fresh pineapples to mobile phones; and massive billboards tout the virtues of condoms and abstinence. Tree-planting campaigns and anti–plastic bag legislation have put the region firmly in the running with the rest of the world to go green. And each day East Africans shake their collective head about the deplorable antics of some of their politicians.

» Area: 1,816,753 sq km

» Highest point: Mt Kilimanjaro (5896m)

» Lowest point: Lake Tanganyika's floor (358m below sea level)

» Famous for: wildebeest migration, mountain gorillas, safaris, dhows, traditional cultures

Ethnic & Political Tensions

Yet, in 2007, Kenya – the regional powerhouse – erupted in postelection ethnic violence, shaking East Africa's upwards-oriented image and sending visitor numbers plummeting. Northern Uganda, although increasingly stable, continues to be plagued by outbreaks of conflict. Opposition party rioting in 2011 injured dozens in Kampala. Parts of Burundi are still shadowed by scattered rebel elements and banditry, and the eastern Democratic Republic of the Congo (DRC; formerly Zaire) remains shaky.

Economic & Social Challenges

East Africa's economy is a mixed picture. Inflation is at low to moderate levels, economies are growing, and tourism is a major money earner; however, all of the five countries covered in this book are ranked in the

Dos & Don'ts

» **Do** support local enterprise: buy directly from the makers.

» **Do** choose safari/trekking operators that treat local communities as equal partners.

» **Do** ask permission before photographing people.

» **Do** take advantage of cultural tourism programs.

» **Don't** engage in indiscriminate gift giving. Donate to sustainable, recognised projects.

» **Don't** buy items made from ivory, skin, shells, etc.

Top Films

» **War/Dance** (2007) A glimpse into northeastern Uganda

» **Kibera Kid** (2006) Life in Nairobi's largest slum

» **Hotel Rwanda** (2004) Story from the Rwandan genocide

» **Africa: The Serengeti** (1994) The annual wildebeest migration

belief systems
(% of population)

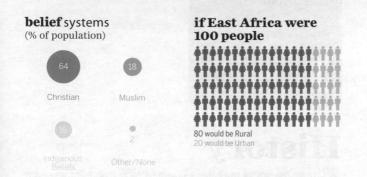

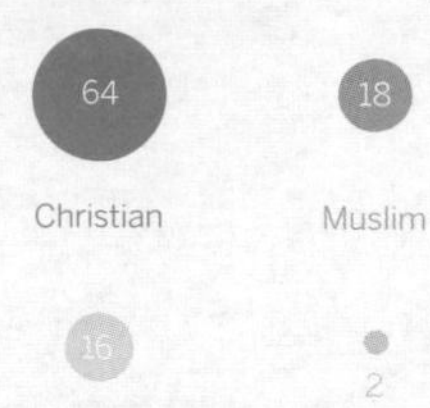

if East Africa were 100 people

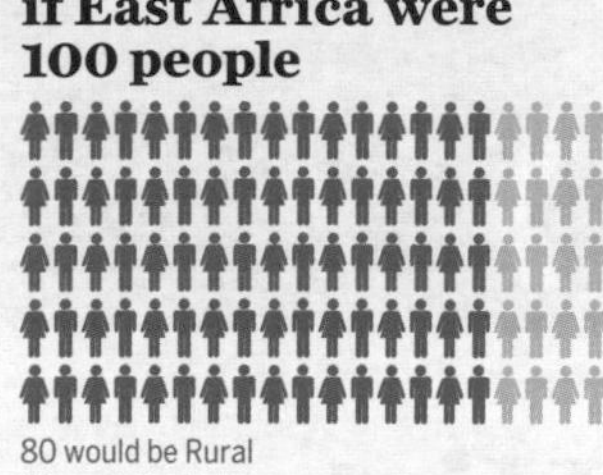

bottom fourth of the global UN Human Development Index. Life expectancy averages around 53 years for the region as a whole. Annual per-capita income levels are just a fraction of what they are in most Western countries. Reliable banking services and savings accounts remain inaccessible for most people, especially rural dwellers, and it's a common scenario for those few students who make it through secondary school to be faced with meagre or no job prospects upon graduation.

These figures are tempered by the extensive informal economy that exists throughout the region, as well as by wide economic variations between rural and urban areas. There are also significant income disparities; Kenya, for example, one of the world's poorest countries, also has as one of the largest gaps between rich and poor. Yet daily life remains a struggle for many.

Another challenge in the region is HIV/AIDS, which, although declining in many areas, has left over two million children orphans. Malaria also claims the lives of countless East Africans daily. Rates of secondary school attendance remain low throughout the region (the highest attendance rate by far is in Kenya, at 40%), and corruption is rampant.

GDP per capita in East Africa

» Burundi US$300

» Kenya US$1600

» Rwanda US$1100

» Tanzania US$1400

» Uganda US$1300

Hope for the Future

As East Africa's countries celebrate their 50 year anniversaries of independence, many hurdles remain. Yet despite the challenges, there are so many encouraging stories, especially at the village and community level. It is here where investment in education and health, successful micro-lending schemes, income from cultural tourism programs and other ventures, combined with East Africans' renowned resilience, ingenuity and humour, have turned prospects for the future from bleak to bright.

Top Books

» **The River Between** (Ngũgĩ wa Thiong'o)

» **Abyssinian Chronicles** (Moses Isegawa)

Song of Lawino (Okot p'Bitek)

» **Tropical Fish: Stories Out of Entebbe** (Doreen Baingana)

» **A Grain of Wheat** (Ngũgĩ wa Thiong'o)

» **Land Without Thunder** (Grace Ogot)

» **The Gunny Sack** (MG Vassanji)

Top Resources

» **The East African** (www.theeastafrican.co.ke) Regional English-language weekly

» **BBC's Focus on Africa** (www.bbc.co.uk/africa) Wide-ranging East Africa coverage

History

East Africa has one of the longest documented human histories of any region in the world. Home to some of humankind's earliest ancestors, it later received steady waves of migration from elsewhere on the continent, as well as arrivals from the Arabian Peninsula and from the Orient. East Africa's modern face has been shaped by these influxes, and further defined by the legacies of colonialism and of the independence struggle.

For travellers, the many threads of East Africa's long history are still very much in evidence – from Oldupai (Olduvai) Gorge, with its fascinating fossil finds, to the winding lanes and ornate lintels of old Swahili settlements such as Lamu and Zanzibar, to the bustling coastal dhow ports, Portuguese-era garrisons and colonial-era architecture. All of these threads are tied together by the rich tribal cultures that are the region's lifeblood.

Portuguese influence is still seen in East Africa's architecture, customs and language. The origin of the Swahili word *gereza* (jail), from Portuguese *igreja* (church), dates to the days when Portuguese forts contained both in the same compound.

The Dawn of Mankind

Ancient hominid (humanlike) skulls and footprints, some over three million years old, have been found at various sites in East Africa, including at Oldupai Gorge in Tanzania and Lake Turkana in Kenya. Although similarly ancient traces have also been found elsewhere on the continent, the East African section of the Great Rift Valley is popularly considered the 'cradle of humanity'.

By about one million years ago, these early ancestors had come to resemble modern humans, and had spread well beyond East Africa, including as far as Europe and Asia. Roughly 100,000 years ago, and possibly earlier, Homo sapiens – modern man – had arrived on the scene.

The earliest evidence of modern-day East Africans dates to around 10,000 years ago, when much of the region was home to Khoisan-speaking hunter-gatherer communities. On the western fringes of East Africa, including parts of the area that is now Rwanda and Burundi, there were also small populations of various so-called Pygmy groups.

TIMELINE

c 25 million BC

Tectonic plates collide and the East African plains buckle. Formation of the Great Rift Valley begins, as do changes that result ultimately in formation of Kilimanjaro and other volcanoes.

c 3.5 million BC

Fossils found at Lake Turkana (Kenya) and at Laetoli (Tanzania) show that hominid (humanlike) creatures wandered the East African plains over three million years ago.

c 100 BC

The first Bantu-speakers arrive in the region, part of a series of great population migrations that continue to shape the face of modern-day East Africa.

The Great Migrations

Beginning between 3000 and 5000 years ago, a series of migrations began that were to indelibly shape the face of East Africa. Cushitic- and Nilotic-speaking peoples from the north and Bantu-speakers from the west converged on the Khoisan and other peoples already in the area, creating over the centuries the rich tribal mosaic that is East Africa today.

The first to arrive were Cushitic-speaking farmers and cattle herders who made their way to the region from present-day Ethiopia, and settled both inland and along the coast. They moved mostly in small family groups, and brought with them traditions that are still practiced by their descendents, including the Iraqw around Tanzania's Lake Manyara and the Gabbra and Rendille in northern Kenya.

The next major influx began around 1000 BC when Bantu-speaking peoples from West Africa's Niger Delta area began moving eastwards, arriving in East Africa around the 1st century BC. Thanks to their advanced agricultural skills and knowledge of ironworking and steel production – which gave them a great advantage in cultivating land and establishing settlements – these Bantu-speakers were able to absorb many of the Cushitic- and Khoisan-speakers who were already in the region, as well as the Pygmy populations around the Great Lakes. Soon, they became East Africa's most populous ethnolinguistic family – a status which they continue to hold today.

A final wave of migration began somewhat later when smaller groups of Nilotic peoples began to arrive in East Africa from what is now southern Sudan. This influx continued through to the 18th century, with the main movements taking place in the 15th and 16th centuries. Most of these Nilotic peoples – whose descendants include the present-day Maasai and Turkana – were pastoralists, and many settled in the less fertile areas of southern Kenya and northern Tanzania where their large herds would have sufficient grazing space.

Today, the population diversity resulting from these migrations is one of the most fascinating aspects of travel in East Africa.

Swahili Ruins

- Kilwa Kisiwani (Tanzania)
- Kaole Ruins (Tanzania)
- Gede Ruins (Kenya)
- Jumba la Mtwana (Kenya)
- Takwa Ruins (Kenya)
- Mnarani (Kenya)

'...Two days' sail beyond, there lies the...last market-town of the continent of Azania, which is called Rhapta... in which there is ivory in great quantity, and tortoise-shell...' *(Periplus of the Erythraean Sea)*

Monsoon Winds

As these migrations were taking place in the interior, coastal areas were being shaped by far different influences. Azania, as the East African coast was known to the ancient Greeks, was an important trading post as early as 400 BC, and had likely been inhabited even before then by small groups of Cushitic peoples, and by Bantu-speakers. The *Periplus of the Erythraean Sea,* a navigator's guide written in the 1st century AD, mentions Raphta as the southernmost trading port. Although its location remains a mystery, it is believed to have been somewhere along the

c 750–1200 AD

Monsoon winds push Arab trading ships to the East African coast and Swahili civilisation is born. Settlements are established at Lamu, Gede, Kilwa and elsewhere along the coast.

1331

Moroccan traveller Ibn Battuta visits Kilwa (Tanzania) and finds a flourishing town of 10,000 to 20,000 residents, with a grand palace, mosque, inn and slave market.

JOHN WARBURTON-LEE/ALAMY ©

» Great Mosque, Kilwa Kisiwani (p193), Tanzania

15th Century

The king of Malindi sends the Chinese emperor a giraffe. Vasco da Gama reaches East Africa en route to the Orient, stopping at Mombasa and Malindi before continuing to India.

Kenyan or Tanzanian coast, possibly on the mainland opposite Manda or Paté Islands (north of Lamu), or further south near the Pangani or Rufiji estuaries.

Trade seems to have grown steadily throughout the early part of the first millennium. Permanent settlements were established as traders, first from the Mediterranean and later from Arabia and Persia, came ashore on the winds of the monsoon and began to intermix with the indigenous peoples, gradually giving rise to Swahili language and culture. The traders from Arabia also brought Islam, which by the 11th century had become entrenched.

Between the 13th and 15th centuries these coastal settlements – including those at Shanga (on Paté Island), Gede, Lamu and Mombasa (all in present-day Kenya) and on the Zanzibar Archipelago and at Kilwa Kisiwani (both in Tanzania) – flourished, with trade in ivory, gold and other goods extending as far away as India and China.

Historical Unesco World Heritage Sites

- Sacred Mijikenda Kaya Forests (Kenya)
- Kasubi Tombs (Uganda)
- Lamu Old Town (Kenya)
- Fort Jesus (Kenya)
- Kolo-Kondoa Rock Art Sites (Tanzania)
- Kilwa Kisiwani & Songo Mnara (Tanzania)
- Zanzibar's Stone Town (Tanzania)

Expeditioning Europeans

The first European to reach East Africa was the intrepid Portuguese explorer Vasco da Gama, who arrived in 1498, en route to the Orient. Within three decades, the Portuguese had disrupted the old trading networks and subdued the entire coast, building forts at various places, including Kilwa and Mombasa. Portuguese control lasted until the early 18th century, when they were displaced by Arabs from Oman.

As the Omani Arabs solidified their foothold, they began to turn their sights westwards, developing powerful trade routes that stretched inland as far as Lake Tanganyika and Central Africa. Commerce grew at such a pace that in the 1840s, the Sultan of Oman moved his capital from Muscat to Zanzibar Island.

The slave trade also grew rapidly during this period, driven in part by demand from European plantation holders on the Indian Ocean islands of Réunion and Mauritius. Soon slave traders, including the notorious Tippu Tip, had established stations at Tabora (Tanzania) and other inland towns. By the mid-19th century, the Zanzibar Archipelago had become the largest slave entrepôt along the East African coast, with nearly 50,000 slaves, abducted from as far away as Lake Tanganyika, passing through Zanzibar's market each year.

Colonial Control

In addition to reports of the horrors of the still-ongoing regional slave trade, tales of the attractions of East Africa also made their way back to Europe, and Western interests were piqued. In 1890, Germany and Great Britain signed an agreement defining 'spheres of influence' for themselves, which formally established a British protectorate over the

c 1400–1700

In several waves, small bands of nomadic cattle herders migrate south from the Sudan into the Rift Valley – ancestors of the Maasai who today live in Kenya and Tanzania.

1850–1870

Zanzibar's slave market becomes the largest in East Africa. According to some estimates, up to 50,000 slaves passed through its gates each year.

» Slave monument, Zanzibar (p58), Tanzania

1890

Britain and Germany create 'spheres of influence'. Zanzibar becomes a British 'protectorate'. After WWI, the German area of Rwanda-Urundi (later to be Rwanda and Burundi) comes under Belgian control.

SWAHILI

The word Swahili ('of the coast', from the Arabic word *sāhil*) refers both to the Swahili language, as well as to the Islamic culture of the peoples inhabiting the East African coast from Mogadishu (Somalia) in the north down to Mozambique in the south. Both language and culture are a rich mixture of Bantu, Arabic, Persian and Asian influences.

Although Swahili culture began to develop in the early part of the first millennium AD, it was not until the 18th century, with the ascendancy of the Omani Arabs on Zanzibar, that it came into its own. Swahili's role as a lingua franca was solidified as it spread throughout East and Central Africa along the great trade caravan routes. European missionaries and explorers soon adopted the language as their main means of communicating with locals. In the second half of the 19th century, missionaries, notably the German Johann Ludwig Krapf, also began applying the Roman alphabet. Prior to this, Swahili had been written exclusively in Arabic script.

Zanzibar Archipelago. Most of what is now mainland Tanzania, as well as Rwanda and Burundi, came under German control as German East Africa (later Tanganyika), while the British took Kenya and Uganda.

The 19th century was also the era of various European explorers, including Gustav Fischer (a German whose party was virtually annihilated by the Maasai at Hell's Gate on Lake Naivasha in 1882), Joseph Thomson (a Scot who reached Lake Victoria via the Rift Valley lakes and the Aberdare Highlands in 1883), and Count Teleki von Szek (an Austrian who explored the Lake Turkana region and Mt Kenya in 1887). Anglican bishop James Hannington set out in 1885 to establish a diocese in Uganda, but was killed when he reached the Nile. Other explorers included Burton and Speke, who were sent to Lake Tanganyika in 1858 by the Royal Geographical Society, and the famous Henry Morton Stanley and David Livingstone.

By the turn of the 20th century, Europeans had firmly established a presence in East Africa. Both the British and German colonial administrations were busy building railways and roads to open their colonies to commerce, establishing hospitals and schools, and encouraging the influx of Christian missionaries. Kenya's fertile and climatically favourable highlands proved eminently suitable for European farmers to colonise. In Tanganyika, by contrast, large areas were unable to support agriculture and were plagued by the tsetse fly, which made cattle grazing and dairy farming impossible.

1905–7

In the Matumbi Hills near Kilwa (Tanzania), the mystic Kinjikitile stirs African labourers to rise up against their German overlords in what became known as the Maji Maji rebellion.

1952

The Mau Mau rebellion begins as a protest against colonial land-grabbing in Kikuyu lands. By the time it was suppressed, thousands of Kikuyu had been killed or put into detention camps.

1961–63

Following a period of increasing discontent with colonial rule, the countries of East Africa gain independence, with Tanganyika (now Tanzania) leading the way in December 1961.

1978–79

Ugandan dictator Idi Amin invades Tanzania, burning villages along the Kagera River believed to harbour Ugandan rebels. Tanzania's army marches to Kampala to topple Amin and restore Milton Obote to power.

Independence

As the European presence in Africa solidified, discontent with colonial rule grew and demands for independence became more insistent. In the 1950s and early 1960s, the various nationalist movements coalesced and gained force across East Africa, culminating in the granting of independence to Tanzania (1961), Uganda, Rwanda and Burundi (all in 1962), and Kenya (1963). In Kenya, the path to independence was violent and protracted, with some of the underlying issues reflected in the country's current political difficulties; in Tanzania and Uganda the immediate preindependence years were relatively peaceful, while in Rwanda and Burundi, long-existing tribal rivalries were a major issue – the effects of which are still being felt today.

THE SLAVE TRADE

Slavery has been practised in Africa throughout recorded history, but its greatest expansion in East Africa came with the rise of Islam, which prohibits the enslavement of Muslims. Demands of European plantation holders on Réunion and Mauritius were another catalyst, particularly during the late 18th century.

Initially, slaves were taken from coastal regions and shipped to Arabia, Persia and the Indian Ocean islands. Kilwa Kisiwani, off Tanzania's southern coast, was a major export gateway. As demand increased, traders made their way inland, and during the 18th and 19th centuries, slaves were being brought from as far away as Malawi and the Congo. By the 19th century, with the rise of the Omani Arabs, Zanzibar island had eclipsed Kilwa Kisiwani as East Africa's major slave-trading depot. According to some estimates, by the 1860s from 10,000 to as many as 50,000 slaves were passing through Zanzibar's market each year. Overall, close to 600,000 slaves were sold through Zanzibar between 1830 and 1873, when a treaty with Britain paved the way for the trade's ultimate halt in the region in the early 20th century.

As well as the human horrors, the slave trade caused major social upheavals. In the south of present-day Tanzania, it fanned up inter-clan warfare as ruthless entrepreneurs raided neighbouring tribes for slaves. In other areas, it promoted increased social stratification and altered settlement patterns. Some tribes began to build fortified settlements encircled by trenches, while others concentrated their populations in towns as self defence. Another major societal change was the gradual shift in the nature of chieftaincy from religiously based to a position resting on military power or wealth.

The slave trade also served as an impetus for European missionary activity in East Africa, prompting the establishment of the first mission stations and missionary penetration of the interior. A tireless campaigner against the horrors of slavery was Scottish missionary-explorer David Livingstone (1813–74), whose efforts, combined with the attention attracted by his funeral, were an important influence mobilising British initiatives to halt human trafficking in the region.

1984

Kenya reports its first AIDS case. Within a decade, an estimated 800,000 people are infected with HIV.

1994

The presidents of Rwanda and Burundi are killed when their plane is shot down during landing, unleashing the Rwandan genocide, leaving more than one million dead in its wake.

7 August 1998

Within minutes of each another, Al-Qaeda truck bombs explode at the American embassies in Nairobi and Dar es Salaam, killing and injuring dozens.

2004

Uganda's aggressive anti-AIDS campaign begins to show results, as adult prevalence rates fall to about 6%, down from about 18% around a decade earlier.

Kenya

In Kenya, the European influx increased rapidly during the first half of the 20th century, so that by the 1950s there were about 80,000 settlers in the country. Much of the land that was expropriated for their farms came from the homelands of the Kikuyu people. The Kikuyu responded by forming an opposition political association in 1920, and by instigating the Mau Mau rebellion in the 1950s, which marked a major turning point in Kenyan politics.

Zamani: A Survey of East African History, edited by renowned Kenyan historian BA Ogot with JA Kieran, is a classic introduction to the region's precolonial and colonial history from an African perspective.

Tanganyika

In Tanganyika, the unpopular German administration continued until the end of WWI, when the League of Nations mandated the area to the British, and Rwanda and Burundi to the Belgians. British rule was equally unpopular, with the Brits neglecting development of Tanganyika in favour of the more lucrative and fertile options available in Kenya and Uganda. Political consciousness soon began to coalesce in the form of farmers' unions and cooperatives through which popular demands were expressed. By the mid-20th century, there were over 400 such cooperatives, which soon joined to form the Tanganyika Africa Association (TAA), a lobbying group for the nationalist cause based in Dar es Salaam.

Uganda

In Uganda, the British tended to favour the recruitment of the powerful Buganda people for the civil service. Members of other tribes, unable to acquire responsible jobs in the colonial administration or to make inroads into the Buganda-dominated commercial sector, were forced to seek other ways of joining the mainstream. The Acholi and Lango, for example, chose the army and became the tribal majority in the military. As resentment grew, the seeds were planted for the intertribal conflicts that were to tear Uganda apart following independence.

Rwanda & Burundi

In Rwanda and Burundi, the period of colonial rule was characterised by increasing power and privilege of the Tutsi. The Belgians administrators found it convenient to rule indirectly through Tutsi chiefs and their princes, and the Tutsi had a monopoly on the missionary-run educational system. As a result, long-existing tensions between the Tutsi and Hutu were exacerbated, igniting the spark that was later to explode in the 1994 Rwanda genocide.

For more about the independence movements, and the history of each country since independence, see the individual country chapters.

Modern Historical Sites

- Kigali Memorial Centre (Kigali, Uganda)
- National Museum (Dar es Salaam, Tanzania)
- Arusha Declaration Museum (Arusha, Tanzania)
- National Museum (Nairobi, Kenya)
- National Museum (Kampala, Uganda)
- Nyerere Museum (Butiama, Tanzania)

Dec 2007–Jan 2008

Kenya is wracked by postelection violence as hundreds are killed and thousands displaced from their homes in the Rift Valley and central areas.

2008

Kilimanjaro's rapidly diminishing snows are predicted to disappear entirely by 2020. Climate change is also linked to an increase in malaria and other vector-borne diseases.

mid-2011

Overshadowed by regional strife and fears of giving up national sovereignty, the goal of achieving political federation among members of the East African Community by 2015 stalls completely.

10 September 2011

In one of the region's worst shipping disasters, the grossly overloaded MV *Spice Islander* sinks between Tanzania's Zanzibar and Pemba islands, killing at least 200 people.

Life in East Africa

Daily Life & Customs

It's a wild place, the East African bush, and hospitality counts because it has to. You never know if you'll soon be the one on the asking end – whether for a cup of water, a meal or a roof over your head for the night – and strangers are accordingly welcomed as family. In a region where it is commonplace for a 10km walk to get you to the nearest water source, the nearest medical clinic or the nearest primary school, time takes on an altogether different dimension. Daily rhythms are determined by the sun and the seasons, and arriving is the most important thing, not when or how. *Nitafika* (I will arrive). *Safiri salama* (Travel in peace). *Umefika* (You have arrived). *Karibu* (Welcome). Additional words are not necessary.

No monthly social security cheques arrive in the mail in East Africa, so community life is essential – for support in times of sickness and for the ageing, as well as in ensuring a proper upbringing for the young people. Mourning is a community affair, as is celebrating. It would be unheard of not to attend the funeral of your mother's second cousin once removed, just as it would be equally unheard of to miss celebrating the wedding of your father's stepbrother's neighbour. Salaried jobs are scarce, and if you're one of the lucky few to have found one, it's expected that you'll share your good fortune with the extended family. Throughout East African society, 'I' and 'me' are very much out, while 'our' and 'we' are in.

In all aspects of daily life, emphasis is on the necessary. If you do attend that funeral, forget bringing flowers; a bag of rice, or money, would be a more appropriate way of showing your solidarity with the bereaved.

AIDS IN EAST AFRICA

Together with malaria, AIDS is the leading cause of death in sub-Saharan Africa, and East Africa is no exception. In Uganda alone, there are nearly one million AIDS orphans under 17 years of age. The figures elsewhere in the region are just as sobering.

Encouragingly, AIDS awareness has improved in the region; East African governments now discuss the situation openly, and you'll notice AIDS-related billboards in Dar es Salaam, Nairobi, Kampala and elsewhere. Yet at the grassroots level in many areas, the stigma remains and, especially away from urban centres, real discussion remains limited. AIDS-related deaths are often kept quiet, with tuberculosis used euphemistically as a socially acceptable catch-all diagnosis. And many AIDS clinics and counselling centres still operate anonymously; if a sign were hung out, many victims wouldn't enter for fear of being recognised. In one study in Kenya, over half of the women surveyed who had acquired HIV hadn't told their partners because they feared being beaten or abandoned.

FEMALE GENITAL MUTILATION

Female genital mutilation (FGM), often euphemistically referred to as female circumcision, is the partial or total removal of the female external genitalia. In Kenya, an estimated one-third of women, most in the northeast, near Somalia, have undergone FGM. In Tanzania, the figures are estimated at between 10% and 18%, while in Uganda, it's about 5%.

FGM is usually carried out for reasons of cultural or gender identity, and it is entrenched in tribal life in some areas. Longstanding traditional beliefs about hygiene, aesthetics and health also play a role in the continuance of FGM. Yet among the very real risks of the procedure are infection, shock and haemorrhage, as well as lifelong complications and pain with menstruation, urination, intercourse and childbirth. For women who have had infibulation – in which all or part of the external genitalia are removed, and the vaginal opening then narrowed and stitched together – unassisted childbirth is impossible, and many women and children die as a consequence.

Since the mid-1990s there have been major efforts to reduce the incidence of the practice, with slow but real progress. In both Kenya and Tanzania, FGM has been declared illegal, although the number of prosecutions are small and the practice continues in many areas. Several nongovernmental women's organisations, in Kenya in particular, have taken a leading role in bringing FGM to the forefront of media discussion. There is also a growing movement towards alternative rites that offer the chance to maintain traditions while minimising the health complications, such as the practice of *ntanira na mugambo* (circumcision through words).

In Uganda, FGM was finally banned by the government in 2009, with penalties of 10 years imprisonment for violators (or life, if the girl dies), although enforcement of this is still a concern. The main area where FGM is still practiced is in northeastern Uganda, near the border with Kenya.

At all levels of society, invisible social hierarchies lend life a sense of order. Age-based groups play a central role among many tribes, and the elderly and those in positions of authority are respected. Men rule the roost in the working world and, at least symbolically, in the family as well. Although women arguably form the backbone of the economy throughout the region – with most juggling child-rearing plus work on the family farm or in an office – they are frequently marginalised when it comes to education and politics. Some positive contrasts to this situation are found in Kenya, which is notable for its abundance of nongovernment organisations, many headed by women, and in Uganda, where women play prominent roles in educational and literary circles.

Former Kenyan president Jomo Kenyatta once argued that female genital mutilation (FGM) was such an integral part of initiation rites and Kikuyu identity that its abolition would destroy the tribal system.

With the exception of Tanzania, where local chieftaincies were abolished following independence, tribal identity and structures are strong. This sometimes comes with disastrous consequences, as seen in the Rwandan genocide in 1994 and in the 2007 postelection violence in Kenya. Otherwise, clashes between traditional and modern lifestyles are generally fairly low profile.

Multicultural Melting Pot

Almost since the dawn of humankind, outsiders have been arriving in East Africa and have been assimilated into its seething, simmering and endlessly fascinating cultural melting pot. From the Bantu-, Nilotic- and Cushitic-speaking groups that made their way to the region during the early migrations, to Arab and Asian traders, to colonial-era Europeans, a long stream of migrants have left their footprints. Today, the region's modern face reflects this rich fusion of influences, with 300-plus tribal groups, as well as small but economically significant pockets of Asians,

Arabs and Europeans all rubbing shoulders. For more on some of the major groups, see Tribal Cultures chapter (p583).

While national identities have become entrenched over the past half-century of independence, tribal loyalties also remain strong in many areas. The highest-profile conflicts resulting from intertribal clashes have been in Rwanda, where longstanding tensions exploded in 1994, leading to a brutal genocide which still scars the nation; in Burundi, where intertribal conflicts culminated in a long civil war; and, most recently, in Kenya, where the 2007 presidential elections were marred by interethnic violence. At the other end of the spectrum is Tanzania, which has earned a name for itself for its remarkably harmonious society, and its success in forging tolerance and unity out of diversity.

Although intrareligious (primarily Christian-Muslim) frictions exist, they are at a generally low level, and not a major factor in contemporary East African politics.

BRIDES

Negotiations of bride price still play a major role in marriages in the region. Although cash is becoming an increasingly common replacement, cattle are still coveted in many areas.

Sports

Football (soccer) dominates sporting headlines throughout the region, and matches always draw large and enthusiastic crowds. Kenya's national team, the Harambee Stars, regularly participates in pan-African competitions and World Cup qualifiers; there are also occasional appearances by Uganda's Kobs and Rwanda's Amavubi (Wasps). A new national stadium in Dar es Salaam and enthusiastic backing from the president are giving Tanzania's Taifa Stars an improved profile.

On the international sports stage, Kenya regularly dominates in long-distance running competitions.

The East African Safari Rally (www.eastafricansafarirally.com), which has been held annually since 1953, passes through Kenya, Uganda and Tanzania along public roadways, and attracts an international collection of drivers with their vintage (pre-1971) automobiles. Just as rugged, if not more so, is the Tour d'Afrique (www.tourdafrique.com) bicycle race that passes through East Africa (Kenya and Tanzania) en route between Cairo (Egypt) and Cape Town (South Africa).

Bao

It's not exactly sport, but *bao* (also known as *kombe, mweso* and by various other names) is one of East Africa's favourite pastimes. It's played throughout the region, but it is especially popular on the Zanzibar Archipelago and elsewhere along the coast, where you'll see men in their *kanzu* (white robe-like outer garment) and *kofia* (hat) huddled around a board watching two opponents play. The rules vary somewhat from place to place, but the game always involves trying to capture the pebbles or seeds of your opponent, which are set out on a board with rows of small hollows. Anything can substitute for a board, from finely carved wood to a flattened area of sand on the beach, and playing well is something of a patiently acquired art form.

Religion

The vibrant spirituality that pervades the African continent fills East Africa as well. The major religions in the region are Christianity and Islam, with Islam especially prevalent in coastal areas. There are also a sizeable number of adherents of traditional religions, as well as small communities of Hindus, Sikhs and Jains.

Christianity

The first Christian missionaries reached East Africa in the mid-19th century. Since then the region has been the site of extensive missionary activity, and today most of the major denominations are represented, including Lutherans, Catholics, Seventh Day Adventists and Baptists. In many areas, mission stations have been the major, and in some cases the only, channels for development assistance. This is particularly so with health care and education, with missions still sometimes providing the only schools and medical facilities in remote areas.

In addition to the main denominations, there is also an increasing number of home-grown African sects, especially in Kenya. Factors that are often cited for their growth include cultural resurgence, an ongoing struggle against neo-colonialism and the alienation felt by many jobseekers who migrate to urban centres far from their homes.

Church services throughout East Africa are invariably very colourful and packed to overflowing. Even if you can't understand the language, it's worth going to listen to the unaccompanied choral singing, which East Africans do with such beauty and precision.

Islam

Islam was founded in the early 7th century by the Prophet Mohammed. By the time of his death, the new religion had begun to spread throughout the Arabian peninsula, from where it was then carried in all directions over the subsequent centuries, including along the East African coast, where it is today flourishing, although – in typical East African fashion – in a considerably less dogmatic form than in other parts of the world.

The five pillars of Islam that guide Muslims in their daily lives:

Haj (pilgrimage) It is the duty of every Muslim who is fit and can afford it to make the pilgrimage to Mecca at least once.

Sala (prayer, sometimes written *salat*) This is the obligation of prayer, done five times daily when muezzins call the faithful to pray, facing Mecca and ideally in a mosque.

NAMING

In Swahili-speaking areas of East Africa, it's common for a woman to drop her own name, and become known as *Mama* followed by the name of her oldest son (or daughter, if she has no sons).

CONDUCT IN EAST AFRICA

East Africa comfortably mixes a generally conservative outlook on life with a great deal of tolerance and openness towards foreigners, and meeting locals is one of the highlights of regional travel. Following are a few tips to smooth the way.

» While most East Africans are likely to be too polite to tell you so directly, they'll be privately shaking their head about travellers doing things like not wearing enough clothing or sporting tatty clothes. Especially along the Muslim coast, cover up your shoulders and legs, and avoid plunging necklines and skin-tight fits.

» Pleasantries count. Even if you're just asking for directions, take time to greet the other person. Handshake etiquette is also worth learning, and best picked up by observation. In many areas, East Africans often continue holding hands for several minutes after meeting, or even throughout an entire conversation.

» Don't eat or pass things with the left hand.

» Respect authority; losing your patience or undermining an official's authority will get you nowhere, while deference and a good-natured demeanour will see you through most situations.

» Avoid criticising the government of your host country as well as offending locals with public nudity, open anger and public displays of affection (between people of the same or opposite sex).

» When visiting a rural area, seek out the chief or local elders to announce your presence, and ask permission before setting up a tent or wandering through a village – it will rarely be refused.

» Receive gifts with both hands, or with the right hand while touching the left hand to your right elbow. Giving a gift? Don't be surprised if the appreciation isn't expressed verbally.

Sawm (fasting) Ramadan commemorates the revelation of the Qur'an to Mohammed and is the month when Muslims fast from dawn to dusk.
Shahada (the profession of faith) 'There is no God but Allah, and Mohammed is his Prophet' is the fundamental tenet of Islam.
Zakat (alms) Giving to the poor is an essential part of Islamic social teaching.

Most East African Muslims are Sunnis, with a small minority of Shiites, primarily among the Asian community. The most influential of the various Shiite sects represented are the Ismailis, followers of the Aga Khan.

Life Expectancy

» Burundi – 51 years

» Kenya – 55 years

» Rwanda – 51 years

» Tanzania – 56 years

» Uganda – 53 years

Traditional Religions

The natural and spiritual worlds are part of the same continuum in East Africa, and mountain peaks, lakes, forests, certain trees and other natural features are viewed by many as dwellings of the supreme being or of the ancestors.

Most local traditional beliefs acknowledge the existence of a supreme deity. Many also hold that communication with this deity is possible through the intercession of the ancestors. The ancestors are thus accordingly honoured, and viewed as playing a strong role in protecting the tribe and family. Maintaining proper relations is essential for general well being. However, among the Maasai, the Kikuyu and several other tribes, there is no tradition of ancestor worship, with the supreme deity (known as Ngai or Enkai) the sole focus of devotion.

Traditional medicine in East Africa is closely intertwined with traditional religion, with practitioners using divining implements, prayers, chanting and dance to facilitate communication with the spirit world.

Tribal Cultures

East Africa has a rich mosaic of tribal cultures, with over 300 different groups in an area roughly one-fourth of the size of Australia. Their traditions are expressed through splendid ceremonial attire, pulsating dance rhythms, refined artistry and highly organised community structures, and experiencing these will likely be a highlight of your travels. Following are short profiles of several groups in the region.

Akamba

The Akamba, who live east of Nairobi towards Tsavo National Park, first migrated here from the south about 200 years ago in search of food. Because their own low-altitude land was poor, they were forced to barter for food stocks from the neighbouring Maasai and Kikuyu peoples. Soon, they acquired a reputation as savvy traders, with business dealings extending from the coast inland to Lake Victoria and north to Lake Turkana. Renowned also for their martial prowess, many Akamba were drafted into Britain's WWI army, and today they are still well represented among Kenyan defence and law enforcement brigades.

In the 1930s, the British colonial administration settled large numbers of white farmers in traditional Akamba lands and tried to limit the number of cattle the Akamba could own by confiscating them. In protest, the Akamba formed the Ukamba Members Association, which marched en masse to Nairobi and squatted peacefully at Kariokor Market until their cattle were returned. Large numbers of Akamba were subsequently dispossessed to make way for Tsavo National Park.

All Akamba go through initiation rites at about the age of 12, and have the same age-based groups common to many of the region's peoples. Young parents are known as 'junior elders' (*mwanake* for men, *mwiitu* for women) and are responsible for the maintenance and upkeep of the village. They later become 'medium elders' *(nthele),* and then 'full elders' *(atumia ma kivalo),* with responsibility for death ceremonies and administering the law. The last stage of a person's life is that of 'senior elder' *(atumia ma kisuka),* with responsibility for holy places.

Baganda

Uganda's largest tribal group, the Baganda, comprise almost 20% of the population and are the source of the country's name ('Land of the Baganda'; their kingdom is known as Buganda). Although today the Baganda are spread throughout the country, their traditional lands are in the areas north and northwest of Lake Victoria, including Kampala. Due to significant missionary activity most Baganda are Christian, although animist traditions persist.

The Baganda, together with the neighbouring Haya, have a historical reputation as one of East Africa's most highly organised tribes. Their traditional political system was based around the absolute power of the *kabaka* (king), who ruled through district chiefs. This system reached its zenith during the 19th century, when the Baganda came to dominate various neighbouring groups, including the Nilotic Iteso (who now comprise about 8% of Uganda's population). Baganda influence was solidified during the colonial era, with the British favouring their recruitment to the civil service. During the chaotic Obote/Amin years of the late 1960s and early 1970s, the Bagandan monarchy was abolished; it was restored in 1993, although with no political power.

El-Molo

The Cushitic-speaking El-Molo are a small tribe, numbering less than 4000. Historically the El-Molo were one of the region's more distinct groups, but in recent times they have been forced to adapt or relinquish many of their old customs in order to survive, and intermarriage with other tribes is common.

The El-Molo, whose ancestral home is on two small islands in the middle of Kenya's Lake Turkana, traditionally subsisted on fish, supplemented by the occasional crocodile, turtle, hippopotamus or bird. Over the years an ill-balanced diet and the effects of too much fluoride began to take their toll. The El-Molo became increasingly susceptible to disease and, thus weakened, to attacks from stronger tribes. Their numbers plummeted.

Today, the El-Molo face an uncertain future. While some continue to eke out a living from the lake, others have turned to cattle herding or work in the tourism industry. Commercial fishing supplements their traditional subsistence and larger, more permanent settlements in Loyangalani, on Lake Turkana's southeastern shores, have replaced the El-Molo's traditional dome-shaped island homes.

Haya

The Haya, who live west of Lake Victoria around Bukoba, have both Bantu and Nilotic roots, and are one of the largest tribes in Tanzania. They have a rich history, and in the precolonial era boasted one of the most highly developed early societies on the continent.

At the heart of traditional Haya society were eight different states or kingdoms, each headed by a powerful and often despotic *mukama* (ruler) who ruled in part by divine right. Order was maintained through a system of chiefs and officials, assisted by an age group–based army. With the rise of European influence in the region, this era of Haya history came to an end. The various groups began to splinter, and many chiefs were replaced by persons considered more malleable and sympathetic to colonial interests.

Resentment of these propped-up leaders was strong, spurring the Haya to regroup and form the Bukoba Bahaya Union in 1924. This association was initially directed towards local political reform but soon

AGE-BASED GROUPS SETS

Age-based groups (in which all youths of the same age belong to a group, and pass through the various stages of life and their associated rituals together) continue to play an important role in tribal life throughout much of East Africa. Each group has its own leader and community responsibilities, and definition of the age-based groups is often highly refined. Among the Sukuma, for example, who live in the area south of Lake Victoria, each age-based group traditionally had its own system for counting from one to 10, with the system understood by others within the group, but not by members of other groups. Among the Maasai, who have one of the most highly stratified age-group systems in the region, males are organised into age groups and further into sub-groups, with inter-group rivalries and relationships one of the defining features of daily life.

FOREST DWELLERS

The clash between traditional and Western ways of life in East Africa is particularly apparent among the region's hunter-gatherer and forest-dwelling peoples. These include the Twa, who live in the western forests of Rwanda and Burundi, where they comprise less than 1% of the overall population, and the Hadzabe, in north-central Tanzania around Lake Eyasi. Typically, these communities are among the most marginalised in East African society.

For the Twa and the Hadzabe, loss of land and forest means loss of their only resource base. With the rise of commercial logging, the ongoing clearing of forests in favour of agricultural land, and the establishment of parks and conservation areas, the forest resources and wildlife on which they depend have dramatically decreased. Additional pressures come from hunting and poaching, and from nomadic pastoralists (many of whom in turn have been evicted from their own traditional areas) seeking grazing lands for their cattle. The Hadzabe say that the once-plentiful wildlife in their traditional hunting areas is now gone, and that many days they return empty-handed from their daily search for meat. Others lament the fact that once-prized skills such as animal tracking and knowledge of local plants are being relegated to irrelevance.

Although some Hadzabe have turned to tourism and craft-making for subsistence, the benefits of this are sporadic. Some now only hunt for the benefit of tourists, and others have given up their traditional lifestyle completely. In Rwanda, the Twa have begun mobilising to gain increased political influence and greater access to health care and education. However, throughout the region, it will take more time before these people are given a real voice.

developed into the more influential and broad-based African Association. Together with similar groups established elsewhere in Tanzania, it constituted one of the country's earliest political movements and was an important force in the drive towards independence.

Kalenjin

The Kalenjin have age-set groups into which a man is initiated after circumcision. Administration of the law is carried out at the *kok* (an informal court led by the clan's elders).

The Kalenjin are one of Kenya's largest groups. Together with the Kikuyu, Luo, Luyha and Kamba, they account for about 70% of the country's population. Although often viewed as a single ethnic entity, the term 'Kalenjin' was actually coined in the 1950s to refer to a loose collection of several different Nilotic groups, including the Kipsigis, Nandi, Marakwet, Pokot and Tugen (former Kenyan president Daniel arap Moi's people). These groups speak different dialects of the same language (Nandi), but otherwise have distinct traditions and lifestyles. Due to the influence of arap Moi, the Kalenjin have amassed considerable political power in Kenya. They are also known for their female herbalist doctors, and for their many world-class runners.

The traditional homeland of the various Kalenjin peoples is along the western edge of the central Rift Valley area, including Kericho, Eldoret, Kitale, Baringo and the land surrounding Mt Elgon. Originally pastoralists, Kalenjin today are known primarily as farmers. An exception to this are the cattle-loving Kipsigi, whose cattle rustling continues to cause friction between them and neighbouring tribes.

The Nandi, who are the second largest of the Kalenjin communities, and comprise about one-third of all Kalenjin, settled in the Nandi Hills between the 16th and 17th centuries, where they prospered after learning agricultural techniques from the Luo and Luyha. They had a formidable military reputation and, in the late 19th century, managed to delay construction of the Uganda railway for more than a decade until Koitalel, their chief, was killed.

Karamojong

The marginalised Karamojong, at home in Karamoja, in northeastern Uganda, are one of East Africa's most insulated, beleaguered and colourful tribes. As with the Samburu, Maasai and other Nilotic pastoralist peoples, life for the Karamojong centres around cattle, which are kept at night in the centre of the family living compound and grazed by day on the surrounding plains. Cattle are the main measure of wealth, ownership is a mark of adulthood, and cattle raiding and warfare are central parts of the culture. When cattle are grazed in dry-season camps away from the family homestead, the Karamojong warriors tending them live on blood from live cattle, milk and sometimes meat. In times of scarcity, protection of the herd is considered so important that milk is reserved for calves and children.

The Karamojong have long been subjected to often heavy-handed government pressure to abandon their pastoralist lifestyle; their plight has been exacerbated by periodic famines, and by the loss of traditional dry-season grazing areas with the formation of Kidepo Valley National Park in the 1960s. While current Ugandan president Yoweri Museveni has permitted the Karamojong to keep arms to protect themselves against raids from other groups, including the Turkana in neighbouring Kenya, government expeditions targeted at halting cattle raiding continue. These raids and expeditions, combined with easy access to weapons from neighbouring Sudan and a breakdown of law and order, have made the Karamoja area off-limits to outsiders in recent years.

KIKUYU GOD

The Kikuyu god, Ngai, is believed to reside on Mt Kenya, and many Kikuyu homes are still oriented to face the sacred peak.

Kikuyu

The Kikuyu, who comprise about 20% of Kenya's population and are the country's largest tribal group, have their heartland surrounding Mt Kenya. They are Bantu peoples who are believed to have migrated into the area from the east and northeast from around the 16th century onwards, and to have undergone several periods of intermarriage and splintering. According to Kikuyu oral traditions, there are nine original *mwaki* (clans), each tracing its origins back to male and female progenitors known as Kikuyu and Mumbi. The administration of these clans, each of which is made up of many family groups *(nyumba),* was originally overseen by a council of elders, with great significance placed on the roles of the witch doctor, medicine man and blacksmith.

Instead of circumcision, the Luo traditionally extracted four to six teeth at initiation. It's still common to see Luo elders with several pegs missing.

Initiation rites consist of ritual circumcision for boys and female genital mutilation for girls, though the latter is becoming less common. The practice was a source of particular conflict between the Kikuyu and Western missionaries during the late 19th and early 20th centuries. The issue eventually became linked with the independence struggle, and the establishment of independent Kikuyu schools.

The Kikuyu are also known for the opposition association they formed in the 1920s to protest European seizure of large areas of their lands, and for their subsequent instigation of the Mau Mau rebellion in the 1950s. Due to the influence of Jomo Kenyatta, Kenya's first president, the Kikuyu today are disproportionately represented in business and government (President Mwai Kibaki is a Kikuyu). This has proved to be a source of ongoing friction with other groups, and a persistent stumbling block on Kenya's path to national integration.

Luo

The Luo live on the northeastern shores of Lake Victoria. They began their migration to the area from Sudan around the 15th century. Although their numbers are relatively small in Tanzania, in Kenya they comprise about 12% of the population and are the country's third largest tribal group.

During the independence struggle, many of Kenya's leading politicians and trade unionists were Luo, including Tom Mboya (assassinated in 1969) and former vice-president Jaramogi Oginga Odinga, and they continue to form the backbone of the Kenyan political opposition. Kenya's current prime minister, Raila Odinga, is a Luo.

The Luo have had an important influence on the East African musical scene. They are notable especially for their contribution to the highly popular *benga* style, which has since been adopted by musicians from many other tribes. For more information about *benga,* see p632.

The Luo were originally cattle herders, but the devastating effects of rinderpest in the 1890s forced them to adopt fishing and subsistence agriculture, which are now the main sources of livelihood of most Luo today. Luo family groups consist of the man, his wife or wives, and their sons and daughters-in-law. The family unit is part of a larger grouping of families or *dhoot* (clan), several of which make up *ogandi* (a group of geographically related people), each led by a *ruoth* (chief). Traditional Luo living compounds are enclosed by fences, and include separate huts for the man and for each wife and son. The Luo consider age, wealth and respect as converging, with the result that elders control family resources and represent the family to the outside world.

Maasai

Although comprising less than 5% of the population in Kenya and Tanzania, it is the Maasai, more than any other tribe, who have become for many the quintessential face of 'tribal' East Africa. With a reputation (often exaggerated) as fierce warriors, and of having a proud demeanour, the Maasai have insisted on maintaining their ethnic identity and traditional lifestyle, often in the face of great government opposition. Today, Maasai life continues to be inextricably bound with that of their large cattle herds, which they graze in Tanzania–Kenya border areas.

The Maasai are Nilotic people who first migrated to the region from Sudan about 1000 years ago. They eventually came to dominate a large area of what is now central Kenya, until the late 19th century when their numbers were decimated by famine and disease, and their cattle herds routed by rinderpest.

BODY ART

The Maasai's artistic traditions are most vividly seen in their striking body decoration and beaded ornaments. Women are famous for their magnificent beaded plate-like necklaces, while men typically wear the red-checked shuka (blanket) and carry a distinctive balled club.

LAND PRESSURES

During the colonial era in Kenya, it was largely Maasai land that was taken for European colonisation through two controversial treaties. The creation of Serengeti National Park in Tanzania and the continuing colonial annexation of Maasai territory put much of the remaining traditional grazing lands of the Maasai off-limits. During subsequent years, as populations of both the Maasai and their cattle increased, pressure for land became intense and conflict with the authorities was constant. Government-sponsored resettlement programs have met with only limited success, as Maasai traditions scorn agriculture and land ownership.

One consequence of this competition for land is that many Maasai ceremonial traditions can no longer be fulfilled. Part of the ceremony where a man becomes a *moran* (warrior) involves a group of young men around the age of 14 going out and building a small livestock camp after their circumcision ceremony. They then live alone there for up to eight years before returning to the village to marry. Today, while the tradition and will survive, land is often unavailable.

THE SWAHILI

The East African coast is home to the Swahili ('People of the Coast'), descendants of Bantu-Arab traders who share a common language and traditions. Although generally not regarded as a single tribal group, the Swahili have for centuries had their own distinct societal structures, and consider themselves to be a single civilisation.

Swahili culture first began to take on a defined form around the 11th century, with the rise of Islam. Today most Swahili are adherents of Islam, although it's generally a more liberal version than that practised in the Middle East. Thanks to this Islamic identity, the Swahili have traditionally considered themselves as historically and morally distinct from peoples in the interior, and with links eastwards towards the rest of the Islamic world.

Swahili festivals follow the Islamic calendar. The year begins with Eid al-Fitr, a celebration of feasting and almsgiving to mark the end of Ramadan fasting. The old Persian new year's purification ritual of Nauroz or Mwaka was also traditionally celebrated, with the parading of a bull counter clockwise through town followed by its slaughter and several days of dancing and feasting. In many areas, Nauroz has now become merged with Eid al-Fitr and is no longer celebrated. The festival of *maulidi* (marking the birth of the Prophet) is another Swahili festival, marked by decorated mosques and colourful street processions.

Throughout the year in Swahili communities, the hands and feet of brides and married women are often adorned with henna painting – intricate designs made with a paste from leaves of the henna plant.

The World of the Swahili by John Middleton is a good place to start for anyone wanting to learn more about Swahili life and culture.

While tourism provides an income to an increasing number of Maasai, the benefits are not widespread. In recent years many Maasai have moved to the cities or coastal resorts, becoming guards for restaurants and hotels.

The Samburu, who live directly north of Mt Kenya, are closely related to the Maasai linguistically and culturally.

Makonde

The Makonde are famed throughout East Africa and beyond for their highly refined ebony woodcarvings. The tribe has its origins in northern Mozambique, where many Makonde still live; although in recent years a subtle split has begun to develop between the group's Tanzanian and Mozambican branches. Today, most Tanzanian Makonde live in southeastern Tanzania on the Makonde plateau, although many members of the carving community have since migrated to Dar es Salaam.

The Makonde are matrilineal. Although customs are gradually changing, children and inheritances normally belong to the woman, and it's still common for husbands to move to the villages of their wives after marriage. Makonde settlements are widely scattered (possibly a remnant of the days when the Makonde sought to evade slave raids), and there is no tradition of a unified political system. Despite this, a healthy sense of tribal identity has managed to survive. Makonde villages are typically governed by a hereditary chief and a council of elders. The Makonde traditionally practised body scarring, and many elders still sport facial markings and (for women) wooden lip plugs.

Because of their remote location, the Makonde have succeeded in remaining largely insulated from colonial and postcolonial influences. They are known in particular for their steady resistance to Islam. Today, most Makonde follow traditional religions, with the complex spirit world given its fullest expression in their carvings.

Pare

The Bantu-speaking Pare inhabit the Pare mountains in northeastern Tanzania, where they migrated several centuries ago from the Taita Hills area of southern Kenya.

The Pare are one of Tanzania's most educated groups. Despite their small numbers, they have been highly influential in shaping Tanzania's recent history. In the 1940s they formed the Wapare Union, which played an important role in the independence drive.

The Pare are also known for their rich oral traditions, and for their elaborate rituals centring on the dead. Near most villages are sacred areas in which skulls of tribal chiefs are kept. When people die, they are believed to inhabit a netherworld between the land of the living and the spirit world. If they are allowed to remain in this state, ill fate will befall their descendants. As a result, rituals allowing the deceased to pass peacefully into the world of the ancestors hold great significance. Traditional Pare beliefs hold that when an adult male dies, others in his lineage will die as well until the cause of his death has been found and 'appeased.' Many of the possible reasons for death have to do with disturbances in moral relations within the lineage or in the village, or with sorcery.

Among the Pare, a deceased male's ghost influences male descendants for as long as the ghost's name is remembered. Daughters, too, are dependent on their father's goodwill. Yet, since property and status are transmitted through the male line, a father's ghost only has influence over his daughter's descendants until her death.

Sukuma & Nyamwezi

The Sukuma, Bantu speakers from southern Lake Victoria, comprise almost 15% of Tanzania's total population, although it is only relatively recently that they have come to view themselves as a single entity. They are closely related to the Nyamwezi, Tanzania's second largest tribal group around Tabora.

The Sukuma are renowned for their drumming, and for their dancing. Lively meetings between their two competing dance societies, the Bagika and the Bagulu, are a focal point of tribal life.

The Sukuma are also known for their highly structured form of village organisation in which each settlement is subdivided into chiefdoms ruled by a *ntemi* (chief) in collaboration with a council of elders. Divisions of land and labour are made by village committees consisting of similarly aged members from each family in the village. These age-based groups perform numerous roles, ranging from assisting with the building of new houses to farming and other community-oriented work. As a result of this system, which gives most families at least a representational role in many village activities, Sukuma often view houses and land as communal property.

DANCES

Among the most famous Sukuma dances are the *banungule* (hyena dance) and the *bazwilili bayeye* (snake and porcupine dance). Before beginning, dancers are treated with traditional medicaments as protection from injury. It's not unheard of for the animals, too, to be given a spot of something to calm their tempers.

Turkana

The colourful Turkana are a Nilotic people who live in the harsh desert country of northwestern Kenya where they migrated from southern Sudan and northeastern Uganda. Although the Turkana only emerged as a distinct tribal group during the early to mid-19th century, they are notable today for their strong sense of tribal identification. The Turkana are closely related linguistically and culturally to Uganda's Karamojong.

Like the Samburu and the Maasai (with whom they are also linguistically linked), the Turkana are primarily cattle herders, although in recent years increasing numbers have turned to fishing and subsistence farming. Some also earn a livelihood through basket weaving and producing other crafts for the tourism industry. Personal relationships based on the exchange of cattle, and built up by each herd owner during the course of a lifetime, are of critical importance in Turkana society and function as a social security net during times of need.

Swahili's role as a lingua franca was solidified as it spread throughout East and Central Africa along the great trade caravan routes. Today it is spoken in more countries and by more people than any other language in sub-Saharan Africa.

The Turkana are famous for their striking appearance and traditional garb. Turkana men cover part of their hair with mud, which is then painted blue and decorated with ostrich and other feathers. Despite the intense heat of the Turkana lands, the main garment is a woollen blanket, often with garish checks. Turkana accessories include a stool carved out of a single piece of wood, a wooden fighting staff and a wrist knife. Tattooing is another hallmark of Turkana life. Witch doctors and prophets are held in high regard, and scars on the lower stomach are usually a sign of a witch doctor's attempt to cast out an undesirable spirit. Traditionally, Turkana men were tattooed on the shoulder and upper arm for killing an enemy – the right shoulder for killing a man, the left for a woman.

In addition to personal adornment, other important forms of artistic expression include finely crafted carvings and refined acappella singing. Ceremonies play a less significant role among the Turkana than among many of their neighbours, and they do not practice circumcision or female genital mutilation.

Environment

The Land

Straddling the equator, edged to the east by the Indian Ocean and to the west by a chain of Rift Valley lakes, East Africa is as diverse geographically and environmentally as it is culturally.

Great Rift Valley

Africa's Great Rift Valley is one of Africa's defining landforms and this great gouge in the planet cuts a swathe through the heart of East Africa. It was formed between 30 and eight million years ago, when the tectonic plates that comprise the African and Eurasian landmasses collided and then diverged again. As the plates moved apart, massive tablets of the earth's crust collapsed between them, resulting over the millennia in the escarpments, ravines, flatlands and lakes that mark much of East Africa today.

The Rift Valley is part of the Afro-Arabian rift system that stretches 5500km from the salty shores of the Dead Sea to the palm trees of Mozambique. The East African section of the Rift Valley consists of two branches formed where the main rift system divides north of Kenya's Lake Turkana. The western branch, or Western Rift Valley, makes its way past Lake Albert in Uganda through Rwanda and Burundi down to Lake Tanganyika, after which it meanders southeast to Lake Nyasa. Seismic and volcanic disturbances still occur throughout the western branch. The eastern branch, known as the Eastern or Gregory Rift, runs south from Lake Turkana past Lake Natron and Lake Manyara in Tanzania before joining again with the Western Rift in northern Malawi.

The Rift created Africa's highest mountains, among them Mt Kilimanjaro, Mt Kenya, Uganda's Rwenzori Mountains and the DRC's Virunga Range. Most began as volcanos and most are now extinct, but no fewer than 30 remain active, among them the DRC's Nyiragongo volcano (p498). Other places where the escarpments of the Rift Valley are particularly impressive include Kenya's Rift Valley Province, the Nkuruman Escarpment east of Kenya's Masai Mara National Reserve, and the terrain around Ngorongoro Conservation Area and Lake Manyara National Park in Tanzania.

Forest Cover

» Tanzania – 39.9%

» Kenya – 6.2%

» Uganda – 8.4%

» Rwanda – 9.5%

» Burundi – 5.9%

» DRC – 58.9%

The Savannah

The African savannah is a quintessentially African landform, so much so that it covers an estimated two-thirds of the African land mass. Savannah is usually located in a broad swathe surrounding tropical rainforest and its sweeping plains are home to some of the richest concentrations of wildlife on earth. The term itself refers to a grasslands ecosystem. While trees may be (and usually are) present, such trees do not, under the strict definition of the term, form a closed canopy. Wet and dry seasons (the latter often with regenerating and/or devastating wildfires) are also typical of Africa's savannah regions.

In East Africa, the most famous sweeps of savannah are found in Tanzania's Serengeti National Park and Kenya's Masai Mara National Reserve.

Mangroves

- Wasini Island, Kenya
- Mida Creek, Kenya
- Zanzibar Archipelago, Tanzania
- Pemba, Tanzania
- Tanga, Tanzania
- Mafia Island Marine Park, Tanzania

Forests

East Africa's forests border the great rainforest systems of central Africa which once formed part of the mighty Guineo–Congolian forest ecosystem. The most intact stands of rainforest are found in places like the Rwenzori Mountains National Park in southwestern Uganda and the DRC's Virunga range, although important blocks of rainforest still exist in Rwanda and Burundi; in the latter two countries, the pressure on forests from soaring populations is particularly acute. Kenya has few forests, although the Kakamega Forest shows what most of Western Kenya must have once looked like, while the Arabuko Sokoke Forest Reserve is the largest surviving tract of coastal forest in East Africa. There are also small patches of tropical rainforest in Tanzania's Eastern Arc mountains, such as the Usambara Mountains.

Lakes

Lake Victoria, which is shared between Uganda, Tanzania and Kenya, is Africa's largest freshwater lake (and the second-largest by area in the world after the US's Lake Superior). Its surface covers an area of over 68,000 sq km. Water levels fluctuate widely, depending largely on the rains, with depths never more than 80m and more often lower than 10m. More than 90% of the lake falls within Tanzanian or Ugandan territory. Lake Victoria is also considered one of the sources of the Nile.

Lake Tanganyika is the world's longest freshwater lake and is estimated to have the second-largest volume of freshwater in the world (after Lake Baikal in Siberia), with 45% belonging to the DRC and 41% to Tanzania.

Lake Nyasa (also known as Lake Malawi), Africa's third-largest and second-deepest freshwater lake, is the Rift Valley's southernmost lake. Its waters reportedly contain more fish species than any other freshwater lake on earth.

Besides providing fertile soil, the volcanic deposits of the Rift Valley have created alkaline waters in most Rift Valley lakes. Its largest is a sea of jade, otherwise known by the more boring name of Lake Turkana (p305), which straddles the Ethiopian border in the north; Lake Turkana is the world's third-largest salt lake. Other important alkaline lakes include Bogoria (p257), Nakuru (p256), Elmenteita (p254) and Natron

THREATS TO LAKE VICTORIA

Lake Victoria is one of Africa's most endangered lakes. A fast-growing population around the lake's shoreline has caused massive environmental problems such as siltation, sedimentation and toxic pollution (primarily pesticides and untreated sewage). Then there are Nile perch (introduced 50 years ago to combat mosquitoes), which eventually thrived, growing to over 200kg in size and becoming every fishing boat captain's dream. Horrifyingly, the ravenous perch have wiped out over 300 species of smaller tropical fish unique to the lake.

But outstripping many of these problems as the major threat to the lake has been the invasion of water hyacinth since the late 1980s. This has been a particular problem in the Winam Gulf, a 100km-long, 50km-wide arm of the lake which falls within Kenyan territory. The millions of dollars ploughed into solving the problem largely rid the gulf of hyacinth by 2005. However, heavy rains in 2006, and the subsequent return of hyacinth, showed that the gulf is still highly susceptible to the hyacinth's clutches.

(p135). These shallow soda lakes, formed by the valley's lack of decent drainage, experience high evaporation rates, which further concentrates the alkalinity. The strangely soapy and smelly waters are, however, the perfect environment for the growth of microscopic blue-green algae, which in turn feed lesser flamingos, tiny crustaceans (food for greater flamingos) and insect larvae (food for soda-resistant fish). In 2011, Kenya's Rift Valley lake system (primarily Lakes Nakuru, Elmenteita and Bogoria) was inscribed on Unesco's list of World Heritage Sites.

Wildlife

East Africa is arguably the premier wildlife-watching destination on earth. The wildlife that most visitors come to see ranges from the 'Big Five' (lions, buffaloes, elephants, leopards and rhinos) to lesser profile animals such as zebras, hippos, giraffes, wildebeests and antelopes, plus major populations of primates. All these are not only impressive to watch but also essential linchpins in a beautifully complex natural web where each species has its own niche.

In addition to the large animals, which are present in such high concentration and diversity, other players include over 60,000 insect species, several dozen types of reptiles and amphibians, many snake species and abundant marine life, both in the Indian Ocean, and inland. Completing the picture are close to 1500 different types of birds, including many rare birds – Tanzania, Kenya and Uganda are each home to more than 1000 species.

For a survey of the region's major wildlife species, see p597. For more on the regions primate species, see p627, while for advice on tracking East Africa's highly endangered eastern mountain gorillas, turn to p32.

BIG FIVE

Few visitors to East Africa know that the term 'Big Five' was coined by white hunters for those five species deemed most dangerous to hunt.

Endangered Species

Many of East Africa's most important species have become endangered over the past few decades because of poisoning, the ongoing destruction of their natural habitat, and merciless poaching for ivory, skins, horn and bush meat.

Elephants

Although elephants are not currently considered endangered, their story has been a conservation cause celebre for decades. In the 1970s and 1980s, the numbers of African elephants plummeted from an estimated 1.3 million to around 500,000 thanks to widespread poaching. In Kenya, the epicentre of the poaching holocaust, elephant numbers fell from 45,000 in 1976 to just 5400 in 1988. The slaughter ended only in 1989 when the trade in ivory was banned under the Convention for International Trade in Endangered Species (CITES). When the ban was established, world raw ivory prices plummeted by 90%, and the market for poaching and smuggling was radically reduced. Although illegal poaching continues, the ivory ban remains an overwhelming success, so much so that in some areas elephant populations have grown to unsustainable levels – in Kenya's Amboseli National Park, for example, numbers have doubled in the past decade alone.

For more information on the fight to save elephants in East Africa and further afield, contact **Save the Elephants** (www.savetheelephants.org). And to visit one of the most distinguished elephant research programs in Africa, see p241.

For the best places to see elephants, see p14.

BOOKS

Peter Matthiessen's classic *The Tree Where Man Was Born* is an evocative and beautifully written 1960s picture of East Africa's physical, environmental and cultural make-up. His novel *Sand Rivers* (1981), a timeless account of a foot safari through the Selous Game Reserve, is less known but just as brilliant.

Black Rhinoceros

These inoffensive vegetarians are armed with impressive horns that have made them the target of both white hunters and poachers; rhino numbers plummeted to the brink of extinction during the 20th century and the illegal trade in rhino horns is still driven by their use in traditional medicines in Asian countries and the demand for dagger handles in Yemen. Despite having turned the situation around from the desperate lows of the 1980s, wildlife authorities in East Africa are again battling a recent upsurge in rhino poaching.

There are two species of rhino – black and white – both of which are predominantly found in savannah regions. The black rhino is probably East Africa's most endangered large mammal – the black rhino population plummeted by over 97% between 1960 and 1992, with the lowpoint reached in 1995 with just 2410 thought to remain in the wild. By the end of 2010, numbers were thought to have rebounded to 4800. Kenya has East Africa's largest share, with an estimated 630 black rhinos surviving in the wild.

Black Rhino Hotspots

Lake Nakuru National Park, Kenya

Ngorongoro Conservation Area, Tanzania

Selous Game Reserve, Tanzania

Tsavo West National Park, Kenya

Nairobi National Park, Kenya

Laikipia Plateau, Kenya

Lions

Because lions are the easiest of the big cats to observe, few people realise that lions face an extremely uncertain future. A century ago, more than 200,000 lions roamed Africa. Now, fewer than 30,000 are thought to remain and lions have disappeared from 80% of their historical range, according to **Panthera** (www.panthera.org), the leading cat conservation NGO based in New York. More than half of the continent's total population resides in Tanzania, while in Kenya lion numbers have reached critical levels: less than 2000 lions are thought to remain in the country.

Across their range, numbers are falling alarmingly, thanks primarily to human encroachment and habitat loss. The poisoning of lions, either in retaliation for lions killing livestock or encroaching onto farming lands, has also reached dangerous levels, to the extent that some lion conservationists predict that the lion could become regionally extinct in Kenya within 20 years.

Living With Lions (www.livingwithlions.org) is one Kenyan organisation fighting to protect lions and is an important source of information. **Wildlife Direct** (wildlifedirect.org) is another useful source of information, particularly on the threat posed by poisoning. For a fascinating insight into an innovative approach to lion conservation in the Amboseli region, see the boxed text on p242.

For some of the best places to see lions, leopards and cheetahs, see p14.

There is no finer resource on Africa's wild cats than *Cats of Africa* by L Hunter. It is an authoritative but highly readable book covering their behaviour, conservation and ecology, with superb photos by G Hinde. The author is the president of Panthera (www.panthera.org), the leading cat conservation NGO.

Grevy's Zebra

Kenya (along with neighbouring Ethiopia) is home to the last surviving wild populations of Grevy's zebra. In the 1970s, approximately 15,000 Grevy's zebras were thought to survive in the wild. Just 2500 are estimated to remain and less than 1% of the Grevy zebra's historical range lies within protected areas. Distinguished from other zebra species by having narrow stripes and bellies free from stripes, the Grevy's zebra is found in the Lewa Wildlife Conservancy (p307), Ol Peteja Conservancy (see the boxed text, p303) and the Samburu, Buffalo Springs and Shaba National Reserves (p308).

Rothschild Giraffe

The most endangered of the nine giraffe subspecies, the Rothschild giraffe has recently been hauled back from the brink of extinction. At the forefront of the fight to save the Rothschild giraffe (which, unlike other subspecies, has distinctive white 'stockings' with no orange-and-black markings below the knee) has been the Giraffe Centre (p222) in Nairobi. Rothschild giraffes are making a comeback with populations having been reintroduced into the wild at Lake Nakuru and Ruma National Parks (both in Kenya). There's also a small population in Uganda's Murchison Falls National Park.

African Wild Dog

The **IUCN Redlist of Threatened Species** (www.iucnredlist.org) lists the African wild dog as endangered, with no more than 5500 left on the continent (of which less than half are mature individuals). Most range across southern Africa, but southern Tanzania does have East Africa's most important regional populations. Your best chance of seeing the species is in Selous Game Reserve, while they're also found in Ruaha National Park. Reports occasionally surface of African wild dogs in Kenya's Tsavo East National Park, but Kenya's only significant population is found on the Laikipia Plateau (see the boxed text, p303).

Environmental Issues

East Africa is confronting some pressing environmental issues including deforestation, desertification, poaching, threats to endangered species and the impacts of tourism. The ongoing debate over whether conservation should be in public or private hands is also a hot topic.

CATTLE-FREE NATIONAL PARKS?

Nothing seems to disappoint visitors to East Africa's national parks more than the sight of herders shepherding their livestock to water sources within park boundaries. In the words of former Kenya Wildlife Service head, Dr Richard Leakey: 'People don't pay a lot of money to see cattle'. The issue is, however, a complicated one.

On the one hand, what you are seeing is far from a natural African environment. For thousands of years people, and their herds of cattle, lived happily (and sustainably) alongside the wildlife, and their actions helped to shape the landscapes of East Africa. But with the advent of conservation and national parks, many of East Africa's tribal peoples, particularly pastoralists such as the Maasai and Samburu, have found themselves and their cattle excluded from their ancestral lands, often with little or no compensation or alternative incomes provided (although of course some do now make a living through tourism and conservation). Having been pushed onto marginal lands and with limited access to alternative water sources in times of drought, many have been forced to forgo their traditional livelihoods and have taken to leading sedentary lifestyles. Those who continue as herders have little choice but to overgraze their lands. This position is passionately argued in the excellent (if dated) book *No Man's Land: An Investigative Journey Through Kenya and Tanzania* (2003) by George Monbiot.

At the same time, tourism is a major (and much-needed) source of revenue for East African countries and most visitors want to experience a natural wilderness – on the surface at least, the national parks, reserves and private conservancies appear to provide this Eden-esque slice of Africa. And even where the parks have been artificially carved out at the expense of tribal peoples, East Africa's population numbers are such that it remains questionable whether allowing herders and their livestock to graze within park boundaries would alleviate the pressures on over-exploited land and traditional cultures, or would instead simply lead to the degradation of Kenya's last remaining areas of relatively pristine wilderness.

Deforestation

More than half of Africa's forests have been destroyed over the last century, and forest destruction continues on a large scale in parts of East Africa where forest areas today represent only a fraction of the region's original forest cover. On the Zanzibar Archipelago, for example, only about 5% of the dense tropical forest that once blanketed the islands still remains. In sections of the long Eastern Arc chain, which sweeps from southern Kenya down towards central Tanzania, forest depletion has caused such serious erosion that entire villages have had to be shifted to lower areas. In densely populated Rwanda and Burundi, many previously forested areas have been completely cleared to make way for agriculture.

Native hardwood such as ebony and mahogany is often used to make the popular carved wooden statue souvenirs sold in East Africa. Though this industry supports thousands of local families who may otherwise be without an income, it also consumes an estimated 80,000 trees annually. The World Wide Fund for Nature (WWF) and Unesco campaigned to promote the use of common, faster-growing trees, and many handicraft cooperatives now use wood taken from forests managed by the Forest Stewardship Council. If you buy a carving, ask if the wood is sourced from managed forests.

WEBSITE

Eastern Arc Mountains Information Source (www.easternarc.org) is an information clearinghouse for the many environmental and community-based projects being undertaken in the Eastern Arc range in Kenya and Tanzania.

Tourism

Unregulated tourism and development also pose serious threats to East Africa's ecosystems. In northern and eastern Zanzibar, for example, new hotels are being built at a rapid rate, without sufficient provision for waste disposal and maintenance of environmental equilibrium. Inappropriate visitor use is another aspect of the issue; prime examples are the tyre tracks criss-crossing off-road areas of Kenya's Masai Mara National Reserve, the litter found along some popular trekking routes on Mt Kilimanjaro, and the often rampant use of firewood by visitors and tour operators alike.

One positive development has been the rise of community-based conservation as tour operators, funding organisations and others recognise that East Africa's protected areas are unlikely to succeed in the long term unless local people obtain real benefits.

Among the most impressive projects are the Lewa Wildlife Conservancy (p307), near Isiolo in Kenya, and the private conservancies of the Laikipia Plateau (see the boxed text, p303), also in Kenya. Another project to watch is the **Mara Conservancy** (www.maratriangle.org), a non-profit organisation that manages the Mara Triangle sector of the Masai Mara National Reserve.

Wildlife & Habitat

David Lukas

Think of East Africa and the word 'safari' comes to mind, but travel west from the big wildlife parks of Tanzania and Kenya and you cross through a world of gorgeous lakes and rivers before ascending into a mystical realm of snowy, cloud-draped peaks that straddle Africa's continental divide. Many parts of the verdant western region remain relatively unknown and are seldom visited, providing welcome respite from overbooked safaris and lodges to the east. But no matter where you travel, East Africa – home to a dazzling number and variety of animals – is sure to amaze.

Wildebeest, Serengeti National Park (p142), Tanzania

Big Cats

In terms of behaviour, the six common cats of East Africa are little more than souped-up housecats; it's just that some weigh half as much as a horse and others travel along as fast as a speeding car. With their excellent vision and keen hearing, cats are superb hunters. If you stumble across a big cat making its kill, you won't easily forget the energy and ferocity of this life-and-death struggle.

Lion

1 *Weight 120-150kg (female), 150-225kg (male); length 210-275cm (female), 240-350cm (male)* Those lions sprawled out lazily in the shade are actually Africa's most feared predators. Equipped with teeth that tear effortlessly through bone and tendon, they can take down an animal as large as a bull giraffe. Each group of adults (a pride) is based around generations of females who do all the hunting; the swaggering males fight among themselves and eat what the females catch.

Cheetah

2 *Weight 40-60kg; length 200-220cm* The cheetah is a world-class sprinter. Although it reaches speeds of 112km/h, the cheetah runs out of steam after 300m and must cool down for 30 minutes before hunting again. This speed comes at another cost – the cheetah is so well adapted for running that it lacks the strength and teeth to defend its food or cubs from attack by other large predators.

Leopard

3 *Weight 30-60kg (female), 40-90kg (male); length 170-300cm* More common than you realise, the leopard relies on expert camouflage techniques to stay hidden. During the day you might only spot one reclining in a tree after it twitches its tail, but at night there is no mistaking their bone-chilling groans.

1

3

2

1

3

IGNACIO PALACIOS/LONELY PLANET IMAGES ©

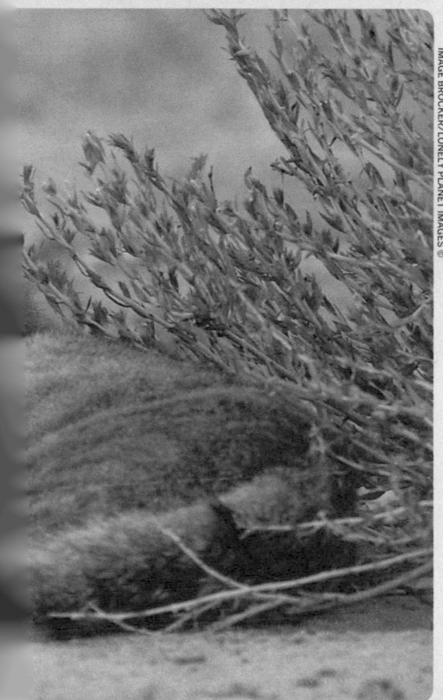

IMAGE BROCKER/LONELY PLANET IMAGES ©

Small Cats

While big cats get the lion's share of attention from tourists, East Africa's small cats are equally interesting though much harder to spot. You won't find these cats chasing down gazelles or wildebeest, instead look for them slinking around in search of rodents or making incredible leaps to snatch birds out of the air.

Caracal

1 *Weight 8-19kg; length 80-120cm* The caracal is a gorgeous tawny cat with long, pointy ears. This African version of the northern lynx has jacked-up hind legs like a feline dragster. These beanpole kickers enable this slender cat to make vertical leaps of 3m and swat birds out of the air.

Serval

2 *Weight 6-18kg; length 90-130cm* Twice as large as a housecat, with towering legs and large ears, the beautifully spotted serval is highly adapted for walking in tall grass and making prodigious leaps to catch rodents and birds. This elegant cat is often observed hunting in the daytime.

Wildcat

3 *Weight 3-6.5kg; length 65-100cm* Readily found on the outskirts of villages, or wherever there are abundant mice and rats, the wildcat looks like a common tabby and is in fact the direct ancestor of the domesticated housecat. The wildcat is best identified by its unmarked rufous ears and longish legs.

Ground Primates

East Africa is the evolutionary cradle of primate diversity, giving rise to over 30 species of monkeys, apes and prosimians (the 'primitive' ancestors of modern primates), all of which have dextrous hands and feet.

1

Mountain Gorilla

1 *Weight 70-115kg (female), 160-210kg (male); length 140-185cm* Gorilla-viewing is a big draw in Uganda and Rwanda, so expect some effort or expense getting a coveted slot on a tour into gorilla habitat. Seems like a hassle? Just wait until you're face-to-face with a massive silverback male on his home turf and nothing else will matter!

Chimpanzee

2 *Weight 25-40kg; length 60-90cm* Travelling to the forests of western East Africa to see chimpanzees may take you off the beaten path, but it's hard to deny the allure of these uncannily human-like primates, with deep intelligence and emotion lurking behind their eerily familiar deep-set eyes. Researchers at Gombe and Mahale Mountains National Parks are making startling discoveries about chimp behaviour.

3

Vervet Monkey

3 *Weight 4-8kg; length 90-140cm* Each troop of vervets is composed of females who defend home ranges passed down from generation to generation, and males who fight each other for bragging rights and access to females. Check out the extraordinary blue and scarlet colours their sexual organs take on when they are aroused.

Olive Baboon

4 *Weight 11-30kg (female), 22-50kg (male); length 95-180cm* Although the formidable olive baboon has 5cm-long fangs and can kill a leopard, its best defence may be its ability to run up trees and shower intruders with liquid excrement.

ARIADNE VAN ZANDBERGEN/LONELY PLANET IMAGES ©

2

GERRY ELLIS/MINDEN PICTURES/CORBIS ©

1

3

2

ARIADNE VAN ZANDBERG/LONELY PLANET IMAGES ©

DLILLC/CORBIS ©

Arboreal Primates

Forest primates are a diverse group that live entirely in trees. These agile, long-limbed primates generally stay in the upper canopy where they search for leaves and arboreal fruits. It might take the expert eyes of a professional guide to help you find some of these species.

Black-and-White Colobus

1 *Weight 10-23kg; length 115-165cm* Also known as the guereza, the black-and-white colobus is one of East Africa's most popular primates due to the flowing white bonnets of hair across its black body. Like all colobus, this agile primate has a hook-shaped hand so it can swing through the trees with the greatest of ease. When two troops run into each other expect to see a real show.

Blue Monkey

2 *Weight 4-12kg; length 100-170cm* These long-tailed monkeys are widespread primates that have adapted to many forested habitats throughout sub-Saharan Africa, including some of the forested parks in Tanzania where they are among the easiest monkeys to spot. These versatile monkeys live in large social groups that spend their entire lives among trees.

Greater Galago

3 *Weight 550-2000g; length 55-100cm* A cat-sized nocturnal creature with a dog-like face, the greater galago belongs to a group of prosimians that have changed very little in 60 million years. Best known for its frequent bawling cries (hence the common name 'bushbaby'), the galago would be rarely seen except that it readily visits feeding stations at many popular safari lodges. Living in a world of darkness, galagos communicate with each other through scent and sound.

Cud-Chewing Mammals

Africa is arguably most famous for its astounding variety of ungulates – hoofed mammals that include everything from buffaloes to giraffes. In this large family, the cud-chewing antelope are particularly numerous, with 40 different species in East Africa alone.

Wildebeest

1 *Weight 140-290kg; length 230-340cm* Few animals evoke the spirit of the African plain like the wildebeest. Over one million gather in vast, constantly moving herds on the Serengeti.

Thomson's Gazelle

2 *Weight 15-35kg; length 95-150cm* Lanky and exceptionally alert, the long-legged Thomson's gazelle is built for speed. The 400,000 living on the Serengeti Plains migrate with wildebeest and zebras.

African Buffalo

3 *Weight 250-850kg; length 220-420cm* Imagine a big cow with curling horns, and you have the African buffalo. Fortunately, they're usually docile – an angry or injured buffalo is an extremely dangerous animal.

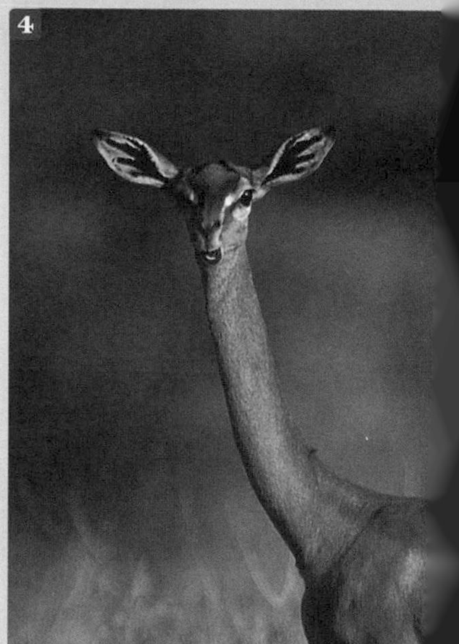

Gerenuk

4 *Weight 30-50kg; length 160-200cm* The gerenuk is one of the strangest creatures you'll ever see – a tall slender gazelle with a giraffe-like neck that stands on its hind legs to reach 2m-high branches.

Uganda Kob

5 *Weight 60-120kg; length 170-200cm* Kob gather in great numbers on the flood plains of Uganda, where males fight and show off their curved horns in front of gathered females.

2

IGNACIO PALACIOS/LONELY PLANET IMAGES ©

3

IGNACIO PALACIOS/LONELY PLANET IMAGES ©

1

DOUGLAS STEAKLEY/LONELY PLANET IMAGES ©

4

IGNACIO PALACIOS/LONELY PLANET IMAGES ©

IGNACIO PALACIOS/LONELY PLANET IMAGES ©

MITCH REARDON/LONELY PLANET IMAGES ©

Hoofed Mammals

The continent has a surprising diversity of hoofed animals that have been at home here for millions of years. Those that don't chew cuds can be seen over a much broader range of habitats than the cud-chewing antelope. Without human intervention, Africa would be ruled by elephants, zebras, hippos and warthogs.

African Elephant

1 *Weight 2200-3500kg (female), 4000-6300kg (male); height 2.4-3.4m (female), 3-4m (male)* No one argues with a bull elephant. Bull elephants are commonly referred to as 'the king of beasts,' but elephant society is actually ruled by a lineage of elder females who lead each group along traditional migration routes between watering holes.

Giraffe

2 *Weight 450-1200kg (female), 1800-2000kg (male); height 3.5-5.2m* The 5m-tall giraffe does such a good job reaching up to grab mouthfuls of leaves on high branches that stretching down to get a drink of water is difficult. Though they stroll along casually, they can outrun any predator.

Black Rhinoceros

3 *Weight 700-1400kg; length 350-450cm* Pity the black rhinoceros for having a horn that is worth more than gold. Once widespread and abundant on open plains south of the Sahara, the slow-moving rhino has been poached to the brink of extinction. Even worse, females may only give birth once every five years.

Plains Zebra

4 *Weight 175-320kg; length 260-300cm* My oh my, those plains zebras sure have wicked stripes. Although each animal is as distinctly marked as a fingerprint, scientists still aren't sure what function these patterns serve.

More Hoofed Mammals

This sampling of miscellaneous hoofed animals highlights the astonishing diversity in this major group of African wildlife. Every visitor wants to see elephants and giraffes, but don't pass up a chance to watch hyraxes or warthogs.

Hippopotamus

1 *Weight 510-3200kg; length 320-400cm* The hippopotamus is one strange creature. Designed like a big grey floating beanbag with tiny legs, the 3000kg hippo spends all its time in or very near water, chowing down on aquatic plants. Placid? No way! Hippos display a tremendous ferocity and strength when provoked.

Warthog

2 *Weight 45-75kg (female), 60-150kg (male); length 140-200cm* Despite their fearsome appearance and sinister tusks, only the largest male warthogs are safe from lions, cheetahs and hyenas. To protect themselves when attacked, most warthogs run for burrows, then back in while slashing wildly with their tusks.

Rock Hyrax

3 *Weight 1.8-5.5kg; length 40-60cm* It doesn't seem like it, but those funny tailless squirrels you see lounging around on rocks are an ancient cousin to the elephant. You won't see some of the features that rock hyraxes share with their larger kin, but look for tusks when one yawns.

1

3

CHRISTER FREDRIKSSON/LONELY PLANET IMAGES ©

2

ARIADNE VAN ZANDBERGEN/LONELY PLANET IMAGES ©

1

3

JOE MCDONALD/CORBIS ©

ARIADNE VAN ZANDBERGEN/LONELY PLANET IMAGES ©

Carnivores

It is a sign of Africa's ecological richness that the continent supports a remarkable variety of predators. When it comes to predators, expect the unexpected and you'll return home with a lifetime of memories!

Spotted Hyena

1 *Weight 40-90kg; length 125-215cm* Living in packs ruled by females that grow penis-like sexual organs, these savage fighters use their bone-crushing jaws to disembowel terrified prey on the run or to do battle with lions.

Golden Jackal

2 *Weight 6-15kg; length 85-130cm* Through a combination of sheer fierceness and bluff, the trim little jackal manages to fill its belly while holding hungry vultures and hyenas at bay.

Banded Mongoose

3 *Weight 1.5-2kg; length 45-75cm* Bounding across the savannah on their morning foraging excursions, family groups search for delicious snacks like toads, scorpions and slugs.

Hunting Dog

4 *Weight 20-35kg; length 100-150cm* Organised in complex hierarchies maintained by rules of conduct, these social canids are incredibly efficient hunters, running in packs of 20 to 60 to chase down antelope and other animals. Sadly, these beautiful dogs are now highly endangered.

Ratel

5 *Weight 7-16kg; length 75-100cm* Some Africans say they would rather face a lion than a ratel, and even lions relinquish their kill when a ratel shows up. Also known as 'honey badger,' the ratel finds its favourite food by following honey guides (birds that lead the badger to beehives).

1

ADRIAN BAILEY/LONELY PLANET IMAGES ©

4

ARIADNE VAN ZANDBERGEN/LONELY PLANET IMAGES ©

2

CHRISTER FREDRIKSSON/LONELY PLANET IMAGES ©

3

ARIADNE VAN ZANDBERGEN/LONELY PLANET IMAGES ©

Birds of Prey

East Africa has nearly 100 species of hawks, eagles, vultures and owls. More than 40 species have been spotted within a single park, making these some of the best places in the world to see an incredible variety of birds of prey.

African Fish Eagle

1 *Length 75cm* This replica of the American bald eagle presents an imposing appearance but is most familiar for its loud, ringing vocalisations that have become known as 'the voice of Africa.'

Secretary Bird

2 *Length 100cm* With the body of an eagle and the legs of a crane, the secretary bird stands at 1.3m tall and walks up to 20km a day in search of vipers, cobras and other snakes, which it kills with lightning speed and agility. This idiosyncratic, grey-bodied raptor is commonly seen striding across the savannah.

White-Backed Vulture

3 *Length 80cm* Mingling around carcasses with lions, hyenas and jackals, vultures use their sheer numbers to compete for scraps of flesh and bone.

Bateleur

4 *Length 60cm* French for 'tightrope-walker,' bateleur refers to this bird's distinctive low-flying aerial acrobatics. At close hand, look for its bold colour pattern and scarlet face.

Augur Buzzard

5 *Length 55cm* Perhaps the most common raptor in the region, the augur buzzard occupies a wide range of wild and cultivated habitats. They hunt by floating motionlessly in the air then swooping down quickly to catch unwary critters.

1

ARIADNE VAN ZANDBERGEN/LONELY PLANET IMAGES ©

4

IGNACIO PALACIOS/LONELY PLANET IMAGES ©

2

ARIADNE VAN ZANDBERGEN/LONELY PLANET IMAGES ©

3

ARIADNE VAN ZANDBERGEN/LONELY PLANET IMAGES ©

Other Birds

Birdwatchers from all over the world visit East Africa in search of the region's 1400 species of birds, an astounding number by any measure and including birds of every shape and colour imaginable.

Ostrich

1 *Length 200-270cm* Standing at 270cm and weighing upwards of 130kg, these ancient flightless birds escape predators by running away at 70km/h or lying flat on the ground to resemble a pile of dirt.

Lilac-Breasted Roller

2 *Length 40cm* Nearly everyone on safari gets to know the gorgeously coloured lilac-breasted roller. The roller gets its name from its tendency to 'roll' from side to side in flight as a way of showing off its iridescent blues, purples and greens.

Shoebill

3 *Length 124cm* The reclusive shoebill is one of the most highly sought-after birds in East Africa, where it lurks in undisturbed swamps. Looking somewhat like a stout-bodied stork with an ugly old clog stuck on its face, the shoebill baffles scientists because it has no clear relative in the bird world.

Lesser Flamingo

4 *Length 100cm* Coloured deep rose-pink and gathering by the hundreds of thousands on shimmering salt lakes, the lesser flamingo creates one of Africa's most dramatic wildlife spectacles when they fly in formation or perform synchronised courtship.

Grey-Crowned Crane

5 *Length 100cm* Uganda's national bird is extremely elegant. Topped with a frilly yellow bonnet, this blue-grey crane dances wildly and shows off its red throat pouch during the breeding season.

Habitats

Nearly all the wildlife in East Africa occupies a specific type of habitat, and you will hear rangers and fellow travellers refer to these habitats repeatedly as they describe where to search for animals. If this is your first time in East Africa some of these habitats and their seasonal rhythms take some getting used to, but your wildlife-viewing experiences will be greatly enhanced if you learn how to recognise them and the animals you might expect to find in each one.

Savannah

1 Savannah is *the* classic East African landscape – broad rolling grasslands dotted with lone acacia trees. The openness and vastness of this landscape makes it a perfect home for large herds of grazing animals, and fast-sprinting predators like cheetahs. Shaped by fire and grazing animals, savannah is a dynamic habitat in constant flux with its adjacent woodlands. One of the best places in the world for exploring African savannah is found at Serengeti National Park.

Woodland

2 Tanzania is the only place in East Africa where you'll find dry woodlands, locally known as *miombo*. This important habitat provides homes for many birds, small mammals and insects. Here the trees form a continuous canopy that offers shelter from predators and harsh sunlight, and is a fantastic place to search for wildlife. In places where fingers of woodland mingle with savannah, animals such as leopards and antelope often gather to find shade and places to rest during the day. During the dry season, fires and elephants can wreak havoc on these woodlands, fragmenting large tracts of forest habitat into patches. Ruaha National Park in Tanzania is a great place to explore a wide diversity of mixed savannah and *miombo* habitats.

Right
1. Masai Mara National Reserve (p261), Kenya **2.** Tanzania woodland

IGNACIO PALACIOS/LONELY PLANET IMAGES ©

LUDOVIC MAISANT/CORBIS ©

High Mountains

3 High mountains are such a rare habitat in East Africa that the massive extinct volcanoes of Mts Kilimanjaro, Kenya and Elgon, and the remarkable highlands of the Rwenzori Mountains, stand out dramatically in the landscape. These isolated peaks are islands of montane forest, ethereal bogs, giant heathers, and moorlands perched high above the surrounding lowlands. The few animals that survive here are uniquely adapted to these bizarre landscapes.

Semiarid Desert

4 Much of eastern and northern Kenya and parts of northeastern Tanzania see so little rainfall that shrubs and hardy grasses, rather than trees, are the dominant vegetation. This is not the classic landscape that many visitors come to see, and it doesn't seem like a great place for wildlife, but the patient observer will be richly rewarded. While it's true that the lack of water restricts larger animals such as zebras, gazelles and antelope to waterholes, this habitat explodes with plant and animal life whenever it rains. Tsavo East National Park in Kenya is a massive and gorgeous region of semiarid wilderness.

Left

3. Mt Kenya National Park (p291), Kenya **4.** Tsavo East National Park (p247), Kenya

White rhinos, Lake Nakuru National Park (p256), Kenya

National Parks & Reserves

History

The idea of setting aside protected areas began during colonial times when the authorities set aside areas for protection, and in many cases this meant forcibly evicting the local peoples from their traditional lands. Enforcement of any vague notions of conservation that lay behind the reserves was often lax, and local anger was fuelled by the fact that many parks were set aside as hunting reserves for white hunters with anything but conservation on their minds.

Many of these hunters, having pushed some species to the brink of extinction, later became conservationists and by the middle of the 20th-century, the push was on to establish the national parks and reserves that we see today.

Visiting National Parks & Reserves

Throughout this book, we have covered the parks and reserves in detail. In the case of the major parks and reserves, we've also included a Practical Tip box to sum up the park in a nutshell, from the wildlife you're likely to see to helpful details such as the best gates by which to enter.

Tanzania

With more than one-third of Tanzanian territory locked away as a national park, wildlife reserve or marine park, Tanzania has the widest selection of protected areas to choose from. That doesn't mean that they have their entry system sorted – at the time of writing, the best advice is to bring sufficient US dollars cash to pay for your park entry fees *and* a Visa credit card.

Park entry fees range from US$20/5 per adult/child per 24 hours for Rubondo Island or Katavi national parks up to US$100/20 for Gombe National Park. There is an additional charge for all vehicles at all parks and reserves.

For more information on Tanzania's parks and reserves, see p201.

Kenya

Kenya has 22 national parks, plus numerous marine parks and national reserves. Entry is, in theory at least, unified under a safaricard system, which can be purchased at the Kenya Wildlife Service offices in Nairobi and Mombasa. In practice, the safaricard system is in use only for Nairobi, Lake Nakuru, Aberdare, Amboseli and Tsavo national parks. The remaining parks still work on a cash system, with US dollars, euros and Kenyan shillings all accepted.

Entry to some marine parks start at US$15/10 per adult/child per 24 hours, with mainland parks starting at US$20/10 and going as high as

Major National Parks & Reserves of East Africa

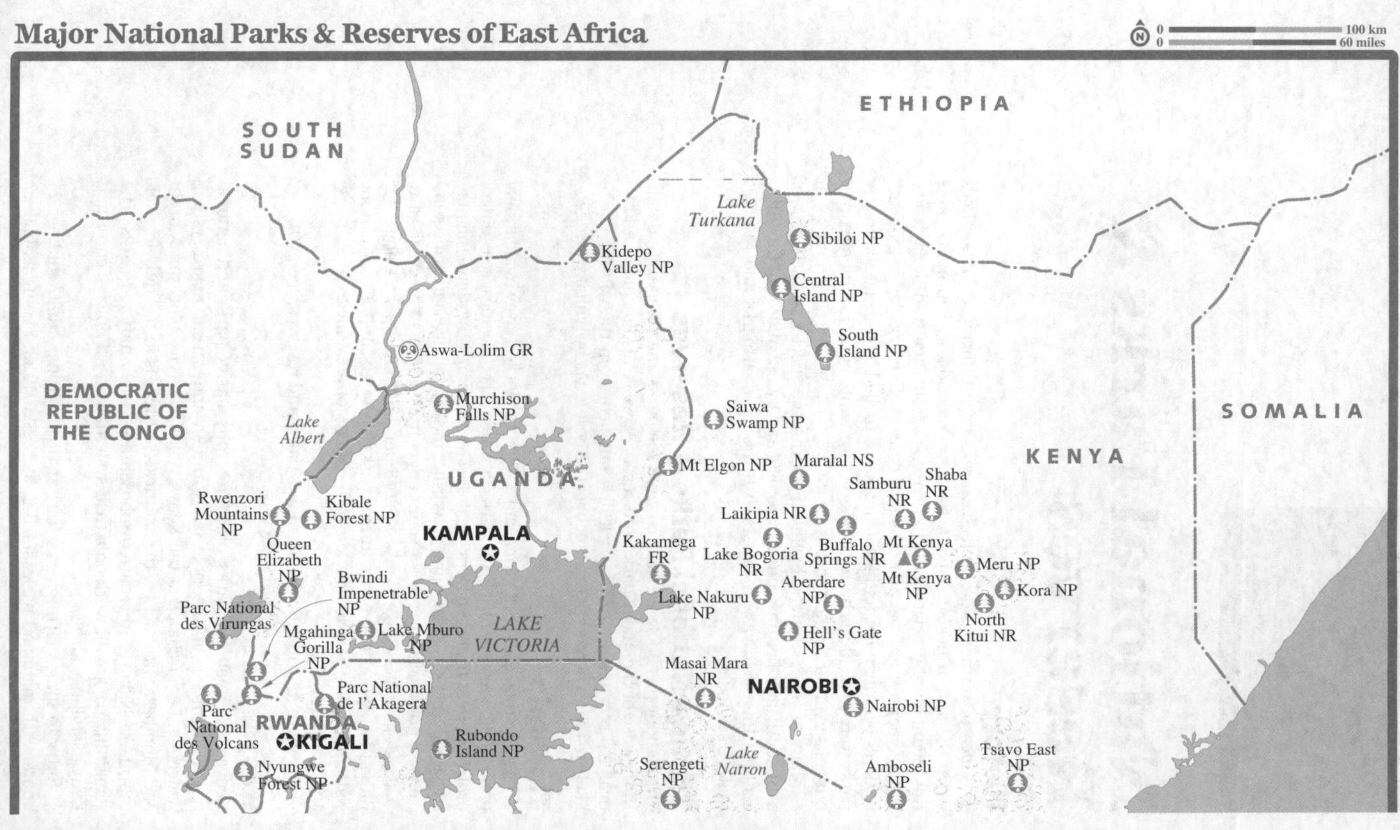

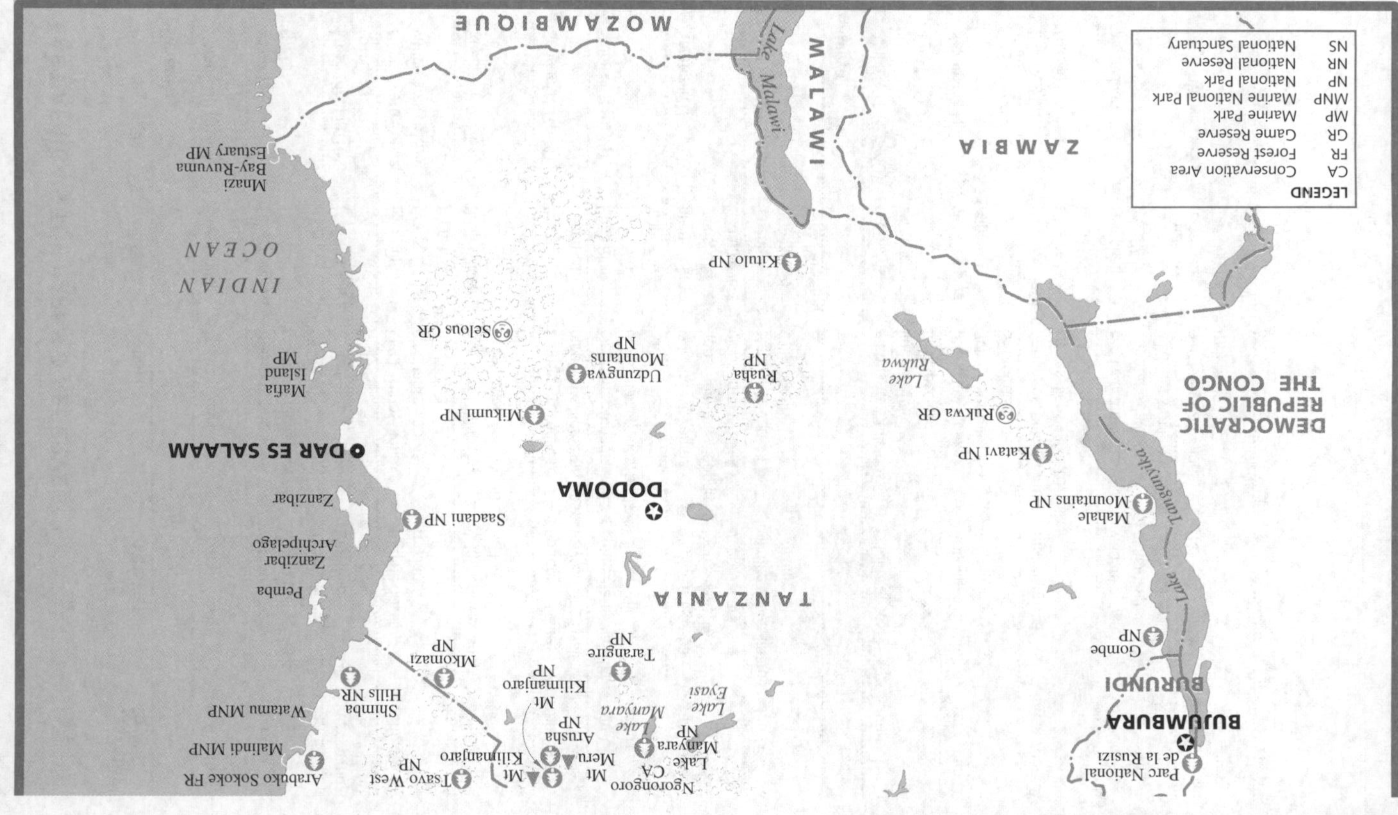
MOZAMBIQUE
MALAWI
ZAMBIA
TANZANIA
DEMOCRATIC REPUBLIC OF THE CONGO
BURUNDI
BUJUMBURA
DODOMA
DAR ES SALAAM
INDIAN OCEAN
Lake Malawi
Lake Tanganyika
Lake Rukwa
Lake Eyasi
Lake Manyara
Mnazi Bay-Ruvuma Estuary MP
Mafia Island MP
Zanzibar
Zanzibar Archipelago
Pemba
Watamu MNP
Malindi MNP
Arabuko Sokoke FR
Shimba Hills NR
Tsavo West NP
Mt Kilimanjaro
Mt Kilimanjaro NP
Mkomazi NP
Saadani NP
Selous GR
Mikumi NP
Udzungwa Mountains NP
Ruaha NP
Kitulo NP
Rukwa GR
Katavi NP
Mahale Mountains NP
Gombe NP
Parc National de la Rusizi
Ngorongoro CA
Lake Manyara NP
Mt Meru
Arusha NP
Tarangire NP
LEGEND
CA Conservation Area
FR Forest Reserve
GR Game Reserve
MP Marine Park
MNP Marine National Park
NP National Park
NR National Reserve
NS National Sanctuary

EAST AFRICA'S TOP PARKS & RESERVES

PARK/RESERVE	HABITATS	WILDLIFE	ACTIVITIES	BEST TIME TO VISIT
Tanzania				
Gombe NP (p165)	Lake Tanganyika, forest	chimpanzees	chimp tracking	year-round
Lake Manyara NP (p133)	Lake Manyara	tree-climbing lions, hippos, hyenas, leopard, elephants	wildlife drives, walking & cycling in nearby areas	Jun-Feb
Mt Kilimanjaro NP (p111)	Mt Kilimanjaro	buffaloes, elephants, leopard	trekking	year-round
Ngorongoro Conservation Area (p137)	Ngorongoro Crater, Crater Highlands	black rhinos, lions, elephants, zebras, flamingos	wildlife drives, trekking	Jun-Feb
Ruaha NP (p176)	Ruaha River	elephants, hippos, giraffes, cheetahs, > 400 bird species	wildlife drives, short walks	Jul-Oct
Saadani NP (p94)	Wami River, beach	hippos, crocodiles, elephants, lions, giraffes	boating, wildlife drives, beach walks	Jun-Feb
Selous GR (p188)	Rufiji River, lakes, woodland	elephants, hippos, wild dogs, black rhinos, birds	boat safaris, walking, wildlife drives	Jun-Oct, Jan-Feb
Serengeti NP (p142)	plains & grasslands, Grumeti & Mara rivers	wildebeest, zebras, lions, cheetahs, leopard, elephants, giraffes	wildlife drives, balloon safaris, walking in border areas	year-round
Tarangire NP (p131)	Tarangire River, woodland, baobabs	elephants, zebras, wildebeest	wildlife drives, limited walking	Jun-Oct
Kenya				
Amboseli NP (p240)	dry plains, scrub forest	elephants, buffaloes, lions, antelope, > 370 bird species	wildlife drives	Jun-Oct
Kakamega FR (p274)	virgin tropical rainforest	red-tailed monkeys, flying squirrels, about 330 bird species	walking, birdwatching	year-round
Lake Nakuru NP (p256)	hilly grassland, alkaline lakeland	flamingos, black & white rhinos, lions, leopard, >400 bird species	wildlife drives	year-round
Masai Mara NR (p261)	savannah, grassland	Big Five, antelope, cheetahs, hyenas, wildebeest migration	wildlife drives, ballooning	Jul-Oct
Mt Kenya NP (p291)	rainforest, moorland, glacial mountain	elephants, buffaloes, mountain flora	trekking, climbing	Jan-Feb, Aug-Sep

PARK/RESERVE	HABITATS	WILDLIFE	ACTIVITIES	BEST TIME TO VISIT
Nairobi NP (p221)	open plains with urban backdrop	black rhinos, lions, leopard, cheetahs, giraffes, >400 bird species	wildlife drives	year-round
Tsavo West & East NPs (p243 & p247)	plains, ancient volcanic cones	Big Five, cheetahs, giraffes, hippos, crocodiles, around 500 bird species	rock climbing, wildlife drives	year-round
Uganda				
Bwindi Impenetrable NP (p437)	primeval tropical forest	eastern mountain gorillas	gorilla tracking, birdwatching	May-Sep
Kibale Forest NP (p423)	lush forest	highest density of primates in Africa, including chimpanzee, red colobus & L'Hoest's monkey	chimp tracking, forest elephant viewing	May-Aug
Mgahinga Gorilla NP (p450)	volcanoes	eastern mountain gorillas, golden monkeys, elephants	gorilla tracking, visiting Twa (Batwa) villages,birdwatching	Jun-Sep
Murchison Falls NP (p460)	thundering falls, the Victoria Nile	elephants, hippos, crocodiles, lions, leopard, hyenas, Rothschild giraffes, Ugandan kob, >460 bird species	launch trip, wildlife drives, birdwatching	year-round
Queen Elizabeth NP (p432)	lakes, gorges, savannah	hippos, elephants, lions, leopard, chimpanzees, 611 recorded bird species	launch trip, chimp tracking, birdwatching	year-round
Rwenzori Mountains NP (p428)	Africa's highest mountain range	blue monkeys, chimpanzees, Rwenzori red duiker, 241 recorded bird species	trekking	Jun-Aug
Rwanda & the DRC				
Parc National des Volcans (p519)	towering volcanoes	eastern mountain gorillas, golden monkeys	gorilla & golden monkey tracking, volcano climbing	May-Sep
Nyungwe Forest NP (p535)	one of Africa's oldest rainforests, waterfalls	chimpanzees, Angolan colobus monkeys, about 275 bird species	chimp & colobus monkey tracking	May-Sep
Parc National des Virungas, the DRC (p497)	volcanoes, dense rainforest	eastern mountain gorillas, chimpanzees, forest elephants, okapis	gorilla & chimp tracking, volcano climbing	May-Sep

US$80/45 for the Masai Mara National Reserve in high season. Vehicles cost extra, with US$10 per day the norm.

For more information on Kenya's parks and reserves, see p360.

Protected Areas of Country

- Tanzania 38.4%
- Kenya 12.7%
- Uganda 26.3%
- Rwanda 7.6%
- Burundi 5.6%
- DRC 8.4%

Uganda

More than one-quarter of Uganda is protected in some form, with a particularly rich concentration in the country's southwest; 20% of park fees go directly to local communities. Most national parks charge US$35/20 per adult/child per 24 hours, with additional charges for vehicles, nature walks and ranger-guides. Conveniently, payments can be made in Ugandan shillings, dollars, euros and pounds in cash or travellers cheques (1% commission). And remember that if you're here to track gorillas, the US$350 to US$500 permit fee includes park entry fees; see p482 for more on obtaining permits for gorilla tracking in Uganda.

For more information on Uganda's national parks, see p482.

Rwanda & the DRC

Rwanda has three national parks worthy of the name and entry fees, depending on the reason for your visit. A permit to track the gorillas in the Parc National des Volcans costs US$750, which includes park entry fees. Tracking chimpanzees (US$90) or golden monkeys (US$100) is considerably cheaper, while wildlife drives generally cost US$30. Payments are usually made in cash, and preferably in US dollars. See p32 for more on obtaining permits for gorilla tracking in Rwanda.

In the DRC's Parc National des Virungas, chimpanzee tracking costs US$100, climbing the Nyiragongo Volcano costs US$200, while gorilla tracking goes for a bargain US$400.

Primates

East Africa is a hotspot for primate diversity, an evolutionary cauldron from which forest monkeys spread out onto the plains, and from which the great apes and we humans developed. Represented in East Africa today are the 'primitive' bushbabies (or galagos), gorilla and chimpanzee, two species of baboon and 17 species of monkey. The most widespread primate species in East Africa include the olive baboon (which can gather in troops of 150) and vervet monkey.

For a detailed look at the complicated process of primate habituation, see the boxed text on p482.

Mountain Gorillas

Gorillas are the largest of the great apes and share 97% of their biological make-up with humans. Gorillas used to inhabit a swathe of land that cut right across central Africa, but the last remaining eastern mountain gorillas number just over 700, divided between two 300-plus populations in the forests of Uganda's Bwindi Impenetrable National Park and on the slopes of the Virunga volcanoes, encompassing Uganda's Mgahinga Gorilla National Park, Rwanda's Parc National des Volcans and the DRC's Parc National des Virungas.

For advice on visiting East Africa's mountain gorillas, see p482.

Primate Books

- *The Year of the Gorilla* (1964), George Schaller
- *Gorillas in the Mist* (1983), Dian Fossey
- *A Primate's Memoir* (2004), Robert Sapolsky
- *Among the Great Apes* (2010), Paul Raffaele

Daily Life

Gorillas spend 30% of their day feeding, 30% moving and foraging, and the remainder resting. They spend most of their time on the ground, moving around on all fours but standing up to reach for food. Gorillas are vegetarians and their diet consists mainly of bamboo shoots, giant thistles and wild celery, all of which contain water and allow the gorillas to survive without drinking for long periods of time. A silverback can eat his way through more than 30kg of bamboo a day.

A group's dominant silverback dictates movements for the day, and at night each gorilla makes its own nest. Gorillas usually travel about 1km a day, unless they have met another group in which case they may move further.

Families

Gorillas generally live in family groups of varying sizes, usually including one to two older silverback males, younger blackback males, females and infants. Most groups contain between 10 and 15 gorillas, but they can exceed 40. The two largest habituated family groups (one in Rwanda, the other in the DRC) at the time of writing had 32 members.

There are strong bonds between individuals and status is usually linked to age. Silverbacks are at the top of the hierarchy, then females with infants or ties to the silverbacks, then blackbacks and other females. Most gorillas leave the group when they reach maturity, which helps prevent interbreeding among such a small population.

Conflict

Gorillas are relatively placid primates and serious confrontations are rare, although violence can flare if there's a challenge for supremacy between silverbacks. Conflicts are mostly kept to shows of strength and vocal disputes.

Conflict between groups is also uncommon, as gorillas aren't territorial; if two groups meet, there's usually lots of display and bravado on the part of silverbacks, including mock charges. Often the whole group joins in and it's at this point that young adult females may choose to switch allegiance.

If gorillas do fight, injuries can be very serious as these animals have long canine teeth and silverbacks pack a punch estimated at eight times stronger than a heavyweight boxer. If a dominant male is driven from a group by another silverback, it's likely the new leader will kill all the young infants to establish his mating rights.

Gorilla Websites

» International Gorilla Conservation Programme (IGCP; www.igcp.org)

» Dian Fossey Gorilla Fund International (www.gorillafund.org)

» African Wildlife Foundation: Adopt a Gorilla (www.awf.org/content/action/detail/3602)

» IUCN Redlist of Threatened Species (www.iucnredlist.org)

Communication

Gorillas communicate in a variety of ways, including facial expressions, gestures and around two dozen vocalisations. Adult males use barks and roars during confrontations or to coordinate the movement of their groups to a different area. Postures and gestures form an important element of intimidation and it's possible for a clash to be diffused by a display of teeth-baring, stiff-legging and charging.

Friendly communication is an important part of group bonding and includes grunts of pleasure. Upon finding food, gorillas will grunt or bark to alert other members of the group.

No mountain gorillas have ever been successfully reared in captivity, contributing to the precarious nature of their existence.

Biology

Gorillas are the largest primates in the world and mountain gorillas are the largest of the three gorilla species; adult male mountain gorillas weigh as much as 200kg (440lb). Females are about half this size.

Males reach maturity between eight and 15 years, their backs turning silver as they enter their teens, while females enter adulthood at the earlier age of eight. Conception is possible for about three days each month, and once a female has conceived for the first time, she spends most of her life pregnant or nursing.

The duration of a gorilla pregnancy is about 8½ months. Newborn infants are highly dependent on adults, and a young infant will rarely leave its mother's arms during its first six months. In its second year, a young gorilla begins to interact with other members of the group and starts to feed itself. Infant gorillas and silverbacks often form a bond, and it's not uncommon for a silverback to adopt an infant if its mother dies. This distinguishes gorillas from other primates, where child-rearing

BEST PRIMATE PARKS

We've covered the best places to see mountain gorillas and chimpanzees in this chapter, but if your passion is primates and you're eager to see as many species as possible, we recommend the following:

» Kibale Forest National Park (p423), Uganda, with 13 primate species

» Nyungwe Forest National Park (p535), Rwanda, with 13 primate species

» Bwindi Impenetrable National Park (p437), Uganda, with 11 primate species

» Semuliki National Park (p424), Uganda, with nine primate species

» Queen Elizabeth National Park (p432), Uganda, with nine primate species

» Kakamega Forest Reserve (p276), Kenya, with seven primate species

WHERE TO SEE OTHER PRIMATES

SPECIES	LOCATION
Angolan colobus	Nyungwe Forest NP (p535), Rwanda Diani Beach (p332), Kenya
Black-and-white colobus	Lake Nakuru NP (p256), Kenya Saiwa Swamp NP (p280), Kenya Mt Elgon NP (p281), Kenya
De Brazza's monkey	Kakamega Forest Reserve (p276), Kenya Saiwa Swamp NP (p280), Kenya Mt Elgon NP (p281), Kenya Semuliki NP (p424), Uganda
Dent's monkey	Nyungwe Forest NP (p535), Rwanda
Golden monkey	Mgahinga Gorilla National Park (p451), Uganda Nyungwe Forest NP (p535), Rwanda Parc National des Volcans (p519), Rwanda
Greater galago (bushbaby)	Nyungwe Forest NP (p535), Rwanda Jozani Forest (p84), Zanzibar, Tanzania
Grey-cheeked mangabey	Nyungwe Forest NP (p535), Rwanda Kibale Forest NP (p423), Uganda
L'Hoest's monkey	Nyungwe Forest NP (p535), Rwanda Kibale Forest NP (p423), Uganda Queen Elizabeth NP (p432), Uganda Bwindi Impenetrable NP (p437), Uganda
Potto	Nyungwe Forest NP (p535), Rwanda Kakamega Forest Reserve (p276), Kenya
Red colobus	Jozani Forest (p84), Zanzibar, Tanzania Kibale Forest NP (p423), Uganda
Sykes' monkey	Mt Kenya NP (p291), Kenya Arabuko Sokoke Forest (p341), Kenya Jozani Forest (p84), Zanzibar, Tanzania

duties are left to females. From about three years, young gorillas become quite independent and build their own nests.

Mountain gorillas are distinguished from their more widespread lowland relatives by longer hair, broader chests and wider jaws. The most obvious thing that sets the gorillas in Bwindi apart from those of the Virungas is that they are less shaggy, most likely due to the lower altitude.

Conservation Status

Mountain gorilla numbers have held firm over the past decade despite the widely publicised execution-style killings of seven gorillas in the DRC's Parc National des Virunga in 2007, ongoing threats from instability in the DRC, poaching, the Ebola and Marburg viruses and the trade in bush meat. Even so, the IUCN Redlist of Threatened Species lists the eastern mountain gorilla as endangered.

Chimpanzees

Chimpanzees are the animal world's closest living relative to humans, with whom they share 99% of their genetic make-up.

Families

Communities of between nine and 120 forage in territories protected by males that spend their entire lives on ancestral turf in shifting hierarchies. Females disperse to other communities. Smaller family groups within these larger communities range from three to eight members.

Status is big among chimps; males constantly vie to dominate a clan for the benefits it confers. For example, being the alpha male means you get to monopolise the sex scene (a challenge since females are promiscuous). But other male chimps may gang up and try to oust the alpha male, so he relies on a network of buddies for help and rewards them with, for example, a share of the meat taken on hunts. Squabbling among lesser ranks goes on all the time, and all males must maintain allegiances and friendships throughout their lives. When two adults fight, a third party may bring the rivals together for a reconciliation, which inevitably involves mutual grooming. But they also use deception to lure a rival to reconciliation then punish him for past transgressions.

Chimp Hotspots

- Gombe NP, Tanzania
- Mahale Mountains NP, Tanzania
- Murchison Falls NP, Uganda
- Kibale Forest NP, Uganda
- Toro-Semliki WR, Uganda
- Nyungwe Forest NP, Rwanda
- Parc National des Virungas, the DRC

Behaviour

So much of what we know about chimpanzees comes as a result of decades of research at Tanzania's Gombe National Park (p165), and the research has revealed a fascinating picture.

Young chimps laugh, turn somersaults, tickle each other, play tag and cry real tears, but the life of an adult chimp is a serious business – adults mount hunts for red colobus and other species, while murder is a fact of chimpanzee life.

Among chimpanzees, food traditions and the use of tools vary greatly from area to area: famous examples include using rocks to break open nutshells and stems to extract termites from holes. Other behaviour that varies between chimp 'cultures' includes using moss to soak up drinking water; using a leaf as a napkin; making cushions to sit on; and eating medicinal plants when feeling unwell. Chimps also sit and gaze at waterfalls, and break into frenzied drumming and hooting during rainstorms.

Conservation Status

Even though chimpanzees are the most widespread of Africa's primates, the IUCN Redlist of Threatened Species lists the chimpanzee as endangered. This is largely due to rampant habitat loss, human encroachment and hunting for bush meat.

The Arts

Swahili-Style Architecture

East Africa is an architectural treasure trove, with its colonial-era buildings and religious architecture, including both churches and mosques. The real highlights, however, are the old town areas of Zanzibar and Lamu (both Unesco World Heritage Sites) and of Mombasa, all of which display mesmerising combinations of Indian, Arabic, European and African characteristics in their buildings and street layouts.

In Lamu, Pate and elsewhere along the coast, Swahili architecture predominates. At the simplest level, Swahili dwellings are plain rectangular mud and thatch constructions, set in clusters and divided by small, sandy paths. More elaborate stone houses are traditionally constructed of coral and wood along a north–south axis, with flat roofs and a small open courtyard in the centre, which serves as the main source of light.

The various quarters or neighbourhoods in Swahili towns are symbolically united by a central mosque, usually referred to as the *msikiti wa Ijumaa* (Friday mosque). In a sharp break with Islamic architectural custom elsewhere, traditional Swahili mosques don't have minarets; the muezzin gives the call to prayer from inside the mosque, generally with the help of a loudspeaker.

Rwanda has a small but notable film festival, spearheaded by Rwandan filmmaker Eric Kabera. It is centred in Kigali, with screenings also in villages outside the capital.

Cinema

East Africa's long languishing and traditionally under-funded film industry received a major boost with the opening of the **Zanzibar International Film Festival** (ZIFF; www.ziff.or.tz), which has been held annually on Zanzibar island since 1998, and continues to be one of the region's premier cultural events. The festival serves as a venue for artists from the Indian Ocean basin and beyond, and has had several local prize winners, including *Maangamizi: The Ancient One,* shot in Tanzania and co-directed by Tanzanian Martin M'hando. M'hando is also known for his film, *Mama Tumaini* (Women of Hope). Other regional winners have included *Makaburi Yatasema* (Only the Stones are Talking), a film about AIDS and directed by Chande Omar Omar, and *Fimbo ya Baba* (Father's Stick), a 2006 Chande Omar Omar production also focusing on AIDS. In 2005 Tanzania's Beatrix Mugishawe won acclaim (and two prizes) for *Tumaini,* which focuses on AIDS orphans.

Rwandan Eric Kabera is known worldwide for *Keepers of Memory,* as well as *100 Days* (produced together with Nick Hughes) and *Through My Eyes,* both sobering documentaries of the Rwandan genocide and its aftermath, and both also ZIFF award winners.

East African Literature

East Africa's first-known Swahili manuscript is an epic poem dating from 1728 and written in Arabic script. However, it wasn't until the second half of the 20th century – once Swahili had become established as a regional language – that Swahili prose began to develop. One of the best known authors from this period was Tanzanian poet and writer Shaaban Robert (1909–62), who spearheaded development of a modern Swahili prose style. Among his works are the autobiographical *Maisha yangu* (My Life), and several collections of folk tales.

In more recent years there has been a flowering of English-language titles by East African writers, including *Weep Not, Child* and *Detained: A Prison Writer's Diary,* both by Kenyan Ngũgĩ wa Thiong'o; *Song of Lawino* by Ugandan Okot p'Bitek; *Abyssinian Chronicles* by Ugandan Moses Isegawa; and *Desertion* by Zanzibari Abdulrazak Gurnah. See the individual country chapters for more on these and other authors.

There is also a rich but often overlooked body of English-language literature by East African women, particularly in Uganda. Some names to watch out for include Mary Karooro Okurut, whose *A Woman's Voice: An Anthology of Short Stories by Ugandan Women* provides a good overview of the work of some of Uganda's female writers. Another name to look for is that of the internationally recognised Kenyan writer Grace Ogot, known in particular for *The Promised Land.*

MUSIC WEBSITES

For more on East African music, see www.eastafricanmusic.com, which provides a broad overview of the region's music; for more on kanga sayings, see www.glcom.com/hassan/kanga.html and www.mwambao.com/methali.htm, both of which provide a sampling of what is being said around you.

Ngoma: Music & Dance

Congolese Roots

The single greatest influence on the modern East African music scene has been the Congolese bands that began playing in Dar es Salaam and Nairobi in the early 1960s, and which brought the styles of rumba and soukous into the East African context. Among the best known is Orchestre Super Matimila, which was propelled to fame by the late Congolese-born Remmy Ongala ('Dr Remmy'). Many of Ongala's songs (most are in Swahili) are commentaries on contemporary themes such as AIDS, poverty and hunger, and he was a major force over the decades in popularising music from the region beyond Africa's borders. Another of the Congolese bands is Samba Mapangala's Orchestra Virunga. Mapangala, a Congolese vocalist, first gained a footing in Uganda in the mid-1970s with a group known as Les Kinois before moving to Nairobi and forming Orchestra Virunga.

As Swahili lyrics replaced the original vocals, a distinct East African rumba style was born. Its proponents include Simba Wanyika (together with offshoot Les Wanyika), which had its roots in Tanzania but gained fame in the nightclubs of Nairobi.

Benga

In the 1970s Kenyan benga music rose to prominence on the regional music scene. It originated among the Luo of western Kenya and is characterised by its clear electric guitar licks and bounding bass rhythms. Its ethnic roots were maintained, however, with the guitar taking the place of the traditional *nyatiti* (folk lyre), and the bass guitar replacing the

CRAFT SHOPPING

Craft shopping is one of the many pleasures of travel in East Africa. You'll encounter a wide selection of crafts in the region, ranging from basketry and woodcarvings to textiles, paintings and jewellery. While there's plenty of cheap, low-quality work available, with a bit of looking and comparison shopping you should be able to find high-quality work at reasonable prices. When checking for quality, consider the attention given to detail and the overall craftsmanship; with textiles, spread them out to check for flaws or uneven cuts. Always try to buy crafts and souvenirs directly from those who make them; artists' cooperatives are always a good bet.

MAKONDE WOODCARVINGS

Among the most common Makonde carving styles are those with *ujamaa* motifs, and those known as *shetani,* which embody images from the spirit world. *Ujamaa* carvings are designed as a totem pole or 'tree of life' containing interlaced human and animal figures around a common ancestor. Each generation is connected to those that preceded it, and gives support to those that follow. Tree of life carvings often reach several metres in height, and are almost always made from a single piece of wood. *Shetani* carvings are much more abstract, and even grotesque, with the emphasis on challenging viewers to new interpretations while giving the carver's imagination free reign.

drum, which originally was played by the *nyatiti* player with a toe ring. One of the best-known proponents of benga has been DO Misiani, whose group Shirati Jazz has been popular since the 1960s.

Dance

Throughout East Africa, dance plays a vital role in community life, although masked dance is not as common in most parts of the region as it is in West Africa. A wide variety of drums and rhythms are used depending on the occasion, with many dances serving as expressions of thanks and praise, or as a means of communicating with the ancestors or telling a story. East Africa's most famous dance group is the globally acclaimed Les Tambourinaires du Burundi.

Kanga, Kikoi & Handicrafts

Women throughout East Africa wear brightly coloured lengths of printed cotton cloth, typically with Swahili sayings printed along the edge and known as *kanga* in Kenya, Tanzania and parts of Uganda. Many of the sayings are social commentary or messages – often indirectly worded, or containing puns and double meanings – that are communicated by the woman wearing the *kanga,* generally to other women. Others are simply a local form of advertising, such as those bearing the logo of political parties.

In coastal areas, you'll also see the *kikoi,* which is made of a thicker textured cotton, usually featuring striped or plaid patterns, and traditionally worn by men. Also common are batik-print cottons depicting everyday scenes, animal motifs or geometrical patterns.

Jewellery, especially beaded jewellery, is particularly beautiful among the Maasai and the Turkana. It is worn in ceremonies as well as in everyday life, and often indicates the wearer's wealth and marital status.

Basketry and woven items – all of which have highly functional roles in local society – also make lovely souvenirs.

Visual Arts

East Africa is renowned for its exceptional figurative art, especially that of Tanzania's Makonde who are acclaimed throughout the region for their skill at bringing blocks of hard African blackwood (*Dalbergia melanoxylon* or, in Swahili, *mpingo*) to life in often highly fanciful depictions.

In comparison with woodcarving, painting has a fairly low profile in East Africa. One of the more popular styles is Tanzania's Tingatinga painting, which takes its name from the self-taught artist Edward Saidi Tingatinga, who began the style in the 1960s. Tingatinga paintings are traditionally composed in a square format, and feature brightly coloured animal motifs set against a monochrome background.

ART WEBSITES

For dozens of links on art in Africa, including many on East Africa, see the listings on Columbia University's Art and Archaeology of Africa page (www.columbia.edu/cu/lweb/indiv/africa/cuvl/AfArt.html).

A Taste of East Africa

It's easy to travel in East Africa thinking that the region subsists on rice or ugali (one of the main staples) and sauce. But hunt around, as there are some real treats to be discovered. Cuisine is best along the coast, with savoury seafood dishes and an abundance of spices. Inland, watch out for grilled-meat kebabs and tilapia (Nile perch). Throughout the region, the warm hospitality and lively local atmosphere will be the highlights of your eating experiences.

The Street Food Scene

Whether for the taste or simply the ambience, the street-food scene is one of the region's highlights. Throughout East Africa vendors hawk grilled maize, or deep-fried yams seasoned with a squeeze of lemon juice and a dash of chilli powder. Along the coast *pweza* (octopus) kebabs sizzle over the coals, and women squat near large, piping-hot pots of sweet *uji* (millet porridge). Other East African streetside favourites include *sambusas* (deep-fried pastry triangles stuffed with spiced mince meat), but be sure they haven't been sitting around too long, *maandazi* (semi-sweet doughnut-like products) and *chipsi mayai* (a puffy omelette with chips mixed in). *Nyama choma* (seasoned barbecued meat) is found throughout the region but is especially popular in Kenya.

UROJO

Urojo is a filling, delicious soup with *kachori* (spicy potatoes), mango, limes, coconut, cassava chips, salad and sometimes *pili-pili* (hot pepper). Originally from Zanzibar, it's widely available along the coast.

Ugali & Other Staples

One of the most common staples in East Africa is ugali (a thick, filling dough-like mass made from maize or cassava flour, or both); it's known as *posho* in Uganda. Around Lake Victoria, the staple is just as likely to be *matoke* (cooked plantains), while along the coast, women shred coconuts with a *mbuzi* (literally, 'goat' – a wooden stool with a protruding neck with a sharp metal edge) and prepare rice with coconut milk. Whatever the staple, it's always accompanied by a sauce, usually with a piece of meat floating around in it.

Three meals a day is the norm, with the main meal eaten at midday and breakfast frequently nothing more than tea or instant coffee and packaged white bread. In remote areas, many places are closed in the evening and street food is often the only option.

Vegetarian Cuisine

While there isn't much in East Africa that is specifically billed as 'vegetarian', there are many vegie options, and you can find cooked rice and beans almost everywhere. The main challenges are keeping dietary variety and balance and getting enough protein. In larger towns, Indian restaurants are wonderful for vegetarian meals. Elsewhere, try asking Indian shop owners if they have any suggestions; many will also be able to help you find fresh yoghurt. Peanuts and cashews are widely available, and fresh fruits and vegetables are abundant. Seafood eaters will have no problems along the coast or near the lakes; even in inland areas fish is often available from rivers and streams. Most tour operators are willing to cater to special dietary requests, such as vegetarian, kosher or halal, with advance notice.

Drinks

Water & Juices

Tap water is best avoided; also be wary of ice and fruit juices that may have been diluted with unpurified water. Bottled water is widely available, except in remote areas, where it's worth carrying a filter or purification tablets.

Sodas (soft drinks) are found almost everywhere. Freshly squeezed juices, especially pineapple, sugar cane and orange, are a treat, although check whether they have been mixed with safe water. Local milkshakes are also worth hunting for – fresh juice, chilled milk and syrup. Also refreshing, and never a worry hygienically, is the juice of the *dafu* (green) coconut. Western-style supermarkets sell imported fruit juices.

Coffee & Tea

Although East Africa exports high-quality coffee and tea, what's usually available locally is far inferior, and instant coffee is the norm. Both tea and coffee are generally drunk with lots of milk and sugar. On the coast, sip a smooth spiced tea (chai masala) or sample a coffee sold by vendors strolling the streets carrying a freshly brewed pot in one hand, cups and spoons in the other.

Coffee Coastal Style

Especially along the coast, coffee vendors carry around a stack of coffee cups and a piping-hot kettle on a long handle with coals fastened underneath. They let you know they're coming by clacking together their metal coffee cups.

Beer & Wine

Among the most common beers are the locally brewed Tusker, Primus and Kilimanjaro, and South Africa's Castle Lager, which is also produced locally. Many locals prefer their beer warm, especially in Kenya, so getting a cold beer can be a task.

Kenya and Tanzania have fledgling wine industries. Good-quality South African wines are readily available in major cities.

Locally produced home brews (fermented mixtures made with bananas or millet and sugar) are widely available. However, avoid anything distilled; in addition to being illegal, it's also often lethal.

DINING LEXICON

» *biryani* – casserole of spices, rice and meat; common along the coast

» *kiti moto* – fried or roasted pork bits, sold by the kilogram, served with salad and fried plantain, and eaten at an informal 'kiti moto' stand

» *mchuzi* – sauce, sometimes with bits of beef and vegetables

» *mishikaki* – marinated, grilled-meat kebab

» *mkate* – bread; *mkate wa kumimina* (sesame seed bread) is particularly good, and found along the coast

» *mtindi* – cultured milk, usually sold in small bags and delicious on a hot day

» *ndizi* – banana; available in dozens of varieties

» *pilau* – spiced rice cooked in broth with bits of seafood or meat and vegetables; a coastal speciality

» *pili-pili* – hot pepper

» *vitambua* – small rice cakes resembling tiny, thick pancakes

» *wali na kuku/samaki/nyama/maharagwe* – cooked white rice with chicken/fish/meat/beans

DINING EAST AFRICAN STYLE

If you're invited to join in a meal, the first step is hand washing. Your hostess will bring around a bowl and water jug; hold your hands over the bowl while she pours water over them. Sometimes soap is provided, and a towel for drying off.

At the centre of the meal will be ugali (a thick, filling dough-like mass made from maize or cassava flour, or both) or some other similar staple, which is normally taken with the right hand from a communal pot, rolled into a small ball with the fingers, dipped into a sauce and eaten. Eating with your hand is a bit of an art and may seem awkward at first, but after a few tries it will start to feel more natural.

The underlying element in all meal invitations is solidarity between the hosts and the guests, and the various customs, such as eating out of a communal dish, are simply expressions of this. If you receive an invitation to eat but aren't hungry, it's OK to explain that you have just eaten. However, still share a few bites of the meal in order to demonstrate your solidarity with the hosts, and to express your appreciation.

Don't be worried if you can't finish what's on your plate; this shows that you have been satisfied. But try to avoid being the one who takes the last handful from the communal bowl, as your hosts may think that they haven't provided enough.

Except for fruit, desserts are rarely served; meals conclude with another round of hand washing.

Dining Out

Hotelis & Night Markets

For dining local-style, find a local eatery, known as *hoteli* in Swahili-speaking areas. The day's menu, rarely costing more than US$1, is usually written on a chalkboard. Rivalling *hoteli* for local atmosphere are the bustling night markets, where vendors set up grills along the roadside and sell *nyama choma* (seasoned barbeque meat) and other street food.

Restaurants

For Western-style meals, cities and main towns will have an array of restaurants, most moderately priced compared with their European counterparts. Every capital city has at least one Chinese restaurant. In many parts of East Africa, especially along the coast, around Lake Victoria and in Uganda, there's also usually a selection of Indian cuisine, found both at inexpensive eateries serving Indian snacks, as well as in pricier restaurants.

Avoid handling or eating food with the left hand; in many areas, it's even considered impolite to give someone something with the left hand.

SELF-CATERING

Supermarkets in main towns sell imported products, such as canned meat, fish and cheese.

Local Customs & Traditions

Meals connected with any sort of social occasion are usually drawn-out affairs for which the women of the household will have spent several days preparing. Typical East African style is to eat with the right hand from communal dishes in the centre of the table. Although food is shared, it's not customary to share drinks. Children generally eat separately.

Street snacks and meals-on-the-run are common. European-style restaurant dining, while readily available in major cities, is not an entrenched part of local culture. More common are meal-centred gatherings at home, or perhaps at a rented hall, to celebrate special occasions.

Lunch is served between noon and 2.30pm, and dinner from about 6.30pm or 7pm to 10pm. The smaller the town, the earlier its dining establishments are likely to close; after about 7pm in rural areas it can be hard to find alternatives to street food. During Ramadan, many restaurants in coastal areas close completely during daylight fasting hours.

Survival Guide

SAFE TRAVEL 638
COMMON DANGERS 638
Banditry 638
Crime 638
Road Accidents. 638
Scams 638
COUNTRY-BY-COUNTRY 639
Tanzania. 639
Kenya 639
Uganda. 639
Democratic Republic of the Congo (DRC). 639
Rwanda 639
Burundi 639

DIRECTORY A–Z . . . 640
Accommodation. 640
Activities 641
Bargaining 642
Business Hours 642
Electricity 643
Food 643
Gay & Lesbian Travellers 643
Insurance. 643
Internet Access. 643
Legal Matters 644
Maps. 644
Money. 645
Photography 645
Public Holidays. 646
Solo Travellers. 646
Telephone 646
Time 646
Toilets. 646
Travellers with Disabilities. 647
Visas. 647
Volunteering 648
Women Travellers. 648
Work 649

TRANSPORT 650
GETTING THERE & AWAY. 650
GETTING AROUND. 652

HEALTH 657
BEFORE YOU GO 657
Insurance. 657
IN EAST AFRICA 657
Availability & Cost of Health Care 657
Infectious Diseases 658
Traveller's Diarrhoea 660
Environmental Hazards. . .661

LANGUAGE 663
SWAHILI. 663
Basics. 663
Accomodation. 664
Directions 664
Eating & Drinking. 664
Emergencies 665
Shopping & Services. . . . 665
Time, Dates & Numbers 666
Transport. 666
FRENCH. 667
GLOSSARY. 668

Safe Travel

It's difficult to generalise about safety in East Africa. While there are large risks in some areas, other places are extremely safe. The list of potential dangers may sound daunting, but remember that the majority of visitors to the region never experience any difficulties, and the best approach is to always be alert without being paranoid.

COMMON DANGERS

Banditry

Banditry tends to occur in quite localised areas – northern Kenya, northeastern Uganda, rural Burundi and the DRC are the most common trouble-spots, but these areas are well-known and easily avoided. Always check the international travel advisories and make detailed enquiries locally – expats, police and local guides are usually reliable sources – before setting out.

Crime

Petty theft is a risk throughout East Africa, primarily in capital cities and tourist areas. The risks are especially high in crowded settings (markets, public transport, and bus and train stations) or in isolated areas (dark streets or deserted beaches). Muggings and violent crime are less frequent but nonetheless do occur. By following a few simple precautions, you'll minimise the risks.

» Avoid isolated areas, including beaches, at any time of day, but especially at night.

» In cities, especially Nairobi (Kenya), be alert for hustlers who will try any ploy to get you into a back alley and away from the watching eyes of onlookers.

» Don't tempt people by flaunting your wealth. Avoid external money pouches, dangling backpacks and camera bags, and leave jewellery, fancy watches, electronics and the like at home.

» When out walking, keep a small amount of cash separate from your other money and handy, so that you don't pull out large wads of bills for making purchases.

» Try not to look lost, even if you are. Walk purposefully and confidently, and don't refer to this guidebook or a map while on the street.

» Take particular care when arriving for the first time at a bus station, particularly in places such as Nairobi and Arusha (Tanzania). Try to spot the taxi area before disembarking, and make a beeline for it.

» Store valuables in a hotel safe, if there's a reliable one, ideally inside a lockable pouch.

» Keep the windows up in vehicles when stopped in traffic, and keep your bags out of sight.

» On buses and trains, never accept food or drink from fellow passengers. Also avoid travelling at night.

Road Accidents

Perhaps the most widespread threat to your safety comes from travelling on the region's roads. Road conditions vary, but driving standards are almost universally poor and high speeds are common.

Tips for minimising the risk of becoming a road statistic include:

» Never travel at night.

» It's better to go with a full-sized bus than a minibus.

» If travelling in a matatu (usually a minivan), never take the seat next to the driver.

Scams

The region's thieves have invented numerous ways to separate you from your money. Most are deceptively simple, and equally simple to avoid.

» Be sceptical of anyone who approaches you familiarly on the street; for example, someone who approaches you on the street saying 'Remember me?' or claiming to be collecting donations for school fees. Your money has a better chance of reaching those most in need when channelled through registered charities or churches.

GOVERNMENT TRAVEL ADVICE

The following government websites offer travel advisories and information for travellers:

Australian Department of Foreign Affairs & Trade (www.smartraveller.gov.au)

Canadian Department of Foreign Affairs & International Trade (www.voyage.gc.ca)

French Ministere des Affaires Etrangeres Europeennes (www.diplomatie.gouv.fr/fr/conseils-aux-voyageurs_909/index.html)

Italian Ministero degli Affari Esteri (www.viaggiaresicuri.mae.aci.it in Italian)

UK Foreign & Commonwealth Office (www.fco.gov.uk)

US Department of State (www.travel.state.gov)

» You're walking along a busy city street, and suddenly find your way blocked by someone. Before you know it, his buddy has come up behind you and relieved you of your wallet, and they both disappear into the crowds.

» Someone strikes up a conversation and tries to sell you marijuana (*bangi* or *ganja*). Before can shake them loose, police officers (sometimes legitimate, sometimes not) appear and insist that you pay a huge fine for being involved in the purchase of illegal drugs. Insist on going to the nearest police station before paying anything, and whittle the bribe down as low as you can.

» Your taxi driver passes a police officer, and is stopped for not wearing his seatbelt. The police officer takes the driver's keys, and you need to pay the officer to get the keys back to access your luggage in the trunk. The 'fine' is then divvied up among all the accomplices. Always take taxis from hotels or established ranks.

» A smooth-talker befriends you and his friend just happens to have a taxi. When you get in, you're soon joined by his buddies, who then force you to turn over your ATM card and PIN, and ride with them to various ATMs around the city until your account is emptied. Only take taxis from established ranks, and avoid getting into taxis with a 'friend' of the driver or someone else already in it.

COUNTRY-BY-COUNTRY

Tanzania

Although you should take all the usual precautions, Tanzania is one of the safest countries in the region. Muggings and petty thefts do occur, especially in Dar es Salaam and Zanzibar, while touts can be a particular annoyance in Arusha, Mbeya and Zanzibar.

Kenya

Nairobi is notorious for muggings and more serious crime, but the situation has improved and the greatest dangers are relatively easy to avoid. Crime can be a problem in Mombasa and other coastal areas, especially beach resorts. Northern Kenya has an ongoing problem with banditry (see boxed text, p311). The problem is particularly acute close to the Somali border where kidnappings have occurred; see the boxed text p347. For detailed advice on travelling safely in Kenya, see p367.

Uganda

Uganda is generally safe for foreign travellers and Kampala is one of the region's safer large cities. The main threats come from bandits in the Karamojong area of far northeastern Uganda (see boxed text, p471) and the border areas of the country's far northwest.

For detailed advice on travelling safely in Uganda, see p487.

Democratic Republic of the Congo (DRC)

The DRC's reputation for violence is well known. Always check the security situation carefully and be aware that things can change rapidly in this troubled corner of Africa. At the time of writing, the small areas of eastern DRC covered in this guide were considered relatively safe, at least by Congolese standards. For detailed advice on travelling safely in the DRC, see p501.

Rwanda

Few visitors to Rwanda experience any problems, although you should take the usual safety precautions. You should also always check the prevailing security situation close to Rwanda's borders with Burundi and the DRC.

Burundi

The security situation for visitors to Burundi has improved recently, although the country remains subject to political instability and violence. Bujumbura has a reputation for street crime, while most rural areas remain off-limits; the road from Bujumbura north to the Rwandan border is considered fairly safe. For detailed advice on travelling safely in Burundi, see p566.

Directory A–Z

This chapter contains general regional travel information. For country-specific details, see the Directory sections in the country chapters.

Accommodation

Accommodation ranges from no-frills rooms with communal bucket bath to some of Africa's most luxurious safari lodges.

Camping

» There are campsites in most national parks and in or near many major towns. In some rural tourist areas, local villagers maintain camping grounds. Facilities range from none at all to full service, with hot showers and cooking areas.

» Except for the national parks (where camping fees are often much higher), prices average US$5 to US$10 per person per night.

» Camping away from established sites is not advisable; in rural areas, ask the village head or elders before pitching your tent. The exceptions to this are in Rwanda and Burundi, where camping options range from limited to nonexistent.

» In coastal areas, bungalows or *bandas* (simple wooden or thatched huts, often with only a mattress and mosquito net) offer an alternative to camping.

BOOK YOUR STAY ONLINE

For more accommodation reviews by Lonely Planet authors, check out http://hotels.lonelyplanet.com. You'll find independent reviews, as well as recommendations on the best places to stay. Best of all, you can book online.

Hostels, Guesthouses & Budget Hotels

» True hostels are rare, but mission hostels and guesthouses are scattered throughout the region. While intended primarily for missionaries and aid-organisation staff, they're generally happy to accommodate travellers if space is available. Most are clean, safe and good value.

» In budget guesthouses and hotels, you generally get what you pay for, though there's the occasional good deal. The cheapest ones (every town will have one) are poorly ventilated cement-block rooms with reasonably clean sheets, shared toilets, cold showers or a bucket bath, mosquito net, sometimes a fan and often only a token lock on the door. Rates for this type of place average from US$5 per room per night. A few dollars more will get you a somewhat more comfortable room, often with a bathroom (although not always with running or hot water).

» Many budget places double as brothels, and at many of the cheapest ones, solo women travellers are likely to feel uncomfortable. For peace and quiet, guesthouses without bars are the best choice.

» Backpackers and dormitory-style places aren't as common as in southern Africa, but there are a few, with prices slightly higher than you'd pay for a room in a basic guesthouse.

Hotels, Lodges & Luxury Safari Camps

» Larger towns will have one or several midrange hotels, most with private bathroom, hot water and a fan or an air-conditioner. Facilities range from faded to good value, and prices range from US$25 to US$100 per person.

» Major tourist areas also have a good selection of top-end accommodation, with prices ranging from about US$100 to US$300 or more per person per night. On the safari circuits, top-end prices are generally all-inclusive.

» National parks often have 'permanent tented camps' or 'luxury tented camps'. These offer comfortable beds in canvas tents, usually with private toilet, screened windows and most of the comforts of a hotel room, but with a wilderness feel. 'Mobile' or 'fly' camps are temporary camps set up for several nights, or for one season, and used for

ACCOMMODATION PRICES

The following price ranges refer to a standard double room in high season, except as noted otherwise.

» **$** less than US$50

» **$$** US$50 to $150

» **$$$** more than US$150

» Except for low-budget local guesthouses (where you get a room only), prices listed here include private bathroom and continental breakfast (coffee or tea, bread, jam and sometimes an egg).

» Many lodges and luxury camps around the parks quote all-inclusive prices, which means accommodation and full board plus excursions such as wildlife drives, short guided walks or boat safaris. Park entry fees are generally excluded.

» Camping prices are per person, except as noted.

walking safaris or a more intimate bush experience away from the main tented camp.

Activities

Following is some general information about diving and hiking in East Africa. See the country chapter Directories for overviews of country-specific activities.

Diving & Snorkelling

If you want to learn to dive, or to refresh your skills, East Africa is a rewarding if somewhat pricey place to do this. The main areas are the Zanzibar and Mafia archipelagos in Tanzania and the coast south of Mombasa, around Malindi and the Lamu archipelago, in Kenya. All areas have an array of operators and courses.

Be sure to allow a sufficient surface interval between the conclusion of your final dive and any onward flights. The Professional Association of Dive Instructors (PADI) recommends at least 12 hours, or more if you have been doing daily multiple dives for several days. Another consideration is insurance, which you should arrange before coming to East Africa. Many policies exclude diving, so you'll likely need to pay a bit extra, but it's well worth it in comparison with the bills you will need to foot should something go wrong.

DIVE OPERATORS & SAFETY

When choosing a dive operator, quality rather than cost should be the priority. Consider the operator's experience and qualifications; the knowledge and competence of staff; and the condition of equipment and frequency of maintenance. Assess whether the overall attitude is serious and professional, and ask about safety precautions: radios, oxygen, boat reliability and back-up engines, emergency evacuation procedures, first-aid kits, safety flares and life jackets. On longer dives, do you get an energising meal, or just tea and biscuits?

There are decompression chambers in Matemwe on Zanzibar's east coast, in Mombasa (although this latter one is an army facility, and not always available to the general public) and in Johannesburg (South Africa). Also check the **Divers Alert Network Southern Africa** (DAN; www.dansa.org) website, which includes Tanzania and Kenya, and has a list of Zanzibar- and Pemba-based operators that are part of DAN. If you dive with an operator that isn't affiliated with DAN, it's highly recommended to take out insurance coverage with DAN.

SAFE DIVING

» Possess a current diving certification card from a recognised scuba diving instructional agency.

» Be sure you are healthy and feel comfortable diving.

» Obtain reliable information on conditions (eg from local dive operators).

» Dive only at sites within your realm of experience.

» Be aware of seasonal changes in sites and dive conditions, and equip yourself accordingly.

Hiking & Trekking

Almost all hikes and climbs in the region require local

PRACTICALITIES

» **Discount cards** An International Student Identity Card (ISIC) or the graduate equivalent is occasionally useful for discounts on train fares, airline tickets and entry charges to museums and archaeological sites.

» **Newspapers** *The East African* (weekly). For a pan-African focus: BBC's *Focus on Africa; Business Africa;* and *Africa Today*. For environmental issues: *Africa Geographic*. For ornithology: *Africa: Birds & Birding*.

» **Radio** Kenya, Uganda and Tanzania: government-run national broadcasters with radio and TV transmissions in English. BBC's World Service and Deutsche Welle transmit in English and Swahili.

» **Weights & measures** Metric system

RESPONSIBLE DIVING

Wherever you dive, consider the following tips, and help preserve the ecology and beauty of the reefs:

» Never use anchors on a reef, and take care not to ground boats on coral.

» Avoid touching or standing on living marine organisms or dragging equipment across a reef. Polyps can be damaged by even the gentlest contact. If you must hold on to a reef, only touch exposed rock or dead coral.

» Be conscious of your fins. Even without contact, the surge from fin strokes near a reef can damage delicate organisms. Take care not to kick up clouds of sand, which can smother organisms.

» Practise and maintain proper buoyancy control. Major damage can be done by divers descending too fast and colliding with a reef.

» Take great care in underwater caves. Spend as little time within them as possible, as your air bubbles may be caught within the roof and thereby leave organisms high and dry. Take turns inspecting the interior of a small cave.

» Resist the temptation to collect or buy corals or shells – which you'll frequently be offered by vendors on the beaches – or to loot marine archaeological sites (mainly shipwrecks).

» Ensure that you take home all your rubbish and any litter you may find as well. Plastics in particular are a serious threat to marine life.

» Do not feed fish.

» Minimise your disturbance of marine animals, and never ride on the backs of turtles or attempt to touch dolphins.

guides, and some require a full range of clothing, from lightweight for the semitropical conditions at lower altitudes to full winter gear for the high summits. Waterproof clothing and equipment is important at any altitude and season.

Bargaining

Bargaining is expected by vendors in tourist areas, except in a limited number of fixed-price shops. However, away from tourist areas and for nontourist items, the price quoted will often be the 'real' price, so don't automatically assume that the quote you've been given is too high.

Where bargaining is appropriate, if you pay the first price asked – whether due to ignorance or guilt about how much you have compared with locals – you'll probably be considered naive. You'll also be doing fellow travellers a disservice by creating the impression that all foreigners are willing to pay any named price. Paying consistently above the curve can also contribute to goods being priced out of the reach of locals.

While there are no set rules for bargaining, it should be conducted in a friendly and spirited manner; losing your temper or becoming aggressive or frustrated will be counterproductive. In any transaction, the vendor's aim is to identify the highest price you will pay, while your aim is to find the lowest price at which the vendor will sell. Before starting, shop around to get a feel for the 'value' of the item you want, and ask others what they paid. Once you start negotiating, if things seem like a waste of time, politely take your leave. Sometimes sellers will call you back if they think their stubbornness is counterproductive. Few will pass up a sale, however thin the profit. If the vendor won't come down to a price you feel is fair, it means that they aren't making a profit, or that too many high-rolling foreigners have passed through already.

Business Hours

Business hours are only noted in the individual listings when there are major deviations from the following hours:

Banks 8.30am to 3pm or 4pm Monday to Friday, sometimes also 9am to noon Saturday

Drinking 5pm onwards

Tourist information 9am to 5pm Monday to Saturday

Western-style restaurants lunch noon to 2.30pm, dinner 6.30pm to 10pm

Local Restaurants 7.30am to 8pm Monday to Saturday

Shops 8.30am to 5.30pm Monday to Friday, 8.30am to 1pm Saturday.

Many shops and offices close for one to two hours between noon and 2pm and, especially in coastal areas, on Friday afternoons for mosque services. Supermarkets in major cities are often open on Saturday afternoon and Sunday for a few hours around midday.

Electricity

220-250V/50Hz

220-230v/50hz

Food

For more on East African cuisine, see p634. Price ranges used in individual listings are:

» **$** less than US$5
» **$$** US$5 to $10
» **$$$** more than US$10

Gay & Lesbian Travellers

Officially, male homosexuality is illegal in Tanzania and Kenya. While prosecutions rarely occur, discretion is advised as gay sexual relationships are culturally taboo, and public displays of affection, whether between people of the same or opposite sex, are frowned upon. In Uganda, homophobics have become increasingly vocal in recent times. This said, it is unlikely that gay travellers will experience any particular difficulties.

Initial contacts include **Purple Roofs** (www.purpleroofs.com), which lists gay or gay-friendly tour companies in the region, and **Gay2Afrika** (www.gay2afrika.com), with a range of regional tours.

Insurance

Taking out travel insurance covering theft, loss and medical problems is highly recommended. Some tips include the following:

» Shop around before choosing a policy, as those designed for short package tours in Europe may not be suitable for East Africa.
» Read the fine print: some policies specifically exclude 'dangerous activities', which can mean scuba diving, motorcycling and even trekking. A locally acquired motorcycle licence isn't valid under some policies.
» Most policies valid in East Africa require you to pay on the spot and claim later, so keep all documentation.
» Most importantly, check that the policy covers an emergency flight home or at least medical evacuation to Western-standard health facilities, and understand in advance the procedures you need to follow in an emergency.
» Before heading to East Africa, consider taking out a membership with one of the following, both of which operate 24-hour air ambulance services and offer emergency medical evacuation within East Africa:
» **African Medical & Research Foundation** (Amref; www.amref.org) Nairobi emergency lines (☎254-20-315454/5, 254-20-600 2299, 254-733-639088, 254-722-314239); Nairobi head office (☎254-20-699 3000) A two-month membership costs US$25/50 for evacuations within a 500km/1000km radius of Nairobi. The 1000km membership encompasses the entire East African region, except for southernmost Tanzania around Songea, Tunduru and Mtwara.
» **First Air Responder** (www.firstairresponder.com) Dar es Salaam head office (☎022-276 0087/8, emergency 0754-777073, 0754-777100, 0784-555911; info@firstairresponder.com); Arusha branch office (☎0732-972283, emergency 0754-510197) A two-week/one-month membership costs US$20/35 and entitles you to emergency evacuation within Tanzania and Kenya as well as local ground support in the vicinity of Dar es Salaam, Arusha and several other Tanzanian cities.
» Worldwide travel insurance is available at www.lonelyplanet.com/travel_services. You can buy, extend and claim online anytime, even if you're already on the road.

Internet Access

» There are internet cafes in all capitals and major towns. In rural areas, connections remain spotty.
» Prices average US$1 per hour; truly fast connections are rare.
» Many business-class hotels and cafes have wireless access points. Connections are possible at some but not all safari camps.

RESPONSIBLE TREKKING

The huge number of visitors in some of East Africa's wilderness and trekking areas are beginning to take their toll. Mt Kilimanjaro is a prime example, although there are many others. Following are some tips for helping to preserve the region's delicate ecosystems and beauty:

» Carry out all your rubbish, and make an effort to carry out rubbish left by others. Sanitary napkins, tampons, condoms and toilet paper should be carried out despite the inconvenience. They burn and decompose poorly.

» Minimise waste by taking minimal packaging and no more food than you will need. Take reusable containers or stuff sacks.

» Contamination of water sources by human faeces can lead to the transmission of all sorts of nasties. Where there is a toilet, use it. Where there is none (as is the case in many of the region's trekking areas), bury your waste. Dig a small hole 15cm (6in) deep and at least 100m (320ft) from any watercourse. Cover the waste with soil and a rock. In snow, dig down to the soil. Also ensure that these guidelines are applied to a portable toilet tent if one is being used by a large trekking party.

» Don't use detergents or toothpaste in or near watercourses, even if they are biodegradable. For personal washing, use biodegradable soap (best purchased at home) and a water container at least 50m (160ft) away from the watercourse. Disperse the waste water widely to allow the soil to filter it fully. Wash cooking utensils 50m (160ft) from watercourses using a scourer, sand or snow instead of detergent.

» Hillsides and mountain slopes, especially at high altitudes, are prone to erosion. Stick to existing trails, and avoid short cuts. If a well-used trail passes through a mud patch, walk through the mud so as not to increase the size of the patch. Avoid removing the plant life that keeps topsoils in place.

» Don't depend on open fires for cooking. The cutting of wood for fires in popular trekking areas such as Kilimanjaro can cause rapid deforestation. Cook on a light-weight kerosene, alcohol or Shellite (white gas) stove and avoid those powered by disposable butane gas canisters.

» If you are trekking with a guide and porters, supply stoves for the whole team. In cold conditions, ensure that all members are outfitted with enough clothing so that fires are not a necessity for warmth. If you patronise local accommodation, try to select places that don't use wood fires to heat water or cook food.

» Ensure that you fully extinguish a fire after use. Spread the embers and flood them with water.

» If you will be in East Africa for a while, consider buying a USB stick from one of the main mobile providers (US$20 to US$75), which you can then load with airtime and plug into your laptop.

Legal Matters

Apart from traffic offences such as speeding and driving without a seatbelt (mandatory in many areas for driver and front-seat passengers), the main area to watch out for is drug use and possession. Marijuana *(bangi* or *ganja)* is widely available in places such as Nairobi, Dar es Salaam and Zanzibar, and is frequently offered to tourists, invariably part of a set-up involving the police or fake police. If you're caught, expect to pay a large bribe to avoid arrest or imprisonment.

If you're arrested for whatever reason, you can request to call your embassy, but the help they can give you will be limited.

If you get robbed, most insurance companies require a police report before they'll reimburse you. You can get these at the nearest police station, though it's usually a time-consuming process.

Maps

» Nelles *Tanzania, Rwanda, Burundi*

» Nelles *Kenya*

» Nelles *Uganda*

» Bartholomew's *Kenya & Tanzania*

» Hallwag *Kenya & Tanzania* (also includes Uganda, Rwanda and Burundi).

» Michelin *Africa: Central & South* (covers most of the region on a smaller scale)

Money

Bring a mix of dollars or euros cash (large and small

denominations); a credit card (Visa is most widely accepted) for withdrawing money from ATMs; and some travellers cheques as an emergency standby (although note that these are generally changeable in major cities only, and with very high commissions).

ATMs

There are ATMs in all capital cities and most major towns (except for Rwanda and Burundi, where they are found almost exclusively in the capital cities). They take Visa, MasterCard or both (Visa only in Rwanda). Some banks in Kenya, Tanzania and Uganda also have machines linked to the Plus and Cirrus networks. However, despite their growing use, ATMs are out of order or out of cash with enough frequency that you should always have some sort of back-up funds. There are few ATMs away from major routes.

Black Market

Except for in Burundi, there is essentially no black market for foreign currency. Nevertheless, you'll still get shady characters sidling up beside you in Nairobi, Dar es Salaam and major tourist areas, trying to get you to change money and promising enticing rates. It's invariably a setup; changing on the street should be avoided.

Cash

US dollars, followed by euros, are the most convenient foreign currencies and get the best rates. Other major currencies are readily accepted in major cities, but often not elsewhere, or at less favourable rates. You'll get higher rates for larger denomination bills (US$50 and US$100 notes), but carry a supply of smaller denomination notes as well, as change can be difficult to find. Throughout the region, the only US dollar notes that are accepted for exchange are those from 2006 or newer.

Credit Cards

Visa and MasterCard can be used for some top-end hotels and a few tour operators, especially in major towns and in Kenya. However, they're best viewed as a stand-by unless you've confirmed things in advance with the establishment. In Rwanda and Burundi, you'll need to rely almost exclusively on cash, although a few banks in major cities give cash advances against a credit card with a high commission. Some places, especially in Tanzania, attach a commission of about 5% to 10% to credit card payments.

Exchanging Money

You can change cash with a minimum of hassle at banks or foreign exchange (forex) bureaus in major towns and cities; rates and commissions vary, so it pays to shop around. In addition to regular banking hours, most forex bureaus are also open on Saturday mornings. Outside banking hours and away from an ATM, ask shop owners if they can help you out, rather than changing with someone on the street (which should always be avoided). It's better to say something like 'The banks are closed; do you know someone who could help me out?' rather than directly asking if they will change money.

Tipping

Tipping generally isn't practised in small, local establishments. But in major towns, upmarket places and anywhere frequented by tourists, tips are expected. If a service charge hasn't been included, either round out the bill or calculate about 10%.

Travellers Cheques

Throughout the region, travellers cheques can be changed either not at all (as in Rwanda and Burundi) or only in major cities, with high commissions and with great difficulty. They should not be relied upon. Where they can be changed, rates are lower than for cash. American Express and Thomas Cook are the most widely recognised; get your cheques in US dollars or euros. Bring a range of denominations because some banks charge a per-cheque levy. Carry the *original* purchase receipt with you (and separately from the cheques), as many banks and forex bureaus ask to see it.

Direct payment with travellers cheques for accommodation and services is almost never accepted. If your cheques are stolen, getting replacements while still in the region is generally not possible.

Photography

Admission Fees

Expect to pay an additional admission fee to various parks and sights if you are toting photography or video equipment.

Equipment

Nairobi has the best selection of camera equipment, followed by Dar es Salaam and Kampala, though it's best to bring what you'll need, including extra memory chips, with you.

Many internet cafes and speciality shops can help with transferring digital images to storage devices. It's a good idea to carry a USB converter for memory cards if you want to burn your photos onto CDs or DVDs, as many internet cafes don't have card reader slots.

Whatever equipment you carry, be sure to keep it well protected against dust. Lonely Planet's *Travel Photography: A Guide to Taking Better Pictures* by Richard I'Anson is full of helpful tips for taking photographs while on the road.

Photographing People

Always ask permission before photographing people, and always respect their wishes. In many tourist areas, locals will ask for a fee before allowing you to photograph them, which is fair enough, though rates can be high. If you promise to give someone a photo, follow through with it, as your promise will be taken seriously.

Restrictions

Avoid taking pictures of anything connected with the government or the military, including army barracks, land or people anywhere close to army barracks, government offices, post offices, banks, ports, train stations, airports, bridges and dams.

Some locals may object if you take pictures of their place of worship (this includes natural features with traditional religious significance), so always ask first.

Public Holidays

For national holidays see the country chapter Directories.

In Tanzania, parts of Kenya and Uganda, major Islamic holidays are also celebrated as public holidays. The dates depend on the moon and fall about 11 days earlier each year. The most important ones include the following:

Eid al-Kebir (Eid al-Haji) Commemorates the moment when Abraham was about to sacrifice his son in obedience to God's command, only to have God intercede at the last moment and substitute a ram. It coincides with the end of the pilgrimage (*hajj*) to Mecca.

Eid al-Fitr The end of Ramadan, and East Africa's most important Islamic celebration; celebrated as a two-day holiday in many areas.

Eid al-Moulid (Maulidi) The birthday of the Prophet Mohammed.

Ramadan The annual 30-day fast when adherents do not eat or drink from sunrise to sunset.

Approximate dates for these events are shown below. Although Ramadan is not a public holiday, restaurants are often closed during this time in coastal areas.

PUBLIC HOLIDAYS

EVENT	2012	2013	2014
Ramadan begins	20 Jul	9 July	28 Jun
Eid al-Fitr (end of Ramadan, two-day holiday)	19 Aug	8 Aug	28 Jul
Eid al-Kebir (Eid al-Haji)	26 Oct	15 Oct	4 Oct
Eid al-Moulid	4 Feb	24 Jan	13 Jan

Solo Travellers

While you may be a minor curiosity in rural areas, especially solo women travellers, there are no particular problems with travelling solo in East Africa, whether you're male or female. Times when it is advantageous to join a group are for safaris and treks – when going in a group can be a significant cost saver – and when going out at night. If you go out alone at night, take taxis and use extra caution, especially in urban and tourist areas. Whatever the time of day, avoid isolating situations, including isolated stretches of beach. Also see the Women Travellers sections, p648 and p638.

Telephone

Mobile Phones

The mobile network reaches most areas of the region. Most companies sell prepaid starter packages for about US$2, and top-up cards are on sale at shops everywhere. Although several mobile companies have a presence throughout the region (meaning you can keep the same SIM card in different countries), it's cheaper to buy a local SIM card when you cross the border. Local SIM cards can be used in European and Australian phones. Other phones must be set to roaming.

Phone Codes

Throughout the region, except in Rwanda and Burundi, area codes must be used whenever you dial long-distance. In this guidebook, codes are included in all listings.

Time

Time in Kenya, Uganda and Tanzania is GMT/UTC plus three hours year-round; in Rwanda and Burundi it's GMT/UTC plus two hours.

Toilets

Toilets vary from standard long drops to full-flush luxury conveniences. Most midrange and top-end hotels sport flushable sit-down types, although at the lower end of the price range, toilet seats are a rare commodity.

COUNTRY CODES

Burundi	☎257
DRC	☎243
Kenya	☎254
Rwanda	☎250
Tanzania	☎255
Uganda	☎256

Budget guesthouses often have squat toilets, sometimes equipped with a flush mechanism, otherwise with a bucket and scoop.

Toilets with running water are a rarity outside major hotels. If you see a bucket with water nearby, use it for flushing. Paper (you'll invariably need to supply your own) should be deposited in the can that's usually in the corner.

Many of the upmarket bush camps have 'dry' toilets – just a fancy version of the long drop with a Western-style seat perched on the top.

Travellers with Disabilities

While there are few facilities specifically for the disabled, East Africans are generally quite accommodating, and willing to offer whatever assistance they can as long as they understand what you need. Disabled travel is becoming increasingly common on the Kenyan and Tanzanian safari circuits, and several tour operators listed in the Safaris chapter (p24) cater to disabled travellers. Some considerations:

» While some newer lodges have wheelchair-accessible rooms, few hotels have lifts, many have narrow stairwells and there are generally no grips or rails in bathrooms.

» Many park lodges and camps are built on ground level. However, access paths, in an attempt to maintain a natural environment, are sometimes rough or rocky, and rooms or tents raised. It's best to inquire about access before booking.

» As far as we know, there are no Braille signboards at any parks or museums, nor any facilities for deaf travellers.

» In most places, taxis are small sedans. Minibuses are widely available in Kenya, Tanzania and Uganda, and can be chartered for transport and customised safaris. Large or wide-door vehicles can also be arranged through car-hire agencies in major cities, and often with safari operators as well.

In general, Kenya and northern Tanzania are probably the easiest destinations, and safari companies in these areas often have experience taking disabled people on safari. Helpful contacts include the following:

Accessible Journeys (www.disabilitytravel.com)

Access-Able Travel Source (www.access-able.com)

Mobility International (www.miusa.org)

National Information Communication Awareness Network (www.nican.com.au)

Holiday Care (www.tourismforall.org.uk)

Visas

» It's best to arrange visas in advance, although currently all countries in the region except Rwanda are issuing visas at the airport. Kenya, Tanzania and Uganda also issue visas at most land borders. Regulations change frequently so call the relevant embassy for an update. Many international airlines require you to have a visa before boarding the plane to East Africa.

» Once in East Africa, a single-entry visa for Kenya, Tanzania or Uganda allows you to visit either of the other two countries (assuming you've met their visa requirements and have been issued a visa) and then return to the original country without having to apply for second visa for the original country. Thus, if you're in Tanzania on a single-entry visa, you can go to Kenya (assuming you also have a Kenyan visa), and then return to Tanzania without needing a new Tanzanian visa. This doesn't apply to Rwanda and Burundi, so if you will be including visits to these or other African countries in your regional itinerary, it saves money to get a multiple-entry visa at the outset. Note that visas issued at airports and land borders are usually for single entry only.

SWAHILI TIME

In Swahili-speaking areas, locals use the Swahili system of telling time, in which the first hour is *saa moja (asubuhi),* corresponding with 7am. Counting begins again with *saa moja (jioni),* the first hour in the evening, corresponding with 7pm. Although most will switch to the international clock when speaking English with foreigners, confusion sometimes occurs, so ask people to confirm whether they are using *saa za kizungu* (international time) or *saa za kiswahili* (Swahili time). Signboards with opening hours are often posted in Swahili time.

ON TIME IN EAST AFRICA

While the discussion of time makes everything sound quite official and precise, when all is said and done, time is a very different concept in East Africa than in many parts of the West. Buses that are going 'now' rarely leave until they're full, regardless of how much engine revving takes place in the meantime. Agreed-upon times for appointments are treated as very approximate concepts. A meeting set for 9am today could just as likely happen at 11am, or that afternoon, or even the next day. Getting upset when things don't go like clockwork is generally counterproductive. The best way to get things done efficiently is to stay relaxed, treat the person you're dealing with as a person, inquire how their family is going or how their children are doing at school, and take the time to listen to the answer. Then, sit back, wait and be patient – you'll usually get where you're going or what you're hoping for, but on East Africa's time rather than yours.

» At most borders and at airport immigration, visa fees must be paid in US dollars cash.

» Ensure that your passport has plenty of blank pages for entry and exit stamps, and is valid for at least six months after the conclusion of your planned travels.

» Carry extra passport-sized photos for visa applications.

» Proof of an onward ticket or sufficient funds is rarely required if you apply for a visa at land borders. It's occasionally requested at airports in the region, but generally only if you give immigration officials reason to doubt that you'll leave.

Volunteering

There are various opportunities for volunteering, generally teaching, or in environmental or health work; these are almost always best arranged prior to arriving in East Africa.

Some places to start your search are listed following. See the country chapter directories for country-specific listings.

Camps International (www.campsinternational.com)

Coordinating Committee for International Voluntary Service (www.ccivs.org)

Earthwatch (www.earthwatch.org)

Frontier (www.frontier.ac.uk)

Global Volunteer Network (www.globalvolunteernetwork.org)

Idealist.org (www.idealist.org)

International Volunteer HQ (www.volunteerhq.org)

International Volunteer Programs Association (www.volunteerinternational.org)

i-to-i (www.i-to-i.com)

Peace Corps (www.peacecorps.gov)

ResponsibleTravel.com (www.responsibletravel.com)

Travel Tree (www.traveltree.co.uk)

Volunteer Abroad (www.goabroad.com/volunteer-abroad)

Voluntary Service Overseas (VSO; www.vso.org.uk)

Volunteers for Peace (www.vfp.org)

Working Abroad (www.workingabroad.com)

Worldwide Experience (www.worldwideexperience.com)

Worldwide Volunteering (www.wwv.org.uk)

Women Travellers

East Africa (especially Kenya, Tanzania and Uganda) is a relatively easy region to travel in, either solo or with other women, especially when compared with parts of North Africa, South America and certain Western countries. You're not likely to encounter any more specifically gender-related problems than you would elsewhere in the world and, more often than not, you'll meet only warmth, hospitality and sisterly regard, and find that you receive kindness and special treatment that you probably wouldn't be shown if you were a male traveller. That said, you'll inevitably attract some attention, especially if you're travelling alone, and there are some areas where caution is essential. Following are some tips:

» Dressing modestly is the single most successful strategy for minimising unwanted attention. Wear trousers or a long skirt, and a conservative top with sleeves. Tucking your hair under a cap or scarf, or tying it back, also helps.

» Use common sense, trust your instincts and take the usual precautions when out and about. Try to avoid walking alone at night. Avoid isolated areas at all times, and be particularly cautious on beaches, many of which can become isolated very quickly. Hassling tends to be worse in tourist areas along the Kenyan coast than elsewhere in the region. While most of it is limited to verbal hassles, and many travellers – female and male – travel in this area without incident, take extra care here about where you go alone.

» If you find yourself with an unwanted suitor, creative

approaches are usually fairly effective. For example, explain that your husband (whether real or fictitious) or a large group of friends will be arriving imminently at that very place. Creative approaches are also usually effective in dealing with the inevitable curiosity that you'll meet as to why you might not have children and a husband, or if you do have them, why they are not with you. The easiest response to the question of why you aren't married is to explain that you are still young (*bado kijana* in Swahili), which, whether you are or not, will at least have some humour value. Just saying '*bado*' ('not yet') to questions about marriage or children should also do the trick. As for why your family isn't with you, you can always explain that you will be meeting them later.

» Seek out local women, as this can enrich your trip tremendously. Good places to try include tourist offices, government departments or even your hotel, where at least some of the staff are likely to be formally educated young to middle-aged women. In rural areas, starting points include women teachers at a local school, or staff at a health centre.

» In mixed-race situations in some areas of the region – specifically if you're a black woman with a white male – some East Africans may assume that you're a prostitute. Taking taxis if you go out at night and ignoring any comments are among the tactics that may help minimise problems here.

» Arrange tour and trekking guides through a reputable hotel or travel agency. Avoid freelance guides who approach you on the street.

In Rwanda and Burundi, verbal hassles, hisses and the like tend to be more common than elsewhere in the region, although things rarely go further than this. The best strategy – in addition to following the preceding tips – is to ignore hissing and catcalls; don't worry about being rude, and don't feel the need to explain yourself. Due to the overall unstable security situation, especially in Burundi, you'll need to take particular care in more remote areas, but this applies to travellers of whatever gender.

A limited selection of tampons is available at pharmacies or large supermarkets in major towns throughout the region. Elsewhere, the choice is usually limited to pads. Ladies will likely come to appreciate the benefits of Western-style consumer testing when using local sanitary products.

Work

» The most likely areas for employment are the safari industry, tourism, scuba diving and teaching. For safari-, diving- and tourism-related positions, competition is stiff and the best way to land something is to get to know someone already working in the business. Also check safari operator and lodge websites, some of which advertise vacant positions.

» Work and residency permits generally must be arranged through the employer or sponsoring organisation; residency permits normally should be applied for before arriving in the region. Be prepared for lots of bureaucracy.

» Most teaching positions are voluntary, and best arranged through voluntary agencies or mission organisations at home. Also start your search from home for international staff positions aid agencies. There are numerous opportunities, especially in Kenya, Uganda and Burundi. However, most organisations require applicants to go through their head office.

Transport

GETTING THERE & AWAY

This chapter covers getting to East Africa from elsewhere in the world. For travel between and around East African countries, and for border-crossing information, see the Transport sections in the individual country chapters.

Flights and tours can be booked online at www.lonelyplanet.com/travel_services.

Air

Airports

Nairobi (Kenya) is East Africa's major air hub, and the best destination for finding special airfares. Other major airports include Dar es Salaam and Kilimanjaro in Tanzania, and Entebbe in Uganda. There are also international airports in Kigali (Rwanda), Bujumbura (Burundi) and Zanzibar (Tanzania), and it's worth checking out cheap charter flights to Mombasa (Kenya) from Europe.

Airlines

The following airlines fly to/from East Africa. For connections between East African countries, see the Getting There & Away information in the Transport sections of the country chapters.

Air Madagascar (www.airmadagascar.com) Antananarivo (Madagascar) to Nairobi.

Air Malawi (www.airmalawi.com) Blantyre and Lilongwe to Dar es Salaam.

Air Mauritius (www.airmauritius.com) Mauritius to Nairobi.

Air Uganda (www.air-uganda.com) Juba (South Sudan) to Entebbe, and then to Dar es Salaam, Zanzibar, Nairobi, Mombasa and Kigali.

British Airways (www.britishairways.com) London to Nairobi, Dar es Salaam and Entebbe.

Egypt Air (www.egyptair.com.eg) Cairo to Nairobi, Dar es Salaam, Entebbe and Kigali.

Emirates (www.emirates.com) Dubai to Nairobi, Dar es Salaam and Entebbe.

Ethiopian Airlines (www.ethiopianairlines.com) Abidjan, Lagos, Douala, Cairo, Rome, New York, Washington, DC, Mumbai, Bangkok and many other cities to Addis Ababa, and then onward connections to all major East African airports.

Gulf Air (www.gulfairco.com) Bahrain to Nairobi and Entebbe.

Kenya Airways (www.kenya-airways.com) Abidjan, Cairo, Douala, Harare, Johannesburg, Khartoum, Lilongwe, London, New York, Mumbai, Hong Kong, Bangkok, Guangzhou and many other cities to Nairobi, with onward connections to all East African capitals and Zanzibar.

KLM (www.klm.com) Amsterdam to Nairobi, Dar es Salaam, Kilimanjaro and Entebbe.

Linhas Aéreas de Moçambique (www.lam.co.mz) Maputo to Nairobi and Dar es Salaam via Pemba (Mozambique).

Monarch (www.monarch.co.uk) London to Mombasa.

Qatar Airways (www.qatarairways.com) Doha to Nairobi, Dar es Salaam, Entebbe and Kigali.

RwandAir (www.rwandair.com) Johannesburg, Libreville, Brazzaville, Dubai and Brussels to Kigali.

SN Brussels Airline (www.flysn.com) Brussels to Entebbe, Nairobi, Kigali and Bujumbura.

South African Airways (www.flysaa.com) Johannesburg to Dar es Salaam, Nairobi, Entebbe and Kigali.

Swiss International Airlines (www.swiss.com) Zurich to Dar es Salaam and Nairobi.

Thomson Airways (http://flights.thomson.co.uk) London to Mombasa.

Turkish Airlines (www.turkishairlines.com) Istanbul to Nairobi and Dar es Salaam.

Virgin Atlantic Airways (www.virgin-atlantic.com) London to Nairobi.

Tickets

» Airfares from Europe and North America to East Africa are highest in December and January, and again from June

CLIMATE CHANGE & TRAVEL

Every form of transport that relies on carbon-based fuel generates CO_2, the main cause of human-induced climate change. Modern travel is dependent on aeroplanes, which might use less fuel per kilometre per person than most cars but travel much greater distances. The altitude at which aircraft emit gases (including CO_2) and particles also contributes to their climate change impact. Many websites offer 'carbon calculators' that allow people to estimate the carbon emissions generated by their journey and, for those who wish to do so, to offset the impact of the greenhouse gases emitted with contributions to portfolios of climate-friendly initiatives throughout the world. Lonely Planet offsets the carbon footprint of all staff and author travel.

through August. They're lowest from March through May, except around the Easter holidays.

» London is the main discount airfare hub, and a good place to look for special deals, especially to Nairobi.

» When planning your trip, consider buying an open-jaw ticket, which enables you to fly into one country and out of another. This often works out more cheaply and more environmentally friendly than booking a standard return flight in and out of one city, plus a connecting regional flight.

» Charter flights are generally cheaper than scheduled flights, and are also worth considering. Some come as part of a package that includes accommodation, but most charter companies sell 'flight only' tickets.

Lake

The main lake ferry connections to/from East Africa are between Malawi and Tanzania on Lake Nyasa (see p210), and between Zambia and Tanzania on Lake Tanganyika (see p211).

Land

Several possibilities for combining East Africa travels with overland travel elsewhere in Africa are outlined here. For more on driving your own vehicle to the region, check out the *Adventure Motorcycling Handbook* by Chris Scott et al (useful especially if you're combining the Sahara and West Africa with East Africa) and *Africa by Road* by Bob Swain and Paula Snyder.

North & West Africa

For information on trans-Saharan routes, see Lonely Planet's *West Africa*, and check the website of **Chris Scott** (www.sahara-overland.com). Once through West Africa, most travellers fly from Douala (Cameroon) over the Central African Republic and Democratic Republic of the Congo (the DRC) via Addis Ababa to any of the East African capitals, from where you can continue overland.

Northeast Africa

The Nile route through northeast Africa goes from Egypt into Sudan (via Lake Nasser, and then on to Khartoum). From Khartoum, it's straightforward to make your way to Ethiopia, and then into Kenya. Note, however, that going in the other direction, Ethiopian visas are currently not being issued in Kenya.

There are regular flights between Juba (South Sudan) and Entebbe. However, arranging permission to travel by land between Sudan and South Sudan is very difficult. For all travel involving routings in Sudan and South Sudan, get an update on the security situation before setting your plans.

Southern Africa

The main gateways between southern and East Africa are Zambia and Malawi, both of which are readily reached from elsewhere in southern Africa. Once in Zambia, head to Kapiri Mposhi where you can get the Tanzania–Zambia Railway (Tazara) northeast to Mbeya (Tanzania). From Mbeya, continue by road or rail towards Dar es Salaam, and then by road towards Mombasa and Nairobi. Another route from Zambia goes to Mpulungu on the Zambian shore of Lake Tanganyika, from where you can travel by steamer to Kigoma. From Kigoma, head by rail east to Dar es Salaam or northeast by road towards Lake Victoria, Uganda and western Kenya.

From Malawi, after entering East Africa at Songwe River Bridge (at the Tanzanian border), head by bus to Mbeya and continue as outlined above.

For Burundi, options include following the route outlined earlier from Mpulungu to Kigoma, from where you can continue by boat or overland to Bujumbura, travel through Burundi, Rwanda and Uganda, and on into Kenya or Tanzania.

Overland travel into East Africa from Mozambique is detailed on p208.

Tours

Organised tours can be low-budget affairs, where you

travel in an 'overland truck' with 15 to 30 other people and some drivers/leaders, carrying tents and other equipment, buying food along the way, and cooking and eating as a group. At the other end of the spectrum are individually tailored tours, ranging in price from reasonable to very expensive.

Following is a small sampling of tour companies operating in East Africa. For locally based safari companies, see town listings in the country chapters.

Australia & New Zealand

African Wildlife Safaris (www.africanwildlifesafaris.com.au) Customised itineraries in East and southern Africa.

Classic Safari Company (www.classicsafaricompany.com.au) Upmarket customised itineraries in Kenya, Tanzania and Uganda.

Peregrine Travel (www.peregrineadventures.com) Everything from overland truck tours to upscale wildlife safaris and chimpanzee tracking. Also family safaris.

South Africa

Africa Travel Co (www.wildlifeadventures.co.za) Overland tours combining East and southern Africa.

Wild Frontiers (www.wildfrontiers.com) A range of itineraries in Kenya, Tanzania, Uganda, Rwanda and the DRC, including gorilla tracking tours.

UK

Abercrombie & Kent (www.abercrombiekent.co.uk) Customised tours and safaris, including chimpanzee tracking.

Africa-in-Focus (www.africa-in-focus.com) East and southern Africa overland tours and safaris.

African Initiatives (www.african-initiatives.org.uk) Fair-traded safaris in northern Tanzania.

Baobab Travel (www.baobabtravel.com) A culturally responsible operator with itineraries in Kenya and Tanzania.

Camps International (www.campsinternational.com) Community-focused budget itineraries in Tanzania and Kenya.

Dragoman (www.dragoman.com) East Africa overland tours.

Expert Africa (www.expertafrica.com) A long-standing, experienced operator with a wide selection of itineraries in Tanzania, Kenya and Rwanda.

Responsible Travel.com (www.responsibletravel.com) Matches you up with ecologically and culturally responsible tour operators to plan an itinerary.

Safari Drive (www.safaridrive.com) Self-drive safaris, primarily in northern Tanzania and Kenya.

Tribes Travel (www.tribes.co.uk) Fair-traded safaris and treks in Tanzania, Kenya, Uganda and Rwanda, including gorilla tracking.

USA & Canada

Abercrombie & Kent (www.abercrombiekent.com) Customised tours and safaris.

Africa Adventure Company (www.africa-adventure.com) Upscale specialist safaris in Kenya, Tanzania, Uganda and Rwanda.

African Horizons (www.africanhorizons.com) A small operator offering various packages throughout East Africa.

Deeper Africa (www.deeperafrica.com) Socially responsible, upmarket safaris in Kenya and Tanzania, and gorilla tracking in Uganda and Rwanda.

Eco-Resorts (www.eco-resorts.com) Socially responsible itineraries in Kenya, Tanzania and Rwanda.

Explorateur Voyages (www.explorateur.qc.ca, in French) Itineraries in Kenya, Tanzania, Uganda and Rwanda.

Good Earth (www.goodearthtours.com) Itineraries in Tanzania, Kenya and Uganda, with detours also to Rwanda.

International Expeditions (www.ietravel.com) Naturalist-oriented safaris in Kenya, Tanzania and Uganda.

Mountain Madness (www.mountainmadness.com) Upmarket treks on Mt Kilimanjaro and Mt Kenya.

Thomson Family Adventures (www.familyadventures.com) Family-friendly northern Tanzania safaris and Kilimanjaro treks.

GETTING AROUND

For specifics of getting around each country, see the Transport sections in the country chapters.

Air

While air service within East Africa is relatively reliable, cancellations and delays should still be expected at any time. Always reconfirm your ticket, and allow cushion time between regional and intercontinental flights.

Airlines in East Africa

For airlines flying within East Africa, see the Transport sections in the country chapters.

Bicycle

Cycling is an enjoyable, adventurous way to explore East Africa. When planning your trip, consider the following:

- Main sealed roads aren't good for cycling, as there's usually no shoulder and traffic moves dangerously fast.
- Distances are very long, often with nothing in between. Consider picking a base, and doing exploratory trips from there.
- Cycling is best well away from urban areas, in the early morning and late afternoon

hours, and in the cooler, dry season between June and August.

» When calculating daily distances, plan on taking a break from the midday heat, and don't count on covering as much territory each day as you might in a northern European climate.

» Mountain bikes are best for flexibility and local terrain, and should be brought from home. While single-speed bicycles (and occasionally mountain bikes) can be rented in many towns (ask hotel staff or inquire at the local bicycle repair stand), they're only suitable for short rides.

» Other planning considerations include water (carry at least 4L), rampaging motorists (a small rear-view mirror is a worthwhile investment), sleeping (bring a tent) and punctures (thorn trees are a problem in some areas).

» Bring sufficient spares (including several spare inner tubes, a spare tyre and plenty of tube patches), and be proficient at repairs.

» Bicycles can be transported on minibuses and buses (though for express or luxury buses, you may need to make advance arrangements with the driver to stow your bike in the hold). There's also no problem or additional cost to bring your bicycle on any of the region's lake or coastal ferries. Cycling isn't permitted in national parks or wildlife reserves.

» As elsewhere in the world, don't leave your bike unattended unless it's locked, and secure all removable pieces. Taking your bike into a hotel room is generally no problem (and is a good idea).

» A recommended contact is the US-based **International Bicycle Fund** (www.ibike.org/bikeafrica), a socially conscious, low-budget organisation that arranges tours in East Africa and provides information.

Boat

» On the Tanzanian section of Lake Victoria, there are passenger boats connecting Mwanza (Tanzania) with Bukoba, Ukerewe Island and various lakeside villages. In the Kenyan section of the lake, small boats connect the mainland around Mbita Point with the Mfangano, Rusinga and Takawiri Islands. In Uganda, small boats connect mainland villages with the Ssese Islands; there are also regular cargo boats from Kampala to Mwanza that accept passengers.

» On Lake Tanganyika, a passenger ferry connects Kigoma (Tanzania) with Mpulungu (Zambia). Also see the Burundi and DRC sections under Sea & Lake on p210.

DHOW TRAVEL

With their billowing sails and graceful forms, dhows (ancient Arabic sailing vessels) have become a symbol of East Africa for adventure travellers. Yet, despite their romantic reputation, the realities can be quite different. Before undertaking a longer journey, test things out with a short sunset or afternoon sail. Coastal hotels are good contacts for arranging reliable dhow travel. If you decide to give a local dhow a try, keep the following tips in mind:

» Be prepared for rough conditions. There are no facilities on board, except possibly a toilet hanging off the stern. Sailings are wind and tide dependent, and departures are often predawn.

» Journeys often take much longer than anticipated; bring extra water and sufficient food.

» Sun block, a hat and a covering are essential, as is waterproofing for your luggage and a rain jacket.

» Boats capsize and people are killed each year. Avoid overloaded boats and don't set sail in bad weather.

» Travel with the winds, which blow from south to north from approximately July to September and north to south from approximately November to late February.

Note that what Westerners refer to as dhows are called either *jahazi* or *mashua* by most Swahili speakers. *Jahazi* are large, lateen-sailed boats. *Mashua* are smaller, and often with proportionately wider hulls and a motor. The *dau* has a sloped stem and stern. On lakes and inland waterways, the *mtumbwi* (dugout canoe) is in common use. Coastal areas, especially Zanzibar's east-coast beaches, are good places to see *ngalawa* (outrigger canoes).

» On Lake Nyasa, the main route is between Mbamba Bay and Itungi (both in Tanzania), via numerous lakeside villages. There's also a boat between Mbamba Bay and Nkhata Bay (Malawi).

» The main coastal routes are between Dar es Salaam, Zanzibar and Pemba (see the Tanzania chapter for more information), and the short run between the coast and the Lamu archipelago (Kenya).

Bus

Buses are the most useful type of public transport. They're usually faster than trains or trucks, and safer and more comfortable than minibuses. In Kenya and Tanzania, you sometimes have the choice of going by 'luxury' or 'ordinary' bus. Luxury buses are more comfortable and more expensive, although not always quicker than ordinary buses. Some also have the dubious advantage of a video system, usually playing bad movies at full volume for the entire trip. Uganda has mostly ordinary buses, although there are luxury buses on some cross-border routes. There are a few full-size buses in Rwanda and Burundi, although, especially in Burundi, minibuses are the rule.

For details of routes and fares, see the Transport sections in the country chapters.

Car & Motorcycle

Touring East Africa by car or motorcycle is quite feasible, although it's generally only an option used by those already living in the region with local driving knowledge and access to their own vehicle, as rentals are expensive.

Throughout East Africa, main roads are sealed and in reasonable states of repair. In rural areas, they range from decent to terrible, especially in the wet season when many secondary routes become impassable. Trips in remote areas require 4WD; motorcycles generally aren't permitted in national parks.

Whether you drive your own or a rental vehicle, expect stops at checkpoints where police and border officials will ask to see your driving licence, insurance paperwork and vehicle papers.

Bring Your Own Vehicle

» To bring your own vehicle into East Africa, you'll need to arrange a *carnet de passage*. This document allows you to take a vehicle duty-free into a country where duties would normally be payable. It guarantees that if a vehicle is taken into a country but not exported, the organisation that issued the *carnet* will accept responsibility for payment of import duties (generally between 100% and 150% of the new value of the vehicle). The *carnet* should also specify any expensive spare parts that you'll be carrying.

» To get a *carnet*, contact your national motoring organisation at home, which will give you an indemnity form for completion by either a bank or an insurance company. Once you have deposited a bond with a bank or paid an insurance premium, the motoring organisation will issue the *carnet*. The cost of the *carnet* itself is minimal; allow at least a week to complete the process.

» For longer trips, in addition to a *carnet* and mechanical knowledge, bring along a good collection of spares.

Driving Licence

If you're taking your own vehicle or are considering hiring one in East Africa, arrange an International Driving Permit (IDP) before leaving home. They're available at minimal cost through your national motoring organisation.

Fuel & Spare Parts

» Fuel costs in the region average US$1.60 per litre of petrol or diesel. Filling and repair stations are readily available in major towns but scarce elsewhere. In many areas, diesel is easier to find than petrol.

» Top your tank up at every opportunity and carry basic spares. For travel in remote areas and in national parks, also carry jerry cans with extra fuel.

» Petrol sold on the roadside is unreliable, as it's often di-

BUS SAFETY

Public transport is a fine (and often the only) choice for getting around East Africa, but be savvy when using local buses and minibuses.

» Never accept food and drink from fellow passengers, even if it appears to be sealed.

» Avoid night travel, especially on long-distance routes such as Nairobi–Kampala.

» Be especially wary of pick-pockets on minibuses, and when boarding.

» At bus stations, keep your luggage compact and your valuables well-concealed.

» Road safety is a major issue. Get advice from the country chapters of this book, and locally, about the best (safest) bus lines, and stick to established lines.

For more on safe travel, see p638.

luted with water or kerosene. Diluting is also a common problem at established petrol stations in much of the region, so ask around locally before tanking up.

Hire

Car, 4WD and motorcycle hire is expensive throughout East Africa, averaging US$100 to US$200 per day for a 4WD. Few agencies offer unlimited kilometres, and many require that you take a chauffeur (which is a good idea anyway). For self-drive rentals, you'll need a driving licence and often also an IDP. If you'll be crossing any borders, you'll need to arrange the necessary paperwork with the hire agency in advance.

Insurance

Throughout the region, liability insurance must generally be bought at the border upon entry. While cost and quality vary, in many cases you may find that you are effectively travelling uninsured, as there's often no way to collect on the insurance. With vehicle rentals, even if you're covered from other sources, it's recommended to take the full coverage offered by hire companies.

Road Rules

Tanzania, Kenya and Uganda follow the British keep-left traffic system. In Rwanda and Burundi, driving is on the right-hand side. At roundabouts throughout the region, traffic already in the roundabout has the right of way.

Road Conditions & Hazards

» Nighttime road travel isn't recommended anywhere; if you must drive at night, be alert for stopped vehicles in the roadway without lights or hazard warnings.

» If you're not used to driving in Africa, watch for pedestrians, children and animals, as well as for oncoming vehicles on the wrong side of the road. Especially in rural areas, remember that many people have never driven themselves and are not aware of necessary braking distances and similar concepts; moderate your speed accordingly.

» Tree branches on the road are the local version of flares or hazard lights and mean there's a stopped vehicle, crater-sized pothole or similar calamity ahead.

» Passing (including on curves or other areas with poor visibility) is common practice and a frequent cause of accidents.

Hitching

Hitching may be your only option in remote areas, although it's rare that you'll get a free ride unless you're lucky enough to be offered a lift by resident expats, well-off locals or aid workers; even then, at least offer to make a contribution for petrol on longer journeys, or to pick up a meal tab. To flag down a vehicle, hold out your hand at about waist level and wave it up and down, with the palm to the ground; the common Western gesture of holding out your thumb isn't used.

A word of warning about taking lifts in private cars: smuggling across borders is common practice, and if whatever is being smuggled is found, you may be arrested even though you knew nothing about it. Most travellers manage to convince police that they were merely hitching a ride (passport stamps are a good indication of this), but the convincing can take a long time.

As in other parts of the world, hitching is never entirely safe, and we don't recommend it. Those travellers who decide to hitch should understand that they are taking a potentially serious risk. If you do hitch, you'll be safer doing so in pairs and letting someone know of your plans.

Local Transport

Minibus

» Most East Africans rely heavily on minibuses for transport. They're called matatus in Kenya, dalla-dallas in Tanzania, and taxis or matatus in Uganda.

» Except in Rwanda and Burundi, minibuses are invariably packed to the bursting point, and this – combined with excessive speed, poor maintenance and driver recklessness – means that they're not the safest way of getting around. In fact, they can be downright dangerous, and newspaper reports of matatu and dalla-dalla crashes are a regular feature. In Rwanda and Burundi, travelling in minibuses is generally safer.

» If you have a large backpack, think twice about boarding, especially at rush hour, when it will make the already crowded conditions even more uncomfortable for others.

Taxi

In Kenya, northern Tanzania and Uganda, shared taxis operate on some routes. These officially take between five and nine passengers, depending on size, leave when full and are usually faster, though more expensive, than bus travel. They're marginally more comfortable than minibuses but have their share of accidents too. Private taxis for hire are found in all major towns.

Motorcycle taxis (boda-boda in Kenya, Tanzania and Uganda, *moto-taxi* in Rwanda, Burundi and the DRC) are also widely available, at a fraction of the cost of standard vehicle taxis.

Truck

» In remote areas, trucks may be the only form of transport, and they're invariably the cheapest. For most regular runs there will be a 'fare', which is more or less

TRAVEL TIP

Use only reliable hotel taxis, or those from established ranks, and avoid freelancers (known in Swahili-speaking areas as 'taxi bubu'). Also avoid taking matatus, dalla-dallas, boda-bodas and the like after dark.

fixed and is what the locals pay. It's usually equivalent to, or a bit less than, the bus fare for the same route. For a place in the cab, expect to pay about twice what it costs to travel on top of the load.

» Many truck lifts are arranged the night before departure at the 'truck park' – a compound or dust patch that you'll find in most towns. Ask around for a truck that's going your way, and be prepared to wait, especially on remote routes where there may be trucks leaving only once or twice a week.

For longer trips, ask what to do about food and drink, and bring plenty of snacks and extra drinking water – enough for yourself and to share.

Tours

For safari and trekking operators, and local tour operators, see the country chapters. Many of the companies listed in this guidebook can also organise local itineraries in addition to your safari or trek.

Train

» The main passenger lines are the Nairobi–Mombasa route (Kenya), the Tazara 'express' line from Dar es Salaam to Mbeya (Tanzania), and the meandering Central line connecting Dar es Salaam with Kigoma (Tanzania).

» First class costs about double what the bus would cost but is well worth it for the additional comfort. Second class is reasonably comfortable, but the savings over first class are marginal. Economy-class travel is cheap, crowded and uncomfortable. There are no assigned seats, and for long trips you'll probably wind up sitting and sleeping on the floor. Reservations for first class are best made as early as possible, although sometimes you'll get lucky and be able to book a cabin on the day of travel.

» In all classes, keep an eye on your luggage, especially at stops. In first and second class, make sure the window is jammed shut at night to avoid the possibility of someone entering when the train stops (there's usually a piece of wood provided for this), and keep your cabin door shut.

» Food and drink (mainly soft drinks) are available on trains and from station vendors, but bring extra food and water. Have plenty of small change handy.

Health

If you stay up to date with your vaccinations and take basic preventive measures, you'd be unlucky to succumb to most of the health hazards covered here. The exception is malaria, which is a real risk throughout much of East Africa.

BEFORE YOU GO

Predeparture planning will save you trouble later.

» Get a check-up from your dentist and doctor if you have any regular medication or chronic illness (eg high blood pressure or asthma).

» Organise spare contact lenses and glasses (and take your optical prescription with you).

» Get a first-aid and medical kit together and arrange necessary vaccinations. Get an International Certificate of Vaccination ('yellow booklet') listing vaccinations you have received.

» Carry medications in their original (labelled) containers. If carrying syringes or needles, have a physician's letter documenting their medical necessity.

Insurance

Check whether your insurance plan will make payments directly to providers or reimburse you later for overseas health expenditures. Most doctors in East Africa expect cash payment.

Ensure that your travel insurance will cover any emergency transport required to get you at least as far as Nairobi (Kenya), or, preferably, home, by air and with a medical attendant if necessary. Consider temporary membership with the **African Medical & Research Foundation** (Amref; www.amref.org) Nairobi emergency lines (☎254-20-315454/5, 254-20-600 2299, 254-733-639088, 254-722-314239); Nairobi head office (☎254-20-699 3000), which provides air evacuation in medical emergencies for most of East Africa; or **First Air Responder** (www.firstairresponder.com), which provides emergency air evacuation in Tanzania and Kenya. See p643 for further details.

IN EAST AFRICA

Availability & Cost of Health Care

Good, Western-style medical care is available in Nairobi (which is the main medical hub for the region and the main regional destination for medical evacuations), and to a lesser extent in Dar es Salaam. Elsewhere, reasonable to good care is available in larger towns, and in some mission stations, though availability is patchy off the beaten track. Private or mission-run clinics and hospitals are generally better equipped than government ones. If you fall ill in an unfamiliar area, ask staff at top-end hotels or resident expatriates where the best nearby medical facilities are; in an emergency, contact your embassy. Most towns have at least one clinic where you can get an inexpensive malaria test and, if necessary, treatment. With dental treatment, there is often an increased risk of hepatitis B and HIV transmission via poorly sterilised equipment.

Most drugs can be purchased over the counter in East Africa, without a prescription. However, there are often problems with ineffectiveness, eg if the drugs are counterfeit, or if they have been improperly stored. Most drugs are available in capital cities, but almost none in remote villages. Bring all drugs for chronic diseases from home.

There can be a high risk of contracting HIV from infected blood if you receive a blood transfusion. To minimise this risk, seek out treatment in reputable clinics. The **BloodCare Foundation** (www.bloodcare.org.uk) is a useful source of safe, screened blood, which can be transported to any part of the world within 24 hours.

RECOMMENDED VACCINATIONS

Check **World Health Organization** (www.who.int/en/) recommendations for travel vaccinations, and check **Centers for Disease Control & Prevention** (www.cdc.gov) recommendations for East Africa. Yellow fever is required for all visitors to Rwanda and the DRC, and recommended for elsewhere in the region. Also peruse the following government travel-health websites:

» Australia – www.smartraveller.gov.au

» Canada – www.phac-aspc.gc.ca/tmp-pmv/index.html

» UK – www.nhs.uk/nhsengland/Healthcareabroad/pages/Healthcareabroad.aspx

» USA – www.cdc.gov/travel

Infectious Diseases

With basic preventive measures, it's unlikely that you'll succumb to any of the following.

Bilharzia (Schistosomiasis)

This disease is spread by flukes (minute worms) that are carried by a species of freshwater snail. Don't paddle or swim in any freshwater lakes or slow-running rivers anywhere in East Africa unless you have reliable confirmation that they are bilharzia-free. A blood test can detect antibodies if you might have been exposed, and treatment is possible in specialist travel clinics. If not treated the infection can cause kidney failure or permanent bowel damage.

Cholera

Cholera is spread via contaminated drinking water. The main symptom is profuse watery diarrhoea, which causes debilitation if fluids are not replaced quickly. An oral cholera vaccine is available but is not particularly effective. Pay close attention to good drinking water and by avoiding potentially contaminated food. Treatment is by fluid replacement (orally or via a drip), but sometimes antibiotics are needed. Self-treatment is not advised.

Diphtheria

Found throughout East Africa, diphtheria is spread through close respiratory contact. Vaccination is recommended for those likely to be in close contact with the local population in infected areas and is more important for long stays than for short-term trips.

Filariasis

Tiny worms migrating in the lymphatic system cause filariasis. The bite from an infected mosquito spreads the infection. Symptoms include localised itching and swelling of the legs and/or genitalia. Treatment is available.

Hepatitis A

Hepatitis A is spread through contaminated food (particularly shellfish) and water. It causes jaundice, and although rarely fatal, it can cause prolonged lethargy and delayed recovery. If you've had hepatitis A, don't drink alcohol for up to six months afterwards; once you've recovered, there won't be long-term problems. Early symptoms include dark urine and a yellow colour to the whites of the eyes, sometimes with fever and abdominal pain. Hepatitis A vaccine (Avaxim, VAQTA, Havrix) gives protection for up to a year; a booster after a year gives 10-year protection. Hepatitis A and typhoid vaccines can also be given as a single-dose vaccine (hepatyrix or viatim).

Hepatitis B

Hepatitis B is spread through infected blood, contaminated needles and sexual intercourse. It can also be spread from an infected mother to the baby during childbirth. It affects the liver, causing jaundice and occasionally liver failure. Most people recover completely, but some might be chronic carriers of the virus, which could lead eventually to cirrhosis or liver cancer. Those visiting high-risk areas for long periods or those with increased social or occupational risk should be immunised.

HIV

Human immunodeficiency virus (HIV), the virus that causes acquired immune deficiency syndrome (AIDS), is an enormous problem throughout East Africa. It's spread through infected blood and blood products, by sexual intercourse with an infected partner and from an infected mother to her baby during childbirth and breastfeeding. It can be spread through 'blood to blood' contacts, such as with contaminated instruments during medical, dental, acupuncture and other body-piercing procedures, and through sharing used intravenous needles. If you think you might have been infected with HIV, a blood test is necessary; a three-month gap after exposure and before testing is required to allow antibodies to appear in the blood.

Malaria

Malaria is endemic throughout East Africa (except at altitudes higher than 2000m, where risk of transmission is low). The disease is caused by a parasite in the bloodstream spread via the bite of the female Anopheles mosquito. There are several types of malaria, with falciparum malaria the most dangerous type and the predominant form in the region. Infection rates vary with climate and season. Rates are higher during the rainy season, but the risk exists year-round. It is extremely important to take preventive measures, even just for short visits.

There is no vaccination against malaria (yet). However, several different drugs are used for prevention with new ones in the pipeline. Up-to-date advice from a travel-health clinic is essential. The pattern of drug-resistant malaria changes rapidly, so what was advised several years ago might no longer be current.

SYMPTOMS

Malaria's early stages include headaches, fevers, generalised aches and pains, and malaise, which could be mistaken for flu. Other symptoms can include abdominal pain, diarrhoea and a cough. Anyone who develops a fever while in East Africa or within two weeks after departure should assume malarial infection until blood tests prove negative, even if you have been taking antimalarial medication. If not treated, the next stage could develop within 24 hours, particularly if falciparum malaria is the parasite: jaundice, then reduced consciousness and coma (also known as cerebral malaria) followed by death. Treatment in hospital is essential; the death rate might still be as high as 10% even in the best intensive-care facilities.

SIDE EFFECTS & RISKS

Many travellers are under the impression that malaria is a mild illness, that treatment is always easy and successful and that taking antimalarial drugs causes more illness through side effects than actually getting malaria. Unfortunately, this is not true. Side effects of the medication depend on the drug taken. Doxycycline can cause heartburn and indigestion; mefloquine (Lariam) can cause anxiety attacks, insomnia and nightmares and (rarely) severe psychiatric disorders; chloroquine can cause nausea and hair loss; and proguanil can cause mouth ulcers. These side effects are not universal and can be minimised by taking medication correctly, eg with food. Also, some people should not take a particular antimalarial drug – for example, people with epilepsy should avoid mefloquine, and doxycycline should not be taken by pregnant women or children younger than 12.

If you decide against taking antimalarial drugs, you must understand the risks and be obsessive about avoiding mosquito bites. Use nets and insect repellent, and report any fever or flu-like symptoms to a doctor as soon as possible. Malaria in pregnancy frequently results in miscarriage or premature labour and the risks to both mother and foetus during pregnancy are considerable. Travel in East Africa when pregnant should be carefully considered.

STAND-BY TREATMENT

Carrying emergency stand-by treatment is essential for travel in remote areas. Seek your doctor's advice as to recommended medicines and dosages. However, this should be viewed as emergency treatment only and not as routine self-medication, and should only be used if you will be far from medical facilities and have been advised about the symptoms of malaria and how to use the medication. If you resort to emergency self-treatment, seek medical advice as soon as possible to confirm whether the treatment has been successful. In particular, you want to avoid contracting cerebral malaria, which can be fatal within 24 hours. Self-diagnostic kits, which can identify malaria in the blood from a finger prick, are available in the West and are worth buying.

ANTIMALARIAL A TO D

» **A** – Awareness of the risk. No medication is totally effective, but protection of up to 95% is achievable with most drugs, as long as other measures have been taken.

» **B** – Bites: avoid at all costs. Sleep in a screened room, use mosquito spray or coils and sleep under a permethrin-impregnated net at night. Cover up at night with long trousers and long sleeves, preferably with permethrin-treated clothing. Apply repellent to all areas of exposed skin in the evenings.

» **C** – Chemical prevention (ie antimalarial drugs) is usually needed in malarial areas. Expert advice is needed as resistance patterns change and new drugs are in development. Most antimalarial drugs need to be started at least a week in advance and continued for four weeks after the last exposure to malaria.

» **D** – Diagnosis. If you have a fever or flu-like illness within a year of travel to a malarial area, malaria is a possibility; immediate medical attention is necessary.

Meningococcal Meningitis

Meningococcal infection is spread through close respiratory contact and is most likely contracted in crowded situations. Infection is uncommon in travellers. Vaccination is particularly recommended for long stays and is especially important towards the end of the dry season. Symptoms include fever, severe headache, neck stiffness and a red rash. Immediate medical treatment is necessary.

The ACWY vaccine is recommended for all travellers in sub-Saharan Africa. This vaccine is different from the meningococcal meningitis C vaccine given to children and adolescents in some countries; it is safe to be given both types of vaccine.

Rabies

Rabies is spread by receiving the bites or licks of an infected animal on broken skin. It is always fatal once the clinical symptoms start (which might be months after an infected bite), so postbite vaccination should be given as soon as possible. Postbite vaccination (whether or not you've been vaccinated before the bite) prevents the virus from spreading to the central nervous system. Animal handlers should be vaccinated, as should those travelling to remote areas where a reliable source of postbite vaccine is not available. Three preventive injections are needed over a month. If you haven't been vaccinated you will need a course of five injections starting 24 hours or as soon as possible after being exposed. If you have been vaccinated, you will need fewer postbite injections, and have more time to seek medical help.

Rift Valley Fever

This fever is spread occasionally via mosquito bites. The symptoms are of a fever and flu-like illness; and the good news is, it's rarely fatal.

Trypanosomiasis (Sleeping Sickness)

Spread via the bite of the tsetse fly. It causes headache, fever and eventually coma. If you have these symptoms and have negative malaria tests, have yourself evaluated by a reputable clinic, where you should also be able to obtain treatment.

Tuberculosis (TB)

TB is spread through close respiratory contact and occasionally through infected milk or milk products. The BCG vaccine is recommended for those likely to be mixing closely with the local population, although it only provides moderate protection. It's more important for long stays than for short-term visits. Inoculation with the BCG vaccine is not available in all countries, but it is given routinely to many children in developing nations. It is a live vaccine and should not be given to pregnant women or immunocompromised individuals.

TB can be asymptomatic, only being picked up on a routine chest X-ray. Alternatively, it can cause a cough, weight loss or fever, months or even years after exposure.

Typhoid

This is spread through food or water contaminated by infected human faeces. The first symptom is usually a fever or a pink rash on the abdomen. Sometimes septicaemia (blood poisoning) can occur. A typhoid vaccine (typhim Vi, typherix) will give protection for three years. In some countries, the oral vaccine Vivotif is also available. Antibiotics are usually given as treatment, and death is rare unless septicaemia occurs.

Yellow Fever

Tanzania, Kenya, Uganda and Burundi no longer officially require you to carry a certificate of yellow fever vaccination unless you're arriving from an infected area (which includes from anywhere in East Africa). However, it's still sometimes asked for at some borders, and is a requirement in some neighbouring countries, including Rwanda. The vaccine is recommended for most visitors to Africa by the **Centers for Disease Control & Prevention** (www.cdc.gov). Also, there is always the possibility that a traveller without a legally required, up-to-date certificate will be vaccinated and detained in isolation at the port of arrival for up to 10 days, or possibly even repatriated.

Yellow fever is spread by infected mosquitoes. Symptoms range from a flu-like illness to severe hepatitis (liver inflammation), jaundice and death. The yellow fever vaccination must be given at a designated clinic and is valid for 10 years. It is a live vaccine and must not be given to immunocompromised or pregnant travellers.

TSETSE FLIES

Tsetse flies can be unwelcome safari companions in some areas, delivering painful, swelling bites. To minimise the nuisance, wear thick, long-sleeved shirts and trousers in khaki or other drab shades, and avoid bright, contrasting and very dark clothing. The flies are also attracted by heat (eg the heat of a running car motor), so if you're idling, keep the windows rolled up.

Traveller's Diarrhoea

Diarrhoea is the most common travel-related illness.

Sometimes dietary changes, such as increased spices or oils, are the cause. To help prevent diarrhoea, avoid tap water unless you're sure it's safe to drink; only eat fresh fruits or vegetables if cooked or peeled; and be wary of dairy products that might contain unpasteurised milk. Although freshly cooked food can often be a safe option, plates or serving utensils might be dirty, so be selective when eating food from street vendors (make sure that cooked food is piping hot all the way through).

If you develop diarrhoea, be sure to drink plenty of fluids, preferably lots of an oral rehydration solution containing water, and some salt and sugar. A few loose stools don't require treatment, but if you start having more than four or five stools a day, you should start taking an antibiotic (usually a quinoline drug, such as ciprofloxacin or norfloxacin) and an antidiarrhoeal agent (such as loperamide) if you are not within easy reach of a toilet. If diarrhoea is bloody, persists for more than 72 hours or is accompanied by fever, shaking chills or severe abdominal pain, you should seek medical attention.

Amoebic Dysentery

Contracted by consuming contaminated food and water, amoebic dysentery causes blood and mucus in the faeces. It can be relatively mild and tends to come on gradually, but seek medical advice if you think you have the illness, as it won't clear up without treatment (which is with specific antibiotics).

Giardiasis

This, like amoebic dysentery, is also caused by ingesting contaminated food or water. The illness usually appears a week or more after you have been exposed to the offending parasite. Giardiasis might cause only a short-lived bout of typical traveller's diarrhoea, but it can also cause persistent diarrhoea. Ideally, seek medical advice if you suspect you have giardiasis, but if you are in a remote area you could start a course of antibiotics, with medical follow-up when feasible.

Environmental Hazards

Altitude Sickness

The lack of oxygen at high altitudes (over 2500m) affects most people to some extent. Symptoms of Acute Mountain Sickness (AMS) usually develop in the first 24 hours at altitude but may be delayed up to three weeks. Mild symptoms are headache, lethargy, dizziness, difficulty sleeping and loss of appetite. Severe symptoms are breathlessness, a dry, irritated cough (followed by the production of pink, frothy sputum), severe headache, lack of coordination, confusion, vomiting, irrational behaviour, drowsiness and unconsciousness. There's no rule as to what is too high: AMS can be fatal at 3000m, but 3500m to 4500m is the usual range when it can cause problems. *Symptoms should never be ignored;* trekkers die every year on East Africa's mountains, notably Mt Kilimanjaro.

Treat mild symptoms by resting at the same altitude until you have recovered, usually a day or two. Paracetamol or aspirin can be taken for headaches. If symptoms persist or grow worse, however, immediate descent is necessary; even 500m can help. Drug treatments should never be used to avoid descent or to enable further ascent. Diamox (acetazolamide) reduces the headache of AMS and helps the body acclimatise to the lack of oxygen. It is only available on prescription.

Suggestions for preventing acute mountain sickness:

» Ascend slowly. On Mt Kilimanjaro, this means choosing one of the longer routes (eg Machame) that allow for a more gradual ascent, and taking the option offered by most operators to sleep two nights at the same location. On Mt Kenya, it means spending at least three nights on the ascent.

» Sleep at a lower altitude than the greatest height reached during the day if possible ('climb high, sleep low').

» Drink extra fluids. Monitor hydration by ensuring that urine is clear and plentiful.

» Eat light, high-carbohydrate meals for more energy.

» Avoid alcohol, sedatives and tobacco.

Heat Exhaustion

This condition occurs following heavy sweating and excessive fluid loss with inadequate replacement of fluids and salt, and is particularly common in hot climates when taking unaccustomed exercise before full acclimatisation. Symptoms include headache, dizziness and tiredness. Dehydration is already happening by the time you feel thirsty – aim to drink sufficient water to produce pale, diluted urine. Self-treatment requires fluid replacement with water and/or fruit juice, and cooling by cold water and fans. Treatment of the salt-loss component consists of consuming salty fluids, as in soup, and adding a little more table salt to foods than usual.

Insect Bites & Stings

Mosquitoes might not always carry malaria or dengue fever, but they (and other insects) can cause irritation and infected bites. To avoid these, take the same precautions as you would for avoiding malaria (see p658). Use DEET-based insect repellents. Excellent clothing treatments are also available, and mosquitoes that land on the treated clothing will die.

Bee and wasp stings cause real problems only

to those who have a severe allergy to the stings (anaphylaxis). If you are one of these people, carry an 'epipen' – an adrenaline (epinephrine) injection, which you can give yourself. This could save your life.

Scorpions are frequently found in arid or dry climates. They can cause a painful bite that is sometimes life threatening. If bitten by a scorpion, seek immediate medical assistance.

Bed bugs are often found in hostels and cheap hotels. They lead to very itchy, lumpy bites. Spraying the mattress with crawling insect killer after changing bedding will get rid of them.

Scabies is also frequently found in cheap accommodation. These tiny mites live in the skin, particularly between the fingers. They cause an intensely itchy rash. The itch is easily treated with malathion and permethrin lotion from a pharmacy; other members of the household also need treatment to avoid spreading scabies, even if they do not show any symptoms.

Snake Bites

Avoid getting bitten! Do not walk barefoot, or stick your hand into holes or cracks. However, 50% of those bitten by venomous snakes are not actually injected with poison (envenomed). If you are bitten by a snake, do not panic. Immobilise the bitten limb with a splint (such as a stick) and apply a bandage over the site, with firm pressure, similar to bandaging a sprain. Do not apply a tourniquet, or cut or suck the bite. Get medical help as soon as possible so antivenom can be given if needed. Try to note the snake's appearance to help in treatment.

Water

Don't drink tap water unless it has been boiled, filtered or chemically disinfected (such as with iodine tablets). Never drink from streams, rivers and lakes. Also avoid drinking from pumps and wells; some do bring pure water to the surface, but the presence of animals can contaminate supplies. With bottled water, check that the bottles are properly sealed, and haven't just been refilled with ordinary tap water.

WANT MORE?

For in-depth language information and handy phrases, check out Lonely Planet's *Swahili Phrasebook* or *Africa Phrasebook*. You'll find them at **shop.lonelyplanet.com**, or you can buy Lonely Planet's iPhone phrasebooks at the Apple App Store.

SWAHILI

Swahili, the national language of Tanzania and Kenya, is also one of the most widely spoken African languages and the key language of communication in the East African region. Although the number of speakers of Swahili throughout East Africa is estimated to be well over 50 million, it's the mother tongue of only about 5 million people, and is predominantly used as a second language or a lingua franca by speakers of other African languages. Swahili belongs to the Bantu group of languages from the Niger-Congo family and can be traced back to the first millenium AD. It's hardly surprising that in an area as vast as East Africa many different dialects of Swahili can be found, but you'll be understood if you stick to the standard coastal form, as used in this book.

Most sounds in Swahili have equivalents in English. In our coloured pronunciation guides, ay should be read as in 'say', oh as the 'o' in 'role', dh as the 'th' in 'this' and th as in 'thing'. Note also that the sound ng can be found at the start of words in Swahili, and that Swahili speakers make only a slight distinction between r and l – instead of the hard 'r', try pronouncing a light 'd'. The stressed syllables are indicated with italics.

Basics

Jambo is a pidgin Swahili word, used to greet tourists who are presumed not to understand the language. If people assume you can speak a little Swahili, they might use the following greetings:

Hello. (general)	*Habari?*	ha·*ba*·ree
Hello. (respectful)	*Shikamoo.*	shee·ka·*moh*
Goodbye.	*Tutaonana.*	too·ta·oh·*na*·na

Good ...	*Habari za ...?*	ha·*ba*·ree za ...
morning	*asubuhi*	a·soo·*boo*·hee
afternoon	*mchana*	m·*cha*·na
evening	*jioni*	jee·*oh*·nee

Yes.	*Ndiyo.*	n·*dee*·yoh
No.	*Hapana.*	ha·*pa*·na
Please.	*Tafadhali.*	ta·fa·*dha*·lee
Thank you (very much).	*Asante (sana).*	a·*san*·tay (*sa*·na)
You're welcome.	*Karibu.*	ka·*ree*·boo
Excuse me.	*Samahani.*	sa·ma·*ha*·nee
Sorry.	*Pole.*	*poh*·lay

How are you?
Habari? ha·*ba*·ree

I'm fine.
Nzuri./Salama./Safi. n·*zoo*·ree/sa·*la*·ma/*sa*·fee

If things are just OK, add *tu* too (only) after any of the above replies. If things are really good, add *sana* *sa*·na (very) or *kabisa* ka·*bee*·sa (totally) instead of *tu*.

What's your name?
Jina lako nani? *jee*·na *la*·koh *na*·nee

My name is ...
Jina langu ni ... *jee*·na *lan*·goo nee ...

KEY PATTERNS

To get by in Swahili, mix and match these simple patterns with words of your choice:

When's (the next bus)?
(Basi ijayo) itaondoka lini? — (*ba*·see ee·*ja*·yoh) ee·ta·ohn·*doh*·ka *lee*·nee

Where's (the station)?
(Stesheni) iko wapi? — (stay·*shay*·nee) ee·koh *wa*·pee

How much is (a room)?
(Chumba) ni bei gani? — (choom·ba) nee bay ga·nee

I'm looking for (a hotel).
Natafuta (hoteli). — na·ta·foo·ta (hoh·tay·lee)

Do you have (a map)?
Una (ramani)? — oo·na (ra·ma·nee)

Please bring (the bill).
Lete (bili). — *lay*·tay (*bee*·lee)

I'd like (the menu).
Nataka (menyu). — na·*ta*·ka (*may*·nyoo)

I have (a reservation).
Nina (buking). — *nee*·na (*boo*·keeng)

Do you speak English?
Unasema Kiingereza? — oo·na·*say*·ma kee·een·gay·*ray*·za

I don't understand.
Sielewi. — see·ay·*lay*·wee

Accommodation

Where's a ...?	*... iko wapi?*	... ee·koh *wa*·pee
campsite	*Uwanja wa kambi*	oo·*wan*·ja wa *kam*·bee
guesthouse	*Gesti*	*gay*·stee
hotel	*Hoteli*	hoh·*tay*·lee
youth hostel	*Hosteli ya vijana*	hoh·*stay*·lee ya vee·*ja*·na

Do you have a ... room?	*Kuna chumba kwa ...?*	*koo*·na *choom*·ba kwa ...
double (one bed)	*watu wawili, kitanda kimoja*	*wa*·too wa·*wee*·lee kee·*tan*·da kee·*moh*·ja
single	*mtu mmoja*	m·too m·*moh*·ja
twin (two beds)	*watu wawili, vitanda viwili*	*wa*·too wa·*wee*·lee vee·*tan*·da vee·*wee*·lee

How much is it per ...?	*Ni bei gani kwa ...?*	nee bay *ga*·ne kwa ...
day	*siku*	see·koo
person	*mtu*	*m*·too

bathroom	*bafuni*	ba·*foo*·nee
key	*ufunguo*	oo·foon·*goo*·oh
toilet	*choo*	choh
window	*dirisha*	dee·*ree*·sha

Directions

Where's the ...?
... iko wapi? — ... ee·koh *wa*·pee

What's the address?
Anwani ni nini? — an·*wa*·nee nee *nee*·nee

How do I get there?
Nifikaje? — nee·fee·*ka*·jay

How far is it?
Ni umbali gani? — nee oom·*ba*·lee *ga*·nee

Can you show me (on the map)?
Unaweza kunionyesha (katika ramani)? — oo·na·*way*·za koo·nee·oh·*nyay*·sha (ka·*tee*·ka ra·*ma*·nee)

It's ...	*Iko ...*	ee·koh ...
behind ...	*nyuma ya ...*	*nyoo*·ma ya ...
in front of ...	*mbele ya ...*	m·*bay*·lay ya ...
near ...	*karibu na ...*	ka·*ree*·boo na ...
next to ...	*jirani ya ...*	jee·*ra*·nee ya ...
on the corner	*pembeni*	paym·*bay*·nee
opposite ...	*ng'ambo ya ...*	ng·*am*·boh ya ...
straight ahead	*moja kwa moja*	*moh*·ja kwa *moh*·ja

Turn ...	*Geuza ...*	gay·*oo*·za ...
at the corner	*kwenye kona*	*kway*·nyay *koh*·na
at the traffic lights	*kwenye taa za barabarani*	*kway*·nyay ta za ba·ra·ba·*ra*·nee
left	*kushoto*	koo·*shoh*·toh
right	*kulia*	koo·*lee*·a

Eating & Drinking

I'd like to reserve a table for ...	*Nataka kuhifadhi meza kwa ...*	na·*ta*·ka koo·hee·*fa*·dhee *may*·za kwa ...
(two) people	*watu (wawili)*	*wa*·too (wa·*wee*·lee)
(eight) o'clock	*saa (mbili)*	sa (m·*bee*·lee)

I'd like the menu.
Naomba menyu. — na·*ohm*·ba *may*·nyoo

What would you recommend?
Chakula gani ni kizuri? — cha·*koo*·la *ga*·nee nee kee·*zoo*·ree

Do you have vegetarian food?
Mna chakula bila nyama? — m·na cha·*koo*·la bee·la *nya*·ma

I'll have that.
Nataka hicho. — na·*ta*·ka *hee*·choh

Cheers!
Heri! — *hay*·ree

That was delicious!
Chakula kitamu sana! — cha·*koo*·la kee·*ta*·moo *sa*·na

Please bring the bill.
Lete bili. — *lay*·tay *bee*·lee

I don't eat ...	*Sili ...*	*see*·lee ...
butter	*siagi*	see·*a*·gee
eggs	*mayai*	ma·*ya*·ee
red meat	*nyama*	*nya*·ma

beer	*bia*	*bee*·a
bottle	*chupa*	*choo*·pa
breakfast	*chai ya asubuhi*	*cha*·ee ya a·soo·*boo*·hee
coffee	*kahawa*	ka·*ha*·wa
cold	*baridi*	ba·*ree*·dee
dinner	*chakula cha jioni*	cha·*koo*·la cha jee·*oh*·nee
fish	*samaki*	sa·*ma*·kee
fork	*uma*	*oo*·ma
fruit	*tunda*	*toon*·da
glass	*glesi*	*glay*·see
hot	*joto*	*joh*·toh
juice	*jusi*	*joo*·see
knife	*kisu*	*kee*·soo
lunch	*chakula cha mchana*	cha·*koo*·la cha m·*cha*·na
market	*soko*	*soh*·koh
meat	*nyama*	*nya*·ma
plate	*sahani*	sa·*ha*·nee
restaurant	*mgahawa*	m·ga·*ha*·wa
spoon	*kijiko*	kee·*jee*·koh
tea	*chai*	*cha*·ee
vegetable	*mboga*	m·*boh*·ga
water	*maji*	*ma*·jee
wine	*mvinyo*	m·vee·nyoh

Emergencies

Help!	*Saidia!*	sa·ee·*dee*·a
Go away!	*Toka!*	*toh*·ka

I'm lost.
Nimejipotea. — nee·may·jee·poh·*tay*·a

Call the police.
Waite polisi. — wa·ee·tay poh·*lee*·see

Call a doctor.
Mwite daktari. — m·*wee*·tay dak·*ta*·ree

I'm sick.
Mimi ni mgonjwa. — *mee*·mee nee m·*gohn*·jwa

It hurts here.
Inauma hapa. — ee·na·*oo*·ma *ha*·pa

I'm allergic to (antibiotics).
Nina mzio wa (viuavijasumu). — *nee*·na m·*zee*·oh wa (vee·oo·a·vee·ja·*soo*·moo)

Where's the toilet?
Choo kiko wapi? — choh *kee*·koh *wa*·pee

Shopping & Services

I'd like to buy ...
Nataka kununua ... — na·*ta*·ka koo·noo·*noo*·a ...

I'm just looking.
Naangalia tu. — na·an·ga·*lee*·a too

Can I look at it?
Naomba nione. — na·*ohm*·ba nee·*oh*·nay

I don't like it.
Sipendi. — see·*payn*·dee

How much is it?
Ni bei gani? — ni bay *ga*·nee

That's too expensive.
Ni ghali mno. — nee *ga*·lee *m*·noh

Please lower the price.
Punguza bei. — poon·*goo*·za bay

There's a mistake in the bill.
Kuna kosa kwenye bili. — koo·na koh·sa kwayn·yay bee·lee

ATM	*mashine ya kutolea pesa*	ma·*shee*·nay ya koo·toh·*lay*·a *pay*·sa
post office	*posta*	*poh*·sta
public phone	*simu ya mtaani*	*see*·moo ya m·*ta*·nee
tourist office	*ofisi ya watalii*	o·*fee*·see ya wa·ta·*lee*

Signs

Mahali Pa Kuingia	Entrance
Mahali Pa Kutoka	Exit
Imefunguliwa	Open
Imefungwa	Closed
Maelezo	Information
Ni Marufuku	Prohibited
Choo/Msalani	Toilets
Wanaume	Men
Wanawake	Women

Time, Dates & Numbers

The Swahili time system starts six hours later than the international one – it begins at sunrise (about 6am year-round). So, *saa mbili* sa m·*bee*·lee (lit: clocks two) means '2 o'clock Swahili time' and '8 o'clock European time'.

What time is it?
Ni saa ngapi? nee sa n·*ga*·pee

It's (10) o'clock.
Ni saa (nne). nee sa (*n*·nay)

Half past (10).
Ni saa (nne) na nusu. nee sa (*n*·nay) na *noo*·soo

morning	*asubuhi*	a·soo·*boo*·hee
afternoon	*mchana*	m·*cha*·na
evening	*jioni*	jee·*oh*·nee
yesterday	*jana*	*ja*·na
today	*leo*	*lay*·oh
tomorrow	*kesho*	*kay*·shoh

Monday	*Jumatatu*	joo·ma·*ta*·too
Tuesday	*Jumanne*	joo·ma·*n*·nay
Wednesday	*Jumatano*	joo·ma·*ta*·noh
Thursday	*Alhamisi*	al·ha·*mee*·see
Friday	*Ijumaa*	ee·joo·*ma*
Saturday	*Jumamosi*	joo·ma·*moh*·see
Sunday	*Jumapili*	joo·ma·*pee*·lee

1	*moja*	*moh*·ja
2	*mbili*	m·*bee*·lee
3	*tatu*	*ta*·too
4	*nne*	*n*·nay
5	*tano*	*ta*·noh
6	*sita*	*see*·ta
7	*saba*	*sa*·ba
8	*nane*	*na*·nay
9	*tisa*	*tee*·sa
10	*kumi*	*koo*·mee
20	*ishirini*	ee·shee·*ree*·nee
30	*thelathini*	thay·la·*thee*·nee
40	*arobaini*	a·roh·ba·*ee*·nee
50	*hamsini*	ham·*see*·nee
60	*sitini*	see·*tee*·nee
70	*sabini*	sa·*bee*·nee
80	*themanini*	thay·ma·*nee*·nee
90	*tisini*	tee·*see*·nee
100	*mia moja*	*mee*·a *moh*·ja
1000	*elfu*	*ayl*·foo

Question Words

What?	*Nini?*	*nee*·nee
When?	*Wakati?*	wa·*ka*·tee
Where?	*Wapi?*	*wa*·pee
Who?	*Nani?*	*na*·nee

Transport

Which ... goes to (Mbeya)?	*... ipi huenda (Mbeya)?*	... *ee*·pee hoo·*ayn*·da (m·*bay*·a)
bus	*Basi*	*ba*·see
ferry	*Kivuko*	kee·*voo*·koh
minibus	*Daladala* (Tan) *Matatu* (Ken)	da·la·*da*·la/ ma·*ta*·too
train	*Treni*	*tray*·nee

When's the ... bus?	*Basi ... itaondoka lini?*	*ba*·see ... ee·ta·ohn·*doh*·ka *lee*·nee
first	*ya kwanza*	ya *kwan*·za
last	*ya mwisho*	ya *mwee*·shoh
next	*ijayo*	ee·*ja*·yoh

A ... ticket to (Iringa).	*Tiketi moja ya ... kwenda (Iringa).*	tee·*kay*·tee *moh*·ja ya ... *kwayn*·da (ee·*reen*·ga)
1st-class	*daraja la kwanza*	da·*ra*·ja la *kwan*·za
2nd-class	*daraja la pili*	da·*ra*·ja la *pee*·lee
one-way	*kwenda tu*	*kwayn*·da too
return	*kwenda na kurudi*	*kwayn*·da na koo·*roo*·dee

What time does it get to (Kisuma)?
Itafika (Kisumu) saa ngapi? ee·ta·*fee*·ka (kee·*soo*·moo) sa n·*ga*·pee

Does it stop at (Tanga)?
Linasimama (Tanga)? lee·na·see·*ma*·ma (*tan*·ga)

I'd like to get off at (Bagamoyo).
Nataka kushusha (Bagamoyo). na·*ta*·ka koo·*shoo*·sha (ba·ga·*moh*·yoh)

I'd like to hire a ...	*Nataka kukodi ...*	na·*ta*·ka koo·*koh*·dee ...
4WD	*forbaifor*	*fohr*·ba·ee·fohr
bicycle	*baisikeli*	ba·ee·see·*kay*·lee
car	*gari*	*ga*·ree
motorbike	*pikipiki*	pee·kee·*pee*·kee

regular	*kawaida*	ka·wa·*ee*·da
unleaded	*isiyo na risasi*	ee·see·yoh na ree·*sa*·see

Is this the road to (Embu)?
Hii ni barabara kwenda (Embu)? — hee nee ba·ra·*ba*·ra *kwayn*·da (aym·boo)

Where's a petrol station?
Kituo cha mafuta kiko wapi? — kee·*too*·oh cha ma·*foo*·ta *kee*·ko *wa*·pee

(How long) Can I park here?
Naweza kuegesha hapa (kwa muda gani)? — na·*way*·za koo·ay·*gay*·sha *ha*·pa (kwa *moo*·da *ga*·ni)

I need a mechanic.
Nahitaji fundi. — na·hee·*ta*·jee *foon*·dee

I have a flat tyre.
Nina pancha. — *nee*·na *pan*·cha

I've run out of petrol.
Mafuta yamekwisha. — ma·*foo*·ta ya·may·*kwee*·sha

FRENCH

French is the official language in Burundi (along with Kirundi), the Democratic Republic of Congo (with four local languages – Swahili, Kikongo, Tshiluba and Lingala) and Rwanda (along with the English and the national language, Kinyarwanda).

French has nasal vowels (represented in our pronunciation guides by o or u followed by an almost inaudible nasal consonant sound m, n or ng). Note also the 'funny' *u* (ew in our guides) and the deep-in-the-throat *r*. The last syllable in a word is lightly stressed.

Hello.	*Bonjour.*	bon·zhoor
Goodbye.	*Au revoir.*	o·rer·vwa
Excuse me.	*Excusez-moi.*	ek·skew·zay·mwa
Sorry.	*Pardon.*	par·don
Yes./No.	*Oui./Non.*	wee/non
Please.	*S'il vous plaît.*	seel voo play
Thank you.	*Merci.*	mair·see
You're welcome.	*De rien.*	der ree·en

How are you?
Comment allez-vous? — ko·mon ta·lay·voo

Fine, and you?
Bien, merci. Et vous? — byun mair·see ay voo

What's your name?
Comment vous appelez-vous? — ko·mon voo·za·play voo

My name is ...
Je m'appelle ... — zher ma·pel ...

Do you speak English?
Parlez-vous anglais? — par·lay·voo ong·glay

I don't understand.
Je ne comprends pas. — zher ner kom·pron pa

What time Is It?
Quelle heure est-il? — kel er ay til

How much is it?
C'est combien? — say kom·byun

Where are the toilets?
Où sont les toilettes? — oo son lay twa·let

Can you show me (on the map)?
Pouvez-vous m'indiquer (sur la carte)? — poo·vay·voo mun·dee·kay (sewr la kart)

I'm lost.
Je suis perdu/perdue. — zhe swee·pair·dew (m/f)

Help!
Au secours! — o skoor

Leave me alone!
Fichez-moi la paix! — fee·shay·mwa la pay

Call a doctor.
Appelez un médecin. — a·play un mayd·sun

Call the police.
Appelez la police. — a·play la po·lees

I'm ill.
Je suis malade. — zher swee ma·lad

What's the local speciality?
Quelle est la spécialité locale? — kel ay la spay·sya·lee·tay lo·kal

Cheers!
Santé! — son·tay

a ... room	*une chambre ...*	ewn shom·brer ...
single	*à un lit*	a un lee
double	*avec un grand lit*	a·vek un gron lee

a ... ticket	*un billet ...*	un bee·yay ...
one-way	*simple*	sum·pler
return	*aller et retour*	a·lay ay rer·toor

1	*un*	un
2	*deux*	der
3	*trois*	trwa
4	*quatre*	ka·trer
5	*cinq*	sungk
6	*six*	sees
7	*sept*	set
8	*huit*	weet
9	*neuf*	nerf
10	*dix*	dees
20	*vingt*	vung
30	*trente*	tront
40	*quarante*	ka·ront
50	*cinquante*	sung·kont
60	*soixante*	swa·sont
70	*soixante-dix*	swa·son·dees
80	*quatre-vingts*	ka·trer·vung
90	*quatre-vingt-dix*	ka·trer·vung·dees
100	*cent*	son
1000	*mille*	meel

GLOSSARY

The following is a list of words and acronyms from Burundi (B), the Democratic Republic of the Congo (C), Kenya (K), Rwanda (R), Tanzania (T) and Uganda (U) that appear in this book. For a glossary of food and drink terms, see p635.

askari – security guard, watchman

ASP (T) – Afro-Shirazi Party on Zanzibar Archipelago

banda – thatched-roof hut with wooden or earthen walls; simple wooden and stone-built accommodation

bangi – marijuana; also ganja

bao – a board game widely played in East Africa

baraza – the stone seats seen along the outside walls of houses in the Stone Towns of Zanzibar and Lamu, used for chatting and relaxing

benga (K) – musical style originating among the Luo in western Kenya, and characterised by its electric guitar licks and bounding bass rhythms

Big Five, the – the five archetypal large African mammals: lion, buffalo, elephant, leopard and rhino

boda-boda (U) – bicycle taxi

boma – a living compound; in colonial times, a government administrative office

bui-bui – black cover-all garment worn by some Islamic women outside the home

CCM (T) – Chama Cha Mapinduzi (Party of the Revolution); Tanzania's governing political party

chai – tea; bribe

Cites – Convention on International Trade in Endangered Species

CUF (T)– Civic United Front; Tanzania's main opposition party

dalla-dalla (T) – minibus

dhow – traditional Arabic sailing vessel, common along the coast

duka – small shop or kiosk

fly camp – a camp away from the main tented camps or lodges, for the purpose of enjoying a more authentic bush experience

flycatcher (T) – used mainly in Arusha and Moshi to mean a tout working to get you to go on safari with 'his' particular operator, from whom he knows he can get a commission. We assume the name comes from a comparison with the sticky-sweet paper used to lure flies to land (and then get irretrievably stuck) – similar to the plight of a hapless traveller who succumbs to a flycatcher's promises and then is 'stuck' (ie, with their money and time lost in a fraudulent safari deal)

forex – foreign exchange bureau

gacaca (R) – traditional tribunal headed by village elders

ganja – see *bangi*

gof – volcanic crater

hoteli – small informal restaurant

injera – unleavened bread

Interahamwe (R) – Hutu militia

kabaka (U) – king

kanga – printed cotton wraparound, incorporating a Swahili proverb, worn by Tanzanian women

karibu – Swahili for welcome

kikoi – printed cotton wraparound traditionally worn by men in coastal areas

KWS (K) – Kenya Wildlife Service

lingala – Congolese dance music; also *soukous*

makuti – palm thatching

manyatta (K) – Maasai or Samburu livestock camp often surrounded by a circle of thorn bushes

matatu (K) – minibus

Maulid – birth of the prophet Mohammed and Muslim feast day, celebrated in many areas of East Africa

mihrab – prayer niche in a mosque showing the direction of Mecca

miraa – bundles of leafy twigs and shoots that are chewed as a stimulant and appetite-suppressant

moran (K) – Maasai or Samburu warrior

mpingo – African blackwood

murram – dirt or partly gravelled road

mwami (B; R)– king

mzungu – white person, foreigner (plural wazungu)

NCA (T) – Ngorongoro Conservation Area

Ngai – Kikuyu god

ngoma – dance and drumming

NRA (U) – National Resistance Army

NRM (U) – National Resistance Movement

nyatiti – traditional folk lyre

panga – machete, carried by many people in the east African countryside

papasi (T) – literally 'tick'; used on the Zanzibar Archipelago to refer to street touts

RMS (U) – Rwenzori Mountaineering Services

RPF (R) – Rwandan Patriotic Front

shamba – small farm or plot of land

shetani – literally, demon or something supernatural; in art, a style of carving embodying images from the spirit world

shuka – tie-dyed sarong

soukous – see *lingala*

taarab (T) – Zanzibari music combining African, Arabic and Indian influences

Tanapa (T) – Tanzania National Parks Authority

TANU (T) – Tanganyika African National Union

taxi-motor – motorcycle taxi

tilapia – Nile perch

TTB (T) – Tanzania Tourist Board

Ucota – Uganda Community Tourism Association

uhuru – freedom or independence

ujamaa (T) – familyhood, togetherness

Unguja (T) – Swahili name for Zanzibar Island

UWA (U) – Uganda Wildlife Authority

ZIFF (T) – Zanzibar International Film Festival

ZNP – Zanzibar Nationalist Party

ZPPP – Zanzibar & Pemba People's Party

behind the scenes

SEND US YOUR FEEDBACK

We love to hear from travellers – your comments keep us on our toes and help make our books better. Our well-travelled team reads every word on what you loved or loathed about this book. Although we cannot reply individually to postal submissions, we always guarantee that your feedback goes straight to the appropriate authors, in time for the next edition. Each person who sends us information is thanked in the next edition – the most useful submissions are rewarded with a selection of digital PDF chapters.

Visit **lonelyplanet.com/contact** to submit your updates and suggestions or to ask for help. Our award-winning website also features inspirational travel stories, news and discussions.

Note: We may edit, reproduce and incorporate your comments in Lonely Planet products such as guidebooks, websites and digital products, so let us know if you don't want your comments reproduced or your name acknowledged. For a copy of our privacy policy visit lonelyplanet.com/privacy.

OUR READERS

Many thanks to the travellers who used the last edition and wrote to us with helpful hints, useful advice and interesting anecdotes:

Chris Adam, James Argent, Rosemary Armao, Morten Broberg, Al Bruce, James Burton, Allan Cole, Christine Cooper, Lewis Cunningham, Jill Daines & Michael Gasper, Jelly De Jong, William Deed, Robbert Dijkstra, Khalin Driver, Annelie Eddy, Tina Fistravec, Catherine Fraser, Anita Geertsen, Gijs Gunterman, Stefanie Haehnel, Markus Hesper, Gavin Hickey, Guy Hindley, Marco Hoffmann, Annedee Jaeger, Naz Khakoo, Terry Kita, Frederik Køhlert, Marloes Krom, Stefan Lausch, Jonathan Levitt, Christine Markiw, Izzy Marks, Erica Meadows, Anna Miller, Keith Mitchell, Jenny Nakata, Sarit Nathwani, Paige Newman, Armando Nogueira, Bettina Ortmann, Belen Oton, Nathan Page, David Pap, Richard Raeon, Michele Ragazzini, Guy Raven & Carolein Kuijpers, Jeppe Robert, Stef Russell, Adam Sandell, Vera Scheepens, Robert Sheal, Lenke Slegers, Karen Spizer, Vidar Stefansson, Mark Stivers, Nick Thomas, Lesley Thompson, Christos Venturas, Albert Vilanova, Natalia Wadood, Sofie Wambeke, Daniel Wapp.

AUTHOR THANKS

Mary Fitzpatrick

I'd like to thank Anthony, Trent and Dean for being such great coauthors, and for all their help with tips and information. Many thanks also to David, Sam, Will and everyone else at Lonely Planet. My biggest thanks goes to Rick, Christopher and Dominic for their fine company, unflagging patience and wonderful good humour while this book was being researched and written.

Anthony Ham

Special thanks to Peter Ndirangu, my driver and guide who quickly became a friend; he taught me so much about Kenya. Thanks to Dr Darcy Ogada (Nairobi), Dea and Lisa Shupbach (Lake Naivasha), Philip Briggs, Leela Hazzah, Lisette Gelber, Eric Kesoi and Kamunu Saitoti (Selenkay Conservancy). Back home, my three wonderful girls (Marina, Carlota and Valentina) endure my absences with good grace and welcome me home with unbridled joy. One day, I will take you here.

Trent Holden

First up, thanks to Tim Bewer and Anne-Marie Weeden for the invaluable tips and contacts in Uganda. Big thanks to Robert Brierley, Debbie Willis, Cam McLeay, guys from

UWA, Jimmy my boda-boda driver, Jason, Miha, Fred, John Hunwick and everyone who helped out along the way. Also huge thanks to David Carroll for giving me a shot on this book. Finally, sending all my love to my family (including the newest addition, baby Samantha), and my girlfriend Kate.

Dean Starnes

It would be wrong not to acknowledge the legacy of work from previous editions, the assistance from my fellow authors and the hard work by the team at Lonely Planet. Big ups to Greg Bakunzi, Emmanuel Munganga Rufubya, Augustin Ndikuriyo and Cai Tjeenk Willink for their kind assistance. The company of Andrew Mendelssohn, Alison Mollon, LuAnne Cadd and my wife, Debbie Starnes, vastly improved long trips. At home my Mum and Dad, as always, held down the fort.

ACKNOWLEDGMENTS

Climate map data adapted from Peel MC, Finlayson BL & McMahon TA (2007) 'Updated World Map of the Köppen-Geiger Climate Classification', *Hydrology and Earth System Sciences*, 11, 163344.

Cover photograph: Giraffe and elephants near Mt Kilimanjaro; DLILLC, Corbis. Many of the images in this guide are available for licensing from Lonely Planet Images: www.lonelyplanetimages.com.

This Book

This 9th edition of Lonely Planet's *East Africa* guidebook was researched and written by Mary Fitzpatrick, Anthony Ham, Trent Holden and Dean Starnes, and included research by Stuart Butler and Tim Bewer. The Wildlife & Habitat chapter was written by David Lukas. The previous edition was written by Mary Fitzpatrick, Tim Bewer and Matthew Firestone. This guidebook was commissioned in Lonely Planet's Melbourne office, and produced by the following:

Commissioning Editors David Carroll, Sam Trafford, Will Gourlay
Coordinating Editors Gabrielle Innes, Karyn Noble
Coordinating Cartographer Jolyon Philcox
Coordinating Layout Designer Joseph Spanti
Managing Editors Barbara Delissen, Brigitte Ellemor
Managing Cartographers Amanda Sierp, Adrian Persoglia
Managing Layout Designers Chris Girdler, Jane Hart
Assisting Editors Nigel Chin, Carly Hall, Shawn Low, Erin Richards, Gabrielle Stefanos, Helen Yeates
Assisting Cartographers Anita Banh, Joelene Kowalski, Jennifer Johnston, Jacqueline Nguyen
Cover Research Naomi Parker
Internal Image Research Claire Gibson
Language Content Annelies Mertens, Branislava Vladisavljevic
Thanks to Elin Berglund, Lucy Birchley, Ryan Evans, Anna Metcalfe, Anthony Phelan, Gerard Walker, Trent Paton

A

Aberdare National Park 287-9, **288**
Acacia Camp 235
accommodation 640-1, *see also individual locations*
activities 17-18, 641-2, *see also individual activities*
African buffaloes 606, **607**
African fish eagles 615, **614**
African Queen, The 463, 479
African wild cats 14, 544, 594, 598, 601, **598-601**
African wild dogs 595
Afro-Shirazi Party (ASP) 198
AIDS 478, 571, 576, 578
air travel
  Burundi 567
  Kenya 370-1, 372
  Rwanda 554, 555
  Tanzania 206, 211-12
  to/from East Africa 650-1
  Uganda 489, 491
  within East Africa 652
airline offices
  Burundi 567
  Kenya 372
  Rwanda 554
  Tanzania 211-12
  Uganda 489
airports
  Burundi 567
  Kenya 370
  Rwanda 554
  Tanzania 206
  Uganda 489
Akamba people 583
al-Qaeda 356, 357, 576
al-Shabab 477
altitude sickness 661
Amabeere Cave 422-3
Amakula Kampala International Film Festival 385

000 Map pages
000 Photo pages

Amani Nature Reserve 99-100
Amboseli National Park 9, 240-3, **241**, **9**
Amin, Idi 382, 383, 389, 471-2, 474
amoebic dysentery 661
animals, *see* wildlife, *individual animals*, *individual locations*
Annan, Kofi 357
antelopes 248, 360, 544
Anti-Gay Bill 477
Arab colonisation 574
Arabuko Sokoke Forest Reserve 341-2
archaeological sites, *see also* ruins
  Oldupai Gorge 140
  Kondoa Rock-Art Sites 149-50
architecture 352, 631
area codes 646, 647
art galleries
  Tanzania 115
  Uganda 395
arts 631-3, *see also individual arts*
  festivals 385
  Kenya 358
  Rwanda 549-50
  Tanzania 200
  Uganda 479-80
Arusha 114-27, **116**
Arusha Declaration 198
Arusha National Park 127-8, **128**
Association of Uganda Tour Operators 25
ATMs 645
  Burundi 566
  Democratic Republic of the Congo (DRC) 501
  Kenya 366
  Rwanda 552
  Tanzania 205
  Uganda 486
augur buzzards 615

B

Babati 149
baboons 602, 627
Bagamoyo 92
Baganda people 583-4
Bagaza, Jean-Baptiste 565
Bagosora, Colonel Theoneste 546
Bahati, David 477
balloon safaris 31, 254, 263, 364
banded mongooses 613, **612-13**
banditry 367, 638
bao 580, 668
Baragoi 316
bargaining 487, 642
basketry *see* handicrafts
bat-eared foxes 469, 481
bateleurs 615, **614**
bathrooms 646-7
Batwa people, *see* Twa people
Bawi 85
beaches 2-3
  Bawi 85
  Bongoyo 57
  children 37
  Coco Beach 52, **16**
  Dar es Salaam 57-8
  Diani Beach 332-6, **332**
  Entebbe 399
  Fumba 84
  Gisenyi 525-30, **527**
  highlights 16, 38, 39, 332
  Jambiani 82
  Jimbizi Beach 192
  Kizimkazi 83-4
  Lake Tanganyika 11, **11**
  Malindi 342-6
  Matemwe 78-9
  Matvilla Beach 152
  Mbuyuni Beach 89
  Michamvi Peninsula 81-2
  Nungwi 76-8
  Paje 80-1
  Pongwe 80
  Saga Beach 559, **11**
  Shela 353-4
  Ssese Islands 455-7
  Takaungu 339
  Tanzania 57-8
  Tiwi Beach 331, **332**
  Vumawimbi Beach 91
  Watamu 339-41
  Zanzibar 75-84
beer 483, 635
Belgian colonisation 519, 534, 548, 565, 577
Besigye, Kizza 476
bicycle travel, *see* cycling
Big Five 20, 216, 359, 378, 593
Bigodi Wetland Sanctuary 423-4
bilharzia 658
Binaisa, Godfrey 471, 473
birds 615-18, **615-18**, *see also individual birds*
  books 479
birdwatching
  Bigodi Wetland Sanctuary 423
  Busingiro 466-7
  Kaniyo Pabidi 466
  Kenya 240, 259
  Lake Baringo 259-60
  Nyungwe Forest National Park 538
  Parc National de l'Akagera 543-4
  Parc National des Volcans 523
  Rubondo Island National Park 157
  Rwanda 523, 538, 543-4, 551

Sinet Delta 240
Tanzania 157, 202
Uganda 402, 423, 466-7, 481, 483
Bisesero 541
Biya, Paul 546
black market 645
black rhinos 594, 609, **609**
Kenya 222, 243, 256, 263, 284, 287, 303, 308, 359, 362
Rwanda 544
Tanzania 138, 188, 544
black-and-white colobus monkeys 605, **604**
Kenya 251, 257, 280, 281, 332
Tanzania 164
Uganda 421, 424, 426, 458, 466
Blixen, Karen 217, 222-3, 247
blue monkeys 605, **605**
Democratic Republic of the Congo (DRC) 499
Uganda 423, 451
boat safaris 30-1, 251
boat travel 651, 653-4, *see also* dhow travel, ferry travel, sailing
Kenya 372-3, 375
Tanzania 212
Uganda 491
boda-boda travel 372, 375, 397, 492
Bongoyo 57
books 479, 571, 593, *see also* literature
African wild cats 594
elephants 241
history & politics 480
primates 627
wildlife 479
border crossings
Burundi 567-8
Democratic Republic of the Congo (DRC) 502
Kenya 283, 489-90
Rwanda 554-5
Tanzania 206-10
Uganda 489-91
British colonisation 574-5, 577, 583
budget 12
Budongo Forest Reserve 465-7
Buffalo Springs National Reserve 308, **310**
buffaloes, African 606, **607**
Kenya 302, 308, 330, 359
Rwanda 544
Tanzania 111, 127, 130, 131, 133, 138, 142, 166, 167, 171, 176, 188
Uganda 412, 423, 424, 426, 432, 457, 461, 467, 469, 481
Buggala Island 455-6
Bujumbura 558-64, **560**
accommodation 559-61
activities 559
drinking 562-3
emergency services 563
food 561-2
internet access 563
medical services 563
money 563
postal services 563
shopping 563
sights 559
tourist information 563
travel agencies 563
travel to/from 563
travel within 564
Bukoba 158-60, **159**
bungee jumping 407-8
Burton 575
Burundi 39, 557-68, **558**
accommodation 566
border crossings 567-8
business hours 566
climate 557
consulates 566
culture 557, 565-6
economy 566
embassies 566
environment 566
highlights 558
history 564-5
holidays 566
money 566
nature 557
planning information 557
public holidays 566
safe travel 563, 566-7
telephone services 567
travel seasons 557
travel to/from 567-8
travel within 568
vacations 566
visas 567
Burundian Civil War 557, 565, 580
bus travel 654
Burundi 567
Kenya 371-2, 373
Rwanda 555, 556
Tanzania 206-10, 212-13
Uganda 489-90, 491
bushbabies 605, **604-5**
bushwalking, *see* hiking
business hours 642, *see also individual countries*
Butare 530-3, **531**
butterflies 84, 276, 341, 403, 423, 458, 537
Buyoya, Major Pierre 565
buzzards, augur 615
Bwejuu 81
Bwindi Impenetrable National Park 10, 33-4, 437-43

C

camel safaris 31, 314, 315
Cameron, David 365
canoe safaris 30-1, 128, 133
car travel 13, 654-5
Burundi 568
driving licences 213, 374, 492, 654
hire 655
insurance 655
road accidents 638
road rules 655
Kenya 371, 373-5
Rwanda 555
Tanzania 213
Uganda 491-2
caracals 259, 601, **600**
cash 205, 645, *see also* money
cats, African wild 14, 544, 594, 598-601, **598-601**
caves
Kenya 246, 281, 297, 337
Rwanda 516
Uganda 422-3
cell phones 646
Central Highlands 283-305, **284**
Central Island National Park 319
Chake Chake 87-9, **88**
Chama Cha Mapinduzi (CCM) 146, 198
Changuu 84-5
cheetahs 14, 598, **599**
Kenya 222, 243, 248, 263, 308
Tanzania 131, 142, 176, 200
Uganda 469, 481
Cherangani Hills 318
children, travel with 36-7
chimpanzee tracking 499
Democratic Republic of the Congo (DRC) 499
Rwanda 535, 536, 537, 538
Uganda 423, 426, 434, 466, 481
chimpanzees 14, 602, 629-30, **603**
Democratic Republic of the Congo (DRC) 497
Kenya 303
Ngamba Island Chimpanzee Sanctuary 401-2
Tanzania 158, 160, 165, 166
Uganda 398, 401-2, 423, 432, 437, 458, 465, 467, 481
Chogoria 305
cholera 658
Christianity 411, 580-1
chukudus 498
Chumbe Island Coral Park 85

Chutes de la Karera 564
cinema 631
  festivals 385
  Uganda 393-4, 479
climate 12, 17-18, *see also individual countries*
climate change 577, 651
climbing, *see also* hiking, trekking
  Kenya 254, 364
  Rwanda 523-4
Coco Beach 52, **16**
coffee 635
  tours 105
colobus monkey tracking 536-7
colobus monkeys 605, **604**
community projects 485, *see also* volunteering
conservation
  chimpanzees 630
  gorillas 629
consulates, *see individual countries*
costs 12
courses 204, 366, 486
cows 452
cranes, grey-crowned 617
Crater Lakes 421-2
credit cards 645
  Rwanda 552
  Tanzania 205
  Uganda 487
crime 638
crocodiles 263, 303
Cultural Tourism Programs 123, 171
culture 570, 578-82
  tribal groups 583-90
currency 13
customs regulations 578-82
Cyangugu 540
cycling 652-3
  Kenya 364
  safaris 30
  Tanzania 202-3
  Tour d'Afrique 580

D

dalla-dalla 214
dance 633
  Rwanda 549
  Uganda 480
dangers 213, 638-9, *see also* safe travel
  hitching 655
Dar es Salaam 46-56, **48, 50**
  accommodation 46-7
  cultural tourism 52
  dangers 53
  drinking 52
  emergency services 53
  entertainment 52
  immigration office 53
  internet access 53
  media 53
  medical services 53
  money 53-4
  postal services 54
  shopping 52-3
  sights 46
  telephone services 54
  travel to/from 54-6
  travel within 56
deforestation 596
Democratic Republic of the Congo (DRC) 39, 493-502, **494**
  climate 493
  culture 493
  election 501
  highlights 494
  history 500-1
  money 501
  nature 493
  planning information 493
  safe travel 501-2
  telephone services 502
  travel seasons 493
  travel to/from 502
  visas 502
dhow travel 212, 350, 653
Diani Beach 332-6, **332**
diarrhoea 660-1
digital photography 645-6
diphtheria 658
disabilities, travellers with 369, 647
diving 16, 641, 642
  Kenya 340, 364
  Tanzania 67
Dodoma 146-9, **148**
dogs, hunting 613
dolphins 83
Donkey Sanctuary 347-8
DRC, *see* Democratic Republic of Congo
drinks 635
driving, *see* car travel
driving licences 654
  Kenya 374
  Tanzania 213
  Uganda 492

E

eagles, African fish 615, **614**
East African Safari Rally 580
economy 570-1
Eldoret 276-9, **277**
electricity 643
elephants 9, 14, 302, 359-60, 593, 609, **608**
Eliye Springs 319-20
Elizabeth II, Queen 289
El-Molo people 584
Elsa's Grave 303-4
embassies, *see individual countries*
emergencies 665, *see also individual locations*
endangered species 359-60, 593-5
Engaruka 136
Entebbe 398-401, **400**
environment 591-6
  Burundi 566
  Kenya 358-62
  Rwanda 550
  Tanzania 200-1
  Uganda 480-3
environmental issues 595-6
  Kenya 361-2
  Lake Victoria 592
  Rwanda 550
equator 403
European colonisation 575
events 17-18
exchange rates
  Kenya 216
  Rwanda 504
  Tanzania 43
  Uganda 378
exchanging money 645

F

female genital mutilation 579
Ferguson's Gulf 320
ferry travel
  Rwanda 556
  Tanzania 212
  Uganda 491
Festival of the Dhow Countries 18
festivals 17-18, *see also individual locations*
  film 385, 631
filariasis 658
films 570, 631
  festivals 385, 631
  Rwanda 549-50
Fischer, Gustav 575
flamingos 259, 617, **616**
flycatchers 119
food 634-6, 643, *see also individual locations*
  customs 636
  language 664-5
Forces for the Defence of Democracy (FDD) 565

000 Map pages
000 Photo pages

forests 592
Fort Portal 417-21, **420**
Forum for Democratic Change (FDC) 476
Fossey, Dian 521, 524
French language 667
Fungu Yasini 57

G

Gadaffi, Colonel 472
Gandhi, Mahatma 405
gay travellers 204, 486, 643
- Anti-Gay Bill 477

gazelles 606, **607**
Gede Ruins 342
genocide
- Burundi 565
- Rwanda 513, 533-4, 541, 546, 550, 576

gerenuk 606, **606**
German colonialism 574-5
giardiasis 661
Giraffe Centre 222
giraffes 222, 302, 360, 595, 609, **609**
Gisenyi 525-30, **527**
Gitega 564
Githongo, John 356
golden jackals 613, **613**
golden monkeys 14, 523
Goma 494-7, **496**
Gombe National Park 165
Gorilla Naming Ceremony 17, 523
gorilla tracking
- Democratic Republic of the Congo (DRC) 498-9
- habitutation 482
- permits 438, 450
- Rwanda 520-3
- Uganda 437-8, 450-1, 481

gorillas 14, 602, 627-9, **602-3**
- internet resources 628

Gorillas in the Mist 521, 550
Great Rift Valley 591
Great War of Africa 501
greater galago 605, **604-5**
Grevy's zebra 594
grey-crowned cranes 617
Gulu 467-468

H

Habyarimana, Juvenal 565
Hadzabe people 585
handicrafts 480, 633
Hannington, James 575
Haya people 584-5
health 657-62
- insurance 657
- internet resources 658
- vaccinations 658
- water 662

heat exhaustion 661
Hell's Gate National Park 253-4, **253**
Hemingway, Ernest 463
hepatitis 658
hiking 15, 102, 641-2, *see also* climbing, trekking
- Congo Nile trail 529
- Rwanda 551
- safaris 30
- Tanzania 203
- Usambara Mountains 100

hippos 263, 289, 610, **610-11**
history 15, 572-7, *see also individual countries*
hitching 655
- Tanzania 213
- Uganda 492

HIV 478, 571, 658
Hoima 459-60
holidays 646
Homa 271
honey badgers 613
Hotel Rwanda 549
hunting dogs 613
Huye 530-3, **531**
hyenas 613, **612**
hyraxes 610, **610**

I

Ibikorwa rusangi 564
Il Ngwesi 308
independence 576
independent safaris 31
insect bites 661-2
insurance 643, 655
International Camel Derby 18
International Criminal Tribunal for Rwanda (ICTR) 548
internet access 643-4
internet resources 13, 571
Iringa 173-6, **174**
Isiolo 305, **309**
Islam 581
islands 15
- Buggala Island 455-6
- off Dar es Salaam 57
- off Zanzibar 84-5
- Ssese Islands 455-7

itineraries 19-23
- safaris 28-9

J

jackals 613, **613**
Jambiani 82
Jewish Abayudaya community 411
Jinja 403-11
- accommodation 408-10
- activities 405-8
- drinking 410
- food 410
- sights 405
- tourist information 410
- travel to/from 410
- travel within 411

Jozani Forest 84
Juba Peace Talks 476
Jumba la Mtwana 338
Jumbe, Aboud 198

K

Kabale 443-4, **444**
Kabila, Joseph 501
Kabila, Laurent 547
Kabwoya Wildlife Reserve 467
Kagame, Paul 545, 547
Kakamega Forest 274-6, **275**
Kalenjin people 585
Kampala 379-98, **382**, **386-7**, **398**
- accommodation 385-90
- activities 379-84
- dangers 379
- drinking 392-3
- emergency services 395
- entertainment 393-4
- festivals & events 385
- food 390-2
- internet access 395
- medical services 395
- money 395-6
- postal services 396
- shopping 394-5
- sights 379-84
- tourist information 396
- tours 384-5
- travel agencies 396
- travel to/from 396-7
- travel within 397-8

Karamojong people 586
Karatu 136-7
Kasavubu, Joseph 500
Kasese 427-8
Katavi National Park 167-8
Kato, David 477
Katonga Wildlife Reserve 426-7
kaya 336
Kayibanda, Gregoire 545
Kendwa 78
Kenya 38, 215-376, **218-19**, **262**
- accommodation 362-4
- activities 364
- budget 216

Kenya *continued*
- business hours 364
- climate 215
- consulates 364-5
- cultural tips 216
- culture 215, 357-8
- customs regulations 364
- disabilities, travellers with 369
- economy 357
- embassies 364-5
- environment 358-62
- exchange rates 216
- food 229-32
- gay travellers 365
- highlights 218-19
- history 355-7
- internet access 365
- itineraries 216
- legal matters 366
- lesbian travellers 365
- literature 358
- maps 366
- money 366
- music 359
- nature 215
- planning information 215-16
- postal services 367
- public holidays 367
- religion 358
- safaris 228, 327
- safe travel 367-8
- telephone services 368-9
- transport 216
- travel seasons 215
- travel to/from 370-2
- travel within 239-40, 372-6
- visas 369-70
- volunteering 370
- wildlife 359-60

Kenya African Democratic Union (KADU) 355
Kenya African National Union (KANU) 355-6
Kenya Land Freedom Army 355
Kenyan African Movement (KAU) 355
Kenyan Association of Tour Operators 25
Kenyan Coast 320-54, **321**
Kenyatta, Jomo 355, 579
Kenyatta, Uhuru 356
Kenya Wildlife Service 361
Kericho 272-74
Kibaki, Mwai 356-7
Kibale Forest National Park 423-4
Kibera 229
Kibuye 540-2
Kidepo Valley National Park 469-70
Kigali 505-15, **508**
- accommodation 509-11
- drinking 513
- emergency services 514
- entertainment 513
- food 511-12
- history 506
- internet access 514
- maps 514
- medical services 514
- money 514
- postal services 514
- shopping 513-14
- sights 506-7
- tourist information 514
- tours 508
- travel agencies 514
- travel to/from 514-15
- travel within 515

Kigoma 162-5, **164**
Kigomasha 91-2
Kihingami Wetland 422
Kikuyu people 586
Kilifi 338-9
Kilwa Kisiwani 193-4
Kilwa Masoko 192-3, **192**
King Leopold 500
King Mutara III 534
Kisii 272
Kisoro 448-50, **449**
Kisumu 266-71, **267**
Kitale 279, **280**
Kitgum 468
Kiwengwa 79-80
Kiweni 90
Kizimkazi 83-4
kob, Uganda 606
kombe 580
Kondoa Rock-Art Sites 149-51
Kony, Joseph 475-6
Kwita Izina 17, 523

L

Laikipia Plateau 303
lakes 592
- Crater Lakes 421-2
- Lake Albert 467
- Lake Baringo 259-61, **260**
- Lake Bogoria National Reserve 257-9, **260**
- Lake Bunyonyi 445-8
- Lake Elmenteita 254
- Lake Eyasi 141-2
- Lake Kasenda 422
- Lake Kifuruka 422
- Lake Kivu 526
- Lake Manyara National Park 133-5
- Lake Mburo National Park 453-4
- Lake Mutanda 450
- Lake Naivasha 250-3, **252**
- Lake Nakuru National Park 256, **258**
- Lake Natron 135-6
- Lake Nkuruba 421
- Lake Nyasa 182-4
- Lake Nyinabulitwa 421-2

Lake Tanganyika 11, 169, **11**
Lake Victoria 151, 266-71, **151**
- environmental issues 592

Lamu 9, 346-53, **348**, **9**
language 663-9
- courses 204, 366, 486
- French 667
- Rwanda 504
- Swahili 575
- Uganda 378

Last King of Scotland, The 479
Leakey, Dr Richard 361
legal matters 204, 644
leopards 14, 598, **598**
Leopold, King 500
lesbian travellers 204, 486, 643
- Anti-Gay Bill 477

Les Tambourinaires du Burundi 562
lesser flamingos 617, **616**
Lewa Wildlife Conservancy 307
life expectancy 582
lilac-breasted rollers 617, **617**
lions 14, 242, 360, 432, 594, 598, **598-9**
literature 631-2, *see also* books
- Kenya 358
- Uganda 479

Livingstone, Dr David 61, 575, 576
Lodwar 319
long-horned Ankole cows 452
Longonot National Park 249-50
Lord's Resistance Army (LRA) 475
Loyangalani 316-17
Lule, Yusuf 473
Lumumba, Patrice 500
Luo people 586-7
Lushoto 100-2, **101**

M

Maasai people 587-8
Mabamba Swamp Wetlands 402
Mabira Forest Reserve 403
Mafia 186-8, **187**

000 Map pages
000 Photo pages

Mafia Island Marine Park 188
Mahale Mountains National Park 165-7
Mai Mai 501
Maji Maji Rebellion 184
Makambako 178
Makonde people 588-9
Makunduchi 83
malaria 658-9
Malindi 342-6, **344**
Malindi Marine National Park 342-3
Manda Island 354
Manda Toto Island 354
mangroves 592
maps 644
Marafa 343
Maralal 313, **314**
Maralal International Camel Derby 315
Marangu 110-11
Marich 317-20
Marsabit 311-13
Marsabit National Park 313, **313**
Masai Mara National Reserve 8, 261-6, **264-5**, **618**
Masaka 454-5
Masasi 197
Masindi 458-9
Matemwe 78-9
Matiba, Kenneth 355-6
Mau Mau rebellion 355, 577
Mbale 411-12
Mbarara 452
Mbeya 179-81
Mbudya 57
measures 641
medical services 657
Menai Bay 84
meningococcal meningtis 660
Meru 301-2
Meru National Park 302-5, **304**
Mgahinga Gorilla National Park 34, 450-2
Michamvi Peninsula 81-2
Mida Creek 341
Mikindani 196-7
Mikumi National Park 171
Mikumi Town 171-3
minibuses 655
Misali 89
Mkame Ndume (Pujini) Ruins 89
Mkoani 90
Mnarani 339
Mnemba 85
mobile phones 646
Mobutu, Joseph 500-1
Moi, Daniel arap 355-6, 585
Mombasa 320-30, **322**, **324-5**
activities 320-3
dangers 329
drinking 328
emergency services 329
entertainment 328
events 323
festivals 323
food 327-8
internet access 329
medical services 329
money 329
safaris 327
shopping 328-9
tourist information 329
tours 327
travel to/from 329-30
travel within 330
Mombasa Triathlon 323
Mombo 103
money 12, 13, 641, 645
mongooses 613, **612**
monkeys, *see individual species*
Morogoro 169-70, **170**
Moshi 103-10, **106**
motorcycle travel 654-5
hire 655
road rules 655
Rwanda 555
Uganda 491-2
moto-taxis 556
mountain biking 364, 372, 653
mountain gorillas 33-4, 35, 39, 602, 627-9, **602-3**
Democratic Republic of the Congo (DRC) 498, 499
Rwanda 515, 519-21
Uganda 437, 448, 450, 482
Mpanda 167
Mpanga Forest Reserve 403
Mt Elgon National Park 281-3, 412-14, **282**
Mt Kenya 298, **295**
Mt Kenya National Park 291-7, **292**, **619**
Mt Kilimanjaro 6, 111-14, 115, **112**, **6-7**
Mt Meru 129-31
Mtae 102
Mtwara 194-6, **195**
Muheza 98
Murchison Falls National Park 460-5, **462**
Musanze 515-19, **516-17**
museums, *see also* national museums
Baden-Powell Museum 284
National Museum of Rwanda 532
Uganda Museum 379
Museveni, Janet 477
Museveni, Yoweri 475, 545, 586
music 632-3
Kenya 358, 359
Les Tambourinaires du Burundi 562
Tanzania 200
Uganda 480
Musoma 151-2
Mutara III, King 534
Mwaluganje Elephant Sanctuary 334
Mwambutsa, Mwami 564
Mwanza 152-6, **154**
mweso 580

N

Nairobi 217-40, **220-1**, **224-5**, **237**, **238**
accommodation 223-9
drinking 232-3
emergency services 235-6
entertainment 234
festivals & events 223
internet access 236
medical services 236
money 236
postal services 236
safe travel 233
shopping 234-5
sights 217-23
telephone services 236
tourist information 235-7
travel agencies 237
travel to/from 236, 237-9
travel within 239-40
Nairobi National Park 221-2, **230-1**
Nakuru 255-6, **256**
Nanyuki 297-301, **300**
Naro Moru 297
Narok 261
National Alliance Rainbow Coalition (NARC) 356
National Liberation Forces (NLF) 565
national museums
Kenya 217
Rwanda 532
Tanzania 46
national parks & reserves 202, 621-6, **622-3**
Aberdare National Park 287-9
Amani Nature Reserve 99-100
Amboseli National Park 240-3
Arabuko Sokoke Forest Reserve 341-2
Arusha National Park 127-9
Budongo Forest Reserve 465-7
Buffalo Springs National Reserve 308
Bwindi Impenetrable National Park 10, 33-4, 437-43

national Parks & Reserves *continued*
  Central Island National Park 319
  Gombe National Park 165
  Hell's Gate National Park 253-4
  Kabwoya Wildlife Reserve 467
  Katavi National Park 167-8
  Katonga Wildlife Reserve 426-7
  Kenya 360-1
  Kibale Forest National Park 423-4
  Kidepo Valley National Park 469-70
  Lake Bogoria National Reserve 257-9
  Lake Manyara National Park 133-5
  Lake Nakuru National Park 256
  Longonot National Park 249-50
  Mahale Mountains National Park 165-7
  Malindi Marine National Park 342-3
  Marsabit National Park 313
  Masai Mara National Reserve 261-6
  Mgahinga Gorilla National Park 450-2
  Mikumi National Park 171
  Mpanga Forest Reserve 403
  Mt Elgon National Park 281-3, 412-14
  Mt Kenya National Park 291-7
  Mt Kilimanjaro National Park 111-14, 115
  Murchison Falls National Park 460-5
  Nairobi National Park 221-2
  Ndere Island National Park 268
  Ngezi Vumawimbi Forest Reserve 91
  Nyungwe Forest National Park 11, 535-40
  Parc National de l'Akagera 542-5
  Parc National des Virungas 497-500
  Parc National des Volcans 519-25
  Queen Elizabeth National Park 432-7
  Ruaha National Park 176-8
  Rubondo Island National Park 157-8
  Ruma National Park 271
  Rwanda 550
  Rwenzori Mountains National Park 428-32
  Saadani National Park 94-5
  Saiwa Swamp National Park 280-1
  Samburu National Reserve 308-11
  Selous Game Reserve 188-92
  Semuliki National Park 424-5
  Serengeti National Park 6, 142-6
  Shaba National Reserve 308
  Shimba Hills National Reserve 330-1
  Sibiloi National Park 318
  South Island National Park 317
  Tanzania 200
  Tarangire National Park 131-3
  Toro-Semliki Wildlife Reserve 425-6
  Tsavo East National Park 247-9
  Tsavo West National Park 243-7
  Uganda 482-3
  Watamu Marine National Park 340
National Resistance Army (NRA) 475
National Resistance Council (NRC) 475
National Resistance Movement (NRM) 476
Ndadaye, Melchior 565
Ndayizeye, Domitien 565
Ndere Island National Park 268
Ndoto Mountains 312
Nelson Mandela Stadium 478
Netanyahu, Benjamin 473
newspapers 641
  Kenya 362
  Tanzania 203
  Uganda 484
Ngamba Island Chimpanzee Sanctuary 401-2
Ngezi Vumawimbi Forest Reserve 91
Ngorongoro Conservation Area 137-41, **138**
Ngorongoro Crater 137-40
  trekking 139-40
Ngulia Rhino Sanctuary 243
Nile River 405
Ningaba, Colonel Sylvestre 565
Njombe 178-9
Nkurunziza, Pierre 565
Northern Kenya 305-20, **306**
Northern Tanzania 103-46, **104**
Ntaryamira, Cyprien 546, 565
Ntibantunganya, Sylvestre 565
Nungwi 76-8
Nyabisindu 534-5
Nyahururu 289-91, **290**
Nyamwezi people 589
Nyanza 534-5
Nyerere, Julius 198, 472
Nyeri 283-6
Nyero Rockpaintings 416
Nyiragongo Volcano 498, **11**
Nyungwe Forest National Park 11, 535-40, **11**

O

Obama, Barack 477
Obote, Dr Milton 382-3, 471-5, 575
Odinga, Raila 357, 365, 587
Okello, General Tito 473, 545
Okello, John 198
Ol Doinyo Lengai 140
opening hours 642
Operation Entebbe 473
Operation Iron Fist 476
Organisation for African Unity (OAU) 472
ostriches 617, **616**

P

Paje 80-1
Palestine Liberation Organization (PLO) 473
Pangani 95-6
Pangavini 57
papasi 65
Parc National de l'Akagera 542-5
Parc National de Nyungwe 11, 535-40, **11**
Parc National des Virungas 35, 497-500
Parc National des Volcans 34-5, 519-25, **522**
Pare people 589
passports 648
Paté Island 354
Pemba 85-91, **86**
Pemba flying foxes 91
permits 34-5
photography 645-6
planning, *see also individual countries*
  budgeting 12
  calendar of events 17-18
  children 36-7
  East Africa basics 12-13
  East Africa's regions 38-9
  internet resources 13
  itineraries 19-23
  safaris 24-31
  travel seasons 12, 17-18
plants 200-1, 591-2
poaching 247
politics 570-1
Pongwe 80
population 570, 579-80
Portuguese colonisation 574
postal services, *see individual locations*
primates 602-5, 627-30, **602-5**
primate tracking 14
  Rwanda 551
  Uganda 10
public holidays 646
  Burundi 566
  Kenya 367
  Rwanda 552-3

000 Map pages
000 Photo pages

Tanzania 205
Uganda 487
Pugu Hills 56-7
pupil's pass 369

Q

Queen Elizabeth II 289
Queen Elizabeth National Park 432-7, **433**

R

rabies 660
radio 641
Kenya 362
Tanzania 203
Uganda 484
Ras Mkumbuu 89
ratels 613
religion 571, 580-2
Kenya 358
Rwanda 549
Tanzania 200
Uganda 479
rhinos 14, 303, 359, 457
Ngulia Rhino Sanctuary 243
rift valley fever 660
Rift Valley 249-60, **250**
rock hyraxes 610, **610**
Rothschild giraffes 222, 595, *see also* giraffes
Ruaha National Park 176-8
Rubia, Charles 355-6
Rubondo Island National Park 157-8
Ruhengeri 515-19, **516-17**
ruins 15
Engaruka 136
Gede Ruins 342
Jumba la Mtwana 338
Kilwa Kisiwani 193-4
Mkame Ndume (Pujini) 89
Mnarani 339
Ras Mkumbuu 89
Ruma National Park 271
Rwanda 39, 503-56, **505**
accommodation 550-1
activities 551
border crossings 554-5
budget 504
climate 503
cultural tips 504
culture 503, 548-9
currency 504
drinking 550
economy 549
environment 550
environmental issues 550
exchange rates 504
festivals 551
food 550
highlights 505
history 545-8
internet access 551
itineraries 504
language 504
maps 552
money 504, 552
nature 503
planning information 503-4
plastic bags, ban of 555
population 549
postal services 552
provincial renaming 552
public holidays 552-3
religion 549
safaris 556
safe travel 553
telephone services 553
time 553
tourist information 553
tours 556
travel seasons 503
travel to/from 554-5
travel within 555-6
visas 504, 554
work 554
Rwanda Development Board (RDB) 553
Rwandan Patriotic Front (RPF) 545
Rwenzori Mountains National Park 428-32, **428**

S

Saadani National Park 94-5
Saba Saba 356
safari operators 54, 126
safaris 24-31
balloon safaris 31, 254, 263, 364
boat safaris 30-1, 251
camel safaris 31, 314, 315
canoe safaris 30-1, 128, 133
cycling safaris 30
hiking safaris 30
independent safaris 31
itineraries 28-9
Kenya 228, 327
Rwanda 556
Tanzania 54, 126
Uganda 483
vehicle safaris 30
safe travel 36, 638-9
Burundi 563, 566-7
bus travel 654
car travel 213
Democratic Republic of the Congo (DRC) 501-2
hitching 655
Kenya 233, 311, 347, 367-8
Rwanda 553
Uganda 471, 487
Saga Beach 559, **11**
sailing 335
Saiwa Swamp National Park 280-1
Samburu National Reserve 308-11, **310**
savannahs 591-2, 618, **618**
schistosomiasis 658
secretary birds 615, **615**
Selous Game Reserve 188-92, **189**
Semuliki National Park 424-5
Serengeti National Park 6, 142-6, **144**
servals 601, **601**
Shaba National Reserve 308
Shela 353-4
Shimba Hills National Reserve 330-1
Shimoni Island 336-8
shoebills 617, **617**
Sibiloi National Park 318
Sipi Falls 414-16
slave trade 574, 576
snake bites 662
snorkelling 16, 641
Kenya 337, 364
Tanzania 57, 65, 84, 88, 90
solo travellers 646
Sometimes in April 550
Songea 184-5
Soni 103
Source Du Nil 564
South Island National Park 317
sports 549, 580
spotted hyenas 613, **612**
Ssemogerere, Paul 476
Ssese Islands 455-7
Stanley, Henry Morton 559, 575
Stone Town 8, **62**, **8**
Sukuma people 589
Sumbawanga 168-9
Swahili 663-7
architecture 352, 631
culture 575, 588
literature 631-2
Szek, Count Teleki von 575

T

taarab music 73
Tabora 161-2, **162**
Takaungu 339
Tanga 96-8, **98**
Tanganyika Africa Association (TAA) 198, 577
Tanganyika African National Union (TANU) 198

Tanzania 38, 42-214, **44-5**, **147**, **161**, **172**, **186**
accommodation 46-7, 201
activities 202-3
budget 43
climate 42
consulates 203-4
cultural tips 43
culture 42, 199-200
currency 203
customs regulations 203
embassies 203-4
environment 200-1
exchange rates 43
food 47-52
highlights 44-5
history 197-9
internet access 204
itineraries 43
legal matters 204
maps 204
money 204-5
national parks & reserves 201
nature 42
planning information 42-3
plants 200-1
religion 200
transport 43
travel seasons 42
travel to/from 206-11
travel within 211-14
visas 206
volunteering 206
wildlife 200
Tanzanian Association of Tour Operators 25
taxis 655, 656
tea 274, 635
telephone services 646
terrorism 356
theft 638
Thiong'o, Ngũgĩ wa 358, 571, 632
Thomson, Joseph 575
Thomson's Falls 289-91, **290**
Thomson's gazelles 606, **607**
time 646, 647, 648
tipping 27, 645
Kenya 367
Rwanda 552
Tanzania 205
Uganda 487
Tiwi Beach 331, **332**
toilets 646-7

Toro-Semliki Wildlife Reserve 425-6
Tour d'Afrique 580
tourist information
Burundi 563
Democratic Republic of the Congo (DRC) 497
Kenya 368
Rwanda 514, 553
Tanzania 206
Uganda 396
tours 651-2, 656, *see also* safaris
coffee 108
cultural 150, 160
walking 351
train travel 214, 656
travellers cheques 645
travel to/from East Africa 650-2
travel within East Africa 652-6
trekking 15, 641-2, 644, *see also* climbing, hiking
Kenya 296, 318, 364, 365
Mt Elgon 412-14
Mt Kilimanjaro 111-14, 115, 120
Mt Meru 129-31
Ngorongoro Crater Highlands 139-40
Nyungwe Forest National Park 537-8
Parc National des Volcans 523
Rwanda 551
Rwenzori Mountains National Park 428-9, 430-1
Tanzania 110, 203
volcanoes 451
tribal groups 579-80, 583-90
trucks 655-6
trypanosomiasis 660
Tsavo East National Park 247-9, **244-5**, **619**
Tsavo West National Park 243-7, **244-5**
tsetse flies 660
Tshisekedi, Etienne 501
tuberculosis 660
Tukuyu 181-2
Tumbe 90
Tunduru 185
Turkana Massacre 474
Turkana people 589-90
turtles 340
TV 362, 484
Twa people 585
Democratic Republic of the Congo (DRC) 495
Uganda 425, 439, 445, 446, 451
typhoid 660

U

Uganda 39, 377-492, **380-1**, **404**, **418-19**, **458**
accommodation 484
activities 484
budget 378
business hours 484-5
children, travel with 485
climate 377
consulates 485-6
cultural tips 378
culture 377, 477-8
currency 378
drinking 483
embassies 485-6
environment 480-3
exchange rates 378
food 483
gay travellers 486
highlights 380-1
history 471-7
internet access 486
itineraries 378
language 378
language courses 486
lesbian travellers 486
maps 486
money 378, 486
nature 377
planning information 377-8
postal services 487
public holidays 487
religion 479
safe travel 471, 487
sport 478-9
telephone services 487-8
transport 378
travel seasons 377
travel to/from 489-91
travel within 491-2
visas 378, 488
volunteering 488-9
Uganda kob 606
Uganda People's Congress (UPC) 471
Ukerewe 157
UN Assistance Mission for Rwanda (UNAMIR) 546
Unesco World Heritage Sites 574
Unguja Ukuu 84
Usambara Mountains 98-103

V

vacations, *see* public holidays
vegetarian travellers 634-5
vehicle safaris 30
vervet monkeys 602, **602**
visas 13, 647-8
Burundi 567

000 Map pages
000 Photo pages

Democratic Republic of the Congo (DRC) 502
Kenya 369-70
Rwanda 504, 554
Tanzania 206
Uganda 378, 488
Voi 249
volcanoes 451
Democratic Republic of the Congo (DRC) 11
Rwanda 523
Uganda 451
Volcanoes National Park 34-5, 519-25, **522**
volunteering 648
Kenya 370
Tanzania 105, 206
Uganda 488-9
vultures, white-backed 615, **615**

W

Waivimenya Bay 402-3
walking, *see* hiking
walking tours 351
Wambaa 89
warthogs 610, **611**
Wasini Island 336-8
Watamu 339-41
Watamu Marine National Park 340
water sports 354, 364
waterbucks 302
waterfalls 564
weather 12, 17-18, *see also individual countries*
websites, *see* internet resources
weights 641
Western Tanzania 160-9, **161**
Westlands **234**
Wete 90
white-backed vultures 615, **615**
white-water rafting
Kenya 364
Uganda 10, 405-6
wild cats 14, 544, 594, 598-601, **598-601**
wildebeest 606, **597**, **606**
annual migration 17-18
wildlife 8, 14, 593, 597-620
Kenya 359-60
Rwanda 538, 544, 551
Tanzania 200
Uganda 480-1
wine 635
women in East Africa 579
women travellers 648-9
work 649
World War I 577
World War II 501

Y

yellow fever 660

Z

Zanzibar 58-75, **60**
accommodation 66-70
activities 65
dangers 73
diving 67
drinking 72
entertainment 72
festivals 68
food 70-2
internet access 73
medical services 73
money 73
postal services 73
shopping 72-3
sights 59-65
tour operators 74
tours 65-6
travel agencies 74
travel to/from 74
travel within 74-5
Zanzibar and Pemba People's Party (ZPPP) 198
Zanzibar Archipelago 58-85, **59**
Zanzibar International Film Festival 631
Zanzibar Nationalist Party (ZNP) 198
zebras 302, 594, 609, **608**
Ziwa Rhino Sanctuary 457

how to use this book

These symbols will help you find the listings you want:

- Sights
- Beaches
- Activities
- Courses
- Tours
- Festivals & Events
- Sleeping
- Eating
- Drinking
- Entertainment
- Shopping
- Information/ Transport

These symbols give you the vital information for each listing:

- Telephone Numbers
- Opening Hours
- Parking
- Nonsmoking
- Air-Conditioning
- Internet Access
- Wi-Fi Access
- Swimming Pool
- Vegetarian Selection
- English-Language Menu
- Family-Friendly
- Pet-Friendly
- Bus
- Ferry
- Tram
- Train

Reviews are organised by author preference.

Look out for these icons:

TOP CHOICE Our author's recommendation

FREE No payment required

A green or sustainable option

Our authors have nominated these places as demonstrating a strong commitment to sustainability – for example by supporting local communities and producers, operating in an environmentally friendly way, or supporting conservation projects.

Map Legend

Sights
- Beach
- Buddhist
- Castle
- Christian
- Hindu
- Islamic
- Jewish
- Monument
- Museum/Gallery
- Ruin
- Winery/Vineyard
- Zoo
- Other Sight

Activities, Courses & Tours
- Diving/Snorkelling
- Canoeing/Kayaking
- Skiing
- Surfing
- Swimming/Pool
- Walking
- Windsurfing
- Other Activity/ Course/Tour

Sleeping
- Sleeping
- Camping

Eating
- Eating

Drinking
- Drinking
- Cafe

Entertainment
- Entertainment

Shopping
- Shopping

Information
- Bank
- Embassy/ Consulate
- Hospital/Medical
- Internet
- Police
- Post Office
- Telephone
- Toilet
- Tourist Information
- Other Information

Transport
- Airport
- Border Crossing
- Bus
- Cable Car/ Funicular
- Cycling
- Ferry
- Metro
- Monorail
- Parking
- Petrol Station
- Taxi
- Train/Railway
- Tram
- Other Transport

Routes
- Tollway
- Freeway
- Primary
- Secondary
- Tertiary
- Lane
- Unsealed Road
- Plaza/Mall
- Steps
- Tunnel
- Pedestrian Overpass
- Walking Tour
- Walking Tour Detour
- Path

Geographic
- Hut/Shelter
- Lighthouse
- Lookout
- Mountain/Volcano
- Oasis
- Park
- Pass
- Picnic Area
- Waterfall

Population
- Capital (National)
- Capital (State/Province)
- City/Large Town
- Town/Village

Boundaries
- International
- State/Province
- Disputed
- Regional/Suburb
- Marine Park
- Cliff
- Wall

Hydrography
- River, Creek
- Intermittent River
- Swamp/Mangrove
- Reef
- Canal
- Water
- Dry/Salt/ Intermittent Lake
- Glacier

Areas
- Beach/Desert
- Cemetery (Christian)
- Cemetery (Other)
- Park/Forest
- Sportsground
- Sight (Building)
- Top Sight (Building)

Contributing Author

David Lukas wrote the Wildife & Habitat chapter. David is a freelance naturalist who lives next to Yosemite National Park in California. He writes extensively about the world's wildlife, and has contributed wildlife chapters for eight African Lonely Planet guides ranging from *Ethiopia* to *South Africa*.

OUR STORY

A beat-up old car, a few dollars in the pocket and a sense of adventure. In 1972 that's all Tony and Maureen Wheeler needed for the trip of a lifetime – across Europe and Asia overland to Australia. It took several months, and at the end – broke but inspired – they sat at their kitchen table writing and stapling together their first travel guide, *Across Asia on the Cheap*. Within a week they'd sold 1500 copies. Lonely Planet was born.

Today, Lonely Planet has offices in Melbourne, London and Oakland, with more than 600 staff and writers. We share Tony's belief that 'a great guidebook should do three things: inform, educate and amuse'.

OUR WRITERS

Mary Fitzpatrick

Coordinating Author, Tanzania Mary's love affair with East Africa began almost two decades ago, when she travelled from Mozambique to Tanzania to climb Mt Kilimanjaro. Since then she has returned countless times, including to study Swahili. A travel writer for more than 15 years, Mary has authored and coauthored numerous Lonely Planet titles, including *Tanzania*. She is currently based in Tanzania. Mary also wrote the Welcome to East Africa, 11 Top Experiences, Need to Know, Safaris, Countries at a Glance, East Africa Today, History, Life in East Africa, Tribal Cultures, The Arts and A Taste of East Africa chapters.

Read more about Mary at:
lonelyplanet.com/members/mary

Anthony Ham

Kenya Anthony has spent the last decade in North and West Africa, exploring the Sahara with Tuareg nomads and tracking down endangered elephant herds from the Malian Sahel to remote corners of southern Chad. In addition to coordinating Lonely Planet's *West Africa*, *Africa* and *Libya* guides, Anthony writes and photographs for numerous publications. Anthony also wrote the If You Like, Month by Month, Itineraries, Gorilla Tracking, Travel with Children, Environment, National Parks & Reserves, Primates and Safe Travel chapters.

Read more about Anthony at
lonelyplanet.com/members/anthonyha

Trent Holden

Uganda On his first sojourn into Africa as a Lonely Planet author, Trent was thrilled to be assigned to Uganda – one of his favourite destinations in the world. It's a place he loves not only for its incredible diversity but for some of the lushest landscapes he's seen in his travels. Trent is a freelance writer and editor from Melbourne and this is his sixth book for Lonely Planet, having coauthored other titles including *India* and *Nepal*.

Dean Starnes

Rwanda, Burundi, Detour: Democratic Republic of the Congo Dean first backpacked through East Africa in 2004 – racing camels in Maralal, rafting the Nile in Jinja and falling off the map in Rwanda. Since then he has returned to Africa multiple times, coauthoring the *Ethiopia* (4th edition) and *Kenya* (8th edition) guide. Dean relished the chance to finally climb DRC's Nyiragongo Volcano for this book. When he's not writing for Lonely Planet, Dean lives in New Zealand with his wife.

OVER PAGE MORE WRITERS

Published by Lonely Planet Publications Pty Ltd
ABN 36 005 607 983
9th edition – July 2012
ISBN 978 1 74179 672-8

10 9 8 7 6 5 4 3 2 1
Printed in China